The Gospel of According to St. Luke

Luke 1:41-50 . . . . [illegible]
Luke 2:1-14 . . . . [illegible]
Luke 2:15-20 . . . . I, 107-124
Luke 2:21 . . . . I, 186-195
Luke 2:33-40 . . . . I, 163-185
Luke 3:42-50 . . . . I, 235-253
Luke 3:1-6 . . . . I, 71-98
Luke 4:1-13 . . . . II, 1-36
Luke 5:1-11 . . . . III, 214-225
Luke 5:12-15 . . . . I, 287-313
Luke 5:17-26 . . . . IV, 177-200
Luke 6:36-42 . . . . III, 84-104
Luke 7:2-10 . . . . I, 287-313
Luke 7:11-16 . . . . IV, 112-132
Luke 7:18-27 . . . . I, 28-49
Luke 8:4-15 . . . . I, 386-403
Luke 8:22-25 . . . . I, 314-327
Luke 8:41-56 . . . . IV, 306-328
Luke 9:10-17 . . . . II, 100-128
Luke 9:28-36 . . . . II, 37-73
Luke 10:23-37 . . . . IV, 22-71
Luke 10:25-28 . . . . IV, 153-176
Luke 11:14-28 . . . . II, 74-99
Luke 14:1-11 . . . . IV, 133-152
Luke 14:16-24 . . . . III, 164-189
Luke 15:1-10 . . . . III, 190-213
Luke 16:1-9 . . . . III, 320-340
Luke 17:11-19 . . . . IV, 72-86
Luke 18:9-14 . . . . III, 356-372
Luke 18:31-43 . . . . I, 404-428
Luke 19:29-38 . . . . II, 157-184
Luke 19:41-47 . . . . III, 341-355
Luke 21:25-33 . . . . I, 1-27
Luke 24:12 . . . . II, 211-264

The Gospel of According to St. John

John 1:1-14 . . . . I, 125-162
John 1:19-28 . . . . I, 50-70
John 2:1-11 . . . . I, 254-286
John 4:46-53 . . . . IV, 240-264
John 6:1-15 . . . . II, 100-128
John 6:56-59 . . . . III, 105-163
John 8:46 . . . . II,129-156
John 10:11-16 . . . . II, 290-320
John 12:12-16 . . . . II, 157-184
John 14:23-31 . . . . III, 1-57
John 15:26-16:4 . . . . II, 441-460
John 16:5-14 . . . . II, 337-371
John 16:16-22 . . . . II, 321-336
John 16:23-30 . . . . II, 372-409
John 18:33-37 . . . . IV, 446-459
John 20:1-18 . . . . II, 211-264
John 20:19-31 . . . . II, 265-289

THE SUNDAY SERMONS OF THE GREAT FATHERS

VOLUME TWO

From the First Sunday in Lent to the Sunday after the Ascension

TRANSLATED AND EDITED BY

M. F. TOAL, D.D.

P.O. Box 612 Swedesboro, NJ 08085

Library of Congress Cataloging-in-Publication Data

Patristic homilies on the Gospels.
The Sunday sermons of the great Fathers: a manual of preaching, spiritual reading, and meditation / translated and edited by M. F. Toal.
p. cm.
Originally published Patristic homilies on the Gospels. Chicago: Regnery, 1955-1963.
Contains Saint Thomas Aquinas' Catena aurea.
Includes bibliographical references and indexes.
Contents: v. 1. From the first Sunday of Advent to Quinquagesima—v. 2. From the first Sunday in Lent to the Sunday after the Ascension—v. 3. From Pentecost to the tenth Sunday after Pentecost—v. 4. From the eleventh Sunday after Pentecost to the twenty-fourth and last Sunday after Pentecost.
ISBN 1-886412-14-6 (set: alk. paper). — ISBN 1-886412-15-4 (v. 1: alk. paper). — ISBN 1-886412-16-2 (v. 2: alk. paper). — ISBN 1-886412-17-0 (v. 3: alk. paper). — ISBN 1-886412-18-9 (v. 4: alk paper)
1. Bible. N.T. Gospels—Sermons. 2. Sermons, English. 3. Church year sermons. 4. Bible. N.T. Gospels—Commentaries. 5. Fathers of the church. I. Toal, M. F. II. Thomas, Aquinas. Saint, 1225?-1274. Catena aurea. English. III. Title.
BS2555.A2T6 1997
252'.011 —dc21 96-44004
CIP

2 3 4 5 6 7 8 9 10 Printing/Year 00 99 98

For information write Preservation Press:
P.O. Box 612, Swedesboro, NJ 08085

TO

OUR LADY OF WALSINGHAM

WHO KEPT ALL THESE THINGS IN HER HEART

FOREWORD TO THE FIRST VOLUME

THE author of the present work has had as his purpose to put into the hands of his fellow priests material of incomparable value, in a form easy of access, with a view to aiding them in the sacred ministry of preaching. This apostolic ministry is the one on which all else depends in the mission of the Church for the salvation of souls.

A large portion of it will always consist in homilies on the Gospels of the Sundays and Principal Feasts. Father Toal, in this first volume, has in view this sector of the preacher's work. For the Gospel of each Sunday and Feast he has brought together from the most reliable sources, and translated, all that he thought to be best and most useful in the homilies and expositions of the Fathers and of the Angel of the Schools.

Nothing more suited to his noble purpose could be conceived. The word of God contained in Scripture, and especially in the Gospels, has been given to the Church for the instruction of men. Sacred Tradition guided by the Spirit of God has expounded it in the writings of the Holy Fathers and Doctors.

Father Toal has placed in the easiest possible reach of the busy priest this treasure house of sacred lore, this quintessence of the doctrine of Tradition on each Gospel. What he supplies may, of course, not be all that may be usefully known in relation to it, but it is, and by long odds, the most important thing. A sermon well prepared on the matter here supplied cannot fail to be learned, solid, simple and effective.

What more can be said in praise of the utility of Father Toal's contribution? We shall all be grateful to him, and *his reward will indeed be great* (Mt. v. 12).

MICHAEL BROWNE, O.P.
Master of the Sacred
Apostolic Palace

Vatican
24 *November*, 1954

BIBLIOGRAPHY AND ABBREVIATIONS

Bibliotheca Patrum Concionatoria of P. Francois Combefis O.P. Paris 1681	BPC
Migne's Patrologiae Cursus Completus	
Series Graeca. Edition Paris 1886. Vols. 161	PG
Series Latina. Edition Paris 1844–66. Vols. 221	PL
Corpus Scriptorum Ecclesiasticorum Latinorum	CSEL
Catena Aurea Sancti Thomae	
Editio Joannis Nicolae O.P. Lyons 1686	CA
(A complete edition in English of the Catena Aurea is in course of preparation.—Ed.)	
Catena Sexaginta-quinque Graecorum Patrum in Lucam, Quae Quatuor simul Evangelistarum introduxit Explicationem. Luce ac latinitate donata a Balthasare Corderio Soc. Jesu. Antwerp 1628	Catena GP
Catena Patrum Graecorum in S. Joannem, ex antiquissimo Graeco codice MS nuncprimum in lucem edita, a Balthasare Corderio Soc. Jesu. Antwerp 1630	Catena GP
Graffin, Patrologia Syriaca	GPS
Vossio, Sti Ephraem Syri Opera Omnia, Cologne 1616	Vossio S. Eph.
Graffin, Patrologia Orientalis	GPO
Denzinger, Enchiridion Symbolorum 1928	Denz.
Enchiridion Biblicum, 1954	EB
Dictionnaire de Theologie Catholique	DTC
Clavis Patrum Latinorum, Sacris Erudiri III, 1051	Clavis
Pour Revaloriser Migne, Tables Rectificatives, par Mgr. Glorieux, Lille 1952	PRM
Etude, Textes, G. Morin, Maredsous 1913	
Faure, Glossarium	
A Glossary of Later Latin to A.D. 600, compiled by Alexander Souter, Oxford 1949	GLL
Mediaeval Latin Word List, Baxter and Johnson, Oxford 1947	
Texts and Studies	
Altaner, Patrologie, 1951	

Note on the Arrangement of This Book

For each Sunday or Feast Day in the book there is given the Gospel of the Day, and after that the parallel passages from other gospels where such passages exist. In every case these are followed by an exposition of the Gospel taken from the Catena Aurea of St Thomas Aquinas, which in turn is followed by a selection of sermons on the Gospel.

CONTENTS

	Page
FOREWORD TO THE FIRST VOLUME	vii
FIRST SUNDAY OF LENT	1
SECOND SUNDAY OF LENT	37
THIRD SUNDAY OF LENT	74
FOURTH SUNDAY OF LENT	100
PASSION SUNDAY	129
PALM SUNDAY	157
IN THE HOLY NIGHT OF THE PASCH	185
EASTER SUNDAY	211
LOW SUNDAY	265
SECOND SUNDAY AFTER EASTER	290
THIRD SUNDAY AFTER EASTER	321
FOURTH SUNDAY AFTER EASTER	337
FIFTH SUNDAY AFTER EASTER AND THE ROGATION DAYS	372
ASCENSION DAY	410
SUNDAY WITHIN THE OCTAVE OF THE ASCENSION	441
INDEX	461

FIRST SUNDAY OF LENT

I. St Ambrose: The Acceptable Time

II. St Ambrose: The Season of Penance

III. St John Chrysostom: Exposition of Today's Gospel

IV. St Cyril of Alexandria: The Preparation for the Pasch

V. St Leo the Great: Lent the Season of Purification

VI. St Gregory the Great: On the Gospel of the Sunday

THE GOSPEL OF THE SUNDAY

Matthew iv. 1–11

At that time, Jesus was led by the Spirit into the desert, to be tempted by the devil. And when he had fasted forty days and forty nights, afterwards he was hungry. And the tempter coming said to him: If thou be the Son of God, command that these stones be made bread. Who answered and said: It is written, *not in bread alone doth man live, but in every word that proceedeth from the mouth of God*. Then the devil took him up into the holy city, and set him upon the pinnacle of the temple, and said to him: if thou be the Son of God, cast thyself down, for it is written: *That he hath given his angels charge over thee, and in their hands shall they bear thee up, lest perhaps thou dash thy foot against a stone*. Jesus said to him: It is written again: *Thou shalt not tempt the Lord thy God*. Again the devil took him up into a very high mountain, and showed him all the kingdoms of the world, and the glory of them, and said to him: All these will I give thee, if falling down thou wilt adore me. Then Jesus saith to him: Begone Satan: For it is written: *The Lord thy God shalt thou adore, and him only shalt thou serve*. Then the devil left him; and behold angels came and ministered to him.

PARALLEL GOSPELS

Mark i. 12–13

And immediately the Spirit drove him out into the desert. And he was in the desert forty days and forty

Luke iv. 1–13

And Jesus being full of the Holy Ghost, returned from the Jordan, and was led by the Spirit into the nights, and was tempted by Satan; and he was with beasts, and the angels ministered to him.

desert, for the space of forty days; and was tempted by the devil. And he ate nothing in those days; and when they were ended he was hungry. And the devil said to him: If thou be the Son of God, say to this stone that it be made bread. And Jesus answered him: It is written, *that man liveth not by bread alone, but by every word of God.* And the devil led him into a high mountain, and showed him all the kingdoms of the world in a moment of time; and he said to him: To thee will I give all this power, and the glory of them; for to me they are delivered, and to whom I will, I give them. If thou therefore wilt adore before me, all shall be thine. And Jesus answering said to him: It is written: *Thou shalt adore the Lord thy God, and him only shalt thou serve.* And he brought him to Jerusalem, and set him on a pinnacle of the temple, and he said to him: If thou be the Son of God, cast thyself from hence. For it is written, that *he hath given his angels charge over thee, that they keep thee.* And that *in their hands they shall bear thee up, lest perhaps thou dash thy foot against a stone.* And Jesus answering said to him: It is said: *Thou shalt not tempt the Lord thy God.* And all the temptation being ended, the devil departed from him for a time.

Exposition from the Catena Aurea

1. *Then Jesus was led by the Spirit into the desert . . .*

Chrysostom, *Opus Imp., Hom.* 5: When the Lord had been baptized in water by John he was then led by the Spirit into the desert, to be baptized in the fire of temptation. Hence is it said: *Then Jesus was led . . . to be tempted by the devil. Then,* i.e., when the Father had proclaimed Him from heaven, saying: *This is my beloved son.*

Chrysostom, *Hom.* 13 *in Matt.*: Who therefore among you who is even more tempted after baptism should not be troubled. It is for this you have received arms: not to stand at ease, but to fight. God will not then ward you off from temptation; and this He does for many reasons. First, that you may so learn that you are now stronger. Then, lest you be exalted by the greatness of His gifts. Thirdly, that the devil may receive proof you have wholly renounced him. Fourthly, that by this trial you may become yet stronger. Fifthly, that you may receive an indication of the treasure you have received: for the devil would not so pursue you, to tempt you, did he not see that you had now come to a higher dignity.

HILARY, *in Matt. ii*: The temptations of the devil are specially directed against those who have been sanctified: for victory over the just is more desirable to him. GREGORY, *hom* 16 *on the Gospels*: Some are disposed to hesitate as to what spirit it was led Jesus into the desert, because of the words: *Then the devil took him into the holy city*. But it may correctly and without any question be accepted, that we may believe that He was led by the Holy Spirit, so that by His own Spirit He should be led where the evil spirit would find Him; to tempt Him.

AUGUSTINE, *The Trinity IV*, 13: Why did He allow Himself to be tempted? That He might as our Mediator help us to overcome temptations; not alone by assisting us, but also by His example. CHRYSOSTOM, *Op. Imp*: He is *led* by the Holy Spirit, not as a lower being is led under the command of a greater; for not he alone is said to be led who is led by the power of another, but he also who is convinced by the reasoned persuasions of another; as was said of Andrew: *He findeth first his brother, Simon, . . . and brought him to Jesus* (Jn. i. 41). JEROME, *in Matt.*: He is not however led as one unwilling, or as a captive, but led by the desire to combat.

CHRYSOSTOM, *ex Op. Imp*: The devil goes out against man to tempt him. But since the devil cannot attack Christ, Christ goes out towards the devil. Hence we read: *To be tempted by the devil.* GREGORY, *as above*: We must keep in mind that temptation is brought to fulfilment by three stages: suggestion, delight, consent. And we in temptation generally fall through delight, and then through consent; for being begotten of the sin of the flesh we bear within us that through which we suffer conflict. But God, Incarnate in the womb of a Virgin, came into the world without sin, and so suffers no conflict within Himself. He could therefore be tempted by suggestion, but the delight of sin could never touch His mind. So all these temptations of the devil were from without, not from within Him.

CHRYSOSTOM, *Hom.* 13 *in Matt.*: It is when he sees us alone that the devil especially harasses us with temptation. So was it that seeing the woman without her husband he tempted her in the beginning. Accordingly, an opportunity in which to tempt Jesus is provided for the devil when Jesus is *led into the desert*.

GLOSS: This is the desert between Jerusalem and Jericho, where robbers were at this time wont to hide; and it is called Damin, *the place of blood*, because of the blood robbers had shed there. Again, when a certain man had gone down from Jerusalem to Jericho, it is recorded of him that *he fell among robbers*: this being a figure of Adam, who was overcome and wounded by the demons. It was fitting therefore that Christ should defeat the devil there where the devil is said, figuratively, to have defeated man.

CHRYSOSTOM, *ex Op. Imp*: Not alone is Christ led by the Spirit into the desert, but so likewise are all the sons of God who have within them the Holy Spirit. For they are not content to sit idle; the Holy Spirit urges them, to take on some great task, such as to go out into the desert; going as it were to encounter the devil; for there injustice, in which the devil delights, is to be found. For all good is outside the world and the flesh, since it is not according to the will of the world or of the flesh. So to such a desert all the sons of God go out, that they may be tempted. For example, if you should resolve not to marry, the Holy Spirit leads thee into the desert; that is, outside the boundaries of the world and of the flesh, to be tempted by the concupiscence of the flesh. For how can he be tempted by desire who is all day with his wife? We must know that the sons of God are not tempted by the devil, unless they have gone out into the desert. The sons of the devil, held fast in the world, and by the flesh, yield and are brought to naught. A good man, if he have a wife, does not commit fornication, but is content with his wife; but the wicked, though he possess a wife, commits fornication, not content with his wife. And so it is you will observe with all things. The sons of the devil do not go out against the devil, to be tempted. Why should he go forth to combat who desires not to win? But they that are worthier, the sons of God, they go out against him, beyond the limits of the flesh, because they seek the glory of victory. And so in this sense also Christ went out against the devil; to be tested by him.

CHRYSOSTOM, *Hom.* 13 *in Matt.*: That you may learn how great a good is fasting, and how effective a shield against the devil, and also, that after receiving baptism it behoves us not to incline towards pleasure, but towards mortification, He fasted; not because He needed to, but to teach us. CHRYSOSTOM, *ex Op Imp*: And that He might lay down the length of our Lenten fast, He fasted for forty days and forty nights. CHRYSOSTOM, *hom. in Matt.*: He did not prolong His fast beyond that of Moses and Elias, lest His taking on of our flesh might seem a thing not to be believed.

GREGORY: He, the Author of all things, for forty days tasted no food. Let us likewise, as far as we are able, afflict our flesh by abstinence during the season of Lent. A fast of forty days is observed, since the perfection of the Decalogue is completed by the four books of the Holy Gospel; ten multiplied by four being forty. Or, again: because this mortal body is made up from four elements; and because of its pleasures we are bound by the commandments of the Lord, made known in the Decalogue, it is therefore fitting that we who through the desires of the flesh despise the commands of God should chastise this same flesh four times ten times.

Or, as by the Law men had to offer up tithes of their possessions, so ought we strive to offer tithes of our days. For from the first Sunday of Lent, until the joys of the Paschal feast, there are six weeks, which are two and forty days, from which, since the six days of Sunday are subtracted from the fast, there remain but thirty-six days. Since the year continues for three hundred and sixty-five days, we do penance for thirty-six days, as though offering to God a tenth of our year.

AUGUSTINE, *Book* 83 *de Quaest.* 81: Or, again: The whole purpose of wisdom is to know the creature and the Creator. The Trinity is the Creator, Father, Son, and Holy Ghost. The creature is partly invisible; as the soul, to which a threefold activity is assigned; for we are commanded by God to love in a threefold way: with thy whole heart, thy whole soul, and all thy mind; partly visible: as the body, to which a quaternary property belongs: heat and cold, liquid and dry. The number ten, therefore, which pervades all life, enlarged four times, that is, multiplied by the number that pertains to the body, because through the body government is administered, makes the number forty; whose corresponding divisors added together make fifty. For one and two and four and five and eight and ten, which are parts of the quadragenary number, added together are fifty. Accordingly, the time in which we grieve and mourn is represented by the quadragenary number. The state of blessedness, in which shall be our joy, is represented by the celebration of Quinquagesima; that is, from Easter to Pentecost.

AUGUSTINE, *Sermon 6 in Lent*: Not because Christ, after He had received the baptism of John, began at once to fast, must we believe that a rule of observance was given us; that when the baptism of Christ is received it is necessary to fast. But when the contest with the tempter grows sharp, then must we fast, so that the body may discharge the Christian duty of warfare against the world, by penance, and the soul seek victory in humiliation. CHRYSOSTOM, *ex Op. Imp*: But the Lord knew the mind of the devil, that he wished to try Him. For he had heard of Him when Christ was born into the world; the angels had proclaimed Him, the Shepherds borne witness, the Magi had come to adore Him, and John later had pointed Him out. Hence the Lord went towards him, not as God, but as man; rather indeed as God and man. For it was not the nature of man to fast forty days; nor of God to eat at times. Hence He fasted, lest He be clearly seen to be God, and so put an end to the devil's hope of tempting Him, and thus prevent His victory over him. Hence there follows: *afterwards he was hungry*.

V. 2. *And when he had fasted forty days and forty nights, afterwards . . .*

HILARY *in Matt.* ii: For He was hungry *after* forty days; not *during* the forty days. Accordingly, when the Lord hungered, it was not that the consequences of his abstinence overtook Him, but that He surrendered the Man Christ to the order of His nature. For not by God was the devil to be overcome, but by flesh; which circumstance reveals that, at the completion of the forty days during which He would, following on His Passion, remain in the world, he would again hunger: for the salvation of men; at which time He bore back to the Father the gift He awaited, namely, the humanity He had assumed.

V. 3. *And the tempter said to him: If thou be the Son of God . . .*

And the tempter coming said to Him: If thou be the Son of God. CHRYSOSTOM. *ex Op. Imp*: For the devil had despaired, seeing Christ fasting for forty days; but perceiving that afterwards He was hungry, he began to hope again; and so there follows: *and the tempter coming . . .* If therefore you have fasted, and you suffer temptation, do not say to yourself, 'I have lost the fruit of my fasting.' For if your fast has not availed that you be not tempted, it will yet avail that you be not overcome in temptation.

GREGORY: But looking at the actual order of the temptation, let us see how wondrously we have been freed from temptation. For the ancient enemy tempted the first man by gluttony, when he persuaded him to eat the forbidden fruit of the tree; by vain glory, when he said, *you shall be as Gods* (Gen. iii, 5); by avarice, when he said: *knowing good and evil.* For avarice is not solely the desire of money, but also of pride of place, when dignity is sought without measure. By these means he laid low the first man; by the same means was he defeated by the Second Man. For he tempted through gluttony, when he said: *command that these stones be made bread*; by vainglory, when he said: *If thou be the Son of God*; by greed of place, when he showed Him the kingdoms of the world, saying: *all these will I give thee.*

AMBROSE *on Luke, iv.* 18: He made a beginning there where he had already overcome, namely, with gluttony; hence he said: *If thou be the Son of God, command that these stones be made bread.* What is the meaning of such a beginning, unless that he already knew that the Son of God was to come? But that He had come, in the infirmity of a body, he did not suspect. So in one sense his speech is a seeking for information; in another it is the speech of one who tempts. So he here both professes to believe in God, and seeks at the same time to deceive a man.

HILARY: In tempting Him therefore he lays down that condition, as to the thing to be done, whereby he would acknowledge in God the Might of His Power, from the changing of stones into bread; and in man, by offering the delight of bread, would make sport of the prolonged suffering of the man who was hungry. JEROME: But you are held fast by two contrary things, O demon: if it is in His power to make stones into bread, then in vain do you tempt Him Who has such power; if He cannot do this, you seek in vain to know if He be the Son of God.

CHRYSOSTOM, *ex Op. Imp*: Just as the devil blinds all men, so now he is, invisibly, blinded by Christ. After forty days he sees one Who hungers; and throughout forty days he has not formed an idea of who it is that now hungers. When he inclined to think He is not the Son of God, he did not consider that that

Mighty Champion would condescend to the things that are lowly. A weak man cannot rise up to the things of the mighty. More then from this, that for so many days He had not hungered, ought he to have known that He was God, than from this, that after so many days He was hungry, that He was man. He should the more readily have known He was God, because through so many days He had not hungered, than that He was man, because after forty days He was hungry. But you will say: Moses and Elias fasted forty days, and they were men. But they while they fasted and persevered were hungry. He for forty days was not hungry, but only *afterwards*. Not to eat, and to hunger, is part of human infirmity. Not to hunger, belongs to the divine nature.

V. 4. *Who answered and said: It is written . . .*

JEROME: It was the purpose of Christ to triumph by means of humility. LEO, *Sermon I in Quad*: And so He overcame the enemy by the testimonies of the Law, not by the strength of His Might; and for this end: that He might the more honour man, and punish yet more his enemy since the enemy of the human race would be punished, not as it were by God, but by man. Hence: *Who answered and said: It is written: Not in bread alone doth man live, but in every word that proceedeth from the mouth of God.*

GREGORY: So the Lord, when tempted by the devil, made answer in the precepts of the Divine Word. And He that could cast His enemy down to the abyss, showed not His Power, that He might give us an example: so that as often as we suffer from evil men, we may be turned rather towards the words of divine truth than towards vengeance.

CHRYSOSTOM, *ex Op. Imp*: He did not say: Not in bread alone do I live, lest it appear to be said of Himself; but, not in bread alone doth man live, so that the devil might say: if He is the Son of God, He conceals Himself, so that He reveals not His Power; if He is a man, He acts astutely, so that He reveals not that He cannot do this. RHABANUS MAURUS: He took this testimony from Deuteronomy. If anyone therefore does not eat of the Word of God, the same shall not live; for as the human body cannot live without earthly bread, so the soul cannot live without the Word of God. A word is said to proceed from the mouth of God when He makes His Will known through the Sacred Scripture.

V. 5. *Then the devil took him up into the Holy City . . .*

CHRYSOSTOM, *ex Op. Imp*: Since the devil could not, from Christ's answer, learn with certainty whether Christ was God or man, he drew Him on to another temptation; saying to himself: This man, who is not overcome by hunger, though he is not the Son of God, is yet a holy man. For men who are holy are able to resist hunger. Yet even when they defeat the cravings of the flesh they fall through vain glory. So he began to tempt him through vain glory. Accordingly there follows: *The devil took him up . . .*

JEROME: This taking up does not result from the weakness of Our

Lord, but from the pride of His enemy, who believed that the will of the Saviour was subject to need. RHABANUS: Jerusalem was called the Holy City. The Temple of God was there, and the Holy of Holies, and worship according to the Law of Moses. REMIGIUS: By which it is shown that the devil lies in wait for the faithful even in holy places.

GREGORY: When we read it written down, that God made Man was *taken up* into the Holy City, men's ears are grievously shocked. But the devil is the head of all evil men. Why then should we be shocked if He suffers Himself to be led to a high mountain by the devil, Who permitted Himself to be crucified by his followers? GLOSS: The devil ever leads up to *high places*, through vain glory, that he may then cast us down. So there follows: *And set him upon the pinnacle of the temple.*

REMIGIUS: The pinnacle was the seat of the Doctors. The temple did not possess a high roof ridge or summit, such as our houses possess, but was flat on top, after the manner of Palestinian houses. And in the temple itself there were three stories. You must know that the pinnacle was placed on the floor, and on each floor there was a pinnacle. Whichever pinnacle therefore he set Him upon, we know that he set Him upon one from which he could fall down. GLOSS: Note that all these things took place in a bodily manner. For if we compare the words it will seem very likely that the devil appeared in the form of a man.

CHRYSOSTOM, *as above*: But you may say: How could he set Him bodily above the temple in the sight of all? But perhaps the devil so took Him up that He might be seen by all, but He, unknown to the devil, so disposed that He was seen by no one. GLOSS: Since he was seeking to deceive Him through vain glory he set Him upon a pinnacle of the temple; for in the seat of the Doctors he had already deceived many by this temptation; and so he thought that This Man, when placed there, might be caught by pride. Accordingly he says:

V. 6. *And said to him: If thou be the Son of God, cast thyself down . . .* JEROME: In all the temptations the devil strives to find out if He is the Son of God. But he says, *cast thyself* down; for the voice of the devil, by which he seeks ever that man shall fall, can persuade men to cast themselves down, but cannot cast them down. CHRYSOSTOM, *as above*: How could he learn through this suggestion whether Christ was the Son of God or not? For to leap through the air is not a work proper to the Son of God; for it is a useless thing to do. If then anyone should, through being urged in this way, so fly, he would do this only from foolish vanity, and so would belong to the devil rather than to God. If therefore it suffices to a prudent man to be what he is, and if he has no need to appear other than he is, how much more the Son of God, Whom no man may know as He is in Himself?

AMBROSE *in Luke IV*: But as Satan changes himself into an angel of light, and even from the holy Scriptures prepares snares for Christians, so now he uses the testimonies of

Scripture, not to instruct, but to deceive. So there follows: *For it is written: That he hath given his angels charge over thee.* JEROME: This we read in the ninetieth psalm; but there the prophecy was not spoken of Christ, but of the just man; so the devil has quoted the Scriptures dishonestly.

CHRYSOSTOM, *ex Op. Imp*: For indeed the Son of God is not borne up by the hands of angels; rather it is He that sustains the angels; and if He should be borne up by the hands of angels, it is not, as though He were a creature, *lest he dash his foot against a stone*, but out of reverence; because He is the Lord. O Devil, since you have read that the Son of God is borne up by hands, have you not also read that, *he shall walk upon the asp and the basilisk*? But he quotes the first passage out of evil pride; he is silent regarding the second because he is cunning.

CHRYSOSTOM, *Hom.* 13 *in Matt.*: Observe how the Scriptural testimonies are correctly quoted by the Lord, but with evil intent by the devil. For it is not because it was written that, *he hath give his angels charge of thee*, that any one is thereby counselled to cast himself down, and destroy himself. GLOSS: So it must be explained in this way. The Scripture says of any good man that, *he has given the angels*, that is, the ministry of spirits, *charge over him*, so that *in their hands*, that is, by their aid, they shall *bear him up*, and protect him, for fear he *dash his foot*, that is, the desires of his soul, *against a stone*, that is, against the Law, which was inscribed on tables of stone. Or, by a stone is signified every occasion of sin and fall from grace.

RHABANUS: Let us observe that Our Saviour, though He allowed Himself to be set upon a pinnacle of the temple, refused to cast Himself down at his command; giving us an example that whosoever should tell us to go upwards, along the way of truth, we ought to obey. But should anyone wish us to cast ourselves down, from the heights of truth and virtue to the depths of sin and vice, let us not listen to him. JEROME: He breaks the false arrows of the devil, which he drew from the Scriptures, upon the true shield of the Scriptures. Hence we have:

V. 7. *Jesus said to him: It is written again: Thou shalt not tempt . . .*

HILARY *in Matt.* 3: Crushing the artifices of the devil He shows Himself as God and Lord: CHRYSOSTOM, *ex Op. Imp*: He did not say: Thou shalt not tempt Me, the Lord Thy God, but: *Thou shalt not tempt the Lord thy God*; which every man of God tempted by the devil could have said: since whoever tempts a man of God tempts God. RHABANUS: Or again: it was suggested to Him, as to a man, that He should seek by some sign to test the power of the Lord. THEODOTUS: For he tempts God who unreasonably exposes himself to danger. JEROME: And let us note that the Lord draws His answers only from the Book of Deuteronomy; that He might set forth the mysteries of the second law.

V. 8. *Again the devil took him up into a very high mountain . . .*

CHRYSOSTOM, *ex Op. Imp*: The devil, still in doubt, because of the second answer, goes on to the third temptation. Christ had broken the net of gluttony, turned aside that of vainglory. Now he tries the snare of avarice: *And the devil took etc.*; which the devil, going all about the earth, knew was higher than all other mountains. For the higher the mountain, the wider the extent of the earth that is seen; hence: *and showed him all the kingdoms of the world, and the glory of them.* He so showed him, not that he could see the kingdoms themselves, or their cities, or peoples, or their silver and gold, but rather the parts of the earth in which each kingdom or city lay. As for example, if going up to some very high place, I, with finger extended, say to you: see, there is Rome, or Alexandria. I do not so show it that you see the cities themselves, but the part of the earth in which they are situated. So could the devil point out to Christ each single place, and unfold by word the glory and state of each kingdom. For that is also said to be shown which is unfolded to the understanding.

ORIGEN, *Hom.* 30 *on Luke*: Or, again: We must not think that in showing Him the kingdoms of the world he showed Him, for example, the kingdoms of the Persians, and of the Jews. But he showed Him his own kingdoms, as he reigned in the world that is, how some are ruled by fornication, some by avarice. REMIGIUS: He describes gold, silver, precious stones, and temporal goods, as, *the glory of them.* RHABANUS: These things the devil showed to the Lord, not that he could increase the extent of what He before saw, or reveal to Him what He knew not, but, laying before Him the vanity of worldly pomp, which he loved, and declaring it in words to be beautiful and desirable, he sought to awaken in Christ the love of it. GLOSS: Who looked upon it, not with the eye of desire, as we do, but as physicians look without danger upon bodily infirmities.

V. 9. *And said to him: all these will I give thee.*

JEROME: Arrogant and full of pride, he speaks from boastfulness. For *he* could not give all these kingdoms; since we know that many holy men were made kings by God. CHRYSOSTOM, *ex Op. Imp*: But the things that are acquired wrongly, by iniquity, throughout the world; as, for example, riches acquired by theft or by perjury, these the devil bestows. The devil therefore may give riches, not however to whom he wills, but to those who desire to receive them from him.

REMIGIUS: Remarkable is the empty folly of the devil. He promises to give earthly kingdoms to Him Who, on His own followers, bestows heavenly ones; and the glory of the world on Him Who is the Lord of heavenly glory. AMBROSE: But ambition has its peculiar tribulations. For, that it may lord it over others, it must first be subservient; it bows itself down in submission, that it may rule in honour; and in striving to be raised higher sinks ever lower. Hence aptly follows: *If falling down thou wilt adore me.* GLOSS: See here the ancient pride of the devil. For as in the beginning he desired to make himself equal with God, so here he seeks to usurp the worship that is due to God, saying: *if falling down thou wilt adore me.* He therefore that will adore the devil falls down before him.

V. 10. *Then Jesus saith to him: Begone, Satan.*

CHRYSOSTOM, *ex Op. Imp*: By which he puts an end to the devil's tempting, so that he proceeds no further. JEROME: Not in the same sense, as many think, were Peter and Satan rebuked. For to Peter was said: *Go behind me, Satan* (Mt. xvi, 23); that is, walk behind me, you who are not in accord with My Will. This other hears the words: *Begone, Satan*; to him, *behind Me*, is not said, so that here one may understand the words: *depart into everlasting fire*, which was prepared for thee and thy angels.[1] REMIGIUS: Or, according to other codices: *Go behind* (vade retro), remember, and think upon, the wretchedness you have fallen into.

CHRYSOSTOM. *ex Op. Imp*: See how when Christ suffered the affront of the temptations, the devil saying to him: *if thou be the Son of God, cast thyself down*, He was not troubled, nor did He rebuke the devil. But now, when the devil dares to usurp the honour due to God, He hardens His heart and rebukes him, saying: *begone, Satan*; so that from this example we may learn to bear with courage the injuries done to us, but never to endure to hear injuries against the honour of God. For to be patient in one's own afflictions is praiseworthy; but to pass over affronts to God is a grievous impiety.

JEROME: The devil, in saying to the Saviour: if *falling down . . .*, hears instead that he rather should adore Him, as his Lord and God. AUGUSTINE, *serm. contra Arianorum*, 29: Hence there follows: *for it is written: The Lord thy God thou shalt adore, and him only shalt thou serve.* The Trinity is indeed the Lord our God, to Which alone we owe the service of our adoration. AUGUSTINE, *City of God* 10, 1: By the word *service* we understand, the honour due to God. The word *latria*, wherever it is translated in the Holy Scriptures, is interpreted as service. But the service which is rendered to men (and in accordance with which the Apostle bade servants be subject to their masters) is expressed by another Greek word, *dulia*. But *latria*, however, always, or so frequently that it is almost always, means the subjection that relates to the worship of God.

CHRYSOSTOM, *ex Op. Imp*: The devil, as can reasonably be supposed, withdrew; though not as it were in obedience to the command, but because the divinity of Christ, and the Holy Spirit that was within Him, drove him from thence. Hence follows: *then the devil left Him.* What affords us personal consolation is that the devil tempts those who serve God, not as long as he wills, but only as Christ permits. Though He permits him for a while to tempt them, because of our weakness He banishes him.

V. 11. *Then the devil left him; and behold angels came and ministered to him.*

AUGUSTINE, *City of God*, IX, 21: But after His temptations the good angels, who are feared by the unclean spirits, ministered to the Lord, and through this it became more and more apparent to the demons how great He was. Hence: *And behold angels came and ministered to him.* CHRYSOSTOM, *ex Op. Imp*: He did not say, and *the angels descending*, that he might show they were ever present on the earth for His service, but that on this occasion, at the word of the Lord, they withdrew that they might give place to the devil, lest he, seeing the angels round about Him, would not dare approach. In what manner they ministered to Him it is impossible to know: whether in healing infirmities, or in the purification of souls, or in the banishment of evil spirits; hence, while He appeared to perform these signs, they were being wrought by them. But it is plain that not because of His need did they minister to Him, but in reverence to His Majesty. For it is not said that they assisted, but that they ministered to Him.

GREGORY: In these events both natures of the One Person are revealed. For it is as man that the devil tempts Him; and the Same is God to Whom the angels minister.

CHRYSOSTOM, *ex Op. Imp*: Now let us briefly recall what is the meaning of the temptations. To fast is to abstain from an evil thing; that you hunger means the desire of it; its enjoyment is bread. He therefore who changes sin into his pleasure, changes stone into bread. Let him then make answer to the devil, that not in the sole enjoyment of pleasure does man live, but in the observance of the commandments of God. When however someone has become puffed up, believing himself holy, he is as it were taken up above the temple; and when he thinks he is standing upon the summit of holiness, he has been set upon a pinnacle of the temple.

And this temptation follows the first, because the overcoming of temptation causes pride, and so may cause boasting. You see how Christ of His own Will fasted; yet the devil took Him up into the temple. You also freely practise a praiseworthy self-denial, but do not flatter yourself that you are then raised to the summit of holiness. Turn from the pride of the heart and you will not then come to ruin of the soul. The ascent of the mountain is the going up towards the heights of riches, and to the glory of this world which leads on to pride of heart. For when you have set your heart on riches: which is to go up into a high mountain: you begin to think of ways and means to acquire them; and it is then that the prince of this world will show you the glory of his kingdom. Thirdly, he will furnish you with motives why you must, to attain them, serve him, and neglect the service of God and of virtue.

HILARY: Here we are shown that we too, when we have repulsed the devil, and crushed his head under our heel, shall not want for the ministry of angels, and the friendly aid of the heavenly powers. AUGUSTINE, *The Harmony of the Gospels*: Luke has also recorded these temptations, but not in the same order. So it is uncertain which of the two latter temptations took place first. Whether the kingdoms of the earth were first shown, and afterwards He was set upon a pinnacle of the temple, or vice-versa. It is not however a point of consequence as long as it is plain that both events took place. GLOSS: But that which Luke states seems more in accord with the facts; Matthew relates the temptations according to what was done to Adam.

I. ST AMBROSE, BISHOP AND DOCTOR

The Acceptable Time[2]

1. Behold, Dearly Beloved, the sacred days are drawing near, *the acceptable time*, of which it is written: *Behold, now is the acceptable time; behold, now is the day of salvation* (II Cor. vi. 2). And so you must be more earnest in prayer and in almsgiving, in fasting and in watching. He that till now has given alms, in these days let him give more; for as water quencheth a flaming fire, so does almsgiving wipe out sin (Eccles. iii. 33). He that till now fasted and prayed, let him fast and pray still more: for there are certain sins which are *not cast out, except by prayer and fasting* (Mt. xvii. 20).

Should anyone cherish anger towards another, let him forgive from his heart. Should anyone take unjustly what belongs to another, let him restore it; and if not fourfold, at least that which he has taken; if he desires God to be merciful to himself (Lk. xix. 8). And though a Christian should abstain at all times from cursings and revilings, from oaths, from excessive laughter, and from idle words, he must do this especially in these holy days, which are set apart so that, during these forty days, he may by penance wipe out the sins of the whole year.

2. Let you believe, and believe firmly, that if in these days you have made a thorough confession of your sins, and done penance as we have told you, you shall receive from Our Most Merciful Lord the pardon of all your offences; as did the Ninivites, who earned deliverance from their afflictions by doing penance in sackcloth and ashes (Jn. iii). So you also, following their example, if you cry out with all your heart to the Lord, you will invoke His Mercy on you, so that serene and joyful you will celebrate the day of the Lord's Resurrection, and, thus blessed, you will after this life cross over to your heavenly home, by the grace of Our Lord Jesus Christ, Who with the Father and the Holy Ghost livest and reignest, world without end. Amen.

II. ST AMBROSE, BISHOP AND DOCTOR

The Season of Penance[3]

1. Behold, now is the appointed time, in which you must confess your sins to God, and to the priest, and by prayer and by fasting, by tears and by almsgiving, wipe them away. Why should a sinner be ashamed to make known his sins, since they are already known and manifest to God, and to His angels, and even to the blessed in heaven? Confession delivers the soul from death. Confession opens the door to heaven. Confession brings us hope of salvation. Because of this the

Scripture says: *First tell thy iniquities, that you may be justified* (Is. xliii. 26). Here we are shown that the man will not be saved who, during his life, does not confess his sins. Neither will that confession deliver you which is made without true repentance. For true repentance is grief of heart and sorrow of soul because of the evils a man has committed. True repentance causes us to grieve over our offences, and to grieve over them with the firm intention of never committing them again.

2. And though every day a man lives may rightly be a day of repentance, yet is it in these days more becoming, more appropriate, to confess our sins, to fast, and to give alms to the poor; since in these days you may wash clean the sins of the whole year. Therefore I counsel all of you, and I exhort each one of you singly, to repair whatever you know within your soul is blameworthy. Whosoever among you discerns within himself what is unworthy in a Christian, let him correct it; and where he has given less than his due, as where he has not faithfully paid his tithes. What does it mean to give tithes faithfully, but that no man should offer to God, either of his grain, or of his wine, or of the fruit of his trees, or of his sheep, or from his herds, or from his business, or even from the chase, what is defective or stunted. For of all substance the Lord bestows on a man, a tenth part He reserves to Himself. So it is not lawful to keep what the Lord has reserved to Himself. To thee He has given nine parts; for Himself He reserved a tenth. And if you do not give God His tenth part, God will take your nine parts from you.

Again, if anyone knows in his own heart that he has taken something unjustly from another, let him make amends by restoring what he has unjustly taken. For he that will not render to God His tenth, which He reserved to Himself, and to another man what he took from him unjustly, such a man no longer fears God, and does not know the meaning of true repentance, or of true confession of his sins.

3. Such a man cannot give an honest alms. It is good then, Brethren, to render to God what is His, and to your neighbour what belongs to him; so that when you give alms from the fruits of your own honest labour, you may obtain pardon of your sins, according to the word of God: *Redeem thou thy sins with alms, and thy iniquities with works of mercy to the poor* (Dan. iv. 24). And you should further know: *that as water quencheth a flaming fire, alms resisteth sins* (Ecclus. iii. 23).

And this you ought to do, since each according to his means should give to the needy; that is, he that has much should give much, and he that has but little ought to give a little; as the holy Tobias taught his son: *Give alms out of thy substance, and turn not away thy face from the poor: for so will it come to pass that the face of the Lord shall not be turned away from thee. According to thy ability be merciful. If thou have much give abundantly: if thou have little, take care to bestow willingly even a little. For thus thou storest up to thyself a good reward for the day of necessity* (Tob. iv. 7–10).

And with what earnestness, with what eagerness, should not the Christian give alms, so that he may hear at the day of judgement the words: *For I was hungry, and you gave me to eat; I was thirsty and you gave me to drink; I was a stranger, and you took me in: naked, and you covered me: sick, and you visited me: I was in prison and you came to me. Come, ye blessed of my Father* (Mt. xxv. 34–6). And if you will not do these works of mercy which I here recall to your minds, then on that day shall you hear: *Depart from me, ye cursed, into everlasting fire.*

4. Since these days will come I dare not refrain from speaking to you of the danger, of the great evil, that hangs over this multitude of people. Yet, if you do these works, He will say to you: *Come, ye blessed of My Father.* And what kind of Christian is it who will not fast, at least till nones,[4] during this season? Recall how the Ninivites required even of children at the breast that they too should fast, and their flocks and herds likewise, that all might be delivered from the danger that threatened them. What kind of Christian is he who though well and able refuses to fast with Moses, with Elias, and with the Lord? They will say: We cannot both work and fast. They cannot because they will not. Then let them work less that they may fast more. I warn you and I exhort you in the Lord, that none among you, unless a sick person or a child, eat or drink before the hour of nones, except on Sundays.

5. I counsel you also that he who is near the church, and can come, should hear Mass each day. And that he who can should come each evening to the recitation of matins. Let those who live far from the church try to come to matins each Sunday; that is, men and women, the young and old, and all except the sick; but let one or two remain at home to safeguard the house.

6. Let husband and wife live singly till the octave of the Pasch. Let him who has hate in his heart, or anger, against another, put it wholly from him; if he wishes to be saved. And every Sunday all Christians should offer Mass and communicate;[5] excepting those whom the priest has advised not to communicate. I counsel you that during Lent you should offer and communicate every day, or, as I said, at least every Sunday. And therefore let you lead a pure and holy life, so that you may be worthy to approach to Holy Communion. And you must understand that whatever it is that you deny yourself through fasting must be given entirely to the poor, not kept back for yourselves.

7. May Almighty God grant that you keep before you what I have told you, and that you fulfil it in deed; so that at the end of this life, and at the close of your labours, you may enter into eternal rest. May He grant you this Who created you, and sought at the price of His own blood to redeem you, Who livest and reignest world without end. Amen.

III. St John Chrysostom, Bishop and Doctor

Exposition of the Gospel[6]

Then Jesus was led by the Spirit into the desert, to be tempted by the devil.

Then! When? After the Descent of the Holy Spirit. After the Voice speaking from above had said: *This is my beloved Son, in whom I am well pleased* (Mt. iii. 17). And since he did everything in order to teach us, and suffered everything for the same reason, so here also He willed to be led by the Spirit into the desert, to meet the devil in combat, and so that no one should be shocked if, after receiving baptism, he suffers even severer temptations: as though something strange had happened; but that he may learn to stand firm and endure with fortitude what happens according to the ordinary rule of our life.

This is the reason you received arms; not to stand at ease, but to fight. And God will not prevent temptations from rushing against you. And this first that you may learn how stronger you are now than before. Then that you learn prudence; so as not to be overbold because of the greatness of the gifts you have received: for temptation will steady you. Thirdly, so that the evil demon, who is uncertain whether you have renounced him or not, may not be left in doubt, through this test of temptation, that you have abandoned him, and wholly renounced him. Fourthly, that you may become stronger, and more tempered than steel. And fifthly, that you may receive a kind of indication of how precious is the treasure you have been given. For the devil would not have attacked you had he not seen you now held in honour. It was because of this he attacked Adam, because he saw he was given great dignity. For this reason he attacked Job, because he saw him raised up and honoured by the God of all. It was because of this He Himself says: *Pray that ye enter not into temptation* (Mt. xxvi. 41).

For this reason the Evangelist speaks of Jesus as, not going, but as being *led*; and this was according to the design of our salvation: implying that we are not as it were to leap into temptation, but, if we are led there, to stand firm against it. And consider where it was the Spirit led Jesus. Not into a city, nor into the market place, but into the desert. For since He wished to attract the evil spirit, He gives him occasion, not alone from his hunger, but also from the place. For then especially will the devil attack us, when he sees us alone and separated from each other. It was in this way he attempted the woman in the beginning: approaching as she was alone, and her husband absent. For when he sees us in the company of others, and united, he does not dare attack us. For this special reason should we come frequently together: so that it shall be more difficult for the devil to attack us.

The devil therefore finds Him in the desert, in a pathless wilderness. For that it was a wilderness Mark conveys to us by the words: *And he was with beasts*. Consider with what craft and purpose of mind he draws near; and the opportunity he is seeking. He draws near to a Person who is not now fasting, but enduring hunger. He fasts that you may learn how efficacious fasting is, and what a weapon it is against the devil; and that after our baptism we should give ourselves, not to pleasures, not to drunkenness, not to the delights of the table, but to fasting. For this reason He fasted; not because He had need to fast, but to teach us. For before we were purified through baptism the pleasures of the stomach led us to sin. It is as if a physician, who has restored a sick man to health should command him to avoid what had brought on his sickness. So likewise did He introduce fasting after baptism.

For it was the intemperance of the stomach that drove Adam from Paradise, and provoked the Flood in the days of Noah, and sent thunderbolts against Sodom. And though they also committed fornication, yet the root of either chastisement was here; as Ezechias also tells us where he says: *Behold this was the iniquity of Sodom thy sister, fulness of bread, and abundance, and they were lifted up, and committed abominations* (Ezech. xvi. 49). And the Jews also; it was when they were filled with the delights of food that they then fell into and committed their greatest sins.

2. So He fasts for forty days, pointing out to us the remedy for our salvation. Nor does He exceed this length of time, lest the strangeness of the wonder discredit the truth of His plan for our salvation. This was not to be feared here, since both Moses and Elias, strengthened by the power of God, were also enabled to endure fasting for this great length of time. Had He gone beyond this time His taking flesh might then appear unbelievable to many.

When He had therefore fasted for forty days and for forty nights, and afterwards was hungry, He gave an opportunity to the devil to draw near, so that He might teach us through this encounter how we are to overcome and defeat him. This a wrestler also does. For in order to teach his pupils how to win he himself engages in contests with others, demonstrating on the actual bodies of others that they may learn how to gain the mastery. This is what took place here. For, desiring to draw the devil into contest, He made His hunger known to him. He met him as he approached, and meeting him, with the skill which He alone possessed, He once, twice, and a third time, threw His enemy to the ground.

But lest we should in passing too quickly over these victories take away your rightful profit in them, let us begin at the first encounter. Since he was hungry it was written: *The tempter coming said to him: if thou be the Son of God, command that these stones be made bread.* For since he had heard a Voice from heaven saying: *This is my beloved Son*, and had also heard John testifying such great things about Him, and then saw Him hungry, he was puzzled. For he could not believe that this was just a mere man, because of all that had been said about Him. But neither could he believe that He was the Son of God, since he sees that he suffers hunger. So being doubtful in mind he speaks with two voices as it were. Just as when he drew near to Adam in the beginning he pretended to things that were not true, that he might find out what was true, so here also, since he did not know clearly the deeply veiled mystery of the design of our Redemption, nor who this Person was Who stood before him, he began to weave other nets, by means of which he might learn what was now hidden and obscure to him.

And what does he say? *If thou be the Son of God, command that these stones be made bread.* He does not say: Since you are hungry, but, *If thou be the Son of God*: thinking to flatter Him. And so he makes no reference to His hunger; lest he might seem to bring it against Him, to mock Him with it. For not knowing the immensity of the divine plan he thought that this *might* be a reproach to Him. So in the manner of a flatterer he makes mention only of His dignity.

What did Christ say? Putting down his pride, He shows him that there was nothing humiliating in what He suffered, and nothing unworthy of His wisdom; which the devil, flattering Him, had passed over in silence. And this He now brings forward, and puts before him, saying: *Not in bread alone doth man live*.

So the devil begins with the stomach's need. Note carefully with me the astuteness of this malign spirit, and from what point he begins his attack, and how he leaves out nothing of his craft. He begins where he had overthrown the First Man, immersing him in unending afflictions. From here he again weaves his snares. I am speaking of the incontinence of the stomach. One hears from many foolish men of the countless miseries brought about by hunger. But Christ shows us that a man of virtue cannot be compelled by the tyranny of this appetite to do what it is not fitting to do, but will rather endure hunger and not obey its command; teaching us that in nothing should we obey the devil.

And since the First Man had violated the law in this way, committing also an offence against God, He here teaches us very carefully that even though that which the devil tells us to do may not be a transgression, yet even then we should never obey him. And why do I say transgression? For should the demons counsel what is useful, even so, He tells us, we must not heed them. For this reason He forbade those demons to speak who were proclaiming Him, as *the Holy One of God* (Lk. iv. 35). Paul rebuked them in the same way, though what they cried out was profitable to salvation (Acts xvi. 18). He rebuked them all the more, thwarting their designs against us: though speaking salutary truths: and closing their mouths and imposing silence on them he drove them away. So neither did Christ agree here to what he said. And what does He say? *Not in bread alone doth man live*. What He means here is that God is able, even by a word, to feed the hungry; and for this He quotes the testimony of the Old Testament. In this way He teaches us that though we may hunger, though we may suffer, we must never depart from God.

3. But some of you may say: he ought to have known Who the Lord was. To this I answer: why, and for what reason? For the devil did not say this as though he might himself come to believe, but, as he seemed to think, that he might lead the Lord into unbelief. So had he deceived the First Man, and confused him, so that he did not firmly trust in God. For he promised them what was contrary to what God had said to them, filling them with empty hopes, leading them on to infidelity, and so cheated them out of the happiness they possessed. But Christ shows him that neither to the devil, nor to the Jews who afterwards were

of the same mind as the devil, would He give a sign: instructing us also that at all times, and even though we were able to work a sign, we should never do it without a purpose, without a sufficient reason; and never at any time, even though subjected to violence, should we obey the devil.

And what does this accursed being do when he is defeated? Unable to persuade Christ to do his will, though He was now suffering hunger, he makes another attempt. Now he says: *If thou be the Son of God, cast thyself down. For it is written: That he hath given his angels charge over thee, and in their hands they shall bear thee up, lest perhaps thou dash thy foot against a stone.* Why does he begin each temptation with the words: *If thou be the Son of God*? What he did before he now does again. For just as formerly he spoke against God by the words, *In what day soever you shall eat thereof, your eyes shall be opened* (Gen. iii. 5): hoping to show by these words that they had been deceived and defrauded and had received no favour, so here he hints at the same thing, saying as it were: 'He called you Son to no purpose, and He tricked you undeservedly. But if this is not so, then you must show us you have such power.' And as Christ had answered him from the Scriptures, so he also quotes the testimony of a prophet.

How then does Christ answer? He is not indignant, nor was He provoked; but with great mildness He again replies from the Scriptures; saying: *Thou shalt not tempt the Lord thy God*, so that He may teach us that we are to overcome the devil, not by wonders, but by patience and long-suffering; and that we should never do anything for display alone, or for the desire of vain glory. But observe the devil's folly even in the testimony he quoted. For while the Lord quotes the Scriptures with great precision, those he made use of he employed foolishly and ineptly; and neither were they suited to his purpose. For it does not follow that because it was written, *That he had given his angels charge over thee*, He was to be persuaded to cast Himself headlong below. Besides, this was not said of the Lord. However, He did not notice this, though the devil had used the words offensively, and in a manner contrary to their meaning. No one asks this of the Son of God; it is purely the suggestion of the devil and his demons that He should throw Himself down; it is the way of God to uplift those who have fallen. For if He were to reveal His power He would not do so by foolishly throwing Himself down, but rather by raising others up. But it is the natural activity of the hosts of evil to throw themselves down headlong into the pit. For so the leader among them everywhere does.

But even when this was said Christ still did not reveal Himself, but goes on to speak as a man. Saying, *Not by bread alone*, and also, *Thou shalt not tempt the Lord thy God*, are not the words of anyone intending to reveal who he is, but the words rather of one who says that he is but one among men. Nor should it surprise you that in speaking to Christ the devil should as it were shift his ground. For just as pugilists, when they receive a deadly blow stagger about half-blinded and covered with blood, so likewise the devil, stunned by the first, and then by the second blow, says at random whatever comes to his mind, and comes again on to the third encounter.

Again the devil took him up into a very high mountain, and showed him all the kingdoms . . . and said: All these will I give thee, if falling down thou dost adore me. Then Jesus said to him: Begone, Satan: for it is written, the Lord thy God thou shalt adore, and him only shalt thou serve. Because he here sinned against the Father, saying that all that belonged to the Father was his; putting himself forward as God and Creator of the universe, the Lord rebukes him. But even then not severely, but simply with the words: *Begone, Satan.* A command rather than a castigation. For as soon as He said to him: *Begone*, He caused him to disappear. For he brought forward no other temptations.

4. And how, you may ask, does Luke say: *All the temptations being ended*? To me it seems that having recorded the principal temptations he may be said to have recorded them all; as if in this number the rest were included. For the evils that hold within themselves endless others are, to be a slave to gluttony, to labour for vainglory, to be possessed by a mad craving for riches. And so this accursed one, reflecting that the strongest of all was this insatiable craving for riches, placed it last of all. And though from the beginning he was eager to come to this temptation, he kept it till the end: as being the most efficacious of them all. For this seems to be a rule of his method of warfare, to keep to the last those things that seem most apt to undo man. This he did also with Job. And so having commenced with the motives that seemed weaker, he goes on to the stronger.

How are we to overcome this wickedness? As Christ has taught us; by turning to God: so that we shall never give way because of hunger, placing our trust in Him Who can feed us with a word; never, even in the enjoyment of the good things we have received, let us tempt the Giver, but being satisfied with the glory that is on high, let us attach no importance to the glory of men, and turn away from what is beyond our present needs. For nothing so places us under the power of the devil as avarice and the passion for gain. And this we may see from what now follows. For there are those who say: all these will I give thee, if falling down thou wilt adore. These persons are men, by nature, but they have become the instruments of the devil. For even then he attacked Him, not alone by himself, but through certain others; and this Luke tells us when he said: *the devil departed from Him for a time*, showing that later he approached Him, by means of the tools he had prepared for himself.

And behold angels came and ministered to him. For while the attack was going on He did not permit them to appear, so as not to drive away the quarry. But after He had confuted him, in all things, and put him to flight, they then appear; so that you may also learn that, like Him, after you have overcome, angels will receive you, applauding what you have done, and ministering to you. So likewise did the angels receive Lazarus, and after the furnace of poverty, hunger and distress, they carried him to eternal peace. For as I have said to you,

Christ now shows us many of the things that we shall afterwards enjoy.

Since all these things were done for you, let you imitate them and also strive to overcome. And should one of the servants of the devil come near you, one who is like to him in mind, and would reproach you, saying: if you are a great and wonderful person, move this mountain. Be not troubled, and do not let yourself be carried away by fury, but reply with calmness, giving that answer which you have just now heard your Lord make: *Thou shalt not tempt the Lord thy God.*

And should he, while offering you power and glory, and an infinity of riches, command that you adore him, resist him boldly. For this the devil has attempted, not alone against the common Lord of us all, but he brings these same devices to bear against each single one of the Lord's servants, and not merely in the wilderness, or upon the mountains, but in the cities, and in the market-place, and in the very courts of justice, and not by himself alone, but by means of men who are like to us by nature.

What therefore must we do? We must wholly deny him all belief; stop up our ears against him, and regard this seducer with hate. And the more he promises the more must we avoid him. This he did with Eve. For when he had filled her with false promises, it was then he utterly ruined her, and brought unending misery upon her. He is an unpitying enemy, and he has set himself implacably to war against us. We do not seek our own salvation so eagerly as he seeks our ruin. Let us turn away from him, and not in word only but in deed. And let us do none of the things that give him pleasure. In this way all we do shall be pleasing to God.

For the devil makes many promises: not with a mind to give us anything, but so as to take from us what we have. He promises from what he has stolen, that he may deprive us of justice and the kingdom of heaven; laying treasures in the earth like traps and snares, that by means of them he may deprive us of the treasures of heaven. He desires to see us rich here on earth, that he may not see us rich in heaven. And if he cannot by means of riches deprive us of our inheritance, he will try another way; as he did with the blessed Job. For when he saw that riches did not harm him, he wove a snare from poverty, hoping to catch him with that. What could have been more foolish? For he who bore wealth with moderation, much more could he bear want. And he who is not eager for riches when they are at his hand will not be eager for them when they are not there. And such was this blessed man, who through poverty became even more blessed.

The evil spirit had indeed the power to take his riches from him; but he could not take from him the love of God: rather he made it more fervent. And when he had stripped him of all he possessed, he grieved to see him abounding in yet greater riches. So he knew not what to do to him; for he saw that the more injuries he heaped on him the stronger he became. So having tried everything else, and proved that nothing availed, he had recourse to that ancient weapon, his wife; and she, putting on the mask of woe, sadly and tragically goes over the tale of his misfortunes, and pretends to help him with her evil counsel, so that he may be delivered from his miseries (Job ii. 9). But neither could he undo him by this means. For that greatly-to-be-admired man saw the bait in the trap, and with much prudence closed the mouth of the woman speaking at the devil's instigation.

5. And this we also must do; even should he speak to us through the mouth of our own brother, or friend, or wife, or any such person through whom he may speak what is not worthy. Let us receive no counsel from such persons, but rather because of their evil advice turn away from them. For the devil does in fact employ such means. He will cloak himself in the mask of sympathy, and feigning friendship will pour into our ears words more deadly than any poison. To soothe that he may hurt is the way of the devil. To chastise that He may bring us to greater good is the way of the Lord. So when things are going easily amid full and plenty then let us beware. And those that live in sin should ever be fearful; especially when they suffer no affliction. But when, a little at a time, God exacts punishment from us, he is making our own reparation lighter. But when He patiently suffers each single offense He is reserving for us a grievous chastisement: should we keep on offending Him. And if chastisement is necessary for the just, how much more is it needed for the unjust?

Recall with what patience God suffered Pharaoh to continue in his evil doing, but at the end of his crimes he received a supreme chastisement. Of how many crimes was Nabuchodonosor guilty; yet he too suffered for them all in the end? And Dives, self-indulgent in life, was for this especially punished, because he had suffered nothing here, and departed to suffer for what he had done there where, in the midst of torments, no remedy can ever come.

Yet there are those so foolish and dull that they long only for the things of the present; saying such senseless things as: 'Let me enjoy now what I have; later I shall think about what is not certain. Let me indulge my appetite. I want to enjoy myself. Give me today, and you may keep tomorrow.' What folly! They who say such things, in what way do they differ from goats and swine? For if the prophet did not regard as men those who neighed after their neighbour's wife (Jer. v. 8), who shall blame us if we consider those men as more senseless than swine and donkeys who speak of such things as uncertain which are clearer than what the eye sees.

For if you will believe nothing else, consider the devils in their torment; they who do and say nothing except towards our destruction? For you will not deny that they stop at nothing to add to our own heedlessness; striving to take from us the fear of hell, and to make us cease believing in the judgement to come? And though they do this, yet, at times, wailing and crying aloud, they make known the torments they suffer there. Why do they speak in this way, and speak too against their own inclinations? For no other reason but they are compelled, by a greater torment. For of their own will they would not confess that they are forced to suffer, and by men who are dead (i.e. *at the tombs of the martyrs*), or admit that they suffer anything at all. And why do I say this to you? Because the devils proclaim there is a hell; they who would have you believe there is no hell. But you who now enjoy such honour, who are made partakers in the most sacred *mysteries*, you not alone imitate them, you have even become worse than them.

But you will say: who has ever come from hell and told us these things? Who has ever come from heaven and told us that there is a God, Who has made all things? That we have a soul: whence was that made known to us? For if you only believe the things you see, you may then doubt about God and the angels, and about the mind and the soul, and in that way all teaching will be emptied of its truth. If you believe what you take in by your senses, then all the more should you believe in the invisible world rather than in the visible. And if what I say seems contradictory, it is nevertheless true; and may without question be accepted by intelligent men. For our eyes are often deceived, not with regard to invisible things: for as to these they cannot judge: but in the things that men seem to see; their accuracy being disturbed by distance, by distractions, by anger, by care, and countless other things. But the reflections of the soul, especially if it has received the light of the divine Scriptures, will arrive at a more accurate and certain judgement of things.

Let us then not foolishly deceive ourselves. Let us not build the fire higher against ourselves, because of the senseless manner of our lives: fruit in turn of these false ideas. For if there is no judgement, and if we need give no account of our misdeeds, then neither shall we receive a reward for all our toil. Consider therefore where such blasphemies lead you, when you say that God Who is Just and Merciful places no value on your toil and labour. How can such a thing be true? If there were no other proof consider this in the light of what happens within your own home, and then reflect how lacking in sense it is? For should you be a master, and cruel and inhuman beyond measure, and less kindly than the beasts would you not, if you were dying, provide for a loving and faithful servant? Would you not give him his freedom, and a gift of money, and, departing as you are from this world, so that you cannot be of help to him, would you not make provision for him through your heirs, directing them to do this, and seeking by every means that he shall not be left unrewarded?

You then who are so evil are yet thoughtful and humane towards your servant; will that infinite goodness and mercy which is God leave unrewarded and uncrowned His servants Peter and Paul and James and John and all those who day after day have for His sake suffered hunger, been bound with chains and beaten, buffeted by the sea, thrown to wild beasts, given over to death, and uncountable other afflictions? The judge at the Games declares who is the Olympic winner, and crowns him. The master rewards the servant, the king the soldier, and each man the one who serves him, and according to what he possesses.

But shall it be said of God alone that after such toils and labours He pays nothing, great or little, but leaves His just and faithful servants, who have practised every virtue, in the same condition as the adulterer, the parricide, the murderer, the despoiler of graves? How can this be possible?

And if there be nothing after our departure from here, and if our existence is bounded within the limits of this present life, then the one and the other are in the same condition; or rather not the same: for if, as you say, they all fare alike, then they do not all fare alike. For those first mentioned have suffered torments, while the rest have lived in pleasure. What tyrannical cruel inhuman barbarous master has ever so treated his servants and dependants? You see then how absurd such reasoning is; and to what it leads? And even if you have learned of this in no other way than by this reflection, put away these wicked ideas. Fly from evil and strive after virtue. Then you will learn that what is important to us does not come to an end at the boundaries of this present life.

And if someone should say to you, who that has come from there has told us these things, say to him in reply: Who among men? No one. For if a man had come he would not be believed: for fear he had exaggerated, and added to what he had learned. But the Lord of Angels has told us the truth regarding all this. What need have we that any man should tell us, when He that will be our Judge has been here amongst us, proclaiming each day to men, that He made hell, and that He has also prepared a kingdom for the just, and of all this He gave us the clearest proof?

And if He is not to judge us, then neither should He have punished us here on earth. And this, how can this also be right? That He should punish some, and others not at all? For if God is not an acceptor of persons, and this is true, why then does He punish this man, and let that other go free? This raises a greater difficulty than the preceding question. But, should you sincerely desire me to answer it, we shall try and make it clear to you.

What is the answer? He does not in this life exact punishment for all offences, so that men shall not lose faith in the resurrection and in the judgement to come: as though all things were already judged. And neither does He suffer that all shall go unpunished: lest men begin to think that there is no over-ruling Providence. But He both punishes, and does not punish. Through those He punishes He makes clear to us that those who have not been punished in this life will receive it in the life to come. And through those He does not punish in this life, He prepares your mind to believe that after this life there is a tribunal which men shall indeed fear.

For if He took no account whatever of our past deeds, He would not in this life either punish or give rewards. But you can see yourselves how he has spread forth the elements and given us the sun's light. He has laid down the earth, poured out the seas, opened wide the heavens, appointed the recurring motions of the moon, and established the unchanging laws of the seasons. By His word all things are harmoniously ordered in their courses. For it is by that unwearied Hand that our own nature, and the natures of all unthinking things, creeping things and those that walk and fly and swim, and those that dwell in the swamps, in the brooks and rivers, in the mountains, in the forests, amid the rocks and caves, in the air, the fields, the plants, seeds, trees, both of the wild and of the garden, fruit-bearing and without fruit, and all things else, are made to serve the need of our daily life, and not our needs only, but they give us also the means whereby we may show mercy to others, and thus render service to Him.

Beholding this so wondrous divine Providence, though we have recounted but little of it, can you dare to say that He, Who has had such care for you, will yet fail you in the time of your supreme need, and leave you in death to rest with asses and with swine? And this after He has crowned you with such great dignity, making you the equal of the angels, and will He, after all your pains and sufferings, finally abandon you? How can this accord with right reason? Why, though we should be silent with regard to these things the very stones would cry out, so clear and reasonable are they: clearer even than the very light of day!

Taking all these things into account, and believing them in our heart: namely, that after this present life we are to stand before a fearful tribunal, that we shall render an account of all we have done, that we shall receive sentence and suffer punishment if we remain in our sins, or that on the other hand we shall receive a crown and countless other good things, if for this brief present time we have a care for our own souls, let us put to silence those who dare to say, to proclaim, what is contrary to this belief, and let us walk the paths of virtue, so that drawing near with a confident heart to that tribunal, we may receive of the good things He has promised us, by the grace and mercy of Our Lord Jesus Christ, to Whom be honour and glory now and forever. Amen.

IV. St Cyril of Alexandria, Bishop and Doctor

The Preparation for the Pasch[7]

1. Behold! this wondrous and most profitable time of our Pasch is now approaching, when, after we have shaken off the oppressive burthen of our sins, we shall freely take upon us the saving yoke of the Divine Word come down from heaven; and taught by the mild and salutary words of Emmanuel, we shall no longer labour or be burthened. And coming together in the churches in common joyfulness let us lift up our voices in holy harmony, and give humble thanks to Christ the Saviour of all men, Who has cleansed us of the ancient stain that clung to us from of old, from our first parent's sin, and let us cry out what was so truly said in times past: *Christ hath redeemed us from the curse of the law, being made a curse for us* (Gal. iii. 13).

Since we were because of the evil will of the devil sent forth from Paradise and its joy, and heard because of the just anger of God that sorrowful decree: *Dust thou art, and unto dust thou shalt return* (Gen. iii. 19), and since we were caught in the snare of that diabolical tyranny, unhappy that we were, we dared not raise our eyes to heaven for mercy. Where was the way of salvation for those who longed for it? What means of pardon was there for those who had broken the command of the Lord? There was only the clemency of God: the mercy and compassion that belong to that unseen and unutterable majesty.

So therefore He sent His Son as our Saviour and Redeemer, Who alone had power to free mankind from the hands of the devil. And with infinite kindness and goodness the Only Begotten Son of the Father, equal to Him in power and majesty, Co-Eternal with Him Who had begotten Him, Creator and Artificer of heaven and earth, of angels and of men, *thought it not robbery to be equal with God: but emptied himself, taking the form of a servant* (Phil. ii. 6), took upon Himself our likeness, made in all things as we are, sin alone excepted, that through Himself He might redeem us all, and bring us to God the Father freed from all defilement and stain.

For this purpose He suffered hunger, and fasted for a certain time, that He might be for us the beginning of our salvation, and the model of a blameless life. So let us also make fasting the prelude of our holy celebrations. *Therefore let us feast, not with the old leaven, nor with the leaven of malice and wickedness; but with the unleavened bread of sincerity and truth* (I Cor. v. 8). And should we keep ourselves pure and chaste, steadfastly adhering to a way of life that pleases God, we shall as not unprofitable servants hear in due time these words: *Well done, good and faithful servant, because thou hast been faithful over a few things, I will place thee over many* (Mt. xxv. 23). For the fruits of their fasting shall not fail for those who hope in Him. Nor will they ever hear those dreadful words that were spoken to the Jews: *Not such a fast have I chosen, saith the Lord.* For thus he denounces them in the words of Isaias, and most justly: *You fast, and with your fist you strike the humble. What is your fasting to me?* (Is. lviii. 4: Septuagint).

It is required of us therefore that our life should be good in all ways; that fasting is but added to our own clear and joyful virtue, the sure means of immortality, the worthy pledge of the kingdom of heaven, and the strong and unshakeable foundation of eternal life. And because of this it becomes us that: *Cleansing ourselves from all defilement of the flesh and of the spirit, we perfect our sanctification in the fear of God* (II Cor. vii. 1). And so with confidence and without fear we then shall stand before the Tribunal of Christ, clothed in shining garments, and cry out to Him: *Behold we come to thee: for thou art the Lord our God* (Jer. iii. 22).

2. And when the people of Israel did not confess this, they heard once more the voice of God, speaking through the voice of Isaiah: *Woe to the sinful nation, a people laden with iniquity, a wicked seed, ungracious children! They have forsaken the Lord, they have blasphemed the Holy One of Israel, they are gone away backwards. For what shall I strike you more, you that increase transgression?* (Is. i. 4). They were indifferent to the wonders wrought by the Saviour; and neither did they

receive with awe the divine testimonies He wrought; on the contrary they insulted Him, declaring that, *This man casteth not out devils but by Beelzebub, the prince of devils* (Mt. xii. 24).

O God-hating madness! O monstrous impiety! *They have not known nor understood: they walk on in darkness; they go astray from the least to the greatest of them* (Ps. lxxxi. 5). If you know not what is written of Him, if you understand not the testimonies of the holy prophets, why do you boast, setting yourselves up as the custodians of the Law? When have you seen that fulfilled which was prophesied of old? *Then shall the eyes of the blind be opened, and the ears of the deaf shall be unstopped. Then shall the lame man leap as a hart, and the tongue of the dumb shall be free?* (Is. xxxv. 5, 6). Will you forever remain hoping that Emmanuel will come? And looking for the things that you have seen fulfilled? Does nothing of all that you see move you to wonder? Rather you seek to cover up what is known and proclaimed to all. Will you keep on shutting your eyes and closing your ears to the wonders Christ has wrought? For your contradictions have you been sorely repaid! For now you possess no more the outward tokens of your beliefs; without fatherland, without altar, you wander scattered everywhere upon the face of the earth.

Hear ye then one among you who has still retained a right judgement, that which Baruch proclaimed: *How happeneth, O Israel, that thou art in thy enemies' land? Thou art grown old in a strange country, thou art defiled with the dead: thou art counted with them that go down into hell. Thou hast forsaken the fountains of wisdom* (Bar. iii. 10–12). You have no answer to what has been said against you. You have no longer the power of plain speech: even to Truth itself you answer with sophisms. Listen then to what was fittingly said by the Just Judge of all men: *Behold all you that kindle a fire, walk in the light of the fire, and in the flames which you have kindled* (Is. l. 11).

You have placed upon a Cross the Lord of glory and the Maker of the Universe; and you thought that Life could, by you, be shrouded in death. You have not known, neither have you understood, that immortality which was prepared for the nature of man. Yet this Our Lord Jesus Christ went down to hell, and defeating it, He commanded as their Lord those who were in bonds: *Go forth*; and to those who were in darkness: *Reveal yourselves* (Is. lix. 9: Septuagint). And on the third day He returned to life, leaving the abode of the dead, and then, rejoicing in what He had accomplished, commanded His Disciples: *Going therefore, teach ye all nations; baptizing them in the name of the Father, and of the Son, and of the Holy Ghost* (Mt. xxviii. 19).

Profiting then by such teachers, let us resolve to be obedient to them alone, and to be subject to them; and being instructed by them in truth, and having also the perfect teaching of the divine Scriptures, let us, in the words of Moses, cry out to Our Redeemer and Saviour: *Who is like to Thee among the strong, O Lord? Who is like to thee, glorious in holiness?* (Ex. xv. 11). And again: *Who is as Thee, taking away iniquity, and overlooking injustice?* (Deut. xxxiv. 7: Septuagint).

Let no imposter therefore seduce you from the true faith. Let us tread the royal way, turning neither to the left nor to the right. Let us preserve our faith intact, untarnished by deceit, or by heretical contention; following always in the way of the true service of God. Let us confess the Consubstantial Trinity of the Father and the Son and the Holy Ghost. For this the Holy Scriptures have given us from above. Let us proclaim the Lord Who became man for us, born of the Virgin Mary Mother of God. Let us say to Him in the words of the Scriptures: *My lord and My God* (Jn. xx. 28).

Thus putting our lives in order, and cleansing ourselves of the stains of our former sins by an upright and devout manner of living, purified and without blemish, blameless and without reproof, let us show the tenderness of a father to the orphaned, let us bestow on the widow care such as becomes the sanctified; and in a word let us love our neighbour, and drive out from our own soul every iniquity.

Let us shelter in our homes the needy and the homeless, so that sharing with the poor that which God has given us for our own lives, clothing the naked, and in general adorning ourselves with everything that is pleasing to God, we may be able to come to the joy of the good things He has promised us.

Beginning the holy Quadragesima on the nineteenth of February, the week of the saving Pasch on the twenty-fourth of the month of March, we shall bring to an end our fast on the twenty-ninth day of the same month of March, at the close of the evening, according to the evangelical proclamation, celebrating then the festival, at the rising dawn of the Lord's Day on the thirtieth of the same month, and then going on thereafter to the seven weeks of the holy Pentecost.

In this way we shall come to inherit the kingdom of heaven in Christ Jesus Our Lord, through Whom and with Whom, may there be glory and honour to the Father, for ever and ever. Amen.

V. St Leo, Pope and Doctor

Lent the Season of Purification[8]

Synopsis:

I. That Lent has been instituted that we may profitably purify our souls from sin.

II. We should strive earnestly after virtue during this time; purchasing it by our own effort.

III. The devil weaves snares even from our devotion; the sequence and meaning of his temptations against Christ are explained.

IV. Concerning the perverted abstinence of the Manichees.

V. These fast on the first and second days of the week, in honour of the sun and moon; and withhold themselves from the participation of the Blood of Christ etc.

VI. Sanctify Lent with good works.

I. At the commencement of my sermon to you Beloved Brethren, on this the greatest and most sacred of the fasts, what more fitting opening than to begin with the words of the Apostle, in whom Christ spoke, and declare again what has just been read to you: *Behold, now is the acceptable time; behold, now is the day of salvation* (II Cor. vi. 2). For though there is no season that is not filled with the divine gifts, and though at each moment we have, through His grace, access to the Divine Mercy, yet now is the time in which the souls of all men should be stirred with greater fervour towards spiritual perfection, and inspired with greater confidence: now when the return of that day on which we were redeemed invites us once more to the fulfilment of all our sacred duties, so that purified in body and soul we may celebrate the supreme Mystery of the Passion of Our Lord. Indeed, such unending reverence and unceasing devotion is due to these so sacred *mysteries*, that such should we ever be in the Presence of God as we now are obliged to be for the worthy celebration of the Paschal Feast.

But since there are few that have this strength of soul, and since, because of the weakness of our flesh, the more severe observance is relaxed, and since the manifold duties of the present life take up so much of our care, it will happen that even the most devout of heart are stained with the dust of earth. Accordingly, with great solicitude has this divine means been given us, so that these forty days of reflection may assist us to restore the purity of our souls, and so that during them we may by good works make satisfaction for our past sins, and by devout mortification purge outselves of them.

II. As we are therefore beginning this sacred season, dedicated to the purification of the soul, let us be careful to fulfil the Apostolic command that *we cleanse ourselves from all defilement of the flesh and of the spirit* (II Cor. vii. 11), so that restraining the conflict that exists between the one and the other substance, the soul, which in the Providence of God is meant to be the ruler of the body, may regain the dignity of its rightful authority, so that, giving offence to no man, we may not incur the contumely of evil-mongers. With just contempt shall we be tormented by those who have no faith, and from our wickedness evil tongues will draw weapons to wound religion, if the way of life of those who fast be not in accord with what is needed in true self denial. For the sum total of our fasting does not consist in merely abstaining from food. In vain do we deny our body food if we do not withhold our heart from iniquity, and restrain our lips that they speak no evil.

We must then so moderate our rightful use of food that our other desires may be subject to the same rule. For this is also a time for gentleness and patience, a time of peace and serenity, in which having put away all stains of evil doing we strive after steadfastness in what is good. Now is the time when generous Christian souls forgive offences, pay no heed to insults, and wipe out the memory of past injuries. Now let the Christian soul exercise itself in the armour of justice, on the right hand and on the left, so that amid honour and dishonour, evil report and good, the praise of men will not make proud the virtue that is well rooted, the conscience that has peace, nor dishonour cast it down. The moderation of those who worship God is not melancholy, but blameless.

Neither should we now hear sound of discord coming from those to whom the consolations of holy joy are never wanting. And when you are engaged in works of mercy, do not fear a lessening of your own earthly possessions. Christian poverty is ever rich; for that which it possesses is greater than that which it does not possess. Neither should he fear to work on in poverty to whom it has been given to possess all things in the Lord of all things.

They therefore who desire to do good works let them not fear that they shall be without the means; since even for giving two farthings, the generosity of the poor widow of the Gospel was glorified (Lk. xxi. 2); and even the free gift of a cup of cold water shall not be without its reward (Mt. x. 42). By their desires we shall know the measure of the good will of the just; and he that has a heart ever open to pity will never lack means to help those in need. We learn this from that holy widow Sareptha who, in a time of famine, placed before the blessed Elias all that she had, and that was but food sufficient for a day; and, putting the prophet's hunger before her own, she gave without hesitation her handful of meal and her drop of oil (III Kings xvii. 18). But she was not left to want for that which she had so piously bestowed: and in the vessels which charity had emptied there arose a fresh source of abundance, so that the amount of what she had had was not made less by the charity that had not feared to go wanting.

III. Be you certain, Dearly Beloved, that the devil, the enemy of all virtue, will look with envy upon these pious practices, to which we trust you freely give yourselves; and he will bring against them all the force of his malice, so that from piety itself he may weave snares against piety: so that those he could not destroy through despair he will seek to undo through vain glory. For standing close at hand to all our actions is the iniquity of pride; and vanity lies ever in wait for virtue: for it rarely happens that the praise of men is not given to those who live worthy lives, unless, as was written, *He that glorieth, let him glory in the Lord* (II Cor. x. 17).

But whose purpose will that most wicked enemy not dare to attack? Whose self denial does he not seek to undo, when, as we so clearly see from today's Gospel, he attempted his deceits even against the Saviour of the world? For being astonished by this fast of forty days, he brazenly tries to learn whether this power of continence has been given to Him or is His own; and so he dares to attempt to discover by trickery whether Christ was a creature, as was His body.

Accordingly, he seeks by guile to find out, first, whether or not Our Lord was Himself the Creator of all things, and could therefore change the nature of earthly things into what he willed? Secondly, whether under the appearance of human flesh the Divinity lay concealed: to Whom it would be a simple thing to pass through the air, and bear His earthly members through the void? But since it was the Lord's desire to defeat him by the justice of a true man, rather than by the power of His Divinity, to this end then did he direct the subtlety of the third temptation: to test this Man, in whom the signs of divine power had now ceased, with the lust of dominion, and by promising Him the kingdoms of this world endeavour to lead Him to the worship of himself. The wisdom of God makes folly of the artifices of the devil. But the arrogant enemy, seeing but a man, such as he had once before overcome, does not hesitate to pursue his evil intent against Him Who was to die for the world.

IV. Let us therefore, Dearly Beloved, be watchful against the deceits of the devil, not alone against the enticements of gluttony, but even in our very purpose of fasting. For he who knew how by means of food to bring death upon all men knows how to injure us even by our fast; and, by using his Manichean servants, inflict on us a grievous injury. For just as by a serpent he brought it about that what was forbidden was eaten, so by them he persuades men to shun what is lawful.

Abstinence is truly praiseworthy; since by accustoming us to a modest diet it restrains the appetite from luxuries. But woe to their teaching, according to which a man sins by fasting! For they condemn the nature of creatures in affront to their Creator; and declare that those who eat of them are defiled by such things: whose author, they say, is not God but the devil. For there is no substance whatever that is evil; nor is there any substance evil by its nature. For the Good Creator has made all things; and One is the Maker of all things; *Who made heaven and earth, the sea, and all things that are in it* (Ps. cxlv. 6).

And whatsoever is given to man as food and as drink is clean and holy; of whatever kind it may be. But if it is indulged in with unmeasured appetite it will dishonour both those that eat it and those that drink it; yet it is not the nature of the food that defiles us: *For all things*, as the Apostle says, *are clean to the clean: but to them that are defiled, and to unbelievers, nothing is clean: but both their mind and their conscience are defiled* (Titus i. 15).

V. But you, Dearly Beloved, the holy offspring of the Catholic Mother, Whom the Spirit of God has taught in the School of Truth, use your freedom of action with right reason, knowing that it is good to abstain, even from what is lawful; and when you must practise self denial, so abstain from food as merely putting aside its use, not as condemning its nature. And so you will not allow yourselves in any way to be infected by the error of those who are completely defiled by their own observance of it; *Serving the creature rather than the Creator* (Rom. i. 25); and dedicating their own stupid observance to the lights of heaven. For they have decreed for themselves days of fasting, on the first and second days of the week, in honour of the sun and moon, and, twice-impious in their single act of blasphemy, and twice-sacrilegious, they have decreed this fast both in honour of the stars and to show their contempt of the Lord's Resurrection.

For they recoil from the Mystery of Human Redemption, and they believe not in Christ Our Lord, and that He was truly born, in the true flesh of our nature, that He truly suffered, that He was truly buried, and that He truly rose again. And for this reason they darken the day of our joy with the gloom of their own fast. Yet so as to conceal their faithlessness they dare to take part in our assemblies, but refrain from the fellowship of the sacred mysteries; but now and then, since they must not entirely conceal themselves they receive into their unworthy mouths the Body of Christ; but the Blood of the Redemption they wholly refuse to drink.

We make this known to Your Sanctity so that by these indications persons of this kind may be discovered by you; and if their sacrilegious deceptions are observed, let them be banished from the communion of the sanctified. For the blessed Apostle Paul has given timely warning to the Church concerning such people, where he says: *Now I beseech you, brethren, to mark them who make dissensions and offences contrary to the doctrine which you have learned, and avoid them. For they that are such, serve not Christ Our Lord, but their own belly; and by pleasing speeches and good words, seduce the hearts of the innocent* (Rom. xvi. 17).

VI. Being now sufficiently instructed against this error by these warnings, which, Dearly Beloved, we have often spoken in your hearing, enter then with pious devotion upon these holy days of Lent; and prepare for yourselves the works of mercy, that you may merit the Divine Mercy. Extinguish the fires of anger, wipe away all hate, love the bond of unity, give way to each other in the simplicity of true humility.

Rule your servants with justice, and likewise all who are subject to you; and let none of them be tormented, either by prison or by chains. Let there be an end to vengeance. Let offences be forgiven. Let harshness be changed to mildness, disdain to gentleness, discord into peace. Let us all make trial of being modest, let all be gentle, all be kind: so that our fasting may be pleasing to God. To Him we shall offer a true sacrifice of self denial and devotion if we keep ourselves from all iniquity; being helped in all things by Almighty God, Who with the Son and Holy Ghost is One in Divinity, One in Majesty, for ever and ever. Amen.

VI. St Gregory the Great, Pope and Doctor

Given to the People in the Basilica of Saint John, which is called The Constantinian, on the First Sunday of Lent

THE GOSPEL OF THE SUNDAY[9]

1. There are some persons who ask by which spirit was it that Jesus was led into the desert, and they are uncertain because of these words: *The devil took him up into the holy city*; and also by: *The devil took him up*

into a very high mountain. But it is rightly and without question accepted, and may be believed, that He was led by the Holy Spirit into the desert; that His own Spirit led Him there where the spirit of evil would find Him to tempt Him. But observe that when it is said that the God-Man was taken up by the devil into a very high mountain, or into the Holy City, that this the mind turns away from believing, and human ears are horrified at hearing it. Yet when we reflect upon the other things that were done against Him we can well see that these are not incredible.

Without doubt the devil is the head of all evildoers; and the wicked are the members of this head. Was not Pilate a member of the devil? Were not the persecuting Jews, and the soldiers who crucified Jesus, members of the devil? Why then should we be astonished if He allows Himself to be taken up into a mountain by the devil, when He suffered Himself to be crucified by his members? And is it not also fitting that He chose to be tempted Who had come that He might suffer death? It was indeed fitting, that as He had come to undo our death by His own, He would also overcome our temptations in His temptations.

We should keep in mind that temptation is accomplished in three stages: by suggestion, by delight, by consent. And we, when we are tempted, generally fall through pleasure or delight, and also by consent; for since we are begotten through the sin of the flesh, we bear within us that whereby we now suffer conflict. But God Who became Incarnate in the womb of the Virgin entered into this world without sin, and had within Him no source of this conflict. He therefore could be tempted by suggestion; but the delight of sin could take no hold on his mind. And so all this diabolic temptation was from without; not from within.

2. But, dwelling on the sequence of the temptations, let us consider through what greatness we are delivered from temptation. Our ancient enemy set himself against the First Man, our parent, with three temptations; for he tempted him by gluttony, by vain glory, and by avarice; and tempting him defeated him: for by consenting to the temptation he placed himself under the power of the devil.

He tempted him through gluttony when he put before him the forbidden fruit of the tree, and persuaded him to eat it. He tempted him by vain glory when he said: *Ye will be as Gods* (Gen. iii. 5). And he tempted him from the heights of avarice when he said: *knowing good and evil.* For there is an avarice not alone of money, but of grandeur. Rightly is it called avarice when exaltation is desired above all moderation. For if the seizure of honour did not pertain to avarice Paul would never have said: *Who thought it not robbery to be equal to God* (Phil. ii. 6). In this the devil led our parent to pride, by provoking in him the greed of human grandeur.

3. But by the very means by which he laid low the First Man, by these same did he himself succumb to the Second Man. For he tempted Him by gluttony when he said:

Command that these stones be made bread. He tempted Him by vain glory when he said: *If thou be the Son of God, cast thyself down*. By greed of dominion when he showed him all the kingdoms of the earth, and said: *All these will I give thee, if falling down thou wilt adore me*. But by these very means by which he gloried in defeating the First Man, was he overcome by the Second; so that defeated he goes out from our hearts by that very way through which, once forcing an entrance, he was wont to hold us in slavery.

There is, Dearly Beloved, yet another thing we must consider in this temptation of Our Lord; namely, that the Lord when tempted by the devil answers in words from the holy Scripture; that He Who, by that Word which He is, could have cast the tempter into the pit, does not reveal His Majesty, but answers only according to the precepts of the Divine Words. He did this to give us an example of patience, that we also, as often as we suffer anything from an evil person, may be moved to remembrance of what He taught us, rather than to the desire of revenge. Reflect how great is the patience of God, and how great our own impatience! Should we be provoked by injury or by attack we fly to anger; and we either avenge ourselves as best we can, or threaten what we cannot. But consider how the Lord endures the enmity of the devil, and makes answer only in words of gentleness. He suffered him whom He could have chastized; and in this also is He to be glorified, that He overcame His enemy, not by destroying him, but by patiently enduring him for the time.

4. Let us observe what follows; namely, that the devil leaving Him, angels minister to Him. From this what do we learn, if not the twofold nature of the One Person? For it is a man the devil tempts; and the same Person is God to Whom angels minister. We recognize then our own nature in Him; for unless the devil saw Him as man he would not have tempted Him. We venerate in Him His own divinity; for unless He were God of all, angels would not have come and ministered to Him.

5. And since the Gospel reading refers to these present days: for we who are now at the beginning of the season of Lent have just heard the Gospel account of the forty days fast: we must consider for ourselves, why it is this abstinence is observed for forty days? For Moses also fasted forty days, that he might receive the Law (Ex. xxxiv. 28). Elias in the desert fasted for forty days (III Kings xix. 8). And He Who is the Author of all men, coming amongst men, went entirely without food *for forty days and forty nights*. And we, as far as we are able, must also endeavour to mortify our bodies by abstinence during this yearly time of Lent.

Why is the number forty observed if not that the excellence of the Decalogue is perfected by the Four Books of the Gospel? For as ten multiplied by four make forty, so we perfectly fulfil the precepts of the Decalogue when we faithfully observe the Four Books of the Holy Gospels. From this another thing may be learned. In this mortal body we are composed of four elements; and it is because of this same body we are made subject to God's Commandments. The Commands of the Law are given to us in the Decalogue. And since it is through the desires of the body we have despised the Commandments of the Decalogue, it is just that we chastize this same flesh four times ten times.

And if you wish there is yet another thing to be understood from this time of Lent. From this present day till the joyful solemnities of Easter there are six weeks; that is, two and forty days. From which if you subtract the six Sundays there remain six and thirty days of abstinence. And since a year continues throughout three hundred and sixty-five days, we, when we mortify ourselves for thirty-six days, give to the Lord a tithe as it were of our year; so that we who have lived for ourselves throughout the year we have received, may, during His tenth of it, die to Our Maker through abstinence.

And so, Dearly Beloved, as it was commanded in the Law to offer tithes of all things, so let you offer Him a tithe of your days. Let each one mortify his own body, as far as his strength allows, and let him weaken its desires, and lower the pride of its evil lusts, so that he may become, in the words of Paul, *a living sacrifice* (Rom. xii. 1). A man is both living and a sacrifice when he has died to the desires of his body, though he has not departed from this life. It is the pleasure-loving body that leads us into sin; mortification leads us back to forgiveness. The parent of our death sinned against the commandments of our life, because of the fruit of the forbidden tree. We therefore who because of eating have fallen from the joy of paradise may, as far as we are able, return to it once more through fasting.

6. But let no one believe that fasting alone is sufficient; for the Lord tells us by the mouth of the prophet: *Is not this rather the fast that I have chosen?* And then continues: *Deal thy bread to the hungry, and bring the needy and the harbourless into thy house: when thou shalt see one naked, cover him, and despise not thy own flesh* (Is. lviii. 6, 7). The Lord therefore blesses that fast which uplifts our hands in almsgiving before His eyes, which is joined to the love of our neighbour, and founded on compassion. That which you deny yourself let you therefore give to another; so that that by which your body is weakened, may refresh the body of your hungry neighbour.

Because of this the Lord says to us through His prophet: *When you fasted and mourned, did you keep a fast unto me? And when you did eat and drink, did you not eat for yourselves, and drink for yourselves?* (Zach. vii. 5, 6). He eats and drinks for himself who enjoys the food of the body: which is the common gift of the Creator: without a thought for those in need. And each one fasts for himself if that which he denies himself for a time he gives, not to the needy, but saves that he may later offer it to his own stomach. Hence was it said by the prophet Joel: *Sanctify ye a fast* (Joel i. 14; ii. 15). To sanctify a fast is to offer to God a worthy mortification of the body: provided we are worthy in other respects also. Let anger cease, and quarrelling end. In vain do you deny the flesh when the soul is unchecked in its evil delights; for the Lord has warned us by the prophet: *Behold in the day of your fast your own will is found; behold you fast for debates and strife, and strike wickedly with your fist, and you exact from all your debtors* (Is. lviii. 3).

Though he who demands back from his neighbours what he gave them commits no injustice, yet it is fitting that whoever mortifies himself in penance should deny himself even what is justly his due. And so by doing penance ourselves, and humbled by others, we shall obtain from God pardon for what we have done unjustly, if for love of Him we let go our hold of what is rightly ours; by the grace and aid of Our Lord Jesus Christ, Who reigns with the Father and the Holy Ghost for ever. Amen.

NOTES

[1] Cf. PL 26, 32.

[2] PL 17, Sermo 17. Serm I for Lent.

[3] Pl 17, Sermo 25. Serm. 9 for Lent.

[4] i.e., until about 3 p.m., when the principal meal was eaten.

[5] *Omnes Christiani omni Dominica debent offere et communicare.*

[6] PG 57, hom. 13.

[7] PG 77, col. 850. *Homilia Paschalis* XXI.

[8] PL 54, col. 274; Sermo. 4 de Quad.

[9] PL 76, 1134, Sermo. 16.

SECOND SUNDAY OF LENT

I. St Ephraem: On the Transfiguration of Our Lord and Saviour Jesus Christ

II. St John Chrysostom: The Transfiguration of Christ, and Against Usury

III. St Augustine: The Kingdom of Christ

IV. St Cyril of Alexandria: On the Transfiguration of the Lord our God and our Saviour Jesus Christ

V. St Leo the Great: The Purposes of the Transfiguration

THE GOSPEL OF THE SUNDAY

Matthew xvii. 1–9

At that time Jesus taketh unto him Peter and James, and John his brother, and bringeth them up into a high mountain apart: And he was transfigured before them. And his face did shine as the sun: and his garments became white as snow. And behold there appeared to them Moses and Elias talking with him. And Peter answering, said to Jesus: Lord, it is good for us to be here: if thou wilt let us make here three tabernacles, one for thee, and one for Moses, and one for Elias. And as he was yet speaking, behold a bright cloud overshadowed them. And lo, a voice out of the cloud, saying: This is my beloved Son, in whom I am well pleased: hear ye him. And the disciples hearing, fell upon their face, and were very much afraid. And Jesus came and touched them: and said to them, Arise, and fear not. And they lifting up their eyes saw no one but only Jesus. And as they came down from the mountain, Jesus charged them, saying: Tell the vision to no man, till the Son of man be risen from the dead.

PARALLEL GOSPELS

Mark ix. 1–12

And after six days Jesus taketh with him Peter and James and John, and leadeth them up into an high mountain apart by themselves, and was

Luke ix. 28–36

And it came to pass about eight days after these words, that he took Peter, and James, and John, and went up into a mountain to pray. And transfigured before them. And his garments became shining and exceeding white as snow, so as no fuller upon earth can make white. And there appeared to them Elias with Moses; and they were talking with Jesus. And Peter answering, said to Jesus: Rabbi, it is good for us to be here: and let us make three tabernacles, one for thee, and one for Moses, and one for Elias. For he knew not what he said: for they were struck with fear. And there was a cloud overshadowing them: and a voice came out of the cloud, saying: This is my most beloved Son; hear ye him. And immediately looking about, they saw no man any more, but Jesus only with them. And as they came down from the mountain, he charged them not to tell any man what things they had seen, till the Son of man shall be risen again from the dead. And they kept the word to themselves; questioning together what that should mean, when he shall be risen from the dead. And they asked him, saying: Why then do the Pharisees and Scribes say that Elias must come first? Who answering, said to them: Elias, when he shall come first, shall restore all things; and as it is written of the Son of man, that he must suffer many things and be despised. But I say to you that Elias also is come, and they have done to him whatsoever they would, as it is written of him.

whilst he prayed, the shape of his countenance was altered, and his raiment became white and glittering. And behold two men were talking with him. And they were Moses and Elias, appearing in majesty. And they spoke of his decease that he should accomplish in Jerusalem. But Peter and they that were with him were heavy with sleep. And waking, they saw his glory, and the two men that stood with him. And it came to pass, that as they were departing from him, Peter saith to Jesus: Master, it is good for us to be here; and let us make three tabernacles, one for thee, and one for Moses, and one for Elias; not knowing what he said. And as he spoke these things, there came a cloud, and overshadowed them; and they were afraid, when they entered into the cloud. And a voice came out of the cloud, saying: This is my beloved Son; hear him. And whilst the voice was uttered, Jesus was found alone. And they held their peace, and told no man in those days any of these things which they had seen.

Exposition from the Catena Aurea

V. 1. *And after six days . . .* (Matt. xvii. 1–9).

Remigius: The glory of the vision of Himself which He had promised His Disciples, He here fulfilled in this Transfiguration, which took place six days later, upon a mountain; hence is it said: *And after six days.* Jerome: It may be asked how it is that He took them up after *six* days, when Luke speaks of *eight*? But the answer is simple: for here the six intervening days are counted, there the previous day and the last are added.

CHRYSOSTOM, *Hom.* 57 *in Matthew*: Therefore it was not immediately following on the promise that He leads them upwards, but after six days: that the other disciples might not suffer what was but human, that is, any impulse of envy. Or, that being filled during the space of these days, they who were to be taken up, with a more fervid desire, they would approach it with a more earnest mind. RHABANUS: Rightly did he reveal this glory after six days; for the resurrection to come will be after the six ages. ORIGEN: Or, because in six days was the whole visible world created. He who rises above the things of this world, can ascend the high mountain, and look upon the glory of the Word of God.

CHRYSOSTOM: He therefore took those three: since they were greater than the others. Observe how Matthew does not suppress the names of those that were preferred before him; neither also does John, who speaks with great praise of Peter; for the band of the Apostles was free of all envy and vainglory. HILARY *on Matt. XVII*: Three being taken up who were by descent from three: Sem, Cham, and Japhet, the future choice of the people is shown. RHABANUS: Or, He took but three Disciples with Him, since many are called but few are chosen; or, because they who now in a pure heart hold fast to faith in the Blessed Trinity shall then rejoice in its eternal vision.

REMIGIUS: The Lord, being about to reveal the splendour of His glory to His Disciples, brought them to a high mountain; hence there follows: *and bringeth them up into a high mountain apart*; in which event He teaches us that it is necessary for all who desire to look upon the glory of God that they lie not down amid base pleasures, but that they be uplifted to heavenly things; and that He might show His Disciples that they must not seek the light of His glory in the dark of this world, but in the Kingdom of heavenly blessedness. They are taken upwards *apart*; because men that are holy are separated with their whole heart and by the eagerness of their faith from evildoers; and they shall be completely separated from them in the future; Or, because many are called but few are chosen.

V. 2. *And He was transfigured before them . . .*

JEROME: Such as He shall be in the judgement to come, so did He appear to His Apostles. But let no one think that He put off His earthly form and outward appearance, or that He lost the reality of His Body, and that He took on a spiritual one. How He was transformed the Evangelist describes, saying: *His face did shine as the sun: and his garments became as white as snow*. When the brightness of His Face is spoken of, and the whiteness of His garments described, His substance is not made to disappear, but becomes transformed by glory. Without doubt the Lord was transfigured into the likeness of that glory in which He shall afterwards come into His Kingdom. The transfiguration added splendour; it did not take away

His outward appearance. Should it be the case that the body became spiritual, were the garments then also changed, which were *white*, as another Evangelist says, *as no fuller on earth can make white*? But it was corporeal, and subject to touch, and not a spiritual and ethereal substance, which deceives the senses and is seen only in an unreal appearance.

REMIGIUS: If the face of the Lord shone as the sun, and if *the just shall shine as the sun* (Mt. xiii. 43), is the glory of the servants then equal to the glory of the Master? By no means. But as there is nothing shines so splendidly as the sun, to give us a figure of the resurrection that is to come, the face of the Lord, and the countenance of the just are both said to have the brightness of the sun.

ORIGEN: Mystically, when one has passed beyond the six days, as we explained, he shall see the transfigured Christ before the eyes of his soul. For the Word of God has various forms, and appears to each one according to the manner He knows is best suited to the one who sees; and to no one does He show Himself in a manner above their comprehension. Here he does not simply say: *He was transformed*; but, *He was transformed before them*. For in the Gospels Jesus is simply seen by those who do not, by the practise of virtue, ascend to the sacred mountain of wisdom; but to those who do ascend there He is no longer known as man, but is understood as God the Word.

Jesus therefore is transfigured *before them*; and not before those who are down below, following an earthly manner of life. But they before whom He is transfigured have been made children of God, and to them He is revealed as the sun of justice; and His garments become white as light: which are the words and sayings in which Jesus is clothed, according to what the Apostles tell us of Him. GLOSS (*apud Anselm*): Or the garments of Christ mean the saints, of whom Isaias says: *Thou shalt be clothed with all these as with an ornament* (Is. xlix. 18). And they are compared to snow because they are shining white with virtue, and purified of all fever of vice.

V. 3. *And behold there appeared to them Moses and Elias talking with them.*

CHRYSOSTOM: And this happened for many reasons; of which this is the first: because the multitude had been saying He was Elias or Jeremias or one of the prophets He here took to Himself the chief persons among the prophets, so that from this also they might see what difference lay between the Master and His servants. Another reason is: the Jews continually accused Jesus of being a violator of the Law, and a blasphemer, and of taking to Himself the glory of the Father. That He may be shown guiltless of these accusations He brings before them two persons who had been preeminent in regard to both those things. For Moses had given the Law, and Elias had been filled with zeal for the glory of the Father.

Another reason was that they might learn that He had power over life and death, and for this He brought Moses before them: who had departed this life by way of death, and Elias who had not yet suffered death. The Evangelist reveals another reason, namely: to manifest the glory of the Cross, and to comfort Peter and the other Disciples who were fearful of the Passion. For *they spoke*, as another Evangelist says, *of his decease that he should accomplish in Jerusalem* (Lk. ix. 13). And so He brings before them these two who had challenged death for the things that were pleasing to God, and on behalf of the people who believed in Him. For both of their own will had faced tyrants; Moses confronting Pharao, and Elias Achab. And lastly He brings them before them so that the Disciples might be emulous of their special qualities: that they might become gentle, like Moses, and zealous for the glory of God, like Elias.

HILARY: That only Moses and Elias are present from all the multitude of the saints means that Christ in His Kingdom will stand between the Law and the Prophets; for He shall judge Israel in the presence of those by whom He was made known to the people of Israel. ORIGEN: For where any one discerns a spiritual significance in the Law, or Christ's wisdom hidden in the prophets, such a one sees Moses and Elias in glory with Jesus.

JEROME: Let us note that He refused to give a sign from heaven to the Scribes and Pharisees asking Him for one; but here He gives a sign from heaven so that He may increase the Apostles' faith: Elias descending whither he had ascended, and Moses rising from the dead; just as Achaz was bidden by Isaias to seek a sign from on high, or from hell (Is. vii).

V. 4. *And Peter answering said to Jesus: Lord, it is good for us to be here.* ORIGEN: What the fervent Peter said follows: *Lord* etc. Because he had heard that the Lord must go to Jerusalem he was still fearful for Christ. But since his reproof he does not again dare to say: *Be merciful to Thyself*, but indirectly he conveys the same state of mind by other means. For when he sees this place of solitude and quiet he thinks that, from its situation, here would be a suitable place to remain. He desires even to remain there always, and so he speaks of dwelling places, saying: *Let us make here three tabernacles.* For he thought that if they did this the Lord would not go to Jerusalem; and if He did not go up to Jerusalem He would not die. There, he knew, the Scribes lay in wait for Him. And He thought also to himself how they had Elias with them: he that had caused fire to descend upon the mountain (IV Kings i); and Moses, who had entered the midst of the cloud, and spoken with God (Ex. xxiv. 33). They would be well hidden here, so that none of the persecutors would know where they were.

REMIGIUS: Or again; having seen the majesty of the Lord, and the glory of His two servants, Peter was so overjoyed that he became oblivious of earthly things, and desired to remain there for ever. If Peter was so enraptured then, what delight, what sweetness, shall we taste beholding the King in His beauty, and dwelling amid the choirs of the angels and saints? Yet, saying, *Lord, if thou wilt*, Peter reveals the obedience of a humble and devoted servant.

JEROME: You err, Peter, and as another Evangelist says, *you know not what you say* (Lk. ix. 33). Do not seek for three tabernacles, since one is the dwelling place of the Gospel: in which are summed up both the Law and the Prophets. But if you do seek for three tabernacles, do not place the servants on the same level with their Master. But make three tabernacles; rather, make but one, for the Father, Son, and Holy Ghost: so that as one is their Divinity, so let one be their tabernacle, and let that one be in thy own breast.

REMIGIUS: He erred also in that he wished that the Kingdom of the Elect, which the Lord had promised to bestow in heaven, might be established on earth. He erred again, forgetting that both he and his companions were mortal, and without tasting death he sought to mount to eternal glory. RHABANUS: And in this—that he thought dwellings should be erected in the celestial life, in which no house was necessary—since it was written: *And I saw no temple therein* (Apoc. xxi. 22).

V. 5. *And as he was yet speaking, behold a bright cloud overshadowed . . .*

JEROME: They who had thought to erect an earthly covering above them, made from branches, or tents, were now covered beneath the shelter of a bright cloud. So we have: *And as he was speaking . . .* CHRYSOSTOM: When the Lord threatens, He comes in the darkness of a cloud, as on Sinai (Ex. xix). But here, since He wished not to chastise but to teach, a *bright cloud* appears.

ORIGEN: The *bright cloud* overshadowing the just men is the Paternal Power, or may it not be the Holy Spirit? I venture to say that our Saviour is also a *bright cloud*, which overshadows the Gospel and the Law and the Prophets; as they understand who see His light in the Gospel and in the Law and in the Prophets. JEROME: Because Peter had questioned Him foolishly, he did not deserve an answer from the Lord. But the Father answers for the Son, that the word of the Lord might be fulfilled: *He that hath sent me, hath given testimony of me* (Jn. v. 37).

CHRYSOSTOM: Neither Elias nor Moses spoke, but the Father who is greater than all speaks from out the cloud: that the Disciples may believe that this voice was from God. For God has always appeared in a cloud; as was written: *Clouds and darkness are round about him* (Ps. xcvi. 2); and this is what was said: *And lo, a voice out of the cloud.*

JEROME: The voice of the Father is heard speaking from heaven, giving testimony to the Son, and, his error now corrected, teaching Peter the truth; and indeed through Peter the other Apostles. So it continues, saying: *This is my beloved Son.* For Him let you build a tabernacle. Him you must obey. He is My Son; these My servants. And with you they also must prepare in the depths of their hearts a dwelling for the Lord. CHRYSOSTOM: Fear not then, Peter. If God is Mighty, Mighty also is His Son. If Beloved, fear not; for no one forsakes him he loves. Nor do you love Him as the Father loves. Nor does He love Him solely because He begot Him, but also because He is One in Will with Him. For there follows: *In whom I am well pleased*; as if to say: In Whom is My rest and My delight. For all things of the Father He fulfils with care, and One is His Will with the Father's. So if He wills the Cross do not gainsay Him.

HILARY: The voice from the cloud then proclaims: That this is the Son, this is the Beloved, this is the One in Whom He is well pleased, this also is the One we must hear; declaring to us: *Hear ye him*; for He is a Worthy Teacher of such precepts, Who has confirmed by this example (*the living presence of Moses sharing His glory though departed this life*) the glory of the heavenly kingdom after the loss of this world, after carrying the Cross, and after the death of the body.

REMIGIUS: Therefore He says: *Hear ye him*, as though saying: Let the shadows of the Law and the Prophetic figures now depart; follow ye the shining Light of the Gospel. Or He says: *Hear ye him*, to show that He it was Whom Moses had foretold when he said: *The Lord thy God will raise up to thee a PROPHET of thy nation and of thy brethren like unto me: him thou shalt hear*. So the Lord has testimonies from all sides: from heaven the Voice of the Father, Elias from Paradise, Moses from hell, from among men the Apostles, so that in the name of Jesus every knee should bend, of those that are in heaven, on earth, and under the earth (Phil. ii. 10).

ORIGEN: The Voice out of the cloud speaks either to Moses and Elias, who have long desired to see the Son of God, and hear Him; or It speaks to the Disciples. GLOSS: We must note that the mystery of the second re-birth, that namely which will take place in the resurrection, when the body will be raised again, rightly agrees with the mystery of the first, which takes place in Baptism, where the soul is restored to life. For in the Baptism of Christ the operation of the whole Trinity is revealed to us: for there was the Son Incarnate, the Holy Spirit under the form of a dove, and the Father made known by His Voice. And so in the Transfiguration, which mystically signifies the second re-birth, the whole Trinity appears: the Father in the Voice, the Son in man, the Holy Spirit in a cloud. If it be asked why the Holy Spirit was first shown through a dove, but here by a cloud, the answer is that He indicates His gifts through fitting forms. He bestows innocence in Baptism, symbolized by the bird of purity; He will give glory and refreshment in the resurrection: refreshment is symbolized by the *cloud*; the glory of the rising bodies by the *brightness* of the cloud.

V. *And the disciples hearing, fell upon their face, and were afraid . . .*

JEROME: They were afraid for three reasons; either because they knew they had erred in the past, or because the bright cloud had covered them, or because they heard the Voice of God the Father speaking. For human frailty cannot endure the sight of such great glory, and so trembling in body and soul falls to the earth. For to the degree a man seeks the higher things, to the same degree he falls back to lower things, should he be unmindful of his own nature (*mensura*).

REMIGIUS: That the holy Apostles fall on their faces shows their sanctity: because the holy are described as falling upon their faces, the wicked as falling backwards. CHRYSOSTOM: But at the Baptism of Christ the same voice was heard, yet none from the crowd present suffered any such effect; how then was it that the Disciples upon the mountain fell upon their faces? Because the solitude and the height and the silence were very great, and the transfiguration filled them with awe, and the light was bright and shining, and there was a cloud round about them. Because of all this they were overcome with fear and wonder.

V. 7. *And Jesus came and touched them: and said to them, Arise.*

JEROME: Since they were lying prone on the earth, unable to rise, He spoke gently to them, and touched them, and at His touch fear left them, and their trembling limbs again became strong. And this is what is here related: *And Jesus came and touched them.* And those he had healed by the touch of His Hand He healed also by His command. For there then follows: *And he said to them, Arise, and fear not.* He first casts out fear, that He may then give them His teaching.

V. 8. *And they lifting up their eyes saw no one but only Jesus.*

This was a deliberate sequence of events. For had Moses and Elias remained with the Lord, it would have appeared uncertain to whom the Voice of the Father had given testimony. For when the cloud had passed they saw Jesus standing there, and that Moses and Elias had disappeared. For after the shadow of the Law and of the Prophets had disappeared (which had covered the Apostles as with a garment) both the one and the other are found in the Gospel. Then there follows:

V. 9. *And as they came down from the mountain, Jesus charged them.*

Because of the greatness of the event He did not wish it to be spread among the people: lest it should not be believed, and lest after such a vision of glory, the Cross that was to follow might prove a stone of stumbling to the minds of simple people. REMIGIUS: Or lest the people, should they come to learn of the greatness of His dignity, interfere with the divine ordering of His Passion, by opposing the Chief Priests, and thus the redemption of the human race should be delayed. HILARY: He imposed silence on them as to what they had seen, until when, filled with the Holy Ghost, they should be witnesses of the things of the spirit.

I. ST EPHRAEM, CONFESSOR AND DOCTOR

On the Transfiguration of Our Lord and God and Saviour Jesus Christ[1]

The harvest comes joyfully from the fields, and a yield that is rich and pleasant from the vine; and from the Scriptures teaching that is lifegiving and salutary. The fields have but one season of harvest; but from the Scripture there gushes forth a stream of saving doctrine. The field when reaped lies idle, and at rest, and the branches when the vine is stripped lie withered and dead. The Scriptures are garnered each day, yet the years of its interpreters never come to an end; and the clusters of its vines, which in it are those of hope, though also gathered each day, are likewise without end. Let us therefore come to this field, and take our delight of its life-giving furrows; and let us reap there the wheat of life, that is, the words of Our Lord Jesus Christ.

And after six days Jesus taketh unto Him Peter and James, and John his brother, and bringeth them up into a high mountain apart: and He was transfigured before them. And His face did shine as the sun: and His garments became white as snow. For the men whom He had said would not taste death until they should see the form and the foreshadowing of His Coming are these three Apostles, whom having taken with Him He brought to a mountain, and showed them in what manner He was to come on the last day: in the glory of His Divinity, and in the Body of His Humanity.

He led them up to the mountain that He might also reveal to them Who this Son is, and Whose Son is He. For when He asked them: *Whom do men say that the Son of man is*, they said to Him: *Some Elias; some others Jeremias, or one of the prophets*. And so He led them up into a high mountain, and showed them that He was not Elias, but the God of Elias; that neither was He Jeremias, but He that had sanctified Jeremias in his mother's womb; that neither was He one of the prophets, but the Lord of the prophets, and He that had sent them.

And He showed them also that He was the Creator of heaven and earth, and the Lord of the living and the dead; for He spoke to the heavens, and they sent down Elias; He made a sign to the earth, and raised Moses to life again. And He brought them to Sinai, that He might show them He was the Son of God, and begotten of the Father before all ages, and last of all taking flesh from the Virgin Mary, and, in a manner which He knows, was born without seed in an ineffable manner, without stain whatsoever of her virginity. For where God wills it, the order of nature is superseded. For God the Word dwelt in the womb of the Virgin: and the fire of His Divinity consumed not the members of the virginal body; and in that dwelling place she kept watch over him for the space of nine months. He dwelt in the womb of the Virgin, not despising our nature; and from it God came forth clothed in human flesh, that He might redeem us.

He took them up into a high mountain apart, that He might also show them the glory of His Divinity, and that He might declare Himself the Redeemer of Israel, as He had foretold by the prophets, and so that they would not be scandalized in Him when they would see Him in the Passion He had taken upon Himself; and which for our sakes He was about to suffer in His human nature. For they knew that He was man; but they knew not that He was God. They knew Him as the Son of Mary, and as a man sharing their daily life in the world. On the mountain He revealed to them that He was the Son of God, and Himself God. For they knew that He hungered and that He ate; that He thirsted and that He drank; that He laboured and that

He took rest, that He felt need of sleep and that He slept, that He feared and that He sweated. And all this belonged not to His divine nature, but only to His humanity; and therefore He led them to the mountain, so that the Father may with His own voice call Him Son, and that He may show that He is in truth His Son, and God.

He took them therefore up to the mountain, that He might show them His Kingdom, before they witnessed His suffering and death; and His glory before His ignominy: so that when He was made a prisoner, and condemned by the Jews, they might understand that He was not crucified by them because of His own powerlessness, but because it had pleased Him of His goodness to suffer, for the salvation of the world.

He brought them up to the mountain that He might also show them, before His Resurrection, the glory of His Divinity, so that when He had risen from the dead they might then know that He had not received this glory as the reward of His labour, and as one who had it not; but that He had had it from all eternity, together with the Father and the Holy Spirit; as He had already said when He came of His own will to suffer: *Now glorify me, O Father, with thyself, with the glory which I had, before the world was, with thee* (Jn. xvii. 9). It was therefore this glory of His Divinity, which was hidden and veiled to humanity, that He revealed to the Apostles on the mountain. For they beheld His Face shining as the sun, and His garments white as snow.

The Disciples upon the mountain beheld two suns, one, to which they were accustomed, shining in the sky, and Another, to which they were unaccustomed; one which shone down on them, and from the firmament gave light to the whole world, and One which then shone for them alone, which was the Face of Jesus *before them*. And His garments appeared to them white as light: for the glory of His Divinity poured forth from His whole body, and all His members radiated light. His Face shone, not as the face of Moses, from without; from His Face the glory of His Divinity poured forth, yet remained with Him. From Himself came His own light, and was contained within Him. For it did not spread out from elsewhere, and fall on Him; it did not come slantwise to adorn Him. Neither did He receive it, to use for a while, nor did He reveal to them the unfathomable depths of His glory, but only as much as the pupils of their eyes could take in and distinguish.

And there appeared to them Moses and Elias talking with him. And this was the manner of their speech with Him. They gave thanks to Him that their own words had been fulfilled, and together with them the words of all the prophets. They adored Him for the salvation He had wrought in the world for mankind, and because He had in truth fulfilled the mystery which they had themselves foretold. The Prophets therefore were filled with joy, and the Apostles likewise, in their ascent of the mountain. The prophets rejoiced because they had seen His Humanity, which they had not known. And the Apostles rejoiced because they had seen the glory of the Divinity, which they had not known.

And when they heard the voice of

the Father, giving testimony of the Son, they learnt through this that which till now had been obscure to them: that humanity had been assumed by Him. And together with His Father's Voice the glory of His own Body gave testimony to Him, shining resplendent because of That within Him which partakes of the Divinity, unchangeably and without confusion. And this was confirmed by three witnesses: by the Voice of the Father, and by the presences of Moses and Elias, who stood by Him as servants. And they looked, the one upon the other, the Prophets upon the Apostles, the Apostles upon the Prophets. They looked upon each other, the Princes of the Old and the Princes of the New Testament. Moses the holy man looks upon Simon the Sanctified. The servant of the Father looks upon the vicar of the Son. The one had divided the sea, so that the people might walk in the midst of the waves (Ex. xiv). The other made a tabernacle, that he might build a church.

The virgin of the old Testament looks upon the virgin of the New: Elias looks upon John. He who had ascended into heaven in a fiery chariot looks upon him who had rested his head upon a Burning Breast (IV Kings ii; Jn. xiii. 21). His mountain became a figure of the Church; and in Himself Jesus has united the Two Testaments, which the Church receives, revealing to us that He is the Giver of both. The one received His divine secrets; the other has proclaimed the visible glory of His works.

And so Simon says: *Lord, it is good for us to be here*. What is it you say, O Simon? If we should remain here, who would fulfil the words of the Prophets? Who confirm the tidings of the Heralds? Who accomplish the mysteries of the Just? If we should remain here, then that prophecy: *They have pierced my hands and my feet* (Ps. xxi. 17), in whom would it be fulfilled? Or that other: *They parted my garments among them, and upon my vesture they cast lots* (Ps. xxi. 19), to whom would it then pertain? *And they gave me gall for my food, and in my thirst they gave me vinegar to drink* (Ps. lxviii. 22), to whom would these words apply? And the words: *Free among the dead*, who would make them true? (Ps. lxxxvii. 6).

If we should remain here who would tear up the writ against Adam, and who would pay his debt? And who would give him back his garment of glory? If we should remain here how would the things I have told you be fulfilled? How would the Church be built upon you, Peter? And the Keys of the Kingdom of Heaven, how would you receive them from Me? Whom would you bind? Whom would you loose? If we should remain here all these things will remain unfulfilled which were spoken of by the Prophets.

Then he said: *Let us make here three dwelling-places, one for thee, and one for Moses, and one for Elias.* Simon was sent to build the Church in the world, and he wishes to build three dwellings upon a mountain: for he still continues to speak with Christ as one speaks with a man, placing Him on a level with Moses and Elias. But immediately the Lord shows him that He has no need of dwelling-places. For He it was who concealed His dwelling-place in a cloud among their forefathers in the wilderness throughout forty years (Num. ix. 10). For as He was speaking to them *a bright cloud* overshadowed them. Behold, O Simon, a dwelling-place made without hands; a dwelling-place that protects you from the heat, and that is without any darkness: a dwelling-place that shines as the sun. And to the great wonder of the Disciples, behold a Voice, Which proceeds from the Father, is heard from the cloud, saying: *This is my beloved Son, in whom I am well pleased: hear ye him.*

The Father having spoken Moses returns to his own place and Elias to his fatherland; and the Apostles fall down with their faces to the earth; and Jesus stands alone, since only in Him were these words fulfilled. The Prophets are gone, and the Apostles lie prone upon the earth, for it is not in any of these that the words are fulfilled which the Father spoke: *This is my beloved Son in whom I am well pleased. Hear ye him.*

The Father teaches them that the Dispensation of Moses had been fulfilled; and now they must hearken to the voice of His Son. For the former, as a servant, had spoken that which he was commanded; and that which was told him he had made known: and in like manner all the Prophets, until He had come in place of them, namely, Jesus, Who is the Son, not a servant of His household, the Lord, not a slave, the Ruler, not one subject to rule, the Lawgiver, not one subject to the law; His Son by nature, not by adoption.

Accordingly, the Father makes manifest upon the mountain what was yet obscure to the Apostles regarding the divinity of His Son. He Who is signifies to them *Who* He is. The Father by His voice gives testimony to His Son; and at the sound of His voice the Apostles fall prone upon the ground. Since it was awesome as the thunder, and as the earth trembled at His voice, so likewise they sink down upon the earth. It told them that the Father had come nigh them, and had called Him Son Who by His voice had comforted them. For as that dread voice of the Father cast them prone upon the earth, so the voice of the Son caused them to rise up again by the power of His divinity. Which, since It dwells in His flesh, is united unchangeably to Him: Both dwell within the one hypostasis, and in the one Person abide without separation and without commingling.

Nor did He appear as Moses, outwardly beautiful, but shone as God; for it was from the light of the glory of His countenance that the face of Moses was clothed with beauty. But Jesus shone forth in His own Body, as the sun in the midst of its rays; from the glory of His divinity. The Father indeed cried out: *This is My beloved Son, in whom I am well pleased, Hear ye him.* He is not separate from the glory of the divinity of His Son. For One is the Nature of the Father, and of the Son, together with the Holy Ghost: One is the Power, One the Essence, One the Kingdom, and it calls Him with one voice, by a name that is simple, but of a glory that is fearful.

And Mary called Him her Son, Who was undivided by His human body from the glory of His Divinity: since One is God, seen in this world in our body. His glory reveals His divine nature, which is from the Father; and His body reveals His human nature, which is from Mary. Both natures have united, and, without change and without commingling, have been joined together in one hypostasis or person. The Same is the Only-begotten of the Father Who is the Only-begotten of Mary. And he who separates them is himself separated from His Kingdom; and he who commingles His natures into one will have no part in His life. He that denies that Mary gave birth to God shall not see the glory of His divinity; and whosoever denies that He was clothed in flesh Who was free from the stain of every sin shall be shut out from salvation, and from the life which is given by His Body.

The events of His life, and His own divine powers, teach those who can learn that He is true God, and His sufferings openly proclaim Him true man. And if this does not convince those who are weak and foolish of mind, they shall suffer punishment on the day of His dread judgement. For if He were not flesh, for what reason did Mary bring Him forth? And if He was not God, who then did Gabriel call Lord?

If He was not flesh, who then lay in the manger? If He was not God, to whom did the angels coming on earth give glory?

If He was not man, who was wrapped in swaddling clothes? If He was not God, whom then did the Shepherds adore?

If He was not man, whom did Joseph circumcize? And if He was not God, in whose honour did a new star appear in the heavens?

If He was not man, whom did Mary nourish at the breast? And if He were not God, to whom did the Magi offer gifts?

If He was not man, whom did Simeon take in His arms? And if He was not God, to whom did Simeon say: *Dismiss me in peace*?

If He was not man, whom did Joseph take and fly with him into Egypt? And if He was not God, in whom was the prophecy fulfilled: *Out of Egypt have I called my son*? (Mt. ii. 15; Os. xi. 1).

If He was not man, whom did John baptize? And if He was not God, of whom did the Father from heaven say: *This is my beloved Son, in whom I am well pleased*? (Mt. iii. 17).

If He was not man, who fasted and hungered in the desert? And if He was not God, to whom did the descending angels minister?

If He was not man, who was invited to the wedding feast at Cana of Galilee? And if He was not God, who changed the water into wine?

If He was not man, in whose hands were the loaves of bread placed? And if He were not God, who fed and filled from five barley loaves and two fishes the multitude in the desert, five thousand men, not counting the women and children?

If He was not a man, who slept in the boat? And if He were not God, who was it rebuked the winds and the sea?

If He was not man, who was it ate with Simon the Pharisee? And if He were not God, who forgave the woman her sins?

If He was not a man, who sat by the well weary from the journey? And if He was not God, who gave the Samaritan woman the water of life; and who rebuked her, she that had already five husbands?

If He was not of our flesh, who

wore the garments of a man? And if He were not God, who then was it that wrought signs and wonders?

If He was not a man, who spat upon the earth, and made mud from the clay? And if He were not God, who caused eyes to see because of the clay? (Jn. ix).

If He was not man, who wept at the tomb of Lazarus? And if He were not God, who by his command alone called forth the four days dead?

If He was not a man, who was it sat upon an ass's colt? And if He were not God, before whom did the crowd march to give Him glory?

If He was not a man, whom did the Jews make prisoner? And if He were not God, who commanded the earth, and it threw them flat to the ground?

If He was not a man, who was beaten with blows? And if He were not God, who healed the ear which Peter had cut off, and who restored it to its place?

If He was not a man, whose face was spat upon? And if He were not God, who breathed the Holy Spirit upon the faces of the Apostles (Jn. xx. 22).

If He was not a man, who was it stood before Pilate at the judgement seat? And if He were not God, who caused the wife of Pilate to suffer many things in a dream?

If He was not a man, upon whose garments did the soldiers cast lots, dividing them amongst them? And if He were not God, for what reason did the sun grow dark above the Cross?

If He was not a man, who was it hung upon a cross? And if He were not God, who moved the earth from its foundations?

If He was not a man, whose hands were pierced by the nails? And if He were not God, how was the veil of the temple rent in two, and the rocks split asunder, and the graves opened?

If He was not a man, who cried out: *My God, My God, why hast Thou abandoned me?* And if He were not God, who then hath said: *Father forgive them, for they know not what they do*?

If He was not man, who hung with thieves upon a cross? And if He were not God, for what cause did He say: *This day thou shalt be with me in paradise*?

If He was not man, to whom did they offer gall and vinegar? And if He were not God, at whose voice did they shake and tremble? (Ps. lxxvi. 19).

If He was not a man, whose side was opened by a lance, *and there came out blood and water*? (Jn. xix. 34). And if He were not God, who *hath broken the gates of hell, and burst the iron bars*? (Ps. cvi. 16). And by whose command did the dead that slept in their graves come forth?

If He was not a man, whom did the Apostles behold in the Upper Room? And if He was not God, in what manner did He enter, *the doors being closed*?

If He was not a man, in whose hand did Thomas feel the wounds of the nails and the lance? And if He was not God, to whom did Thomas cry out saying: *My Lord and My God*?

If He was not a man, who ate food by the sea of Tiberiades? And if He were not God, at whose command was the net filled with fishes?

If He was not man, whom did the Apostles and the Angels see received into the heavens? If He was not God, to whom were the heavens opened, whom did the powers adore in fear and trembling, and to whom had the Father said: *Sit thou on my right hand,* and the rest which follows? (Ps. cix. 1). If He were not both God and man, then is our salvation a false thing; and false likewise the voices of the prophets. But the prophets have spoken what is true, and their testimonies are far from falsehood of any kind. For they spoke that which they were bidden to speak, and through them the Holy Spirit spoke. For which reason the chaste John, who leaned upon that burning Breast, confirming the voices of the prophets, and discoursing of the divinity, teaches us in His Gospel, saying: *In the beginning was the Word, and the Word was with God, and the Word was God. All things were made by Him: and without Him was made nothing that was made. And the Word was made flesh, and dwelt among us;* Who is God the Word from God, and the Only-begotten Son of the Father, Who is consubstantial with the Father, Who is, from Him Who is: the Word before all ages: ineffably and before all ages Begotten of the Father without a mother; the Same in these last days is born without a father, God Incarnate, from a daughter of men, from the Virgin Mary; taking flesh from Her, and from Her made man, which He was not, remaining God, which He was, that He might redeem the world.

And He is Christ the Son of God: the Only-begotten of the Father, the Only-begotten of His Mother. And I confess that the Same is perfect God and perfect man, Who in His two natures is acknowledged to be indivisibly, unchangeably, and without confusion, united in the one *hypostasis* or person; clothed in living flesh, and having a soul that is endowed with reason and understanding, subject in all things to the same afflictions as ourselves, sin alone excepted.

The Same is of both earth and heaven: of time and eternity; Who began, and is without beginning; free of time, yet subject to time; created and Uncreated; impassible, and capable of suffering; God and man; perfect as either one or the other; One sharing two natures, and in two natures One. One the Person of the Father, and one the Person of the Son, and one the Person of the Holy Ghost. One the Godhead, one the Majesty, one the Kingdom in three Persons or Hypostases.

So let us give glory to the Holy Unity in Trinity, and to the Holy Trinity in Unity! In Which the Father has declared from heaven: *This is My beloved Son, in whom I am well pleased: Hear ye him.* This the Most Holy Catholic Church professes. In this same Holy Trinity She baptizes unto eternal life. She venerates the Same with equality of honour; and confesses the Same without division, and without separation; and without superstition adores, proclaims, and glorifies the same Holy Trinity.

To that Unity in three Persons, to the Father, Son, and Holy Ghost, glory, thanksgiving, honour, power, and glory, now and for ever. Amen.

II. St John Chrysostom, Bishop and Doctor

The Transfiguration of Christ[2] *(and Against Usury)*

Matthew xvi. 28; xvii. 1–9. 1. Since the Lord had said many things concerning the dangers that awaited Him, and had spoken of His passion and death, and of the putting to death of His Disciples, and had told them of the many severe trials that would come upon them in this life, and were now close at hand, and told them also of the many good things laid up for their hope and expectation: such as that they who lose their life shall find it, and that He shall come in the glory of the Father and give us our reward; and since He also wished to show them what that glory would be like in which He would appear, that they might see it with their own eyes and understand it as far as was possible to them, He shows it to them in this present life, and He shows it also so that they might not continue to grieve over their own death, and over the Lord's death, especially Peter, who particularly was fearful. And what does He do?

After He had spoken to them of Hell, and of His Kingdom: for when He said: *He that findeth his life, shall lose it, and he that shall lose his life for me, shall find it* (Mt. x. 39); and also: *He will render to every man according to his works* (Mt. xvi. 27). He spoke of both these things: and when He had spoken of them He revealed His kingdom to them; but not however the kingdom of darkness. Why was this? Had they been different, grosser men, the other would certainly have been necessary; but since they were tried and worthy men He now strengthens them with this vision of His Glory. And this was not the sole reason for what He did; but it was the most becoming to Him. Yet He does not pass over the other kingdom; for He frequently brings the realities of hell before their eyes, as when He brought before them the picture of Lazarus, and when He reminded them of the man who had extorted the hundred pence, and also of the man who was clothed in filthy garments, and of many others (Lk. 16; Mt. xviii. 22).

And after six days Jesus taketh unto him Peter and James, and John his brother. Elsewhere it is written: *And after eight days* (Lk. ix. 28). But one Evangelist does not contradict the other, but rather fully agrees with him. For one counts the day on which He spoke, and also the day on which He brought them up, the other only the intervening days. And I would like you to take note of how modest Matthew is; not withholding the names of those who were honoured above himself. And this John often does, carefully recording the special praises of Peter. For this holy company of men was ever free of envy and vain glory.

The Transfiguration of Christ. Taking with Him His chief Disciples He leads them up into a high mountain apart. And He was transfigured before them. And His face did shine as the sun, and His garments became white as snow. And behold there appeared to them Moses and Elias, talking with Him. Why did He bring only these Disciples? Because they excelled the others; Peter in the manner of His wholehearted love for Christ, John in that he was himself greatly beloved, James because together with his brother he had answered: *We can drink of the chalice* (Mt. xx. 22), and not for this answer alone, but also because of his good works, and for other things, and because, in the end, he did what he said he would do. For so zealous and impressive did he seem to the Jews that Herod believed he did them the greatest favour putting him to death (Acts xii).

But why did He not lead them up to the mountain straight away? So that the other Disciples might not suffer, as was but human. For the same reason He does not mention by name those who are to ascend. For the others would also greatly desire to follow them, to see such glory, and would have suffered greatly were they not permitted. For though this was revealed to them in a corporeal manner, yet it was an event that would have awakened the greatest desire to see. But why did He foretell it? So that foretelling it they might be forewarned and more prepared for the Vision, and with the passing of the days their minds would become more alert and more vigilant, being filled with an eager desire to see it.

And why did He bring Moses and Elias before them? Many reasons can be given, of which this is the principal one: because of what the multitude were saying, some that Christ was Elias, others that He was Jeremiah, and others that He was one of the ancient prophets (Mt. xvi. 14). So He brings the chief Disciples there, that they might learn how great was the difference between the Master and the servant; and also because Peter deserved to be rewarded for confessing that Christ was the Son of God.

There is yet another reason. Because of those who said He broke the Law, and called Him a blasphemer, in that He took to Himself glory that belonged, not to Him, but to the Father, and who said of Him: *This man is not of God, who keepeth not the sabbath* (Jn. ix. 16); and also: *For a good work we stone thee not, but for blasphemy; and because thou, being a man, makest thyself God* (Jn. x. 33). That He might show that both accusations arose from malice, and that neither applied to Him, and that He neither violated the Law, nor took glory that was not His when He declared Himself equal to the Father, He brings before them these two men who had been pre-eminent in either regard. For Moses had given them the Law; and the Jews would be unable to believe that He would lightly suffer the Law to be violated as they imagined, or that He would do reverence to an enemy of the Law he had himself given them. Elias too was filled with zeal for the glory of God. And were Christ an enemy of God, and had He falsely declared Himself God, and equal to the Father, Elias would never have stood beside Him, and shown Him reverence.

2. *Why Moses and Elias were present at the Transfiguration. The wonders wrought by Peter have converted the world.*

Besides these reasons we must speak of another. What is this? That they might learn He had power over life and death; and that He has power equally over those in heaven and those on earth. And so He brings before them the one who had died, and one that had not yet died. The Evangelist gives a fifth reason also: for it is fifth in number. And what is this? That He might show them the glory of the Cross, and bring comfort to Peter and the others who went in fear of His Passion, and raise their courage. For when these men appeared they were not silent, but spoke with Him of the glory He was to accomplish in Jerusalem,[3] that is, of His Passion and Cross; for so they always speak of it.

Not alone did He encourage them in this way, but also through the example of the virtue of both these men: which He wished them to imitate. For He had said: *If any man will come after me, let him take up his cross and follow me*, and because of this He brought before the Apostles men who had pleased God, and who, on behalf of the people entrusted to them, had faced a thousand deaths. Both had lost their life, and found it. For both the one and the other had courageously withstood a tyrant: one the Egyptian, the other Achab; and this on behalf of a people who were both ungrateful and disobedient. And they were placed in this danger through those whose salvation they were defending; and each that He might withdraw them from idolatry.

And both were simple unlearned men. One was slow of speech and weak of voice (Ex. iv. 10). The other a rough countryman. And both were men who had despised the riches of this world. For Moses possessed nothing. And Elias had nothing but his sheepskin. And this too when they were yet under the Old Law, and had not the privilege of seeing signs and wonders. And though Moses had divided the sea in two, Peter had walked upon the waters, and could move mountains, and had healed many diseased persons, and put evil spirits to flight, and had wrought extraordinary miracles by the very shadow of his body, and had changed the world. And if Elias had raised a dead man to life, these raised thousands, though they had not yet received the Holy Spirit.

He brought these men before them for this reason also. He wished them to imitate their courage of soul, and their steadfastness in leading their people; and so that they might be gentle as Moses, and possessed of the zeal of Elias, and as devoted as both were. For one of them, on behalf of the Jewish people, had for two years suffered hunger, and the other had prayed to God: *Either forgive them this trespass, or strike me out of the book that thou hast written* (III Kings xvii. 1; Ex. xxxii. 31, 32). He brought all this before their mind through this Vision. He brought these before them in glory; and not alone that they might be as they were, but that they might surpass them. When for example they had said: *Shall we command fire to come down from heaven*, recalling Elias who had done this (Lk. ix. 54). He had answered: *You know not of what spirit you are*; exhorting them to the forgiveness of injuries, because of the difference of their gifts.

Do not think we speak of Elias as someone imperfect (Lk. ix. 54). We are not saying this: for he was a truly perfect man. But in those days, when the mind of man was less formed, they were in need rather of simpler instruction. In this sense Moses also was perfect; but more is required of the Apostles than from him. *For unless your justice abound more than that of the Scribes and Pharisees, you shall not enter into the kingdom of heaven* (Mt. v. 20). For they have not alone gone into Egypt, but into the whole world, which is more dangerously and more wickedly disposed than Egypt. They were to speak not before Pharao, but to wage war against the devil, and the very kingdom of wickedness. For the purpose of their warfare was that they should bind up the evil one, and deprive him of his weapons. And this they have done; and not by dividing the sea, but, by the rod of Jesse, dividing the great deep of wickedness which is troubled by far fiercer tempests.

See how many and how great are the evils which would inflict terror on men; death, poverty, infamy, and a thousand others, which they feared more than the Jews of old feared the Red Sea. Nevertheless He encourages them to face them all, and to cross over them as it were with every confidence, as though they were on dry land. That He might uplift their courage against all such dangers He here brings before them those two men who were such shining lights of the Old Testament.

What does the impulsive Peter say? *It is good for us to be here?* For since he had heard that the Lord was to go up to Jerusalem, and to suffer there, he had been in great fear. But after the reproof he had received he dared not again approach Him, and say: *Far be it from thee*. But still in the grip of fear he hints at this same desire, using other words. And now he sees a mountain place, a great remote wilderness, and he thinks to himself that because of the nature of the place they would be secure there; and this not alone because of the place, but because he hoped they might never again go near Jerusalem. He wished to remain here always. And so he speaks of dwelling places. For if this is done we shall not go up to Jerusalem. And if we do not go up there, He will not die. For there, He had said, the Scribes lay in wait to attack them. But he does not dare to say these things aloud. Yet wishing to bring them about he says confidently: *It is good for us to be here*, where Moses and Elias are with us: Elias who had called down fire from heaven upon the mountain, and Moses who had entered the darkness of the cloud, when he had spoken with God (IV Kings i. 10; Ex. xix. 6); and no one will know where we are.

3. You see here the fervent lover of Christ? Do not notice the circuitous manner of his speech, but consider how fervent, how great, was his love for Christ. And to show that when he said this he did not in saying it fear for himself, hear what he says when Christ foretold his own death and the snares that were prepared for him: *I will lay down my life for thee: although I should die with thee, I will not deny thee* (Jn. xiii. 37; Mk. xiv. 31). See how in the midst of danger he cared little for his own life. For though surrounded by a crowd of people, not alone did he not take flight, but drawing a sword he cut off the ear of the servant of the high priest. So he was not considering himself, but rather was in fear for his Master.

Then, having spoken so boldly, he recollects himself, and fearing that he might again be rebuked he says: *If thou wilt let us make here three tabernacles, one for thee, and one for Moses, and one for Elias.* What sayest thou, Peter? Did you not, a while ago, place Him far above His servants? Why now do you name Him together with His servants? See how imperfect they were prior to His crucifixion? For the Father had revealed knowledge to Peter, but not for long did he remember that revelation: for he was tormented by fear, and not alone by that fear of which I have already spoken, but also by another which had arisen from this vision. And indeed the other Evangelists, when they spoke of this, declared that the confusion of mind by which he was troubled when he said these words arose from this latter fear. Mark indeed says: *For he knew not what he said: for they were struck with a great fear.* Luke, even after he had recorded the words: *Let us make three tabernacles*, immediately adds: *Not knowing what he said* (Mk. ix. 5; Lk. ix. 33). Then, showing that both he and the others were overcome by heavy sleep, he says: *They were heavy with sleep. And waking, they saw His glory*; describing as sleep the stupor that came upon them at such a vision. For as eyes may be dimmed by a too great light, so had it happened to them. For it was not now the night, but the day; yet the splendour of this glory was too great for their eyes.

Then what happens? The Lord does not speak, nor does Moses, or Elias: but He Who is greater than all of them, and more worthy of belief, the Father, He speaks from out the cloud. Why from out the cloud? Because so does God always appear: *For darkness and clouds are round about Him*; and again: *Who makest the clouds thy chariot*; and again: *Behold the Lord will ascend upon a swift cloud*; and: *And a cloud received him out of their sight*; and: *One like the Son of man came with the clouds of heaven* (Ps. xcvi. 2; ciii. 3; Is. xix. 1; Acts i. 9; Dan. vii. 13).

That they might therefore believe that the voice was from God Himself it came from thence, and it was a *bright* cloud; for, *as he was yet speaking a bright cloud overshadowed them. And lo, a voice out of the cloud, saying: This is my beloved Son, in whom I am well pleased: hear ye him.* But when He threatened He spoke from out a *dark* cloud, as in Sion: *Moses went to the dark cloud wherein God was*; and the prophet, speaking of threatenings, says: *Dark waters in the clouds of the air* (Ex. xx. 31; Ps. xvii. 12). But here, since He wishes not to terrify but to teach, it is a *bright* cloud.

And Peter said: *Let us make three tabernacles.* But He shows them a dwelling not made with hands. There was smoke and steam as from a furnace; here is light ineffable, and a Voice. Then that He might show that He was speaking not simply of one of the three, but of Christ alone, when the Voice finished speaking, Moses and Elias had departed. For had it spoken merely of any one of them, He would not have remained alone, the two others departing.

[Why then did the cloud not overshadow Christ alone, and not all together? Had it overshadowed Christ alone, then it might be thought that it was Christ Himself that had spoken. And so the

Evangelist, that he might confirm this, says that the voice came from out the cloud, that is, from God. (*Excerpt found in two codices.*)]

And what did this Voice say? *This is my beloved Son.* If He is the Beloved, fear not, Peter. You should now know both of His power and His majesty, and be confident of His resurrection; but since you do not know these things, then at least take courage from the Voice of His Father. For if the Father is all powerful, so likewise is the Son. Do not then be fearful of dangers. But if this will not reassure you, remember this at least that He is His Son, and His Beloved! *For*, says He: *This is my beloved Son.* If He is His beloved, be not afraid. For no one casts off the one he loves. Be not troubled then: however much you love Him, you do not love Him as His own Father loves Him.

In whom I am well pleased. He not alone loves Him because He has begotten Him, but because He is equal to Him in all things, and because Their will is one. Twofold then, nay, threefold, is the ground of His love: because He is the Son, because He is the Beloved, and because in Him He is well pleased. And what does this mean: *In whom I am well pleased*? It is as if He said, in Whom I take my rest, in Whom I delight, Who is equal to Me in all things, Who is of one Will with the Father, and while yet His Son, is One in all things with Him Who has begotten Him. *Hear ye Him*, He says. So that if He wills to be crucified, seek not to oppose Him.

4. *And hearing this, they fell upon their face, and were much afraid. And Jesus came and touched them: and said to them, Arise, and fear not. And they lifting up their eyes saw no one but Jesus.* How was it they were stricken when they heard these words? For before this happening a similar voice had spoken above the Jordan; there had been crowds present, yet no one had suffered anything. And later again, when they said that the sound of the voice was caused by the thunder, neither did anyone then suffer anything (Jn. xii. 28, 29). How then was it that the Apostles fell prostrate upon the mountain? Because here there was a vast solitude, and a lonely height, and a great stillness, and a transfiguration full of awe, and overpowering light, and a cloud spread all about them. All this awakened in them an immense fear. Terror assailed them from every side, and full of dread they fall prone upon the earth, in adoration.

But in a moment, lest fear if too prolonged might wipe out the memory of what had taken place, He delivers them from their fear; and He is seen to be alone, as He bids them that they tell no man what they have seen, till He was risen from the dead. For, *as they came down from the mountain, Jesus charged them, saying: Tell the vision to no man, till the Son of man be risen from the dead.* For the more striking were the things told of Him, the more difficult of belief were they to many people; and hence the scandal of the Cross grew greater.

So He bound them to silence, and not merely this, but He again spoke of His passion, as though it were the reason why He bade them be silent. But He did not tell them that they must never tell of this to anyone, but that they should not tell it until He had risen from the dead. And in this

He was silent as to what was painful, and spoke only of what was joyful And afterwards, what then? Would they not suffer scandal? Far from it. He was now concerned only with the time preceding His passion; for after that they were reassured by the Holy Spirit, and they had the witness of great signs, pressing their proof upon them; and all that they then spoke was readily believable, since events would proclaim His power more clearly than any trumpet; nor would any stumbling block stand in their way.

How glorious the second coming of Christ! No one was ever more blessed than the Apostles, and especially those three who were thought worthy of being overshadowed by the cloud together with the Lord. But if we will it, we also shall see Christ, not as they saw Him upon the mountain, but in yet greater glory: for not in this way will He come at the end of the world. For then, for His Disciples, He tempered the revelation of His glory to the measure they could endure to see. But in the last days He will come in the true glory of the Father; and not alone will He be accompanied by Moses and Elias, but by the whole host of heaven, by the Archangels, the Cherubim, and by an infinite multitude of every degree. And not with a cloud about His Head, but clothed with the heavens.

It shall be as when the judges publicly give sentence, and those who stand about their seat draw aside the veils and allow them to be seen by all, so shall all men look on Him enthroned. And mankind will stand before Him, and He will pronounce sentence, and to some He will say: *Come ye blessed of My Father: for I was hungry and you gave me to eat.* And to others He will say: *Well done, good and faithful servant, because thou hast been faithful over a few things, I will place thee over many.* But to others He will say: *Depart from me, you cursed, into everlasting fire which was prepared for the devil and his angels.* And to yet others: *Wicked and slothful servant!* (Mt. xxv. 34, 21, 41, 26). And some He will set apart, and deliver to the torturers. And others He will have bound hand and foot, and cast out into exterior darkness; and after the ax the furnace will receive them. And they that are discarded from the net will also fall down into it.

Then shall the Just shine as the sun (Mt. xiii. 43). Yea, more than the sun. This was said, not because their light shall be like that of the sun, but since there is no other light so splendid He sought by this example to make known the future glory of the blessed. For when the Evangelist, in speaking of the mountain, said *He shone* as the sun, he spoke in this way for a like reason. For the Disciples falling prone to the ground proved this light was greater than that used in the comparison. For were the light indeed wondrous, yet still only like the light of the sun, they would easily have endured it, and would not have fallen down. The Just therefore shall shine as the sun, and more gloriously than the sun; but sinners shall suffer most grievous torments.

Then shall there be no need of proofs, or of testimony, or of witnesses; for He that is the Judge is also each of these things: He is witness, proof, and judge. For He sees all things clearly. *All things are naked and open to his eyes* (Heb. iv. 13). And no rich man will appear there, and no poor man, no ignorant, no mighty, no weak, no wise, no foolish, no slave, no freeman. For all these appearances will be at an end, and there shall only be trial of our misdeeds. For if in our courts a man be tried for oppression or for murder, whoever he may be, whether governor or consul, or whatever you will, all these symbols of his greatness disappear, and if he is guilty he suffers the extreme penalty. Much more so will it be on that day.

4. *Virtue is easy to bear; Iniquity a burthen.* That this may not happen to us, let us, I beseech you, put away our soiled garments, and let us put on the armour of light, and the glory of God will enfold us. How can His commands be heavy? What is there in them that is not easy? Hear what the prophet says, and see how light they are: *Is this such a fast as I have chosen: for a man to afflict his soul for a day? Is this it, to wind his head about like a circle, and to spread sackcloth and ashes? Wilt thou call this a fast, and a day acceptable to the Lord? Loose rather the bonds of iniquity, undo the bonds that are oppressive* (Is. lviii. 5, 6). See the wisdom of the prophet. He first puts before us what is hard, and then puts it aside and exhorts us to seek salvation by easier means; making clear to us that God demands of us not achievements but obedience.

Then to show that virtue is not difficult, but that evil is a burthen, He makes this clear from their very names. For iniquity is a bond and a tie; virtue is deliverance and freedom from them. *Undo every unjust contract*, referring here to deeds of loans and interest. *Let them that are broken go free*; those who are tormented, for such is a debtor: when he sees his creditor his spirit is broken, and he fears him more than a wild beast. *And bring the needy and the harbourless into thy house; when thou shalt see one naked, cover him, and despise not thy own flesh.*

In the previous discourse, speaking of rewards, we showed what riches are prepared for the Just. Now let us see whether any one of the divine precepts is difficult or beyond our power to fulfil? We shall find nothing of the sort, but rather all to the contrary: that every thing relating to the practise of virtue is easy, while all that relates to wickedness is a grievous burthen. For what is more burthensome than making loans, and to be ever concerned with interest and agreements, and searching for securities, and being in fear and trembling over guarantees, and about the principal, the deeds, the interest, the guarantors? Such are the cares of this world. The security that seems so carefully established is full of mistrust, and the most insecure of all things. But to show mercy is easy, and frees a man from all anxiety.

Let us then not make a traffic of other peoples' misfortunes; nor put to interest what belongs to mercy. I know well there are many who will give no ear to what I say. But what is to be gained by my keeping silent? For though I should be silent, and disturb no one with my words, I cannot by my silence deliver you from punishment. Rather the opposite will happen; for punishment would be increased, and not you alone, but I also would be punished. What good are soothing words, since they help us not at all to do good; rather they but do you harm? Where is the good in causing pleasure by my words if in the end they bring you affliction? What does it profit to soothe the ear, and lead the soul to death?

So we must sorrow here lest there we receive torment. For a grave evil, grave indeed, and crying out for remedy, has entered the Church. For those who are bidden not to lay up treasure, even from honest toil, but rather to open their houses to those in need, are now growing rich out of the poverty of others; making up plausible schemes of robbery, of well-concealed avarice. Do not speak to me about the laws of the land; for even the publican observes the law of the land, but he is punished by it notwithstanding. And we shall suffer the same unless we cease from plundering the needy; cease from shameless usury, and from taking advantage from poverty and from need. For this you received wealth, that you may help those in need; not oppress them. But you, pretending to give help, inflict greater misery, and sell them benevolence at interest.

Sell it: I do not forbid you: but for the kingdom of heaven! And take no small return: such as the monthly hundredth, for such a deed; but only for that life which is immortal! Why be poor and needy? Why be timorous, and sell your great possessions cheaply, giving them away for money, when you should hold out for an enduring Kingdom? Why, casting God aside, do you only look for human gain? Why do you turn from One Who is rich, neglecting Him Who would reward you, and deal only with those who show you no gratitude? For He desires to enrich you; these others begrudge paying you back. They will hardly pay you the interest; He will repay you a hundred fold, and give you also life eternal. The one repays you with insults and with infamy; the Other with praise, and with words of good omen. The one only envies you; the Other prepares a crown for you. The one scarcely repays you now; the Other pays you both now and in the hereafter. How many have lost the principal for the sake of the interest? How many have fallen into great misery through usury? How many have brought total poverty both on themselves and on others because of this monstrous greed?

6. Do not tell me that so and so is grateful for your loan, and accepts it joyfully! That has happened because of your inhumanity. Abraham gave his wife to the barbarians, trying to make himself agreeable to them; but through fear of Pharaoh, not joyfully (Gen. xii. 13). So too the poor man in need; since you do not deem him worthy of free help he is forced to be grateful for your cruelty. You are like a man who delivers another from danger but demands payment for it. No, no! you say, it is not so. What do you mean? No, no? When you deliver a man from great danger you do not demand money; but when you deliver him from a less evil you treat him with this inhumanity? Can you not see what grievous punishment this will bring on you? Have you not heard that even in the Old Law this was forbidden? And what is the excuse many make? When I make

a profit I give something to the poor! Be silent, man! God wants no part in such profits. Do not try to deceive the law. Far better give nothing to the poor than to give to them out of such gains. For oftentimes money that is the fruit of honest toil you make evil because of gains of this kind; as if one should force an honoured womb to bring forth scorpions.

And why am I speaking to you of the law of God? Do you not speak among yourselves of usury as sordid? And if you who gain by it so speak of it, think of the sentence God will pronounce on it. And if you ask the public law makers you will learn that they hold it a shameful thing. In fact it is forbidden to anyone who holds a public office, or belongs to the Senate, to degrade themselves by such gain: for there is a law which applies to them forbidding it. How then can it be other than an abhorrent thing, if you do not attribute such honour to the kingdom of heaven as the lawmakers do to the Roman Senate; and give less honour to heaven than to earth, and feel no shame for such unworthiness! What greater folly than for a man to sow seed without soil, without rain, without a plough! It is from this they reap tares, for burning, who let their minds be occupied with such sorry husbandry.

The Evils of Usury. Are there not enough ways of earning a livelihood? Are there not those of the land, of flocks and herds, the crafts, the skilled care of one's own patrimony? Why do you foolishly gather thorns to no good end? But, you will say, the fruits of the earth are liable to so many risks: to hail, to disease, to floods? But not to so many as moneylending. For in the one case whatever happens damages only the yield; the principal, namely, the land, remains secure. But in this other business many have lost their all. And even before that happens they live in constant anxiety. They never enjoy their own. Even when the interest comes in such a man is not then happy. He frets because the interest has not yet equalled the principal, and before this has yielded its evil fruit in full: changing interest into principal: he is striving to make it bring forth fruit again, and so forces it that it too may bring forth its own untimely brood of the viper.

Such are the moneylenders gains; which, more sharply than the viper, will rend and devour unhappy souls. This is *the bond of iniquity* (Is. lviii. 5), this is the twisted knot of *oppressive bargaining*. I give, he will say, not that you may receive, but that you may give me more! And God bids us not to receive back what is given, but: *Lend*, He says, *hoping for nothing thereby* (Lk. vi. 35). You seek back more than you have given; and what you did not give you have forced him who has received your loan to regard as a debt owing to you. And you think in this way to increase your substance, when instead you are, as return for your capital, but kindling an inextinguishable fire for yourself.

That this may not come to pass let us make an end of the wicked and unjust profit of usury. Let us cut away this pernicious womb. Let us dry up this deadly source of evil, and seek for the gains which alone are true and worthy. And what are they? Hear Paul telling us: *Godliness with contentment is great gain* (I Tim. vi. 6). Let us enrich ourselves with this wealth alone, so that we may have peace in this life, and in the next life attain to what is perfect, by the grace and mercy of Jesus Christ Our Lord, to Whom with the Father and the Holy Spirit be there glory and honour now and for ever. Amen.

III. St Augustine, Bishop and Doctor

The Kingdom of Christ

Matthew xvii. 1–8. 1. *The Kingdom of Christ.* We must read and discuss, Dearly Beloved, this vision which the Lord manifested upon the mountain. For it was of this He had said: *Amen I say to you, there are some of them that stand here, that shall not taste death, till they see the Son of man coming in his kingdom* (Mt. xvi. 28). Then begins the lesson just read: *When he had said this, after six days Jesus taketh unto him Peter and James, and John his brother, and bringeth them up into a high mountain apart.* These three were the *some* of whom He had said: *There were some* of them who should not taste death till they see *the Son of man coming in his kingdom.*

Now here is no trivial subject of inquiry. For this mountain is not the limit of His Kingdom. What is a mountain to Him to Whom the heavens belong? And this we not alone read is so, but in a manner we see it with the eyes of the soul. What He here calls His Kingdom, in many other places He calls the Kingdom of Heaven. But the Kingdom of Heaven is the Kingdom of the Blessed. *For the heavens show forth the glory of God* (Ps. xviii. 1). And of these heavens it goes on to say in the psalm: *There are no speeches nor languages where their voices are not heard. Their sound hath gone forth into all the earth: and their words unto the ends of the earth.* Whose words but the words of the heavens? Therefore of the Apostles, and of all faithful preachers of God's word. The heavens shall reign with Him Who made the heavens. Now behold what took place, that this might be revealed to us.

2. *The Significance of the Lord's Transfiguration. The Garments of Christ.* The Lord Jesus shone bright as the sun, and His garments became white as snow, and speaking together with Him were Moses and Elias. Jesus Himself shone resplendent as the sun: signifying that He is *the light which enlightens every man coming into this world.* What the sun is to the eyes of the body, this Light is to the eyes of the soul. And what that is to the bodies of men, This is to their hearts.

His garments are His Church. And garments, unless they are properly sustained, fall off. And of these garments, Paul was as it were but the outward hem. For he says of himself: *I am the least of the Apostles* (I Cor. xv. 9). And in another place: *I am the last of the Apostles* (I Cor. iv. 9). Now in a garment the hem is the last and the least part of it. And as that woman who suffered an issue of blood was healed by the Lord when she touched the hem of His garment, so the Church which came from the Gentiles was saved by the preaching of Paul (Lk. viii. 44).

What wonder that the Church is symbolized by shining garments, when we hear the prophet Isaias say: *If your sins be as scarlet, they shall be made white as snow* (Is. i. 18). Moses and Elias, the Law and the Prophets, what do they avail unless they speak together with the Lord? Unless they give testimony of the Lord, who will read the Law or the Prophets? See how concisely the Apostle states this. *For by the law is the knowledge of sin. But now without the law the justice of God is made manifest.* Behold the Sun! *Being witnessed by the law and the prophets* (Rom. iii. 20). Behold Its splendour!

3. *The Desire of Peter.* Peter sees It, and, as a man savouring human delights, says: *Lord it is good for us to be here.* Wearied of the multitudes he had come upon the solitude of the mountain. Here he was close to Christ, the Bread of his soul. Why go away, to travail and to suffer, when he could live here in holy love of God; and because of this in holiness also of life? He longed for happiness, so he goes on: *If thou wilt, let us make here three tabernacles, one for thee, one for Moses, and one for Elias.*

To this the Lord makes no reply; yet Peter receives an answer. For while he was speaking a bright cloud came and overshadowed them. He wished to make three tabernacles. The heavenly answer shows we have but One; which human understanding would divide. Christ the Word of God, God's Word in the Law, God's Word in the Prophets. And why, Peter, do you seek to divide them? Ought you not rather unite them? You prepare for three; know that there is but One.

4. *The Voice from the Cloud. The Prostration of the Disciples.* As the cloud overshadowed them, and in manner formed for them one tabernacle, a Voice spoke from out the cloud, saying: *This is my beloved Son.* Moses was there, and Elias. The Voice did not say: These are my beloved sons. For One only is the Son; others are adopted. It is He that is commended to them: He from Whom the Law and the prophets derive their glory. *This,* It says, *is my beloved Son, in whom I am well pleased: hear ye him.* You have heard Him in the prophets; you heard Him in the Law. And where have you not heard Him?

When they hear this they fall to the ground. Here now we are shown that in the Church is the Kingdom of God. Here is the Lord; here is the Law; and here the Prophets. But the Lord as Lord; in Moses the Law, in Elias the Prophets, but both as servants and ministers. They are as vessels; He is the spring. Moses and the Prophets wrote and spoke; but it was from Him they were filled when they gave forth.

5. *The raising up of the Disciples. When raised up they see only Jesus. God Himself is our Promised Reward.*

The Lord put forth His hand and wakened them as they lay there. Then, *they saw only Jesus.* What does this mean? You heard when the Epistle was being read to you, that we now see, *through a glass in a dark manner; but then face to face.* And that tongues shall cease when that which we hope for has come to pass (I Cor. xiii. 12, 8, 9). That they fall to the ground means therefore that we die; for it was said to the body: *Dust thou art, and into dust thou shalt return* (Gen. iii. 19). When the Lord thus raised them up He signified our resurrection.

After the Resurrection what does the Law avail you? And what the Prophets? And so Elias is seen no more, nor Moses. But to you remains: *In the beginning was the Word, and the Word was with God, and the Word was God.* He remains that God may be all in all (I Cor. xv. 28). Moses will be there; but now not the Law. There we shall see Elias; but not as a prophet. For both the Law and the Prophets but served to give testimony to Christ: that He was to suffer, and that on the third day He would rise again, and that He would enter into His glory (Lk. xxiv. 44–7). And there shall be fulfilled that which He promised to those who love Him: *He that loveth me, shall be loved of my Father: and I will love Him* (Jn. xiv. 21).

And then, as though it were said, since You love him, what will You give him? He says: *I will show myself to him.* Wondrous gift, and wondrous promise! God has laid up for you as reward, not something that is His, but His very Self. You are eager for gain, will not what Christ has promised you be enough? You may consider yourself rich; but if you have not God, what have you? Another may be poor; but if He has God, what is it he has not?

6. *Salvation must be won through charity towards others.* Go down, Peter: you long to remain in the peace of the mountain; go down, preach the word, dwelling upon it continually, welcome or unwelcome; bring home wrong-doing, confirm the waverer, rebuke the sinner, with all patience and doctrine (II Tim. iv. 2). Struggle, labour hard, suffer what torments may come, so that through the brightness and beauty of holy labours, fulfilled through charity, you may come to possess what is signified by the shining garments of the Lord. For when we read to you the words of the Apostle in praise of charity we heard: *Seeketh not her own.* She seeks not her own, since she gives away that which she possesses.

In another place this same is said, but could there be harmful: unless you understand it. For the Apostle, instructing the faithful, the members of Christ, in this same rule of charity, says: *Let no man seek his own, but that which is another's* (I Cor. x. 21). Greed hearing this would get ready its deceits, that on the pretext of helping another, it may cheat him; and in *this* way seek not its own, but that which is another's.

Let greed restrain itself, and let justice appear; let us pay heed, and let us seek to understand. To charity was it said: *Let no man seek his own, but that which is another's.* But you, greedy man, if you continue as you are, and make use of this teaching so as to covet what is another's, may you lose what you have! You desire, since I know you well, to have both your own and what is another's. And you practise deceit that you may gain what is another's. Then may you be the prey of robbery, and lose what you have. You seek, not what is yours, but rather take away what belongs to another. If you do this, you do not do well. Listen then, greedy one; pay heed: the Apostle explains to you more fully in another place that which he has here said: *Let no man seek his own, but that which is another's*. Of himself he says: *I also in all things please all men, not seeking that which is profitable to myself, but to many; that they may be saved* (I Cor. x. 33).

This lesson Peter had not yet grasped, when he sought to stay with Jesus upon the mountain. He was keeping it for you, Peter, until after His death. Now however He says: Go down upon the earth, and labour there, and be a servant upon the earth, and upon the earth be despised, and crucified. Life came down, that it might be slain; the Bread, that It might hunger. The Way came down, that It might be wearied on the journey; the Fountain, that It might thirst: and do you refuse to labour? *Seek not your own.* Abide in love, preach the truth; then will you reach heaven, where you shall find peace.

Turning then to the Lord our God, the Father Almighty, in pureness of heart, let us as best we can give thanks with all our hearts; beseeching Him that in His Goodness He will graciously hear our prayers, and by His power drive evil from our thoughts and actions, increase our faith, guide our minds, grant to us His holy inspirations, and bring us unending joy, through His Son Our Lord and Saviour Jesus Christ. Amen.

IV. St Cyril of Alexandria

Given at Ephesus, in the Greater Church dedicated to Mary
On the Transfiguration of the Lord, Our God and Our Saviour Jesus Christ[5]

They who are skilled in combat are pleased by the plaudits of the spectators, and urged on by the hope of rewards to the victory of their calling. They however who aspire to divine rewards, and thirst for a share in that which is laid up for the blessed, gladly face the contests which are endured for love of Christ. They live blameless lives, not clinging to sloth, which merits no reward; neither do they yield to unworthy cowardice, but bear themselves manfully against all temptation, making light of the attacks of their persecutors; believing that to suffer for the Lord is a great gain. For they are mindful of what the Blessed Paul has said, *that the sufferings of this time are not worthy to be compared with the glory to come, that shall be revealed in us* (Rom. viii. 18).

Behold therefore the all beautiful disposition of things Our Lord Jesus Christ now arranges for the profit and edification of His holy Apostles. For He says to them: *If any man will come after me, let him deny himself, and take up his cross, and follow me. For he that will save his life, shall lose it: and he that shall lose his life for my sake, shall find it* (Mt. xvi. 24, 25).

The precept is a salutary one, worthy of the sanctified; one which leads to heavenly glory, and conducting us to a joyful destiny. For the will to suffer for Christ shall not go unrewarded; nay, more, it will bring us the joy of eternal life and glory. But it was to be expected that the Disciples, who were not yet endowed with power from on high (Lk. xxiv. 49), would succumb to human foolishness and, thinking within themselves, would say: 'How can anyone deny *himself*? How can one who has lost his life find it again? What comparable reward can be given to those who have suffered this loss? And also, in what kind of reward will he share?'

That He may remove such thoughts and words from their minds, and as it were change them, and uplift them to largeness of soul, awakening within them a desire for the glory He is to bestow on them, He says: *I say to you, there are some of them that stand here, that shall not taste death, till they see the Son of man coming in his kingdom* (Mt. xvi. 28). Was it that the duration of their life was to be lengthened, so as to reach those days, after which, coming down from heaven at the end of ages, He will restore to the saints the kingdom that was prepared for them? And this also He could well do. For He can do all things; nor is there any thing that cannot be done by His almighty command. But he calls His kingdom this vision of His glory, in which He shall presently be seen; and in which He shall shine before them as the sun upon the earth.

For He shall come in the glory of God the Father; not in the lowliness that belongs to us. How then will He make them spectators of this wonder, those to whom He promised this? He goes up into a high mountain, taking with Him the three He had chosen from among them. There He becomes transfigured into a Being of wondrous glory, so that even His garments seemed to shine, as though He were clothed with light. Then Moses and Elias appear, standing beside Him, and speaking of His death on the Cross which was to take place in Jerusalem; speaking, that is, of the mystery of the plan of our Redemption through His Body and Saving Passion, which was, as I say, to be accomplished on the Cross.

For it was true that the Law of Moses and the words of the Prophets had foreshadowed the mystery of Christ; the Law in types and figures as well as by its written Table, the Prophets foretelling *at sundry times and in diverse manners* that He would appear, and in our likeness, and that for the salvation of men, and for their eternal life, He would not refuse the death of the Cross. Therefore Moses and Elias stood by Him, and spoke with Him, and this was done to show that the Law and the Prophets were as it were in attendance on Our Lord Jesus Christ, making it plain that He was the Master of both the Law and the Prophets, and that He was by them proclaimed in unison. For what the Law declared, the Prophets confirmed. And this was, I believe, because the most saintly Moses conferred together with the holiest of the Prophets; and this was Elias.

We may make here yet another reflection. Since among the people there were some who said that He was Elias, and others that He was Jeremiah, and others that He was one of the Prophets (Mt. xvi. 14). He brings before them the greatest among these, so that they might see through this how great was the difference between the Master and the servant. And after this we may make yet another reflection. Since they were constantly accusing Him of transgressing the Law, and also had called Him a blasphemer, who claimed glory that belonged not to Him but to the Father, saying of Him: *This man is not of God, who keepeth not the Sabbath* (Jn. ix. 16); and again: *For a good work we stone thee not, but for blasphemy; and because that thou, being a man, makest thyself God* (Jn. x. 33); that He might show that both charges arose out of malice, and that He was guilty of neither, and also that that which He did was not a breaking of the Law, nor a taking of honour that did not belong to Him: because He said He was equal to the Father: He brings before them these two men, who were pre-eminent both as to the Law and among the Prophets. For Moses had given them the Law, and the Jews might well know that he would not overlook any violation of the Law, such as they imagined. Neither could he have honoured one who had transgressed the Law he had given them. Furthermore Elias was a man filled with zeal for the glory of God. And should Christ be an enemy of God, and had He declared Himself equal to the Father, and if He was not what He said, and if He did not do what was just, Elias would not have stood beside Him and reverenced Him.

To these another reason may be added. What is that? That they may know He had power over both life and death; and dominion over those who were above and those beneath. And so He brought before them one who still lived, and one who had died. And when they both appeared they were not silent, but spoke together with Him of His coming glory, which was to be fulfilled in Jerusalem: namely, of His Passion and Cross, and, by means of them, of His Resurrection also.

But the blessed Disciples sleep for a little while, as when Christ was giving Himself to prayer. Providentially they fulfil this human need. Then when they wakened they became witnesses of this wondrous holy transfiguration. The blessed Peter, thinking that the day of the kingdom of God had come, longed to remain there in the mountain; and not knowing what he was saying declared, that they must build there three dwelling places.

But it was not the hour of the ending of the world; neither in our own day shall the sanctified be partakers of the future hope promised them. For says Paul: *Who will reform the body of our lowliness, made like to the body of his glory* (Phil. iii. 21), that is, Christ's. Since therefore the divine plan of our redemption was yet but at its beginning, and not yet fulfilled, how could it be that Christ, Who had come into the world because of love, would abandon His desire to suffer for it? For He redeemed this our earthly nature when He died in our body; and rising from the dead He set it free.

Therefore Peter knew not what he was saying. Furthermore, besides this wondrous and mysterious vision of the glory of Christ, something else took place, which was both profitable and likewise necessary to strengthen belief in Himself, not alone in His Disciples, but in us also. For from on high came the voice of God the Father, saying: *This is my beloved Son, in whom I am well pleased: hear ye him. And when it had ended they found no one only Jesus.*

What has the stiff-necked Jew to say to this; arrogant and contradictory that he is, with a heart that will receive no counsel? Behold, in the presence of Moses, the Father commands the holy Apostles, that they hearken to Christ. For had He willed that they should obey the laws of Moses He would have said: 'Obey Moses, and keep the Law.' But this God and the Father does not say. But with Moses standing there, and with him Elias His prophet, He commands them rather that they should obey Christ. Lest some should pervert the truth by saying that the Father bade them *hear Moses*, and not the Christ the Saviour of us all, the Evangelist (Luke) of necessity has noted, saying, that when the voice was stilled *Jesus* was found *alone*.

When therefore God the Father commanded the holy Apostles, speaking as it were from out the clouds, and saying, *hear ye Him*, Moses had already departed, and Elias also was no longer there; and there was only Christ. Therefore it was He Whom He commanded them to hear. For He is the fulfilment of both the Law and the Prophets. And it was because of this that He said to the Jews: *For if you did believe Moses, you would perhaps believe me also; for he wrote of me* (Jn. v. 46).

Since therefore they continue to reject the words of the truly wise Moses, and to disregard what was said by the holy prophets, rightly are they deprived of, and shut out from, the rewards which were promised to their forefathers. *For obedience is better than sacrifices: and to hearken rather than to offer the fat of rams*, as it is written (I Kings xv. 22).

And such is the state of the Jews in these things. But for us who have acknowledged His Coming all good things are prepared, through Christ and in Him, through Whom and with Whom let there be glory and honour to God the Father, together with the Holy Ghost, for ever and ever. Amen.

V. St Leo the Great, Pope and Doctor

Given to the People on the Saturday preceding the Second Sunday of Lent

THE PURPOSES OF THE TRANSFIGURATION[6]

Synopsis:

I. That True Faith confesses that Christ is both God and man; and this in Peter was rewarded by the giving of great authority.
II. That for this especially was Christ transfigured: that He might give proof of the power and the reality of His Body.
III. That He might also remove the scandal of the Cross; and confirm the expectations of His Church.
IV. And reveal the Harmony which exists between the Old and the New Testaments regarding Christ, by the visible presences of Moses and Elias.
V. That Peter's desire was inordinate but not unworthy.
VI. *This is my beloved Son* is explained.
VII. *Hear ye him* is dwelt upon.
VIII. By this testimony of the Father the infirmity of spirit in all men is raised up and strengthened.

I. The Gospel lesson, Most Dearly Beloved, which has by means of our bodily ears reached inwards to the ears of our soul, invites us to seek for an understanding of this wondrous mystery. To this we shall by the assistance of God's grace the more readily attain if we recall to mind what was related a little earlier. For Jesus Christ the Saviour of all mankind, when He founded the faith which draws sinners to repentance and restores the dead to life, instructed His Disciples, both by word of doctrine, and by the signs and wonders He wrought, to this end: that they believe that the same Christ was both the Only Begotten Son of God and the Son of man. For one of these truths, without the other, avails not to salvation; and it was equally perilous to believe that the Lord Jesus Christ was God only, and without humanity, or man only, without Divinity: since both must in like manner be confessed; for as God possessed true humanity, so to the Man there belonged true Divinity.

The Lord therefore, that He might confirm the most saving knowledge of this Truth, questioned His Disciples as to what, amid the varying opinions of others, they believed concerning Him? Whereupon Peter the Apostle, rising above what was corporeal, and transcending what was human, and not looking only to the substance of Flesh and Blood, saw with the eyes of his soul, and through the revelation of the Father on high, the Son of the Living God; and confessed the glory of His Divinity.

So greatly pleasing was his sublime faith, that, rewarded with the ioy of the divine blessing, he receives a sacred steadfastness as of an indestructible rock, founded upon which the Church would overcome the gates of hell, and the rule of death; and in the binding and loosing of all things whatsoever, that alone would be approved in heaven which had been approved by the will of Peter.

II. But the sublimity of this wondrous knowledge was to be based on the mystery of His lower nature, lest the faith of the Apostle, uplifted to the glory of confessing the Divinity of Christ, might come to think that the reception of our infirmity would be unworthy of God, and incompatible with His impassible nature, and might thus begin to believe that, in Him, this lesser nature was already glorified: so that it could neither be touched by affliction nor be overcome by death. So, when the Lord says He must go up to Jerusalem, and suffer many things there, from the Scribes and Ancients and Chief Priests, and be put to death, and on the third day rise again (Mt. xvi. 21; xx. 17–19); when the Blessed Peter, who given light from on high had confessed the Son of God, had, as he thought, rejected with earnest if unmeasured loathing the insult of their expected mockery, and the shame of this fearful death, the Lord corrected him with a mild rebuke, and then awakened in him the desire to suffer with Him in this Passion.

For the words of the Saviour, following on Peter's remark, had inspired this, and had taught them all that they who wish to come after Him must deny themselves, and must consider the loss of earthly things as nothing, because of their hope of eternal rewards: for he would save his life who feared not to lay it down for Christ's sake (Mt. xvi. 25; cf. Jn. x. 18). So therefore that the Apostles might come to possess the strength of this blessed steadfastness, and with all their heart, and that they might be without fear in the cruel presence of the Cross which He was to take upon Himself, and that they might not feel humiliated by His public execution, nor think themselves put to shame by the patience with which He was so to endure the torment of His Passion that He would not in death lose the glory of His Majesty, *He took unto him Peter and James, and John his brother*, and going up with them to a high mountain apart He showed them the splendour of His glory. For though they had witnessed in Him the power of the Divinity, yet they had not begun to know the power of the Body with which the Divinity was clothed.

And for this reason He had personally and clearly promised that some among the Disciples who had stood about Him would not taste death until they had seen the Son of man *coming in His Kingdom* (Mt. xvi. 28), that is, till they had seen Him clothed in the royal dignity that rightly belonged to the human nature He had assumed, and which He now wished to make visible to these three men. For while they remained in the body they could never look upon and behold that unspeakable and inaccessible vision of the Divinity which is laid up for the clean of heart unto life everlasting.

III. And so in the presence of these chosen witnesses the Lord unveils His glory, and clothes with such splendour the Body which is His in common with all other men that His Face shines as the sun and His garments appear white as snow. By this transfiguration He desired, first, to remove from the hearts of His Disciples the scandal of the Cross, and then that the lowliness of his voluntary Passion might not trouble the faith of those to whom He now reveals the perfection of His hidden glory. And with no less providence He confirms the hope of His Church, so that It may know what it is for which the Body of Christ has been given in exchange, and so that Its members may also be taught to look for that glory which here shone forth in Its Head. The Lord had told them of this when He spoke of the might of His Coming. *Then shall the just shine as the sun in the kingdom of their Father* (Mt. xiii. 43). The blessed Apostle Paul testifying to this truth declares: *For I reckon that the sufferings of this time are not worthy to be compared to the glory to come, that shall be revealed in us* (Rom. viii. 18). And again: *For you are dead; and your life is hid with Christ in God. When Christ shall appear, who is your life, then you also shall appear with him in glory* (Col. iii. 3).

IV. To confirm the minds of His Apostles, and to lead them to all knowledge, He adds to this wonder another lesson. For Moses and Elias —the Law and the Prophets—appear, talking with the Lord, so that in the presence of these five men would be fulfilled what had been declared: that, *In the mouth of two or three witnesses every word shall stand* (Deut. xix. 15). What more stable, more steadfast, than the Word, in Whose proclaiming the trumpets of the Old and the New Testaments sound in concert: the witness of the ancient writings, in harmony with the Gospel teaching. For the pages of either Covenant agree one with the other. And He Whom the signs that preceded had promised under the veil of mysteries is now revealed clear and distinct in the brightness of this present glory. It was because of this the blessed John says: *The Law was given by Moses; grace and truth came by Jesus Christ* (Jn. i. 17); in Whom are fulfilled the promise of the prophecies, and the significance of what the Law prescribed: while by His Presence He teaches us that the prophecies were true, and by His grace makes possible what He commands us to do.

V. The Apostle Peter, exalted by the revelation of these mysteries, turning from the world, and rejecting what belonged to this earth, is seized in a sort of ecstasy with a desire for things eternal; and now filled with the joy of this whole vision he expressed his longing to dwell here with Christ, where he had been gladdened by the revelation of His glory. And so he says: *Lord, it is good for us to be here: if thou wilt let us make here three tabernacles, one for thee, and one for Moses, and one for Elias.* But to this suggestion the Lord makes no answer: implying not that it was unworthy, but that it was at variance with the divine purpose. For the world could only be saved by the death of Christ, and the Lord's attitude in this is a challenge to the faith of the believing, reminding them that though we may not doubt the promises of future happiness, yet we must understand that, amid the trials of this life, we are to beg for patience rather than for glory: for the joys of heaven cannot come before the times of our trial.

VI. And while Peter was speaking a bright cloud overshadowed them, and behold a voice from the cloud spoke, and said: *This is my beloved son, in whom I am well pleased: hear ye him.* The Father was indeed present in the Son, and in that brightness of the Lord, which He tempered to the eyes of the Disciples, the nature of the Father was not separated from His Only-Begotten. But to put before them the separateness of either Divine Person, as the splendour of His Body revealed the Son to their sight so the Father was proclaimed to their ears by the voice from out the cloud; and hearing his voice the Disciples fall on their faces in great fear. And they feared, not alone because of the Divine Majesty of the Father, but also because of the Majesty of the Son: for with their heightened perception they perceive the Divinity common to them both: and as in their faith there was no uncertainty, so neither in their fear was there any distinction.

Wide and multifold then was this testimony, and more is learned from the profundity of the words than from the sound of the voice. For when the Father says: *This is my beloved son, in whom I am well pleased; hear ye him*, do we not plainly hear: *This is my beloved son,* Who is from Me, and with Me, before time was? For He Who begot Him was not before Him Whom He begot; nor was He Who was

Begotten after Him Who begot Him. *This is my beloved son*, Whom Divinity does not separate from Me, nor might divide Us, nor eternity set Us apart. *This is my beloved son*, not adopted, but Mine; Begotten of Me, not elsewhere made; not made like to me from another nature, but born of My Being and Equal with Me. *This is my beloved son*, through whom were all things made, and without Whom nothing was made; for all that I make He likewise makes; and whatsoever I do He immediately and without separation from Me also does (Jn. v. 19). For the Son is in the Father, and the Father is in the Son: nor is Our Oneness ever divided (Jn. xiv. 10; x. 38). And though I Who have begotten am One Person, and He the Begotten is Another, yet it is not lawful to think concerning Him other than that which you may think concerning Me. *This is my beloved son*, Who sought not by robbery that equality with Me which is His, nor did He usurp it (Phil. ii. 6); but while remaining in the nature of My Divinity bowed down His unchangeable Divinity, even to the taking on Himself of the nature of a servant, so that He might bring to fulfilment Our common plan for the redemption of mankind.

VII. Without delay therefore hear Him Whom in all things I am well pleased; in preaching Whom I am made known; in Whose lowliness I am glorified; for He is the Truth and the Life, He is My power, My wisdom. *Hear ye him* Whom the mysteries of the Law foretold; Whom the mouths of the Prophets proclaimed. *Hear ye him* Whose Blood has redeemed the world; Who has chained the demon, and taken from him what he held; Who has blotted out the deed of sin, the covenant of evildoing. *Hear ye him* Who opens the way to heaven, and through the humiliation of His Cross prepared for you a way to ascend to His kingdom.

Why do you fear to be redeemed? Why tremble at being healed of your wounds? Let that be done which I willing Christ wills. Put away bodily fear, and arm yourselves with steadfast faith: for it is unfitting you should fear, in the Passion of your Saviour, what, by His gift to you, you shall not fear in your own end.

VIII. These words, Beloved, were spoken for the profit, not alone of those who heard them with their bodily ears, but in these three Apostles the whole Church learns what their eyes saw and their ears heard. Let the faith of all men be strengthened by means of the preaching of the most holy Gospel; and let no one be ashamed of the Cross of Christ, through which He redeemed the world. And because of this let no man fear to suffer for justice' sake, or doubt of the fulfilment of His promises: for it is through toil we come to rest, and through death we cross over to life. Since He has taken upon Himself all the infirmity of our humanity, in Him we shall overcome what He has overcome, and receive what He has promised, provided that we persevere in faith and love of Him. And so, Beloved, that we may do what He has told us to do, and bear our trials in patience, we should have ever in our ears the voice of the Father telling us: *This is my beloved son, in whom I am well pleased: hear ye him*, Who with the Father and the Holy Ghost liveth and reigneth world without end. Amen.

NOTES

[1] Vossio, St Ephraem, 686; John xvii. 19. [2] PG 58, Homs. 56. 57.

[3] *Glory* has δόξαν in Chrysostom; which is found in four codices (medieval). The Vulgate in Luke, has (ἔξοδον) *excessum*, which means death. It may be Chrysostom's reading of what Christ would accomplish by His death.

[4] PL 38, Sermo. 78.

[5] PG 77, col. 1009, hom. 9.

[6] PL 54, 308, Sermo. 51.

THIRD SUNDAY OF LENT

I. St Ambrose: On Lent

II. St Ambrose: On the Gospel

III. St Cyril of Alexandria: Exposition of the Gospel

IV. St Leo the Great: The Purpose of Lent

V. St Maximus: The Significance of Lent

VI. St Bruno: The Kingdom of Evil

THE GOSPEL OF THE SUNDAY

Luke xi. 14–28

At that time Jesus was casting out a devil, and the same was dumb: and when he had cast out the devil, the dumb spoke: and the multitudes were in admiration at it: But some of them said: He casteth out devils by Beelzebub, the prince of devils. And others tempting, asked of him a sign from heaven. But he seeing their thoughts, said to them: every kingdom divided against itself, shall be brought to desolation, and house upon house shall fall. And if Satan also be divided against himself, how shall his kingdom stand? because you say, that through Beelzebub I cast out devils. Now if I cast out devils by Beelzebub; by whom do your children cast them out? Therefore they shall be your judges. But if I by the finger of God cast out devils; doubtless the kingdom of God is come upon you. When a strong man armed keepeth his court, those things are in peace which he possesseth. But if a stronger than he come upon him, and overcome him; he will take away all his armour wherein he trusted, and will distribute his spoils. He that is not with me, is against me; and he that gathereth not with me, scattereth. When the unclean spirit is gone out of a man, he walketh through places without water, seeking rest; and not finding, he saith: I will return into my house whence I came out. And when he is come, he findeth it swept and garnished. Then he goeth and taketh with him seven other spirits more wicked than himself, and entering in they dwell there. And the last state of that man becomes worse than the first. And it came to pass, as he spoke these things, a certain woman from the crowd, lifting up her voice, said to him: Blessed is the womb that bore thee, and the paps that gave thee suck. But he said: Yea rather, blessed are they who hear the word of God, and keep it.

PARALLEL GOSPELS

Matthew xii. 22–37

Then was offered to him one possessed with a devil, blind and dumb: and he healed him, so that he spoke and saw. And all the multitudes were amazed, and said: Is not this the Son of David? But the Pharisees hearing it, said: This man casteth not out devils but by Beelzebub the prince of devils. And Jesus knowing their thoughts, said to them: Every kingdom divided against itself shall be made desolate: and every city or house divided against itself shall not stand. And if Satan cast out Satan, he is divided against himself: how then shall his kingdom stand? And if I by Beelzebub cast out devils, by whom do your children cast them out? Therefore they shall be your judges. But if I by the spirit of God cast out devils, then is the kingdom of God come upon you. Or how can any one enter into the house of the strong, and rifle his goods, unless he first bind the strong? and then he will rifle his house. He that is not with me, is against me: and he that gathereth not with me, scattereth. Therefore I say to you: Every sin and blasphemy shall be forgiven men, but the blasphemy of the Spirit shall not be forgiven. And whosoever shall speak a word against the Son of man, it shall be forgiven him: but he that shall speak against the Holy Ghost, it shall not be forgiven him, neither in this world, nor in the world to come. Either make the tree good and its fruit good: or make the tree evil, and its fruit evil. For by the fruit the tree is known. O generation of vipers, how can you speak good

Matthew xii. 43–5

And when an unclean spirit is gone out of a man he walketh through dry places seeking rest, and findeth none. Then he saith: I will return into my house from whence I came out. And coming he findeth it empty, swept, and garnished. Then he goeth, and taketh with him seven other spirits more wicked than himself, and they enter in and dwell there: and the last state of that man is made worst than the first. So shall it be also to this wicked generation.

Mark iii. 20–30

And they come to a house, and the multitude cometh together again, so that they could not so much as eat bread. And when his friends had heard of it, they went out to lay hold on him. For they said: He is become mad. And the scribes who were come down from Jerusalem, said: He hath Beelzebub, and by the prince of devils he casteth out devils. And after he hath called them together, he said to them in parables: How can Satan cast out Satan? And if a kingdom be divided against itself, that kingdom cannot stand. And if a house be divided against itself, that house cannot stand, but hath an end. No man can enter into the house of a strong man and rob him of his goods, unless he first bind the strong man, and then shall he plunder his house. Amen I say to you, that all sins shall be forgiven unto the sons of men, and the blasphemies wherewith they shall blaspheme. But he that shall blaspheme things, whereas you are evil? for out of the abundance of the heart the mouth speaketh. A good man out of a good treasure bringeth forth good things: and an evil man out of an evil treasure bringeth forth evil things. But I say unto you, that every idle word that men shall speak, they shall render an account for it in the day of judgement. For by thy words thou shalt be justified, and by thy words thou shalt be condemned.

against the Holy Ghost, shall never have forgiveness, but shall be guilty of an everlasting sin. Because they said: He hath an unclean spirit.

Exposition from the Catena Aurea

V. 14. *And he was casting out a devil, and the same was dumb.*

GLOSS: The Lord had just promised that the *Good Spirit would be given to them that ask him*; whose goodness He reveals to them by the following miracle; hence we have: *And He was . . .*

THEOPHYLACTUS: *Kophos*, which the Latins translate by *mutus* (dumb) is a term used to describe a dumb man; it is also used to describe one who does not hear; but more correctly it means one who can neither hear nor speak. If a man cannot hear from birth, of necessity he will be dumb. For we only speak that which we have learned to say through hearing. Should he through some misfortune lose his hearing, this will not prevent him from speaking. But the man who was brought to the Lord was both deaf and dumb.

TITUS BOSTRENSIS *in Matt. Cat. G.P*: Because it is he who inflicts this infirmity, so that the word of God may not be heard, it is the devil whom he calls a dumb spirit, or a deaf one. For the demons by taking away the natural power of the senses, interfere with the hearing of the soul; and so Christ comes, both that He may cast out the devil, and that we may hear the word of truth. For He heals one man, so that He may give to all men a foretaste of human salvation. Hence there follows: *And when He . . .*

BEDE: But in Matthew it is recorded that the possessed man was blind as well as dumb. Three wonders therefore were wrought in this one man: the blind was given sight, the dumb speaks, and he that was possessed was delivered of an evil spirit. This is daily renewed in the conversion of the faithful; for being first freed of a demon they then look upon the Light of the Faith, and their lips that before kept silence are now opened in praise of God.

CYRIL: When He had worked this wonder the multitudes were filled with awe, and they began to extol Him with such praise as belonged to God. Hence: *The multitudes were in admiration of him.* The multitudes, who appear to have been but poorly instructed, were ever in admiration of what He did, but the Scribes and Pharisees sought rather to contradict Him and to twist the significance of His wonders by a perverse interpretation: as though they were not the works of God but of an evil spirit. Hence we have:

V. 15. *But some of them said: He casteth out devils by Beelzebub.*

Beelzebub was the god of Acheron: for *Beel* is actually Baal. *Zebub* means 'of the flies'. He is called Beelzebub, Lord of the Flies, from the foul office which they were wont to attribute to the prince of the demons.

V. 16. *And others tempting him, asked of him a sign from heaven.*

CYRIL, *Catena G.P*: Some others, urged on by the sharp goad of envy, sought of Him a sign from heaven. As though they said: 'Although you cast forth a demon from a man, that is no sign of a divine work. For we have not seen from you any sign like to those of former days. Moses led our people through the midst of the sea. Josue his successor held the sun back before Gabon. But you have done no such wonders.' That they sought a sign from Him indicates that they were thinking such thoughts about Christ.

V. 17. *But He seeing their thoughts, said to them . . .*

CYRIL, *Catena G.P*:[1] The Pharisees dared not reveal their suspicions to the multitudes, since they were so unfounded. But they turned them over in their minds. Hence we have: *But He seeing their thoughts . . . said: Every kingdom divided against itself . . .*

BEDE: He gave an answer, not to their words, but to their thoughts, so that by this they should be compelled to believe in His power Who could read even the secrets of the heart.

CYRIL, *as above*: He did not answer them from the Scriptures: for they paid no heed to them, except to interpret them falsely: but He answers them from circumstances which are common among men. For a house or a city that is divided within itself soon falls to nothing; and the same is true of a kingdom: though there is nothing seems so strong as a kingdom. But on the other hand concord gives strength to kingdoms, and to the homes of their subjects. If I then by the aid of a demon cast out demons there is division among them, and their power is passing away. Hence:

V. 18. *And if Satan also be divided against himself . . .*

For Satan does not war against himself. Neither does he oppose his own accomplices; rather does he uphold what is his own dominion. It follows then that it must be by divine power that I cast down Satan.

AMBROSE: By this also does He show that His own Kingdom is indivisible and everlasting; and so He declares that they do not belong to His everlasting kingdom who do not place their hope in Christ, but believe He casts out demons by the prince of demons: which applies to the Jewish people also. For how can the kingdom of the Jews be everlasting when Jesus Who was begotten under the Law is rejected by the people of the

Law? So in part the belief of the Jewish people turns on itself, and so doing becomes divided, and being divided is brought to nothing. But the Kingdom of the Church shall remain for ever, because the whole Church is one body.

BEDE: Neither is the Kingdom of the Father, Son, and Holy Ghost divided for it will endure in eternal unchangeableness. Let the Arians cease then from saying the Son is less than the Father, and the Holy Spirit less than the Son; for Their Kingdom is One, and One Their divine majesty. CHRYSOSTOM, *Hom.* 42 *in Matt.*: This is the first answer. He then gives the second: which refers to His Disciples. He says to them:

V. 19. *Now if I cast out devils by Beelzebub, by whom do your children . . .?*

He does not say, My Disciples, but *your children* (i.e. sons): wishing to soften their anger. CYRIL: For the Disciples of Christ were Jews, and born from Jews according to the flesh. And from Christ had they received power over evil spirits; and those who were oppressed by them they delivered in His Name. Since therefore your sons crush Satan in *My Name*, is it not grievous folly to say I hold My Power from Satan? Let you be judged by the faith of your own sons. Hence: *Therefore they shall be your judges.* CHRYSOSTOM: Since they though sprung from you obey Me it is evident they will condemn those who are contrary to Me.

BEDE: Or, He means by, *your children*, the exorcists of their own people who cast out devils by the invocation of the Name of God; as though saying: If the casting forth of evil spirits wrought by your sons is due to God, and not to the power of demons, why then has the same result wrought by Me not the same cause? *Therefore they shall be your judges*, not by the exercise of authority, but because of the comparison; for they attribute the casting forth of the evil spirits to the power of God, you to Beelzebub the prince of the evil spirits. CYRIL: Seeing what you say is tainted with calumny it is then evident that it is by the Spirit of God that I cast out evil spirits.

V. 20. *But if I by the finger of God cast out devils; doubtless the kingdom . . .*

AUGUSTINE, *Harm. of the Gospels*, 2, 38: That Luke says *by the finger of God*, where Matthew says *by the Spirit of God*, does not imply that he does not mean the same thing; rather he adds something: that we may learn in what way we are to understand *the finger of God* when we meet it in the Scriptures.

AUGUSTINE, *Quaest. Evangel.*, 2, 17: The Holy Ghost is called the *Finger of God* because of the distribution, wrought by Him, of the gifts each one receives: whether men or angels: for by none of our members is distribution more indicated than by the fingers. CYRIL, *Catena Pat. Graec.*, 13, 2: Or, the Holy Ghost is called the *Finger of God* because the Son is called the *Hand* and *Arm of God*; for by Him the Father does all things. As the finger therefore is not separated from the hand, but is joined naturally to it, so is the

Holy Ghost joined consubstantially to the Son, and through Him the Son does all things.

AMBROSE: Nor must you assume, because of this comparison, that He possesses but a portion of the divine power; for there is no division of an indivisible thing, and accordingly the term is to be used to refer, not to a division of power, but to the nature of the divine unity.

ATHANASIUS, *Contra Arianos*, *Or.* 2: Here the Lord in virtue of His humanity refuses not to declare that He is less than the Holy Ghost, saying that it was by the Holy Ghost He cast out devils; as if to say: human nature, unaided by the Holy Ghost, is not sufficient to cast out evil spirits.

CYRIL: And so fittingly is it said, *The kingdom of God is come upon you*; that is, if I, being a man, cast out devils by the power of the Holy Ghost, in Me human nature is enriched, and the kingdom of heaven is come.

CHRYSOSTOM: He says, *upon you*, that He may draw them to Him. As though to say: if favourable things come to you, why do you question good fortune?

AMBROSE: At the same time He shows that the power of the Holy Ghost, in which is the kingdom of God, is imperial so to speak. We also, in whom the Holy Spirit dwells, are a kingly habitation.

TITUS: Or He says: The kingdom of heaven is come upon you so that it may be understood that it has come against you, not for you: for the Second Coming of Christ must be dreaded by all who do not believe.

V. 21. *When a strong man armed keepeth his court, these things . . .*

CYRIL: It was necessary for many reasons to refute the words of His detractors, so He used now a clear illustration, which showed, to whoever was willing to see, that He overcomes the prince of this world by His own strength, saying: *When a strong man . . .*

CHRYSOSTOM: He describes the devil as a *strong man*, not because he is such by nature, but referring to his ancient tyranny: which our own weakness brought about.

CYRIL: For before the coming of the saviour he enjoyed great power; seizing another's flock, that of the Most High God, and driving it as it were into his own fold.

THEOPHYLACTUS: His arms are sins of every kind, trusting in which he wars against all men. BEDE: He describes the world as being the camp of him who is set fast in evil doing; and in which, till the coming of the Saviour, he held sway: since in the hearts of the unbelieving he ruled untroubled. But Christ, by a power stronger than his own, delivered all men, and cast him out: Hence:

V. 22: *But if a stronger than he come upon him, and overcome him; he . . .*

CYRIL: And when the Word of the Most High, the Giver of all strength, and the Lord of all power, was made man, He attacked him, and took away his armour. BEDE: The deceits and frauds of incorporeal evil are therefore his armour; his spoils, the souls he deceives. CYRIL: For those he had long held in error and in ignorance of God were now by His Apostles brought to the knowledge of truth, and led to God through believing in His Son. BASIL, *Catena G.P*: He also distributed his spoils by handing the faithful over to the care of the angels, so that men may be saved (cf. Is. 18). BEDE: Christ as Victor also distributes His spoils, in sign of His victory; for leading captivity captive He gave gifts to men: appointing some Apostles, some Evangelists, others Prophets, and others Pastors and Doctors (Eph. iv. 11).

V. 23. *He that is not with me, is against me . . .*

CHRYSOSTOM: Then He puts forward a fourth explanation when He adds: *He that is not with me, is against me.* As much as to say: I desire to bring men to God; Satan desires the opposite. How then does he who does not work with me, but scatters what I do, become so helpful to Me, that together with Me he casts out demons? Then follows: *He that gathereth not with me, scattereth.*

CYRIL, *Hom.* 44 *in Matt.*: As though He says: I come that I may gather together the scattered children of God; and this Satan, since he is opposed to Me, seeks to scatter what I come to gather together and save. How then can he who seeks to undo my work be giving me help? CHRYSOSTOM: And if he who does not work with Me is an adversary, how much more so is he who opposes Me? To me He seems to refer here in a veiled manner to the Jews themselves, classifying them with the demons: for they had begun to work against Him, striving to disperse those He was bringing together.

V. 24. *When the unclean spirit is gone out of a man . . .*

CYRIL: After saying these things the Lord then shows how it came about that the Jews fell into such errors concerning Christ, saying: *When etc.* That this refers to the Jews Matthew shows when he says: *So shall it be also to this wicked generation* (Mt. xii. 45). For while they were in Egypt, living after the manner of the Egyptians, an unclean spirit dwelt in them, which was driven out of them when they sacrificed a lamb, a figure of Christ; and sprinkled with its blood they escaped the Destroying Angel.

AMBROSE: So the whole Jewish nation is likened to one man, from whom, because of the Law, an unclean spirit had gone forth. But because the devil could find no rest among the Gentiles: whose hearts which before were dry and hard, but after baptism had begun to soften from the dew of the Spirit, because of faith in Christ (for Christ is the undoing of unclean spirits): he then returns to the Jewish people. So there follows: *And not finding, he saith: I will return into my house whence I came out.* ORIGEN: That is, to those who are of Israel; whom he sees have now retained nothing of God within them, having forsaken, and no longer dwelling, in His house. Hence:

V. 25. *And when he is come, he findeth it swept and garnished . . .*

AMBROSE: Garnished with a superficial, legalistic cleanness, but more than ever stained of heart. For it has neither restrained nor washed away its fierceness in the stream of the sacred spring: so deservedly did the unclean return to it, bringing with it seven wickeder spirits.

V. 26. *Then he goeth and taketh with him seven other spirits more wicked.*

For with evil mind it has sinned against the *week of the Law*, and the mystery of the *eighth day* (Dan. xix. 27).[2] And so as the grace of the sevenfold Spirit is multiplied in us, on them is heaped every injury of the spirits of evil. For the whole, or totality, is often signified by this number. (For on the seventh day God ended His work and rested: Gen. ii. 2.)

CHRYSOSTOM: The evil spirits that now dwell in the souls of the Jews are worse than in former times. For then they raged against the Prophets, now they insult the very Lord of the Prophets. And so they suffered greater afflictions from Titus and Vespasian than they had endured in Egypt and Babylon. So there follows: *And the last state of that man becomes worse than the first.* For then they were still protected by Providence, and received the grace of the Holy Spirit; they are now deprived of this also. And because of this virtue is rarer among them and their suffering is more intense, and the tyranny of the demons more cruel. CYRIL: And so their last state is worse than the first, in accordance with the saying of the Apostle: *It had been better for them not to have known the way of justice, than after they had known it, to turn back* (II Pet. ii. 2).

BEDE: This can also be understood of any heretic or schismatic, or even of a bad Catholic, out of whom the unclean spirit had gone at baptism, and had walked through places without water; that is, the insidious Betrayer searches the hearts of the believing faithful, which have been purified of the corruption of evil thoughts, to find if there be any among them he may lead into the ways of evil. He says: *I will return into my house whence I came out*, and from this we learn that we must be very careful, lest through our own neglect the fault we thought dead within us return unawares.

But he finds—the faithful—swept and garnished; that is, purified by the grace of baptism from the stains of sin, yet without any great eagerness in good works. By the seven more wicked spirits he takes with him He means all the vices. They are said to be more wicked because he will bring with him not alone these seven vices, which are opposed to the seven virtues, but he will pretend in his hypocrisy to possess these seven virtues also.

CHRYSOSTOM: Let us accept as said to us as well as to them the words which follow: *And the last state of that man becomes worse than the first.* For if we who have been given light, and delivered from our former miseries, return again to the same iniquity, then more grievous shall be the guilt of the sins that follow.

BEDE: This may also be taken to mean simply that the Lord added this to distinguish the works of Satan from His own; namely, that He seeks ever to make clean what was defiled, while Satan is ever seeking to soil what has been made clean; and by yet greater impurities.

V. 27. *And it came to pass, as he spoke these things, a certain woman* . . .

BEDE: In the midst of the provocation and the blaspheming of the Scribes and Pharisees a certain woman with wondrous faith proclaimed the Lord's Incarnation. *And it came to pass . . . a certain woman lifting up her voice, said to him: Blessed is the womb that bore thee* . . . In this she put to shame both the calumny of those who stood about her, and the unbelief of future heretics. For as the Jews, blaspheming the works of the Holy Spirit, denied He was the true Son of God and consubstantial with the Father, so later heretics, denying that the Blessed Mary ever Virgin gave the substance of His Flesh to the Only Begotten God, Who by the power of the Holy Spirit was about to come into the world, said that we ought not to confess that He was true Son of man and consubstantial with His Mother.

But if the Body of the Word of God, born of the flesh of a Virgin Mother, is said to be a stranger to her, then there is no reason for proclaiming blessed the womb that bore Him and the breasts that gave Him suck. For why should He be believed to be nourished by her milk from whose seed it is denied He was conceived, since, according to the physicians, either fluid is said to flow from the same source? But He called blessed, not alone Her who had merited to give birth bodily to the Word of God, but likewise all those who, from the hearing that is of faith, spiritually conceive the same Word, and are in labour through good works to bring it forth, and nourish it as it were, either in their own hearts, or in the hearts of their neighbour. For their follows:

V. 28. *But he said: Yea, rather, blessed are they who hear the word of* . . .

CHRYSOSTOM: He did not say this as repudiating His Mother, but to show that His Birth would have been no gain to her unless she were also good and faithful in all things. Certainly if it would have been no gain to her that, though not possessing virtue, Christ should be born of her, much less will it avail us that we have a virtuous father or brother or son but are ourselves far from virtue.

BEDE: But this same Mother of God, and for this also Blessed, that she became instrument of the incarnation of the Word, was yet more Blessed in this, that she remained an undying keeper of the ever to be loved Word. In this saying He strikes at the wise ones among the Jews; who sought neither to hear nor to keep the Word of God, but rather to deny it, and to blaspheme it.

I. ST AMBROSE, BISHOP AND DOCTOR

On Lent[3]

1. Give thanks, Brethren to the Divine Mercy Which has brought you safely half-way through the season of Lent. For this favour they

give praise to God, thankfully and with devotion, who in these days have striven to live in the manner in which they were instructed at the beginning of Lent; that is, those who, coming with eagerness to the Church, have sought with sighs and tears, in daily fasting and almsdeeds, to obtain the forgiveness of their sins.

2. They however who have neglected this duty, that is to say, those who have not fasted daily, or given alms, or those who were indifferent or unmoved in prayer, they have no reason to rejoice, but cause rather, unhappy that they are, for mourning. Yet let them not mourn as if they had no hope; for He Who could give back sight to the man blind from birth (Jn. ix. 1), can likewise change those who now are lukewarm and indifferent into souls fervent and zealous in His service, if with their whole heart they desire to be converted unto Him.

Let such persons therefore, that is, those living in uncleanness of heart, or those who cherish hatred in their hearts against another, or those who take unjustly what belongs to another, or cling inordinately to what is theirs, let such persons acknowledge their own blindness of heart, and let them draw near to the Divine Physician that they may be restored to sight.

3. Would that you might seek the medicine of the soul when you have sinned, as you seek that of the body when you are ill in the flesh. Who now in this so great assembly were he condemned, not to be put to death, but to be deprived of his sight only, would not give all he possessed to escape the danger? And if you so fear the death of the flesh, why do you not fear more the death of the spirit, especially since the pains of death, that is, of the body, are but of an hour, whilst the death of the soul, that is, its punishment and its grieving, has no end? And if you love the eyes of your body, that you soon will lose in death, why do you not love those eyes of the soul by which you may see your Lord and your God for ever?

4. Labour therefore, Beloved Children in the Lord, labour while it is yet day; for as Christ Our Lord says, *The night cometh, when no man can work* (Jn. ix. 4). Daytime is this present life; night is death, and the time that follows death. If after this life there is no more freedom to work, as The Truth tells us, why then does every man not labour while yet there is time; that is, while he yet lives in this world?

Be fearful, Brethren, of this death, of which the Saviour says: *The night cometh, when no man can work.* All those who now work evil are without fear of this death, and because of this when they depart from this life they shall encounter everlasting death. Labour while yet ye live, and particularly in these days; fasting from dainty fare, withholding yourselves at all time from evil works. For those that abstain from food, but do not withhold themselves from wickedness, are like to the devil, who while he eats not, yet never ceases from evildoing. And lastly, you must know that what you deny yourself in fasting, you must give to heaven in the poor.

5. Fulfil in work, Brethren, the lesson of this day's sermon; lest there

come upon you the chastisement of the Jews. For they said to the blind man: *Be thou his disciple* (Jn. ix. 28). What does being a disciple of Christ mean if not to be an imitator of His compassion, and a follower of His truth and humility? But they said this meaning to curse the man. Instead it is a truly great blessing, to which may you also attain, by His grace Who liveth and reigneth world without end. Amen.

II. St Ambrose, Bishop and Doctor

Exposition of the Gospel[4]

Every kingdom divided against itself, shall be brought to desolation, and house upon house shall fall.

The cause of this saying was because our Lord was accused of casting out devils by the power of Beelzebub, the prince of devils; so that He might show that His own kingdom is one and everlasting. And rightly did He also answer Pilate: *My kingdom is not of this world* (Jn. xviii. 36). And so He tells them that those who do not place their trust in Christ, and who believe that He casts out devils through the power of the prince of the devils, do not belong to His eternal kingdom. And this refers to the Jewish people who, in afflictions of this kind, seek the help of the devil to cast out the devil.

For how can a kingdom remain undivided when its faith is destroyed? For, since the Jewish people is subject to the Law, and Christ also as man was born under the Law, how can the kingdom of the Jews, which derives from the Law, endure when this same people divided the law into parts; when Christ Who was promised under the Law was rejected by the people of the law? So in part the faith of the Jewish people turns against itself, and so turning becomes divided, and by being divided it is brought to nothing. And therefore the kingdom of the Church shall endure for ever; for being one faith, it is one body: For there is *One Lord, one faith, one baptism*; *One God and Father of all, Who is above all, and through all, and in us all* (Eph. iv. 5, 6).

How great the foolishness of the impious belief, that though the Son of God had taken flesh to crush the unclean spirits, and take away the armour of the prince of this world, and had also given power to men to destroy the spirits of evil, distributing his spoils in sign of triumph, some should seek the help and protection of the power of the devil; since it is by the *Finger of God*, or as Matthew says, by the *Spirit of God* that devils are cast out? (Mt. xii. 28). From this we are to understand that His kingdom is as it were the inseparable Body of the Divinity; since Christ is the *right hand of God*, and the Spirit, under the figure of a finger, seems to express to us the notion of the Oneness Being of the Divinity.

Since His Body is One, shall His kingdom not seem to be one? *For*, as you have read, *in him dwelleth all the fulness of the divinity corporally* (Col. ii. 9). And what you may not deny of the Father you ought not deny of the Spirit. Nor should a certain part appear as the instrument of power, because of this comparison with our members; for there is no division of an indivisible thing, and because of this the use of the term *finger* is to be referred to the reality of their unity, not to a division of power. For the Right Hand of God also says: *I and the Father are one* (Jn. x. 30). Yet though divinity is undivided, the person is distinct and separate.

When however the Spirit is called *Finger* operative power is signified; for the Holy Spirit, equally with the Father and the Son, is the holy Operator of the divine works. For David says: *I will behold thy heavens, the work of thy fingers* (Ps. viii. 4). And in the thirty-second psalm: *And all the power of them by the spirit of his mouth.* And Paul says: *But all these things one and the same spirit worketh, dividing to everyone according as he will* (I Cor. xii. 11). And when He says:

But if I by the finger cast out devils; doubtless the kingdom of God is come upon you, saying this He shows that there is a certain royal dominion of the Holy Spirit, which is the Kingdom of God. We in whom the Spirit abides have also within us a royal dwelling. So on a later occasion He says: *The kingdom of God is within you* (Lk. xvii. 21). We must therefore consider the Holy Spirit as being an equal sharer of the Divinity, and of the Divine Power, and of the Divine Majesty; because *the Lord is a Spirit: and where the Spirit of the Lord is there is liberty* (II Cor. iii. 17).

When the unclean spirit is gone out of a man, he walketh through places without water, seeking rest, and not finding. It cannot be doubted that this was said of the Jewish People, whom in the preceding words the Lord severed from His Kingdom. And from this we are to understand that heretics and schismatics are also severed from the Kingdom of God, and from the Church. And so He makes it clearly evident that every assembly of heretics and schismatics belongs, not to God, but to the unclean spirit. Accordingly, the whole Jewish People is compared to a man from whom, through the Law, an unclean spirit has gone forth.

But because he could find no resting place among the nations and Gentiles, because of their faith in Christ (for Christ is the undoing of the unclean spirits; for He has cooled the fiery darts of the enemy against the hearts of the Gentiles, which before were dry and hard, but which now have begun to be soft from the dew of the Holy Spirit in baptism) he returns to the Jewish People, which had been swept and garnished to a legalistic but superficial cleanness, yet remained ever more stained in its inward soul. For it had not begun either to restrain or to cleanse its fierceness in the sacred stream of baptism. And so not without reason did the unclean spirit return to it; bringing with him *seven other spirits more wicked than himself*; for in this impious purpose he warred against the *week* of the Law, and the mystery of the *eighth day*.

And as the grace of the sevenfold Spirit is multiplied on us, so on them is heaped every violence of the spirits of evil; for totality is often signified by this number; for it was on the seventh day that, having finished the work of creation, God rested (Gen. ii. 2). Because of this we also have: *Therefore the barren hath borne many* (hepta), *and she that had many children is weakened* (I King ii. 5).[5]

Chap. 12: 10–12. *And whosoever speaketh a word against the Son of man, it shall be forgiven him: but to him that shall blaspheme against the Holy Ghost, it shall not be forgiven him.* We understand that Christ is truly the Son of man, Who was conceived of the Holy Ghost, and born of the Virgin; that the Virgin is His sole earthly Parent. Is the Holy Ghost then preferred before Christ, so that though sinning against Him we yet receive pardon, but if we sin against the Holy Spirit we shall not obtain pardon? There is no question of comparison, no discussion of degree, where there is but oneness of power; for *the Lord is great, and of his greatness there is no end* (Ps. cxliv. 3). If therefore we believe that Oneness belongs to the Trinity, then so does indivisible might, and undivided action; which is seen from what follows. For since it was elsewhere said: *The Father will give to you what you shall say*, here we have added: *For the Holy Ghost shall teach you in the same hour what you must say.* So if action relates to this Unity, so does offence. But let us return to what we proposed.

Here it seems to some that we are to understand that the same Christ is both Son of man and Holy Spirit: saving the distinction of Persons and their Oneness of Nature; for One and the Same Spirit is both God and the Man Christ, as we find written: *The breath of our mouth Christ the Lord* (Lam. iv. 20). The Same is Holy; for as the Father is God, and the Son is God, and the Father is Lord, and Lord also is the Son, so also Holy is the Father, Holy the Son, Holy the Spirit. Accordingly, the Cherubim and Seraphim with unwearying voices exclaim: *Holy, Holy, Holy*, that by this threefold name the Trinity may be signified.

If then Christ is both, what is the reason for the distinction, unless that we may know that it is not lawful for us to deny the Divinity of Christ? And what was it that was demanded of us in the persecutions but that we should deny that Christ was God? And so whosoever does not confess that God is in Christ, and that Christ is in God and from God, will not be deserving of pardon. And whosoever does not also confess that Christ came in the flesh is not of God; for he who has denied the Man has denied the God: because God is in the Man, and Christ as Man is in God. Amen.

III. St Cyril of Alexandria, Bishop and Doctor

Exposition of the Gospel[6]

And he was casting out a devil, and the same was dumb. The man here spoken of as being without certain senses we would describe as speechless; for his nature was not afflicted. He suffered rather from a trick of the devil, by whom his tongue was as it were tied. So he needed to be brought forward by others: since without a voice he could not plead for himself. For this reason the Lord does not inquire into his faith, but straightaway cures his affliction; *and the multitude were in admiration at it.*

And when the man had been delivered, and the miracle wrought, the people began to praise Christ, with praise such as befitted God.

But some of them, the Evangelist says: (and these were from the Scribes and Pharisees, whose hearts were filled with desperation and jealousy) made as though to regard what had happened as simply a stage in the course of the disease. For seeking to detract from the wonders He wrought by divine power, they began to attribute them to the power of the devil; for through him it was, they said, that the Lord cast out devils.

And thus Christ, though He had as it were cast into the abyss the spirits of evil whom He had forced unwilling from the bodies they possessed, and where they had dared to rule; and though for this He was worthy indeed of praise, yet He did not escape the tongues of those who love to belittle, and those of evil speaking men. For twisting the miracle into a crime they say: *He casteth out devils by Beelzebub.*

And others tempting him, asked of him a sign from heaven. Others urged by the goad of jealousy asked of Him a sign from heaven, almost saying: 'You have driven out an evil spirit from a man, but that is no great wonder. And neither does this show you have divine power. We have seen nothing yet like the miracles of old. Show us something that no one can doubt is from above. Moses led the people through the midst of the sea; making the deep passable for them. With a wand he struck the rock, and made it the mother of streams: springs rushing from the hard stone. And his successor halted the sun before Gabaon; and the moon above the valley of Ajalon (Jos. xii. 12). He held back the Jordan, and put a barrier before its rushing waters.' For these men to ask a sign can only mean, that they were turning thoughts of this kind over in their minds as they watched Him. How did Christ answer them?

But he seeing their thoughts, said to them: Every kingdom divided . . . First He shows that He is God by this, that He knows what they had been murmuring among themselves: for He had known their thoughts. For since suspicions of this kind were shameful, and also because they feared the people, they did not give tongue to their grievance against Him, but limited themselves to turning it over in their mind. Then that He might divert their minds from this grievous impiety He answers them, not from the Scriptures: for they paid no heed to them, rather they tried to twist their meaning: but from what is commonly agreed to happen among men.

For, He says, a city, and even a house, if it be divided against itself will soon come to nothing; the same is true of a kingdom: than which men think there is nothing stronger. If I therefore, having in me the power of a demon, by this demon cast out other demons, the kingdom of the demons is divided; whose power if they oppose each other will soon pass away. For it is the union of its people makes a kingdom strong. A house too is strong when its members are no way in conflict with each other. The kingdom of Beelzebub then also remains strong, unless it seeks to do that which works against itself. How then does Satan drive out Satan? It is unlikely that it is of their own will evil spirits are driven from men. For Satan does not fight against Satan, nor direct attacks against his own followers; rather he gives aid to his own kingdom. You must then believe that it is by divine power I crush Satan.[7]

They dared, this perverse assembly of wicked Pharisees, to accuse Emmanuel of crime. They dared to slander his honour; and blasphemously they repeat that upheld by the power of Beelzebub He cast the evil spirits out of the afflicted. For this, in times past, Emmanuel had rebuked the unrestrained mouths of the Jews, by the mouth of Osee His Prophet. *Woe to them*, He said, *for they have departed from me: they shall be wasted because they have transgressed against me. And I have redeemed them! But against me they have spoken lies* (Os. vii. 13).

If I cast out devils by Beelzebub; by whom do your children cast them out? The blessed Disciples were Jews, and born of Jews. They had received power from God against unclean spirits; and those who were tormented by them they had delivered by the invocation of the Name of Jesus Christ. If then, He says, your sons crush Satan in My Name, striking down his followers, and driving them headlong from the bodies they afflict, how can it be anything but plain blasphemy on your part, coupled with great ignorance, if any among you say that I receive My power from Beelzebub? Your own sons' testimony condemns you: for they, after they had received My authority and My power, put Satan to flight, driving him out against his will from those he had possessed; while you say that it is by *his* power I work My miracles!

But if I by the Finger of God cast out devils; doubtless the kingdom of God is come upon you. Since what you say is not true, rather a worthless fabrication, darkened further by slander, it is manifest therefore that it is by the Finger of God that I cast out demons. He calls the Holy Ghost the *Finger of God*. Christ Himself is called the *Hand* and the *Arm of God* (Ps. xliii. 4; Is. liii. 1): because through Him the Father does all things. And the Son in turn works through the Spirit. As the finger is joined to the hand, not separate from it, but joined naturally to it, so the Holy Spirit, sharing the same nature as the Son, is joined naturally to Him; though He proceeds from God the Father. For, as I have said, the Son works all things through His Consubstantial Spirit.[8] Now however as man, He says, by reason of My divine purpose, I cast forth devils by the *Finger of God*. For the Jews, weak and corrupt of mind as they were, could not have endured it had He said He cast out devils by His own Spirit. And note here, I beseech you, that as the Father works His wonders through the Son, it is the Spirit that accomplishes them; but as One and the Same is their Nature, so one likewise is their operation.

Since then the adversaries of the Holy Spirit are driven on every side towards the truth, let them reject the vomit of the deceivers, and turning again to God let them seek from Him the Light of truth, which He being kind and merciful will grant them. If therefore, He says, becoming a man like you, I cast out devils by the Spirit of God, it follows that the nature of man, beginning with Me, has grown rich from the heavenly kingdom. For it has acquired glory in crushing Satan, and in rebuking the unclean spirits. This is the meaning of, *the Kingdom of God is come upon you.*

And when a strong man armed keepeth his court, these things are in peace that he possesseth. Since it was necessary for many reasons that He should answer remarks of this kind He here uses a clear and striking illustration by which they may see, they who desire to see, that He has truly overcome the prince of this world, and as it were unnerved him, and taken from him the strength he once had, and given his possessions to His own friends. For, He says, as long as he had power, and kept guard over what he had, he feared no violence. But if someone stronger suddenly attack him, and overwhelm him, he is then defenceless.

This is a parable based on what happens among men; but the same has befallen the devil, the hater of good, who, before the Coming of the Saviour, did indeed enjoy great power, seizing on the flocks that were manifestly not his, but belonged to the God of all things; shutting them in, and as it were keeping them in his own fold. Then later the Word of God, the Giver of all strength, the Lord of Hosts, being made man, assaulted him and deprived him of his armour, and gave to others all that he had possessed. For those he had held fast in atheism and error are now through the holy Apostles called to the knowledge of Truth, and because of their belief in His Son they have been restored once more to the Father.

He that is not with me, is against me; and he that gathereth not with me, scattereth. For I have come, He says, that I may snatch everyone from the hands of the devil, that I may deliver those who were captives, give light to those in darkness, raise up the fallen, heal the bruised, and gather together in one the children of God he has scattered. But it is otherwise with Satan, who is not with Me, but strives to scatter what has been delivered and gathered together. How then should he who is at war with all I do give help to Me against himself? Is it not great folly to believe that this could happen? And how it came to happen to the Jews to fall into such thoughts He then goes on to explain.

When the unclean spirit is gone out of a man, he walketh through places without water. That this similitude is directed against the Jews Matthew has already told us where He says: *So shall it be also to this wicked generation.* For while they were in servitude in Egypt, living after the manners and customs of the Egyptians, and abounding in every impurity, the unclean spirit began to dwell in them. Afterwards, by the mercy of God they were delivered through Moses, and had the Law as their guide and teacher, and through this they were led to the knowledge of the True God, and the impure and evil spirit was cast out from them. Then sacrificing a lamb, the figure of Christ, and being sprinkled with its blood, they escaped the Destroying Angel. But because they refused to believe in Christ, and turned from their Redeemer, the spirit of evil has again possessed them, and has enslaved them more cruelly than before. For he found their heart empty, and void of all concern for the things of God, and wholly taken up with the flesh, and so he took up his abode in them. For just as the Holy Spirit, when He finds the heart of man free of all uncleanness, enters in and abides there, and there takes His rest, so the unclean spirit takes up his abode in the souls of the wicked. For they are, as I say, empty of all virtue. And in this way it comes to pass that the last state of Israel is worse than the first. For, as the Saviour's Disciple says: *It had been better for them not to have known the way of justice, than after they have known it, to turn back from the holy commandment which was delivered to them. For that of the true proverb has happened to them: The dog is returned to his vomit: and the sow that has washed to her wallowing in the mire* (II Pet. ii. 21, 22).

And from what they afterwards dared to do, it is plain to see that they have swallowed their vomit, and turned again to wallow in their ancient mire, and relapsed into the errors of Egypt. For the evil spirit has again entered them, and their last state has become worse than their first; in accordance with the words of our Saviour, Who with the Father and the Holy Ghost lives and reigns world without end. Amen.

IV. St Leo the Great, Pope and Doctor

The Purposes of Lent[9]

Synopsis:

I. During the season of Lent we are to strive with greater zeal to cleanse our souls from the blemishes of our past life; from which no one is free.

II. To fasting let us join purity of conscience, the harmony of peace, and generous almsgiving: and from these duties there is no one exempt.

III. We should put away the spirit of pride and of revenge, with the aid of mildness and humility.

I. *The earth*, Dearly Beloved, is indeed always *filled with the mercy of the Lord* (Ps. xxxii. 5), and it is the teaching of nature itself to all who believe, that God is to be adored, since heaven and earth, the sea, and all things that are in them, proclaim the goodness and might of their Creator. And the wondrous beauty of the stars, and of all creatures that serve Him, call for a giving of thanks from that creature who is endowed with reason. And now a more earnest purification of our hearts is asked of us, as once again we draw near to those special days in which we so solemnly recall the mystery of man's redemption, and which in ordered sequence precede the Paschal Festival.

For though the life of many among you is at all times without stain, and the regular practice of good works commends many of you to God, yet not for this reason are we so to trust to the healthiness of our conscience, that we may think that, though we dwell in the midst of temptations and occasions of sin, we cannot fall into anything which could injure it. For the most worthy prophet says, *Who can say, my heart is clean; I am free from sin?* (Prov. xx. 9). And again: *Who can understand sins? From my secret ones cleanse me, O Lord: and from those of others spare thy servant* (Ps. xviii. 13).

But if, as experience proves to us, such is the state of the soul of those who resist evil desires, who struggle against the impulses of anger, and who restrain their most secret thoughts, so that never is anything found in their hearts that may be blamed, and yet are often unaware of their own secret sins, or troubled by those of others, let them then carefully consider during this time what are the blemishes, what the weaknesses, how grievous the effects of past sins, for which a stronger medicine may be needed: that they may not be found strangers to that mystery *by which the works of the devil are destroyed* (I Jn. iii. 8).

For this is the special nature of the Paschal Festival, that the whole Church rejoice in the forgiveness of sin, which has place not alone in those who are reborn in holy baptism, but also in those long since numbered among the adopted children of God. For though the baptism of regeneration causes men to be reborn, since there is in all men a need for daily renewal against the rusting of our nature, and since in every state of soul there is no one who ought not to be better, all should therefore strive that on the day of Redemption no one shall be found in his former sins.

II. That therefore, Dearly Beloved, which it becomes every Christian to do at all times, let it be done now more earnestly and more devoutly, so that the apostolic institution of Lent may be fulfilled by your abstinence: not alone in refraining from food, but especially in refraining from wickedness. For since this self denial is practised to this end, that men may be drawn away from that which kindles the desires of the flesh, no form of self denial should be more practised than to keep ourselves at all times from unworthy desires, and to abstain from unworthy actions.

Nor are the sick dispensed from this devotion; and neither are the infirm excused from it; for health of soul can be found even in a weak and useless body: if where before was an abode of wickedness the beginnings of virtue are now made strong. For this the sickness of the poor body is enough: indeed it often will exceed the measure of our voluntary suffering: provided that the soul does its part, and that that which has no delight in bodily feasting will neither feast on iniquity.

Nothing is more profitably joined to worthy and holy fasting than almsgiving, which includes many works of piety under the single name of mercy, so that in this the good will of all the faithful may be equal, though their means may not be. For nothing ever can so stand in the way of the love we owe both to God and to man, that it is not free at all times to be of good will. For according to what the angels said, *Glory to God in the highest, and on earth peace to men of good will*, whosoever is joined in charity to others, and has mercy on those who are in suffering, from any cause whatever, he shall be blessed, not alone with the virtue of good will, but also with the gift of peace.

For the works of compassion are most profitable, and in their very variety they bring this gain to all true Christians, that in the giving of alms not alone have the rich their part, but those also of the middle state of means, and even the poor; and they who are not alike in their power to give, may yet be alike in the good dispositions of their hearts.

For when, under the eyes of the Lord, many gave of their abundance to the Temple treasury, a certain widow put in two brass farthings, and merited to be crowned by this special testimony of Jesus Christ: that in her humble fulfillment of her duty, her offering was worthy of being praised above all that others had given; though compared to their rich offerings, to whom much still remained, hers was indeed poor, but it was her all.

Should anyone then be so poor that he cannot give even two farthings to one in want, in the precepts of the Lord he still has that by which he can fulfil the demands of good will. For he who gives a cup of cold water to a poor man who thirsts shall receive a reward for his deed (Mt. x. 42; Lk. xxi. 2; Mk. xii. 40). Such are the simple means the Lord provides, in order that his servants shall be able to win the kingdom of heaven, so that even the giving of a drink of water, whose enjoyment is free and open to all, will not go without its reward. And so that no poverty shall stand in the way, an example of mercy is given us from simple cold water: so that even he shall not think he will go without his reward who has not the price of the wood to warm the water. And not for nothing does the Lord also warn us that this cup be given in His Name. For things which of themselves are without value become precious through faith; and that which is given without faith, however precious it may be, is still empty of all virtue unto justice.

III. As you are about to celebrate the Paschal Festival, Dearly Beloved, let you so exercise yourselves in these sacred abstinences, that you may approach the most holy feast free from every disorder. Let the spirit of pride, from which all sins have come, be driven out by the spirit of humility; and let those who are puffed up with arrogance become mild through forbearance. Let those whom some insult has provoked, becoming reconciled, seek earnestly to return to the peace of friendship: *To no man rendering evil for evil* (Rom. xii. 17), and, *forgiving one another, as Christ also hath forgiven you* (Col. iii. 13), wiping out human enmities in peace.

And if there be any among those subject to you who have earned bonds or imprisonment, let them in mercy be pardoned: that we who are in daily need of pardon may not be slow in forgiving others. For when we say to the Lord our Father: *Forgive us our trespasses, as we forgive them who trespass against us*, there can be no doubt whatever, that when we pardon the offences of others against us we prepare the way for the divine mercy towards ourselves, by the grace of our Lord Jesus Christ, Who with the Father and the Holy Ghost lives and reigns world without end. Amen.

V. St Maximus, Bishop and Father of the Church

The Time of Lent[10]

We must accept with all reverence, Brethren, the sacred days of Lent, and not repine because of the length of the season; for the longer the days of our fasting, the greater the grounds of our forgiveness; the longer the time of our self-denial, the greater the price paid for our soul's salvation; the severer the treatment of our wounds, the more sure the healing of our offences. For God Who is the Physician of our souls has instituted an appropriate time; sufficient for the just to make reparation, and for sinners to ask for mercy; the one praying for peace, the other imploring pardon.

For the days of Lent are suited to our purposes; not short, so that we may plead in prayer; not long, for our need to gain merit. For in this fast of forty days any offence may be wiped out, and the severity of any judge softened. The time may be long and tedious for the man who neither pleads for his sins, nor hopes for forgiveness. For he who despairs will neither confess his sin, nor hope in the mercy of the Judge.

Holy and salutary therefore is the time of Lent, in which the Judge is moved to mercy, the sinner to repentance, and the just to peace. For in these days the Divinity is wont to be more merciful, the sinner to repent, and grace to be earned. All things are now prepared: the heavens to pardon, the sinner to confess, the tongue to plead.

Mystical and salutary is this number, forty. For when in the beginning the iniquity of man covered the face of the earth, God, dissolving the clouds of heaven for the space of this number of days, covered the whole earth with a flood. You see then already that in this time the Mystery is put before us in Figure. For as it then rained for forty days, to cleanse the world, so now does it also. Yet the deluge of those days must be called a mercy; in that through it iniquity was crushed, and justness upheld. For it took place out of mercy: to deliver the just, and that the wicked might no longer sin. We see clearly it was through mercy it came; as a sort of baptism, in which the face of the earth was renewed: that is, so that man who wallowed in the dreadful sin of abandoned men might come to grace in the dwelling of Noah, and so that he who was then an abode of iniquity, might become a dwelling of holiness.

The Flood of those days was, as I say, a Figure of baptism. For that was then prefigured which is now fulfilled; that is, just as when the fountains of water overflowed, iniquity was imperilled, and justness alone reigned: sin was swept into the abyss, and holiness upraised to heaven. Then, as I said, that was prefigured which now is fulfilled in Christ's Church. For as Noah was saved in the Ark, while the iniquity of men was drowned in the Flood, so by the waters of baptism the Church is borne close to heaven, all the superstitions of idols overthrown, and the faith reigns on earth which came forth from the Ark of the Saviour.

Holy and dedicated is this time of forty days, which immediately from the beginning began to divide the just from the unjust; and by a kind of judgement separate the good from the bad. And this takes place even in our time of forty days. For in these forty days the good are divided from the bad: that is, the chaste from the unchaste, the temperate from the intemperate, the Christian from the heathen. The wicked, as I say, are separated from the good: that is, the sinner from the just man, the devil from the saint, the heretic from the faithful. For those others are lost, as in the Flood, in the disaster of this world, while the Church alone, with all its virtues, is like the Ark sustained above the deep.

And so we, though we also are sinners, announce to you, as the blessed Noah in his time, the coming destruction of the world. And we tell you that they alone shall escape who find shelter in the bosom of the threefold Ark of the Faith. For threefold is the Ark of the Church: since it contains within it the Mystery of the Trinity. For when the Scripture relates that the Ark had *a middle and a third storey*, it is showing us that the Church is adorned by the threefold Presence of the Trinity. And so like Noah we announce to you the coming end of the world, and we warn all men to take refuge in this House. And as Noah received his children into the Ark, so do we also earnestly desire to receive our children into this Ark. And he who desires to dwell with us in this House is our child.

But someone will say, that Scripture has left us no account of the words of Noah's announcement to men. Know that though he was silent as to speech he spoke aloud in work; his tongue was still, but the work of his hands cried out. For certainly while he was engaged on his extraordinary task, and one never before heard of, he was warning all men that he was preparing a new dwelling against an unheard of danger to come (Gen. vi. 14; Eccli. xliv. 17; I Pet. iii. 20; Mt. xxiv. 37). He spoke therefore in his work; and what he was saying to men was the saying of Our Lord in the Gospel: *If you do not believe me, believe in my works* (Jn. x. 38), and believing you may escape the danger, by the assistance of Our Lord Jesus Christ, Who with the Father and the Holy Ghost liveth and reigneth world without end. Amen.

VI. Saint Bruno, Abbot

The Kingdom of Evil[11]

Luke xi. 14. The Blessed Evangelist Matthew tells us, that this man was not alone dumb but blind also. And blind is every man who follows not after that Light Which says: *I am the Light of the world; he that followeth Me walketh not in darkness, but shall have the Light of life* (Jn. viii. 12). And he is indeed dumb who confesses not his sins, and who knows not how to open his mouth to the praise of God.

And he hath a demon within him who persists in any grave sin. And because of this the Apostle admonishes us, where he says: *Let not sin therefore reign in your mortal body* (Rom. vi. 12). For as long as sin remains in a man, for so long is he bound and captive and possessed by the devil. Such a man, blind and dumb, if he be offered to the Lord, if he be converted to penance, the Lord shall straightaway heal him; so that the evil spirit being driven out of him he may speak and see.

But let him not, as before, speak idle and vain things, but what is holy and of the Spirit, as becometh a Christian. Nor let him look upon vain things with the eyes of his body; but with the eyes of his soul let him contemplate the Light of life and truth.

But some of them said: *He casteth out devils by Beelzebub, the prince of devils.* Of these the Evangelist Matthew says: *But the Pharisees hearing it, said: this man casteth not out devils but by Beelzebub the prince of devils.* For the more the Pharisees appear to be better and wiser than the rest, so much the more often are they goaded by an ever greater jealousy against the Lord. But who, O Pharisees, has taught you this? For only because you are the disciples of Beelzebub could you say such things in his praise. You see Jesus raising the dead, giving light to the blind, cleansing the lepers, and curing every kind of infirmity and disease, and you say that He casts out devils by the power of Beelzebub? When did Beelzebub, the Lord of the Flies, ever do such things?

And others tempting, asked of him a sign from heaven. Another Evangelist relates what answer the Lord gave to these men; saying to them: *An evil and adulterous generation seeketh a sign: and a sign shall not be given it, but the sign of Jonas the prophet. For as Jonas was in the whale's belly three days and three nights: so shall the Son of man be in the heart of the earth three days and three nights* (Mt. xii. 39). Let this sign suffice for you; nor will any other sign be given to you, either from heaven or from the earth. Great and wondrous is this sign: that He Who holds all things in His Hands allowed himself to be in the power of men for three days and three nights. For what does it mean to be in the heart of the earth if not to be subject to the passions, to the power, to the evil will, of sinners? Because of this the Lord also answered Pilate: *Thou shouldst not have any power against me, unless it were given thee from above* (Jn. x. 11). And as heaven means the Just, so likewise earth signifies sinners.

But he seeing their thoughts, said to them: Every kingdom divided against shall be brought to desolation, and house upon house shall fall. And if Satan also be divided against himself, how shall his kingdom stand? because you say, that through Beelzebub I cast out devils. With a very clear illustration He confutes those who said that He was casting out devils by Beelzebub. For if it is as they say, then Beelzebub has wholly lost his power, his leadership, and his kingdom. For if the spirits of evil were waging war against each other, they would have had little or no power against man.

Rather what is worse than this holds; for there are scarcely to be found any number of men imbued with such unity of purpose in doing good, as the devils possess in doing evil. For though they are endless, innumerable, yet in this they are one, that they seek to do nothing but what is evil. If then they had not this concord in wickedness, and desired to be converted to penance, and could do so, then indeed would the kingdom of Beelzebub be brought to desolation; for this is what we see take places in other kingdoms. It is not therefore as these *others* say; and Satan does not cast out Satan; rather do all in his kingdom give aid to each other in all that they do.

For this same reason was it said by the Lord, through the mouth of Job, concerning the devil: *His body is like molten shields, shut close up with scales pressing upon one another. One is joined to another and they hold one another fast, and shall not be separated* (Job. xli. 6, 8). By these words He makes clear that the spirits of evil have, between them, such harmony of purpose that in no way can they be separated one from another. For by the *body* of the devil is understood the whole array of the malignant spirits. And because of their strength these same malign spirits are spoken of as *molten shields*, and they are described as *scales pressing upon one another*, and as, *holding one another fast*, and as being *joined to one another*, because of this surpassing unity and concord which they possess in every kind of malice and desire of evil-doing. Would indeed if it could be that this so great unity and harmony might be broken, and the kingdom of evil be destroyed!

Now if I cast out devils by Beelzebub; by whom do your children cast them out? If, He says, you have such thoughts against Me, what then do you say of My Disciples? I know that you who say such abominable things of the Master will not think well of His Disciples. For earlier He had declared: *If they have called the master of the house Beelzebub, how much more them of his household?* (Mt. x. 25). The Apostles are spoken of as sons of the Pharisees, since they also, and all who were accustomed to believe in the resurrection, which the Pharisees preached, were wont to look upon the Pharisees as fathers and teachers. For which reason they also may be considered as belonging to that sect: for this sect was better than the others; though it too was in many respects not worthy. And likewise in the Acts of the Apostles Paul is recorded as crying out: *I am a Pharisee: the son of Pharisees; concerning the hope and resurrection of the dead I am called in question* (Acts xxiv. 6). This therefore is why the Disciples of Christ are spoken of as sons of the Pharisees. And so Our Lord says: *Therefore they shall be your judges*. For they shall sit on twelve thrones, judging the twelve tribes of Israel.

But if I by the Finger of God cast out devils; doubtless the kingdom of God is come upon you. What this means another Evangelist tells us, saying: *If I by the Spirit of God cast out devils* (Mt. xii. 28): which is indeed true, and may not be doubted: therefore *is the kingdom of God come upon you*. For where the Spirit of God is, there also is the Kingdom of God. The Holy Ghost is called the *Finger of God*, because of the multiple division of graces. For in no part of the body do we find such division as in the fingers. And this is as if He had said: I indeed cast out devils in the Spirit and Power of God; since they are subject to me, since they are powerless to withstand me, since I hold them tied, and keep them bound.

But when a strong man armed keepeth his court, these things are in peace which he possesseth. But if a stronger than he come upon him, and overcome him etc. For the devil was strong; but I am stronger. I have entered his court; I have come into this world which he has held as though it were his own house; and the time draws near for the prince of this world to be cast forth. I have bound him; I have broken his armour; and the unhappy people he held captive I have delivered from his bondage. He is not therefore *with Me*; nor does he gather with Me; neither does he cast out devils together with Me; nor does he heal men, as I do; nor does he gather in the flocks, nor lead them to the living pastures, which I am doing. What then does he do? Do you wish to hear? He scatters, he harries, he kills, he drags down to death and eternal damnation whomsoever he can. For this is the meaning of those words: *He that is not with me, is against me; and he that gathereth not with me, scattereth.*

When the unclean spirit is gone out of a man etc. The Lord spoke to us this similitude that He might show us that the evil and adulterous generation of the Jews, because of their hard and unrepentant hearts, would be condemned, not alone by the Ninivites, but also and rightly by the other Gentiles. Since this impious generation knew not that it should repent, but daily became more wicked, its last state was worse than its first. And this they themselves likewise implied when they said of Our Saviour: *His blood be upon us and upon our children* (Mt. xxvii. 35). So shall it be unto this most wicked generation as it was to this man who was possessed by an unclean spirit:

For when the unclean spirit is gone out of a man, he walketh through places without water, seeking rest; and not finding . . . For the unclean spirit enters easily into a man, and easily goes out from him. For as often as a man, either in thought or in action, does something that is wicked, the devil is present with him. But should he begin to repent from his heart, the devil will leave him. And going out he walks through dry and waterless places, tempting those that are free of the sap of malice and of lust, and in whom *he finds no rest*; since he seeks what is corrupt and moist. And for this was it written of him: *He sleepeth under the shadow, in the covert of the reed, and in moist places* (Job xl. 16); in which reference the genitals are signified. *Then he saith: I will return into my house whence I came out.* Because he could find no foothold in the good he turns back to the wicked. For the devil may tempt the good, but he cannot find rest in them; for he is shaken violently, and upset, and driven out, now by their prayers, now by their tears of repentance, and now by their almsgiving and similar good works.

And when he is come, he findeth it empty (Matt. xii. 43). *Empty*, since he finds there no charity, nor true faith, nor humility, nor patience, nor justice, nor mercy, nor any of the other things with which the souls of the saints are furnished. How does he find it? *Swept and garnished*: he finds it as he desires to find it. He finds it *swept clean* by evil brushes, and *garnished* with evil furnishings; evil brushes that sweep out the virtues, and leave the vices; evil brushes that scatter dust upon the floor, and do not sweep it out. It is lust, fornication, pleasure, pride, avarice, discord, and all uncleanness, which are the furnishings of the devil. With these adornments he finds it garnished.

Then he goeth and taketh with him seven other spirits more wicked than himself, and entering in they dwell there. It is not enough for him that he possesses the house alone; he seeks companions: the place is spacious: it needs many dwellers there. But who are these seven spirits? Why also are they seven? Why are they more wicked than himself? Because seven are the gifts of the Holy Ghost, by means of which every soul is converted to faith in Christ, and defended against the contrary evils. Therefore the unclean spirit takes unto him those seven wickeder, contrary, spirits, with which he defends the house against the virtues.

Namely, opposing the spirit of stupidity to the spirit of wisdom; the spirit of revolt and unreason to the spirit of understanding; the spirit of rashness to the spirit of counsel; the spirit of inconstancy and fear to the spirit of fortitude; the spirit of ignorance to the spirit of knowledge; the spirit of impiety to the spirit of piety; the spirit of contempt and hate to the spirit of the fear of the Lord.

Unhappy the soul where these seven evil spirits dwell, and wherein they rule. For these are, in a certain way, worse than the one who brought them there; since it is they who in this life corrupt souls; while he, after this life, torments them. He opens the door; they, once entered, lay waste and destroy everything within. He tempts; they kill. He can tempt and vex a man; but without these others he cannot kill the soul. And so they are worse than he is; for they injure more grievously than he can. He, tempting and persuading, is truly wicked; they by doing and destroying are yet more wicked. To the one the Apostle delivered a man, *for the destruction of the flesh*; but of these others he says: *Let not sin therefore reign in your mortal body* (I Cor. v. 5; Rom. vi. 12). It is no wonder then that the last state of this man is worse than the first; since he is first oppressed by the one, and then following this by the seven other demons.

And as he spoke these things, a certain woman from the crowd, lifting up her voice, said to him: Blessed is the womb that bore thee, and the paps that gave thee suck. This is as if He said: Blessed indeed is My Mother, and blessed the womb that bore Me. But not for this is She blessed: because She is My Mother. Neither is the womb blessed because it bore Me. But both are blessed because She heard the word of God, and hearing it, believed; and believing, She safeguarded it. For had she not done this, She would neither be blessed, nor My Mother.

Turning then to the Lord Our God, the Father Almighty, let us as best we can give thanks with all our hearts; beseeching Him that in His Goodness He will graciously hear our prayers, and by His Power drive evil from our thoughts and actions, increase our faith, guide our minds, grant us His holy inspirations, and bring us to everlasting joy, through His Son Our Lord and Saviour Jesus Christ. Amen.

NOTES

[1] PG 72, col. 701 note.

[2] Dan. xix. 27. We know from the frequent testimony of both Greek and Latin Fathers that by the *eighth day* (*octave mysterium*) is meant the Blessed Resurrection and the New Dispensation of grace; as, e.g., Gregory Ny. in Psalm vi; Hilary in Prolog. in Ps.; August. Cassiod. in Psalmos; also from the words of Ambrose himself: 'The Resurrection was accomplished on the eighth day; hence many psalms are inscribed for the Octave, e.g.: vi and

xi'; and 'in the octonory number is the fulness of perfection', cf. on Luke xiii. 10, 11. *Vide* PL 15; Note c.

[3] PL 17, col. 664. Serm. 29, Quad. VI.

[4] PL 15. Expos. in Lucam Lib. VII, 91–5.

[5] LXX (ἑπτα). [6] PG 72, col. 699.

[7] This paragraph is not given by Combefio, in his translation from Cat. Cardinal Mazarini in Luke.

[8] *Τῶ τῆς ὁμοουσιότητος λόγῳ*

[9] PL 54, c. 285 Serm. 44, Quad. VI.

[10] PL 57, c. 573, Serm. 20 in Quad VI.

[11] PL 165, cols. 794 and 183.

FOURTH SUNDAY OF LENT

I. Origen: The Mystery of the Loaves and Fishes

II. St Cyprian: On Good Works and Almsdeeds

III. St Hilary: On the Gospel

IV. St Augustine: Exposition of the Gospel

V. St Leo the Great: The Spirit of Lent

THE GOSPEL OF THE SUNDAY

John vi. 1–15

At that time, Jesus went over the sea of Galilee, which is that of Tiberias. And a great multitude followed him, because they saw the miracles which he did on them that were diseased. Jesus therefore went up into a mountain, and there he sat with his disciples. Now the pasch, the festival day of the Jews, was near at hand. When Jesus therefore had lifted up his eyes, and seen that a very great multitude cometh to him, he said to Philip: whence shall we buy bread, that these may eat? And this he said to try him; for he himself knew what he would do. Philip answered him: two hundred pennyworth of bread is not sufficient for them, that every one may take a little. One of his disciples, Andrew, the brother of Simon Peter, saith to him: There is a boy here that hath five barley loaves, and two fishes; but what are these among so many? Then Jesus said: Make the men sit down. Now there was much grass in the place. The men therefore sat down, in number about five thousand. And Jesus took the loaves: and when he had given thanks, he distributed to them that were set down. In like manner also of the fishes, as much as they would.

And when they were filled, he said to his disciples: Gather up the fragments that remain, lest they be lost. They gathered up therefore, and filled twelve baskets with the fragments of the five barley loaves, which remained over and above to them that had eaten. Now these men, when they had seen what a miracle Jesus had done, said: This is of a truth the prophet, that is to come into the world. Jesus therefore, when he knew they would come to take him by force, and make him king, fled again into the mountains himself alone.

PARALLEL GOSPELS

Matthew xiv. 13–21

Which when Jesus had heard, he retired from thence by a boat, into a desert place apart, and the multitudes having heard of it, followed him on foot out of the cities. And he coming forth saw a great multitude, and had compassion on them, and healed their sick. And when it was evening, his disciples came to him, saying: This is a desert place, and the hour is now past: send away the multitudes, that going into the towns, they may buy themselves victuals. But Jesus said to them, They have no need to go: give you them to eat. They answered him: We have not here, but five loaves, and two fishes. He said to them: Bring them hither to me. And when he had commanded the multitudes to sit down upon the grass, he took the five loaves and the two fishes, and looking up to heaven, he blessed, and brake, and gave the loaves to his disciples, and the disciples to the multitudes. And they did all eat, and were filled. And they took up what remained, twelve full baskets of fragments. And the number of them that did eat was five thousand men, besides women and children.

Mark vi. 30–44

And the Apostles coming together unto Jesus, related to him all things that they had done and taught. And he said to them: Come apart into a desert place, and rest a little. For there were many coming and going: and they had not so much as time to eat. And going up into a ship, they went into a desert place apart. And they saw them going away, and many knew: and they ran flocking thither on foot from all the cities, and were there before them. And Jesus going out saw a great multitude: and he had compassion on them, because they were as sheep not having a shepherd, and he began to teach them many things. And when the day was now far spent, his disciples came to him, saying: This is a desert place, and the hour is now past: send them away, that going into the next villages and towns, they may buy themselves meat to eat. And he answering said to them: Give you them to eat. And they said to him: Let us go and buy bread for two hundred pence, and we will give them to eat. And he saith to them: How many loaves have you? Go and see. And when they knew, they say: Five, and two fishes. And he commanded them that he should make them all sit down by companies upon the green grass. And they sat down in ranks, by hundreds and by fifties. And when he had taken the five loaves, and the two fishes: looking up to heaven, he blessed, and broke the loaves, and gave to his disciples to set before them: and the two fishes he divided among them all. And they did all eat, and had their fill. And they took up the leavings, twelve full baskets of fragments, and of the fishes. And they that did eat, were five thousand men.

Luke ix. 10–17

And the Apostles, when they were returned, told him all they had done. And taking them, he went aside into a desert place, apart, which belongeth to Bethsaida. Which when the people knew, they followed him; and he received them, and spoke to them of the kingdom of God, and healed them who had need of healing. Now the day began to decline. And the twelve came and said to him: send away the multitude, that going into the towns and villages round about, they may lodge and get victuals; for we are here in a desert place. But he said to them: Give you them to eat. And they said: We have no more than five loaves and two fishes; unless perhaps we should go and buy food for all this multitude. Now there were about five thousand men. And he said to his disciples: Make them sit down by fifties in a company. And they did so; and made them all sit down. And taking the five loaves and two fishes, he looked up to heaven, and blessed them; and he broke, and distributed to his disciples, to set before the multitude. And they did all eat, and were filled. And there were taken up of fragments that remained to them, twelve baskets.

Exposition from the Catena Aurea

John vi. 1–16

V. 1. *After these things Jesus went over the sea of Galilee etc. . .*

Chrysostom, *Hom.* 42 *in John*: Just as javelins when they meet with something strong and unyielding rebound with great force against those who thrust them, but when nothing opposes them they fall down and lie still, so is it that when we resist men of violence with violence, they rage the more; but should we yield, we calm their fury. And so Christ calmed the fury which had arisen from the preceding discourses, by retiring into Galilee; but not to the same districts as when He had come up from Jerusalem. For he did not go into Cana of Galilee, but crossed over the sea. Hence is it related: *After these things Jesus went over etc.*

Alcuin: This sea is called by a variety of names by reason of the diversity of places. In this place it is called the sea of Galilee, because of the province; it is called the sea of Tiberias, because of the city of that name. It is called a sea, not because its waters were salt, but after the manner of the Hebrews, who called large bodies of waters seas. The Lord frequently crossed this sea, that He might impart His Teaching to the peoples dwelling beyond it.

V. 2. *And a great multitude followed him because they saw the miracles etc.*

THEOPHYLACTUS: For he preaches from place to place, testing the dispositions of the peoples; rendering more eager and sollicitous the men of every city; hence: *And a great multitude followed him.* ALCUIN: And this because He gave sight to the blind, and did other similar things. And we must keep in mind that those whom He healed in body, He likewise renewed in soul.

CHRYSOSTOM, as above, *sparsim in princ:* Though delighting in His teaching they were moved more by His miracles. But *signs*, as Paul says, *are not for believers, but unbelievers* (I Cor. xiv. 22). They were wiser of whom Matthew says: *The people were in admiration at His doctrine* (Mt. vii. 28). But why does he not relate the miracles they saw Him working? This Evangelist desires to devote the great part of his Gospel to the *discourses* of the Lord. For there follows:

V. 3. *Jesus therefore went up into a mountain and sat there with His Disciples.*

He went up into a mountain because of the sign that was to follow. That the Disciples alone ascended with Him is the fault of the crowd, which failed to follow Him. He went up that He might also teach us to seek quiet, apart from the noise and tumult of men: and that solitude is more suited to the pursuit of wisdom. For there follows:

V. 4. *Now the pasch, the festival day of the Jews, was near at hand.*

See how the Evangelist tells us nothing of the miracles of Christ during a whole year other than that He healed the paralytic, the son of the Ruler. For he was not trying to make a record of all of them, but narrating a few among the many; and these the striking ones. Why did He not go up to Jerusalem for the Feast? Because He had begun gradually to undo the Law; taking occasion from the wickedness of the Jews.

THEOPHYLACTUS: Since the Jews were wont to follow Him, taking this opportunity of their absence He shuts out the Law; thus conveying to those who were observant that the Truth being now come all *figures* were at an end; and that He was not so subject to the Law that He must observe the festivals of the Law. And note that this was not a feast of Christ, but of the Jewish people.

BEDE, *in Mark* 5: If any one carefully studies the words of the Evangelist, he will easily learn that there was a space of one year between the beheading of John the Baptist and the Passion of Our Lord. For since Matthew says (xiv. 13) that when Jesus heard of it He retired *into a desert place, apart*, and there fed the multitude. And John says that the pasch of the Jews was near at hand when He fed the multitudes. It is therefore clearly indicated that John's beheading took place close to the Festival. With the passing of the space of one year Christ was put to death; at the time of the same Festival.

V. 5. *When Jesus therefore had lifted up his eyes etc.*

THEOPHYLACTUS: The Evangelist says: *When he had lifted up his eyes*, that we might learn that He did not turn His eyes this way and that, but sat recollectedly giving His attention to His Disciples.

CHRYSOSTOM: For He did not sit idly with His Disciples, but studiously conversing with them; holding their attention upon Himself. Then, raising His eyes He saw the multitudes coming towards Him. On whose behalf did He question Philip? For He knew which among the Disciples of His gathering most needed instruction. Such a one was Philip, who was afterwards to say: *Lord, show us the Father, and it is enough for us* (Jn. xiv. 8). And He first instructs him. For if He had simply wrought the miracle, the sign would not have seemed so striking. So now He makes him proclaim their lack of food, that they might the more clearly perceive the greatness of the miracle. And so there follows:

V. 6. *And this he said to try him; for he himself knew what he would do.*

This He did, not because He did not know what Philip would say, but said it as men will. Just as when it was said: *He that searcheth the hearts* (Rom. viii. 27), does not mean the searching of ignorance, but of true knowledge; so when the Evangelist says that He said this *to try him* (Philip), he means merely that the Lord knew perfectly. And it can also be said that He made this man more sure, inducing in him by this questioning a more precise memory of the miracle. For this reason also the Evangelist, lest you suspect any thing out of place because of the simplicity of the remark, adds: *For he himself knew what he would do.*

ALCUIN: He asks therefore, not that He might learn what He knew not, but that Philip might learn the dullness of his own faith, which, he himself could not know, but his Master knew, and strengthened by performing this miracle. THEOPHYLACTUS: Or also that He might reveal this fact to others; not as though He Himself did not see into Philip's soul.

AUGUSTINE, *Harmony of the Four Gospels*, 2: 46, 96: For if the Lord, according to the narration of John, seeing the multitudes asked Philip, with a view to trying him, whence food might be found for them, a difficulty might be raised whether that was true which the others narrated; namely: that the Disciples first said to the Lord that He should send away the multitudes. To whom, according to Matthew, He replies: *They have no need to go, give you them to eat* (xiv. 16). Accordingly, we must understand that the Lord after these words looked upon the multitude, and then said to Philip that which John relates; but which the others have omitted, viz.: *Whence shall we buy bread, that these may eat?*

CHRYSOSTOM: Or those are one set of events and these are another; and both did not take place at the same time. THEOPHYLACTUS: The Lord therefore, testing Philip to see if he had faith, found him still subject to human impressions; as is plain from what follows:

V. 7. *Philip answered him: two hundred pennyworth of bread is not etc.*

ALCUIN: In which he discloses his slowness of faith. For if he had perfectly understood his Creator he would not have been mistrustful regarding the generosity of His power.

AUGUSTINE, *Harm. of F.G.*, 2: 46, 96: But that which Philip, according to John, here answered, this same Mark records as having been said by all the Disciples: desiring by this to be understood as saying that Philip had answered as the mouthpiece of the others: although he may have employed the plural number for the singular, as was frequent.

THEOPHYLACTUS: And the Lord found Andrew like to Philip; though considering the matter from a higher point of view than Philip. For there follows:

V. 8 and 9. *One of his Disciples, Andrew, the brother of Simon Peter etc.*

CHRYSOSTOM: I believe that Andrew did not speak without a reason, but because he knew of the miracle Eliseus had wrought with the barley loaves. For the prophet had fed one hundred men with twenty loaves (IV Kings iv). His mind therefore rose somewhat higher; but he did not rise to the heights, as appears from what follows: *But what are these among so many?* For he reckoned that he who was wont to perform miracles would make fewer from the few, and more from the greater number. But this was not so. For He could as easily feed the multitudes from a few loaves as from many. For He needed no subject matter. But, lest created things seem outside the power of His wisdom, He uses created things to work His wonders.

THEOPHYLACTUS: The Manicheans are confuted, who say that bread and all such created things are from an evil God; because Jesus Christ the Son of the Good God multiplied the loaves. For if created things were evil, He that was Good would not have multiplied them.

AUGUSTINE, *as above*: What Andrew, according to John, here says relating to the five loaves and the two fishes, the others (Evangelists), using the plural number for a single person, relate as coming from the Disciples generally.

CHRYSOSTOM: Let us here learn, we who give ourselves to pleasure, what was the food of these truly great and admirable men; and the amount of it they brought with them; and the plainness of their table. And before the loaves were multiplied He bade them sit down, that you may learn that the things that are not are as the things that are, as Paul says: *And calleth those things that are not, as those that are* (Rom. iv. 17). For there follows:

V. 10. *Then Jesus said: Make the men sit down etc.*

ALCUIN: We say the men literally lay down; reclining in the manner of the ancients: *There was much grass in the place.*

THEOPHYLACTUS: That is, green grass. For it was the paschal time, which took place in the first month of the Spring. There follows: *The men therefore sat down, in number about five thousand.* Only the men were counted by the Evangelist, as was the custom of the Law. For Moses numbered the people from the age of twenty upwards, no mention being made of women (Num. i): implying that everyone who was twenty years old, and fit to bear arms, is worthy and honourable before God. Then follows:

V. 11. *And Jesus took the loaves: and when he had given thanks etc.*

CHRYSOSTOM, *Hom.* 41 *as above*: Why was it He did not pray when He was about to heal the paralytic, and when raising the dead, or when calming the sea, but prays here, giving thanks? It was to teach us that those who are about to eat should give thanks to God. But elsewhere, especially in lesser matters, to teach us that it was not because of need He did pray. For had He had need to pray, then much more would He have done so in greater matters. Since He works by His own authority, it is evident that He here prays accommodating Himself to us. And also since a great multitude was assembled, it was necessary to convince them that His Coming was in accord with the Will of the Father. So, when He wrought a miracle in private He did not pray; but when in the presence of many persons He prayed, lest they believe He was contrary to God.

HILARY, *De Trin.* III, 6: Five loaves are accordingly placed before the multitude, and broken in pieces; the new increase flowing imperceptibly from the hands breaking the fragments; the bread from which they are broken not growing less, while the portions broken off continue to fill the hand that is breaking them. Neither sense nor sight can follow the progress of the wondrous operation. That is now which was not; that is seen which is not comprehended; what alone remains is to believe that God can do all things.

AUGUSTINE, *Tr.* 24 *in John*: For from the same source from which He multiplies the fields from a few grains, He has, in His own hands, multiplied five loaves. For the power was in the hands of Christ; the five loaves were as seeds: not indeed cast into the earth, but multiplied by Him Who made the earth.

CHRYSOSTOM: See how great is the difference between Master and servant. For the prophets, receiving power as it were by measure, wrought their wonders accordingly. Christ, holding all power in His hands, brings forth in overflowing abundance. Then follows:

VV. 12, 13: *And when they were filled, he said to his disciples . . .*

This was no vain display, but lest the people think that what had taken place was an illusion. For this reason also He wrought the miracle from means found at hand. But why did He give the fragments to the Disciples, and not to the people, to bring away with them? Because He especially desired to instruct those who were to be Teachers of the whole world. And I am astonished, not alone at the great quantity of bread He made, but at the precise quantity that remained: that He caused that which remained over to be neither more nor less but what He willed, namely, twelve baskets, which is the number of the Apostles.

THEOPHYLACTUS: From the miracle we learn that we are not to be mean-spirited in helping need. BEDE: The multitude were astonished when they saw this sign; for they had not yet come to know that He was God; and so the Evangelist adds:

V. 14. *Now these men, when they had seen what a miracle Jesus had done . . .*

Because they were unspiritual men, and understood things in an earthly manner, when they saw the wonder Jesus had wrought they said: *This is of a truth the prophet that is to come into the world.* ALCUIN: Not yet filled with faith they speak of the Lord as the Prophet, since they knew not yet to call Him God. But they had already gained much from the miracle, they who distinguishing Him from other men now began to call Him the Prophet; for they knew that the prophets, among this people, were wont to work wonders. Neither did they err calling Him prophet, since the Lord had called Himself a prophet, saying: *It cannot be that a prophet perish outside Jerusalem* (Lk. xiii. 33).

AUGUSTINE, *Tr.* 24 *in John*: As Christ is an Angel, and the Lord of the Angels, so also is He a Prophet, and the Lord of the prophets. For in this that while present amongst us He announced tidings, He is an Angel; and in that He foretold things to come, He is a prophet; for this, that the Word was made Flesh, He is Lord both of the Angels and of the prophets: for without the Word of God there was no prophet.

CHRYSOSTOM: From this that they say, *that is to come into the world*, it is apparent that they expected some pre-eminent prophet; and so what is here said: *This is of a truth the prophet* (which has in the Greek the definite article) is said to show that He is outstanding among all the prophets.

AUGUSTINE, *as above*: But we must here consider what is said: for since God is not of such substance as the eye can see, and the miracles by which He rules the world, and has care of every creature in it, are unnoticed by reason of their repetition, He reserved to Himself certain things which He would do in due time in a manner outside the course and order of nature, so that they would wonder and be astonished at seeing not great but unusual things, who are unmoved by things daily seen. For the government of the world is a greater miracle than feeding five thousand men from five loaves; yet at the former no one wonders, the latter astonishes all men: not as a greater wonder, but as a rarer. Yet it is not enough to consider this only in the miracles of Christ; for the Lord is on His Mountain, the Word of God is on high; not now in lowliness, nor lightly to be passed over.

ALCUIN: The troubled world is mystically indicated by the word *sea*. As soon as Christ draws near to the sea of our mortality in His birth, walks on it in dying, crosses over it by rising from the dead, the multitudes of the faithful, gathered from either people, follow him by believing Him, and imitating His example.

BEDE: Then did the Lord ascend the mountain, when He ascended into heaven; symbolized by the mountain. ALCUIN: That He went into the higher regions together with His Disciples, leaving the multitude below, indicates to us, that the lesser precepts are to be given to the simple, the higher to the more perfect. That He fed them at the approach of the Pasch signifies, that whosoever desires to be nourished by the Bread of the Divine Word, and by the Body and Blood of the Lord, should make a spiritual Pasch; that is, pass over from the vices to the virtues. The eyes of the Lord are truly spiritual gifts, which He mercifully bestows on His Elect, whenever He turns His eye upon them: that is, when He bestows on us the rewards of filial piety.

AUGUSTINE, *Book* 83 *Quest*. 61: The five barley loaves signify the Old Law; *either* because the Law was given to the not yet spiritually minded, but still carnally minded Jews; that is, given over to the five senses of the body (the crowd also numbered five thousand men), *or*, because the Law itself was given through Moses. For Moses wrote the Five Books. And that the loaves were made from barley truly signifies the Law, which was so given that the vital food of the soul might be concealed under corporeal mysteries. For the inner fruit of the barley is close held within a strong husk. Or, this people was not yet detached from carnal desiring, which like the barley husk clung fast to the soul.

BEDE: Barley is the nourishment of beasts of burden, and the food of slaves; and the Old Law was given to slaves and to beasts of burden. AUGUSTINE, *as above*: to signify the two types of persons by whom this people were ruled: the kingly, namely, and the sacerdotal; both of which types prefigure Our Lord, for He fulfilled both. ALCUIN: Or the two fishes signify the sayings or writings of the Prophets and Psalmsists; and while the quinary number relates to the five senses of the body, the thousand relates to perfection. They therefore who seek to rule perfectly over their five senses are called men (*viri*), from that strength which effeminate softness does not corrupt, living chastely and soberly, and meriting to be refreshed by the sweetness of heavenly wisdom.

AUGUSTINE, *Tr*. 24 *In John*: The boy who had this food was perhaps the Jewish people, who, with a boy's understanding, bore these things, and did not partake of them. For those things which they carried, being sealed, burdened them; but opened, nourished them.

BEDE: Well did He say: *What are these among so many?* For the Old Law availed little until He took it into His hands; that is, fulfilled it in deed, and at length taught them how it must be spiritually understood: for the Law of itself brought no one to perfection.[1] AUGUSTINE, *as above*: By breaking, the loaves were multiplied. For the Five Books of Moses were made into many books, when they were expounded by as it were breaking them up and examining them.

AUGUSTINE, *Bk*. 83, *Q*. 61: The Lord by as it were breaking and opening what was hard and fast closed in the Law filled His Disciples, when after His Resurrection He opened the Scriptures to their understanding.

AUGUSTINE, *Tr.* 24 *in John*: But because the ignorance of the people was in respect of the Law, this testing by the Lord revealed the ignorance of the Disciple. They reclined upon grass, because they had only a carnal discernment, and found contentment only in the things of the flesh; and *all flesh is grass* (Is. x. 46). But they are filled with the Bread of the Lord who fulfill in work what they have heard with their ears.

AUGUSTINE, *as above*: What are the fragments but that which the people could not eat? What remains to us except that the more hidden things of the understanding, which the multitude cannot absorb, shall be entrusted to those who are capable of receiving them, and able, as the Apostles were, to teach them to others? For this were twelve baskets filled.

ALCUIN: Servile tasks are fulfilled with baskets. Baskets therefore are the Apostles, and their imitators, who though they appear contemptible in this present life, are yet filled interiorly with the riches of the spiritual mysteries. The Apostles are said to have been baskets, because by means of the Apostles the faith of the Holy Trinity was to be preached in the four quarters of the world. That He willed not to make new loaves, but increased those brought to Him, signifies that He did not reject the ancient Scriptures, but that opening them out He now made them clear.

I. ORIGEN, PRIEST AND CONFESSOR

A Mystical Exposition of the Gospel[2]

And when it was evening, his disciples came to him, saying: this is a desert place, and the hour is now past: send away the multitudes, that going into the towns, they may buy themselves victuals (Matt. xiv. 15).

And observe, Dearly Beloved, that when Our Lord was about to give the bread of benediction to the Disciples, who were to set it before the people, He first heals the sick, so that being restored to health they might become partakers of the bread of blessing; for they who are still infirm cannot receive the bread of the blessing of Jesus. But should anyone, hearing the words: *But let a man prove himself: and so let him eat of that bread, and drink of the chalice* (I Cor. xi. 28), and the rest which follows, does not harken to them, but rashly partakes of the bread of the Lord, and drinks of His Chalice, he will become weak or sick; or, if I may so speak, be stricken by the sleep of death, by reason of the power of that Bread.

And when evening was come His Disciples came to Him, that is, at the end of the world, concerning which it is lawful to say that which we find in the Epistle of John: *It is the last hour* (I Jn. ii. 18). And they, not yet knowing what the Word is about to do, say to Him: *This is a desert place*; seeing in many souls an emptiness of God, of the Law, and of the Word. And they add this: *And the hour is now past*: that is, the special times of the Law and of the Prophets have now ended.

But perhaps they said this referring to the news they had just heard, that because of the beheading of John, both the Law, and the Prophets, who had continued till John, had now come to an end. The hour accordingly, they say, is now past, and there is no food; because the former times are no more, in which those who are in the desert, following Thee, may serve the Law and the Prophets.

The Disciples also say to Him: Send away the multitudes, so that each one, if he cannot reach the cities, may buy food in the villages or less important places. The Disciples said this because of the breaking down of the letter of the Law; and because the Prophets had ceased they were without hope that the multitudes could find some new and wondrous food.

But see what Jesus answers to His Disciples, only not crying it aloud, and openly declaring it: 'You think that if the multitudes, hungering for food, go away from Me, they will find it in the villages rather than with Me; in the assemblies of men, not of their own fellow-citizens, but of the villages, rather than had they remained with Me? But I declare to you that they are not in need of that which you think they need: they have no need to go away: but of that of which you think they have no need, namely, Myself: as though I could not feed them: of this, contrary to what you are seeking, they have need. Since therefore I have taught you, making you capable of giving the nourishment of the soul to those who are in need of it: give, you that have followed Me, that which they may eat. You have the power, received from Me, to give food to the people; whom, if you have been observant, you will understand that much more have I the power to feed them; and neither ought you to have said: *Send away the multitudes that they may buy themselves victuals*.'

Jesus therefore, because of that which He gave to His Disciples, the power of nourishing others, said: *Give you them to eat*. They however, while not denying that they can bestow bread, but thinking that what they have is too little and insufficient to feed those who had followed Jesus, and not reflecting that Jesus, taking a loaf, that is, the word, could extend it as He wished, rendering it sufficient to provide for all whom He wished to give to eat, say: *We have not here, but five loaves, and two fishes;* obscurely signifying perhaps that the five loaves are the visible words of the Scriptures, and for this reason correspond to the five senses; and the two fishes the word, either spoken by the mouth, or that conceived in the heart, which are the garnishing as it were of the sensible things stored within the Scriptures; or perhaps the words that have come to them with reference to the Father and the Son. And for this He, after His Resurrection, partook of fish with them; accepting a portion from His Disciples, and approving, as far as they could tell it to Him, the theology of the Father.

We have therefore, as far as we could, tried to explain the significance of what was said concerning the five loaves and the two fishes. It is likely however, that those who are better able than us to reason can provide a better and fuller understanding regarding these five loaves and two fishes. But we must note that in Matthew, Mark, and Luke, the Disciples say that they have five loaves and two fishes; not indicating whether the loaves are wheaten or barley loaves. Only John says they are barley loaves; from which perhaps it may be deduced that the Disciples in the Gospel of John did not say it either, but that with him they said: *there is a boy here that hath five barley loaves, and two fishes.* And as long as the five barley loaves and the two fishes were not brought to Jesus they do not begin to increase or be multiplied, or have power to feed the multitude.

But when the Saviour had taken them, He first looked up to heaven, drawing down from there as it were, along the rays of His sight, the power that was to be commingled with the loaves and fishes, by which five thousand people would be fed. And then He blessed the five loaves and the fishes by His word, by His blessing increasing them, and multiplying them; then, thirdly, breaking and dividing them in pieces He gave them to His Disciples to set before the people. Then they distributed the bread and fish so that all might eat and be filled; and some of the blessed loaves they could not finish. For there remained so much over from the people; which however remained not to the people, but to the Disciples, so that they were able to gather up what remained of the broken pieces, and put them in baskets; which they filled to the number of the twelve tribes of Egypt.

In the psalms it is written of Joseph: *His hands had served in baskets* (Ps. lxxx. 7); and of the Disciples of Jesus, that they, the twelve, I believe, gathered up of the remainder of the broken bread twelve baskets: not half-filled; but full. And with the Disciples of Jesus, as the Teachers of the Multitudes, now and until the end of the world, remain *the twelve baskets of fragments* of the Living Bread, which the multitudes could not eat.

They who ate of the five loaves, which were before the twelve basketfuls remained, have affinity with the quinary number. For they who had eaten of the five loaves had begun to discern things hidden; since they were fed by Him Who had looked up to heaven, and Who had blessed and broke them; and they were not women or children, but men. For, unless I am mistaken, there are degrees in food perceivable by the senses, so that some may be for those who have *put away the things of a child* (I Cor. xiii. 11), and some for those who are still children, and carnal-minded in Christ.

And we have said these things because of the words: *And the number of them that did eat, was five thousand men, besides women and children*; which provides a certain ambiguity. For either they who ate were five thousand men, and no one ate who was a child or a woman, or the men only numbered five thousand and the women and children were not counted. So some, as we say, understand the words to mean, that there were no women or children among those who were fed and made full from the five loaves and two fishes.

But someone will say that since many ate, and were made partakers of the loaves of blessing according to their standing and influence, some there were who merited to be in this number, like those from twenty years upwards as recorded in the Book of Numbers (Num. i. 3), and were men in Israel, and others who were not entitled to this standing and enumeration, as the women and children. Explain the children to me, allegorically, according to the saying: *And I, Brethren, could not speak to you as unto spiritual, but as unto carnal* (I Cor. iii. 1); and again the women, according to the words: *I desire that I may present you all as a chaste virgin to Christ* (II Cor. xi. 2); and the men, according to the words: *When I became a man, I put away the things of a child* (I Cor. xiii. 11).

Let us not pass over without explanation the passage: *And when he had commanded the multitudes to sit down upon the grass, he took the five loaves and the two fishes, and looking up to heaven, he blessed, and brake, and gave the loaves to his disciples, and the disciples to the multitude: and they did all eat.* What does this mean, that He commanded all the people to sit down upon the grass, and what can we understand here that is worthy of Jesus's command in this place? I believe that He ordered the people to sit down upon the grass because of what is said in Isaias: *all flesh is grass* (Is. xl. 6); that is, to humble the flesh, to make subject *the arrogance of the flesh* (Rom. viii. 16); so that each one may become a partaker of the loaves to which Jesus gave His blessing.

Then since various are the groupings of those who need the nourishment of Jesus, since all are not nourished by the same words, it was, I think, because of this Mark has written: *And he commanded them that they should make them all sit down by companies upon the green grass, and they sat down in ranks, by hundreds and by fifties.* And Luke: *And he said to his disciples: Make them sit down by fifties in a company.* For it was necessary for those who were to regain their strength through the food of Jesus, either to belong to the companies of a hundred, which is a sacred number, and consecrated to God through union; or in the order of the fifties, which number contains remission, according to the mystery of the Jubilee, which occurs in each fiftieth year, or to the mystery of the feast of Pentecost, which is the fiftieth day.

I believe that the twelve baskets mean the Apostles, to whom it was said: *You shall sit on twelve seats judging the twelve tribes of Israel* (Mt. ix. 28; Lk. xxii. 32). And, as anyone may say, there is a mystery in the throne of the one judging the tribe of Ruben, and the throne of the one judging the tribe of Simeon, and again in regard to the tribe of Judah, and so on with the others; and likewise regarding the basket of the tribe of Simeon, of Ruben, of Levi. But it is not the aim of our present discourse to turn so far aside from our purpose, that we may gather up what may be said concerning the twelve tribes, together and singly, and expound who is each tribe of Israel. Amen.

II. St Cyprian, Bishop and Martyr

On Good Works and Almsdeeds[3]

Manifold and wonderful, Dearly Beloved Brethren, are the divine favours by means of which the rich and inexhaustible divine mercy labours, and never ceases to labour, for our salvation. For this cause the

Father has sent His Son, that He might redeem us, giving us life, and preserving us in it; and that He might make us children of God the Son willed to be sent, and to become the Son of man. He stooped down to us, that He might raise up a people who before lay prone. He was wounded, that He might heal our wounds. He became Himself a servant, that He might deliver the enslaved. He submitted to death, that He might confer immortality on mortal men.

Such are the great and manifold gifts of the divine mercy. But yet more, what providence is this, and what clemency, that there has been provided for us a special means whereby we may win salvation, so that on man once redeemed yet ever more anxious care is bestowed to preserve him? For when the Lord at His Coming healed the wounds that afflicted Adam, and cured him of the ancient poison of the serpent, He gave a law to man restored, and bade him sin no more, lest to him who sins a greater ill befall. We have been drawn together, and enclosed as it were in a narrow space, by this rule of blamelessness. Nor had the weakness and folly of frail humanity anything that could help it had not the divine clemency, again making known to us the ways of justice and mercy, opened to us a certain way of guarding our soul's health, so that whatever the stains we may have contracted after our baptism, we may wash them away by the giving of alms.

The Holy Spirit speaks to us in the Sacred Scriptures and says: *By mercy and faith sins are purged away* (Prov. xv. 27). Not indeed those offences that were committed before (baptism): for they are purged away by the blood and sanctification of Christ. And again He says: *As water quencheth a flaming fire, and alms resisteth sins* (Ecclus. iii. 33). Here also is it shown to us, and proved, that as the fire of hell is put out by the laver of saving water, so is the flame of evil-doing extinguished by good works and almsdeeds. And since but once is forgiveness of sin bestowed by baptism, yet steadfast and uninterrupted almsgiving bestows on us again as in baptism, the remission of our offences.

This the Lord also teaches us in the Gospel. For when the Disciples were criticized for eating with unwashed hands He defended them, and said: *He that made that which is without, made also that which is within. But give alms, and behold, all things are clean unto you* (Lk. xi. 40); teaching us and showing, that it is not the hands that must be washed, but our hearts; and that we must be at pains to remove inward rather than outward stains: for he who has purified himself inwardly has also begun to purify himself exteriorly; for when the soul is made clean, the skin and body begin likewise to be made clean. And again, warning us and teaching us whence we can be made clean, He adds: that we must give alms. He Who is Himself merciful teaches us and exhorts us to be merciful; and because He seeks to save those whom He has at a great price redeemed, He shows how those who after baptism have become defiled can again be made clean.

Let us then, Dearly Beloved, acknowledge this healthful gift of the divine clemency, and let us who are never free of some wound in our conscience cure our souls, purifying and cleansing them of sin by the aid of these spiritual remedies. Do not let anyone flatter himself that he has a pure and stainless heart, so that, confiding in his blamelessness, he considers he has no need to apply a remedy to his wounds; for it was written: *Who can say: my heart is clean: I am pure from sin?* (Prov. xx. 29). And again John, in his Epistle, states and declares: *If we say that we have no sin, we deceive ourselves and the truth is not in us* (I Jn. i. 8).

But if there can be no one without sin, and if anyone who says he is blameless is either conceited or a fool, how necessary then, how considerate, the divine mercy which, knowing that to those who were healed there will afterwards come fresh wounds, has given us these saving remedies to heal us and take care of our wounds again.

Finally, Dearly Beloved, never has the divine warning ceased and grown silent, since in the Holy Scriptures, both of the Old and the New Testament, the people of God are ever and in all places urged to do works of mercy; and whosoever is instructed unto the hope of the kingdom of heaven is bidden in the prophesying and exhortation of the Holy Spirit to give alms. God ordained and commanded Isaiah: *Cry*, He says, *cease not, lift up thy voice like a trumpet, and shew the people their wicked doings, and the house of Jacob their sins* (Is. lviii. 1). And when He commanded him to reproach them for their sinfulness, and when in the full force of His wrath He had made known their iniquities, and had declared that neither by entreaties nor by prayers nor by fasting could they make satisfaction for their sins, nor could they by clothing themselves in sackcloth and ashes soften the anger of God, yet, in the end, proving to us that God can be appeased by almsgiving alone, He goes on to say: *Deal thy bread to the hungry, and bring the needy and the harbourless into thy house: when thou shalt see one naked, cover him, and despise not thy own flesh. Then shall thy light break forth as the morning, and thy health shall speedily arise, and thy justice shall go before thy face, and the glory of the Lord shall gather thee up. Then shalt thou call, and the Lord shall hear: thou shalt cry, and he shall say, Here I am* (Is. lviii. 7–9).

The means to propitiate God are given us in God's very words. The divine teachings make clear to us what sinners must do: make satisfaction to God by good works; and that sins are purged away by the rewards of mercy. And in Solomon we read: *Shut up alms in the heart of the poor, and it shall obtain help for thee against all evil* (Ecclus. xxix. 15). And again: *He that stoppeth his ear against the cry of the poor, shall also cry himself and not be heard* (Prov. xxi. 13).

Nor will the man who could have been merciful, and was not, receive mercy from God; nor will he, even through prayer, win anything from the divine compassion, who hardened his own heart to the prayer of the poor. The Holy Spirit has declared this to us in the psalms, saying: *Blessed is he that understands concerning the needy and the poor, for in the day of evil the Lord shall deliver him* (Ps. xl. 2).

Daniel, mindful of these warnings, when Nabuchodonosor was terrified by his evil dream, offered him this means of receiving divine help to prevent the disaster, saying to him: *Wherefore, O King, let my counsel be acceptable to thee, and redeem thou thy sins with alms, and thy iniquities with works of mercy to the poor: perhaps he will forgive thy offences* (Dan. iv. 24). But the king paying no heed to his counsel suffered the afflictions and disasters of his dream, when he could have avoided them and escaped them had he redeemed his sins with almsgiving.

And the Angel Raphael bears witness to the same, and exhorts us to give alms freely and generously, saying to us: *Prayer is good with fasting and almsdeeds; for alms delivereth from death, and the same purgeth away sins* (Tob. xii. 8, 9). He shows us that prayer and fasting is not enough, and that they are to be assisted by almsdeeds; that supplication alone avails little to obtain what we ask, unless joined to good works and acts of mercy. The Angel reveals, and makes clear to us, and confirms to us, that our requests become efficacious through almsgiving, that our life shall be delivered from dangers by almsgiving, that our soul shall be delivered from death through almsgiving.

And, Dearly Beloved, we do not say this to you without being able to confirm from the witness of Truth what the Angel Raphael made known to us. For his testimony is confirmed from an event fully recorded in the Acts of the Apostles, which proves to us that we can be freed, not alone from the second, but even from the first death, by means of almsgiving.

When Tabitha, who was much given to good works and almsgiving, became ill and died (Acts ix. 36–41), Peter was summoned to her lifeless body. And when he with apostolic zeal had come in great haste, there round about stood the widows, weeping and praying, who showed him the cloaks and tunics and all the garments they had in the times past received from her. They pleaded for the departed, not alone with their voices, but also with her own good works.

Peter believed that what was so asked for might be obtained, and that the help of Christ would not be wanting to the widows: for he too had been clothed as the widows had been. When therefore he had gone on his knees and prayed, and, as a fitting advocate of the poor and of the widows, had offered to the Lord the prayers entrusted to him, he cried out: *Tabitha, in the Name of Jesus Christ, arise.* Nor did He Who had said in the Gospel: *Anything you shall ask in My Name I will give to you*, fail Peter. For immediately He came to his aid. And because of this death is suspended, and the spirit restored, and to the wonder and admiration of them all, the revived body is reawakened once more to the light of this world. So much could the rewards of merit achieve, so much did good works avail. She who had generously given the means to sustain life to the widows in need merited through the prayers of the widows to be recalled to life.

Accordingly, Dearly Beloved, the Teacher of our life and the Master of eternal salvation, while giving life to the multitude of the faithful, and providing for ever for those restored to life, has in the Gospel, among His divine commandments and heavenly precepts, ordered and prescribed for nothing more urgently than that we be unceasing in the giving of alms; not to cling tightly to our earthly possessions, but rather to lay up treasure in heaven. *Sell*, He says, *what you possess and give alms* (Lk. xii. 33). And again: *Lay not up to yourselves treasures on earth: where the rust, and moth consume, and where thieves break through and steal. But lay up to yourselves treasures in heaven: where neither the rust nor the moth doth consume, and where thieves do not break through, nor steal* (Mt. vi. 19–21).

And when He would show them how a man who has already fulfilled the Law may become truly perfect He says: *If thou wilt be perfect, go sell what thou hast, and give to the poor, and thou shalt have treasure in heaven: and come follow me*. Again, in another place, He declares that if a man is seeking to purchase the grace of heaven, and to acquire eternal salvation, let him sell all he has, and with the price of his whole patrimony let him purchase this precious pearl, that is, life eternal, whose cost was the blood of Christ: *The kingdom of heaven, He says, is like to a merchant seeking good pearls. Who when he had found one pearl of great price, went his way, and sold all that he had, and bought it* (Mt. xiii. 45, 46).

Should you be fearful and apprehensive lest starting to give generously in good works, your own patrimony being consumed in doing good to others you may yourself perhaps be reduced to want: as to that have no fear, have no anxiety. That cannot be consumed from which the needs of Christ are supplied, wherewith the work of heaven is fulfilled. And I do not say this on my own authority simply, but declare it to you on the truth of the Holy Scriptures, and on the authority of the divine promise. For the Holy Spirit, speaking through the mouth of Solomon, says: *He that giveth to the poor, shall not want; he that turneth away his face shall be in great need* (Prov. xxviii. 27); showing that the merciful and those who do good to others cannot want; but rather that the mean and the empty handed shall hereafter come to hunger.

Again the Blessed Apostle Paul, filled with the grace of the Lord's inspiration, says: *And he that ministereth seed to the sower, will both give you bread to eat, and will multiply your seed, and increase the growth of the fruits of your justice, that you may be enriched in all things.* And again: *The administration of this office doth not only supply the wants of the saints, but aboundeth also by many thanksgivings in the Lord* (II Cor. ix. 10, 12); since, while thanks are offered to God for our almsdeeds and good works by the prayers of the poor, the patrimony of the one who gives is at the same time enlarged by the recompense of God.

And the Lord in the Gospel, looking then into the hearts of men of this kind, and with prophetic voice giving warning to the faithless and unbelieving, testifies to us, saying: *Be not solicitous therefore, saying, What shall we eat: or what shall we drink, or wherewith shall we be clothed? For after all these things do the heathens seek. For your Father knoweth that you have need of all these things. Seek ye therefore first the kingdom of God, and his justice, and all these things shall be added unto you* (Mt. vi. 31–3). He declares that all these things shall be added and bestowed upon those who seek the kingdom of God and His justice. It is those who in His Church have laboured in doing good works that, the Lord says, shall on the day of judgement be received into the kingdom of heaven.

Neither should this consideration, Dearly Beloved, restrain you, or keep a Christian from good and virtuous works: namely, the belief that he is excused out of consideration for his own children, since in spiritual givings he ought to have Christ in mind, Who has openly declared that it is He who receives them; and also that it is the Lord, not our fellow servants, whom we are to favour above our own children, as He has warned and taught us. *He that loveth father or mother, He says, more than me, is not worthy of me; and he that loveth son or daughter more than me, is not worthy of me* (Mt. x. 37).

And in the Book of Deuteronomy similar things are written, to strengthen our faith and our love of God: *Who hath said to his father, and to his mother: I do not know you; and their own children they have not known. These have kept thy word, and observed thy covenant* (Deut. xxxiii. 9). For if we love God with our whole heart we must not put either parent or child before God. This John, in his Epistle, also lays down: that the charity of God is not in those whom we see unwilling to show mercy to the poor: *He that hath,* He says, *the substance of this world, and shall see his brother in need, and shall shut up his bowels from him: how doth the charity of God abide in Him?* (I Jn. iii. 17). For if we lend to God by giving alms to the poor, and if we give to Christ what we give to the least of His brethren, there is no reason why a man should prefer earthly to heavenly things, or put human before divine things.

And as to your children, be a father to them such as was Tobias. To these pledges of your love give profitable and salutary counsels, such as he gave his son. Tell your children that which he told his son, saying: *Hearken therefore, my children, to your father: serve the Lord in truth, and seek to do the things that please him: and command your children that they do justice and almsdeeds, and that they be mindful of God, and bless him at all times in truth* (Tob. xiv. 10, 11). And again: *And all the days of thy life, Beloved Son, have God in thy mind: and take heed thou never consent to sin, nor transgress the commandments of the Lord our God. Give alms out of thy substance, and turn not away thy face from any poor person: for so it shall come to pass that the face of the Lord shall not be turned from thee. According to thy ability be merciful. If thou have much give abundantly: if thou have little take care even so to bestow willingly a little. For thus thou storest up to thyself a good reward for the day of necessity. For alms deliver from all sin, and from death, and will not suffer the soul to go into darkness* (Tob. iv. 6–11).

Christ has given us His precepts; He has taught us what His servants must do; and has promised rewards to those who do good works, and threatened with chastisements the barren. He has set forth His judgement. He has foretold that in which we shall be judged. What justification can they have who do nothing? What is to be said for those who are barren of every good work? And if the servant will not do that which he was commanded, the Lord shall do that which He has threatened, as when He said: *When the Son of man shall come in his majesty, and all the angels with him, then shall he sit upon the seat of his majesty: And all nations shall be gathered together before him, and he shall separate them one from another, as the shepherd separateth the sheep from the goats: And he shall set the sheep on his right hand, but the goats on his left. Then shall the king say to them that shall be on his right hand: Come, ye blessed of my Father, possess you the kingdom prepared for you from the foundation of the world.*

For I was hungry, and you gave me to eat: I was thirsty, and you gave me to drink; I was a stranger, and you took me in: naked, and you covered me; sick, and you visited me; I was in prison, and you came to me. Then shall the just answer him, saying: Lord, when did we see thee hungry, and fed thee; thirsty, and gave thee drink? And when did we see thee a stranger, and took thee in? or naked, and covered thee?

And the king answering shall say to them: Amen I say to you, as long as you did it to one of these my least brethren, you did it to me. Then he shall say to them also that shall be on his left hand: depart from me, you cursed, into everlasting fire which was prepared for the devil and his angels.

For I was hungry, and you gave me not to eat: I was thirsty, and you gave me not to drink. I was a stranger, and you took me not in: naked, and you covered me not: sick and in prison, and you did not visit me.

Then they also shall answer him, saying: Lord, when did we see thee hungry, or thirsty, or a stranger, or naked, or sick, or in prison, and did not minister to thee? Then He shall answer them, saying: Amen I say to you, as long as you did it not to one of these least, neither did you do it to me. And these shall go into everlasting punishment: but the just, into life everlasting (Mt. xxv. 31–46).

What more could Christ tell us? In what other way could He more earnestly arouse us to works of justice or mercy, than by telling us that what is given to the needy and the poor is given to Him; and that *He* is offended when the poor or the needy are denied? So that he who in the Church is not moved by the distress of a brother may be moved beholding Christ in him; and that he who has no thought for a fellow servant in poverty and need will have a thought for the Lord dwelling in the one from whom he turns away.

What, Dearly Beloved, shall be the glory of those who labour in doing good? How great and full their joy when the Lord begins to number His own people; bestowing on our merits and good works the rewards He had promised: giving heavenly joys for earthly: eternal for temporal: great things in exchange for little ones; and to present us to the Father, to Whom He has restored us by His sanctifying power, and to bestow on us the eternity and immortality He has regained for us; giving us life through His own blood, leading us exiles again into paradise, and in truth and fidelity to His promises opening to us the kingdom of heaven?

Keep these promises steadfastly before your minds. Grasp them with full confidence. Let them be loved with your whole heart. Let them be purchased by the generosity of your unceasing good works. A glorious and divine thing is it, Dearly Beloved, to give alms in the Name of Christ, a great source of comfort to the faithful, a sure defence of our soul's safety, the bulwark of our hope, the protection of our faith, a healer of sin, something placed within the power of the one who uses it, something great, something simple, a crown of peace without the dangers of persecution, a true gift of God and the greatest, a necessity for the weak, a glory of the strong, and aided by which the Christian attains to grace of soul, merits the favourable judgement of Christ, and may regard God as a debtor to himself.

Let us strive promptly and generously for this crown of the works of mercy. Let us enter this contest of good will; at which God and Christ are present. And let us who have begun to rise above this life and this world not dally on our journey because of any earthly desire. If the day (*of the contest*), whether it be a day of homecoming, or a day of persecution, shall find us contesting, swift, ready, the Lord will not fail to give us the reward of our merits. In a time of peace He will give those who have won a garland of white (*lilies*) for their good works; in a time of persecution He will join to it a purple one (*of roses and violets*) as a reward for their suffering. Amen.

III. St Hilary, Bishop and Doctor

The Passing of The Law[4]

The times of the Law being now at an end, and buried together with John, his disciples then came: from the Law to the Gospel, and told the Lord what had happened. And so the Law being ended, the Word of God, embarking on a ship, enters the Church, and passes over into a desert place; abandoning His association with Israel to enter into hearts yet empty of the knowledge of God. The people hearing this followed the Lord out of the city into the desert; that is, withdrawing from the Synagogue to the Church. And He seeing the multitude had compassion on it, and healed all their sick and infirm; that is, cleansed the bodies and souls beset with the lassitude of unbelief, that they might understand the new Gospel.

And when the Disciples urged Him to send away the people, to buy food in the neighbouring villages, He replied to them, that: *They have no need to go*; showing, that those He healed were not in want of the food of the doctrine of the Law, and had no need to return to Judea to buy it. So He bids His Apostles feed them. Did He not know they had nothing to give? Did He not know, He Who saw the secrets of men's hearts, how much the Apostles had for themselves? But all this had a symbolic purpose, now to be unfolded. For it had not yet been given to the Apostles to prepare, and to minister, the heavenly bread, the food of eternal life. Their reply opened the way to an ordered exposition of spiritual teaching. For they answered that they had only five loaves and two fishes: for till now they had been nourished from the five loaves; that is, from the five books of the Law, and by the two fishes, that is, by the preaching of the prophets and of John. For in the works of the Law, as from bread, there was life; and the preaching of John and the prophets refreshed as with water the true hope of human life. It was these therefore, since they were nurtured in them, that the Apostles at first carried with them; from them the preaching of the Gospel is shown to have been foretold, and, rising from these sources, its own perfection grows in ever increasing richness.

And so, taking the loaves and fishes, the Lord looked up to heaven, then blessed and broke them, giving thanks to the Father that, after the Law and the Prophets, He is Himself become the Evangelical Bread. And when He had commanded the people to sit down on the grass, not to lie prone on the earth, but to sit upheld by the Law, each one spread his own good works, like the grass of the earth, under him. The bread is also given to the Apostles, because it is through them the gifts of the divine grace are to be given. Then the people ate of the five loaves and the two fishes, and were filled. And of the fragments of the bread and of the fishes, after all who had sat down were satisfied, there remained over enough to fill twelve baskets: that is, the hunger of the multitude is satisfied by the word of God coming to them from the teaching of the Law and the Prophets; and the abundance of the divine goodness, kept in reserve for the people of the Gentiles, has overflowed from the source of eternal Food unto the filling of the Twelve Apostles.

And the number of those who ate is, we find, the same as that of those who were to believe. For, as we learn from the Book of the Acts, out of the numbers of the people of Israel five thousand believed (Acts iv. 4). For the miracle of these things extends even to the measure of the reason that underlies them. The bread together with the fishes broken for the feeding of the people increased to the need of the number of people who believed, and to the number of Apostles chosen to be filled with heavenly graces: so that the quantity conformed to the number, and the number to the quantity, and so that the reason contained within them might, under the guidance of the divine power, be linked with the outward circumstances of the effect that was to follow.

The wonder of this deed surpasses human understanding. And while often things are done which the mind can grasp but words cannot explain, in these things even the acuteness of the mind to perceive is at a loss: astonished at the very thought of the complexity of this unseen action. For taking in His hands the five loaves, the Lord looks up to heaven, and acknowledges His glory from Whom He Himself was: not that He needed to look upon the Father with the eyes of His Body, but that those who stood about him might know from Whom He had received such power. He then gives the bread to His Disciples. The five loaves are not multiplied into many loaves; but to the portions broken off succeed other portions, which pass unnoticed from the hands breaking them. The substance progressively increases, whether at the place that served for tables, or in the hands of those taking it, or in the mouth of those who ate it, I know not.

Wonder not that the fountains run, that *there are grapes in the vines*, and that wine comes forth from the grapes; and that all the resources of this world come to us in a certain yearly and unwearied motion; for this so great yield of loaves proclaims the Maker of all this, by Whom the quantity of the substance He has touched is so increased. Under this visible work we have an invisible making; and the Lord of heaven's mysteries works the miracle of this mystery before us. And the Power of Him Who makes surpasses all nature; and the nature of that power far exceeds our understanding of what He does; and all that remains is the Mystery of His power, Who with the Father and the Holy Ghost liveth and reigneth world without end. Amen.

IV. St Augustine, Bishop and Doctor

Exposition of the Gospel[5]

1. The miracles Our Lord wrought are truly divine. And, through what is visible, they lead the mind to the knowledge of God. For since He is not a substance the eye can see, and the wonders by which He rules the world and cares for every creature in it pass unnoticed, because of their repetition, so that scarce anyone troubles to reflect on the wondrous and astounding perfection in each single grain of seed, in accord with this very care He reserved certain things, which in due time He would accomplish, in a manner outside the usual course and order of nature, so that they to whom things daily seen evoke no wonder might be awakened to wonder, seeing, not great, but unusual things.

For the daily ordering of this whole world is a greater wonder than the feeding of five thousand men from five loaves. Yet at the one no one is astonished, at the other all men marvel; not as at a greater happening, but as at a rarer. For Who is it feeds the whole world but He Who from a few grains brings forth the harvest? He wrought then as God. For from that source whence He multiplies the fields from a few seeds, He has here multiplied the five loaves. For Divine Power was in Christ's hands; these five loaves were as seeds, not indeed cast into the earth, but multiplied by Him Who made the earth.

Here is a work brought close to our senses, by which to lift up the mind; and placed before our eyes, to exercise our understanding, so that through the works we see we may begin to give our soul to the unseen God, and with minds uplifted towards faith, and purified by faith, we may also begin to long to know Him invisibly Whom though Unseen we have come to know from the things that are visible.

2. But it is not enough to dwell with wonder on the miracles Christ has wrought. We must also ask the miracles what is it they tell us of Christ: for they have, if we understand it, their own manner of speech. For as Christ is the Word of God, any deed of the Word is a sermon to us. So since we have seen how great this miracle is, let us also see how deep it is. Let us not delight in it only from without, but seek also to learn its inward mystery. For this outward sign we wonder at holds something great within.

We have seen, we have looked upon something mighty, something wondrous, and wholly divine, which only God could do. We praise the Doer because of the deed. But just as when we handle a beautiful book, it is not enough to praise the skill of the scribe, that he has made the letters all evenly, equal and well-formed, unless we also read what by means of them he makes known to us. So here also, he who but looks at the outward event is moved by the perfection of what was done to praise the Doer; but he who understands is as he who reads. You look at a painting one way, you look at a book in another. When you see a picture, you have seen it all; but when you have seen a book, that is not all: you are minded to read as well. For when you see a book, and let us say you do not know how to read, you will then ask: what are we to suppose is written here? Just as when you see anything you ask what it is? He from whom you look to learn what it is you have seen, is likely to describe to you something else. For his eyes see one thing, yours another. You see the letters, as he does. But you do not know what they mean, as he does. You see them, and admire them. He sees them, and admires them, reads and understands them. Since we have seen and praised, let us now read and understand.

3. The Lord is on the mountain (cf. II Pet. i. 18). Let us here understand much more, that the Lord on the mountain is the *Word on high*. And so what took place on the mountain is not as it were hidden in lowliness, nor to be lightly passed by, but to be contemplated with reverence. He saw the multitudes. He knew they were hungry, and in pity He feeds them; and not alone because of His goodness, but also because of His power. For what would goodness alone avail, when there was no bread, so that the hungry people might be fed? Unless His power supported His goodness, the multitude would remain unfed and hungry.

And the Disciples, who with the Lord were also hungry, were anxious to feed the people, that they might not continue in hunger; but they had not the means to feed them. The Lord asks them where they could buy bread to feed the multitude. And the Scripture adds, *and this he said to try him*: meaning the Disciple Philip, to whom He had put the question. He himself knew what He would do. Why did He try, if not that He may show the Disciple's ignorance? And it may be that in disclosing the Disciple's ignorance, He signified something. This will appear when the actual mystery of the five loaves has begun to speak to us, and to show us what it means. For there we shall see why the Lord wished at this moment to disclose the ignorance of His Disciple, asking him what He already knew. For sometimes we ask when we do not know: wanting to hear so as to learn. And sometimes we ask what we know: wanting to find out if the one we ask knows. The Lord already knew in both cases. He knew what He asked: for He knew what He Himself would do. And He knew that Philip did not know what He asked him. Why then did He ask, if not to disclose the latter's ignorance? And why He did this, we shall, as I said, later see.

4. *Andrew said: There is a boy here that hath five barley loaves and two fishes, but what are these among so many?* When Philip who had been asked had said that two hundred pennyworth of bread would not be enough to feed so great a multitude, a certain boy there was carrying five barley loaves and two fishes. Then Jesus said to make the men sit down. *Now there was much grass in the place. The men therefore sat down, in number about five thousand. And Jesus took the loaves: and gave thanks*; and He commanded, and the bread was broken, and was set before those who were sitting down. Not now five loaves, but what He had added Who had made what was multiplied. *In like manner also of the fishes, as much as they would.* And not alone was the multitude fed, but fragments were left over; and these He bade them gather up, lest they be wasted; *and they filled twelve baskets with the fragments of the five barley loaves.*

5. Let us briefly review these events in order. By the five barley loaves we are to understand the Five Books of Moses; and with reason are they barley loaves, not wheaten; for they relate to the Old Testament. You know from the nature of barley that only with effort do we reach its inner fruit. For this is covered with a husk of chaff, and the chaff is so close fitting and tenacious that it is not easily removed. Such is the letter of the Old Testament: clothed in a vesture of corporeal rites; but should anyone reach to its inward marrow, he eats and is satisfied.

A certain boy therefore was carrying five barley loaves and two fishes. Should we ask who the boy was, the answer is that perhaps he stands for the Jewish People, who with a boy's understanding carried, but did not eat them. For that which they carried sealed up, burthened them; opened out, they fed from them.

The two fishes seem to us to signify the two exalted types of the Old Testament, the Priest and the King; who were anointed to sanctify and to rule the people. And He Whom they prefigured came in time, in the divine secret revealed in Christ; in time He came Who was signified in the marrow of the barley, and was concealed by its husk. He came Who in Himself alone fulfils both figures; that of Priest, and that of King; as Priest through the Victim Which offers Itself to God on our behalf; as King, because we are ruled by Him; and the things that were carried close sealed are now opened out. Thanks be to Him! He has fulfilled in Himself all that was promised in the Old Testament.

And He commanded the loaves to be broken; and in being broken they are multiplied. Nothing is more true! For the Five great Books of Moses, how many books did they become when they were broken up by expounding them, that is, by discussing them? But since the ignorance of the first people was concealed in this barley, of the first people was it said: *But even until this day, when Moses is read, the veil is upon their heart* (II Cor. iii. 15). For the veil was not yet taken away, because Christ had not yet come; nor had the veil of the Temple yet been rent by Him as He hung upon His Cross. As the ignorance of the people was due to the Law, so the *trying* of the Lord made clear the ignorance of the Disciple.

6. Nothing then is done without purpose. All things convey something; but they require that we understand them. And so also the number of people fed; they signify the people who were placed under the Law. For why were they five thousand, if not because they were under the Law, which Law is discovered in the Five Books of Moses? So also was it for this reason the sick came from under the five porches, and were not healed. But He cured the sick man there (Jn. v. 2–9) Who here feeds a multitude from five loaves. And they also reclined on grass; and so they savoured of the flesh, and were content only with carnal things: for, *all flesh is grass* (Is. xl. 6).

And what are these fragments but that which the people were unable to eat? These are to be understood as the truths which are more obscure to the understanding, and which the multitude cannot grasp. What then is to be done but entrust these higher truths of the mind, which the multitude cannot comprehend, to those who are fit both to grasp them and to teach them to others: as were the Apostles? And for this reason *twelve baskets* were filled.

This, since it was a truly great miracle, was wondrously done; and since it is also a great spiritual reality, was profitably done. They who saw it were astonished; but we who hear of it do not greatly wonder. For it was wrought that they might see; it was written down that we might believe. What their eyes did for them faith does for us. For we have seen with the soul what we could not with our eyes. And we are placed above them; since of us it was written: *Blessed are they that have not seen, and have believed* (Jn. xx. 29). I shall add this: that we perhaps have grasped what this multitude did not understand. And we have been truly fed: in that we have been enabled to reach to the marrow of the barley.

7. And these men who saw this, what did they think? *These men*, he says, *when they had seen what a miracle Jesus had done, said: This is of a truth the Prophet*. Perhaps they still thought He was a prophet, because they had been lying on grass. He was the Lord of the Prophets, the Fulfiller of the Prophets, the Sanctifier of the Prophets, but also a Prophet. For to Moses was it said: *I will raise up to them a prophet like to thee* (Deut. xviii. 15). Like him in the flesh, but not like him in glory. And that this promise of the Lord is to be understood of Christ is clearly set forth and read in the Acts of the Apostles (Acts vii. 37). And of Himself the Lord says: *A prophet hath no honour in his own country* (Jn. iv. 4). The Lord is a Prophet, and the Lord is the Word of God, and without the Word of God no prophet prophesies. The Word of God is with the Prophets, and the Word of God is a Prophet. Past ages received Prophets: men inspired and filled with the Word of God; we have received a Prophet Who is the Word of God.

And as Christ the Prophet is Lord of the Prophets, so the Angel Christ is Lord of the Angels. For He is spoken of as the Angel of the Great Council (Is. ix. 6: Septuagint). Yet what does the Prophet elsewhere say? That not an ambassador, not an angel, but that He himself coming shall save them (Is. lxiii. 9; xxxv. 9); that is, that He will not send someone representing Him to save them, nor will He send an angel, but will come Himself. Who will come? The Angel Himself. Certainly not by means of an Angel, unless that as Lord of the Angels He is thus also an Angel. For Angels mean *announcers*. Had Christ announced nothing He would not be called an Angel. Had Christ not prophesied He would not be called a Prophet. He has urged us to faith, and to lay firm hold on eternal life. Present amongst us He announced great tidings, and foretold what was to come. In that while present here He announced to us He was an Angel. In that He foretold the future He was a prophet. In that He is the Word of God made Flesh He is Lord both of the Prophets and of the Angels. Amen.

V. St Leo the Great, Pope and Doctor

The Spirit of Lent[6]

Synopsis:

I. How man co-operates with grace, that he may be inwardly renewed; which is necessary for all men.
II. There are few adversity does not weaken, or prosperity inflate.
III. The duty of repentance is laid on all men.
IV. Sins are wiped out most of all by almsdeeds.

1. Apostolic teaching, Beloved, exhorts us that *we put off the old man with his deeds* (Eph. iv. 22; Col. iii. 9), and renew ourselves from day to day by a holy manner of life. For if we are the temple of God, and if the Holy Spirit is a Dweller in our souls, as the Apostle says: *You are the temple of the living God* (II Cor. vi. 16); we must then strive with all vigilance that the dwelling of our heart be not unworthy of so great a Guest. And just as in houses made with hands, we see to it with praiseworthy diligence that whatever may be damaged, either through the rain coming in, or by the wind in storms, or by age itself, is promptly and carefully repaired, so must we with unceasing concern take care that nothing disordered be found in our souls, that nothing unclean be found there. For though this dwelling of ours does not endure without the support of its Maker, nor would the structure be safe without the watchful care of the Builder, nevertheless, since we are rational stones, and living material, the Hand of our Maker has so fashioned us, that even he who is being repaired may cooperate with His Maker.

Let human obedience then not withdraw itself from the grace of God, nor turn away from That Good without which it cannot be good. And should it find in the fulfilment of His commands something that is difficult to accomplish or beyond its powers, let it not remain apart, but turn rather to Him Who commands us, and Who has laid on us this precept that He may both help us and awaken in us the desire of Him, as the prophet tells us: *Cast thy care upon the Lord, and he shall sustain thee* (Ps. liv. 23). Or perhaps there is someone who prides himself beyond due measure, and who imagines himself to be so untouched, so unblemished, that he has now no need to renew himself? Such a belief is wholly deceiving, and he will grow old in folly without end whosoever believes that amid the temptations of this life he is safe from all injury to his soul. All things are filled with dangers, filled with snares. Desires inflame us, allurements lie in wait for us, the love of gain beguiles us, losses frighten us, bitter are the tongues of detractors, and not always true the lips of those who praise us. There hate rages against us; here the false friend cheats us; so that it is easier to avoid discord, than to shun deceit.

II. But in holding fast to virtue, so faltering is our control, so uncertain our discernment, that though a man may observe with the utmost fidelity the lines between what is good and what is bad, it is difficult for the person of upright conscience to escape the wounding tongue of the slanderer, or for one who loves justice to avoid the reproaches of the wicked. For just as when the human mind turns itself to the consideration of the variety of human affairs, what obscurities confront it, how many the errors that arise from false notions, so that even the simple stating of contrary ideas gives rise to quarrelling? For though there is no one who believes in his heart that there is any time or place in this world which is outside the care of the divine providence, or that the outcome of human affairs depends on the power of the stars—which power does not exist—but believes rather that all things are ordered by the most just and kind will of the Most High King; as it is written: *All the ways of the Lord are mercy and truth* (Ps. xxiv. 10), yet, when certain things do not go as we wish, and because of an error in human judgement the cause of iniquity sometimes defeats what is just, it will go hard that even great souls are not troubled, and forced to murmur some unlawful complaint. Even the most worthy prophet David confesses he is troubled, even to the point of danger, by such trials. *My feet*, he says, *were almost moved; my steps had well nigh slipped. Because I was jealous of the wicked, seeing the peace of sinners* (Ps. lxxii. 2).

And since there are few so steadfast that no trial disturbs them, and since not merely bad fortune, but good also, corrupts many among the faithful, we must use earnest care in treating the wounds by which our human mortality has been injured. And so let us run briefly through these dangers with which the world is filled, since the Scripture says: *Who can say: my heart is clean, I am pure from sin?* (Prov. xx. 9). And let each one think within himself of the forgiveness he has need of for his sins, and of the medicine he needs for the restoration of his soul.

III. When, Dearly Beloved, should we more fittingly have recourse to the divine remedies than when, by the very law of time, we are once again reminded of the mysteries of our redemption? And that we may the more worthily commemorate them, let us earnestly prepare ourselves by this forty days of abstinence. And not alone do they, necessarily and profitably, take to themselves this safeguard of charity who are by the regeneration of baptism to enter into newness of life by means of the mystery of Christ's death and Resurrection, but also all who are reborn: the first that they may receive what they do not yet possess, the latter, to protect what they received. For as the Apostle says: *He that thinketh himself to stand, let him take heed lest he fall* (I Cor. x. 11), no one is sustained by such strength of mind that he can be certain of his own constancy in virtue.

Let us then, Dearly Beloved, observe these venerable practices of this most acceptable time, and with anxious care clean the windows of our soul. For however chastely and soberly we live in this mortal life, we shall yet be soiled by some dust in the course of our earthly journey, and the brightness of our soul, formed to God's image and likeness, is not so remote from the smoke of every vanity, that it will be unclouded by any stain, and need never to be polished. And if this is needed for even the most guarded souls, how much more is it needed for those who pass almost the whole year in carelessness and perhaps in total neglect? Let us with all charity remind such as these not to flatter themselves, because we cannot see into their consciences, since not even the walls of houses, nor remoteness of place, can conceal anything from the eyes of God. And not alone are thoughts and actions known to Him, but all that shall yet be thought and done (Rom. iv. 13). Such is the knowledge of the Supreme Judge, such the power of His sight, to Whom all that is solid is open, all that is secret is laid bare, to Whom things hidden are clear, to Whom the dumb answer, the silence cries out, and the soul speaks without voice.

Let no one despise the patience of God's goodness because his own sins go unpunished (Rom. ii. 4); and think that because he has not felt His wrath he has not offended God. The days of grace of this mortal life are not prolonged, nor the time allotted to the foolish of heart before they cross over to the pains of eternal punishment, unless while justice holds its hand they seek for the medicine of penance.

IV. Let us then take refuge in the ever present mercy of God, and, so that we may with becoming reverence celebrate the holy Pasch of the Lord, let all the faithful seek to make holy their own hearts. Let harshness give place to mildness, let wrath grow gentle, forgive one another your offences, and let him who seeks to be forgiven be not himself a seeker of vengeance. For when we say: *Forgive us our debts, as we also forgive our debtors* (Mt. vi. 12), we bind ourselves in the most enduring bonds unless we fulfil what we profess. And if the most sacred contract of this prayer has not in every respect been fulfilled, let every man now at least examine his conscience, and gain the pardon of his own sins by forgiving those of others.

For when the Lord says: *If you will forgive men their offences, your heavenly Father will forgive you also your offences* (Mt. vi. 14; xviii. 35; Lk. vi. 37), what he is here asking is close to each one of us: for the sentence of the Judge will depend on the clemency of the suppliant. For the Just and Merciful Receiver of the prayers of men has laid it down, that our own generosity is the measure of

His fairness to ourselves; so that he will not treat with strict justness those whom He finds not eager for revenge. And generosity is becoming to kind and gentle souls. Nothing is more fitting than that a man imitate His Maker, and that as best he can he is a doer of the works of God. For when the hungry are fed, the naked clothed, the sick assisted, are not the hands that minister but completing the help God gives, and is not the generosity of the giver also a gift from God?

He Who has no need of a helper to perform His works of mercy, so orders His own omnipotence that it is by means of men He comes to the aid of men. And rightly do we give thanks to God for the ministers of that Charity whose works of mercy are seen in His servants. It was because of this the Lord Himself said to His Disciples: *So let your light shine before men, that they may see your good works, and glorify your father who is in heaven* (Mt. v. 16); Who with the same Father and the Holy Ghost lives and reigns God for ever and ever. Amen.

NOTES

[1] More fully cf. Bede, PL 92, col. 707.

[2] PG 13, 902, in Matt. xiv. 15.

[3] PL 4, 601. Concerning this work St Jerome says, *Ep. to Pammachius*, 'Of how great is the power of mercy, and of what are its rewards, the Blessed Cyprian treats in his noble work *On Good Works and Almsdeeds* (*De opere et Eleemosynis*)—and confirms the counsel of Daniel, who told the impious king, if he would hearken, he could be saved by deeds of mercy to the poor.'

It is a short work of twenty-six paragraphs, of which a little over half is given here. What is omitted is restatements of themes already treated, and which if included would lengthen the homily beyond the scope of the present work. The substance, in its own form, of the work is here. Apart from its other qualities this elevated discourse is a perfect example of pure and simple Gospel preaching; without rationalizing, and without going outside the limits of the revealed Word of God. —Ed.

[4] PL 9, c. 999. [5] PL 35, Tr. 24.

[6] PL 54, Col. 281.

PASSION SUNDAY

I. St John Chrysostom: On the Respect Due to the Church of God; and to the Sacred Mysteries

II. St Augustine: I Who are of God?

III. St Leo the Great: On Faith in the Divinity and Humanity of Christ

IV. St Leo the Great: The Fruits of the Passion

V. St Gregory the Great: The Patience of Christ

THE GOSPEL OF THE SUNDAY

John viii. 46

At that time Jesus said to the multitudes of the Jews: Which of you shall convince me of sin? If I say the truth to you, why do you not believe me? He that is of God, heareth the words of God. Therefore you hear them not.

The Jews therefore answered, and said to him: Do not we say well that thou art a Samaritan, and hast a devil? Jesus answered: I have not a devil: but I honour my Father, and you have dishonoured me. But I seek not my own glory: there is one that seeketh and judgeth. Amen, amen, I say to you: If any man keep my word, he shall not see death for ever.

The Jews therefore said: Now we know that thou hast a devil. Abraham is dead, and the prophets; and thou sayest: If any man keep my word, he shall not taste death for ever. Art thou greater than our father Abraham, who is dead? and the prophets are dead. Whom dost thou make thyself?

Jesus answered: If I glorify myself, my glory is nothing. It is my Father that glorifieth me, of whom you say that he is your God. And you have not known him, but I know him. And if I shall say that I know him not, I shall be like you, a liar. But I do know him, and do keep his word. Abraham your father rejoiced that he might see my day: he saw it and was glad.

The Jews therefore said to him: Thou art not yet fifty years old, and hast thou seen Abraham? Jesus said to them: Amen, amen, I say to you, before Abraham was made, I am.

They took up stones therefore to cast at him. But Jesus hid himself, and went out of the temple.

Exposition from the Catena Aurea

John viii. 46–59. V. 46. *Which of you shall accuse me of sin? etc.*

Theophylactus: As though saying: If you are the children of God you should hate sinners. If therefore you can accuse Me, Whom you hate, of sin, it is plain that you justly hate Me. But if none among you can accuse Me of sin, it is also evident that it is because of the truth you hate me. Because of what truth? Wholly because He had said that He was the Son of God; which is most true.

Origen, *in John*: Christ spoke these words with supreme confidence; for none of mankind could confidently declare this save Our Lord, *who did no sin*. I consider that the saying, *which of you*, was said, not alone of those who stood by, but of all mankind; as if He had openly said: What man of your race, or who is there, whomsoever he may be, can accuse Me of sin, or convict Me of any fault? For I know that there is no one.[1]

Gregory, *in Hom*. 18 *in Evang*: Consider the mildness of God. He had come to forgive sins, and He said: *Which of you* etc? He did not disdain to show from reason that He Who had come to justify sinners by the power of His divinity was Himself without sin. Hence follows:

V. 47. *He that is of God, heareth the words of God; therefore you etc.*

Augustine, *Tract* 43 *in John*: Consider not the nature, but the sin; sinners (*isti*) are from God, yet not of God. In their nature they are from God, in their evil they are not of God. The nature that God made good sinned; by yielding assent to the persuasion of the devil it became corrupted. This was said to those who were not alone corrupted by sin, for this was common to all, but to those of whom it was known beforehand that they would also refuse to believe in that faith by which they could be freed of the bond of their sins.

Gregory: Let each one then ask himself whether he hears the word of God with the ear of his heart, and understands whence it comes. For there are some who do not deign to hear the precepts of God, even with the ears of their body. And there are some who do indeed hear them with their ears, but embrace none of them with the desire of their soul. And some there are who freely receive the words of God, so that they are moved even to tears; but when the tears are over they return to their evil-doing. These of a certainty do not hear the words of God; because they depise them in deed.

V. 48. *The Jews therefore answered, and said to him etc.*

Chrysostom, *Hom*. 53 *in John*: When the Lord spoke some sublime truth, this, to the Jews, who were wholly without understanding, seemed madness; as appears from the answer they here made Him: *Do not we say well that thou art a Samaritan, and hast a devil?*

Origen: But it is fitting to ask how, since the Samaritans deny a future life, and neither did they believe in the survival of the soul, did they dare to call the Saviour a Samaritan: He Who had taught so much and so often concerning the resurrection and the judgement to come? But perhaps they said this meaning only to insult Him; since that which they believed He does not teach.

ALCUIN: For the Samaritans (a people whom the Israelites hated), ten of the Tribes having been taken captive, still occupied their land.

ORIGEN: It pleased some of them to think that He was of the same opinion as the Samaritans; that nothing of man remained after death; and that to please the Jews he spoke mendaciously of the resurrection and of eternal life. For they were wont to say of Him that He had a demon, because of His words, which transcended human understanding, in which He declared that God was His Father, and that He was Himself come down from heaven, and that He was the Bread of life, Which was far more perfect than the manna, and that He who would eat of this Bread would live for ever, and other things of this kind, or, on account of their suspicions; for many of them believed He cast out demons by the power of Beelzebub, the prince of the demons.

THEOPHYLACTUS: Or they called Him a Samaritan as though He were a destroyer of the Hebrew observances; as for example, the Sabbath. For the Samaritans did not live entirely according to the Jewish ritual. From this that he revealed to them what they were thinking they suspected Him of having a devil. When it was they had said He was a Samaritan the Evangelist no where tells us. From which it is plain that the Evangelist omitted many things.

GREGORY: Observe that God, while receiving insults, does not answer the injurious words. For there follows:

V. 49. *Jesus answered: I have not a devil: but I honour my father etc.*

What is indicated to us by this if not that at the time we are being falsely accused by our neighbour we should be silent with regard to their own undoubted evil doing; lest the office of true correction be changed into an instrument of anger?

CHRYSOSTOM: And we must note that where it was His duty to teach them, and take away their pride, He was sharp. But where however He had Himself to endure their offensiveness He showed great mildness: teaching us to uphold that which pertains to God, and despise what relates to ourselves.

AUGUSTINE, *Tr.* 43 *in John*: And let us first imitate His patience as a man, so that we may partake of his power. But although He was reviled, He answered not His revilers; yet it fell to Him to deny one thing. They accused Him of two things: that *He was a Samaritan*, and that *He had a devil.* He did not say: I am not a Samaritan; for Samaritan is interpreted to mean guardian: and He knew that He was our Defender. For if it was His task to redeem us, was it not His duty to preserve us? Then lastly, He is indeed the Samaritan who draws near to the injured, and bestows His comfort on them.

ORIGEN, *as above*: The Lord also, and in a way other than that of Paul, wished to become all things to all men, that He might gain all (I Cor. ix. 22), and so He did not say that He was not a Samaritan. I believe that of Jesus alone may it be said: *I have not a devil etc.*; and that also which comes later: *For the prince of this world cometh, and in me he hath not anything* (Jn. xiv. 30); for even those that are considered the very least among sins are attributed to the demons.

AUGUSTINE, *as above*: Then after such an affront He has only this to say of His own glory: *I honour my Father*, as though saying: Lest you should think me proud I declare Whom I do honour. THEOPHYLACTUS: He honoured the Father, vindicating Him, and not suffering that murderers and liars should call themselves the true sons of God.

ORIGEN: Only Christ truly honours the Father, for no man who honours anything whatsoever of the things which are not honoured by God, honours God. GREGORY: But as whoever uses zeal in God's service is defamed by the evil, the Lord gave us in His own Person an example of patience when He says, *but you have dishonoured me*. AUGUSTINE: As though saying: I do what I ought to; but you do not do what you ought to.

ORIGEN: This speech, *you have dishonoured me*, was not said to them alone, but to all who do evil, offering insult to Christ, Who is Justice Itself; and to all who offend wisdom, since Christ is likewise Wisdom Itself, and similarly of other things.[3]

GREGORY: By His example he teaches us what we are to do against injuries, when He goes on:

V. 50. *But I seek not my own glory: there is one that seeketh . . .*

CHRYSOSTOM: As though to say: Because I honour My Father I have said these things to you, and because of this you dishonour Me. But I am indifferent to this dishonour. But because of what I have heard from you, you shall render an account to Him. ORIGEN: God seeks the glory of Christ in all who receive Him; and this He shall find in those who work in accord with the means of justice planted within them. But when He does not find it, He will punish those in whom He has not found the glory of His Son. Hence: *There is one that seeketh and judgeth.*

AUGUSTINE: Who does He here mean but the Father? How then does He elsewhere say: *For neither doth the Father judge any man, but hath given all judgement to the Son* (Jn. v. 22). But observe that sometimes judgement stands for damnation, but that here He means to indicate a difference, as though He said: It is My Father Who will distinguish between My glory and yours. You glorify yourselves after the manner of this world; but I am not of this world. He distinguishes the glory of the Son from the glory of all men (Jn. xvii. 10). For it is not because He was made man that He is to be compared to us. We are men of sin. He is without sin, although He took upon Himself *the form of a servant*. For who is it can speak fittingly of the words: *In the beginning was the Word*?

ORIGEN: Or again, if it were truly said by the Saviour that, *all my things are thine* (John xvii. 10), it is evident that the judgement of the Son is also the judgement of the Father. GREGORY: As the perversity of evil men increases, preaching should not grow less, rather must it be increased. Hence the Lord, after being accused of having a demon, bestows yet more generously on them the graces of His Teaching, saying:

V. 51. *Amen, amen, I say to you: If any man keep my word, He shall . . .*

AUGUSTINE: *He shall not see* is said to convey the meaning of, 'he shall not experience'. For since He Who was to die was speaking with those who were also to die, what does He mean by the words, *If any man keep my word he shall not see death forever*, if not that the Lord was contemplating another death, from which He had come to deliver us: eternal death, the death of damnation in the company of the devil and of his angels? This is true death; this other is but a crossing-over.

ORIGEN: And so this saying: *If any man keep my word etc.* is to be understood as though He said: If any man shall keep my light, he shall not be in darkness. That He says, *for ever*, must be taken in its ordinary sense; so that this is the understanding of the words: *If any man keep my word* for ever, *he shall not see death for ever*; because as long as a man keeps the word of Jesus, so long shall he not taste death. When therefore someone is inert as regards observing His word, and, becoming negligent in keeping it, ceases to obey it, from that time shall he taste death; not in another, but in himself. So therefore, taught by the Saviour, to the prophet asking: *Who is the man that shall live, and not see death?* (Ps. lxxxviii. 49) we can answer: He that keepeth the word of Christ.

CHRYSOSTOM: *Keep* means, not alone by faith, but also by a pure life. In a veiled manner He also infers that they can do nothing to Him. For if he who keeps His word shall not die for ever, much more shall He not die for ever.

V. 52. *The Jews therefore said: Now we know that thou hast a devil etc.*

GREGORY: As it must be that the good grow better through injuries, so the wicked become more reprobate because of the favours granted them. For when they heard the words He had spoken to them the Jews again blaspheme. For it is said: *They said therefore etc.*

ORIGEN: Those who believe in the Scriptures comprehend that what is done by men beyond the capacity of reason does not happen without the help of demons. The Jews therefore believed that Jesus had spoken by the power of the demons when He said: *If any man keep my word* etc. . . . This happened to them because they did not discern the power of God; for here He makes known to them a death of a kind inimical to reason: by which evildoers perish. They, thinking that He was speaking of ordinary death, insult Him because of what He had said; as though Moses and the Prophets were not dead. Hence follows:

V. 53. *Art thou greater than our father Abraham, who is dead? etc.*

Since there is a certain difference between *taste* death and *see* death; for they, as inaccurate listeners quoting Our Lord's words, for, *not see death*, say, *shall not taste death*. For the Lord in that He is Living Bread can be tasted (Ps. xxxiii. 9); in that He is Wisdom, He is of visible beauty (Wisd. viii. 2); so likewise His adversary, death, can be tasted, and can be seen. When therefore a man stands in that place of the understanding, through Jesus, he shall not taste death, if he safeguards that state; according to the words: *Of them that stand* HERE, *that shall not taste death* (Mt. xvi. 28). When a man therefore has received the teaching of the Lord, and kept it, he shall not see death.

CHRYSOSTOM: Again, out of vain glory they speak about their ancestry. Hence we have: *Art thou greater etc?* They could also say: Are you greater than God, Whose words they have died who heard them? But they do not say this, because they regarded Him as even less than Abraham.

ORIGEN: For they saw not that He Who was born of the Virgin is greater, not alone than Abraham, but than anyone born of woman. Nor did the Jews say what was true in saying: *Abraham is dead*; for he heard the word of God, and kept it. And you may say the same also of the Prophets, of whom they remark: *And the Prophets are dead.* For they kept the word of the Son of God; when word was made unto Osee (Os. i. 1), or to Isaiah (Is. ii. 1), or to Jeremiah (Jer. xiv. 1). Nor was any word made to anyone of these, save that Word which was *in the beginning with God.*)[4]; which if any man has kept, the prophets have kept. They therefore spoke a falsehood in this: *We know thou hast a devil*; and in this also: *Abraham is dead, and the Prophets.*[5]

GREGORY: For since they were held fast in eternal death, and saw not that death to which they clung, and had eyes only for the death of the flesh, they were blind to the words of truth. And so they ask: *Whom dost thou make thyself?* THEOPHYLACTUS: As though they say: You who are of no importance, the son of a Galilean carpenter, how do you take to yourself such honour? BEDE: *Whom does thou make thyself?* That is, because of what merit or dignity do you wish to be believed? Abraham died in the body, but his soul was still living. But greater is the death of the soul that will be mastered for ever, than that of the body which at some time or other will dissolve.

ORIGEN: This was the speech of blind men: since Jesus did not make Himself what He was, but received it from the Father. Hence follows:

V. 54. *Jesus answered: If I glorify myself, my glory is nothing etc.*

CHRYSOSTOM: He said this only because of their opinion of Him; as also upon another occasion: *If I bear witness of myself, my witness is not true* (Jn. v. 31). BEDE: By these words He shows us that the glory of the present time is nothing.

AUGUSTINE, *Tr.* 43: He said this because of their remark: *Whom dost thou make thyself?* For He refers His glory to the Father; from Whom He is. Hence He goes on: *It is my Father that glorifieth me.* On this saying the Arians have spoken falsely of our Faith, saying: See, the Father is the greater, since He it is Who gives glory to the Son. Heretics, have you not heard the Son also saying, that He gives glory to the Father? (Jn. xiv. 13; Mt. iii; Mt. xvii; Jn. xii. 28).

ALCUIN: The Father glorified the Son at the time of His baptism, and on the mountain, and before the time of His Passion, when a voice spoke to Him in the presence of the multitude, and after His passion when He raised Him again, and placed Him on the right hand of His own Majesty.

CHRYSOSTOM: But He added: *Of whom you say that he is your God.* For He wished to show, that not alone did they not know Him as Father, but that they knew not God. THEOPHYLACTUS: For if they had truly known the Father, they would honour His Son. But they despise God also, Whose Law had forbidden murder, when they cried out against Christ. Hence He continues:

V. 55. *And you have not known him, but I know him. And if I, etc.*

ALCUIN: As though saying: You in a carnal minded manner call Him your God; you serve Him for temporal rewards; and you have not known Him, as He must be known. You have not known how to serve Him in the spirit.

AUGUSTINE: Some heretics say that the God announced in the Old Testament is not the Father of Christ, but some chief among the angels, whom I know not. Against these He calls Him Father Whom they say is their God, and Whom they have not known: for if they had known Him they would have received His Son. But of Himself He adds: *But I know him.* To those who judge in the wisdom of the flesh, at times He could here seem to be presuming. But the appearance of presumption may not be avoided, lest truth be overlooked; for which reason He goes on: *And if I shall say that I know him not, I shall be like to you, a liar.*

CHRYSOSTOM: As though He says: just as you in saying you know Him lie, so should I likewise lie if I say I know Him not. But the greatest proof that He was sent by Him is that which follows: *But I do know him.*

THEOPHYLACTUS: Possessing this knowledge wholly and naturally: for that which I am the Father is also. Since therefore I know myself, I also know Him. He provides a sign that He does know Him, when He adds: *And do keep his word*; describing His commandments as, *His word.* But some interpret what is here said: *And keep his word*, as, I retain the nature of His Substance: for the same is the nature of the substance of the Father and the Son; and therefore I know the Father; for (they say) *and* is taken here to mean 'since'; so that the sense is: Since I keep His word.

AUGUSTINE: As His Son He was wont to speak the word of the Father; and He was the Word of the Father, that was spoken to men.

CHRYSOSTOM: And because they had said: *Art thou greater than our father Abraham?* saying nothing of death, He goes on, in the words that follow, to show that He is greater than Abraham:

V. 56. *Abraham your father rejoiced that he might see my day etc.*

THEOPHYLACTUS: He regarded *my day* as a day to be longed for, and full of joy; not any day, or the day of anyone. AUGUSTINE: He did not fear it, but, *Rejoiced that He might see it*; and believing, *he* truly *rejoiced*, while hoping, *that he might see*, by understanding, *my day*. It may be uncertain whether He here spoke of the temporal day of the Lord, in which He was to come in the Flesh, or of the day of the Lord that knows no rising and knows no setting. But I do not doubt that Father Abraham knew the whole; for he said to the servant whom he sent: *Put thy hand under my thigh, and swear to me by the God of heaven* (Gen. xxiv. 12). What therefore was this oath if not a signifying that the God of heaven would come in the flesh from the race of Abraham?

GREGORY, *Hom.* 18: Then also did Abraham see the day of the Lord, when He received as guests the three angels who prefigured the supreme Trinity. CHRYSOSTOM: Or He calls the day of the Cross His day; which Abraham prefigured in the offering both of Isaac and of the ram: showing by this, that not against His own will did He come to His passion, and showing also that they are not kindred to Abraham should they grieve over that in which he rejoiced. AUGUSTINE: What joy of heart beholding the enduring Word, His splendour shining in holy minds, abiding God with the Father, yet in time to come to us, clothed in our flesh though never receding from the Bosom of the Father! GREGORY: The carnal minds of the Jews, listening to the words of Christ, do not raise their eyes above His Flesh: since in Him they are regarding only the years of His Flesh; hence:

V. 57. *The Jews therefore said to him: Thou art not yet fifty years old . . .*

As though they said: many are the courses of the years since Abraham died, and how did he see thy day? For they understood Him in a carnal sense. THEOPHYLACTUS: Christ was then about thirty-three years old. Why then did they not say: you are not yet forty years old, instead of *fifty*? A question of this kind is superfluous: for they mentioned the years simply as they occurred to them. But some may answer that when they mention *fifty years*, they are, out of reverence, referring to the Jubilee; in which captives were set free, and every man returned to his former possessions (Lev. xxv. 10).

V. 58. *Jesus said to them: Amen, Amen, I say to you, before Abraham was . . .*

GREGORY: Whom Our Saviour kindly turned from the consideration of His Flesh to the contemplation of His Divinity; hence follows: *Before Abraham was made, I am.* For *before* belongs to past time; *I am* to the present. And since the Divinity has not past time nor future, but possesses uninterrupted existence, He does not say: Before Abraham was I was, but, *before Abraham was made, I am*; according to the words: I AM WHO AM (Ex. iii. 14). Therefore both before and after Abraham He had existence, Who could draw near us through the manifestation of His Presence, or depart along the way of life.

AUGUSTINE: Because Abraham was a creature He did not say *before Abraham was*, but, *before he was made*; nor did He say *I was made*; for, *In the beginning was the Word*. GREGORY: But the minds of the unbelievers, unable to endure these words which spoke of eternity, which they could not grasp, sought to overwhelm Him. Hence:

V. 59. *They took up stones therefore to cast at him . . .*

AUGUSTINE: To what did such hardness of heart run if not to its like, that is, to stones? Because after He had fulfilled, by teaching them, all things which related to Him, they throw stones at Him, He leaves them; as not receiving correction. Hence follows: *But Jesus hid himself, and went out of the temple*. He did not hide himself in a corner of the Temple, as though He were afraid, or take refuge in some dwelling-house, or turn aside behind some column or wall; but, by heavenly power, making Himself invisible to those who lay in wait for Him, He passed through their midst.

GREGORY: He Who could had He wished to wield the power of His Divinity by the silent command of His mind have frozen them in their assault, or crushed them by the chastisement of sudden death. But He Who came to suffer sought not to exercise judgement.

AUGUSTINE: He taught us patience rather than the exercise of power. ALCUIN: He fled also because the hour of His passion was not yet come; and because this was not the kind of death He had chosen. AUGUSTINE: Therefore, as a man He fled from the stones; but woe to them from whose stony hearts God has taken flight.

BEDE: Mystically, a man throws as many stones at Jesus as he takes unto himself evil thoughts; and if he proceeds to dwell on them, He then, as far as it depends on him, destroys Jesus. GREGORY: What does the Lord signify by hiding himself if not that Truth is hidden from those who despise to follow after His words? For Truth flies from the mind which it finds not humble. What does this example tell us if not that even when we can resist them let us rather humbly turn away from the anger of the proud.

I. ST JOHN CHRYSOSTOM, BISHOP AND DOCTOR

On the Respect Due to the Church of God, and to the Sacred Mysteries[6]

Very few have come here today. Whatever is the reason? We celebrate the Feast of the Martyrs, and nobody comes? The length of the road makes them reluctant; or rather it is not the length of the road that prevents them from coming, but their own laziness. For just as nothing stops an earnest man, one whose soul is upright and awake, so anything at all will stand in the way of the half-hearted and the lazy.

The Martyrs gave their blood for the truth, and you are not able to think little of a brief stretch of road? They gave their life for Christ, and you are reluctant to make a small journey for Him? The Martyrs' Commemoration, and you sit in sloth and indifference! It is but right that you should be present; to see the devil overcome, the Martyrs triumphant, God glorified, and the Church crowned with honour.

But, you will say to me, I am a sinner. I cannot come. Then if you are a sinner, come, that you may cease to be one! Tell me, who is there among men without sin? Do you not know that even those close to the altar are wrapped in sins? For they are clothed with flesh, enfolded in a body: as we also who are sitting and teaching upon this throne are entangled in sin. But not because of this do we despair of the kindness of God; and neither do we look on Him as inhuman. And for this reason has the Lord disposed that those who serve the altar shall also be subject to these afflictions: so that from what they too suffer they may learn to have a fellow feeling for others.

How absurd and foolish is it that should a harper, or a dancer, or any one of these kind of people, invite us to his house, we would go there with all haste, and thank him for having invited us, and spend almost half the day there; paying attention only to him. But when God is speaking to us through His holy Prophets and Apostles we yawn, and we scratch, and we turn this way and that!

And at the circus, without a roof above them to keep off the rain, the crowds stand there crazy, the rain pouring down on them, and the wind blowing it in their faces, and they think nothing of the cold or the rain or the distance, and nothing will keep them from going there, and nothing will keep them at home! But to go to the Church, a shower, or the mud on the road, is a serious obstacle!

And if they are asked who were Amos or Abdias, or what was the number of the Prophets or of the Apostles, they cannot open their mouths. But if it is a question of horses, or charioteers, their eloquence surpasses that of the poets and orators. And how, may I ask you, are we to put up with this? I have warned you time and again that you should not go to the theatre. You heard me, but you have not obeyed me. You have gone to the theatre, and taken no notice of my words to you. Are you not ashamed to come now and hear them again?

But, you will say to me, I have heard, and not obeyed; how can I come again and listen? Well this you do understand, that you have not obeyed; and now you are ashamed, you blush, and though no one has corrected you, you have corrected yourselves, you know what I say is true and certain and even without my presence my words yet troubled your conscience. You have not obeyed me? So much the more reason have you for coming to Church, to listen again; and then you will obey.

If you take a medicine, and it does not purify you, will you not try it again another day? Suppose, O Man, a tree-feller wishes to cut down an oak. He takes an axe. Then he cuts the roots. And when he has struck one blow, and the tree does not fall, will he not add another blow? And a fourth, and a fifth, and a tenth? Let you do the same. And I am saying these things to you, not to make you still more lazy, but to make you more alert.

You have entered the Church, O Man; you have been held worthy of the company of Christ. Go not out from it: unless you be sent. For if you go out from it without being sent you will be asked the reason; as if you were a runaway. You spend the whole day on things which relate to the body, and you cannot give a couple of hours to the needs of the soul? You go often to the theatre. And you will not leave there till they send you away. But when you come to the Church you rush out before the divine mysteries are ended. Be fearful of Him Who has said: *He that despiseth anything, shall by it be despised* (Prov. xiii. 13).

Were you to stand in the presence of the king you would not even dare to smile. But when you stand in the presence of the Lord of all, you do not stand there in fear and trembling, you laugh, provoking him to anger? Do you not see that by this conduct you provoke Him more than by your very sins? God is not wont to be as angry against those who sin as against those who, when they have sinned, feel neither sorrow nor regret.

And you, O Man, standing about in the Church, with a mind only for the attractions of the women, are you not horrified, offering such an insult to the temple of God? Do you regard the Church of God as a house of ill fame, and of less repute than the market place? For there you would be ashamed, and afraid, to be seen staring at a woman so curiously. But in the very temple of God, while He is speaking to you, and threatening you with punishment, you dare to do such things during the very time in which you are hearing that such things are not to be done? And are you not shocked, or troubled in your soul, at making your eyes and your heart the workshop of evil doing? Better for a man to be blind than use his eyes to do this.

Think, O Man, of Who it is Who is close to thee in this tremendous sacrifice, and of who it is with whom you are to call upon God; that is, of the Cherubim, the Seraphim, and the other heavenly powers. Remember who are celebrating, together with you, the worship of God. This will suffice to make you recollected in spirit, when you reflect that while enfolded in a body, and clothed in flesh, you have been made worthy, together with the incorporeal powers, to praise the common Lord of all.

Do not then take part in this holy praise, in these sacred mysteries, with a dissipated soul. Let not your thoughts during this time be occupied with worldly things. Rather, casting all earthly things from your mind, and being wholly turned towards heaven, and as though you were raised on wings as the Seraphim, and were standing at the very threshold of His glory, offer your holy praise to God for all He has done.

Because of this are we bidden to stand worthily during the time of the divine sacrifice, so that while still on earth we may raise to heaven our dragging thoughts, so that shaking off that dissoluteness which comes from the affairs of this life, we may be enabled to awaken our souls to the presence of God. It is not a question of the hands and feet of the body, for we are speaking here not of runners or gymnasts; but we desire by these words to raise up the powers of our inner thoughts, brought low through temptation. For at the time of the Divine Supper, Brethren, it is not men alone who raise that tremendous cry, for even the Angels are bowed down before the Lord, and the Archangels are in prayer; for them too it is a fitting help, and a helpful Offering.

And as men spread branches of palm before kings, meaning by this to remind them of mercy and compassion, so likewise the angels, bearing before them instead of branches the Body of the Lord, pray to the Lord on behalf of mankind, and all but saying: We beseech Thee on behalf of those whom before Thou didst deign to so love, that for them thou gavest up thy own spirit! We supplicate Thee for those for whom Thou didst shed Thy Blood! We pray to Thee for these for whom Thou hast given Thy body in sacrifice!

Let each one consider within himself what faults he must remedy in himself, what good work he may yet do, what sin he may wipe out from his soul, so that by this he may become better. And if he finds that he has made progress in this excellent market, through fasting, and is aware that there is need for much care for his wounds, then let him draw near. If however he remains neglectful of himself, and has only his fasting to show, and makes no progress in other directions, then let him remain outside, and let him return only when all his sins are cleansed. He who does not fast, offering as a reason the weakness of his body, may fittingly receive pardon. But he who will not correct his evil ways cannot be excused in the same way.

And what shall we do if the Lord requires of us an account of this neglectfulness of conduct in our assemblies? For well you know that oftentimes, while the Lord Himself is speaking to us through the mouth of His prophet, we turn away to hold prolonged and frequent conversations with our neighbour, and on things that have nothing to do with us. Putting aside all our other sins, should He exact punishment for this conduct what hope of salvation have we? Do not regard this as a little sin; for if you wish to see how evil it is, consider this same offence in relation to men, and you will see the magnitude of your folly. Should some prince or person of superior station speak with you, would you dare to turn away to begin a conversation with a servant; and here you perceive what your offence is, doing this very thing in the presence of God. If this other were a powerful person, he would seek satisfaction for the insult offered. But God, Who is offended each day by many and by grievous sins, and not by one man only, but by nearly all men, forbears and endures in patience.

And when you seek to placate the anger of an earthly king, do you not come all together, with your wives and your children, and sometimes you deliver from punishment someone who has been condemned by the anger of the king. But to placate the King of heaven, and to deliver from His wrath, not one, or two, or three, or a hundred, but all the sinners of the world, you do not hasten together, all of you, so that God, being appeased by your common prayers, forgives your offences, and remits the punishment due to them. You stay away.

I would like to know then, what they are doing who so neglect the assemblies of the faithful, and keep away from this sacred table? I know but too well. They are either talking about vain and idle things, or immersed in worldly things. The time used in either case is without justification, and merits severe correction. As to the first there is no need to prove it in words. Nor can they be excused who put forward the excuse of family affairs, and of the needs that arise from them; for it is plain that they do not esteem spiritual and heavenly things above those of this world. For what servant, I ask you, attends to the things of his own house before fulfilling those of his master?

How absurd is it therefore that among men, where authority is but a mere name, such reverence and obedience should be shown to masters, while to Him Who is not alone Our Master, but the Lord of all Powers, we do not offer even such reverence as we give our own equals? Would that it were possible that I might set before your eyes the souls of such men, and you would see how stained and unworthy they are, how profligate, how weak and earthly? Would that I might open to you their hearts, they who cut themselves off from the sacred assembly! Would that you might penetrate into their consciences, then would you clearly see with how many wounds it is afflicted, how many the thorns that are there!

For just as soil that is not touched by the hand of the farmer goes wild and becomes unlovely, so likewise the soul that goes without spiritual cultivation brings forth weeds and thistles. For if we who each day hear the teaching of the prophets and apostles, singing from our hearts the songs of Holy Scripture, can scarce contain our own fiery hearts, scarce hold in check our own angers, scarce free ourselves from the poison of envy, scarce master our own concupiscence, scarce restrain these wild beasts, what hope of salvation have they who never use these saving medicines, never listen to the divine teaching?

For just as he who leaves behind a place of safety will stray in every direction, and he who goes without a light in darkness will strike against many things, so he who falls into forgetfulness of the fear of God will be given over without ceasing to cares and pains and anxieties. And as when God is with us and protects us, sadness is banished from us; so, leaving Him, and abandoning ourselves to forgetfulness of Him, our soul is split in two, and our heart afflicted with sorrow, and those who torment us laugh at us, so that even the very careless, because they are tormented by all, return quickly whence they set out. *Thy own wickedness shall reprove thee, and thy apostasy shall rebuke thee* (Jer. ii. 19). For abandonment is a form of divine providence. For while He cares for and provides for us, He is despised. He then lets go of us, and forsakes us, to the end that being undone by their own neglect, they who had despised Him now become more diligent.

I believe that many of those who long ago forsook us, and deserted to the gatherings of iniquity, today are present among us. And I wish that I might know them with certainty, that I might cast them forth from this sacred abode, not that they might remain shut out, but that having mended their ways they might return again. Just as fathers, should their sons provoke them, are wont to drive them from the house, and forbid them the table; not indeed that they may for ever be deprived of these things, but that being so reproved they may become better, because of this, and may be restored with due honour to the paternal inheritance.

This shepherds too are wont to practise. For they separate the sheep with mange from those that are healthy, and when they are cured of the disease they return to the flock; and so the rest are not infected. It is for this reason we desire to know them. And though we cannot tell them with our eyes, these words of ours mark them; and where it touches their conscience, it will readily persuade them to withdraw themselves in secret, teaching them that he alone is of the household who reveals a disposition worthy of the Christian way of living: just as he who while living unworthily becomes a partaker of this sacred Supper, though he approaches hither in the body, yet is he cast out, and more truly sent forth than those who have been shut out, and who may not partake of the sacred table.

For these latter have been excluded according to God's laws, and while remaining without have yet a good hope of presently returning; and if they seek to amend their faults, they can return again with a pure conscience to the Church from whence they were banished. But they who have stained themselves, and have been warned that they must not return before being purified of the blemish of their sins, and then conduct themselves shamelessly, make more grevious their wound. For there is no sin so grevious as shamelessness after sin committed.

Many partake of the Sacred Mysteries but once in the year; others twice, others oftener. Who among these are we to praise? They who come once? Or they who come oftener? Or those who come less frequently? Neither those who come once nor they who come oftener, nor they who come more rarely, but they who come with a clean heart, with unclouded conscience, with a manner of life that is without reproach. Let such as these approach: they who are not of this kind, let them not come even once, for they take judgement and damnation unto themselves. For as food that has the power to nourish, if it enter into one who has a stomach infected with disease, injures and aggravates everything, and becomes a cause rather than a remedy for sickness, so is it with this tremendous Mystery.

Will you partake of this spiritual table, the table of the King, and then soil your body again with filth? Do you anoint it with ointments, and then fill it up with foulness? Do you consider that it suffices for the forgiveness of the sins of the whole year if you at each returning year partake of communion, and then at the end of the week give yourself again to your former conduct?

Tell me this. If you after forty days were restored to health again from a serious illness, should you return again to those things that earlier had brought on your sickness, would you not squander uselessly all your former efforts? And if the things of the body are spoiled in this way, how much more the things that depend on our own free will and decision? And if there be bitterness in your mouth, you do not eat even the simplest food: how then, I ask you, when there is so great foulness in your soul do you dare to partake of the Sacred Mysteries? What forgiveness is there for this? For the Apostle says: *Whosoever shall eat this bread, or drink the chalice of the Lord unworthily, shall be guilty of the body and of the blood of the Lord* (I Cor. xi. 29); that is, he shall have the same guilt, and the same punishment, as those who crucified Christ. For as those butchers became guilty of His Blood, so likewise are they who partake unworthily of the Eucharist. For as he who has torn the royal purple, or bespattered it with mud, has equally insulted the one who wears it, so those who take to themselves the Body of the Lord, and receive It with an impure soul, treat Him with the same mockery as they who dishonour the royal apparel.

The Jews put Him to death upon a cross; they who receive Him with unworthy hearts dishonour Him. Therefore, though the sins may be diverse, the affront is the same. This troubles many of you, this confounds many, this gnaws at the conscience of many who listen to me; and not alone the consciences of you who hear me, but even more than you, it troubles our conscience who speak to you. For this teaching is for every man: for all have the same afflictions, and for this reason I set before you the common remedies. This is the doing of the divine benevolence: that he who speaks, and he who listens, share the same nature and are subject to the same laws: so each alike is guilty who offends them. And why is this? That he may correct with moderation; that he may be prompt to bestow forgiveness on those who have sinned; that mindful of his own infirmity he will not make his rebuke unendurable.

If therefore there is one among you of those who gather together with you in the Church who is a fornicator, and you observe him approaching the sacred mysteries, say to the dispenser of them: This man is unworthy of the mysteries: exclude him who is unworthy of our sanctities. For if such a man is not worthy *to declare the justices of God* (Ps. xlix. 16), consider how he adds to his punishment should he touch the sacred table; and not alone he, but you also who countenance him. For He said not: 'and you committed adultery'; but: *and with adulterers thou hast been a partaker* (Ps. xlix. 18).

Save us, what an evil, to cover up the rottenness of another! For the Lord says that you make yourself a sharer of the retribution that will come to them; and rightly too. For the other had the excuse of passion; though this is no justification for pardon. You had not even this. Why then, since you shared not in his pleasure, do you make yourself an associate and a partaker of his punishment? Neither let you make to me that remark which is laden with selfishness: What is it to me? I mind my own affairs. For then do you best care for your own affairs, if you care for them by helping the need of your neighbour; as Paul has also said: *Let no man seek his own, but that which is another's* (I Cor. x. 24), so that he may thus find what *is* his own. For when one who has sinned sees that all turn away from him, he will then come to see that his sin is something evil and reprehensible. But should he see that others do not consider his conduct to be unworthy, and accept him without complaint, and even encourage and abet him, then will the approval of others, abetting his own corrupt soul corrupt also the judgement of his conscience.

Many, not submitting to these grave corrections have after their return among us been very indignant, and have complained that we turned them away from the Sacred Table and shut them out from Communion. And so I am forced to speak of these things, so that you may understand that I do not turn away, but seek to unite; nor do I repel or exclude, but seek rather by trials to help you. For the fear of chastisement falling on the consciences of those who do wrong destroys and consumes sin as fire touching wax, and while it remains there preserves the soul clean and undefiled, and thus brings us to a greater degree of confidence. And just as the physician who ministers bitter medicine to those whom food disgusts drives out distressing poisons and helps to revive the lost appetite, so that our accustomed food is eaten with even greater appetite, so does he who uses sharp words, and helps to purify the evil thoughts of the heart, and lift the heavy burden of sin, allowing the conscience to breathe, and thus prepares the soul to taste with even greater delight the precious Body of the Lord.

Rightly then has the blessed Paul told us: *Obey your prelates and be subject to them. For they watch as being to render an account of your souls* (Heb. xiii. 17). You no doubt carefully look after your own affairs, and if they are well ordered you have no account to render for those of others. But a priest, though his own life should be well ordered, yet, if he has not an earnest care for yours also will go down to Gehenna with the reprobate. And often, though not betrayed by sins of his own, he perishes because of those of others.

And since we have spoken sharply to those who partake unworthily of the Sacred Mysteries, it is necessary that we speak also to you who minister them, that you may dispense those Gifts with great carefulness: for otherwise your chastisement will not be light. For should you while knowing that a man is unworthy permit him to partake of the Sacred Table, his blood will be required at your hands. And should he be a general of the imperial army, or a Prefect, or even one whose head is encircled by the imperial diadem, and should he approach while unworthy, forbid him. Yours is a higher authority than his. Take care not to provoke the Lord, by not purifying His Body.

Do not offer a sword in place of food. And should such a man, because of his infirmity, approach so that he may take part, fear not to forbid him. Fear the Lord God, not man. If you fear a man, he will scorn you; and you will anger God. If you fear God you will be dear to him, and revered by men. Should you fear of yourself to do this, then send him to me. I shall not suffer him to attempt to do this. I would give up life itself first, rather than communicate the Blood of the Lord to the unworthy. Far better to be deprived of one's own life, for God's sake, than to save that life, and be deprived of God; to Whom be honour, praise and glory now and for ever. Amen.

II. St Augustine, Bishop and Doctor

Who are of God?[7]

Which of you shall convince me of sin? And how shall I convince you and *your father (the devil)? If I say the truth to you, why do you not believe me,* if it is not because you are the sons of the devil?

He that is of God, heareth the words of God: therefore you hear them not, because you are not of God. Here again consider, not nature, but moral defect. And so these men *are* of God, and *are not* of God: by nature *of God*, by sin *not of God.* I beseech you note this carefully: in the Gospel you possess the means whereby you are made safe against the wicked and poisonous errors of heretics.

For the Manichean is wont to say of these words: 'See, there are two natures, one good, the other bad; the Lord says it. What does the Lord say? *Therefore you hear them not, because you are not of God.* The Lord said these words. What then, he says, have you to say to this?

Listen to what I have to say. They are both *of God*, and *not of God*; by nature they are *of God*, because of sin they are *not of God*. Their nature, which is good because it is *of God* sinned of its own free will, giving assent to diabolic persuasion, and became corrupt; and so needs a Healer, because it is infirm. That is what I have to say.

But to you it may appear impossible that they are both *of* God, and *not* of God. Learn that it is not impossible. They are of God, and not of God; just as they are both children of Abraham, and not children of Abraham. Here is the text; there is nothing you can say against it.

Listen to the Lord Himself. He said to them: *I know that you are the children of Abraham* (v. 37). Would the Lord speak falsely? Far from it. Then, is it true what the Lord has said? It is true. Is it true therefore that these men were children of Abraham? It is. Hear Him now as He denies this.

He Who said: *You are the children of Abraham*, the Same has denied that they are children of Abraham. *If you be the children of Abraham*, He says, *do the works of Abraham. But now you seek to kill me, a man who have spoken the truth to you, which I have heard of God. This Abraham did not. You do the works of your father*, that is, of the devil.

How then were they children of Abraham, and not children of Abraham? He shows that in the case of these men that they were both: they were children of Abraham, because of their birth; and they were not children of Abraham, because of the evil of diabolic deceit. So give ear then to our God and Lord: they were of Him, and they were not of Him. How were they *of* God? Because He had created the man from whom they were born. How were they of God? Because He is the Author of nature, He is the Creator of body and soul. How then are they *not of* God? Because by their own will they have become evil. They are not His, because, imitating the devil, they have become the children of the devil.

The Lord then comes to man the sinner. You hear the two titles: man and sinner. What is man, is of God; the sinner, is not of God. Let sin and nature be held apart: let nature be known as that for which the Creator is to be praised, and sin as that for which the Physician is to be called upon. So, when the Lord said: *He that is of God, heareth the words of God. Therefore you hear them not, because you are not of God*, He was not touching on the faults of their natures, and neither has He found some nature among men, over and above His own body and soul, not corrupted by sin. But since He foreknew who would believe, He said these were of God: since by adoption in their regeneration they would be born again of God (cf. Mt. xix. 28). It is to these His words apply: *He that is of God, heareth the words of God.*

That which follows: *Therefore you hear them not, because you are not of God*, was said to those who were not alone corrupted by sin, for this was an evil common to all men, but of those of whom it was foreknown that they would not believe by the faith through which alone they could be delivered from the bond of sin. And so He knew that those to whom He said such things would stick fast in that because of which they were of the devil; that is, in their sins, and that they would die unrepentant: in which they resembled him; and that neither would they come to the regeneration in which they would become children of God, that is, born of God, by Whom they were created men. It was in accord with this predestination the Lord spoke: not that He had found some men who through regeneration were now of God, or who because of their nature were already not of God. Amen.

III. St Leo the Great, Pope and Doctor

Faith in the Divinity and Humanity of Christ[8]

Synopsis:

I. That in this time of the greater fasts Christians should, through mortification, prepare for the Pasch.

II. They must guard not alone virtue, but also Faith: especially in the Divinity and Humanity of Christ.

III. That by almsdeeds, and especially by forgiving offences against them, are they to be reconciled to Christ.

I. Among all the Christian solemnities the Paschal Mystery holds, we know, chief place, Dearly Beloved; for which indeed, that we may worthily and rightly celebrate it, the practises of the whole preceding year prepare us. But earnest devotion is required of us especially in these days which are, as we are aware, close to this most sublime mystery of the divine mercy. So it was right that the holy Apostles, inspired by the Holy Spirit, should ordain that during these days we are to observe severer fasts: so that we also, by a common sharing of Christ's Cross, might suffer a little of what He endured for us, as the Apostle says: *If we suffer with him, we shall also be glorified in him* (Rom. viii. 17; II Tim. ii. 12). For where there is a sharing of the passion of the Lord, there is a sure and certain expectation of our promised happiness.

There is no one, Dearly Beloved, to whom, because of the state of the times, this fellowship of glory is denied: as though the tranquillity of peace gave us no opportunity for the practise of heroic virtue! For the Apostle foretold us that: *All that will live godly in Christ Jesus, shall suffer persecutions* (II Tim. iii. 12). So, where men live in Christ there shall be no lack of the trials of the persecutions. The Lord Himself, in his exhortations, says to us: *He that taketh not up his cross, and followeth me, is not worthy of me* (Mt. x. 38). Nor should we doubt that these words were directed, not only to the Disciples of Christ, but to all the faithful who, in those with Him, are all taught unto salvation.

And as at all times[9] we must live worthily, so at all times must we bear the Cross: which for each one is rightly called *his*, for it is borne by each one in his own way and measure. The *name* persecution is one word; but not one is the reason of the fight; and as a rule there is greater danger in the hidden betrayer, than in the open foe. The blessed Job, taught by the alternating good and bad fortune of the world, has wisely and piously said: *Is not the life of man upon earth a warfare?* (Job vii. 1). For the faithful soul is oppressed not alone by the pain and torments of the body, but even should the bodily members be untouched, the soul is troubled by grave illness should it be weakened by the pleasures of the flesh.

But when the flesh lusts against the spirit, and the spirit against the flesh, the rational soul is supported by the Cross of Christ; nor does it when seduced by evil desires consent to evil doing, for it is pierced and held fast by the nails of continence, and by the fear of God. And so for those who are steadfast in virtue, there will be, through the instigation of the devil, no lack of enmity on the part of those who are unlike them; and they whose wicked life becomes yet more reprobate in contrast with the just will readily burst forth in hatred against them.

Iniquity dwells not in peace with virtue; drunkenness hates sobriety; falsehood has nothing in common with truthfulness. Pride has no regard for humility, wantonness for modesty, greed for generosity. And this division awakens such enduring conflicts that though it may outwardly seem to subside, yet never does it cease from troubling the inmost soul of the just in heart, so that it is indeed true that, *all who will live godly in Christ Jesus, shall suffer persecutions*; and true as well that all this life is a warfare. Let each faithful soul, learning from his own experiences, arm himself with the Cross of Christ, that he may be found worthy of Christ.

II. The guile of the devil, Dearly Beloved, against those who strive in this contest for the rewards of heaven, especially lies in wait to undo the faith of those whose virtue he cannot overthrow. For whoever is led away from the path of the true faith, and changed to another, his whole journey is an apostasy; and the further he travels from the Catholic light, the nearer he comes to the darkness of death.

This has happened in our own days to some who through carelessness have caught the infection of an ancient madness, from the evil spirit of an error long since confuted and condemned; and who dare to deny that in Christ there is a twofold nature, either by not accepting the truth of the Incarnation, or that the Divinity became flesh: so that, according to the Manichean, where there was no passion there is no Resurrection, or, according to Apollinaris, the very Godhead of the Word has become subject to change and to suffering.

To listen to such teaching, to pour it into the ears of Christian people, what is it if not to seek to overthrow the very foundations of our religion, and to deny that the true Son of God is true Son of man, in Whom alone was the restoration of man to his former state testified to by the Law, promised by the Prophets, and announced by all the signs of the Old Testament; so that we may not doubt of the fulfilment, at the time appointed, of that great mystery of the Divine Mercy, so often and so long foreshadowed, which was to benefit all ages?

Whence is it that, because *the Word was made flesh*, the one person in Christ belongs to both God and man, so that in none of His actions is there a separation between the one nature and the other; yet Evangelical truth repeatedly confesses that He is the Son of man Whom it proclaims is the Son of God, so that though of the things which it records, some belong to His Divinity, and some to His humanity, yet both the one and the other are commemorated under the name of the Son of man: so that the faith which was to believe that Our Lord Jesus Christ, born of the Virgin Mary, was at the same time both God and man, might not hesitate in confessing either humanity in God or Godhead in man; and that the true lowliness of the assumed man was in the Word, and the true Majesty of the assuming Godhead in our flesh.

III. Since, as you will remember, Dearly Beloved, I have frequently instructed you in this matter, these words in which we have briefly discoursed on the Incarnation of the Word will suffice for the occasion of the Paschal Feast, for which we must prepare ourselves with purity of heart. And now I wish to awaken your devotion in regard to that which the season requires of us: that you beautify your holy and salutary fasting with works of piety. And since we are especially to labour for the pardon of our sins, you can make sure of the unfailing divine mercy if you likewise, in respect of those subject to you, change every offence into a pardon.

For it is but fitting that the members of the Church of God should come together for this so great festival in gentleness and harmony of spirit; and that the harshness of punishments, which now are tempered even in the public courts, should be mitigated much more in the hearts of Christians; rather should the solicitude of the sanctified be intent upon this: that no one suffer cold, that no one hunger, that no one shall be in want, that no one be left to pine away in sorrow, that no one be bound in chains, that the gaol shall hold no prisoner.

For however great the causes of offence, yet, between man and man, we should rather keep in mind not so much the enormity of the offence, as the fact that we share a common nature; so that with what mercy a man shall judge another, he shall obtain mercy from God Who will judge him. For, *Blessed are the merciful: for they shall obtain mercy* (Mt. v. 7), from God: Who liveth and reigneth world without end. Amen.

IV. St Leo the Great, Pope and Doctor

The Fruits of the Passion[10]

Synopsis:

I. That Justice might be preserved Christ fought, not alone by His divine power, but also through the body of our lowliness.
II. What is now fulfilled was of old foreshadowed; and one and the same is the faith of all mankind.
III. That the union of Christ with His Body, natural and mystical, is indissoluble.
IV. The Christian must above all things strive for this: to imitate his Head.
V. Only the Ritual commandments are changed: grace is given for all moral precepts.
VI. Christ brings forth to Himself many children through Baptism; in which there is a clear figure of His Death and Resurrection.
VII. Each merit of the Christian is to the glory of Christ, Who rules and works in those He nourishes with His Body.

I. The glory of the Lord's Passion, Dearly Beloved, of which we promised to speak today also, is especially to be honoured in the mystery of His lowliness, by which He has redeemed and taught us all: so that from where our price was paid charity might also spring up. For the Omnipotence of the Son of God, in which through one and the same essence He is equal with the Father, could have, by a simple act of His Will, saved us from the power of the devil, were it not more perfectly in accord with the divine plan, that the hostility of our wicked enemy should be undone through that which he had undone; and that we should be restored by means of that same nature through which slavery was imposed on man.

For the Evangelist, saying that, *The Word was made Flesh, and dwelt amongst us*, and the Apostle saying, *That God was in Christ, reconciling the world to himself* (II Cor. v. 19), shows us, that the Only-Begotten Son of the Most High Father entered into such a union with our human lowliness, that, though taking to Himself the substance of our soul and body, He yet remained One and the Same Son of God; raising up our nature, not His: for it was lowliness that was raised up, not power: in such a manner that when the creature was joined to its Creator, nothing of the divinity was absent from what He assumed, and nothing of humanity in Him Who assumed it.

II. This plan of God's justice and mercy, though veiled in times past, was yet not so hidden as to be concealed from the minds of the saints who lived good lives from the beginning to the Lord's Coming. For the salvation that Christ was to bring us, was promised both in the words of the Prophets and in the meaning of events; and received not alone by those who foretold it, but by all who believed them. For one is the faith which sanctifies the just of all ages, and the same is the hope of the faithful, whatever we confess was accomplished, or our forefathers prayed might come to pass, through Jesus Christ, the Mediator of God and man (I Tim. ii. 5).

Nor is there any difference as between Jew and Gentile. For, as the Apostle says, *Circumcision is nothing, and uncircumcision is nothing; but the observance of the commandments of God* (I Cor. vii. 19). And if we observe those in perfect faith, they shall make us true children of Abraham; that is, perfect Christians, as the same Apostle says: *For as many of you have been baptized in Christ, have put on Christ. There is neither Jew nor Greek: there is neither bond nor free: there is neither male nor female. For you are all one in Christ Jesus. And if you be Christ's, then you are the seed of Abraham, heirs according to the promise* (Gal. iii. 27–9).

III. There is then no doubt, Dearly Beloved, that human nature was taken into such close union with Him by the Son of God, that Christ is not alone in the Man Who is the *firstborn of every creature* (Col. i. 15), but one and the same in all the sanctified. And as the Head cannot be separate from Its members so neither can the members from their Head. And though it is not in this life but in the life eternal that God *shall be all in all* (I Cor. xv. 28), yet even now He dwells within His Temple, the Church, as He promised, saying: *Behold I am with you all days, even to the consummation of the world* (Mt. xxviii. 20). And this the Apostle echoes when he says: *He is the head of the body, the Church, who is the beginning, the firstborn from the dead: that in all things he may hold the primacy: because in him it hath well pleased the Father, that all fulness should dwell; and through him to reconcile all things unto himself* (Col. i. 18–20).

IV. What is here made known to our hearts by these and like testimonies, but that in all things we are to be remade in His likeness Who, remaining by nature God, did not hold it beneath Him to be seen as a servant? For though without taint of sin, He took upon Him all the infirmities which arose from sin, so that He knew hunger and thirst, weariness and the need of sleep, sorrow and tears, and bore to the end the most bitter torments: for no one could be freed from the net of death unless He, in Whom our nature was free of taint, suffered Himself to be put to death at the hands of the wicked.

And it was from this that the Son of God Our Saviour gave those who believed in Him both a faith and an example; that they might receive the one by regeneration, and follow the other by imitating Him. This the Blessed Apostle Peter teaches, saying: *Christ suffered for us, leaving you an example that you should follow his steps. Who did no sin, neither was guile found in his mouth. Who, when he was reviled, did not revile: when he suffered, he threatened not: but delivered himself to him that judged him unjustly. Who his own self bore our sins in his body upon the tree: that we being dead to sins, should live to justice* (I Pet. ii. 21–4).

V. As therefore there is no one among the faithful, Dearly Beloved, to whom the gifts of grace are denied, so neither is there any among them not subject to the Christian rule of life. For though the harshness of the Symbolic Law has been taken away, yet the gain from free obedience of the will has increased, as John the Evangelist says *For the law was given by Moses; grace and truth came by Jesus Christ* (Jn. i. 17). For everything that belonged to the Law, whether as to circumcision, or to the different offerings, or to the observance of the sabbath, all gave testimony to Christ, and foretold the grace of Christ.

And He is the end of the Law (Rom. x. 4), not in that he brings it to nothing, but in that He fulfils it. And though He is the Author of both the New and the Old. He brought the mystical significance of the Figures and the Promises to an end, in that He fulfilled the promises, and caused the prophecies to cease, since He Who had been foretold had now come. But in the moral order there was no change in the precepts of the Old Law; rather were many of them enlarged through the Gospel teaching, that they might be clearer and more perfect teaching us salvation than they were when promising us a Saviour.

VI. So all these things which the Son of God taught and did to restore the world we now know, not alone from the history of what is past, but also from the power of what is done in the present. He it is Who, Born of the Holy Ghost from the Virgin Mary, by this same Breath of Life makes fruitful His own unspotted Church; so that from the birth of baptism an unending multitude are born to God, of whom it is said: *Who are born, not of blood, nor of the will of the flesh, nor of the will of man, but of God* (Jn. i. 15).

He it is in Whom the Seed of Abraham is blessed, by the adoption of the whole world, making the Patriarch the father of the nations (Gen. xxii. 18). The children of the promise being born, not of the flesh, but of faith. He it is Who choosing no nation forms from every nation under heaven one flock of sanctified sheep, and each day fulfils what He promised: *And other sheep I have, that are not of this fold: them also I must bring, and they shall hear my voice, and there shall be one fold and one shepherd* (Jn. x. 16). For though it is to Blessed Peter in chief he says: *Feed my sheep* (Jn. xxi. 17), yet is it by the One Lord that care is taken of all the shepherds also. And those who come to the Rock He feeds on such sweet and joyful pastures that unending numbers of His sheep, grown strong and fat on His love, have not hesitated to lay down their life for the Name of their Shepherd, as the Good

Shepherd did not hesitate to lay down His life for His sheep (Jn. x. 17).

He it is in Whom suffers not alone the glorious courage of the martyrs, but all the new-born in the birth of their faith. For when they renounce the devil, and believe in God; when they pass over from their old life to the new; when they put aside the nature of the earthly man, and put on that of heaven, there comes between a sort of death, and a sort of likeness to the resurrection, so that he who puts on Christ, and whom Christ puts on, is not now the same as before the laver of baptism: the body of the man new born in faith is now the Body of Christ Crucified.

VII. This is the change of the Right Hand of the Most High (Ps. lxxvi. 11), Who worketh all in all (I Cor. xii. 6), that we may know it is He Who is the Author of the good works that follow from the worthy life of each one of the faithful; giving thanks to the mercy of God, Who so adorns the whole Body of the Church with His unending gifts of grace, so that through manifold rays the same splendid Light shines everywhere; nor can the merit of any Christian be other than the glory of Christ. This is that true light which enlightens and sanctifies every man. This it is which delivers us from the power of darkness, and translates us into the Kingdom of the Son of God (Col. i. 13).

This it is which uplifts the desires of the soul through newness of life, and extinguishes the desires of the flesh. This it is by means of which the Lord's Pasch is celebrated in the unleavened bread of sincerity and truth (I Cor. v. 8); by which the new creature is filled and nourished from the Lord Himself: as long as he has put away the old leaven of wickedness. For this alone is the fruit of the Communion of the Body and Blood of Christ, that we pass over into That which we receive, and bear with us in all things, both in our soul and in our body, Him in Whom we have died, been buried, and risen again, as the Apostle tells us: *For you are dead; and your life is hid with Christ in God. When Christ shall appear, who is your life, then you also shall appear with Him in glory* (Col. iii. 3); Who with the Father and the Holy Ghost liveth and reigneth for ever and ever. Amen.

V. St Gregory the Great, Pope and Doctor

Given to the People on Passion Sunday, in The Basilica of the Holy Apostle Peter

The Patience of Christ[11]

1. Recall to mind, Dearest Brethren, the patience of God. He had come to forgive sin, and He said: *Which of you shall convince me of sin?* He did not disdain to make clear to us that He was not Himself a sinner: He Who had come to justify sinners by the power of His divinity. But truly fearful is that which follows. *He that is of God, heareth the words of God. Therefore you hear them not, because you are not of God.* If he who

is of God can hear the words of God, and he who is not of God cannot hear them, then let each one ask himself whether or not he hears the word of God in the ears of his heart, and he will then know to whom he belongs.

The Truth bids us long for our heavenly home, and to tread under foot the desires of the body, to turn from the glory of this world, not to desire what is another's, to be generous with what is ours. Let each one then reflect within himself, whether this voice of God has become loud in the ear of his own heart, and then he will know if he belongs with God. For there are some who do not trouble to listen to the commands of God even with their bodily ears. And some who do listen to God's words, but do not lay hold of them with any desire of the soul. And there are some who freely receive God's words, and are even moved to tears by them. But when their tears are dry they go back again to their evil ways. They do not in truth hear the words who take no thought to put them into practice.

Recall then to mind, Dearest Brethren, the life of your own soul, and with serious concern dwell upon that which has come forth from the mouth of Truth Itself: *Therefore you hear them not, because you are not of God.* And that which the Truth says of the reprobate (Jews), they themselves prove from their own deeds. For there follows: *The Jews therefore answered, and said to him: Do not we say well that thou art a Samaritan, and hast a devil?*

2. Let us hear what the Lord replies after receiving such an insult. *I have not a devil: but I honour my Father, and you have dishonoured me.* The word *Samaritan* means *Guardian.* And He is truly the Guardian of whom the psalmist says: *Unless the Lord keep the city. he watches in vain that keepeth it* (Ps. cxxvi. 1), and of whom it was said by the mouth of Isaias: *Watchman, what of the night? Watchman, what of the night?* the Lord replies, not, I am not a Samaritan, but: *I have not a demon.* There were two accusations made against Him: the one He denies; His silence regarding the other means He accepts it as true.

For He had come as the Guardian of the human race; and had He said He was not a Samaritan He would have denied He was a Guardian. What He passed over in silence, therefore, He acknowledged; He rejects with patience what He had heard falsely declared. And what is He here rebuking by these words if not our pride, which, should it be censured ever so slightly, replies with injuries more cruel than it received. It works what evil it can in revenge, and what it cannot do it threatens.

See the Lord receiving the insult, and He is not angered, nor does He reply with injurious words: He Who had He replied to those who said these words that, It is you who have a demon, would have answered what was true; for were they not filled with a demon they would not have spoken such wicked things against God! But He Who is Truth Itself, accepting the insult, did not say in answer even what was true: lest it should appear, not that He had answered what was indeed true, but that being provoked He had returned the insult.

And what are we here taught but

that whenever we receive false accusations against ourselves from our neighbour, we should be silent, even about their own real faults: lest we turn the duty of correction into a weapon of anger? But since those who have a zeal for the things of God shall ever be calumniated by evil men, the Lord offers us Himself as an example of patience, when He says: *I honour my Father, and you have dishonoured me*. And besides this He teaches us by His example what we should do in face of such things, when He goes on: *I seek not my own glory: there is one that seeketh and judgeth*.

We know that it is written, that the Father has given all judgement to the Son, and yet, Behold the Same Son receives injuries, but seeks not His own glory. The injuries offered to Him He leaves to be judged by His Father: to teach us how important it is that we should be patient, when even He who is to judge us does not seek to be revenged. And when the perversity of the wicked increases, preaching is not to be lessened, it is even to be increased. This the Lord warns us to do by His example, when, after they said that He was possessed by a devil, He poured out yet more generously the riches of His Teaching, saying: *Amen, amen, I say to you: if any man keep my word, he shall not see death for ever*.

Since it must be that the good become better through suffering persecution, so do the wicked become worse through the good that is done them. For these here, when they heard His words in answer, again say: *Now we know thou hast a devil*. For since they clung blindly to eternal death, they did not see the death to which they clung: they had eyes only for the death of the body, and were blind to the words of Truth, crying out: *Abraham is dead, and the prophets; and thou sayest: If any man keep my word, he shall not taste death for ever*. In this they put Abraham and the prophets above the Truth Itself; worshipping them almost. Here we are plainly shown, that they who know not God, give false honour to God's servants.

3. And let us take note that the Lord saw they resisted Him with open insult, and yet ceased not with untiring voice to preach to them, saying: *Abraham your father rejoiced that he might see my day; he saw it and was glad* (Gen. xviii. 1). Abraham did in truth see the day of the Lord when, in a figure of the Blessed Trinity, He received the three angels as guests. And when He was receiving them, He spoke to the three as to one; for though in the Persons of the Trinity there is number, there is but Oneness in the Nature of Their Divinity.

But the carnal minds of those who stand around Him do not lift their eyes above His Flesh, and they consider in Him only the years of His Body; and they say: *Thou art not yet fifty years old, and hast thou seen Abraham?* Our Redeemer then gently turns them from the appearance of His Humanity, and leads them to the contemplation of His Divinity, saying: *Amen, amen, I say to you, before Abraham was made, I am*. *Before*, relates to past time; *I am*, to the present. And since His Divinity has neither past nor future, but only unchanging existence, He does not say: Before Abraham was, I was; but: *Before Abraham was made, I am*. For this reason was it said of old to Moses: I AM WHO AM. And again: *Say to the children of Israel: HE WHO IS, hath sent me to you* (Ex. iii. 14).

Therefore, both before and after Abraham, He Who was could both come near us by the manifestation of His Presence, or depart from us by the way of life. The Truth exists for ever; for nothing begins in a time prior to it, and nothing is brought to an end after it. But the minds of those unbelievers, unable to endure these words that spoke to them of eternity, rush to stone Him; trying to overwhelm Him Whom they could not understand.

4. What the Lord did in reply to the fury of those who stoned Him we have been told; for immediately there follows: *Jesus hid himself, and went out of the temple*. It is a thing that greatly arouses our wonder, Dearest Brethren, why the Lord should turn away from His persecutors by hiding Himself; He Who had He willed to use His divine power could have frozen them in their assault by the silent command of His mind, or overwhelmed them for ever by the sudden chastisement of death? But since He came to suffer, He willed not to exercise judgement.

And in the hour of His passion He had truly shown what He could do, yet suffered that which He came to endure. For when He said to His persecutors who came seeking Him: *I am he* (Jn. xviii. 6), with His voice alone He struck down their pride, and laid them all prostrate upon the earth. He then Who on this occasion could have escaped the hands of those who stoned Him without hiding Himself, why does He hide Himself if not that our Redeemer, being made a man among men, tells us some things by His words, and yet others by His example? What does He here tell us by His example but that we should humbly turn aside from those who, *in their anger worketh pride* (Prov. xxi. 24); even when we are able to resist them. And for this same reason Paul also tells us: *Give not place unto wrath* (Rom. xii. 19).

Let man then carefully consider with what great humility he should fly from the anger of his neighbour, when God, hiding Himself, turned away from the fury of those who raged against Him. Let no one then rise in anger against the injuries he receives; let no one give back injury for injury. For, imitating God, it is more glorious to turn away in silence from insult, than to triumph over it by answering in kind.

5. But the proud in heart will say: 'It is a dishonourable thing that a man who has received an insult should take it in silence. For whoever sees you receive an insult, and keeping silent, will not believe you are exercising patience, but rather admitting guilt.' But how do such words arise in us against the virtue of patience if not because we have our minds fixed on this lower world, and care nothing about pleasing Him Who looks down on us from heaven? If we have received injury, let us give ourselves to reflection on the words of God: *I seek not my own glory: there is one that seeketh and judgeth.*

This which was written of the Lord: that *He hid himself*, can be understood in another sense. He had preached many things to the Jews; but they had mocked the words of His Teaching. And because of it they became even more perverse: going so far as to stone Him. What does the Lord then teach us by hiding Himself, if not that Truth hides Herself from those who continue to despise Her words? For Truth flies from the soul it does not find humble.

How many are there even now who execrate the Jews for not hearing the words of God; yet, what they were, whom they reprove, in regard to believing, that are they themselves in regard to the works of grace? They listen to the teachings of God, they see His miracles, but they refuse to change their evil ways. Behold He calls us, and we refuse to return to Him! Behold He waits for us, and we ignore His patience! While there is yet time, Brethren, let each one of you forsake his own way of evil, and let Him stand in great fear of the patience of God, lest later he may be unable to escape His wrath Whose mildness he now despises; Who with the Father and the Holy Ghost lives and reigns world without end. Amen.

NOTES

[1] PG 14, 646–79.

[2] PG 59, col. 301, hom. 55.

[3] Cf. col. 662 in Text cited.

[4] Cf. Text cited, n. 1.

[5] PG 14, cols. 678, 674.

[6] PG 63, cols. 623–32.

[7] PL 35, col. 1705; Tr. 42, 14.

[8] PL 54, col. 294. Sermo. 9 in Quad. 2: 12.

[9] For *temporis* some codices have *corporis*; which the Roman Breviary uses. The latter word however seems unsuited to the text; and at variance with the context, and with the parallelism between, all pursuing virtue—always following Jesus—and, at all times bearing the Cross, to this end. Cf. Matt. x. 38.

[10] PL 54, col. 353. Sermo. 63 on The Passion of The Lord XII. Given on Wednesday—*feria quarta*.

[11] PL 76, col. 1149, sermo. 18.

PALM SUNDAY

I. Origen: Christ's Entry into Jerusalem

II. St Ambrose: The Colt a Figure of the Gentiles

III. St Jerome: The Meaning of the Gospel

IV. St John Chrysostom: Lessons of Today's Gospel

V. St Leo The Great: Passion of Our Lord

THE GOSPEL OF THE SUNDAY

Matthew xxi. 1–9

At that time when they drew nigh to Jerusalem, and were come to Bethphage, unto Mount Olivet, then Jesus sent two disciples, saying to them: Go ye into the village that is over against you, and immediately you shall find an ass tied, and a colt with her: loose them and bring them to me. And if any man shall say anything to you, say ye, that the Lord hath need of them: and forthwith he shall let them go.

Now all this was done that it might be fulfilled which was spoken by the prophet, saying: Tell ye the daughter of Sion: Behold thy king cometh to thee, meek, and sitting upon an ass, and a colt the foal of her that is used to the yoke. And the disciples going, did as Jesus commanded them. And they brought the ass and the colt, and laid their garments upon them, and made him sit thereon.

And a very great multitude spread their garments in the way: and others cut boughs from the trees, and strewed them in the way: and the multitudes that went before and that followed, cried, saying: Hosanna to the Son of David: Blessed is he that cometh in the name of the Lord: Hosanna in the highest.

PARALLEL GOSPELS

Mark xi. 1–10

And when they were drawing near to Jerusalem and to Bethania at the mount of Olives, he sendeth two of his disciples, and saith to them: Go ye into the village that is over

Luke xix. 29–38

And it came to pass, when he was come nigh to Bethphage and Bethania, unto the mount called Olivet, he sent two of his disciples, saying: Go ye into the town which is over against you, and immediately at your coming in thither, you shall find a colt tied, upon which no man yet hath sat: loose him, and bring him. And if any man shall say to you, What are you doing? say ye that the Lord hath need of him: and immediately he will let him come hither.

And going their way, they found the colt tied before the gate without, in the meeting of two ways: and they loose him. And some of them that stood there, said to them: What do you loosing the colt? Who said to them as Jesus had commanded them; and they let him go with them. And they brought the colt to Jesus; and they lay their garments on him, and he sat upon him. And many spread their garments in the way: and others cut down boughs from the trees, and strewed them in the way. And they that went before and they that followed, cried, saying: Hosanna, blessed is he that cometh in the name of the Lord. Blessed be the kingdom of our father David that cometh: Hosanna in the highest.

against you, at your entering into which you shall find the colt of an ass tied, on which no man ever hath sitten: loose him and bring him hither. And if any man shall ask you: Why do you loose him? you shall say thus unto him: because the Lord hath need of his service.

And they that were sent, went their way, and found the colt standing, as he had said unto them. And as they were loosing the colt, the owners thereof said to them: why loose you the colt? But they said: Because the Lord hath need of him. And they brought him to Jesus. And casting their garments on the colt, they set Jesus thereon.

John xii. 12–16

And on the next day, a great multitude that was come to the festival day, when they had heard that Jesus was coming to Jerusalem, took branches of palm trees, and went forth to meet him, and cried: Hosanna, blessed is he that cometh in the name of the Lord, the king of Israel. And Jesus found a young ass, and sat upon it, as it is written: Fear not, daughter of Sion: behold, thy king cometh, sitting on an ass's colt.

These things his disciples did not know at first; but when Jesus was glorified, then they remembered that these things were written of him, and that they had done these things to him.

Exposition from the Catena Aurea

V. 1. *And when they drew nigh to Jerusalem, and were come . . .*

Remigius: The Evangelist had previously narrated that *Jesus* had *departed from Galilee*, and had begun *going up to Jerusalem*. After this he stops to narrate what Jesus had done on the way, and then going on with his previous purpose says: *And when they drew nigh* etc. Bethphage was a little village belonging to the priests, about a mile from Jerusalem, and situated on the Mount of Olives. For the priests, who were wont to serve on certain days in the Temple, when they had completed their turn came out here to wait. Likewise those who had discharged their duty rested here: for it was a precept of the Law, that on the Sabbath no one should journey more than a mile.

ORIGEN, *Tr.* 14 *in Matt*: For this reason Bethphage is interpreted as the House of the Jawbones: for in the Law the jawbone was the particular portion of the priests.[1]

V. 2. *Saying to them: Go ye into the village etc...*

CHRYSOSTOM, *Super Matt. Hom.* 37 *ex Op. Imperf*: He did not say to His Disciples, say ye that his own Lord hath need of them, or your Lord: that they might understand that He alone is the Lord, and not alone of animals, but of all men. For sinners, in their external state, belong to Him: but of their own free will they belong to the devil.

CHRYSOSTOM, *Hom.* 67 *in Matt*: Do not consider what here happened as being of little moment. For who persuaded the owners of the beasts, so that they agreed not to oppose Him, to submit in silence and let them go? And in this also He instructed His Disciples: for He could have checked the Jews, but He willed not to. He also teaches that whatsoever be asked of them they should give. For if they who knew not Christ so yielded, much more should His Disciples give up all things.

V. 3. *And forthwith he will etc.*

CHRYSOSTOM, *ex Op. Imp*: That He said, *and forthwith he will let them go*, must be understood to imply that the animal, as soon as He had entered into Jerusalem, was returned by Christ to its own master . . .

GLOSS: Or that the owner of the beasts forthwith let them go, freeing them for the service of the Lord. The testimony of a prophet is joined to this event, that it may be shown that the Lord had fulfilled all things which were written of Him; but the Scribes and Pharisees, blinded by envy, would not understand that which they read. And so there follows:

V. 4. *Now all this was done that it might be fulfilled etc.*

CHRYSOSTOM, *ex Op. Imp*: For the prophet, namely Zachariah, knowing the malice of the Jews, that they were to contradict Christ as He was going up to the Temple, forewarned them that they would recognize their king by this sign, saying:

V. 5. *Tell ye the daughter of Sion etc...*

RHABANUS: The title *Daughter of Jerusalem* was historically used to describe the City of Jerusalem, which is situated on Mount Sion. Mystically it means the Church of the Faithful, belonging to the heavenly Jerusalem.

CHRYSOSTOM, *ex Op. Imp*: *Behold* is the phrase of one who is making something clear, that is, consider the works of His power, not in their outward but in their spiritual meaning. For the prophet lived long before, yet he said, *Behold*, that he might make clear that He of Whom he was speaking, even before He was born, was already your King. When therefore you shall see Him, do not say: *We have no king but Caesar. He cometh to thee*, that He may save thee: if you will understand. If you will not He cometh against thee. *Meek*, that He might not be feared because of His majesty, but loved for His gentleness. He comes therefore, not seated upon a golden chariot, or resplendent in purple, or mounted upon a fiery horse, eager for contention and strife, but upon a she-ass, the friend of tranquillity and peace. Hence we have: *Sitting upon an ass*.

AUGUSTINE, *Harmony of the Four Gospels*, 2, 66. The account of the Evangelist is in this somewhat different from the prophetic testimony. For Matthew so uses this latter as saying that the prophet made mention of the ass. But this is not so, either according to what John has recorded, or according to the ecclesiastical codices which bear the name of the Septuagint. To me the cause of this difference appears to be because Matthew is said to have written in Hebrew.[2] But it is evident that the translation which is called the Septuagint is in some things different from that which they who know that tongue find in the Hebrew, as also those individual scholars who have translated these same Hebrew books.

And if you ask the reason for this difference I consider that nothing is more probable than that these seventy translated by the aid of that Spirit by Whom that which they were translating had been uttered; which is confirmed by their own wondrous harmony, for which they are praised. Accordingly, these translators, while in no way departing from what God intended and Whose words these are, and while varying in some things, they desire nothing else than to show us the actual event, which to our delight we observe to be related with common accord, and with a certain diversity, by the four Evangelists. By this it is made clear to us that there is no fabrication, should one of them relate something in a manner that is different, yet in no way departs from His purpose with Whom he must be in agreement.

To know this is profitable in regard to style, to guard against deceptions; and to faith itself, lest we should think that truth is defended by a form as it were of consecrated words: to the extent that God gave us not alone the truth, but also the words which are to be spoken of it; since rather the truth is held to be so far above the words, that we should have no need whatever to inquire about them, if we could know the revelation without them, as God knows it, and His angels know it in Him.

V. 6. *And the disciples going, did as Jesus commanded them.*

The other Evangelists are silent regarding the ass. Nor should the reader be concerned if Matthew were silent regarding the colt, as they were regarding the ass. How much less cause have we for concern that one so spoke of the ass: concerning which the rest were silent: yet as not to pass over in silence the colt, concerning which the others have spoken. For where it may be gathered that both were employed there is no discord; even though one should mention one and another the other. How much less is the danger of conflict when one mentions one, and another mentions both?[3]

V. 7. *And they brought the ass . . . and made him sit thereon.*

JEROME: It would seem that the Lord could not have rode on both animals in the short space of the journey. Since the simple record contains an impossibility, or unseemliness, let us devote ourselves to the higher, that is, to the mystical interpretation of them. REMIGIUS: Though it could have happened that the Lord rode upon each animal.

CHRYSOSTOM, *Hom.* 67 *in Matt*: It seems to me that He rode upon the ass, not alone because of the divine mystery, but that He might also furnish us with a rule of holy wisdom. He shows here that it is not necessary to travel on horseback; that it suffices to use an ass, and that we should be contented with what is sufficient for our needs. But let you ask the Jews: What king has ever entered Jerusalem riding upon an ass? They can tell you of none save Him.

V. 8. *And a very great multitude spread their garments in the way . . .*

JEROME: The crowds then that had come out from Jericho, and had followed the Saviour, laid their garments before His path, and spread branches of trees in His way. And so there follows: *A very great multitude etc.*; under the feet of the ass, lest it might stumble somewhere upon a stone, or tread upon a thorn, or slip on the uneven road. *And others cut boughs from the trees, and strewed them in the way*; that is from the fruitbearing trees with which the Mount of Olives was planted. And when they had done all this they offered also the tribute of their voices. Hence there follows:

V. 9. *And the multitudes . . . cried, saying: Hosanna to the son of . . .*

What *Hosanna* means I shall now briefly explain. In psalm 117, which manifestly was written concerning the Coming of the Saviour, among other things we also read this verse: *O Lord save me: O Lord give good success. Blessed is he that cometh in the name of the Lord.* In place of what is given in the Septuagint: *Ὦ Κύριε σῶσον δή*, that is, *O Lord save me*, we read in the Hebrew: ANNA ADONAI OSIANNA, which Symmachus has clearly interpreted to say: *I beseech Thee, O Lord, save me, I beseech Thee.* Therefore let no one thing that the saying is made up from the two phrases, the Greek and the Hebrew; rather is it wholly Hebrew.

REMIGIUS: And is composed from a complete phrase and an incomplete one. For OSI in Latin means *Salva*, save, or *Salvifica*, deliver: ANNA among them (the Hebrews) is the cry of one beseeching. For with them one who beseeches says ANNA, as among Latins one in pain cries, *heu*!

JEROME: For it signifies that the Coming of Christ is the salvation of the world. Hence follows: *Blessed is he that cometh in the name of the*

Lord; which Our Lord also confirms in the Gospel, John v. 43. REMIGIUS: Because as in all his good works He sought not His own but the glory of the Father.

GLOSS: And the meaning is, *Blessed*, that is, may He be glorified; *that cometh*, that is, Who has become Incarnate; *in the name of the Lord*, that is, of the Father, glorifying Him. Again they repeat, *Hosanna*, that is, *Save me, I beseech Thee*; and they determine where they wish to be as saved, *in the highest*, that is, in heaven, not upon the earth.

JEROME: Or through this that there is added Hosanna, that is, salvation *in the highest*, it is clearly indicated that the Coming of Christ means the salvation, not alone of men, but of the whole world, linking earthly with heavenly things (cf. Phil. ii. 10). ORIGEN, *Hom. in Matt*: Or they praise the humanity of Christ in that they cry out: *Hosanna to the son of David: Blessed is he that cometh in the name of the Lord*. And His complete restoration to the House of God, in that they cry: *Hosanna in the highest*.

CHRYSOSTOM. *ex Op. Imp*: Some interpret Hosanna as also meaning glory; others as meaning redemption. And both glory is due to Him, and redemption belongs to Him Who has redeemed all men. HILARY: For the words of praise clearly express the power of redemption that is in Him. They call Him *son of David*, in Whom they confess the inheritance of an eternal kingdom.

CHRYSOSTOM, *ex Op. Imp. Hom.* 37: Never before had the Lord made use of the services of beasts of burthen, or placed about Himself as ornaments the green foliage of trees, except on this occasion, when going up to Jerusalem to fulfil His passion. For He stirred up the Jews, who beheld this and envied it, not that they might do that which previously they were not willing to do, but that they might do that which previously they desired to do. Opportunity therefore was given to them; not a change of purpose.

JEROME: But, mystically, the Lord draws nigh to Jerusalem; going out from Jericho, with a very great multitude following him; returning as a great man endowed with much riches (the salvation of those who believed in Him), He desires to enter the City of peace, and the abode of the vision of God. And He came to Bethphage, that is, to the *House of Jawbones* (see note 1) which was a figure of praise of God, and was situated on Mount Olivet: by which is signified the light of knowledge, and rest from toil and pain. By the village that was *over against* the Apostles, this world is signified: for it was against the Apostles, and neither did it wish to submit to the yoke of true doctrine.

REMIGIUS: The Lord then sends the Disciples from Mount Olivet to the village; as from the primitive Church He sent His preachers into the world. And He sent two, because of the two orders of preachers; which the Apostle makes clear when he says: *He who wrought in Peter to the apostleship of the circumcision, wrought in me also among the Gentiles* (Gal. ii. 8); or because there are two precepts of charity; or because there are two testaments; or because of the letter and the spirit.

JEROME: Or because of the theoretical and the practical; that is, knowledge and good works. The ass which was used to the yoke, and subdued, and had born the yoke of the Law, is interpreted to mean the Synagogue. The ass's colt, wanton and unbroken, stands for the people of the Gentiles: for Judea in respect to God is the mother of the Gentiles. RHABANUS: Hence Matthew, who wrote his Gospel for the Jews, alone relates that the ass was brought to the Lord, that he might show that the salvation of this same Jewish people must not be despaired of, providing they repent.

CHRYSOSTOM, *ex Op. Imp. Hom.* 37: Because of certain resemblances men are likened to these animals; not knowing God, nor the Son of God. For this is an unclean animal, and more unintelligent than other beasts of burthen, stupid and weak and ignoble, and toiling under a load. Such men were, before the Coming of Christ: soiled by every passion, unreasoning, without sense in their speech, foolish in their neglect of God—for what greater folly than to despise their Creator as though He were a creature, and to adore the work of their own hands, as if it were their Maker—weak of soul; ignoble because, forgetful of their heavenly origin, they had become slaves of their passions and of the demons. Laden, because they suffered under the burden of pagan darkness and superstition, laid on them either by the demons or by the Pharisees.

The ass was *tied*, that is, held by the chains of diabolical superstition, so that it had no freedom to go whither it willed. For before we can sin we have freedom of will, to follow or not after the will of the devil, according as we wish. But if we once have sinned we have bound ourselves to his service, and cannot free ourselves of our own power. As a ship with a broken helm is led hither and thither at the sway of the storm, so man, when he loses the aid of divine grace through sin, does not that which he wishes, but what the devil wishes. And if God does not deliver him by the strong hand of His mercy he will remain till death in the bonds of his sins. And so He commands His Disciples: *Loose them*, namely, by means of your teaching, and through your miracles: because all, Jews and Gentiles, have been freed by the Apostles. *And bring them to me*; that is, convert them to the blessedness of My Kingdom.

ORIGEN, *Hom. in Matt. xvi.* 16: Whence it was that ascending to heaven He commanded His Disciples, that they should forgive sins, giving them the Holy Ghost (Jn. xx. 22, 23). Those now loosed from their sins, and going forward in grace, and sustained by the divinity of the Word, are found worthy of being returned to the place from which He had brought them: but not now to their former tasks, but to preach there the Son of God. And this is the meaning of: *And forthwith he will let them go.*

HILARY: Or, by the ass and its colt is signified the twofold calling of the Gentiles. For the Samaritans, who served God in accordance with certain rites of their own, are here signified by the ass. The colt signifies the Gentiles, who were still wild and unbroken. And so two are sent to free those who are still in the bonds of superstition: for through Philip Samaria believed, and through Peter Cornelius was brought to Christ as the first fruits of the Gentiles.

REMIGIUS: As was then said to the Apostles: *If any man shall say anything to you, say ye, that the Lord hath need of them*, so now preachers are commanded that, though enmity seek to oppose them, they should not desist from preaching the Gospel.

JEROME: The garments of the Apostles laid upon the beast may mean either the teaching of Christian virtues, the explanation of the Scriptures, or the variety of the truths of the Church; with which if the soul be not adorned and clothed, it shall not merit to bear the Lord.

REMIGIUS: The Lord riding on an ass went towards Jerusalem, because as the Ruler Who guides either the Holy Church or the soul of each believer, He both guides their life in this world, and afterwards leads them to the sight of their heavenly country. The Apostles and the other teachers of the Church laid their garments upon the ass: because the faith they received from Christ they gave to the Gentiles.

But the multitudes spread their garments *in the way*: because those believing from the Circumcision rejected the faith given them by the Law. *They cut boughs from the trees*: because they received from the prophets, as from green trees, proofs concerning Christ. Or, the multitudes who spread their garments in the way represent the martyrs, who gave their garments, that is, their bodies, which are as it were the clothing of their souls, for Christ. Or they are signified who mortify their own bodies by self denial. They who cut boughs from the trees are they who desire to learn the sayings and deeds of the Holy Fathers: for their own salvation and that of their children.

JEROME: His words: *The multitudes that went before and that followed*, showed that both peoples, those who believed in the Lord before the Gospel, and those who believed after, with one voice praise and confess the Lord. CHRYSOSTOM, *as above*: The former in prophesy acclaiming the Christ Who was to come; the latter giving praise acclaim the now fulfilled Coming of Christ.

I. ORIGEN, PRIEST AND CONFESSOR

Christ's Entry into Jerusalem[4]

Matthew xxi. 1–9. *And when they drew nigh to Jerusalem.* Mark in this same place writes as follows: *And when they were drawing near to Jerusalem and to Bethania on the mount of Olives*, and continues: *And immediately he will let him come hither.* Luke relates this also in the words: *When he was come nigh to Bethphage and Bethania*, continuing until: *You shall say thus unto him, because the Lord hath need of his service.*

It is worth while in such places in the Gospel to apply our minds to the meaning and purpose of the writers, and to consider why, after they had related the wonders and portents of the Saviour's actions, they should also record these things which reveal nothing of this sort. It is understandable that the Evangelists should commemorate the restoration of sight to the blind man, the healing of the paralytic, the raising of the dead, the cleansing of the lepers, in order that those who would read their writings might be strengthened in Jesus.

But what purpose had they in mind in this place in which it is recounted, that after Jesus had with His Disciples drawn near to Jerusalem, and had come to Bethphage close to Mount Olivet, He sent two Disciples with the command that they should loose and bring to Him an ass that was tied, together with its colt; He Who frequently made long journeys by foot, and did not refuse to complete His sojourn here on foot, as when He had come to Jerusalem, and passing through Samaria arrived at the well, and being weary from the road had sat down by it? And what did Jesus also mean when He bade them loose the ass that was tied, and the colt with her, telling them to answer any man who asked them: *Why do you loose him?* to answer *that the Lord hath need of them: and forthwith he will let them go*?

That He the Lord should have need of an ass and a colt which before that were tied reveals to us something that is worthy of His greatness. Zacharias the prophet, the son of Barachias, increases the difficulty of the question, having uttered a prophecy concerning these things, which is worthy of our consideration, in which remarkable things are said, in these words: *Rejoice greatly, O Daughter of Sion, shout for joy, O Daughter of Jerusalem. BEHOLD THY KING will come to thee, the just and saviour; he is poor, and riding upon an ass, and upon a colt the foal of an ass.*

Should you wish to learn from the prophet why the Daughter of Sion ought to rejoice because of the things foretold her, hear him further: *And I will destroy the chariot out of Ephraim, and the horse out of Jerusalem, and the bow for war shall be broken; and he shall speak peace to the Gentiles, and his power shall be from sea to sea, and from the rivers even to the end of the earth. Thou also by the blood of thy testament hast sent forth thy prisoners out of the pit, wherein is no water. Return to the strong hold, ye prisoners of hope, I will render thee double as I declare today* (Zach. ix. 9; x. 12).

But lest our discourse to you run on too long, we shall leave to him who so wishes to compare this prophecy with the Gospel narrative, and inquire into whatever is contained there. But we have noticed that the prophecy has not been set out by Matthew, or by John, in the same words. For it is not the same thing to say: *Rejoice greatly, O Daughter of Jerusalem*, as to say: *Tell ye the daughter of Sion.* And after the words: *Behold thy king will come to thee*, and before the word *meek*, the words which the prophet adds, *The just and Saviour*, have been left out by Matthew. Again in place of, *riding upon an ass, and a colt the foal of her that is used to the yoke*, the prophet has, *riding upon an ass, and a colt the foal of an ass*, or as some have it, *a young colt*. John in this place has, *sitting on an ass's colt*, instead of, *sitting upon an ass*. But he however, implying that here there is need of inquiry, comments: *These things his disciples did not know at first*.

But should anyone ask how must the Daughter of Sion greatly rejoice, and why should the Daughter of Jerusalem shout for joy, as the prophet has proclaimed, because He was coming riding upon an ass, and a young colt, when a little later He would weep seeing Jerusalem, *that killest the prophets*, and all that follows (Lk. xiii. 14). See if you can tell whether Sion whom he calls His Daughter and whom he bids rejoice, and Jerusalem, also His Daughter, and whom he commands to cry out for joy, are not those heavenly beings of whom it is written in the epistle to the Hebrews: *But you are come to Mount Sion, and to the city of the living God, the heavenly Jerusalem, and to the company of many thousands of angels* (Heb. xii. 22): or to that which is referred to in the epistle to the Galatians: *But that Jerusalem, which is above, is free: which is our mother?* (Gal. iv. 26).

And see also if these actions of the Saviour are not symbolical: loosing by means of the Apostles the beasts of burden from their bonds; that is, those who from this people or from the Gentiles who would confess His faith. For the ancient Synagogue, the ass, was bound and held fast by its sins; and bound also with it was the colt, namely, the people lately newborn from among the Gentiles, and as the Saviour draws near, and the way opens to the heavenly Jerusalem, He commands that both shall be freed by the teaching of His Disciples, to whom He had given the Holy Spirit in these words: *Receive ye the Holy Ghost. Whose sins you shall forgive, they are forgiven them; and whose sins you shall retain, they are retained* (Jn. xx. 22, 23).

And ever since the Disciples, whom He made *fit ministers of the New Testament, not in the letter, but in the spirit* (II Cor. iii. 6), loosening the ass that was tied, and the colt, bring them to Jesus, Who wills to use as his carriage those who by means of His true and genuine Disciples have been freed from their ancient bonds. And it truly becomes the Son of God, since He is human, to have need of this kind of the ass that was tied, and of the colt that was tied with it; for His need was that, seated upon them He might rather refresh from toil and restore those upon whom He sat, than that they should give rest to Him.

But someone will ask, how the things we have said agree with what follows, *And forthwith he will let them go*; or as Mark tells it: *And immediately he will let him come hither*? The question answers itself, if you reflect upon the letting go of the two beasts according to Matthew or of the colt according to Mark. It is manifest that there was no other Lord of the beasts which were bound save our *One Lord Jesus, by whom are all things* (I Cor. viii. 6), whom none would oppose from among those who said: *What do you loosing the colt?* or other like question. For that no one would oppose them the Saviour had foretold when He said: *And if any man shall say anything to you, say ye, that the Lord hath need of them*; or as Luke says: *And if any man shall ask you: Why do you loose him? you shall say thus unto him: Because the Lord hath need of his service*.

You will also ask if the Saviour after He had mounted upon the beasts, or upon the one, and had come to Jerusalem, had any special mission to be accomplished which needed to be done there; as according to what is actually passed over in silence, yet indicated though not openly, there was something which the ass and the colt were to perform. The order of the Beatitudes, as they are set down by Matthew, suggested this to me, in which, after the sentence: *Blessed are the poor in spirit: for theirs is the kingdom of heaven*, this was written: *Blessed are the meek: for they shall possess the land*. Observe here that to the first among the Blessed belongs the Kingdom of heaven, then those who shall possess the land; not as though they are to be on it for all time: for after they have been comforted and because they have hungered and thirsted after justice, and been filled with it, and have received mercy, and seen God, and have been called Children of God, they shall be restored again to the Kingdom of heaven.

And if an ass and a colt, upon which the Saviour rode, chance to be put before us, take care not to be scandalized at the comparison between those who have sustained Christ, and dumb beasts of burden. Something of this kind perhaps the prophet had in mind when he said that he was a beast, not literally, but before God, or before His Anointed, in these words: *I am become as a beast before thee* (Ps. lxxii. 23). For before the Majesty of God, and before His Word, not alone are we as beasts, but they also who are wiser and more intelligent than we are. Compared with the power of mind of Our Shepherd we are His sheep; for the mind of even the wisest of men compared with the wisdom which is in the Word is remoter from it than the mind of an ass or a colt or of a sheep is from that of a man.

And such are the ass and the colt which, carrying Jesus, go up to Jerusalem. But after they have come there they are no longer a beast of burden and its colt but now, transformed and enriched, made sharers of the divinity of the Word and of His sublime doctrine, and changed by the Lord, they may, for the glory of God, be returned to the place whence they were loosed; receiving this as a reward for carrying Him, that they are sent back to their former place but not to their former service. For being freed from their bonds, and honoured by carrying Christ, Our Lord Jesus Christ would not send them back again to bondage, and to baser tasks than that which they fulfilled when they had borne on their backs the Son of God.

And because of this mystery, and because of the events which are recorded with it, it is but fitting that the Daughter of Sion should greatly rejoice, and increase the fruit of joy, which is the fruit of the Spirit (Gal. v. 22), and that the Daughter of Jerusalem should *shout for joy*. For her king has come to her, the *just* and *Saviour*, not simply saving, but saving with justice and judgement, and preparing for salvation those who were to obtain it.

He came to Jerusalem and to Sion, meek, and sitting upon an ass, and upon a young colt, as we have already declared to you; visiting Israel, destroying the chariots of Ephraim, which are likened to the chariots of Pharaoh, *when He overthrew the chariots of Pharaoh, and all his host into the sea* (Ex. xv. 5; Ps. cxxxv. 15). Again He came, destroying the beast of war, the horse out of Jerusalem, that He might prepare peace for Israel, restoring the sheep which were lost; and, that He might obtain peace for Jerusalem, to bring back her children who had been driven forth. And how could this not be an event worthy of great rejoicing, that the King, the meek, the *Just and Saviour*, was thus to come to Jerusalem? When every bow of war was to be broken, so that no more should *the wicked bend their bows, and have prepared their arrows in the quiver: to shoot in the dark the upright of heart* (Ps. x. 3). Then shall there be peace and great numbers among those that believe and win salvation from among the Gentiles, the Saviour ruling *from sea to sea, and from the rivers even unto the end of the earth.*

Should anyone wish to interpret Sion and the Daughter of Jerusalem as meaning simply the people to whom the Saviour came, he can say that the Word bids the Daughter of Sion rejoice, and the Daughter of Jerusalem to proclaim. And if some do not comply with the command of His wishes, not doing the things that are worthy of joy, not accepting the command to proclaim Him, they have themselves given cause why they should suffer what they have suffered; so that it may truly be said of them: *To you the Gospel ought to be announced: but since you judge yourselves unworthy, behold we turn to the Gentiles* (Acts xiii. 46).

It should be known also that the five editions of Zachary we have seen, together with the Septuagint and Aquila, have: *He is meek, and riding upon an ass* (beast of burthen), *and a young colt*; or, *upon an ass* (asinam), *and an ass colt.* In Theodosius however we find: *He is obedient and riding upon an ass* (asinam), *and a colt the son of an ass.* In Symmachus: *He is poor, and riding upon an ass* (asinam), *and a colt the son of the ass.* In the fifth edition: *He is poor riding upon a yoked ass* (subjugalem), *and a colt the son of asses.* Someone may be able to adapt these variations to the narrative by a study of this portion of the Gospel; since gentle, and obedient, and poor the Saviour was as He entered Jerusalem. For while *being rich* yet was He poor, so that those who listen to Him, Who hears us, may through His poverty become rich (cf. II Cor. viii. 9).

We note that Matthew speaks of Bethphage, Mark of Bethania, and Luke of Bethphage and Bethania. These events took place upon a mount which is called Olivet. Bethphage, which means the House of Jawbones, was a villa belonging to the priests. Bethania means House of Obedience. They are brought to the House of Obedience who were loosed from their bonds, that there Jesus might sit upon them, and to the House of Jawbones; which name is taken from the Book of Judges, in which the Spring of the Jawbone is mentioned (Judges xv. 19) in which Samson quenched his thirst, or perhaps it represents the mystery of patience in which our Lord enjoins on us that *if a man strike thee on thy right cheek* you should then turn to him the other (Mt. v. 39). Bethphage then is, we may say, a symbol of their patience who attain to salvation; hence Jesus seated himself upon those whom the Disciples, at His command, had delivered from bonds. The mount is the Mount of Olives, the Church, where those within it, because they are fertile and fruit-bearing, declare: *But I, as a fruitful olive tree in the House of God, have hoped in the mercy of God*. And they who have been taught the beginnings of the Faith are, *as olive plants, around about thy table*, as His sons and children (Ps. cxxvii. 3).

If we turn to the consideration of the Two Disciples whom Jesus sent to bring the ass that was tied, and the colt with her, so that untied they might bring them to Him, may we not say that these stand for the two Disciples Peter and Paul, who gave to each other *the right hand of fellowship* (Gal. ii. 9), that Peter should go unto the Circumcision: to those bound to the yoke of the Law: and Paul to the colt that was unbroken: the Gentiles. Before Jesus came both the ass and the colt were in the village where they were tied: not in the City. And the Disciples loosed both and brought them to Jesus. Again, if you regard the two Disciples allegorically you will then say that one of them is of the order of those who minister to the Circumcision, the other to the Gentiles, and between them (those bidden by Jesus to loose who were to be loosed) is a fellowship of work and mind. So to anyone saying to them as they loosed, *Why loose you the colt*, or *anything*, they reply: we declare to you that the Lord has need of those who till now were in bonds. He has need of them that He may be seated upon them who are loosed from their sins, and have obtained forgiveness. For upon those who are still tied, *and fast bound with the ropes of their sins* (Prov. v. 22), upon these Jesus does not sit.

Now according to Mark and Luke we read: *You shall find a colt tied, upon which no man yet hath sat*. For nothing based on reason, or conformable to man's nature, had penetrated and taken firm hold of the colt of the Gentiles. And happy was he upon whom till now nothing based on reason had been established that God should come to rest upon him: the Word, the Son of God, so that guided by His Hand upon the reins he might reach to the Jerusalem of God. Let us dwell upon these things here put before us. And let he who is endowed with more understanding, and who receives more grace, bring to light more and better considerations upon it, and such as are more adapted to the ears of those who thirst for the clear truth of the Gospel.

And the Disciples going did as Jesus commanded them. And they brought the ass and the colt, and laid their garments upon them etc. Mark however relates the event in these words: *And going their way they found the colt tied before the gate without, in the meeting of the two ways: and they loose them*, and then he continues on till the words: *Blessed be the kingdom of our father David that cometh: peace* (Vulgate, *Hosanna*) *in the highest*. Luke however has: *And they that were sent, went their way, and found the cold standing, as he had said unto them*, and the rest which follows until the words: *If these shall hold their peace, the stones will cry out* (V. 40).

After what we have already said regarding the Two Disciples who were sent to loose the ass, and the colt that was with it, and after what we have added on this passage, we shall here expound that which is now before us, where it is related that His two Disciples going and doing as the Saviour had told them bring to Him the ass and the colt. And these they did not leave uncovered, but clothed and adorned them with the garments which were their own covering, so that the Word of God alone might be placed and take His rest upon the ass and the colt, now adorned with the clothing of those who taught them truth, guiding as with a rein the animals which were now freed of their bonds, and bearing Him.

And Jesus sat upon the garments of those who by their preaching instructed both the ass and the colt (the Circumcision and the Gentiles), and since it was fitting that every one should offer some thing to the meek King Who came riding upon an ass, and upon a colt, a very great multitude entered with Jesus into Jerusalem, who also manifested the fruit of their acceptance of the Saviour, when they spread their garments and every adornment they possessed before the ass and the colt on which He sat.

Along the way the ass and the colt followed to Jerusalem the great multitude placed their garments, so that the ass and the colt might go up to Jerusalem through places that were free of earth and earthly things, and unstained by its dust. And besides the two Disciples, and the great multitude, who spread their garments in the way, a third group is mentioned. Others adorned the way along which Jesus ascended to Jerusalem mounted upon these animals. This adorning was made with branches cut from trees, and spread on the ground on either side of the garments. Unless this is in fact a fourth group. For one was the group of Disciples who freed the animals. Another was the ass and the colt. A third was the very great crowd. And the fourth then was composed of those who cut boughs from the trees, *and strewed them in the way*. Besides these you may see here a fifth and a sixth group, from those that went before Jesus, and those that followed after.

But they who went before Him you may say are drawn from the saints and prophets who lived before His Coming; they who follow, from the Apostles and from the Just who joined Him after the Coming of the Word. And they who went before Him, and they who followed, proclaimed the same thing, for all together in one united voice they cry, proclaiming the humanity of the Saviour: *Hosanna to the son of David*; and His Second Coming in this canticle: *Blessed is he that cometh in the name of the Lord*; and His complete restoration to the House of God in the greeting: *Hosanna in the highest*. Amen.

II. St Ambrose, Bishop and Doctor

The Colt a Figure of the Gentiles[5]

Strikingly does the Lord go up to the Temple; for having turned from the Jews He will now abide in the hearts of the Gentiles. For that temple is the true one in which the Lord is adored, not in the letter but in the spirit. That is the temple of God which is based on the truths of the Christian faith, not on a structure of stone. Accordingly they who hate Him are passed by; and they who will love Him are preferred before them.

And for this He comes to the Mount of Olives, that by His heavenly strength He may plant the *young olives, whose mother is that Jerusalem, which is above* (Gal. iv. 26). Upon this mountain He is the heavenly husbandman; so that all who are planted in the House of God may one by one declare: *But I, as a fruitful olive tree in the house of God, have hoped in the mercy of God for ever* (Ps. li. 10).

And perhaps Christ is Himself the mountain. Who other than He could bring forth such fruitful olive trees; not such as bend under the weight of their fruit, but those which by the fulness of the Spirit abound with Gentiles? He it is by Whom we go up, and to Whom we ascend. He is the Door, He is the Way; Who is opened, and Who opens; on which they must knock who are to enter, and Who is adored by those that are found worthy.

And He was in a village, and a colt was tied there and an ass; it could not be loosed save by the command of the Lord. An apostolic hand loosed it. Such was the means, such the life, such the grace. Be you of such a kind: that you also may loose those that are bound.

Now let us ponder who they were, who, discovered in sin, were cast out of paradise, and banished to a village. And see how Life recalls those whom death had driven forth. And so we read, according to Matthew, *an ass* and *a colt*, so that as in the person of two human beings each sex was driven out, in the two animals either sex is recalled. Consequently in the mother ass we have a figure of Eve who erred; in the colt a figure of the people of the Gentiles. And He is seated on the colt of the ass; and rightly, *on which no man ever hath sitten*: because no man before Christ had called the people of the Gentiles into the Church. And Mark too has the same: *Upon which no man yet hath sat*. It was however held fast tied by the bonds of unbelief, in bondage to an evil master, enslaved by falsehood: but he had no just claim to dominion whom guilt, not nature, had made master. And because of this when *Lord* is said, One only is held true Lord: for there are many gods and many lords; but for us there is but One Lord and One God. And though He is not named as Lord, yet is it indicated, not by conjunction of a person, but through community of nature.

Mark introduces the beast as, *bound before the gate without*: for whosoever is outside of Christ is without in the way; but he that is in Christ is not outside in the way. *In the meeting of two ways*, he adds, where he is the certain possession of no one; and there is no stall, no roof, no manger. Unhappy the servitude with none but uncertain rights: for he that has no master will have many. Strangers will tie him fast, to make him theirs. Another frees him, that he may keep him for himself; so He makes acquaintance with harsher gifts than fetters.

And it was not without design that two Disciples are sent: Peter to Cornelius, Paul to the rest (Acts x. 23; xiii. 2). And so the persons sent are not named, only the number of them is made known. Should you ask if anyone were sent by name, let him think of Philip, whom the Spirit sent to Gaza on the occasion of his baptizing the eunuch of Queen Candace, and who sowed the word of God from Azoto *through all the cities unto Caesarea* (Acts viii. 26, 40).

Nor should we fail to note that He declared that they would then return: for they had to be formed in soul who would preach the Lord Jesus to every nation. And they who accordingly were sent, did they, while freeing the colt, speak in their own name? Far from it; they said only what the Lord had told them; that you may learn that the faith is spread among the nations of the Gentiles, not through your eloquence, but by the word of God; not by your name, but in the Name of Christ: and that before this divine authority the powers of evil, who have usurped dominion over the nations, give way and withdraw.

For which reason also was it that the Apostles spread their garments before the path of Christ, and doing this anticipated the honour shown to the preaching of the Gospel. For in the divine Scriptures garments frequently symbolize deeds showing power or moral excellence; which would by their own particular virtue so soften pagan hardness, that they would through friendly dispositions win them the assistance of a safe and favoured road.

It was not for pleasure the Lord of the world was borne a public spectacle upon the back of an ass, but that He might by the Mystery within Him caparison the inner chambers of our soul, and as a Mystic Rider occupy an interior seat in the depths of our hearts, penetrating there as it were by a certain substance of His divinity, guiding the steps of the soul, restraining the wantonness of the flesh, so that made gentle by the hand of kindness He might then wholly rule in the hearts of the Gentiles.

Happy they who have welcomed this Rider in their inmost heart! Happy they whose mouth the reins of the heavenly Word hold fast, so that it may not be loosened by a multitude of words. What is this rein, Brethren? Who shall teach me in what manner it restrains, or opens, the mouths of men? He has told me of this rein who said: *And for me, that speech may be given to me, that I may open my mouth with confidence* (Eph. vi. 19).

Speech therefore is the rein, speech the goad; and on that account it is hard for thee to kick against the goad. Thus He has here taught us to open our heart, to endure the goad, to bear the yoke. May He also teach us to put up with the restraint of others' loquacity. For rarer is the power of silence than that of speech. May he wholly instruct us Who was as one dumb, Who opened not His mouth against betrayal (Ps. xxxvii. 14), Who stood ready for the scourges (Ps. xxxvii. 18), and refused not the stripes, so that God may find prepared in us a fitting resting-place. Amen.

III. St Jerome, Priest and Doctor

The Meaning of the Gospel[6]

Matthew xxi. 1–9. *And when they drew nigh to Jerusalem.* He goes out From Jericho, drawing with Him from there a great multitude; and having given back sight to the blind, He draws near to Jerusalem. He comes back Great (cf. Mt. v. 19), enriched with mighty rewards (I Cor. ix. 18; Apoc. xxii. 12): the salvation of those who have believed in Him; and eager to enter the Tower of the Watchman, the place of the vision of God, the City of peace.

And when they had drawn near to Jerusalem, and had come to Bethphage, to the House of the Jawbones (a villa belonging to the priests, and a figure of praise to God, situated on Mount Olivet; in which we have a figure of the lamp of knowledge, and of rest from weariness and toil) He sent two of His Disciples; that is, knowledge and work (Θεωρητικὸν καὶ ἐργαστικὸν),[2] that they might go into the village.

He said to them: *Go ye into the village that is over against you.* For it was against the Apostles; and unwilling to accept the yoke of their teaching. *And immediately*, He says, *you shall find an ass tied, and a colt with her: loose them and bring them to me.* For the ass was tied with the manifold bonds of sin. The colt, wanton and unbroken, was with its mother; and according to Luke, was subject, not to one error, or to one doctrine, but to many *masters* (Lk. xix. 33). And yet the many *masters* who had claimed unlawful ownership of him, when they see the True Master, and His servants whom He had sent to free them, has come, they do not dare to oppose Him. Who this ass is, and who the colt, we shall set out in what follows.

Now all this was done that it might be fulfilled . . . This prophecy is found written in the prophet Zachary; of which we shall speak, in its proper place, if our days of life permit. Now we shall say briefly, that literally He could not ride on both animals in that short stretch of way. He either rode on the ass, and the colt was riderless; or if He sat upon the colt, which is more founded, the ass was led free. And therefore since the actual record of the fact savours of the impossible or the unseemly, let us apply ourselves to a higher interpretation; namely: that by this ass we are to understand the Synagogue, which was tamed, and broken to the yoke, and had borne the yoke of the Law. The colt of the ass, wanton and unbroken, is the people of the Gentiles, upon whom Christ sat; and that He had sent His two Disciples to them: the one to the Circumcision, and the other to the Gentiles.

And the disciples going, did as Jesus commanded . . . This colt and the ass, upon which the Apostles laid their garments, that Jesus might ride softly, were naked before the Coming of the Saviour, and, without covering, suffered from cold; and many sought to establish possession of them. But after they had received the clothing of the Apostle, and were made more seemly, they have the Lord as their Rider. The Apostolic clothing can be understood to mean, either the teaching of virtue, or the explanation of the Scriptures, or the variety of the Church's teachings; with which if a soul be not clothed and adorned it cannot merit to have Jesus seated in it.

And a very great multitude spread their garments in the way. Observe the differences between the persons represented. The Apostles lay their garments upon the ass; the crowd as lesser in degree, spread theirs before the feet of the ass; lest it should anywhere stumble on a stone, or tread on a thorn, or its foot slip into a hole.

And others cut boughs . . . and strewed them in the way. They cut branches from the fruitbearing trees with which the Mount of Olives was planted, and spread them in the way; so as to make the crooked ways straight, and the rough ways smooth, that Christ the Conqueror of sin might walk straightly and safely into the hearts of the faithful.

And the multitudes that went before and that followed . . . Since the literal order of events is manifest, let us treat of the mystical order. The crowds which had come out from Jericho, and had followed the Saviour and His Disciples, when they saw the ass's colt, which before was tied, now free and adorned with the clothing of the Apostles, and saw the Lord Jesus sitting upon it, spread their garments under Him, and strewed branches of trees in His path. And when they had done all that was to be done by their hands, they offered also the tribute of their voices; and going before and following after they cry, not in a brief and wordless confession, but with all their might: *Hosanna to the son of David. Blessed is he that cometh in the name of the Lord.*

In saying: *The multitudes that went before and that followed,* he shows that the peoples who preceded the Gospel and they who after the preaching of the Gospel believed in the Lord, with one harmonious voice give praise to Jesus, and after the example of the parable recorded earlier, of the workers who were called at different hours, they also receive the common reward of faith.

And as to the meaning of what follows: *Hosanna to the son of David,* you may remember, that many years ago I spoke of this in a short letter to Damasus, then Bishop of the city of Rome, and shall now again briefly touch on it. In the hundreth and seventeenth psalm, which manifestly was written concerning the Coming of the Saviour, among other things we also find this: *The stone which the builders rejected; the same is become the head of the corner. This is the Lord's doing; and it is wonderful in our eyes. This is the day which the Lord hath made: let us be glad and rejoice therein.*

And immediately there follows: *O Lord, save me: O Lord, give me good success. Blessed be he that cometh in the name of the Lord* etc. Where we read in the Septuagint: O Lord, save us (*O Domine, salvum fac*), in the Hebrew we read: ANNA ADONAI OSIANNA; which Symmachus has clearly rendered as saying: I beseech Thee, O Lord, save us, do, I beseech Thee.

Let no one therefore think these words are made up from two phrases, a Greek and a Hebrew, and that it is a composite utterance; for it is wholly Hebrew, and signifies that the Coming of Christ is the Salvation of the world. Hence there follows: *Blessed is he that cometh in the name of the Lord.* The Saviour also confirms this Himself in His Gospel, saying: *I am come in the name of my Father, and you receive me not: if another shall come in his own name, him you will receive* (Jn. v. 43)

And through what follows: *Hosanna in the highest*, it is distinctly indicated, that the Coming of Christ is for the salvation, not alone of men, but of the whole world: joining the things of earth to those that are above: so *that in the Name of Jesus every knee should bend, of those that are in heaven, on earth, and under the earth* (Phil. ii. 10). Amen.

IV. St John Chrysostom, Bishop and Doctor

Lessons of Today's Gospel[8]

The Lord had often entered Jerusalem; but never before with such solemnity. What then was the reason for this? The other occasions were at the beginning of His Divine Mission; neither was He yet well known, nor had his time to suffer yet come. For this reason He would then mingle freely with the people: seeking rather to remain unknown. And had He shown Himself in this manner then, He would have excited no great interest; and His enemies would have been roused to greater anger.

But when He had given sufficient proof of His power, and the Cross was at the very doors, He revealed Himself more clearly, and did publicly whatever might stir up the things that were to come. This could have happened at the beginning, but done in that way it would not have been of advantage, nor expedient. But see with me how many miracles there have been; how many prophecies fulfilled.

He said: *You shall find an ass.* He foretells that no will oppose them; and that those who would hear them would say nothing. This was no light condemnation of the Jews, that He persuades men who knew Him not at all, and whom He had not seen, to give up without a word what was theirs, and this through His Disciples. Yet this people refused to obey Him when He performed signs and wonders in their presence.

Do not look upon what happened on this occasion as being of slight importance. For Who was it persuaded them not to oppose the Disciples when their property was taken from them: poor men that they were, and tillers of the soil? What am I saying, not to oppose them? Not even to answer, or, at least, having answered then to fall silent and yield? For both facts are alike wonderful; that they said nothing when their beasts were taken away, and that when they heard that the Lord had need of them they yielded and did not oppose them; especially since they did not see the Lord Himself, but only His Disciples. From this He teaches us that He could have restrained the Jews, even against their will, when they were getting ready to lay hands on Him; and could have stricken them dumb. But He willed not to. From this He likewise teaches His Disciples, that whatsoever He might ask of them they should give. Even should He bid them give up life itself, even that must not be denied. For if these obeyed Him who knew Him not, much more should they be prepared to give up all things for Him.

Added to this He was fulfilling a twofold prophecy: the one in word, the other in deed. And that which He fulfilled in deed, He fulfilled sitting upon an ass; and that in word was the prophecy of Zacharias; for he had said: *The king will come riding upon an ass*. And riding thus He gave a beginning to another prophecy which prefigured the things to come by what He was now doing. How, and in what way? He foretold the calling of the unclean Gentiles; namely, that He would take His rest upon them; that they would come to Him, and would follow Him. And so prophecy gives way to prophecy.

But it does not seem to me that it was for this alone He rode upon the ass; but that He might also give us examples of holy wisdom. For not alone does He fulfil the prophecies, not alone did He plant the word of truth, but also in these happenings He gave us guidance regarding our lives, providing us with a rule of conduct for every need; teaching us by every means how to live worthily.

And so when He was about to be born He did not seek out a splendid home, nor look for a rich and illustrious mother, but for a poor woman, one whose husband was a carpenter. And He was born in a stable, and placed in a manger. And when He chose His Apostles, He did not choose scholars and wise men, nor rich men and high born, but poor men, of poor families, and everywhere unknown. And for His food, now He provides loaves made from barley, now He sends His Disciples to buy something in the market. His bed was of reeds, His clothing what was plain and in common use. House He had none. When He had need to go from place to place He went on foot, and so journeying grew weary. And when He sat down He had no need of throne or cushion, but sat upon the ground, sometimes on a mount, sometimes by a well; and not only by a well, but alone, as when He spoke to the Samaritan woman.

Again, giving us a right measure in grief, when He must mourn, He weeps a little; everywhere giving us, as I say, measures and standards; showing us how far we should go, and where we should stop. And so now, since it happens that some being weak will have need of a beast of burden, here too he lays down a measure, showing us there is no need of horse or mule, but that we should use an ass; and that everywhere we should confine ourselves to what we need. Let us consider this prophecy; one of words and one of deeds. What then is this prophecy? It is this:

Behold thy king will come to thee, and sitting upon an ass, and a colt the foal of her that is used to the yoke; not drawn in a chariot like other kings; not demanding a tribute, nor surrounded by officers and guards; and in this also showing meekness. Then ask the Jews: What king has ever entered Jerusalem riding upon an ass? There is none that they can say save This One.

And this, I say, He did, signifying the things that are to come. For by the colt the Church is signified; and also the new people, who before were unclean, but became clean as soon as Jesus had rested on them. And note with me how everywhere the allegory is continued. For it is the Disciples that loose the beasts. And it is through the Apostles that both we and they have been called to the faith, and through the Apostles have we been brought to Jesus. And because the glory of our calling has made these others envious, so the ass is seen to follow the colt. For after Christ has been seated upon the Gentiles, moved by jealousy they also will come. Of this Paul has warned us, saying: *That blindness in part has happened in Israel, until the fulness of the Gentiles should come in: and so all Israel should be saved* (Rom. xi. 25, 26). That this is a prophecy is plain from what has already been said. Otherwise the prophet would not have troubled to tell us the condition of the ass.

But not alone are these things foretold, but also that the Apostles would bring them without difficulty. For as no man here opposes them: preventing them: so in the Apostles' bringing in of the Gentiles not one of those who before had claimed dominion over them could withstand them.

Neither did the Lord sit upon an unclothed colt; but upon one covered by the garments of the Apostles. For they, after they find the colt, give up all things; as Paul has written: *But I most gladly will spend and be spent myself for your souls* (II Cor. xii. 15). And observe also the obedience of the colt, which though untamed and unbroken to the rein was now well behaved. This also was a prophecy of what was to come; foretelling the submissiveness of the Gentiles, and their ready turning to right order. For the words: *Loose them and bring them to me*, disposed all things towards due order: so that what was disordered might be brought to order, and what was unclean might thence forward become clean.

But observe the baseness of the Jews. So many wonders had He wrought, yet they remained indifferent; but seeing a multitude gathered, then they marvelled. *And when he was come into Jerusalem, the whole city was moved, saying: Who is this? and the people said: This is Jesus the prophet, from Nazareth of Galilee.* And when they thought themselves to be saying something great, even then their mind was commonplace, and base, and earthy. He was doing these things, not for display, but, as I say, to fulfil the prophecy, and at the same time to teach us holy wisdom. And also to comfort His Disciples, now grieving because of His death, showing them that it was of His own free will that He was to suffer.

And note the accuracy of the prophet; how he has foretold everything. David foretold some things, and Zachary others. So let us also do these things: let us cry out in hymns, and let us give our garments to those who bear Him. For of what shall we be worthy if, when others have covered with their garments the ass upon which He sat, and others have spread their clothing before His feet, we see Him naked who are not called upon to shed our garments, but to give a little, and yet do not show even this sign of zeal?

They walk before Him and follow after Him, but should He draw near to us we repel Him. How grievous the chastisement, the punishment, such conduct merits? The Lord in His need turns to you. You do not even wish to hear His petition; you reproach Him, you rebuke Him; and this too after you have been hearing such words as these. And if in the giving of a loaf or a little money you are so mean and so harsh, what would you be like if you had to give up everything?

You have seen the spendthrifts in the theatre, how much they squander on harlots? You do not bestow in alms even the half of this, nor the least part of it. Should the devil bid you to give to any chance comer, and even though you are fostering hell's fire, you give. But let Christ command you to give to someone in need, promising you a kingdom, not alone do you not give, you insult; you prefer to obey the devil, that he may punish you, than to obey Christ, and earn salvation.

What folly could be greater? The one offers you hell; the Other heaven. Yet you leave the One, and run to the other. And you repulse Him as He comes to you: He to Whom from afar you pray. And this is just as if a king, clad in the royal purple, and offering you a diadem, could not gain your good will; while a thief brandishing a sword at you, and threatening you with death, can do so easily.

Reflecting on these things, Beloved, let us even now open our eyes and be watchful. I am ashamed to speak of alms since I have spoken so often on this theme; but without any great fruit from my exhortations. You have given more, but not as much as I have need of. I see that you sow, but not with a generous hand. And because of this I fear you shall reap but sparingly!

To prove that you sow but sparingly let us, if you will, estimate who are the more numerous in the city, the rich or the poor; and who are neither rich nor poor but hold a place in between? A tenth part of the city is rich, a tenth are the poor who possess nothing; the rest hold the middle place. Let us then divide the whole city among the poor, and you will see what a shameful state of things exists. For the rich are few. They who come next are many. The poor are far fewer than these. And though there are many who feed the poor, yet many go hungry to sleep. And this not because the rich have not the wherewith to feed them, but because they are hard and unfeeling. For were the rich and those next to them to apportion amongst them those who are in need of food and clothing, you would scarcely find one poor person to be helped for fifty or even a hundred of the rest. And though there are many who can help, yet day by day the poor go wanting.

And that you may learn the inhumanity of these others, while the Church has the income of but one of the rich, and even of one of the medium rich, think of how many widows, how many virgins, she daily provides for: the number has reached three thousand. Add to those the needy she succours each day; those held in prison, the sick in the hospitals, the others who are getting on well, the pilgrims, the maimed, those who serve the altar, and those who come daily needing food and clothing. And yet her substance in no way grows less. And so were there only ten rich men prepared to give to the full, there would be no poor.

What then, you will say, would remain for our children? The principal would remain, and the income would be increased; for you would then have laid up treasure in heaven. And should you not wish to do this, then give a half, a third, or a fourth, or a fifth, or a tenth. For by God's favour it is possible for this our city to feed the poor of ten cities.

And if you wish let us reckon this up; nay, there is no need to reckon. For it is obvious how easily this could be done. See how often, and how much, one family does not hesitate to spend on a public occasion; and scarcely notices the cost? If one of the rich were to do this in the service of the poor, in one brief moment he would seize heaven.

What excuse have you, therefore, what shadow of excuse, when from that which departing from here we must leave behind we do not give as generously to the poor as others bestow on public display; and this when we could gain so much by doing so? And even were we to be in this world for ever we ought not to be sparing in this so worthy giving. But when in a little while we must go, borne naked hence, what plea have we to offer, we who from what flows into us give nothing to the poor and the hungry?

I am not urging you to give up your capital; not that I am reluctant, but because I see that you are, exceedingly so! And so I do not ask you. But spend of your returns. Gather no wealth from them. Let it suffice for you that you have a return from your money, flowing to you as from a fountain; make the poor sharers of this, and be a good steward of the things which God has given thee.

But, you will say, I pay my taxes. Is it because of this then you are scornful; that no one demands your help? You do not dare to oppose the one who compels you, and torments you: and that whether the earth bears a crop or not: but to the One that is Meek, and asks of you only when the earth is fruitful, you do not answer, even with a word? And who will deliver you from these intolerable punishments? There is no one who can. For if in the first case you pay up quickly, because of the punishments for non-payment, then reflect that here even severer punishments await you: not merely to be bound, not simply to be thrown in prison, but to *depart into eternal fire*.

Let us then because of this pay these taxes first. For great is the facility for payment, and greater still the reward; and the greater our means the greater the punishment should we act unworthily. For a punishment shall come upon you that will have no end. But if you offer me as an excuse the needs of the men who are fighting for you against the barbarian, there is here also an army, of the poor, who wage war and fight on your behalf. For when they receive from you, by their prayers they win the favour of God for you; and in placating Him they repulse the assaults, not of the barbarians, but of the devils. They overcome the violence of the evil one, and do not permit him to attack unceasingly; and they weaken his strength.

When therefore you see those soldiers fighting daily on your behalf with the devil by their prayers, demand from yourself a good contribution: their food. For their king being *mild* He has laid it on no one to *demand* it from you, desiring that you give it freely; and even though you pay little by little, He accepts it. And if being in difficulties you do not pay it for a long time, He will not press him that has not.

Let us not then abuse His patience. Let us treasure up for ourselves, not wrath, but salvation; not death, but life; not penalties and punishment, but honour and a crown. There is no need here to pay the cost of the transport of your offerings; no need here to labour to turn them into money. If you but lay them down, the Lord will raise them to heaven. He will Himself make the transaction profitable for you. There is no need here to find someone to carry what you have offered. Offer it, and straightaway your offering ascends to heaven; not that by it soldiers may be fed, but that it may be laid up for you with greater profit. Here below whatever you pay you cannot recover; there you shall receive it again, with great honour, and receive greater and spiritual profits. Here what is given is demanded; there it is a loan, capital, a debt. For God has given you a bond: *He that hath mercy of the poor, lendeth to the Lord* (Prov. xix. 17).

He gave you also a pledge and a security, though He is God. What kind of a pledge? The things of the present life; visible things, spiritual things, the beginnings of that which is to come. Why then do you hesitate; why are you reluctant, when you have received so many and such things, and look forward to so many? For what you have received are these: He gave you a body, and He placed a soul in it. You alone on the earth has He honoured with reason. He has given you the use of whatever is visible; and bestowed on you the knowledge of Himself. He gave up His Son for you. He has given you a baptism that bears with it many gifts, and a holy table, and promised you a kingdom, and things which cannot be described.

So much have you received, and so much are you yet to receive, and yet you are sparing of money that will perish? And what excuse will you have? You look at your children, and you make excuses because of them. Teach these also to seek the same kind of gain. For if you have your capital placed at interest, and your debtor is an upright man, you would certainly prefer to leave a bond to your child instead of gold, so that he would thus have a safe return, and not be forced to seek others with whom to place it. Give such a deed to your children now, and leave them God as their debtor. You do not sell your fields, but leave them to your children: that they may have an income, and so that the increase of the property comes to them. Do you fear to leave them *this* deed: so much more fruitful than any field, or any yield whatever? What great folly, what madness, would this be! And this when you know that leaving it to them, you yet bring it with you when you go from here. For such things being spiritual have in them a great fruitfulness.

Let us then not be poor in spirit; nor without mercy towards ourselves. But let us invest in this worthy enterprise: so that we may both bring it with us when we depart this life, and still leave it to our children; and so doing we shall attain to the things that are to come by the grace and mercy of Our Lord Jesus Christ, to Whom with the

Father and the Holy Ghost let there be glory honour and majesty now and for ever world without end. Amen.

V. St Leo the Great, Pope and Doctor

On the Passion of our Lord[9]

Synopsis:

I. How weak the human understanding in presence of divine mysteries?
II. Belief in the Incarnation is taught us through the Creed. The steadfastness of Peter's faith; because of which the Rock Peter was made the Foundation of the Church.
III. The devil deceived by his own wickedness. Christ's prayer for His enemies brought them, through Peter's preaching, to faith.
IV. That Christ died for all sinners. Judas also could have obtained pardon had he not hastened to the noose.
V. By the will of the Jews Christ's death was cruel; but wondrous by His power Who died.

I. The Festival of the Passion, Dearly Beloved, so earnestly looked forward to, so desired of all men, is now here; and it does not suffer us to remain silent in face of the exultation rising from our joy of soul. For though it is not easy, time after time, to speak in a fitting and worthy manner upon this same solemnity, yet it is not lawful for the priest to withhold from the ears of the faithful the ministry of his word upon this so great mystery of the divine compassion: since this subject, in that it is unutterable, gives matter without end for speaking; nor may what we say fall short, for of what we speak never can there be enough.

Let human weakness bow down before the glory of God. May it ever find itself unequal to the task of unfolding the works of the divine mercy. Let us labour in our understanding. Let us remain poor in talent, and wanting in the power of words. It is good for us to learn how little we truly know of the Majesty of God. For the prophet tells us: *Seek ye the Lord and be strengthened: seek his face for evermore* (Ps. civ. 4). So no one may presume that he has found all that he is seeking; lest he cease to be close to Him who has ceased to draw near Him.

And among all the works of God, before which the mind grows faint with awe, which so rejoices yet overwhelms the soul as the Passion of our Saviour? For as often as we dwell, as best we can, upon His Omnipotence, which He shares with the Father in one and the same nature, more wondrous does His lowliness seem to us than His power; and with more difficulty do we grasp His emptying Himself of the divine Majesty, than His sublime uplifting of the form of a servant. Yet it helps us greatly to understand, that while One is the Creator, one the created—One the inviolable Divinity, one the suffering flesh—what belongs to either nature meets in the single Person: so that whether in might or in suffering His the humiliation Whose also the glory.

II. By this rule of faith, which we learn from the beginning of the Creed on the authority of Apostolic

Teaching, we confess, that the Lord Jesus Christ, Whom we declare to be the Only Son of God, the Father Almighty, was also born of the Holy Ghost from the Virgin Mary. Nor do we deny His Majesty when we believe that He was crucified and died, and that on the third day He rose again. For His divinity together with His humanity has fulfilled all that was required of God and of man: yet so that while the impassible was present in the passible, Power was not diminished by infirmity, nor infirmity swallowed up by Power.

With reason was the blessed Apostle Peter praised for his confession of this unity: he who, when the Lord asked whom did the Disciples say He was, quickly forestalling the words of all the rest, said: *Thou art the Christ the Son of the living God.* And this he saw, not through anyone of flesh and blood telling him, for their telling it could have but hindered his inward seeing, but through the Spirit of the Father, working in his own believing heart, so that, while he was being prepared for the ruling of the universal Church, he might first learn what he was to teach, and might hear, as a reward for his firmness in the faith he was to teach: *Thou art Peter, and upon this rock I will build my Church, and the gates of hell shall not prevail against it* (Mt. xvi. 16).

For this the strong Christian faith which, built upon an indestructible rock, fears not the gates of death, confesses One Lord Jesus Christ Who is both True God and true man; believing that the Same is the Virgin's Son Who is the Author of the mother; that the Same was born at the end of ages Who is the Author of all times; that the Same is both Lord of all Majesty and one of the race of mortal men; and, that He Who is without Sin *in the likeness of sinful flesh* was offered up in behalf of sinners.

III. That He might deliver man from the bonds of the death-bringing transgression, He concealed the power of His Majesty from the fury of the devil (cf. I Cor. ii. 8), and offered him instead the infirmity of our lowliness. For had this proud and cruel enemy known the plan of God's mercy, he would have striven rather to temper with mildness the hearts of the Jews than to inflame them with evil hate, so that he might not lose the slavery of all his captives, while he pursued the liberty of the One Who owed him nothing.

And so he was tricked by his own wickedness. He inflicted a torment on the Son of God which was changed into a medicine for all the sons of men. He shed innocent Blood, Which then became both the price and the drink which restored the world. The Lord took upon Himself what He had freely chosen. He suffered upon Himself the impious hands of those who raged against Him, who while intent on their dreadful crime yet served the plan of the Redeemer. And such was the tenderness of His love, even for those who put Him to death, that from the Cross He begged His Father, not that He be revenged, but that they might be forgiven; crying out, *Father, forgive them, for they know not what they do* (Lk. xxiii. 34).

And it was certainly through the power of this intercession that the hearts of many of those who had cried, *His blood be upon us and upon our children* (Mt. xxvii. 25), were changed to repentance at the preaching of the Apostle Peter, so that in one day there were baptized *about three thousand* of the Jews (Acts ii. 41), and they became all of *one heart and one soul* (Acts iv. 32); ready to give their lives for Him for Whose crucifixion they had clamoured.

IV. The traitor Judas did not attain to this mercy, for *the son of perdition* (Jn. xvii. 12), at whose right hand the devil had stood (Ps. cviii. 6), had before this died in despair; even while Christ was fulfilling the mystery of the general redemption. Even he perhaps might have obtained this forgiveness, had he not hastened to the gallowstree; for the Lord died for all evildoers. But nothing ever of the warnings of the Saviour's mercy found place in that wicked heart: at one time given over to petty cheating, and then committed to this dread parricidal traffic.

On these impious ears in vain had fallen the words of the Lord, declaring: *I am not come to call the just, but sinners* (Mt. ix. 13); or the words: *I came not to call the just, but sinners to penance* (Lk. v. 32). Neither had he given thought to the clemency of Christ, Who ministered not alone to the infirmities of the body, but healed likewise the wounds of the injured soul; as in His words to the paralytic: *Be of good heart, son, thy sins are forgiven thee* (Mt. ix. 3); and to the woman brought before Him who was an adultress: *Neither will I condemn thee, Go, and now sin no more* (Jn. viii. 11), so that He might show throughout all His works that in this Coming He had appeared, not as the Judge of the world, but as its Saviour. But the Godless betrayer, shutting his mind to all these things, turned upon himself, not with a mind to repent, but in the madness of self-destruction: so that this man who had sold the Author of life to the executioners of His death, even in the act of dying sinned *unto the increase* of his own eternal punishment.

V. This, therefore, which false witnesses, which bloodstained rulers, which impious priests, have done to the Lord Jesus Christ by means of a coward judge and the aid of the imperial soldiery, must be both lovingly embraced, and repudiated with horror, for all ages to come. For the Cross of the Lord, an instrument of torture in the intention of the Jews, is become glorious in the might of the Crucified. The multitude raged against one man; Christ had compassion on all men. What was inflicted through cruelty was suffered by majesty: so that in the permitting of the evil deed, the purpose of the eternal will might be accomplished.

For this reason the whole order of events, as narrated so fully in the Gospel, must be so accepted by the faithful; that while believing in what was done when the passion of Christ was being fulfilled, we may come to understand that in Christ, not alone were our sins remitted, but there was set here before us the perfect model of love. But that we may with God's help expound this more at length, we shall keep this part of our sermon till the fourth hour of the sabbath. By the grace of God and the aid of your good prayers we hope to fulfil this promise, through Christ Jesus Our Lord, Who with the Father and the Holy Ghost will reign for ever. Amen.

NOTES

[1] Possibly because of the injunction given to Moses and Aaron, for priests. Lev. xi. 3; and relating especially to beasts which have not the hoof divided, and chew the cud, Deut. xiv. 7; figures of *meditating* on the Law of God, and of the *discernment* of good and evil.

[2] In the Hebrew Zacharias speaks of a *chamor asinum*, or male ass. The Greek translators of Matthew have *ὄνον*, which as in English means ass, male or female. The Vulgate renders it *asinam*. The Septuagint records Zacharias as speaking of *ὑποξύγιον πῶλον ὄνον; ὑποξύγιον* meaning *beast of burden*. It may be that the mystic parallelism, latent in the prophecy, here comes clearer, with the near approach of salvation to the Gentiles.

[3] CSEL 43, p. 228 *seq*.

[4] PG 13, in Matt. xvi. 14–18.

[5] CSEL 32, 4. Bk. 9 in Luke; PL 15, col. 1795. This homily is a most striking and authoritative testimony to the intrinsic power of the word of God, spoken in the preaching of the Gospel; at once an encouragement to human diffidence, and an inducement to preach it correctly, steadfastly and worthily, however imperfect the human instrument. Its power cannot be defeated nor its message controverted.

[6] PL 26, III, 21.

[7] The contemplative and the active.

[8] PG 58, Hom. 67 in Matt.

[9] PL 54, Sermo. 62, *De passione Domini* XI. To some it may seem contradictory that the Saint speaks of the Commemoration of the Passion as a festival, and says it delights the soul. But the day of His Death was the day of our deliverance, and so a day of joy; hence also, in the belief of the faithful: Good Friday.

IN THE HOLY NIGHT OF THE PASCH

I. St Amphilochius of Iconium: The Solemnity and Burial of Our Saviour

II. St Augustine: On the Vigil of Easter

III. St Augustine: Watchfulness Against the Devil

IV. St John Chrysostom: Against Drunkenness

V. St Leo the Great: For the Resurrection of the Lord

VI. The Venerable Bede: The Giving of Peace

THE GOSPEL OF HOLY SATURDAY

Matthew xxviii. 1–7

And in the end of the sabbath, when it began to dawn towards the first day of the week, came Mary Magdalen and the other Mary, to see the sepulchre. And behold there was a great earthquake. For an angel of the Lord descended from heaven, and coming, rolled back the stone, and sat upon it. And his countenance was as lightning, and his raiment as snow. And for fear of him, the guards were struck with terror, and became as dead men. And the angel answering said to the women: Fear not you, for I know that you seek Jesus who was crucified. He is not here, for he is risen, as he said. Come, and see the place where the Lord was laid. And going quickly, tell ye his disciples that he is risen: and behold he will go before you into Galilee; there you shall see him. Lo, I have foretold it to you.

Exposition from the Catena Aurea

V. 1. *And in the end of the sabbath, when it began to dawn.*

Augustine, *Serm. on the Resurrection*: After the blows and the mockery, after the gall and the drink of vinegar, after the agony and the wounds of the cross, the new Body, returning more beautiful than before, has risen again from its grave; the latent life returning from its setting, and the salvation that was laid up for us in His death now appears.[1]

Augustine, *Harmony of the Gospels*, III, 24, 65: A question here rises which we may not lightly pass over: as to the hour at which the women came to the tomb. For when Matthew tells us that: *In the end of the sabbath, when it began to dawn towards the first day of the week*, what does Mark mean when he says: *And very early in the morning, the first day of the week, they come to the sepulchre?* Now, by the first part of the night, which is here called evening (*vespere*), Matthew desired to refer to this very night at the close of which they came to the tomb. Since they were prevented by the sabbath from coming earlier, he calls night the time in which it began to be lawful for them to do whatever they did in the course of that night. The words therefore: *In the end of the sabbath* (*vespere autem sabbathi*) are used, as though he would say: In the night of the day of the sabbath; that is, in the night following the day of the sabbath.

His words express this. For he goes on: *When it began to dawn towards the first day of the week*; and this could not be the case if by the words, *end of the sabbath* (*vespere*) we were to understand only the first brief part of the night; that is, merely the beginning of the night. For it was not the actual beginning of the night, that began to dawn towards the first day of the week, but the night itself; which began to end with the break of day. It is a frequent practice of Holy Scripture to signify the whole by the part. By evening (*vespere*) the Evangelist signifies the whole night: whose extremity is the first light of day. They therefore came to the tomb as it began to dawn.[2]

BEDE *in Matthew*: Or again; That it was said, namely: that *in the evening of the sabbath, as it began to dawn towards the first day of the week, the women came to see the sepulchre*, must be understood to mean that they began to come in the evening, but that they arrived at the sepulchre as the first day of the week was breaking; that is, in the evening they prepared the sweet spices, with which they desired to anoint the body of the Lord, but brought them to the tomb in the morning; which Matthew relates a little obscurely, for the sake of brevity; but the other Evangelists show more clearly in what order the events took place.

For the Lord being buried on the sixth day, the women, returned from the tomb, got ready the spices and ointments for as long as it was permissible for them to work. On the sabbath they rested, according to the commandment of the Law; and as Luke expressly tells us. But when the sabbath had passed, and with the night drawing on, the time to work returned. Eager in their devotion, they *bought spices* (according to Mark) of which they had prepared an insufficient quantity, so that *coming they might anoint Jesus, and very early in the morning they come to the sepulchre*.

JEROME, *in Matthew*: That different times concerning the women are referred to in the Gospels is not a sign of untruth, as the impious assert, but the dutiful service of loving devotion; since they repeatedly go and return, and cannot endure to stay for long, or afar, from the tomb of their Lord.

REMIGIUS: We should mark how Matthew, mystically speaking, seeks to impress on us what greatness this most blessed night receives from the glory of the Lord's Resurrection and triumph over death. Accordingly, he said: *And in the end of the sabbath etc.* For since the usual ordering of time has it that evening does not lighten into day, but rather darkens into night, he shows by his words that the Lord made this whole night joyful and shining by the light of His own Resurrection.[3]

BEDE: From the beginning of earthly creation until now, the course of time has been so divided that day precedes the night; because man, fallen through sin from the light of paradise, has turned away into the toils and darkness of this world. But now most fittingly does day follow night, since through faith in the Resurrection we are, through the bounty of Christ, brought back from the shadow of death and the darkness of sin to the light of life.[4]

SEVERIANUS, *Sermon on the passion*:[5] It is the sabbath that began to be given light: for the sabbath is illumined by Christ, not abolished. *I am not come*, He says, *to destroy the Law, but to fulfil* (Mt. v. 17). It is enlightened so that in the day of the Lord it may shine; that grows clear in the Church which grows dark in the Synagogue: the Jews seeking to obscure it.

Then follows: *There came Mary Magdalen and the other Mary, to see the sepulchre.* At length woman hastens to receive forgiveness, who early had hastened to sin. She who had begun unfaith in paradise, hastens to begin faith at the sepulchre.[6] She hastened to receive life from death, who had taken death from life. The Evangelist does not say, they came, but *Mary came* (*non dixit venerunt, sed venit*); under the one name two came: in mystery, not in grammar. She came, but also *the other*; that woman might be changed, not in name, but in soul; in excellence, not in sex. *Came Mary Magdalen and the other Mary.*

The women, who are a figure of the churches, precede the Apostles to the tomb of the Lord; Mary, namely, and Mary: as she came so also *the other*: the other as she: Mary the Mother of Christ, *the other Mary* also. The one name is repeated for the two women, because here the Church, arising from two peoples (that is, from the Jews and from the Gentiles), is prefigured as one coming from the two peoples.

Mary came to the tomb, as to the womb of the Resurrection: that Christ Who was born from a womb of flesh might be born again from the tomb of faith; and that He Whom sealed virginity had born into this present life, the sealed tomb would give forth to life eternal. It is a token of Divinity, that He should leave the virgin womb inviolate after childbirth; and come forth in His Body from the tomb that was sealed.[7]

V. 2. *And there was a great earthquake . . .*

JEROME: Our Lord, One and the Same the Son of God and of man, according to the natures both of the divinity and of man, sets up now a sign of His Majesty, now one of His lowliness. And so in this present place, though it is a man who was crucified and buried, yet what took place, apart from Him, shows that He was the Son of God (the sun darkening, the earth trembling etc.).

HILARY, *in Matthew*: The earthquake signifies the power of the Resurrection; for the sting of death now crushed, and the dark places made light by the rising up of the Lord of Hosts, hell is shaken by alarm.

CHRYSOSTOM, *Hom.* 90 *in Matthew*: Or, the earth was shaken so that the women might be aroused and awakened from sleep. For they had come to anoint His Body, and as they were about to do this during the night, it is possible that some slept.

BEDE, *as above*: That a great earthquake took place at the Resurrection of the Lord (and also while He lay dying upon the Cross), signifies that earthly hearts must first be shaken to repentance through faith in His Passion and Resurrection: stirred up by a most salutary fear.

SEVERIANUS, *as above*: If the earth so trembled when the Lord arose for the forgiveness of the sanctified, how will it not tremble when He shall arise for the punishment of the wicked? As the prophet says: *Thou hast caused judgement to be heard from heaven: the earth trembled and was still* (Ps. lxxv. 9). And how shall he endure the presence of the Lord, who could not sustain the presence of an angel? For there follows: *For an angel of the Lord descended from heaven.* For Christ rising from the dead, and death dying, heavenly intercourse is restored to the people of earth; and to woman who had held deathly converse with the devil, life-giving speech is made now by an angel.

HILARY: It is a sign of the clemency of the Father, that, His Son rising from hell He should send down the ministry of the heavenly powers. And so this is the first sign of the Resurrection, in that by a kind of favour of the Will of the Father the Resurrection is made known.

BEDE: For since Christ is both God and man, never, amid his human activities is He without the ministry that is due to the Lord of Angels. There follows: *And coming, rolled back the stone.* Not that he may open a way for the Lord to come forth: but that he might open to the eyes of men evidences of His going forth, already accomplished. For He Who while yet mortal, in being born, could enter this world leaving sealed the womb of the Virgin, now immortal could, rising up from the still sealed tomb, go forth from the world.

REMIGIUS: Rolling back the stone signifies the opening out of the mysteries of Christ, which had been concealed under the Law. And the Law had been written on stone, and so is typified by the stone.

SEVERIANUS, *as above*: He did not write, rolled (*volvit*), but, *rolled back the stone* (*revolvit lapidem*); for the stone rolled to, proved His death; rolled back, it became the proclaimer of His Resurrection. Here the order of things is changed: the tomb devours death, not the Dead; the abode of death becomes the dwelling place of Life. We learn of a new kind of womb: which receives the dead, and brings forth the living.

And sat upon it. He in whom there was no weariness, I say, sits down; but he sits as a Doctor of the faith, as a Teacher of the Resurrection. And he sat upon a stone, so that the stability of his seat might give steadfastness to those who would believe. The Angel placed upon a rock the foundation of faith; upon which Christ was to build His Church.

Or the stone of the sepulchre can mean death: by which all men were held down. By this therefore that the angel sat upon the stone is signified, that Christ by His own power has conquered death.

BEDE: And rightly did that angel stand who foretold the Coming of the Lord into the world; that by standing he would show that the Lord would come to wage war against the prince of this world. But the Herald of the Resurrection is recorded as sitting, that sitting he might signify that the Lord, having overthrown the author of death, would now ascend to the throne of His everlasting kingdom. He sat upon a stone rolled back, by which the entrance to the tomb had been closed, that he might teach that the Lord had thrown down the gates of hell by His own power.

AUGUSTINE, *Harmony of the Gospels* 3, 24, 63: It is a puzzle how, according to Matthew, the angel was sitting outside upon the stone rolled back from the tomb, while Mark says that the women entering in to the tomb saw an angel sitting within the sepulchre, on the right hand side, unless we understand either that Matthew was silent regarding the angel they saw when they went in, and that Mark said nothing of the angel they saw sitting outside on the stone. So that they saw two angels, and learned from the two, and from each singly, what they had said concerning Jesus.

At all events we should accept what Mark says: *and entering into the sepulchre*, as meaning, entering into a kind of enclosure; that is, a space in front of the rock from which the tomb had been cut out, which was surrounded by a fence, and that they saw the same angel sitting within this space, on the right hand side, who, as Matthew says, was seated upon the stone.

V. 3. *And his countenance was as lightning, and his raiment white . . .*

SEVERIANUS, *as above*: The brightness of his countenance is distinguished from that of his garments. His face is compared to the lightning, his garments to snow: for lightning is from heaven, snow from the earth. And so the prophet says: *Praise the Lord from the earth; fire, hail, snow* (Ps. cxlviii. 7). The splendour of his heavenly nature is shown in his countenance; in his garments the cheerfulness of human companionship is signified. And the appearance of the angel is so regulated, that human eyes can both perceive the pleasing beauty of his garments, and, because of the brightness of his countenance, tremble and stand in awe at the message of his Author.

THE SAME, *in the sermon following*: Why does he wear a garment who has no need of clothing? The angel prefigures to us our future state of body, our own perfection, our own appearance at the resurrection, when man will be clothed in the splendour of his own risen body. JEROME: The angel by his shining garment signifies also the glory of the Triumphant Saviour.

GREGORY, *in Hom. Paschal*: Or, in the lightning is the terror of awe; in the snow the soothing of what is white. For as the Omnipotent God is both terrifying to sinners, and the Comfort of the just, rightly is His Angel, the Witness of the Resurrection, shown to us with countenance as the lightning, and with garments shining white: that by his appearance he may both terrify the wicked, and console the just.

V. 4. *And for fear of him the guards were struck with terror . . .*

RHABANUS MAURUS: They who are without the confidence of love were terrified by the force of their fear; and they who believed not in the truth of the Resurrection are become as dead men.

SEVERIANUS: From motives of cruelty, not from the desire to do Him reverence, they place guards around the tomb. He cannot stand upright whom conscience has forsaken, and guilt throws to the ground. Hence is it that the angel strikes these men down, the wicked, and speaks to and comforts the good. Then follows:

V. 5. *And the angel answering, said to the women: fear not you . . .*

JEROME: The guards struck by fear lie senseless and as dead men; yet the angel did not seek to comfort them, but the pious women, saying to them: *Fear you not*; as if to say: Let them fear in whom there is no faith, but you, because you seek Jesus Who was crucified, hear you that He is risen, and that He has fulfilled what He promised. Hence there follows: *for I know that you seek Jesus who was crucified.*

SEVERIANUS: For it was one that had been crucified and put to death they were seeking. The storm of His passion had shaken their faith, and the weight of temptation lay on them, as they looked for the Lord of heaven in a tomb.

V. 6. *He is not here, for he is risen, as he said.*

RHABANUS MAURUS: He is not here in the Flesh of His Body, Who is no where absent in the Presence of His Majesty; *for he is risen, as he said.* CHRYSOSTOM, *Hom.* 90 *in Matthew*: As though he says: Though you believe me not, recall to your minds His own words. Then there follows another proof when he says: *Come, and see the place where the Lord was laid.*

SEVERIANUS: The Angel therefore announces His Name, makes mention of His Cross, and speaks of His Passion; and then of His Resurrection, and then also confesses He is the Lord. And if after such torments, and after His burial, an angel acknowledges Him as Lord, why should any man think that God became less through His humanity, or that He was without power in His Passion?

He speaks of Him as crucified, and shows them the place where the Lord was laid, lest another, and not Him, might be believed to be risen from the dead. And if the Lord returns in the same Flesh, and gives us proof of His Resurrection, why should any man believe he will himself return in another flesh? Shall the servant disdain his own flesh, when the Lord did not exchange from ours?

V. 7. *And going quickly, tell ye his disciples that he is risen . . .*

RHABANUS: Not to you alone was the great joy bestowed: to hold the secret in your heart: you must make it known to all who love Him. Hence we have: *And going quickly, tell ye . . .* SEVERIANUS: As though he says: Return to your husband, O woman now healed, and persuade him to believe, you who before persuaded him to unbelief. Tell the man of this sign of the Resurrection, whom once you counselled to his ruin.

And behold he will go before you into Galilee. CHRYSOSTOM, *as above*: He says this, snatching them out of danger, so that fear may not disturb their faith. JEROME: Mystically, He will go before ye *into Galilee*; that is, into the wallow of the Gentiles, where before was error, a slippery place, where the foot had no secure and stable hold. Then follows: *There you shall see him. Lo, I have foretold it to you.* BEDE: Fittingly is it in Galilee the Disciples see the Lord, Who now has passed over from death to life, from mortality to immortality. For Galilee means *passing over*. Happy women, who merited to make known to others the triumph of the Resurrection. Happier still the souls, who in the day of judgement, when the wicked are stricken with fear and trembling, shall have merited to enter in to the joy of Resurrection!

I. ST AMPHILOCHIUS OF ICONIUM

For Holy Saturday[8]

The Solemnity of the Burial of Our Saviour

1. Let us commemorate today the solemnity of the burial of Our Saviour. He has undone the bonds of death of those who were in hell, filled hell with His splendour, and roused from sleep those lying there; and we on earth rejoice exultant, recalling to mind His Resurrection, and now we fear death no more, for it shall not prevail against immortality. *Because thou wilt not*, says the Scripture, *give thy holy one to see corruption* (Ps. xv. 10).

It may be that the Jews and the Greeks will laugh at our wisdom; the former looking for another Christ, the latter bringing their own hopes to an end in the grave; of whom the prophet has rightly said: *And their sepulchres shall be their houses for ever* (Ps. xlviii. 12). They now laugh, but they shall weep: for they shall weep when they look upon Him *Whom they have pierced* (Zach. xii. 10), and tormented with injuries. We now weep, but our grief will be tempered with joy.

Death has seized Our Lord Jesus Christ; but shall not keep its hold on Life. It swallowed Him; it swallowed Him, not knowing Him: but, with Him, it will give up many. Of His own will He is now held; tomorrow, He shall rise again, and hell shall be emptied. Yesterday, on the Cross, He darkened the sun's light, and behold in full day it was as night; today death has lost its dominion; suffering itself a kind of death. Yesterday the earth mourned, contemplating the evil hate of the Jews, and in sadness clothed itself in a garment of darkness. Today, *the people that walked in darkness have seen a great light* (Is. ix. 2).

Yesterday the earth trembled, as though it would dissolve, threatening to swallow those who dwelt in it; and the mountains were cleft asunder, the rocks were split, the Temple appeared as though naked, and as though it were a living being threw off its veil; seeking as it were to show by what had happened to itself that its holy places were no longer sacred to the Lord. They that suffered these things were lifeless, without mind. The elements mourned, as though it wanted little for them to dissolve in chaos, and bring disaster on the world, were it not that they could see the purpose of their Maker: namely, that of His own will He suffered.

2. O new and unheard of happening! He is stretched out upon a Cross Who by His word *stretched out the heavens* (Is. li. 13). He is held fast in bonds Who has *set the sand a bound for the sea* (Jer. v. 22). He is given gall to drink Who has given us wells of honey. He is crowned with thorns Who has crowned the earth with flowers. With a reed they struck His Head Who of old struck Egypt with ten plagues, and submerged the head of Pharaoh in the waves. That countenance was spat upon at which the Cherubim dare not gaze. Yet, while suffering these things He prayed for His tormentors, saying: *Father, forgive them, for they know not what they do* (Lk. xxiii. 34).

He overcame evil by goodness. Christ undertook the defence of those who put Him to death: eager to gather them into His net; annulling the charge, and pleading their ignorance. Made the sport of their drunken frenzy, He submitted without bitterness. He suffered their drunkenness, and in His love for mankind called them to repentance. What more could He do?

Profiting nothing from that goodness, they enclose Him in a tomb Whom creation cannot contain. They seal the tomb, safe-guarding our deliverance; and fearing He would rise again, they station soldiers to watch the sepulchre. Who has ever seen the dead placed under watch? Or rather, who has ever seen a dead body treated as an enemy? Who has ever seen one struck by death causing fear to those who have slain him? Who fears his enemy, once he has killed him? And who will not forget his enmity when sated by the death of his adversary?

Why do you still fear Him, ye Jews, Him Whom you have done away with? Why do you dread Him Whom you have slain? Why do you still dread Him Who has gone forth from among the living? Why do you fear the dead? Why do you still fight with One Whom you have crucified? His slaughter has made you safe: rest secure. If it is a mere man who has died, he will not rise again. If it is a mere man has died, then there is no truth in those words of His: *Destroy this temple, and in three days I will raise it up.*

If He was a mere man, then death will keep him. If He was a mere man, what need to seal His tomb: is it not useless? Wait till the third day, and see the disproof of His madness? Cease to labour in vain, and you will see what comes to pass. Cease to rage against the truth. Do not try to wage war against

God, inflicting wounds only on yourself. Cease offering insults to the Sun of justice: thinking you can put out its light. Cease I say, and do not try to seal up the fountain of life.

Do not begin to make difficulties for yourself. Do not speak of guards. Have no traffic with corruption; and the bribing of those who keep watch. Do not attempt what is foolish; nor spend what you have in impiety; nor imagine that you will defeat God. Do not give money to the soldiers, to say this and not that. Do not set a crowd to watch the tomb. Put not your trust in armour. The Resurrection will not be stopped by force of arms; nor impeded by seals; nor put down by soldiers; nor concealed by bribes. Rather it shall be believed in.

Have you not seen Lazarus a little while ago throw off death as though it were a sleep? Have you not seen him come forth, clothed in his cerements, at the words: *Come forth*? Have you not seen the dead obedient to His voice when He bade him come: and the winding sheet did not prevent Him? Have you not seen how His voice restored a man already dissolving in death? He Who did that can also do this. He Who raised His own servant, much more shall He Himself be raised up. He Who gave life again to a body already corrupting shall not leave Himself in death.

The great blindness of the Jews, who, beholding these wonders, yet could not see: For, *they have eyes and see not*! For, *the god of this world hath blinded the minds of unbelievers, that the light of the Gospel may not shine unto them* (Ps. cxiii. 5; II Cor. iv. 4). But let us for a time leave these unhappy ones in their unbelief, and let us, while contemplating in spirit the tomb of our Saviour, say with the faithful Mary: They have taken away our Lord, and we know not where they have laid Him. To Him and to the Father Undefiled, together with the Holy Spirit, be there glory for ever and ever. Amen.

II. St Augustine, Bishop and Doctor

The Vigil of Easter[9]

Sacred Vigils. How they are to be celebrated. The Blessed Paul, exhorting us to imitate him, among many other things which are indications of his own virtue, speaks also of: *frequent watchings* (II Cor. xi. 27). How much the more eagerly should we keep watch during this vigil, the mother of all the sacred vigils, when the whole world watches? Not the world of which it was written: *If any man love the world, the charity of the Father is not in him. For all that is in the world, is the concupiscence of the flesh, and the concupiscence of the eyes, and the pride of life, which is not of the Father* (I Jn. ii. 15).

The devils and their angels rule that world; that is, the children of unbelief. Against these we wage war, as the same Apostle tells us where he says: *For our wrestling is not against flesh and blood; but against principalities and powers, against the rulers of the world of this darkness* (Eph. vi. 12). And we also, till now, were darkness, but now we are light in the Lord (Eph. v. 8). And so by the light of our vigils let us stand firm against the rulers of darkness.

It is not that world then which watches during this vigil, but this, of which it was said: *For God indeed was in Christ, reconciling the world to himself, not imputing to them their sins* (II Cor. v. 19). Nevertheless, so great is the splendour of this vigil throughout the whole world, that they also are, bodily, compelled to watch who are, not simply sleeping, but wholly buried in tartarean iniquity. They also watch this night, during which what was long ago foretold is now made visible:[10] *And night shall be light as the day* (Ps. cxxxviii. 12). This has place in the hearts of the just, to whom it was said: *For you were heretofore darkness, but now light in the Lord* (Eph. v. 8). This has place for all who take part; both those whose eyes are on the Lord, and those who do not praise Him.

This night then the whole world keeps vigil: the world that hates Him, and the world restored to Him. The one, now delivered, watches that it may give praise to its deliverer; the other, now condemned, that it may blaspheme its Judge. The one keeps watch, fervent and loving in the mind of the just; the other, weeping and gnashing its teeth. Love inspires one, hate the other; the Christian rules one, diabolic envy the other. Thus, without knowing, even our enemy teaches us how we should keep watch for our own sake, when he, because of us, keeps watch who envies us.

Yet many there are among those in no way signed with the Name of Christ who are in sorrow, many in shame. And many who draw near to faith sleep not through fear of God. For many reasons the holy solemnity rouses them. How then shall he not keep watch rejoicing who is a friend of Christ, when he who is His enemy watches though in suffering? How the Christian should be on fire to keep watch for this so great glory of Christ, when the Pagan is ashamed to sleep? How fitting it is that he who has entered this great House should keep watch in this solemnity, when he already keeps watch who is arranging to enter? Let us then watch and pray: that both within and without we may celebrate this vigil. God speaks to us in the holy Scriptural readings. Let us speak to Him in our prayers. If we listen obediently to His voice, He to Whom we pray dwells within us.

Turning then to the Lord our God, the Father Almighty, let us as best we can give thanks with all our hearts, beseeching Him that in His Goodness He will mercifully hear our prayers, and by His grace drive evil from our thoughts and actions, increase our faith, guide our minds, grant us His holy inspirations, and bring us to joy without end, through His Son our Lord and Saviour Jesus Christ. Amen.

III. St Augustine, Bishop and Doctor

Watchfulness Against the Devil[11]

We must keep watch against the devil. The devil and his angels are the rulers of this world. They dwell in a certain element of the air. The devil is rejected from the heart of the just.

Though the very solemnity of this holy night, Dearly Beloved, incites you to watch and pray, nevertheless our own customary exhortation is due to you, in order that the shepherd's voice may rouse from sleep his flock in the Lord, against the jealous and threatening powers and rulers of darkness, as though against wild beasts of the night. *For our wrestling is not against flesh and blood*, as the Apostle says; that is, against weak men in a mortal body; *but against principalities and powers, against the rulers of the world of this darkness, against the spirit of wickedness in the high places* (Eph. vi. 12).

You are not on this account to think that the devil and his angels, to whom the Apostle refers in these words, are the rulers of the world of which it is written: *And the world was made by him* (Jn. i. 10). For when he called them, *rulers of this world*, that no one might think it was the world spoken of in many places in Scripture by the name, *heaven and earth*, he at once added, as though explaining this, *of this darkness*; that is, of the unbelieving. For this reason he says to those who believe: *You were heretofore darkness, but now light in the Lord* (Eph. v. 8).

These spirits of wickedness are therefore in the world above us; not where the stars in their order shine out, nor where the holy angels dwell but in a murky dwelling of this lower world, where clouds are formed; for it is written: *Who covereth the heaven with clouds* (Ps. cxlvi. 8). Where birds also fly; for they too are called, *the flying creatures of the heavens* (Ps. xlix. 11). It is in these heavens then, not in the serenity of the upper heavens, that these most evil spirits dwell; against whom we are told is our spiritual warfare, so that when we overcome the angels of evil, we may enjoy the reward we are to share with the good angels for an unbroken eternity.

So in another place the same Apostle, speaking of the dark dominion of the devil, says: *When you walked according to the spirit of this world, obeying the ruler of the kingdom of the lower heaven, the spirit which even now is working on the children of unbelief* (Eph. ii. 2). That then which is the spirit of this world, the same are the rulers of the world. And as he has shown there what it is he calls the world, *the children of unbelief*, so here also, when he adds: *Of this darkness*. And he whom he here calls: *The ruler of the kingdom of the lower heaven*, the same in this other place is called: *The spirits of wickedness in the high places*.

So thanks be to the Lord our God, Who has delivered us from the power of darkness, and brought us into the kingdom of the Son Whom He loves (Col. i. 12, 13). Separated then from this darkness by the light of His Gospel, and delivered from these powers of evil through His Precious Blood, let you watch and pray so that you may not enter into temptation (Matt. xxvi. 41). For whosoever among you has that faith which works by charity (Gal. v. 6), the prince of this world is cast forth from your hearts (Jn. xii. 31). But outside, he goes about like a roaring lion, seeking whom he may devour (I Pet. v. 8).

Do not then yield place to the devil, whatever the quarter he seeks to enter by. But suffer Him to dwell within you, and against him, Who through suffering for your sake cast him forth. For when he ruled you,

you were then *darkness*, but now you are *light in the Lord. Walk then as children of the light.* Watch then in this Mother Light (cf. Gal. iv. 26)[12] against the darkness, and the rulers of it, and from the bosom of this Mother Light pray you to the *Father of lights* (Jas. i. 17).

Turning then to the Lord our God, the Father Almighty, let us as best we can give thanks with all our hearts, beseeching Him that in His Goodness He will mercifully hear our prayers, and by His grace drive evil from our thoughts and actions, increase our faith, guide our minds, grant us His holy inspirations, and bring us to joy without end, through His Son our Lord and Saviour Jesus Christ. Amen.

IV. St John Chrysostom, Bishop and Doctor

Sermon Given on the Great and Holy Night of the Pasch

Against Drunkards[13]

1. We have finished with the duty of fasting; let us not however finish with the fruits of fasting. For we can put aside the obligation of fasting, and yet gather the fruits of it. The weariness of the struggle has passed; but let the eagerness of doing what is right not leave us. The fast has ended, but the service of God remains; rather fasting has not ended. But do not be afraid. I did not say this because I am going to impose another Lent on you, but solely that I may speak of another virtue. Bodily fast has ended; but the discipline of the spirit has not ended. This latter is more desirable than the first; and the first was instituted because of this.

For as when you were fasting I used to say to you, that there could be one among you who, while he fasted, was not fasting; so now I say that it can be that one fasts by not fasting. Perhaps you think I am speaking in riddles; and so I shall explain. How can it be that one who is fasting does not fast? When a person abstains from food but not from sin. How can it be that one who is not fasting yet fasts? When he partakes of food, but tastes nothing of sin. This latter fast is better than the other: not alone better, but easier.

In the season of the other fasting many would plead weakness of body, the severe gnawing of hunger. I am covered with sores, one says, I cannot endure the fast. To drink water kills *me*. Vegetables *I* cannot digest. Many have I heard saying these sort of things. But against this fast nothing of the kind can be said. Enjoy the bath. Take your place at the table. Take wine, but drink it in moderation. You may also eat meat; there is nothing to prevent you. You can enjoy all things: abstain only from sin.

See how easy for everyone is this fasting? You will not plead here weakness of body; for right doing is the health of the soul. For one who has not tasted wine can yet be inebriated: and one can still be sober though drinking wine. And what it means to be inebriated while drinking no wine let us hear from the prophet who has said: *Be drunk, and not with wine: stagger, and not with drunkenness* (Is. xxix. 9). And how can a man be drunk without wine? When you do not temper the pure wine of the passions with Christian moderation. Another can be drinking wine, and yet not be drunk; and if it were not so Paul would not have laid this on Timothy, writing to him in these words: *Use a little wine for thy stomach's sake, and thy frequent infirmities* (I Tim. v. 23).

Drunkenness is nothing other than the degradation of the natural powers of the mind, the undoing of reason, the impoverishment of the soul, the emptying of the mind. And these consequences come not alone from that inebriation that is caused by wine, but also from the intoxication that is caused by anger and unlawful desires. For just as lack of sleep causes unrest, and causes weariness, and causes depression, and brings on evil humour, and though the cause of it varies, the consequences and the distress are all the same, so wine causes drunkenness, it also awakens lust, and leads to a corrupted heart; and though the causes may vary, the suffering and weakness that follow are one and the same.

Let us keep ourselves from drunkenness. I do not say: let us abstain from wine; but let us abstain from drunkenness. Wine does not make a man drunk: for it is a creature of God, and no creature of God works evil. It is the deliberate evil will that is the cause of drunkenness. And that you may know that one may be inebriated in another way than by wine alone, hear what Paul says: *And be not drunk with wine* (Eph. v. 18), showing that a man may become inebriated by yet other means. *Be not drunk with wine, wherein is luxury*. Behold how in a few words he has put together the whole accusation against drunkenness.

What does this mean: *Be not drunk with wine, wherein is luxury*? We call those young men profligate, who as soon as they receive their paternal inheritance straightaway set about wasting it all, taking no thought of to whom or when it should be given; but without discrimination they distribute precious garments, silver, gold, and all they have inherited, among the worthless and among prostitutes. Such is drunkenness; which, as in the case of the young man, invades the mind of the inebriated, and having reduced reason to a state of slavery, forces it to scatter without measure or without care all the wealth of the soul and of the senses.

He who is inebriated knows not what must be said, and what must be passed over in silence. His mouth is ever open, and babbles away from beginning to end; there is no bar to make it fast, no door to his lips. The drunkard no longer knows how to place words in their right order; he is unable to employ the riches of his mind. He knows not how to put this aside, to lay out that; everything is given over to wastefulness and extravagance. Drunkenness is deliberate insanity, a betrayal of the mind. Drunkenness is a calamity of folly, a sickness that is mocked at, a deliberately embraced spirit of evil, and worse than madness itself.

The Picture of Drunkenness. Do you wish to understand how the drunkard is lower than one possessed by a devil? With one that is possessed by an evil spirit we sympathize; this other we loathe. We grieve for the one, but with the other we are angry and indignant. And why? Because the infirmity of the one is a disaster, that of the other is due to his own conduct. There the treachery of the enemy has entered, here the treachery of one's own mind. And the same things happen to the drunkard as to the possessed. Both wander about in the same way. Both are out of their senses. Both fall down the same way. Both roll the pupils of their eyes. Both will lie gasping prone upon the earth, foaming and dribbling from the mouth, their breath filled with an intolerable foul odour. A man in this state is unpleasant to his friends, and a laughing-stock to his enemies, an object of contempt to those subject to him, unpleasing to his wife, hateful to all, and more troublesome than the very beasts. The dumb beasts drink only when they are thirsty, and their desire arises from their need. But the drunkard in his intemperance goes beyond them in his desire, and seems more lacking in reason than the beasts that are without reason.

But what is more unendurable than this is that a disease so abounding in evils, that brings with it so many disasters, is not even considered an offence; and because of this attitude, at the tables of the rich, there will even be a struggle, a contest, over this indecency; and they will strive with one another to see who will degrade himself the most, who will provoke the most laughter, who will cause the greater damage to his nerves, who will destroy his powers the more effectively, who will most provoke the anger of their common Lord. And this diabolic strife and contest can be seen by all.

The drunkard is more wretched than the dead: for he that is dead is deprived of his senses, and can no more do either good or evil. But the drunkard is ready for every evil, and with the soul buried in the body as in a tomb, he carries about with him a body that is dead. You see then how he is more wretched than one possessed; more senseless than the dead? Do you wish that I tell you something worse than all this? The drunkard shall not enter into the kingdom of heaven. Who says so? Paul. *Do not err: neither fornicators, nor idolators, nor adulterers, nor the effeminate, nor liers with mankind, nor thieves, nor covetous, nor drunkards, shall possess the kingdom of God* (I Cor. vi. 9, 10).

You hear with what kind of people he has placed them? With the shameless, the fornicators, the idolators, adulterers, detractors, the avaricious, with thieves. Someone then may say: is a drunkard and a shameless person the same? Is a drunkard and an idolator the same? Do not ask me these things, good man. I have read to you the laws of God. Do not seek the reason of them from me. Ask Paul. He will give you an answer. I cannot tell you whether he will be placed in punishment with these or separate from them. But this I can confidently declare: that it is certain that the drunkard no less than the idolator shall be shut out from the kingdom of heaven. If that is certain, why then ask me for an explanation of the degree of the sin? Since he shall remain without the gate, since he shall be deprived of salvation, if he is condemned to hell, why hold out to me a measure for sin, and weights and scales?

Drunkenness, dearest brethren, is a fearful thing, and wholly disastrous. I do not direct my words against you. Far from it. I believe that your soul is free of this poison, and of this misfortune; and it is a proof of your soundness that you are gathered here, that you have come with eagerness, that you hear me with attention. For no one who is drunk with wine is eager for the word of God: *Be not drunk with wine, wherein is luxury: but be ye filled with the holy spirit.* This inebriation is to be praised. Steep your soul in this intoxication of the spirit, so that you may not sleep in drunkenness. Fill your soul and your thoughts with it, so that this shameless disorder shall find no place in you.

And because of this he did not say: Be sharers in the Spirit, but, *be ye filled with the holy Spirit.* Fill your soul with the Spirit, as though it were a cup, so that the devil can find no place to enter. We are not simply to partake of the Spirit, but to be filled with it; in psalms and hymns, and spiritual canticles, as today you are filled; and for which reason I am confident of your temperance. For we possess a wondrous cup of intoxication; it is a cup of inebriation, that brings about moderation, not paralysis. And of what kind is this cup? It is a spiritual cup: the immaculate cup of the Blood of the Lord. This cup causes no drunkenness, brings on no paralysis. For it does not undo our powers; but awakens our powers. It does not destroy the nerves; rather it tones the nerves. For it brings sobriety. It makes us respected by the angels, honoured by men, and loved by God.

See what David says of this spiritual cup put before us at this table: *Thou hast prepared a table before me, against them that afflict me. Thou hast anointed my head with oil; and my chalice which inebriates me, how goodly is it!* (Ps. xxii. 5). And lest you, hearing the word *inebriates*, be surprised and think it to be the same as that which produces infirmity of body, he adds, that it is wonderful and strengthening. It is a new kind of drunkenness, that gives strength, and makes men strong and powerful: for it flows from the spiritual rock. Here there is no degradation of the mind, but an enlargement of the powers of the soul.

2. Let us then be drunk with this wine; but let us abstain from that other, so that we shall not dishonour this solemnity. For not alone on earth is this day celebrated, but also in heaven. Today there is joy on earth, and today there is joy in heaven: for if there is joy both in heaven and on earth at one sinner being converted, how much more joy shall there be in heaven when the whole world is taken from the hands of the devil? Now the angels exult, now the archangels rejoice, and the cherubim and seraphim together with us celebrate this holy feast. And they are not ashamed of their fellow servants, but rejoice with us at our good fortune; and though the gift we have received from God is ours alone, yet our joy is shared by them.

And why do I speak only of our fellow servants? The same Lord who is both ours and theirs does no disdain to celebrate this feast with us. What am I saying: does not disdain? For He says: *With desire I have desired to eat this pasch with you* (Lk. xxii. 15). And if He desired to celebrate the Pasch with us, without doubt He desires to celebrate the Resurrection also. When therefore the angels rejoice, and the archangels, and the Lord of all the heavenly Hosts, celebrate this feast with us, what reason can remain for sadness? *There is no distinction of persons in the participation of the Mysteries.*

3. Let no poor person grieve, because of his poverty; for this is a festival of the soul. Let no rich person take pride in his abundance, for money can not add to the joy of this day. In the Feasts that are celebrated outside us, in the world of men, where there is much strong wine, where the tables are laden, and men eat to satiety, where there is shamelessness and laughter, and every suggestion of Satan, the poor man may well be sad, and the rich man merry. And why? Because the rich man spreads before himself a splendid table, and enjoys his delights to the full; the poor man, through his poverty, spreads before him nothing at all of this magnificence.

Here there is nothing of this. One is the table that is prepared for rich and poor alike. And though a man may be rich, yet to this table he can give nothing. And should another be poor, he shall have no less honour because of his poverty in regard to the things which here belong to all. For this favour is from God, and what wonder that it should be for the rich and the poor alike? For the same is the table that is prepared for the poor man, sitting waiting for an alms, as for the Emperor adorned with the diadem, and clad in the royal purple, to whom the rule of the world is given. Such are the gifts of God; and He gives, not according to dignity, but according to the will and the mind of each.

To this table therefore let the poor man and the Emperor come with equal confidence, and with equal profit; and here more often the poor man will be the richer. And why? Because the Emperor is involved in a thousand affairs, and like a ship is tossed hither and thither, and brought close to many sins. But the poor man has to think solely of his need for food, and his life is passed in tranquillity and freedom from responsibility, like a ship secure in harbour; and so he approaches much more confidently to the sacred table.

Again, in the feasts of the outside world the poor may be sad and unhappy, the rich festive and rejoicing; and not because of food only, but also because of dress. For what happens with regard to food happens also with regard to clothing. For when a needy man sees a rich one clad in fine clothing, he is stricken, and fancies himself the unhappiest of men. But here this is taken away: for all alike are clothed with the one saving garment: *For as many of you as have been baptized in Christ, have put on Christ* (Gal. iii. 27).

Let us then not shame this sacred day with drunkenness; for the Lord has honoured us all alike, rich and poor, masters and servants; but rather let us repay the Lord for His goodness towards us; and the most perfect thanksgiving is a pure manner of life, and a sober mind. For this Festival and for this solemn gathering there is need neither of wealth nor display, but of the riches of the mind, riches of the will. Such are the riches that here are for sale. Nothing is sold here that relates to the body; only the hearing of the divine teaching, the prayers of the Fathers, the blessings of the priests, harmony, peace, and union of soul. The gifts are spiritual, and spiritual also the price; which may we all receive, through the grace and mercy of Our Lord Jesus Christ, to whom with the Father and the Holy Ghost be glory and honour for ever and ever. Amen.

V. St Leo, Pope and Doctor

On the Resurrection of the Lord I; Given on Holy Saturday in the Night Watch of the Pasch[14]

Synopsis:

I. We must take care that the Fruits of our Fast are not wasted; so that they who have died with Christ may also rise with Him.

II. That the Days of Burial were shortened because of the Disciples.

III. That Christ gave many proofs of the Truth of His Resurrection.

IV. What change took place in the Body of Christ because of His Resurrection.

V. That the Christian, placing no value on earthly things, should hold firmly to heavenly.

VI. Each one must be watchful that after the Paschal Festivity he will not again return to the seductions of sin.

I. In our last sermon, Dearly Beloved, we instructed you, and not, I think, unfittingly, in the sharing of the Cross of Christ, so that the Paschal mystery may enter into the very life of the faithful, and so that what we honour in the festival we may practise in our daily conduct. You have yourselves proved how profitable this is, and you have learned from the practice of your faith how much long fasting and frequent prayer and generous almsgiving profit both soul and body. There is scarcely one among you who has not been enriched by these practices, and who has not stored away in the depths of his soul something in which he may indeed rejoice.

But these gains are to be cared for with constant watchfulness, lest in relaxing our efforts the devil, because of our inattention, should steal from us what God's grace has brought us. Since then, by this fast of forty days, we wished to bring it about, that during the time of our Lord's Passion we might feel a little of his sufferings, so now must we strive to become sharers of Christ's Resurrection, and while yet in this mortal body that we may *pass over* from death to Life. For to any man who is changed from one condition to another, to cease to be what he was forms an end; and to begin to be what he was not is a beginning. But it is important to what end a man lives or dies. For there is a death which causes life, and a life which causes death; and no where save in this fleeting world are both sought for together: so that upon our present life depends the difference in our future rewards.

We must then die to the devil, and live to God; depart from evil doing, that we may rise again to justness. Let the past be buried, that a new life may rise up. And since, as Truth Itself tells us, *no man can serve two masters* (Mt. vi. 24), let our master be the Lord Who has lifted up the fallen to glory, not that other who has brought those who stood upright to ruin.

II. Now since the Apostle says: *The first man was of the earth, earthly; the second man from heaven, heavenly. Such as is the earthly, such are the earthly: and such as is the heavenly, such also are they that are heavenly. Therefore as we have borne the image of the earthly, let us also bear the image of the heavenly* (I Cor. xv. 47, 49), we should greatly rejoice in this exchange, through which we have been translated from the baseness of what is earthly to a heavenly dignity, by His unspeakable mercy Who, to raise us up to His dignity, descended to our lowliness; and this that He might not alone take on Himself our body, but also the sinful state of our nature: so that divine impassibility might suffer what human frailty so unhappily endures.

So then, that prolonged sadness might not afflict the troubled minds of His Disciples, with a wondrous promptness He cut short the promised time of the three days; so that though the number of the days remained, the time was shortened; by joining the last part of the first day and first part of the third day to the entire second day. And so the Resurrection of our Saviour brought it about that Christ's soul should not be long detained in hell, nor His Body in the sepulchre. And so swift was the revivifying of His uncorrupted Body, that we have here the appearance of sleep rather than of death: for the Divinity which departed not from either substance of His assumed humanity, joined together by Its power what by Its power it had sundered.

III. Then follow the many proofs on which would rest the authority of the faith that was to be preached to the whole world. And though the rolling back of the stone, the emptying cf the sepulchre, the laying aside of the winding sheet, and the angels' telling of what had happened, abundantly established the reality of the Lord's Resurrection, nevertheless He manifested Himself clearly to the eyes both of the Apostles and of the holy women; not alone speaking together with them, coming into their midst, and eating with them, but also permitting Himself to be felt by the cautious curious touch of those to whom doubt still clung.

For this He entered in among the Disciples, the doors being closed (Jn. xx. 19), and with His breath gave them the Holy Spirit; and giving light to their minds, He revealed to them the hidden things of the Sacred Scriptures (Lk. xxiv. 27). And He showed them the wounds in His side, and the place where the nails had been, and all the signs of His so recent passion (Jn. xx. 27), so that they might know that there remained in Him what belonged to the human as well as to the divine nature;[15] that we may know that the Word is not that which the Body is, that we may confess that the Only Son of God is both the Word and the Flesh.

IV. The Apostle Paul, the Teacher of the Gentiles, Dearly Beloved, is in accord with this belief when he says: *Although we have known Christ according to the flesh; but now we know Him so no longer* (II Cor. v. 16). For the Resurrection of our Lord was not the end of His Body, it was Its change; and its nature was not consumed in the increase of its perfection. Its quality was changed, the nature did not fade; and the Body which could suffer crucifixion became impassible; what could be killed, became immortal; what could be wounded, invulnerable. And rightly is it said that the Body of Christ is no longer known in that state in which we knew it: for there remains in It nothing that can suffer, nothing that is weak, so that It is Itself in essence, but not Itself in glory.

And what wonder that he should say this of the Body of Christ, when he says it of all Christians: *And so henceforth we know no man according to the flesh* (II Cor. v. 16). For in that moment in which He Who is the image of all that we hope for went on before us, a beginning of our own resurrection in Christ took place in Him Who died for us all. We do not hesitate in doubt, nor falter in uncertain expectation; but receiving the beginnings of the promise we perceive already, with the eyes of our faith, the things that are to come; and rejoicing in this raising up of our nature, even now we take hold of that in which we believe.

V. Therefore, do not let the beauty of earthly things take possession of us, nor let earthly delight turn our gaze from heavenly things to itself. Let us regard as done with things which for the most part are in truth no more; and let the soul, intent on what endures, fix there its hopes where what is offered us is everlasting. For though we are *saved by hope* (Rom. viii. 24), and still bear this weak mortal flesh, rightly are we said *not to be in the flesh*, if the desires of the body no longer rule us; and rightly do we renounce even the name of that whose will we no longer obey.

And so when the Apostle elsewhere says: *Make not provision for the flesh in its desires* (Rom. xiii. 14), let us not think that is forbidden which is healthful to us, and which our weakness needs. But since we are not to obey all our desires, nor gratify every wish of the body, we must understand that here we are being taught that we are to practise moderation, and that to the body, which is placed subject to the rule of the soul, we should neither give what is superfluous, nor deny what is necessary.

Because of this the same Apostle says: *For no man ever hateth his own flesh: but nourishes and cherishes it* (Eph. v. 29): not that it may do evil do we nourish and defend it, but that it may fulfil its due purpose, so that nature refreshed may continue the course of its life; that the baser instincts may not wickedly and perversely prevail over the higher, or the higher yield to the baser; and so, with evil ruling in the soul, it becomes a slave where it ought to be the master.

VI. Let the people of God (i.e., *Christians*) acknowledge then that they are *a new creature in Christ* (II Cor. v. 17), and let them watchfully learn from Whom it was received, and Whom it is they have received. Let the things that were made new not return to their former insecurity, nor let him who has put his hand to the plough turn aside from his task: let him pay heed to what he is sowing, not look back to what he has left behind him. Let no one sink back to that from which he rose up; and even should he lie sick through some infirmity, let him earnestly long to be healed and restored to strength.

For this is the way of salvation, and the beginning of our own resurrection which began in Christ, so that, as amid the hazards of this life we shall avoid neither lapses nor falls, the feet of those who walk along it may be guided from uncertain to what is safe ground; since, as the Scripture tells us: *With the Lord shall the steps of a man be directed, and he shall like well his way. When he shall fall he shall not be bruised, for the Lord putteth his hand under him* (Ps. xxxvi. 23, 24).

This thought, Dearly Beloved, must be kept before us, and not for the Paschal Festival alone, but for the sanctification of all our life. And to this end should the present stirring up of our heart be directed, that what has delighted the souls of the faithful, during this brief time of abstinence, may become a habit, may remain unclouded in your mind; and that if any thing evil has crept into our life, let it be wiped out by speedy repentance. And since the cure of a long standing disease is slow and difficult, the more recent the wound, the more promptly let remedies be applied to it; so that at all times rising afresh from our defeats, we may merit to attain to the glorious resurrection of an incorruptible body, in Christ Jesus our Lord, Who with the Father and the Holy Ghost lives and reigns, world without end. Amen.

VI. Venerable Bede, Priest and Doctor

For the Vigil of Easter[16]

The Giving of Peace

Luke xxiv; John xx. Our Lord and Redeemer, gradually and at intervals, revealed to His Disciples and to others the wonder of His Resurrection from the dead. Foi such was the greatness of this miracle, that the human souls of mortal men could not take it in all at once. Thinking therefore of the simple people who were seeking Him, He shows those coming to the tomb, the holy women fervent in their love, and also the men, first, *the stone rolled back*, and then, *laid by themselves*, His Body being taken away, *the linen cloths* in which It had been wrapped.

Next, to the holy women, who had sought Him more carefully and had been terrified by what they had learned about Him, He gave a vision of angels, who made clear to them the fact of His Resurrection. Then last of all, the fame of His accomplished Resurrection thus preceding Him, the Lord of Hosts and the King of Glory. Himself appearing, He shows them how great was the power which had triumphed over the death He had just tasted.

Altogether, by what we learn from the account in the Gospel narrative, on the day He arose from the dead He appeared five times to the sight of men. First to Mary Magdalen, at the tomb when He addressed to her the words: as she desired to embrace His Feet: *Do not touch me, for I am not ascended to my Father.* Then to the two women who came running from the sepulchre to tell the Disciples what they had learned from the angel regarding the fulfilment of the Resurrection; of whom Matthew writes: *They came up and took hold of his feet, and adored him.*

In the evening of the same day He appeared to two Disciples on the road to Emmaus, who, inviting Him to take supper with them, then recognized Him in the breaking of the bread. He appeared also to Peter. When or where this took place the Evangelist (Luke) does not say; but nevertheless he does not pass over the fact that it did take place, for writing down that the two above-mentioned Disciples, as soon as they recognized the Lord at Emmaus, went back that same hour to Jerusalem, and found the eleven gathered there, and those with them, who said: *The Lord is risen indeed, and hath appeared to Simon.* And then the Evangelist adds: *And they told what things were done in the way; and how they knew him in the breaking of the bread.*

And immediately following he adds His fifth appearance; from which, while it was being read, we learned as follows: *Now while they were speaking these things, Jesus stood in the midst of them, and saith to them: Peace be to you; it is I, fear not.* Here we must note, and carefully commit to memory, that while the Disciples were actually speaking of Him the Lord deigned to stand in the midst of them, and grant them a vision of His Presence. For this is what He elsewhere promised to all the faithful when he said: *Where there are two or three gathered together in my name, there I am in the midst of them.* That which He does at all times through the presence of His loving kindness, He wishes yet again to make clear to us; to confirm the steadfastness of faith, by the vision of His bodily presence.

We must trust to His goodness that this also happens to us, even though we are far lower than the Apostles; so that as often as we are gathered in His Name, He is in the midst of us. For His name is Jesus: that is, He is our Saviour. And when we come together to speak of obtaining our salvation, then we are gathered together in His Name. Nor should we ever doubt that He is present among those who gather together to speak of the things he loves; and the more truly shall this be, the more we believe with our hearts what we profess with our lips.

Next we must take note that when the Saviour appears in the midst of the Disciples, He immediately bestows on them the joys of peace; repeating now in the fulfilled glory of His immortality, that which He had committed to them as the special pledge of their salvation, when He was Himself about to undergo his passion; saying to them: *Peace I leave with you, my peace I give unto you* (Jn. xvi. 27).

And likewise when He was born, the Angels whom the Shepherds saw immediately proclaim the favour of this gift to men; praising God and saying: *Glory to God in the highest; and on earth peace to men of good will* (Lk. ii. 14): for the whole divine mission of our Redeemer in the flesh was to restore peace to the world. It was for this He became man, for this He suffered, for this He rose from the dead: that by appeasing Him He might bring us back to the peace of God, who by offending God have incurred His anger. And because of this rightly did the prophet speak of Him as: *The Father of the world to come, and the prince of peace* (Is. ix. 6). And the Apostle, writing of Him to those converted from the Gentiles, says: *And coming, he preached peace to you that were afar off, and peace to them that were near. For by him we have access both in one Spirit to the Father* (Eph. ii).

But when the Lord appeared in their midst the Disciples were troubled and afraid, and thought they were seeing a spirit. They knew it was the Lord Who appeared, but they thought they saw Him, not in the substance of His Body, but of His Soul; that is, that they were looking at, not His Body which they knew was dead and buried, and now risen from the dead, but that they had before their eyes the spirit which before it left the body He had commended into the hands of His Father. But their most kind Master, by the grace of His consolation and exhortation, mercifully removed this error from their minds, and at the same time the fear that had struck them at this new and unknown vision.

Why are you troubled, He says, *and why do thoughts arise in your hearts? See my hands and feet, that it is I myself*. Not without purpose did He bid them see and examine His hands and feet rather than His face: which they knew equally well: but so that they who would see the places of the nails, by which He had been fastened to the Cross, would then begin to understand that not alone were they seeing that it was a body, but that it was the Body of the Lord, Which they knew had been crucified.

And because of this well did John, recording His remembrance of this appearance, tell that He also showed the Apostles *His side*, which had been pierced by a soldier, so that the more testimony they learned of His widely known passion and death, the more certain would be the belief with which they would rejoice because of His now fulfilled Resurrection, and His triumph over death. And so that He might in every way render certain their faith in the Resurrection, He showed them His Body, not alone for their eyes to see, but for their hands to touch, and by this made plain to them that it was immortal, saying: *Handle and see, for a spirit hath not flesh and bones, as you see me to have*.

For seeing that they were to preach the glory of His Resurrection, they should be able to tell us also, and without any uncertainty, what it is we are to hope for regarding the appearance of our risen body. It is because of this that with great confidence the blessed apostle John appeals to his hearers, to follow after the hidden things of truth and faith, of which he had learned, saying: *That which was from the beginning, which we have heard, which we have seen with our eyes, which we have looked upon, and our hands have handled, of the word of life* (I Jn. i. 1).

The Gentiles are wont in this place to lay snares of deception before the simple trustfulness of our faith, by saying: Are you not rash to trust that the Christ Whom you worship can bring back your bodies imperishable from the dust: He Who did not even conceal the signs of death that were upon that body which you say was raised from the dead; and who could not heal the scars of the wounds He received upon the Cross?

To whom we answer, that Christ, since He is the Omnipotent God, and as He promised, has both recalled to life, as He willed, His own body, Which by dying He had put off, and raised our bodies from corruption to incorruption, from death to life, from the dust of the earth to everlasting glory. He could have shown It to His Disciples with the wounds of His Passion healed, yet, because of the divine purpose of the Incarnation, He chose to retain upon it these tokens of His Passion.

First, manifestly, so that the Disciples who saw them would know that it was not a spirit, without a body, but a living body which they held; and would preach to the world an assured faith in the fulfilment of the Resurrection, and an assured hope in the resurrection of all mankind. Then, that Our Lord and God, Jesus Christ, Who in His humility intercedes for us with the Father, may, displaying the scars of His wounds, perpetually show to Him how much He has suffered for the salvation of men; and in this wonderful and ineffable way remind Him without ceasing Who cannot forget, and Who is ever ready to have compassion on us, how just it is that He should have compassion on men, of whose nature, of whose pain and suffering, the Son of God Himself has become a Sharer, and in fighting for whom He has by dying submitted Himself to the power of death.

Thirdly, that all the elect who have been received into perpetual happiness, seeing upon their Lord and God these signs of His passion, may never cease to give thanks to Him through Whose death they now live; and so that by the voice of the whole Church that may be fulfilled of which the prophet sings in the psalm: *The mercies of the Lord I will sing for ever* (Ps. lxxxviii. 1).

Lastly, so that at the Judgement the reprobate may also see these same tokens of the passion; as it was written: *They shall look on him whom they pierced* (Jn. xix. 37); and may then understand that they have been most justly condemned; and not alone they who laid impious hands upon Him, but they also who despised His graces, or had not troubled to accept those He offered them; or they who strove with yet greater malice to destroy and to corrupt these same graces, through hatred and persecution of those who did receive them.

Faith in the Resurrection does not err; and neither are we deceived in our hope of resurrection; for God the Father has both raised the Lord, and will raise us up also by His power (I Cor. vi. 14). This the same Apostle elsewhere declared. *And if the spirit of him*, he says, *that raised up Jesus from the dead, dwell in you; he that raised up Jesus Christ from the dead, shall quicken also your mortal bodies, because of His Spirit that dwelleth in you* (Rom. viii. 11).

This was said especially of the elect; since *we shall all indeed rise: but we shall not all be changed* (I Cor. xv. 51); only those who are now ruled by the indwelling Spirit shall then be raised, by a yet greater grace of the same Spirit, to the happiness of eternal life. So the Lord, to confirm their faith in His Resurrection, showed Himself Living to His Disciples, spoke to them words of consolation, and showed them the marks of His passion: to touch as well as to see.

But their weak hearts could not yet grasp the wonder of such power, and they begin to be astonished with the joy of what they see, rather than to believe what they were being taught. And so that no trace of doubt would remain in their minds, the Lord taking their food also ate it before them; so if they had not believed the evidence of their eyes, and the touch of their fingers, now, seeing him eat earthly food, they would come to know that what had appeared among them was truly man.

In this connection, Dearly Beloved, we must avoid the foolish heresy of the Corinthians; namely, that no one will unwisely think that the Body of the Lord, and the Mediator of God, Which had risen from the dead, had need of the sustenance of food; or that after the resurrection our own bodies, in their spiritual life and existence, need to be nourished with bodily food; since the contemplation of the divine glory in no way permits that we suffer either hunger or thirst or the want of any earthly good. And so the most ardent lover of that life, steadfast in his devotion, joyful in his hope of God, declares: *As for me, I will appear before thy sight in justice: I shall be satisfied when thy glory shall appear* (Ps. xvi. 15). And Philip, filled with the same love, says: *Lord, show us the Father, and it is enough for us* (Jn. xiv. 8).

Therefore let us simply and devoutly believe, that the Body of our Lord, risen from the dead and now to die no more, had no need of food, though retaining the power to eat. And so when it was a fitting time of day for taking food He asked them to give Him food to eat; and they offer it to Him Who had no need of earthly sustenance, such as mortal bodies have; and as water thrown upon the fire, so presently was the food consumed by His spiritual power.

And we must believe that after their resurrection our bodies also shall be endowed with heavenly glory: that they shall have power to do what they will, and shall be free to reach to wherever they may wish; but since we shall then have no need or profit from eating, in no way whatever shall that immortal world make use of earthly food: that world wherein the children of the Resurrection have no other food or drink than true life and salvation, joy, peace, and every good, as we read in the psalmist who says: *Blessed are they who dwell in thy house, O Lord: they shall praise thee for ever and ever* (Ps. lxxxiii. 5). And again: *The God of Sion shall be seen in Sion.* Because of this, the Apostle, writing of the hidden things of that world, says: *When God will be all in all* (I Cor. xv).

Having finished His meal the Lord goes on to add further words of counsel, saying: *These are the words which I spoke to you, while I was yet with you*; that is, while I was like you, in a body that could suffer and die: *That all things needs must be fulfilled, which are written in the law of Moses, and in the prophets, and in the psalms, concerning me*. The Master of Truth takes away every shadow of *figure*, and everywhere confirms the claims of the Reality. He is seen, He is touched, He eats food: a sermon of encouragement is contained in each act of His. And lest it be thought that His testimony alone did not suffice, He also brings before them the authority of Moses, and of the Prophets, who had prefigured in their writings His Incarnation, His Passion, and His Resurrection. And lest the Apostles be slow in understanding their mystical words, He also opens their minds, that they might understand them. And this done He permits nothing of their former state of doubt to remain in their minds; nor did He then cease to give them proofs of His Passion and Resurrection. For there follows:

And he said to them: Thus it is written, and thus it behoved Christ to suffer, and to rise again from the dead, the third day: and that penance and remission of sin should be preached in his name, unto all nations. So it was necessary that Christ suffer, and rise again; because it was impossible for the world to be saved unless God came as man, Who, appearing in the nature of man, would teach men how to serve God, and Who, submitting to death, as man would triumph over it by divine power; and thus awaken in those who believed in Him a contempt for death, and kindle in them a certain hope of resurrection and of life everlasting.

For in what way could men be more truly encouraged to believe in the glory to come, and to strive for eternal life, than by knowing that God Himself had become a Sharer of their humanity and their mortality? In what other way could they be more efficaciously appealed to, to suffer evils of every kind for the sake of salvation, than by learning that their own Creator had undergone at the hands of impious men infamy of every kind; and, even the sentence of death itself? For what reason could they more fittingly accept the hope of resurrection, than through remembering that they had been cleansed and sanctified by His sacraments, and made one in His Body Who, tasting death on their behalf, speedily offered them an example of rising from the dead?

It was then necessary that Christ should suffer, and rise again from the dead the third day, and that, as He says, penance and the forgiveness of sin be preached in His Name to all nations. For this it was necessary that first the blood of Christ should be shed for the salvation of the world, and that afterwards by His Resurrection and Ascension He should open the gates of heaven to men.

And so at last they were sent forth who would preach the word of life to all the nations of the earth, and would minister to them the sacraments whereby men could be saved, and so reach to the joys of their heavenly fatherland, by the help of the Mediator of God and men, the man Jesus Christ, Who lives and reigns with the Father, in the Unity of the Holy Ghost, God, world without end. Amen.

NOTES

[1] This quotation cannot be verified in any of the Saint's Paschal sermons. Combefis says it is found in the third of the Easter sermons of St Chrysostom, but neither is it there, nor among the *Spuria* under his name. In the second of these latter there is however a significant attestation; namely, 'that in the death of Christ life overcame the signs of death. The Blessed John says that this was observed with regard to the Body also, in that His legs were not broken; which has likewise a spiritual significance; namely: that in Him authority remained undefeated, and accordingly corruption did not attack His Body . . . since it was of divine generation, and was not subject as men to destruction.' PG 59, *Spuria* in Pasch II.

[2] Cf. CSEL III, 24, 65.

[3] What is here attributed by the saintly author to Remigius, and unspecified, is found verbatim, in the same context as the citation from Bede which follows.

[4] Cf. PL 92. In Matthew iv, *in fine*.

[5] These citations under the name of Severianus, Bishop of Gabbala, rival and contemporary of Chrysostom, do not belong to him, but to Sermons 74 and 75 on the Resurrection by St Peter Chrysologus, Archbishop (of Ravenna) and Doctor of the Church, from which they are taken verbatim: consequence necessarily of some copyist's error. The citations are wholly Latin (and classical) in style and content.

[6] PL 52, col. 409, footnote b.

[7] PL 52, col. 412, note q.

[8] PG 39, Oratio V, col. 89.

[9] PL 38, Sermo. 219.

[10] This refers to the public illuminations on this night; ordered first by Constantine the Great, who was said to have turned the *night into day* by the splendour of the illuminations which he imposed everywhere throughout the empire.

[11] PL 38, Sermo. 222.

[12] The Church.

[13] PG 50 On the Pasch.

[14] PL 54, Sermo. 71.

[15] Cf. Denzinger 143, Ep. ad Flavianum; also 283, Symb. Toletan.

[16] PL 54, II Hom., 2 in Vig. Paschae, col. 139.

EASTER SUNDAY

I. St Ambrose: The Sunday of the Resurrection

II. St Gregory Nazianzenus: On The Holy Easter I

III. St John Chrysostom: The Fruits of Christ's Resurrection

IV. St Augustine: To Those Baptised the Previous Day

V. St Augustine: Peace Be To You

VI. St Augustine: To Children, on the Holy Sacrifice

VII. St Proclus: On the Holy Pasch

VIII. St Leo the Great: On the Resurrection of the Lord II

IX. St Maximus: The Prayer of the Good Thief

X. St Gregory the Great: The Mystery of the Resurrection

XI. St Gregory Nazianzenus: On the Holy Easter II

THE GOSPEL OF THE SUNDAY

Mark xvi. 1–8

And when the sabbath was passed, Mary Magdalen, and Mary the Mother of James, and Salome, bought sweet spices, that coming, they might anoint Jesus. And very early in the morning, the first day of the week, they come to the sepulchre, the sun being now risen. And they said one to another: Who shall roll us back the stone from the door of the sepulchre? And looking, they saw the stone rolled back. For it was very great. And entering in to the sepulchre, they saw a young man sitting on the right side, clothed with a white robe: and they were astonished. Who saith to them: Be not affrighted; you seek Jesus of Nazareth, who was crucified: he is risen, he is not here, behold the place where they laid him. But go, tell his disciples and Peter that he goeth before you into Galilee; there you shall see him, as he told you.

PARALLEL GOSPELS

Matthew xxviii. 1–10

And in the end of the sabbath, when it began to dawn towards the first

Luke xxiv. 12

And on the first day of the week, very early in the morning, they day of the week, came Mary Magdalen and the other Mary, to see the sepulchre. And behold there was a great earthquake. For an angel of the Lord descended from heaven, and coming, rolled back the stone, and sat upon it. And his countenance was as lightning, and his raiment as snow. And for fear of him, the guards were struck with terror, and became as dead men. And the angel answering, said to the women: Fear not you; for I know that you seek Jesus who was crucified. He is not here, for he is risen, as he said. Come, and see the place where the Lord was laid. And going quickly, tell ye his disciples that he is risen: and behold he will go before you into Galilee; there you shall see him. Lo, I have foretold it to you. And they went out quickly from the sepulchre with fear and great joy, running to tell his disciples. And behold Jesus met them, saying: All hail. But they came up and took hold of his feet, and adored him. Then Jesus said to them: Fear not. Go, tell my brethren that they go into Galilee, where they shall see me.

came to the sepulchre, bringing the spices which they had prepared. And they found the stone rolled back from the sepulchre. And going in, they found not the body of the Lord Jesus. And it came to pass, as they were astonished in their mind at this, two men stood by them, in shining apparel. And as they were afraid, and bowed down their countenance towards the ground, they said unto them: Why seek you the living with the dead? He is not here, but is risen. Remember how he spoke unto you, when he was yet in Galilee, saying: The Son of man must be delivered into the hands of sinful men, and be crucified, and the third day rise again. And they remembered his words. And going back from the sepulchre, they told all these things to the eleven, and to all the rest. And it was Mary Magdalen, and Joanna, and Mary of James, and the other women that were with them, who told these things to the apostles. And these words seemed to them as idle tales; and they did not believe them. But Peter rising up, ran to the sepulchre, and stooping down, he saw the linen cloths laid by themselves; and went away wondering in himself at that which was come to pass.

John xx. 1–18

And on the first day of the week, Mary Magdalen cometh early, when it was yet dark, unto the sepulchre; and she saw the stone taken away from the sepulchre. She ran, therefore, and cometh to Simon Peter, and to the other disciple whom Jesus loved, and saith to them: They have taken away the Lord out of the sepulchre, and we know not where they have laid him. Peter therefore went out, and that other disciple, and they came to the sepulchre. And they both ran together, and that other disciple did outrun Peter, and came first to the sepulchre. And when he stooped down, he saw the linen cloths lying. And the napkin that had been about his head, not lying with the linen cloths, but apart, wrapped up into one place. Then that other disciple also went in, who came first to the sepulchre: and he saw, and believed. For as yet they knew not the scripture, that he must rise again from the dead. The disciples therefore departed again to their home. But Mary stood at the sepulchre without, weeping. Now as she was weeping, she stooped down, and looked into the sepulchre. And she saw two angels in white, sitting, one at the head, and one at the feet, where the body of Jesus had been laid. They say to her: Woman, why weepest thou? She saith to them: Because they have taken away my Lord; and I know not where they have laid him. When she had thus said, she turned herself back, and saw Jesus standing; and she knew not that it was Jesus. Jesus saith to her: Woman, why weepest thou? whom seekest thou? She, thinking that it was the gardener, saith to him: Sir, if thou hast taken him hence, tell me where thou hast laid him, and I will take him away. Jesus saith to her: Mary. She turning, saith to him: Rabboni (which is to say, Master). Jesus saith to her: Do not touch me, for I am not yet ascended to my Father. But go to my brethren, and say to them: I ascend to my Father and to your Father, to my God and your God. Mary Magdalen cometh, and telleth the disciples: I have seen the Lord, and these things he said to me.

Exposition from the Catena Aurea

V. 1. *And when the sabbath was over . . .*

Jerome, *in Mark, in h.c.*: After the sadness of the sabbath a day of happiness now shines forth, which holds the primacy among all days, the First Light shining upon it; and upon it the Lord rises triumphant from the dead. Whence is it written: *And when the sabbath was past, Mary Magdalen, and Mary the mother of James, and Salome, bought sweet spices, that coming, they might anoint Jesus.*[1]

Gloss: For as soon as the Lord was laid in the tomb, since it was lawful to work till sunset, the holy women prepared ointments, as Luke says. And because they could not complete their task foı lack of time, as soon as the sabbath ended, that is, as the sun was setting, they were again free to continue their work, and they hastened to buy spices, as Mark here says, so that coming early they might anoint the body of Jesus; nor were they able on the evening of the sabbath, as darkness fell, to approach the tomb; hence there follows:

V. 2. *And very early in the morning, the first day . . .*

Severianus: With feminine devotion they here hasten to the tomb, the holy women who come bringing not faith to the Living, but ointments for the Dead,[2] and that they may prepare the tribute of their grief for the One who was buried, not to make ready for the joys of the divine triumph for the One now rising.

Theophylactus: For they were not sensible of the greatness and merit of the divinity of Christ. They came to anoint the body of Christ according to the custom of the Jews, that it might remain fragrant, and so that it would not begin to dissolve: for the spices have a drying effect, and absorb the moisture of the body; hence they preserve it incorrupt.

GREGORY, *Hom.* 21 *in Evang*: But we who believe in Him Who has died, we come with ointments to His tomb when we seek the Lord, filled with the odours of virtue, and with the fame of good works.

And very early in the morning . . .

AUGUSTINE, *Harmony of the Gospels III*, 24, 65: What Luke calls *very early in the morning*, and John, *early, when it was yet dark*, Mark is read as saying: *very early in the morning, the sun being now risen*, that is, when the sky begins to whiten in the east; which in any case takes place around the time the sun begins to rise. For it is its glow which is wont to be given the name *aurora* (daybreak); and he is not contradicting the evangelist who says: *when it was yet dark*. For as day breaks the more the light grows the more the remaining darkness fades. Neither are we to take the words, *very early in the morning, the sun being now risen*, to mean that the sun was already visible above the horizon, but as meaning that the sun was drawing close to that quarter of the sky; that is, the sun now rising begins to lighten the sky.

JEROME: *Very early*, therefore, he says, where another Evangelist says, *very early in the morning*; the time between the darkness of the night and the brightness of the day. In which time the salvation of the human race appeared as the sun: His blessed nearness must be announced (*in the Church*), which, as it rises, sends before it a roseate aurora, that the eye prepared by the grace of this shining glow may see, when the hour of the Lord's Resurrection has shone out; that the whole Church, after the example of the holy women, might then sing the praises of Christ, when by the proof of His Resurrection He has awakened mankind from sleep, when He has given them life, and poured into them the light of belief.

BEDE: As it was *very early in the morning* that the women, according to the account, came to the tomb, a great eagerness of life is implied; and so, mystically, an example is given us of how, scattering the darkness of the vices, and with our face to the light, we should be earnest in offering to the Lord the odour of our good works, and the sweetness of our prayer.

THEOPHYLACTUS: He says, *The first day of the week*; that is, the first of the seven days: for the seven days are called a sabbath, and this was the first of them. BEDE: Or, the first day after the sabbath, that is, the day of rest; which they observed on the seventh day.

V. 3. *And they said one to another: Who shall roll us back . . .*

SEVERIANUS: Your heart was sealed, your eyes were shut, and so you saw not before you the splendour of the wide open tomb. For there follows:

V. 4. *And looking, they saw the stone rolled back from the door.*

BEDE: How the stone was rolled back Matthew sufficiently explains

(Matt. 28). This rolling back of the stone mystically suggests the unlocking of the Mysteries of Christ, which were concealed by the covering of the Law: for the Law was written on stone. There follows: *For it was very great.* SEVERIANUS: Great in size, yet greater in significance than in size, which sufficed to shut in and cover the Body of the Creator of the world.

GREGORY: The holy women who came with sweet spices beheld the angels: for those souls see the citizens of heaven who in the odour of virtue come in desire to the Lord.

V. 5. *And entering in to the sepulchre, they saw . . .*

THEOPHYLACTUS: Do not be astonished should Matthew say that the angel was sitting upon a stone, and Mark that the women, *entering into the sepulchre saw a young man sitting on the right hand side.* For he whom they first saw sitting upon the stone, the same they also saw afterwards inside the sepulchre.

AUGUSTINE, *Harmony of the Gospels III*, 24, 63: Or we are to understand that Matthew was silent regarding that angel whom the women saw on entering into the sepulchre, and Mark as to the one they saw without, sitting upon the stone; that they saw two angels, and learned from each, singly, what the angels had said concerning Jesus. Or we ought certainly to accept, *going into the sepulchre*, as meaning, into a certain part of the garden in which, it is reasonable to infer, there was then an enclosed part, giving a certain small space in front of the rock from which a place for burial had been hewn; and that they beheld the same angel *sitting on the right side* whom Matthew says was sitting upon the stone.

THEOPHYLACTUS: There are some who say that the women spoken of by Matthew are other than those spoken of by Mark; but Mary Magdalen followed them all, having in her heart both fervent haste and ardent love.

SEVERIANUS: The holy women therefore enter into the sepulchre, that, buried with Christ, they may rise with Christ from the tomb. They see a young man, that they may see the age of our resurrection: for resurrection knows no old age; and where man is neither born or dies, there age allows of no loss, nor does it need to gain: whence is it they see *a young man*, not an old one, not an infant, but one in the joyous time of life.

BEDE: They saw a young man sitting on the right side, that is, on the southern side of that place where He was laid. For the Body lying prone had the Head to the west, the right side must therefore be to the south. GREGORY: What is signified by the left side if not the present life? And what by the right if not life everlasting? Therefore, because Our Redeemer had now passed over beyond the infirmity of this present life, rightly does the Angel who had come to announce His eternal life sit at the right side.

SEVERIANUS, *as above* (i.e. Chrysologus): They see the young man sitting at the right side also because resurrection has no part with the left. They also see him, *clothed with a white robe*. This robe came from no mortal fleece, but from lifegiving Power, and shone with heavenly light, as the prophet says: *Thou art clothed with light as with a garment* (Ps. ciii. 2); and as was said of the Just: *Then shall the just shine as the sun* (Mt. xiii. 43).

GREGORY: Or, he appeared *clothed with a white robe*, because he has announced the joys of our great Feast: for the shining whiteness of the garment proclaims the splendour of our solemnity. JEROME: The enemy now put to flight, and the kingdom restored, the shining white garment is that of true joy: for the King of Peace is sought and found and never given up. This young man therefore reveals the nature of the resurrection to those who fear death. *And* because of this *they were astonished*; because *the eye has not seen, nor the ear heard, neither hath it entered into the heart of man, what things God had prepared for them that love him* (I Cor. ii. 9).

V. 6. *Who saith to them: Be not affrighted . . .*

GREGORY: As if to say: Let them be affrighted who love not the coming of the heavenly citizens; and let them fear exceedingly who because they are ruled by carnal desires despair of being able to enter their company. But you, why should you fear, you who now see your own fellow citizens? JEROME: For where there is love, there is no fear. What were they frightened of who had found Him Whom they sought?

GREGORY: But let us hear what the Angel goes on to say. *You seek Jesus of Nazareth*. Jesus in the Latin language is interpreted to mean Saviour. But then there could have been many called Jesus, in name, but not in the reality. Accordingly, the place also is added, so that it may be clear of what Jesus he is speaking, namely: *of Nazareth*. And he immediately adds their motive: *Who was crucified*.

THEOPHYLACTUS: For he was not ashamed of the Cross: for in this is the salvation of men, and of the blessed Powers. JEROME: For the bitter root of the cross has disappeared; the Flower of Life has come forth in fruit; that is, He Who lay in death has risen in glory; whence he here adds: *He is risen, he is not here*. GREGORY: *He is not here*, is said of His Presence in the Flesh Who was everywhere present in His Majesty.

THEOPHYLACTUS: And as if he were saying: If you look for proof of His Resurrection, he adds: *Behold the place where they laid him*. For it was for this he had rolled the stone back: to show the place. JEROME: Immortality is shown to mortal men, that we may make fitting thanks, and that we may understand what we have been, and know what we shall be.

V. 7. *But go, tell his disciples and Peter that he goeth . . .*

The women are told to tell the Apostles: because through a woman death had been promulgated; and through a woman Life now rising again. He says especially, *and Peter*: for since the latter had thrice denied

His Master he regards himself as unworthy of being His Disciple; but past sins hurt not, when they please not.

Gregory: Had the Angel not mentioned him by name who had denied the Master he would not have dared to come into the midst of the Disciples. He is therefore invited by name, so that he shall not despair because of his denial.

Augustine, *Harmony of the Four Gospels, III*, 25, 79: That he said: *He goeth before you into Galilee*, seems to mean that Jesus was not to show Himself to His Disciples except in Galilee. This manifestation however Mark himself does not record who has told us that He showed Himself first to Mary Magdalen, and after this to the two Disciples who were going to the village; all of which took place in Jerusalem on the day of the Resurrection. Then he comes to the final manifestation, which took place we know on Mount Olivet, not far from Jerusalem. Therefore nowhere does Mark commemorate the fulfilment of what he testifies the angel had foretold.

(80): Matthew on the other hand speaks of no other place whatever, where the Disciples had seen the Lord after His Resurrection, excepting Galilee, as the angel had foretold. But though it is not stated when this was to be, or whether before He was seen by them elsewhere, and though Matthew tells us that the Disciples *went into Galilee unto the mountain*, he does not tell us on what day, or the order of the events he is narrating, yet he does not contradict the accounts of the other Evangelists; but gives us ground for understanding and accepting them. But the fact that the Lord sent word that He was to be seen, not where He was first to show Himself, but in Galilee, where He was afterwards seen, makes all who believe in Him eager to find out in what mystical sense are we to understand this saying.

Gregory: For Galilee is interpreted as meaning, *passing-over* (*transmigratio*). For now our Redeemer has crossed over from death to life, from His Passion to His Resurrection. And if we now cross over from evil-doing to the heights of virtuous living, afterwards we shall joyfully behold the glory of His Resurrection. He therefore Who is announced from the sepulchre is seen in that crossing over: because He Who is acknowledged in the mortification of the flesh is to be seen in the crossing over of the soul.

Jerome: A saying brief in its words, but a promise immense in its significance. There is the fountain of our joy, and the source that was prepared of our eternal salvation. There are gathered the multitudes that were dispersed; and the contrite of heart are healed. *There*, he says, *you shall see him*; but not as you have seen Him.

Augustine, *as above, III*, 25, 86: The words, *there you shall see him* etc., signify also that the grace of Christ was to pass over from the people of Israel to the Gentiles, and that the Apostles' preaching would never be received by them unless the Lord going before them prepares the way in their hearts. *I will go before you into Galilee; there you shall see him*, that is, there you shall find His members.

I. St Ambrose, Bishop and Doctor

The Sunday of the Resurrection[3]

1. You have heard, Brethren, that the holy women who came with sweet spices to the sepulchre saw there an angel; for the Evangelist says: *And entering into the sepulchre; they saw a young man sitting on the right side*. Who this young man was another Evangelist (Matthew) tells, so that you may not be confused: *For an angel of the Lord descended from heaven, and coming, rolled back the stone, and sat upon it*. Mary Magdalen however, who loved the Lord more dearly, for she had remained at the sepulchre weeping, saw the Lord first of all of them, and told the Apostles. For the Evangelist John says: *But Mary Magdalen coming tells the disciples: I have seen the Lord, and these things he said to me*. Through this we are counselled that we should come seeking the Lord laden with sweet spices, that is, with the spices of virtue and good works.

2. There are some, Dearly Beloved, who seem to be seeking the Lord, but since they are slothful, and strangers to virtue, they do not deserve to find Him; nor, when found, to see Him. What however were these holy women seeking at the tomb, if not the Body of the Lord Jesus? And you, what is it you are seeking in the Church if not Jesus, that is, the Saviour? But if you wish to find Him, *the sun being now risen*, then come as these women came; that is, let there be no darkness of evil in your hearts; for the desires of the flesh, and works that are evil, are darkness. They in whose hearts there is darkness of this kind see not the light, and understand not Christ; for Christ is the Light.

Therefore, drive the darkness from you, brethren; that is, all sinful desires, and all evil works, and provide yourselves with sweet spices, that is, earnest prayer, saying with the psalmist: *Let my prayer, O Lord, be directed as incense in thy sight* (Ps. cxl. 2).

3. Take further note of what you have heard read: namely, that Mary Magdalen, persevering by the tomb, found Him Whom she had been seeking; *For he that shall persevere unto the end, he shall be saved* (Mt. x. 22). Accordingly it is necessary that you drive evil from you, and so it is expedient for you that you persevere steadfastly in whatever good you have begun, if you desire to see the Lord and come to your heavenly home.

4. Now since you are celebrating the holy Pasch, you should know, brethren, what the Pasch is. Pasch means, *the crossing-over*; and so the Festival is called by this name. For it was on this day that the Children of Israel crossed over out of Egypt, and the Son of God crossed over from this world to His Father. What gain is it to celebrate the Pasch unless you imitate Him Whom you worship; that is, unless you cross over from Egypt, that is, from the darkness of evildoing to the light of

virtue, and from the love of this world to the love of your heavenly home?

For there are many who celebrate this holy festival, and honour this solemnity, and yet do so unworthily and because of their own wickedness: because they will not cross over from this world to their Father, that is, they will not cross over from the desires of this world, and from bodily delights, to the love of heaven. O unhappy Christians, who still remain in Egypt, that is, under the power of the devil, and taking delight in this evil!

Because of these things I warn you, Brethren, that you must celebrate the Pasch worthily, that is, that you *cross over*. Whosoever among you who are in sin, and celebrate this festival, let you cross over from evil doing to the life of virtue. Whosoever among you are just-living, let you pass from virtue to virtue; so that there shall be none among you who has not *crossed over*.

5. And as the Jews, when they celebrated the Pasch were wont to eat unleavened bread during these seven days, so every Christian who eats the flesh of the True Lamb, which is Christ, should live in a simple and holy manner all the days of his life: which continue throughout seven days. Be careful that the *old leaven* no longer remains in you, Brethren, as the Apostle warns us, where he says: *Purge out the old leaven* (I Cor. v. 7); that is, your former manner of life. For if you turn from all evil, which is signified by the *old leaven*, and faithfully observe what you promised in your Baptism, then you will be indeed *true Christians*. May He grant you this Who lives and reigns for ever and ever. Amen.

II. St Gregory Nazianzenus

On the Holy Pasch (*And his own Reluctance*)

I. This is the Day of the Resurrection; and for me a fitting beginning. Let us be all united in heart, and let us give glory to God on this solemn festival (Is. lxvi. 5). Let us address as brothers even those who hate us, as also those who love us, and have helped us, and have suffered anything on our behalf. Let us forgive all things in the Resurrection. Let us forgive one another: I who have suffered this honourable violence, and you who have inflicted it; should you be angry with me because of my reluctance (i.e., *to accept the priestly dignity*). For it may be that my reluctance is more acceptable to God than the readiness of others. For it is good to be retiring, even with God, as Moses was (Ex. iv. 13), and after him Jeremias; and then to run obediently when He calls, as Aaron did, and Isaias (Jer. i. 6; Ex. iv. 27; Is. vi. 8), provided that the one and the other are done in a right spirit: the one because of one's own weakness, the other because of the Majesty of Him Who calls.

II. The divine mystery (*ordination to the Priesthood*) hath anointed me.[5] For a while I withdrew from the mystery, to reflect and to look into my own heart. Again I unite myself with the mystery: bringing with me this great day as the shining support of my own timidity and weakness, so that He Who on this day rose from the dead may give life to my spirit also, and clothe me with the *new man* (Eph. iv. 23, 24); and may he also bestow me on the new creatures; that is, on those *who are born of God*, as a good moulder of them and teacher for Christ: one both ready to die with Him, and one now rising together with Him.

III. Yesterday the Lamb was slain, and the doorposts sprinkled with His Blood; while Egypt mourned for her firstborn. But the Destroying Angel and his sacrificial knife, fearful and terrifying, passed over us (Ex. 12): for we were protected by the Precious Blood. This day we have wholly departed from Egypt, and from Pharaoh its cruel tyrant, and his oppressive overseers; we are freed from labouring with bricks and straw (Ex. 5), and no one forbids us celebrate the festival of our *passing over*, our Pasch, and to celebrate, *not with the leaven of malice, and wickedness, but with the unleavened bread of sincerity and truth* (I Cor. v. 8), and carrying with us nothing of the ancient and evil leaven of Egypt.

IV. Yesterday I was crucified with Christ; today I am glorified with Him. Yesterday I died with Him; today I am given life with Him. Yesterday I was buried with Him; today I rise again with Him. Today let us offer Him (cf. Ex. xxiii. 15; xxxiv. 20; Deut. xvi. 16) Who has suffered and Who has risen for us—you think perhaps I was about to say, gold, or silver, or precious things, or shining stones of rare price, the frail material of this earth, which will remain here, and of which the wicked and those who are slaves of earthly things and of the prince of this world possess the greatest part—rather, let us offer Him ourselves, which to God is the most precious and becoming of gifts. Let us offer to His Image what is made in the image and likeness of this Image. And let us make recognition of our own dignity. Let us give honour to Him in Whose Likeness we were made. Let us dwell upon the wonder of this mystery, that we may understand for what Christ has died.

V. Let us become like Christ, since Christ became like us. Let us become Gods because of Him, since He for us became man. He took upon Himself a low degree that He might give us a higher one. He became poor, that through His poverty we might become rich (II Cor. viii. 9). He took upon Himself the form of a servant (Phil. ii. 7) that we might be delivered from slavery (Rom. viii. 21). He came down that we might rise up. He was tempted that we might learn to overcome. He was despised that we might be given honour. He died that He might save us from death. He ascended to heaven that we who lie prone in sin may be lifted up to Him.

Let each one of you give all to Him: offer all to Him Who gave Himself in exchange for us: as the price of our Redemption (Mt. xvi. 22; xx. 28). But should anyone come to understand this mystery in Christ, and that what He did He has done for him, he shall give nothing unless he gives his own self.

VI. And the Good Shepherd, He Who laid down His life for you, offers you a second shepherd (e.g., *himself, as coadjutor to his father, the elder Gregory*); for this is what he, your own good shepherd, hopes for you, and prays and begs for you who are his care; and he becomes the staff of your old age, and the staff of your souls (Tob. x. 4). To this inanimate temple[6] he adds a living one; to this soaring splendid shrine he adds this other poor one (*himself*), which, whatever it may be, was also raised with much toil and labour: would that I could say that it was worthy of that labour!

And all that is his he has given you. O worthy generosity! Rather, that I may speak more truly, O paternal love! His age, and his youth, a temple and a priest, the Testator and the heir; and the words on which you are nourished: not idle words, rashly and lightly poured out upon the air, going over the minds of those who listen, but those the Spirit writes, and engraves on tables of stone, and upon *the fleshy tables of the heart* (Ezech. xxxv. 26; II Cor. iii. 2, 3); and not lightly written there, and easily erased, but written deep, and not with ink, but with the grace of God.

VII. All this then this venerable Father Abraham (*Gregory the Elder*) offers you, this patriarch, the beloved and revered head, a dwelling-place of goodness, a true measure of virtue, a model of the priesthood, who this day offers to God a willing sacrifice, his only son: who is of the Promise (Gen. xxii; Gal. iii. 16). Let you, for your part, offer in a true spirit to God and to us due submission, as to your shepherds; you who dwell *in a place of pasture*, and are *reared on the waters of refreshment* (Ps. xxii. 1, 2), and knowing your shepherd, and being known by him, follow him when he calls as your shepherd, entering freely by the door.

Follow no strange shepherd; climbing like a thief and a robber into the fold. Pay no heed to strange voices; deceiving you and cutting you off from the truth, scattering you upon the mountains, and into the deserts, and among dangers, and through places where the Lord does not come (Ezech. xxxiv. 5, 6), seeking to lead you far from the true faith—which is in the Father, Son, and Holy Ghost, Whose Voice you have heard, and may you ever hear!—plundering you through false and corrupted teaching, and seducing you from your First and True Shepherd.

Let us all then, shepherds and flock, pasture and be pastured, far from such evil as this, as from rank and poisoned herbiage; and may we all ever be one in Jesus Christ, both now and in the peace of that life beyond. To Him be glory and honour for ever and ever. Amen.

III. St John Chrysostom, Bishop and Doctor

The Fruits of Christ's Resurrection[7]

Let us celebrate this greatest and most shining feast, in which the Lord has risen from the dead. Let us celebrate it with joy, and in equal measure with devotion. For the Lord has risen, and together with

Him He has raised the whole world. He has risen, because He has broken the bonds of death.

Adam sinned, and died. Christ did not sin; yet he died. This is strange and wondrous: the one sinned and died, the Other sinned not, yet He died. And why was this? So that by His aid Who did not sin he might be freed from the grasp of death who had sinned and died. So will it happen with regard to money. Oftentimes a man will owe a debt, and not having the means to pay he is put in bonds. Another who owes no debt, and has the means to pay, will deliver him who is liable to punishment. So did it happen with Adam. Adam was a debtor, and was held in bonds by the devil. But he had not the means to pay his debt. Christ was not a debtor, nor was he under the power of the devil, but He had the means to pay this debt. He came, and for the one held prisoner by the devil suffered death, to deliver him.

You behold the wondrous work of the Redemption? We were dead: by a twofold death, and we awaited a twofold resurrection. He died a single death, and so rose by a single Resurrection. What do these things mean? Adam, I repeat, died in both body and soul; he died by sin, he died by nature. *In what day soever thou shalt eat of it, thou shalt die the death* (Gen. ii. 17). But in that day he did not die in his nature; but he died by sin. The first death was of the soul; afterwards came that of the body.

But when you hear of the death of the soul, do not imagine that the soul dies; for the soul is immortal. The death of the soul is sin, and eternal punishment. Because of this Christ says: *Fear ye not them that kill the body, and are not able to kill the soul: but rather fear him that can destroy both soul and body in hell* (Mt. x. 8). He who is destroyed continues to be; but outside the sight of Him Who has destroyed him.

But as I said, there is a twofold death; and so twofold must be our resurrection. In Christ there was but one death. For Christ did not sin; but for us He suffered this single death. For He was not subject to death, since He was never a debtor to sin, and so neither was He liable to death. And so from a single death He rose in a single Resurrection from the dead. But we who have died a twofold death rise by a twofold resurrection. Until now we have risen by one resurrection: that is from sin. For we were buried with Him in baptism, and we have risen with Him through baptism. This resurrection is deliverance from our sins; the second is the resurrection of the body. He has given us the greater: we await the lesser. The first is greater than the second. For it is a greater thing to be delivered from our sins than for the body to see resurrection. Through this the body fell: because it sinned. If then this was the cause of its fall, to be freed from sin is the cause of its rising again.

We have risen in the greater resurrection: throwing off the greater death of sin, and putting off the old garment; so we need not despair regarding the lesser one. By this resurrection we rose when we were baptized; as these here who yesterday were found worthy of baptism; the dear lambs! The day before yesterday Christ was crucified; but as night passed He rose again today. And they on the day before yesterday were still held fast by sin; but together with Him they have risen. He died in the body, and in the body He rose again. They died through sin, and they have risen again, delivered from sin.

And as now in this time of spring the earth brings forth roses and violets and other flowers; and the rains make the fields yet more lovely, you do not think that the rains cause the flowers to spring up, nor that the earth of its own power brings forth, but that it is by God's command the seed brings forth. And in the beginning water brought forth also animals that moved; for Scripture says: *Let the waters bring forth the creeping creature having life* (Gen. i. 20). And the command was fulfilled, and the substance without life brought forth living creatures. So now the waters bring forth, not reptiles however, but divine spiritual gifts. The waters have brought forth fish that were dumb and void of reason; now they bring forth spiritual fish endowed with reason: fish such as the Apostle caught: *Come ye after me, He says, and I will make you fishers of men* (Mt. iv. 19). This is the fishing He spoke off. A new kind indeed; for they who are wont to fish draw fish out of the water, but we throw them into the water; and that is how we fish!

Once under the Jewish Law there was a pool. Listen to what the pool could do, so as to learn of the poverty of the Law, and understand the richness of the Church. The pool was full of water, and at certain times an angel would descend and move the waters. And at the moving of the waters one sick man would enter the pool and be healed. And only one person was healed each year, and then the grace ended; not because of the poverty of the One Who bestowed the grace, but because of the infirmity of those who received it. Then an angel descended into the pond, and moved its waters, and one person was healed. The Lord of the angels descended into the Jordan, and moved the waters, and healed the whole world.

In the first case he who next descended into the pool, following the first, received no healing; for the grace was given to the Jewish sick. Here, after the first the second is healed, and after the second the third, and after the third the fourth, and even were ten, or a hundred, or ten thousand, or were you to plunge the whole world into the pool, you will not consume the grace, nor exhaust the gift, nor soil the stream. A new way of purification! For it is not of the body. For in bodily purification the more the water cleanses the more it becomes soiled. Here the more the water washes the cleaner it becomes.

Consider how great a gift this is! And treasure the greatness of this gift, O man! It is not lawful for you to live indifferently. Seek with all diligence to know the law to which you are subject. This life is a struggle and a warfare, and one who is fighting restrains himself in everything. Do you wish that I tell you a good and worthy way of doing what is just? Put out of your mind the things which seem to you of no importance but which yet bring about sin. For among our actions some are sinful, and some not sinful in themselves yet the cause of sin. So laughter of its nature is not a sin, but becomes sinful if indulged in beyond measure. For from laughter comes coarse jesting, from jesting arises obscenity in word, from that comes obscenity in deeds, and from evil deeds comes punishment and retribution.

Therefore first take out the root, that you may then remove the whole disease. For if we are watchful regarding the things that are indifferent we shall never fall into what is forbidden. Again, to look upon a woman may seem to many an indifferent thing; yet from this arises lustful desire, and from desire comes fornication, and from fornication chastisement and retribution. So also to live richly and delicately does not seem a very grave thing; yet from this comes excess, and from excess arises a thousand other evils. Let us therefore root out the beginnings of sin. Let us exercise ourselves daily in self-discipline.

For seven days continuously we shall gather here together, and we shall set before you a spiritual table; so that by our efforts you may taste of the divine wisdom, each day instructing you, and arming you against the devil. For now he fiercely assails us; for the greater the gift, so much greater will be the assault against us. For if the devil seeing even one enter paradise cannot bear it, tell me how can he endure to see so many in heaven. You have aroused this fierce beast; but do not fear! You have received greater power, a sharper sword. Pierce the serpent with it. God suffers the demon to rage against you; that you may learn by trial the force of your own strength. And as when a very good trainer of the gymnasium accepts some weak and wretched athlete, and when he has massaged him, taught him, and strengthened his body, he does not allow him to remain idle, but bids him enter the contests, so as to learn from experience what strength he has acquired. So has Christ also done. He could have removed the enemy from our midst, but that you may learn the superiority of His grace, the greatness of the spiritual strength you have received in your baptism, he allows him to attack you, giving you at the same time the opportunity to gain for yourself many victories.

For this reason, during the coming seven days, profit by these instructions, so as to learn how to stand firmly in the contest. We might call the days that follow spiritual nuptials; for in nuptials the adornments of the bridal chamber remain for seven days. And so we lay it upon you that for the coming seven days you assist at these spiritual nuptials. In the world however, after the seven days, every thing is put away; but here, should you wish it, you may remain for all your days in this sacred bridal chamber. And in earthly nuptials also, after a month or two, the spouse is not so lovable to her bridegroom. Here it is not so; for the more time passes the greater becomes the love of the bridegroom, the sweeter His embraces, the closer the spiritual union; provided we are watchful and in earnest.

In earthly nuptials after youth comes age. Here should you desire it youth begins again: a youth without end. A great grace; but it shall be greater if we deserve it. Paul was great when he was baptized; how much greater did he not become? When he began to preach he confounded the Jews. Later he was rapt up to Paradise, and ascended to the third heaven. So we may also increase in the grace given us at baptism: if we will. And this grace increases through doing good, becoming yet more perfect, and giving us yet greater beauty of soul.

And should this happen to us, with confidence shall we enter the dwelling of the Bridegroom, and there enjoy the things He has prepared for those who love Him. May it be granted to each one of us to reach this happiness, through the grace and mercy of our Lord Jesus Christ, to Whom, with the Father and the Holy Ghost, be there glory and adoration, world without end. Amen.

IV. St Augustine, Bishop and Doctor

To the People and to the Children, or, To those Baptized This Day[8]

I. *Grace is given to the Baptized. The Just to be imitated, not the wicked.* Today we address our words to those reborn and baptized in Christ Jesus; and to you all in them, and to them in you. You have been made members of the Body of Christ! If you but reflect upon what you have become all your bones will cry out: *Lord, who is like to thee* (Ps. xliv. 10). For this divine condescension cannot be truly understood, and human thought and language fails us, that without previous merit on your part this free gift has come to you. And for this do we call it a grace: because it is given gratis. And what grace is this? That you are now members of Christ, Children of God; that you are brothers of the Only-Begotten!

But if He is the Only-Begotten, how can you be His brothers, unless it is that He *is* the Only-Begotten by nature, and you have *become* His brothers through grace. Therefore, because you have been made members of Christ I must warn you; for I fear dangers for you, and not alone from those who are pagans, not alone from the Jews, and not so much from the heretics as from bad Catholics. Choose from among the people of God (*the Christians*) those you would imitate. For if you wish to imitate the multitude, you shall then not be among the few who shall enter in *by the narrow way*. Withhold yourself from fornication, from theft, from fraud, from perjury, from things unlawful, from quarrels. Put drunkenness from you. Let you dread adultery as you would death; not the death that parts soul and body, but that in which both body and soul burn for ever.

II. *The devil makes light of the sins of the flesh, though they are grievous and mortal.* My brethren, my sons, my daughters, my sisters, I know the devil does his part, and never ceases to whisper in the heart of those he holds fast in bonds. I know that to fornicators, to adulterers, who are not content with their own wives, he says that the sins of the flesh are not grievous. Against such whispering we must hold before our minds the Incarnation of Christ. It is through the enticements of the flesh the enemy deceives the Christian; making light of what is grave sin, mild what is fierce, sweet what is bitter.

But what does it avail that Satan makes light of what Christ has shown us is grave? Is this some new thing the devil has made up for the believing Christian? 'There is no grave sin in what you do! Do you sin in the flesh or in the spirit? The sin of the flesh is easily forgiven; that God pardons without difficulty. What great evil is there in it?' No. He is using that deception wherein he said: *Eat and you shall be as Gods: no, you shall not die the death!* For God had said: *In what day soever thou shalt eat of it, thou shalt die the death* (Gen. iii. 4, 5; ii. 17).

The commandment of God was ignored. And they gave ear to the persuasions of the devil. Then they learned that the word of God was true: false the trickery of the devil. And what did it avail, I ask you, when the woman said: *The serpent deceived me*? What did her excuse avail? If her excuse was valid, why did condemnation follow?

III. *The Incontinent are corrected and excommunicated. Any woman with whom a man consorts besides his wife is a harlot.* And so I declare to you, my brethren, my sons, who possess wives, that you know no other woman. And you who have them not, and who desire to marry, preserve yourselves uncorrupted; as you desire to find them uncorrupted. You who have vowed yourselves in chastity to God, do not look back. Behold I declare to you, behold I cry out to you, I do that which I must: God has set me here as a preacher, not as an avenger. Yet, where he can, where there is opportunity, where it is given us, where we know, we rebuke, we reprove, we anathematize, we excommunicate!

Yet it is not we who correct you. Why so? Because *neither he that planteth is anything, nor he that watereth; but God that giveth the increase* (I Cor. iii. 7). And now while I am speaking to you, whilst I warn you, what does it avail unless God listens to my prayers for you, and works something in you; that is, in your souls? I say but a few words to you, I commend you to God, and waken fear in those who are baptized, and I seek to build you up. You are members of Christ: listen then, not to me, but to the Apostle. *Shall I then*, he says, *take the members of Christ, and make them the members of a harlot?* (I Cor. vi. 15).

But, someone will say: I know not who: she is not a harlot I have, she is my concubine. O holy bishop are you making a harlot of my concubine? What have *I* said? It is the Apostle says this; and am I then guilty of calumny? I would like to think you are sane: why rage against me as if you were mad? You who say this: have you a wife? I have, you say. Very well: then, whether you wish it or not, she who sleeps with you other than your wife, is as I have said, a harlot. Off now, and tell her that the bishop has insulted you! You have a lawful wife, and another sleeps with you: whoever she is, she is, as I have just said, a harlot! And your wife, she is faithful to you, and knows no other man but you, and seeks to know no other. Since she is chaste, why do you give yourself to fornication? If she has but you alone, what right have you to two? But, you will say: my concubine is my own slave; am I going to the wife of another? Do I go to a common harlot? May I not do as I please in my own house? I tell you, you may not. And they who do this will go to hell, and burn in everlasting fire!

IV. *The Correction of Morals is not to be Deferred.* And here let me open my lips to speak and say: let such persons correct their lives while they still have life; lest afterwards they should wish to and may not. For death comes soon; and then there will be no one to correct you, but there will be someone to cast you into the fire. And when that last hour will come you know not, and yet you say: I shall correct myself.

When will you correct yourself, when will you change your way of life? Tomorrow, you say. Ah, how often you say tomorrow, tomorrow (*crās, crās*)! You sound like a crow! Pay heed now to what I say. While you are crying out in that corvine tone, disaster is rushing to meet you. For the crow, whose voice you imitate, went out from the Ark, and never returned! You, brother, let you return to the Church, of which the Ark was but a figure.

Hearken to me, O you baptized; hear me, O you reborn in Christ's blood! I beseech you by the Name that has been invoked upon you, by this altar to which you have come, by the Sacraments you have received, and by the future Judgement of the living and dead, I beseech you, I adjure you in the Name of Christ, that you imitate not those whom you know to be such as these are; so that there may remain in you His holy grace Who refused to descend from the Cross, but willed to rise again from the tomb!

Turning then to the Lord our God, the Father Almighty, let us as best we can give thanks with all our hearts, beseeching Him that in His Goodness He will mercifully hear our prayers, and by His grace drive evil from our thoughts and actions, increase our faith, guide our minds, grant us His holy inspirations, and bring us to joy without end, through His Son our Lord and Saviour Jesus Christ. Amen.

V. St Augustine, Bishop and Doctor

Peace Be To You,[9] *The Mystical Body*

Jesus stood in the midst of them, and saith to them: Peace be to you (Luke xxiv. 36).

I. *The Heresy of the Manicheans.* The Lord, as you have heard, appeared to His Disciples after His Resurrection, and greeted them, saying: *Peace be to you.* This is indeed peace, and the salutation of Salvation; for salutation receives its name from salvation. And what better than that Salvation Itself should greet mankind?

For Christ is our Salvation. For He is our Salvation Who was wounded for us, and fastened with nails to the Wood, and taken down from the Wood, and laid in the sepulchre. But He rose from the sepulchre; and though His wounds were healed the scars remained. For this He judged expedient for His Disciples: that He should keep His scars to heal the wounds of their soul.

What wounds are these? The wounds of their unbelief. For He

appeared before their eyes, showing them a true body; and they believed they saw a spirit. No light wound of the soul this. And they who continued in this wounded state have caused a malignant heresy. And do not let us think that because they were healed so quickly that the Disciples were not wounded.

Let your Charity consider how had they remained in this wounded state, thinking that His buried Body had not risen, and that a spirit in the likeness of a body deceived their human eyes, had they remained in this belief, rather, had they remained in this unbelief, we should be grieving, not for their wounds, but for their death!

II. *The Hesitation of the Disciples.* But what is the Lord Jesus saying? *Why are you troubled, and why do thoughts arise in your hearts?* If thoughts arise in your hearts the thoughts are from the earth. It is good for man, not that thoughts should rise up in his heart, but that his heart should rise up: whither the Apostle would raise the hearts of the faithful to whom he said: *If you be risen with Christ, seek the things that are above; where Christ is sitting at the right hand of God; mind the things that are above, not the things that are upon the earth. For you are dead; and your life is hid with Christ in God. When Christ shall appear, who is your life, then you also shall appear with him in glory* (Col. iii. 1–4).

In what glory? The glory of the Resurrection. In what glory? Listen to the Apostle speaking of this body: *It is sown in dishonour, it shall rise in glory* (I Cor. xv. 43). The Apostles were unwilling to give this glory to their Master, their Christ, their Lord; they had not begun to believe He could raise His Body from the dead; they did not believe even their own eyes, and when they saw His Body they supposed it was a spirit they saw. Yet we believe those who preach Him to us, though they do not show Him. And they did not believe Christ, showing Himself to them.

A grievous wound: let the remedy of the scars appear! *Why are you troubled, and why do thoughts arise in your hearts? See my hands and my feet,* where I was fastened by the nails. *Handle, and see.* You see, and you do not see. *Handle, and see.* See what? That *a spirit hath not flesh and bones, as you see me to have. And when he had said this,* so it is written, *he showed them his hands and feet.*

III. *How they were persuaded to believe. And while they were yet hesitant and wondering for joy.* They were now joyful, yet their hesitation remained. For something had taken place which was incredible; yet it had taken place. Is it incredible now that the body of Christ has risen from the tomb? The whole healed world believes it: and he who believes not remains unhealed. Then it was incredible: and they were brought to believe not alone through their eyes, but through their hands, so that faith might enter their heart by way of their senses, so that the faith thus entering their heart might be preached throughout the world, to those who would neither see nor touch Him, and yet without hesitation would believe in Him.

Have you here, He says, *anything to eat?* How much the Good Builder adds to the edifice of our faith? He suffered no hunger, yet He asked for food. And He ate for the occasion, not because of need. And then the Apostles acknowledge that His Body is real; and the world acknowledges It from their preaching.

IV. *Against the Manicheans.* If by chance there are heretics who still believe in their hearts that Christ showed Himself to their eyes, but not the true Body of Christ, let them now put that belief aside, and let the Gospel persuade them. We reprove them for thinking this: He will condemn them if they continue to think it. Who are you who do not believe that a body laid in the tomb could not rise again? If you are a Manichean, you do not believe He was crucified, because you do not believe He was born; you then proclaim that all that He showed was false.

He showed what was false; you however say only what is true? You do not lie with your tongue; but He lied with His Body? Then you consider that He appeared to men's eyes what He was not; that He was a spirit, not a body. Listen to Him: He loves you, do not have Him damn you. Listen to Him speaking. See! He is addressing you, you unhappy one, He is speaking to you! What has troubled you, and why do thoughts arise in your heart? *See!* He is saying, *my hands and feet. Handle, and see: for a spirit hath not flesh and bones, as you see me to have.* The Truth said this; and He was deceiving us? It was a body, it was flesh; what had been buried appeared. Let hesitation end; let it give way to becoming praise.

Christ awakens faith. He shows Himself then to His Disciples. What is He, Himself? The Head of the Church. The Church that was to be throughout the world He foresaw; the Disciples did not yet see it. He showed them its Head; He promised them the Body. For He now adds what is to follow: *These are the words which I spoke to you, while I was yet with you.* What does this mean: *While I was yet with you?* Was He not *with them* while He was speaking to them?

What then does this mean: *While I was yet with you?* While I was with you as *mortal man*, which I am no longer. I was *with you* when I was about to die. What does *with you* mean? I Who was to die was with you who were to die. Now I am with you no longer; for I shall die no more, with those who are to die. It is this, then, *which I spoke to you.* What?

V. *That all things must needs be fulfilled, which are written in the Law, and the Prophets, and the Psalms, concerning me.* I said to you that all things must be fulfilled. *Then He opened their minds.* Come then, Lord! Use Thy keys, open that we may understand! Behold you tell us all things, and you are not believed! You are supposed to be a spirit; you are handled, you are touched, and they still hesitate who touch you! You instruct them from the Scriptures, and yet they do not understand. Their hearts are closed; open them and enter there. He does this: *Then he opened their minds.* Open, O Lord, open the heart that still doubts concerning Christ! Open *his* mind who believes that Christ was a spirit: *Then he opened their minds, that they might understand the Scriptures.*

The Future Church is promised to all nations. Christ is distinguished from the Apostles: The Church from us.

And he said to them. What did He say? *Thus it is written, and thus it was necessary.* What was necessary? For *Christ to suffer, and rise again from the dead, the third day.* This they have seen. They have seen Him suffering; they have seen Him hanging on the Cross, they were seeing Him in their midst after His Resurrection from the dead, living. What therefore was it they did not see? His Body; that is, the Church. They saw Him; Her they did not see. They saw the Bridegroom; the Bride lay still concealed. Let Her also come forth. *Thus it is written, and thus it behoveth Christ to suffer, and to rise again from the dead, the third day.* This is the Bridegroom.

VI. What of the Bride? *And that penance and remission of sin should be preached in his name, unto all nations, beginning at Jerusalem.* The Disciples had not yet seen this: they did not yet see the Church among all the nations; beginning from Jerusalem. The Head they had seen: concerning the Body they believed the Head. Because of what they had seen they believed what they had not yet seen. And we are like them. We see something they saw not; and there is something they saw that we do not see. What do we see that they did not see? The Church throughout the nations. What do we not see which they saw? Christ in the Flesh. And as they saw Him, and believed in His Body, so we see His Body, and believe in Its Head.

May what we have both seen help each of us! Christ seen in the Flesh helps them: so that they believe in the Church to come. The Church Visible helps us: so that we believe Christ arose from the dead. Their faith was made full; ours also is made full. Their faith was made full seeing the Head; ours seeing the Body. The Whole Christ became known to them; and so has He become known to us. But He was not wholly seen by them; nor is He wholly seen by us. By them the Head was seen, the Body believed; by us the Body is seen, the Head believed. Yet to no one is Christ wanting. He is complete in all; though His Body is still incomplete.

They believed, and through them many believed in Jerusalem; Judea believed, Samaria believed. Let members be added; let the building be raised upon the foundations: *For other foundation no man can lay, but that which is laid: which is Christ Jesus* (I Cor. iii. 11). Let the Jews rage! Let them be filled with jealousy. Let Stephen be stoned. Let Saul hold the garments of those who stone him: Saul the future Apostle Paul! Let Stephen be put to death; let the Church in Jerusalem suffer persecution. And from there let the burning brands go forth, and increase, and flame out! For in a manner the brands were kindled in the Church at Jerusalem by the Holy Spirit: where they had but one heart and one soul for God (Acts iv. 32). And when Stephen was stoned the whole Body suffered persecution: the brands were scattered, and the world caught fire.

VII. *Saul is changed into a Preacher of the Gospel.* Then following after these happenings, the raging Saul receives letters from the Chief Priests, and, burning with fury, breathing slaughter, thirsting for blood, he begins his journey, to seize as many as he can and bring them bound to punishment, and sate himself with the blood he has shed. But where is God? Where is Christ? Where is He Who crowned Stephen? Where but in heaven? May He now look down on Saul, and laugh at him as he rages, and call to him from the heavens: *Saul, Saul, why persecutest thou Me?* I am in heaven: you are on earth: yet you are persecuting Me! My Head you do not touch: but you are crushing My members. Why are you doing this? What do you gain? *It is hard for thee to kick against the goad* (Acts ix. 5).[10] Kick as you will: you but torment yourself. So put aside your rage; take hold of your sanity. Put aside your evil purpose: look for good counsel.

At the words he was thrown to the ground. Who was thrown to the ground? The persecutor. See! At a word he is laid low. Why are you on this journey? Whom do you rage against? Those you pursued you will now follow; for those you persecuted you will now suffer persecution. He rises up a preacher who was thrown down a persecutor. He has heard the voice of the Lord. He was blinded: but only in the body, that his soul might receive light. He was led to Ananias; he was instructed in many things. He was baptized; and came forth an Apostle. Speak now: preach, preach Christ, spread the Gospel, O good ram! so long a wolf! Behold him; take note of him who once raged cruelly: *But God forbid that I should glory, save in the cross of Our Lord Jesus Christ; by whom the world is crucified to me, and I to the world* (Gal. vi. 14).

Spread the Gospel: spread with your tongue what you have conceived in your heart. Let the Gentiles hear you! Let the Gentiles believe! Let the Gentiles blossom forth! Let the Spouse be born to the Lord, empurpled with the blood of martyrs! And from her how many come? How many members adhere to the Head, and now hold fast to Him, and believe? They were baptized, and yet others shall be baptized, and after us yet others shall come!

Then, I say, at the end of the world the stones will adhere to the foundation, living stones, holy stones, so that the whole edifice may be built up from that Church, yes, from this very Church which now sings the new canticle, while the house is a-building; for so has it the psalm thus named: *When the House was Built after the Captivity*. And what does it say? *Sing ye to the Lord a new canticle; sing to the Lord all the earth* (Ps. xcv. 1).

How great a House! And when will it sing the new canticle? While it is being built. And when will it be dedicated? At the end of the world. Its foundations have already been dedicated: because He ascending into heaven *dieth no more*. When we also have risen, and shall die no more, then shall we be dedicated.

Turning then to the Lord our God, the Father Almighty, let us as best we can give thanks with all our hearts, beseeching Him that in His Goodness He will mercifully hear our prayers, and by His grace drive evil from our thoughts and actions, increase our faith, guide our minds, grant us His holy inspirations, and bring us to joy without end, through His Son our Lord and Saviour Jesus Christ. Amen.

VI. St Augustine, Bishop and Doctor

To Children, on The Holy Sacrifice[11]

1. I have not forgotten my promise. For I promised you, those who were baptized, a sermon in which I would explain to you the mystery of the Lord's Table: which you now see before you, and of which last night you became partakers. For you must know what it is you have received, what it is you are about to receive, what it is you should receive every day.

This Bread you see on the altar, consecrated by the word of God, is Christ's Body. This chalice, or rather, what the chalice holds, is Christ's Blood. By them Christ the Lord wishes to bestow on us His Body and His Blood, Which He shed for you unto the forgiveness of sins.

If you have received them worthily, you are what you have received. For the Apostle says: *For we, being many, are one bread, one body; all that partake of one bread* (I Cor. x. 17). So did he explain the mystery of the Lord's Table: *One bread, one body; all that partake of one bread.* He puts before you here how much we are to love unity. For this Bread, was it made out of one grain of wheat? Were there not many grains?

But, before they came to make the bread, they were separated. After they had been ground in the mill, they were united together by water. For unless wheat is ground, and mixed together with water, it will not take the shape we know as bread. So you also, you who have been as it were ground in a mill: by the grace of exorcism, and the humiliation of fasting. Then came Baptism, and water; and you were sprinkled with it, so that you came to be like the bread.

But, there can be no bread without a fire. What does the fire stand for? Confirmation. For the oil of chrism is the symbol of the Holy Ghost: our Fire. Pay careful attention to the Acts of the Apostles when they are being read: for we begin now to read this book. Today we commence reading the book called the Acts of the Apostles.[12] Whoever wants to thrive in goodness, has the means to do so. When you all come together to the church, put away vanities: be very attentive to the reading of the Scriptures. *We* are *your* books.

Pay attention then, and keep your eyes open; for at Pentecost the Holy Ghost will come. And this is how He will come. He will show Himself as tongues of fire. For He will kindle charity in us: by which we shall earnestly love God, and think little of the world and our chaff will be burned away, and our hearts purified like gold. The Holy Spirit then comes as the fire after the water: and you are made into the bread which is the Body of Christ. And in this way we are taught about unity.

Consider the holy mysteries in their due order. First, after the Prayers, you are exhorted to *lift up your hearts*. This is fitting for the members of Christ. For if you have become the *members* of Christ where then is your *Head*? Members have a head. If the head did not lead the way, the members would not follow! Whither has *your* Head gone?

What is it you recite in the Creed? '*The third day He rose again from the dead. He ascended into heaven, and sits at the right hand of God the Father Almighty. Our* Head then is in heaven. So, when we say: *Sursum corda*: Lift up your hearts; you answer: *Habemus ad Dominum*: We have raised them to the Lord.

And do not think it is by your power, by your merits, that your heart is raised up to the Lord: for to have your heart lifted up is God's gift to you. So when the people have answered: *Habemus ad Dominum*: *We have raised them to the Lord*, the Bishop, or the Priest, who is offering the Sacrifice goes on to say: *Gratias agamus Domino Deo nostro*: *Let us give thanks to the Lord our God*; because our heart is raised up. We are giving thanks, because, unless He gave us this gift, our heart would be upon this earth. And you bear witness that *Dignum et justum est*, that *it is just and fitting*, that we should give Him thanks Who has caused us to raise our hearts to our Head in heaven.

Then, after the consecration of the Sacrifice, where He wishes us also to be His Sacrifice—as we have shown where it was explained before this that we also are a sacrifice (*offering*) to God, and that this is a sign of what we are[13]—so when the consecration is completed we say the Lord's Prayer,[14] which you have received (from God), and which you have recited.[15] After this is said: *Pax vobiscum*: *Peace be unto you*; and then Christians salute each other with a holy kiss. This is a sign of peace: so that as we do with our lips so should our consciences be. That is, as your lips approach your brother's, so must your heart not draw back from his heart.

Great indeed are the Holy Mysteries, and very great. Do you wish to know how great we are to consider them? The Apostle says: *Whosoever shall eat this bread, or drink the chalice of the Lord unworthily, shall be guilty of the Body and of the Blood of the Lord* (I Cor. xi. 27). What does it mean to receive *unworthily*? To receive laughing; or to receive with contempt? Do not hold that as the unworthy thing, for the reason that you see it. What you see passes away; but what it stands for, and you do not see, does not pass away; that remains.

And when you have received, and have eaten, and have consumed the Body of Christ; is the Body of Christ then consumed? Is the Church of Christ consumed? Are the members of Christ consumed? Far from it! Here they are made clean: there they are crowned. What is here made known to us will remain for ever, though it seems to pass away. Receive then having yourselves in mind: that you may be united in heart; that your heart may be ever above. For what you hope for is not on the earth, but in heaven. Let your faith in God be strong; and let it be acceptable to God. Because in this life you believe that which you do not now see, in the life to come you will see Him, and you shall have joy without end. Amen.

VII. St Proclus, Patriarch of Constantinople

On the Holy Pasch[16]

I. Glorious is our Paschal Festival; and truly splendid this great assembly of the Christian people. And within this holy mystery are contained things both old and new. The celebration of this week, or rather its joyfulness, is shared by such a multitude, that not alone does man rejoice on earth, but even the powers of heaven are united with us in joyful celebration of Christ's Resurrection.[17] For now the Angels, and the hosts of the Archangels, also keep holiday this day, and stand waiting for the triumphant return from this earth of Christ Our Lord, Who is King of heaven. And the multitude of the Blessed likewise rejoice, proclaiming the Christ Who was begotten before the day star rose (Ps. cix. 3). The earth rejoices, now washed by divine blood. The sea rejoices, honoured as it was by His Feet upon its waters. And ever more let each soul rejoice, who is born again of water and the Holy Ghost; and at last set free from the ancient curse!

II. With such great joy does Christ fill our hearts this day by His Resurrection, not alone because He gives us the gladness of this day, but because He has also given us salvation through His Passion, immortality through His Death, healing for our wounds, and resurrection from our fall! And long ago, Beloved, this Paschal Mystery, begun in Egypt, was symbolically pointed out to us in the Old Law, in the sacrifice of the lamb. And now, in the Gospel, let us celebrate the Resurrection of the Lamb: our Pasch.

Then a lamb of the flock was slain, as the Law laid down (Ex. xii); now Christ, the Lamb of God, is offered up. There a sheep from the sheepfold; here, in place of the sheep, the Good Shepherd lays down His life for His sheep. There the sprinkled blood upon the doorposts was a sign of deliverance for the people of God; here the precious Blood of Christ was poured out for the deliverance of the whole world: that we might be forgiven our sins. There the firstborn of Egypt were slain; here the manifold children of sinners are made clean confessing the Lamb. There Pharao and his fearful host were drowned in the sea; here the spiritual Pharao with all His people are immersed in the deep of baptism. There the children of the Hebrews, crossing over the Red Sea, sang their song of victory to their Deliverer, singing: *Let us sing to the Lord: for he is gloriously magnified* (Ex. xv. 1); here those found worthy of baptism sing their song of victory, singing: *One Holy, One Lord Jesus Christ, in the glory of God the Father.*[18]

The prophet also sings: *The Lord hath reigned, he is clothed with beauty* (Ps. xcii. 1). The Hebrews, after the crossing of the Red Sea, ate manna in the desert; now, those who have come forth from the waters of baptism eat bread that came down from heaven. For His is the Voice that says: *I am the living bread, which cometh down from heaven* (Jn. vi. 31).

III. Rightly then does Paul exclaim: *Now all these things happened to them in figure: and they are written for our correction, upon whom the ends of the world are come* (I Cor. x. 11). The Jews plainly erred in not recognizing the reality: *For if they had known it, they would never have crucified the Lord of glory* (I Cor. ii. 8). But unhappy that they were, they did not understand that the figure served only till the reality came. For a sculptor preparing for the king a statue of gold or silver or bronze, first makes a model of his statue in clay. And he is careful to preserve his clay model, until he has completed the real statue, from gold or silver or perhaps bronze: it being of the utmost necessity to him as the artificer. The statue made, the clay model is broken up; as useless and unnecessary. So the Jews, before the Reality came amongst men, rightly preserved the figures of what was to come. But after Our Lord Jesus Christ appeared, He Who said: *I am the light of the world; I am the truth and the life; I am the resurrection* (Jn. viii. 12; xiv. 6; xi. 25), it is folly for them to cling to the figures; which no longer have even this value, that they are types and figures.

And so let the Jews, fighting against the will of God, make an end of offering a dumb sheep for the redemption of their people; for now the Spiritual Lamb, the Son of God, Who takes away the sins of the world, has been offered for us, and has delivered us out of the hands of the destroyer. Let them say farewell to the old leaven; and let them receive instead the new unleavened Bread of Truth. Let them eat no more of *the wild lettuce* (Ex. xii. 8): for Christ has taken bitter gall for us, that He might then mingle sweetness in the fountains which heal us. Let us then feast; *but not with the old leaven, nor with the leaven of malice and wickedness; but with the unleavened bread of sincerity and truth* (I Cor. v. 8), so that after our departure from this life, we may together with the angels give praise to the Lord of glory, singing with them: *The Lord hath reigned: he is clothed with beauty* (Ps. xcii. 1). To Him be Glory and Honour and Adoration for ever. Amen.

VIII. St Leo the Great, Pope and Doctor

On the Resurrection of the Lord II[19]

Synopsis:

I. That Christ's Cross is both a *sacrament* and an example.
II. In the Incarnation our nature was assumed by the Word, so that He might pay it as a price.
III. We are buried, and rise again, with Christ: and strengthened by Christ abiding with us on earth; and invited to reign with Him in glory.
IV. The power and example of the Cross, by which we are armed against evil desires, is everywhere present to us.
V. We must strive towards heavenly things, through contempt of earthly; holding fast to faith in the two-fold nature in Christ.
VI. Through the *passing-over* of Christ, which refers only to our nature, we are prepared for passing over to heaven.
VII. The Eutychians, who deny Christ possessed our nature, have no share in the Paschal Feast.

I. The Gospel narrative, Dearly Beloved, describes for us the whole Paschal mystery; and thus, by way of our bodily ears, it has reached the ears of the soul, so that there are none amongst us who have not formed a picture of what took place. For the account of this divinely inspired history shows clearly with what impiety our Lord Jesus Christ was betrayed, with what kind of judgement He was condemned, with what cruelty He was crucified, and with what glory raised from the dead.

But to this account we must add the sermon our office requires of us; since I feel that you, with devout expectation, claim from us that which is due to you also by custom; namely, that to the solemn reading of the Lesson there be added the exhortation of the priest. So that there may be in the ears of the faithful no grounds for ignorance, the seed of the word of God, which consists in the preaching of the Gospel, ought to be cultivated in your heart, so that removing the thorns and briars which might smother it, the young and tender shoots of holy knowledge and just desires may be free to bear fruit.

For the Cross of Christ, which was dedicated to the salvation of mortal man, is both a sacrament and an example; a sacrament, in which the divine power is made known; an example, by means of which devotion is kindled among men; for to those freed from the yoke of slavery their redemption also brings them this: that they may imitate it. For if human wisdom takes such pride in its errors, so that each one copies the notions, the manners, all the ideas, of the one he has chosen as guide, what share have we in the Name of Christ if we are not wholly united with Him Who is, as He has taught us, *The way and the truth and the life* (Jn. xiv. 6)? The Way of holy living; the Truth of divine teaching: and the Life of happiness without end.

II. Since the whole human race had fallen in our First Parents, the mercy of God willed, through His Only-Begotten Son Jesus Christ, to help the creature He had made in His own image and likeness; so that the restoration of their nature would not be done outside of that nature; and so that their second state should be raised higher than the dignity they possessed from the beginning.

Happy indeed would man be had he not fallen from what God made him; yet happier should he persevere in what God has re-made him. It was a great honour that Christ should take his form; yet more that man should have the nature that is in Christ. For that Nature has taken us to itself (which condescends to whatever measure of kindness It wills, yet not to the point of change) which would neither lose what was His in ours, nor what was ours in His; which so made One Person of divinity and humanity in Himself, that in the ordering within Him of both infirmity and power, His Body did not become impassible because of His divinity, nor could His divinity come to suffer through His Body.

That Nature raised us up, which would not break off the branch of our race from the common way, and would shut out the contagion of sin that passed to every man. Weakness and mortality, which were not sin but the chastisement of sin, were taken on Himself in punishment, that they might be as a price paid by the Redeemer of the world. What in all men is the effect of sin, in Christ is a mystery of loving kindness. Free of the debt, He gave Himself to this most cruel debtor; and suffered Jewish hands to torture His immaculate Flesh, in service to the devil. So this He willed to remain mortal, until the Resurrection; so that, to those who believe in Him, neither persecution should seem insurmountable, nor death terrifying. And since there could be no doubt of His sharing our nature, neither can there be doubt of our sharing His glory.

III. If then, Dearly Beloved, if without faltering we believe in our hearts what we confess with our lips, then have we in Christ been crucified, we have died with Him, we have been buried with Him, and with Him have risen again on the third day. Because of this the Apostle says: *If you be risen with Christ, seek the things that are above; where Christ Jesus is sitting at the right hand of God. Mind the things that are above, not the things that are upon the earth. For you are dead; and your life is hid with Christ in God* (Col. iii. 1–4).

And that the hearts of the faithful may know that they have the means by which, putting away the desires of the world, they may be raised to heavenly wisdom, the Lord promises us His own Presence, saying: *Behold I am with you all days, even to the consummation of the world* (Mt. xxviii. 20). For it was not without design the Holy Ghost said, through the mouth of Isaias: *Behold a virgin shall conceive, and bear a son, and his name shall be called Emmanuel, which being interpreted, is God with us* (Is. vii. 14; Mt. ii. 23). Jesus is therefore fulfilling the promise of His Name, and He Who ascends to heaven does not abandon His adopted children. He Who sits at the right hand of the Father, the Same dwells in all the faithful; and He Who invites us to the glory of heaven, confirms us in patience here on earth.

IV. Let us then be not led astray by vanities, nor falter when things are hard for us; in the one case deceit will flatter us, in the other our difficulties but grow worse. But since *the earth is full of the mercy of the Lord* (Ps. xxxii. 5), everywhere the victory of the Lord is with us, that the words may be fulfilled which say: *Have confidence, I have overcome the world* (Jn. xvi. 33). Whether we are fighting the claims of the world, or the lusts of the flesh, or the darts of the heretics, let us at all times arm ourselves with the Lord's Cross. And if we in the sincerity of truth keep from ourselves the leaven of our old wickedness, the Paschal Feast will never end for us. For in all the changes of this life, filled as they are with so many kinds of suffering, we must keep in mind what the Apostle teaches us: *Let this mind be in you, which was also in Christ Jesus; who being in the form of God, thought it not robbery to be equal with God: but emptied himself, taking the form of a servant, being made in the likeness of men, and in habit found as a man. He humbled himself, becoming obedient unto death, even to the death of the Cross. For which cause God also hath exalted him, and hath given him a name which is above all names: that in the name of Jesus every knee should bow, of those that are in heaven, on earth, and under the earth: and that every tongue should confess, that the Lord Jesus Christ is in the glory of God the Father* (Phil. ii. 5–11).

If, he says, you understand the mystery of the Great Compassion, and if you grasp what the Only Begotten Son of God has done for the salvation of men, let this be in your mind, which was also in Christ Jesus, whose lowliness let none of those who are rich despise, and none who are high born scorn. For no human good fortune can reach the height where it will not feel itself shamed that God, while continuing in the form of God, thought it not unworthy of Him to take on Himself the nature of a slave.

V. Imitate what He has done; love what He has loved, and finding in you the grace of God, love your own nature again in Him. For as He did not lose His riches in poverty, nor His glory in lowliness, nor immortality in death, so you also, following in these same footsteps, in these very footprints, hold earthly things as nothing, that you may acquire what is heavenly. To take up the Cross is death to covetousness, the end of vices, a turning away from vanity, the renunciation of all error. For they who are without shame, the lustful, the proud in heart, the greedy, have no part in the Pasch of the Lord; yet none of these are so far from this feast as heretics, and those above all who hold false beliefs concerning the Incarnation of the Word: either by lessening what belongs to the divinity, or by emptying out what belongs to His humanity.

For the Son of God is true God, having wholly from the Father that which the Father is; not subject to time through a beginning, or to alteration by change; neither separated from Unity, nor separate from Omnipotence; the eternal Only-Begotten Son of the Eternal Father; so that the soul informed by faith believing in the Father, the Son, and the Holy Ghost, does not, within the Same Essence of the One Godhead, divide Unity into degrees of relationship, or confound the Trinity with Oneness (*individuality*).

But it is not enough to know the Son of God only in the nature of the Father, unless we also acknowledge Him in our own: though not as withdrawing from what is His as God. For that emptying of Himself which He gave as the price of human redemption, was a dispensation of divine mercy, not a deprivation of the divine majesty. For since in the eternal design of God, *there was no other name under heaven given to men, whereby we must be saved* (Acts iv. 12), He Who was invisible made His own a nature that was visible; the Timeless what was temporal; the Impassible that which could suffer; and this not so that power could be eclipsed in weakness, but that our weakness might pass over to unchanging strength.

VI. For this reason this Festival, which we call the Pasch, is by the Hebrews called *Phase*; that is, *Passing-over*; as the Evangelist tells us, where he says: *Before the festival day of the Pasch, Jesus knowing that his hour was come, that he would pass out of this world to the Father* (Jn. xiii. 1). And to which nature did this coming *Passing-over* belong but to ours; for the Father was inseparably in the Son, and the Son in the Father?

But since the Word and the Flesh are the One Person, we do not separate what was assumed from the One Who assumes, and the honour of the one upraised is spoken of as being an *increase* of Him Who upraised us (Col. ii. 19), as the Apostle says in the words we recalled to you: *For which cause God also hath exalted him, and hath given him a name which is above all names.* Here it is the raising up of the humanity He assumed that is praised; that He is Co-eternal in the glory of the Divinity, Who in His Passion remained God Indivisible.

That they may have part in this unspeakable blessing, the Lord Himself prepares for His faithful children a blessed *passing-over*, when, as the time of His Passion drew near, He began to pray; and not alone, for His Apostles and Disciples, but also for the whole Church, saying: *And not for them only do I pray, but for them also who through their word shall believe in me; that they all may be one, as thou, Father, in me, and I in thee, that they also may be one in us* (Jn. xvii. 20, 21).

VII. Of this *oneness* with Him they can have no part who deny that human nature remains in the Son of God, Who is God; who are enemies of this saving Mystery; and exiles from the Paschal Feast. For since they deny the Gospel, and contradict the Creed, they cannot celebrate it with us. And though they dare to lay claim to the name of Christian, yet every creature, Whose Head is Christ, scorns them. But you, rightly exulting in this sacred Day, and devoutly rejoicing, admit no falsehood to the sacred truth, and doubt neither Christ's Birth in the flesh, nor His Passion or death, or the Resurrection of His Body; since, without separation of Him from His Divinity, you acknowledge that Christ was truly born of the Virgin Mary, that He was truly nailed to the wood of the Cross, truly laid in His Body in the sepulchre, truly Christ in the glory of the Resurrection, and truly sits at the right hand of the Majesty of the Father. From whence also we look, as the Apostle says: *For the Saviour, Our Lord Jesus Christ, who will reform the body of our lowness, made like to the body of his glory* (Phil. iii. 20, 21). Who lives and reigns with the Father and the Holy Ghost for ever and ever. Amen.

IX. St Maximus, Bishop and Father

The Prayer of the Good Thief[20]

Synopsis:

In this feast of Christ's Resurrection, we especially rejoice that, by the Mystery of this new sacrament, our sins are taken away; heaven given back to us, paradise restored. The faith of the Good Thief upon his cross has helped the whole world. The Prayer of Christ for His executioners.

Most fittingly does the world rejoice, with great gladness, upon this day; for with Christ returning from the dead the hope of resurrection has everywhere been awakened in the hearts of men. For it is but right that when the Lord of creation triumphs, the creatures He has made should also rejoice. This day the heavens rejoice, for now at length they see the earth, defiled by sin, made clean in the Blood of the Lord. The multitudes of the hosts of heaven rejoice, for their king has overthrown in battle the hosts of the prince of evil. The sun rejoices, and now with unceasing thankfulness holds back by its joyful beams that woeful darkness that overshadowed it as Christ was dying. And together with them we too above all others must rejoice, for whom the Only-Begotten Son of God, Who also is True God, clothed Himself in our flesh, that through that flesh He might come to the Cross, by the Cross suffer death, and through death despoil the kingdom of hell. Should we not rejoice: we whose sins the mystery of this new sacrament has taken away, to whom heaven is given, paradise restored?

And as He drew near His end, the Lord Himself says to the Thief then hanging on his cross: he whose faith, neither Christ's torment, nor his own, had weakened: *Amen, I say to you, this day thou shalt be with me in paradise*. For the Thief had said to Him: *Lord, remember me when thou shalt come into thy kingdom* (Lk. xxiii). How admirable this faith, Brethren: that a thief who had been judged unworthy of this life, should amid his torments nourish the hope of life eternal, and believe, that this could be given to him by One Who also was being crucified? And how justly does the believing Thief receive the favour of such a promise: he who, in that hour when the Apostles scattered in fear, had confessed the Kingdom of God? And the merit of this one confession wipes away all his past sins; in that brief moment whatever crimes he had committed, throughout all the years of his life, were now forgiven.

Nor did the blood he shed in his robberies condemn him before God: for he believed that the Blood of Christ was shed for a Kingdom, not for a punishment. And that this death was a gain for all men, there can, Beloved Brethren, be no possible doubt. For who can despair of God's grace, when the Thief was forgiven; should he unite the faith of the Thief with his own humble prayer for pardon?

We have yet another shining example of the Lord's most loving kindness, and because of it, let us, putting away all fear, and all deadly despair, place our trust in the unspeakable generosity of Our Redeemer. For when, condemned by the Godless, Christ hung upon the Cross, and the Jews in their evil rage mocked at Him they had crucified, in the midst of His agony, this kind Petitioner prayed to His Almighty Father for His executioners, and said: *Father, forgive them, for they know not what they do*.

And though in His hands was the judgement of both the living and the dead, He implored pardon for those who were then perishing in sin; and this, I believe, that He might show us beyond any manner of doubt, that He forgave them their awful crime, and that His Father would also spare them, if they, putting away their unbelief, would come together in Christ's Name. For who can doubt the effect of that prayer, where He Who is Goodness asks help for those in misery? *They know not*, He says, *what they do*. The Jews knew well that they were shedding the blood of an innocent man; but they did not know that the guilt of all men was being washed away in that Blood. They knew they were punishing Christ by this most bitter torment of the Cross; but they did not know that it was through this Cross the Son of God would triumph. They knew He would die; but they did not know He would rise again. So, well might the Lord declare: *They know not what they do*.

For they knew not, the Jews, of what immense goodness their very wickedness was the instrument. But the Lord, in the knowledge of His own majesty, has compassion on their human errors, and knowing how great the joy that would follow these torments, while He yet endured them, forgives the crime of those who were crucifying Him: willing that His death would give life to His slayers, and be the condemnation of those who would perish. Returning from hell He seeks His Apostles, so that He might show them, that within Him there was both the power of divinity, and the reality of our flesh.

Because of this, Brethren, let us rejoice in Christ, now risen from the dead. Let us hold firmly, that He has recalled this Flesh from the sepulchre that we may merit to have part in that wondrous common heritage: namely, the grace of the Apostles, and the Resurrection of the Lord, by the help of this Same Lord Who with the Father and the Holy Ghost lives and reigns world without end. Amen.

X. St Gregory the Great, Pope and Doctor

Given to the People in the Basilica of the Blessed Virgin Mary, on the Holy Day of the Resurrection

The Mystery of the Resurrection[21]

1. It has been my custom, beloved brethren, to speak to you on many of the Gospel readings, by means of a sermon I had already dictated for you. But since I have been unable, because of the weakness of my throat, to read to you myself what I had prepared, I notice that some among you listen somewhat indifferently. So, contrary to my usual practice, I shall for the future make the effort during the sacred solemnities of the Mass to explain the Gospel, not through a sermon I have dictated, but by speaking directly to you myself.

So for the future it shall be the rule for me to speak to you in this way. For the words which are spoken directly to sluggish souls awaken them more readily than a sermon that is read to them; moving them by that touch as it were of authority, so that they listen with more attention. I am not, as I well know, competent to fulfil this office: but let your charity make good what my ignorance denies me. For I have in mind Him Who has said: *Open thy mouth wide, and I will fill it* (Ps. lxxx. 11). We all have in mind a *good work*, and it will be *perfected* by His divine assistance (II Tim. iii. 17). And also, this great solemnity of the Sunday of the Resurrection gives us a fitting occasion for speaking to you: for it would indeed be unfitting that the tongue of our body should be silent in the praises that are due this day; that day on which the Body of our Author rose again from the dead.

2. You have heard, Beloved, how the holy women who had followed the Lord came to His tomb, bringing with them sweet spices, so that with tender affection they might tend Him in death Whom they had loved in life. And this tells us something which we should observe in the life of our holy Church. And it is important we give attention to what here took place: to see what we must do to imitate them. And we also, who believe in Him Who died, truly come with sweet spices to His tomb, when we come seeking the Lord, bringing with us the sweet odour of virtue, and the credit of good works.

But these women who came bringing sweet spices beheld angels. And this signifies that those souls who, because of their holy love, come seeking the Lord, bearing the sweet spices of virtue, shall also see the citizens of heaven. And let us also take note of what it means that the angel is seen sitting *on the right side*. For what does the left side mean but this present life; and the right hand side, if not life eternal? Because of this it is written in the Canticle of Canticles: *His left hand is under my head, and his right hand shall embrace me* (Cant. ii. 6).

And so, since Our Redeemer has now *passed over* beyond the mortality of this present life, rightly does the Angel, who had come to announce His entry into eternal life, sit *at the right side*. And he came clothed in white: for he was announcing the joy of this our present solemnity. For the whiteness of his garments signifies the glory of our great Feast. Should we say ours or His? That we may speak truly let us say that it is both ours and His. For this day of our Redeemer's Resurrection is also our day of great joy; for it has restored us to immortality. It is also a day of joy for the angels: for restoring us to heaven, it has filled up again the number of its citizens. On this our festival day, and His, an angel appeared, clothed in white robes, because they are rejoicing that because we are restored to heaven the losses their heavenly home had suffered are now made good.

3. But let us hear what is said to the women who came? *Be not affrighted!* As though he said to them: Let them fear who love not the coming of the heavenly citizens. Let them fear who, steeped in bodily desires, have no hope of belonging to them. But you, why should you fear, meeting your own? Matthew also, describing the appearance of the Angel, says of him: *And his countenance was as lightning, and his raiment as snow* (Mt. xxviii. 3). Lightning awakens dread and fear; the white radiance of snow is soothing. For Almighty God is both terrifying to sinners, and comforting to those who are good. Rightly then is the Angel, the Witness of the Resurrection, revealed to us with countenance like the lightning, and his garments white as snow: so that even by his appearance he might awaken fear in the reprobate, and bring consolation to the just.

And rightly also, for the same reason, there went before the Lord's People in the desert, a column of fire by night, and a column of smoke by day (Ex. xiii. 21, 22). For in fire there is fear; but in the cloud of smoke the comforting assurance of what we can see: day also meaning the life of the just, and night the life of sinners. Because of this Paul, speaking to converted sinners, says: *For you were heretofore darkness, but now light in the Lord* (Eph. v. 8). So a pillar of cloud was set before them by day, and a pillar of fire by night: because Almighty God shall appear mild of countenance to the just, but fearful to the wicked. Coming to judge us, He shall comfort the one by the mildness of His countenance, and terrify the other with the severity of His justice.

4. Now let us hear what the angel says. *You seek Jesus of Nazareth.* Jesus, in the Latin tongue, is *saving*; that is, *Saviour*. Then however many were called Jesus, by name, not because of the reality it means. So the place is added, to make clear of what Jesus he is speaking: *Of Nazareth.* And to this he adds the reason they seek Him: *Who was crucified.* And then he goes on: *He is risen, he is not here.* That He was not there was said only of His Bodily Presence; for no where is He absent in the power of His divinity. *But go,* he continues, *tell his disciples and Peter, that he goeth before you into Galilee.*

Now we have to ask ourselves, why did he, speaking of the Disciples, single out Peter by name? But, had the Angel not referred to him in this way, Peter would never have dared to appear again among the Apostles. He is bidden then by name to come, so that he will not despair because of his denial of Christ. And here we must ask ourselves, why did Almighty God permit the one He had placed over the whole Church to be frightened by the voice of a maid servant, and even to deny Christ Himself? This we know was a great dispensation of the divine mercy, so that he who was to be the shepherd of the Church might learn, through his own fall, to have compassion on others. God therefore first shows him to himself, and then places him over others: to learn through his own weakness how to bear mercifully with the weakness of others.

5. And well did he say of Our Redeemer that: *He goeth before you into Galilee; there you shall see him, as he told you.* For Galilee means, *passing-over*. And now our Redeemer has passed over from His suffering to His Resurrection, from death to life, from punishment to glory, from mortality to immortality. And, after His Resurrection, His Disciples first see Him in Galilee; as afterwards, filled with joy, we also shall see the glory of the Resurrection, if we now pass over from the ways of sin to the heights of holy living. He therefore Who is announced to us from the tomb is shown to us by crossing over: for He Whom we acknowledge in the denial of our flesh is seen in the passing over of our soul. Because of the solemnity of the day, we have gone briefly over these points in our explanation of the Gospel. Let us now speak in more detail of this same solemnity.

6. There are two lives; one of which we knew, the other we did not know of. The one is mortal, the

other immortal; the one linked with human infirmity, the other to incorruption; one is marked for death, the other for resurrection. The Mediator between God and man, the Man Jesus Christ, came, and took upon Himself the one, and revealed to us the other. The one He endured by dying; the other He revealed when He rose from the dead. Had He then foretold to us, who knew His mortal life, the Resurrection of His Body, and had not visibly shown it to us, who would believe in His promises? So, becoming Man, He shows Himself in our flesh; of His own will He suffered death; by His own power He rose from the dead; and by this proof He showed us that which He promises as a reward.

But perhaps some one will say: Of course *He* rose: for being God *He* could not be held in death. So, to give light to our understanding, to strengthen our weakness, He willed to give us proof, and not of *His* Resurrection only. In that hour He died alone; but He did not rise alone from the dead. For it is written: *And many bodies of the saints that had slept arose* (Mt. xxvii. 52). He has therefore taken away the argument of those who do not believe.

And let no one say: No man can hope that that will happen to him which the God-man proved to us in His Body; for here we learn that men did rise again with God, and we do not doubt that these were truly men. If then we are the members of our Redeemer, let us look forward to that which we know was fulfilled in our Head. Even if we should be diffident, we ought to hope that what we have heard of His worthier members will be fulfilled also in us His meanest members.

7. And here there comes to mind what the Jews, insulting the Crucified Son of God, cried out: *If he be the king of Israel, let him come down from the cross, and we will believe him.* Had He, yielding to their insults, then come down from the Cross, He would not have proved to us the power of patience. He waited for the little time left, He bore with their insults, He submitted to their mockery, He continued patient, and evoked our admiration; and He Who refused to descend from the Cross, rose again from the sepulchre. More did it matter so to rise from the sepulchre than to descend from the Cross. A far greater thing was it to overcome death by rising from the sepulchre, than to preserve life by descending from the Cross.

And when the Jews saw that despite their insults He would not descend from the Cross, and when they saw Him dying, they rejoiced; thinking they had overcome Him, and caused His Name to be forgotten. But now through all the world His Name has grown in honour, because of the death whereby this faithless people thought they had caused Him to be forgotten. And He Whom they rejoiced over as slain, they grieved over when He was dead: for they know it was through death He had come to His glory.

The deeds of Samson, related in the Book of Judges, foreshadowed this Day (Judges xvi. 1–3). For when Samson went into Gaza, the city of the Philistines, they, learning he had come in, immediately surrounded the city and placed guards before the gates; and they rejoiced because they had Samuel in their power. What Samson did we know. At midnight he took the gates of the city, and carried them to the top of a hill outside. Whom does Samson symbolize, Beloved, in this, if not our Redeemer? What does Gaza symbolize, if not the gates of hell? And what the Philistines, if not the perfidy of the Jews, who seeing the Lord dead, and His Body in the sepulchre, placed guards before it; rejoicing that they had Him in their power, and that He Whom the Author of life had glorified was now enclosed by the gates of hell: as they had rejoiced when they thought they had captured Samson in Gaza.

But in the middle of the night Samson, not alone went forth from the city, but also bore off its gates, as our Redeemer, rising before day, not alone went forth free from hell, but also destroyed the very gates of hell. He took away the gates, and mounted with them to the top of a hill; for by His Resurrection He bore off the gates of hell, and by His Ascension He mounted to the kingdom of heaven.

Let us, Beloved, love with all our hearts this glorious Resurrection, which was first made known to us by a Figure, and then made known in deed; and for love of it let us be prepared to die. See how in the Resurrection of our Author we have come to know His ministering angels as our own fellow citizens. Let us hasten on to that great assembly of these fellow citizens. Let us, since we cannot see them face to face, join ourselves to them in heart and desire. Let us cross over from evildoing to virtue, that we may merit to see our Redeemer in Galilee. May Almighty God help us to that life which is our desire: He Who for us delivered His only Son to death, Jesus Christ our Lord, Who with Him reigns One with the Holy Ghost, for ever and ever. Amen.

XI. St Gregory Nazianzenus, Bishop and Doctor

On The Holy Pasch II[22]

I. *I will stand upon my watch* (Hab. ii. 1), said the great Habacuc. And today I will stand beside him, because of the power and the vision given me by the Holy Spirit, and I shall watch and I shall learn what is to be seen and what is to be said. And I have taken my stand, and I have watched. And behold, a man coming seated upon the clouds, of wondrous dignity, his face as the face of an angel, and his garments shining as the lightning flashing (Judges xiii. 6). And he stretched his hand towards the East, and cried with a great voice. And his voice was as the voice of a trumpet; and round about him was a multitude of the heavenly host. And he said: This Day has salvation come to the world, the visible and the unseen world. Christ is risen from the dead. Rise ye with Him! Christ has returned to Himself; return ye likewise.[23] Christ is delivered from the grave; free yourselves from the bonds of sin. The gates of hell are opened, death is defeated, the old Adam discarded, the new has come. If any man lives in Christ, he is a new being: be ye renewed!

These things he proclaimed; as

before when Christ appeared to us at His Birth, and all together with him sang: *Glory to God in the highest; and on earth peace to men of good will!* And together with them I also proclaim these same tidings to you; and would that I were given the voice of an angel, that I might be heard through all the earth.

II. The Pasch of the Lord, the Pasch, and in honour of the Blessed Trinity I again proclaim it: The Pasch! This for us is the Feast of Feasts, the Festival of Festivals; as far above all the rest as the sun above the stars; not alone those related to the earth and to men, but even to those of Christ Himself, and celebrated in His honour. Beautiful indeed were the white garments of yesterday, and the splendid illuminations both public and in private in which we all, men of almost every sort and rank, delighted as the night was lit up with great fires, resembling that great fire which flashes from the heavens, and in its splendour shines on all the world, and that above the heavens, shining in the angelic nature, as next to that Nature Which is in the Trinity, Which is The First, and from which all light comes, partaking of that undivided Light; and for this to be revered. But more beautiful is this day, and more resplendent. For yesterday's light was as the outer chamber of the Great Light now shining, and but the prelude of our rejoicing. Today we celebrate the Resurrection itself; not now as something to be hoped for, but as come to pass, and uniting in itself the whole world.

Let each one of us then, during this time, bring here and offer to God as our Festival Gift, some fruit of our lives, whether great or small: provided it is one of the spiritual gifts that are pleasing to God, which each of us has in his power to offer. For the gifts that are truly worthy of God not even the angels can offer: even these the first of all creatures, intelligent, pure beings, who see and proclaim His Glory in heaven; if even they are equal to the full measure of Its praise.

And we for our part shall offer our discourse: the best and the most worthy thing we possess, and this especially because we also shall praise the Word for His Goodness to us His rational creatures. I shall begin from this. For I cannot do otherwise when my lips offer their sacrifice concerning the Great Sacrifice, and concerning this the greatest of days, than turn to God and make my beginning from Him. And you, let you therefore cleanse your hearts, and give ear, and understand, all you who delight in these things; for this discourse concerns God and divine things, so that you may go from here filled with a delight that does not pass away. Our discourse to you will be complete, yet concise; for I would not wish to pain you because of its deficiencies, nor weary you by its length.

III. God always was, is, and ever shall be;[24] or rather ever *is*. For *was* and *shall be* are but portions of our time, and share its fleeting nature. But He forever *is*. And it is by this verb He names Himself, when He spoke with Moses on the mountain top (Ex. iii. 13). For all that is He holds within Him, having neither beginning nor any end; an infinite boundless sea of being, transcending all notion either of time or of nature, of Which the mind catches but shadows, and these dim and according to our small measure, and not from that which He is within Himself, but from what is without Him, one picture derived from another, forming together a sort of semblance of the truth, which flies before we can grasp it, and before we can look closely at it escapes us; so shining on that in us which guides us, and that too when purified, as the swift unstaying flash of the lightning on our eyes; and this so that It may, as I believe, draw us to Itself by the little we have grasped (for what is wholly incomprehensible can neither be hoped for, nor striven for); and in the measure that we have not grasped It, It awakens our wonder, and because of our wonder is It the more earnestly desired, and what is desired purifies us, and what in us is purified is made like to God. And when that comes to pass He speaks to us as to friends, God (if I may use a somewhat bold phrase) being united to us, and acknowledging us as Gods, even as He knows those who are known to Him (Jn. x. 15; I Cor. xiii. 12).

Boundless then is the Divinity, and difficult to contemplate; and this alone is all we can grasp of It: that It is boundless; though one might think that because Its nature is simple It is either wholly incomprehensible, or wholly comprehensible. What this simplicity of Its nature is, let us now enquire. For certain it is that this simplicity is not itself Its nature, just as complexity is not the nature of complex things.

IV. When the mind considers this boundlessness from two points; that is, beginning and end—for what is outside these and not contained is Infinity—when the mind contemplates the depth above, not having place where it may rest itself and dwell on these shadows of God, it describes the Infinite and the Unattainable that confronts it as the Unbeginning. And when it considers the depths below, and the future, it calls It the Indestructible and the Immortal. For eternity is neither time, nor part of time; for it cannot be measured. As time is to us, measured by the sun's motion, this Eternity is to the Everlasting: something coextensive with eternal things, a timelike motion and interval as it were. This is all that I may now say concerning God; as it is not the appropriate time for this question: for my discourse is on the Plan of the Divine Redemption, not on the Nature of God.

And when I say God I mean the Father and the Son and the Holy Ghost; for the Divinity does not overflow beyond These Three—setting up as it were a community of gods—and neither is It more restricted than to These Three; lest we be condemned for a defective idea of the Divinity; narrow like the Jews, to uphold Its Oneness, or excessive, like the Greeks. For on either hand the evil is the same. Thus the Holy of Holies, veiled even to the Seraphim, is adored with a threefold sanctification addressed to the One Dominion, the One Divinity; as one before us has so sublimely and so perfectly reasoned.[25]

V. But since it did not suffice to this Goodness to be moved only by the act of Self-contemplation, and since good must go forth and diffuse itself, that many may share it (for this is the supreme quality of Goodness) It first brought forth the angelic and heavenly powers; and this conception was a work wrought by the Word, and perfected by the Spirit. And so the Secondary Splendours were made, as the ministers of the First Splendour. These we must suppose were either intelligent spirits, or fire of an immaterial and incorporeal nature, or some such nature near to what we say. I must however say of them, that they are inviolable by evil, and disposed only towards what is good, as standing before God, and shone upon by the first rays of God—for lesser creatures here below receive only His secondary beams. But I should say rather, not inviolable, by evil, but, difficult to move, and this I am forced to say because of the one who was called the Lightbearer (*Lucifer*) for his splendour, who now because of his pride has become and is called Darkness, and, through him, the apostate powers also, who because of their turning away from good are now instruments of evil, and its agents among us.

VI. And so the world of reason was made by Him; as far as I am able to consider such matters, examining these great things with my poor understanding. And when His first creation was established, He conceived another world, material and visible: that made up of the heavens and the earth, and of what lies between them; wondrous in the perfection of each part, and still more wondrous when we consider the harmony and unity of the whole, each part fitting perfectly to each, and every part of all of it uniting to form the perfection of the one world. And this He did to show He could create, not alone what was like to Himself in nature, but what was wholly unlike to Him. For like to Him are the natures which are intelligent, and which perceive by the mind alone; wholly unlike Him are those subject to sense; and of these those most unlike Him are those which are void both of life and of motion.

VII. Mind, therefore, and senseless things, thus separate from one another, stood each within their own limits, showing forth in themselves the power of the creating Word, silent praisers and proclaiming heralds of His mighty work. There was as yet no blending of the one with the other, nor any commingling of these opposites to reveal a yet higher wisdom and abundance through these natures. Not yet was the full richness of His Goodness made known. This the Creating Word now willed to do; and made from both; that is, from the visible and the invisible, one living creature, Man.

Taking a body from the earth, He breathed in it the breath of life (Gen. i. 27; ii. 7) (which the Word knew as an intelligent soul and image of God) as a sort of other world, great in little, and set it upon this earth, a new angel, a commingled adorer, beholding the visible creation, knowing something of the invisible; king of all things upon the earth, but subject to heaven; of the earth and of heaven; fleeting yet undying; seen and yet understanding; placed midway between lowliness and greatness, the same creature being both body and spirit: spirit, with a view to grace;

body, for its exaltation: the one that he might continue without change, the other that he might suffer, so that through suffering he might be corrected, and learn, should he become vainglorious because of his greatness. A living being, dwelling here, then permitted to go to another place; and as complete fulfilment of this mystery, made like to God by reason of its inclination towards God. For it is to this I think that the slight measure of the truth we possess tends: that we should both see and feel the splendour of God, that is worthy of Him who has both made us and will unmake us, so that He may make us again yet more sublimely.

VIII. This being He placed in Paradise, whatever this Paradise may have been (endowing him with free will, that good might be his of his own free choice, as it is His Who sowed the seeds of it) tending the immortal trees; the divine purposes, the lesser ones as well as the greater ones; naked and unashamed, living a life of perfect simplicity, without clothing and without shelter; for it was fitting that he should be like this who first was made. And He laid on him a law; as material on which to exercise his free will. This law was a commandment, decreeing the trees he might make use of, and the one he might not. And this was the tree of knowledge; not because it was from the beginning evil, or that it was forbidden out of envy (let not the enemies of God here wag their tongues, or imitate the serpent), but good if partaken of in due time. To me this tree was contemplation, as I understand contemplation, safe only for those to attempt who have arrived at a more perfect manner of life, not good for the more simple souls, not for those yet strong in earthly appetites; just as solid food is not suited to those of tender age, who have need rather of milk. Then through the devil's envy (Wisd. ii. 24), and through the woman's wanton folly, which as the weaker caused her to fall, she, as the more persuasive, seduced the man (alas for my weakness; for that of my father is mine), and he, unmindful of the commandment laid upon him, consented to the bitter fruit; and for his sin was banished from the trees of life, from Paradise as well as from God; and put on himself garments of skin, a thicker flesh as it were, mortal and rebellious. And this was the first thing he learned: his own shame. And he hid himself from God. He gained something too: death, and the cutting off of sin, that evil might not live for ever. So his chastisement became a mercy; for it is in mercy, I am convinced, that God inflicts chastisements.

IX. And first being chastened in many ways, since his sins were manifold, springing up from the root of evil, and by a variety of causes was he chastened, and at various times, by word and by law, by prophets, and by benefits, by plagues, floods, fire, war, victory, defeat, by signs from heaven and by signs in the air, upon the earth, and upon the sea, by the unexpected vicissitudes of men and cities and nations all combining to this end: that wickedness might be exterminated. He then began to be in need of a stronger remedy, for his evils were growing worse: mutual slaughter, adulteries, perjuries, crimes against nature, and then the first and last of all evils, idolatry, and the transferring of worship from God to creatures. And since these called for a greater divine aid, they also received a Creator.

This was the Word, the Son of God, Who is before all ages, Invisible, Incorporeal, the Beginning of the beginning, Light from Light, the Source of Life, and of immortality, the Imprint of the Pattern, the Immoveable Seal, the Unchanging Image, the Measure of the Father and His Word, He, I say, came to His own image, and there for the sake of our flesh took Flesh, and for my soul's salvation joined Himself to a rational soul, and through like purified like, becoming man in all things; sin alone excepted. He was conceived by the Virgin, who by the Spirit had been prepared beforehand, in both body and soul; (for it was fitting that generation should be honoured, and that virginity should be yet more honoured) He came forth God together with that which He had assumed: one from two contrary things, flesh namely, and Spirit; One of which bestowed divinity, the other received it.

O new and unheard of commingling! O strange and wondrous union! He Who is, begins to be; He Who is uncreated, is brought forth! The Unconfined is contained within a reasoning soul, placed between Divinity and gross flesh. He Who gives riches, becomes poor. For He becomes poor in my flesh, that I may be enriched in His Divinity. He Who is full, empties Himself; for a time He empties Himself of His glory, that I may share of His fulness. What are the riches of His Goodness? What is this mystery that is round about me? I received His image within me, and I did not guard it. He takes to Himself my body, that He may save the image, and give immortality to the body. He bestows on us a new relationship, more wondrous by far than the first. In that He gave us what was a better nature; in this He takes to Himself what is worse. This act is more Godlike than the first; to men of understanding it is a sublimer action.

X. But perhaps some among you, more impatient and eager for the Feast, will say, 'Where is this leading to? Spur your horse to the goal! Speak to us about the Festival, and why we are sitting here today.' That is what I shall do, though I have begun from a somewhat more exalted starting-point; being forced to do so both by reason and by inclination. Nor will there be any harm if we also add a few words on the name itself of the Pasch; for the sake of those who love what is good and beautiful, for this will be acceptable to their ears.

This Pasch, this great and venerable Feast, is by the Hebrews called in their language Phaska; and it is evident the word means *passing-over*: historically recalling their flight from Egypt to the Land of Canaan. But if we consider the word in a spiritual sense it refers to our progress and ascent from lower things to higher, and to the land of promise. And we find that what often happens in many places in Scripture, that certain words change from being obscure and become clearer in meaning, and from being harsh become refined, has taken place here. For some people, thinking that this is the name of the Saving Passion, in consequence altered the spelling, putting P for Ph, and k for ch (literally, changing Phi and Kappa into Pi and Chi), and made a Greek word of it (Paskein, to suffer) and called the day The Pasch. Use confirmed this, helped by people's ears; to which this had a more devout sound.

XI. But before our time the Apostle has said, that the whole law was but a shadow of things purposed and to come (Heb. x. 1). And before this, when God was instructing Moses, when He was laying down laws concerning these things, He said: *Look that you do all things in accordance with the pattern shown thee on the mountain* (Ex. xxv. 20); that is, showing him things visible to the eye which were as it were the shadow and outline of the things they could not see. And I believe that no detail was laid down without its purpose, without reason, nor anything mean or unworthy of God as Lawmaker, or of Moses as His minister, or of the ministry of Moses; though it is difficult to discover the meaning behind each shadow and figure down to each detail, such as those concerning the Tabernacle, its measurements and material, the Levites and Priests who bore it, as well as all that was laid down concerning sacrifices and purifications and offerings; though these were clear but only to those who were like Moses in virtue, or who resembled him in knowledge.

For on the mountain itself God is seen by men; on the one hand by His own descent from His heavenly dwelling, on the other through raising men up from their own earthly lowliness, so that He Who is incomprehensible may in some degree, and so far as it is safe, be conceived by our mortal nature. For in no other way except by His divine aid can our dense body and fettered mind come to know God. Moreover, it is evident that all are not held worthy of the same rank or position; in relation to Him but one of one place, and one of another, according, as I believe, to the degree of purification of each single one. Some were wholly forbidden to draw near, and only permitted to hear the Voice coming from on high;[26] these were like the beasts, in their way of life, and unworthy of sharing in the divine mysteries.

XII. We however taking a middle way between those who are of a denser mind, and those who are withdrawn and contemplative, so that we are neither dull or indifferent, nor yet more exact than is needed, and so fall short of or turn away from our true purpose (for the one manner is Jewish and unbecoming, the other the manner of a dreamer and soothsayer, and both to be rejected) shall treat of these things as best we can; not in any unusual manner, or one likely to appear ridiculous to the people. This is what we believe: that since we fell through original sin, and were brought down through our guilty pleasures, even to idolatry and to lawless bloodshed, it was necessary that we be again restored through the merciful compassion of God the Father Who would not suffer that such a work of His Hands as man be lost to Him.

How then were we to be reformed; what was to be done? The

sharper remedy of the surgeon was to be put aside, as not persuasive, and which also would, because of our long standing pride, only aggravate our condition; so it was by a gentle and kind method that we were to be restored. For a young tree bent one way will not endure to be suddenly bent the other way, or withstand violence from the hand that bends it (for so it will rather be broken than made straight); nor will a fiery horse, rising in age, endure the restraint of the bit without coaxing and gentle handling. And so the Law is given to us, as a help, as a space between God and idols, drawing us away from the one and towards the Other. And it yields to us a little in the beginning, that it may gain us the more. It allows us sacrifices for a time, that God may thereafter be established, when, in a suitable time, He will do away with sacrifices, in His wisdom gradually withdrawing them, and changing our dispositions, and leading us, now formed and exercised in obedience, to the way of the Gospel.

XIII. So the written law was given to us, and for these reasons, leading us to Christ; and for me this is the purpose of the sacrifices. And that you may understand the depth of the wisdom of God, and the riches of His unsearchable judgements, He did not leave them as wholly profane, or profitless, and consisting only of blood. But that Great and, if I may say so, in respect of Its first nature, Unsacrificeable Victim was commingled with the sacrifices of the Law, and not for a small part of the race, nor for a time, but as an everlasting Sacrifice for the whole world.

And so *a lamb was chosen* (Ex. xii. 3), because of its innocence, and as the clothing of our original nakedness. For such is the Victim that is offered for us: the Garment of our immortality, in fact and in name. A perfect victim, and not alone because of His Divinity, than which nothing is more perfect, but also because of what He assumed and anointed with His Divinity, which became as that Which anointed it, and, if I may say so, an equal with God. A male victim, as offered for Adam, or rather as the Stronger offered for the strong; since the latter had fallen into sin, and especially because there is in Him nothing womanly, nothing unmanly; and then by natural force and power He burst forth from the maternal and virginal bonds and, as Isaias announces, a male child was born from the prophetess (Is. viii. 3). And *of a year old*, as the Sun of Justice (Mal. iv. 2), coming forth from heaven, and circumscribed by a visible nature, and turned towards Himself. And *a blessed crown of goodness*,[27] Equal and like to Himself from on every side; but also giving life to the circle of the virtues, gently blended and intermingled one with another, as love and due order require. Blameless and *unblemished*, the Healer of our defects, and of the vices and stains that come from sin. For though He has borne our infirmities and carried our sorrows (Is. liii. 4), yet He Himself suffered none of these things that needed to be healed in us. He was tempted in all things as we are, without sin (Heb. iv. 15). For he that persecuted the Light shining in the darkness, did not comprehend It (Jn. i. 5).

XIV. *The custom of the First Month* is established (Is. xii. 2 *et seqq.*), or rather, a beginning of months; whether there was one before among the Jews from the beginning, or this began then, and because of the Mystery this was made the First. And *the Tenth of this month*; for this is the most complete number, and of units is the first perfect unit, and the parent of perfection. And it is observed until *the fifth day*; perhaps because my Victim is the Purifier of the five senses, by which we have fallen, and around which is this warfare: since they are vulnerable to the goad of sin.

And the victim was chosen, not alone from among the lambs, but also from among the lower kind of animals which *are on the left* (Mt. xxv. 33); for He is offered, not alone for the just, but also for sinners; and perhaps even more for those: since we have greater need of mercy. Nor is it to be wondered at that a lamb is required for each house; but if it has it not, then let families join together as needed. For it is best that each one should as far as possible make a beginning of perfection within himself, and offer himself as his own living sacrifice to the God Who has called him, and be devoted to God at all times and in all places. And if that cannot be, then let him be close to those who are kindred in virtue, and like us in our dispositions. For this rule seems to me to mean, that, where there is need, those nearest us should be sharers of our sacrifice.

XV. Then comes the Sacred Night, that is, of this present life now flowing, and enemy of that night into which the primeval darkness dissolves itself, and all things return to light, and the world which before was in disorder is now restored to order and form. Here we fly from Egypt, from dark persecuting sin, from Pharaoh the unseen tyrant, and from the cruel taskmasters; ascending to a world above this one, and we are freed from clay and the toil of making bricks, and from the straw and from the weakness of our own bodies; which in many is not made strong for all their strawlike calculations.

Then the Lamb is slain, and word and deed are sealed with the precious blood; that is, our way of life and our actions, the sideposts of our doors: I mean of the movements and thoughts of our minds, which are opened and closed by contemplation, since there is a limit even to thoughts. Then the last and most grievous plague descends on the persecutors, one worthy of night, and Egypt mourns the firstborn of her thoughts and actions (which are also called in the Scriptures the Seed of the Chaldeans, taken away and oppressed, and the Children of Babylon dashed against the rocks (Judith v. 6; Ps. cxxxvi. 9), and the air is filled with the cry of the Egyptians, and their destroyer passes us by in fear and reverence of our anointing.

Then for seven days there is no leaven (this is the most mystical of numbers and related to this world);[28] that is, the old and sour wickedness (not that which is life-giving, and makes bread) so that we shall not lay up for ourselves any of the Egyptian (leavened) paste (Ex. xii. 19), nor any of the impious teaching of the Pharisees (Mt. xvi. 6).

XVI. Let them mourn! We shall eat of the Lamb, and *in the evening* (Ex. xii. 18), for Christ's Passion came at the end of ages. And it was in the evening He shared His Mystery with His Disciples, undoing the darkness of sin. And we shall eat it, *not boiled in water, but roasted at the fire*, that our teaching may contain nothing impious, nothing diluted, or what may be easily undone; but that it may be well compacted together and stable, and purfiied by cleansing fire, free of what is superfluous, not over-subtle; and let us be helped by Him, as by those *live coals* (Is. vi. 6), enlightening and purifying our mind, which come from Him Who came *to cast fire upon the earth* (Lk. xii. 49), and also to hasten its kindling, so as to destroy our evil habits.

Whatsoever then that is solid and nutritious in the word, let it be eaten with the inward and hidden parts of the mind, and given over to spiritual digestion, *from the head even to the feet*; that is, from the first reflections on the Divinity to the last thoughts on the Incarnation. Neither let us carry anything with us, *neither shall there remain anything of it until morning*; since many of our mysteries cannot be carried to those outside; nor is there beyond this night any other purification, and putting off is not to be commended in those who become sharers of the Word. For just as it is pleasing to God (Eph. iv. 26) that your anger does not endure for the course of the day, but that it goes down before the sun goes down, whether you take this in the literal or the mystical sense—for it is not safe for us that the Sun of Justice should go down on our anger—so we also should not let such food remain through the night, or lay it aside for the morrow.

And whatever is of bone, and hard to penetrate in thought, let it not be broken; that is, badly interpreted or expressed (for let me say that in the Passion of Christ, according to the narrative, not a bone of Jesus was broken, and this though His executioners were eager for His death: because of the sabbath) nor should it be cast out to be snapped up, lest what is *holy be given to dogs*: that is, to those who tear the word to pieces, just as the shining pearl of the word should also not *be cast before swine* (Mt. vii. 6), but *let it be consumed by fire*, with which the burnt offerings were also consumed: being refined and preserved by the Spirit, *that searcheth all things*, and not perishing upon the waters like the calf's head which Israel had hastily made for itself, and which was scattered in dust upon the waters in reproach for their hardness of heart.

XVII. And it would not be right for us to pass over the manner of this eating; for the Law does not, but deals with it even in detail. Let us eat the victim *in haste*, eating it *with unleavened bread*, and *with wild lettuces*, having our loins girt, having shoes on our feet, and lastly, leaning on staves like old men. *In haste*, lest we fall into that error against which Lot was divinely warned (Gen. xix. 17 *et seqq.*): that we *look not back, nor stay in all that country about*, but that we save ourselves in the mountain, lest we be overtaken by the strange fire of Sodom, and because of our turning back to wickedness, which may arise through dallying, be turned into a pillar of salt. *With wild lettuces*; for a life that is lived in accord with God is bitter and arduous, especially to those who are beginning it, but more sublime than a life of pleasure. For though the new yoke is easy and the burden light (Mt. xi. 30), as you have heard, this is because of the hope and the reward, which far outweigh the sufferings of this life. If it were not so who could not say that the Gospel is more grievous and toilsome than the demands of the Law? For while the Law forbids the outcome of sinful acts, we are blamed for the causes, as if they were also acts.

The Law says: *Thou shalt not commit adultery* (Ex. xx. 14); but you may not even desire, awakening desire by intent and curious looks. *Thou shalt not kill*, says the Law. You on the contrary may not even return a blow, but must rather turn the other cheek to the smiter (Mt. v. 39). How much closer to holy wisdom is this rather than the other? *Thou shalt not bear false witness*; you may not swear at all (Mt. v. 34), neither a great oath nor a small one: for an oath is the begetter of perjury. *Join not house to house*, it says, *nor lay field to field* (Is. v. 8), oppressing the poor; but you of your own will give away what you have justly acquired, and deprive yourselves for the sake of the poor (Mt. xix. 21), so that you freely take up the Cross and follow to where there is treasure unseen (Mk. x. 21).

XVIII. Let the loins of irrational animals be loose and unbound, for they are without the reason that can dominate pleasure (though they know the right measure of natural inclination) but let that part of you which is the centre of natural inclination, and which neighs (Jer. v. 8) (for by this term Scriptures reproves shameful passion) be restrained by the girdle of moderation, so that, *being mortified in your members which are upon the earth* (Col. iii. 5), you may eat the Pasch in purity; putting on the girdle of John, the precursor of the Great Announcer of Truth (Mt. iii. 4). And I know of another girdle, I mean a virile and martial one, from which the Euzones of Syria take their name, and also certain Monozones, concerning which God said to Job: *Gird up thy loins like a man* (Job xxxviii. 3), and give a manly answer.

David also gloried that he was girt with the strength of God (Ps. xvii. 33), and also speaks of God being clothed with strength, and as having *girded himself* (Ps. xcii. 1), against the impious: unless someone prefers that these words refer to the fulness of His power, and its moderation; as in this sense He is said to be, *clothed with light as with a garment* (Ps. ciii. 2). For who can bear His unveiled Majesty and Light? What, may I ask, is common to loins and to truth? And what does Paul mean when he says: *Stand therefore having your loins girt about with truth* (Eph. vi. 14)? Is it that contemplation perhaps is to restrain concupiscence, and not allow it to be carried elsewhere? For he who is disposed to sensual love has not the same capacity for other delights.

XIX. And as to shoes. Let him who will tread the holy ground trodden by divine feet *put off the shoes from his feet*, like Moses on the mountain (Ex. iii. 5), that he may bring there nothing dead: nothing to come between man and God.

Thus must any disciple go who is sent to preach the Gospel (Lk. x. 3), frugally and simply, since, besides carrying neither money, nor a staff, nor two coats, he should also be without shoes, that his feet may appear beautiful who bears the good tidings and every other good (Is. lii. 7). But he who flies from Egypt, and the things of Egypt, let him have shoes on his feet, that he may go unharmed from other things, especially from the serpents and scorpions that abound in Egypt; so that he may not be wounded by those who lie in wait for the heel (Gen. iii. 15), and which we are bidden to tread underfoot (Lk. x. 19).

Concerning *the staff*, and its meaning, this is what I believe. There is a staff used for support, and another used by shepherds and teachers, to correct the sheep that have reason, and keep them on the right way. Here the law prescribes the staff, to lean on it, that you may not stumble in your mind when you hear of God's Blood, and of His Passion and death; and that you may not wander away from God when you speak of God; but that without hesitation and without shame you may eat the Body and drink the Blood, if you possess the desire of eternal life, not disbelieving His words concerning His Flesh, nor faltering at those of His Passion. Lean on this, steadfast and strong, and so prepared you shall be in nothing shaken by your adversaries, nor swept along persuaded by their words. Stand in thy high place, your feet standing in the courts of Jerusalem (Ps. cxxi. 2), firm on the *rock*, so that you falter not in your steps towards God (I Cor. x. 4).

XX. What sayest thou? Thus has it pleased Him that you should come forth out of Egypt, out of the iron furnace; (Deut. iv. 20); that you may leave the impious worship of many gods which flourished there, and be led by Moses and by his laws and military rule. I give you certain advice; not mine, or rather, mine also, if you consider it spiritually. Borrow from the Egyptians vessels of silver and gold (Ex. xi. 2); with these begin your journey, prepare yourself for the road with alien goods, or rather with thy own. The wages of thy servitude are owing to thee; the wages of thy brick-making; act cleverly for your part in seeking payment; take plenty. Follow your reason. You have suffered grievous toil there, wrestling with clay, that is, with this difficult and impure body, raising cities, alien to you and fleeting, whose memory perishes with their sound.

What then? Shall you come out from there with nothing, without wages? Why so? Will you leave to the Egyptians and to the power of your adversaries what they wickedly acquired, and will spend more wickedly? These things are not theirs. They robbed them; they have sacrilegiously plundered what is His Who has said: *Thy silver is mine, and the gold is mine, saith the Lord of hosts, and I will give it to whomsoever I shall choose* (Agg. ii. 9; Dan. iv. 15). Yesterday they possessed it; for it was permitted them. Today the Lord offers it and gives it to you: that you may use it well unto salvation. Let us make to ourselves friends from the Mammon of iniquity, that when we fail they may receive us in the time of judgement (Lk. xvi. 9).

XXI. If you are a Rachel, or a Liah, a patriarchal and great soul, steal the idols of your father wherever you find them (Gen. xxxi. 19); not to keep, but to destroy them. If you are a wise Israelite, remove them to the Land of Promise; and let the persecutor grieve over them, and from the deceit practised on himself, let him learn not to oppress and enslave his betters. If you do this, and come out of Egypt, know that you will be guided by a pillar of cloud by day, and a pillar of fire by night (Ex. xiii. 22). The desert shall be tamed for you, and the sea divided, Pharaoh shall be drowned beneath the waves, it shall rain bread, the rock become a fountain, Amalek overcome, and not by arms alone, but by the conquering hands of the just uplifted in prayer, and forming at the same time the unconquerable Sign of the Cross (Ex. xiv. 21; xiv. 28; xvi. 15; xvii. 6; xvii. 10, 11).

The river shall be cut off, the sun stand still, the moon held back, walls thrown down without the machinery of war, hornets go before you to make a way for Israel and hold the Gentiles (Jos. iii. 15, 16; x. 13; vi. 20; xxiv. 12). All the other events which after these, and together with these, belong to history (that this account may not be too long) shall happen to you, as a favour from God.

And such is the Feast you celebrate this day; and in this way I would have you, as best you can, celebrate both His Birth and His Death Who was both born and Who died for you. This is the Mystery of your Pasch. This the Law foreshadowed; this Christ fulfilled: He Who was the Destroyer of the letter and the Perfector of the Spirit, Who in His sufferings taught us how to suffer, and in His glorification (*Resurrection*) enables us to become partakers of His glory.

XXII. There is something else to be considered; a certain question, neglected by many, but which in my opinion should be carefully studied. To whom was that Blood offered which was shed for us, and for what purpose was it shed; this great and precious Blood of our God Who was both Priest and Victim? For we were held in bondage by the Wicked One, sold under the dominion of sin, receiving instead the pleasure of wickedness. But if the price of redemption is paid to the one who holds the bond, to whom, I ask, was it offered here, and why? If to the Wicked One: then alas for the loss of it! If the thief receives, not alone from God, but also God Himself as ransom, it would have been more equitable to have saved the payment of so great a price in exchange for his tyranny. But if it was paid to the Father first, how was this done? For we were not held in bondage by Him. And again, why should the Blood of His only-Begotten Son be acceptable to the Father, Who would not accept Isaac when he was offered by his father, but instead changed the sacrifice, substituting a ram in place of the rational victim? (Gen. xxii. 11).

Is it not plain that the Father accepted It, but that He neither demanded It, nor had need of it; but because of the Plan of the Redemption, and because it was required that man be restored to sanctity by means of the humanity assumed by

God, so that, tyranny being overcome by a man's strength, He might deliver us, and bring us back to Himself by means of His Son, Who did all this for the honour of the Father Whom in all things He obeys?[29] This we have said of Christ; and more we shall pass over in reverent silence. The brazen serpent that was hung up as a remedy against the serpent's bite (Num. xxi. 8) was not a figure of Him suffering for us, but a contrasting figure (*antitupos*). And it healed those who looked upon it, not because it was believed to be living, but because it was believed to be dead, and its power at an end, and also that the powers subject to it were dead with it; as was but fitting. And what fitting epitaph shall we sing over it? *O death where is thy victory? O death where is thy sting?* (I Cor. xv. 55). By the Cross thou art overthrown. The Author of life has brought thee down to death. Thou art lifeless, dead, without movement, inert, though you keep the form of a serpent, hanging publicly on high.

XXIII. Let us partake of the Pasch, which even now is a Figure, though more clear than that of old (for the Pasch of the Law was, I venture to say, an obscurer figure of the Figure); later it shall be still more perfect, purer, when, namely, the Word shall drink it with us *new* in the kingdom of His Father (Mt. xxvi. 29); making plain to us what He now teaches us less clearly. For that is always new which but now is becoming known. What that drink is, and what that enjoyment, it is for us to learn, and for Him to teach; sharing His doctrine with His Disciples. For teaching is food; and the food of Him Who teaches. Come then, and let us also be partakers of the Law, but not according to its letter, but according to the Gospel; not imperfectly, but perfectly; not for a time, but for eternity.

Let us have as our capital, not the earthly Jerusalem, but the Heavenly City: not that, I say, now trodden under the feet of armies (Lk. xxi. 20–4), but that glorified by the angels. Let us not sacrifice lambs, nor young calves, sprouting horns and hooves (Ps. lxviii. 32), of which many parts are dead and without feeling, but let us offer to God a sacrifice of praise upon His heavenly altar, together with His heavenly choirs (Ps. xlix. 14). Let us pass through the first veil, and draw near the second, and look upon the Holy of Holies (Heb. x. 20, *seqq.*). And shall I say what is still greater? Let us sacrifice ourselves to God; more, let us sacrifice each day and each action. Let us accept all things for the Word; in suffering let us imitate His suffering; in blood let us honour His Blood; let us be prepared to mount even to the Cross. Though most painful yet sweet are the nails. For far more desirable than delight with others is to suffer with Christ, to suffer for Christ.

XXIV. If you are a Simon of Cyrene, take up the Cross and follow (Mk. xv. 21). If you are crucified together with Him as a thief, as a just man acknowledge thy God (Lk. xxiii. 42). If He for your sake, and because of your sin, was numbered with the wicked (Is. liii. 12), let you then become just for Him. Adore Him Who was crucified for you; though you also be crucified.

Make some profit out of your wickedness; with death buy salvation: enter Paradise with Jesus, that you may understand *from whence thou art fallen* (Apoc. ii. 5). Think of the glories there, and let the murderer and his blasphemies perish without.

If you are a Joseph of Arimathea, beg the Body from him who crucified it (Lk. xxiii. 50); make yours that which *cleanseth us from all sin* (1 Jn. i. 7). If you are a Nicodemus, who worshipped God by night, anoint Him with spices for burial (Jn. xix. 39). If you be a Mary, or the *other Mary*, or a Salome, or a Joanna, weep for Him in the early morning. Be first to see the stone rolled back; and perhaps you will also see the angels, and even Jesus Himself. Say something to Him: hear His voice. But should you hear: *Do not touch me* (Jn. xx. 17), stand afar off: adore the Word; do not grieve; for He knows those by whom He must be seen first.

Celebrate the Feast of the Resurrection. Help Eve: the first to fall; the first to greet Christ, and to tell of Him to the Disciples. Be like Peter, or John; hasten to the sepulchre, running one against the other, striving in worthy rivalry (Jn. xx. 3 *seqq.*). And if overtaken, then win by zeal: not stooped down, *looking into* the sepulchre, but *going in*. And if like Thomas you were not among the Disciples to whom Jesus appeared, when you do see Him be not faithless. Or if faithless, at least believe others who tell you of Him; and if you do not believe them either, then at least trust the print of the nails. Should He descend into hell (I Pet. iii. 19), go with Him. Learn there also of the mysteries of Christ; what is the purpose of this second descent, what is the plan of it: appearing there did He save all, or, there also, those only who believed?

XXV. And if He ascend to heaven, ascend with Him; be among the angels who accompany Him upwards, or among those who receive Him. Bid the gates *be lifted up* (Ps. xxiii. 7, 9), and become higher, that He may enter in Who through His Passion has become greater. Answer those who doubt because His Body now bears the marks of His Passion, which He had not coming down; and to those who ask: *Who is this king of glory*, let you answer: *The Lord who is strong and mighty*, both in all that He has ever done and does, and now also in this present battle and triumph for man: To the twofold doubt of the questioner, give a twofold answer.

And if they wonder, saying, as in the dramatic words of Isaiah: *Who is this that cometh from Edom* (Is. lxiii. 1), and from earthly things, or, How are His garments Who is without body or blood red like a winepresser who has trodden the filled winepress? Tell of the loveliness of the garment of His Body that suffered, made beautiful by His Passion, made glorious by His Divinity, than which nothing can be more lovely, nothing more loved.

XXVI. What will these slanderers say to us against this, these bitter opponents of His Divinity, those betrayers of everything that is good and praiseworthy, those darkeners of the Light, those blind to wisdom, for whom Christ died in vain, thankless, images of the Evil One? Do you reproach God for His Goodness? Because of this do you belittle Him, because of this is He lowly, because He the Good Shepherd came to seek the sheep that was lost? He who laid down His life for His sheep (Jn. x. 11), Who came to the mountain tops where you were wont to sacrifice (Os. iv. 13), and found the erring one, and took it upon His shoulders, on which He also bore the Cross, and having borne it back restored it to the life above, and placed it among those who had not strayed?

Because He lit a candle, His own Flesh, and swept the house (Lk. xv. 8), cleansing the world of sin, and looked for the coin, the royal image defaced with passion, and because the coin was found He calls together His friends, the Heavenly Powers, and makes them sharers of His joy, as before He made known to them the divine plan of Redemption? Because this most splendid Light follows the light that went before, that the Word should come after the Voice (*crying in the desert*) the Bridegroom follow the Bridegroom's friend, preparing for the Lord a people ready, baptizing them in water in preparation for the Spirit? Do you reproach God with these things? Do you think Him less because of this? And that He puts on a towel, and washes the feet of His Disciples, and shows them that lowliness is the best way to become exalted (Mt. xxiii. 12), because He humbles Himself to the soul that is bent to the ground, that He may raise with Himself the one fallen under sin? How is it you do not accuse Him because He eats with publicans, sat at table with them, made Disciples of them, that He also might make a little profit? What profit? The salvation of sinners. If you do then you must blame the physician for stooping down to the suffering, for enduring evil smells, that he may give health to the sick; and likewise the man who moved by pity stoops down that he may, as the Law allows, raise the beast fallen into the pit? (Deut. xxii. 4).

XXVII. He was sent, but as Man; for He was of two natures: since He hungered and thirsted and was weary and grieved and wept, as nature moved Him. And though He were sent as God, what then? Consider His sending (Gal. iv. 4) as the Good Will of the Father, to Which He refers all that is His; both as honouring His Eternal Beginning, and lest He should seem opposed to God. For on the one hand it is said of Him that He was betrayed, and on the other that He gave Himself up; that He was recalled to life by the Father, and taken up by Him, and again that He raised Himself from the dead, and that He ascended into heaven (Eph. iv. 8). The one relates to the Good Will, the other to His own authority. You speak only of what lessens Him; what exalts Him you ignore. You comment on the facts of His suffering; but you do not add that He did so *of His own will.*

And what the Word suffers even now! By some He is honoured as God, and submerged in Him;[30] by others He is despised as Flesh, and separated from Him. With whom shall He be the more angry, or rather, whom shall He forgive: those who wickedly seek to contract Him, or those who wish to lessen Him? The one ought to distinguish, the other unite; the one as to number, the other as to Divinity. Are you scandalized at His Flesh? So also were the Jews. Do you call Him a Samaritan, and other things I shall not repeat? (Jn. viii. 48). Do you deny His Divinity? This not even the demons did. In this you go beyond the perversity of the Jews, and the incredulity of the demons. The former held that the name Son means equality in rank; and they acknowledged Him as God by Whom they were driven forth (Mk. v. 7, 14 *et seqq.*); for they were convinced by what they suffered. But you neither admit His equality, nor confess His Divinity. It would be better for you you were circumcised, and even a demon, to say something fantastic, than to think and speak so wickedly, so impiously, while uncircumcised and sound in mind. But this war we wage against such men is best ended by their return, however late, to a better state of mind, if they will; and if they will not, and remain as they are, let it be but for a time. However, we fear nothing, when, with the Trinity we fight for the Trinity.

XXVIII. We must now sum up our discourse to you. We were created for happiness: we were made happy when we were first made. We were given Paradise: to enjoy its delight. We received a commandment: that obeying it we might win merit, not that He knew not what was to be, but as laying down the law of free will. Through envy we were deceived. We were cast forth because we had broken the law. We hungered, because we did not deny ourselves: being defeated and overcome by the Tree of Knowledge. For the Commandment was with us from our beginning, being in a manner an unvarying guide to our soul, and a restraint upon pleasure; and to it we were reasonably made subject, so that we might regain by keeping it what we had lost by not keeping it. That we might live we needed a God Incarnate, and dying for us. We died with Him, that we might be cleansed of our sin. We rose with Him, because we died with Him. And with Him shall we be glorified, because we have risen with Him.

XXIX. Many indeed are the wondrous happenings of that time: God hanging from a Cross, the sun made dark, and again flaming out; for it was fitting that creation should mourn with its Creator. The Temple Veil rent, blood and water flowing from His side: the one as from a man, the other as from what was above man; the earth shaken, the rocks shattered because of the Rock; the dead risen to bear witness to the final and universal resurrection of the dead. The happenings at the Sepulchre, and after the Sepulchre, who can fittingly recount them? Yet no one of them can be compared to the miracle of my salvation. A few drops of blood renew the whole world, and do for all men what the rennet does for the milk: joining us and binding us together.

XXX. But, O Pasch, great and holy, purifier of all the world!—For I shall speak to thee as to one living—O Word of God and Light and Life and Wisdom and Power! I rejoice in all Thy Names. O Child of That Great Mind, Its Desire and

Its Image! O Word conceived, and Man beheld, Who bearest all things, bound together by the power of Thy Word! Receive now this our discourse, not as First-fruits, but as perhaps the last offering I shall make to Thee,[31] as an act of thanksgiving, and as a supplication, that we suffer no affliction beyond the necessary and sacred cares to which we have dedicated our life. Restrain in us the tyranny of the body (Thou seest, O Lord, how great it is, and how it bows me down) or Thy own sentence, if we are to be condemned by Thee. But should we attain to what we desire, and are received into everlasting dwellings, there also shall we speedily offer thankful gifts to Thee, upon Thy holy altar, O Father, and Word, and Holy Spirit, since to Thee belongs all glory, honour, and majesty through endless ages. Amen.

NOTES

[1] Comment. on Mark: unauthentic, anonymous of the fifth century, PRM 30.

[2] From Sermon 92 of St Peter Chrysologus. Secn. 5 of preceding section: not the work of Severianus.

[3] PL 17, col. 671. Sermo. 34.

[4] PG 35, col. 395. Oratio Prima; in which he speaks to the people for the first time after his flight, which followed on his ordination to the Priesthood, which he had accepted with great reluctance.

[5] In the glossary of Later Latin, *mysterium*, *sacramentum*, and *sacrificium*, were, we learn, used frequently to signify the same thing. The realities spoken of were clearly understood by the people; the terminology became fixed only in the course of subsequent definitions. Here the meaning is always apparent from the context.

[6] St Gregory's father, Gregory also, to whom he has now returned as coadjutor, or assisting priest, had restored the church at Nazianzen with great splendour; surmounting it by a great dome.

[7] PG 50, On the Pasch, Col. 437.

[8] PL 38, Col. 1093, Sermo. 224.

[9] PL 38, col. 657, Sermo. 116.

[10] A possible reference to Proverbs xxx. 31, which *no one can resist.*

[11] PL 38, col. 1099, Sermo. 227.

[12] In sermon 315 we read also: that *The Book of the Acts of the Apostles* begins to be read from the Sunday of the Pasch, as is the custom of the Church.

[13] An obscure place, which we have rendered according to the context; using the variants Migne supplies.

[14] Prior to St Gregory's putting it in its present place in the Canon.

[15] The impression is conveyed that this little sermon is being spoken to the children, before they receive Holy Communion, or as they are about to receive It.

[16] PG 57, col. 795.

[17] The Festival, begun with the illuminations of the preceding evening, was kept up the whole week; of which reminders still continue in the Divine Office of the Breviary, in which the Paschal *ferias* are celebrated, and the Paschal mystery recalled.

[18] Chorus from the Liturgy of St John Chrysostom.

[19] PL 57, col. 390, Sermo. 72. This sermon, apart from its profound

yet clear reaffirmation of the doctrine of the Incarnation, is rather an instruction on the way of perfection.

[20] PL 57, col. 613, Sermo. 39.

[21] PL 76, col. 1169, Sermo. 21.

[22] PG 36, col. 623, Oratio 45. On the Holy Pasch II. This is the last sermon composed by St Gregory Nazianzenus, and for this reason is placed last among the Paschal Homilies; as *On the Holy Pasch I* was the first. It is one of the very greatest of the Patristic Homilies, a synthesis of the whole Plan of the Incarnation; from its foreshadowing in the Old Testament to its perfect fulfilment in Christ's Resurrection, and in the Gospel. The exordium of the discourse is in the Biblical style, and describes, as though seen in a vision, the appearance of the Angel of the Resurrection. Taking his stand, at the hour of his watch, he waits to see what shall be said to him. The preacher opens his sublime discourse by putting into the mouth of the Angel words that announce the fact of the Resurrection, and the significance and blessing of this wonder, after the manner in which the Angel of the Nativity announced to the shepherds the good tidings of Christ's Birth, and its significance to men. His purpose is to show the greatness of the Feast, and the perfect fulfilment of the Paschal Figures of the Old Testament, and in detail those governing the slaying and eating of the lamb in Exodus Chapter Twelve; applying them to Christ, and to those who become one with Him, or desire to, in the Christian life. The penetration and discernment of this sublime and most eloquent discourse proclaim it an authoritative and most learned recounting of Divine Tradition.

[23] To the pristine glory that was man's.

[24] This passage, to the end of Chapter nine, occurs verbatim in Sermon 38, on The Birthday of Christ. Whether this is due to the holy author, or to the amanuenses, is not known.

[25] St Athanasius: *Quia sicut singillatim unamquamque personam Deum et (ac) Dominum confiteri Christiana veritate compellimur, ita aut tres deos aut dominos dicere Catholica religione prohibemur.* Athanasian Creed. Denzinger 39.

[26] Here possibly he is referring to Exodus Chapter Nineteen; though in general he is referring to Ex. xxv to end of book.

[27] The idea of a year is taken from the sun; that of the crown, from the year: for the year is a circle with four seasons; and from the circle is inferred equality. So Christ is the Crown adorning the minds of those who believe. *Thou shalt bless the crown* etc., Ps. lxiv. 12, i.e., the year when Christ, moved by goodness, was declaring the Gospel to the poor, as Isaiah had foretold: *To proclaim the acceptable year of the Lord* (Is. lxi. 2). Christ in His Humanity is the Crown of Justice, composed of all the virtues, without end to His Goodness: Which is equal on every side.

[28] We are to relinquish the leaven for seven days (Exod. xii. 15); that is, be without sin for the whole week of this life. The number of seven days means the passage of time, which revolves in weeks. The number is mystical also because it is virgin, and symbolizes virginity, and the angelic life; for it alone, as arithmeticians teach, of all the numbers within the decade is neither

a multiple nor a measure; and also because it contains within itself the 4 and the 3: the Four Elements of the world, and their Creator the Blessed Trinity. He calls it related to the world, because the world was made in seven days (Nicetas, Bishop, 335–414 A.D.). St Augustine says the number seven often stands for the universe, because it is made up of four, which as 2 and 2 is altogether even, and three, which is altogether uneven (*City of God* xxxi, 11).

[29] Theologians observe that there is a twofold kind of Redemption; one, 'in which the price is paid to him who holds the captive, who is bought back from him by money'. The other, 'in which another undertakes to suffer on behalf of the guilty one, as a favour to this one'. So Christ suffered to be crucified for us; and thus through His Passion nothing was given to the devil. Further, the Blood of Christ was offered to the Father, 'not that He might be pleased by the shedding of the Blood of His Only-Begotten Son', but as *showing* that the Son, of His own will, had taken on Himself man's guilt, and had suffered death to redeem man, and restore him to the grace of God, and repair the injury offered to the Divine Majesty. Footnote (11) Greek Text, PG 36, col. 653.

[30] Namely, by Sabellius, who, while honouring the Son as God, joins Him as one Person with the Father; the allusion following is to the heresy of Arius.

[31] This was the Saint's last discourse, and so a final, and in the circumstances prophetical, offering of his fruitfulness in preaching the Gospel.

LOW SUNDAY

I. St John Chrysostom: The Authority and Dignity of the Priesthood

II. St Augustine: Christian Compassion

III. St Gregory the Great: The Power of Binding and Loosing
The Judgement and Resurrection

THE GOSPEL OF THE SUNDAY

John xx. 19–31

At that time, when it was late that same day, the first of the week, and the doors were shut, where the disciples were gathered together, for fear of the Jews, Jesus came and stood in the midst, and said to them: Peace be to you. And when he had said this, he showed them his hands and his side. The disciples therefore were glad, when they saw the Lord. He said therefore to them again: Peace be to you. As the Father hath sent me, I also send you. When he had said this, he breathed on them; and he said to them: Receive ye the Holy Ghost. Whose sins you shall forgive, they are forgiven them; and whose sins you shall retain, they are retained.

Now Thomas, one of the twelve, who is called Didymus, was not with them when Jesus came. The other disciples therefore said to him: We have seen the Lord. But he said to them: Except I shall see in his hands the print of the nails, and put my finger into the place of the nails, and put my hand into his side, I will not believe. And after eight days again his disciples were within, and Thomas with them. Jesus cometh, the doors being shut, and stood in the midst, and said: Peace be to you. Then he saith to Thomas: Put in thy finger hither, and see my hands; and bring hither thy hand, and put it into my side; and be not faithless, but believing. Thomas answered, and said to him: My Lord, and my God.

Jesus saith to him: Because thou hast seen me, Thomas, thou hast believed: blessed are they that have not seen, and have believed. Many other signs also did Jesus in the sight of his disciples, which are not written in this book. But these are written, that you may believe that Jesus is the Christ, the Son of God: and that believing, you may have life in his name.

Exposition from the Catena Aurea

V. 19. *Now when it was late that same evening etc.*

Chrysostom, *Hom.* 85 *in John*: The Disciples hearing what Mary announced, it would follow that they would either not believe her, or that, accepting what she said, would grieve that He had not deemed them worthy of this vision. So that they would not brood over this He did not suffer even one day to pass, now that they knew He was risen, and would be eager to see Him, and because they were afraid, when *it was evening*, He stood in the midst of them, *where they were gathered together, for fear of the Jews.*

Bede: The weakness of the Apostles is disclosed in this circumstance; gathered together behind closed doors through fear of the Jews: in fear of whom they had earlier been dispersed. *Jesus came and stood in the midst.* And He came, *when it was late*; for obviously at that hour their fear would be greatest.

Theophylactus: Or because He waited till all were assembled: *The doors being shut*; so that He might show He had risen in the same way: while the stone still lay sealing the tomb.

Augustine, *in Paschal sermon*: Some are so puzzled by this circumstance as almost to be endangered; setting the preconceptions of their own reasoning against the divine wonders. For they argue in this way: If it was a true body, if that rose from the tomb which had hung upon the Cross, how could it enter through closed doors? If you understand how, there is no miracle. Where reason falls short, there is the *building* of faith (cf. I Cor. iii. 9).

Augustine, *Tr.* 121 *in John*: Where divinity was, closed doors did not stand in the way of the Body's substance. For He could enter, though they were not open, in whose Birth the virginity of His Mother remained inviolate.

Chrysostom, *as above*: But the wonder was why they did not take him to be a phantom. It was because the holy woman, coming just before, had awakened great faith in them. Also, He showed His countenance to them very clearly, and His voice steadied their wavering minds; and so there follows: *And He said to them: Peace be to you*; that is, Be not troubled. In this saying He reminds them of the words He had spoken to them before the Crucifixion: *My peace I leave you*; and again: *That you may have peace* (Jn. xiv. 20; xvi. 33).

V. 20. *And when he had said this etc.*

Gregory, *Ser.* 76 *in Ev*: And because the faith of those who were looking at him was wavering with regard to that Body, which they could see, He there and then showed them His hands and His side. Hence: *And when he had said this he shewed them . . .* For nails had pierced His hands, and a spear had opened His side. The scars of His wounds there serve to heal the hearts of the doubting.

CHRYSOSTOM, *as above*: And what He had said to them before His passion: *But I will see you again, and your heart shall rejoice* (Jn. xvi. 22), is now fulfilled in deed. Hence: *The disciples therefore were glad, when they saw the Lord.*

AUGUSTINE, *City of God*, 22; 19: The brightness in which *the just* shall shine as the sun in the kingdom of their Father, we must believe to have been concealed rather than absent from the body of Christ when he rose from the dead: for the weak and human eye could not endure it, and it was His purpose that He should be so scrutinized by His followers that they should recognize Him.

CHRYSOSTOM: All these things led them to a very secure faith. Since there was deadly war between them and the Jews He frequently repeats to them the greeting of peace. So there follows: *He said therefore to them again: Peace be to you.* BEDE: The repetition is a confirmation. Or He repeats it because the virtue of Charity is twofold; or because He is our peace, *Who hath made both one* (Eph. ii. 14).

CHRYSOSTOM: At the same time He shows them the efficacy of the Cross, through which He has brought an end to all sorrowing, and brought us good; and this is peace. To the women he had earlier announced joy: for that sex had been cursed and was in sorrow through the Lord saying: *In sorrow shalt thou bring forth* (Gen. iii. 16). Now all prohibiting ordinances being removed, and what remained made straight, the Gospel continues:

V. 21. *He said therefore . . . As the Father hath sent me . . .*

GREGORY: The Father sent the Son Whom He has decreed shall take flesh for the redemption of the human race. And so He says: *As the Father hath sent me etc*; that is, when I send you amid the scandals of the world, I love you with that same love with which the Father loved Me upon Whom he imposed this burden of suffering. AUGUSTINE, 121 *in John*: We know that the Son is equal to the Father; but here we recognize the words of the Mediator. He shows Himself as standing in between by saying: *He sends me*; and *I send you.*

CHRYSOSTOM: And so He uplifts their hearts, both by what had been accomplished, and by the dignity of the One Who now sends them forth. And He no longer makes appeal to the Father, but of His own authority gives them power. Hence:

V. 22. *When he had said this, he breathed on them; and he said . . .*

AUGUSTINE, *On the Trinity;* 4, 20: That corporeal breath was not the substance of the Holy Spirit, but a showing, by this fitting outward sign, that the Holy Spirit proceeds not alone from the Father, but also from the Son. Who would be so foolish as to say that the Spirit which He here bestows upon them by breathing is one, and another that Spirit He promised to send them after He had ascended to heaven?

GREGORY: Why was it given to the Disciples on earth first, and sent from heaven afterwards, if not because two are the precepts of charity; namely: the love of God, and the love of our neighbour. On earth the Spirit is given that we may love our neighbour; It is given from heaven that we may love God. Therefore since charity is one, and its precepts two, so One is the Holy Spirit, and its givings two; the first by the Lord as He dwelt on earth, afterwards it is given from heaven. For it is through the love of our neighbour that we learn how we are to come to the love of God.

CHRYSOSTOM: Some say that He did not give the Spirit but prepared them to receive the Holy Spirit by breathing on them. For if Daniel was bereft of strength beholding an angel, what would they not have felt receiving this unspeakable grace, had He not first prepared His Disciples? They are not mistaken however who say they received a certain reality of spiritual power; not such as to raise the dead and work wonders, but such as to forgive sins. Hence there follows:

V. 23. *Whose sins you shall forgive, they are forgiven them . . . etc.*

AUGUSTINE, 121 *in John*: The charity of the Church, which is poured forth in our hearts by the Holy Ghost (Rom. v. 5), forgives the sins of those who are partakers of it; of those who are not partakers it retains. Accordingly, after He said: *Receive ye the Holy Ghost*, He goes on to speak the words relating to the forgiving and retaining of sins.

GREGORY: We must keep in mind that those who formerly had the Holy Spirit received it that they might live holy lives, and help some others by their preaching. These received it openly after the Lord's Resurrection, that they might help, not a few, but many. It is pleasing to contemplate these Disciples, led to such a height of glory, called to such burthens of humility. Behold now they have become, not alone fearless regarding themselves, but sharers in the authority of the heavenly Judge; so that on behalf of God they withhold forgiveness for the sins of some, and pardon those of others. Their place in the Church the Bishops now hold; and they who succeed to their power of ruling receive authority to bind and loose. Great indeed is the honour; but great likewise the burthens of that honour. And truly grievous is it, that one who knows not how to rule himself, should become the judge of the life of another.

CHRYSOSTOM, *Homs.* 85 *and* 86 *in John*: For the priest, though his own life be well-ordered, who does not exercise with due diligence his responsibility towards others shall go with the wicked to hell. Knowing well therefore the greatness of their danger, give them every respect, even though they should not be very holy persons. For it is not fitting that they should be judged by those placed subject to them. And should their own life be not worthy, in no way will they injure you in regard to the things committed to them by God; for neither priest, nor angel, nor archangel can do anything to what is given to you by God; for the Father, Son, and Holy Ghost arrange all things. The priest but lends his hand and tongue. For it would not be just that because of another's evil life they should suffer harm who approach in faith to the symbols of our salvation. All the Disciples had now gathered together, and only Thomas was missing; through the dispersion which had taken place. Hence:

V. 24. *Now Thomas, one of the twelve, who is called Didymus . . .*

ALCUIN: Didymus (*geminus*) means twofold or doubting, because of his heart that was hesitant in believing. Thomas means *abyss*; for with sure faith he penetrated to the depths of the divinity.

GREGORY: It was not by chance that this chosen Disciple was then absent. For the supreme mercy in a wondrous manner ordered that the doubting Disciple, as he touched the wounds in the flesh of His Master, healed in us the wounds of our unbelief. More does the doubt of Thomas help us to believe, than the faith of the Disciples who believed. For when he, through touching, is brought to believe, our soul, putting all doubt aside, is made firm in faith.

BEDE: It may be asked why does this Evangelist say that Thomas *was not with them*, seeing that Luke writes that the two Disciples who went to Emmaus found, on returning to Jersualem, *the eleven* gathered together? But we are given to understand that there had been a certain interval of time during which Thomas had gone out, and it was then that Jesus coming stood in the midst of them.

CHRYSOSTOM, *Hom.* 86 *in John*: As to give belief carelessly and simply is a sign of an easy disposition, so, to question excessively is a sign of a slow intelligence. Of this latter Thomas is accused. For when the Apostles say, *we have seen the Lord*, he did not believe; not so much doubting them as thinking such a thing impossible. So there follows:

V. 25. *The other disciples therefore said to him: We have seen . . .*

For being ruder than the rest he sought that testimony which is the crudest of all; that, namely, of touch: not believing even his own eyes. And so it was not enough for him to say: *Except I shall see*, but he also adds: *And put my finger etc.*

V. 26. *And after eight days again his disciples were within . . .*

CHRYSOSTOM: Consider the clemency of the Master; how for merely one soul He shows Himself and His wounds, and draws near to save one. And yet the Disciples who had spoken were worthy of belief, and so was He Who had promised. Yet because Thomas alone asked for yet more proofs Christ does not deny him. He does not straightaway appear to him, but *after eight days*; so that being in the meanwhile instructed by the Disciples, he might be aroused to a greater desire, and in the future be more believing. Hence follows: . . . *And Thomas with them. Jesus cometh, the doors being shut . . .*

AUGUSTINE, in *Paschal serm*: You seek of me, saying: If He enters, *the doors being shut*, where is the substance of His Body? And I shall answer: If He walked on the waters, where was the weight of His Body?

The Lord did this as Lord. Has He then, because He is risen, ceased to be Lord?

CHRYSOSTOM: And so Jesus is standing in their midst, and He does not wait to be questioned by Thomas; but, to show that He was present even when he [Thomas] used certain words to his fellow-Disciples, He uses the same words. And first He rebukes or reproaches him; for, saying to Thomas:

V. 27. *Put in thy finger hither, and see my hands,*

He added: *And be not faithless, but believing.* See how his doubt was due to lack of faith, before they had received the Holy Ghost; afterwards it was not so, and for the future they were steadfast. But it is fitting to ask how an incorruptible body retained the print of the nails? But be not troubled. What took place was a mark of condescension: that you might learn that this was He Who was crucified.

AUGUSTINE, *De Symb.* 2, 8: He could, had He wished, have removed all trace of every wound from His risen and glorified Body; but He knew why He had retained the scars in His Body. For as He showed them to Thomas, who continued to doubt until he should see and touch them, so likewise was He to show the wounds to His enemies. Not that He might say to them, as to Thomas: *Because thou hast seen, thou hast believed*, but that convincing them the Truth may say: Behold the Man Whom you crucified: See the wounds you inflicted on Him: Look upon the side you pierced, since it was through you, and because of you, it was opened; and yet you have not wished to enter.

AUGUSTINE, *City of God*, 22, 20: But in some manner, I know not how, we are so moved by love of the Blessed Martyrs, that in that Kingdom we desire to see in their bodies the scars of the wounds they have suffered for the Name of Christ. And perhaps we shall see them; for in them there shall be no deformity, but only honour; and there shall shine out a certain beauty of virtue; in their body, but not of their body.

And though many of the members of the Martyrs have been cut off and taken from them, they shall not lack these members to whom it was said: *A hair of your head shall not perish* (Lk. xxi. 18). And if it please Him in the future world that the traces of their precious wounds shall be seen in their glorified flesh, then, where members were struck or cut that they might be severed, there the scars shall be visible, and the members shall not be lost but restored to them. For though every injury that has happened to the body shall not be then visible, these are no more to be called injuries, but honours.

GREGORY: The Lord offered that flesh to be touched which He had brought into their midst, *the doors being shut*, in which He puts before us two, and according to human reasoning, widely contradictory things; when after His Resurrection He showed us a body that was both incorruptible and palpable. For it must be that what can be touched is corruptible, and that may not be touched which is incorruptible. He therefore shows Himself both incorruptible and palpable; that He might truly show us that after His Resurrection His Body was still of the same nature, but now partaker of another glory.

GREGORY, *Morals*, 13, 3: Our body likewise, through the glory of that Resurrection, will indeed be rarified as a consequence of spiritual power, but palpable because of the reality of its nature; not, as Eutychius writes, impalpable, and more rarefied than the air or the winds.

AUGUSTINE, *Tr.* 121 *in John*: Thomas saw and touched a man, and confessed Him the God Whom he had neither seen nor touched. And through that which he saw and touched, he, putting aside all doubt, now believed. Hence:

V. 28. *Thomas answered, and said to him: My Lord, and my God.*

THEOPHYLACTUS: He who had first disbelieved, after he touched His side showed himself to be an excellent theologian. For he set forth the twofold nature and the Oneness of the Person of Christ. For in saying, *My Lord*, he confessed to the Human Nature. Saying, *My God*, he confessed the Divine; and that the one and the same Being was both God and Lord.

V. 29. *Jesus saith to him: Because thou hast seen me, Thomas . . .*

AUGUSTINE, *Tr.* 121 *in John*: He does not say, because thou hast touched Me, but *because thou hast seen me*; since the power of vision pertains in a general way to all the senses, and by it the other four are wont to be implied; as when we say: 'Listen and see how good it sounds'; 'smell and see how good it smells'; 'taste and see how good it tastes'; 'feel and see how warm it is'. And so here the Lord says: *Put in thy finger, and see my hands.* What else does He say but: 'feel and see'. For he had not eyes in his finger. Therefore, whether by seeing or by touching, He says this: *Because thou hast seen, thou hast believed*; though it could be said that the Disciple did not dare to touch Him, when He offered Himself to be touched.

GREGORY: But when the Apostle says: *Faith is the substance of things to be hoped for, the evidence of things that appear not* (Heb. xi. 1), it is indeed evident, that what does appear confers, not faith, but *knowledge*. Thomas therefore, since he saw, and since he touched, why does He say to him: *Because thou hast seen, thou hast believed*? Because he sees one thing and believes another. He sees man; he confesses God.

What follows gives *us* great joy: *Blessed are they that have not seen, and have believed.* In these words we more particularly are meant; since we hold Him fast in our hearts, Whom we have not seen in the Flesh; provided we accompany our faith with good works. For he truly believes, who shows what he believes in the good works he practises.

AUGUSTINE, *Tr.* 121 *in John*: He uses the words in the sense of time past; as though that were fulfilled which in His Providence He had known would come to pass. CHRYSOSTOM: Should anyone say: 'Would that I had lived in those days, and had seen Christ working His wonders', let him recall these words: *Blessed are they that have not seen, and have believed.*

THEOPHYLACTUS: He also includes in this the Disciples who believed; although they had neither touched the place of the nails or His side.

CHRYSOSTOM: Because John had spoken of fewer incidents than the other Evangelists, he adds:

V. 30. *Many other signs also did Jesus in the sight of his disciples, which are not written in this book.*

But neither did the others write all down, but only that which sufficed to awaken faith in those who heard. And here he seems to me to be speaking of those signs which Jesus did after the Resurrection, and it was for this reason he says, *in the sight of his disciples*, with whom alone He had conversed after His Resurrection. Then, that you may learn that these signs were not done for the benefit of the Disciples alone, he adds;

V. 31. *But these are written, that you may believe that Jesus is the Christ, the Son of God.*

In this he speaks to all men generally. And that he may show that, not to Him, in Whom we believe, but to us is it a gain to believe, he adds: *And that believing, you may have life in his name;* that is, through Jesus. For He is Life.

I. ST JOHN CHRYSOSTOM, BISHOP AND DOCTOR[2]

The Authority and Dignity of the Priesthood[3]

Mary related to them the vision she had seen, and the words she had heard; and by this they were comforted. Since it was likely that the Disciples on hearing these things would either not believe the holy woman, or believing would grieve that they had not been thought worthy of a vision, though He had promised that they were to see him in Galilee, so lest they be troubled thinking this He did not let even the day pass, but having awakened their longing through knowing He was risen, and from what they heard from the holy woman, and when they would be all eagerness to see Him, and fearful as well (which made their longing greater), when it was evening He appeared in their midst, and in a truly wondrous manner.

Why did He appear to them in the evening? Because it was probable that they would then be most fearful. But the wonder is why they did not think He was a phantom. For He came of a sudden, and while the doors were shut. This was certainly because the holy woman had prepared them beforehand; giving them great confidence. Besides, He presented Himself clearly, and with a mild countenance. He had not come by day, so that they might all be gathered together. For their amazement was indeed great. He did not knock at the door, but all at once stood among them, and showed them His hands and His side, and at the same time His voice calmed their troubled minds as He said to them: *Peace be to you*; that is: Be not troubled; recalling what He had said to them just before His Crucifixion: *Peace I leave with you*, and also, *In Me you may have peace. In the world you shall have distress* (Jn. xiv. 27).

The Disciples were glad when they saw the Lord. Behold how His words are now truly fulfilled! For that which He said before His Crucifixion: *I shall see you again, and your heart shall rejoice; and your joy no man shall take from you* (Jn. xvi. 22), has now in this moment come to pass. All this wrought in them a most exact faith. And since they were engaged in deadly warfare with the Jews He repeats frequently the words: *Peace be to you*; bestowing this grace to comfort them in the war.

These were the first words He said to them after His Resurrection, (and because of this Paul also everywhere says, *Grace be to you, and peace*). But to the women He gave joy (Mt. xxviii. 9); for that sex was in sorrow, and on them He bestows joy first. Aptly does He announce peace to the men, because of their warfare; and joy to women, because of their sorrow. Then His own sufferings ended He recounts the fruits of the Cross; and these are *peace*. For since all things that stood in its way are now banished, and He has won a glorious victory, and has restored all things to right order, He says to them:

As the Father hath sent me, I also send you. You shall encounter no difficulty, both because of what has been accomplished, and because of My authority Who send you. Here He uplifts their souls, and made clear to them the ground of their confidence, if they are willing to take His work upon them. And now no longer calling upon the Father, but of His own authority, He bestows on them this power. For *He breathed on them; and he said to them: Receive ye the Holy Ghost. Whose sins you shall forgive, they are forgiven them; and whose sins you shall retain, they are retained.* For as a king sending forth His governors gives them power to put a man in prison, or free him from prison, so Christ sending these forth gave them this power.

But why does He say, *If I go not, He (the Comforter) will not come to you* (Jn. xvi. 7), and yet give them this Spirit? Some say that He did not give them the Spirit, but disposed them for receiving it by breathing on them. For if Daniel was struck with fear at the sight of an angel (Dan. viii. 17), what would these men have not suffered had they received such an unspeakable favour, unless He had first prepared them for it while they were His Disciples? And so He did not say: You have received the Holy Ghost, but: *Receive ye the Holy Ghost.*

Yet a man will not err who says they received some spiritual power and grace; not so as to raise the dead and perform wonders, but so as to forgive sins. For the gifts of the Spirit are manifold. And so He goes on: *Whose sins you shall forgive they are forgiven them; and whose sins you shall retain, they are retained*, indicating what kind of power He was bestowing. Later however, after fifty days, they received the power of miracles. And accordingly He says: *You shall receive the power of the Holy Ghost coming upon you, and you shall be witnesses unto me in Jerusalem, and in all Judea.* They became witnesses through signs and wonders;

for ineffable the grace of the Spirit, and manifold His gift.

This has come to pass that you may learn that One is the Authority and the Gift of the Father, Son, and Holy Ghost. How then is it that, *no man comes to the Son, except the Father draw Him*? (Jn. vi. 44). But this is shown to be also the property of the Son; for He says: *I am the way: No man cometh to the Father but by me* (Jn. xiv. 6). And see also how the same belongs to the Holy Ghost; for *No man can say the Lord Jesus, but by the Holy Ghost* (I Cor. xii. 3). And again we see that the Apostles are said to have been given to the Church, now by the Father, now by the Son, and now by the Holy Ghost; and that the *diversities of grace* belong equally to the Father, to the Son, and to the Holy Ghost.

Let us then do all things that we may have the Spirit of God within us. And let us treat with reverence those to whose hands the work of the Spirit has been entrusted. For great is the dignity of the priesthood. *Whose sins you shall forgive*, He says, *they are forgiven*; and because of this Paul says: *Obey your prelates, and be subject to them* (Heb. xiii. 7), and hold them in great reverence. For you have but the care of what concerns yourself; and if you look well after that you will not be held accountable for what others do. But the priest, even should he order his own life in a fitting manner, yet does not scrupulously have due care for both your life, and the lives of those about him, shall go with the wicked into everlasting fire; and so he oftentimes while not failing in his own conduct will perish because of yours, if he has not done all that belonged to him to do.

Knowing then the greatness of their danger, treat them with much consideration, for as Paul goes on to say: *They watch for your souls*; and not simply this, but as *having to render an account* of them. Because of this you must treat them with honour. And should you join with others to insult them, then neither will your own affairs prosper. For as long as the helmsman is in good heart those on board are safe. But if he is grieved by their abuse, and by their hostile behaviour, he can neither keep a good watch, nor perform his task properly, and unwillingly involves them in many disasters. And so likewise the priest. If he is held in honour by you, he will be able to take care of what relates to yourselves. But if you throw them into depondency, weakening their hands, and making them easily overcome, you expose both them and yourselves to the waves, however courageous they may be.

Remember what Christ said of the Jews: *The Scribes and the Pharisees have seated themselves in the chair of Moses* (Mt. xxiii. 2, 3). Now we can say that the priests are seated, not upon the chair of Moses, but upon the chair of Christ. For it is from Him they have received their teaching. Because of this, Paul says: *For Christ therefore we are ambassadors, God as it were exhorting by us* (II Cor. v. 20).

You see that in the case of those who judge in the world outside that all are subject to them; even those who may be superior to them in family, in conduct, or in intelligence. Yet out of respect for the King, who gives him his authority they do not consider this, but uphold the authority of the king, whoever the person who exercises it. And if there is such respect where a man gives authority, are we to slight the authority of one who is appointed by God? And shall we despise his authority, and abuse him, and humiliate him with constant faultfinding? And though forbidden to judge our brethren, we sharpen our tongues against the priests.

And how can this be pardoned; when paying no attention to the beam in your own eye, you are very concerned with the speck of dust in another's eye? Do you not understand that judging others in this manner you are preparing a more difficult judgement for yourself? And I am saying this to you, not as excusing those who may exercise the priesthood unworthily: for such as these I weep and sorrow exceedingly: nevertheless I declare that it is not fitting that they be judged by those they rule; especially by the ruder kind. And though their conduct may be greatly criticized, you, if you pay heed to yourself, will suffer no harm from them in regard to the things entrusted to them by God. For if he made use of the voice of an ass to speak, and bestowed spiritual blessings by means of a soothsayer; because of the Jews, working by the mouth of a dumb beast, and by the unclean tongue of Balaam how much more for you who are worthy, even though the priests be wholly unworthy, will He do all things, and send His Holy Spirit upon you?

And neither does a mind that is pure draw down grace because of its purity; it is the divine favour that does all: *For all things, it says, are yours, whether it be Paul, or Apollo, or Cephas* (I Cor. iii. 22). For what the priest has had entrusted to him it is God alone Who bestows; and however much human wisdom may help us, it will ever appear less than grace. And I say this, not that you may be careless with regard to your own life, but so that should those who have the spiritual care of you be neglectful of their conduct, you whom they guide may not heap up evils for yourselves.

But why do I say priests? For neither an angel, nor an archangel, can do anything in regard to what is given us by God. It is the Father, Son, and Holy Ghost Who disposes of all things: the priest but lends his tongue, and puts forth his hand. For it would not be just that, because of the wickedness of another, they should suffer injury who draw near in faith to the symbols of our salvation.

Keeping all these things before our mind, let us both fear God, and hold His priests in reverence; showing them every respect, to the end that, through our own worthy manner of living, and because of our obedience to them, we may receive from God a great reward, by the grace and kindness of Our Lord Jesus Christ, to Whom with the Father and the Holy Ghost be there honour, glory, and empire, now and forever, world without end. Amen.

II. St Augustine, Bishop and Doctor

For Sunday the Octave of the Pasch[4]

Christian Compassion

1. *The mind of the Christian should be directed towards the future life.* Today is for us a day of unending joy, within a great mystery. For not as this day will pass shall that life pass away which this day signifies. Therefore, Brethren, we exhort you, we beseech you, in the Name of Our Lord Jesus Christ, through Whom our sins were forgiven, Who willed that His Blood be our price, Who deigned to make us His brothers, we who are unworthy to be called His servants, that as you are Christians, and bear His Name upon your brow and upon your heart, let all your mind be directed towards that life alone which we shall share with the angels; where there shall be unending peace, eternal joy, unceasing happiness, no disorder, no sadness, no death.

This life no one can know save those who have made trial of it; and they cannot make trial of it unless they believe. For should you ask that we show you what God has promised you we cannot. But you have heard how the Gospel of John ended: *Blessed are they that have not seen, and have believed.* You desire to see, and so do I. Let us together believe, and together we shall see. Let us not set ourselves against the word of God. For is it fitting that Christ should now come down from heaven, and show us His wounds? And so He deigned to show them to this faithless Disciple, that He might reprove the doubting, and instruct those who would believe.

2. *The Mystery of the Seventh and Eight day. The Kingdom of Christ and of the Sanctified on earth after the severance of the Wicked. The celebration of the Sabbath by the Sanctified on earth.*

This eighth day therefore signifies the new life at the end of the world; the seventh the future rest of the sanctified on earth.[5] For the Lord will reign with His holy ones, as the Scriptures say, and He shall have here a Church whither no one evil will enter, cut off from and purified of every taint of wickedness, of which the draught of one hundred and fifty-three fishes is a sign: of which I have, as far as I remember, at some time treated.

For the Church shall first here appear in great splendour and honour and power. Then it shall not be possible to deceive, to lie, to conceal the wolf under sheep's clothing. *For the Lord will come*, as it is written, *who will both bring to light the hidden things of darkness, and make manifest the counsels of the heart; and than shall every man have praise from God* (I Cor. iv. 5). The wicked therefore shall not be there. For they shall already be cut off. The multitude of the sanctified will appear as winnowed grain heaped upon the threshing floor; and thus will be gathered into the heavenly barn of life everlasting. For as wheat, where it is threshed there also is it winnowed; and the place where the corn has been threshed, that it may be stripped from the straw, is adorned by the comely appearance of the winnowed grain. For after the winnowing we see on one side of the threshing floor the heap of chaff, and on the other the mass of wheat. Whither the chaff goes we already know, as well as how the grain gives joy to the husbandmen.

Therefore as the corn appears on the threshing floor before it is separated from the straw, and as after so much labour there is joy at the sight of the heaped up mass of the grain, which was concealed by the chaff, and not seen while being threshed out; then gathered into the barn and stored away; so in that world you shall see how this threshing floor is treaded; but the chaff is so close to the wheat, that this cannot be seen because it is not yet winnowed. Accordingly, after the winnowing of the last judgement the heap of the sanctified shall appear, shining in virtue, strong in their merits, and proclaiming the mercies of their Saviour.

And this will be the seventh day. The first day as it were being all time from Adam until Noah, the second from Noah to Abraham, and the third, as Matthew's Gospel divides it, from Abraham to David. The fourth from David to the Babylonian transmigration, the fifth from the transmigration to the Coming of Our Lord Jesus Christ. The sixth therefore is counted from the Coming of Our Lord: we are in the sixth day. And so as in Genesis man on the sixth day was formed in *the image and likeness* of God, so we also in this time, upon as it were the sixth day of the whole of time, are reborn in Baptism; that we may receive again the image and likeness of Our Maker.

But when the sixth day has passed, the Sanctified and the Holy unto God will celebrate the Sabbath, and there shall be rest after the winnowing. But after the seventh day, when the splendid heap, the glory and the merit of the Sanctified, has appeared upon the threshing floor, we shall enter into that life, and into that rest of which it is said: *That eye hath not seen, nor ear heard, neither hath it entered into the heart of man, what things God hath prepared for them that love him* (I Cor. ii. 9).

Then we as it were return to the beginning. For as these seven days end, the eighth then becomes as it were the first: so when the seven ages of this passing world are ended and complete, we shall return to that blessed happiness and immortality from which man has fallen. And concerning this question, the number seven multiplied seven times makes forty-nine; and one being added, as though to return again to the beginning, we have fifty: which number is celebrated by us in mystery till Pentecost. This is seen again by another reckoning, in the distribution of the number forty, to which is added a denarius as wages. Both reckonings come to the quinquagenary number; which multiplied three times, because of the Trinity, makes one hundred and fifty. Adding three, as token and witness both of the multiplication and of the Trinity, by this number of one hundred and fifty-three fishes we understand the Church.

3. *He praises the works of mercy.* In the meanwhile, till we reach that rest, *in this time* in which we now suffer, and while we are in this night, as long as we see not what we hope

for, while we journey in this desert, until we come to the heavenly Jerusalem, as to the Land flowing with milk and honey, let us therefore, since trials will not cease, let us labour well in good works. Let there be medicine ever at hand, to heal as it were our daily wounds. And there is medicine in the good works of almsgiving. For if you wish to receive mercy from God, let you be merciful. If you as man, deny humanity to man, God will deny you divinity: that is, the incorruption of immortality by which He makes us God.

God has no need of you: but you have need of God. He seeks nothing of you, to be happy: but unless you receive it from Him, you cannot possess happiness. I do not know if you would dare to complain were you to receive from Him Who made all things something perfect which He had created. But He gives you, not something of what He has made, but Himself for your delight: He, the Creator of all things. For what of all He has made can be more perfect, more wondrous, than Him Who made it?

And why has He given it to you? Because of your merits? If you seek for what you merit, think of your sins. Hear the sentence God spoke against sinners: *Dust thou art, and into dust thou shalt return* (Gen. iii. 19); for when the commandment was given, a warning preceded it: *In what day soever thou shalt it eat of it, thou shalt die the death* (Gen. ii. 17). If you seek the reward of your sins, what is there but punishment? So forget your merits, lest they awaken terror in your soul; or rather, do not forget them: lest through pride you drive mercy away.

Let us make ourselves acceptable to God, Brethren, by our works of corporal mercy. *O praise ye the Lord, for he is good: for his mercy endureth for ever* (Ps. cxvii. 29). Give praise to God: since He shows us mercy, and desires to forgive the sins of those that praise Him. But let you offer Him sacrifice. Have compassion on man, O man, and God will have compassion on you. You are a man, and the other is a man: two who are unhappy. God is not unhappy; He is merciful. If the unhappy have not compassion on the unhappy, how can he ask for mercy from Him Who shall never know unhappiness?

Pay heed to what I say, Brethren. Whoever is wanting in mercy towards another who has, for example, suffered some disaster, is wanting in feeling for such a man as long as he has himself suffered no disaster. Should it come his own way he will then, should he see another suffer, think of his own past misery and be touched by a fellow feeling. And so he in whom a common humanity awakened no compassion will be moved by a common bond of suffering. How readily that man helps a slave who has been himself a slave? How readily he sympathizes with a servant defrauded of his wages who has been himself a servant? How deeply he grieves for a father mourning his son who grieves himself for the same cause? And so kinship of suffering has power to soften every hardness of the human heart.

If then you who have been in sorrow, or are fearful lest it come upon you—for as long as you live in this world you should be fearful of what you have felt not, and think of what you may suffer, and consider what you are—if then mindful of your own past sufferings, and fearful of what may come, you have no compassion on one in misery and needing your assistance, do you expect Him Whom misery touches not to have compassion on you? You give nothing from what you have received from God, yet you look to God for that which He has never received from you?

4. *Our Deeds of Mercy should surpass our Sins. Mercy is Twofold.*

You my Brethren, who are now about to return to your homes, and whom we shall scarcely ever see again, except on some great occasion, let you be merciful: let you do the works of mercy, for those of sin abound. For there is no other resting place, no other way, where we may restore ourselves, and come to God and be reconciled to Him Whom we have so dangerously offended. We are to appear before His Face. There let our good works speak for us. Let them speak louder than our sins. For whichever prevails will lead us, either to eternal punishment if our sins deserve it, or to eternal rest if our good works have earned it.

Within the Church mercy is twofold. One is that in which no one need give either of his money or his labour. The other that which demands of us the service of our hands and the giving of our money. That which requires neither alms nor effort has its place in the soul: that you forgive those who offend you. The treasure from which you bestow this alms is in your own heart: there unfold it in the presence of God. Here no man will say: Bring out your purse, open your money box, unlock your barn. And neither will any man say to you: Come, walk, run, hurry, intercede for me, speak, visit, work. Remaining in the same place, cast out from your heart what you hold against your brother: at no cost, with no labour, you perform a work of mercy; by kindness alone, moved only by the impulse of compassion.

For if we should say: Give what you possess to the poor, we should appear to be unfeeling. Now however we are mild and easy when we say: Give from where your treasure is not lessened; forgive that you may be forgiven. Let us also say: give and it shall be given unto you. In His commandments the Lord joined these two together, and they describe the two kinds of mercy. *Forgive, and you shall be forgiven:* the mercy of the one who forgives. *Give, and it shall be given to you* (Lk. vi. 37): the mercy of the almsgiver.

See if God does not give us more. You forgave a man in that in which a man offended you who are a man. God forgives you in that in which you a man offended God. Do you think it is the same, for a man to offend God and to offend a man? And so He gives you more: because you forgave that in which a man offended you. He forgave that by which God was offended. And note another mercy of the divine grace.

You give bread. He gives salvation. You give a cup of something to a thirsty man. He gives you the cup of His own wisdom. Are they to be compared: what you give, and what you receive? See how treasure is to be gained. If anyone wishes to be a moneylender, we do not altogether forbid him. But let the money be lent to Him Who being rich returns more and better things, and to Whom also everything belongs that you give Him, whereby you receive back more and better than you gave Him.

5. *Alms to be given with Humility and Cheerfulness.* This I also counsel Your Sanctity,[6] that you may know that he fulfils this twofold mercy, who so bestows something on the poor that he bestows it on himself. For there is needed of us, not alone kindness in the gift, but humility in the giving. I do not understand, Brethren, the mind of the man who, as the hand of the giver touches the hand of the receiver, gives to the poor man as though he were giving to all humanity and infirmity. For though one may give and one may receive, both the giver and the one to whom he gives are joined together. And it is not misfortune joins them together, but their common lowliness.

Abundance shall be yours, and your children's, if God so wills. But of this earthly abundance He makes no mention: which you see is liable to so many disasters. A treasure lies quietly in your house; but it does not suffer its owner to be at rest. He is in fear of thieves. He is in fear of housebreakers; of an unfaithful servant; of a neighbour who is both wicked and powerful. The more he has, the more he fears. But if you give it to God in His poor, you will not lose it, and you may rest secure; for He will mind it for you in heaven, Who gives you what you need here on earth.

Or perhaps you fear that Christ will lose what you have entrusted to Him? Does not every man select a faithful steward from among his household, to whom he will entrust his money? This man, though he has not the power to steal it has yet the power to lose it. What more boundless than the faithfulness of Christ? What stronger than His omnipotence? Nor can He steal it from you: for He gave it to you in the hope that you would give it to Him. Nor can He lose anything: since He holds the world in His Hand.

You nourish your body when you partake of the love-feasts (*agape*).[7] From this that what is given is ours and is given by us we seem to give to ourselves; yet that only is given which God has given us. It is also good that you should distribute alms with your own hand: this is greatly pleasing to God. He Himself receives it, and will give it back to you, Who before He owed it to you gave it to you, that you might give it to Him. To the duty of almsgiving should be joined the duty of distributing them. When you can earn a twofold reward, why forego one of them?

Let him who has not the means to give to all the poor, give according to his means; and with cheerfulness: *For God loveth a cheerful giver* (II Cor. ix. 7). We are taught that we must secure the Kingdom whatever the price. Let no one say who has but twopence that he is not rich enough to buy it. For with just so much did the widow in the Gospel buy it (Lk. xxi. 2).

6. *Holy Days.* The Festival Days are now at an end,[8] and these now follow that are given over to daily meetings, demands, disputes. Let you be careful, Brethren, how you pass your life amid these things. From the quiet of these days you

should draw in gentleness of spirit; not brood over plans for future strife. For there *are* men who use these days for this purpose: to plan roguery, to be put in practise when the days are past. We implore of you, that you live becomingly; and as knowing that you are to render to God an account of your whole life; and not only of these past fifteen days!

I confess lastly that I owe you an explanation of the Scriptural questions I mentioned yesterday, but for lack of time did not explain. But as both civil and public law allow of demands even of money, in the coming days let you demand this of me: but as a Christian right. Now all are here for the solemnity; after these days may the love of the Holy Scripture lead you to demand of me what I promised. For He Who gives it to you, gives it to you through me: indeed, it is He Who gives it to us all.

From the Apostle I have learned: *Render to all men their dues. Tribute, to whom tribute is due: custom, to whom custom: fear, to whom fear: honour, to whom honour. Owe no man anything, but to love one another* (Rom. xiii. 7, 8). Only love is to be rendered at all times: there is no one free of that debt. But what I owe I shall render, Brethren, in the Lord's Name. But I declare to you that I shall not render it to the indifferent; but only to those who come demanding payment!

Turning then to the Lord our God, the Father Almighty, let us as best we can give thanks with all our hearts, beseeching Him that in His goodness He will mercifully hear our prayers, and by His grace drive evil from our thoughts and actions, increase our faith, guide our minds, grant us His holy inspirations, and bring us to joy without end, through His Son our Lord and Saviour Jesus Christ.

III. St Gregory, Pope and Doctor

The Power of Binding and Loosing,[9] *the Judgement and Resurrection*

Given to the People in the Basilica of the Blessed John, which is called the Constantiniana, *on the Octave of the Pasch*

John xx. 19–31. 1. The first question that strikes the mind in the Lesson of this Gospel is this: how after the Resurrection was the Lord's Body a true body, since It entered in among the Disciples *the doors being shut*? But we must know that if the divine action can be understood by the mind, then it is no matter of wonder; and neither would our faith have any merit if human reason could provide the proof of it. But we are to consider these actions of Our Redeemer, which cannot in themselves be in any way comprehended, in the light of other divine works, so that our faith in these wondrous happenings may increase through remembering things that are yet more wonderful.

For this Body of the Lord, which entered in among the Disciples though the doors were closed, is the same which at His Birth came forth to human eyes from the closed womb of the Virgin. What wonder therefore that, now risen from the dead, and about to enter into eternal life, He should enter in while yet the doors are closed, Who coming into this world to die came forth from the unopened womb of the Virgin?

But since the faith of those beholding that Body, which could be seen, remained doubtful, He straightaway showed them His hands and His side; allowing them to touch the flesh He had brought into the room through the closed doors. In this He puts before us two wondrous, and, according to human reason, widely contradictory things; showing us that following His Resurrection His Body is both incorruptible and yet capable of being touched. For it must be that what can be touched is perishable, and what cannot be touched is imperishable.

But in a wondrous but incomprehensible manner Our Redeemer reveals to us a Body which, since His Resurrection, is both palpable and imperishable, so that by showing us that it is imperishable He would draw us towards our reward; and by showing that it is palpable confirm our faith. He therefore showed Himself as both imperishable, yet palpable, that He might truly prove that since His Resurrection from the dead His Body was still of the same nature, but partaking of another glory.

2. *He said to them: Peace be to you. As the Father hath sent me, I also send you.* That is, as the Father has sent Me Who am God, so I also as Man send you who are men. The Father sends the Son: ordaining He shall become Incarnate for the Redemption of all mankind. He willed that He should come into this world to suffer; yet He loves the Son Whom He destined to suffering. And the Lord choosing His Apostles sends *them* into the world; not to taste the joys of this world, but for the same end as He was sent: that they might suffer.

And so as the Son loved by the Father was yet sent by Him to suffer, so the Disciples loved by our Lord are yet sent by Him into the world to suffer. And so rightly does He say: *As the Father hath sent me, I also send you*; that is, with the same love do I love you when I send you amid the snares of the persecutors, as the Father loves Me Whom He caused to come here to suffer.

Though we may also understand this passage in the sense that He *is sent* in accordance with the nature of the Divinity. For in that He is born of the Father the Son is said to be sent by the Father. For the Son also says He will send the Holy Spirit: Who though Co-Equal with the Father and the Son did not become Incarnate, saying: *When the Paraclete cometh, whom I will send you from the Father* (Jn. xv. 26). For if we are to understand that to be sent means only to become Incarnate, then we may not say the Holy Spirit was sent, since He did not become Incarnate. *His* sending is that *procession* in which He proceeds from both Father and Son. So as the Holy Spirit is said to be sent because *He proceeds*, so the Son may rightly be said to be sent because He is Begotten.

3. *When he had said this, he breathed on them; and he said to them: Receive ye the Holy Ghost.* Here we should ask why Our Lord gave the Holy Ghost once while on earth, and once from His throne in

heaven? In no other place is the Holy Ghost openly shown as given, except now where He is received through being breathed on, and later when He is shown descending from heaven in the form of *diverse tongues*. Why then is He first given to the Disciples here on earth, and afterwards sent down from heaven, if not because the precepts of charity are twofold: The love of God, and the love of our neighbour. As Charity then is one, and its precepts two, so the Spirit is one, but Its giving is twofold. First by the Lord while on earth, and afterwards coming down from heaven: for it is through the love of our neighbour that we learn how we are to come to the love of God. Because of this the same John says: *He that loveth not his brother, whom he seeth, how can he love God whom he seeth not?* (Jn. iv. 20).

And even before this time the same Holy Spirit was in the hearts of the Disciples, that they might believe, but He was not given by a visible giving till after the Resurrection. For this was it written: *As yet the Spirit was not given, because Jesus was not yet glorified* (Jn. vii. 29). And also through Moses was it said: *They sucked honey from the rock, and oil from the hardest stone* (Deut. xxxii. 13). For nowhere is this related, even if you were to read the entire Old Testament. For nowhere did the people suck oil from the rock, and nowhere did they suck honey from stone. But because, as Paul says: *The rock was Christ* (I Cor. x. 4), they did indeed suck honey from the rock who saw His signs and wonders. They sucked oil from the firm stone when after His Resurrection they were anointed by the outpouring of the Holy Spirit. It was therefore as a suffering rock that the Lord still mortal showed His Disciples the sweetness of His signs and wonders. But the Firm Rock pours forth oil, as now, Immortal after His Resurrection, by His breath the gift of His holy anointing is poured forth.

4. Of this oil was it said by the prophet: *The yoke shall putrefy at the presence of the oil* (Is. x. 27). We were in truth under the yoke of the demonic tyranny, but we have been anointed by the oil of the Holy Spirit. And because He has anointed us with the grace of freedom, the yoke of the demon's tyranny has putrefied; as Paul bears witness when he says: *Where the spirit of the Lord is, there is liberty* (II Cor. iii. 17). But we must keep in mind that they who, before this, had received the Holy Spirit, that they might themselves live holy lives, and help some by their preaching, received it openly now after the Resurrection that they might help, not some, but many. So, in giving them the Holy Spirit was it said: *Whose sins you shall forgive, they are forgiven them; and whose sins you shall retain, they are retained.*

It delights us to see to what heights of glory are they led who were called to take on them such burthens of obedience. For not alone are they become sure of their own salvation, but they receive also the power of undoing the evil dominion in which others are held. And they receive the power of the heavenly Judge, that in the Name of God they may forgive sin in some, and retain it in others. So it was fitting that they should be raised up by God, who for God consented to be so greatly humbled. See how they who fear the stern justice of God are now judges of souls; and they who themselves stood in fear of damnation may now free or condemn others.

5. The Bishops now hold their place in the Church. They receive the power of binding and loosing who succeed to their office of ruling. A great honour, but great is the burthen of that honour. For it is hard that one who knows not how to rule his own life should be the judge of another's. And often it happens that he holds this place of judgement whose own life ill becomes the place he fills. And often it will happen, that he either condemns the innocent, or while himself guilty free others. Often his judgement in binding and loosing is not in accord with the merits of the case. From this it will happen that by this he deprives himself of the power of binding and loosing, when he exercises it, not for the good of his subjects, but for his own ends.

Often it will happen that a pastor is moved either by favour or by dislike of some neighbour. They cannot worthily judge those subject to them who are influenced in the causes of their subjects either by hate or by fear. Rightly does the prophet say: *They killed souls which should not die; and they saved souls alive which should not live* (Ezech. xiii. 19). For he causes death to one who should not die who condemns an innocent man. And he tries to give life to one who should die who endeavours to deliver the guilty from punishment.

6. Cases are therefore to be carefully considered, and then let the power of binding and loosing be exercised. Let the fault be disclosed which has taken place, or what repentance has followed the fault, so that the sentence of the pastor may absolve those whom Almighty God has touched by the grace of repentance. Then shall the absolution of the one who judges be effective, when it accords with the Will of the Hidden Judge. This the raising of the man four days dead signifies, showing us namely, that first the Lord called the dead man and gave him life, saying: *Lazarus, come forth* (Jn. xi. 13); and after he came forth living he was loosed by the Disciples, as it is written: *And when he came forth who had been bound with winding bands, He said to his disciples: Loose him, and let him go*. See how the Disciples loose him now living whom the Master had restored to life. For had the Disciples unbound the dead Lazarus, they would have revealed corruption rather than living power.

Because of this reflection we must carefully keep before our minds, that we are to absolve by our pastoral authority those we know our Author has brought back to life by means of His revivifying grace. And this revivifying is seen even before the act of reconcilement, in the very confession of our sins. Because of this He said to the dead Lazarus, not: Return to life; but: *Come forth*. For every sinner hides within himself; buried within his very spirit, as long as he covers up his guilt within his own conscience. But he who is dead *comes forth* when a sinner freely confesses his own sins.

To Lazarus then was it said: *Come forth*. As though He said to someone dead in sin: Why hide your guilt within your conscience? Come forth now by confessing, you who lie hid within yourself by refusing. And so let the dead come forth, that is, let the sinner confess his sin. And as he comes forth let the Disciples loose him from his bands; as pastors of the Church take away the punishment he merited who has not been ashamed to confess what he has done.

I have spoken thus briefly of the manner of binding and loosing, so that pastors of the Church shall be at pains to use with great discretion the power to bind and to loose. But whether the pastor binds justly or unjustly, the sentence of the pastor is to be feared by his flock, lest the one who is subject to it, though perhaps unjustly bound, may then deserve sentence for another sin. Therefore let the pastor be fearful lest without due care he either bind or loose. But he that is under the care of the pastor, let him also be fearful lest he be bound, though unjustly. Neither let him rashly question the judgement of the pastor, lest, though unjustly bound, from the angry resentment of his complaint sin may arise where there was no sin. But as we have said these things to you by way of digression, let us now return to the order of our exposition of the Gospel.

7. *Now Thomas, one of the twelve, who is called Didymus, was not with them when Jesus came.* This one Disciple was absent, and on his return hears what has happened, but refuses to believe what he hears. The Lord comes again, and offers to the unbelieving Disciple His side that he may touch it, showing him His hands; and by the sight of the scars of His wounds heals the wound of his unbelieving. What, Dearly Beloved, what do you perceive in all this? Do you believe that this took place by chance; that this chosen Disciple should be missing at this time, that coming in later he hears of these things, and that hearing he doubts them, and doubting he touches the Lord, and that while touching Him he believed? Not by chance, but by divine arrangement, did this come to pass. For the divine clemency acted in this so wondrous manner that the doubting Disciple, when he touched the wounds in the Body of His Master, healed in us the wounds of our unbelief. For more did the unfaith of Thomas profit us, than the faith of the believing Disciples; for when he through touching is brought back to faith, our soul, setting all doubt aside, is made steadfast in faith.

So the Lord of a certainty suffered His Disciple to doubt after His own Resurrection, yet He did not abandon him to doubt; just as before His own nativity He willed that Mary should have a spouse, who however did not attain to his nuptials. For so the Disciple through his doubting and touching, became a witness to the truth of His Resurrection; as the Spouse became the guardian of the spotless virginity of His Mother.

8. He touched, and he exclaimed: *My Lord, and my God. Jesus saith to him: Because thou hast seen me, Thomas, thou hast believed: Blessed are they that have not seen, and have believed.* When Paul the Apostle says: *Faith is the substance of things to be hoped for, the evidence of things that appear not* (Heb. xi. 1), it is plain to us that faith is the evidence of those things which cannot appear. For

the things which do appear bring about, not faith, but knowledge. Then while Thomas looked, while he touched, why did He say to Him: *Because thou hast seen me, thou hast believed*? But he saw one thing, and believed another. The Godhead could not be seen by mortal man. And so seeing man, he confesses God, saying: *My Lord, and my God.* Seeing then he believed; he who as he carefully scrutinizes a true man, exclaims that He is the God, Whom he could not see.

9. What follows rejoices us exceedingly: *Blessed are they they have not seen, and have believed.* These words refer especially to us: who hold Him fast in our souls Whom we have not seen with our eyes. We are referred to, but only when to faith we join good works. He truly believes who practises what he believes. While on the other hand Paul says of those who believe in name only: *They profess that they know God, but in their works they deny him* (Titus i. 16). And concerning this James says: *Faith without works is dead* (Jas. ii. 26). And because of this the Lord said to the blessed Job, regarding the ancient enemy of the human race: *Behold he will drink up a river, and not wonder: and he trusteth that the Jordan may run into his mouth* (Job xl. 18). And who is meant by the river if not the flowing stream of the human race? The race that flows from the beginning unto the end; and like water runs from the river of humanity to its appointed end.

What is the Jordan but a figure of those who are baptized? For as the Author of our Redemption deigned to be baptized in the Jordan, so by the name Jordan is signified the multitude of those who are protected within the sacrament of baptism. The ancient enemy of mankind, therefore, drank up the human race, because from the beginning of the world until the coming of the Redeemer, a few of the elect escaping, he dragged mankind down into the maw of his own iniquity. Rightly then is it said of him: *Behold he will drink up a river, and not wonder*; for he holds it as nothing when he snatches up the unbelieving.

But what follows is truly grievous: *And he trusteth that the Jordan may run into his mouth*; for after he has overcome all who have not believed from the beginning of the world, even now he is confident he can make his own those also who believe. For by the mouth of his deadly persuasions he daily devours those whose wicked life is opposed to the faith they confess.

10. Fear this, Dearly Beloved, with all your mind; and dwell upon it with anxiety of soul. Behold how we are now celebrating the Paschal Feast. But we must live in such a way that we may deserve to take part in the everlasting Pasch. All the feasts we celebrate here come quickly to an end. Take care, you who have shared in these holy celebrations, that you may not be shut out from the eternal celebrations. What gain is it to us to take part in the feasts of men if we are to take no part in the feasts of the angels? This present solemnity is but the shadow of that which is to come. And for this do we celebrate it each year, that we may be brought to that joy which comes, not every

year, but goes on without end. By celebrating the one at the appointed season, the longing for the other is renewed afresh in our mind. By the renewal of our earthly joy, the soul grows fervent and eager for the joys of eternity, so that through the shadow of the joy it contemplates on earth it may come to the possession of its reality in heaven.

Therefore, Brethren, put your life and your manner of living in order. Consider beforehand how terrible He shall appear in judgement who has risen mild of countenance from the dead. For on that dread day of His Judgement when He shall appear with His angels and archangels, with His thrones and dominations, with His princes and His powers, while the heavens shall burn, and all creation stricken with fear of His wrath. Keep before your mind this so fearful Judge. Fear His Coming, so that when He comes you may be able to look upon Him, not in fear, but in confidence. He is now to be feared, so that then we shall not fear Him. Let the fear of Him make you eager in doing good. Let fear of Him keep your soul from evil. Believe me, Brethren, the more we are now in earnest to keep ourselves free from sin, the more confident shall we then be in His Presence.

11. For it is certain that if one among you, together with his opponent, were to appear before me tomorrow in the courts, he would pass maybe the whole night without sleeping, turning over in his fevered, anxious mind what he could say for himself, what he could say to objections against him; fearful that he may find me severe, fearful lest I find him guilty. And who am I, and what am I? Soon after being a mortal man I shall be a worm, and after a worm dust. If then you so greatly fear the judgement of what is but dust, with what anxiety should you look upon, with what fear behold, the judgement seat of His awful majesty?

12. As there are some who are in doubt concerning the resurrection of the body—and we shall teach more accurately regarding this truth if we also answer the questions hidden in your hearts—we must now say a few words on faith in the Resurrection. For many doubting the Resurrection, as we also at one time, when they see in the earth the body reduced to corruption and bones to dust lose hope that flesh and bone can again be renewed from this dust. And so pondering within themselves they say: When shall man be restored from the dust? How can ashes be brought again to life? To which we briefly answer: that for God to restore what was is far less than to create what was not. And what great wonder should it be that He renews man from the dust Who created all things from nothing? It is more wondrous by far, that He should make heaven and earth from nothing that previously existed, than that He should restore man from the earth.

But we look at the ashes, and the mind despairs of it being able ever again, to become flesh, and seeks by its reason to form a notion of the power of the divine operation. They who so think and speak in their own hearts do so because to them the daily round of wonders that God performs have become as nothing because of their repetition. For see how in a single grain of the smallest seed is hidden the whole mass of that great tree that is to rise from it. Let us put before our mind the wonder of any tree you will; and let us consider from what did this begin which is now so great. Beyond any doubt we shall find that its beginning was from some tiny seed. Let us consider now where in this little grain of seed is the strength of the wood concealed, and the toughness of the root, the abundance of its sap and fragrance, the richness of its fruits, the greenness of its leaves? For when we touch it the seed seems without strength. Whence then comes the strength of the wood? It is not resistant. Whence then the toughness of the root? It is not sweet. Then from where does the sweetness of its fruit come? Smell it, it has no odour. Whence the odour that smells so sweet in the fruit? There is no trace of green in it. From where then does the green of its leaves come? All these things are hidden together in the seed; yet they do not come forth together from the seed. From the seed a root comes; and from the root a young shoot. From the plant the fruit comes; and in the fruit the seed is born. So we may say then that in the seed the seed is also hidden.

What wonder is it then that He should bring back from the dust our bones and nerves and flesh and hair Who from a tiny seed builds wood and leaves and fruit into the splendour that is a tree? So when the mind, doubting the possibility of the Resurrection, asks how it can be, then let questions of such a kind be put to it regarding that which continually takes place, and which the mind still cannot understand, so that when it cannot grasp what it sees it may believe what it hears, from the promise of the divine majesty.

Reflect then within you, Dearly Beloved Brethren, upon those promised gifts which last for ever; and turn from those which pass away with time, as from things already given up. Hasten with all zeal towards the glory of that Resurrection which Truth has manifested to you in Himself. Fly from those earthly things that shut you out from your Maker; for the more detached the soul is in its love for the Mediator of God and man, the higher will it reach towards the vision of the Omnipotent God, Who with the Son and Holy Ghost lives and reigns God for ever and ever. Amen.

NOTES

[1] Cf. PL Sermo. 247, par. 2 *prope init.*

[2] After the long series of seasonal homilies, for Lent and Paschal time, the Fathers appear in this Sunday to have turned their minds to giving, together with their homily on the Gospel, careful detailed teachings on particular questions, which relate to the manner of Christian living. So the three homilies for this Sunday, which are really sermons rather than homilies, because of their definite theme, treat respectively of: St John Chrysostom, The fitting use of the Power of Binding and Loosing, together with respect for Sacerdotal authority and dignity. St Augustine, Christian Almsgiving, and the Twofold Love of our Neighbour; St Gregory, on Faith in the Resurrection of the Body. We are listening

here, as indeed elsewhere in the preaching of the Fathers, to words containing the oral teaching of Christ, *handed down* to us through these so august and so authoritative channels; words and discourses which reformed, and formed anew, the pagan social structure, and delivered the Christian people from the influence of the pagan and material notions of human conduct and belief.

[3] PG 59, Sermon 85.

[4] PL 38, Sermo. 259.

[5] Regarding the mystery of the eight day and seventh day, referred to at the beginning of paragraph 2, the word *on earth* (*in terra*) is added on the authority of a Vatican MS (PL 38, col. 1197, note (a) at foot of page). However as to this kingdom, outside of that of the blessed and on the sabbath of the saints, which some held would last a thousand years, Augustine speaks again later, repudiating this opinion, and saying of it: 'This opinion might be tolerated if it proposed only spiritual delights during this time; and we were once of this opinion ourselves', *City of God*, 20, 7. And again later: 'We ourselves shall be the seventh day, when we shall be restored again with His blessing and sanctification . . . the seventh day shall be our sabbath, whose end shall not be the evening, but the Lord's Day, as the eighth eternal day, made holy by the Resurrection of Christ, prefiguring the eternal rest of both body and soul', Book 22, Ch. 30.

[6] *Your Sanctity*, *Your Holiness*, *Your Charity*, etc., used as titles of address to Emperor, Clergy, nuns, congregations (fourth century on), GLL 363.

[7] *Agape*, love feasts or gifts; provided by the richer Christians for the poorer.

[8] Fifteen days; i.e., seven before the Paschal Day and seven after; on which days, by a Law of Theodosius, all disputes and contentions ceased.

[9] PL 76, Sermo. 26. A wonderful discourse of pastoral instruction.

SECOND SUNDAY AFTER EASTER

I. St John Chrysostom: On the Gospel

II. St Augustine: On the Shepherd, the Thief, and the Hireling

III. St Cyril of Alexandria: The Good Shepherd

IV. St Gregory the Great: The Unfading Pastures: the Christian Hope

THE GOSPEL OF THE SUNDAY

John x. 11–16

At that time: Jesus said to the Pharisees: I am the good shepherd. The good shepherd giveth his life for his sheep. But the hireling, and he that is not the shepherd, whose own the sheep are not, seeth the wolf coming and leaveth the sheep, and flieth: and the wolf catcheth, and scattereth the sheep: and the hireling flieth, because he is a hireling: and he hath no care for the sheep.

I am the good shepherd; and I know mine, and mine know me. As the Father knoweth me, and I know the Father: and I lay down my life for my sheep. And other sheep I have, that are not of this fold: them also I must bring, and they shall hear my voice, and there shall be one fold and one shepherd.

Exposition from the Catena Aurea

V. 11. *I am the good shepherd. The good shepherd giveth his life . . .*

Augustine, *Tr.* 46 *in John*: The Lord has opened out two things, which He had already revealed but which were still somewhat obscure. In the first place we learn that He is the Door. Now He shows us that He is the Shepherd, when He says: *I am the Good Shepherd.*

Earlier he had said, *entered in by the door*. If then He is the Door, how does He enter in through Himself? Since He knows the Father through Himself, we know the Father through Him, so He enters the sheepfold through Himself, but we enter it through Him. We, because we preach Christ, enter in by the Door; but Christ preaches Himself: for light reveals itself as well as other things. If the rulers of the Church, who are sons, are shepherds, how is there but One Shepherd, unless they be the members of the One Shepherd?

(*Tr.* 47) And that he is a shepherd He gave to His members as a gift:

for Peter also is a shepherd, and the other Apostles were shepherds; and so likewise are all worthy bishops. But none amongst us calls himself a door. This He reserved strictly to Himself. He would not have added *good* (to *Shepherd*) unless there were also wicked shepherds. These are the thieves and robbers, or certainly, as more frequent, the *hirelings*.

GREGORY, *Hom.* 14 *in Gosp*: And He adds the character of that goodness we are to imitate, saying: *The good shepherd giveth his life for his sheep*. He has accomplished what He taught us: He has shown us what He commanded us to do. He laid down His own life for His sheep, that within our mystery He might change His Body and Blood into food, and nourish the sheep He had redeemed with the food of His own Flesh. He has shown us the way we must follow, despite fear of death. He has laid down the pattern to which we must conform ourselves. The first duty laid on us is to use our worldly goods in mercy for the needs of His sheep, and then, if necessary, give even our lives for them. He that will not give of his substance for his sheep, how shall he lay down his life for them?

AUGUSTINE, *Tr.* 47: Not Christ alone has done this. Yet if they did it who are His members, the Same Who is one with them has done this. For this He could do without them, but without Him they could not do it.

AUGUSTINE, *Serm.* 138, *Contra Donat*: What was Peter? What was Paul? What were the rest of the Apostles? What were the holy bishops and martyrs who followed close after them? They were all *good shepherds*; not alone because they shed their blood, but because they shed it for their sheep, and not in pride but in love. For some there are among the heretics who, because of their evil doings and their errors, have suffered some vexations, flatter themselves with claims of martyrdom, so that whitewashed as it were by this they more readily plunder: for they are wolves. But not all who submit their bodies to suffering, even to the flames, are to be held as having shed their blood for their sheep; rather they may have shed it against the salvation of their sheep, for as the Apostle says: *If I should deliver my body to be burned, and have not charity, it profiteth me nothing* (I Cor. xiii. 3). And how can he have the faintest charity in him who, though shown to be at fault, has yet no love for that unity commending which the Lord chose to speak, not of many shepherds, but of One; saying, *I am the good shepherd.*[2]

CHRYSOSTOM, 59 *in John*: He then goes on to speak of His passion, making clear to them that this was to be suffered for the salvation of the world, and that He submitted to it of His own will. Then he points out to them the marks of the hireling, and those also of the true shepherd, when He says:

V. 12. *But the hireling, and he that is not a shepherd . . .*

GREGORY: There are some who because they love earthly privileges more than their flock rightly forfeit the name of shepherd. For he is to be called, not a shepherd, but a hireling who feeds his flock in the Lord from no love of them but for earthly gain. A hireling is one who holds indeed the place of a shepherd, but seeks not for the riches of souls. He desires only worldly favours, and takes delight in the dignities of his office.

AUGUSTINE, *Serm.* 187, *par.* 9: He is not seeking God in the Church; he is seeking something else. If he were seeking God he would be chaste; for the soul has God for its lawful spouse. But He who is seeking from God something that is other than God is not seeking God chastely.

GREGORY: Whether he is a shepherd or a hireling cannot be truly known unless a time of trial arise. For as a rule in times of peace both shepherd and hireling alike remain watching their flocks. It is only when the wolf comes that each one shows the purpose for which he has been standing guard over his flock.

AUGUSTINE, *as above*: The wolf is the devil, and those who follow after him. For of these was it said that outwardly they are dressed in sheep's clothing, but that inwardly they are ravening wolves.

AUGUSTINE, *Tr.* 46 *in John, par.* 8: Behold, as a wolf seizes a sheep by the throat so the devil persuades one of the faithful to yield to adultery. And such a one must be excommunicated. But if he is excommunicated, he will be an enemy, he will lie in wait for you, he will injure when he can. You keep silent, you do not correct him. You have seen the wolf coming, and you have fled. You have stood fast in the body: you have fled in the soul. For our feelings are the movements of our soul. Gladness is the outpouring of the soul; sadness, the shrinking of the soul; great desire, a going forward of the soul; fear, the flight of the soul.

GREGORY: The wolf comes for the sheep likewise when some lawless person or robber oppresses any among the faithful, or those who are poor. But he who seemed to be a shepherd, and was not, abandons the sheep and flies. For fearing danger to himself from the wolf he does not dare to stand fast against his lawlessness. He flies, not by yielding ground, but by withholding his consolations. For against such things the hireling is not aroused by any feeling of zeal; for since he is concerned only with outward gains, he bears indifferently the inward losses of his flock. And so we have:

V. 13. *And the hireling flieth, because he is a hireling . . .*

The sole reason therefore why the hireling takes flight is because he is a hireling. It is as though He said: To stand fast amid the dangers that threaten the sheep is not to be looked for from one who while he pastures the sheep yet does not love them, but thinks only of worldly gain. And so he is fearful of withstanding dangers lest he lose what he loves.

AUGUSTINE, *Tr.* 46 *in John*: But if the Apostles were not hirelings, but shepherds, why did they fly when they suffered persecution? And the Lord saying: *And when they shall persecute you in this city: flee into another* (Mt. x. 23)? May the Lord fittingly answer this question? Let us knock; there is one *Who openeth* the door. AUGUSTINE *ad Honoratus, Ep.* 108: Let the servants of Christ, the ministers of His Word, and of His sacraments, flee from city to city whenever one of them is especially sought for by persecutors; but so that the Church is not abandoned by those who are not thus pursued. But when the danger is common to all, that is, to bishops and clergy and to the laity, let those who need the help of others be not abandoned by those whose help they need. Therefore, either let all pass over to a place of safety, or else let those who must of necessity remain be not abandoned by those through whom their need for the rites of the Church are to be fulfilled.

The ministers of the Church, therefore, must then fly, under pressure of persecution, from those places in which we dwell when there is either no people of Christ there to whom we must minister, or when the needed ministry can be fulfilled by others who have not the same reason for flight. But when the people remain, and the ministers take to flight, and their ministry is withdrawn, what then have we but that condemnable flight of hirelings who *have no care for the sheep*.

AUGUSTINE, *Tr.* 46: Among the good are numbered the door, the doorkeeper, the shepherd, and the sheep. Among the wicked, thieves and robbers, hirelings, and the wolf. AUGUSTINE, *Serm.* 137, 5: The shepherd must be loved, we must beware of the robber, and suffer the hireling. As long as he sees not the wolf, the thief, or the robber, so long is the hireling of use. But should he see them he flies.

AUGUSTINE, *Tr.* 47: Nor is he called a hireling unless he receives payment from the one who hires him. Sons patiently wait for the eternal inheritance of the Father. The hireling is impatient for the temporal wage of his hirer. Yet the divine glory of Christ is made known to men through the tongues of both the one and the other. He therefore does injury, not when he tells good tidings, but when He does what is evil. Gather the grape cluster; beware of the thorn. For the clusters, growing up from the root of the vine, sometimes hang amid thorns. For many within the Church preach Christ, while pursuing earthly gain; and yet through them the voice of Christ is heard, and the sheep follow: not indeed the voice of the hireling, but the voice of the shepherd spoken through the hireling.

V. 14. *I am the good shepherd; and I know mine, and mine know me.*

CHRYSOSTOM, *Hom. in John* 60: Having pointed out the marks of the true shepherd the Lord indicates two kinds of plunderers: the one a thief, who kills and robs, the other who does not prevent such things. By the one He refers to certain seditious persons; by the other he reproves the teachers of the Jews, who care nothing for the flocks entrusted to them. But from both Christ has distinguished Himself: from those who come to plunder by saying: *I am come that they may have life* (verse 10); from those who make nothing of the robbery of the wolves, by this that He laid down His life for His sheep. And so summing up, as it were, He continues: *I am the good shepherd*.

But because just before He had

said that the sheep hear the voice of the shepherd, and follow him, so that no one may say: What then of those who do not believe in You? He goes on to add: *And I know mine, and mine know me.* This Paul also makes evident, saying: *God hath not cast away his people, which he foreknew* (Rom. xi. 2).

GREGORY: As if He openly declared: I love my sheep, and they loving Me follow Me. For he who loves not the truth is yet far from knowing it. THEOPHYLACTUS: From this you may seek out the difference between the shepherd and the hireling. For the hireling does not know the sheep: for he rarely visits them. But the shepherd knows his sheep, being ever concerned for them.

V. 15. *As the Father knoweth me, and I know the Father . . .*

CHRYSOSTOM, *as above*: Then so that you may not consider the measure of the knowledge between Christ and His sheep to be equal He adds: *As the Father knoweth . . .* As though saying: I indeed know Him as He knows Me. Here there is equality of knowing. There there is not; for He continues: *and I lay down my life for my sheep.*

GREGORY: As though openly saying: It is agreed that I know the Father, and am known by the Father, because *I lay down my life for my sheep*; that is, I show how much I love the Father by the love through which I die for my sheep. CHRYSOSTOM: He also says this to show that He is not an impostor. For the Apostle likewise, when he wished to show that he was a true teacher, brought forward, as proof against the false apostles, his *stripes and his deaths* (II Cor. xi. 23).

THEOPHYLACTUS: For the corrupters of the faith do not expose their lives for their flocks, but like the hirelings they abandon those who followed them. But the Lord, that these latter might not be taken, said: *Let these go their way* (Jn. xviii. 8).

V. 16. *And other sheep I have, that are not . . .*

GREGORY: Because He had come to redeem not alone the Jews but also the people of the Gentiles, He adds: *And other sheep I have etc.*

AUGUSTINE, *serm.* 138; 5: For He had been speaking to the first fold of the family of the fleshly Israel. But there were others of the family of the faith of this Israel, and they were without; they were among the Gentiles, predestined, not yet gathered in. They are not therefore of this fold; because they are not of the family of the fleshly Israel. But they shall be of this fold, for there follows: *Them also I must bring.*

CHRYSOSTOM: He shows that both were scattered, and without shepherds. There follows: *And they shall hear my voice.* As if to say: Why wonder if these shall follow Me, and hear My voice, when you shall see those others follow Me, and listening to My voice? Then He foretells their future union: *And there shall be one fold and one shepherd.*

GREGORY: As though from the two flocks He has made one sheepfold; for He has joined the Jewish and the

Gentile peoples together in faith in Him. THEOPHYLACTUS: For the seal of baptism is the same on all: One Shepherd, the Word of God. Let the Manicheans therefore pay heed: since One is the Fold, and One the Shepherd, of both the Old and the New Testament.

AUGUSTINE, *Tr.* 47: What means then: *I was not sent but to the sheep that are lost of the house of Israel* (Mt. xv. 24), if not that only to the Jewish people does He reveal His bodily presence? To the Gentiles however He does not Himself go; but He sends.

CHRYSOSTOM: The word *must* here does not mean necessity; but is indicative of that which shall truly come to pass.

I. ST JOHN CHRYSOSTOM, BISHOP AND DOCTOR[2]

John x. 11–14. It is a grave thing, Beloved, a grave thing indeed to have the care of a church; it is a task that needs a measure of love and courage as great as that of which Christ spoke, so that a man may lay down his life for his flock, may never abandon them, and may boldly face the wolf. It is in this the shepherd differs from the hireling. For the latter, indifferent to the sheep, is ever watchful of his own safety; while the former, regardless of his own safety, seeks that of his sheep.

And having indicated to them the signs of the true shepherd, He tells them of the two kinds of despoilers. One is the thief, who kills and steals. The other does not himself destroy, but should these things take place, he does not prevent them. By the one He refers to the followers of a certain Theudas; by the other He exposes the teachers of the Jews, who had no concern for the sheep that were entrusted to them. And because of this of old Ezechias had reproached them, saying: *Woe to the shepherds of Israel! That fed themselves: should not the flocks be fed by the shepherds?* (Ezech. xxxiv. 2). But they did the opposite; which is wickedness of the worst kind, and the cause of all other evils. And because of this he says: they have not led back those that strayed, nor sought for those that were lost, nor bound up those that were broken, nor healed those that were sick, because they fed themselves and did not feed my sheep.

And this Paul also says, in other words: *For all seek the things that are their own; not the things that are Jesus Christ's* (Phil. ii. 21), and again: *Let no man seek his own; but that which is another's* (I Cor. x. 24). From both kinds (of despoilers) Christ distinguishes himself. From those that come to plunder by saying: *I am come that they may have life, and may have it more abundantly* (v. 10); and from those who care nothing whether the sheep are taken by the wolves, by not deserting them, and by laying down His life that they may not perish. For when they sought to put Him to death He neither withdrew His teaching, or betrayed those believing in Him; but stood firm, and chose to die.

And so everywhere He says: *I am the good shepherd.* Then because His words seemed to be without testimony (for the words, *I lay down my life* were fulfilled a little later; the words, *that they may have life, and have it more abundantly*, were to come to pass after their departure from this life) what does He do? He proves the one by the other; namely, in that He gave His own life He will also give life. This Paul also teaches: *For if, when we were enemies, we were reconciled to God by the death of His Son; much more, being reconciled, shall we be saved by his life* (Rom. v. 10). And again, in another place: *He that spared not even his own Son but delivered him up for us all, how hath he not also, with him, given us all things?* (Rom. viii. 32).

But why do they not say to Him as they said before: *Thou givest testimony of thyself: thy testimony is not true?* (Jn. viii. 13). Because he had often forced them to be silent; and because He was less interrupted as through His miracles people drew near to Him with greater confidence. Then, because He had just said: *And the sheep hear his voice, and follow him* (v. 3), lest anyone should say: What of those who do not believe in Him? hear what He adds: *And I know my sheep, and my sheep know me*. This Paul also indicated: *God hath not cast away his people, which he foreknew* (Rom. xi. 2); and also Moses: *The Lord knoweth who are his* (II Tim. ii. 19; Num. xvi. 5): those, he says, whom He foreknew.

Then that you might not think their knowledge equal, hear how He corrects this by what follows: *I know mine*, He says, *and mine know me*. But their knowing is not equal. But where is there equal knowledge? In the Father and in Me. For, *as the Father knoweth me, and I know the Father*. For unless He wished to assert this, why did he bring it forward? For the reason that frequently He placed Himself as one among the many, and so that no one would therefore think that He knew the Father as man, He adds: *As the Father knoweth me, and I know the Father*. Thus I know Him precisely as He knows Me. Accordingly He said: *No one knoweth who the Son is, but the Father; and who the Father is, but the Son* (Lk. x. 22), indicating a certain special knowledge, such as no one else could attain to. *I lay down my life for my sheep*. This He says frequently, showing that He is not an uncertain person. In the same way the Apostle, when he wished to prove that he was a true teacher, and was defending himself against certain pretended apostles, he appealed to his *stripes* and *his deaths*, saying: *In stripes above measure, in deaths often* (II Cor. xi. 23). For should He say: 'I am light, I am life', it would seem to the foolish that He was speaking from vanity. But to say: I am ready to lay down my life awakened no envy. Because of this they do not here say to Him, *Thou givest testimony of thyself: thy testimony is not true*. For His words reveal a tender concern for them, as though He were indeed prepared to give Himself for those who were ready to stone Him.

2. Because of this He here makes a timely reference to the Gentiles. *And other sheep I have, that are not of this fold: them also I must bring*. Notice however that the word *must* which He here uses does not imply necessity, but indicates something that will of a certainty come to pass; as though He had said: Why wonder if these follow Me, and if they shall hear My voice? For when you shall see others following Me, and hearkening to

my voice, then will you be much more astonished.

And do not be troubled because He says: *That are not of this fold.* For the distinction arises only from the Law, as Paul says: *Circumcision is nothing, and uncircumcision is nothing* (I Cor. vii. 19).

And *them also I must bring.* He shows that both flocks were scattered, and that both the one and the other are without shepherds, for the Good Shepherd had not yet come.

Then He proclaims their future union: *And there shall be one fold.* And this same Paul has also declared: *That he might make the two in himself into one new man* (Eph. ii. 15); through Jesus Christ Our Lord, to Whom be praise and honour and glory for ever and ever. Amen.

II. St Augustine, Bishop and Doctor[3]

On the Shepherd, the Thief, and the Hireling[4]

John x. 1–16; Ch. i. *The health of the members* (of Christ's Body) *is in unity and love.*

Through your faith you are aware, Dearly Beloved Brethren, and I know that because of this you have been taught by the Master from heaven in Whom you have placed your hope, that Our Lord Jesus Christ, Who has just suffered for us, and risen again, is the Head of the Church, and that the Church is His Body, and that in His Body the unity of the members, and the bond of their mutual love, is as it were the token of its health. And whosoever has grown cold in charity, has grown weak in the Body of Christ. But He Who has raised up our Head is able also to heal our infirm members: provided they are not cut off by too grievous wickedness, but remain with the Body till they are healed. For all who adhere to the Body still have hope of healing; but they who have been cut off can neither be treated nor healed.

Since then He is the Head of the Church, and the Church is His Body, the whole Christ is then both Head and Body. He is now risen. And so we have our Head in heaven. Our Head intercedes for us. Our Head, without stain and immortal, now makes intercession with God for our sins, so that at the end of the world, we also being risen, and partaking of His heavenly glory, may follow our Head. For where the Head is, there also are the other members. And whilst here, we are His members; let us then be filled with hope that we shall follow our Head.

Ch. ii. *The Unity of Christ and His Members.* For consider, Brethren, the love of this Our Head. He is now in heaven, yet while the Church suffers here on earth, He too suffers here. Here Christ hungers, here He thirsts, here He is naked, here He is a stranger, He is sick, He is in prison. All that His Body here suffers, He has said that He suffers. And on the last day, setting this His Body at the right hand side, and the rest, by whom He is now despised, on the left, He will say to those on the right hand: *Come, ye blessed of my Father, possess you the kingdom prepared for you from the foundation of the world* (Mt. xxv. 34). And in reward for what? *For I was hungry, and you gave me to eat*; and so He goes on to the rest, as though it were He Who had received: so much so that they, not understanding Him, answer and say: *Lord, when did we see thee hungry, a stranger, or in prison?* And He will say to them: *As long as you did it to one of these my least brethren, you did it to me.*

For so also in our own body is the head above, and the feet on earth. Yet in any crowd when men press close together should someone tread on your foot, does not your head say, 'you are treading on my foot'. No one has trodden on your head, or on your tongue; it is above in safety, no harm has come to it, and yet, because of the bond of love, there is a oneness from your head down to your feet, the tongue does not consider itself apart from the foot, but says: 'you are standing on me' when no one has touched it. Therefore just as the tongue, which no one has touched, says, 'you are standing on my foot', so Christ, Whom no one has touched, says: *I was hungry, and you gave me to eat.* And how does He conclude? *These shall go into everlasting punishment: but the just, into life everlasting.*

Ch. iii. *Christ is the Door. Peter unknown to himself is weak.*

Now when Our Lord was speaking on this occasion He said He was the Shepherd, and He said also that He was the Door. You may read both words there: *I am the door*, and, *I am the shepherd.* In the Head He is the Door; He is the Shepherd in the Body. For He said to Peter, on whom alone He built His Church: *Peter, lovest thou me?* He answered: *Lord, I love thee. Feed my sheep.* And a third time He asks: *Peter, lovest thou me?* Peter was grieved that He had asked him a third time (Jn. xxi. 15–17): as though He were looking at the conscience of a betrayer, and saw not the faith of the one who confessed Him.

But He had always known him. He knew him even when Peter knew not his very self. He had not then known himself when he said, *I am ready to go with thee, even to death* (Lk. xxii. 33). And how weak he was he knew not. And this will happen often with the sick, that a sick man does not know what is the matter with him, while the physician does: though it is the sick man who is suffering from the illness, and not the physician. The physician can tell what is happening to another better than the one who is ill can describe what is happening to himself. Peter was then the sick man; the Lord was the physician. The one said he had strength; when he had none. The Other, touching his pulse, says that he is going to deny Him three times. And so it came to pass, as the Physician had foretold; not as the sick man had believed (Lk. xxii. 33, 34, 55–61).

And so after the Resurrection the Lord asks him; not as though He knew not with what fervour he would confess his love of Christ, but so that by a threefold confession of love he might cancel the threefold denial of fear.

Ch. iv. *What is asked of Peter? To enter the Sheepfold by the Door.*

The Lord accordingly asks Peter: *Peter, lovest thou me?* as it were saying: what will you give Me, what will you offer Me, since you love Me? What was Peter to put before His Lord, now risen from the dead, and ascending to heaven, to sit at the right hand of the Father? As though He said: You will give Me this, you will offer this to Me, if you love Me, that you feed My sheep, that you go in by the Door, that you do not climb in another way.

While the Gospel was being read you heard the words: *He that entereth in by the door is the shepherd of the sheep; he that climbeth up another way, the same is a thief and a robber; he cometh not, but for to steal, and to kill, and to destroy*. Who is this who enters in by the door? He who enters in through Christ. Who is this? He who associates himself with the passion of Christ; He who has learned the humility of Christ; so that he has learned that though God has become man for us, man himself is not God, but man. For he who desires to appear as God, when he is but man, is no follower of Him, Who while being God, became man.

To you it is not said: be something less than you are; but rather, learn what you are. Know that you are weak, know that you are a man, know that you are a sinner; know that it is He Who sanctifies you; know that you are stained by sin. Let the blemish in your soul be made manifest in your confession, and you shall belong to the flock of Christ. For the confession of your sins invites the Physician to heal you; just as when he who is sick says, 'I am well', he desires no help from the physician.

Did not the Pharisee and the Publican go up into the Temple? The one boasted of how strong his soul was; the other showed his wounds to the Physician. The one said: *God, I give thee thanks that I am not as is this Publican* (Lk. xviii. 11). He set himself far above the other man. And so if the Publican had been strong of soul, the Pharisee would have envied him; for he would have no one above whom he might set himself. In what state of soul did he come who was so ill-disposed? Surely not in a healthy state; and though he declared how strong he was, yet he went down unhealed. But the other, with downcast eyes, not daring to raise them towards heaven, beat his breast, saying: *O God, be merciful to me a sinner*.

And what does the Lord say? *Amen I say to you, that the Publican went down into his house justified, rather than the Pharisee: because every one that exalteth himself, shall be humbled: and he that humbleth himself, shall be exalted*. They therefore who exalt themselves seek to climb into the Sheepfold by *another way*; while they who humble themselves enter the Door. And so of the one He says: *he entereth in*; of the other that: *he climbeth up*. He that climbs up, you perceive, who is seeking the high places, does not enter in but falls. But he who bows himself down that he may enter through the Door, he does not fall; and what is more he is a shepherd.

Ch. v. *The three persons who come to the sheepfold: the shepherd, the thief, the hireling. The shepherd is to be loved, the hireling suffered, the thief guarded against.*

But the Lord speaks of three persons, and we must consider them carefully as they are in the Gospel: the persons of the shepherd, of the hireling, and of the thief. While it was being read I presume that you noticed that He was describing a shepherd, that He described the hireling, and He described the thief. The shepherd, He said, entered in by the door, and laid down his life for his sheep. The thief and the robber, He said, climb in by another way. The hireling, He said, should he see a wolf, or even a thief, flies; because he has no concern for the sheep; for he is a hireling, not a shepherd.

This first enters by the door, because he is the shepherd; this other climbs in another way, because he is a thief; and this last seeing those coming who are going to steal the sheep is afraid and runs away, because he has no care for the sheep; for he is a hireling. When we have learned who these three persons are, Your Sanctity has found those whom you should love, those whom you must bear with, and those of whom you must beware. The shepherd you must love, the hireling you must suffer, against the thief you must be on your guard.

There are men in the Church of whom the Apostle says that they preach the Gospel because of their circumstances, seeking from men the things that are theirs (Phil. ii. 21): money, honour, or human praise. They preach the Gospel, seeking gain by any means; seeking not so much the salvation of those to whom they preach as their own advantage. But he who hears the word of salvation from him who has not himself gained salvation, should he believe in the One Whom he preaches, not placing his hopes in the one through whom salvation is preached, he that preaches shall suffer loss; he to whom he preaches shall gain.

Ch. vi. *The words of Christ against the Pharisees apply also to the wicked shepherds in the Church. There is one Church formed from Jew and Gentile.*

The Gospel records Our Lord as saying of the Pharisees, that *they sat upon the chair of Moses*. The Lord did not here refer only to them; as though He would send those who would believe in Christ to the school of the Jews, that they might there learn which is the way to the kingdom of heaven. Did the Lord not come to found His own Church, and separate, as wheat from the chaff, those of the Jews who believed rightly, and hoped rightly, and lived worthily; and to make one wall of the circumcision, to which He would join another wall from the uncircumcision of the Gentiles; of which two walls, coming together from different directions, He would himself be the Corner-stone? Did not the same Lord then say of those two peoples who were to be one: *Other sheep I have, which are not of this fold*? He was speaking of the Jews: *Them also*, He says, *I must bring, that there may be one fold, and one shepherd*.

Whence also were there two ships, from which He called His Disciples. They stood for the two peoples, when they cast their nets and took such a great draught of fishes that their nets almost broke: *and filled both the ships* (Lk. v. 2–7). The two ships signify the One Church; but made from the two peoples, joined together in Christ through coming from different directions. This the two wives, Leah and Rachel, who had a common husband, also signify (Gen. xix). The two blind men who sat by the way side and to whom the Lord gave sight also stand for these two peoples. And if you consider the Scriptures carefully you will find that two Churches, which are not two but one, are signified in many places. And to this end does the Corner-stone serve: to make one out of two. And to this likewise the Shepherd: that from the two flocks he may make one.

Therefore the Lord Who was to teach the Church, and in addition to that of the Jews was to have his own school, as we now see, would he send those believing in Him to the Jews to be taught? But by the names of the Scribes and Pharisees He implied that in His Church there would be certain ones who would speak but would not perform (what they teach): for Moses prefigured His own Person; and accordingly, when he spoke to the people he placed a veil before him (II Cor. iii. 13): because as long as those subject to the Law were given over to bodily delights and pleasures, and looked for an earthly kingdom, a veil was set before their face so that they might not discern Christ in the Scriptures. For when after the passion of Christ the veil was taken away, the secret places of the temple were exposed to view.

When therefore He hung upon the Cross the veil of the temple was rent from top to bottom. And the Apostle Paul openly tells us: *When they shall be converted to the Lord, the veil shall be taken away.* He however who has not been converted to the Lord, even though he reads the law of Moses, *the veil is laid upon their heart*, as the Apostle says. When therefore the Lord wished to prefigure certain future figures in the Church, what does He say: *The scribes and the Pharisees have seated themselves on the chair of Moses: whatsoever they say, do ye; but according to their works, do ye not* (Mt. xxvii. 51; II Cor. iii. 16, 15; Mt. xxiii. 2, 3).

Ch. vii. *Evil living clerics strive to undo the Gospel when through their example they lead lay persons to sin.*

When wicked clerics hear what is here spoken against them, they desire to change its meaning. For I have heard that some have wished to misconstrue the meaning of this sentence. Would they not if they could delete it from the Gospel? But since they cannot delete it, they endeavour to change its meaning. But the grace and mercy of God assists us, and does not suffer them to do so: for He has hedged in His words with truth, and balanced them, so that should anyone wish to cut anything from them, or insert something by a dishonest reading or interpretation, he that has a conscience may join to the Scripture what was severed from the Scripture, and read what preceded it and what followed it, and he will find the meaning the other sought to render falsely.

What then do you think these say of those persons of whom it was said: *What they shall say to you, do*? That it is in truth addressed to lay persons. For a lay man who desires to live worthily, what does he say to himself when he sees an unworthy cleric? 'The Lord said: *What they shall say, do; what they do, do not.* Let me walk the way of the Lord: not follow the example of this man. Let me hear from him, not his own words, but God's. I shall follow God; let him follow his own evil desires. For if I am to defend myself before God by saying, 'Lord, I saw thy cleric living in wickedness, and because of that I have lived wickedly! will He not say to me: "Wicked servant, have you not heard Me say: *What they shall say to you, do ye; what they do, do ye not*?"'

An evil living lay person, on the other hand, an unbeliever, who does not belong to the flock of Christ, who belongs not with Christ's wheat, who is permitted on the threshing floor only as chaff is permitted there, what does he say to himself when he has begun to feel the correction of the word of God? 'Off with you: why talk to me? Even the bishops, even the clergy, do not observe this; and you want to force me to practise it.' He is not looking for a defender of his bad conduct, but for a companion in punishment. For he whose conduct he has chosen to copy will never defend him in the day of judgement. For as all whom the devil seduces, he seduces, not that they may reign with him, but that they may be damned with him: so all who follow after the wicked are seeking companions for themselves in hell, not clients for the kingdom of heaven.

Ch. vii. *The perverted interpretation of the Gospel.*

How then do they twist the meaning of this sentence, when to the evil-living is it said: rightly did the Lord say, *What they say to you, do; what they do, do ye not*. 'It *was* rightly said,' they say. 'For it was said to you, that you may do what we say; but that you may not do what we do. For we offer sacrifice; it is not lawful for you.' See the perverted ingenuity of these men: what am I saying? of these hirelings. For were they shepherds they would not say such things. And so the Lord, that He might shut the mouth of such as these, went on and said: *They sit upon the chair of Moses: whatsoever they shall say to you, do; whatsoever they do, do ye not; for they say, and do not.*

What does He mean, Brethren? Were He speaking of offering sacrifice would He have said: *For they say, and do not*? For they do offer sacrifice; they do make offerings to God. What is this they say, and do not? Hear what follows: *For they bind heavy and insupportable burdens, and lay them on men's shoulders; but with a finger of their own they will not move them*. He openly rebukes them, describes and points them out. But they, when they thus seek to pervert the meaning of this sentence very plainly show they are seeking in the Church nothing but their own advantage; and that they do not read the Gospel: for had they known of this page, and had read it all, they would never have dared to say this.

9. *That there are in the Church evil shepherds who are similar to the Pharisees. Which shepherd is a hireling, which chaste. The chaste wife.*

But observe even more plainly that the Church has within it persons of this kind; in case anyone says to you: 'He was talking about the Pharisees, He was speaking of the Scribes, He was speaking of the Jews: the Church has no such persons within her.' Who then are they of whom the Lord says: *Not every one that saith to me, Lord, Lord, shall enter into the kingdom of heaven*? (Mt. vii. 21). And adds: *Many will say to me in that day: Lord, Lord, have we not prophesied in thy name, and done many miracles in thy name, and in thy name we have eaten and drunk?* Was it the Jews did this is the name of Christ? It is very plain that He is speaking of those who bear the Name of Christ.

But what follows? *And then I will profess unto them, I never knew you: depart from me, you that work iniquity.* Hear the Apostle grieving because of such persons. He says that there are some who preach the Gospel out of charity; some for their own gain, of whom he says: *They preach the Gospel, but not sincerely* (Phil. i. 17). A worthy thing; but they are not worthy. What they preach is praiseworthy; but they are not praiseworthy who preach it. And why are they not worthy? Because whosever is seeking in the Church for another thing, is not seeking God.

Were he seeking for God he would be chaste: for the soul has God for its lawful spouse. Whoever seeks from God something other than God does not chastely seek God. Consider, Brethren, how if a wife loves her husband because he is rich, she is not chaste. For she loves not her husband, but her husband's gold. If she loves her husband, she loves him though he may be poor, she loves him with nothing. For if she loves him because he is rich, what (human chances being what they are) if he loses the protection of the law and of a sudden has nothing? She gives him up perhaps; for what she loved was not her husband, but what was his. But if she truly loves her husband, she loves him even more when he is poor; because she loves him with compassion.

Ch. ix–x. *God must be chastely sought for.*

But, however, Brethren, Our God never can be poor. He is rich; it is He made all things; heaven and earth, the sea and the angels. All that we behold in the heavens, all that we do not behold, He has made. Yet we should not love these riches, but Him Who made them. For He has promised you only Himself. Discover something more precious and He will give it to you. The earth is beautiful, the heavens and the angels; but more beautiful is He Who made them. They therefore who speak of God, while loving God; who speak of God, because of God, feed His sheep, and they are not hirelings.

Our Lord Jesus Christ demanded this chastity of the soul when He said to Peter: *Peter, lovest thou me?* What does this mean: *Lovest thou me?* Art thou chaste? Thy heart is not adulterous? It is not your own ends you are seeking in the Church, but mine? If then you are such a man, and you love me, *feed my sheep.* For then you will not be a hireling; you will be a shepherd.

11. *In what manner hirelings are profitable. Shepherds few, hirelings many.*

They did not speak from worthy hearts whom the Apostle laments. What did he say? *But what then? So that by all means, whether by occasion, or by truth, Christ be preached.* He tolerates the presence of hirelings. The shepherd speaks of Christ from truth; the hireling speaks of him because of his circumstances: while seeking something else. Yet the one preaches Christ, and the other preaches Christ. Listen to the voice of the shepherd Paul: *Whether by occasion, or by truth, Christ be preached.* Himself a true shepherd he was willing that there should be hirelings. For they work where they can: they are profitable according to their measure. But when for other purposes the Apostle looked for those whom the weaker brethren might imitate, he says: *For this cause have I sent to you Timothy, who will put you in mind of my ways* (I Cor. iv. 17).

And what does he mean by this? That I have sent you a shepherd, who will put you in mind of my ways; that is, who as I walk so shall he walk. And sending them this shepherd, what does he say? *For I have no man so of the same mind, who with sincere affection is sollicitous for you.* Did he not have many with him? But what comes after? *For all seek the things that are their own; not the things that are Jesus Christ's* (Phil. ii. 20, 21); that is, 'I desired to send you a shepherd; there are many hirelings: but it was not fitting that a hireling be sent.' A hireling is to be sent for other tasks, and other ends; but for the ends that Paul desired a shepherd was needed. And among the many hirelings he scarce found one shepherd: for shepherds are few, hirelings many.

But what is it that is said of hirelings? *Amen, amen, I say to you, they have received their reward* (Mt. vi. 2). But what does the Apostle say of the shepherd? *If any man therefore shall cleanse himself from these, he shall be a vessel unto honour, sanctified and profitable to the Lord, prepared unto every good work* (II Tim. ii. 21). Not *prepared unto* certain works, and unprepared unto others, but prepared unto every good work. These things I have said regarding shepherd.

Ch. x–xii. *The fleeing hireling, Donatists, wolves and robbers.*

Let us now speak of hirelings. *The hireling when he sees the wolf coming, flieth.* The Lord said this. Why? *Because he hath no care for the sheep.* The hireling then is profitable until he sees the wolf, and as long as he does not see the robbers. When he sees them he flies. And who is there among the hirelings who does not fly from the Church when he sees the wolf and the thief? Wolves abound; thieves abound. These are they who climb up another way. Who are they who climb up? They are those of the Donatists' faction who desire to make havoc of Christ's flock. They climb in by another way. They do not enter in through Christ; for they are not humble. Because they are proud, they climb up. What does this mean, *they climb up*? They have grown insolent. From where do they climb up? By *another way*. From this they wish to be named by their way.

They who are not in unity are of another way; and by this way they climb up; that is, they have become insolent, and desire to plunder the sheep. Observe how they climb up. 'We,' they say, 'we sanctify, we justify, we make righteous.' Behold how they have climbed up. But he that exalteth himself shall be humbled . . . (Lk. xiv. 11). The Lord Our God is able to humble them.

Now the wolf is the devil, and they that follow him; and he lies in wait to deceive. For it is said that they are clothed in the skins of sheep, but that inwardly they are ravening wolves (Mt. vii. 13). Should the hireling be aware of someone speaking evil, or thinking it to the peril of his own soul, or who commits some criminal or obscene thing, and, seeing that he is someone of importance in the Church, from whom he hopes for some personal gain, he keeps silent. And when he sees a man perishing in sin, sees the wolf close upon him, sees him held fast by the throat, dragged to torment, he does not tell him, 'you are committing sin'; he does not correct him for fear he may lose his own advantages. This then is *when he sees the wolf coming and flieth*; when he does not tell him: 'you are acting wickedly.' This is flight, not of the body, but of the soul. He though standing there in body, flies in his soul; since he sees a sinner and does not say to him, 'you are committing sin'; since he is even aiding and abetting him.

Ch. xi–xiii. *The grapes gathered from thorns.* My dear Brethren, does any priest or bishop come up here, and say other from this high place (*pulpit* or *tribune*) than that the possessions of others must not be taken, that you practise no deception, that you yield to no wickedness? They cannot speak otherwise who sit in the chair of Moses, and it is this that speaks through them, not they that speak. What then is the meaning of the words: *Do men gather grapes of thorns*, and, *every tree is known by its fruits* (Mt. vii. 16; xii. 33). Can a Pharisee utter good tidings? A Pharisee is a thorn; how do I gather grapes from thorns? Because Thou, O Lord, hast said: *What they say to you, do; what they do, do ye not.*

Did you bid me gather grapes from thorns when you said: *Do men gather grapes from thorns?* The Lord will answer you: I did not bid you gather grapes from thorns; but see, note well, whether the vine, as sometimes happens, when it wanders about upon the ground, is not perhaps entangled among thorns? For we sometimes find this, Brethren, a vine planted over a hedge of thorns, and throwing out its branches entangles them in the thorns of the hedge, and the clusters hang amid the thorns. And he that sees them gathers the grapes, not indeed from the thorns, but from the vine entangled in the thorn.

In this way they are thorns (*the Pharisees*). But sitting in the chair of Moses the vine enfolds them; and the clusters, that is, good tidings, good teachings, hang about them. Let you gather the grapes; the thorns will not pierce you, since you read, *Whatsoever they say to you, do; what they do, do ye not.* Their works are thorns; their words the grapes: but they are from the vine, that is, from the chair of Moses.

14. *The hirelings fly when they favour the wicked. Augustine not a hireling.*

These then fly when they see the wolf; when they see a thief. It was this that I had begun to say; that from this high place they can say nothing other than, 'labour well, do not commit perjury, do not tell lies, do not cheat any one'. But at times men's lives are so bad that on the matter of wresting a farm from another man, they will seek advice from a bishop; and counsel of similar kind is sought from him.

Sometimes it has happened to us: we speak from experience: otherwise we would not believe it. Many ask of us evil counsels, counsels of lying, of cheating; thinking to please us by such things.

But in the Name of Christ, if what we say be pleasing to God, no such person has tempted us, and found in us what he was seeking. For by His good will Who has called us we are shepherds, not hirelings. But what is it the Apostle says? *To me it is a very small thing to be judged by you, or by man's day; but neither do I judge my own self. For I am not conscious to myself of anything, yet am I not thereby satisfied: but he that judgeth me is the Lord* (I Cor. iv. 3, 4). My conscience therefore is not good because you praise it. For how can you praise what you cannot see? Let Him praise it Who sees it. Let Him also correct it, should He see there what offends His sight.

From this I do not say that we are sound in every respect. But we beat our breast, and say to God: 'Be merciful unto us, lest we fall into sin.' Nevertheless I do believe, for I speak in His Presence, that I seek nothing from you but your salvation; and I grieve without ceasing over the sins of our brethren, and suffer with them, and are tormented in our soul, and on occasions we correct them: rather we never cease to correct them. All of you who remember that of which I am speaking are witnesses of how often we have corrected our sinful brethren, and strongly corrected them.

Ch. xii–xv. *What account must the shepherd give of his sheep?*

I shall now speak of my relationship with your Holiness. In Christ's Name you are the people of God, you are the Catholic people, you are the members of Christ: you are not cut off from Unity. You have been united with the members of the Apostles; you have a share in the memorials of the holy martyrs, which are to be found everywhere throughout the world; and you are a part of our own care, so that we must give an account of you. And what our whole account is you know. Lord, Thou knowest why I have spoken. Thou knowest that I have not kept silent. Thou knowest in what spirit I have spoken. Thou knowest that I have wept before Thee when I had spoken and was not listened to. This I believe to be the whole of my account. For the Holy Spirit has given us confidence through Ezechiel the prophet. You know the words spoken concerning the watchman:

O son of man, he says, *I have made thee a watchman to the house of Israel. When I say to the wicked: O wicked man, thou shalt surely die: if thou dost not speak*: that is (for I speak to thee that you may speak); *if thou dost not sound the trumpet, the sword will come and cut him off*; that is, what I have threatened the sinner: *that wicked man shall die in his iniquity, and I will require his blood at the hand of the watchman*. Why? Because he did not speak. *But if the watchman see the sword coming, and sound the trumpet. Then he that heareth the sound of the trumpet, and doth not look to himself*; that is, does not correct his way of living, so that he shall not receive that punishment which God is threatening, *the sword will come, and cut him off, whoever he may be; he shall die in his iniquity: but thou hast delivered thy soul* (Ezech. xxxiii. 7).

And in that place in the Gospel what else than this did He tell His servant, when He said: *Lord, I know that thou art a difficult or hard man; thou reapest where thou hast not sown, and gatherest where thou hast not strewed. And being afraid I went and hid thy talent in the earth: behold here thou hast that which is thine.* And He answers: *Wicked and slothful servant*: and the more so because you know that I am a severe man, who reap where I have not sown, and gather where I have not strewn. My very greed ought to have taught you that I look for profit on my money; *Thou oughtest therefore to have given my money to the bankers, and at my coming I should have demanded my own with interest* (Mt. xxiv. 27; Lk. xix. 20–7). Did *He* say: Thou oughtest to have *given*, and thou oughtest to have demanded? Therefore, it is we who give; He is to come Who will demand of us. Pray, that He find us ready!

Turning then to the Lord Our God, the Father Almighty, let us as best we can give thanks with all our hearts, beseeching Him that in His Goodness He will mercifully hear our prayers, and by His grace drive evil from our thoughts and actions, increase our faith, guide our minds, grant us His holy inspirations, and bring us to joy without end, through His Son Our Lord and Saviour Jesus Christ. Amen.

III. St Cyril of Alexandria, Bishop and Doctor

John x. 11–13. *I am the Good Shepherd.* Since he had already very clearly shown what evil had followed from the ancient deceptions of the false prophets and false shepherds, he makes clear to them the present fruits of His Coming amongst them, and, defeating them by comparing their respective flocks, and winning His victory by truth, He cries out aloud: *I am the good shepherd.* It is in vain then, He says, that you plot against Me, since you can by no means separate Me from my care for My sheep, in no way convict Me; and strive not to number Me among the number of those who do this. And what is good you say is evil; and you think that a man filled with self-love is able to give judgement in accordance with the mind of the Lawgiver. And so He rebukes them, unworthy Teachers of the Law, as wholly contemptuous of the commandments of Moses, as ignorant of the purpose of His dwelling amongst us, so that the prophet Isaias is found to be speaking the truth concerning them: *Woe to you that call evil good, and good evil: who put bitter for sweet, and sweet for bitter; that put darkness for light, and light for darkness* (Is. xv. 20).

For are they not found to be doing this who seek to put in darkness that True Light which is Our Lord Jesus Christ, when they dare to place our Good Shepherd among the number of those shepherds falsely called, and even below them. For they who then ruled the people held in great esteem those who claimed to have a divine message, and they tried under the protection of the name of prophet to plunder the credulous, and turn them from the truth, seeking to make them obey their will rather than God's. Semeias the Elamite at any rate, putting forward his falsehoods dared to rise against the glory of Jeremiah. And though Sedecia (the king) held the latter in bonds, and the other in honour, yet he came to the reward of his lying. But the unhappy Pharisees, now far exceeding the impiety of their forbears, and filled with a greater audacity, do not yield to Christ what they give to false teachers. For what do they say to those who are eager to hear him: *He hath a devil, and is mad: why hear you him?* (Jn. x. 20).

And for the same reason He also says of them through the prophet Isaias: *Woe to them, for they have departed from me. They shall be wasted because they have transgressed against me; and I redeemed them: and they have spoken lies against me.* And again: *Their princes shall fall by the sword, for the rage of their tongue* (Os. vii. 13, 16). How are they not then worthy of every punishment who sharpen their bold tongues in this manner against Him, so that they dare to say against Him words that are fitting only for such as they are, or permit such words to be heard even in casual conversation.

The good shepherd giveth his life for his sheep; but the hireling, and he that is not the shepherd, whose own the sheep are not, seeth the wolf coming and leaveth the sheep, and flieth: and the wolf catcheth, and scattereth the sheep: and the hireling flieth, because he is a hireling: and he hath no care for the sheep.

Having very skilfully replied to the verbosity of some of His hearers, and set the perfection of his own actions against their lawless conduct, and shown that they are as robbers who climb into the sheepfold by *another way*, and that He is their True Shepherd, He passes on to the rulers of the Jews, and shows that His authority is greater than that of the Pharisees. And he shows this by a very simple comparison. For He contrasts His own watchfulness and love with their neglect, and points out that they are without concern for their flock, while he declares that His own care for them reaches to the point where He is prepared to lay down His life for them all.

He shows in what manner a shepherd may be proved good; and He teaches that he must be prepared to give up his life fighting in defence of his sheep, which was fulfilled in Christ. For man has departed from the love of God, and fallen into sin, and, because of this was, I say, excluded from the divine abode of paradise, and when he was weakened by that disaster, he yielded to the devil tempting him to sin, and death following that sin he became the prey of fierce and ravenous wolves. But after Christ was announced as the True Shepherd of all men, *He laid down his life for us* (I Jn. iii. 16), fighting for us against that pack of inhuman beasts. He bore the Cross for us, that by His own death He might destroy death. He was condemned for us, that He might deliver all of us from the sentence of punishment: the tyranny of sin being overthrown by our faith: fastening to the Cross the decree that stood against us, as it is written (Col. ii. 14).

Therefore as the father of sin had as it were shut up the sheep in hell, *giving them to death to feed on*, as is written in the psalms (Ps. xlviii. 15), He died for us as truly Good, and truly our Shepherd, so that the dark shadow of death driven away He might join us to the company of the blessed in heaven; and in exchange for abodes that lie far in the depths of the pit, and in the hidden places of the sea, grant us mansions in His Father's House above. Because of this He says to us in another place: *Fear not, little flock, for it hath pleased your Father to give you a kingdom* (Lk. xii. 32).

Up to this point we have spoken of Christ; let us speak now of those others. To the eyes of just men they will appear as nothing other than mercenaries, and false shepherds, craven, betrayers, falterers, and men who have never troubled themselves concerning the salvation of their sheep, cautiously seeking in every direction for what appears pleasing to every one. And according to the words of the Saviour they are in truth hirelings; for the sheep are not theirs, but Christ's, Who hired them in the beginning, and selected them to fill the highest places as rulers and priests of the Jewish people, and who without care for these poor creatures betrayed their sheep to the wolves, in what manner we shall now briefly recount.

For in the earliest times the manifold peoples of the Jews looked upon God alone as their king, and paid to Him the drachma of sacrifice, and the custom of the tribute, in token of their citizenship. But their came upon them a certain fierce wolf: a man of another race, who reduced them to slavery, subjecting them to the yoke of an earthly king, carrying them off and forcing them into a strange and lawless way of life, exacting tribute from them, and plundering the kingdom of God. Broken down by misery they were compelled to obey the laws of the tyrant. There came a stranger to the authority of God: that is, to the tribe to which was assigned the priesthood, and to whom the office of judging and giving justice had been given by God: altering all this, and enforcing his will by violence, putting his own image on the coins, and employing every kind of tyranny.

Against this intolerable oppression the shepherds were not watchful. They saw the wolf coming, and leaving their flocks they fled; for the flocks were not theirs; neither did they call on Him Who was able to defend them, Who had delivered them out of the servitude of Babylon, Who had overthrown the Assyrian, Who had by the hand of His Angel slain one hundred and eighty-five thousands of the strangers (IV Kings xix. 35). That this subjection to an alien rule undid in no small degree the devotion of Israel to God you may learn from this happening. When Pilate reproached the Jews for their incredible rashness, crying out for the crucifixion of the Lord, He challenged them, saying: *Shall I crucify your king?* They, casting off their duty to God, breaking the bond of their ancient rule, and as it were subjecting themselves to a new yoke, brazenly cry out: *We have no king but Caesar.*

And all that they did and cried out seemed acceptable to their own rulers, who therefore must be regarded as the cause of all their miseries. They are condemned and rightly as betrayers of their flocks, as unworthy, as cowards, refusing completely to defend, or to fight for the flocks entrusted to them. And for this God has rebuked them, saying: *The pastors have done foolishly, and have not sought the Lord: therefore have they not understood, and all their flock is scattered* (Jer. x. 21). From these happenings it is shown that Christ is the True Shepherd of His flocks, and that these others are corrupters and pests rather than good shepherds, and far from worthy of true praise.

I am the good shepherd. He exults again, as a Victor, and as triumphant over the rule of the Jews, not by the testimony of a few, but proclaimed aloud by the visible evidence of things. For after he had compared his own actions with the evildoing of the false prophets, showing that His works and their wondrous consequences are more potent than their falsehoods (for they came among their flock only that they might steal, and kill, and lay waste, and in their speech they are given over to lying, and they utter nothing that is just; but He came, not alone that He may give life to His sheep, but that they may have it more abundantly), and well and truly does he cry out: *I am the good shepherd*, showing in this way that a shepherd who is truly good, is prepared to die for his sheep, and freely lays down His life for them, but that the hireling and the stranger placed over them is a runaway and a coward, or whatever you will. And seeing that He knows that He is Himself this shepherd, Who will lay down His life for His sheep, rightly does He again exclaim: *I am the good shepherd.*

For He must prevail over all, Who *in all things holds the primacy* (Col. i. 18), so that the psalmist will be seen to have spoken truly concerning Him when he said: *That thou mayest be justified in thy words, and mayest overcome when thou art judged* (Ps. l. 6). In addition to what has been said this must be explained. For I believe that the Lord putting before the Jewish people the things that are to be to their advantage, warns them, not alone by His own words, but also from the sayings of the prophets, that they may understand, and know clearly, what is plain to the mind, that He it is Who is their True Shepherd; these others being no longer what they were. For it was a possibility that should they not believe His words, they would though unwillingly give assent to those of the prophets.

He therefore says: *I am the good shepherd*, recalling to the minds of the Jews that which was said by the voice of Ezechiel. For this is what he says concerning Christ and concerning those to whom the care of the Jews had been given: *Thus saith the Lord God: Woe to the shepherds of Israel, that fed themselves: should not the flocks be fed by the shepherd? You ate the milk, and you clothed yourselves with the wool, and you killed that which was fat: but my flock you did not feed. The weak you have not strengthened, and that which was sick you have not healed, that which was broken you have not bound up, and that which was driven away you have not brought again, neither have you sought that which was lost: but you ruled over them with vigour, and with a high hand. And my sheep were scattered, because there was no shepherd: and they became the prey of all the beasts of the field, and were scattered. My sheep have wandered in every mountain, and in every high hill: and my flocks were scattered upon the face of the earth, and there was none that sought them, none, I say, that sought them* (Ezech. xxxiv. 3).

For one thing only filled the minds of the Jewish Teachers: the love of gain, the desire to grow rich on the offerings of those subject to them, to exact tribute. For what might be of advantage to their people, or of help to those subject to them, they had no concern. And so He Who is indeed the Good Shepherd again says of them: *Thus saith the Lord: Behold I myself come upon the Shepherds, and I will require my flock at their hands, and I will cause them to cease from feeding the flock any more, and I will deliver my flock from their mouth, and it shall no more be meat for them.*

Again, a little later He says: *AND I WILL SET UP ONE SHEPHERD OVER THEM, and he shall feed them, and he shall be their shepherd. And I the Lord will be their God: and my servant David the prince in the midst of them: I the Lord have spoken it. And I will make a covenant of peace with them, and will cause the evil beasts to cease out of the land: and they that dwell in the wilderness shall sleep secure in the forests. I will make them a blessing round about my hill: and I will send down the rain in its season, there shall be showers of blessing. And the tree of the field shall yield its fruit, and the earth shall yield her increase.*

From these words the Lord most clearly manifests that the impious rabble of the Pharisees shall be removed from the pastoral care of the Jewish people, and that after them Christ, Born according to the flesh from the seed of David, will rule the reasoning flocks of the believers. For He has made a Testament of Peace through Him, the divine Evangelical announcement, bringing us to friendship with God, and laying up for us the kingdom of heaven. Through Him likewise the rain of blessing, that is, the first fruits of the Spirit, which renders fertile as the fields the souls on which it falls. And because the Pharisees did no little injury to their flocks, not even feeding them, suffering them to be hurt in various ways, while Christ delivers them, and shows that He is the Giver and the Distributor of blessings from above, so rightly therefore is that seen to be true which He now confesses: *I am the good shepherd.*

Let no one take scandal that God and the Father should call Him a servant, Who from the seed of David became man, though by nature God and His True Son. But let him rather remember that He emptied Himself of His glory, taking the form of a servant. And having taken the form of a servant He is therefore by God and the Father called by the name of a servant.

And I know mine, and mine know me. As the Father knoweth me, and I know the Father.

Someone may say that the Lord here wishes to say nothing more than that He will reveal Himself to His own, and that without effort on their part He will bestow the knowledge of Himself on those who believe in Him, and that He will know His own, and implying that to know Him would not be unprofitable to those to whom it should happen. For what can we say is better than to know God? But since what is said here requires a closer examination, especially because He added: *As the Father knoweth me, and I know the Father*, we must explain the meaning of these words. For I believe that no one will venture to say that anyone can possess such knowledge of Christ as is in God and the Father concerning Him. For only the Father knows His Only-Begotten, and He is known only by His Only Begotten, according to the words of Our Saviour: *No one knoweth the Son, but the Father: neither doth any one know the Father, but the Son* (Mt. xi. 27). For that the Father is God, and that the Son likewise is True God we know and believe. What that ineffable nature is in Its Essence is above our capacity, or that of any created being.

How then shall we know Him as the Father knows His Son? One must consider in what way does He affirm that He will know us, and will be known by us, as the Father knows Him and He knows the Father. We must accordingly carefully investigate what explanation we can give to those words which is not opposed to what has been previously said. I shall not withhold what I have come to believe; others however are free to accept this or not. I believe that knowing here does not mean knowledge, but is to be taken rather as meaning familiarity or relationship, arising from nature or kinship, or that which results from a participation of honour and grace. The Greeks were wont to call known (*friends*) not alone their connexions, but even their brothers by blood. From this we understand how Sacred Scripture accepts knowledge (of a person) as meaning relationship. For the Lord says somewhere of those who were in no way related to Him: *Many will say to me in that day*, that is, on the Day of Judgement, *Lord, Lord, have we not cast out devils, and done many miracles in thy Name? And then I will profess unto them: I never knew you* (Mt. vii. 22, 23).

And if knowing meant knowledge in its full sense, how could He not know them to Whom *all things are naked and open to His eyes* (Heb. iv. 13; Dan. xiii. 42); and Who knows all things *before they come to pass?*[6] Therefore, not alone is it absurd but impious also to suppose that there were some whom God did not know; rather must we hold that here He says that He has no bond of relationship with them whatever. I do not know them, He says, as persons zealous of virtue, or as holding my words in reverence; nor are they persons joined to me by the bond of good works. In the same way was it said to the most wise Moses: *I know thee before all the others, and thou hast found grace with me*, saying as it were: you are related to Me above all the rest, and I shall endow you with much grace. I say this not as denying that this passage is to be taken as referring to the power of knowing, but as interpreting it in the manner most suited to our reasoning.

Accordingly He says: *I know mine, and mine know me. As the Father knoweth me, and I know the Father*; that is, I shall belong to my sheep, and they will be joined to me, in the same way as the Father belongs to me, and I am joined to the Father. For in the manner in which the Lord and Father knows His only and truly Begotten Son, and the fruit of His Substance, and as the Son knows the Father, holding Him as True God, and as drawing His own Being from Him, in the same way we, being assigned to Him as His, are said to be of His family, and are called His children; as He has said: *Behold I and my children, whom the Lord hath given me for a sign* (Is. viii. 18). We are indeed His kindred (Acts xvii. 29), and we bear the name of the Son, and, because of Him that of the Father; since though Begotten of God, and truly God, He has become man, taking upon Himself our nature, if you except all sin.

Then how are we *the offspring of God*, and in what manner are we *partakers of the divine nature*? (II Pet. i. 4). We possess a measure of His glory, not alone from this that Christ desired to receive us as His kindred, but also because the power of this relationship is manifest in us. For though the Word of God is divine by nature, even in our flesh, and though He remains God by nature, we are His kindred because He has taken our flesh. Similar therefore is the manner of our relationship. For as He belongs to the Father, and because of Their identity of nature the Father is joined to Him, so we also in that He has become man are regarded as belonging to Him, and He in a like manner is united to us. Through Him as through an intermediary are we united to the Father. For Christ is as it were a boundary between the supreme divine nature and that of humanity; both being in Him; and containing within Himself things that are so distantly separate; and He is joined to God the Father as being by nature God, and to men in that He is true man.

But someone may say: Do you not see that what you say may lead to danger? For if we are to think that He, in that He is man, knows His own, that is, enters into relationship with His sheep, who shall remain without the flock? For all men will then be His friends, in as much as they are men as He also is a man. What significance then has the word *my*? Or what is there set apart for His sheep? For if we are all joined to Him by this common bond, what shall those who are closer to Him receive?

To this we must answer, that the manner in which we are joined to Him is common to all, both those who know Him and those who know Him not. For He became man, not as showing favour to some and not to others, but out of compassion for our whole fallen nature. But this bond of kinship will avail nothing to those who offend Him through disobedience and pride; but a special reward will be given to those who love Him. For just as the motive of the resurrection extends to all men, because of the Resurrection of Our Saviour, who together with Himself has raised up the nature of all men, yet this will avail nothing to those who love sin, since they shall be cast into hell; their life being restored to them only that they may be punished. But it shall be a great gain to those who have followed the chosen way of life. For they shall receive, together with the resurrection, the gift of joys that are beyond the mind of man to conceive.

In the same way I believe that the plan of this relationship includes all men, both good and bad, but it is not given in equal measure to all. To those who believe in Him He will be the source of true relationship, and the beginning of every reward; but to those who do not He shall stand as the most dreadful reproach of their impiety and ingratitude. Let whosoever that wishes consider which of these two choices, the former or the latter, are the better?

One must observe how true and

consistent the sentence is; each part is disposed in due and fitting order. For He did not say: My sheep know Me, and I know Mine, but places Himself as first knowing His own sheep; then He says He is known by them. If you take this knowing for true knowledge (*eidesis-scientia*), as we said in the beginning, you will understand the sentence in this way: We did not know of Him first; He first knew us. And therefore Paul, writing to those who were converted from the Gentiles says something of this sort: *For which cause be mindful that you, being heretofore Gentiles in the flesh, who are called uncircumcision by that which is called circumcision in the flesh, made by hands; that you were at that time without Christ, being aliens from the conversation of Israel, and strangers to the testament, having no hope of the promise, and without God in this world. But now in Christ Jesus, you, who sometime were afar off, are made nigh by the blood of Christ* (Eph. ii. 11–13).

Out of His immeasurable kindness Christ drew nigh to the Gentiles; and foreknew us rather than was known by us. Taking this knowing for familiarity and relationship, we say again: It was not we who made a beginning in this, but God, the only-Begotten of God. For we did not lay hold of the nature of the divinity, but He Who is by nature God *took hold of the seed of Abraham*, as Paul says (Heb. ii. 16), and became man, so that in all things being made like to His brethren, sin excepted, He might receive him into relationship who had not of himself this privilege, namely, man. And so of necessity He says that He first knows us; then that we know Him.

And I lay down my life for my sheep. He here vows that He is prepared in every way to fight and to face danger on behalf of his friends and kindred; confirming by this emphatic repetition of His intention that He is indeed the Good Shepherd. For they who abandon the sheep to the wolves are rightly named cowards and hirelings. But he who is prepared to defend them, so that he does not falter even in face of death, is with just reason called a good shepherd.

But when He says, *I lay down my life for my sheep* because I am a good shepherd He is rebuking the Pharisees, and giving us to understand that they will reach that point of fury against Him as to bring about His death Who should not suffer it, and that He shall be held worthy of praise and admiration for all He has done, and for His wisdom and prudence in feeding His flock. And we must keep in mind that Christ did not suffer death for us unwillingly; rather He seems to walk towards it of His own will, though He could with ease have avoided suffering had He wished not to suffer. Therefore, in that He freely and of His own will suffered for our sakes, we behold the greatness of His love and goodness towards us.

And other sheep I have, that are not of this fold: them also I must bring, and they shall hear my voice, and there shall be one fold and one shepherd.

In divers ways He smites the unruly Pharisees; and here He lets them take note that they are about to be deprived of the care of His sheep, which He shall Himself now rule. He signifies that mingling the flocks of the Gentiles with those of good will from among the people of Israel, He shall rule not alone the Jews, but shall spread the glory of His Light over the whole earth, and from on all sides shall call the peoples to the knowledge of God; desiring that He shall be known, not alone in Israel, as from the beginning, but proposing to all men under heaven the knowledge of the True God.

That Christ is the Gentiles' Instructor in the knowledge of God is plain to see (Gal. iii. 24); for the Scriptures are filled with testimonies concerning Him, which it is but fitting we should briefly recall, leaving their close study to the more learned; but bringing before you two or three quotations from the prophets I shall speak of them in turn.

In one place God the Father says of Him: *Behold I have given him for a witness to the people, for a leader and a master to the Gentiles* (Is. lv. 4). He has declared that Christ is the Teacher of the Gentiles unto salvation, teaching them that whereby they shall be saved. And the divine psalmist calls them as it were into one company, inviting all men under the sun to the heavenly celebrations: *O clap your hands*, He says, *all ye nations: shout unto God with the voice of joy*. And should any wish to search for the reason of this great and shining feast he will find it where He clearly says: *For God is the King of all the earth: sing ye wisely* (Ps. xlvi. 1, 8, 9). And in another place He speaks of the Lord as announcing to all the nations: *Hear these things, all ye nations: Give ear, all ye inhabitants of the world. All you that are earthborn, and you sons of men: both rich and poor together. My mouth shall speak wisdom: and the mediation of my heart understanding* (Ps. xlviii. 2–4). Speaking in this way we learn of that which Christ shall teach.

Accordingly, returning again to the Gospel, the Lord clearly foretells that the hosts of the Gentiles shall be joined together with those who shall be converted from Jerusalem. But someone may say, closely examining the meaning of this passage, that the Saviour, conversing with the leaders of the Jews, and speaking to men whose hearts were poisoned with hate and envy, here speaks in mysteries. For why, I ask, was it necessary that such men should know that He was to rule the Gentiles, and that He would bring into His sheepfold His sheep which are outside of Judea?

What shall we say to this? What are we to answer? That not as to friends did He impart these mysteries, and neither did He make this revelation without purpose; for He knew that He would help them, as much as was possible to Him; for this was decreed, though the minds of those who heard Him were hard and intractable and not disposed to obedience. But since He knew that they paid heed to the writings of Moses and to the words of the holy prophets, and that the prophets had announced many times that Christ would as it were gather in the Gentiles to the knowledge of God, consequently setting before them as proof that which was announced and foretold of old, He clearly tells them that He is about to call in the sheep which are outside the fold of Israel; so that they may now believe that it is He Whom the prophets and the holy men of old had spoken of. Amen.

IV. St Gregory, Pope and Doctor[7]

Given to the People in the Basilica of Blessed Peter the Apostle on the Second Sunday after Easter

The Unfading Pastures: The Christian Hope

Lesson, John x. 11–16. 1. You have heard, Beloved Brethren, in the reading of the Gospel, an instruction regarding yourselves; you have heard also the danger to which we shepherds are subject. For He Who is good, not through grace given to Him, but by nature, says: *I am the good shepherd.* And putting before us the character of that goodness we must imitate He adds: *The good shepherd giveth his life for his sheep.*

He has done what He commended; He has given us an example in what He bade us do. The Good Shepherd has laid down His life for His sheep, so that in our sacrament He might change His own Body and Blood, and nourish with the food of His Flesh the sheep He had redeemed.

The way has been shown us that without fear of death we must follow; the example set before us we must copy. Our first duty is to pledge our earthly goods in mercy to His sheep; and then, if need be, give up our soul for these same sheep. From this first duty, which is also the least, we come to the last, and the greatest. But since the soul whereby we live is incomparably more precious than the earthly goods outside us, how shall he give up his soul for His sheep who will not surrender his earthly possessions for them?

And there are some shepherds who, loving their earthly possessions more than their sheep, rightly forfeit the name of shepherd. And of these He immediately says: *But the hireling, and he that is not the shepherd, whose own the sheep are not, seeth the wolf coming, and leaveth the sheep, and flieth.*

2. He is called not a shepherd but a hireling who feeds His flock in the Lord, not from an inward love, but for earthly gain. He is a hireling who, holding the place of shepherd, seeks not the gain of souls; who hungers for earthly privileges, revels in the dignity of his office, waxes fat on its temporal rewards, and takes delight in the respect men show to him. For these are the wages of the hireling; that he may have what he worked for here below, while taking care of the sheep, but afterwards be a stranger to the inheritance of his flock.

2. Whether a man is indeed a shepherd, or but a hireling, can only be known when a time of trial comes. For in times of peace, just as the true shepherd is wont to stay by his flocks, so likewise does the hireling. But should a wolf appear each will reveal with what mind he had been taking care of the flock. For a wolf descends upon the flock whenever some lawless person or robber oppresses those of the faithful who are poor and lowly. Then the one who seemed to be a shepherd, and was not, leaves the sheep and flies; for since he is fearful of danger from it for himself, he does not dare to stand firm against the injustice.

He flies, not by giving ground,

but by withholding his help. He flies, because he sees injustice and says nothing. He flies, because he takes refuge in silence. To such as these was it said: *You have not gone up to face the enemy, nor have you set up a wall for the house of Israel, to stand in battle in the day of the Lord* (Ezech. xiii. 5). For to go up and face the enemy means to oppose with the free voice of reason any power whatsoever that is acting wickedly. And we set up a wall, and we stand fast in the day of the Lord for the house of Israel, whenever by the authority of justice we defend the unoffending faithful against the unjustice of the irreligious. This the hireling will not do; for when he sees the wolf coming he flies.

3. But there is another wolf who daily and without ceasing tears, not at our bodies, but at our souls; namely, that evil spirit who prowls about watching the sheepfold of the faithful, and seeking the death of souls. And of this wolf he immediately adds: *And the wolf catcheth and scattereth the sheep*. The wolf comes, and the hireling flies, when the malignant spirit tears at the souls of the faithful by temptation, and he who holds the shepherd's place has no feelings of anxiety. The souls are perishing while he takes his delight in the comforts of this world.

The wolf catches and scatters the sheep when he seduces one person by means of lust, inflames another with avarice, swells another through pride, destroys another through anger, provokes another by envy, overthrows this one by fraud. The wolf then as it were scatters the flock when the devil kills the members of the faithful by means of temptations. But against these things a hireling is kindled by no zeal, aroused by no fervour of love; for as he looks only for outward gain, he is indifferent to the interior damage suffered by his flock. And for this has He added: *The hireling flieth, because he is a hireling: and he hath no care for the sheep*.

The sole reason why the hireling flies is because he is a hireling. As if He were openly to say: He cannot stand fast in the face of danger to his flock who ministers to his flock, not because He loves his sheep, but because he is looking for earthly profit. For as long as he is held in honour, and as long as he takes delight in temporal advantages, he will hesitate to stand against danger, lest he lose what he loves.

But seeing that Our Redeemer has held up to us the defects of the false shepherd, He then sets before us a model on which we should form ourselves, saying: *I am the good shepherd*. And He goes on: *And I know mine*, that is, I love mine, *and mine know me*. As if He were openly saying: Those who love give themselves for others. For he who does not love the truth is still without knowledge of it.

4. As you have heard then, Dearest Brethren, the danger to which we are liable, reflect on the danger to which in the Lord's words you also are subject. Reflect whether you are His sheep. Reflect whether or not you know Him. Consider whether you know the light of truth. You know, I affirm, not through faith, but through love. You will know, I say, not from faith, but from charity. For he who tells us thus, John the Evangelist, bears wit-

ness, saying: *He who saith that he knoweth him, and keepeth not his commandments, is a liar* (I Jn. ii. 4). For this reason the Lord here also adds: *As the Father knoweth me, and I know the Father: and I lay down my life for my sheep.* As if openly saying: By this is it shown that I know the Father, and am known by him, because I lay down my life for my sheep; that is, by that love whereby I die for my sheep I show the measure of my love for my Father.

But because He had come to redeem, not alone the Jews, but the Gentiles also, He adds: *And other sheep I have, that are not of this fold: them also I must bring, and they shall hear my voice, and there shall be one fold and one shepherd.* The Lord had our redemption, we who came from the Gentiles, in mind when He was saying that *He must bring* the other sheep. This you see fulfilled daily, Brethren; this fact you witness this day in the reconcilement of the Gentiles to the bosom of the Church. For He has as it were made one sheepfold from the two flocks: He has made the Jewish and the Gentile people one, through faith in Him; to which Paul bears witness, saying: *For he is our peace, who hath made both one* (Eph. ii. 14). For when He chooses the just from either nation for life eternal, He leads His sheep into His own sheepfold.

5. And of these sheep He later truly says: *My sheep hear my voice: and I know them, and they follow me, and I give them life everlasting* (v. 27). And earlier He says concerning them: *By me, if any man enter in, he shall be saved; and he shall go in, and go out and shall find pastures* (v. 9). He shall go in to faith, and go out by sight (II Cor. v. 7); from belief to contemplation; and pasture he shall find in the everlasting refreshment of the soul. His sheep therefore shall find pasture; for whosoever follows Him with *a sincere heart* (I Pet. i. 22) is nourished on pastures of unfading greenness.

But what are the pastures of these sheep if not the hidden delights of the evergreen paradise? For the pastures of the Elect are the ever present countenance of God, Who while He is unfadingly contemplated by the soul, nourishes it without ceasing by the food of life eternal. In these pastures they are satiated with the fulness of eternity who turned aside from the snares of earthly gratifications. There shall be the singing choirs of angels: there the company of the citizens of heaven. There the sweet solemnity of the blessed returning from the weariness of this earthly pilgrimage. There shall be the far-seeing company of the prophets; the number of the Apostles who shall sit in judgement; there the uncountable host of triumphant martyrs: there the greater shall be our joy, the more we have suffered here below. There shall be the steadfast men, the strength of whose manhood the delights of this world could not soften; there the holy women who triumphed over both the world and their sex; there the youths who here below in their lives surpassed their years; there the Elders whom age had here enfeebled, yet they ceased not from works of virtue and of mercy.

6. Let us then, Dearest Brethren, seek this pasture where we shall share in the joy of so many friends. Let their joyfulness invite us to the feast.

We know that if anywhere there should be a market-day, or people gathering together for the dedication of a church, for which word has been sent out, we would all hasten together to be there, and each in turn would be eager to be present for the solemn occasion, and would feel he had suffered a great loss did he not share this common rejoicing. Here it is the rejoicing of all the chosen people of heaven, all rejoicing with one another in their coming together, and yet we, lukewarm as we are towards that eternal love, burn with no desire for it, seek not to be present at so great a solemnity. We deprive ourselves of everlasting blessedness, and we are happy!

Let us, Brethren, enkindle our soul as a light. Let faith grow fervent in what it has believed. Let our desires grow eager for the things of heaven; and thus to love is already to go there. Let no adversity turn us away from the joy of this inward fulfilment; for when any one has resolved to go to a determined place, whatever the roughness of the way, it does not alter his desire. Let no smiling good fortune entice us away; for he is a foolish traveller who, beholding on his way a pleasant meadow, forgets to go on in the way he was going.

Let the soul therefore long with desire for its heavenly home. Let it grasp at nothing in this world; for well we know that it will quickly let go. So, if we are truly sheep of the Heavenly Shepherd, if we do not linger attached to the delights of the way, we shall be filled to satiety when we shall arrive in the eternal pastures; by the help of Our Lord Jesus Christ Who with the Father and the Holy Spirit liveth and reigneth world without end. Amen.

NOTES

[1] A reference to a public conference with the Donatists (*Collatio*) in the year 411, in which they were finally confuted.

[2] PG 59, Col. 327. Serm. 60.

[3] The three following homilies, or expositions, form a symposium of the most venerable authority, on the theme of the Good Shepherd. The Figure of the Good Shepherd is the most perfect human image revealed to us of the whole divine mystery or plan of our restoration to God by means of the Word Incarnate: the most complete, the tenderest, the most authoritative.

For the Word Incarnate is the Good Shepherd. And He in turn has established and perpetuated His Office among men till the end of time; Supreme in Peter, and in his lawful Successor, and with him in those who as bishops and Successors of the other Apostles are the divinely instituted Shepherds of the particular churches; and committed in turn by the Church to the priest who, by the authority of his bishop, is given the pastoral care of the souls of a portion of the flock.

The three homilies consider the Office from three complementary standpoints: St Augustine, the Office as it was unfolded in the teaching of the Incarnate Word; St Cyril, as foreshadowed in Old Testament revelation and tradition; St Gregory, as it is actually fulfilled by imperfect human instruments, and its final and perfect fulfilment.

The discourses would appear to apply more to the shepherds than to the flocks. But they were spoken by their holy and venerable authors to the people; and their example suffices. What is especially striking in them is the extraordinary precision (as well as profundity) of their witness regarding this supreme point of Sacred Tradition, and the wisdom (particularly in the most wise Gregory) of its setting forth in simple human terms. Ed.

[4] PL 38. Serm. 137.

[5] PG 73, Book VI.

[6] Exodus xxii (xxxii). 12. Not verifiable, even in lxx.

[7] PL 76. Serm. 14.

THIRD SUNDAY AFTER EASTER

I. St John Chrysostom: Explanation of the Gospel

II. St Augustine: A Little While

III. St Cyril of Alexandria: Christian Hope: The Promised Joy

IV. The Venerable Bede: I Will See You Again: the Christian's Hope

THE GOSPEL OF THE SUNDAY

John xvi. 16–22

At that time: Jesus said to his disciples: A little while, and now you shall not see me; and again a little while, and you shall see me: because I go to the Father. Then some of his disciples said one to another: What is this that he saith to us: A little while, and you shall not see me; and again a little while, and you shall see me, and, because I go to the Father? They said therefore: What is this that he saith, a little while? we know not what he speaketh. And Jesus knew that they had a mind to ask him; and he said to them: of this do you inquire among yourselves, because I said: A little while, and you shall not see me; and again a little while, and you shall see me? Amen, amen, I say to you, that you shall lament and weep, but the world shall rejoice; and you shall be made sorrowful, but your sorrow shall be turned into joy. A woman, when she is in labour, hath sorrow, because her hour is come; but when she hath brought forth the child, she remembereth no more the anguish, for joy that a man is born into the world. So also you now indeed have sorrow; but I will see you again, and your heart shall rejoice; and your joy no man shall take from you.

Exposition from the Catena Aurea

V. 16. *A little while, and now you shall not see me.*

Chrysostom, 79 *in John*: After the Lord had encouraged the Disciples, because of what He had promised them through the Holy Spirit, He again saddens their spirits by saying: *A little while etc.* This He does that He may as it were harden their spirits to the hearing of painful things, so that they shall bear up well against the coming separation from Him; for nothing is so wont to calm a soul which grieves, and which is held fast by sorrow as to repeat again and again the words which cause the sorrow.[1]

BEDE: For He says: *A little while, and now you shall not see me*. For that night He was taken by the Jews, and the next day He was crucified, and on that evening He was buried, and shut away from human eyes.

CHRYSOSTOM: If any one should carefully consider them, these are words of consolation: *because I go to the Father*. For they are meant to show that He will not perish; but that His death is but a (*translatio*) removal from earth to heaven. And He adds another consolation when He says: *And again a little while, and you shall see me*; showing that, since He will return again, the separation will be but for a little while, and that their meeting again shall be without end.

AUGUSTINE, *Tr.* 101 *in John*: But these words of the Lord were obscure to the Disciples, prior to the fulfilment of what was said in them; so there follows:

V. 17. *Then some of his disciples said one to another: what is this . . .*

CHRYSOSTOM: They did not understand what He said, either because of their grief, which pushed out of their minds the significance of what He was saying, or because of the obscurity of what He said; and thus He seemed to utter contrary things, which were not in reality contradictory. For, they say, if we shall see Thee, how then is it that you are going away? And if you do go, how then shall we see Thee? So they say to Him:

V. 18. *What is this that he saith, a little while? We know not . . .*

AUGUSTINE, *as above*: Because, a little while before—verse 10—He had said, not, *a little while*, but merely: *I go to the Father*, He had seemed to speak in simple terms to them. What was then obscure to them, and presently explained, is now made clear to us also. For after a little while He suffered, and they did not see Him; and then after a little while He rose again, and they saw Him. He said: *And you shall see me no longer*; meaning that they never again would see the *mortal* Christ.

ALCUIN: Or, for *a little while* you shall not see me; that is, for the three days in which He lay in the sepulchre and *again* it will be another *little while* until you shall see me; that is, these forty days, from His Passion to His Ascension, in which He frequently appeared to them. And so for that little while you shall see me; *for I go to the Father*: I shall not always remain bodily upon the earth, but shall, in this humanity I have assumed, ascend to heaven.

V. 19. *And Jesus knew that they had a mind to ask him; and he said . . .*

The kind Master, knowing their ignorance, answers them according to their doubts, as it were explaining what He had said.

V. 20. *Amen, amen, I say to you, that you shall lament and weep:*

AUGUSTINE, *as above*: This can be taken to mean that the Disciples were grief stricken because of Christ's death; and then made joyful by His

Resurrection. But the world, and by this I mean the enemies who had slain Christ, then indeed rejoiced, at Christ's death, while the Disciples sorrowed. So we have: *But the world shall rejoice: and you shall be made sorrowful, but your sorrow shall be turned into joy*.

ALCUIN: These words of Christ are meant for all the faithful, who amid the trials and afflictions of this present life strive to reach to the joy of heaven. But while the just now weep, the world rejoices: for it takes its joy in the present, having no hope of the joys of the life to come. CHRYSOSTOM: Then showing that grief will bring forth joy, and that sorrow is but fleeting, while their happiness will be without end, He puts before them an example from our own nature.

V. 21. *A woman, when she is in labour, hath sorrow, because . . .*

AUGUSTINE, *as above*: This parable does not seem difficult to understand, for its application is known to us; and He has Himself explained to us why He used it. For there follows: *So also you now indeed have sorrow; but I will see you again, and your heart shall rejoice.* Sadness is compared to travail, joy to actual birth; which is always greater when a manchild, not a female child, is born. In saying: *And your joy no man shall take from you*, He means that to which the Apostle refers: *Christ rising again from the dead, dieth now no more* (Rom. vi. 19), for Jesus is Himself their joy.

CHRYSOSTOM, *as above*: Here He also hints at some mystery, that He has Himself also eased the pangs of death, causing a new man to be born of them. And He also said that the woman would not alone have no more anguish, but that she will not even remember the anguish she had: so great is the joy that comes. So shall it be with the blessed. And the woman rejoices, not because a man has come into the world, but because *she* has brought forth a child. He did not say *a child is born*, but *that a man is born again into the world*; obscurely referring to His own Resurrection.

AUGUSTINE: I think that the words: *A little while and you shall not see me, and again a little while and you shall see me*, are best understood of the vision and glory to come: of which we have spoken earlier. For the *little while* is this whole span of time in which this present world revolves. When He added: *Because I go to the Father*, He is referring to the first part of the previous sentence, namely: *A little while and you shall not see me*; and not to the other half of it where He says: *And again a little while, and you shall see me*. For His going to the Father would mean they would not see Him. And so to those who were then seeing Him in the Body He says: *A little while and you shall not see me*: for He was about to go to His Father, and from thence forward they would not again see Him as the mortal man they were seeing while He spoke these words. What He added here, namely: *And again a little while, and you shall see me*, He promises to the whole Church. This little while seems long while it is endured by us; but when it is over, then we shall see how little it was.

BEDE: The woman spoken of is the Holy Church; fruitful in all good works, and bearing spiritual children to God. This woman, while she is bringing forth; that is, while in this world she keeps steadfast in the ways of virtue, though tried and afflicted on every side, sorrows for this reason, that her hour is come; for no one hates their own flesh (Eph. v. 29).

AUGUSTINE: But neither let us be joyless in the bringing forth of this object of our desire; but let us be as the Apostle says, *rejoicing in hope*; for even the woman in labour, to whom we are compared, is more joyful over the child now coming to her, than grieving over her present pain.

BEDE: *But when she hath brought forth the child*; that is, when she has overcome pain in the contest of her travail and attained the palm of victory, *she remembereth no more the anguish*, that went before, *for joy* of the reward received, *that man is born into the world*. For as the woman rejoices that a man child is born into this world, so is the Church filled with exultation at the multitude of the faithful born to eternal life.

BEDE: Nor should it appear to you strange that he is called born who has departed from this life. For as a man is said to be born when coming forth from his mother's womb he enters into the light of day, so may he be said to be born who from the bonds of the flesh is uplifted to that light which is eternal. So the commemorations of the saints are not called funeral ceremonies, but birth day festivities (*Natalitia*).

V. 22. *So also you now indeed have sorrow; but I shall see you again.*

ALCUIN: That He said, *I will see you again* means, I shall take you to myself. Or, *I will see you again*; that is, I shall appear again for you to see Me; *and your heart shall rejoice*.

AUGUSTINE: The Church is now in labour, longing for this fruit of all her labour; then shall She bring forth, beholding It. And therefore a Man-child: since it is towards this Fruit of her eager longing that all her actions are directed. For He alone is free; because He is desired in Himself, and not in relation to some other end. To Him her actions are directed. To this end is directed whatsoever good she does. For there is the end which contents us: and which therefore shall be eternal. For there is no end that can content us, save that of which there is no end. Of this Object then, which alone fulfils all our desiring, rightly are we told: *Your joy no man shall take from you* (here again, possibly, referring to the Mystical Body of Christ, born of the Church, the woman in labour. Ed.).

I. ST JOHN CHRYSOSTOM, BISHOP AND DOCTOR

Explanation of the Gospel[2]

John xviii. 16–22. Nothing so depresses a mind that is faint-hearted and in sorrow, as hearing over and over the words which have caused its sorrow. Why then did Christ, after He had said, *I go away*, and again, *I will not now speak many things* (xiv. 28, 30), return to these same words and say: *A little while, and you shall not see me*; and, *Because*

I go to him that sent me? When He had comforted by what He had told them of the Holy Spirit, He again discourages them. Why is this? He does it to test their courage, and to make it more resolute, and He is seeking to harden them strongly against the hearing of painful things, so that they shall bear manfully their coming separation from Himself; for when they had exercised their minds on His words, they would the more easily face the reality.

And if you look at it closely, His saying that He was going to the Father was also a consolation. For He tells them by this, that He is not going to perish; that His death is but a passing over. And He adds another consolation. For not alone did He say, *A little while and you shall not see me*, but He says also, *a little while and you shall see me*; showing them He will come again, and that their separation will be but for a while, and that their meeting then would be forever.

But they did not understand this; indeed in this whole matter one may well wonder how they doubted, as though they had heard nothing; seeing they had heard it so frequently. How then was it that they did not understand? It was either because of their grief, as I think (for that put out of their mind the memory of what they had heard), or else because of the obscurity of what was said. For He seemed to utter things contrary to each other, but which in fact were not contrary. If we shall see You, they say, how can You be going away? And if You go away, how shall we see You? And so they say: *We know not what he speaketh*.

That He was about to go away they knew. They did not know that after a little while He would come to them again. It was because of this He reproached them; for not knowing what He said. And in His desire to secure firmly in their minds what He had taught them regarding His own death, what does He say? *Amen, amen, I say to you, that you shall lament and weep*: because of His Cross and death: *But the world shall rejoice*. For since they desired it, they were easily led to believe that He would not die; and then hearing that He would die they were in doubt, not understanding what a *little while* meant. *You shall weep and lament*, He says, *but your sorrow shall be turned into joy*.

Then after He has shown that joy will come after their sorrow, and that grief brings forth gladness, and that the first is but for a little while, and the latter without end, He puts before them a natural example; and what does He say? *A woman, when she is in labour, hath sorrow*. The prophets have frequently used this example: comparing sadness to the pains of childbirth. This is what He means. Pain like travail will come upon you; but the pains of childbirth are the cause of joy: here confirming His own words regarding the coming Resurrection, as well as showing that the going from this world is like going from the womb into splendid light. As though He said: Wonder not if through pain I lead you to such great gain; for a mother, that she may be a mother, passes through a like suffering.

Here something mystical is also indicated; that He has also eased the pains of death, and has disposed that from them a *new man* shall be born. And He said, not alone do the pangs come to an end, but that they will not even be remembered: so great is the joy that will follow them. And so shall it be with the saints. And a woman does not rejoice because a man child has come into the world, but because a son is born to her. For did she rejoice for the first reason, there is no reason why they who are barren should not rejoice because sons are born to others. Why then does He say this? Because He makes use of this example only to show that their sorrow is but passing, their joy enduring for ever; to show that death is but a passing over to life, and that great is the reward of these birth pangs.

Neither did He say: *that a* child *is born into the world*, but, *that a man is born*. Here it seems to me He is alluding to His own Resurrection; that He is about to be born, not from that birth which brings forth death, but unto a Kingdom. And therefore He does not say, because a son is born to her, but because *a Man is born into the world. So you also now indeed have sorrow; but I will see you again, and your sorrow shall be turned into joy*. And then, to show that He shall die no more, He says: *And your joy no man shall take from you*; through the grace and mercy of Our Lord Jesus Christ, to Whom with the Father and the Holy Ghost, be honour, praise and glory, for ever and ever. Amen.

II. St Augustine, Bishop and Doctor

A Little While[3]

John xvi. 16–22. 1. These words of the Lord where He says: *A little while and you shall not see me, and again a little while and you shall see me*, were so obscure to the Disciples, before that took place of which He speaks, that questioning each other as to the meaning of what He says, they confessed that they did not know. For the Gospel continues: *Then some of his disciples said one to another: what is this that he saith to us: A little while, and now you shall not see me, and again a little while, and you shall see me, and, because I go to the Father? They said therefore: What is this that he saith, a little while? We know not what he speaketh.*

This is what troubled them, that He said, *A little while, and you shall not see me, and again a little while and you shall see me*. For in the words that preceded this gospel He had not said, *A little while*, but had said, *I go to the Father; and you shall see me no longer* (v. 10); and He appears as speaking quite plainly, nor did they need to ask each other anything regarding this saying. But now, what was obscure to them, and was soon after made plain to them, is very plain to us also. For after a little while He suffered, and they did not see Him. And again after a little while He arose, and they saw Him.

He said the words, *and you shall see me no longer*, because He wished by the use of the phrase *no longer* to be understood as meaning they would see Him no more; and how this is to be taken we have explained where He said that the Holy Spirit *will convince the world of justice, because I go to the Father; and you shall see me no longer* (*Tr.* 95); because they shall see the *mortal* Christ no more.

2. And Jesus knew, as the Evangelist goes on to say, *that they had a mind to ask him; and he said to them: Of this do you enquire among yourselves, because I said: A little while, and you shall not see me; and again a little while, and you shall see me. Amen, amen I say to you, that you shall lament and weep, but the world shall rejoice: and you shall be made sorrowful, but your sorrow shall be turned into joy.* And this can be taken to mean that the Disciples were stricken with grief at the death of the Lord, and then immediately made joyful by His Resurrection: but the world, and by the world He means the enemies by whom Christ was crucified, were truly made joyful by the slaying of Christ at the time when the Disciples were sorrowing.

By the expression *world* we can understand the wickedness of this world; that is, of the men who love this world. For this same reason James the Apostle says in his Epistle: *Whosoever therefore will be a friend of this world, becometh an enemy of God*; from which enmity it arose that they spared not His only-Begotten Son.

3. Then He goes on and says: *A woman, when she is in labour, hath sorrow, because her hour is come; but when she hath brought forth the child, she remembereth no more the anguish, for joy that a man is born into the world. So also you now indeed have sorrow; but I will see you again, and your heart shall rejoice; and your joy no man shall take from you.* Neither does this similitude appear to be difficult to understand; for its explanation is added, He Himself giving us the key to what was said. Travail is compared with sadness, birth with joy; which is wont to be greater when a man child, not a girl, is born. Because He adds, *and your joy no man shall take from you*: for Jesus is Himself their joy: that is signified which the Apostle says: *Christ rising from the dead, dieth now no more* (Rom. vi. 9).

4. Up to this point of this chapter of the Gospel which we are today expounding everything has gone smoothly, and has been as it were easy to understand. But close attention is needed for what follows. For what does He mean by these words, *And in that day you shall not ask me anything* (v. 23)? The verb to ask, which is employed here, means not alone to beg, but also to question; and the Greek gospel, from which this was translated, has a verb of a similar kind, which can be understood in both senses (*erotesete*), so that the ambiguity is not removed in this way; though were it resolved, not on that account would no question remain. For we read that after His Resurrection the Lord Christ was both *questioned* and *asked.* For He was questioned by His Disciples, as He was about to ascend into heaven, when He would be proclaimed, and when would the kingdom of Israel come; and when He was already in heaven He was besought by the holy Stephen to receive his spirit (Acts i. 6). And who will venture to say or think that Christ, who was asked while dwelling on earth, must not be asked sitting upon His heavenly throne? That while man should beseech Him while mortal on earth, as immortal He must not be asked? Rather, Dearly Beloved, let us beg of Him to undo the knot of this question, illuminating our souls to

enable us to discover what it is He says.

5. For I think that the words: *I will see you again, and your heart shall rejoice; and your joy no man shall take from you*, are not to be referred to the time in which He rose from the dead, and when He showed them His Body to see and to touch, but rather to that time when He had said: *He that loveth me, shall be loved of my Father: and I will love him, and will manifest myself to him* (Jn. xiv. 21). For He had already arisen; He had already shown Himself to them in the flesh; He was already sitting at the right hand of the Father, when the same Apostle, John, whose Gospel this is, said in his Epistle: *Dearly beloved, we are now the sons of God; and it hath not yet appeared what we shall be* (1 Jn. iii. 2).

This vision is not for this life, but for the future; not temporal, but eternal. *Now this is eternal life*, says that Life, *that they may know thee*, He says, *the only true God, and Jesus Christ, whom thou hast sent* (Jn. xvii. 3). And of this vision and knowledge the Apostle says: *We see now through a glass in a dark manner; but then face to face: Now I know in part; but then I shall know even as I am known* (I Cor. xiii. 12, 13).

Now the Church is in travail, longing for this fruit of all Her labour. Then She shall bring forth in the vision of it. Now she is groaning and in labour; then She shall bring forth in joy. Now She brings forth in prayer; then She shall bring forth in praise. And accordingly it is a Man child; since it is towards this fruit of Her eager longing that all the tasks of her activity are directed. For He alone is free of every bond; for He is desired of Himself, and not in relation to another end. All her actions are in service to Him; for what is worthily done is directed towards Him; because it is done for His sake; He is to be had and to be held, because of Himself, not because of another beyond Him. Here then is the end that contents us. Therefore it shall be eternal; for no end will suffice us, if it be not the One of which there is no end. It was this thought inspired Philip when he said: *Show us the Father, and it is enough for us*. And in that showing the Son promises us Himself also, saying: *Do you not believe, that I am in the Father, and the Father in me?* (Jn. xiv. 8, 10). Of this object of our desire therefore that alone contents us have we most fittingly been told: *Your joy no man shall take from you!*

6. From what we have just now said we can, I think, better understand the words, *A little while, and now you shall not see me; and again a little while, and you shall see me*. For the *little while* is the whole span of time in which this world revolves; whence this same Evangelist says in his Epistle: *It is the last hour* (I Jn. ii. 18). For it is because of this He added: *Because I go to the Father*, which is to be related to the previous sentence where He says: *A little while, and now you shall not see me*; not to one that follows it: *And again a little while, and you shall see me*. For by going to the Father He was to bring it about that they would not see Him. And for this reason He did not say He was about to die, and be withdrawn from their eyes till He would rise again from the dead, but that He was about to go to

the Father; which He did after He had risen, and when after dwelling with them forty days He ascended into heaven.

Therefore He says: *A little while, and now you shall not see me*, to those who were then seeing Him in bodily form; because He was about to go to His Father, and from thence forward they would never see Him again in that *mortal form* in which they beheld Him while He was saying these things to them. What He has added: *And again a little while, and you shall see me*, He promised to the whole Church: as He promised the whole Church: *Behold I am with you all days, even to the consummation of the world* (Mt. xxviii. 20).

The Lord does not delay the fulfilling of what He promised. A little while, and we shall see Him, where we shall have nothing more to ask; where we need question Him no more: for there shall remain nothing more to be desired, nothing hidden to be looked for. This *little while* appears long to us, since it still endures; when it has ended then we shall see how little it was. Let our joy then be not such as the world's is, of which it is said: *The world shall rejoice*. Neither let us be sorrowful and joyless in the bringing forth of that which we desire; but let us be, as the Apostle says: *Rejoicing in hope, patient in tribulation* (Rom. xii. 2); for she who is in labour, to whom we are likened, has more joy of the offspring now about to be born to her, than sorrow because of her present pain. But let this be the end of our discourse: for that which follows contains a most difficult question, and neither may it be briefly treated if it is to be, should the Lord will it, satisfactorily expounded.

III. St Cyril of Alexandria, Bishop and Doctor

Christian Hope: the Promised Joy[4]

A little while, and now you shall not see me; and again a little while, and you shall see me: because I go to the Father.

Since He had said a little before this that He would reveal to them through His Holy Spirit all things whatsoever that were necessary and profitable to them, He also tells them of His passion, and that then would come His ascension into heaven; after which would follow that most necessary descent of the Spirit. Returning now to the Father, there would be no more mutual converse, in the flesh, with His holy Apostles. He uses but few words, lessening in this way the sharpness of their sorrow. For He knew, He knew that His Disciples were to face no simple fears, and that they were about to be tested by the most piercing grief, awaiting in dread grave and unendurable evils, when it came to pass that the Saviour, ascending to His Father in heaven, would leave them alone.

Because of this, I believe, He does not say to them openly that He is about to die, and that the fury of the Jews was about to break upon Him, but most kindly, mingling great delicacy with His words, He shows them that the sufferings of His passion will swiftly be followed by the joy of His Resurrection; saying to them: *A little while, and you shall not see me; and again a little while, and you shall see me.* For the time of His death was now at hand, when the Lord would be taken from the sight of His Disciples; and indeed for a little time, until, destroying the power of hell, and opening the gates of darkness to those who dwelt there, He would again raise up His temple (Jn. ii. 19). And this accomplished, again appearing to His Disciples, He promises that He will remain with them all the days of this world, as it is written (Mt. xxviii. 20). For though absent in the Flesh, having placed Himself before the Father for our sake, and sitting at the right hand of His Begetter, He dwells in the Just through His Spirit, and remains for ever one with His saints: for He has promised that He will not leave them orphans (Jn. xiv. 18).

There is indeed but little time between now and His passion. *A little while*, He says, *and you shall not see me*: for He shall be hidden for a little while in death: *and again a little while, and you shall see me.* For in three days He lives again; having *preached to those spirits that were in prison* (I Pet. iii. 19). For in this way he gave the most complete manifestation of His love for men: that He saved not alone those still dwelling upon earth, but descended to proclaim their freedom to those who had passed from this life and were sitting in darkness and in the depths of the abyss (Lk. i. 79).

Observe also in what manner He speaks of His passion, and of His Resurrection. *A little while, and you shall not see me; and again a little while, and you shall see me.* But adding: *Because I go to the Father*, He is silent as to all the rest. For He does not indicate how long he will remain there, or when He will return, or for what cause. For it is not, according to the words of the Saviour Himself, for us to know the times or the moments which *the Father hath put in his own power* (Acts i. 6–7).

Then some of his disciples said one to another: what is this that he saith to us: a little while, and you shall not see me; and again a little while, and you shall see me, and, because I go to the Father? They said therefore: What is this that he saith, a little while? We know not what he speaketh.

Not understanding His words, the divinely chosen Apostles speak with each other as to the meaning of them: this, *A little while*: and, *again a little while*; and they begin to doubt also the words, *You shall not see me.* But Christ anticipates their eagerness to question Him; opportunely showing once again that, as God, He knows their hearts, and what takes place there, and even what is in the very depths of their soul, as well as if it were uttered by their tongues. For what, I ask, can be hidden from Him before Whom *all things are naked*? (Heb. iv. 13). And therefore He says, from out the lips of one of His holy ones: *Who is this that concealeth counsel, and holdeth words in his heart, and thinketh to conceal them from me?* (Job xlii. 3).[5] Truly He helps them by every means, and putting before them the opportunity, makes Himself the fosterer of a steadfast and unwavering faith.

And Jesus knew that they had a mind to ask; and he said to them: of this do you inquire among yourselves, because I said: a little while, and you shall not see me; and again a little while, and you shall see me? Amen, amen I say to you, that you shall lament and weep, but the world shall rejoice; and you shall be made sorrowful, but your sorrow shall be turned into joy.

In response to their eagerness to know what the words of the Saviour might mean He speaks more openly of His passion, and of what He is about to undergo, and this He also grants them to foresee; and most profitably. And it was not to inflict sorrow prematurely upon them that He told them these things, but that by this knowledge they might be prepared and strengthened against the fear that would assail them. For an attack whose coming is awaited is not as severe as one wholly unexpected.

When therefore, You, O true and beloved Disciples, shall see your Lord and Master patient under the blows and insults of Jewish violence, then shall you weep and mourn, but the world shall rejoice; that is, they who have no mind for the things that are pleasing to God, but only for the gratifications of this world. Here again He points out that the base and wicked rabble among the Jews, the evil and impious group of those who held rule, namely, the Scribes and Pharisees, smouldering with hate from the thrusts of the Saviour, would mock at Him; now saying: *If thou be the Son of God, come down from the cross*; and now: *Thou that destroyest the temple of God, and in three days dost rebuild it: save thy own self* (Mt. xxvii. 42, 40). For it was such brazen utterances as these came from the abominable mouths of the Jews.

But while the worldlings are doing and saying such things, you, He says, shall lament, but you will not endure this for long. For your sorrow will be turned into joy. I shall rise again, and I shall take away all cause of sorrow, and I shall put an end to your tears, and call you to unending joy of soul. For the joy of the blessed is without end. For Christ lives for ever, and the death of all men has been undone through Him. But it is right to keep in mind that worldly men in their turn will be forever in affliction. For if through Christ dying in the flesh His Disciples were filled with sorrow, and because of what caused their grief the world rejoiced, but since death and corruption are now wholly overcome, and Our Saviour risen from the dead, the mourning of the just is changed to joy, but the joy of the worldling is changed to sorrow.

A woman, when she is in labour, hath sorrow, because her hour is come; but when she hath brought forth the child, she remembereth no more the anguish, for joy that a man is born into the world. So also you now indeed have sorrow; but I will see you again, and your heart shall rejoice; and your joy no man shall take from you.

He increases the grounds of their consolation, and by various discourses provides them with the means of turning aside the sharpness of their sorrow. For see here how by a very natural example He encourages them to bear themselves bravely, and not to let either suffering or grief weaken them; for these shall be wholly changed into joy. For, He says, the fruit of the sharp birth pangs is a new-born child; and without the pains of labour mothers do not receive the joy of children. But should they from the beginning reject the pains of labour, and refuse to bear the fruit of the womb, and put aside the offer of nuptials, then they would never be mothers, and the thrice longed for and ever to be desired possession would be forfeited because of cowardice.

For this same reason your suffering shall not be without reward. For you shall rejoice when you see the wondrous Guest born a Child into that world, incorruptible and indestructible. He is of course speaking of Himself. For He says that everlasting and indestructible shall be our joy in Him. For according to the voice of Paul, rather, according to Truth itself: *He died once; He dieth now no more* (Rom. vi. 10). Ever enduring therefore is the joy that comes from Him, and with good cause. For if Christ's death has brought us sadness, who shall take our joy from us, we who know that He now lives, and shall so remain without end, the Prince and Giver of our spiritual good things. From the holy no man takes joy away, according to the words of Our Saviour; but it was straightaway taken from those who nailed Him to the cross. But His suffering ended, they must inevitably suffer grief who believed that because of it they should be happy.

IV. The Venerable Bede, Priest and Doctor[6]

I Will See You Again:[7] *the Christian's Hope*

Let us with true joy of soul, Beloved Brethren, take to our hearts the promises of happiness made to us by our Lord Jesus Christ; and let us strive with all our hearts, that we may be found worthy to receive them. For what can be more comforting to the soul than to hear that we may attain a happiness that will be without end? Let us note, that though the whole context of this Gospel applies to those who heard these things from the Lord while in His presence, a part of it concerns us also who have come to the faith after the Lord's Passion and Resurrection. And so His words: *A little while, and now you shall not see me; and again a little while and you shall see me: because I go to the Father*, apply immediately to those who were found worthy to be His Disciples while He was yet preaching in His Body; who after the sorrow of His passion, were made joyful beholding His Resurrection and Ascension into heaven. For since He said these things on that night in which He was betrayed, it was but a little while: that is, the remainder of that day, and that portion of the next till the hour when they began not to see Him. For in that night He was taken by the Jews, and on the following day He was crucified; and when it was evening He was taken down from the Cross, and shut away from the eyes of men within a narrow tomb.

And again a little while and they saw Him; for on the third day He rose from the dead, and by many proofs showed Himself to them during forty days. He adds the reason why it was that in a little time they would not see Him, and again a little while and they would see Him, when He said: *Because I go to the Father*. As though He openly said: And after a little while I shall be hidden from your eyes, within the enclosure of a tomb; and in another little while I shall appear, to be seen by you: having by then overcome the power of death; for it will then be time to return to My Father: for the purpose for which I became man is completed with the triumph of My Resurrection.

But the words: *A little while, and you shall not see me; and again a little while and you shall see me*, can be understood in yet another way. The time in which they would not see Him was but a little time; namely, the three days in which He would lie in the tomb; and again it would be but a little while till they would see Him again: namely, during the forty days following His Passion and until His Resurrection when He frequently appeared to them. But that He added the words: *Because I go to the Father*, relates however, according to this interpretation, in a special way to the words which preceded those; namely: *And again a little while, and you shall see me*. As though He were to say openly: For this reason you shall in a little while see me risen from the dead, because I am not always to remain bodily upon the earth, but, in the Humanity I have assumed, I shall ascend to heaven.

These words of the Lord apply as we have said especially to those who were able to behold His Resurrection. What He goes on to explain to those who have a mind to ask Him; namely: *Amen, amen I say to you, that you shall lament and weep, but the world shall rejoice; and you shall be made sorrowful, but your sorrow shall be turned into joy*, relates both to them and to the condition of the whole Church. And the lovers of Christ began indeed to lament and weep when they saw Him taken by His enemies, bound, led before the Council, condemned, scourged, held up to mockery, and at the end crucified, pierced by a lance, and buried. The lovers of the world began to rejoice: they whom the Lord called the world, because of their base thoughts; for He Whom they could not even bear to see, they had delivered to a most shameful death. The Disciples were filled with grief when the Lord lay stretched in death; but their sorrow was changed to joy upon hearing of His Resurrection. And in the presence of the might of His Ascension they began to praise and bless the Lord, uplifted by a yet greater joy; as the Evangelist Luke tells us (Lk. xxiv. 53).

These words of the Lord relate to all the faithful, who strive amid the tears and pain of this present life to reach to eternal joy. With reason do they lament and weep and are sorrowful during this present life; for they are not yet able to see Him Whom they love. For they know that as long as they are in the body they are wanderers from their own people and from their own true country; for they doubt not that it is through toil and struggle they are to reach their crown. Their sorrow shall be changed into joy when, the contest of this life at an end, they shall receive the reward of eternal life of whom the Psalmist sings: *They that sow in tears, shall reap in joy* (Ps. cxxv. 5).

But while the faithful lament and weep the world will rejoice; for rightly is it only in this present life that they will have any joy whatever, who place no hope in the joys of another life, or who are without hope that they can attain to them. This can be understood especially of the persecutors of the Christian faith: for having tormented and slain the martyrs they rejoiced that they had conquered. But not for long; for the martyrs being crowned in secret, these others suffered eternal chastisement, both for their unbelief and for their murders. To these was it said in divine reproof, by the mouth of the prophet: *Behold my servants shall rejoice, and you shall be confounded. Behold my servants shall praise for joyfulness of heart, and you shall cry for sorrow of heart, and shall howl for grief of spirit* (Is. lxv. 14).

Then follows: *A woman when she is in labour, hath sorrow, because her hour is come.* He speaks of the Holy Church as the woman, because of her fruitfulness in all good, and because she never ceases to bring forth children to God. And of her elsewhere is it said: *The kingdom of heaven is likened to a leaven, which a woman took and hid in three measures of meal, until the whole was leavened* (Mt. xiii. 33; Lk. xiii. 21). The woman takes the leaven, as the Church takes from the Lord the divine gift of faith and love. She hides this in three measures of flour until the whole is leavened; as she has ministered the word of life in Asia, Africa, and Europe, until all the earth is set on fire with the love of the kingdom of heaven. He shows that He belongs to the members of this Woman who in sorrow declares to certain persons who were falling away from the purity of the Faith: *My little children, of whom I am in labour again, until Christ be formed in you* (Gal. iv. 19). They testify they are her members who inflamed with heavenly desires cry out in praise of their Creator: *From thy fear, O Lord, we have conceived and brought forth, and have been as it were in labour, and have brought forth wind. But this woman when she is in labour hath sorrow, because her hour is come; but when she hath brought forth the child, she remembereth no more the anguish, for joy that a man is born into the world* (Is. xxvi. 17). For as long as she is steadfast in this world in advancing in virtue, she will never cease to be harassed by the trials of the world; but when she has overcome in the contest of her labours, and attained to the palm of victory, she remembers no more the anguish that is now ended because of her joy in the reward received. *For the sufferings of this time are not worthy to be compared with the glory to come, that shall be received in us* (Rom. viii. 18).

She remembers no more, He says, the anguish, *for joy that a man is born into the world.* For as the woman rejoices that a man is born into the world, so also is the Church filled with becoming exultation at the birth of the Christian people into life eternal; because of whose birth she now grieves and is in labour, as a woman who brings forth in this present life. Nor should it seem strange to anyone that he is said to be born who departs from the present life. For just as he is said to be born who comes forth from his mother's womb into this light of ours, so also may he most justly be said to be born who delivered of the bonds of the flesh is uplifted to light eternal. For this reason is it the custom of the Church to call those days in which the passing of the Martyrs and Confessors of Christ is commemorated, not funeral celebrations, but Birth Festivals, or *Natalitia*. The Lord then goes on to explain this figure of the woman He has put before us.

So also you now indeed have sorrow; but I will see you again, and your heart shall rejoice; and your joy no man shall take from you. This is easily understood of the Disciples; for they had to mourn over the slain and buried Christ; but after the glory of the Resurrection, they *were glad when they saw the Lord.* And their joy no one takes from them; for though in the days that followed they suffered persecution and torment for Christ's Name, yet they suffered these things gladly: for they were inflamed with the hope of resurrection and the hope of seeing Him. Indeed, *they counted it all joy* when they met with trials of every kind (Jas. i. 2). For even when they were scourged by the chiefs of the priests, *They went from,* as it is written, *rejoicing that they were accounted worthy to suffer reproach for the name of Christ* (Acts v. 41).

Their joy no one takes from them; for by suffering such things for the sake of Christ they merited to reign with Christ forever. And the whole Church likewise, amid the trials and labours of this present life, goes steadily forward to the reward of eternal joy; as the Apostle bears witness: *That through many tribulations we must enter into the kingdom of God* (Acts xiv. 21).

When He said: *I will see you again, and your heart shall rejoice*, He meant: I will see you; I will snatch you from the jaws of your enemies; I will crown you as victors; I will prove to you that I was ever with you as a witness while you fought. For when would He not see His own, especially in the midst of trials, since He has promised to be with them all the days of this world? And as the faithful died in the midst of their sufferings, their torturers believed that they were without divine aid; saying: *Where is their God?* For this, one such as these, hedged about with torments, cries out: *Behold, O Lord, my afflictions, because the enemy is lifted up* (Lam. i. 9); which is as if he were openly to say: Since the enemy who torments me raises his head in pride against thy lowly ones, sustain us by thy help, O Triumphant Creator; prove to us when our enemies are defeated and driven off that thou hast seen our struggles, and that they were pleasing to Thee. So after their tribulation the Lord sees the Elect when, the enemy condemned, He gives them the reward of their patience.

We can interpret the words: *I will see you again,* as though He said: I shall appear to you who now see me; as He said to Abraham: *Now I know that thou fearest God* (Gen. xxii. 12); just as though He said: Now I have made men know that you fear God, they who till now knew not what was ever known to Me. If then, Brethren, we are afflicted by salutary suffering, if according to the exhortation of the Apostle, *we are patient in tribulation; instant in prayer* (Rom. xii. 12), if with due sorrow we weep for our own errors and for the miseries of our neighbours, the Lord will see us again; that is, He will show Himself to us in the future Who once deigned to see us and bestow on us the knowledge of His Faith. He will see us that He may crown us Who once saw us that He might call us. He will see us and our heart will rejoice, and our joy no man shall take from us; for this is the sole and true reward of those who sorrow for God's sake; to rejoice for ever in His sight.

This reward on high He promised when He said: *Blessed are the clean of heart: for they shall see God* (Mt. v. 8). The psalmist longed for this reward when He cried: *My soul hath thirsteth after the strong living God; when shall I come and appear before the face of the living God?* (Ps. xli. 3). This the Apostle rejoiced that with others like him he might receive; who though conscious of his own struggles could yet confidently proclaim: *We see now through a glass in a dark manner; but then face to face* (I Cor. xiii. 12). Relying on God let us also truly seek to lay hold of this reward, until we come to see Him Who is the Help of those who fight, and the Reward of those who win, Jesus Christ our Lord, Who with the Father and the Holy Ghost liveth and reigneth world without end. Amen.

NOTES

[1] Homily 79 in John (in princ.), PG 59.

[2] PG 59, hom. 79 in John.

[3] PL 35, Tract 101 in John.

[4] PG 74 in John xi. 2.

[5] The Septuagint has here *me* for *se*.

[6] The Venerable Bede recapitulates Sacred Tradition on this Gospel and goes on to throw light on the mystical knowledge within John xiv. 21 (concerning the Vision of Christ).

[7] PL 94, Bk. II, hom. 5.

FOURTH SUNDAY AFTER EASTER

I. St Cyprian: The Advantages of Patience

II. St John Chrysostom: The Promise of The Holy Spirit

III. St Augustine: Exposition of the Gospel

IV. St Augustine: The Ascension of Christ's Mystical Body

V. St Cyril of Alexandria: The Mission of The Holy Spirit

THE GOSPEL OF THE SUNDAY

John xvi. 5–14

At that time: Jesus said to his Disciples: I go to him that sent me, and none of you asketh me: Whither goest thou? But because I have spoken these things to you, sorrow hath filled your heart.

But I tell you the truth: it is expedient to you that I go: for if I go not, the Paraclete will not come to you; but if I go, I will send him to you.

And when he is come, he will convince the world of sin, and of justice, and of judgement. Of sin: because they believed not in me. And of justice: because I go to the Father; and you shall see me no longer. And of judgement: because the prince of this world is already judged. I have yet many things to say to you: but you cannot bear them now. But when he, the Spirit of Truth, is come, he will teach you all truth. For he shall not speak of himself; but what things soever he shall hear, he shall speak; and the things that are to come, he shall show you. He shall glorify me; because he shall receive of mine, and shall show it to you.

Exposition from the Catena Aurea

V. 5. *And now I go to him that sent me . . .*

Chrysostom, *Hom.* 77 *in John*: Because sorrow had cast down His Disciples, still not perfected, the Lord raises up their courage, and chides them, saying: *And now I go to him that sent me, and none of you asketh me: whither goest thou?* For when they heard Him say that whoever killed them would think He was doing a service to God, they became so despondent that they had not a word to say to Him. And so He adds:

V. 6. *But because I have spoken these things to you, sorrow . . .*

Even this was a little comfort to them: to know that the Lord knew how deeply they suffered, both over His going from them, and because of the evils they learn they must suffer; not knowing if they could suffer them manfully.

AUGUSTINE, *Tract* 94 *in John*: Or because earlier they had asked Him (xiii. 36) where He was going, and He had answered He was going where they could not come. Now He foretells that He will go in such a way that no one will ask Him where He is going, and this is what He means by the words: *And none of you asketh me* . . . For when He was actually ascending into heaven no one questioned Him with words, but their eyes followed Him upwards.

But the Lord saw what effect His words had on their heart; for not yet possessing that inward comfort they were to receive from the Holy Spirit, they were fearful of losing the visible Presence of Christ. And since they could because of His warning doubt they were to lose Him, their human affections were saddened because they were to be deprived of His Bodily appearance. And so there follows: *Because I have said these things, sorrow hath filled your heart.* But He knew what was best for them; for better for them was that inward vision with which the Holy Spirit was to comfort them. Hence:

V. 7. *But I tell you the truth: it is expedient to you that I go . . .*

CHRYSOSTOM *as above:* As though to say: though it grieve you beyond measure, yet you must accept that it is better for you that I go. How they shall gain He goes on to say: *For if I go not, the Paraclete will not come; but if I go, I will send him to you.*

AUGUSTINE, *The Trinity*, I, 9: He said this, not because of any inequality between the Word of God and the Holy Spirit, but because the presence among them of the Son of man would be an obstacle to the coming of Him Who was not less than He. For He had not emptied Himself as the Son had, taking the form of a servant. It was therefore required that the form of the servant be taken from their sight; for seeing it they supposed that Christ was only that which they beheld with their eyes. Hence: *But if I go, I will send him to you.*

AUGUSTINE, *Tract* 94, 4: Could He not while here on earth send Him Who, as we know, descended on Him at His baptism, and *remained upon him*; indeed from Whom we know He was at no time separable? What then does He mean by saying: *If I go not the Paraclete will not come to you*, but that you cannot receive the Holy Ghost as long as you continue to know Christ as a man. But when Christ departed from them in His Body, not alone was the Holy Spirit present to them, but the Father also, and the Son.

GREGORY, *Moral.* 8, 13: As if He were openly to say: If I do not withdraw My Body from your bodily perception, I cannot through my consoling Spirit lead you to spiritual vision.

AUGUSTINE, *Sermon* 143, 3: The Holy Spirit the Comforter brought us this blessedness, that, the form of a servant, received in the womb of the Virgin Mary, being removed from the eyes of our body, the Lord was revealed to our purified inward vision in that form of God in which He remained equal to the Father, even when He stooped to appear to us in the Flesh.

CHRYSOSTOM: What do they say to this, they who have no proper belief in the Spirit? Is it correct that the Master should go so that the servant may come? What the gain to us is of the Coming of the Holy Spirit He shows when He adds:

V. 8. *And when he is come he will convince the world of sin . . .*

AUGUSTINE, *Tract* 95 *in John*: But did Christ not convince the world? Or was it because Christ spoke only to the people of Israel that He seems not to have convinced the world? But the Holy Ghost, poured out into the hearts of His Disciples spread throughout the world, appears to have corrected, not one people only, but the world. But who is there will venture to say that, by means of the Disciples of Christ, the Holy Ghost corrects the whole world, and that Christ does not correct them, when the Apostle cries out: *Do you seek a proof of Christ that speaketh in me?* (II Cor. xiii. 3).

They then whom the Holy Ghost corrects, Christ also reproves. But He also said: *He will convince the world*, as though He said: He shall pour out His love into your hearts; for fear (by which they would be prevented from daring to reprove the world which raged against them in persecution) being cast out, you will then be free to correct it (II Cor. iii. 17). He then explained what He said:

V. 9. *Of sin: because they have not believed in me . . .*

He sets this sin above all the rest; because while this remains, they are held fast in all the rest; and when this has gone, the rest are forgiven.

AUGUSTINE, *Sermon* 144, 2: Now there is a great difference between believing in Christ, and in believing that Jesus is the Christ. For that He was the Christ even the devils believed; but he believes in Christ who both loves Christ, and hopes in Christ.

AUGUSTINE, *Tract* 95, 2 *in John*: The world is therefore convinced of sin, because it does not believe in Christ; and of justice, the justness of those who believe. For to compare them with the just is to reproach the unjust.

V. 10. *And of justice because I go to the Father.*

Since unbelievers are wont to cry out: How can we believe what we cannot see? the justness of those who do believe needed to be made clearly manifest, *Because I go to the Father: and you shall see me no longer.* For blessed are they who do not see and yet believe. And of those who saw Christ their faith also was praised; but not for this that they believed what they saw, namely, the Son of man. Accordingly, when this *form of a servant* was withdrawn from before their eyes it was then that the saying was wholly fulfilled: *The just man liveth by faith* (Rom. i. 17).

It shall then be by your own justness that the world shall be convinced: since you shall believe in Me Whom you will not see. And when you do see Me, as I shall then be, you will not see Me as you see Me now here among you. That is, you will not see Him as mortal, but as eternal. For by saying, *You shall see me no longer*, He Who is Truth Itself foretold as it were that they would never again see (*this*) Christ.

AUGUSTINE, *Sermon* 144, 3: Or again, they did not believe He was going to the Father. The sin therefore was theirs; the justness was His. That He came to us from the Father was mercy; that whereby He goes to the Father is His justness, according to the words of the Apostle: *For which cause God hath exalted him* (Phil. ii. 9). But if He alone shall go to the Father what profit is this to us? Is it not rather that He is alone in this sense, that Christ is one with all His Members, as the head is with the body? So the world therefore is convinced *of sin* through those persons who will not believe in Christ, and *of justice* by those who shall rise again as members of Christ's Body. Then follows:

V. 11. *And of judgement, because the prince of this world . . .*

That is, the devil, the prince of evil doers, whose heart is only in this world that they love. *Sermon* 143: By the fact that he was cast out he is already judged; and of this *judgement* the world is convicted; for it is useless for one who will not believe in Christ to look instead to the devil, whom not alone have men defeated, but even women and the boys and maidens who were martyred, condemned as he is, that is, outcast, though permitted to attack us outwardly, so that we may be tested.

AUGUSTINE, *Tr.* 95, 4: Or, *he is judged*, since he is committed irrevocably to the chastisement of everlasting fire. And by this judgement the world is convicted, since it is already judged together with its prince, whom, proud and blasphemous as he is, it imitates. So therefore let mankind believe in Christ so that they may not be condemned through his sin of unbelief; by means of which they are held fast in all other sins. Let them pass over to the number of the believing, lest they be condemned by the justness of those whom, as just, they have not imitated. Let them beware of the judgement to come, lest they be condemned together with the prince of this world whom, though he was condemned, they have imitated.

[This is the meaning of *to convince the world*: To show the world that those things are true which it did not wish to believe were so. For it did not wish to believe that the Saviour came from God. But the Saviour, after He had restored justice, did not delay in returning to Him Who had sent Him. And by so returning there He proved that it was from there He had come; because *no man hath ascended into heaven but he that descended from heaven, the Son of man who is in heaven.* John iii. 13, from (Augustine) Quaest. ex N. & V. Tests, n. 89. *See note* 1.]

CHRYSOSTOM: Or again: *he will convince the world of sin*, that is, He will cut off all their excuses and will show them they have sinned, in not believing in Me, when they shall see the ineffable graces of the Holy Spirit given at the invocation of My Name.

AUGUSTINE, *Questions of the Old and New Testaments*, 89: In this way also shall the Holy Spirit convince the world of sin, in that He will work wonders in the name of the Saviour Who was condemned by the world. But the Saviour, justice now restored, does not delay in returning to Him Who had sent Him, and by returning He proved from where it was He had come; because of this there follows: *And of justice: because I go to the Father.*[1] CHRYSOSTOM: That is, because My going to the Father will be a proof of the blameless justice of My life, that they may no longer be able to say: *This man is a sinner, and not of God* (Jn. ix. 24, 23). Again, since I have overcome My enemy, (and had He been a sinner He could not have overthrown him), they cannot say that I have a devil, and that I am a seducer. And since through Me he was condemned, they shall come to learn that afterwards they will trample on him; and they will come to see clearly the fact of My Resurrection: for he was powerless to hold Me.

AUGUSTINE, *Questions etc.* 89: The demons seeing souls ascend from hell to heaven knew that the prince of this world had been judged; that in the contest with the Saviour he had lost all right to what he had held till then. This they saw as the Saviour ascended, but with the descent of the Holy Spirit upon the Apostles these things were clearly and openly revealed.

V. 12. *I have yet many things to say to you; but you cannot etc.*

THEOPHYLACTUS: Since the Lord had said a little before this (v. 7), *it is expedient for you that I go*, He now enlarges this by saying: *I have yet many things to say to you; but you cannot bear them now.*

AUGUSTINE, *Tr.* 97 *in John*: For all heretics try to justify the effrontery of their own vapourings, when the common sense of mankind scorns them, by taking advantage of this sentence of the Gospel; as if these were the things which the disciples could not bear, and that the Holy Spirit had taught things which even the unclean spirit was ashamed to teach and proclaim. But (*Tract* 96, 5) the evil teachings that no human modesty could permit are one thing; the truths which the limited human mind can grasp are another. The one are to be found in those whose bodies are unchaste, the others are far removed from all bodies. (*Tract* 96, 1) Which of us will presume to say that he can grasp what they could not? And because of this neither is it to be expected that they can be expounded by me.

But, someone will say, many could bear what Peter could not, just as many could bear to be crowned with martyrdom, which Peter then could not; especially as the Holy Spirit has now been sent, Who had not then been sent. But do we know what these *things* were which He wished to tell them? It seems to me a very foolish thing to say that the Disciples could not bear to hear the sublime things which we find in the Apostolic Epistles, which were written later, and which the Lord is not recorded as having told them. But men of perverted belief cannot bear what is found in the sacred Scriptures concerning the Catholic faith, just as we cannot endure their own sacrilegious absurdities: for what does *cannot bear them* mean but that the mind cannot bear to consider them in patience? For what believer, or what catechumen, who even before he receives the Holy Spirit in Baptism will not patiently read and accept, even if he does not understand them, what was written after the Ascension of Our Lord?

But someone will say (*Tract* 97, 1): Have spiritual men nothing in their teaching on which they are silent to those who are carnal minded, but speak openly of only to those that are spiritual?[3] There is no need for some secrets of our teaching to be concealed from the young in faith, and to be spoken of to the older ones apart. For men who are spiritual ought not wholly to pass over in silence things spiritual; because the Catholic Faith is to be preached to all men.[5] Yet neither should they so explain them that, striving to reduce them to the understanding of those who are incapable of taking them in, they may more likely awaken in them a dislike for their discourse upon some truth, than to bring them to perceive the truth of the discourse.

Let us not therefore (*Tract* 97, 1) believe that these words of Our Lord refer to I know not what secrets, which, though the teacher could utter them, the disciple would not be able to bear them; but to those very truths which in the teaching of religion we speak of to all men whatsoever. If Christ were to speak to us as He speaks to His angels what men could bear it, even though they were spiritually minded, such as the Apostles were not? For whatever can be known of creation is less than nothing compared with what can be known of the Creator Himself; and who is silent concerning Him?

Who is there (*Tract* 96, 4) while living in this body can know all truth, for the Apostle says: *We know in part*? But since, through the Holy Spirit, it happens that we come also to that fulness (*of knowledge*) of which the same Apostle speaks.

Tract 96, 5: Who is there that dwells in this body which corrupts and oppresses the soul (Wisd. ix. 15) can know all truth; as the Apostle says: *We know in part*? (I Cor. xiii). But because we are sanctified by the Holy Spirit it comes to pass that we are brought also to that fulness of which the same Apostle says: *Then we shall see face to face*. Our Lord did not refer only to what is known in this life when He said: *But when he, the Spirit of truth, is come, he will teach you all truth*, or, *he will lead you to all truth*; by this phrase we should understand that the fulness of truth is reserved for us to the life that is to come. *Tract* 97, 1: The Holy Spirit now teaches the faithful as much as each one can grasp of spiritual things, and at the same time enkindles in their hearts a yet greater desire for them.

DIDYMUS, I, 2: Or He says that those who heard His words were not yet able to bear all that they were afterwards capable of enduring for His Name's sake; and so revealing some truths now He postpones till later those which were of greater importance: which they could not then bear, until He should as Our Head have given us an example by means of His Cross. For being still subject to the pattern of the Law, to shadows and images, they were still unable to come to terms with the reality of which the Law was but the shadow. But when the Spirit of truth has come He will lead you to all truth, by His teaching and instruction, bringing you over from the dead letter of the Law to the vivifying Life in Which the reality of all Scripture is alone found.[2]

V. 13. *But when He, the Spirit of truth, is come, he will teach you . . .*

CHRYSOSTOM: And so because He had said: *you cannot bear them now*, and, *the Holy Spirit will lead you to all truth*, lest they should suppose on hearing this that the Holy Spirit was greater than Himself, He also adds: *He shall not speak of himself; but what things soever he shall hear, he shall speak.*

AUGUSTINE, *Tract* 99, 1, *in John*: This is like what He said earlier of Himself: *I cannot of myself do anything. As I hear, so I judge* (Jn. v. 30). This we can take as spoken of Himself as man. Therefore (*par.* 2, *near end*) since the Holy Spirit did not, by taking on the nature of any creature, become a creature, how is this saying of the Lord to be understood concerning Him: *He shall not speak of himself; but what things soever he shall hear, he shall speak*? We must (*par.* 4, *in medio*) accept the words as to understand by them that He does not derive existence from Himself. (The Father alone proceeds from no one.) For the Son is born of the Father; and the Holy Ghost proceeds from the Father. It would take much too long to explain, and it would be rash to define, in what lies the difference between *proceeding* and *being born*. He does not speak of Himself because He *is* not of Himself. But what He hears He speaks. He hears from Him from Whom He proceeds. With Him to hear is to know; to know is *to be*. And so because He *is* not of Himself, but from Him from Whom He proceeds, from Whom He has Being, from Whom knowledge, and therefore from Whom hearing, which is none other than knowledge. And so (*par.* 5, *near end*) forever does the Holy Spirit hear, because forever does He know. From Him therefore has He heard, hears, and shall hear, from Whom He is.

DIDYMUS, *on the Holy Spirit, as above, par.* 34: Therefore did He say: *He shall not speak of himself*; that is, not without Me, and without Mine and My Father's authority. Because He is not from Himself, but from the Father and Me. For this Being Which is and Which speaks proceeds to Him from the Father and from Me. *I speak the truth*; that is, I inspire the things He utters, since He is the Spirit of Truth.

But to speak and to give utterance in the Trinity is not to be understood after the manner of our nature, but after the manner of incorporeal natures, and especially That of the Trinity, Which implants its will in the hearts of the believing, and of those who are worthy to receive it (*par.* 36). For the Father to speak, and for the Son to hear, is but an indication of the unanimity of Nature of both Father and Son. The Holy Spirit likewise, Who is the Spirit of Truth, and the Spirit of Wisdom, cannot, when the Son speaks, hear that which it knew not: since He *is That* which was spoken by the Son, namely, the Truth proceeding from the Truth: the Comforter flowing forth from the Comforter, God the Spirit of Truth proceeding from God. Lastly, lest any one should set Him apart from the will and the company of the Father and the Son, it was written: *But what he shall hear he shall speak.*

AUGUSTINE, *The Trinity*, 2, 13: But it does not follow from this that the Holy Spirit is less than God; for this was said because of His proceeding from the Father.

AUGUSTINE, *Tract* 99, 5, *in John*: Nor may it be brought forward that the future tense is employed. For this hearing is sempiternal: since the knowing is from all eternity. In regard to what is eternal, without beginning and without end, you may use whatever tense you will. For though that unchanging Nature does not admit of *was* and *will be*, but only of *is*, yet, because of the changeableness of the times in which our mortality dwells, we may truthfully say was and is and will be; *was*, because He never was not; *will be*, because He never shall not be; *is*, because He is forever.

DIDYMUS, *as above*, 38: By the Spirit of Truth also a certain knowledge of future events is given to holy men. And through this the Prophets, filled with the Holy Spirit, foretold and saw as though present things that were yet to come. Hence: *And the things that are to come, he shall show you.*

BEDE: It is well known that many persons who were filled with the Holy Spirit had knowledge of things to come. But as many who were remarkable for virtue had yet no knowledge of future things, these words: *And the things to come, he shall show you*, can be understood to mean that He will bring to your minds the joys of your heavenly home. He did however tell to the Apostles things that were to come: the evils, namely, they were to suffer in confessing Christ, and also the good things they were to receive because of these same evils.

CHRYSOSTOM: In this way He uplifted their minds; for there is nothing of which men are so eager to know as future events. And by this He delivered them from anxiety, making clear to them that since He had foretold the dangers they were to meet, they would not come upon them unawares. Then, indicating that He had spoken all the truth to which the Holy Spirit will lead them, He added:

V. 14. *He shall glorify me; because he shall receive of mine.*

AUGUSTINE, *Tract* 100, 1: Namely, by pouring out His charity into the hearts of the faithful, and making them spiritual, He showed them how there was equality between the Father and the Son, Whom before this they had known as man, and Whom they thought of as a man like other men. Or else that they being filled, through this very charity, with courage, and casting fear aside, proclaimed Christ to men; and thus His fame went forth to all the world. For that which they were to do in the Holy Spirit, this same, He said, would be the doing of the Holy Spirit.

CHRYSOSTOM: And because the Lord had said: *One is your master, Christ* (Mt. xxiii. 8), so that they might also receive the Holy Spirit, He adds: *Because he shall receive of mine, and shall show it to you.*

DIDYMUS, *as above*, 36, 37: The word to *receive* must be understood in a manner becoming to the divine nature. For as the Son in giving is not deprived of that which He gives, nor in giving does He give to His own loss, so likewise the Holy Spirit does not receive that which before He had not. For if He were to receive what before He had not, the gift being then given to another, the Giver is less by that gift. So therefore we must understand that the Holy Spirit receives from the Son that which belongs to Their nature, and does not mean that there is one substance giving and one receiving, but one substance only. In the same manner the Son is said to receive from the Father that wherein He also subsists. For the Son is nothing other than that which He receives from the Father; and the Holy Spirit has no other substance but that which is given Him by the Son.

AUGUSTINE, *Tract* 100, 4: Hear with Catholic ears, and take in with Catholic minds, the words: *He shall receive of mine, and shall show it to you.* For it does not follow from these words, as some heretics have supposed, that the Holy Spirit is less than the Son, that as it were by gradations of nature the Son receives from the Father, and the Holy Spirit from the Son. He Himself, solving the question, explains why it is He said this, saying:

V. 15. *All things whatsoever the Father hath, are mine.*

DIDYMUS, 38: As though He said: Though the Spirit of Truth proceeds from the Father, yet all things that the Father has are mine, and the Spirit of the Father is My Spirit, and shall receive of Mine. Take care however lest when these things are said you fall into the error of mind of thinking that these are things or possessions owned by the Father and by the Son. That which the Father has by reason of His substance (*nature*), namely, eternity, unchangeableness, goodness, these also the Son possesses. Let us be wary of the petty sophisms of the logicians. For they say: Therefore, the Father is also the Son, and the Son the Father. Had He said: All things which God hath are mine, impiety might have had an excuse for raising its head. But since He said: *All things the Father hath are mine*, by using the name Father He declared Himself the Son, and He Who is the Son does not lay claim to the Fatherhood, although He too, by the grace of adoption, is the Father of many saints.

HILARY, *The Trinity*, *Book* 8: The Lord therefore has not left it in uncertainty whether the Paraclete Spirit is to be thought to be from the Father, or from the Son. For He receives from the Son, because He is sent by Him, and He proceeds from the Father. And I ask you if it be the same things to receive from the

Son as to proceed from the Father? There is no doubt that to proceed from the Son must be considered as one and the same thing as to receive from the Father. For when He says, *all things whatsoever the Father hath are mine*, and therefore said that He shall receive of His, He teaches us that what is received from Him must be received from the Father also, since all that the Father has is His. This unity is without diversity: nor does it make a difference from whom anything is received, for what is written as given by the Son is given also by the Father.[3]

I. St Cyprian, Bishop and Martyr

On the Advantages of Patience[4]

1. Since, Dearly Beloved, I am to speak to you of patience, and make known to you its usefulness and its advantages, where can I better begin than by saying that I can see that even at this present moment you will need patience, that you may listen to me. For without patience you will be unable either to listen to me or to learn anything from me. For preaching and instruction unto salvation are received with fruit only when listened to in patience. And, Beloved Brethren, among the varied ways along which the Church is divinely guided towards heaven, I do not find any more profitable to this present life, or more helpful in obtaining future glory, than that we, who with reverential fear and devotion place our trust in what the Lord has taught us, should hold most carefully to patience.

2. *The Wisdom of this World.* There are certain philosophers who profess that they also are devoted to patience. But their patience is as false as their wisdom. For how can anyone be patient or truly wise who knows nothing of the wisdom or of the patience of God: for He has Himself warned us of this where He speaks of those who appear to themselves to be wise in this world: *I will destroy the wisdom of the wise, and the prudence of the prudent I will reject* (I Cor. i. 19; Is. xxix. 14). The blessed Paul, who was filled with the Holy Spirit, and who was sent to call and to instruct the Gentiles, also bears witness to this, and teaches us, saying: *Beware lest any man cheat you by philosophy, and vain deceit* (Col. ii. 8). And in another place he says: Let no man deceive himself: *If any man among you seem to be wise in this world, let him become a fool, that he may be wise. For the wisdom of this world is foolishness with God. For it is written: I will catch the wise in their own craftiness.* And again: *The Lord knoweth the thoughts of the wise, that they are vain* (I Cor. iii. 20). And so if their wisdom is not true, neither is their patience. For he is truly patient who is meek and humble. But we see no philosophers who are either meek or humble; but rather only such as are very satisfied with themselves. And since they are pleased with themselves: and displeasing to God: it is plain that wherever you find this arrogant proclaiming of an assumed freedom of conduct, and the unbecoming vanity of the half covered breast, you will find no true patience.

3. *Virtue does not consist in Words but in Deeds.* But we, Dearly Beloved, who love wisdom not in word but in deed, and profess it, not by our dress but by our lives, we whose minds are intent on the virtue that is within rather than on its outward semblance, who talk not of lofty things but live them, as becomes servants and worshippers of God, let us show forth in humility of spirit the patience we learn from our heavenly teachers. Here is a virtue we may share with God. For it is from Him that patience comes: in Him its glory and its dignity have their source, in Him as its Author patience has its greatness and its beginning. And what is precious in the eyes of God must be held in honour by men; what the Divine Majesty loves it commends to us. If God is our Lord and our Father let us strive after the patience of our Lord and Master; for servants should imitate their masters, as sons should be like their fathers.

4. *Patience ripens all.* How great, how wondrous, the patience of God, Who while enduring with so much forbearance the godless temples, the images of clay, and the accursed abominations set up by men in contempt of His Honour and Majesty, yet makes day begin and His light to shine upon the good and upon the bad; and as He waters this earth with showers He excludes no one from their benefit, bestowing the bounty of His rain alike upon the just and upon the unjust? We can see with what serene patience and impartiality the seasons at His command serve both the innocent and the guilty, the Godfearing and the Godless, those who give thanks and the thankless. The elements wait on them, the winds blow for them, the streams flow, the harvest abounds, the vines mature, the trees become laden with apples, the woods come out in leaf, and the field in flowers. And though we provoke God by frequent, nay, by continuous offences, He restrains His wrath and waits in patience for that destined day of retribution.

For though He has the power to punish He chooses rather to go on in patience, forbearing in mildness, putting off the day, so that, if it is possible, the long continuing evil-doing may at length be changed, that man, surrounded as he is by the evil contagion of error and of crime, may turn at last to God; as He tells us Himself, where He says: *I desire not the death of the wicked, but rather that he turn from his ways and live* (Ezech. xxxiii. 11). And again: *Return to me, saith the Lord* (Mal. iii. 7). And again: *Return to the Lord your God: for he is gracious and merciful, patient and rich in mercy, and willingly forgiving towards our wickedness* (Joel ii. 13).

And this the blessed Paul also proclaims to us, where he calls upon the sinner to repent, and says: *Or despisest thou the riches of his goodness, and patience, and long-suffering? Knowest thou not, that the benignity of God leadeth thee to penance? But according to thy hardness and impenitent heart, thou treasurest up to thyself wrath, against the day of wrath, and revelation of the just judgement of God* (Rom. ii. 4–6). He tells us that the judgement of God is just, because it is slow in coming, because it is long and often deferred, so that through the enduring patience of God man may give thought to the life to come. And then when repentance for sin can no longer avail him, punishment is inflicted on the sinner.

5. *Patience is of God.* And that we may more fully understand, Beloved Brethren, that patience is a thing of God, and that he who is patient and gentle and mild is an imitator of God the Father, when the Lord in His Gospel was giving His precepts for our salvation, and communicating His divine counsels to His Disciples, to instruct them in the way of perfection, He declared to them: *You have heard it that it hath been said, Thou shalt love thy neighbour, and hate thy enemy. But I say to you, Love your enemies: do good to them that hate you: and pray for them that persecute and calumniate you: that you may be the children of your father who is in heaven, who maketh his sun to rise upon the good, and bad, and raineth upon the just and the unjust. For if you love them that love you, what reward shall you have: do not even the publicans know this? And if you salute your brethren only, what do you more? Do not also the heathens do this? Be you perfect therefore, as also your heavenly Father is perfect* (Mt. v. 43–8). So, He says, shall the children of God become perfect; so, He shows and teaches, renewed through being spiritually reborn shall they come to fulfilment, provided that the patience of God the Father remain in us, that the divine likeness, which we lost through the sin of Adam, may again be seen in us, shining forth in our deeds. What glory to become like unto God! How wondrous, how great, a happiness to merit the virtue which we praise in God!

6. *Christ did not teach us in Words only.* And neither did Jesus Christ, Beloved Brethren, Who was our Lord and our God, teach us only by His words; for these He fulfilled in His deeds. And because He had said that He had come down to do the will of His Father, among the other signs He showed us in proof of His divine power, in His unvarying forbearance He showed also the patience of His heavenly Father. And so from the beginning of His Coming every action of His is accompanied by patience as by an attendant; and first of all, though coming down from the glory of heaven to this earth, the Son of God did not refuse to put on the body of a man, and, though Himself without sin, to take upon Him the sins of others. And putting aside for a time His own immortality, He chose to endure our mortality, so that though He was without stain He might yet suffer death for the salvation of sinners.

The Lord is baptized by His servant; and He Who was to purify us of sin does not think it beneath Him to wash His Body in the baptism of regeneration. He by Whom others are fed fasts for forty days. He goes without food, and He suffers hunger, that they who were hungry for the word and for grace might be filled with bread from heaven. He confuted the devil who tried to tempt Him, and, using only words, was content simply to frustrate the enemy. He ruled His Disciples, not with the authority of a master over servants, but Mild and Gentle He loved them as a brother. He stooped even to the washing of the feet of the Apostles that by His own example He might teach them, that as the Lord was among His servants so should they be among their fellow servants and equals.

Nor need we wonder that He should do this among the dutiful, when with prolonged patience He suffered Judas to the end; taking food with one who was His enemy; knowing who it was within His own household that plotted against Him, yet not denouncing him, not refusing the kiss of the betrayer. What patience and what serenity in bearing with the Jews! By His gentle words He turned them from unbelief to faith. He answered with mildness those who contradicted Him; suffered the overbearing with clemency; yielded humbly to those who tormented Him, desiring even to the hour of His Cross and Passion to unite with Him these who were ever the slayers of the Prophets and rebels against God.

7. And even in His very Passion and Crucifixion, before they had come to the shedding of His Blood and the final cruelty of His death, what infamies of reproach did He not patiently endure, what revilings, what mockeries; so that He Who a little before had healed with His spittle the eyes of a blind man was spat upon by those who insulted Him. He was scourged in Whose Name and by Whose servants the devil and his angels are scourged. He who crowns the martyrs with unfading garlands was Himself crowned with thorns. They struck Him on the face with the palms of their hands Who gives the palm of victory to those who endure to the end. He Who clothes others with the garment of everlasting life was stripped of His earthly garments. They gave Him gall Who gives us the food of heaven. He was given vinegar to drink Who has given us the cup of salvation. He the Just One, the Innocent, nay, more, Innocence Itself, He Who *is* Justice, was reputed among thieves, and Truth Itself was surrounded by false witnesses. The Judge of all men was placed standing before an earthly judge. The Word of God was led wordless to be sacrificed.

And when the heavens were fearful at sight of the Lord upon the Cross, and when the elements were thrown into confusion, and the earth trembled, and night shut out day, and the sun withdrew its beams and veiled its eyes, so as not to be compelled to look upon the crime of the Jews, He did not speak, He did not move; not even in His very agony did He speak of His own divine majesty. He bore with everything, patiently and steadfastly to the end: so that in Christ patience might have its perfect fulfilment.

8. And after all this He still receives His slayers, should they be converted and come to Him: He Who is kind and forbearing to save us, and with salutary patience closes His Church to no one. And those who oppose Him, who blaspheme him, who were enemies of His Name, should they repent of their sins, not alone will He admit them to pardon, He will admit them also to a share in the rewards of the kingdom of heaven. What can one tell that is more kind, more patient, than this? Even he who has shed Christ's blood is through Christ's blood given life everlasting. So wondrous, so sublime, is the patience of God! And had it not been so wondrous and so sublime the Church

would not have had Paul also as an Apostle.

9. And if, Dearly Beloved, we too live in Christ, if we put Him on as a garment, if He is the way of our salvation, let us, Who walk in Christ's saving footsteps, also follow Christ's example; as the Apostle John teaches us where he says: *He that saith he abideth in him, ought himself to walk, even as he walked* (I Jn. ii. 6). And Peter upon whom, by the favour of Christ, the Church was founded lays this down in his Epistle: *For unto this are you called: because Christ also suffered for us, leaving you an example that you should follow in his steps. Who did no sin, neither was guile found in his mouth. Who, when he was reviled, did not revile: when he suffered, he threatened not: but delivered himself to him that judged him unjustly* (I Pet. ii. 21).

10. (13). The saving rule given to us by our Lord and Master is, that *he that shall persevere unto the end, he shall be saved* (Mt. x. 12). And again: *If you continue in my word, you shall be my disciples indeed, and you shall know the truth, and the truth shall make you free* (Jn. viii. 51). We must endure, and we must persevere, Dearly Beloved, so that while possessing the hope of truth and of freedom, we may attain to the reality of truth and freedom, and in that we are Christians lies the ground of our faith and of our hope. But that our faith and hope may bear fruit, we have need of patience. For we are not striving for the glory of this, but of the future life; as the Apostle reminds us when he says: *For we are saved by hope. But hope that is seen is not hope. For what a man seeth, why doth he hope for? But if we hope for that which we see not, we wait for it with patience* (Rom. viii. 24). And so patience and expectation are needed, that we may bring to fulness what we have begun, and that we may receive what we look forward to: with faith and hope because of the promises of God.

And because of this the same Apostle, in another place, teaches those who are virtuous and right-living, and who lay up their treasure in heaven, by the mounting-up of divine interest, that they must also be patient, saying to them: *Therefore, whilst we have time, let us work good to all men, but especially to those who are of the household of the faith. In doing good, let us not fail. For in due time we shall reap, not failing* (Gal. vi. 9). He urged them not to cease from doing good because of impatience; that no one, because he is distracted or overcome by temptation, should turn aside from the road of praise and of glory: and this also lest they lose the merits of past good works, and lest those begun may no longer bear fruit; for it is written: *The justice of the just shall not deliver him, in what day soever he shall sin* (Ezech. xxxiii. 12). And again: *Hold fast that which thou hast, that no man take thy crown* (Apoc. iii. 11). His words encourage us to persevere in courage and in patience, so that whosoever is striving for the crown of glory, now close at hand, shall be crowned by being steadfast in patience.

11 (14). *The Power of Patience against Evil.* And patience, Dearly Beloved, not alone keeps watch over what is good, it will also drive away evil. Aided by the Holy

Spirit, and keeping close to the divine and heavenly powers, it wars from the fortress of its own virtue against the weaknesses and lust of the flesh and of the body, whereby the soul is assaulted and overcome. Let us think for a moment of a few out of the many temptations: that from this few the rest may be understood. Adultery is a mortal crime, and so is fraud, and the killing of a man. If the heart is strong and steadfast in patience, the body that is sanctified and a temple of God will not be polluted by adultery, nor will innocence that is dedicated to virtue be soiled by the touch of fraud, nor will the hand that has borne the Eucharist be stained by the sword or by blood.

12 (15). *Patience and the Foundation of Charity.* Charity is the bond of brotherhood, the foundation of peace, the anchor and stay of unity. It is greater than faith and hope. It is higher than good works and martyrdoms. It will abide with us for ever with God in His Kingdom of heaven. But take patience from it, and forsaken it will not long continue. Take from it the power to *bear* and to *endure*, and it remains without root and without strength. And so when the Apostle spoke of charity he joined it to both patience and endurance. *Charity*, he says, *is patient, is kind; charity envieth not, is not puffed up; is not provoked to anger, thinketh no evil, loveth all things, believeth all things, hopeth all things, endureth all things* (I Cor. xiii. 4–7). He shows that it can strongly persevere because it knows how to endure all things. And in another place: *Supporting one another in charity; careful to keep the unity of the Spirit in the bond of peace* (Eph. iv. 2). He proved that neither unity nor peace can survive unless brothers support each other with mutual forbearance, and protect the bond of union by having patience one with another.

13 (16). And then what next? That you do not swear, that you curse not, that you do not demand back what was taken from you, that when you receive a blow you turn the other cheek to the smiter, that you forgive to a brother who has offended you, not merely seven times, but seventy times seven, and that you forgive all offences whatsoever, that you love your enemies, that you pray for those who injure you and persecute you. Can you do these things if you have not steadfastness in patience and the power of enduring? We see this fulfilled in Stephen, who when being put to death by the Jews, by violence and with stoning, pleaded not for vengeance against his slayers but for their forgiveness, crying out: *Lord, lay not this sin to their charge* (Acts vii. 59). It was fitting that the first martyr for Christ should be such a man, who, as the forerunner of all who as martyrs were to follow the example of his glorious death, was not alone a preacher of the Passion of Christ, but was also an imitator of His most gentle patience.

And what shall I say of anger, of discord, of strife: things which should have no place in the Christian heart? Let there be patience in the breast, and these things will have no place there! And should they try to enter they will speedily be excluded, and will depart, so that God may continue to have a peaceful abode in the heart where it pleases

Him to dwell. And so the Apostle counsels us, and teaches us, telling us: *Grieve not the Holy Spirit of God; whereby you are sealed unto the day of redemption. Let all bitterness, and anger, and indignation, and clamour, and blasphemy, be put away from you* (Eph. iv. 30). For if the Christian has left behind him rage and carnal striving, as one who comes in out of a stormy sea, and now within the harbour of Christ begins to be mild and gentle, he must permit neither anger nor discord to enter his breast; for he may neither hate anyone nor render evil for evil.

14 (17). *Patience in Bodily Afflictions.* Patience is necessary also that we may endure the various miseries of the flesh, and the sharp recurring afflictions of the body which weary and torment mankind each day of our lives. For ever since the first sin of disobedience, together with immortality, strength left our bodies, and since infirmity came with death, and since strength cannot return till immortality is restored, it is in this weakness and frailty that we have always to struggle and to fight. And we cannot sustain this struggle, this warfare, unless by the strength of patience.

And since we are to be proved and tested we have to endure much pain; and various kinds of trials are inflicted on us: by the loss of our possessions, by the heat of fever, by the pain of wounds, by the loss of our dear ones. And nothing will show more clearly the difference between good men and bad than the manner in which, in affliction, the wicked will complain and blaspheme in impatience, while the good man is proved by his patience; as it is written: *In thy sorrow endure, and in thy humiliations keep patience. For gold and silver are tried in the fire, but acceptable men in the furnace of humiliation* (Ecclus. ii. 4).

15 (19). *Evils of Impatience.* So that the good of patience may shine out even more, let us, Dearly Beloved, consider and compare what impatience leads to. For as patience is the gift of Christ, so impatience is an affliction of the devil. And just as he will be found patient in whom Christ dwells and abides, so he is ever impatient whose soul is in the keeping of the wickedness of the devil. Let us consider the commencement of all this. The devil bore with impatience that God was above himself, and that man was made in the image and likeness of God. Because of the first sin he perished in the beginning, and then ruined man. Adam failed to hold fast in patience to the divine favours he had received; and unable to endure the divine command of the forbidden food fell to death. And Cain was so impatient of his brother's gifts and sacrifices that he slew him. And Esau, impatient for a meal of lentils, lost his birthright, which then passed from the elder to the younger son.

And why in spite of the divine favours was the Jewish people so unbelieving and so ungrateful? Was it not because of the sin of impatience that they from the first turned away from God, unable to endure the delay while Moses spoke with God? And they dared to ask for profane gods, so that they came even to call a calf's head, and an image of clay, the *guide of their journey* (Ps. lxxix. 10). Nor did they cease from their impatience, since, ever impatient of the divine warnings, of the divine mildness, putting their prophets and certain just men to death, they rush on even to the crime of the Cross, and to the Blood of the Lord.

Even within the Church impatience has made heretics, and, after the manner of the Jews, has driven them on to war against charity and the peace of Christ, and to hostile raging hatreds. And so, without speaking of every single example, everything whatsoever which patience by its labour raises to the glory of God, impatience brings down in ruins.

16 (20). *The Merits of Patience.* And thus, Dearly Beloved, having carefully considered both the good of patience andthe evils of impatience, let us with all watchfulness keep a firm hold on patience, by which we abide in Christ, so that together with Christ we may come to God: a patience that is manifold, generous, not taken up with petty things, and not enclosed within narrow limits. The power of patience spreads far and wide. Its richness and its generosity come forth from a source which has indeed but one name, but abounding in channels it flows forth by many ways to the praise and honour of God; nor can anything we do serve the divine glory, unless all our actions draw from this source steadfastness to complete them.

It is patience that commends us to God, and keeps us close to Him. It is patience that calms anger, restrains the tongue, controls the mind, safeguards peace, governs the manner in which we serve God, breaks down the onslaught of lust, lowers the swelling of pride, puts out the fires of enmity, curbs the arrogance of the rich, comforts the poor in their need, protects the blessed integrity of maidens, the steadfast virtue of the widow, the mutual love of spouses.

Patience makes men humble in prosperity, courageous in adversity, mild in the face of injuries and contempt. It teaches us how to forgive promptly those who offend us; and should we offend teaches us to plead long and earnestly for pardon. It withstands temptation, it endures persecution, it brings sufferings as well as martydoms to their perfect fulfilment. It is patience which makes firm the foundations of our faith. It is patience which subtly brings about the increase in our hope. It is patience which directs the mind to an awareness of what we are doing so that as we walk forward we may keep to the way of Christ. As long as we imitate the patience of our Father, this will enable us to continue to be Children of God.

17(21). But since I know, Dearly Beloved, that many because of the pain and the burthen of the injuries that oppress them are eager to be revenged on those who rage against them and torment them, and are not disposed to postpone to the final day the avenging of their wrongs, we exhort you to take to yourselves this blessing of patience; that placed as we are amid the storms of this changing world, and exposed to the persecutions of Jews and of Gentiles, and even of heretics, let us await in patience the day of the divine vengeance, and not rush on with fretful haste to avenge our sufferings, since it is written: *Expect me, saith the Lord, in the day of my resurrection that is to come, for my judgement is to assemble the Gentiles, and to gather the kingdoms; and to pour upon them my indignation* (Soph. iii. 8).

The Lord commands us to wait, and to endure with steadfast patience the coming day of the divine retribution. And in the Apocalypse He also says: *Seal not the words of the prophecy of this book: for the time is at hand. He that hurteth, let him hurt still: and he that is filthy, let him be filthy still, and he that is just, let him be justified still, and he that is holy, let him be sanctified still. Behold, I come quickly, and my reward is with me, to render to every man according to his works* (Apoc. xxii. 10–12). Because of this, even the Martyrs, their grief bursting forth from them, pressing forward and crying out for vengeance for their blood, are commanded to wait a little longer, and to show patience till the days are at an end and the number of the martyrs is complete. *And when*, he said, *he had opened the fifth seal, I saw under the altar the souls of them that were slain for the word of God, and for the testimony which they held. And they cried out with a loud voice, saying: How long, O Lord (holy and true) dost thou not judge and revenge our blood on them that dwell on the earth? and single white robes were given to every one of them; and it was said to them, that they should rest for a little time, till their fellow servants, and their brethren, who are to be slain, even as they, should be filled up* (Apoc. vi. 9–11).

18 (22). And in what manner the divine vengeance for the blood of the just shall come the Holy Spirit declares by the mouth of the prophet Malachy, where he says: *Behold the day of the Lord comes as a burning furnace; and all the proud, and all that do wickedness shall be as stubble: and the day that cometh shall set them afire, saith the Lord of hosts* (Mal. iv. 1). And the same we read in the psalms. *God shall come manifestly: our God shall come, and shall not keep silence. A fire shall burn before him: and a mighty tempest shall be round about him. He shall call from heaven above, and the earth, to judge his people. Gather ye together his saints to him: who set his covenant before sacrifices. And the heavens shall declare his justice: for God is judge* (Ps. xlix. 3–6).

And Isaias foretells the same. *For behold the Lord will come with fire, and his chariots are like a whirlwind, to render his wrath in indignation, and his rebuke with flames of fire. For the Lord shall judge by fire, and by his sword unto all flesh* (Is. lxvi. 15). And again: *The Lord God of Hosts shall go forth and shall threaten war, and stir up zeal; he shall cry out upon his enemies with strength. I have been silent, shall I keep silent for ever?* (Is. xlii. 13).

19 (23). Who is this Who says He has kept silence, but will not keep silence for ever? It is He Who was truly led as a sheep to the slaughter; and Who as a lamb silent before the shearer opened not his mouth. It is He Who did not cry out, and Whose voice was not heard in the streets (Is. liii. 7; xlii. 2). It was He Who was not rebellious, Who did not defend Himself: for He offered His back to the scourgers, and his cheeks to the hands that struck him, and turned not away his face from the foulness of their spittle. It is indeed He Who when accused by the High Priests and Elders answered

not; and Who before Pilate *answered never a word so the Governor wondered exceedingly*. It is He Who though silent in His Passion shall not be silent in His divine vengeance. This is He: our God! Not the God of all men, but of the faithful, and of those who believe in Him, Who when He comes, at His Second Coming, shall appear openly and shall not keep silence. For though He first came hidden in lowliness, in the might of His Power He shall come openly.

20 (24). Let us wait for Him, dearly Beloved, our Judge and our Avenger; Who shall revenge, together with Himself, the people of His Church and the number of all the just from the beginning of the world. Let him who is impatient and eager for vengeance remember, that He Who shall avenge us is Himself unavenged. God the Father has decreed that His Son shall be adored, and, mindful of the divine command, Paul the Apostle teaches us and declares: *God hath exalted him, and hath given him a name which is above all names: that in the name of Jesus every knee should bow, of those that are in heaven, on earth, and under the earth* (Phil. ii. 9–10). And the Angel in the Apocalypse resisted John when he wishes to adore him, and said to him: *See thou do it not: for I am thy fellow servant, and of thy brethren. Adore the Lord Jesus* (Apoc. xxii. 9).

How wondrous the Lord Jesus and how great His patience! That He Who is adored in heaven should remain unavenged on earth! Let us, Beloved Brethren, in our suffering and persecutions be mindful of His patience. Let us offer Him a submission filled with expectation of His Coming! Let us not rush forward in irreverent and unbecoming haste, to be revenged before our Lord: servants as we are! Let us rather stand fast and labour on, keeping watch with all our hearts; and let us observe the commandments of the Lord, steadfast to endure all things, so that when that day of wrath and vengeance shall come, we may not be punished with the wicked and with the sinful, but may be crowned with the just and with those who fear the Lord. Amen.

II. St John Chrysostom, Bishop and Doctor

The Promise of the Holy Spirit[5]

John xvi. 5–15. Severe is the effect upon the soul of despondency; and we need much fortitude if we are to resist this feeling with courage, taking from it what may be of profit to us, then putting the rest from us. For despondency has its uses. For when we commit wrong, ourselves or other men, then is it truly a good thing to grieve. But should we fall into the ordinary human misfortunes, then to give way to despondency is of no value whatever. And when despondency shook the not yet confirmed Disciples, see how Christ restored them by a rebuke. For they who had before questioned Him without end; as when Peter said: *Whither goest thou?* And Thomas: *Lord, we know not whither thou goest: and how can we know the way?* And Philip: *Show us the Father* (Jn. xiii. 36; xiv. 5, 8); these men, hearing now that, *they will put you out of the synagogues*, and that men will hate them; and that they who killed them, *will think they do a service to God*, became so despondent that they were wordless, and had nothing to say to Him.

And He reproached them for this, and said to them: *I told you not these things from the beginning, because I was with you. And now I go to him that sent me, and none of you asketh me: Whither goest thou? But because I have spoken these things to you, sorrow hath filled your heart.* For excessive sorrow is a danger to the soul; and a danger that leads to death. Because of it Paul says: *Comfort him lest perhaps such a one be swallowed up with overmuch sorrow* (II Cor. ii. 7).

But, He says, *I told you not these things from the beginning.* Why did He not tell them these things from the beginning? So that no one might say He was as it were guessing from what was wont to happen. And why did He begin to speak of so painful a subject? These things I knew from the beginning, He says, and I did not speak of them, not because I did not know about them, but *because I was with you.* And this He said in a very human way, as though saying: because you were safe, and could ask me for whatever you wished; and also because it was against Me the attacks of the enemy were directed; and there was no need in the beginning to speak of these things.

But did He not tell them these things? Did He not call the Twelve together, and say to them: *You shall be brought before governors and before kings, and they will scourge you in their synagogues* (Mt. x. 18, 19). Why then does He say: *I told you not these things from the beginning*? Though He foretold arrests and scourgings, He had not told them that slaying them would be regarded as so meritorious that it would be held as doing a service to God. This would have caused them the most profound despondency: that they should be regarded as the equal of blasphemers and robbers. Besides, He here also foretold the sufferings they would undergo at the hands of the Gentiles; and told them also, but now more strongly, what they would suffer from the Jews; and that these things were now about to happen.

And now I go to him that sent me, and none of you asketh me: Whither goest thou? But because I have spoken these things to you, sorrow hath filled your heart. It was no small consolation to them that He knew the depth of their despondency. For they were out of their minds with anxiety, because of His going from them, and also through fear of the terrible things that were to come; for they did not know if they could meet them with courage. Why did He not tell them these things afterwards, when they had received the Holy Ghost? That you may learn how extremely worthy they were. For if they did not, though yet unstrengthened by the Holy Spirit, turn away, overwhelmed though they were with sorrow, consider what they would be when filled with grace. For had they then heard these things, and stood firm, we would have said all this was due to the Holy Spirit. Now it is the fruit entirely of their own mind; showing clearly how great was their love of Christ; Who was now testing their yet untried spirit.

But I tell you the truth. See how

He again consoles them. I do not speak to please you, He says; but, though you be grieved beyond measure, it is better that you should hear. You desire that I remain with you; it is better otherwise. It is the duty of a Protector not to spare his friends, in what is to their advantage. *If I go not, the Paraclete will not come to you.* What do they say to this, they who have not a true belief regarding the Spirit? Is it fitting that the Master leaves, that the servant may come? See how great is the dignity of the Spirit?

But if I go, I will send him to you. And to what gain? *When he is come, he will convince the world*; that is, they will not do these things unpunished, when He comes. What has been done already (by Me), is enough to answer them. But when these things are also done by Him, when doctrine is more perfected, and miracles greater, yet more shall they be blamed; seeing so many wonders done in My Name: so that the proof of the Resurrection becomes ever more striking. Now they are able to say, 'this is the son of the carpenter, whose mother and whose father we knew'. But when they see death overcome, evil driven away, the one that was lame from birth now walking upright, demons cast out, the immense outpouring of the Spirit, and all this done at the invocation of My Name, what will they say? The Father has given testimony of Me; the Spirit will also give testimony. He bore witness to Me at the beginning; and once again shall He do this.

What does He mean by, He will convince the world *of sin*? This means He will take away all their excuses, and make clear to them that they have been offending most unforgiveably. *And of justice, because I go to the Father; and you shall see me no longer*; that is, that I have led a life of perfect justice: and the proof is that I go to the Father. For since they were forever accusing Him that He was not of God, and therefore called Him a sinner, and a transgressor of the Law, this ground of reproach will also be taken from them. For if the accusation that I am not of God shows me to be a sinner, then when the Spirit shall show that I have gone thither, and not for a time, but to abide there forever (for this is what *you shall see me no longer* means), what then will they say?

See how by these two means their evil suspicion is removed. For to work miracles is not in the character of a hardened sinner (for a sinner cannot work miracles); neither is it the sign of a sinner that He should dwell with God for ever. And so you can no longer say that This Man is a sinner; or that He is not of God.

And of judgement: because the prince of this world is already judged. Here again He begins to speak of justness; that He has cast down His adversary. This no sinner could do; neither had any just man among men been able to do this. That he was condemned through Me, they shall know who shall hereafter tread upon him; and who shall clearly see the meaning of My Resurrection: the Sign of Him Who has passed sentence upon him. For he could not hold Me. And since they declared that I had a devil, and that I was a deceiver, these things will also be seen as false. For I could not have overcome him had I been subject to him through sin.

But now he is condemned, and cast out.

I have yet many things to say to you: but you cannot bear them now. It seems to Me better that I go; so that you may be enabled to bear them, when I go. What then does this mean? Is the Spirit greater than You; that what we cannot bear now, He will then enable us to bear? Is His power and efficacy the greater? Far from it! For the words He shall speak are Mine. And so He says:

He shall not speak of himself; but what things soever he shall hear, he shall speak; and the things that are to come, he shall show you. He shall glorify me; because he shall receive of mine, and shew it to you. All things whatsoever the Father hath, are mine.

For since He had said, He *will teach you,* and *bring to your mind* (xiv. 26), and console you in affliction (which He has not Himself done), and that *it is expedient for you that I go,* and that He should come, and that now *you are not able to bear* (what I have to say), but then you will be able to bear them, and that He *will guide you to all truth*; and lest hearing all these things, they should think that the Spirit is the Greater, and so fall into grave error, He for this reason tells them that, *He shall receive of mine*; that is, whatever I have said to you, He shall say the same.

When he says, *He shall not speak of himself,* He means, nothing contrary, nothing of His own outside what I say. As for this reason when speaking of Himself He said: *I speak not of myself* (xiv. 10); that is, nothing outside of that which My Father has said; so the same is to be understood regarding the Holy Spirit. The words *of mine* mean: of the things which I know, of my own knowledge. For my knowledge and that of the Holy Spirit is one.

And the things that are to come, he shall show you. He raised up their minds; for the race of mankind are eager for nothing so much as to know the future. It was because of this they asked: *Whither goest thou?* Which is the way? To deliver them from this anxiety He says: He will foretell all things to you, lest they come upon you unawares.

He shall glorify me. How? In My Name He will give you powers. For since upon His coming they will work yet greater wonders, He again emphasises Their equality of honour, and says: *He shall glorify me.*

What means: *He will teach you all truth*? For this also He testifies regarding Him, that He will lead them to all truth. For He, because He was clothed in flesh, and because He wished not to appear as speaking of Himself, and because they did not understand clearly regarding His Resurrection, and were still unformed, and because of the Jews, that they might not appear to punish Him as a transgressor of the Law, He was wont to utter nothing striking regarding Himself,[6] and neither did He openly withdraw them from the Law. But when the Disciples were cut off from the Jews, and set apart from the rest of the people, and many were about to believe, and be cleansed of their sins; and when others spoke about Him, He did not then, fittingly, say any great things concerning Himself.

And therefore it is not to be set down to My ignorance, that I said not the things that I should have said, but rather to the weakness of those who listened. So when He said, *He will teach you all truth,* He added, *He shall not speak of himself.* That the Spirit needed not to be taught, hear what Paul has to say: *So the things that are of God no man knoweth, but the Spirit of God* (I Cor. ii. 11). Just as the spirit of man knows, though not learning from another, so the Holy Spirit *shall receive of mine*; that is, He shall speak in agreement with Me. *All things the Father hath, are mine.* Since therefore these things are mine, He will speak of the things of the Father, if He speaks *of mine*.

But why did the Spirit not come before He had departed? Because the curse was not yet taken away, sin not yet undone, and all men still subject to vengeance, He did not come. It was necessary therefore that this state of enmity should come to an end; that we first be reconciled to God; and then receive this gift. But why does He say: *I will send him to you*? This means: I shall prepare you to receive Him. For how can He be sent Who is everywhere? By this also He makes plain to us the distinction of Persons. For these two reasons has He spoken; and since they would continue to hold fast to Himself, He exhorts them that they should hold fast to the Spirit, that so they might serve Him.

He could have wrought these wonders Himself, but He disposed that the Spirit should work them, for this reason: that they might learn of His dignity. For the Father could have brought into existence all things which are; but the Son has done this that we might learn of His power. So also is it here. For this *He* was made flesh, reserving the inward actions to the Spirit; closing the mouths of those who would seize upon this proof of His unspeakable goodness as a pretext for impiety. For when they say that the Son was made flesh, because He was inferior to the Father, we answer: What then do you say of the Spirit? For He did not take flesh; and you may not on that account say that He is greater than the Son; or that the Son is inferior to Him?

For this reason is the Trinity received in Baptism. For the Father could bring about the whole effect, as could the Son, and the Holy Ghost. But since no man doubts concerning the Father, but there has been doubt concerning the Son, and the Holy Spirit, They have been included in the sacred rite, that from their joint giving of these unspeakable blessings, we may learn of their common glory. For that the Son can of Himself do that which He does together with the Father in baptism, and so likewise the Holy Ghost, listen clearly to these words. For speaking to the Jews He said: *That you may know that the Son of man hath power on earth to forgive sins*; and again: *That you may be the children of light*; and: *And I give them life everlasting*; and later: *That they may have life, and may have it more abundantly* (Jn. xii. 36; x. 28, 10).

Let us consider the Holy Ghost also doing this same thing. Where? *And the manifestation of the Spirit*, it says, *is given to every man unto profit.* He Who gives this, much more does He forgive sin. And again: *It is the Spirit that quickeneth; Shall quicken you because of his Spirit that dwelleth in you;* and: *But the spirit liveth because of justification*; and again: *But if you are led by the Spirit, you are not under the Law. For you have not received the spirit of bondage again in fear; but you have received the Spirit of adoption of sons* (I Cor. xii. 7; Rom. viii. 11; Gal. v. 18; Rom. viii. 15).

And whatever they did in this time, after the Holy Ghost had come, they did in a wondrous manner. Paul, writing to the Corinthians declares: *But you are washed, you are sanctified, in the name of the Lord Jesus Christ, and the Spirit of our God* (I Cor. vi. 11). For they had been hearing many things regarding the Father; and the Son they had seen working His wonders; but of the Holy Spirit they yet knew nothing clearly, such as that He wrought wonders, and would bring them to the fulness of knowledge.

But, as I have said, that the Spirit might not on this account be regarded as the greater, the Lord says: *What things soever he shall hear, he shall speak; and the things that are to come he shall show you.* If this is not true, is it not absurd to say that he will hear them only because of those whom He was instructing? Then, according to you, He was to hear these things only because of the Disciples? What could be more unfounded? And what was He to learn? Had He not Himself already revealed all these things by the mouth of the Prophets? If He is to speak to them regarding the ending of the Law, has this not already been declared? Or of Christ, and of His Divinity and Incarnation, these things had also been spoken of. What remained to be said clearly?

And the things that are to come, he shall show you. Here most of all He reveals the dignity of the Holy Spirit. For to foretell what is to come belongs to God alone. And were He to learn of these things from others, He is no greater than the Prophets. But here Christ is speaking of knowledge in exact conformity with the divine knowledge; other than which the Spirit will not utter. But the words: *He shall receive of mine*, means, either the graces which accompanied my Flesh, or the knowledge which is Mine also; and receiving it, not as needing it, or as learning it from others, but through partaking of One and the same Being.

And why did He speak precisely in this way? Because they had had no instruction concerning the Holy Spirit? He was here preparing them for one thing only: That they should believe in Him, and accept Him, and not resist Him. For since He had said: *One is your teacher, Christ* (Mt. xxiii. 8), so that they might not feel they were unfaithful to Christ in believing in Him, He says: My teaching and His teaching is one; of the things I should have taught you, of these He will speak. Do not think His words will differ from Mine; for His are Mine, and they will confirm what I have taught you. For One is the Will of the Father, and of the Son, and of the Holy Ghost. And this He also wishes for us, as when he said: *That they may be one, as we also are one* (xvii. 11).

There is nothing that compares with unity and harmony; for by it one is made many. For if two or ten are one in mind, each is one no longer; rather each one is multiplied by ten: and in the ten you will find but one, but in each one there are ten. Should they have an enemy, he who attacks one of them finds that it is as if he had attacked ten. And because of this he is defeated. For he meets, not one, but ten opponents. Is one among them in want? But he will not be in want: for he has plenty in his greater part, that is, in the other nine; and the part in need is helped: the lesser part by the greater. Each of them has twenty hands, twenty eyes, as many feet. He sees, not with his own two eyes only, but with those of the others. He is sustained, not merely upon his own two feet, but also on those of the others. He labours, not with his own hands alone, but with the hands of the others who are with him. He has ten lives; for not alone does he have a care for himself, but the others also have a care for him. And if they were a hundred it is the same; except that their power would be greater still.

See for yourself how strong is the bond of love; how it makes one man unconquerable; how one man becomes many men; how one man can even be in many places, the same man in both Rome and Persia. That what nature cannot do, love can. For one part of him will be here, and one there; rather he will be wholly here and wholly there. Should we have a thousand, or two thousand, friends, consider how far his power extends. See what enlargement love bestows; for the wonder lies in this, in making one a thousand. Why should we not enrich ourselves by this power, and make ourselves secure? For this power surpasses all power, and all wealth. This is above health; and greater than anything else a man has. This is the ground of happiness. How long then shall we confine our love to one or two?

Let us consider the matter from the opposite view. Let us suppose there is a man who has no friends (for, *a fool will say: I have no friend*) (Ecclus. xx. 16; LXX). What sort of life is that? For though he may be rich, abounding in wealth and luxury, have endless possessions, yet he is entirely alone and defenceless. It is not so with those who have friends. Though they may be poor they have more resources than the rich; and what a man will not venture to say in his own behalf, a friend will say for him. What he cannot provide by himself he can by another, and more. In this way he owns the means of happiness and security. No great harm can come to one defended by so many spears. The king's guards are not so watchful and diligent as these. They watch through necessity and fear; these through love and kindness, and love is stranger than fear. The king goes in fear even of his own guards. This man has more trust in his friends than in himself; and trusting in them he is afraid of no one.

Let us begin then to acquire these riches. The poor man that he may be comforted in his poverty; the rich man that he may hold his riches in security; the prince that he may rule in safety; the subject that he may have kind rulers. This is the beginning of the rule of mildness; the foundation of gentleness; since even among the beasts those are the most ferocious and wild which do not herd together. It is for this we dwell in cities, and have our market places; that we may mingle with one another. This also Paul laid upon us, saying: *Not forsaking our assembly* (Heb. x. 25). For nothing is as grievous as being alone, and to be friendless and unapproachable.

But what of the monk, you will

say? What of those who dwell in the mountains? They are not without friends. Though they turn away from the common life, they have many companions in the spirit. They are close bound to one another in love; and have withdrawn from the world the better to fulfil this purpose. For contentiousness in the things of the world is the cause of many quarrels. Because of this they retire from it: that they may love more perfectly.

But how can a man have friends if he is alone, you will say? For I desire that as many as possible live in friendship; provided the grounds of their friendship do not alter. For it is not the place makes friends. For the monks have friends who praise them, and who would not praise them if they did not love them. And again, they pray for all men; the greatest proof of their love. It is because of this that we embrace each other at the Sacred Mysteries: that the many may be one. And we make prayer in common for those not initiated; we pray for the sick, for the fruits of the earth, of the land and of the sea. See the power of love; in prayer, in the Mysteries, in all our exhortations!

This is the cause of all good things. If we abide in this with care we shall order all things rightly in our present life, and move onwards to the kingdom which we all desire to reach, by the love and grace of Our Lord Jesus Christ, to Whom with the Father and the Holy Spirit be there glory and honour for ever and ever. Amen.

III. St Augustine, Bishop and Doctor

Exposition of the Gospel[7]

1. John xvi. 5–7. When the Lord Jesus had foretold to His Disciples the persecutions they were to suffer when He had gone from them, He went on to say: *But I told you not these things from the beginning, because I was with you: And now I go to him that sent me*. Here the first thing we must consider is whether he had not already foretold these sufferings? The other Evangelists make it clear that He had foretold these happenings, and previous to the Last Supper (Mt. xxiv. 9; Mk. xiii. 9–13; Lk. xxi. 12–17), at the close of which, as John tells us, He said: *But I told you not these things from the beginning, because I was with you*. The question may be answered in this way. That, they also relate that He was close to the Passion when He said these words. It was not therefore at *the beginning*, while He was with them, that He told them these things. For now He was about to leave them to go to His Father. So, even according to these Evangelists what is here said is true, namely, that *I told you not these things from the beginning*.

But what of our trust in the Gospel of Matthew, who relates that these things were revealed to them by the Lord, not alone on the eve of His Passion, when He desired to take supper with His Disciples, but also at the beginning, when the Apostles were first spoken of by name, and sent forth to do the work of God (Mt. x. 17). What then does He mean when He says in this place: *I told you not these things from the beginning, because I was with you,* but the things He was telling them of the Holy Ghost: that He is to come, and that He will testify to them when they are about to suffer these trials. These things He had not told them from the beginning, because *He* was with them.

2. The comforter therefore, or Advocate (for the Greek word Paraclete may be interpreted by either word) now became necessary, since Christ was leaving them. And as His own presence was their comfort as long as He remained with them, He had not therefore spoken of the Holy Spirit. Now however that He was leaving them, it was necessary to speak of the Spirit's Coming, by Whom it would be brought about, by reason of the charity He would pour into their hearts, that they would preach the word of God without fear. And by reason of His testimony, within them, to Christ, they would also bear witness to Christ. Nor would they be scandalized when their enemies, the Jews, would put them out of the synagogues, and think that they did a service to God by putting them to death; since the charity which was to be poured into their hearts by the Holy Spirit *beareth all things* (Rom. v. 5; I Cor. xiii. 7).

It is here then that His meaning is made clear to us: that He would make them martyrs, that is, witnesses to Him, by means of the Holy Spirit, so that through the working of the Holy Spirit within them they would be able to bear the sharp anguish of every persecution; and that inflamed by this divine fire their hearts would not grow cold in the preaching of the Gospel. *These things*, He says, *I have told you,that when the hour shall come, you may remember that I told you of them.* I have told you these things, not alone because you will suffer such things, but so that you shall not be silent through fear of them, and so you will give testimony of Me. *But I told you not these things from the beginning, because I was with you*; because I was Myself your Comforter, through My Bodily Presence before your eyes, which you could, as children could, take in.

3. *But now I go to him that sent me, and none of you*, He says, *asketh me: Whither goest thou?* He means that He will go from them in such a manner that no one will ask Him about that which they will see taking place openly before their eyes. For earlier they had questioned Him as to where He was going. And He had answered He was going where they could not follow Him (Jn. xiii. 36). Now He says He will leave them in such a manner that none of them will ask Him where He is going. For when He ascended from their midst a cloud received Him; and as He went up to heaven, they did not ask him any questions, but followed Him upwards with their eyes (Acts i. 9–11).

4. *But because I have spoken these things to you, sorrow hath filled your heart*, He says. For He clearly saw the effects His words were producing in their hearts. For since they had not yet within their souls the inward consolation they were to receive through the Holy Spirit, they began now to be fearful of losing what they outwardly beheld of Christ. And

since they could not believe that they were to lose Him, for on this the Truth had spoken, it was their human hearts that began to grieve because they were to see no more His Bodily Presence.

But He knew what was expedient for them. For that inward vision with which the Holy Spirit would comfort them was indeed better. Not that He was as it were to pour some created substance into the bodies of those who shall see Him, but that He shall infuse Himself into the breasts of those who believe. Accordingly He says: *But I tell you the truth: it is expedient to you that I go: for if I go not the Paraclete will not come to you; but if I go, I will send him to you.* As though He said: It is better for you that this outward *form of a servant* be taken from among you. As the Word made Flesh I do in truth dwell amongst you. But I desire that you no longer love me in a bodily manner, and satisfied with this milk, like infants, as it were, look for it always. *It is expedient to you that I go: for if I go not, the Paraclete will not come to you.* If I do not take from you this food of young minds with which I have reared you, you will not come to look for solid food. If you cling in a bodily manner to this Body, you shall not be able to receive the Spirit.

For what does this mean: *If I go not, the Paraclete will not come to you; but if I go, I will send him to you?* Could He not send Him while yet on earth? Who would say that? Or had the Spirit withdrawn from where the Spirit was; or had He so come from the Father that He was no longer with the Father? How was He not capable, while here on earth, of sending Him Whom we know descended upon Him at His baptism, and remained with Him (Jn. i. 32); more, from Whom He was not at any time separable? What then does He mean by: *If I go not the Paraclete will not come to you*, if not that you cannot receive the Spirit as long as you continue to know Christ in the Flesh? Because of this, he who had already received the Spirit, now says: *And if we have known Christ according to the flesh; but now we know him so no longer* (II Cor. v. 16). For even he who spiritually knew the Word made Flesh, did not corporally know the Body of Christ. This then the Good Master meant when he said: *For if I go not, the Paraclete will not come to you; but if I go, I will send him to you.*

5. But though Christ was leaving them bodily, not alone was the Holy Ghost spiritually with them, but the Father also and the Son. For had Christ so left them that the Holy Ghost was not together with Him in them but rather in His place, what then became of His promise: *Behold I am with you all days, even to the consummation of the world* (Mt. xxviii. 20); for though He had promised He would send them the Holy Spirit, so also had He promised He would be with them for ever. And since from being earthly minded they were to become spiritual, it would follow that they were then to possess more abundantly the Father, Son, and Holy Ghost.

For we must believe that the Father is in no one without the Son and Holy Ghost, or the Father and the Son without the Holy Ghost, or the Son without the Father and the Holy Ghost, or the Holy Ghost without the Father and the Son, or the Father and the Holy Ghost without the Son; but that where One is there the Trinity One God will be. But the Trinity had to be brought to our minds; that though between them there was no distinction of nature, yet there has been set before us a distinction of Persons, in Whom a distinction of natures can never be discerned by those who have a right understanding.

6. That which follows: *And when he is come, he will convince the world of sin, and of justice, and of judgement; of sin because they believed not in me; and of justice, because I go to the Father; and you shall see me no longer; and of judgement, because the prince of this world is already judged*: as though not to believe in Christ alone was sin; and as though it were justness in us not to see Christ; and as though this is judgement: that the prince of this world, that is, the devil, is already judged; all this is extremely obscure, and must not be briefly treated in this discourse, lest through brevity it become more obscure, and so must rather be left for another sermon: to be explained to you as the Lord shall help us. Amen.

IV. St Augustine, Bishop and Doctor

The Ascension of Christ's Mystical Body[8]

John xvi. 8–11. I. *Why the world is reproached for the sin of unbelief.* When Our Lord and Saviour Jesus Christ had spoken at length of the Coming of the Holy Ghost, Whom He promised to send into the world, and did send, among many other things He said: *He will convince the world of sin, and of justice, and of judgement.* And when He had said this He did not then pass on to something else, but condescended to explain this more fully. *Of sin,* He said, *because they believe not in me: and of justice, because I go to the Father; and of judgement, because the prince of this world is already judged.*

There arises therefore within us a desire to understand why it is that the Holy Ghost should correct the world for this sin only: of not believing in Christ: as though this were the only sin that men commit. And if it is plain that besides the sin of unbelief men commit many other sins, why does the Holy Ghost rebuke the world for this alone? Is it that all other sins remain unforgiven because of unbelief, and forgiven when we believe: that God as it were holds this against us above all the rest, so that the rest remain unforgiven as long as man in his pride refuses to believe in an humble God? For so it is written: *God resisteth the proud, and giveth grace to the humble* (Jas. iv. 6). For the grace of God is a gift of God. But the greatest gift is the Holy Ghost Himself: and so for this He is called grace. For since all have sinned, all have needed the glory of God (Rom. iii. 23). For sin entered into this world through one man (and through sin death, in whom all have sinned (Rom. v. 12); and because of this grace, because it is given gratis. He is therefore freely given, since He is not given in reward after an examination of our merits, but as a gift after our sins are forgiven.

2. *To believe Christ is not to believe in Christ.* The unbelieving, that is,

the lovers of this world, are made to believe in the reality of sin; for it is they who are meant by *the world.* For when He said: *He will convince the world of sin*, the sin is none other than that they have not believed in Christ. And so, should the soul be free of this sin, then no sins will remain upon it, because to the just man who lives in his faith all things are forgiven.

But there is a great difference between a man believing He is Christ, and believing in Christ. For that He is Christ even the demons believed; but the demons did not believe in Christ. *For he believes in Christ who hopes in Christ, and loves Christ.* Should he have faith, but be without hope and without love, he believes that Christ is, but he does not believe in Christ. He therefore who believes in Christ, believing in Christ, Christ comes to him, and he is in a certain manner united to Christ, and made a member of His Body. This cannot be unless hope is added and likewise charity.

3. *Of what justice is the world convinced?* What does He mean when He says: *And of justice: because I go to the Father*? And first we must ask why, if the world is convinced of sin, must it also be convinced of justice? For who can rightly be reproached of justice? Is it that the world is not to be convinced of its own justice, but of the justness of Christ? I do not see what else we can understand; since He says: *Of sin, because they have not believed in me; of justice because I go to the Father.* They have not believed in Him; He goes to the Father. It is a question therefore of their sin, and of His justness.

But why does He speak of justness on this ground only: that He is going to the Father? Was it not out of justice that He also came to us from the Father? Or did He come to us from the Father out of mercy; but because of His justice He goes to the Father?

4. *Wherefore does Christ go to the Father because of justice?* And so, brethren, I believe that it is expedient that in this so profound portion of the Scriptures, in whose words there may perhaps lie hidden something which should rightly be brought to light, let us as it were seek together for it, relying on God, so that we may merit to find it to the profit of our souls. Why then does He call that justice, that He is going to the Father, and not also that He came from the Father?

Is it because He *came* out of mercy, so because of His justice He *goes*; that we too may learn that justice cannot be perfected in us unless we fulfil the demands of mercy; *seeking not our own things, but also the things of others*? And when the Apostle had warned us in this way, He went on to add an example from the Lord Himself: *Let nothing be done through contention, neither by vain glory: but in humility, let each esteem others as better than themselves: each one not considering the things that are his own, but those that are other men's.* Then he adds immediately: *For let this mind be in you, which was also in Christ Jesus: who being in the form of God, thought it not robbery to be equal to God: but emptied himself, taking the form of a servant, being made in the likeness of men, and in habit found as a man: He humbled himself, becoming obedient unto death, even to the death of the cross.*

This is the mercy because of which He came to us from the Father. What then is the justice because of which He goes to the Father? The Apostle goes on to tell us: *For which cause God also hath exalted him, and hath given him a name which is above all names: that in the name of Jesus every knee should bow, of those that are in heaven, on earth, and under the earth: and that every tongue should confess the Lord Jesus Christ is in the glory of God the Father* (Phil. ii. 9–11). This is the justice because of which He goes to the Father.

5. *Christ alone ascends to heaven: One Christ, composed of Head and Members. Christ is one with the Father; In another way He is one with us.*

But if Christ alone goes to the Father, what gain is this to us? To what end is the world convinced of this justice by the Holy Ghost? Yet if He alone does not go to the Father, He would not in another place have said: *And no man ascended into heaven, but he that descended from heaven* (Jn. iii. 13). But Paul the Apostle also says: *But our conversation is in heaven* (Phil. iii. 20). And why is this? Because he also says: *If you be risen with Christ, seek the things that are above; where Christ is sitting at the right hand of God: Mind the things that are above, not the things that are upon the earth. For you are dead; and your life is hid with Christ in God* (Col. iii. 1–3).

How then is it He alone? Does this mean Christ alone, because He is one with all His Members, as a head is one with its body? And what is His Body if not the Church? As the same doctor tells us: *It is you are the Body of Christ; part of His Members* (I Cor. xii. 27).[9] And so since we were fallen, and He for our sake descended from heaven, what do these words mean: *No man has ascended into heaven, except he who has descended*, if not that no man ascends up to heaven who has not been made one with Him, and, as a Member, become hidden within the Body of Him Who has descended from heaven?

And so He said to His Disciples: *Without me you can do nothing* (Jn. xv. 5). For He is One with the Father in one way; He is one with us in another. He is One with the Father in that the Substance of the Father and the Son is One Substance. He is One with the Father in that while *being in the form of God, He thought it not robbery to be equal with God.* He became one with us in that he *emptied himself, taking the form of a servant.* He became one with us through the seed of Abraham, in whom all nations are blessed. And when the Apostle had commented on this, he said: *He saith not*, And to his seeds, *as of many: but as of one*, And to thy seed, *which is Christ* (Gal. iii. 13).

And because we also belong to That Which is Christ: in that we are closely fitted together, making One Body with This Head: Christ is one only. And this also because He said to us: *You are then the seed of Abraham, heirs according to the promise* (Gal. iii. 29). For if the seed of Abraham is one; and that *one* seed of Abraham is only to be understood of Christ; and we also are the seed of Abraham; then this Whole, that is, This Head and This Body, is One Christ.

6. *How Christ's Justice is Ours.* And so we are not to regard our-

selves as separated from that justice of which the Lord Himself speaks where He says: *Of justice, because I go to the Father*. For we also have risen with Christ, and we are joined now with Christ, through faith and hope: but our hope shall be fulfilled in the final resurrection of the dead. And when our hope is fulfilled, then will our justification be also fulfilled. And what we are to hope for the Lord, Who is to fulfil this, has shown us in His own Flesh (that is, in Our Head), in which He rose from the dead, and ascended into heaven. For so it was written: *He was delivered up for our sins, and rose again for our justification* (Rom. v. 25).

The world is then *convinced of sin* in those who do not believe in Christ; and *of justice* in those who rise again among the Members of Christ. For this was it said: *That we might be made the justice of God in him* (II Cor. v. 21). For if justness is not in Him, there is justness in no one. But if it is in Him, He goes, complete with us (Head and Members), to the Father; and this perfect justness will be completed in us. For this reason the world will be convinced of (*the reality of the*) *judgement; because the prince of this world is already judged*: that is, the devil, the prince of the unjust, whose hearts are given over to this world they love; and for this reason they are spoken of as *the world*; just as our resting place shall be in heaven, if we have risen with Christ.

Therefore, as Christ is one with us His Body, so the devil, together with all the wicked of whom he is head, is as it were one with his body. And as we are not separated from that justice because of which He said, *I go to the Father*, so the wicked are not separated from that judgement because of which He said, *the prince of this world is already judged*.

Turning then to the Lord Our God, the Father Almighty, let us as best we can give thanks with all our hearts, beseeching Him that in His goodness He will mercifully hear our prayers, and by his grace drive evil from our thoughts and actions, increase our faith, guide our minds, grant us His holy inspirations, and bring us to joy without end through His Son Our Lord and Saviour Jesus Christ. Amen.

V. St Cyril of Alexandria, Bishop and Doctor

The Mission of the Holy Spirit[10]

All that the Lord had to do on earth was now done; but it was necessary that we should become sharers and *partakers of the divine nature* (II Pet. i. 4) of the Word, or rather, that giving up our old life we should be changed to another, and be reformed in newness of life in a manner pleasing to God. But it was not possible to do this except through the possession and communion of the Holy Spirit. The most fitting and the most appropriate time for the mission of the Holy Spirit, and for His Descent upon us, was that which now opportunely arose, namely, after the going from our midst of Christ Our Saviour.

For as long as Christ remained bodily with those who believed in Him, He appeared to them, I think, as the Giver of every gift. But when it was time, and imperative that He should ascend to His heavenly

Father, then He was to be present to His worshippers by means of the Spirit, and dwell in their hearts by faith, so that possessing Him we might with courage cry: *Abba, Father*, and go forward in every virtue, and as having within us the all powerful Spirit be found strong and invincible against the assaults of men and the snares of the devil.

For is it not easy to show, as well from the Old as from the New Testament, that the Holy Spirit changes the disposition of those in whom He wills to be and to abide, and restores in them a newness of life? For the inspired Samuel, when speaking to Saul, says: *And the spirit of the Lord shall come upon thee, and thou shalt be changed into another man* (I Kings x. 6). But the blessed Paul says: *Now the Lord is a Spirit. And where the Spirit of the Lord is, there is liberty. But we all beholding the glory of the Lord with open face, are transformed into the same image from glory to glory, as by the Spirit of the Lord* (II Cor. iii. 17–18).

See then how the Spirit transforms those in whom He dwells! For He readily turns them away from their taste for earthly things to dwell on those that are in heaven; and from an unmanly cowardice to a courageous state of soul. And we cannot doubt that we shall find the Disciples so changed, and so strengthened by the Spirit, that they were in no way dismayed by the assaults of their persecutors, and holding fast to the love that is in Christ. What the Saviour said then is true: *It is expedient to you that I go*. For it was then the time appointed for the descent of the Spirit.

When He had made it clear to His Disciples that His going to the Father is the fitting time for the mission and the descent upon them of the Spirit, and after He had in this way greatly eased their profound grief, He reveals to them what it is the Paraclete will do. *When he is come*, He says, *he will convince the world of sin, and of justice, and of judgement*. And He clearly teaches us in what form the reproach contained in these sayings will take. But since there are those who cannot readily perceive these things, I feel that I must explain each saying in turn, and state more clearly their meaning.

The reproach of sin is placed first. In what manner will He convince the world? When those who love Christ, that is, the just, are convinced of sin; that is, that He will condemn the world, which means the ignorant and the unbelieving who continue unbelieving, and those held fast by the delights of the world, because of this fact, that they are enslaved by their own vices, and must die because of their offences. For God shall not be a respecter of persons; and to some in this world He will grant His Spirit without just cause, to others He will not grant it at all; but He will have the Paraclete only in those who are worthy of Him, Who in perfect faith worship Him as truly God, confessing that He is the Creator and Lord of the universe. And so what Our Saviour earlier told the Jews: *If you believe not that I am he, you shall die in your sins* (Jn. viii. 24), the Paraclete when He comes will show to be true because of their deeds.

Then He says: *He will convince the world of justice: because I go to the Father; and you shall see me no longer*. For He shall, fittingly, give His wisdom to those who have believed in Christ after His Resurrection, as being, and rightly, justified. For they received Him as True God, though they had not seen Him, and believed that He is enthroned with the Father. For if you recall to mind what Thomas said and did, you will learn that Christ called those blessed who so believe in Him. For while He still doubted the Resurrection of the Son he said: *Except I see in his hands the print of the nails, and put my hand into his side, I will not believe* (Jn. xx. 25). And when, after Christ had suffered him to do this, he then believed, what words did he hear: *Because thou hast seen me, Thomas, thou hast believed: blessed are they that have not seen, and have believed* (Jn. xx. 29).

Rightly then have they been justified who without seeing Him have believed in Christ; but the world will lose the possession of this blessedness, not seeking to possess the justice that comes by faith, preferring to remain in its own wickedness.

We must know that these two reproaches are meant, not for the Jews alone, but rather for every man who shall be stubborn and resistant to the Paraclete. For by the term *world* is meant not alone the man who is endlessly absorbed in seeking pleasure, and does not leave behind the devil's wickedness, but all who are scattered throughout the whole world, and dwell there. So this double reproof is addressed to all men. For Christ has called to salvation not alone the Jews, the seed of Abraham, as in the beginning, but the whole fallen race of Adam. For His grace is without measure; and the gift of faith is offered to the whole world.

The third reproach of the Holy Spirit shall be, as the Saviour tells us, that most merited condemnation of the prince of this world. And how this will come to pass I shall explain. The Paraclete will testify to the glory of Christ, showing that He is indeed the Lord of the universe, and will show the world its error, in that abandoning Him Who is by nature God they have fallen down before and worshipped one who is not by nature God; that is, Satan. For the judgement against him suffices, I believe, to show that such is the case. For he could not have been condemned, and have forfeited his power, nor paid the penalty of his presumption against God, and been cast into the pit of darkness, if he were by nature God, Who sits Enthroned, serene in power and glory.

Now so far is he from being able to preserve his own honour, that it is trodden under the feet of those who are spiritual; I mean the faithful who confess that Christ is God. For they trample on him as he strives to tempt or trouble them. So when you see the swarm of unclean spirits, frightened and driven out by the prayers of such persons, and by the power and operation of the Holy Spirit, can you not then justly say that Satan is condemned? For he is condemned in that he is no longer able to oppress by his power those *who are signed with the Holy Spirit* unto justice and holiness of life, through faith in Christ (Eph. i. 13–15).

How otherwise I ask you have we trodden his power under foot, according to what the psalmist says of every man who rests on the help of the Most High? *Thou shalt walk upon the asp and the basilisk: and thou shalt trample under foot the lion and the dragon* (Ps. xc. 13). Therefore, when the Paraclete from heaven enters the soul of the Just, sent fittingly to them because of their faith, He will then convince the world that it is held fast in its own sins, and deprived of the grace of heaven because they turned from the Redeemer. And also He will reprove the world for falsely accusing of sin those who have believed. For they have indeed been justified; for though they did not behold God as He worked His miracles or as He ascended into heaven, yet they love and honour Him by faith. It was, I believe, with some such thought in mind that the Apostle said: *Who shall accuse against the elect of God? God that justifieth* (Rom. viii. 33). *For the just shall see and rejoice, and all iniquity shall stop its mouth* (Ps. cvi. 42); according to the words of the psalmist: since it can lay nothing to the charge of the Elect Who are crowned with the justice that comes from faith.

He will reprove the world as gone astray, resting its hopes in him who has been so condemned that he has lost all the glory of his former state, and is held as nothing by those who worship God. God then called him *the prince of this world*, not as being so in truth, or as though he possessed the dignity of a ruler inherent in him, but because he holds the glory of this world by fraud and violence, and because he still rules those in error, and because of their own evil wills he exercises authority over them by which, their minds held fast in error,[11] they are themselves inevitably entangled in the bonds of slavery; though it is in their power to escape, by being converted through faith in Christ to the knowledge of the True God. Satan then is but a pretender to the name of prince, and has no natural right to it, and holds it only because of the execrable wickedness of those who have gone astray. Amen.

NOTES

[1] Unauthentic. Possibly work of Ambrosiaster, or various others. PRM 35.

[2] PG 39, 1063, 33.

[3] PL 10, De Trin. Bk. 8, 20.

[4] PL 4, 621. A perfect and sublimely simple Christian discourse. Here is the purest conception of the Christian's life, uttered amid the very fires of persecution; when, at this cost, the Way of Christ was taught and upheld. The flowering of Christian life, the reformation of human society, was without doubt accomplished through these patristic homilies, providing its inspiration and its doctrinal basis; the homilies in turn deriving from the reading and exposition of the Sacred Books, as well as from the Teaching of the Saviour handed down in the Teaching and practice of the Church.

[5] PG 59, Hom. 78 in John.

[6] *οὐδὲν μέγα.*

[7] PL 35, Tract 94, in John.

[8] PL 38, Sermon 144.

[9] St Augustine's version is: *Vos autem estis corpus Christi, et membra ex parte.*

[10] PL 74, *in loco.*

[11] Completely exemplified in the diabolical ideologies of these times; and by the terroristic methods by which they hold fast to power.

FIFTH SUNDAY AFTER EASTER AND THE ROGATION DAYS

I. St Basil the Great: That Prayer is to be Placed Before All Things

II. St Basil the Great: On Prayer

III. St Ambrose: Watch and Pray

IV. St John Chrysostom: Prayer

V. St Augustine: If You Ask the Father Anything in My Name

VI. St Cyril of Alexandria: Confidence in Prayer

VII. The Venerable Bede: The Fathers on Prayer

THE GOSPEL OF THE SUNDAY

John xvi. 23–30

At that time: Jesus said to his disciples: Amen, amen, I say to you: if you ask the Father anything in my name, he will give it to you. Hitherto you have not asked anything in my name. Ask, and you shall receive; that your joy may be made full.

These things I have spoken to you in proverbs. The hour cometh, when I will no more speak to you in proverbs, but will shew you plainly of the Father. In that day you shall ask in my name; and I say not to you that I will ask the Father for you: For the Father himself loveth you, because you have loved me, and have believed that I came out from God. I came forth from the Father, and am come into the world: again I leave the world, and I go to the Father.

His disciples say to him: Behold, now thou speakest plainly, and speakest no proverb. Now we know that thou knowest all things, and thou needest not that any man should ask thee. By this we believe that thou camest forth from God.

Exposition from the Catena Aurea

V. 23: *Amen, Amen, I say to thee.*

Chrysostom, *Hom. 79 in John*: He makes clear to them the power of His Name; for though He is neither seen nor besought, should His Name be invoked before the Father, it produces wonders. Do not think then that because I shall not be dwelling in your midst that I have forsaken you; for my Name will give you even greater protection. Then follows:

V. 24. *Hitherto you have not asked anything in my name . . .*

THEOPHYLACTUS: For when your prayers rising upwards are heard, then will your gladness be made full. CHRYSOSTOM, *as above*: Because the things He said to them remained obscure, He adds:

V. 25: *These things I have spoken to you in proverbs. The hour . . .*

That is, there shall come a time when you shall know all things clearly. (He was speaking of the time after His Resurrection.) *But will show you plainly of the Father.* For throughout forty days He conversed with them all together; speaking of the kingdom of God. Now, He says to them, being in fear you pay no heed to what is said to you. Then however, seeing Me risen from the dead you will be able to take it all in clearly.

THEOPHYLACTUS: Even now He gives them confidence, assuring them that in their trials they shall receive help from above, saying:

V. 26. *In that day you shall ask in my name . . .*

And I declare to you, that so favourably is the Father disposed towards you, that you will no longer need my intercession. So He adds: *And I say not to you, that I will ask the Father for you.*

V. 27. *For the Father himself loveth you . . .*

Yet that they might not turn from the Lord, as no longer being in need of Him, He adds: *Because you have loved me*; as though saying: It is for this the Father is well disposed towards you: because you have loved Me. Therefore should you ever fall away from the love of Me, then shall you fall from the Father's love.

AUGUSTINE, *Tr.* 102, 5 *in John*: Is it that He loves us because we love Him; or rather is it because He loves us that we love Him? This the Evangelist himself answers: *Let us therefore love God, because God hath first loved us* (I Jn. iv. 19). The Father then loves us because we love the Son; since it is from the Father and the Son that we love both the Father and the Son. He loves what He has made; but He would not make in us that which He would love had He not loved us before He wrought it.

HILARY, *De Trin* 6: 31: Perfect faith in the Son has no need of an intercessor with the Father; for since it has come from God it believes, and of itself: proclaiming as it does that He is born of God, and sent by Him, it straightaway merits to be both heard and loved. So there follows: *And because you have believed that I came forth from God.* Accordingly His Nativity and His Coming are signified when He adds:

V. 2: *I came forth from the Father, and am come into the world . . .*

The one event pertains to His Nature, the other to the Dispensation. To have come forth from the Father, and to have come forth from

God, have not the same meaning; since it is one thing to come forth from God in the nature of His Substance, another to come forth from the Father into this world to fulfil the mystery of our salvation. Since then to come forth from God is to share through birth in the being of His nature; how can He be other than God?

CHRYSOSTOM: Because His words concerning the Resurrection comforted them not a little, and likewise hearing Him say He came forth from the Father, and now was returning to Him, He continues to speak of these things: *Again I leave the world, and I go to the Father.* For this was a proof to them they had believed rightly, and would be safe under His protection in the days to come.

AUGUSTINE, *Tr. in John*, 102, 6: He came forth from the Father, because He is of the substance of the Father. He came into this world, for He manifested His Body (which He took from the Virgin) to the world. He left the world by means of a bodily departure, yet not depriving the world of the support of His Presence: for coming forth from the Father He so came to the world that He at the same time departed not from His Father (101, 4). But we read that Our Lord Jesus Christ was both asked questions and prayed to. For about to ascend into heaven He was asked by His Disciples when He would restore the kingdom of Israel? In heaven He was besought by Stephen to receive his spirit (Acts vii. 58). And who will venture to say that while yet mortal He might be besought, but not when immortal? I believe therefore that what He just said: *And in that day you shall not ask me anything* (v. 23), does not refer to the time of His Resurrection, but to that time *when we shall see him as he is* (I John iii). This vision belongs, not to His temporal life, but to the eternal, wherein we shall ask for nothing (101, 6), seek for nothing; for there shall remain nothing to be desired, nothing hidden to be revealed.

ALCUIN: Therefore He says: In the world that is to come *you shall not ask me anything*, but now, while you linger in this pilgrimage of suffering, if you ask the Father for anything, He will give it to you. Accordingly, he continues and says: *Amen, amen, I say to you; if you ask the Father anything in my name, He will give it to you.*

AUGUSTINE, *Tr.* 102 *in John* 2: That He says *anything* is not to be understood as meaning anything whatsoever, but something which has to do with the obtaining of the life of the blessed; for what is asked for to the hindering of our salvation is not asked for in the Name of the Saviour. For when He says, *In my name*, we must understand, not the sound of the letters and syllables, but what is truly and correctly signified by the sound.

Accordingly, he who believes regarding Christ that which is not to be thought of concerning the Only Son of God, does not ask in His Name. But he who believes that which *is* to be held regarding Him, he truly asks in His Name, and shall receive what he is seeking; if he seeks what is not opposed to his own eternal welfare. And he shall receive it when it is fitting that He shall receive it. For there are things which while not denied are yet withheld: to be given in a fitting time.

Likewise we should correctly understand the words: *He will give it to you*, so that by them those favours are to be understood which relate expressly to those who ask. All the sanctified are beyond doubt heard, when they pray, not for anyone, but for themselves; for it was not said simply, *that He will give*, but that, *He will give to you.*

(102, 2). What follows: *Hitherto you have not asked anything in my name*, may be understood in two ways. Either that you have not asked in My name, because you have not known the Name as it is to be known, or because you have not asked *anything*; since in comparison with that which you ought to have asked for, that must be regarded as *nothing* for which you did ask. Therefore, that they may ask in His Name, not for what is nothing, but for the fulness of delight, He goes on: *Ask, and you shall receive; that your joy may be full.* This saying: the fulness of joy: means spiritual not carnal joy; and it will be full when it is so great that nothing can be added to it.

AUGUSTINE, *De Trin.* 1, 2: This is the fulness of our joy, than which there is nothing greater: to enjoy God in the Trinity; in Whose likeness we are made.

AUGUSTINE, *Tr.* 102 *in John* 2: Whatsoever therefore that is asked for which relates to the attainment of this Joy must be asked for in the Name of Christ. The divine mercy shall never disappoint the just who persevere in the desire of that good. Whatsoever else is asked for, nothing is asked for; not that it is really nothing, but that in comparison with this so great joy it is as nothing. Then follows: *These things I have spoken to you in proverbs. The hour cometh, when I will no more speak to you in proverbs.* I would say (102, 3) that the hour of which He is here speaking must be understood of the world to come; when we shall behold Him clearly, *face to face*, as the Apostle says; and that the words: *These things I have spoken to you in proverbs*, relate to what was later said by the Apostle: *We see now through a glass in a dark manner*[4] (I Cor. xiii. 12). *I will show you plainly of the Father*; for the Father shall be seen through the Son. *Neither doth anyone know the Father, but the Son, and he to whom it shall please the Son to reveal him.*

GREGORY, *Morals* 30, 8: He declares that He will speak openly to us concerning the Father; for by the revelation of His own majesty He will show us both the manner in which He came forth, being Equal to Him that begot Him, and the manner in which the Holy Spirit proceeds from Them Both.

AUGUSTINE, *in John; as above*: But this meaning appears to hamper what follows: *In that day you shall ask in my name*: for in the world to come what shall we ask for, since our desire is already *satisfied with good things* (Ps. cii. 5)? For to ask for anything is a sign of need. (102, 4). It remains therefore that Jesus is to be understood as about to change His Disciples from being carnal or animal-minded into spiritual men. A carnal minded man whatever he shall hear concerning the nature of God will understand it in a bodily sense; as he cannot understand It as being other than body (though vast, or immense, or shining, or as beautiful). And so whatever words of wisdom are spoken regarding this incorporeal and unchangeable Substance are proverbs to him; not that he regards them as proverbs, but he thinks of them in the manner of those who are wont to hear proverbs: as not understanding them.

But when he has become spiritual minded he begins to see into all things; though in this life he sees as through a glass, and only in part; yet he perceives through no bodily sense, through no imaginative concept, but by means of a most certain knowledge of his mind understands that God is not body but spirit. And the son speaking so plainly of the Father, it is evident that He who speaks is of the same Substance. Now they who pray, pray in His Name, for by the sound of that Name they mean only the Reality called by this Name. They can think within them that Our Lord Jesus Christ as man intercedes for us, and as God, together with the Father, receives our prayer. I think He implies this when He says: *And I say not to you, that I will ask the Father for you.* Only the eye of a mind that is spiritual can rise to see how it is the Son will not ask the Father, but that Father and Son together receive the prayers of those who pray to them.

V. 29. *His disciples say to him: Behold, now thou speakest plainly . . .*

CHRYSOSTOM, *as above*: Because this especially breathed new life into them: that they were friends of the Father: they thereupon declare they are certain that He knows all things. *Now*, they say, *thou speakest plainly, and speakest no proverb.* AUGUSTINE, 103: But since that hour in which He shall speak to them without proverbs was yet to come, and only promised, why do they say this, if not because the things He knows are to them, who understand them not, still as proverbs; and so little do they understand that they not even see that they do not understand?

V. 30. *Now we know that thou knowest all things . . .*

CHRYSOSTOM, *Hom.* 78, 2: Since His words answer that which was in their minds, they continue: Now we know that thou knowest all things. See how imperfect they were; after seeing so many and such great wonders, they exclaim: *Now we know* . . . saying it too as though conferring a reward on Him. *And thou needest not that any man should ask thee*; that is, without hearing from us Thou dost know what troubles us, and Thou hast given peace to our hearts, telling us that the Father loves us.

AUGUSTINE, 103, 2: What does it mean that they should say to Him Whom they believed knew all things: *Thou needest not that any man should ask thee*, when they should rather have said: Thou needest not to ask any man? Both of which things in fact took place; namely, that the Lord both asked questions, and was asked them. But this is readily explained: for this was for the benefit, not of Him, but of them, whom He questions and by whom He was Himself questioned. For He questioned them, not that He might learn from them, but rather that He might teach them; and they who questioned Him, desiring to learn something from Him, had need to learn certain things from Him Who knew all things. Neither did He need to learn, by their question, that which each wished to learn from Him; for before He was questioned He had known the wish of the questioner. To foreknow the thoughts of men was no great thing for the Lord, but to the newborn (*in Christ*) it was a great wonder; who go on to add: *By this we believe that thou camest forth from God.*

Hilary, *The Trinity*, 6; 34: Because of this they believe that He has come forth from God, namely: that He does the things which only God may do. For when the Lord had said that He both *came forth from God*, and that, *from the Father He had come into this world*, they showed no astonishment at this; for they had frequently heard it before. Accordingly they do not add: And have come from the Father into the world. For they knew already that He was sent by God. But they did not yet know that He came forth from the Father.

Understanding now, because of these words, they then for the first time, when they declare that He now spoke to them without proverbs, begin to turn their minds towards this ineffable mystery of the birth of the Son (par. 35). For not after the manner of a human bringing-forth is God born of God; His is rather a coming forth from God than a bringing forth. He is One from the One; not a portion, not a falling away; it is not a diminution, not an offshoot, not a stretching forth, not an infirmity, but the birth of a living substance from a living substance. It is God coming forth from God; not a creature elected to the name of God. He did not, from nothing, begin to be; but came forth from What *was* forever; and to have *come forth* means birth, not beginning.

Augustine, 103, 2: Lastly He reminds them of their age with regard to the inward man: that it was as yet young and tender.

I. St Basil the Great, Bishop and Doctor

That Prayer is to be placed Before all Things[1]

1. Dearly Beloved, each word and deed of Our Saviour Jesus Christ is for us a lesson in virtue and piety. For this end also did He assume our nature, so that every man and every woman, contemplating as in a picture the practice of all virtue and piety, might strive with all their hearts to imitate His example. For this He bore our body, so that as far as we could we might repeat within us the manner of His Life. And so therefore, when you hear mention of some word or deed of His, take care not to receive it simply as something that incidentally happened, but raise your mind upwards towards the sublimity of what He is teaching, and strive to see what has been mystically handed down to us.

Martha did indeed welcome the Lord; but Mary sat at His feet. In each sister was an earnest good will. Yet note what each does. Martha served Him by preparing what would be needed for the refreshment of His Body; Mary, seated at His feet, listened to His words. The one ministered to the visible man; the other bowed down before the Invisible. And the Lord Who was there as both God and Man was pleased with the good dispositions of both women.

But Martha, busy with her task, cried out to the Lord to speak for her to her sister, that she should come and help her. *Speak to her therefore*, she says, *that she may get up and help me*. But the Lord said to her: *Martha, Martha, thou art careful, and art troubled about many things. But one thing is necessary. Mary hath chosen the best part, which shall not be taken away from her* (Lk. x. 38–42). We have not come here for this purpose, to sit at ease at the table, to fill our stomachs. We are here to nourish you, with the word of truth, and by the contemplation of heavenly mysteries. Yet though He did not turn the one away from her task, He praised the other because of that to which she had devoted herself.

Here we see the two states placed before us by means of the two women; the lower, choosing to serve Him in corporeal ministrations which also is most profitable, and that which, ascending to the contemplation of the sacred mysteries, is the more spiritual. Take these things spiritually, you who listen, and choose that which you wish. And should you choose the way of service, render your service in the Name of Christ. For He said: *As long as you did it to one of these my least brethren, you did it unto me* (Mt. xxv. 40). And so whether you receive the stranger, or feed the poor, or comfort the afflicted, or give help to those who are in need and in pain, or take care of the sick, Christ receives your service as bestowed on Him. But should you choose to imitate Mary, who, putting aside the service of bodily need, ascended to the contemplation of the divine glories, seek truly to do this. Leave the body, leave the tilling of the earth, and the preparation of what is eaten with bread. Sit at the feet of the Lord, and give your mind to His words, that you may become a sharer of the mysteries of the divine nature which Christ reveals. For to contemplate that which Christ teaches is a work above the service of corporal need.

2. You have then, Beloved, received both divine teaching and an example of life. Strive for whichever you will, and be either a servant of the needy of this world, or a zealous lover of the words of Christ. And if it be that you strive after both, then from both gather the fruit of salvation. But the spiritual motive is the first, all the rest come second; *For Mary*, He says, *has chosen the better part*. If then you would enter in to the mysteries of Christ, let you sit by His feet, and receive His Gospel, and abandoning your way of life let you live apart from men and free from all concern; let you have no further thought for your body, and then you will be enabled to enter into mystic converse with Him in contemplation of His truth, and so imitate Mary, and gain the highest glory.

And when you pray, see that you ask not for what is alien to your life, and provoke the Lord. Ask not for money, nor for human glory, nor power, nor for any of the things that pass away. But seek for the kingdom of God, and all that is needed for your body will be provided; as the Lord Himself has said: *Seek ye the kingdom of God, and his justice, and all these things will be added unto you* (Mt. vi. 33).

Twofold, Beloved, are the methods of prayer. One is to give praise to God from a humble heart; the other, the lower, is the prayer of petition. Therefore, when you pray, do not immediately begin with petitions; otherwise you may then be accused of praying to God only when in need. So when you come to pray, leave self behind, leave wife and children. Let the earth go, and rise up to heaven. Leave behind every creature, the visible and the invisible, and begin with the praise and glory of Him Who has made all things. And as often as you offer Him praise be not wandering here and there in your mind. And choose not your words from fables, like the Greeks, but from the holy Scriptures, and say: O Lord, patient and forbearing, I praise Thee because Thou hast spared me who offend Thee daily; giving to all a season for repentance; and because of this Thou art silent, and art patient with us, O Lord, that we may offer glory and praise to Thee who hast care for the salvation of all men. Thou dost help us, now by fear, now by counsel, now through the prophets, and last of all through the coming of Thy Anointed; *For thou hast made us, and not we ourselves* (Ps. xcix. 3).

3. And when you have praised and glorified God from the Scriptures, with all your heart, then begin with humility to say: Lord, I am not worthy to praise Thee, for I have sinned most grievously. And though you may not be conscious of any fault, yet so must you speak to Him. For save God alone there is no one without sin. We commit many sins, and the greater part of them we forget. Because of this the Apostle said: *I am not conscious to myself of anything, yet I am not thereby justified* (I Cor. iv. 4); that is, I have committed many sins, and taken no notice of them. And because of this the prophet also says: *Who can understand sins?* (Ps. xviii. 13). So you do not speak falsely when you say you are a sinner. And if you do know that you are one, you also sin when you say: I am not a sinner. Say rather: I have sinned more than other sinners, for I have broken the commandment which says: *When you have done all things commanded of you, say: we are unprofitable servants; we have done that which we ought to do* (Lk. xvii. 10). So must you think to yourself: *I am a profitless servant.*

And again: *In humility let each esteem others better than himself* (Phil. ii. 3). Pray to the Lord therefore with fear and with humility. And when you pray to Him from a humble heart let you say: I give Thee thanks, O Lord, because Thou hast borne with my sins in patience, and hast left me even till now without chastisement. For I have long deserved to suffer many afflictions; and to be banished from Thy sight; but Thy most clement mercy has borne with me in patience. I thank Thee again, although I am unable to render Thee such thanks as are due Thy mercy.

And when you have fulfilled in turn the duty of praise and of humility, then ask for what you ought to ask for; not for riches, as I said, not for the glory of this earth, not for health of body: for He made you and your health is His care, and He knows which state is profitable to each one, to be healthy or to be infirm. But let you seek, as He has told us, for the kingdom of heaven. For, as I said before, He will provide for your body's needs. For our King is of infinite dignity, and it is unfitting that anyone should ask of Him what is not becoming. Be mindful therefore when you pray that you do not bring upon yourself the anger of God; but seek from Him the things that are worthy of God our King. And when you pray for the things that are worthy of being asked of God, cease not from praying till you receive them. For the Lord has intimated this to us where He says in the Gospel: *Which of you shall have a friend, and shall go to him at midnight, and shall say to him: friend, lend me three loaves, because a friend of mine is come off his journey to me, and I have not what to set before him. And he from within should answer, and say: Trouble me not, the door is now set shut, and my children are with me in bed; I cannot rise and give thee. Yet if he shall continue knocking, I say to you, although he will not rise and give him, because he is his friend; yet because of his importunity, he will rise, and give him as many as he needeth* (Lk. xi. 5–8).

4. Our Lord puts this example before us to teach us that we should be strong and persistent in faith. He takes the example of one man's prayer to another man, that you may learn never to be discouraged, so that when you pray and do not receive the answer to your prayer, you should not cease from praying till you do receive it; provided that, as I said, you ask for what God wishes you to ask. And do not say: I am a sinner, and therefore He does not listen to me. That you may not lose heart on this account He says to us: *Although he will not give him, because he is a friend; yet because of his importunity he will give him as many as he needs.*

So henceforth, if a month goes by, or a year, or three years, or four, or many years, do not give up praying till you receive what you ask for; but ask on in faith, and be at the same time steadfast in doing good. It will happen often that someone in his youth strives earnestly for chastity. Then pleasure begins to undermine his resolution, desires awaken his nature, he grows weak in prayer, wine overcomes his youth, modesty perishes, and the man becomes another man. So we change because we have not with high courage of soul stood firm against our passions. It behoves us therefore to resist all things, yet we must cry out to God, that He may bring us aid.

For if a man through folly gives way to evil desires, and betrays himself to his enemies, God will not aid him, nor hear him, because through sin he has turned away from God. He who hopes to be helped by God should have no part with what is unworthy. But he who does not betray what he owes to God will never be in want of the divine aid. It is just and fitting that in nothing should we be condemned by our own conscience. Only then may we cry out for divine aid and cry earnestly, and not with minds wandering here and there. For one who so prays, not alone shall he continue unheard by God, but he will also provoke the Lord yet more. For if a man stands in the presence of a king, and speaks with him, he will stand there with great trepidation of mind, careful not to let either his eyes or his mind go wandering. With what greater fear and trembling should we stand in the presence of God, having our whole mind intent on Him alone, and on nothing else whatsoever? For He beholds our inward life; not merely the outward one which men see.

Standing then in God's Presence, in a manner truly worthy, and laying before Him all the desires of your heart, cease not to pray till you receive what you ask for. But should your conscience tell you that you are praying unworthily, and should you stand in prayer while your mind goes wandering when you could well pray with recollection, then venture not to stand thus in the presence of the Lord for fear your prayer becomes an offence. Should it be however that your soul has become weak through sin, and that you are unable to pray without distraction, strive with yourself as best you can, striving manfully before the Lord, having your mind steadfast on Him, and calling upon Him, and God will have compassion on you, since it is not because of indifference but through infirmity that you cannot pray as you ought when you kneel before God. Let him who so strives with himself in every good work cease not to pray till he obtains what he asks for; but in making his request let him knock patiently at the door: *For everyone*, He says, *that asketh, receiveth; and he that seeketh, findeth; and to him that knocketh, it shall be opened*; for that which you desire to obtain, what is it but salvation in God?

5. Do you desire to know, Beloved, how the saints endured in patience, and yielded not to despair? The Lord called Abraham when he was still a young man, and brought him out of the land of the Assyrians into Palestine, and said to him: *I shall give this land to thee, and to thy seed after thee, and as the stars of heaven shall thy seed be, which shall not be numbered* (Gen. xiii. 15, 16). And the number of his many years went on, and his nature died, and death stood by his door, and yet he did not say: 'Lord, You promised me many children, and You foretold that I would be the father of many peoples. And the impulses of nature have withered away; and to my wife because of her age nothing remains of the nature of woman. So Your prophecy was false. For what hope have we since we are both old?' But he did not say this, nor did he think it in his heart, but remained unshaken in faith; and while his body grew old, his hope grew young. As his body became weaker and gave him grounds for despairing, his faith gave strength to his soul and his body. 'It is God,' he said, 'who has promised. He is the Lord of nature; otherwise it could not come to pass. It is He Who makes possible what is impossible; for He has made all things; and all that is He changes as He wills.'

Imitate the faith of Abraham. After his nature had withered, and its powers were at an end, then the promise of the Lord took life. Let us consider ourselves, for example. We pray earnestly for a year; and then we cease. We fast for two years; and then we cease to fast. Let us not grow faint in face of the promise of God. For He Who promised this man that his seed would be multiplied has promised us that He will give us what we ask for. For He says: *Come to me, all you that labour, and are burthened, and I will refresh you* (Mt. xi. 28). For when you were far from Him He pitied you as you toiled under the weary burthen of your sins, and called you and relieved you of it, and then gave you rest. And you, have you no faith in Him? Even should we keep silence our conscience would not suffer us. For we do not doubt that He has power to relieve us; but we care not to take upon us His yoke, which is light and sweet; nor enter by the narrow way to the kingdom of heaven; but prefer rather to carry the burthen of our sins, and to walk by the broad way of the pleasures of the senses, and to enter in at the wide gate that leads to destruction.

But, you will say, how often have I prayed, and I have not been answered? Because you have always prayed badly; either without faith, or with a distracted mind, or for the things that were not expedient for you. And if at times you prayed for what was expedient for you, you did not persevere. For it is written: *In patience shall you possess your souls* (Lk. xxi. 19), and again: *He that shall persevere unto the end, he shall be saved* (Mt. x. 22).

6. God sees into the hearts of those who pray. What need then, someone will say, that we should ask God for what we need? Does He not know already what we need? Why then should we pray? God does indeed know what things we need, and with generosity provides all we need for the refreshment of our bodies, and since He is good He sends down His rains upon the just and the unjust alike, and causes His sun to shine upon the good and the bad (Mt. v. 45), even before we ask Him. But faith, and the power of virtue, and the kingdom of heaven, these you will not receive unless you ask for them in labouring and steadfastness.

We must first long for these things. Then when you desire them, you must strive with all your heart to obtain them, seeking them with a sincere heart, with patience, and with faith, not being condemned by your conscience, as praying without attention or without reverence, and so in time, when God wills, you will obtain your request. For He knows better than you when these things are expedient for you. And perhaps He is delaying in giving them to you, designing to keep your attention fixed upon Him; and also that you may know that this is a gift of God, and may safeguard with fear what is given to you. For what we come by with much labour we are zealous to defend; as losing it we lose also our labour; and treating lightly the gift of God we become unworthy of life eternal. For what did it profit Solomon so quickly to receive the gift of wisdom and then lose it?

7. Do not then lose heart if you do not speedily obtain your request. For if it were known to Our Good

Master that were you at once to receive this favour that you would not lose it, He would have been prepared to give it to you unasked. But being concerned for you, He does not do this. For if he who received a single talent, and hid it safely, was condemned because he did not put it to profit, how much more would he have been condemned had he lost it? Keeping this in mind, let us continue to give thanks to the Lord whether we receive speedily or slowly that which we pray for. For all things whatsoever the Lord may do He orders all to the end of our salvation; only let us not through faintheartedness cease from our prayers. It was because of this the Lord spoke the parable of the Widow who persuaded the judge through her steadfastness (Lk. xviii. 2–5): that we also through our steadfastness in prayer may obtain what we ask for.

By this we also show our faith, and our love of God, since though we do not quickly receive what we ask for, yet we remain steadfast in praising Him and giving thanks. Then let us give Him thanks at all times, so that we may be found worthy of receiving His everlasting gifts; since to Him all praise and glory is due for ever and ever. Amen.

II. St Basil the Great, Bishop and Doctor

On Prayer[2]

1. Prayer is not made perfect by uttering syllables, O Brethren, but in the purpose of the soul, and in the just actions of a lifetime. Nor are we to believe that God has need of being reminded through our words. We are not to think that we complete our prayer by murmuring a number of syllables, but rather, O Brethren, by the purpose of our soul, and in deeds of virtue extending into every action and moment of our life. Neither are we to think that God needs the reminder of our spoken words; rather are we to believe that He knows our need whether we ask of Him or not. The ear of God has no need of our cry, since He can see even from the movements of our soul what it is that we seek for. For have you not heard that Moses was heard by the Lord, though he uttered no sound, but besought the Lord through the unspoken groanings of the spirit within him, and the Lord said to Him: *Why cryest thou to me?* (Ex. xiv. 15). And let those who do not keep to the straight path, yet who, because of the length of their prayers, consider themselves as virtuous, take heed of these words: *And when you stretch forth your hands, I will turn away my eyes from you: and when you multiply prayer, I will not hear* (Is. i. 15). For the words of prayer that are simply uttered are of themselves of no avail unless they are sent upwards from a fervent soul.

For even *the Pharisee prayed thus with himself*, but not with God; for, given over to the sin of pride, he thought only of himself. Because of this the Saviour says: *And when you are praying, speak not much, as the heathens; for they think that in their much speaking they may be heard* (Mt. vi. 7), and that: *In the multitude of words there shall not want sin* (Prov. x. 19). This was the cause of

God's turning away His eyes: when they stretch forth their hands in prayer. For the very symbols of their supplication are the occasion of His resentment. It is as if someone should kill the beloved son of another, and then stretch forth to the afflicted father their hands still stained with blood; asking for the right hand of fellowship. Would not the blood of his son, visible on the hand of his slayer, provoke him rather to just anger? And such are the prayers of the Jews. For when they stretch forth their hands in prayer, they but remind God the Father of their sin against His Son. And at every stretching forth of their hands they but make manifest that they are stained with the blood of Christ. For they who persevere in their blindness inherit the blood guilt of their fathers. For they cried out: *His blood be upon us, and upon our children* (Mt. xxvii. 25).

2. Be mindful then of God, O Man, and keep the fear of Him ever in your heart, and join yourself to all men in communion of prayer; for great indeed is their power to appease God. For as long as we live this life in the flesh prayer shall be a powerful aid, and as we journey from here it will be an enduring help on the way to the eternity that awaits us. For as solicitude is a good thing, so likewise to be downcast and despairing, and to doubt of our salvation, are things which hurt the soul.

Therefore place your hope in the goodness of God, and look for His aid; knowing that if we truly and sincerely turn to Him, not alone will He not cast us off for ever, but even as we pray to Him He will say to us: *Here I am* (Is. lviii. 9). For who would do an evil action, or suffer an evil thought, if he believed that God was everywhere, that He is close to those who do such things, and present at every act of ours, and seeing all the counsels of our hearts? Those who answer that they do not see God, or that they do not care what they do, such men, because of this, are but rushing on to an evil state of soul.

Peace is the beginning of the purification of the soul, the tongue freed from speaking of the things of men, the eyes no longer dwelling on the beauty of bodies and the elegance of our surroundings, the hearing not undoing the strength of the soul through listening to melodies that were composed for pleasure, nor through the talk of clever and frivolous men, which more than anything else has power to undo the purpose of the soul. For the mind, when not wasted on outward things, or led astray by the world of the senses, turns inwards on itself, and through this ascends to the thought of God, and lit by that inward beauty becomes unmindful even of nature, and no more troubled by anxiety for its food, or with concern for clothing; at rest from earth's cares, all its zeal is given to gaining the things that are good for ever.

3. Nor should you let the half of your life go without profit to your soul: lost in the insensibility of sleep; but divide the night time between sleep and prayer. And let sleep itself be an act of prayer; for even our sleeping dreams are mostly but echoes of our day time thoughts. What more blessed than that a man as soon as the day dawns should rise

and pray, and worship his Creator with hymns and canticles? And as day begins to brighten to take up our labours, uniting them everywhere to prayer; and with hymns, as with salt, give flavour to our toil. For the solace of hymns brings with it a cheerful and untroubled state of mind.

And before eating let us offer prayer, in thanksgiving for the gifts God now gives us, and for those we are yet to receive; and pray likewise when we have eaten, giving thanks for what we have received, and for the gifts that are promised us.

That is sublime prayer which brings to the soul a clear notion of God; for this is the indwelling of God: through recollection to have God abiding within you. By this we become a temple of God, as long as this state of recollection is not broken by earthly thoughts, or the mind agitated by unlooked for emotions, but turning from all things to God; repelling all feelings that lead to desire, and giving itself to those that lead to virtue.

And what dawn is to others let midnight be to the athlete of the service of God; when the night's peace gives most leisure to the soul, and no sights or sounds enter to trouble the heart. Then the mind, alone with itself and with God, amends itself in the recollection of its sins, giving itself rules that it may avoid evil, and imploring God's help that it may fulfil all that it desires to do.

4. And this the history of Moses also conveys to us; for the happenings relating to him which are recorded there are as it were symbols of man's state in this world. For there events did not proceed at an even pace: now they went well, and now because of failing strength the warriors strove with less power. For when Moses held his arms uplifted, *Israel overcame* (Ps. xxviii. 9). But should his arms drop down, then the Amalec prevailed. This means that when our power of action weakens and falters, then will our ancient enemy prevail against us. But when it is uplifted, and again set upright, our power to see through him becomes stronger. For God uplifts the soul that seeks the things that are above, and lays low the soul that seeks His help to gain the things of the body.

He then who comes to the temple of God, let him speak no evil, nor talk of trifling things, nor shameful things. Away with such things! *In his temple*, as David says, *all shall speak his glory* (Ps. xviii). His angels are present who shall record the words. The Lord is present Who sees the hearts of those who enter. The prayer of each one is open to the sight of God; the prayer of the man who from his heart, or from his understanding, is seeking the things of heaven; and the prayer of the one who speaks the words superficially and as it were with the edges of his lips, while his heart is far from God. And if he does pray he is begging for health of body, or for riches, or for the glory of this world. Not of these things should we speak, but, as the Scripture tells us: *In his temple all shall speak* his *glory*.

But wonder of wonders! *The heavens show forth the glory of God* (Gal. vi. 8). It is the task of the angels to give glory to God. To give glory to the Creator is the whole duty of the entire host of heaven. For every creature, whether it speaks or is silent, whether in heaven or on earth, gives glory to its Maker. We pity the men who hasten from their homes and hurry to the temple as though to receive something; and there pay no heed to the word of God, and, without any discernment of their own inward life, they neither sorrow at the remembrance of their sins, nor have any fear of the judgement, but, smiling and shaking hands with each other they turn the house of prayer into a place of endless gossiping; heedless of what the psalmist solemnly tells us: *In his temple all shall speak his glory*. But you not alone do not speak it, you become a distraction to your neighbour, turning his attention to you. God has no need of thy glory; but He desires that you become worthy to receive His glory. And: *What things a man shall sow, those also shall he reap*.[3]

5. We should give thanks to God for the good things He gives us, and not bear it with bad grace that He measures His giving. Should He grant us to be in union with Him: this we shall receive as a most perfect and joyful gift; should He delay this, let us suffer the loss in patience. For He disposes of our lives more perfectly than we could order them.

The halcyon is a sea bird which nests by the shore, laying its eggs in the sand, and bringing forth its young in the middle of winter; when the sea beats against the land in violent and frequent storms. But during the seven days while the halcyon broods: for it takes but seven days to hatch its young: all winds sink to rest, and the sea grows calm. And as it then is in need of food for its young ones, the most bountiful God grants this little creature another seven days of calm: that it may feed its young. Since all sailors know of this, they give this time the name of the *halcyon days*.

These things are ordered by the Providence of God for the creatures that are without reason, that you may be led to seek of God the things you need for your salvation. And when for this small bird He holds back the great and fearful sea, and bids it be calm in winter, what will He not do for you made in His own image? And if He should so tenderly cherish the halcyon, how much more will He not give you, when you call upon Him with all your Heart?

Let us then be resolved, Brethren, that as in our other needs so also in time of temptation, not to count on human expectations or seek help there, but let us send upwards our entreaties, and with sighs and tears, with earnest prayer, with long watching. And in this manner shall we obtain deliverance from our affliction; rejecting human help as vain, and keeping a firm hope in Him Who alone has power to save us. To Him let us offer glory and adoration, together with the Eternal Father, and the Life-Giving Spirit, now and for ever, world without end. Amen.

III. St Ambrose, Bishop and Doctor

Watch and Pray[4]

Luke xi. 5–13. *Which of you shall have a friend, and go to him at midnight, and shall say to him: Friend, lend me three loaves . . .*

Here is another command to pray always (cf. Lk. xviii. 1); and not alone by day, but also by night. For you see how this man who rose at midnight and asked his friend for three loaves, and with steadfast mind continued to ask him, did not fail in his prayer. And what are these three loaves but the mystical Bread of heaven? And if you love the Lord your God you can earn it, not alone for yourself, but for others also. And who is more your Friend than He Who has given us His Body?

It was of this Friend that David asked for bread in the middle of the night, and received it. For he asked for it when he said: *I rose at midnight to give praise to thee* (Ps. cxviii. 62); and through this he gained those loaves (*the psalms*) which he has set before us to eat. He asked, when he said: *Every night I will wash my bed* (Ps. vi. 7). Neither did he fear he might not waken the Sleeper: Whom he knew was unsleeping. And so, keeping in mind these written words, and ceasing not day and night from prayer, let us implore pardon of our sins.

For if he who was so holy, and burthened with the cares of a kingdom, praised the Lord seven times a day (Ps. cxviii. 164), and was zealous ever at the morning and the evening sacrifice, what must we do; we who should pray even more: for through weakness of body and soul we have sinned more often: so that when we are weary from this earthly road, and faint from our journey through the world, and at the close of life, we may not be left in need of that Bread of spiritual refreshment that gives strength to the heart of man? And the Lord teaches us that we must keep watch, not alone at midnight, but at every moment: for He comes in the evening, and in the second watch, and in the third, and He is wont to knock. *Blessed are those servants, whom the Lord when he cometh, shall find watching* (Lk. xii. 37)

So if you desire that the power of God shall encompass you, and provide for you, you must ever keep watch, for many are the snares that lie in wait for the just, and heavy is the sleep of the body; and if the soul begins to sleep, the power of its virtue is lost. Arise then from your sleep, that you may knock upon the door of Christ, which Paul prayed might be opened to him, beseeching, not alone by his own prayers, but also by the prayers of the people, that he might be helped, so that a door might be opened to him, to speak the mystery of Christ (Col. iv. 3).

And perhaps this is the door that John saw open; for he saw one, and he tells us: *After these things I looked, and behold a door was opened in heaven, and the first voice which I heard, as it were, of a trumpet speaking with me, said: Come up hither, and I will shew thee the things that must be done hereafter* (Apoc. v. 1). A door was therefore opened to John, and opened to Paul: that they might receive bread for us that we might eat. He continued to knock at the door, in season and out of season: so that the Gentiles who were weary from the hardships of the way might be refreshed from the abundance of the Food of heaven.

And in this way was the duty to pray always given to us, and the hope of receiving what we ask for, and the manner in which we are to urge our need. Given first by precept, and then by this example. For He Who promises gives us also the hope of receiving what He promises, so that obedience may be given to His precept, and belief to His promise, Who at sight of human piety grants greater hope in the eternal mercy; providing we ask for what is right and just, so that our prayer may not change into sin.

Paul was unashamed to keep asking for what he desired; so that he might not appear either as doubting God's mercy or as complaining in pride because he had not received what he asked for at his first prayer. *For which thing*, he says, *thrice I besought the Lord* (II Cor. xii. 8), showing us that God when we pray to Him will often not grant our prayer because He judges that what we pray for is not expedient for us, though we believe it a gain. To Whom be honour praise and glory for ever and ever. Amen.

IV. St John Chrysostom, Bishop and Doctor

On Prayer[5]

Prayer is a great good if offered up from a thankful soul; if we are steadfast in it, so that whether we receive or do not receive what we pray for we at all times give thanks to God. For since He will sometimes grant what we ask and sometimes will not, in both cases it is to our gain: for whether you receive or do not receive the answer to your prayer, you have received in not receiving, and whether you succeed or do not succeed, you succeeded by not succeeding in that which you sought. For many times it is more profitable for you not to obtain what you have prayed for. For unless what we ask is expedient for us, it will certainly not be granted to us: so that it is equally a gain to obtain our request and not to obtain it.

Neither should we bear it with bad grace if the answer to our prayer s long delayed. Rather let us because of this show great patience and resignation. For can God not grant our prayers even before we ask Him? But He delays for this reason: that we may offer Him a fitting occasion of honouring us through His divine providence. Whether therefore we receive what we ask for, or do not receive it, let us still continue steadfast in prayer; and let us give thanks not only when we have received, but also when we have not received. For to fail in obtaining the desires of our heart when God so wills it, is not worse than to receive it; for we know not as He does what is profitable to us. And so whether we receive or do not receive, let us at all times give thanks to God, and receive with joy whatever shall seem most pleasing to Him.

For oftentimes God will delay, not as denying our prayer, but in His wisdom seeking rather for our perseverance, and desiring to draw us nearer to Himself; as a loving father when asked by his son for something will often do; withholding consent, and not from the will to refuse, but rather to encourage him in steadfastness.

That our prayers therefore be heard by God they must first come from one who is worthy of receiving. Secondly they should be made in accordance with the laws of God. Thirdly they should be unceasing. Fourthly it is required of us that we pray with earnestness, and not in a worldly manner. Fifthly that we join with Him in bringing them about, by asking only for what is fitting and expedient for us. But just as your prayers will be heard because of the fulfilment of these conditions, so likewise it may arise from these conditions that your requests will not be obtained; even though they who pray are just and worthy souls. For who was more just than Paul. Yet, because he asked for what was not profitable to him, his prayer was denied. *For which thing thrice I besought the Lord,* he tells us, *and he said to me: My grace is sufficient for thee* (II Cor. xii. 8, 9). And who was more just than Moses? Yet neither was his prayer answered, the Lord saying to him: *It is enough: speak no more to me of this matter* (Deut. vi. 3). For when he prayed that he might be allowed to enter the Promised Land the Lord would not grant him his prayer. For it was not expedient.

There is yet another reason that may cause our prayer to go unanswered: namely, that though we pray we yet continue in sin. What did the Lord say to Jeremiah concerning the Jews? *Do not pray for this people: seest thou not what they do?* (Jer. vii. 16, 17). They will not give up their wickedness, He says, and yet you offer prayers for them? But I shall not listen. And if we pray against our enemies, God will not alone not listen to us, but His wrath will fall also on us. Prayer is indeed a medicine. But if we not know how to apply it we cannot profit by its goodness.

How great a thing is perseverance in prayer we learn from the woman of Chanaan, who in the end won from Christ what He had refused her at the request of the Apostles; and this she did through her persevering prayer. But we should ourselves seek pardon for our own personal sins, rather than that others should intercede for us. When we have to appear before men for judgement we need money, and we need to be servile, and to use care and diligence: for a ruler is not always disposed to grant favours, or even a hearing. So first we need to win over his ministers, and those who stand round about him; using money, and employing words in every kind of flattery, so that by their help we may obtain what we seek.

It is not so with God. When we ask Him for something there is no need of intermediaries. And neither is He more disposed to help us because He is asked by others rather than by ourselves. For He desires that we should often seek things from Him; to do this is greatly pleasing to Him. For it is in this alone that He becomes our Debtor: that He is pleased as often as we pray to Him; and gives us freely what we have not loaned Him. And should He see one who is in need praying to Him with fervour, He will Himself pay down for us that which He has not received from us. But should we pray in an indifferent manner, He will be indifferent to our request; not because He does not wish to give, but because our prayer is acceptable only when we pray to Him with all our hearts.

Nor does God put off the granting of our prayers from detestation, or because He is against us. But He does clearly wish, by delaying His giving, to keep us close to Himself; just as fathers, who love their children tenderly, will withhold a gift from children who are lazy and indifferent: to teach them to persevere. And have your prayers been heard? Then give thanks because your prayers have been heard. And have your prayers not been heard? Keep on in prayer that they may be heard. You do not stand in need of persons to speak for you, or of roundabout ways and means, or of winning the help of others by flattery. For though you may be helpless, and without a protector, if you cry out to God Himself you shall most certainly be heard.

For if we come morning noon and night before the eyes of men whom we have offended many times, through this repetition, through this repeated appearance before them, we gradually dissolve their hatred against us. Much more does this happen with God. But He is not so disposed to favour us when prayed to by others on our behalf as He is when we pray for ourselves, even though we should be laden with sin. And let those who pray in an indifferent manner take heed.

And let them not receive it with bad grace should He delay in answering their prayer. For supposing I were to say to you: Pray to God, beseech Him, implore Him, such a person might answer, I have prayed to Him, once, twice, three times, ten times, twenty times, but I received no answer. Then I say: Do not cease from praying to Him till you have. And even then do not cease. Even then continue to pray. And if you do not receive any answer to your prayer, keep praying till you do. And when you have obtained what you prayed for, then give thanks for what you have received.

Many people go into a church, and there they recite endless prayers, and then they go out again without knowing a word of what they said. Their lips moved but the sense of hearing, even the mind, perceived nothing. You who cannot hear your own prayers wish that God will! You will say: But I went on my knees. Yes, but your mind went wandering. Your body was indeed in the church but your mind was outside it. Your lips recited prayers, but your attention was taken up with profit and loss, with business, with exchange, with property, with meeting friends.

For the devil who is full of evil knowing we can do great things by the power of prayer will attack us when we pray so as to deprive us of the fruits of it, and leave us as it were striving in vain. Yet oftentimes at home, lying idle on our beds, we think of nothing at all; but let us begin to pray, and straightaway a thousand thoughts will crowd upon our minds. And in this way it will happen that when our prayer is over we go away without knowing or without hearing what it was we said.

When we see this happen let us

begin our prayer anew. And should it happen again let us begin a third time and a fourth, and let us never give up till we pour out our prayer before God with all fitting reverence and recollection. And when the devil sees we will not give up till we have prayed with due reverence and recollection, he will cease to trouble us, because he sees that his deceits yield him no profit, but only cause us to repeat the praises of God over and over again.

At times it will happen to us, that desiring to speak with some particular person we are so taken up with this purpose that we fail to see others we know who stand nearby: so narrow is the mind that we can then only see this one person with whom we desire to speak. Should we not be much more like this in the presence of God: intent on our prayer, and not allowing our thoughts to wander hither and thither? If the tongue speaks while the mind wanders, thinking of home or of what is going on in the market place, perhaps what is left of our prayer may bring us punishment instead of reward.

For if we in the service of other men must stand long hours waiting, as the soldiers do, who serve and suffer hardships, or those who fulfil lowly tasks, and often without the hope of a reward at the end, should we not wait on the Lord with zeal, from Whom we shall receive a reward greater than all our labours? Those who do not, do they not deserve to be punished? For even if they do not receive what they pray for, is it not a great privilege to speak in loving converse with God?

Prayer is indeed a great and blessed thing, since by means of it we speak with God. Should you speak with a very good man do you not truly draw profit from this? What of the profit of a man who is allowed to speak with God? How unfitting it is that we should command our servants to wait on us at all times, when we do so little in the service of God? You know not, O Man, what is expedient for you. For at times you pray for what is harmful and dangerous. But He Who has a true concern for you disregards your request; yet even before you ask Him, He grants you what you truly need. For if earthly fathers do not give all their children ask for: not because they despise them, but because their concern for them is so deep: how much more will the Lord not do this, Who loves us more than all others, and sees more clearly what is truly for our good?

So when you are weary of prayer, and your prayer is still unanswered, think how often you have heard a poor man pleading for help, and have not answered him. Yet he did not become angry and upbraid you; though you ignored him through callousness, while God does not answer through kindness. If you think you are not to be blamed because you did not heed the prayer of your fellow servant, how can you reproach the Lord Who in His love for him has not answered the prayer of His servant?

And if the blessed David, who was a king, and immersed in cares, and called on from every side, prayed to the Lord seven times in the day, what excuse, what forgiveness, is there for us who are so free, and who yet fail to turn to God in earnest prayer: and when we stand to gain so much? It cannot be, no, it cannot be that a man who prays as he ought, calling on the Lord without ceasing, shall ever fall away! who rouses his mind and soul, and raises himself in spirit to heaven, and in this manner calls upon the Lord, and mindful of his sins pleads with Him to forgive them, begging that He shall be gracious and merciful. While he is so held in holy converse with God, putting aside all earthly desire, he is borne on wings and lifted above all human unrest. For not more do the streams cause the gardens to flower, than the wells of our tears the plant of our prayer; sending it straight upwards to its highest perfection, and bringing him who prays before the very face of the Lord; and from there onwards most surely shall his prayers be heard.

For if while the body is bowed to the ground the mouth babbles idly, and the mind wanders here and there through the house, through the market place, how can such a person say he has prayed before the face of God? He prays before the face of the Lord who contains his soul in every direction, and withdraws it from all that is earthly, and, thrusting aside every human reflection, raises it up towards heaven. For, striving with his whole mind, a man ought so to pray that He calls upon the Lord from a truly repentant soul; not holding forth in loud discourses, not drawing his supplication out to undue length, but speaking in words that are few and simple: for that our prayer be heard depends not on the number of our words but on the fervour of our soul.

We are taught this by the prayer of Anna, the mother of Samuel. For this is how she prayed. *O Lord of hosts, if thou wilt look down on the affiiction of thy handmaid, and will give to thy servant a man child: I will give him to the Lord all the days of his life, and no razor shall come upon his head* (I Kings i. 11). What multitude of words is there here? Yet, because she made this prayer from a fervent and recollected soul, He brought to pass what she longed for, making good what was defective in her nature, opening the womb that was closed, and filling her with confidence, so that she reaped from the sterile womb her unshorn child.

He then who prays should not strain after *long prayers*, but should pray often. For both Christ and Paul teach us to use short but oft repeated prayers, at frequent intervals. For should you stretch your prayer to too great length, often it will happen that, becoming forgetful, you give ready access to the devil to enter your mind and upset you, and lead you away in thought from what you are saying. But if you give yourself to short and frequent prayer, dividing up discreetly the whole time of your prayer, you will easily retain control of your mind; and such prayers as these you will make with great recollection.

Do you wish to learn *watchfulness* in prayer, and *earnestness*, and *recollection*? Then go to Anna, and learn what she did. For they all rose up from the table, but she did not then give herself to sleep nor rest. So to me she seems to have been recollected even at table; to be light of spirit, not weighted with food. Nor did she shed so many tears. For if we though sober and fasting pray in this way only with difficulty, or rather scarce ever pray in this way, much more did she not pray in this manner unless by doing as those who fast at table. Let us, O Men, do reverence to the woman. Let us, I say, reverence her as she pours forth with tears her prayers for a son: we who yawn while we pray for a kingdom!

And reflect with me upon the *devotion* of this woman. *Her voice*, we read, *was not heard at all, only her lips moved.* So let him come to God who desires Him to receive his request; not in softness of spirit, not yawning, not faltering, not half asleep, not distracted. Is it that God cannot grant your prayer until he hears your petition? Or that He knew not the woman's desire till she spoke? Had He granted her this before, then the earnestness of the woman would not have been known, nor her devotion revealed to us, nor would she then have received so great a reward. But now we learn also her wisdom. For see how she answers Heli the Priest, who thought she was drunk with wine. *Count not thy handmaid for one of the daughters of Belial: for out of the abundance of my sorrow have I spoken till now.* It is a sign of a heart truly contrite, when we are not embittered or angry with those who have injured us, and that we even defend them. For nothing so makes the heart wise as suffering and grief borne for God.

It is fitting then that we begin and end each meal with giving thanks to God. He who has made a beginning in this way will never sink to drunkenness and folly, never swell up through gluttony, but will by the preparation of his prayer impose a curb on his senses, and partake in just measure of what is set before him, and doing this fill both soul and body with abundant blessing. For the meal that begins with prayer and ends with prayer shall want for nothing; but more abundant than a spring will yield us an abundance of all that is good. Let us not lose this gain. For it is unfitting that those who serve us should, when they receive a portion of what is set before us, give thanks and withdraw with a blessing on us, while we who enjoy so much do not give the same thanks to God. Because of this neglect many things befall us beyond our expectation, both in public and in private, and this because we are not concerned with the things of the soul first, and then only with worldly affairs. Do you not know that if coming to God you adore Him, and make Him a partner of whatever you do, whatever you may have in hand will prosper.

But have you worldly anxieties? Then because of them hasten here, that you may bring upon yourself the favour of God, and have Him as your Helper, and by His divine aid become invulnerable to the spirits of evil. For if you within yourself, if you share in the common prayer, if you receive help from God, if you go forward defended by his armour, not even the devil has power against you, to say nothing of wicked men seeking to injure and calmuniate you. And if going forth from your house to the market place you find yourself bare of these aids, you will be defenceless against all who threaten you.

And let no one say to me that it cannot happen that a man of the world, taken up with his daily affairs, can go running to the church all day to pray. For he can, and with ease. For though busy in the market place, or engaged in public affairs, he cannot easily run to the Church, yet he can still pray. And this many often do. And when the magistrate is calling out within, threatening, striving, raging, those who stand without, sealed with the sign, breathe a few words of prayer within their heart, and going in they change him and make him gentle, and from being fierce they cause him to become mild; and no circumstances whether of time or of place or lack of silence stood in the way of that prayer.

Nor is there so much need for the voice as for the mind; nor for a stretching forth of hands so much as for a striving of the soul; nor for the outward sign so much as for the inward reality. It was because of this that the prayer of Anna, the mother of Samuel, was heard. Not because she cried out to God with a loud clear voice, but because she cried out so much from within her own heart. *Her voice was not heard at all*, we read, *and the Lord granted her petition.* Let us then make no excuses, saying that it is not easy to pray in the midst of worldly affairs, or that there is no house of prayer close at hand. For wherever you are you may set up your own altar. No place forbids it, and no time prevents it. For though you bend not the knee, nor beat your breast, nor raise hands to heaven, if you will but make known to God your ardent faith you have offered a perfect prayer.

For it is possible even as you go through the market place, and walking alone, to make frequent prayer. It is possible while sitting in your workshop stitching leather to consecrate your heart to God. It is possible for the man who is selling and the man who is buying, for the one going up and the one going down, for the person standing over a pot cooking, to make fervent and frequent prayer though it is not possible to enter a church. For God takes no thought of place. This alone He requires of us: a mind and soul that loves the things of God. Even Paul, not in a place of prayer, but cast into a dungeon, not standing erect, but bent down on his knees: for he was held fast in the stocks to which his knees were fastened: lying there prayed with fervour, and shook his prison, and caused its foundations to tremble, and bound the keeper of the prison, and then he led him to the sacred initiation (Acts xvi).

And Ezechias, far from standing erect, or going upon his knees, but *lying sick unto death* upon his bed, turned his face to the wall. And since he cried fervently to the Lord from a chaste soul the sentence spoken against him was recalled, and he was answered with great kindness by the Lord, and restored to his former health (IV Kings xx). And the Thief stretched out upon a cross for a few words received a heavenly kingdom (Lk. xxiii). And Jeremiah amid squalor and from a prison, and Daniel from the lions' den, and Jonas from the belly of a whale, all cried out to God, and all received favour from on high, and the evils that shadowed them were scattered.

And what must you say when you pray? That which the Chananean woman said; for just as she said: *Have mercy on me: my daughter is grievously tormented by a devil* (Mt. xv. 22), so you also say: Have mercy on me, for my soul is grievously tormented by a devil. For sin is a great demon. He that has a devil finds mercy; the sinner is held in hate. Have mercy on me! The phrase is short; but it holds within it a sea of loving trust; for where there is mercy, there all good things are. Even though you are not within a church, cry out and say: Have mercy on me; and though you move not your lips, cry out in your soul: for even the prayer of the silent is heard by the Lord.

It is not a place that is to be looked for, but the Master of the place. Jeremiah lay in squalor, and the Lord hearkened to his prayer. Job prayed from his dunghill, and the Lord was gracious to him. Jonah was in the belly of a whale, and the Lord listened to his prayer. And you, even if you are in the baths, pray; wherever you are, pray; do not seek for a place to pray in: you yourself are a temple.

The sea lay in the path of the Jews. Behind them were the Egyptians. Between stood Moses, silent. For in great anguish of mind he was praying. And the Lord said to him: *Why criest thou to me?* (Ex. xiv. 15). And you, when temptation shall come against you, fly to God, call upon the Lord. Is He a man that you must find the place where He is, going from one place to another? God is near us always. *Then shalt thou call, and the Lord shall hear, and he shall say: Here I am.* (Is. lviii. 9). Your prayer is scarce ended, and He is offering you a remedy for your need. For if you have a mind free from all impure affections, though you stand in the market place or the street, or are present at a trial, or by the sea, or at an inn, or in your workshop, in a word wherever you may be, by calling on the Lord you can obtain what you ask for.

The Stretching Out of the Hands in Prayer. What is the meaning of stretching out hands in prayer? They have been the instrument of many iniquities, and because of this we are bidden to lift them up, that the ministry of prayer may serve them as a fetter against evildoing, as a withdrawal from iniquity, so that should you be on the point of committing a theft, of oppressing another, of striking him, you may remember that you must raise those hands in pleading before God, and by means of them offer up a spiritual sacrifice. Do not dishonour them; do not deprive them of their office of pleading, by using them in the service of evil. Purify them by almsdeeds, by works of mercy, by protecting those in distress, and thus you will uplift them in prayer. For if you would not raise them in prayer unwashed, much less will you as a just man stain them with sin. For if you fear to pray with unwashed hands, which is a small offence, much more let you fear what is graver. For to pray with unwashed hands is not such a grievous thing; but to uplift them in prayer, stained with innumerable crimes, brings down wrath and destruction.

The Power of Prayer. Do you wish to learn how great is the power of the prayer that is offered by the Church? Peter on a certain occasion was held in prison, bound with many chains. *But prayer was made without ceasing by the Church unto God for him* (Acts xii. 5). And immediately he was delivered from prison. What then was stronger than this prayer, which helped the pillar and the strength of the Church? This is not yet imposed on catechumens; for they have not yet reached this confidence. But it is laid on you, to make intercession for the whole world, for the Church spread to the ends of the earth, and for those who minister in it, and preside over it. And since you fulfil this duty with eagerness, you truly bear witness that great is the power of the prayer offered in the Church with one mind by all the people. For if among men it will happen that when condemned men are being led to death, and the people come forward to plead for them, will not the king, moved by the prayer of so many, set aside the sentence? Much more will our Heavenly King be moved by your prayers, and grant what you ask of Him.

You have heard how Peter was delivered from his prison because prayer was made for him without ceasing by the Church? How much greater a task is it, do you think, for our littleness to go to God, and beseech Him for so many people? For if I have not confidence enough to intercede for myself, much less have I got it for others; this is a task for those who are worthy. Since I also have offended, how am I to plead on behalf of others? That one should pray for many is an act of great faith, and one needing great confidence; but for many together to make intercession for one does not seem a grave task.

We can pray for them also in our own home; but it is not possible to pray there as in the church, where the number of the fathers is large, and where prayer is offered up with one accord. When you pray alone your prayers are not heard in the same way as when you pray with your brethren. For here there is something greater; they are of one mind and one voice; there is the bond of charity, and the prayer of the priests. It is for this reason the priests are there, so that joining their more efficacious prayers to those less strong of the people, they may ascend together with them to heaven. For if the prayer of the Church helped Peter, and delivered that Pillar from the prison, how can you, I ask you, ignore its power? For as the power of love is not broken by distance, neither is the efficacy of prayer. And as the one still links those who are far apart, so too, and from afar, can the other most powerfully help us.

For as Moses, though not present in body at the battle, brought there not less but more aid; for uplifting his hands in prayer he raised up their courage, and made them formidable to their enemies. No right action can be wholly great unless the profit of it is passed on to others. For should you fast, or sleep on the ground, or eat ashes, should you mourn continually, and yet help no one, you have done nothing great. And though many and great were the wonders which Moses wrought, none among them makes him so great as those blessed words which he spoke to the Lord: *Either forgive them this trespass or if thou do not, strike me out of the book thou hast written* (Ex. xxxii. 31, 32). David also reveals this same greatness where he says: *It is I the shepherd that have sinned, I have done wickedly: these that are the sheep, what have they done? Let thy hand be turned against me, and against my father's house* (II Kings xxiv. 17).

Great words, and worthy of a citizen of heaven. The generosity of Paul is even greater: for he prayed that he might be banished from glory for the salvation of others. But Jonas, because he was concerned for his own safety, was brought into danger of his own life; the city stood fast, but he was submerged in the sea. Great too were the other deeds of Moses, but the greatest and crowning glory of that holy soul was that he chose to be blotted out from the book of life for the salvation of the Jews. But the prayer of Paul far surpasses this. For the former did indeed choose to perish with them; the latter prayed, not that he might perish with them, but that they should be saved and he alone be banished from the eternal glory.

It is a good thing therefore to profit by the prayer of the saints; but when we also share in their efforts. If this be wanting, the help of others will avail us nothing: even with this help we may yet perish. For of what help was Jeremiah to the Jews? Did he not three times approach the Lord, and three times heard: *Do not pray for this people: for I will not hear thee* (Jer. vii. 16). And what did Samuel profit Saul, praying for him to the last, grieving over him? What did he profit the Israelites? Did he not declare: *Far from me be this sin against the Lord, that I should cease to pray for you* (I Kings xii. 23). Did they not all perish? *And if these three men, Noah, Daniel, and Job, be in it, they shall deliver their own souls by their justice; they shall deliver neither sons nor daughters, since their iniquity has mounted up* (Ezech. xiv. 14).

What does this mean? Does prayer not help us? It helps us, and exceedingly; but only when we co-operate with it. And if you wish to know how it helps us, consider together with me Cornelius and Tabitha: and listen also to God speaking. *I will protect this city, for my own sake, and for David my servant's sake* (IV Kings xix. 34; Is. xxxvii. 35). But when? In the time of Ezechias the Just. But if the prayers of some of the very wicked then prevailed, why did they not prevail again when Nabuchodonosor came? The Lord said this, but He gave over the city. (IV Kings xxv. 1.) Because wickedness had mounted up. And here also Samuel prayed for the Israelites, and obtained his prayer. But when? When they were also pleasing to the Lord; then did He put their enemies to flight.

But someone will say, what need have I of the prayers of others, since I please God? What is it you say, O Man? Paul did not say, what need have I of prayers. Peter did not say, why do I need prayers; though those who prayed for him were not worthy of him, certainly they were not his equals. Yet you say: what need have I of prayers? *Prayer*, we read, *was made without ceasing by the Church unto God for him*. And immediately he was delivered from his bonds. And you say: what need have I of prayers? You need them for this reason: because you think that you have no need of them.

If God should call us to account for our sloth and indifference while we pray: in that while standing before Him, and speaking with Him, we do not show Him as much honour as servants show their masters, or soldiers their officers, or friends show to friends, for a friend speaking with a friend treats him with consideration, but you, speaking with God of your sins, asking pardon for your so many offences, asking to be forgiven, even while your knees are on the ground, do you not oftentimes carelessly let your mind wander indifferently through the forum, or round the house, while at the same time your mouth babbles idly and to no purpose; and this happens, not once or twice, but frequently; if God should call us to account for this alone, would we be forgiven? Could we put forward any defence? I do not think so. For if God will ask for an account of every idle look, of the evil desires of the mind, of the impure thoughts that enter through our wandering eyes; if the detractions we daily utter shall be brought against us, and the rash judgements by which we condemn our neighbours: having no right to do so: and the deceits by which we set one person against another, now praising a brother in his presence, and speaking as a friend, now speaking against him in his absence; shall we not have to render an account of these other offences also?

And what of envy: for often we are envious even of the good; and not merely of strangers, but of our friends also? And we feel delight when others suffer affliction. And do we not regard their misfortunes as a consolation in our own afflictions? For if we are forbidden to refrain ourselves from earthly and fleeting things, how wretched and unhappy are we who demand these very things of God which He tells us we should give away should we possess them? And if we are bidden to pray, not alone for the believing but also for unbelievers, consider how grievous it is to curse your brother!

What is it you do then, O Man? You seek to draw near to God, that He may be gracious to you, and at the same time invoke evil on another? Unless you forgive you will not be forgiven; and you not alone do not forgive, you ask of God that He too shall not forgive? If he shall not be forgiven who does not forgive, how shall he be forgiven who prays the Lord that He too shall not forgive? For if it is a reproach to have enemies, think how evil it is to curse them. For when you defend yourself, showing why you have enemies, you make accusations against them. And what claim can you offer for forgiveness, slandering them, and at a time when you need mercy for yourself? Have you not come to seek pardon for your own sins? Then let your mind not dwell on those of others, lest you remind God of your own!

For if you have said: Strike my enemy, by this you have closed your own mouth, and deprived your own tongue of freedom. First by bringing on yourself the anger of the Judge. Next you ask for things which are opposed to each other; and opposed to the very nature of prayer. For if you come speaking of forgiveness, how can you then speak of their punishment? We ought rather do the opposite and pray for our enemies, that we may then with more confidence pray for ourselves. For by praying for them: though you have not spoken of your own sins: you have done all that is needed. For if there is nothing more evil than a soul that curses, and nothing more stained than a tongue that utters such evil, why do you not make sure when you pray that you say nothing that will provoke the Lord? Thou art a man; share not the baseness of the serpent. For this have you received your mouth, to serve God, not to bite. Remember of what I warned you, said God: to live in peace and to forgive. You ask me to take part in the undoing of My own commandments? And you would devour your brother, and stain your tongue with blood, like madmen whose teeth are red with their own blood? Think how the devil must laugh and rejoice when he hears such a prayer! How God is angered, and moved to detestation, when you ask such things!

Consider, O Man, Who it is you approach against your neighbour! Do you go to another God? No! You come to Him Who said: *Love your enemies*. How then can you cry out to Him against them? How can you ask of God to undo His own Law? This is not the matter of prayer; no one prays that another be punished, but only that he shall himself be saved! Why then put on the appearance of a suppliant, and use the words of an accuser? When we pray for ourselves we scratch, and we yawn, and we let our minds run in every direction. But when we pray against our enemies we do it with deliberation. For the devil knows that then we are turning the sword against ourselves; so he will neither disturb us nor distract us: that he may injure us the more.

But you will say: I have been injured and made to suffer. Then pray against the devil, who above all others has caused you to suffer. For it is he who has brought forth enemies. But if you pray against your enemies, it is he who wills you so to pray; just as if you pray for your enemies you are praying against him. For he is your implacable enemy, while man, whatever he may do, is your friend and your brother. Why then do you while letting your real enemy go free turn on your own members?

Knowing these things, most dearly beloved, let us be zealous to live according to the commandments and according to the will of the Lord, that we may attain to the Kingdom of heaven, in Christ Jesus Our Lord, to Whom with the Father and the Holy Ghost be honour and glory now and for ever, world without end. Amen.

V. St Augustine, Bishop and Doctor

If you ask the Father Anything in My Name[6]

1. Let us now consider these words of the Lord: *Amen, amen, I say to you: if you ask the Father any thing in my name, he will give it to you*. It had already been said, in the earlier part of this discourse of Our Lord, and for the benefit of those who ask for things from the Father in Christ's Name, and do not receive them, that nothing is to be asked of the Father in the Name of the Saviour which is against the work of our salvation. For when He says, *In my Name*, it is not the sound of the letters and syllables that is here to be considered, but what the sound signifies, and what is to be truly and correctly understood by the sound. So he who thinks that concerning Christ which is not to be thought of about

the only Son of God does not ask in His Name; though in words and syllables he should pronounce the names of Christ: for he asks in his name whom he thinks Christ is. But he who believes in Christ as he should truly asks in His Name and receives what he asks for: provided he asks for what is not opposed to his own eternal salvation.

And he receives what he prays for at a time when it is expedient for him. For certain things are not denied us, but only withheld, to be given to us at a fitting time. In this way are we to understand the words: *He will give it to you*, that by this those favours are meant which are truly expedient for those who pray for them. The sanctified are given their requests when they pray for themselves, not on behalf of others, whether these are friends or enemies or whoever you wish; for He does not simply say, in a general way: *He will give*, but *He will give it to you*.

2. *Hitherto*, He says, *you have not asked anything in my name. Ask, and you shall receive, that your joy may be made full.* That which He speaks of as, *joy made full* is certainly not carnal joy, but spiritual. And when it will be so great that nothing further is to be added to it, then beyond doubt it will be full. Whatever we ask then which relates to the attainment of this joy, this we must ask for in the Name of Christ: if we truly understand divine grace, if we truly seek the life of the Blessed. Whatever else we ask for, nothing is asked for; not in the sense that it is really nothing, but that in comparison with so great a joy whatever else we ask for is as nothing. For of course the man of whom the Apostle spoke is not nothing: *If any man think himself to be some thing, whereas he is nothing* (Gal. vi. 3). But in comparison with a spiritual man, who knows that he is what he is by the grace of God, he who thinks about fruitless things is as nothing.

In this way also we may then correctly understand the words: *Amen, amen, I say to you: if you ask the Father anything in my name, he will give it to you*; that by the word, *anything*, we are not to understand anything whatever, but anything that is not as *nothing* in comparison with the life of the Blessed. And what follows: *Hitherto you have not asked anything in my name*, may be understood in two ways: either that you have not asked in My Name: because you have known My Name as it should not be known, or because you have not asked *anything*; since in comparison with what you ought to have asked, that which you have asked for is to be held as *nothing*.

That they may therefore ask in His Name, not what is *nothing*, but the *fulness of joy*: for if they ask for something other than this, it is as if they asked for nothing: He exhorts them, saying: *Ask, and you shall receive, that your joy may be full*; that is: Ask *this* in My Name: *That your joy may be full*, and you will receive it. For the divine mercy will never deceive His sanctified who persevere in asking for this good.

3. *These things*, He says, *I have spoken to you in proverbs. The hour cometh, when I will no more speak to you in proverbs, but will show you plainly of the Father.* I could say that this hour of which he is speaking is to be understood of that future

time when we shall see him openly, *face to face*, as the blessed Paul says; and that the words: *These things I have spoken to you in proverbs*, mean the same as what was said by the same Apostle: *Now we see through a glass in a dark manner* (I Cor. xiii. 12). But the words, *I will show you*, that the Father shall be seen through the Son, according to what He elsewhere says: *Neither doth any man know the Father, but the Son, and he to whom it shall please the Son to reveal Him* (Mt. xi. 27).

But this meaning seems to stand in the way of what follows: *In that day you shall ask in my name*. For in the world to come, when we have reached the kingdom of heaven, where we shall be like to Him, since we shall see Him as He is (I Jn. iii. 2), what shall we have to ask for, since our desires shall be satisfied with good things? (Ps. cii. 5). Whence is it said in another psalm: *I shall be satisfied when thy glory shall appear* (Ps. xvi. 15). For to ask for something means a need of some kind; and there is such abundance that there will be no need.

4. We must accept then that, as far as I can understand, Jesus is to be understood as having promised His Disciples He would change His followers from worldly minded or carnal men into spiritually minded men; though not yet such as we shall be when we shall have also a spiritual body, but such as he was who said: *We speak wisdom among the perfect*; and: *I could not speak to you as unto spiritual, but as unto carnal;* and: *Now we have received not the spirit of this world, but the Spirit that is of God; that we may know the things that are given us from God. Which things also we speak, not in the learned words of human wisdom, but in the doctrine of the Spirit, comparing spiritual things with spiritual; but the sensual man perceiveth not these things that are of the spirit of God* (I Cor. ii. 16; iii. 1; ii. 12–14).

And so the natural man, not perceiving the things that are derived from the Spirit of God, so hears things that what is told him of the nature of God is grasped by him only in some bodily form, which, however spacious and immense, however shining and beautiful, is yet a body; and so he regards as proverbs whatever Wisdom says of the Substance that is incorporeal and unchangeable. Not that he considers these sayings *are* proverbs, but he thinks of them as they who are used to hearing proverbs think of them; without understanding them.

But when a spiritually minded man begins to examine all such things: he himself is examined by no man: he sees, though in this life as through a glass dimly, yet not in a bodily sense, not by any figment of the imagination, which seizes on, or invents, likenesses of all sorts of bodies, but by means of a most sure discernment of the mind that God is not body but spirit: so clearly does the Son speak to us of the Father, that He Who speaks is seen to be of the same Substance.

Then they who ask, ask in His Name; for by the sound of that Name they understand nothing other than the reality Which is called by this name; nor do they, because of vanity or weakness of mind, imagine the Father to be in one place, and the Son in another, standing before the Father, and praying for us, Each occupying His own space, the Word uttering words on our behalf to Him Whose Word He is, while a definite space interposes between the mouth of the Speaker and the ears of the Hearer, and other such absurdities which those who are animal minded, and those who are carnal minded, make up for themselves in their own hearts.

Whatever notion of this kind comes to spiritually minded men, from our manner of speaking, when they think of God, they drive away, just as you would flies that trouble you, from the inward eyes of the mind, denying them and rejecting them; and find their comfort in the purity of His Light by which, as Witness and Guide, they see as wholly false these same bodily images which force themselves on the inward eye. They can within a certain measure think of Our Lord Jesus as man, interceding for us with the Father, while as God, together with the Father, He hears our prayer. And this I think He hints to us where He says: *And I say not to you, that I will ask the Father for you.* Only the eye of a mind that is spiritual can rise to see how it is that the Son does not ask the Father for us, but that both Father and Son together receive and grant our prayers.

5. *For the Father Himself*, He says, *loveth you, because you have loved me.* Does He love us because we love Him, or rather do we love Him because He loves us? Let the same Evangelist answer from his own Epistle: *We love, because He hath first loved us* (I Jn. iv. 10). From this is it that we love Him: because we are loved by Him. To love God is entirely a gift of God. He gave us the power to love Him Who though we loved Him not yet loved us. And displeasing Him He still loves us, that there might be in us that by which we might begin to please Him.

Nor would we love the Son unless we also loved the Father. The Father loves us because we love the Son; since it is from Father and Son we received the power to love both Father and Son: for the Spirit of them both has poured love into our hearts (Rom. v. 5), through Which Spirit we love both Father and Son, and Which Spirit we love with the Father and the Son. It was God then Who wrought in us the holy love by which we worship God; and He saw that it is good, and for this reason loved what He made. But He would not have wrought in us what He loved had He not loved us before He wrought it.

6. *And you have believed*, He said, *that I came out from God. I came forth from the Father, and am come into the world: again I leave the world, and I go to the Father.* We have truly believed. Nor should it therefore seem incredible, that in thus coming into the world He came from the Father without leaving the Father; and that leaving the world He goes to the Father, yet without abandoning the world. He came from the Father because He is from the Father's Substance. He came into the world in that He showed the world the Body He had assumed from the Virgin. He left the world by a departure of His Body: going to the Father by His Ascension as man, yet not withdrawing from the world the ruling power of His Presence. Amen.

VI. St Cyril of Alexandria, Bishop and Doctor

Confidence in Prayer[7]

John xvi. 23, 24. Jesus tells us that His holy Disciples will be more courageous and more understanding when they would be, as the Scripture says, *Endowed with power from on high* (Lk. xxiv. 49), and that when their minds would be illumined by the torch of the Spirit they would be able to see into all things, even though no longer able to question Him bodily present among them. The Saviour does not say that they would no longer as before need the light of His guidance, but that when they had received His Spirit, when He was dwelling in their hearts, they would not be wanting in any good thing, and their minds would be filled with most perfect knowledge.

And by perfect knowledge we mean that knowledge which is true and undistorted, which withholds itself from thinking or speaking whatever is perverse, and has a right belief in the Holy and Consubstantial Trinity. For though we now as it were see through a glass in a dark manner, and know only in part, as Paul tells us (I Cor. xiii. 12), nevertheless, as long as we adhere carefully to that which has been taught us, and follow close to the mind of the holy and divinely revealed Scriptures, we shall possess a knowledge which is not imperfect, and such as no one may make his own unless first enlightened by the Holy Spirit.

In this way He urges the Disciples to seek for spiritual gifts, and at the same time gives them confidence that, should they ask for them, they will not fail to obtain them; adding the word *Amen*, that He might confirm their belief that should they ask the Father anything they would receive it from Him; He acting as their Mediator and making known their request, and, One with the Father, granting it. For this is what He means by *in my name*; for we cannot draw nigh to God the Father otherwise than through the Son. For it is by Him we have access in the one Spirit to the Father; as it is written (Eph. ii. 8). It was because of this He said: *I am the door; I am the way. No man cometh to the Father, but by me* (Jn. x. 7; xiv. 6). For as the Son is God He, One with the Father, provides good things for His sanctified, and is found to be generous of His Bounty to us.

And regarding this the divine Paul has given us the clearest testimony, where he writes: *Grace to you, and peace from God our Father, and from the Lord Jesus Christ* (Rom. i. 7). And as our Mediator (I Tim. ii. 5) and our High Priest (Heb. iv. 14) and our Advocate (I Jn. ii. 1), He intercedes with the Father for us. He is our assurance in the presence of the Father. Let us then offer our prayers in Christ's Name. For in this way will the Father most readily consent to them, and grant His graces to those who seek them, that receiving them we may rejoice.

Filled therefore with spiritual gifts, and enriched by the fulness of understanding because of His Spirit dwelling within us, let us fight vigorously against every unfitting as well as evil lust, and so doing all things well, and going forward towards every virtue, with fervent zeal, and sustained by all things whatsoever that lead to holiness, let us rejoice exceedingly in the hope of the reward to come, and drawing away from the sadness that rises up from an evil conscience, let us enrich our minds with the joys of Christ.

This grace was not given to those of old. For they did not because of ignorance make use of this manner of prayer. Now it is laid down for us by Christ, and most fittingly. For the time of *making straight* has shone out, and the time of fulfilment been ushered in. For as the Law brought nothing to perfection (Heb. vii. 19), and that justice was incomplete which belonged to it, so also was its manner of prayer. Amen.

VII. The Venerable Bede, Priest and Doctor

The Fathers on Prayer[8]

It may trouble the more timid among those who listen to me to hear at the beginning of this Gospel that the Lord promised His Disciples: *Amen, amen, I say to you, if you ask the Father anything in my name, he will give it to you,* since not alone have we asked the Father many things in the name of Christ and have not received them, but even the Apostle Paul also thrice asked the Lord that he might be delivered of an angel of Satan who troubled him, and did not obtain his request. But the difficulty of this question was made clear at their time in the ancient explanation given by the Fathers who understood that those alone prayed in the name of the Saviour who pray for those things which relate to their eternal salvation. Accordingly, they say, he did not pray in the name of the Saviour when he prayed that he might be freed from the temptation he had received as a safeguard for his humility; for had he failed in this he could not be saved, as he himself declares when he says: *And lest the greatness of the revelations should exalt me, there was given me a sting of my flesh, an angel of Satan, to buffet me* (II Cor. xii. 8, 9).

So as often as our prayers are not heard it will be because we were asking for something opposed to our salvation, and so it was mercifully withheld from us, as in the case of Paul, to whom the answer was given; though he had three times besought the Lord: *My grace is sufficient for you; for power is made perfect in infirmity.* Or else we ask for useful things, and which do relate to our salvation, but we turn from us the ear of the Just Judge by our manner of life, and that happens to us of which Solomon speaks: *He that turneth away his ears from hearing the law, his prayer shall be an abomination . . .* Or while we pray for some who are in the midst of sin, that they may come again to their right mind, and of our own merits we are worthy of being heard, nevertheless their perversity stands in the way of our obtaining what we ask.

It will also sometimes happen that with earnest prayer and devotion we seek for what is wholly salutary, yet do not immediately receive what we ask for, and the answer to our prayer is put off to some future date; just as when on our bended knees we daily pray the Father: *Thy kingdom come*; yet are we to receive this same kingdom, not as soon as we have finished our prayer, but at some suitable time. We know that this is ordered by the kind providence of the Creator, so that, for example, our desires may intensify by the prolongation of our devotion, and by daily increase grow more and more, until at last they come perfectly to possess the joys they seek.

And here we must note that should we pray for sinners, and cannot obtain their conversion, we are not however deprived of the fruit of our prayer. For though they are not worthy of being saved, we shall be given the reward of the love we devoted to them. And so in prayer of this kind that promise of Christ is fulfilled in which He says: *If you ask the Father anything in my name, he will give it to you.* For we should note that He does not simply say, *He will give it*; He says: *He will give it to you.* For though He will not give it to those for whom we pray, He will give us the reward of our charity who intercede with Him for those who were going astray.

Then follows: *Hitherto you have not asked anything in my name.* They had not so far prayed in the name of the Saviour, since while they had the Saviour visibly present in their midst, they had not raised the gaze of their mind towards the invisible gifts of salvation. But our poor infirmity, praying to the Father, does not ask in the name of Jesus, that is, of Our Saviour, when it asks for what is opposed to our salvation; and our prayer is denied, not as the simplicity of the Apostles prevented them from asking for eternal salvation, by the fact of seeing the bodily presence of the Saviour, but impeded rather by our own cupidity from seeing what is God's will. The Lord then goes on to say what it is we must especially pray for, and what beyond all doubt will be given by the Father to those who trustfully persevere in prayer.

Ask, and you shall receive: that your joy may be full. The meaning is: Ask that your joy may be full, and you will receive. He therefore calls the blessedness of eternal peace *full joy*. Passing over in silence the joy of the wicked, by which they purchase eternal sorrow, the just even now have joy in their hope of heaven when for the Lord they endure earthly afflictions. They have joy when taught *by the love of the brotherhood* they learn to rejoice with them that *rejoice; weep with them that weep* (Rom. xii. 15). But joy that is mixed with tears is not full joy. It will be full joy where, with no one weeping, it shall be given to us to rejoice with them that rejoice. So He says: *Ask, and you shall receive: that your joy may be made full.*

It is as though He were to say: Ask of your Father in heaven, not for the fleeting joys of earth, which are ever mingled with sadness, and which all must end, but for that one and only joy that is lessened by no least shadow of change; an eternity of joy which no bound will end. For should you persevere in asking you will beyond any doubt obtain what you ask. Of the fulness of this joy Peter writes: *And believing shall rejoice with joy unspeakable and glorified; receiving the end of your faith, even the salvation of your souls* (I Pet. i. 8, 9).

To ask for joy of such a kind does not only mean begging with earnest words to enter the heavenly glory, but also striving by a worthy life to lay hold of it. For it avails a man nothing to seek heaven by praying well who ceases not from a wicked life, and entangles himself in evil.

These things I have spoken to you in proverbs. The hour cometh when I will no more speak to you in proverbs, but will show you plainly of the Father. He means here that hour when after His passion and resurrection the grace of the Holy Spirit will be given to them. For then being spiritually taught from within, and burning with spiritual love, the more perfectly they received all that is given to mortal men to grasp of the knowledge of the Divinity, the more ardently would they pray for and desire whatever would help them to obtain Its full vision. For this is what He adds:

In that day you shall ask in my name. We may understand here that hour in the future life when He shall openly speak of the Father, that is, when He shall clearly manifest the Father to the elect, when, as Paul says: *we shall see him face to face* (I Cor. xiii. 12). Of this manifestation John also speaks, saying: *Dearly beloved, we are now the sons of God; and it hath not yet appeared what we shall be. We know that when he shall appear, we shall be like to him; because we shall see him as he is* (I Jn. iii. 2).

And when the elect truly ask in the name of Jesus, when they intercede for our infirmity, that we may attain to His salvation, from which amid the snares of enemies we wander far here on earth, this prayer of the elect he most justly promises us, on a day to come: *In that day*, He says, *you shall ask in my name*. They will ask in that day because they are not in the darkness of torment, as in the day of this present life; it is in the light of eternal peace and glory that the prayer of the blessed is poured forth for us.

The spirits of the elect who are now in the heavenly city may also be understood to pray for themselves in the Name of the Saviour, because they long for that time of universal judgement, and for the resurrection of the bodies in which they suffered for Christ. Because of this John says: *I saw under the altar the souls of them that were slain for the word of God, and for the testimony which they held* (Apoc. vi. 9). And they cried with a great voice: *How long, O Lord, holy and true, dost thou not judge and revenge our blood on them that dwell on the earth?* Then he immediately goes on: *And to each one a single white robe was given, and it was said to them that they should rest for a little time, till their fellow servants, and their brethren, should be filled up*. The souls have now each a white robe, since they now dwell alone in joy; when finally the number of the elect is complete they shall be made joyful receiving again their own immortal bodies; then they shall receive two stoles.

And I say not to you, that I will ask the Father for you. For Our Lord Jesus Christ, as God and as man, now alludes to the loftiness of His divinity, now to the lowliness of His humanity. That He says He will not ask the Father for His Disciples was because of the power of His divinity which is consubstantial with the Father, and in Which He is wont, not to ask the Father, but, being asked, to give together with the Father. What He says to Peter: *I have prayed for thee, that thy faith fail not* (Lk. xxii. 32), and the words of John: *We have an advocate with the Father, Jesus Christ, the just* (I Jn. ii. 1), were said of the humanity He assumed because of the Plan of the Redemption, whose Triumph placed before the eyes of the Father makes intercession for our infirmity. In this sense we may also take the words: *And I say not to you, that I will ask the Father for you*; for he speaks, not of the present, *I ask*, but, *I will ask*, of a future time, because, since the blessed are then in perfect peace, there is no longer need to ask anything for them; for they now are given happiness so great that it cannot be increased.

For the Father himself loveth you, because you have loved me, and have believed that I came out from God. We are not to think here that the love and trust of the Disciples preceded the love with which the Father loved them; that human merit precedes the gift of heavenly grace, since the Apostle clearly states: *Or who hath first given to him, and recompense shall be made him? For of him, and by him, and in him, are all things* (Rom. xi. 35, 36), but rather we must understand that the Father had preceded them by His love freely bestowed, and loving them has raised them up to love and believe in His Son; and because they kept their professed faith and love of the Son, with a devout and tender heart, they were rewarded with yet greater gifts of the paternal love.

Nor must we think the Father, without the Son and the Holy Ghost, can love or bestow the gifts of love. Nor again must we think the Son can be loved or believed without the Father and the Holy Ghost. That He says: *The Father himself loveth you*, means that He, together with the Son and Holy Ghost, loves those whom He deems worthy of being loved. And that He adds: *Because you have loved me*, must be understood in the same way; for whoever truly loves the Son, loves Him together with the Father and the Spirit of them both; because the nature of the divinity is inseparable, and one and the same the gifts of Its majesty.

I came forth from the Father, and am come into the world: again I leave the world, and I go to the Father. He came forth from the Father, and came into the world; for He became visible to the world in His humanity Who was invisible with the Father in His divinity. He came forth from the Father, for He appeared to the world, not in that form in which He is equal to the Father, but in the assumed humanity in which He is less than the Father. And He came into the world, for it was in the form of a servant which He took upon Him that He presented Himself to the eyes of those even who were lovers of this world. Again He left the world and returned to the Father; for He withdrew from the eyes of the lovers of this world what they had seen, teaching those who loved Him that they were to believe that He was equal to the Father. He left the world and returned to the Father; for by His Ascension He raised His assumed humanity up to the invisible Glory.

These mystical words were spoken in proverbs, as He Himself testifies. But the Disciples to whom He addressed them were yet so unspiritual that they were far from grasping their profundity, and so perceived neither their hidden meaning nor their own ignorance; considering what had been simply and clearly said to them just as they regard proverbs who do not understand them. And so they go on to reply:

Behold, now thou speakest plainly, and speakest no proverbs. They began to assert then that He was speaking clearly, when they were unable to comprehend the hidden meaning of His words. For they add: *Now we know that thou knowest all things, and thou needest not that any man should ask thee. By this we believe thou camest forth from God.* They tell us clearly that the Lord in speaking to them used especially treat of those subjects of which they delighted to hear, and about which they used to question Him; anticipating them He of His own accord discoursed of these things. So they rightly believe and confess that like God He knows all things, and that as the Son of God He came forth from God. For it is a clear sign of the divinity to know the secrets of the hearts of men, as Solomon testifies, crying out to the Lord: *For thou only knowest the heart of all the children of men* (III Kings viii. 39). On this Jeremiah also says: *But thou, O Lord of Sabbaths, who judgest justly, and triest the reins and the hearts* (Jer. xi. 20).

Nor are these things to be recalled lightly, and in passing, but we must earnestly give our minds to this, My Brethren: that not alone are we to keep our words and actions worthy of the divine scrutiny, but even the secret thoughts of the heart. Let no flame of hate, no rust of envy, reside in the temple of our breast. Let no root of evil, nor words that outrage, rise up from there. Let no plot of wickedness be born there. Be mindful of what the Lord threatened when He said: *I know their works, and their thoughts: I come that I may gather them together* (Is. lxvi. 18).

Putting from us the traces of sin, let us prepare for Him within us an abode where He may dwell Who shall be its final Examiner and Judge. We should know that there are three kinds of evil thoughts. One, those that taint the mind from the deliberate purpose of sinning. Another, those which confuse the mind with the delights of sin, yet do not bring it to consent. Yet another, those that run naturally through the mind, and do not so much draw it to do what is evil as prevent it from dwelling on what is good; as for example, when we idly call to mind pictures of things heard or seen. Their frequent recurrence will trouble the eyes of the soul with the vexatious importunity of flies, and impede rather than shut out the image of spiritual things. Solomon warns us to keep the mind from all such harmful thoughts, saying: *With all watchfulness keep thy heart, because life issueth out of it* (Prov. iv. 23).

With this counsel in mind let us be in earnest, should we sin by consenting within the soul to evil, to wipe this quickly away by confession and by fruits worthy of repentance. If we see ourselves tempted by the delights of sin, let us with repeated prayers and tears drive the evil delight from our mind, with frequent remembrance of its enduring bitterness. And if we have found that we do not of ourselves suffice to drive it from us, let us ask the help of our brethren, so that what we cannot do by our own strength we may achieve by their intercession and counsel. *For the continual prayer of the just man availeth much*; and again as James says immediately before this: *The prayer of faith shall save the sick man, and the Lord shall raise him up: and if he be in sins, they shall be forgiven him* (Jas v. 16, 15).

As we are unable to be wholly free of idle thoughts, let us drive them away as best we can by bringing *good* thoughts into our minds, and especially by frequent consideration of the Scriptures, as the Psalmist counsels us: *O how have I loved thy law, O Lord! It is my mediation all the day* (Ps. cxviii. 97). Let us beseech the divine clemency, which is truly asking in the name of the Saviour, to give us cleanness of heart, and strength to do what is worthy; and above all things let us earnestly recall to mind *that hour* in which the Lord will speak to us no more through the Scriptures, but will speak openly to us of the Father: with Whom He lives and reigns in the Unity of the Holy Ghost for ever and for ever. Amen.

NOTES

[1] PG 31. *Constitutiones Monasticae*, Ch. I.

[2] PG 32, Sermon 9. This is one of twenty-four sermons on morals composed of extracts from the writings of St Basil, and made by Gregory Metaphrastes. Logotheta. This, on prayer, is drawn in good part from Basil's early letter to Gregory Nazianzenus, on the way of seeking spiritual perfection. PG 32, Epistle 2.

[3] A citation, slightly inapposite, from a letter to a friend, Eustathius. *See* note 2.

[4] PL 15, col. 1721.

[5] PG 63, Eclogue on Prayer, II.

[6] PL 35, Tracts in John 102.

[7] PG 74, Cyril on John.

[8] PL 94, Bk. 2, Hom. 7. This homily while adding something from the stream of Sacred Tradition, also bears witness to the established authority and guidance of the Fathers as authoritative and historical exponents of both Scripture and S. Tradition.

ASCENSION DAY

I. St Augustine: On the Day of Our Lord's Ascension

II. St Augustine: The Mystery of the Lord's Ascension

III. St Leo the Great: The Lord's Ascension

IV. St Gregory the Great: Explanations and Reflections on the Ascension

V. St John Chrysostom: Christ's Ascension Man's Exaltation

THE GOSPEL OF THE DAY

Mark xvi. 14–20

At that time: Jesus appeared to the eleven as they sat at table: and he upbraided them with their incredulity and hardness of heart, because they did not believe them who had seen him after he was risen again. And he said to them: Go ye into the whole world, and preach the Gospel to every creature. He that believeth and is baptized, shall be saved: but he that believeth not shall be condemned. And these signs shall follow them that believe: In my name they shall cast out devils: they shall speak with new tongues. They shall take up serpents; and if they shall drink any deadly thing, it shall not hurt them: they shall lay their hands upon the sick, and they shall recover. And the Lord Jesus, after he had spoken to them, was taken up into heaven, and sitteth on the right hand of God. But they going forth preached everywhere: the Lord working withal, and confirming the words with signs that followed.

Exposition from the Catena Aurea

V. 14. *At length he appeared to the eleven as they were at table.*

Gloss: Mark, to complete his narrative of the Gospel, relates this final apparition, in which after His Resurrection Christ appears to His Disciples, saying: *At length he appeared . . .* Gregory, *Hom.* 29 *in Evan*: But we must note what Luke relates in the Acts, saying: *And eating together with them, he commanded them, that they should not depart from Jerusalem*; and a little later, v. 9, he says: *While they looked on, he was raised up*. For He ate and He ascended, that by the act of eating He might make evident the reality of His Flesh. And because of this is it here said: *At length He appeared to them as they were at table.* JEROME: He appeared to the eleven gathered together that they might all be witnesses, and that they might all declare that which together they had seen and heard. Then follows:

And he upbraided them with their incredulity and hardness of heart, because they did not believe them who had seen him after he was risen.

AUGUSTINE: *Harmony of the Gospels*, 3: 25: How is the word *at length* used here? For the last time the Apostles saw the Lord upon the earth was upon the fortieth day after His Resurrection. Why should He then blame them because they had not believed those who had seen Him risen from the dead, seeing they themselves had already seen Him several times since His Resurrection? It remains then to believe that Mark desired to give his own brief account, and said *at length*, because it was the last happening on this particular day, now turning towards night, after the Disciples had returned to Jerusalem from the village and had found the eleven, as Luke tells us, and were speaking with them about the Resurrection of the Lord. But there were there also some who did not believe. While these were sitting at table, as Mark tells us, and talking together of these things, as Luke tells us, the Lord stood in their midst, and said to them: *Peace be to you*, as both Luke and John have related. And among the words which Luke and John tell us He spoke to the Disciples, this upbraiding, of which Mark speaks, is also included.

But again, how is it Mark says that He appeared to the eleven as they were at table, if this time is the beginning of the night of the Lord's Day, since John clearly states (xx. 24) that Thomas was not then with them; whom we believe went out before the Lord entered among them, and after the other two returned from the village had been talking with the eleven, as we find in Luke (xxiv. 33)? But Luke in his narrative gives ground for thinking that while they were speaking of these things Thomas left them and then the Lord came amongst them. But Mark, who says: *At length he appeared to the eleven as they were at table*, compels us to confess that Thomas was there; unless perhaps though one was absent he still wished to speak of them as *the eleven*: for the Apostolic group was referred to by this number before Mathias was elected in the place of Judas. Or if this is hard to accept, let us suppose that after His many appearances, lastly, that is, on the fortieth day, He appeared to the eleven as they sat at table. And since He was now about to leave them, ascending into heaven, He wished on that day particularly to reproach them, because they had not, until they had seen Him themselves, believed the testimony of those who had seen Him risen from the dead; since after His Ascension, when they were preaching the Gospel, even the Gentiles were prepared to believe what they had not seen. For the same Mark after speaking of this upbraiding says:

V. 15. *And he said to them: Go ye into the whole world . . .* and:

V. 16. *He that believeth not shall be condemned.*

Being about to preach this, should they not first be reproved who refused to believe those to whom He had appeared: until they had themselves seen Him?

GREGORY: The Lord rebuked His Disciples as He was about to leave them corporally; as the words He would speak at parting would impress themselves more deeply on the hearts of His hearers. JEROME: He reproached them for their incredulity that credulity might follow. He reproached the hardness of the stony heart, that a heart of flesh filled with love might take its place.

GREGORY: And having reproved their hardness, let us hear what He says admonishing them. For He goes on: *Go ye into the whole world, and preach the Gospel to every creature.* By *every creature* man is meant: for man has being in common with the stones, life with the trees, feeling with the animals, understanding with the angels. The Gospel is preached to every creature when it is preached to man; for he is instructed for whom all things on earth were made, and to whom all things, because of a certain resemblance, are not unlike. By this name *every creature* every nation of the Gentiles may also be meant. For before that He had said: *Go ye not into the way of the Gentiles* (Mt. x. 5). But now He says: *Preach the Gospel to every creature*, so that the preaching of the Apostles, being first rejected by the Jews, would then be preached to our gain; and since it had been rejected by them in pride, it would become a witness of their reprobation.

THEOPHYLACTUS: Or, to every creature, that is, the believing and the unbelieving. Then follows: *He that believeth and is baptized, shall be saved.* It does not suffice to believe: he who believes, and is not yet baptized, but is only a catechumen, has not yet fully acquired salvation. GREGORY: It may be that each of you will say to himself: I have believed; so I shall be saved. He says what is true if together with faith he also does good works; for that is true faith which does not deny in work what it says in word.

But he that believeth not shall be condemned. BEDE: What shall we here say of children who by reason of their age are yet unable to believe. For as to adults there is no question. In the Church of the Saviour children believe through others, as they draw from others those sins which are forgiven them in baptism.[2]

VV. 17 and 18. *And these signs shall follow them . . . they shall take up serpents . . .*

THEOPHYLACTUS: That is, they will destroy serpents, those seen by the mind; according to the words of Luke: *I have given you power to tread upon serpents and scorpions* (Lk. x. 19), spiritually interpreted. It can also be understood of real serpents, as happened to Paul who was unhurt by the viper. *And if they shall drink any deadly thing.* Many such happenings are read in history, and that many of them, protected by the sign of Christ, remained unharmed by poisons they had drunk.

They shall lay their hands upon the sick, and they shall recover.
GREGORY: Is it that we do not believe

because we do not now perform these wonders? But these were needed for the beginning of the Church; for that the faith of those who believed might become strong it had to be nourished by wonders. Because, just as when we plant a vineyard we must water it till we see it flourishing in the soil, and when the vines have begun to take root we no longer water them.

There are certain things concerning these signs and wonders which we should carefully consider. Each day the Church does spiritually that which she then did corporeally by the hands of the Apostles. For when her priests giving the grace of exorcism lay hands on those who believe, and forbid the unclean spirits to dwell in their souls, what is it they do but *cast out devils*? And the faithful, who have put aside the speech of the world and speak of holy things, are speaking *with new tongues*. While they who by their pious encouragement draw evil out of the hearts of others *take up serpents*. And when they hear evil counsels, and yet are not drawn to evil doing, *they drink a deadly thing, and it shall not hurt them*. And they who as often as they see their neighbour grow lax in doing good strengthen them by the example of their own good works, *lay their hands upon the sick* that they may recover. And the more spiritual are these wonders the greater are they; and the greater they are the more, by means of them, not bodies but souls are restored to life.

V. 19. *And the Lord Jesus, after he had spoken to them. . .*

JEROME (on *Go ye into the entire world*): The Lord Jesus, Who had come down from heaven to deliver our nature from its infirmity, the Same has now ascended into heaven. Hence: *And the Lord Jesus*.

AUGUSTINE, *Harm. of Gosp.* 3: 25, 77: From which it is apparent that this was the last discourse He held with them on earth; although it does not appear that we are compelled to accept this. For he does not say: After He had said *these things*, but after He had *spoken* to them. Hence it allows, if need be, that this was not His very final discourse to them, but that all He said to them during these last days could be implied in this sentence: *After he had spoken to them, he was taken up into heaven*.

But because what we have said above more strongly favours that this was the last day, then it must be believed that after the discourse above mentioned, which Mark records, taken with the words which are recorded in the Acts of the Apostles, the Lord was taken up to heaven.

GREGORY: We learned in the Old Testament that Elias was taken up into heaven. But one is the upper heaven (*aethereum*), another the lower (*aereum*). The lower is closer to the earth. Elias was raised up to the lower heaven, that he might swiftly be conducted to some hidden region of the earth where, in great peace of body and soul, he would live until the end of the world, when he again returns that he may pay the debt of nature.

We must also note that Elias is said to have ascended in a chariot, so that it might be clearly manifested to them that a holy man still needs the help of others. But it is not recorded of our Redeemer that He was taken up either in a chariot or by angels: for He Who has made all things by His own power is borne above them all.

But we must consider what Mark adds: *And sitteth on the right hand of God*; since Stephen says: *Behold, I see the heavens opened, and the Son of man standing on the right hand of God* (Acts vii. 55). But to sit is the posture of one giving judgement; to stand of one combating or aiding. Stephen then being in the contest of suffering beholds Him standing Whom he looked on as his helper; but Mark, after His assumption into heaven, describes Him as *sitting*, because after the glory of His assumption He shall at the end be seen as Judge.

AUGUSTINE, *The Creed*: We do not understand this *sitting* therefore in the sense that He is sitting in His human members; as though the Father sits on the left, and the Son on the right; but understand *the right hand* as meaning the power which He as Man receives from God: that He might come to judge Who had first come to suffer judgement. For to sit is understood to mean *dwell*; just as we say of a man, 'he sat in that land for three years'. So we believe Christ abides at the right hand of God the Father. For He is Blessed, and dwells in the blessedness which is called *the right hand of the Father*. For there every one is at the right hand; there is no unhappiness.[3]

V. 20. *But they going forth preached everywhere . . .*

BEDE: As the Evangelist Mark begins his Gospel late, so he continues later in his account of events. For he speaks neither of the Nativity of the Lord, nor of His Infancy, nor of that of His Precursor, but begins from the beginning of the preaching of the Gospel, which was made by John, and continues his narrative till that time in which the Apostles have sown the same word of the Gospel through the whole earth.[4]

GREGORY: What are we to think of these words if not that obedience followed the command, and signs and wonders followed obedience? For the Lord had commanded them: *Go ye into the whole world, and preach the Gospel*; and in the Acts: *You shall be witnesses to the uttermost part of the earth* (Acts i. 8).

But they going forth preached everywhere: the Lord working withal. AUGUSTINE, *Ep.* 80, *to Hesychium*: Why is this preaching said to be fulfilled by the Apostles, since even now there are peoples among whom it has only begun, and in whom it is not yet fulfilled? This command was not so given to the Apostles by the Lord as if they alone, to whom He was then speaking, were to fulfil this so great task. For just as He appears to have said to them alone: *Behold I am with you all days, even to the consummation of the world* (Mt. xxviii. 20), who does not see that He promised this to the whole Church which, as those who die are succeeded by those who are born, shall last from then until the end of the world?

THEOPHYLACTUS: We must keep this before our mind even now: that the word is confirmed by works, as in the times of the Apostles works confirmed their words *by signs that followed.* May it be, O Christ, that our words, which speak of Thy Glory, shall be confirmed by signs and deeds, that we may at last be made perfect, Thou co-operating in all our words and works, for to Thee is the glory both of the words and the works. Amen.

I. St Augustine, Bishop and Doctor

Given in the Leonine Basilica[5]

I. *The Solemnity of the Holy Leontius.* The Lord Jesus, the Only begotten of the Father, Co-eternal with His Parent, like Him Invisible, like Him Omnipotent, as God Equal to Him, became Man for us, as you know, and have received, and hold fast in faith; and though He took to Himself a human form, He did not give up the divine. Omnipotence was veiled; infirmity made manifest. He was born, as you have come to know, that we might be reborn. He died, that we might not die for ever. And straightaway, that is, on the third day, He rose again from the dead; assuring us that we too shall rise on the last day.

He showed Himself to His Disciples: that they might see him with their eyes, and touch Him with their hands; showing them what He had become, and that He had not put off what He always was. For forty days He spoke with them, as you have heard, going in and coming out, eating and drinking together with them; not now from need, but wholly from power, and making plain to them the true nature of His Body: mortal upon the cross, immortal from the grave.

II. This day then we are celebrating the Lord's Ascension. Today there is also a festival proper to this church: the death of the founder of this Basilica of the holy Leontius. But it is fitting that the star be overshadowed by the sun. So let us, as we began, speak rather of the Lord. The good servant rejoices when his Lord is praised.

III. *Belief in the Ascension and its Commemoration over all the earth.* On this day therefore, that is, the fortieth after His Resurrection, the Lord ascended into heaven. We have not seen, but we believe. They who beheld Him proclaimed what they saw, and they have filled the whole earth: *There are no speeches nor languages where their voices are not heard. Their sound hath gone forth into all the earth: and their words unto the ends of the world* (Ps. xviii. 4, 5). And so they have reached even unto us, and awakened us from sleep. And lo! this death is celebrated throughout the world.

IV. *The Prophecy of Christ's Ascension.* Remember the psalm. To whom was it said: *Be thou exalted, O God*? To whom was it said? Was *Be thou exalted* said to the Father, Who never was made lowly? Be Thou exalted: Thou. Who wast enclosed in the womb of a mother. Thou Who wast formed in Her whom Thou made. Thou Who hast lain in a manger. Thou Who as a true Child in the flesh drank milk from the breast. Thou who while borne in Thy Mother's arms sustained the world. Thou whom the venerable Simeon beheld a child, and extolled as Mighty. Thou Whom the Widow Anna saw at the breast, and knew Omnipotent. Thou Who hast hungered because of us, suffered thirst for us, grown weary on the way (but did the Bread of Life hunger, the Fountain thirst, the Way grow weary?). Thou Who hast borne all these things for us. Thou Who hast slept, yet unsleeping watches over Israel. And lastly, Thou Who wast seized, bound, scourged, crowned with thorns, hung upon the Tree, pierced with a lance, died, and was buried. Be Thou exalted, O God!

V. Be Thou exalted, he cries, *exalted above the heavens*: for thou art God. Take Thou Thy seat in heaven Who hung from the Cross. As Judge to come Thou art awaited Who awaited and received judgement. Who could believe this without His help Who raised the needy from the earth, and uplifted the poor from the dunghill? He has raised up His own needy flesh, and placed it with the Princes of His people (Ps. cxii. 7), with whom He shall judge the living and the dead. He has placed this needy flesh with those to whom He said: *You shall sit on twelve seats, judging the twelve tribes of Israel* (Mt. xix. 28).

VI. *The Church The Glory of Christ. Be Thou* therefore *exalted above the heavens, O God!* This has come to pass. It is now fulfilled. Yet we also say of that which was proclaimed of the future: *Be thou exalted above the heavens, O God!* We have not seen it, but we believe. For lo! Before our eyes is now fulfilled that which follows: *Be thou exalted, O God, above the heavens: and thy glory above all the earth.* He cannot believe the first who does not see this. For what does, *And thy glory above all the earth* mean but Thy Church which is spread over all the earth, Thy Spouse spread over all the earth, Thy Bride over all the earth? Thy Beloved, Thy Dove, Thy Consort! She is Thy glory. And the Apostle teaches us this. *The man indeed*, he says, *ought not to cover his head; because he is the image and glory of God. But the woman is the glory of man* (I Cor. xi. 7). If the woman is the glory of man, then the Church is the glory of Christ, Who with the Father and the Holy Ghost lives and reigns world without end. Amen.

II. St Augustine, Bishop and Doctor

The Mystery of the Lord's Ascension[6]

Many are the sacred mysteries stored within the holy Scriptures; whether those we have yet to search for, or those the Lord has deigned to make known to our lowliness, but which time does not allow us to unfold to Your Holiness. For I have come to notice that in these days particularly, the Church is filled with persons who are more eager to leave it than to come there; who find it a burthen should we occasionally speak to you at a little length, and who at the same time should they be held till evening at the dinner table, to which they are hurrying, neither leave nor suffer inconvenience, nor will they without any shame abandon it at any time. Yet, because we cannot cheat those who come here hungry, we shall not pass over in silence, although briefly, the mystery of this day: that Our Lord Jesus Christ, in that Body in which He arose from the dead, has ascended into heaven.

2. *After His Resurrection Christ spoke with His Disciples; to confirm them in their faith. He ascended to heaven, that they might be separated from Him in the Flesh.*

And with just reason because of the weakness of His Disciples: for there were not wanting in that number those whom the devil would tempt to unbelief, so that a certain disciple would have less belief in His living members, in the very outward form in which he had known Him, than in His recent wounds. And so to strengthen them He deigned to live with them after His Resurrection for forty complete days; beginning with the day of His Passion until this last day, coming in and going out, eating and drinking together with them, as the Scripture says; confirming that now, after the Resurrection, He was restored to them Who had been taken from them by the Cross.

This notwithstanding He did not wish to continue to remain before their eyes in the Flesh, nor that they should cling to Him any longer through natural affection. For with that same feeling of attachment because of which Peter was fearful lest He suffer, they desired Him to be always with them in His Bodily Presence. They had grown accustomed to seeing Him with them as their Master, their Comforter, Consoler, Protector; a man like themselves. When they no longer saw Him as such they began to believe in Him though He was absent. He had, as He deigned Himself to say, watched over them as a hen watches over her chickens; for the hen too, because of the frailty of her chickens, also becomes weak. For, as you will call to mind, we see many birds which bring forth their young, but we see no bird become weak with her young save only the hen. And because of this the Lord drew from her this similitude; because of our frailty He too had, by the taking of our flesh, taken on our infirmity.

But now they must be greatly lifted up in their minds, and begin to think of Him in a spiritual manner: as the Word of the Father, God with God, by Whom all things were made; and the Body they beheld did not permit them. He showed Himself to them therefore that they might by conversing during these forty days be confirmed in their faith. But He showed Himself more to withdraw Himself from their eyes; and so that they might begin to learn to think of Him as God, and that He Who on earth had spoken with them as a brother would now as their Lord assist them from heaven.

This the Evangelist John implies; should anyone observe, and consider. For the Lord says: *Let not your heart be troubled. If you loved me*, He says, *you would indeed be glad, because I go to the Father; for the Father is greater than I* (Jn. xiv. 28). And in another place: *I and the Father are one* (Jn. x. 30). And this equality He claims, not by robbery, but by nature: that He might teach this to a certain one of His Disciples who said to Him: *Lord, show us the Father, and it is enough for us.* And He replied: *Philip, have I been so long a time with you, and you have not known the Father? He that seeth me, seeth the Father also* (Jn. xiv. 8, 9).

What does, *Who seeth me*, mean? If it means only the eyes of the flesh, they saw only what they who crucified Him saw. What then does, *Who seeth me*, mean if not who understands Me, who sees Me with the eye of the soul? For it is as the inward ears the Lord had in mind when, though no deaf person stood near Him, He said: *He that hath ears to hear, let him hear* (Mt. xi. 15). Such also is the inward vision of the heart by means of which, if one has seen the Lord, he has seen also the Father; because He is equal to the Father.

3. *The Son of God by Nature equal to the Father, through Mercy became Weak unto death.*

Hear the Apostle, eager to remind us of Christ's mercy, how He became weak for our sakes that He might gather His chickens under His wings, teaching His Disciples so that they also might share the sufferings of the afflicted: they who from their common frailty had risen to a certain steadfastness, since He from His heavenly might had stooped to our infirmity. He said: *Let this mind be in you, which was also in Christ Jesus.* Deign, he tells us, out of compassion for those who are children to imitate the Son of God, *Who being in the form of God.* Now by saying, *Being in the form of God*, He shows Him to be equal to God. For He is not lesser in form (or nature) than He Whose *form* He is. For if it is lesser, it is not the same *form* (of God).

Yet, lest anyone be doubtful, he adds and puts down in writing concerning the Word Itself, thereby closing the mouths of the godless: *Who being in the form of God*, he says, *thought it not robbery to be equal with God.* What, dearest brethren, does the Apostle mean when he says: *Thought it not robbery*? That He is by nature equal with Him. For whom then was equality with God a robbery? For the first man; to whom it was said: *Eat, and you shall be as Gods* (Gen. iii. 5). He wished, by rapine, to raise himself up to equality, and as a punishment forfeited immortality. He for Whom it was not robbery, thought it not robbery to be equal with God. If then He is equal, not by robbery but by nature, their union is one of complete and perfect harmony.

And what did He do? *He emptied himself*, he says, *taking the form of a servant; being made in the likeness of men, and in habit found as a man: he humbled himself, becoming obedient unto death, even to the death of the cross* (Phil. ii. 5–8). It was not enough to speak of His death; he declares to us the kind of death. And why the kind of death? Because there are many who are ready to die; many who will say: I have no fear of death, but I would like to die in my bed, surrounded by my children, my grandchildren, by the tears of my wife. Such persons do not seem to refuse death; but for choosing the kind of death they are punished by fear. And He chose the kind of death: one that was worse than all the rest. As men chose for themselves the better kind of death, so He chose the worst; the one execrated by all Jews. He that is to come to judge the living and the dead did not Himself fear to die, through false witnesses, and by the sentence of a judge. He feared not to die in the ignominy of the Cross, that He might deliver from ignominy all whosoever would believe in Him. And so *He became obedient unto death*; even to the death of the Cross, and, though by nature equal with God and strong in the power of His Might, weak in His tenderness for mankind. Strong so that He could make all things; weak that He might remake all.

4. *Christ wishes to go; that being Absent in the Flesh, they may come to dwell on His Divinity. He is not less the Son of God through His Incarnation*.

Take note therefore of what John says: *If you loved me, you would indeed be glad, because I go to the Father: for the Father is greater than I.* How then is He equal to Him, as the Apostle says? As the Lord Himself says? *I and the Father are one* (Jn. x. 30). And again in another place: *Who sees me, sees the Father* (Jn. xiv. 8, 9). Why then does He say: *The Father is greater than I*? This phrase in the measure the Lord intended to apply it is in a way one of reproach as well as one of consolation. They had thought only for the Man; and were unable to give their minds to God. If the Man should be withdrawn from their eyes and from among them, then they would think of God; and so cutting off the familiar contact which existed between them and the Man, they, in the absence of His Body, would learn to think of His Divinity.

Accordingly He says to them: *If you loved me, you would indeed be glad, because I go to the Father*. Why? So that when I go to the Father you will be able to think of me as equal with the Father. It is for this reason *the Father is greater than I*: for till now you saw Me in the Flesh: till now the Father is greater than I. Consider whether you follow my meaning: they had not yet learned to think of Him as God. I shall put this a little more clearly for our slower brethren. Let those who have already grasped my meaning bear with the slowness of the rest, imitating the patience of the Lord, *Who being in the form of God, humbled himself, becoming obedient unto death.*

If you loved me. If you loved Me you would indeed be glad that I am going to the Father; what else does this mean but that you do not love Me? What is it then that you love? The Body you see. You do not wish It to go from before your eyes. But *if you loved me*: what does He mean by *Me*? *In the beginning was the Word, and the Word was with God, and the Word was God* (Jn. i. 3), as John himself says. If therefore you so loved Me as the One by Whom all things were made, you would indeed be glad that I go to the Father. Why? *Because the Father is greater than I.* For as long as you see Me on earth, the Father is greater than I. Let Me go from before your eyes; let Me take from your sight this mortal Body, assumed because of your own mortality, and you will begin not to see this garment with which in humility I have clothed Myself. Let It be raised up to heaven that you may learn what you are to hope for.

For He did not put off this garment He had willed to put on here below. Had He put It off all men might then despair of the resurrection of their own bodies. He but raised It to heaven. And yet there are those who doubt the resurrection of the body. If God proved this in His own Body, will He deny it to man? For He put it on in mercy; man from the nature of man. And He showed it to them; He confirmed what He said to them, and raised it up. Taken away from their bodily eyes they no longer see Him as man. What was in their hearts that arose from natural affection is now as it were mourned within them.

And they gathered together in one place and began to pray. When ten days had passed He would send the Holy Spirit, to fill them with spiritual love; taking away their earthly affection. In this way He began to make them see how Christ was the Word of God, God with God, by Whom all things were made. They could not be filled with this understanding unless the object of their earthly love should go from before their eyes. And so He said: *If you loved me you would indeed be glad; because I go to the Father; for the Father is greater than I.* As God I am equal to the Father. As man He is greater than I: Equal by nature, greater because of the mercy of His Son. For He humbled Himself; becoming not alone less than Himself, but as the Scriptures say, a little less than the angels (Ps. viii. 6).

He is not less; although with the eyes of the body you see that the Son in taking flesh stepped down in some measure from equality with the Father; from which He yet never departed. But in taking flesh —for He took upon Him a man's body—He was not changed; just as he who puts on a garment is not changed into a garment but within remains his complete self. Should a senator put on a servile dress; should he put on prison dress, because, let us say, clothed as a senator he was unable to enter the prison to comfort someone detained there, because of his compassion he will appear ignoble in appearance. But within he retains the senatorial dignity unimpaired, and indeed the more perfectly the greater the compassion that moved him to put on this outward semblance of baseness.

So too the Lord, while remaining God, while remaining the Word, remaining Wisdom, remaining Majesty, remaining King of heaven and Ruler of earth, while feeding His angels, while everywhere complete, complete in the prophets, complete in all the saints, Whole and entire in the womb of the Virgin, condescends to the taking of our flesh, to join it to Himself as a spouse, so that He might be espoused to the chaste virgin His Church, and as Bridegroom came forth from His chamber.

To fulfil this task, therefore, He became as man less than the Father, while as God He is equal to the Father. Put away from you therefore all unspiritual affection. It is as though He says to His Apostles: You do not wish to let Me go—for every man is reluctant to part with his friend, saying to him as it were: stay yet a while, my heart is refreshed while it sees you—but it is better for you that you no longer see this Body, and that you turn your thoughts to my Divinity. Outwardly I withdraw from you; inwardly I shall fill you with Myself. For is it in the Flesh, and by means of His Flesh, that Christ enters the heart? No! It is in His divinity He takes possession of our soul; in His humanity He outwardly admonishes us, speaking to the heart through the eye. He dwells within us that we may be inwardly changed, and be given life by Him, and be formed on Him: for He is the unformed form of all things that are.

5. *After His Resurrection Christ treats with His Disciples, that He may establish, that in this world we must believe in the Incarnation.*

And so if He spent forty days with His Disciples, He did not without reason spend forty days with them. Perhaps twenty might have been enough; thirty would have sufficed; but forty days is the divine arrangement for this whole world. On occasions we have treated of this point, in relation to the denary number multiplied by four. I shall recall it to those of you who heard Me. The denary number signifies the fulness of wisdom. This wisdom is distributed throughout the four parts of the world; over the whole earth; and the fourfold times are disposed in due order. For the year has four seasons; and the world four cardinal points. Ten then multiplied by four gives us the number forty.

Because of this the Lord fasted for forty days; to show us that as long as we are in the world the faithful must abstain from all corruption. Elias, representing in his person the dignity of prophecy, fasted for forty days (III Kings xix. 8); showing that this is also taught in prophecy. Moses, in his own person standing for the Law, fasted for forty days; showing us that this is taught also in the Law (Ex. xxiv. 28). For forty years the people of Israel were led in the desert (Num. xxxii. 12). For forty days the Ark was tossed upon the Flood; which Ark is a figure of the Church: made from imperishable wood; for imperishable wood are the souls of the saints and the just; which Ark also has within it both clean and unclean animals; for as long as we live in this world, and the Church is made clean by baptism as by a flood, She cannot be without both good and bad; and so the former Ark had within it both clean and unclean animals.

But after Noah emerged from the Ark he offered no sacrifices to God save from the animals that were clean (Gen. vi–viii). From which we are to understand that though in this Ark also there are clean and unclean, after this flood God accepts those only who have made themselves clean. Therefore, brethren, consider all this time you now see passing as but forty days. All this time, as long as men are in this world, the Ark is in the Flood; as long as Christians are baptized and made clean through water, the Ark, which for forty days was tossed upon the waters, is seen upon the waves.

The Lord remaining with His Disciples for forty days deigned by this to show us that belief in the Incarnation is necessary for all men throughout this time; and this is needed because we are weak. If there had been an eye that had seen that, *In the beginning was the Word*, which had seen, which had grasped, which had embraced, which had rejoiced, there would have been no need that the Word should take Flesh and dwell among us. But because the inner eye that could grasp and take delight in Him had been blinded by the dust of sin, there was no way whereby men could come to know the Word; and that He might be sent Whom men before could not see, then afterwards could see, He deigned to become Flesh.

Therefore as the Plan of the Incarnation of Christ, by which we go towards the Lord, is necessary to the faithful in this life, so when we have come to this glorious vision of the Word, this whole fleshly dispensation will no longer be necessary. And so His dwelling on earth for forty days after His Resurrection, that He might show us, that as long as the Ark is seen[7] to toss upon the Flood of this present life, so long shall faith in the Incarnation of Christ be necessary to salvation. Hearken to what I am saying, brethren: Believe in Christ Jesus born of the Virgin Mary, Who was crucified and rose again from the dead.

There is no need to speak of the life after this: that we have already grasped by faith; that we hold fast to; it is indispensable to the weakness of our nature. Remember the love of That Hen which defends our frailty (Mt. xxiii. 37). Think of the beast of mercy of One *who was on his journey*, upon which He lifted up the man who had been left half dead (Lk. x. 30–4). He lifted him up; on what? On His beast of burden. Our flesh is the Lord's beast of burden. Therefore when it shall have passed beyond this present world, what will the Lord say to thee? Because thou hast rightly believed in the Flesh of Christ, now take thy joy in His Majesty and Divinity. The Weak was needed for the weak; the Strong shall be the Friend of the strong.

6. The Future Resurrection of the Body. And you too must put off this same infirmity: according to what you have heard from the Apostle: *For this corruptible body must put on incorruption; and this mortal body immortality. For, flesh and blood cannot possess the kingdom of God* (I Cor. xv. 53, 50). Why can they not possess it? Because this flesh will not rise again? Far from it! The body will rise again; but what shall happen to it? It shall be changed, and it too will become a celestial and angelic body. For have the angels bodies? But this it is that concerns us especially: that this flesh shall rise again, this which dies, and is buried; this which can be seen, can be touched, which has need of food and drink that it may endure, which grows sick, and suffers pain, this will rise again; for the wicked, unto everlasting punishment: for the just, that they may be wholly transformed.

When the body shall be changed what will it then be? It shall be then called a heavenly body; not mortal flesh: *For this corruptible body must put on incorruption; and this mortal body immortality*. They wonder if God Who made all things from nothing makes a heavenly body from flesh! But in the Flesh He made wine from water; and is it astonishing that He shall make a celestial body from flesh? Let you not therefore doubt that God is able to do this thing. Angels, that they might be, were nothing; but by His power they are what they are. He that could make thee when thou were not, can He not restore thee to what thou hast been; and through His own Incarnation can He not give to your faith the reward of His own glory.

And therefore when all these

things have passed away, that shall happen to us of which John tells: *Dearly Beloved, we are now the sons of God; and it hath not yet appeared what we shall be. We know that when he shall appear, we shall be like to him; because we shall see him as he is* (I Jn. iii. 2). Prepare for this vision. Meanwhile, as long as you are in the flesh, believe in Christ Incarnate: and so believe in Him as not to be imagining you have been misled by any falsehood! For does Truth lie? And should He lie, where shall we look for guidance? What shall we do? In whom shall we believe? The Truth therefore, the true Word, true wisdom, the true Power of God: *The Word was made flesh*; true flesh. *Handle and see; for a spirit hath not flesh and bones, as you see me to have* (Lk. xxiv. 39). For they were true bones, true nerves, true wounds; they touched what was true; what was true the mind perceived. A Man was handled, God was perceived; flesh was handled, wisdom perceived; weakness was felt, Might comprehended.

Here is Truth in every respect. Yet thereupon the Body, that is, the Head, went before us into heaven. The other members shall follow afterwards. Why is this? That these members may rest in peace for some time after death, and at their appointed time may all rise again. If the Lord also had willed to rise then from the dead, it would not be in Him we would believe. So He willed to offer to God in Himself, *the first fruits of them that sleep*, so that when you would see what was restored in Him, you would begin to hope for that which is to be given to thee.

All the people of God shall be made equal to the angels, and shall share in their company. Then let no one say to you, brethren: The foolish Christians believe that the body will rise again; Who rises from the dead, or who has ever risen? And who has come from below and told you? Christ came. O wretched, O perverse and foolish human heart! If a man's grandfather should rise from the dead, he would believe in him. The Lord of the world has risen, and he will not believe in Him.

7. *The Mystery of the Trinity.* Hold fast then, brethren, to the true, the genuine Catholic faith. The Son is equal with the Father, the Gift of God the Holy Spirit is equal with the Father, and the Father, Son, and Holy Ghost are one God, not three Gods; not united successively to each other in steps, but united in Majesty, One God. And yet the Son because of us, *the Word was made flesh, and dwelt amongst us. He thought it not robbery to be equal with God, but emptied himself, taking the form of a servant, and in habit found as a man* (Phil. ii. 6, 7).

And that you may know, brethren, that this Trinity is truly equal, and that the words, *the Father is greater than I*, were said only of the body the Lord had put on, why was it never said of the Holy Spirit that He is less than the Father, if not because He had not assumed a body? Note with care what I have said to you. Search the Scriptures, take up any page, read any verse. Never will you find it said that the Holy Spirit is less than God. He therefore was said to be less than the Father Who for our sakes became less, that we through Him might become greater.

Turning then to the Lord our God, the Father Almighty, let us as best we can give thanks with all our hearts, beseeching Him that in His goodness He will mercifully hear our prayers, by His grace drive evil from our thoughts and actions, increase our faith, guide our minds, grant us His holy inspirations, and bring us to joy without end, through His Son our Lord and Saviour Jesus Christ. Amen.

III. St Leo the Great, Pope and Doctor

The Lord's Ascension[8]

Synopsis:

I. Christ's remaining on earth, and the doubt and hesitation of the Disciples, were so ordered that our faith might be confirmed.
II. Great things were laid down for us by Christ in these days.
III. By the touch of His wounds the souls of His Disciples were made firm.
IV. Christ's Ascension filled with joy those His death had saddened, and His Resurrection left doubting. The gifts of Christ outweigh those stolen from us by the devil.

I. After the glorious and blessed Resurrection of our Lord Jesus Christ, whereby in three days He restored that true temple of God which the impiety of the Jews had destroyed, on this day, Dearly Beloved, the number of the sacred forty days was fulfilled, which were ordained by divine providence, and used to the increase of sacred knowledge, so that while the time of Our Lord's Bodily Presence among us was by Him extended by this measure of time, our faith in His Resurrection was strengthened by proofs close linked one with the other.

For the death of Christ had greatly troubled the hearts of the Disciples, and because of the torment of the Cross, the giving up of His Spirit, and the burial of His lifeless Body, a kind of torpor of unbelief had crept over their minds, already weighed down with grief. For when the holy women, as the Gospel tells us, announced that the stone had been rolled back from the sepulchre, and that the tomb was empty of a body, and that angels there were witnesses that *the Lord was alive*, their words, to the Apostles and the other Disciples, seemed like those of deranged persons. The Spirit of Truth would never have allowed this uncertainty, which arose from human infirmity, to enter the hearts of His preachers unless that this faltering anxiety, this anxious hesitancy, might provide a foundation for our faith.

By means of the Apostles divine providence had a care for the trials, the unrest, that would trouble us: we being instructed in them, against the deceits of evil and the arguments of this world's wisdom. Their eyes prepared us, their ears instructed us, their touch confirmed us. Let us give thanks to the divine providence, and likewise to that needed hesitation of the holy fathers. They doubted that we might have no doubt.

II. These days then, Dearly Beloved, which followed, between the

Resurrection of the Lord and His Ascension, were not passed in simple idleness. During them great truths were established, great mysteries revealed. During them the dread of death was taken away, and the immortality not alone of the soul but also of the body made clear. The Lord breathing upon them the Holy Spirit was poured into all the Apostles, and to the Blessed Peter above all the rest was entrusted, first, the Keys of the Kingdom, and next, the care of the Lord's Flock.

During these days to two of the Disciples a third Person, the Lord, is joined as a companion while they journeyed. And that all shadow of doubt might be wiped from our minds, He rebuked the slow-wittedness of those who were fearful and hesitant. Their hearts glowing they conceive the flame of faith, and the souls that were lukewarm now, as the Lord opens the Scriptures to them, begin to burn like fire. And at the Breaking of the Bread the eyes of those who ate with Him were opened. Far happier the opening of *their* eyes, wherein the exaltation of their nature was revealed, than that of our First Parents, on whom was then heaped the shame of what they had done.

III. In the midst of these and other wonders, when the Lord had appeared in their midst and had said to them: *Peace be to you* (Lk. xxiv. 36; Jn. xx. 26), the Disciples began to be greatly troubled by grievous doubts, and, lest they cling to the notions which they then began to turn over in their minds (for they thought they beheld not a body but a ghost) He confutes these thoughts which were contrary to reality, firmly confronting the eyes of the doubters with the marks of the Crucifixion which still remained in His Hands and in His feet, and bids them feel them carefully with their own hands. For these scars of the nails and of the lance had been retained in His Flesh that by means of them the wounds of unbelieving hearts might be healed, so that they would firmly grasp, not from a wavering faith but from sure and certain knowledge, that This Substance, Which had lain in the Sepulchre, was that Which was now about to sit on the Throne of God the Father.

So through all this time, most dearly beloved, which passed between the Resurrection of the Lord and His Ascension into heaven, this was the aim of God's providence, this is taught, this is made known to the eyes and to the hearts of the faithful: that the Lord Jesus Christ, Who had been truly born, and had suffered and died, was to be acknowledged as truly risen from the dead. And so it was that the most blessed Apostles and all the Disciples, who had been fearful because of the outcome of the Cross, and hesitant in their belief in the Resurrection, were now so strengthened by this manifest truth, that upon the Lord's entering into the glory of heaven they were not alone not afflicted with sadness, rather they were filled *with great joy* (Lk. xxiv. 52).

And in truth it was a great and indescribable cause for joy, when, in the presence of the holy multitude, the nature of human kind ascended above the dignity of all the heavenly creatures, rising above the angelic order, above the sublimity of the archangels, with no limit amid all the glory of heaven to the height of its ascent till, received into the company of the Eternal Father, it was made sharer of the Throne of His glory to Whose Nature it was united in the Son.

Therefore, since the Ascension of Christ is our uplifting, and whither the glory of Our Head shall go thither the hope of our body is called, let us then, most dearly beloved, rejoice exceedingly with fitting joy, and let us be glad with devout giving of thanks. For on this day, not alone are we made sure heirs of paradise, but in Christ we have already reached the heights of heaven, and obtained more abundant gifts through the ineffable favour of Christ than we lost through the envy of the devil. For they whom the venom of the enemy cast down from the happiness of their first home, these, made one with Himself, the Son of God has set at the right hand of the Father, with Whom He lives and reigns, in the Unity of the Holy Ghost, God for ever and ever. Amen.

IV. St Gregory the Great, Pope and Doctor

Given to the People in the Basilica of the Blessed Apostle Peter, on the Ascension Day of the Lord[9]

Explanations and Reflections on the Ascension

1. Mark xvi. 14–20. That the Apostles were slow to believe in the Lord's Resurrection happened, not so much because of their weakness of faith, but rather, if I may say so, for the sake of the future firmness of ours. For it was because of their doubting that the fact of the Resurrection was made clear to us by many proofs: and as we read them we must confess that nothing else than their doubt has made us so certain. Of less help to me is Mary Magdalene who believed so readily, than Thomas who doubted so long. For he by his doubting came to touch the scars of the wounds, and removed from our breast the wound of uncertainty.

To set deeper in the mind the truth of the Resurrection we must also take note of what Luke relates, where he says: *And eating together with them, he commanded them, that they should not depart from Jerusalem* (Acts i. 4). And a little later: *While they looked on, he was raised up: and a cloud received him out of their sight* (Acts i. 9). Take note of these words; mark their divine mystery. *Eating together with them He was raised up.* He ate, and He ascended: that by the fact of His eating the truth of His humanity might be made evident.

Mark again records, that before the Lord ascended to heaven He rebuked the Disciples for their hardness of heart, and for their unbelief. What are we to think if not that the Lord then rebuked them for this reason, that as He was leaving them in His Body, the words He would say at parting would more deeply impress themselves on the heart of His hearers? And having rebuked their hardness, let us hear what He goes on to say for their direction: *Go ye into the whole world, and preach the Gospel to every creature.*

2. Was the Holy Gospel, my brethren, to be preached to the

inanimate creation, or to dumb animals, that He should say to the Disciples concerning it: *Preach the gospel to every creature*? But by the words *every creature* He meant man. For there are stones, and they neither live nor feel. There are herbs and plants; they live but do not feel. They live I say, but not because of a soul, but in their freshness; for as Paul says: *Senseless man, that which you sow does not live, unless it first dies* (I Cor. xv. 36). It lives therefore because it dies so as to be given life. There are stones then; but they are not living. There are plants likewise, and they live but do not feel. There are brute beasts; they live, they feel, but they are without understanding. And there are angels; they live, they feel, and they have intelligence.

Man has something in common with *every creature*. He has existence in common with the stones, life with the trees, feeling with animals, understanding with the angels. If therefore man has something in common with every creature, man is in some measure every creature. The Gospel is therefore preached to every creature when it is preached only to man; for he it is plain is being taught for whom all on earth were created: to whom all things, through a certain resemblance, are not unrelated.

But the words *every creature* could also mean every nation of the Gentiles. For some time before this it had been said: *Go ye not into the way of the Gentiles* (Mt. x. 5). Now however it is said: *Preach to every creature*; so that the preaching of the Apostles, first rejected by Judea, might then be preached to our gain; and since they had rejected it in pride, it would then become an aid to their damnation.

But since the Truth has sent His Disciples to preach, what is it that He does but scatter seed upon the earth? And He sows but a little seed; that He may receive the return of many harvests from our faith. But not even in the whole world would such a harvest of believers spring up if upon the rational earth there had not fallen from the hand of God this chosen seed of His preachers.

3. *He that believeth and is baptized, shall be saved: but he that believeth not shall be condemned.* Perhaps each of you will say to himself: I have believed: I shall be saved. He speaks what is true if to faith he joins good works. That is indeed true faith which does not deny in work what it professes in word. For this Paul says of certain false faithful: *They profess that they know God; but in their works they deny him* (Tit. i. 16). For this John also says: *He who saith that he knoweth God, and keepeth not his commandments, is a liar, and the truth is not in him* (I Jn. ii. 4).

Since this is so we must profess the truth of our faith in the manner of our own life. For then shall we be truly faithful when we fulfil in work what we profess in word. On the day of our baptism we promised to renounce all the works and pomps of our ancient enemy. So then let each one of you turn the eyes of his mind to the examination of himself; and should he find that he observes after his baptism what he promised before baptism he may rejoice in the certainty that he truly believes.

But if he is far from fulfilling what he promised, if he has fallen back into evil doing, returned to seeking the delights of this world, let us then see whether he knows how to grieve that he has wandered from the right path. For with the Merciful Judge he is not held to be a betrayer who returns to the truth even after he has betrayed it; for the Omnipotent Judge, while He freely accepts our repentance, even in His judgement hides in darkness that we have wandered from the truth (cf. I Cor. xi. 31).[10]

4. *These signs shall follow them that believe: In my name they shall cast out devils: they shall speak with new tongues. They shall take up serpents; and if they shall drink any deadly thing, it shall not hurt them; they shall lay their hands upon the sick, and they shall recover.*

Is it, my brethren, because we do not these signs that you do not believe? These were needed at the Church's beginning. For that the faith might grow it had need to be nourished by miracles; just as when we plant a vineyard we must water the plants till we see they have begun to grow in the earth, and when they have once taken root we cease to water them. Because of this Paul says: *Wherefore tongues are for a sign: not to believers, but to unbelievers* (I Cor. xiv. 22).

Regarding these signs and wonders we have some things to say, which even now we should consider with close attention. Each day the Catholic Church does in a spiritual manner that which the Apostles did in a bodily manner. For when her priests lay hands on the believing, and by the power of exorcism deny to the evil spirits the power to dwell in these souls, what is it they do but *cast out evil devils*? And when her people everywhere, who have put away the speech of this world, speak now of the sacred mysteries, and proclaim with all their power the praise and glory of their Maker, what is it they do but *speak with new tongues*?

And when by their pious encouragement they take evil out of another's heart, *they are taking up serpents*. And when they hear evil counsels, and yet in no way are they drawn to evil doing, *they drink a deadly thing, and it does not hurt them*. And as often as they see their neighbour grow weak in good works, and hasten with all their power to help them, and to strengthen them by the example of their own good lives, what are they doing if not *laying hands upon the sick*, that they may recover? And wonders such as these, the more spiritual they are the greater they are; and the greater they are the more by means of them souls not bodies are restored again to life. These signs therefore, dearest brethren, if you wish, you also may with divine approval perform.

But true life cannot be obtained by means of these outward signs by those who perform them. For although corporeal works of this kind sometimes do proclaim an inner holiness of life, they do not bring it about. But the spiritual works which are wrought in the soul do not proclaim an inner holiness of life, but they cause it. The former even the wicked may do; only the good may have a part in the latter. Accordingly the Truth says of certain people: *Many will say to me in that day: Lord, Lord, have we not prophesied in thy name, and cast out devils in thy name, and done many miracles in thy name? And then I will profess unto them, that I never knew you: depart from me, you that work iniquity* (Mt. vii. 22, 23; Ps. vi. 9).

Do not then, dearest brethren, love those outward signs which the good may do in common with the reprobate; but give your heart rather to the miracles of piety and divine charity of which we have spoken, and which the more they are inward and hidden the more they are in safety; and for these the greater is their reward with the Lord, the less is their praise among men. Then follows:

5. *And the Lord Jesus, after he had spoken to them, was taken up into heaven, and sitteth on the right hand of God.*

From the Old Testament we learn that Elias was rapt up to heaven. But the upper ethereal heaven is one, another the lower aerial heaven. The aerial is closer to the earth; so we speak of the birds of heaven, because we see them fly in this aerial heaven. Elias was raised up to this heaven that he might swiftly be brought to some hidden region of the earth, where, in great peace of body and soul, he would live till the end of the world, when he would return to pay the debt of nature. For he but postponed death; he did not escape it. But Our Redeemer, as He did not postpone it, but rose above it, and rising from the dead defeated it, ascending into heaven proclaimed the glory of His Resurrection.

Let us note also that Elias is said to have ascended in a chariot; that it might be shown to us that even a holy man has need of the help of others. These manifestations were done by the help of angels; for he could not ascend even to the aerial heaven whom the infirmity of our nature burthened. But we do not read that Our Redeemer was lifted up by angels or in a chariot; for He Who made all things is by His own power borne above them all. Thither He returned, where He had been; and from here He went back to where He had continued to be; for while in His Humanity He ascended to heaven, in His Divinity He was upholding both earth and heaven.

6. As Joseph sold into captivity by his brethren was a figure of the selling of Our Redeemer, so Enoch who was translated, and Elias who was rapt up to the aerial heaven, were figures of the Lord's Ascension. The Lord therefore had both heralds as well as witnesses of His Ascension; one before the Law, and one under the Law: that at some time He would come Who could Himself enter truly into heaven. For this reason the order of the raising up of both the one and the other is marked by a certain progress. For Enoch was *translated* (Gen. v. 24), Elias is spoken of as rapt *up into heaven* (IV Kings ii. 11), that after this He might come Who was neither translated nor rapt up to heaven, but would of His own power enter into heaven.

The Lord has also shown us, both in Himself Who of Himself ascended into heaven, and in their translation who as servants prefigured the Lord's Ascension, that He will bestow cleanness of flesh on those who believe in Him, and that under His Rule the virtue of chastity would flourish. For Enoch had both wife and children, and Elias we read had neither wife nor children. See how by degrees the purity of holiness has grown: shown clearly to us both by means of the servants who were translated, and by the Person of the Lord ascending. For Enoch was translated; and he was begotten of the flesh, and through the flesh begot. Elias was taken up; he was begotten in the flesh, but did not beget. The Lord was assumed into heaven; He was neither begotten of the flesh, nor in the flesh begot.

7. We must next consider the meaning of Mark's words: *And sitteth on the right hand of God*, and with them the words of Stephen, who says: *Behold I see the heavens opened, and the Son of man standing on the right hand of God* (Acts vii. 55). What does it mean that Mark testifies that the Lord is *sitting*, and Stephen that he sees Him *standing*? But you know, Brethren, that to sit is the position of one judging; to stand that of one who fights or gives help. Since our Redeemer is assumed into heaven Mark describes Him, after His Assumption, as *sitting*: for after the glory of His Ascension He will be seen as Judge on the Last Day, and even now He judges all things, and at the end of the world he will come as Judge of all mankind. But Stephen, kneeling in the contest of martyrdom, beholds Him *standing* Whom he looks to as his helper; for He fights for him from heaven that he may triumph over the unbelief of his tormentors on earth.

8. Then follows: *But they going forth preached everywhere: the Lord working withal, and confirming the word with signs that followed.*

What are we to draw from this for our reflection? What must we commit to memory if not that obedience followed His command, and that signs and wonders followed obedience? But since we have by God's help gone briefly over the Gospel lesson, explaining it to you, there still remains the duty of saying something to you regarding this so great solemnity itself.

9. This we must first consider: what does it mean that at the Birth of our Lord angels appear, but we do not read that they appeared clothed *in white garments*, while at the Lord's Ascension the angels who were sent are recorded as appearing *in white garments*? For it is written: *While they looked on, he was raised up: and a cloud received him out of their sight. And while they were beholding him going up to heaven, behold two men stood by them in white garments*. By the words *white garments* a festive state of mind is revealed to us. Why then was it that when the Lord was born the angels did not appear clothed in white garments while they were so clothed at the Lord's Ascension, if not because there was great rejoicing among the angels when the Lord entered into heaven? For when the Lord was born the divinity seemed to be brought low. But at the Lord's Ascension humanity was exalted. And white garments were more becoming for exaltation than for humiliation. Accordingly, at His Assumption the angels are rightly seen clothed *in white garments*: for He Who at His Birth appeared as God made lowly is seen in His Ascension as Man exalted to heaven.

10. But this especially must we reflect upon, dearest brethren, on this great solemnity, that on this day *the handwriting of the decree* of our condemnation was blotted out (Col. ii. 34); the sentence of our death was altered. For that nature to which it had been said: *Dust thou art, and into dust thou shalt return* (Gen. iii. 19), has this day entered heaven. Because of this exaltation of our flesh the blessed Job in figure called the Lord *a bird*. For he beheld that Judaea did not understand the mystery of His Ascension, and he pronounced sentence on its unbelief, saying: *The bird hath not known the path* (Job xxviii. 7).[11] The Lord was rightly called a bird; for He made an earthly body soar to the heavens. He who has not believed that the Lord has ascended into heaven has not known the path of the bird.

Of this solemnity was it said by the psalmist: *Thy magnificence is elevated above the heavens* (Ps. viii. 2). And again He says of it: *God is ascended with jubilee, and the Lord with the sound of the trumpet* (Ps. xlvi. 6). And again: *Thou hast ascended on high, thou hast led captivity captive; thou hast received men in gifts* (Ps. lxvii. 19). Ascending on high he has truly led captivity captive; for our mortality is swallowed up by the power of His immortality. Now He has given gifts to men, for, sending down His Spirit from above, to one He has given the word of wisdom, to another the word of knowledge, to another the gift of miracles, to another the grace of healing, to another diverse kinds of tongues, to another the interpretation of speeches (I Cor. xii. 8). He has therefore given gifts to men.

Of this glory of His Ascension Habacuc also speaks: *The sun was raised up, and the moon continued in its course* (Hab. iii. 11: LXX). Who is meant by the sun if not the Lord, and who by the moon if not the Church? For until the Lord ascended into heaven His holy Church feared the opposition of the world; but after She had been strengthened by His Ascension, She preached openly what She had in secret believed. The Sun then was raised up, and the moon remained in her course, because when the Lord turned towards the heavens, the holy Church flourished in the power of her mission.

And by the mouth of Solomon was it said also of the Church: *Behold he cometh leaping upon the mountains, skipping over the hills* (Cant. ii. 8). For he beheld the mountains of so many good works, and he says: *Behold he cometh leaping upon the mountains*. For in coming to the task of our redemption He made, if I may so speak, certain leaps. Do you desire, dearest brethren, to learn what those leaps were? From heaven He came down to a womb; from the womb to a crib; from the crib to a cross; from the cross to a tomb; from the tomb He returned to heaven. Behold how the Truth, made known in the flesh that He might induce us to run after Him, made for us certain leaps: *For he rejoiced as a giant to run the way* (Ps. xviii. 6), that we from our hearts might cry out to Him: *Draw us after thee; we will run after thee to the odour of thy ointments* (Cant. i. 3).

11. And for this, Dearest Brethren, we must follow Him in our hearts where we believe He has

ascended in His Body. Let us turn away from earthly longings: nothing here below can now delight us whose Father is in heaven. And let us with great seriousness reflect on this. For He Who *mild* of countenance ascended shall be *terrible* when He comes again, and whatsoever He has now commanded with mildness He shall then exact with sternness. So let no one waste this time of repentance allowed us. Let no one neglect to do all he can for his own salvation. The more we now demand of God's patience, before the time of judgement, the more severe shall He be when the time of judgement has come.

Do these things then within your own hearts, Dearest Brethren. Turn these thoughts over in your mind with earnest consideration. For even though your soul still drifts amid the distractions of this world's affairs, nevertheless, from now on make fast to your eternal home the anchor of your hope, and fix the course of your soul by that True Light. Lo! We have heard that the Lord has ascended into heaven. Let us then observe in work what we truly believe. And though still held back in the weakness of our body, let us yet follow Him with the footsteps of love. And He Who gave us this love will not be indifferent to it, Jesus Christ Our Lord Who lives and reigns with God the Father in the Unity of the Holy Ghost, God for ever and ever. Amen.

V. St John Chrysostom, Bishop and Doctor

Christ's Ascension Man's Exaltation[12]

What is it we commemorate this day? It is the great and wondrous munificence of God, Dearly Beloved, which surpasses the power of human understanding, and is worthy of Him from Whom it proceeds. For this day all mankind was restored to God. This day the long warfare, the prolonged estrangement, was ended. This day a wondrous peace returned to us: a peace we had not expected. For who could have hoped that God would be reconciled to man? Not that the Lord is unmerciful, but because the servant was slothful and indifferent; not that the Lord was cruel and vindictive, but because his servant was ungrateful and unrepentant.

Do you wish to learn why we provoked the anger of our most kind and loving Lord? For it is a good thing to know the reason of our primeval estrangement from God, so that when you see us who before were outlaws and enemies now treated with honour, you will be astonished at His clemency Who has so honoured us, and you will be able to see that this change did not come about from any act of ours. And then when you have seen the greatness of the favour done to you, you will not cease from giving thanks to God for the multitude of His mercies to us. Do you wish then to know how it is we have provoked the anger of a Master so generous, so mild, so good, and One Who has ordered all things for our salvation?

For there was a time when He thought to destroy the race of men, and such was his anger against mankind that He wished to destroy all men, together with their wives and children, their asses and oxen, and the whole earth with them. And if you wish I shall repeat His very words that you may hear them: *I will destroy man, whom I have created, from the face of the earth; from man even to the beasts, for it repenteth me that I have made them* (Gen. vi. 7). And that you may understand that He did not hate our nature, but detested rather the wickedness it had done, He Who had said, *I will destroy man, whom I have created*, also said to man: *The end of all flesh is come before me* (v. 3). For had He hated man He would not have spoken with him. You know that He willed not to do what He had threatened, and even made excuses for His servant man, and spoke with Him as with a friend of the same degree, and tells him the reasons for the disaster that is to come; not so that men might come to know the causes, but that by telling them to others they might be rendered more restrained.

But as I have just now been saying to you, so badly did our race conduct itself in the past that it was in danger of being destroyed from the face of the earth. And now, we who before were deemed unfit to dwell upon the earth are raised up to heaven; we who were unworthy of earthly dignity now ascend to a heavenly kingdom, and enter into heaven, and take our place upon a royal throne; and this nature of ours, because of which the Cherubim guarded the gates of Paradise, this day sits high above the Cherubim.

And why has this great and wondrous event come to pass? For what reason have we who have offended against such great mercy, who are seen to be unworthy of earth itself, and have fallen from all primacy and honour, been raised to so sublime a dignity? How has the warfare ended? Why has His anger ceased? What is the cause? For this it is that is wondrous: that peace was made, not by those who provoked without cause the anger of God, but that He, though justly angered, calls us and invites us to peace: *For Christ therefore we are ambassadors*, says the Apostle, *God as it were exhorting by us* (II Cor. v. 20). What does this mean? He is the injured one, yet it is He Who invites us to peace? It is indeed so; for He is God; and because He is, as a loving Father He invites us to come to Him.

How Christ is Mediator. But see Who has come as Mediator. It is the Son of Him Who invites us: not some holy man, not an angel, nor an archangel, not any servant whatever. And what does the Mediator do? The work of a mediator. For when two men are at odds and unwilling to speak to each other, a third then comes and standing between them dissolves the enmity of both one and the other. And so Christ has done. For God was angry with man, and we had turned from God our loving Master, and Christ placing Himself between God and man reconciled both natures.

But in what manner did He make Himself a mediator? By taking upon Himself the punishment the Father must inflict upon us; submitting Himself both to the chastisements decreed against us, and to the humiliations inflicted by us also. Do you wish to learn how He endured both of these? *Christ*, says the Apostle, *hath redeemed us from the curse of the law, being made a curse for us* (Gal. iii. 13). You have seen in what manner He took upon Himself the punishment decreed from above. See also how he has endured the humiliations inflicted by men: *The reproaches of them that reproached thee have fallen upon me* (Ps. lxviii. 10).

Do you perceive in what manner He put an end to enmity, and how He made him who was an enemy into a friend, and pleasing to God; but not before He had paid in full all that was owing, and fulfilled all that was to be done and to be suffered? And the proof of all these good things is the festival of this day. For as He took upon Himself the first-fruits of our nature, so likewise did He take them up to the Lord. And as happens when the fields are filled with corn, and a man gathers a few of the stalks and makes them into a little sheaf, and offering it to God by this little quantity the whole field is blessed, so has Christ done, Who by means of His one Body, and this the First-fruits, has brought it about that the whole race is to be blessed.

And why did He not offer up the whole of our nature? For the reason that he who offers up the whole does not offer the first-fruits. But if he offers up a little part, through this part he causes the whole to be blessed. But, someone will say, if first-fruits are offered then the first man born should be offered: for the first-fruits are those that are begotten first, and first spring up. We are not held to have offered first-fruits, when the first-fruits we have offered, Beloved Brethren, are poor and weak, but when we have offered what is perfect and worthy. Therefore since the former was subject to sin it was not offered, though it came forth the first; but this latter was free of all sin, and this accordingly was offered: for though it was born after, it was the First-fruits.

And that you may know that they are not called first-fruits which came forth first, but those that are worthy and of the best kind, and have reached perfection, I shall bring forward the testimony of the Sacred Scripture. *When you shall enter the land of promise, which the Lord thy God will give thee*, said Moses to his people, *you shall plant in it every kind of fruit tree, bringing forth fruit to eat; for three years its fruit shall be unclean to you; but in the fourth year the fruit shall be holy to the Lord* (Lev. xix. 23, 24). And if the first fruit that was yielded was the first-fruits, then those that were yielded in the first year should have been offered to the Lord. Now he says: *For three years its fruit shall be unclean to you*; leave it lie; for the tree is young, it is weak, and its fruit immature. But, he says, in the fourth year its fruit shall be sacred to the Lord. And observe in this the wisdom of the Lawgiver, Who forbade it to be eaten lest anyone before God Himself should receive the fruit; and forbade that it be offered up so that fruit that was imperfect might not be offered to the Lord. But, he says, let that fruit fall which came first; do not offer it, for it is unworthy of the perfection of Him who is to receive it.

You see then that it is not the first fruit produced that is to be called the first-fruits, but that which is worthy of being offered. We have said this to you because of the Body He offered up. He therefore offered to the Father the first-fruits of our nature, and because of the dignity of the Offerer, and the perfection of What was offered, the Father found the Gift so acceptable that He received It with His own Hands, and placed it close to Himself, saying: *Sit thou at my right hand* (Ps. lxviii. 10).

But to what nature did He say, *sit thou at my right hand*? It was to that which had heard the words: *Dust thou art, and into dust thou shalt return*. But did He not so raise it above the heavens? Did He not upraise it to stand amid the angels? Was not this honour without measure? It ascended above the heavens, it ascended above the angels, it passed upwards beyond the archangels, above the Cherubim, it soared above the Seraphim, higher than all the Powers of heaven, and came to rest only before the Throne of the Lord.

You see how vast the distance from heaven to earth? But let us rather begin from below. You see, do you not, how far it is from hell to the earth? And then from this earth to the heavens? And from the heavens above us to the higher heaven beyond? And from there to the angels, to the archangels, to the heavenly powers, to the royal throne itself? Above this immense intervening void, to the very Summit, has He raised our nature. Consider how low it was, and whither it has ascended. For it was not possible to descend lower than man had descended, or to go higher than Christ had now raised it. And Paul made this clear where he says: *He that descended is the same also that ascended*. And where did He descend? *Into the lower parts of the earth*. But He ascended *above all the heavens* (Eph. iv. 10, 9).

Understand Who ascended, and whose nature, and that it is the same as it was before. Gladly shall I dwell upon the unworthiness of our race, that I may comprehend the honour that has come to us through the loving mercy of the Lord. For we were but dust and ashes; but that was not a fault: it was the weakness of our nature. We became more foolish than the unreasoning beasts. For man *hath been compared to the senseless beasts, and made like to them* (Ps. xlviii. 21). To be like the senseless beasts is to be worse than them. It is their nature to be senseless, and it is natural they remain so. But that creatures which have been adorned with reason should sink to this mindless condition is the fault of our own will. And so when you hear that man has become like to the senseless beasts, do not understand this as saying to us that man is the equal of the beasts, but that it means he has become lower than them; not that we have sunk lower than them, but that though men we have pressed on to a greater senselessness. And this Isaias teaches clearly: *The ox knoweth his master, and the ass his master's crib; but Israel hath not known me* (Is. i. 3).

But let us not be troubled because of our past offences: for *where sin abounded, grace did more abound* (Rom. v. 20). You have seen how we were more foolish than the beasts. Would you know that we are also more irrational than the birds? *The turtle, and the swallow, and the stork, have observed the time of their coming; but my people have not known the time of the Lord* (Jer. viii. 7). See, we are more senseless than asses and oxen, than the birds of the air, the turtle and the swallow. And would you learn yet more of our folly? He sends us to the ants that from them also we may learn wisdom: *Go to the ant*, He says, *and consider her ways, and learn her wisdom* (Prov. vi. 6). We were made pupils of the ant; we who were created in the image and likeness of God. But He Who made us was not the cause of this; it was ourselves, who would not remain in His image and likeness.

And why do I speak of the ant only? We have become even more senseless than the stones. Shall I quote proof of this also? *Let the mountains hear the judgement of the Lord, and the strong foundations of the earth; for the Lord will enter into judgement with his people* (Mich. vi. 2). Thou judgest man, and Thou callest upon the foundations of the earth. Yet, He saith: for men are more senseless than the foundations of the earth. What greater depth of unwisdom can we seek in them, since they are seen to be more stupid than the ass, more senseless than the ox, less understanding than the turtle and the swallow, less wise than the ant, duller than the stones, and are even likened to serpents; for, He says: *The madness of the wicked is according to the likeness of the serpent: the poison of the asps is under their lips* (Ps. lvii. 5; xiii. 3). And what need has He to speak of irrational creatures, since we were also called children of the devil. *For you*, He says, *are children of the devil* (Jn. viii. 44).

Yet though we are senseless and ungrateful, foolish, duller than the stones, so base and unworthy, yet this most abject nature—how shall I utter this, how articulate it, how shall I bring forth the words?—this worthless nature, more senseless than all other creatures, is this day raised above every creature. This day the angels have recovered that which long ago they lost. This day the archangels behold that which they had so long desired to see. This day they behold our nature upon the royal throne, shining in immortal beauty and glory. This the angels had long desired. This the archangels had awaited. And though human nature soared above them in honour, yet they rejoiced because of the good that came to us. For when we suffered punishment they grieved. And though the Cherubim stood guard before Paradise, they yet sorrowed for our unhappiness: just as a servant taking a fellow servant at the bidding of his master, and putting him in prison guards him, yet moved by compassion for his fellow servant he is distressed because of what has happened to him. So did the Cherubim undertake the duty of excluding men from Paradise, while they grieved for their return.

And that you may know they grieved, I shall make it clear from what happens among men. For when you see men having compassion on their fellow servants you cannot doubt that the same is true of the Cherubim. For these heavenly powers are more kind than men. And who among the just does not suffer when other men are punished, even justly, and for manifold sins? And this attitude is worthy of praise; that though they knew of their crimes, and understood that they had greviously offended God; they should yet grieve for them in their hearts. As Moses likewise declared after the sin of idolatry of his people: *Either forgive them this trespass, or, if thou do not, strike me out of the book that thou has written* (Ex. xxxii. 31, 32). What do you mean? You behold their impiety, yet you grieve because they are to be chastized? For this, he says, do I grieve: That they are to be punished; and that they have given just cause for their punishment.

Ezechiel also, beholding the slaughter of his people cried aloud and lamented, saying: *Alas, alas, O Lord God! Wilt thou destroy all the remnant of Israel?* (Ezech. ix. 8). Jeremiah likewise cried out: *Correct me, O Lord, but yet with judgement; and not in thy fury, lest thou bring me to nothing* (Jer. x. 24). And so if Moses, if Ezechiel and Jeremiah, grieved over these sinners, should the Powers of heaven not be moved to pity because of our tribulations? How else are we to understand these words?

That they make our affairs their own, learn what joy is theirs when they see us reconciled to God. And they would not rejoice over this unless before they had grieved. And that they rejoiced is plain to us from Christ's very words: *There shall be joy in heaven*, and on earth, *upon one sinner doing penance* (Lk. xv. 7). So if the angels rejoice upon seeing one sinner restored to God, how can they fail to be filled with the greatest joy when they see the entire nature of man, in its First-fruits, raised up this day to heaven?

Hear again, and from another place, of the joy of the heavenly host because of our return to God's friendship. For when Our Lord was born according to the flesh, seeing that from that moment He had changed from enmity to friendship with mankind: for if He had not He would not have descended among them; seeing this therefore the heavenly choir proclaim: *Glory to God in the highest, and on earth peace to men of good will* (Lk. ii. 14). And that you may know that this was the reason of their giving glory to God: because the earth had received great things, they also add the reason, saying: *On earth peace, to men of good will*: to those who before were declared to be hateful and senseless! See then how the highest praise is offered to God because of others' good tidings, or rather because of their own; for they make our concerns their own!

And would you like to learn how they exulted and rejoiced seeing Christ about to ascend to heaven? Listen to His words telling us how they ascended and descended continually. And this is the very manner of those who are eagerly awaiting some new and wondrous sight. And where is it shown that they were ascending and descending? Listen to His own words: *Then you shall see the heaven opened, and the angels of God ascending and descending upon the Son of man* (Jn. i. 51). This is the way of loving eager hearts; they wait not for the time appointed, but anticipate with delight the appointed hour. And so they keep ascending and descending desiring with loving eagerness to behold this new and wondrous sight: of man appearing in heaven. And it is because of this the angels are everywhere appearing: when He was born, when He rose from the dead, when He ascended into heaven. For, *Behold*, says the Scripture, *two men stood* by them, *in white garments*: their dress proclaiming their joyfulness: and they say to the Disciples: *Ye men of Galilee, why stand you looking up to heaven. This Jesus, who is taken up from you into heaven, shall so come, as you have seen him going into heaven* (Acts i. 10, 9).

Why Angels were seen at the Ascension of the Lord. Here pay careful attention to me. Why did they say these words? Did the Disciples have no eyes? Did they not see what took place? Does not the Evangelist say, that *while they looked on He was raised up*? For what reason therefore did the angels stand by them, telling them that He had ascended into heaven? For two reasons. One was that they were beginning to grieve because Christ had gone from them; for that they did grieve hear what the Lord had said to them: *None of you*, He says, *asketh me: Whither goest thou? But because I have spoken these things to you, sorrow hath filled your heart* (Jn. xvi. 5, 6). For if we suffer when our friends and relatives go from us how could the Disciples not begin to grieve, seeing their Saviour departing from them, He their most mild, most good and gentle Teacher? How could they not feel sorrow? And because of this an angel stood by who tempered the sorrow they felt at His Ascension, by reminding them that He would come again. *For*, he said, *this Jesus who is taken up from you into heaven, shall so come as you have seen him ascending into heaven.*

You are sorrowing, he says, because He was raised up. But sorrow no more, for He will return. And he said this that they might not do what Eliseus did, rending his garment in two when he saw his master taken up to heaven (IV Kings ii. 12); for no one stood by him to tell him that Elias would come again. And so lest they too should do this angels stood by them, and comforted them, and eased the sorrow that filled their hearts.

The Difference between the Ascension of Elias, and that of Christ Our Saviour. This was one reason for the presence of the angels. The other is not lessened because they added the explanation: *He is taken up.* And what is this reason? He was taken up into heaven. Immense the void between; and the power of our vision does not suffice to enable it to see a body taken up into heaven. For just as a bird flying heavenwards, the higher it flies, the more is it withdrawn from our sight, so this Body, the higher it was taken up, the more it was hid from our vision; for the limitation of human sight prevents it reaching to that immense distance. Because of this the angels stood by them, and made clear to them the reality of the Ascension into heaven, so that they would not think that He was taken up only as Elias had been, but that He had truly ascended *into heaven*; and because of this he said: *He is taken up from you into heaven.*

Nor was this added without purpose. Elias was taken up, as though to heaven; for he was a servant. But Jesus was taken up to heaven; for He was the Lord. The one ascended in a chariot; the Other in a cloud. When the servant was called, a chariot was sent; but for the Son a royal throne, and not a throne simply, but the Throne of His Father. For of the Father Isaias says: *Behold the Lord is seated upon a cloud* (Is. xix. 1: LXX). [13] Therefore because the Father sits upon a cloud, so He sends the cloud for His Son. And as Elias ascending let his sheepskin mantle fall upon Eliseus, so Jesus ascending sent down gifts of graces upon His Disciples, constituting them, not one prophet, but into many Eliseuses, and greater and more glorious than he.

Let us then, Beloved Brethren, arise and uplift the eyes of our soul towards that return. For Paul says to us: *He shall come down from heaven, with commandment, and with the voice of an archangel; then we who are alive, who are left, shall be taken up together with them in the clouds to meet Christ, into the air* (I Thess. iv. 15, 16); but not all of us. That we shall not all be rapt up to heaven, but that some shall be taken, and some shall remain, hear what Christ says: *Two women shall be grinding at the mill; one shall be taken, and one shall be left; and two shall be lying in the one bed; one shall be taken, and one shall be left* (Mt. xxiv. 40, 41).[14]

What does this riddle mean? What is hidden in this mystery? By the mill He clearly means all who live in poverty and suffering; by the bed those who abound in wealth and comfort. And desiring to show us that even from among the poor there would be those that would be saved and those that would be lost, He said that from the mill one would be taken, and one left; and of those in their beds one would be taken, and one left; meaning to convey to us that sinners would be left here awaiting chastisement, but that the Just shall be taken up in the clouds.

For as when a king makes his entry into a city, surrounded by his men, those who are just and worthy and secure in his favour go forth from the city to meet him. But the guilty, and those liable to judgement, stay within; awaiting the king's verdict. So when the Lord shall come those that are in His favour shall meet Him in the middle heavens,[15] but the condemned, and those conscious within them of manifold sins, will await His judgement here.

The Humility of Chrysostom. Then shall we also be taken up. In saying *we* I do not count myself among the number of those who shall be taken up. For I am not so devoid of sense and understanding as to forget my own sins. And if I did not fear to mar the joy of this holy festival I would weep bitter tears when I recall to mind these words, and remember my own sins. But since I do not wish to burthen the joyfulness of this day I shall here end my sermon, leaving the joy of this day shining and unclouded in your minds, so that the rich man may not rejoice too greatly in his riches, nor the poor man believe himself unfortunate because he is poor, but that each one of you may do this or do that other thing as his conscience shall tell him. For the happy man is not the rich man, nor the poor man the unhappy man; rather blessed, nay, thrice-blessed is the man who shall be held worthy of being rapt upwards in the clouds, though he be the poorest of all men; as he is truly wretched, yea, thrice-wretched, who shall be numbered among the lost, though he be the richest of all men.

Because of this I say let us who are still under the dominion of sin grieve for ourselves. And let those who live virtuously be of good heart. Let them not alone be of good heart, but let them be of steadfast confidence. But let those others not alone grieve, let them also change their manner of life. For though his life be sinful, it is possible for a man, putting away his sins, to cross over to a life of virtue, and become as those who have lived virtuously from the beginning. And this let us make haste to do. And those who are conscious to themselves of virtuous living, let them persevere in virtue; ever adding to their treasure, and increasing yet more the confidence they already possess.

But we who are fearful and anxious, and conscious within us of manifold offences, let us alter our lives for the better, so that arriving at that confidence these others already possess, we may all together go forth to receive with fitting glory the King of angels, and share in that blessed joy which is in Jesus Christ Our Lord, to Whom, with the Father and the Holy Ghost be there glory and empire for ever and ever. Amen.

NOTES

[1] CSEL, pp. 377 *seq.*

[2] PL 92, 209.

[3] PL 40, *De Symbolo ad Catech;* unauthentic PRM 40.

[4] Cf. PL 92, 300. His text is taken almost literally from St Augustine's *Tractationes in Joannem.*

[5] PL 38, Sermo. 262. *In die Ascensionis Domini* II.

[6] PL 38, Sermo. 264. *De Ascensione Domini* IV.

[7] *docetur*, possibly an incorrect transcription for *videtur*.

[8] PL 54, Sermo. 73, *De Ascensione Domini* I.

[9] PL 76, Hom. 29 in Evang.

[10] Cf. Moralium, Bk. 4, 15, PL. 75.

[11] The Vulgate version is: *Semitam ignoravit avis*, which in English versions, the French and German, is rendered generally as: *The bird hath not known the way.* This rendering does not give a basis for the allegory or figure he is here speaking of. His use of the figure of a bird for Our Lord presupposes, evidently, that the subject is in the verb: and that *avis* is genitive. The Septuagint: *The way knew not the winged creature*, and both the Hebrew verb and context however provide a possible basis for this allegorical interpretation. St Jerome's Interlinear Exposition of Job however affords no basis for the allegory (cf. PL 23, Col. 1441), but it is still of a very striking aptness: the subject being the people of Sodom and Gomorrah, and their cities, chastised and laid waste because of their wickedness.

[12] PG 50. In Ascensione D.N.J.C.

[13] The Vulgate has *ascends* (ascendet).

[14] The Vulgate has, in place of the second figure: *Two shall be in the field.*

[15] Σἰς μέσον τόν ἀέρα

SUNDAY WITHIN THE OCTAVE OF THE ASCENSION

I. St Gaudentius of Brescia: On the Promised Coming of the Paraclete

II. St Augustine: The Paraclete

III. St Leo the Great: The Lord's Ascension

IV. St Caesarius of Arles: On Eating and Drinking the Word of God

V. St Caesarius of Arles: On How the Word of God is to be Received

THE GOSPEL OF THE SUNDAY

John xv. 26–xvi. 4

At that time: Jesus said to His Disciples: When the Paraclete cometh, whom I will send you from the Father, the Spirit of Truth, who proceedeth from the Father, he shall give testimony of me. And you shall give testimony, because you are with me from the beginning. These things have I spoken to you that you may not be scandalized. They will put you out of the synagogues: yea, the hour cometh, that whosoever killeth you, will think that he doth a service to God. And these things will they do to you; because they have not known the Father, nor me. But these things I have told you, that when the hour shall come, you may remember that I told you of them.

Exposition from the Catena Aurea

V. 26. *But when the Paraclete cometh, whom I will send you . . .*

Chrysostom, *Hom.* 76 *in John*: The Disciples might well say to the Lord: If they have heard from Thee words no other man has spoken, if they have seen works which no one else has done, and yet have gained nothing from them, if they have not known the Father and Thee together with Him, why do you send us forth? How are we to be believed? So that they might not be troubled, thinking such thoughts, He consoles them, saying: *When the Paraclete shall come . . . He shall give testimony of me.*[1]

Augustine, *Tr.* 92, 1, *in John*: As though He said: When they saw Me they hated Me, and put Me to death; but the Paraclete shall give such testimony regarding Me, that He will make those believe in Me who do not see Me. And because (93, 1) He shall give testimony of me, you also shall give testimony. Hence: *And you shall give testimony*; He by inspiring your hearts, you proclaiming Him with your voices. (92, 2) And so you shall be enabled to proclaim what you know: *Because you are with me from the beginning*: which now you do not, because you have not within you the fulness of the Spirit. For the charity of God which shall be poured forth in your hearts by the Holy Spirit which shall be given to you (Rom. v. 5) will give you the courage to give testimony. He, giving testimony (92 *in fine*) and forming steadfast witnesses, removes fear from the hearts of Christ's friends, and changes to love the hatred of enemies.

DIDYMUS, *On the Holy Ghost*, 2: He calls the Holy Spirit Who is to come the Comforter, giving Him this name by reason of His work; for He will not alone comfort those He finds worthy, and deliver them from all sorrow and confusion of soul, but He will in very truth bestow upon them a certain incredible joy. Everlasting joy takes up its abode in the hearts where the Holy Spirit shall dwell. This Consoling Spirit is sent to us from the Son, not by means of the ministry of angels, or of prophets or Apostles, but as He must be sent, by the Wisdom and Power of God, having with that same Wisdom and Power identity of Nature. For as the Son that is sent is not cut off from the Father, nor separated from Him, but abides with Him, possessing Him within Himself, so the Holy Spirit, sent by the Son in the manner we have said, does not proceed from the Father as though passing from one place to another. For as the Father is not rooted in one place, since He is above all created things, so neither is the Spirit of Truth enclosed within the bounds of place, since He also is incorporeal, and far excelling even all rational creatures.[2]

CHRYSOSTOM, *as above*: He calls Him, not the Holy Spirit, but the *Spirit of Truth*, that He may show us that He is worthy of our faith; and He says that He *proceedeth from the Father*; that is, that He knew all things; as Christ says also of Himself: *I know whence I came and whither I go* (Jn. viii. 14).

DIDYMUS, *as above*: But though He could have said *from God*, or *from the Omnipotent*, He does not, but says: *From the Father*; not that the Father is other than the same Omnipotent God, but that the Spirit of Truth is said to proceed from Him as from the distinct being and mind of the Father. For when the Son sends the Spirit of Truth, Whom He has called the Comforter, so also does the Father; since it is by the same will of both Father and Son that the Spirit comes.

THEOPHYLACTUS; Elsewhere He says that the Father sends the Holy Spirit; now He says that He will send Him, and by this indicates His equality with the Father. Lest however he should appear as opposed to the Father, as though He should send the Spirit from another and a rival authority, He says: Whom I will send *from the Father*: the Father as it were consenting, and sending with Him. But when you hear that He *proceedeth from the Father*, do not by this understand a mission concluded from without Them, as in the case of ministering spirits; but that He speaks here of a certain singular and distinct mission, that is attributed to the Spirit alone; for procession is the natural mode of being of the Spirit. We must not therefore take proceed as meaning to send, but as expressing His natural mode of being from the Father.

AUGUSTINE, *Tr.* 99, 6 *in John*: Here perhaps someone may ask whether the Holy Ghost proceeds from the Son. For the Son is the Son of the Father alone, and the Father is Father only of the Son: but the Holy Ghost is not the Spirit of one of them, but of Both. On one occasion Our Lord Himself says: *For it is not you that speak, but the Spirit of your Father that speaketh in you* (Mat. x. 20). And again you read in the Apostle: *God hath sent the Spirit of His Son into your hearts* (Gal. iv. 6). Nor do I think (par. 7) He is called the Spirit for any other cause; for if we should be questioned regarding each single Person, we cannot but say that the Father as well as the Son is a spirit. It was fitting that that which they both singly and together are called He also should be called Who is not one or other of them, but in Whom what they possess in common is manifested.

Why then may we not hold that the Holy Ghost also proceeds from the Son, since He is also the Spirit of the Son? For if He did not proceed from Him, He would not after His Resurrection have breathed upon His Disciples, saying: *Receive ye the Holy Ghost*. It is of this power also we must believe the Evangelist was speaking when he says: *For virtue went out from Him, and healed all* (Lk. vi. 19). If then the Holy Ghost proceeds from the Father and the Son, why does the Son say, *Who proceedeth from the Father*, unless that it is just as He is wont to refer what is His to Him from Whom He also has being? For this He said: *My doctrine is not mine, but His that sent me* (Jn. vii. 16). If then it is His doctrine which He yet says is not His but the Father's, how much more should we here understand that the Holy Ghost proceeds from Him also, although He says, *Who proceedeth from the Father*, yet not as though He were also saying: from Me He does not proceed? From Whom then the Son derives that He is God, from the Same the Holy Spirit derives that He proceeds from Him.

Hence it may in some way be understood why the Holy Ghost is not said to be born, but rather to *proceed*; since if He also were to be called Son, He should then be called Son of Both: which would be absurd; since no son is the offspring of two, except of a father and a mother. Far be it from us to consider any such thing between God the Father and God the Son. For neither does a son of men proceed at the same time from both father and mother; for when He proceeds from the father to the mother, he is not then proceeding from the mother (and when he comes to this light from the mother, he is not then proceeding from the father). But the Holy Ghost does not proceed from the Father to the Son, and from the

Son proceed to the sanctifying of the creature, but proceeds at the same time from Both. Neither can we say that the Holy Spirit is not Life: when the Father is life, and the Son is Life. And therefore as the Father has Life within Himself, and also gave it to the Son to have Life within Himself, so has He given the Spirit Life, to proceed from Him as it proceeds from Himself.

Ch. xvi, V. 1. *These things have I spoken to you that you may not . . .*

AUGUSTINE, *in John* 93, 1: Rightly then, after promising them the Holy Spirit, by Whose power working within them they would become witnesses unto Him, He goes on: *These things I have said that you may not be scandalized.* For when the charity of God is poured forth in our hearts by the Holy Spirit Who is given to us (Rom. v. 5), *great peace comes to those who love God* (Ps. cxviii. 16), *so that there is no scandal for them.* Then giving expression in words to that which they were to suffer, He says:

V. 2. *They will put you out of the synagogues . . .*

CHRYSOSTOM: For they (the Jews) had already agreed among themselves, *that if any man should confess him to be the Christ,* he should be put out of the synagogue (Jn. ix. 22).

AUGUSTINE, *Tr.* 93, 2 *continued*: But what harm was it that the Apostles should be put out of the Synagogues of the Jews; for were they not about to cut themselves off from them even if no one should put them out of them? But by this He wished to warn them that the Jews would not receive Christ, Whom they themselves would not abandon. For as there was no other people of God than this seed of Abraham, if they should acknowledge Christ, we should not have here the Churches of Christ, there the Synagogues of the Jews. But since they would not, what is left but that continuing apart from Christ they should put out of the Synagogues those who would not abandon Christ?

And then, after He had said this to them, He added: *Yea, the hour cometh, that whosoever killeth you, will think that he doth a service to God.* These words He added as though to console those who would be driven out from the Synagogues. Would it be that this sundering from the Synagogues would so trouble them that they would prefer to die rather than linger on in this life outside the congregations of the Jews? Be it far from us to think they should be so troubled who sought, not the glory of men, but the glory of God. This then is the meaning of the words, *They will put you out of the Synagogues*: Have no fear of this isolation. Though cut off from their congregations, you shall bring together so many in My Name, that they, in fear lest the Temple and the mysteries of the Old Law be forsaken, shall kill you, and think that in doing so they render a service to God; *having a zeal for God, but not according to knowledge* (Rom. x. 2).

(Par. 4, *in fine*): We must take these words to be said of the Jews, of whom He had said, *They will put you out of the Synagogues.* For the witnesses of Christ, that is, the Martyrs, even if they were killed by the Gentiles, these did not think that they did a service to God, but to their own false deities. But every Jew who killed Christ's preachers thought he did a service to God, in the belief that whoever became converted to Christ would betray Israel. And so, enraged at this, and having a zeal for God, though not according to wisdom, thinking to do a service to God, they put them to death.

CHRYSOSTOM: Then He added for their consolation:

V. 3. *And these things will they do to you; because they have not known the Father, nor me . . .*

As if to say: For your consolation it is enough that you suffer these things for My Father and Me.

AUGUSTINE, *Tr.* 93: Lest however these evils, which were however speedily to pass away, should come of a sudden upon souls which were unaware and unprepared, He for this reason foretells them when He goes on to say:

V. 4. *But these things I have told you, that when the hour cometh . . .*

Their hour was a dark hour, an hour of night; but the night of the Jews has commingled none of its confusion with the Christian day that is now separated from it.

CHRYSOSTOM: He foretold this for yet another reason: that they might not say He did not foresee the future. And this He intimates when He says: *That you may remember what I have told you.* And that they might not say: soothing us He told us only the things that would please us, He indicates to them that it was for this reason He had not told them this from the beginning, saying: *But I told you not these things from the beginning, because I was with you* (v. 5); because you were in My care, and it was lawful for you to question Me when you wished; it was against Me the whole assault was directed. Hence it was not necessary to tell you these things from the beginning. It was for this I did not speak: not because I did not then know of them.

AUGUSTINE, *Tr.* 94 *in John*: But the other three Evangelists show that He foretold these things before the time of the Supper; whereas, according to John, it was when this was over that He spoke of them. Perhaps the question is answered in this way: that they also relate that He was close to His Passion when He spoke of these things. Not, therefore, *from the beginning*, when He was with them. But Matthew records that these things were foretold, not alone on the eve of the Passion, but from the beginning (Mt. x. 17).

What then does He mean when He says: *I told you not these things from the beginning*, if not the things which He here tells them concerning the Holy Ghost; that He is to come upon them, and give testimony, when they shall suffer these evils? These are the things He did not tell them from the beginning, when He was with them, and they possessed the comfort of His Presence. But now that He was about to leave them, it was necessary that He should tell them that He was to come by Whose means it would be that charity would be poured out into their hearts, and they would with confidence preach the Word of God.

CHRYSOSTOM: Or; He had forewarned them that they would suffer torments; but not that their slaying would be regarded as a service to God; which would have greatly terrified them. Or, because He had spoken of the things they must suffer from the Gentiles; but here He tells them of what they must suffer at the hands of the Jews.

I. ST GAUDENTIUS, BISHOP OF BRESCIA

On the Promised Coming of the Paraclete[3]

In His ineffable wisdom the Son of God deigned to communicate step by step to His Disciples an understanding of the truths of His saving faith; for their human hearts could not grasp it all at once. And in the discourses He had already spoken to them He had, as I showed you in my last sermon, made known to them many things concerning the Oneness of His own divinity with that of the Father; making clear that there was no separation between Them; so that even the words He spoke to them were not, He declared, His but the Father's: *And the word which you have heard, is not mine; but the Father's who sent me* (Jn. xiv. 14). In this sentence He makes it abundantly clear that all who reject the teaching of His Only-Begotten Son reject the teaching of the Father also; since the Son says that the words He spoke are not His but the Father's; and from this it follows that if they are the words of the Father, they are also the words of the Son; for He declares: *All things whatsoever the Father hath are mine* (Jn. xvi. 15). And in another place He says to the Father: *And all things are thine, and thine are mine; and I am glorified in them* (Jn. xvii. 10); and this manifestly because of the Oneness of the divine substance; which recognizes nothing as part of it which does not belong to the divine nature.

Now however following on this He immediately lays down that we must believe that the Holy Ghost also shares in this same Oneness, when He foretells that the fulness of His teaching shall be perfected in them by the same Paraclete, declaring: *These things have I spoken to you, abiding with you. But the Paraclete, the Holy Ghost, whom the Father will send in my name, he will teach you all things, and bring all things to your mind, whatsoever I shall have said to you* (Jn. xiv. 25, 26). He deigned by these words to the Blessed Apostles to forewarn them both of His own ascent into heaven after the Passion He was to suffer, and of the descent upon them from heaven of the Holy Spirit, when He said, *These things have I spoken to you, abiding with you. But the Paraclete, the Holy Ghost, whom the Father will send.*

But the Holy Spirit was not in heaven only, and not upon earth; and neither would the Son so ascend into heaven as to forsake the earth; neither did the Father alone possess the throne of Heaven, whither the Son is said to return, and whence the Holy Ghost is said to come. For the most blessed prophet makes this acknowledgement to the Father: *Whither shall I go from thy spirit? Or whither shall I flee from thy face? If I ascend into heaven, thou art there; if I descend into hell, thou art present. If I take my wings early in the morning, and dwell in the uttermost parts of the sea* (Ps. cxxxviii).

If I take wings in the morning, he says, etc. It is well that he has wings, and that taking them he may reach whither he wills. Yet, since he dwelt in a body, in what manner could the prophet ascend into heaven or descend into hell, or reach to the farthest parts of the sea? What manner then of wings has he? The soul of the believer takes to itself wings of faith, so that raised above earthly things, and dwelling wholly in the spirit, *it can comprehend, with all the saints, what is the breadth, and length, and height, and depth of the knowledge of God* (Eph. iii. 18, 19).

But heretics, not possessing these wings of faith, dispute concerning God, and have in mind only the things of earth; and weighed down by the burden of earthly considerations, they are led away from the loftiness of the knowledge of divine things towards that which is carnal and fleeting. Neither can they come to the understanding of that boundless divinity where only the believing soul has access, which perceives, believes, confesses, and proclaims the Unity of the adorable Trinity; and since it cannot fittingly express this in words, in this also is it worthy of praise.

Whither then *shall I go*, he says, *from thy spirit? Or where shall I flee from thy face? If I ascend into heaven, thou art there: if I descend into hell, thou art present. If I take my wings early in the morning, and dwell in the uttermost parts of the sea: even there also thy hand shall lead me; and thy right hand shall hold me.* This confession likewise proclaims the undivided nature of the Trinity. *Whither shall I go*, he says, from Thy Spirit? From Thy Paraclete, that is, Whose fulness the Apostles receiving made known through the mouth of Peter the fulfilment of the divine promise, proclaiming: *This is what was spoken of by the prophet Joel: and in the last days I shall pour out my spirit upon all flesh* (Acts ii. 16, 17).

And whither shall I flee from thy face? From the Son, therefore, Who is the Face of the Father; since the Father is seen in the Son, according to the words of Our Lord and Saviour Himself, Who when Philip besought Him, *Lord, show us the Father, and it is enough for us*, so answered: *Have I been so long a time with you; and have you not known me? Philip, he that seeth me seeth the Father also. How sayest thou. Shew us the Father? Do you not believe that I am in the Father, and the Father in me?* (Jn. xiv. 9).

Neither must the Holy Spirit be regarded as separated from the Father, Whose Spirit He is, nor the Son be believed to be separated from Him Whose Face He is, and Right Hand, and Power, and Wisdom. He does not say: If I ascend into heaven Thy Spirit is there, or Thy Face and Thy Spirit are there, but *Thou*, He says, *art present*; and with Thy Son and with the Holy Ghost; for one and the same everywhere and forever is the divinity of the ever adorable Trinity. But so that a clear faith and separate belief in the Father, Son, and Holy Ghost might be given to those who believe, it is accordingly written that the Father sends both the Son and the Holy Ghost; since neither He Who sends nor He Who is sent can be believed to be God, if there is a place where He is, and a place where He is not.

Let us believe in the Son speaking

to us; since He is the Truth: *I am not alone*, He says, *because the Father is with me* (Jn. viii. 16, 29). And again, speaking of the Holy Spirit: *But*, He says, *if I by the Spirit of God cast out devils* (Mt. ii. 28). And the Evangelist Luke speaking: *But Jesus being full of the Holy Ghost returned from the Jordan* (Lk. iv. 1). Accordingly, since nowhere is the divinity of the Trinity not present, it is part of the divine plan for the redemption of mankind that It is spoken of as both sending and being sent. For otherwise the human mind could not grasp the Father is the Father, and the Son is the Son, and the Holy Ghost is the Holy Ghost, unless it should learn their separateness by the naming of One as sent and One as sending.

And again Faith could not acknowledge the One Divinity of the Father, and of the Son, and of the Holy Ghost, unless it had read that He that was sent was in no way separate from Him Who sent Him. For the Father (as has been said) did not forsake the Son Whom He sent; nor is the Holy Ghost, Who was to guide the Apostles, ever shown as not present with the Father and the Son, so that only the Son of God has become Incarnate. For, as we read, *The Word was made Flesh*; not the Father or the Holy Ghost. Just as the Son of God has fulfilled the mystery of the Incarnation without detracting from the Oneness of the Trinity, this wondrous Omnipotence is witness how the same Son of God has so ascended into heaven with the Body He assumed from among men, that He would remain with His Disciples till the end of the world. *For*, says He, *behold I am with you all days, even to the consummation of the world* (Mt. xxviii. 20); not alone with His Apostles, but also with His Disciples and all whosoever should believe in Him.

We must therefore believe that God exists in no way other than He by His own words proposes Himself to our belief. Now should we regard His works with a disobedient spirit, but honour them with earnest faith, for *the word of the Lord is right, and all his works are done with faithfulness* (Ps. xxxii. 4). If all His works are done with faithfulness, how much more the wondrous work of His most sacred Incarnation? Let us then cease from submitting the Divine Mystery to insulting investigations, while faith is neglected. For the doubtings of the disbelieving, with their idle speculation, leads to no understanding of the works of God, but loses rather the faith that is known to be the guide to salvation and eternal life.

That this excessive probing destroys faith can readily be understood from one kind of divine action: *And God said: be light made. And light was made*. Since I do not come to know that the Creator made it out of nothing unless I believe and confess that He made it, by impious deliberation I call God a liar. Therefore the mind of each single person who believes should accept with love and faith all the works of the Lord, and above all this supreme work of the Incarnation of the Son of God (as the Sacred Scriptures teach us) and proclaim by the loyal obedience of the tongue what it believes with an unwavering heart. *For with the heart we believe unto justice; but, with the mouth, confession is made unto salvation* (Rom. x. 10).

By this that He promised that the fulness of His Teaching would be bestowed by the Holy Spirit He desired that He should be believed equal with Himself in omnipotence. For in the Trinity there is no master and there is no servant; God and an angel; the Creator and the creature. There is that in which they differ, and that in which they are the same: in Person they differ, in Nature they are the same. And yet they are not Gods, but God; for the Oneness of God does not admit of any division.

Lastly Christ says of the Holy Spirit in this same place (John xiv. 25, 26): *Whom the Father will send in my name*; that is, in the Name of God, to proclaim God, namely, as the Son. And for this reason the Son also says of Himself: *I am come in the name of the Father* (Jn. v. 43); and this the Prophet had already foretold of Him; and the children praising Him in the Gospel confirmed it when they cried out: *Blessed is he that cometh in the name of the Lord* (Ps. cxvii. 26; Mt. xxix. 9). And rightly does He come in the Name of the Lord, not in the name of a servant, for He is God. Not in His own Name: for He is the Son; and coming as Son, His Name is that of the Father.

The Son accordingly, I repeat, proclaims of Himself: *I am come in the name of my Father*. But of the Holy Ghost He says: *Whom the Father will send in my name*. And when He decreed that Baptism should be conferred in the Name of the Trinity, He did not say *in the Names of*, but *in the Name of*. For the Father is God, and the Son is God, and the Holy Ghost is God, as I have often made clear to Your Charity from the testimonies of Sacred Scripture; and so One is the Name of the Trinity, One is the Power, and One the Divinity, Which shall endure for ever and ever. Amen.

II. St Augustine, Bishop and Doctor

The Paraclete[4]

John xv. 26, 27. The Lord Jesus Christ, being now near His Passion, and soon to leave them in His Bodily Presence, though in His Spiritual Presence He would be with them till the end of the world, encouraged them in the words He spoke to them after the Supper to bear steadfastly the persecutions of the ungodly; whom He calls *the world*. Yet it was from this world He had, He said, chosen the Disciples (Jn. xv. 19), so that they might know that it was by the favour of God they are what they are; they were what they were because of their own sins.

Then He clearly states the Jews were both His persecutors and theirs, so that it should be very plain to them that these were also meant by the name *world*, which was condemned because it persecuted the saints. And when He said of them that they knew not Him by Whom He had been sent, and that they hated both Father and Son, that is, He that was sent, and He by Whom He was sent: all of which things we have explained to you in the previous discourses: then He comes to this point where He says: *That the word may be fulfilled which is written in their law: They hated me without cause* (v. 25).

Then continuing, as in logical sequence, He adds that which we now undertake to explain to you: *But when the Paraclete cometh, whom I will send you from the Father, the Spirit of truth, who proceedeth from the Father, he shall give testimony of me; and you will give testimony of me, because you are with me from the beginning*. What has this to do with the previous sentence, which says: *But now they have both seen, and hated both me and my father; but that the word may be fulfilled which is written in their law: They hated me without cause*? Is it that when the Paraclete, the Spirit of Truth, comes He will convince those who both see and hate by yet clearer proofs? And in fact at His Coming He did convert some of those who saw, and, until then, hated, to that *faith which worketh by charity* (Gal. v. 6).

Then so that we may understand this let us recall to mind what happened. For on the day of Pentecost the Holy Spirit descended upon the hundred and twenty people who were gathered together, among whom were the Apostles, who, being filled with the Holy Ghost, began to speak in the tongues of every nation, and many of those who hated, astonished at so great a miracle, were changed in heart and were converted (since, when Peter spoke, they saw, because of the great and divine testimony he put forward concerning Christ; that He was shown to be risen from the dead, and to be living, Who was believed by them to have been put to death, and to be among the dead), and they received pardon because of the precious blood so blasphemously and so inhumanly spilled; and were redeemed by the blood they had shed.

For the Blood of Christ was shed for the remission of all sins, so it had the power to forgive also the sins by which it was shed. Having this in mind He therefore said: *They hated me without cause: But when the Paraclete cometh, he shall give testimony of me*: that is to say: they hated Me, and seeing Me they put Me to death: but such will be the testimony the Paraclete shall give of Me, that it will make those who do not see Me believe in Me.

And you, He says, *shall give testimony, because you are with me from the beginning*. The Holy Ghost will give testimony, and you also shall give testimony. For since you were with Me from the beginning, you can preach that which you have seen; and that you do not so now is because you have not yet the fulness of this Spirit. *He shall give testimony of me, and you shall give testimony of me*. And the charity of God that is poured forth into your hearts by the Spirit that will be given to you, shall give you courage to give testimony.

This had indeed been lacking in Peter till then, when terrified at the questioning of the servant maid he had not had the power to give true testimony, but, contrary to his promises, was driven rather by grievous fear to deny him three times. Fear such as this has no place in charity, for true charity casts out fear (Rom. v. 6; I Jn. iv. 18). And thus it was that previous to the Passion of the Lord his servile fear was put to the test by the serving woman. After the Lord's Resurrection his generous love was tested by the Prince of generosity (John xxi. 15); and because of fear then he was terrified, but here restored to calm; there he denies Whom he loved, here he showed his love for Him Whom he had denied.

But even this very love was weak and narrow, till it was enlarged and made strong by the Holy Spirit. And after the fulness of grace was poured into his soul, which before was so lukewarm, the spirit within burned to bear witness to Christ, and unsealed the trembling lips that had withheld the truth, so that while all on whom the Spirit had descended spoke in various tongues, and while the multitude of the Jews stood round about them, he shone out above all the rest in bearing witness to Christ, and confounded those who had slain Him by his witness to the Resurrection (Acts ii. 5).

Should anyone desire to contemplate this so meaningful divine wonder let him read the Acts of the Apostles. There let him with wonder see Peter proclaiming Him for denying Whom he had grieved. There he will see that tongue, changed from cowardliness to confidence, from servitude to freedom, converting to the praise of Christ the tongues of so many that were enemies; of whom one had led him to denial, being unable to stand fast before it. In short, such splendour of grace shone forth in him, such fulness of the Holy Spirit, such weight of most precious truth came forth from his mouth as he preached to them, that he made Jews who were enemies and slayers of Christ, and who formed part of that vast multitude, ready to die for Him; those by whom he had stood in fear of being put to death with Him.

This the Holy Spirit accomplished; promised beforehand, and then sent down upon them. It was these great and wondrous blessings the Lord contemplated when He said: *They have both seen and hated both me and my Father; that the word may be fulfilled which is written in their law, that they have hated me without cause. But when the Paraclete cometh, whom I will send you from the Father, the Spirit of Truth, who proceedeth from the Father, he shall give testimony of me; and you shall give testimony of me.* For He by giving testimony, and by making most courageous witnesses of them, took away fear from Christ's friends, and changed the hate of His enemies to love.

Turning then to the Lord Our God, the Father Almighty, let us as best we can give thanks with all our hearts, beseeching Him that in His goodness He will mercifully hear our prayers, by His grace drive evil from our thoughts and actions, increase our faith, grant us His holy inspirations, and lead us to joy without end, through His Son Our Lord and Saviour Jesus Christ. Amen.

III. St Leo the Great, Pope and Doctor

The Lord's Ascension II[5]

Synopsis:

I. That by the Ascension our joy is made full, and our faith and hope more wondrous.

II. That we might be capable of sharing the blessedness of heaven Christ ascended there; to abide there till the Judgement Day.

III. That our faith is so strengthened by the Ascension that no torment, even against tender maidens, can overcome it.

IV. That through His Ascension Christ became more widely known, and His Divinity brought more closely to men. What the words of the Angel signify.

V. The Ascension of Christ lifts up our own hearts, so that as pilgrims in this life we turn away from earthly things, and seek rather to grow rich in charity, without which we cannot go to Christ.

1. The mystery of our salvation, Beloved, that which the Creator of all things deigned to accomplish at the price of His Own Blood, was, from the day of His corporal birth till the last moment of His Passion, steadfastly accomplished along a divinely decreed path of humiliation. And though while in the form of a servant there shone forth many signs of His Divinity, yet everything He did throughout this time tended to confirm the truth of the humanity He had put on.

But after His Passion, and when He had destroyed the bonds of death, which had lost its power encountering Him in Whom there was no sin, infirmity changed to Might, mortality to Immortality, humiliation to Glory. This the Lord Jesus made clear to the eyes of many, by frequent and clear proofs, until He ended in heaven itself the triumph of the victory He had won over death. And as at Easter time the Resurrection of the Lord was then the cause of our joyful celebration, so His Ascension into heaven is the reason of this day's rejoicing, recalling to mind and fittingly honouring that day on which our poor lowly nature was in the Person of Christ raised above all the hosts of heaven, above the ranks of all the angels, above the sublimity of all the Powers, to the throne of God the Father.

In this order of divine events we are rooted and founded, so that when That was withdrawn from men's sight Which was rightly felt of Itself to claim our reverence, God's grace became yet more wonderful, and faith did not fail, and hope did not falter, and love did not grow cold. For this is the power of worthy souls, this is the glory of those who truly believe, that they believe without faltering what is unseen by the eyes of the body, and there fasten their desires where sight cannot follow.

Where could this devotion arise in our hearts, or how should any man be justified by faith, if our salvation was rooted and founded in things we see with our eyes? It was because of this the Lord said to the man who seemed to doubt the

Resurrection of Christ until by sight and touch he had examined the proofs of the Passion in His Flesh; *Because thou hast seen me*, He says, *thou hast believed; but blessed are they that have not seen, and have believed* (Jn. xx. 29).

II. That we may therefore, Dearly Beloved, be made ready for this blessedness, Our Lord Jesus Christ, after He had disposed in order all that related to the preaching of the Gospel and to the mysteries of the New Testament, was, in the presence of His Disciples, and on the fortieth day after His Resurrection, raised up to heaven. He withdrew for a time His Bodily Presence, for He is to abide at the right hand of the Father, until the times which have been divinely decreed for the multiplication of the children of the Church are accomplished, and then in the same Body in Which He ascended He will come again to judge the living and the dead. And so what was visible in Christ is now veiled in mystery; and that faith might be more perfect and more steadfast, vision was succeeded by revealed truth, whose authority the hearts of the faithful, illumined by light from above, would now begin to follow.

III. This then is the faith which, enlarged by the Lord's Ascension, and made firm by the gifts of the Holy Ghost, neither bonds nor prison, neither exile nor hunger nor fire, neither the fangs of wild beasts, nor the tortures devised by the cruelty of persecutors, have overcome. For this faith men everywhere throughout the world have fought steadfastly even to the shedding of their blood; not alone men, but women also, and beardless boys, and even tender maidens. This faith has cast out demons, banished sickness, raised the dead.

And even the Blessed Apostles, who had been encouraged by so many miracles, and taught by so many discourses, were yet terrified at the cruelty of the Lord's Passion, and had only with much hesitation accepted the reality of His Resurrection, were so greatly uplifted by the Lord's Ascension that whatever before had made them fear now turned their hearts towards joy. For they had turned the whole gaze of their soul upwards to the Divinity of Him Who sits at the Father's right hand. And they were no longer held by the fact of His Bodily Presence from directing their mind's eye towards that Being Who, descending on earth did not leave the Father, and ascending to heaven had not left His Disciples.

IV. It was then, Dearly Beloved, the Son of man, the Son of God, became known in a more perfect, a holier, manner: when He betook Himself to the majestic glory of the Father, and in an ineffable way began to be more present to us in His Divinity, as His humanity became more remote to us. Then a more instructed faith began by way of the soul to draw nigh to that Son Who was equal with the Father, without need to touch and feel the bodily substance in Christ, in which He is less than the Father (Jn. xiv. 28). For though the nature of His glorified Body remains, the faith of the believing began to be called whither the Only-Begotten Who is equal to the Father might be touched and felt, not by our bodily hand, but by the spiritual understanding.

It was because of this the Lord said to Mary Magdalene when she, representing the Church, drew near to touch Him: *Do not touch me, for I am not yet ascended to my Father* (Jn. xx. 17); that is, 'I do not wish you to approach me in a bodily manner, nor that you should know me by the feel of My Flesh; I would have you wait for what is higher; I am preparing for thee what is greater. When I have ascended to My Father then you shall touch me more perfectly and more truly, for you shall know what you touch not, and believe what you do not see.'

And as the Disciples looked upwards and with rapt gaze followed the Lord as He ascended to heaven, two angels in shining white garments stood by them, and said to them: *Ye men of Galilee, why stand you looking up to heaven? This Jesus who is taken up from you into heaven, shall so come, as you have seen him going into heaven* (Acts i. 11). By these words all the children of the Church were taught that they are to believe that Jesus will be seen coming again in that same body in which He ascended, and that likewise we cannot doubt that He to Whom from His Birth angels had ministered, to Him all things are subject. For as an angel announced to the Blessed Virgin that Christ would be conceived of the Holy Ghost, so also was it the voice of the heavenly choir that proclaimed Him to the shepherds New-Born of the Virgin. And as the first testimonies of that told men He had risen from the dead were those of angels from on high, so likewise was it foretold by the ministry of angels that He would come again in the Flesh to judge the world; so that we may know what great powers shall stand about Him when He shall come to judge to Whom so many ministered when He was Himself being judged.

V. Let us then exult, Beloved, with joy of soul, and rejoicing with fitting praise in God's presence, lift up the now free eyes of the soul to that place where Christ abides. Let not earthly things hold here the souls that are called above; let not perishable things fill the hearts that are chosen for eternal things. Let no false allurements hold back those who walk the way of truth. And so should believing souls pass amid these temporal things as knowing they but journey through this world's valley, in which though certain things beguile us we must not feebly yield, but press manfully on our way.

To this the most blessed Apostle Peter exhorts us, and by that love for feeding the sheep of Christ which he received by his own threefold confession of love for the Lord he cries, beseeching us: *Dearly Beloved, I beseech you as strangers and pilgrims, to refrain yourselves from carnal desires which war against the soul* (I Pet. ii. 11). And for whom unless the devil do carnal desires make war; who when souls are striving towards higher things delights to bind them fast to the pleasures of perishable things, and lead them away from those seats from which he himself has fallen?

Against such wiles each believing soul must judiciously stand guard, that he may defeat the enemy in whatever he tries. And there is nothing more efficacious against the wiles of the devil, dearly beloved, than the kindness of forgiveness, and bountifulness in charity, by means of which sin is either avoided or overcome. But this high degree of virtue is not reached until that which is its enemy is rooted out. For what is more inimical to mercy, and to the works of charity, than greed, from whose root arise the fruits of all evil? And unless this be cut at the source it must follow that the thorns and thistles of wickedness will spring up in the field of that heart where this plant of evil flourishes, rather than any plant of true virtue.

Let us then, Most dearly Beloved, stand firm against this so destructive evil, and follow after charity, without which no virtue can flourish; so that we may ascend by that way of love to Christ by which He has come down to us, to Whom with the Father and the Holy Ghost be honour and glory for ever and ever. Amen.

IV. St Caesarius, Bishop of Arles[6]

On Eating and Drinking the Word of God

1. *What it means to hunger after Justice. The Right of the People to ask the Priest for the Word of God.* Among the Beatitudes which Our Lord and Saviour deigned to number in the Gospel, He also included this: *Blessed are they that hunger and thirst after justice: for they shall have their fill* (Mt. v. 6). Happy are they to whom the Lord has deigned to give this exalted hunger, this most desirable thirst. But, Brethren, how does a man hunger after justice? You hunger after justice when you desire gladly and with patience to hear the word of God; for of this food was it said: *They that eat me, shall yet hunger: and they that drink me, shall yet thirst* (Eccli. xxiv. 29). For though it is more perfect to do than to know, yet we must first know what is just before we can do it. He must learn God's will who desires to fulfil it. And therefore he who desires to learn of justice hungers after the knowledge of justice. We must therefore learn of justice, so that afterwards we may merit to fulfil it. If therefore, as we believe, you truly hunger and thirst after justice, in order that this blessedness may, through the grace of God, be fulfilled in you, whenever the word of God is for long withheld from you, let you not wait until such time as we shall preach it to you, but let you eagerly and confidently demand it of us as something that is rightly due to you.

2. *The Obligation of Priests to communicate the Word of God.* If we on the one hand desire always to offer it to you, while you do not desire to seek it from us should we at times be neglectful, we may then perhaps be judged importunate by those who do not know our danger. But they who do know the grave burden laid on priests will understand that even though we preach often, we yet communicate to you less than we are bound to. For the Holy Spirit has testified to priests by the mouth of the prophet: *Cry, cease not.* He does not say, Cry out for many days; but, *Cry, cease not,*

lift up thy voice like a trumpet, and show thy people their wicked doings (Is. lviii. 1). And again: *If thou declare not to the wicked his wicked way, I will require his blood at thy hand* (Ezech. iii. 18). And the Apostle: *Therefore watch, keeping in memory, that for three years I ceased not, with tears to admonish every one of you night and day* (Acts xx. 31). If the Apostle that he might be without blame before God preached night and day the word of God, what will happen to us who rarely, or only after the lapse of many days, provide spiritual pasture for the flock entrusted to us?

Because of this the same Apostle adjures Timothy: *I charge thee, before God and Jesus Christ, who shall judge the living and the dead, by his coming, and his kingdom* (II Tim. iv. 1). And as though he were asked why he begins with such a fearful exhortation, he goes on to say: *Preach the word: be instant in season, out of season: reprove, entreat, rebuke.* What does *in season* and *out of season* mean if not at suitable times to those who desire it, and with urgency to those who are unwilling? The word of God must be offered to those who desire it; it must be urged on those who are averse to it, lest standing before the tribunal of Christ they may declare against us that we did not warn them, and He shall then require their blood at our hands. And so with great fear and trembling we must take thought so that that terrible sentence shall not be pronounced against us which the servant merited to hear who had neglected to double the talent he had received: *Wicked and slothful servant*, he says, *why hast thou not committed my money to the bankers, and at my coming I should have received my own with usury?* (Mt. xxv. 26, 27).

And then what follows? May God deliver us from it! *And the unprofitable servant*, he says, *cast ye out into the exterior darkness; there shall be weeping and gnashing of teeth. Why*, he says, *hast thou not committed my money to the bankers?* By money, dearly beloved, understand only that which is to be preached in the Church. The bankers who should receive the money are none other than the Christian people. For as it shall be for us a grievous sin not to have committed the money of the Lord to the bank of your heart, so likewise no small danger threatens you who are unwilling by means of good works to double what you have received by the words we have preached to you.

3. *This is the Food of the Soul.* Since therefore you are aware both of ours and of your own danger, as often as it shall happen that the word of God is ministered to you tardily, treat this as you would if the substance of your daily food were withheld from your body. For with us the hunger of the soul ought not to be less than that of the body. For the more worthy we know the soul to be, the greater must be our care that it receive the food it needs. For if our body be fed twice each day, why should anyone think it troublesome and uncalled for if the soul that belongs to God is fed but once in seven days. For as the body is restored by this earthly food, so is the soul refreshed by the word of God. And so as often as it is tardily offered to you, awaken us from our sloth and demand what is rightfully yours.

4. *The Priests are as Kine; providing the Milk of the Word of God. The People as Calves, eagerly seeking it.* For in the Church the priests are like the milking kine; the Christian people resemble the calves. For as the cows wander through the fields and the meadows, and go through vineyards and the olive groves, and from the leaves and grass they graze on provide milk for the calves; so priests assiduously reading the word of God on the wide hills of the Scriptures, should from the herbiage they gather provide spiritual milk for their children, so that they may be as Paul, who said: *I gave you milk to drink, not meat* (I Cor. iii. 2). Not unfittingly then, Beloved Brethren, do priests seem to be like the kine. For also as the cow has two udders from which she nourishes her calves, so must priests, from the two udders of the Old and New Testament, provide spiritual food for their people.

Yet, consider, Dearest Brethren, how not alone do kine seek out their young calves, but these also come running to them, and often so buffet them on the udders with their eager heads, that at times, if the calves are big, they seem to lift their mothers from the ground. But this the mothers contentedly suffer; for they desire to see their calves grow strong. And this good priests should also seek after and desire: that their spiritual children should press them with questions regarding their own salvation, so that while divine grace is given to the children who as it were buffet them with questions, a divine reward is being prepared for the priests who thus make known to them the truths of sacred Scriptures.

I tell you this then so that this resemblance may be found both in you and in us. For we are eager to suffer from you this longed for hunger of the soul; so long as we see that your souls grow strong in the love of Christ. And as we must gather the flowers of Scripture to make food for souls, so also should you seek it, and with great eagerness. For as calves beat strongly against the maternal udders, that they may the more freely draw forth the needed food, so should the Christian people seek eagerly from their priests, as from the udders of the Church, to acquire the food of salvation, and the nourishment the soul needs, so that should priests be slow in giving it, and the people too worldly to enquire for it, that may not come to pass which was written: *I will send a famine into the land: not a famine of bread, nor a thirst of water, but of hearing the word of the Lord* (Amos viii. 11).

We trust in the mercy of God that we shall be given a zeal for reading and preaching, and that you will be given an eager desire to hear us, that we may be able to give a good account before the Tribunal of Christ, because of the sermons we have preached, and that you may receive the reward of salvation, because of your obedient hearing of the word of God, and of your perseverance in good works, by the help of Our Lord Jesus Christ, to Whom be honour and glory, now and forever. Amen.

V. St Caesarius, Bishop of Arles

On How the Word of God is to be Received[7]

1. *Paternal sollicitude for the weak in body.* Some days ago, because of those who suffer with their feet, or labour under some bodily weakness, I advised you with fatherly earnestness, and in a manner I besought you, that when the Acts of the Martyrs are read at length, or at all events during certain longer Lessons, that those who were unable to stand should, sitting down, listen with attentive ears, and with humility and in silence, to what was being read. Now there are some among our children who think that all, or at least many who are well in health, may regularly do this. For as soon as the word of God begins to be read they decide to stretch themselves out as if they were in their beds; and would that they do only that, and keeping silence receive the word of God with a devout heart, and not begin to distract themselves with idle gossiping, so that they neither hear what is read, nor let others hear it.

Now, Venerable Brethren, I ask you, and with a father's concern I want to impress upon you, that while the lessons are being read, or while the word of God is being preached, no one is to stretch himself out upon the ground: unless where great weakness compels him to do so, and in that case let him not lie down, but rather sit down, and in this way let him, with a loving heart, take in whatever is being made known to him.

2. *The Word of God is in no way less than the Body of Christ; nor should it be received less worthily.* I ask you, brothers or sisters, tell me: which to you seems the greater, the word of God, or the Body of Christ? If you wish to say what is true you will have to answer that the word of God is not less than the Body of Christ. Therefore just as when the Body of Christ is administered to us, what care do we not use so that nothing of it falls from our hands to the ground, so should we with equal care see that the word of God which is being imparted to us shall not be lost to our soul, while we speak or think of something else. For he who listens carelessly to the word of God is not less guilty than he who through his own inattention suffers the Body of Christ to fall to the ground.

3. *The Preacher is a Giver of Precious Jewels.* Now I would like to know whether if, at the time when the preacher begins to preach to you the word of God, we decided to bestow on you the most precious jewels and earrings and finger rings, would our daughters choose to stay where they are or to come forward to receive them? Without any doubt, and with great good will, they would accept what was offered them. But since we neither can nor ought to offer bodily adornments we are not therefore readily listened to. But it is not just that we who minister to you in spiritual things should not be properly regarded.

Let her who gratefully hears the word of God be certain that she has received earrings for her soul brought down from the heavenly home.

And she who being taught to help those in need holds out her hand to give alms receives a bracelet, placed there by Christ. For as a body given to evil puts on earthly adornments, that for a while it may gratify carnal eyes: to its own loss and that of those who sinfully desire it: so the soul that is spiritually adorned, by means of divine instruction, with the everlasting spiritual pearls of good works, shall be prepared to share the company of the Heavenly Spouse, and enter with Him to the Wedding Feast. So she shall not hear what is written in the Gospels: *Friend, how camest thou in hither not having on a wedding garment*? (Mt. xxii. 12). And that she to whom this was said may, not adorned and not clothed as are the just, merit to hear: *Bind his hands and feet, and cast him into the exterior darkness: there shall be weeping and gnashing of teeth*, rather may she because of her garment of virtue and good works hear these words: *Well done, thou good and faithful servant: enter thou into the joy of thy Lord* (Mt. xxv. 21).

4. *The Preacher is as a Mother who wishes to adorn her Daughter. What reward does he ask of his labour?* I ask you, Daughters, to listen with attention to what we have to say. Should a mother wish to adorn her child, and should she, refusing the adornments, throw herself on the ground and turn this way and that, and will not be quiet so that her mother may adorn her as best she can, may not such a daughter be rightly chastised and scolded? Consider me then as the mother of your souls; who wishes to array you that you may appear *without spot or blemish* before the tribunal of the Eternal Judge? And anxious to provide remedies as well as ornaments for your souls I desire to join together what was sundered, to mend what was torn, to heal what was wounded, to clean what was soiled, to renew what was destroyed, and to adorn what is healthy with spiritual pearls.

I spare not my labour; why should anyone think to accept it with indifference? For since the adornments of the body are bought only at great cost, unless you find someone willing to give them to you, with what thanks should not the spiritual adornments of the soul be received, which though won at no small cost are offered to you without price? For we who offer you heavenly pearls, desire no reward in this life but that we may see you listen freely and with patience to what we preach to you, and that you with God's help and as best you can fulfil our teaching by doing what is good and just.

5. *Conclusion.* Beloved Brethren, and Revered Sisters, do not think we speak to you in this way because you are inattentive to the word of God. For, thanks be to God, my soul is glad and rejoices beyond telling over your good dispositions. We say these things because we desire that you rise to yet better dispositions, even in that which we know you do well. It is for this we presume with paternal anxiety to exhort you in the Lord. Amen.

NOTES

[1] PG 59, pp. 415 *et seq.*

[2] PG 39, Liber de S. Sancto, col. 1056.

[3] PL 20, Sermo. 20.

[4] PL 35, Tract. 92.

[5] PL 54, Sermo. 74, De Ascensione Domini II.

[6] PL 39, App. Sermo. 299; previously attributed to St Augustine. This and the following sermon are examples of the developing popular style of sermon, and while not distinguished by any great powers of exposition they join great tenderness and zeal to their witness of the truths of Tradition as well as of Holy Scripture; notably to the belief that the ministry of the word, and the ministry of the Holy Sacrifice, were the joint essential components of the priest's office, in which he is called to minister to the people.

[7] PL 39, App. Sermo. 300; previously attributed to St Augustine. PRM 39.

INDEX

The following abbreviations have been used: Amb.: Ambrose; Amph.: Amphilocius; Aug.: Augustine; Caes.: Caesarius; Chr.: Chrysostom; Cyl. of A.: Cyril of Alexandria; Cyp.: Cyprian; Gau.: Gaudentius; Gy. Ny.: Gregory of Nyssa; Gy. Gt.: Gregory the Great; Hy.: Hilary; Jer.: Jerome; L. Gt.: Leo the Great; Max.: Maximus; Or.: Origen.

Abraham: and the Word of God, 134; and the prefiguring of Christ's Passion, 136; foresees Day of the Lord, 154; unshaken faith of, 381–382

Absolution, priest's duty, 284

Abstinence, during Lent, 4–5, 91–2

Adam: temptations of, 6, 33; devil's attack on, 16; freed by Christ from death, 222; downfall of, 249

Adversity, effect of on men, 126

Almsgiving, 35, 91, 128, 459; remission of offences by, 13, 14, 113–19; Jer. on our slowness in, 177–80; need for humility and cheerfulness in, 280

Ambrose, St, Bishop and Doctor: on the Season of Penance, 13–15; on Lent, 82–4; on the Casting out of Devils, 84–6; on the Colt a Figure of the Gentiles, 170–2; on the Sunday of the Resurrection, 218–219; 'Watch and Pray', 387–8

Amphilocius of Iconium, St, on the Solemnity of the Burial of our Saviour, 191–3

Ananias, 231

Andrew, St, and the feeding of the five thousand, 105, 125

Angels: proclamation of Christ by, 5; ministering to Lazarus, 20; ministering to Christ, 34, 42; duty of, to give glory to God, 385–6; at our Lord's Ascension, 430; remind the Disciples that Jesus will come again, 438

Anger: no place for in the Christian heart, 351–2

Anna, prayer of, 392

Appolinaris, 148

Apostles: signified by baskets, 109, 112; bidden to feed the people, 119; given understanding of the Resurrection, 209–10

Arians, 78; false sayings of, 135

Ark, the, as a figure of the Church, 94, 227

Ascension, the, 410 ff; of Christ's Mystical Body, Aug. on, 365–8; belief in all over the earth, 415; prophecy of, 415–16; mystery of, Aug. on, 416–24; cause for joy to the sad and doubting, 425–6; Gy. Gt. on, 426–32; Habacuc on, 431; Chr. on, 432–40; L. Gt. on, 452–5

Ass, the, symbolism of, 163–4, 166–7, 173

Augustine, St, Bishop and Doctor: on the Kingdom of Christ, 62–5; on the Feeding of the Five Thousand, 121–5; on the Vigil of Easter, 193–194; on Watchfulness against the Devil, 194–6; To Those Baptized, 225–7; on, Peace Be to You, the Mystical Body, 227–31; To Children, on the Holy Sacrifice, 232–3; on Christian Compassion, 276–81; on the Shepherd, the Thief and the Hireling, 297–307; his refusal to countenance evil in his flock, 306; 'A Little While', 326–9; 'If You Ask the Father Anything in My

Name', 399–402; on Christ's Promise of the Coming of the Holy Spirit, 362–5; on the Ascension of Christ's Mystical Body, 365–8; on Ascension Day, 415–16; on The Mystery of the Lords' Ascension, 416–24; on the Paraclete, 449–51

Avarice: Gy. Gt. on, 6; Christ tempted by, 10; Chr. on, 12; strength of temptation of, 20, 33–4

Baptism: as re-birth, 43; forgiveness of sins bestowed by, 113; as figure of Christ's Death and Resurrection, 151–2; Chr. on, 222; Trinity received in, 359; keeping of promises made, 427–8

Barley loaves, as signifying the Old Testament, 123

Basil the Great, St, Bishop and Doctor: That Prayer is to be Placed before All Things, 377–83; on Prayer, 383–6

Beelzebub, 77, 95, 96; kingdom of, 87

Bede, The Venerable, Priest and Doctor: on the Giving of Peace, 204–210; on the Christian's Hope, 332–336; on the Fathers on Prayer, 404–9

Bethphage, 159, 162, 168, 173

Binding and Loosing, Gy. Gt. on Power of, 281–8

Birth Festivals, 334

Bishops, Gy. Gt. on, 284

Blood of Christ: for whom shed, and why, 257–8

Books, understanding of, 122

Bruno, St, Abbot: on the Kingdom of Evil, 94–8

Burial, Days of, shortened because of the Disciples, 202

Caesarius, St, Bishop of Arles: on Eating and Drinking the Word of God, 456–7; on How the Word of God is to be Received, 458–9

Charity: salvation won through, 64–65; joined to patience and endurance, 351; bountifulness in, 455

Chastisement, God's purpose in, 22; fear of, 144

Chastity: of the soul, 302–3; in a wife, 303

Cherubim, excluding man from Paradise, 436

Children, Aug. to, on the Holy Sacrifice, 232–3

Christ: birth of, 5; refusal to give sign to the devil or to the Jews, 18–19; the Beloved Son, 57; second coming of, 58; as fulfilment of Law and Prophets, 68; as Lord of the Prophets, 107, 124; as Angel and Lord of Angels, 124–5; offended by denial of poor and needy, 117–18; as Word of God, 121, 122; Patience of: as a man, 131, 132; Gy. Gt. on, 152–6; in enduring the Cross, 244; as being without sin, 130; as Justice and Wisdom, 132; His union with our human lowliness, 149–50; indissoluble union of, with His Body, 150; glory of, as merit of the Christian, 152; Divinity and Humanity of, 146–9, 154, 260, 406–7, 420–1; humility of, 155–6, 260; by His life gives us measures and standards, 176; prayer for His enemies, 182–3; death, made wondrous by His power, 183–4; Amph. on Solemnity of His Burial, 191–3; changes in His Body because of Resurrection, 203; mission to restore peace to the world, 205; as our Salvation, 227; opening our minds to understanding, 229; as Head of the Church, 230, 297; assumes nature of man until the Resurrection, 236–7; humanity of, 250; unity with His Members, 297–8; as the Door, 298–9; as the Good Shepherd, 308–9, 310, 314; as known to God, 311–12; our relationship with Him as a man, 312–313; teaches us patience by His actions, 348–9; His justice to others, 367–8; speaks in proverbs, 400–1, 406, 408; became weak for our sakes, 418; as mediator, 433–4; Divinity of, 453; oneness of His Divinity with that of the Father, 446

Christians: striving to imitate Christ, 150–1; need to hold firmly to heavenly things, 203–4; likened to calves, 457
Church, the: Kingdom of God in, 63; expectations of, confirmed by Transfiguration, 70; reasons for attending, 137–9; behaviour in, 139–40, 178–9; richness of, compared with poverty of the Law, 223; throughout the nations, 230; building up of, 231; made from both Jews and Gentiles, 300–1; carrying on work of the Apostles, 413; as the Glory of Christ, 416
Clemency of God, Cyl. of A. on, 26
Clerics. *See* Priests
Cloud, appearance of God in, 42, 48, 56, 63, 71
Colt, the, symbolism of, 163–4, 166–7; Amb. on, 170–2, 173, 176
Comforter, Holy Spirit as, 442
Communion: need to become worthy of, 142–3; exclusion of the unworthy from, 143–4; need for priest to dispense with carefulness, 144–5; Aug. explains, to children, 232–3
Compassion, Christian: Aug. on, 276–81; twofold nature of, within the Church, 279
Confession, Amb. on, 13–14
Confirmation, Aug. explains, to children, 232
Contemplation: not suited to all, 249; spiritual value of, 378
Corinthians, heresy of, 208
Creation, 248
Creed, the, and belief in the Incarnation, 181–2
Cross, the: scandal of, removed by Transfiguration, 70; need for us all to bear, 147; as sacrament and example, 236; power of, to arm us against evil desires, 237–8; Christ's refusal to descend from, 244; ignominy of death on, 419
Cyprian, St, Bishop and Martyr: on Good Works and Almsdeeds, 112–119; on the Advantages of Patience, 346–55
Cyril of Alexandria, St, Bishop and Doctor: on the Preparation for the Pasch, 25–8; on the Transfiguration, 65–8; on the Casting out of Devils, 86–90; on the Good Shepherd, 307–15; on Christian Hope, the Promised Joy, 328–32; on The Mission of the Holy Spirit, 368–71; on Confidence in Prayer, 403–4

Damin, 3–4
David, prophecies of, 177
Death: of the soul, 134; salvation bought with, 259; different kinds of, 418–19
Debtors, and payers of debts, Chr. on, 222
Desert, temptation of Jesus in, 1 ff.
Despondency, Chr. on, 355–6
Deuteronomy, Book of: Jesus draws His answers from, 9
Devil: temptation of Jesus by, 1 ff.; man's temptations by, after baptism, 2–3; misuse of Scriptures by, 8–9; need to resist, 21; speaks to us through mouths of our friends, 22; as head of all evil-doers, 33; as 'a strong man', 79–80, 96; tricked by his own wickedness, 182; Aug. on watchfulness against, 194–6; spiritual strength necessary to withstand attacks of, 224; gifts stolen from us by, 426; and carnal desires, 454
Devils, casting out of, 76 ff.
Devotion, during Lent, 32
Disciples: hesitation in believing Resurrection, 228; persuaded to believe, 228–9; Christ appears to, 273; spiritual power and grace received by, 273; sent by our Lord to suffer, 282; Christ's test of their courage, 325; prepares and strengthens them, 331; promised reward for, 332; comforted by Christ's bodily presence, 417; faith confirmed by touching Christ's wounds, 425
Dives, punishment for self-indulgence, 22
Divinity: of Christ, 45–6, 48–51, 453; boundless nature of, 247

Donatists, 304, 319
Door, Christ as the, 298–9
Drunkenness, Chr. on, 197–9; Paul on, 197, 198

Earthquake, significance of, 187–8
Easter Sunday, 211 ff.
Egypt, flight from, 253, 256
Eighth day, significance of, 276, 289
Elias: fasting by, 7, 15, 17, 34; appearance at Transfiguration, 40–1, 45, 46–7, 53–5, 63, 66; character of, 54; taken up to Heaven, 413–14, 429, 438
Enoch, translation of, 429
Ephraim, St, Confessor and Doctor, on the Transfiguration, 44–51
Eternity, nature of, 247
Eucharist. *See* Communion
Eutychians, heresy of, 239
Eve, devil's attack on, 21
Evil, Bruno on The Kingdom of, 94–8
Evil spirits: harmony amongst, 95–6; seven, 97–8
Evil thoughts, three kinds of, 408
Evils, facing man, 55
Ezechias: on the teachers of the Jews, 295; prayers when sick, 394
Ezechiel: on Christ, and on the Jewish teachers, 310; grief over sinners, 437

Faith: strengthening of, by preaching Gospel, 72; true, need for, 148; one, for all mankind, 150, 342; nature of, 285; Christ's gift of, to whole world, 370; need for persistence in, 380–2; confirmed, by Christ's forty days on earth, 424–5; destroyed by excessive probing, 448; made more wondrous through the Ascension, 452, 453
Fasting: Chr. on, 4, 12, 196; Aug. on, 5; reasons for Christ's fasting, 5; as help in overcoming temptation, 6; Amb. on, 13, 15; Cyl. of A. on, 26; after baptism, 16–17; L. Gt. on, 31; sanctification of, 35–6; and sharing of our Lord's Passion, 147
Finger of God, meaning of, 78–9, 84–5, 88, 96
First Month, custom of, 253
Flood, the, significance of, 93
Food, dangers of delighting in, 17
Forgiveness: man's need of, 127; duty of, towards others, 127; Christ's prayer for, for His enemies, 240–1; efficacious against the devil's wiles, 455
Forty, significance of number, 93
Forty days, significance of, 34–5
Freewill, man endowed with, 249
Friends, importance of, 361–2

Galilee: symbolical meaning of, 217, 243; Sea of, diversity of names of, 102
Garments of Christ, as symbol of Church, 62–3
Gaudentius, St, Bishop of Brescia: on the Promised Coming of the Paraclete, 446–9
Generosity, 128
Gentiles: on the Resurrection, 207; and the true faith, 296–7; their redemption through Christ, 314–315, 318
Gifts, spiritual, pleasing to God, 246
Gluttony, temptation through, 6, 20, 33–4
God: need for turning to, to defeat temptation, 20; justice and mercy of, 150; Majesty of, man's little knowledge of, 181; terrifying to sinners, comforting to good, 242–243; diffused nature of, 247–8; as Lawmaker, 251; our need of, 278; delay in answering prayer, 388–90
Gospel, the: more demanding than the Law, 254–5; perverted interpretation of, 302; to be preached to every nation, 427
Grace, man's co-operation with, 125–126
Grace, the saying of, at meals, 385, 393
Greed, Aug. on, 64
Greeks, defective idea of the Divinity, 247
Gregory the Great, St, Pope and Doctor: on The Temptations in the Desert, 32–6; on the Patience of Christ, 152–6; on the Mystery of

the Resurrection, 241–5; on the Power of Binding and Loosing, the Judgement and the Resurrection, 281–8; on the Unfading Pastures: the Christian Hope, 316–319; Explanations and Reflections on the Ascension, 426–32
Gregory Nazianzenus, St, Bishop and Doctor: on the Holy Pasch (and His Own Reluctance), 219–21

Habacuc, 245; on the Ascension, 431
Halcyon, the, God's provision for, 386
Heaven: we must grow eager for, 319; how far from earth, 435
Hebrews, the: crossing of Red Sea by, 234; and the meaning of Pasch, 238–9. *See also* Jews
Hell: Chr. on belief in, 23–4; realities of, 52; how far from earth, 435
Heretics: claims of martyrdom by, 291; evil teachings of, 341; failure to understand Christ's divinity, 447
Hilary, St, Bishop and Doctor, on the Passing of the Law, 119–21
Hireling, the: Aug. on (and the Thief and the Shepherd), 297–307; tolerated in the Church, 303–4; cowardice of, 305, 308, 309, 316–317
Holy Saturday, 185 ff.
Holy Spirit, the: leading sons of God against the devil, 4; and the teaching of spiritual things, 342–3; Chr. on the Promise of, 355–62; Aug. on, 362–5; Cyl. of A. on, 368–71; as Comforter, 442; Gau. on Promised Coming of the Paraclete, 446–9
Hope, Christian: Gy. Gt. on, 316–19; Aug. on, 329; Cyl. of A. on, 329; Bede on, 332–6; made more wondrous through the Ascension, 452
Hosanna, meaning of, 161–2, 174–5
Humility: virtue of, 92; in prayer, 379; Christ's: His triumph by, 7; misunderstood by us, 260
Hunger, endurance of, 18

Immortality: Cyl. of A. on lack of understanding of, 27
Impatience, evils of, 352–3
Incarnation, the belief in, 181–2; Aug. on, 419, 421
Incontinence, Aug. on, 226
Infinity, nature of, 247
Iniquity, burthen of, 59
Invisible world, Chr. on belief in, 23–4
Isaias, foretells divine vengeance, 354

James, St, and the witnessing of the Transfiguration, 37, 39, 45, 52, 70
Jeremiah: prayers of, 395; grief over sinners, 437
Jerome, St, Priest and Doctor: on the Meaning of Christ's Entry into Jerusalem, 173–5
Jerusalem: Or, on Christ's entry into, 164–70
Jesus. *See* Christ
Jews: sins when filled with the delights of food, 17; as persecutors, 33, 449; and the law of Moses, 67–8; errors in faith of, 78, 80–1, 82, 85, 235, 247; Cyl. of A. on, 89–90; fear of Christ even after His death, 92; condemnation of, 97; refusal to obey Christ, 175; indifference to His wonders, 177; celebration of the Pasch, 219; denial of Christ by, 309; teachers, love of gain among, 311. *See also* Hebrews
Job: on the devil, 95–6; on man's life a warfare, 147; prayers of, 395
John, St, and witnessing of the Transfiguration, 37, 39, 45, 52, 70
John Chrysostom, St, Bishop and Doctor: on Usury, 59–62; on the Transfiguration, 52–9; on the Respect Due to the Church of God, and to the Sacred Mysteries, 137–45; on the Lessons of Christ's Entry into Jerusalem, 175–81; Against Drunkards, 196–201; on the Fruits of Christ's Resurrection, 221–5; on the Authority and Dignity of the Priesthood, 272–5; on the Shepherd and the Hireling, 295–7; 'Yet a Little While', 324–6; on The Promise of the Holy Spirit, 355–62; on Prayer, 388–99; on

Christ's Ascension, and Man's Exaltation, 432–40; humility of, 439–40
Jonah, prayers of, 395
Jordan, River, as figure of the baptized, 286
Joseph, symbolical meaning of his selling, 439
Joy: Christ's announcement of, to woman, 273; our, through the Ascension, 452
Judas, failure to obtain pardon, 183
Judgement, the: Chr. on belief in, 23, 25, 58–9; different meanings of, 132; Gy. Gt. on, 287; period for repentance before, 432; Christ in Heaven until, 453
Justice, Christ convinces world of, 367–8, 369–70
Justness, Christ speaks of, 357–8

Kingdom of Christ: Aug. on, 62; Amb. on, 84–5; severance of heretics from, 85
Knowledge, perfect, 403

Lamb, the, symbolism of, 252, 254
Law, the: signified by barley loaves, 108; Hy. on the passing of, 119–21; foretells grace of Christ, 151; poverty of, compared with riches of Church, 223; given to us as a help, 251–2; Gospel's greater demands, 254–5
Lazarus: received by the angels, 20; and picture of Hell, 52
Laziness of churchgoers, 137–8
Lent: abstinence during, 4–5; L. Gt. on, as Season of Purification, 28–32; Amb. on, 83–4; L. Gt. on the Purposes of, 90–2; Max. on, 92–4; L. Gt. on Spirit of, 125–8
Leo the Great, St, Pope and Doctor: on Lent, the Season of Purification, 28–32; on the Purposes of the Transfiguration, 68–73; on the Purposes of Lent, 90–2; on the Spirit of Lent, 125–8; on Faith in the Divinity and Humanity of Christ, 146–9; on the Fruits of the Passion, 149–52; on the Passion of Our Lord, 181–4; on the Resurrection of the Lord, 201–4, 235–9; on the Lord's Ascension, 424–6, 452–5
Leontius, Holy Solemnity of, 415
Life, future, Christ's mind directed towards, 276
Loaves and fishes, miracle of, 105 ff.; spiritual significance of, 123
Loins, girding of, 255
Love: to be rendered at all times, 281; Chr. on strength of bond of, 361; of God, 402, 407
Low Sunday, 265 ff.

Man: as sinner, 146; creation of, 248–249; unworthiness of, 435–6; raising of, 436
Manicheans, the, 148; L. Gt. on perverted abstinence of, 31; heresies of, 105, 227, 229, 295
Martha and Mary, significance of story of, 378
Mary: and human nature of Jesus, 48–9; denial of, by Jews and heretics, 82; Blessedness of, 98
Mary Magdalene: visit to the tomb, 187, 213, 218; wishes to touch Christ, 454
Maximus, St, Bishop and Father: on the Time of Lent, 92–4; on the Prayer of the Good Thief, 237–41
Mediator, Christ as, 3, 433–4
Mercy: need for acts of, 114–15. *See also* Compassion
Mill, the, symbolism of, 439
Mind, the, wandering during prayers, 391, 392, 398
Miracles: multitudes moved by, 103; what they tell us of Christ, 121; disciples receive power of performing, 273; need of, to nourish faith at Church's beginning, 428–9
Morals, Aug. on correction of, 227
Moses: fasting of, 7, 15, 17, 34; appearance of at Transfiguration, 45, 46–7, 53–4, 63, 66; character of, 54; Five Books of, 108, 123; as God's minister, 251; prayers of, 395; and idolatry of his people, 437

Nabuchodonosor: the suffering of, 22; failure to redeem sins by almsgiving, 114–15

New Testament, in harmony with Old Testament teachings, 71
Ninevites, penance done by, 13
Nourishment, spiritual, 110

Obedience, to priests, 144
Old Testament, in harmony with New Testament teachings, 71
Olivet, Mount, 159, 162, 169, 171, 173
Ordination, Gy. Ny. on, 219–20
Origen, Priest and Confessor: Mystical Exposition of Feeding of the Five Thousand, 109–12; on Christ's Entry into Jerusalem, 164–70

Palm Sunday, 157 ff.
Paraclete. *See* Holy Spirit
Paradise, 249; as pastures of the elect, 318
Pasch, the: L. Gt. on preparations for, 146–7; no distinctions of persons in celebration of, 200; Amb. on meaning of, 218–19; Gy. Ny. on, 219–21, 245–62; Proclus on, 234–5; symbolically pointed out in the old Law, 234, 257, 258; meaning of, 250–1; to the Hebrews, 238–9; the worship of, 261–2
Passion Sunday, 129 ff.
Patience: overcoming of devil by, 19; under provocation, 34; Christ's power of, 131, 132, 244; taught us by Christ, 137; Cyp. on the Advantages of, 346–55; ripens all, 347–8; is of God, 348; power of against Evil, 350–1; and the foundation of charity, 351; in bodily afflictions, 352; merits of, 353–4
Paul, St: on frequent watchings, 193; on war against the devil and his angels, 193, 195; on drunkenness, 197, 198; on the false teacher, 295–296; to those converted from the Gentiles, 314; on the Holy Spirit, 360; prayers in prison, 394; prayer not heard, 404
Peace: Bede, on the Giving of, 204–210; Christ's greeting of, 266, 267, 273; as beginning of soul's purification, 384
Penance, wiping out of sins by, 13, 94
Penetecost: Aug. explains to children, 232; descent of Holy Spirit at, 450
Persecution: of the Christian, 147; makes the good better, 154
Perseverance: Cyp. on, 350; in prayer, 389
Peter, St: and witnessing of the Transfiguration, 37, 39, 41–2, 45, 52, 55, 63, 67, 70, 71; and the raising of Tabitha, 115; on need to follow in Christ's steps, 151; as Foundation of the Church, 181–2; preaching of, 183; weakness of, 298, 450; given courage to shew his love, 451
Pharaoh, final chastisement of, 22, 234
Pharisee, the, and the Publican, 299
Pharisees: words of Christ against, 300; giving to false teachers, 308; Christ's authority greater than, 308
Philip, St: the questioning of, 104, 122; slowness of faith, 104–5
Pilate, Pontius, as member of the devil, 33
Plagues, of Egypt, 253
Poverty, Christian, 30; no bar to giving, 92
Praise, in prayer, 379
Prayer: Basil on, 379–83, 383–6; reasons for, 382; stretching out of hands in, 384, 395; as purpose of the soul, 383; Amb. on, 387–8; communion of, 384; at night, 384–385, 387; Chr. on, 388–99; patience in, when God delays an answer, 388–9, 404–5; reverence and recollection in, 390–1; power of, 395–6; of the saints, 397; our heed of, 397; Aug. on 'If you ask the Father anything in My name', 399–402; to be short and frequent, 392; as a stirring of the soul, 394; place of, immaterial, 395; Cyl. of A. on, 403–4; Bede on 'The Fathers on', 404–9; for sinners, 405; asking for eternal joy, 405–6; against temptation, 408–9
Pride, Chr. on, 12
Priesthood, Chr. on Authority and Dignity of, 272–5
Priests: obedience to, 144; to fear God, not man, 145; responsibility

of, 268; support we can give to, 274; we are to hold in reverence, 275; as instrument of God, 275; unworthy, lead laymen to sin, 301–2; likened to kine, 457
Proclus, St, Patriarch of Constantinople, on the Holy Pasch, 234–5
Prophecy, fulfilling of, in Christ's entry into Jerusalem, 176
Propitiation of God, means of, 114
Prosperity, effect of on men, 126
Proverbs, Christ speaking in, 400–1, 406, 408
Publican, the, and the Pharisee, 299
Punishments, from God, 24
Purification of soul, through observance of Lent, 29
Purpose, behind all happenings, 124

Quinquagesima, celebration of, 5

Raphael, Angel, and plea for almsgiving, 115
Repentance: necessary to confession, 14; to rid man of devil, 97; duty of, 125–7
Resurrection, the: signified in raising of disciples, 63–4; L. Gt. on, 201–4; Christ's proofs of truth of, 202–3; changes in body of Christ, 203; gradual revelation of, 204–5; disciples' fear, 206; our faith and hope in, 207–8; Amb. on, 218–19; twofold, Chr. on, 222; Gy. Gt. on Mystery of, 241–5, 287–8; promise of, to man, 244; our need to believe, 259; of the body, 422–3; proved by God, 419–20; Apostles' doubts of, 426
Reverence, to God, 141
Rogation Days, 372 ff.

Sadness, compared with pains of childbirth, 325, 327
Samaritan, Christ likened to, 130–1, 153
Samson, deeds of, foreshadowing Resurrection, 244–5
Sareptha, lesson learnt from, 30
Saul, Aug. on conversion of, 230–1
Sanctified, the, after the last judgement, 277
Satan, condemnation of, 370–1
Scriptures, the: devil's misuse of, 8–9, 19; Christ's answers through, 34; Eph. on, 44
Sermons, Gy. Gt. on the reading of, 241
Seven, significance of number, 263–4, 277
Seventh day, significance of, 276, 284
Shepherds, witness of Christ by, 5; priests as, 291 ff.; contrasted with hirelings, 292; Chr. on, 295–7; Aug. on, 297–307; evil, similar to Pharisees, 302–3; the Good Shepherd: Cyl. of A. on, 307–15; Gy. Gt. on, 316–19
Shoes, putting off, 255–6
Sin: Christ's innocence of, 130; Chr. on abstention from, 196; L. Gt. on abstention from, 204; as death of the soul, 222; self-discipline to root out beginnings of, 223–4; Christ convinces world of, 339, 357, 369; greatest, lack of belief in Christ, 339, 365
Sleep, as an act of prayer, 384–5
Soldiers, who crucified Jesus, as members of the devil, 33
Solemnity of the Burial of our Saviour: Amph. on, 191–3
Solitude, suited to pursuit of wisdom, 103. *See also* Contemplation
Soul: sin as death of, 83, 222; spiritual cultivation of, 141
Splendours, Secondary, Gy. Ny. on, 248
Staff, the, symbolical meaning of, 256
Stephen, St: stoning of, 230; patience in martyrdom of, 351
Stomach, Chr. on intemperance of, 17, 18
Suffering: kinship of, 278; reward of, 332

Tabitha, raising of, 115
Temple, Christ set on pinnacle of, 8
Temptation: of Christ, in the desert, 1 ff.; meaning of, 12; reasons for suffering, 16; three stages of, 33; to the faithful, 317
Thief, the Good, Max. on, 239–41
Thief, Shepherd, and Hireling, Aug. on, 300

Thomas, St, doubts of, 269–70, 285; faith of, 271, 285–6
Timothy, sending of by Paul, 304
Tithe: the giving of, 14; Lent as, 35
Tobias, teaching his son, 14, 117
Transfiguration, the, 37 ff.
Treasure, in Heaven, laying up, 116
Trinity: Amb. on, 86; received in Baptism, 359; Aug. on Mystery of, 423–4; Gau. on, 447–9; undivided nature of, 447
Truth, hidden from those who despise it, 156

Unbelief, the greatest sin, 339, 365
Unity, Chr. on importance of, 360–1
Usury, Chr. on evils of, 61–2

Vainglory: temptation through, 7–8, 33–4; L. Gt. on, 30
Vices, seven, 81, 97–8
Vigils, Aug. on, 193–4
Virtue: striving after, during Lent, 29–30; easy to bear, 59; not enough without Faith, 148; consisting in Deeds, not Words, 347

'Watch and Pray', Amb. on, 387–8
Widow, giving of farthings by, 92
Wisdom, of this world, not true wisdom, 346
Women, who came to the tomb, 187, 213, 218, 242
Word of God: various forms of, 40; man's hearing and understanding of, 130; Caes. on Eating and Drinking, 455–7; right of people to ask priest for, 455; obligation of priests to communicate, 455–6; Caes. on How to be Received, 458–9
World, the: wonder of daily ordering of, 121; established, nature of, 248; as exemplifying wickedness, 327; meaning the ungodly, 449

'Yet a little while', Chr. on, 324–6; Aug. on, 326–9

Zacharias, prophecy of Christ's entry into Jerusalem, 176

SSAT* & ISEE†

For Private and Independent School Admissions

2013

Table of Contents

A Note to Students: Getting Started ix
A Note to Parents xi
How Do I Use This Book? xii
About the Authors xiii
Available Online xiv

PART ONE: SSAT WORKSHOP

Chapter 1: Inside the SSAT 3
- The SSAT Exam 3
- Scoring 3
- How to Register 4

Chapter 2: SSAT-Specific Verbal Workout: Analogies 5
- The Format 5
- Kaplan 3-Step Method for Analogies 6
- Strong Bridges and Weak Bridges 8
- Six Classic Bridges 9
- Predicting on Three-Term Analogies 10
- Backsolving 11
- Guessing 12
- Practice Questions 14
- Practice Question Answers 16

PART TWO: ISEE WORKSHOP

Chapter 3: Inside the ISEE 19
- The ISEE Exam 19
- Scoring 20
- How to Register 20
- How the ISEE Differs from the SSAT 20

Chapter 4: ISEE-Specific Verbal Workout: Sentence Completions 21
- The Format 21
- Kaplan 4-Step Method for Sentence Completions 22
- Picking Up On Clues 24
- Tackling Hard Questions 25
- Practice Questions 28
- Practice Question Answers 29

Chapter 5: ISEE-Specific Math Workout: Quantitative Comparisons . . . 31
The Format . . . 31
Kaplan's 5 Strategies for QCs . . . 32
Practice Questions . . . 40
Practice Question Answers . . . 41

PART THREE: COMMON CONTENT FOR THE SSAT AND ISEE

Chapter 6: SSAT and ISEE Mastery . . . 45
Using the Test Structure to Your Advantage . . . 45
Approaching SSAT or ISEE Questions . . . 48
Managing Stress . . . 49

Chapter 7: Synonyms . . . 51
The Format . . . 51
Kaplan 3-Step Method for Synonyms . . . 52
Avoiding Pitfalls . . . 53
Vocabulary Techniques . . . 54
Practice Questions . . . 58
Practice Question Answers . . . 60

Chapter 8: Reading Comprehension . . . 61
Reading Strategies . . . 61
SSAT and ISEE Reading Is Different from Everyday Reading . . . 62
Kaplan 4-Step Method for Reading Comprehension . . . 63
Reading Skills in Action . . . 65
Practice Questions . . . 72
Practice Question Answers . . . 73

Chapter 9: The Essay . . . 75
Introduction to the Essay . . . 75
Kaplan 4-Step Method for Writing . . . 76
Pacing . . . 78
Brainstorming in Action . . . 78
Show, Don't Tell . . . 80
Just the Facts . . . 80
Practice Essay . . . 81

Chapter 10: Introduction to SSAT and ISEE Math . . . 85
How to Approach SSAT or ISEE Math . . . 85
Word Problems . . . 90
Percent Increase/Decrease Problems . . . 90
A Word about Calculators . . . 92

Chapter 11: Arithmetic . . . 93

Definitions . . . 93
The Order of Operations . . . 97
Rules for Divisibility . . . 98
Fractions and Decimals . . . 98
Common Percent Equivalencies . . . 101
Exponents and Roots . . . 102
Powers of 10 and Scientific Notation . . . 103
Percents . . . 105
Average, Median, and Mode . . . 106
Ratios, Proportions, and Rates . . . 106
Probability . . . 107
Strange Symbolism and Terminology . . . 108
Practice Questions . . . 109
Practice Question Answers . . . 115

Chapter 12: Algebra . . . 121

Algebra Concepts . . . 121
Working with Equations . . . 125
Working with Inequalities . . . 127
Practice Questions . . . 128
Practice Question Answers . . . 131

Chapter 13: Geometry . . . 135

Lines and Angles . . . 135
Triangles . . . 137
Quadrilaterals . . . 142
Circles . . . 143
Coordinate Geometry . . . 144
Practice Questions . . . 148
Practice Question Answers . . . 157

Chapter 14: Word Problems . . . 163

Translation . . . 163
Symbolism Word Problems . . . 164
Word Problems with Formulas . . . 165
Backdoor Strategies . . . 165
Roman Numeral Word Problems . . . 167
Practice Questions . . . 169
Practice Question Answers . . . 173

Chapter 15: Managing Your Stress 177
The Week before the Test 177
The Days Just before the Test 177
The Night before the Test 178
The Morning of the Test 179
During the Test 179
After the Test 180

PART FOUR: SSAT PRACTICE TESTS AND EXPLANATIONS
SSAT Test Overview 182
Chapter 16: SSAT Practice Test 1: Upper-Level 183
Answers and Explanations 223

Chapter 17: SSAT Practice Test 2: Upper-Level 239
Answers and Explanations 277

Chapter 18: SSAT Practice Test 3: Lower-Level 295
Answers and Explanations 329

Chapter 19: Scoring Your SSAT Practice Test 345
Upper-Level Scores 346
Lower-Level Scores 347

PART FIVE: ISEE PRACTICE TESTS AND EXPLANATIONS
ISEE Test Overview 350
Chapter 20: ISEE Practice Test 1: Upper- and Middle-Level 351
Answers and Explanations 385

Chapter 21: ISEE Practice Test 2: Upper- and Middle-Level 401
Answers and Explanations 437

Chapter 22: ISEE Practice Test 3: Lower-Level 457
Answers and Explanations 489

Chapter 23: Scoring Your ISEE Practice Test 499

PART SIX: LEARNING RESOURCES
Chapter 24: Vocabulary Reference 503
Root List 503
Vocabulary List 514

Chapter 25: 100 Essential Math Concepts 561

Chapter 26: Writing Skills 587

A NOTE TO STUDENTS: GETTING STARTED

In your hands, you have the best test prep available for the SSAT and ISEE, the admissions tests for private and independent schools. This book covers *all levels* of these tests (grades 4–11).

SSAT

- *Upper-level* (for students currently in grades 8–11)
- *Lower-level* (for students currently in grades 5–7)

ISEE

- *Upper-level* (for students currently in grades 8–11)
- *Middle-level* (for students currently in grades 6 and 7)
- *Lower-level* (for students currently in grades 4 and 5)

Since this book covers all levels of the SSAT and ISEE, you will understandably find certain questions too difficult. While you should try your best to solve all of the questions, do not be discouraged if you cannot. Other students in your age group will find these hard to solve as well. Keeping in mind that your test will be scored in relation to other students your age should help relieve some pressure.

Not every topic covered in this book appears on every test level. Quantitative Comparisons, for instance, do not appear on the Lower-level ISEE, though they do appear on the Upper and Middle levels. (They do not appear at all on the SSAT.) At the beginning of each chapter, there is a note indicating what level or test applies to that topic. Keep an eye out for these notes to guide you in your preparation and skip those chapters that are not relevant.

Ideally, you should take a couple of months to work through this book. That gives you enough time before test day to absorb the strategies thoroughly and enough practice so that they become second nature. Do just two or three chapters a week and let the material sink in slowly.

If you don't have a few months for review, however, don't freak out: By working through a chapter or two every day, you can finish this book in a couple of weeks.

Here's how you should approach the review:

1. Read through each chapter completely, learning from the examples and trying the practice questions. Don't just read them: Work through them first as much as you can, before reading the explanation.
2. Read the stress management section in chapter 6 to set the stage for your training and testing success.
3. Take the practice tests for your level under strictly timed conditions. Score your test, find out where you need help, and then review the appropriate chapters.
4. Give yourself a day of rest right before the real exam.

Don't hesitate to take some time off from your SSAT/ISEE preparation when you need to.

Q. It's two days before the SSAT/ISEE and I'm clueless. What I do?

A. First of all, don't panic. If you have only a day or two to prepare, then you won't be able to prepare thoroughly. But that doesn't mean you should give up. There's a lot you can do. First and foremost, get familiar with the test. And if you don't do anything else, take a full-length practice test under reasonably testlike conditions. When you have finished that, check your answers to see what you didn't get right.

Q: The test is tomorrow. Should I stay up all night studying geometry formulas?

A: The best thing to do now is to stay calm. Read chapter 15 to find out the best way to survive—and thrive—on test day.

Q: I don't feel confident. Should I just guess?

A: That depends on whether you're taking the SSAT or the ISEE. The SSAT does penalize you for wrong answers (one-quarter of a point), so you want to be careful, but that doesn't mean you should never guess. If you can rule out at least one answer choice, preferably two, you should guess because you have better odds at guessing correctly. Also, on questions that appear early in a section, more obvious answers will tend to be correct, so you can guess more confidently on those questions. If you're taking the ISEE, you should ALWAYS guess since there's no wrong-answer penalty.

Q: What's the most important thing I can do to get ready quickly?

In addition to basic math and verbal skills, the SSAT/ISEE mainly tests your ability to take the test. So the most important thing you can do is to familiarize yourself with the directions, the question types, the answer grid, and the overall structure. Read everything carefully—many mistakes are the result of simply not reading thoroughly.

Q. So it's okay to panic, right?

A. No! No matter how prepared you are for the test, stress will hurt your performance, and it's really no fun. Stay confident and don't cram. So...breathe, stay calm, and remember: It's just a test.

A NOTE TO PARENTS

Congratulations! By purchasing this book, you have taken the first step toward helping your son or daughter prepare for the SSAT or ISEE and then go on to private school. Each school has a different requirement policy for admissions exams, so check with your schools of interest to find out which test your child should take. These days, many schools accept either test.

How can I help my child prepare for the exam?

This book covers all levels of the SSAT and ISEE: Upper, Middle, and Lower. If your son or daughter is applying to private high school, chances are that he or she already studies well alone. Check on his or her progress regularly as the test date nears.

If your child is at the Middle or Lower level, you may need to get more involved. Sit down together and write out a study plan. To start, your child should take a practice exam under timed conditions as a diagnostic.

Then, once you have identified the areas that need focus, set up specific study activities.

What do the scores mean?

Scores are designed to measure a student's potential performance in private school—not to measure intelligence.

Each level of the test encompasses more than one grade level, but students are graded only against others in their own grade.

What should I know about test day?

A few things you will want to know about test day:

- During the test, your child must remember to mark his or her current grade level on the answer sheet, not the grade he or she will be entering next year.
- No calculators, cell phones, alarm watches, or books will be permitted in the test room.
- Testing normally begins at 9:00 A.M., so students should arrive at the test center by 8:15–8:30 A.M.
- It is possible to get a good score even if some questions are left blank. Many students leave a few questions unanswered.

How Do I Use This Book?

	SSAT	ISEE
All Levels		
(Grades 4–11)	• Chapters 1– 2 • Chapters 6–15 • Chapters 24–26	• Chapters 3–5 • Chapters 6–15 • Chapters 24–26
Lower Level **(Grades 4–7)**	• Chapter 18/Practice Test • P. 347: Scoring the Lower-Level SSAT Practice Test	• Chapter 22/Practice Test • P. 499 Scoring Your ISEE Practice Test
Middle Level* **(Grades 6–7)**		• Chapter 20/Practice Test 1 • Chapter 21 Practice Test 2 • p. 499 Scoring Your ISEE Practice Test
Upper Level **(Grades 8–11)**	• Chapter 16/Practice Test 1 • Chapter 17/Practice Test 2 • P. 346: Scoring Upper-Level SSAT Practice Tests	

* ISEE only

ABOUT THE AUTHORS

Joanna Cohen received her BS in Human Development and Family Studies from Cornell University and her EdM from Harvard University. As an educator, she has taught, conducted research, and written educational materials for students and teachers. Until recently, Ms. Cohen was manager of Kaplan's Pre-College Curriculum.

Darcy L. Galane is the Associate Director of Pre-College Curriculum at Kaplan's Corporate Office. She received a BA from UCLA and began teaching SAT and LSAT classes for Kaplan while earning her JD at the University of Connecticut School of Law. Having taught and written curriculum for most of Kaplan's courses, Ms. Galane has helped thousands of students to raise their scores on standardized tests.

AVAILABLE ONLINE

FOR ANY TEST CHANGES OR LATE-BREAKING DEVELOPMENTS

kaptest.com/publishing

The material in this book is up-to-date at the time of publication. However, the test makers may have instituted changes in the test after this book was published. Be sure to carefully read the materials you receive when you register for the test. If there are any important late-breaking developments—or any changes or corrections to the Kaplan test preparation materials in this book—we will post that information online at **kaptest.com/publishing**.

For customer service, please contact us at **booksupport@kaplan.com.**

| Part One |

SSAT WORKSHOP

CHAPTER 1: INSIDE THE SSAT

THE SSAT EXAM

The SSAT (Secondary School Admission Test) has two tests, one for upper-level students and one for lower-level students.

- Upper-level (for students currently in grades 8–11)
- Lower-level (for students currently in grades 5–7)

Following is a breakdown of the tests. Both levels of the test have the same format.

	Lower-Level	Upper-Level	Time Allowed
Math I	25 questions	25 questions	30 minutes
Verbal	60 questions	60 questions	30 minutes
Reading Comprehension	40 questions	40 questions	40 minutes
Math II	25 questions	25 questions	30 minutes
Essay*	one writing prompt		25 minutes

* The essay will not be scored, nor will it be included with your home report, but it will be sent to the schools to which you are applying.

- All questions have five answer choices, (A) through (E).
- You are not permitted to use calculators, dictionaries, or rulers.
- Bring your own pencils and erasers; they will not be provided.

SCORING

The first thing you might notice with respect to grades is that students from other class years are taking the same test as you. Not to worry! You are graded according to your age. In other words, if you're in 9th grade, you aren't expected to get as many questions right as someone in 11th grade, even though you take the same test. One note of caution: You are scored according to the grade level you report on the answer sheet on test day. Be sure to indicate your current grade level, not the grade for which you are applying.

Given this fact, you can expect to see questions on the test that may be too hard for you. Just remember, you don't need to get every question right to get a great score.

Your score report will include the following:

Scaled scores for Verbal, Math, and Reading in addition to a total scaled score. The scale for the upper-level test is 500–800 (V/Q/R), 1500–2400 (Total). For the lower-level test, the scale is 440–710 (V/Q/R), 1320–2130 (Total).

Percentile ranks for each category. These compare your scores to those of others who have taken the SSAT in the past three years.

Regarding points for each question, each correct answer earns one point. For every wrong answer, one-fourth of a point is deducted, though for questions left blank, nothing is deducted.

Scores are mailed to you and your school two to three weeks after you take the test. Make sure you test early enough in the year that schools will receive your scores by application deadlines.

If you feel that you have not tested well after you leave the test, you have the option of canceling your score. To do so, you must send your request to SSAT by mail, fax, or email (info@ssat.org). This request must be received no later than the Tuesday immediately following the test date. In that case, canceled scores will not be sent to any of your designated score recipients.

HOW TO REGISTER

The SSAT is given eight times per academic year: October, November, December, January, February, March, April, and June. You may register online, by fax, or by mail. For more information, go to the official test site at **ssat.org**.

Phone: (609) 683-4440
Email: info@ssat.org
Fax: 800-442-7728 or (609) 683-4507
Mail: SSAT Registration
CN 5339
Princeton, NJ 08543

CHAPTER 2: SSAT-SPECIFIC VERBAL WORKOUT: ANALOGIES

Analogies appear *only on the SSAT*. If you are not taking the SSAT, you should skip this section.

Analogies may seem frightening because they look pretty weird at first glance. You'll feel better about them as soon as you realize that you speak and think in analogies all the time. Anytime you say, "My sister is like a slug," you're drawing an analogy between your sister and slugs—perhaps your sister is as gross as a slug, or maybe she's as slow as a slug getting out of bed in the morning. That may not be the kind of relationship that will appear on your test, but the thinking is the same.

Once you become familiar with their format, you'll find that Analogy questions are pretty straightforward and very predictable. In fact, prepping often gains you more points on Analogies than on any other Verbal question type. With practice, you can learn to get them right even when you don't know all of the vocabulary words involved.

THE FORMAT

The instructions will tell you to select the pair of words that is *related in the same way* as the two words in the beginning of the question. Those two words are called the *stem words*.

1. Flake is to snow as
   (A) storm is to hail.
   (B) drop is to rain.
   (C) field is to wheat.
   (D) stack is to hay.
   (E) cloud is to fog.

In this example, the answer is (B). A flake is a small unit of snow, just as a drop is a small unit of rain.

Did you get the right answer? If so, how did you determine the right answer? Did you just *feel* that one choice was right, or did you try to figure out how the words in the stem were related, then go through the choices one by one? The Kaplan 3-Step Method will help you handle Analogy questions, even the toughest ones, because you'll approach every question systematically rather than just using instinct. Let's see how it works.

KAPLAN 3-STEP METHOD FOR ANALOGIES

Step 1. Build a bridge.

Step 2. Plug in the answer choices.

Step 3. Adjust your bridge if necessary.

What does it mean to "build a bridge"? A suspension bridge? A steel bridge? No, we're not spanning oceans here; we're filling in ovals on a piece of paper. Wait a minute and it will all make sense. A bridge expresses the relationship between the words in the stem pair, and building a bridge helps you home in on the correct answer quickly and avoid wrong-answer traps. Let's take a closer look to see how it works.

STEP 1: BUILD A BRIDGE

In every Analogy question, there's a strong, definite connection between the two stem words. Your task is to identify this relationship and then look for a similar relationship among the answer pairs.

What's a strong, definite relationship?

- The words *library* and *book* have a strong, definite connection. A library is defined as a place where books are kept. *Library is to book as* could be a question stem.
- The words *library* and *child* do not have a strong, definite connection. A child may or may not have anything to do with a library, and vice versa. *Library is to child* would never be a question stem.

In our original example, a good bridge would be "A flake is a small unit of snow." A bridge is a short sentence that relates the two words in the stem, and every pair of stem words will have a strong bridge that links them.

STEP 2: PLUG IN THE ANSWER CHOICES

You figured out how the words *flake* and *snow* are related. Now you need to determine which answer choice relates words in the same way. Don't just rely on your feeling about the words unless you don't know the vocabulary (more on that later). Go through the choices systematically, building bridges between each word pair as you go. Here's how it would work:

If a *flake* is a small unit of *snow*, then . . .

(A) a *storm* is a small unit of *hail.*
(B) a *drop* is a small unit of *rain.*
(C) a *field* is a small unit of *wheat.*
(D) a *stack* is a small unit of *hay.*
(E) a *cloud* is a small unit of *fog.*

Going through the choices, you can see that only one of them makes sense, (B). At this point, you would be done.

Step 3: Adjust Your Bridge If Necessary

If your bridge is very specific, you won't need to go to step 3, but sometimes you will. For example, if you had the question:

Fish is to gill as

(A) oyster is to shell.
(B) penguin is to wing.
(C) whale is to spout.
(D) mammal is to lung.
(E) dolphin is to flipper.

Let's say you made the bridge "A fish has a gill." Then you went to the choices and plugged in that bridge:

(A) An oyster has a shell.
(B) A penguin has a wing.
(C) A whale has a spout.
(D) A mammal has a lung.
(E) A dolphin has a flipper.

Every choice fits! In this case, the bridge was too general, so you'll need to adjust your bridge.

What would a good adjustment be? Try to articulate to yourself the most specific relationship between the words, because the more specific your bridge is, the fewer choices will match it. A good bridge for this pair might be: "A fish uses a gill to breathe." Now try plugging the bridge into the answer choices.

(A) An oyster uses a shell to breathe.
(B) A penguin uses a wing to breathe.
(C) A whale uses a spout to breathe.
(D) A mammal uses a lung to breathe.
(E) A dolphin uses a flipper to breathe.

It should now be easier to see the correct answer, (D), A mammal uses a lung to breathe.

STRONG BRIDGES AND WEAK BRIDGES

Just to make sure you have your strong and weak bridges straight, try the following exercise. For each phrase, decide whether there is a strong relationship or a weak one.

1. Dog is to canine ____________
2. Dog is to friendly ____________
3. Dog is to kennel ____________
4. Dog is to mammal ____________
5. Dog is to cat ____________
6. Dog is to paw ____________
7. Dog is to puppy ____________
8. Dog is to hound ____________
9. Dog is to bark ____________
10. Dog is to biscuit ____________

ANSWERS TO STRONG/WEAK BRIDGES

1. strong	6. strong
2. weak	7. strong
3. strong	8. strong
4. strong	9. strong
5. weak	10. weak

SIX CLASSIC BRIDGES

There are some bridges that appear on the SSAT over and over again. We call these *Classic Bridges* because no matter what other bridges come and go, these tend to stick around. By getting to know these bridges, you'll be able to identify them quickly, saving yourself a lot of time as you go through Analogy questions.

Bridge Type 1: CHARACTER

One word characterizes the other.
Quarrelsome is to argue [Someone quarrelsome tends to argue.]

Bridge Type 2: LACK

One word describes what someone or something is *not*.
Coward is to bravery [A coward lacks bravery.]

Bridge Type 3: FUNCTION

One word names an object; the other word defines its function.
Scissors is to cut [Scissors are used to cut.]

Bridge Type 4: DEGREE

One word is a greater or lesser degree of the other word.
Deafening is to loud [Something deafening is extremely loud.]

Bridge Type 5: EXAMPLE

One word is an example of the other word.
Measles is to disease [Measles is a type of disease.]

Bridge Type 6: GROUP

One word is made up of several of the other word.
Forest is to trees [A forest is made up of many trees.]

I AM, BY DEFINITION, CONFUSED

"When making a bridge, a good rule of thumb is to relate the words in such a way that you'd be able to insert the phrase *by definition* and the relationship would hold true. A poodle, by definition, is a type of dog. However, a poodle does not, by definition, have a collar. If you can't use *by definition* in the sentence to relate the stem words, your bridge isn't strong and it needs to be reworked."

PREDICTING ON THREE-TERM ANALOGIES

Some Analogies will have three terms in the stem and only one word in each answer choice. For example:

Delight is to grin as dismay is to

(A) frown.
(B) smile.
(C) shrug.
(D) stare.
(E) giggle.

Three-term Analogies aren't very different from two-term Analogies. The key difference is that you need to predict your answer *before* you look at the answer choices. Otherwise, the choices won't make much sense to you! Here's how it works.

First, make your bridge:

A grin shows delight and a —— shows dismay.

Now predict your answer. What might show *dismay*? *Tears,* perhaps, or a *frown*. Look at the answer choices. At this point, the question should be easier than a two-term Analogy, because you already have one of the two words in the answer.

Does a *frown* show dismay?
Does a *smile* show dismay?
Does a *shrug* show dismay?
Does a *stare* show dismay?
Does a *giggle* show dismay?

As you'll see, (A) is the answer: A frown shows dismay. That makes a lot of sense. Can you see how much harder this would have been if you hadn't gone through the steps of building a bridge and predicting the answer? You would likely be staring blankly at five words. Always predict your answer on three-term Analogies, and you'll whiz through them in no time.

Practice your skills of prediction on these stems:

1. Thicket is to bush as grove is to ____.

2. Mason is to brick as carpenter is to ____.

3. Enthusiast is to apathy as miser is to ____.

Now let's see how well you did on predicting:

1. Thicket is to bush as grove is to *tree*.

2. Mason is to brick as carpenter is to *wood*.

3. Enthusiast is to apathy as miser is to *generosity*.

Even with your arsenal of tools, you may run into Analogy questions where you don't know what to do. Perhaps you won't know what a word in the question stem means or how the words relate to one another. What should you do?

There are a few strategies that will really up your chances of getting the question right, even if you're stuck. How cool is that?

WHAT TO DO IF YOU'RE STUCK

- Backsolving
- Educated guessing
- Remembering context
- Using Word Charge

BACKSOLVING

What is backsolving? It may sound like an obscure form of chiropractic medicine, but it's actually just a nifty way of approaching Analogies when you can't answer them directly. So how does it work?

Basically, you skip right past the question stem and head straight for the answer choices. You may be wondering, "How you can figure out the answer without knowing what the question is asking?" Well, you can't necessarily figure out the *answer* right away, but you can start to eliminate *clearly* wrong answer choices, leaving fewer options to choose from. When you rule out choices that you know can't be right, the odds are better that you'll pick the right choice from what's left.

Screwdriver is to tool as
(A) animal is to plant.
(B) garden is to bed.
(C) fertilizer is to soil.
(D) tree is to leaf.
(E) rose is to flower.

Even if you didn't know that a screwdriver is a type of tool, what could you rule out? Well, in (A), there's no logical connection between animal and plant, except that they're both living things. Choice (B), garden is to bed, also sounds somewhat off. You could make the argument that a garden has a bed, but does it have to? What about a hanging garden, or a rock garden? You could rule out (B) as having a weak bridge.

BOTH ARE . . . WRONG!

Watch out for the *Both Are* trap, seen in choice (A) in the screwdriver example: Both *animal* and *plant* are part of a larger group, but there's no connection, by definition, between the words themselves. Bread and bananas are both types of food, but what exactly is their relationship? Bananas aren't a type of bread, a lack of bread, or a function of bread. Watch out for this trap, particularly on harder Analogy questions.

By eliminating even one illogical answer choice, you'll narrow down your choices and have a better chance of getting the question right. Always keep your eye out for *Both Are* traps and *Weak Bridges* as you work through the Analogy section, and you'll rack up lots of points on even the toughest questions.

GUESSING

What if you reach the point where you can't figure out the bridge for the stem words, you can't rule out wrong answer choices, and you want to cry? Well, first of all, don't cry. It's a waste of time and it makes it difficult to read the questions. You have a few options.

Technique 1: Make an Educated Guess

You know the six Classic Bridges. You know they show up often on Analogy questions. So even if you don't know the exact definition of one (or both!) words, you could make an educated guess about the bridge. For example, say you saw this stem:

Word is to philologist as

(A) ______
(B) ______
(C) ______
(D) ______
(E) ______

What might the bridge be? Well, a *philologist* sounds like a type of person (since it ends in *-ologist*), and a *word* is a thing, so maybe a philologist does something with words. Philologist is a tricky word, but you could make a great guess by saying that a philologist studies words, which is exactly right!

Technique 2: Remember the Context

Sometimes a word sounds familiar, but you can't remember why. If that happens, try to think of a place where you may have heard it before. Putting words into context makes it easier to determine their meaning. For example:

Vote is to suffrage as

(A) ______
(B) ______
(C) ______
(D) ______
(E) ______

What does *suffrage* mean? Have you heard of the suffrage movement? Or the suffragists? Think about the word *suffrage* in the context of *voting*. What could the words have to do with each other? Well, suffrage is the right to vote, and the movement to give women the right to vote at the beginning of the 20th century was commonly known as the Suffrage Movement. Just looking at the word *suffrage* in isolation might have left you scratching your head, but putting it in context with the concept of voting could get you back on track and help you home in on the right answer.

Technique 3: Use Word Charge

Some words give you the feeling that they're either positive or negative. Use this sense to help you figure out the bridge between words in the stem when you don't actually know what one of them means—or both!

Decide whether the following words are positive or negative:

1. Cruel (+, –) is to clemency (+, –) as
2. Boorish (+, –) is to polite (+, –) as
3. Animated (+, –) is to ecstatic (+, –) as
4. Annoyed (+, –) is to enraged (+, –) as

So how does Word Charge help you find the right answer? Once you determine the charge of the words in the stem pair, you can look for words in the answer choices that have the same charge relationship. When both words in the stem are either positive or negative, both words in the correct answer choice will have the same charge, too, though it may be the opposite charge from the words in the stem. If one stem word is positive and the other is negative, chances are that the right answer will have the same relationship.

So, what charge does each word above have?

1. (–, +)
2. (–, +)
3. (+, +)
4. (–, –)

PRACTICE QUESTIONS

1. Circumference is to circle as
   (A) diameter is to sphere.
   (B) height is to width.
   (C) side is to hexagon.
   (D) perimeter is to square.
   (E) round is to oval.

2. Write is to paper as paint is to
   (A) board.
   (B) canvas.
   (C) brush.
   (D) palette.
   (E) can.

3. Collar is to shirt as
   (A) toe is to shoe.
   (B) cuff is to trousers.
   (C) waist is to belt.
   (D) hat is to head.
   (E) zipper is to button.

4. Hysteria is to control as
   (A) joke is to laughter.
   (B) feeling is to emotion.
   (C) absurdity is to sense.
   (D) calm is to serenity.
   (E) passion is to insanity.

5. Square is to cube as
   (A) dot is to point.
   (B) angle is to triangle.
   (C) rectangle is to parallelogram.
   (D) hexagon is to octagon.
   (E) circle is to sphere.

6. Shark is to aquatic as
   (A) world is to hungry.
   (B) camel is to terrestrial.
   (C) bird is to winged.
   (D) bat is to blind.
   (E) pig is to hairless.

7. Admonish is to mild as castigate is to
   (A) tepid.
   (B) sweet.
   (C) unbeatable.
   (D) uncertain.
   (E) harsh.

8. Abrupt is to gradual as
   (A) corrupt is to virtuous.
   (B) stirring is to sudden.
   (C) sneaky is to criminal.
   (D) remarkable is to alarming.
   (E) conspicuous is to extreme.

9. Stanza is to poem as
   (A) rhythm is to beat.
   (B) verse is to word.
   (C) movement is to symphony.
   (D) play is to theater.
   (E) column is to journal.

10. Violin is to string as
    (A) harp is to angelic.
    (B) drum is to stick.
    (C) score is to music.
    (D) oboe is to reed.
    (E) bass is to large.

11. Canter is to horse as
    (A) hop is to rabbit.
    (B) halt is to pony.
    (C) hunt is to lion.
    (D) beg is to dog.
    (E) chew is to cow.

12. Baseball is to game as
    (A) hurricane is to storm.
    (B) overcast is to cloud.
    (C) stadium is to sport.
    (D) wind is to tornado.
    (E) conflict is to violence.

13. Rigid is to bend as
    (A) tremulous is to sway.
    (B) incomprehensive is to think.
    (C) immortal is to die.
    (D) lazy is to perspire.
    (E) stiff is to divide.

14. Canine is to wolf as feline is to
    (A) panther.
    (B) pig.
    (C) monkey.
    (D) rat.
    (E) vulture.

15. Rind is to melon as
    (A) skin is to mammal.
    (B) armor is to shield.
    (C) shell is to claw.
    (D) peel is to core.
    (E) pod is to vine.

16. Mile is to length as
    (A) acre is to land.
    (B) inch is to foot.
    (C) kilometer is to race.
    (D) yard is to fabric.
    (E) fathom is to depth.

17. Truthful is to dishonest as arid is to
    (A) sublime.
    (B) aloof.
    (C) innocent.
    (D) moist.
    (E) clear.

18. Tarnish is to silver as
    (A) streak is to glass.
    (B) dirt is to car.
    (C) rust is to iron.
    (D) dull is to wax.
    (E) dust is to wood.

19. Delay is to hasten as
    (A) misunderstand is to dislike.
    (B) undermine is to improve.
    (C) sink is to descend.
    (D) remove is to indict.
    (E) facilitate is to impede.

20. Think is to daydream as walk is to
    (A) stagger.
    (B) crawl.
    (C) meander.
    (D) run.
    (E) prance.

PRACTICE QUESTION ANSWERS

1. D
2. B
3. B
4. C
5. E
6. B
7. E
8. A
9. C
10. D
11. A
12. A
13. C
14. A
15. A
16. E
17. D
18. C
19. E
20. C

| Part Two |

ISEE WORKSHOP

CHAPTER 3: INSIDE THE ISEE

THE ISEE EXAM

The ISEE (Independent School Entrance Exam) has three tests: Upper-level, Middle-level, and Lower-level.

* Upper-level (for students currently in grades 8–11)
* Middle-level (for students currently in grades 6 or 7)
* Lower-level (for students currently in grades 4 or 5)

Following is a breakdown of the tests.

	Lower-Level	Middle-Level	Upper-Level
Verbal Reasoning	34 questions (20 min.)	40 questions (20 min.)	40 questions (20 min.)
Quantitative Reasoning	38 questions (35 min.)	37 questions (35 min.)	37 questions (35 min.)
Reading Comprehension	25 questions (25 min.)	36 questions (35 min.)	36 questions (35 min.)
Mathematics Achievement	30 questions (30 min.)	47 questions (40 min.)	47 questions (40 min.)
Essay*	one writing prompt (30 min.)		

* The essay will not be scored, nor will it be included with your home report, but it will be sent to the schools to which you are applying.

- All questions have four answer choices, (A) through (D).
- You are not permitted to use calculators, dictionaries, or rulers.
- You must bring your own pencils and erasers, as well as black or blue pens for your essay.

SCORING

Scores on the ISEE work similarly to those on the SSAT in that you will be compared against in national and local averages. Your score report for the ISEE will include test scores and diagnostic information. It will also indicate whether your scores are at the expected level given your performance on the Verbal Reasoning and Quantitative Reasoning sections.

As on the SSAT, you are not expected to answer every question. Your test performance is compared only to others in your grade. Unlike with the SSAT, you are not penalized for wrong answers. You will be graded only on the number of correct answers you get.

HOW TO REGISTER

ISEE accepts registration by mail, phone, fax, or online. For more information, go to the official site at **erbtest.org**.

Phone: 800-446-0320
Fax: (919) 682-5775
Mail: ISEE Operations
423 Morris Street
Durham, NC 27701
Email: ISEE@measinc.com

HOW THE ISEE DIFFERS FROM THE SSAT

- On the ISEE, the Verbal section contains Synonym and Sentence Completion questions. On the SSAT, the Verbal section contains Synonym and Analogy Questions.
- On the ISEE, there are Quantitative Comparisons in the Quantitative Reasoning section (Upper and Middle levels only).
- On the ISEE, there is no penalty for a wrong answer. That means it is always in your favor to guess if you're not sure of the answer.
- On the ISEE, there are four answer choices, (A) through (D). On the SSAT, there are five answer choices, (A) through (E).

CHAPTER 4: ISEE-SPECIFIC VERBAL WORKOUT: SENTENCE COMPLETIONS

Sentence Completions appear **on every level of the ISEE.** If you are not taking the ISEE, you should skip this section.

THE FORMAT

Of all the questions in the Verbal Reasoning section, approximately half are Sentence Completions. They're arranged in order of increasing difficulty.

Sentence Completions are "fill-in-the-blank" questions. Each question will have one or two blanks, and you must select the best fit from the four choices provided.

These are probably the easiest of all the Verbal Reasoning question types. Unlike Analogies, they give you some context in which to think about vocabulary words, and unlike Reading Comprehension questions, they require you to focus on only a single sentence at a time.

The directions will look something like this:

Select the word(s) that best fits the meaning of each sentence.

EXAMPLE

Although the tomato looked sweet and ____, it tasted more like a very sour, dried-out old sponge.

(A) arid

(B) juicy

(C) enormous

(D) cloying

A contrast is presented between the way the tomato looked and the way it tasted. It tasted sour and had the texture of dry sponge. Since we were previously told that it looked *sweet* (the opposite of *sour*), we can infer that we need to find the opposite of *dry*. Therefore the tomato must have looked juicy, so (B) is the answer.

KAPLAN 4-STEP METHOD FOR SENTENCE COMPLETIONS

Step 1: Read the sentence carefully, looking for clues.

Step 2: Predict the answer.

Step 3: Pick the best match.

Step 4: Plug in your selection.

Let's take a closer look at each step.

1. Read the Sentence Carefully, Looking for Clues

Think carefully about the sentence before looking at the answer choices. What does the sentence mean? Are there any clue words?

2. Predict the Answer

Take a look at the following examples:

"They say that M&M's do not melt in your hands, but last summer . . ."

"Despite the fact that it was 50 degrees below zero, we were . . . "

"I am so hungry I could . . . "

You could probably fill in the rest of these sentences using words similar to the speaker's own. It's often easy to see the direction in which a sentence is going; that's because the structure and the tone of a sentence can clue you in to its meaning.

Your job for the ISEE Sentence Completion questions is to fill in the missing piece. One way to do this is to anticipate the answer before looking at the answer choices. Clue words and sentence structure (construction and punctuation) can help you determine where a sentence is headed.

Making an exact prediction isn't necessary. If you can even identify the missing word as being positive or negative, that will often be sufficient.

3. Pick the Best Match

Make sure to scan every choice before deciding.

4. Plug in Your Selection

Only one of the four possible answer choices will make sense. However, if you've gone through the four steps and more than one choice still seems possible, don't dwell on it. Try to eliminate at least one choice, guess, and move on. Remember, on the ISEE, a wrong answer will not affect your score.

Using some examples, let's see how Kaplan's 4-Step Method works.

EXAMPLE

Most North American marsupials are ___; at night they forage for food, and during the day they sleep.

(A) fastidious
(B) amiable
(C) monolithic
(D) nocturnal

Read the sentence carefully, looking for clues. The semicolon (;) is a big clue. It tells you that what comes after the semicolon follows the direction of what comes before it. In other words, you're looking for a word that means nighttime activity and daytime rest.

Predict which word should go into the blank.

Compare the answer choices with your prediction. Pick the best match. (A), *fastidious*, has nothing to do with being active at night. Neither does (B), *amiable*, or for that matter (C), *monolithic*. (D), *nocturnal*, however, means to be active at night, so that seems correct.

Check your choice by plugging it into the sentence. "Most North American marsupials are nocturnal; at night they forage for food and during the day they sleep." Sounds pretty good. Finally, scan the other choices to make sure that (D) is indeed the best choice. No other choice works in the sentence, so (D) is right.

EXAMPLE

Juniper skated with such ___ that no one could ___ her talent any longer.

(A) speed . . ascertain
(B) melancholy . . deny
(C) agility . . question
(D) grace . . affirm

Read the sentence carefully, looking for clue words. A major clue here is *such* … *that*. You know that Juniper's skating ability, whether good or bad, has led to everybody agreeing about her talent. So whatever words go into the two blanks, they must agree.

Predict the words that go into the blanks, making sure that whatever goes in the second blank supports the meaning of the first. If Juniper skated well, no one would deny that she has a lot of talent. If she skated terribly, everyone would agree that she had no talent. Don't let the negative structure of the second part of the sentence fool you: It's written as "no one could ——," as opposed to "everyone could ——." Make some predictions about the two missing pieces.

Compare your predictions with each answer choice and pick the best fit. Which two words, when in context, will agree and support each other?

In (A), *speed* and *ascertain* don't make sense together. In (B), *melancholy* and *deny* don't support one another. It doesn't make sense that "no one could *deny* her talent" because she skated sadly, or with *melancholy*. In (C), *agility* and *question* do fit together well. Juniper skates with *agility*, so who could question her ability? In (D), *grace* and *affirm* initially seem to support one another. But remember the negative in the second part of the sentence: " . . . *no one* could —— her talent." It's illogical to say that she skated with such *grace* that "no one could *affirm* her talent." (C) must be the answer.

PICKING UP ON CLUES

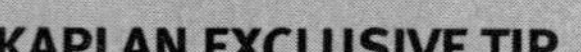

KAPLAN EXCLUSIVE TIP

"Clue words like *and, but, such as, however*, and *although* can indicate where a sentence is heading. Keep your eyes open for these kinds of helpful words."

In order to do well on Sentence Completions, you need to show how a sentence fits together. Clue words will help you do that. The more clues you can find, the clearer the sentence will become. The clearer the sentence, the better your prediction.

What are clue words? There are a variety of clue words. Some will indicate **cause and effect** and others a **contrast,** and some others will **define the missing word.**

EXAMPLES

- Clues that indicate cause and effect:

  Because he was so scared of the dark, we were —— to find him sleeping without a night light.

  As a result of her constant lying, Sheila was —— to trust anyone else.

- Clues that indicate contrast:

  Rita is funny and light-hearted; her twin, Wendy, however is —— and ——.

  Following the wonderful news, Harry's visage changed from an expression of —— to one of ——.

- Clues that define the missing word:

  A loud and tiresome child, he acted particularly —— during the long car trip.

  Smart and witty, Roger was the most —— student in the class.

EXAMPLE

Fiona's bedroom still looks like a ___, despite her efforts to keep it tidy.

In this example, whatever goes into the blank must complete the contrast implied by the word *despite*. You know then, that it must describe the *opposite of tidy*. *Mess* or *sty* would be good predictions.

BE CAREFUL

"A single word can change the meaning of the entire sentence, so make sure to read the sentence carefully."

TACKLING HARD QUESTIONS

Sentence Completions will get more difficult as you go through them, so the last few will be the most difficult. If you get stuck, here are a few tips to help you through:

- Avoid tricky wrong answers.
- Take apart tough sentences.
- Work around tough vocabulary.

Avoid Tricky Wrong Answers

Toward the end of a set, keep your eyes open for tricky answer choices. Avoid these:

- Opposites of the correct answer
- Words that may sound right because they are tough
- Questions with two missing pieces, where one word sounds right but the other doesn't. NOTE: Lower-Level ISEE Sentence Completion questions will have only one blank.

The following would be the 12th question out of a 15-problem set.

EXAMPLE

At first the house seemed frightening with all its cobwebs and creaking shutters, but we soon realized that it was quite ___.

(A) benign
(B) deceptive
(C) affluent
(D) haunted

Read this sentence carefully. If you read it too quickly, it may sound like "The house was really scary with all of those cobwebs and creaking shutters, and we soon realized … it was!" So, you would pick (D), *haunted,* or maybe (B), *deceptive,* when in fact the correct answer is (A), *benign.*

Pick Up the Clues

There are two major Clue Words here, and you should have picked them up right away. The first one, *At first,* indicates that the author perceived something to be one way *at first*—but after taking a second look realized it was different. That leads us to the second Clue Word, *but.* Just as we predicted, the author thought the house was creepy at first *but* then felt differently. We know, therefore, that the word in the blank must be the *opposite,* or at least not the same, as *creepy* or *haunted.*

Don't Pick an Answer Just Because It Sounds Hard

Affluent means wealthy. You might be tempted to choose it because it looks or sounds impressive. But it's thrown in there just to tempt you. Don't choose a word without good reason.

Let's look at a two-blank sentence. The following example is the 15th of a 15-problem set.

EXAMPLE

Screaming and laughing, the students were ___ by their ___ experience on the white-water raft.

(A) amused .. tepid
(B) irritated .. continued
(C) exhilarated .. first
(D) frightened .. secure

TWO-BLANK SENTENCES

"Sentences with two blanks can be easier than those with one blank.

- Try the easier blank first.
- Save time by eliminating all choices that won't work for that blank."

Look at All the Choices

Check out the first blank first. Sometimes you can eliminate one or more answer choices right away if some possibilities don't fit. *Irritated* and/or *frightened* students do not scream and laugh, so eliminate (B) and (D).

Now check the second blank. A *tepid* (or half-hearted) experience wouldn't make a bunch of students scream and laugh, either, so (A) is out. Only (C) fits both of the blanks: The students would laugh and scream due to exhilaration on their first white-water rafting experience.

Take Apart Tough Sentences

Look at the following example, the last question in a 15-question set.

EXAMPLE

The ___ agreement had never been written down but was understood and upheld by the governments of both countries.

(A) tacit
(B) public
(C) distinguished
(D) illegal

What if you were stumped? What if you had no idea which word to pick? Try this method:

Tacit—Hmm, sounds familiar.

Public—Nope. It doesn't sound right in this context.

Distinguished—If it was so distinguished, why was it never written down?

Illegal—Nope. Do governments uphold illegal agreements? That doesn't sound right.

Choice (A) sounds the best. As it turns out, it's also correct. *Tacit* agreements are unspoken or silent ones; they're not expressed or declared openly but instead are implied.

Let's try a complex sentence with two blanks. Remember the rules:

- Try the easier blank first.
- Save time by eliminating all choices that won't work for that blank.

EXAMPLE

The old ___ hated parties and refused to ___ in the festivities.

(A) actor .. direct
(B) curmudgeon .. partake
(C) mediator .. take
(D) surgeon .. place

For the first blank, it's impossible to rule out any choices because an actor, a curmudgeon (especially), a mediator, and a surgeon all have the potential to be old and to hate parties.

Try the second blank and see what can be ruled out. (A) doesn't make any sense; what does *direct* in the festivities mean? It's nonsensical. (B), *partake* makes sense. (C), *take* in the festivities doesn't sound right, and neither does (D), *place* in the festivities. That leaves (B) as the best and only fit. A *curmudgeon* is, by definition, an ornery or grumpy person, so it makes sense that he wouldn't want to *partake* in the festivities.

PRACTICE QUESTIONS

1. The firm employed many lackadaisical employees, who had a(n) ___ approach to their work.

   (A) creative
   (B) independent
   (C) unproductive
   (D) discontented

2. Due to ___ weather, the school closed and ___ all classes.

   (A) cold . . continued
   (B) severe . . cancelled
   (C) humid . . relieved
   (D) frosty . . alleviated

3. Many paleontologists believe that modern birds and crocodiles are the ___ of the ancient dinosaurs.

   (A) descendants
   (B) ancestors
   (C) neologisms
   (D) reptiles

4. Her eyes were wide with ___ as the ship ___ with gold, jewels, and precious metals sailed into port.

   (A) amazement . . arrived
   (B) reason . . purged
   (C) wonder . . laden
   (D) purpose . . meandered

5. It was Mount Vesuvius that erupted and ___ the city of Pompeii in the year 79 C.E.

   (A) desiccated
   (B) decimated
   (C) erected
   (D) detected

6. The determined young cadet ___ every character trait that the ideal soldier should have.

   (A) embodied
   (B) created
   (C) secluded
   (D) vaporized

PRACTICE QUESTION ANSWERS

1. C

Lackadaisical means showing a lack of interest or spirit, being listless or languid. If the firm employed lackadaisical workers, these workers probably had an *unproductive* approach to their work.

2. B

If you tried each of the choices in the first blank, you'd see that they all fit. As for the second blank, only one choice makes sense: Because of *severe* weather, all classes were *cancelled.*

3. A

This question is filled with elements that the test makers hope to fool you with. Both the answer choices and the question itself contain difficult vocabulary (i.e., *neologisms* and *paleontologists*). In addition, the antonym for the correct answer is thrown in as a curve ball. However, the only choice that makes sense is (A), *descendants.* Many paleontologists believe that birds and crocodiles are *descended* from dinosaurs.

4. C

Her eyes could well have been wide with *amazement, reason, wonder,* or *purpose* as the ship sailed in. But the only choice that makes sense when you try to fill in the second blank is that "her eyes were wide with *wonder* as the ship *laden* with gold, jewels, and precious metals sailed into port." The other combinations just don't make sense.

5. B

It's possible to infer from the information in the sentence that Mount Vesuvius is a volcano. Regular hills and mountains don't erupt; only volcanoes do. And volcanoes don't *erect* cities, nor do they *detect* or *desiccate* cities. Indeed, volcanoes are very dangerous because they have the potential to *decimate* cities.

6. A

To *embody* means to personify. (A) is the only choice that works here. The cadet doesn't *create* the characters of an ideal soldier, nor does he *seclude* or for that matter *vaporize* those character traits.

CHAPTER 5: ISEE-SPECIFIC MATH WORKOUT: QUANTITATIVE COMPARISONS

Quantitative Comparisons, or QCs, appear **on only the Upper- and Middle-level ISEE**. If you are not taking one of those tests, you may skip this section.

THE FORMAT

Of the approximately 37 math questions in the Quantitative Reasoning section, about 15 are QCs. In a QC, instead of solving for a particular value, you need to compare two quantities. You'll see two mathematical expressions; one in Column A, the other in Column B. Your job is to compare them.

Some questions include additional information about one or both quantities. This information is centered, unboxed, and essential to making the comparison.

The directions will look something like this:

> In questions 1–10, note the given information, if any, and then compare the quantity in Column A to the quantity in Column B. Next to the number of each question write
>
> (A) if the quantity in Column A is greater.
> (B) if the quantity in Column B is greater.
> (C) if the two quantities are equal.
> (D) if the relationship cannot be determined from the information given.

Three Rules for Choice (D)

Choice (D) is the only choice that represents a relationship that cannot be determined. (A), (B), and (C) all mean that a definite relationship can be found between the quantities in Columns A and B.

There are three things to remember about choice (D):

Rule 1: (D) is rarely correct for the first few QC questions.

Rule 2: (D) is never correct if the two columns contain only numbers.

Rule 3: (D) is correct if there's more than one possible relationship between the two columns.

EXAMPLE

Column A	Column B
$3x$	$2x$

(A) If the quantity in Column A is greater
(B) If the quantity in Column B is greater
(C) If the two quantities are equal
(D) If the relationship cannot be determined from the information given

If x is a positive number, then Column A is larger. If x is equal to zero, then the quantities in Columns A and B are equal. If x is a negative number, then Column B is larger.

There is more than one possible relationship between Columns A and B here, so according to rule 3, (D) is the correct choice. As soon as you realize that there is *more than one* possible relationship, choose (D) and move on.

KAPLAN EXCLUSIVE TIPS

"Compare, don't calculate. There's usually an easier way to solve a QC than to calculate it out."

KAPLAN'S 5 STRATEGIES FOR QCS

The following five strategies will help you to make quick comparisons. The key is to *compare* the values rather than *calculate* them.

Strategy 1: Compare piece by piece.

Strategy 2: Make one column look like the other.

Strategy 3: Do the same thing to both columns.

Strategy 4: Pick numbers.

Strategy 5: Avoid QC traps.

Let's look at each strategy in detail.

Strategy 1: Compare Piece by Piece

This applies to QCs that compare two sums or two products.

EXAMPLE

Column A		Column B
	$a > b > c > d$	
$a + c$		$b + d$

We're given four variables, or "pieces," in the above example, as well as the relationship between these pieces. We're told that *a* is greater than all of the other pieces, while *c* is greater than only *d*, etc. The next step is to compare the value of each piece in each column. If every piece in one column is greater than the corresponding piece in the other column, and if addition is the only mathematical operation involved, the column with the greater individual values ($\boldsymbol{a > b}$ and $\boldsymbol{c > d}$) will have the greater total value ($\boldsymbol{a + c > b + d}$).

In other words, we know from the information given that $a > b$, and $c > d$. Therefore, the first term in Column A, *a*, is greater than its corresponding term in Column B, *b*. Likewise, the second term in Column A, *c*, is greater than *d*, its corresponding term in Column B. Since each individual "piece" in Column A is greater than its corresponding "piece" in Column B, the total value of Column A must be greater. The answer is (A).

Strategy 2: Make One Column Look Like the Other

Use this strategy when the quantities in the two columns look so different that a direct comparison would be impossible.

If the quantities in Column A and B are expressed differently, or if one looks more complicated than the other, try to make a direct comparison easier by changing one column to look more like the other.

Let's try an example in which the quantities in Column A and Column B are expressed differently.

EXAMPLE

Column A	Column B
$2(x + 1)$	$2x + 2$

In the example above, it's difficult to make a direct comparison as the quantities are written. However, if you get rid of the parentheses in Column A so that the quantity more closely resembles that in Column B, you should see the relationship right away. If you multiply to get rid of the parentheses in Column A, you'll end up with $2x + 2$ in both columns. Therefore, the columns are equal in value, and the answer is (C).

This strategy is also useful when one column looks more complicated than the other.

EXAMPLE

Column A	Column B
$\frac{2\sqrt{3}}{\sqrt{6}}$	$\sqrt{2}$

Try simplifying Column A, since it is the more complicated-looking quantity of the two.

1) $\frac{2\sqrt{3}}{\sqrt{6}} = \frac{2\sqrt{3}}{\sqrt{2}\sqrt{3}}$

2) $\frac{2\sqrt{3}}{\sqrt{2}\sqrt{3}} = \frac{2}{\sqrt{2}}$

3) $\frac{2}{\sqrt{2}} = \frac{2}{\sqrt{2}} \times \frac{\sqrt{2}}{\sqrt{2}} = \frac{2\sqrt{2}}{2}$

4) $\frac{2\sqrt{2}}{2} = \sqrt{2}$

By simplifying Column A, we are able to make a direct and easy comparison between the two columns. Column A, when simplified, is equivalent to $\sqrt{2}$, which is the quantity in Column B. Therefore, (C) is the correct answer.

Strategy 3: Do the Same Thing to Both Columns

By adding or subtracting the same amount from both columns, you can often unclutter a comparison and make the relationship more apparent. You can also multiply or divide both columns by the same positive number. This keeps the relationship between the columns the same. If the quantities in both columns are positive, you can square both columns. This also keeps the relationship between the columns the same.

KAPLAN EXCLUSIVE TIPS

"Do not multiply or divide both QC columns by a negative number."

Changing the values, and not just the appearances of the quantities in both columns, is often helpful in tackling QC questions. Set up the problem as an inequality with the two columns as opposing sides of the inequality.

To change the values of the columns, add or subtract the same amount from both columns and multiply or divide by a positive number without changing the absolute relationship. But **be careful.** Remember that the direction of an inequality sign will be reversed if you multiply or divide by a negative number. Since this reversal will alter the relationship between the two columns, avoid multiplying or dividing by a negative number.

You can also square the quantities in both columns when both columns are positive. But **be careful.** Do not square both columns unless you know for certain that both columns are positive. Remember these two things when squaring the quantities in both columns: (1) the direction of an inequality sign can be reversed if one or both quantities are negative, and (2) the inequality sign can be changed to an equals sign if one quantity is positive and the other quantity is negative, with one quantity being the negative of the other. For example, $4 > -5$, yet $4^2 < (-5)^2$, since $16 < 25$. Likewise, $2 > -2$, yet $2^2 = (-2)^2$, since $2^2 = (-2)^2 = 4$.

In the QC below, what could you do to both columns?

EXAMPLE

Column A	Column B
$x > y > 0$	
$\frac{2y+x}{2}$	$y+x$

Try multiplying both columns by 2 to get rid of that fraction in Column A. You're left with $2y + x$ in Column A and $2y + 2x$ in Column B. We know that $2y = 2y$. But what about the relationship between x and $2x$? The centered information tells us that $x > 0$. Therefore, $2x > x$, and Column B is greater than Column A. Choice (B) is the right answer.

In the next QC, what could you do to both columns?

EXAMPLE

Column A	Column B
$\frac{1}{4}+\frac{1}{5}-\frac{1}{3}$	$\frac{1}{2}-\frac{1}{3}+\frac{1}{20}$

Try adding $\frac{1}{3}$ to both sides. If you do this, you'll be left with $\frac{1}{4}+\frac{1}{5}$ in Column A and $\frac{1}{2}+\frac{1}{20}$ in Column B. Now treat this QC like a standard fraction problem. To

KAPLAN EXCLUSIVE TIPS

"When you plug in negative numbers and fractions, remember the following:

- When you square a positive fraction less than 1, the result is a smaller fraction than the original.
- When you square a negative number, the result is a positive number.
- When you square 0 and 1, they remain the same."

find the sums in each column, you must find the lowest common denominator. Upon adding, you get with $\frac{9}{20}$ in Column A and $\frac{11}{20}$ in Column B. Column B is greater than Column A, so the answer is (B).

Strategy 4: Pick Numbers

Substitute numbers into those abstract algebra QCs . Try using a positive, a negative, and zero.

If a QC involves variables, pick numbers to clarify the relationship. Here's what to do:

1. Pick numbers that are easy to work with.
2. Plug in the numbers and calculate the values. What's the relationship between the columns?
3. Pick a different number for each variable and recalculate. See if you get a different relationship.

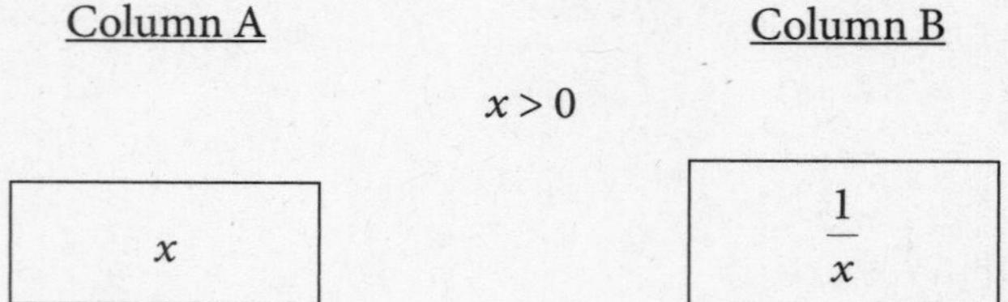

Try choosing a relatively easy number like 1. Plug it in and calculate. If you have calculated correctly, you'll find that Columns A and B are equal, $1 = \frac{1}{1}$. Remember to try another number. Let's try $x = \frac{1}{2}$. If we plug in $\frac{1}{2}$ and recalculate, Column A is now equal to $\frac{1}{2}$, and Column B is equal to 2. The relationship is not the same as before. Therefore, the answer is (D).

Pick Different Kinds of Numbers

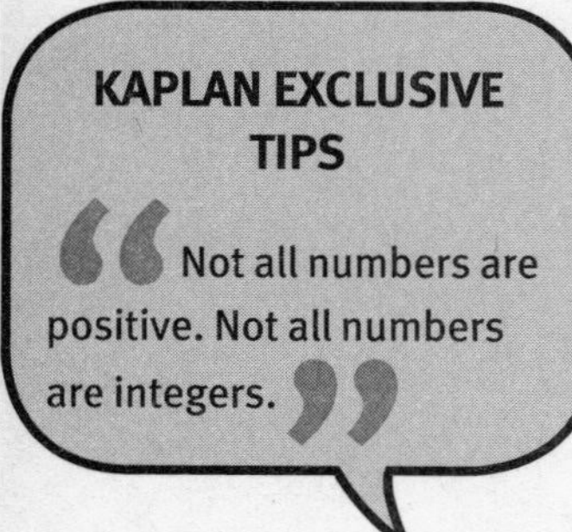

KAPLAN EXCLUSIVE TIPS
"Not all numbers are positive. Not all numbers are integers."

Never assume that all variables represent positive integers. Unless you're told otherwise, as in the case above, variables can be positive or negative, and they can be zero or fractions. Because different kinds of numbers behave differently, you should always choose a different kind of number the second time around. In the example above, we knew that x wasn't a negative number, nor was it zero, so we tried a fraction and discovered that the relationship between the columns did not remain the same.

In the next three examples, we'll choose different kinds of numbers and observe the results. Remember that if there's more than one possible relationship between the two columns, the answer is (D).

EXAMPLE

Column A	Column B
x	$-x$

If $x = 1$, Column A = 1 and Column B = –1.
In this case, Column A is greater

If $x = -1$, Column A = –1 and Column B = 1.
In this case, Column B is greater.

EXAMPLE

$x > 0$

Column A	Column B
x	$\frac{1}{x}$

If $x = 2$, Column A = 2 and Column B = $\frac{1}{2}$.
In this case, Column A is greater.

If $x = \frac{1}{2}$, Column A = $\frac{1}{2}$ and Column B = 2.
In this case, Column B is greater.

EXAMPLE

Column A	Column B
x	x^2

If $x = \frac{1}{2}$, Column A = $\frac{1}{2}$ and Column B = $\frac{1}{4}$.
In this case, Column A is greater.

If $x = 2$, Column A = 2 and Column B = 4.
In this case, Column B is greater.

Strategy 5: Avoid QC Traps

Keep your eyes open for those trick questions designed to fool you into the obvious but wrong answer. Questions are arranged in order of increasing difficulty, so chances are you'll see traps toward the end of the set.

To avoid these nasty traps, always be on your toes. Never assume anything. Be particularly careful toward the end of a QC set.

Don't Be Tricked by Misleading Information

EXAMPLE

Column A		Column B
	Frank weighs more than Hector.	
Frank's height in meters		Hector's height in meters

The test makers are hoping that you'll follow some faulty logic and think, "If Frank is heavier, he must be taller." But that's not necessarily so. The answer in this case would be (D). If you keep your eyes open for these kinds of things, you'll spot them immediately.

Don't Assume

EXAMPLE

Column A		Column B
	$1 + x^2 = 10$	
x		3

A common mistake on QC questions is to assume that variables represent positive integers. We already dealt with these kinds of problems in the Picking Numbers strategy. Remember that positive and negative numbers, as well as fractions and zeros, behave differently.

In the example above, the test makers are hoping you'll assume that $x = 3$, since the square of 3 = 9. But x could also be equal to –3. Because x could be 3 or –3, (D) is the correct answer.

Don't Fall for Look-Alikes

EXAMPLE

Column A	Column B
$\sqrt{4} + \sqrt{4}$	$\sqrt{8}$

Now, 4 + 4 = 8, *but* $\sqrt{4} + \sqrt{4} > \sqrt{8}$! Don't forget the rules of radicals. The test makers are counting on you to rush and look for the obvious choice, (C), that the two quantities are equal. Don't let them fool you. If $a > 0$ and $b > 0$, then $\sqrt{a+b} \neq \sqrt{a} + \sqrt{b}$.

Remember the convention that if x is positive, $\sqrt{x}$ means the positive square root. So $\sqrt{4} + \sqrt{4} = 2 + 2 = 4$. Now we have 4 in Column A and $\sqrt{8}$ in Column B. Since $\sqrt{8} < \sqrt{9}$ and $\sqrt{9} = 3$, $\sqrt{8} < 3 < 4$. Thus, $4 > \sqrt{8}$ and Column A is greater. Because 4 and $\sqrt{8}$ are both positive, you could also show that $4 > \sqrt{8}$ by squaring both 4 and $\sqrt{8}$: $4^2 = 16$ and $(\sqrt{8})^2 = 8$; $16 > 8$, so $4 > \sqrt{8}$. Choice (A) is correct.

PRACTICE QUESTIONS

Directions: In questions 1–9, note the given information, if any, and then compare the quantity in Column A to the quantity in Column B. Next to the number of each question write

(A) if the quantity in Column A is greater.
(B) if the quantity in Column B is greater.
(C) if the two quantities are equal.
(D) if the relationship cannot be determined from the information given.

	Column A	Column B
1.	The average of 106, 117, 123, and 195	The average of 110, 118, 124, and 196

$2x - 6 = 2x + 3x$

	Column A	Column B
2.	x^2	4

$x > 0$
$y > 0$

	Column A	Column B
3.	$x - y$	$y - x$

$x \neq 0$

	Column A	Column B
4.	$\frac{x+2}{3}$	$x + 5$

x is an even integer.

	Column A	Column B
5.	x^2	x^3
6.	$\frac{6+\sqrt{3}}{2}$	$\frac{3+\sqrt{6}}{\sqrt{4}}$
7.	$6 + 10$	$\sqrt{16} + \sqrt{36}$
8.	25% of 65	$65 \times \sqrt{\frac{1}{4}}$

$a > b > c > d$

	Column A	Column B
9.	$a^2 + c$	$b^2 + d$

PRACTICE QUESTION ANSWERS

1. B

Compare piece by piece. The corresponding numbers in Column B are greater than those in Column A. Therefore, the average in Column B must be greater.

2. C

Solve for x in the centered equation. First, subtract $2x$ from both sides. This will leave you with $-6 = 3x$. Divide both sides by 3. Now, $x = -2$. Plug in -2 for x to find the value of x^2 in Column A: $x^2 = (-2)^2 = 4$. The quantities in both columns are equal.

3. D

From the centered information, you know only that the variables x and y must be positive. So plug in some positive integers. If $x = 5$ and $y = 3$, then Column A is $x - y = 5 - 3 = 2$ and Column B is $y - x = 3 - 5 = -2$. In this case, Column A is greater. Now plug in some different numbers. Notice that you have not been given any information about the relationship between x and y. If you were to switch the values that you used on the first try, so that $x = 3$ and $y = 5$, then Column A is $x - y = 3 - 5 = -2$ and Column B is $y - x = 5 - 3 = 2$. Column B is greater. Since more than one relationship between the columns is possible, choice (D) is correct.

4. D

This problem appears to be an obvious candidate for the picking numbers strategy. But be careful with the numbers you choose. Let's plug in 2 for x. Column A is $\frac{2+2}{3}$, or $\frac{4}{3}$, and Column B is $2 + 5$, or 7. Column B is greater. Your next likely step would be to switch your plug-in number from a positive to a negative. Here's where the test makers will mislead you if you aren't careful. By letting $x = -2$, you find that Column A is $\frac{-2+2}{3}$, or 0, while Column B is $-2 + 5$, or 3. Once again, Column B is greater. But what happens if you plug in a negative number considerably further away from 0? If $x = -100$, then Column A is $\frac{-100+2}{3} = \frac{-98}{3}$, or $-32\frac{2}{3}$, and Column B is $-100 + 5$, or -95. In this case, Column A is greater. More than one relationship between the columns is possible.

5. D

This is another picking numbers type of problem. Let's begin by plugging in a positive value for x that is consistent with the centered information. Let $x = 2$. So Column A is $2^2 = 2 \times 2$, or 4, and Column B is $2^3 = 2 \times 2 \times 2$, or 8. In this case, Column B is greater. Now pick a negative value for x that is consistent with the centered information. Let $x = -2$. Now, Column A is $(-2)^2 = (-2) \times (-2) = 4$ and Column B is $(-2)^3 = (-2) \times (-2) \times (-2) = -8$. Column A is greater. Since more than one relationship between the columns is possible, (D) is correct.

6. A

While it is true that every positive number has two square roots—a positive and a negative square root—the convention with the symbol $\sqrt{\ }$ is that if x is positive, $\sqrt{x}$ means the positive square root of x. For example, 16 has the two square roots 4 and -4, while $\sqrt{16}$ means the positive square root of 16, which is 4. Thus, $\sqrt{16} = 4$.

First notice that the denominator $\sqrt{4}$ of Column B is equal to 2. So we're comparing $\frac{6+\sqrt{3}}{2}$ in Column A with $\frac{3+\sqrt{6}}{2}$ in Column B. Now try doing the same thing to both columns. Multiplying both columns by 2 leaves us with $6 + \sqrt{3}$ for Column A and $3 + \sqrt{6}$ for Column B. Next, subtracting 3 from both columns leaves us with $3 + \sqrt{3}$ for Column A and $\sqrt{6}$ for Column B. Now $3 = \sqrt{9}$ and $\sqrt{9}$ is greater than $\sqrt{6}$. So 3 is greater than $\sqrt{6}$. Surely $3 + \sqrt{3}$ (which is what we now have for Column A) is greater than 3. Also, 3 is greater than $\sqrt{6}$, with $\sqrt{6}$ being what we have for Column B. So $3 + \sqrt{3}$ for Column A must be greater than $\sqrt{6}$ for Column B. Choice (A) is correct.

7. A

Just as we saw in the previous question, if x is positive, that means $\sqrt{x}$ is the positive square root of x. In Column A, $6 + 10 = 16$. In Column B, we have $\sqrt{16} + \sqrt{36}$. By convention, $\sqrt{16} = 4$ and $\sqrt{36} = 6$. So $\sqrt{16} + \sqrt{36} = 4 + 6 = 10$. Column A is greater.

8. B

Change one of the columns so you can make a direct comparison. A percentage can be written as a fraction and vice versa. It's generally easier to work with fractions, so convert 25% in Column A to a fraction. The fractional equivalent of 25% is $\frac{1}{4}$. (You convert a percent to a fraction (or decimal) by dividing the percent by 100%, so $25\% = \frac{25\%}{100\%} = \frac{25}{100} = \frac{1}{4}$.)

Therefore, Column A is $\frac{1}{4}$ of 65, or $\frac{65}{4}$. Column B is $65 \times \sqrt{\frac{1}{4}}$. Let's first simplify $\sqrt{\frac{1}{4}} \cdot \sqrt{\frac{1}{4}} = \frac{\sqrt{1}}{\sqrt{4}} = \frac{1}{2}$. So Column B is $65 \times \frac{1}{2}$, or $\frac{65}{2}$. Since $\frac{65}{2}$ is greater than $\frac{65}{4}$, Column B is greater.

9. D

Since the variables could be positive or negative, pick different kinds of numbers for the variables to see if different relationships between the columns are possible. Remember that the values you pick must be consistent with the centered information, which is that $a > b > c > d$.

If $a = 4$, $b = 3$, $c = 2$, and $d = 1$, then the value of Column A is $a^2 + c = 4^2 + 2 = 16 + 2 = 18$, and the value of Column B is $b^2 + d = 3^2 + 1 = 9 + 1 = 10$. Column A is greater. If you pick only positive numbers, then it will always be true that $a^2 + c > b^2 + d$. You could fall for the trap here of thinking that $a^2 + c$ is always greater than $b^2 + d$ if you don't let some or all of the variables be negative. Let $a = -1$, $b = -2$, $c = -3$, and $d = -4$. These values are consistent with the centered information. This time the value of Column A is $a^2 + c = (-1)^2 + (-3) = 1 - 3 = -2$, and the value of Column B is $b^2 + d = (-2)^2 + (-4) = 4 - 4 = 0$. So in this case Column B is greater. More than one relationship between the columns is possible.

| Part Three |

COMMON CONTENT FOR THE SSAT AND ISEE

CHAPTER 6: SSAT AND ISEE MASTERY

Every year, close to 100,000 students take either the SSAT or ISEE for admission to nearly 2,000 independent (private) schools. Although the components of the two tests are remarkably similar, there are some critical differences.

To get a great score on a private school admissions test, you need to to know some key things that have nothing to do with vocabulary words or isosceles triangles. Namely, you need to know how to be a good test taker.

- You need to have a basic understanding of the nature of the test.
- You need to hone your math and verbal skills.
- You need to develop test-taking strategies and techniques.

Having a solid grasp of the content on the test is obviously important. You can't do well if you don't know the material. But it's also just as important to know how the test is set up, what kinds of questions it has, and what kinds of traps it commonly sets. If you don't know these things, you will be at a severe disadvantage on test day.

USING THE TEST STRUCTURE TO YOUR ADVANTAGE

Whether you're taking the SSAT (Secondary School Admission Test) or the ISEE (Independent School Entrance Exam), you'll notice pretty quickly that it is very different from the tests you're used to taking in school. On a school test, you're often told to show your work, spend more time on tough questions (since they're worth more points), and work thoroughly, even if it means taking extra time.

None of these things apply in the world of standardized testing. On your private school admissions test, it won't matter how you answer a question; it only matters what your final answer is. Also, all questions are worth the same number of points, so it's always to your advantage to answer easier questions first to get them out of the way.

The SSAT and ISEE are each given to students in a range of grades, so if you're in 8th grade, for example, you're not expected to get as many questions right as someone in 11th grade (for the Upper-level test). Keep that in mind as you take the test so you won't get discouraged if you find a lot of questions that you can't answer!

To succeed in this unique testing environment, you need to know some fundamentals. Both the SSAT and ISEE have some quirks, so read carefully.

Because the format and directions of the SSAT and ISEE remain relatively unchanged from year to year, you can learn the setup in advance. Then on test day, all you'll have to worry about will be answering each question, not learning how a Synonym question works.

One of the easiest and most useful things you can do to boost your performance is to learn and understand the directions before test day. Since the instructions are always exactly the same, there's no reason to waste your time on the day of the test reading them. Get them straight in your head beforehand, while you go through this book, and you'll be able to skip them during the test.

Skipping Around

You're allowed to skip around as much as you'd like within each section of the SSAT or ISEE. High scorers know this and use it to their advantage. They move through the test efficiently, quickly marking and leaving questions they can't answer immediately, racking up points on questions they do know, then coming back to the tough ones later. They don't dwell on any question, even a hard one, until they've tried every question at least once.

When you see questions that look tough, circle them in your test booklet and skip them for later. Gather points on other questions first. On a second look, some tricky-looking questions can turn out to be much easier than they initially looked. And remember, if you're on the younger side of the testing group within your level, expect to see several questions that you won't be able to answer. The test is intentionally set up this way, so don't let it discourage you.

Guessing—Know Your Test

When should you guess? That's a question we hear from students all the time. It depends on which test you're taking. Read the following information and follow the instructions for your test. Guessing is one of the few areas in which the SSAT and ISEE operate differently, so read carefully!

SSAT: There is a *wrong-answer penalty*. For each answer you get right, you get one point. For each answer you get wrong, one-quarter of a point is deducted from your total score. Does this mean you shouldn't guess? No, not at all. What it means is that you need to be smart about it. Essentially, if you can eliminate at least one—and preferably two—answer choices, it's to your advantage to guess, because you've tipped the odds of guessing correctly in your favor. If you can't eliminate anything, however, you're better off leaving the question blank.

ISEE: There is *no* wrong-answer penalty. That means you should answer every single question on the test, even if you have no idea what it's asking you. The ISEE calculates your score simply by adding up your right answers, so you might as well fill in all those ovals completely. You never know what you might get right by luck!

KAPLAN EXCLUSIVE TIPS

"On the SSAT, guess only if you can eliminate at least one or two answer choices.

On the ISEE, always guess, even if you can't eliminate *anything*."

Gridding—The Answer Grid Has No Heart

Misgridding. It sounds so basic, but it happens all the time: When time is short, it's easy to get confused going back and forth between your test booklet and your answer grid. If you know the answer but misgrid, you won't get any points, so be careful. Don't let it happen to you. Here are some tips to help you avoid making mistakes on the answer grid:

Circle the Questions You Skip

Put a big circle in your test booklet around any question numbers you skip. When you go back, these questions will be easy to locate. Also, if you accidentally skip a box on the grid, you can check your grid against your booklet to see where you went wrong.

CIRCLE BEFORE YOU SKIP

"One common test disaster is filling in all of the questions with the right answers—in the wrong spots. Every time you skip a question, *circle it* in your test book. Make sure that you skip it on the answer grid, too."

Always Circle the Answers You Choose

Circling your answers in the test booklet as you work on each question makes it easier to check your grid against your booklet.

Grid Five or More Answers at Once

Don't transfer your answers to the grid after every question. Do it after every five questions or at the end of each reading passage. That way, you won't keep breaking your concentration. You'll save time and you'll gain accuracy.

Be careful at the end of a section, when time may be running out. You don't want to have your answers in the test booklet and not be able to transfer them to your answer grid because you have run out of time. Make sure to transfer your answers after every five questions or so.

APPROACHING SSAT OR ISEE QUESTIONS

Apart from knowing the setup of the SSAT or ISEE, you need to have a system for attacking the questions. You wouldn't travel around a foreign city without a map, and you shouldn't approach your private school admissions test without a plan, either. Once you know the basics about how each test is set up, you can approach each section more strategically. We recommend the following method for approaching test questions systematically.

Think about the Question Before You Look at the Answer

The people who make the tests love to put distracters among the answer choices. Distracters are answer choices that look like the right answer, but aren't. If you jump right into the answer choices without thinking first about what you're looking for, you're more likely to fall for one of these traps.

Use Backdoor Strategies If Necessary

There are usually a number of ways to get to the right answer on an SSAT or ISEE question. Most of the questions are multiple-choice. That means the answer is right in front of you—you just have to find it. But if you can't figure out the answer in a straightforward way, try other techniques. We'll talk about specific Kaplan Methods such as backsolving, picking numbers, and eliminating wrong answers in later chapters.

Pace Yourself

The SSAT and ISEE give you a lot of questions in a short period of time. In order to get through an entire section, you can't spend too much time on any one question. Keep moving through the test at a good speed; if you run into a hard question, circle it, skip it, and go back later if there's time.

Typically, the questions get harder as you move through a problem set. Ideally, you can work through the easy problems at a brisk, steady clip and use a little more of your time for the harder ones that come at the end of the set.

One caution: Don't completely rush through the easy problems just to save time for the harder ones. These early problems are points in your pocket, and you don't want to work through them in such haste that you end up making careless mistakes.

Locate Quick Points If You're Running Out of Time

Some questions can be done quickly; for instance, some reading questions will ask you to identify the meaning of a particular word in the passage. These can be done at the last minute, even if you haven't read the passage. When you start to run out of time, locate and answer any of the quick points that remain.

When you take the SSAT or ISEE, you have one clear objective in mind: to score as many points as you can. It's that simple. The rest of this book will help you do that.

MANAGING STRESS

The countdown has begun. Your date with the test is looming on the horizon. Anxiety is on the rise. The butterflies in your stomach have gone ballistic. Your thinking is getting cloudy. Maybe you think you won't be ready. Maybe you already know your stuff, but you're going into panic mode anyway. Don't freak! It's possible to tame that anxiety and stress—*before* and *during* the test.

Remember, a little stress is good. Anxiety is a motivation to study. The adrenaline that gets pumped into your bloodstream when you're stressed helps you stay alert and think more clearly. But if you feel that the tension is so great that it's preventing you from using your study time effectively, here are some things you can do to get it under control.

Take Control

Lack of control is a prime cause of stress. Research shows that if you don't have a sense of control over what's happening in your life, you can easily end up feeling helpless and hopeless. Try to identify the sources of the stress you feel. Which sources can you do something about? Can you find ways to reduce the stress you're feeling about any of these sources?

Focus on Your Strengths

Make a list of areas of strength you have that will help you do well on the test. We all have strengths, and recognizing your own is like having reserves of solid gold at Fort Knox. You'll be able to draw on your reserves as you need them, helping you solve difficult questions, maintain confidence, and keep test stress and anxiety at a distance. And every time you recognize a new area of strength, solve a challenging problem, or score well on a practice test, you'll increase your reserves.

Imagine Yourself Succeeding

Close your eyes and imagine yourself in a relaxing situation. Breathe easily and naturally. Now, think of a real-life situation in which you scored well on a test or did well on an assignment. Focus on this success. Now turn your thoughts to the SSAT or ISEE and keep your thoughts and feelings in line with that successful experience. Don't make comparisons between them; just imagine yourself taking the upcoming test with the same feelings of confidence and relaxed control.

Set Realistic Goals

Facing your problem areas gives you some distinct advantages. What do you want to accomplish in the time remaining? Make a list of realistic goals. You can't help but feel more confident when you know you're actively improving your chances of earning a higher test score.

Master Your Physical Well-Being

How well you do on test day doesn't only have to do with how prepared you are. It also has to do with what kind of condition you are in physically.

Exercise Your Frustrations Away

Whether it's jogging, biking, push-ups, or a pickup basketball game, physical exercise will stimulate your mind and body and improve your ability to think and concentrate. A surprising number of students fall out of the habit of regular exercise, ironically because they're spending so much time prepping for exams. A little physical exertion will help to keep your mind and body in sync and sleep better at night.

Avoid Drugs

Using drugs (prescription or recreational) specifically to prepare for and take a big test is definitely self-defeating. (And if they're illegal drugs, you may end up with a bigger problem than the SSAT or ISEE on your hands.) Mild stimulants, such as coffee or cola, can sometimes help as you study, since they keep you alert. On the downside, too much of these can also lead to agitation, restlessness, and insomnia. It all depends on your tolerance for caffeine.

Eat Well

Good nutrition will help you focus and think clearly. Eat plenty of fruits and vegetables; low-fat protein such as fish, skinless poultry, beans, and legumes; and whole grains such as brown rice, whole-wheat bread, and pastas. Don't eat a lot of sugar and high-fat snacks or salty foods.

Keep Breathing

Conscious attention to breathing is an excellent way to manage stress while you're taking the test. Most of the people who get into trouble during tests take shallow breaths: They breathe using only their upper chests and shoulder muscles, and they may even hold their breath for long periods of time. Conversely, those test takers who breathe deeply in a slow, relaxed manner are likely to be in better control during the session.

Stretch

If you find yourself getting spaced out or burned out as you study or take the test, stop for a brief moment and stretch. Flex your feet and arms. Even though you'll be pausing on the test for a moment, it's a moment well spent. Stretching will help to refresh you and refocus your thoughts.

CHAPTER 7: SYNONYMS

Synonyms appear on all levels of the SSAT and ISEE. At its most basic level, a synonym is a word that is similar in meaning to another defined word. *Fast* is a synonym for *quick*. OK, that makes sense. Unfortunately, if synonyms were that easy on the SSAT or ISEE, the tests wouldn't tell admissions officers very much.

THE FORMAT

The synonyms you'll see on your actual test will be much more challenging than the sample above, but they'll all follow the same logic. You'll see a word in capital letters (we call this the *stem word*), and it will be followed by five other words on the SSAT or four on the ISEE). One of them will be the synonym of the given word, and the others will not.

EXAMPLE

AUTHENTIC:

(A) genuine
(B) valuable
(C) ancient
(D) damaged
(E) historical

Which of these words means AUTHENTIC? Maybe you "just knew" that the answer was (A), *genuine,* and maybe you didn't. Either way, you need a method that will work for you on both the easy and the hard Synonym questions. What you need is the . . .

KAPLAN 3-STEP METHOD FOR SYNONYMS

Step 1. Define the stem word.

Step 2. Find the answer choice that best fits your definition.

Step 3. If no choice fits, think of other definitions for the stem word and go through the choices again.

Let's take another look at the previous example, using the Three-Step Method.

STEP 1: DEFINE THE STEM WORD

What does *authentic* mean? Something authentic is something *real,* such as an authentic signature, rather than a forgery. Your definition might look like this: Something authentic can be *proven* to be what it *claims* to be.

STEP 2: FIND THE ANSWER CHOICE THAT BEST FITS YOUR DEFINITION

Go through the answer choices one by one to see which one fits best. Your options are: *genuine, valuable, ancient, damaged,* and *historical.* Something AUTHENTIC could be worth a lot or not much at all, old or new, in good shape or bad, or even recent or historical. The only word that really means the same thing as AUTHENTIC is (A) genuine.

STEP 3: IF NO CHOICE FITS, THINK OF OTHER DEFINITIONS FOR THE STEM WORD AND GO THROUGH THE CHOICES AGAIN

In the previous example, one choice fit, but take a look at another one:

EXAMPLE

GRAVE:

(A) regrettable
(B) unpleasant
(C) serious
(D) careful
(E) lengthy

Say you defined GRAVE as *a burial location.* You looked at the choices and didn't see any words like *tomb* or *coffin.* What to do? Move to step 3 and go back to the stem word, thinking about other definitions. Have you ever heard of a "grave situation"? GRAVE can also mean *serious* or *solemn*, and you can see that (C), *serious*, now fits the bill perfectly. If none of the answer choices seem to work with your definition, there may be a secondary definition you haven't yet considered.

WALK THE WALK

"What if WALK were your stem word. What part of speech is it? It could be the *act of* walking (a verb), or *to take* a walk (the noun). Just look at the answer choices. They'll always be the same part of speech as the stem word. So you'll always know whether to WAVE to Mom or ride the WAVE . . . though she'd probably prefer you do both at once!"

BENE means *good*; SOMN has to do with *sleep*; SCRIB has to do with *writing*; CON means doing something *together*; and VER has to do with *truth*.

Technique 2: Use Your Knowledge of Foreign Languages

Do you study a foreign language? If so, it can help you decode lots of vocabulary words on the SSAT or ISEE, particularly if it's one of the Romance languages (French, Spanish, Italian, Portuguese). Look at the example words below. Do you recognize any foreign language words in them?

- FACILITATE
- DORMANT
- EXPLICATE

Facile means "easy" in French and Italian; *dormir* means "to sleep" in French and Spanish; and *expliquer* means "to explain" in French.

Technique 3: Remember the Context

Sometimes a word might look strange sitting on the page by itself, but if you think about it, you realize you've heard it before in other phrases. If you can put the word into context, such as in a cliché, you're well on your way to deciphering its meaning.

EXAMPLE

GNARLED:

(A) fruitful
(B) dead
(C) twisted
(D) flowering
(E) drooping

What kind of plant have you heard described as *gnarled*? *Trees* are often described as gnarled, particularly old ones. They are knotty and twisted, the kind you think would appear in fairy tales. The answer is (C).

EXAMPLE

ALLEGATION:

(A) evidence
(B) accusation
(C) conservation
(D) foundation
(E) fabrication

What does "making an allegation" mean? *Making an allegation* is accusing someone of committing a crime, a phrase you might have seen on the news or on a police-related TV show. The answer is (B).

EXAMPLE

LAURELS:

(A) vine
(B) honor
(C) lavender
(D) cushion
(E) work

Have you heard the expression *Don't rest on your laurels*? What do you think it might mean? *Don't rest on your laurels* originated in ancient Greece, where heroes were given wreaths of laurel branches to signify their accomplishments. Saying you shouldn't rest on your laurels is the same thing as saying you shouldn't get too comfortable or smug, just enjoying your accomplishment rather than striving for improvement.

Technique 4: Use Word Charge

Even if you know nothing about the word, have never seen it before, don't recognize any prefixes or roots, and can't think of any word it resembles in another language, you can still make a stab at a Synonym question. One useful strategy when you're stumped is Word Charge.

What do we mean by Word Charge? Are some words electric? Or do they spend too much money on credit cards? No, and no. Word charge refers to the *sense* that a word gives you as to whether it's a positive word or a negative one.

VILIFY: This sounds like *villain*, a word most people would say is bad.

GLORIFY: This sounds like *glorious*, a word most people would say is good.

Let's say that VILIFY has a negative charge (–) and GLORIFY has a positive charge (+). On all Synonym questions, the correct answer will have *the same charge as the stem word*, so use your instincts about word charge to help you when you're stuck on a tough word.

Decide whether each of the following words has a positive (+) or negative (–) charge.

AUSPICIOUS ______________
MALADY ______________
NOXIOUS ______________
AMIABLE ______________
BOORISH ______________
MELANCHOLY ______________
HUMANE ______________

Often words that sound harsh have a negative meaning, while smooth-sounding words tend to have positive meanings. If *cantankerous* sounds negative to you, you would be right. It means difficult to handle.

You can also use prefixes and roots to help determine a word's charge. *Mal, de, dis, un, in, im, a,* and *mis* often indicate a negative, while *pro, ben,* and *magn* are often positives.

Not all words sound positive; some sound neutral. But if you can define the charge, you can probably eliminate some answer choices on that basis alone.

Now let's see how you did on identifying the charge of the words listed above.

Auspicious (+) means favorable; a *malady* (–) means an illness; *noxious* (–) means harmful; *amiable* (+) means agreeable; *boorish* (–) means rude; *melancholy* (–) means sadness; and *humane* (+) means kind.

Practice Makes Perfect

Now that you've been through all of the techniques to succeed on Synonym questions, it's time for some practice. Work through the following 20 questions, using the Kaplan 3-Step Method, avoiding pitfalls, and employing vocabulary techniques when you get stuck.

PRACTICE QUESTIONS

1. DISMAL:
   (A) bleak
   (B) crowded
   (C) comfortable
   (D) temporary
   (E) typical

2. HUMID:
   (A) damp
   (B) windy
   (C) hot
   (D) stormy
   (E) hazy

3. DEPORT:
   (A) punish
   (B) banish
   (C) censor
   (D) jail
   (E) praise

4. PEDDLE:
   (A) assemble
   (B) steal
   (C) edit
   (D) deliver
   (E) sell

5. TERMINATE:
   (A) extend
   (B) renew
   (C) end
   (D) sell
   (E) finalize

6. DEARTH:
   (A) explosion
   (B) increase
   (C) shortage
   (D) change
   (E) surplus

7. OBSCURE:
   (A) tragic
   (B) dark
   (C) obligatory
   (D) ignored
   (E) legendary

8. MOURN:
   (A) inaugurate
   (B) celebrate
   (C) greet
   (D) oppose
   (E) grieve

9. RECLUSE:
   (A) artist
   (B) beggar
   (C) lunatic
   (D) scavenger
   (E) hermit

10. HOMAGE:
   (A) youth
   (B) wreath
   (C) respect
   (D) affection
   (E) household

11. HERBIVOROUS:
    (A) huge
    (B) warm-blooded
    (C) endangered
    (D) plant-eating
    (E) intelligent

12. SYNOPSIS:
    (A) summary
    (B) satire
    (C) paragraph
    (D) update
    (E) rebuttal

13. WANTON:
    (A) fantastic
    (B) repeated
    (C) lustful
    (D) careful
    (E) needy

14. IMPERIOUS:
    (A) royal
    (B) friendly
    (C) gusty
    (D) arrogant
    (E) insightful

15. HALLOW:
    (A) revere
    (B) dig
    (C) inhabit
    (D) discover
    (E) release

16. BLISS:
    (A) ecstasy
    (B) escape
    (C) prayer
    (D) terror
    (E) fun

17. INDECENT:
    (A) centralized
    (B) immortal
    (C) improper
    (D) incessant
    (E) recent

18. TANGIBLE:
    (A) unrelated
    (B) glib
    (C) touchable
    (D) tanned
    (E) incapable

19. FEROCITY:
    (A) hardness
    (B) humility
    (C) narrowness
    (D) scarcity
    (E) fierceness

20. TENACIOUS:
    (A) tender
    (B) determined
    (C) temporary
    (D) talkative
    (E) discouraged

PRACTICE QUESTION ANSWERS

1. A
2. A
3. B
4. E
5. C
6. C
7. B
8. E
9. E
10. C
11. D
12. A
13. C
14. D
15. A
16. A
17. C
18. C
19. E
20. B

CHAPTER 8: READING COMPREHENSION

Critical Reading questions appear on all levels of the SSAT and ISEE. The Reading section presents you with five to seven passages (depending on the test and level) and questions that follow. The passages will generally cover topics such as history, science, or literature. For each passage, you'll be asked about the main idea and details presented. You'll only get points for answering questions correctly, not for reading the text thoroughly, so keep your attention on reading as quickly as possible and answering as many questions as you can.

However, remember that if you are in the lower grade within your level, you DON'T need to answer all of the questions—in fact, you don't even need to read all of the passages. You can get a great score even if you don't answer all the questions, so don't sweat it.

READ, DON'T LEARN

"On the SSAT or ISEE, you'll have to read quickly and efficiently. Your goal is not to learn the information presented, or even to think about it very much. Rather, you need to figure out the main point and where to look for any details you might be asked about."

READING STRATEGIES

On the one hand, it's a good thing that you're inherently prepared for this section because you already know how to read. On the other hand, your previous reading experience has the potential to get you into a bit of trouble on this section of the test. Reading habits that may serve you well in school can get in the way on the test.

There are three traps that students commonly fall into on the test.

Trap 1: Reading too slowly

Trap 2: Continually rereading things you do not understand

Trap 3: Spending more time on the passages than on the questions

It is a mistake to approach the reading passages with the intention of understanding them thoroughly. You need to focus on answering the questions, not on getting to know the text.

SSAT AND ISEE READING IS DIFFERENT FROM EVERYDAY READING

This is an important point. You already know how to read, but the way that you read normally may not help you maximize your points on the test. There are three main skills you'll need to employ to ace the Reading Comprehension section:

1. **Summarize:** You'll need to be able to sum up what the passage is all about.
2. **Research:** You'll need to be able to find facts, figures, and names in the passage.
3. **Make inferences:** You'll need to be able to figure out information that isn't directly stated.

How can you make sure you do all of these very official-sounding things? Here are some solid strategies.

1. Look for the Big Idea

Don't read as if you're memorizing everything. Aim to pick up just the gist of the passage—the author's main idea.

2. Pay Attention to Language

The author's choice of words can tell you everything about his or her point of view, attitude, and style.

3. Be a Critical Reader

As you read, ask yourself critical questions: "What's the author's main point? What message is the author trying to get across?"

4. Make It Simple

Despite the fancy language, Reading passages are usually about pretty simple topics. Don't get bogged down by technical language; translate the author's ideas into your *own words*.

5. Keep Moving

Aim to spend no more than one minute reading each passage; remember, just reading the passage won't score you points.

6. Don't Sweat the Details

Don't waste time reading and rereading parts you don't understand. Move swiftly through the passage to answer the questions, which is what really counts.

You've probably realized by now that Kaplan has a multistep method for all the question types on the SSAT and ISEE. It's in your best interest to approach the test as a whole and the individual sections systematically. If you approach every passage the same way, you'll work your way through the Reading Comprehension section efficiently.

KAPLAN 4-STEP METHOD FOR READING COMPREHENSION

Step 1. Read the passage.

Step 2. Decode the question.

Step 3. Research the details.

Step 4. Predict the answer and check the answer choices.

Like the other multistep methods, the Kaplan 4-Step Method for Reading Comprehension requires you to do most of your work before you attempt to answer the questions. It's very tempting to read the questions and immediately jump to the answer choices. Don't do this. The work you do up front will not only save you time in the long run, it will increase your chances of avoiding the tempting wrong answers.

STEP 1: READ THE PASSAGE

The first thing to do is to read the passage. This shouldn't come as a big surprise. And although you don't want to memorize or dissect the passage, you *do* need to read it. If you try to answer the questions without doing so, you're likely to make mistakes. Although you'll learn more about *how* to read the passages later, keep in mind that the main things you want to look for are the **Big Idea** and the **paragraph topics.** Additionally, you'll want to note where the passage seems to be going.

For example, if you saw the following passage (which, admittedly, is a little shorter than the average SSAT or ISEE passage), these are some of the thing you might want to note . . .

The first detective stories, written by Edgar Allan Poe and Sir Arthur Conan Doyle, emerged in the mid-nineteenth century, at a time when there was an enormous public interest in scientific progress. The newspapers of the day continually publicized the latest scientific discoveries, and scientists were acclaimed as the heroes of the age. Poe and Conan Doyle shared this fascination with the step-by-step, logical approach used by scientists in their experiments, and instilled in their detective heroes outstanding powers of scientific reasoning.

This passage is basically about detective stories . . . and science.

The character of Sherlock Holmes, for example, illustrates Conan Doyle's admiration for the scientific mind. In each case that Holmes investigates, he is able to use the most insubstantial evidence to track down his opponent. Using only his restless eye and ingenious reasoning powers, Holmes pieces together the identity of the villain from such unremarkable details as the type of cigar ashes left at the crime scene,

Holmes is an <u>example</u> of a detective hero with a brilliant scientific mind . . .

← **Poe and Conan Doyle seem to be important.**

or the kind of ink used in a handwritten letter. In fact, Holmes's painstaking attention to detail often reminds the reader of Charles Darwin's *On the Origin of the Species*, published some twenty years earlier.

← **Comparison between Holmes and Darwin.**

Again, you'll spend more time later learning how to read the passage. The point here is that the first thing you want to do is read through the entire passage noting the major themes and a few details.

Step 2: Decode the Question

Several questions will follow the passage. And *before* you can answer each question, you'll have to figure out exactly what's being asked. You need to make the question make sense to you.

Which of the following is implied by the statement that Holmes was able to identify the villain based on "unremarkable details"?

(A) Holmes's enemies left no traces at the crime scene.
(B) The character of Holmes was based on Charles Darwin.
(C) Few real detectives would have been capable of solving Holmes's cases.
(D) Holmes was particularly brilliant in powers of detection.
(E) Criminal investigation often involves tedious, time-consuming tasks.

Step 3: Research the Details

This does *not* mean that you should start rereading the passage from the beginning to find the reference to "unremarkable details." Focus your research. Where does the author mention Holmes? You should have noted when you read the passage that the author discusses Holmes in the second paragraph. So scan that paragraph for the reference to "unremarkable details." (Hint: The reference can be found in lines 18–19.)

KAPLAN EXCLUSIVE TIPS

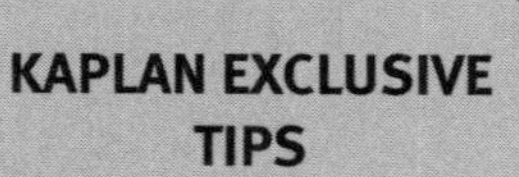

"Don't try to answer questions just from your memory."

Additionally, don't answer questions based on your memory. Go back and do the research. In other words, if you can answer questions based on your memory, you have spent too much time on the passage.

Step 4: Predict the Answer and Check the Answer Choices

When you find the detail in the passage, think about the *purpose* that it serves. Why does the author mention the "unremarkable details"? If you read the lines surrounding the phrase, you'll see that the author talks about how amazing it is that Holmes can solve mysteries based on such little evidence. Therefore, the *reason* the author mentions "unremarkable details" is to show how impressive Holmes is. Now scan your answer choices.

(A) Holmes's enemies left no traces at the crime scene.
(B) The character of Holmes was based on Charles Darwin.
(C) Few real detectives would have been capable of solving Holmes's cases.
(D) Holmes was particularly brilliant in powers of detection.
(E) Criminal investigation often involves tedious, time-consuming tasks.

Answer (D) should leap out at you.

READING SKILLS IN ACTION

Remember earlier in the lesson when we discussed the three key reading skills: summarizing, researching, and making inferences? Let's look at how these skills can help you not only to read the passage but also to answer the questions.

SUMMARIZING

For the purposes of the SSAT and ISEE, *summarizing* means capturing in a single phrase what the *entire* passage is about. Most passages will be followed by a question that deals with the passage as a whole. Wrong answers will include choices that cover only one paragraph or some other subset of the passage. You'll need to recognize the answer choice that deals with the passage as a whole. If you've thought about the Big Idea ahead of time, you're more likely to home in on the correct answer.

The four brightest moons of Jupiter were the first objects in the solar system discovered with the use of the telescope. Their proven existence played a central role in Galileo's famous argument in support of the Copernican model of the solar system, in which the planets are described as revolving around the Sun.

For several hundred years after their discovery by Galileo in 1610, scientific understanding of these moons increased fairly slowly. Observers on Earth succeeded in measuring their approximate diameters, their relative densities, and eventually some of their light-reflecting characteristics. However, the spectacular close-up photographs sent back by the 1979 *Voyager* missions forever changed our impressions of these bodies.

EXAMPLE

Which of the following best tells what this passage is about?

(A) Galileo's invention of the telescope
(B) The discovery of the Galilean moons
(C) Scientific knowledge about Jupiter's four brightest moons
(D) The Copernican model of the solar system
(E) The early history of astronomy

Only one answer choice here sums up the contents of both paragraphs. (B) is just a detail. (A) cannot be correct because Galileo's telescope is not even mentioned. (D) is mentioned only in the first paragraph and is a distortion of the author's point. (E) is too broad in scope.

Only (C) summarizes the entire passage. The passage deals with scientific knowledge about Jupiter's four brightest moons. The four moons are the first thing mentioned in the first paragraph, and the rest of the first paragraph discusses the role they played for Galileo. The second paragraph deals with how the moons were perceived by scientists throughout history. In sum, both paragraphs deal with scientific knowledge about these moons.

Researching

Researching essentially means knowing *where* to look for the details. Generally, if you note your paragraph topics, you should be in pretty good shape to find the details. Once you know where to look, just scan for key phrases found in the question.

A human body can survive without water for several days and without food for as much as several weeks. If breathing stops for as little as three to six minutes, however, death is likely. All animals require a constant supply of oxygen to the body tissues, and especially to the heart or brain. In the human body, the respiratory system performs this function by delivering air containing oxygen to the blood.

Breathing is the most urgent human bodily function.

But respiration in large animals possessing lungs involves more than just breathing. It is a complex process that delivers oxygen to internal tissues while eliminating waste carbon dioxide produced by cells. More specifically, respiration involves two processes known as bulk flow and diffusion. Oxygen and carbon dioxide are moved in bulk through the respiratory and circulatory systems; gaseous diffusion occurs at different points across thin tissue membranes.

Respiration in large animals is a complex process.

Take a look at the previous passage and paragraph topics. The paragraph topics are very general; they just note the gist of the paragraphs. If you saw the following questions, would you know where to find the answers?

EXAMPLE

Which bodily function, according to the passage, is least essential to the survival of the average human being?

(A) Eating
(B) Drinking
(C) Breathing
(D) Blood circulation
(E) The oxygen supply

The first paragraph deals with bodily functions. Lines 2–3 note that food is most expendable.

EXAMPLE

Which part of an animal's body is responsible for producing waste carbon dioxide?

(A) The internal tissues
(B) The circulatory systems
(C) The tissue membranes
(D) The bloodstream
(E) The cells

The second paragraph deals with the complex details of respiration. Carbon dioxide is mentioned in lines 14–15.

Making Inferences

Making an inference means looking for something that is strongly implied but not stated explicitly. In other words, making an inference means *reading between the lines*. What did the author *almost* say, but not say exactly?

Inferences will not stray too far from the language of the text. Wrong answers on Inference questions will often fall beyond the subject matter of the passage.

Children have an amazing talent for learning vocabulary. Between the ages of one and seventeen, the average person learns the meaning of about 80,000 words—about 14 per day. Dictionaries and traditional classroom vocabulary lessons only account for part of this spectacular knowledge growth. More influential are individuals' reading habits and their interaction with people whose vocabularies are larger than their own. Reading shows students how words are used in sentences. Conversation offers several extra benefits that make vocabulary learning engaging—it supplies visual information, offers frequent repetition of new words, and gives students the chance to ask questions.

EXAMPLE

The author of the passage most likely believes that a child is most receptive to learning the meaning of new words at which time?

(A) When the child reaches high school age
(B) When the child is talking to other students
(C) When the child is assigned vocabulary exercises
(D) When the child is regularly told that he or she needs to improve
(E) When vocabulary learning is made interesting

This short passage discusses how children learn vocabulary. The question asks when children are *most* receptive to learning new words. No sentence in the passage states that "children are *most* receptive to learning new words . . ." However, in lines 6–9, the author mentions that reading and conversation are particularly helpful. Lines 10–13 note how conversation makes vocabulary engaging. This is consistent with (E). Nothing in the passage suggests that children learn more at high school age, (A). (B) might be tempting, but it is too specific: There's no reason to believe that talking to students is more helpful than talking to anyone else. (C) contradicts the passage, and (D) is never mentioned at all.

At this point, you have a lot of tools to help you read passages and approach questions. It's a good idea to have a solid understanding of what the questions are, what types of questions you'll see, and how to best approach each one. There are three basic question types in the Reading Comprehension section: **Main Idea, Detail,** and **Inference** questions.

Since you can't exactly deal with questions unless you have an accompanying passage, take one or two minutes to read the following passage. As usual, mark it up. Read it with the goal of answering questions afterwards.

The first truly American art movement was formed by a group of landscape painters that emerged in the early nineteenth century called the Hudson River School. The first works in this style were created by Thomas Cole, Thomas Doughty, and Asher Durand, a trio of painters who worked during the 1820s in the Hudson River Valley and surrounding locations. Heavily influenced by European Romanticism, these painters set out to convey the remoteness and splendor of the American wilderness. The strongly nationalistic tone of their paintings caught the spirit of the times, and within a generation the movement had mushroomed to include landscape painters from all over the United States. Canvases celebrating such typically American scenes as Niagara Falls, Boston Harbor, and the expansion of the railroad into rural Pennsylvania were greeted with enormous popular acclaim.

One factor contributing to the success of the Hudson River School was the rapid growth of American nationalism in the early nineteenth century. The War of 1812 had given the United States a new sense of pride in its identity, and as the nation continued to grow, there was a desire to compete with Europe on both economic and cultural grounds. The vast panoramas of the Hudson River School fit the bill perfectly by providing a new movement in art that was unmistakably American in origin. The Hudson River School also arrived at a time when writers in the United States were turning their attention to the wilderness as a unique aspect of their nationality. The Hudson River

School profited from this nostalgia because they effectively represented the continent the way it used to be. The view that the American character was formed by the frontier experience was widely held, and many writers were concerned about the future of a country that was becoming increasingly urbanized.

In keeping with this nationalistic spirit, even the painting style of the Hudson River School exhibited a strong sense of American identity. Although many of the artists studied in Europe, their paintings show a desire to be free of European artistic rules. Regarding the natural landscape as a direct manifestation of God, the Hudson River School painters attempted to record what they saw as accurately as possible. Unlike European painters who brought to their canvases the styles and techniques of centuries, they sought neither to embellish nor to idealize their scenes, portraying nature with the care and attention to detail of naturalists.

Hopefully, you understood that this passage was about why the Hudson River School became so successful. You should have also noted that the second paragraph addresses how American nationalism contributed to the success of the Hudson River School and the third paragraph discusses how nationalist sentiment was evident in the Hudson River School painting style.

MAIN IDEA QUESTIONS

A **Main Idea** question asks you to summarize the topic of the passage.

Main Idea questions are pretty easy to recognize. They will always ask something general about the passage.

Look for the answer choice that summarizes the entire passage. Rule out choices that are too broad or too narrow.

EXAMPLE

Which of the following best tells what this passage is about?

(A) The history of American landscape painting
(B) Why an art movement caught the public imagination
(C) How European painters influenced the Hudson River School
(D) Why writers began to romanticize the American wilderness
(E) The origins of nationalism in the United States

Do you see which one of these answers describes the entire passage without being too broad or too narrow?

(A) is too broad, as is (E). The passage is not about all American landscape painting; it's about the Hudson River School. Nationalism in the United States is much larger than the role of nationalism in a particular art movement. (C) and (D) are too narrow. European painters did influence the Hudson River School painters, but that wasn't the point of the whole passage. Similarly, writers are mentioned in paragraph 2, but the passage is about an art movement. Only (B) captures the essence of the passage—it's about an art movement that caught the public imagination.

DETAIL QUESTIONS

Detail questions are straightforward—all you've got to do is locate the relevant information in the passage. The key strategy is to **research** the details by relating facts, figures, and names in the question to a *specific* paragraph.

EXAMPLE

Which of the following is not mentioned as one of the reasons for the success of the Hudson River School?

(A) American nationalism increased after the War of 1812.
(B) Americans were nostalgic about the frontier.
(C) Writers began to focus on the wilderness.
(D) The United States wanted to compete with Europe.
(E) City dwellers became concerned about environmental pollution.

Note how the Detail question asks about what is specifically mentioned—or not mentioned.

Scan the passage words or phrases in the answer choices. When you find the references, cross out the answer choices that do appear in the passage. The one left over will be the correct answer.

Four of the five answer choices are mentioned explicitly in the passage. (A) is mentioned in lines 18–22. (B) appears in line 31. (C) shows up in lines 28–29. (D) is mentioned in line 23. Only (E) does not appear in the passage.

Inference Questions

An **Inference** question, like a **Detail** question, asks you to find relevant information in the passage. But once you've located the details, you have to go one step further: You have to figure out the underlying point of a particular phrase or example. Use your inference skills to figure out the author's point. The answer will not be stated, but it will be *strongly implied.*

EXAMPLE

Which of the following best describes what is suggested by the statement that the Hudson River School paintings "fit the bill perfectly" (lines 25–26)?

(A) The paintings depicted famous battle scenes.
(B) The paintings were very successful commercially.
(C) The paintings reflected a new pride in the United States.
(D) The paintings were favorably received in Europe.
(E) The paintings were accurate in their portrayal of nature.

"Suggested" is a classic Inference clue. If something is "suggested," it is not stated outright.

Read the lines surrounding the quote. Summarize the author's point in your mind before you check the answer choices.

First, read the lines surrounding the quote to put the quote in context. Paragraph 2 talks about American pride; that's why Hudson River School paintings "fit the bill." Hudson River School paintings were about America. (C) summarizes the point nicely. Note how this question revolves around the interplay between main idea and details. This detail strengthens the topic of the paragraph, the growing sense of nationalism in America. (A) superficially relates to the War of 1812 but doesn't answer the question. (B), (D), and (E) are way off base.

A Reminder about Timing

Plan to spend approximately one minute reading the passage and roughly a minute to a minute and a half on each question. When you first start practicing, you'll probably find yourself spending more time than that on the passages. That's OK. However, you need to pay attention to your timing and cut the time down to around a minute. If you don't, it will hurt you in the long run.

A WORD ABOUT SCIENCE PASSAGES

"At least one reading passage may deal with a scientific or technical topic. You will NOT be tested on any outside science knowledge, so do not answer the questions based on anything other than the information contained in the passage."

PRACTICE QUESTIONS

Almost everyone enjoys hearing some kind of live music. But few of us realize the complex process that goes into designing the acoustics of concert and lecture halls. In the design of any building where audibility of sound is a major consideration, architects have to carefully match the space and materials they use to the intended purpose of the venue. One problem is that the intensity of sound may build too quickly in an enclosed space. Another problem is that only part of the sound we hear in any large room or auditorium comes directly from the source. Much of it reaches us a fraction of a second later after it has been reflected off the walls, ceiling, and floor as reverberated sound. How much each room reverberates depends upon both its size and the ability of its contents to absorb sound. Too little reverberation can make music sound thin and weak; too much can blur the listener's sense of where one note stops and the next begins.

Consequently, the most important factor in acoustic design is the time it takes for these reverberations to die down altogether, called the reverberation time.

1. Which of the following is the main topic of this passage?

   (A) The challenges of an architect's job
   (B) The differences between speech and music
   (C) The experience of hearing live music
   (D) The role of reverberation in acoustic design
   (E) The construction of large buildings

2. The passage suggests that the "complex process" of acoustic design (line 2) is

   (A) not widely appreciated by the public.
   (B) really a matter of listener sensitivity.
   (C) wholly dependent on the choice of construction materials.
   (D) an engineer's problem, not an architect's.
   (E) most difficult in concert hall construction.

3. According to the passage, audibility of sound is influenced by which of the following factors?

   I. The type of materials used to construct a building
   II. The reflection of sound off a room's ceiling or walls
   III. The size and purpose of a particular room or space

   (A) I only
   (B) II only
   (C) I and II only
   (D) II and III only
   (E) I, II, and III

4. According to the passage, too little reverberation in a concert hall can result in

   (A) a rapid increase in the volume of sound.
   (B) the blurring of details in a piece of music.
   (C) a quiet and insubstantial quality of sound.
   (D) confusion among a listening audience.
   (E) an inaccurate estimate of its reverberation time.

5. Which of the following does the author regard as the most significant consideration in the design of a concert hall?

   (A) An appreciation for music
   (B) An understanding of reverberation time
   (C) The choice of building materials
   (D) The purpose of the venue
   (E) The audience capacity

PRACTICE QUESTION ANSWERS

This passage is a discussion of the challenge of proper acoustic design of concert and lecture halls. The author pays special attention to the problem of fine-tuning reverberated sound, which is the sound that comes to the listener after it has been reflected off the walls, ceiling, and floor.

1. D

Lines 14–22 focus on reverberation, which the author describes as the "most important factor in acoustic design" at the end of the passage.

2. A

Choice (A) is the correct answer because the author says that "few of us realize the complex process that goes into designing the acoustics of concert and lecture halls."

3. E

All three options are mentioned in the passage as factors that affect the acoustics of a building, so (E) is the right answer.

4. C

According to the passage, too little reverberation can make sound thin and weak.

5. B

The final sentence of the passage says that the most important factor in acoustic design is the reverberation time, which makes (B) correct.

CHAPTER 9: THE ESSAY

Both the SSAT and ISEE (all levels) require an essay, though neither one is graded. So why do you need to write it? Well, the essay is a great way for schools to see how you express yourself. The rest of the test tells them how well you perform on a series of standard tasks, but the essay is the one part of the exam where you get to shine as an individual. Schools look closely at your essay, so think of it as part of your application and take it seriously.

So, what do you need to know to write an essay that will stand out? Really, only a few key things. First and most important, stick to the topic. Second, write clearly and logically. And finally, proofread your essay before you finish. Even if you think you have been very careful, you'll undoubtedly find things that you'll want to fix or change.

INTRODUCTION TO THE ESSAY

There are five important things to know about the essay:

1. You'll need to organize your thoughts quickly (you'll have 25 minutes on the SSAT and 30 minutes on the ISEE to write a complete essay).
2. Your essay is limited to two pages.
3. Essay topics will be easy to grasp.
4. What you say is more important than using perfect grammar.
5. Your essay will not be graded.

WHAT'S WRONG WITH THIS PICTURE?

Writing a good essay means following a few key rules about writing. Take a look at the following paragraph and think about what's wrong with it. Use the space below to jot down the problems you notice.

Sample Topic: No good deed goes unpunished.

It always bothers me when people talk about punishment. It's not fair. I mean, there are some kids out there who do really good things, even though people don't notice them. In my opinion, everyone spends too much time talking about whether or not there is enough punishment in the world. We should really be talking about more important things like the environment . . .

PLEASE JUST ANSWER THE QUESTION, MA'AM.

"The Golden Rule of essay writing is to stick to the topic. You don't need to be very creative; all you need to do is stay on course and write clearly, giving examples to support your points."

Common Pitfalls in Essay Writing

What's wrong with the paragraph you just read? The biggest problem is that it goes off topic. Granted, you're only seeing the beginning of the essay, but you can tell from the way it ends that the author is about to go off on a tangent about the environment instead of discussing the topic. Remember, *always* stay on course.

What else is wrong with the sample paragraph? You might have noticed that it sounds very casual, almost like a conversation. Phrases such as "I mean" and "In my opinion" give the essay a tone that's too familiar and too emotional. While you always want to present your opinion, you should do it in a detached, formal way, as if writing a newspaper article. Try to avoid "I" statements in your essay writing.

How can you avoid making these types of mistakes? How can you make sure you don't get sidetracked while you write or repeat yourself? Kaplan has an easy method that you should follow when you write your essay. By following each and every step, you'll be guaranteed to create an organized, clear essay.

KAPLAN 4-STEP METHOD FOR WRITING

Step 1. Brainstorm.

Step 2. Make an outline.

Step 3. Write your essay.

Step 4. Proofread.

The Kaplan Method might sound pretty general, a lot like the essays you've written for school. In fact, the essay is the part of the test that most closely resembles the work you do in school. However, the essay follows a much more specific format than most essays assigned in school, and you don't have a lot of time to do it, so it's very important that you follow all four steps. Let's break them down.

Step 1: Brainstorm

When you start to brainstorm for ideas, first think about the topic. With the sample topic No good deed goes unpunished, your thinking might go like this: I believe that people are rewarded for good deeds, not punished. Okay, what examples can I use to support this point of view?

It's important that you're clear in your head about what your stance is *before* you start to organize your essay. Once you start to put your examples together, you don't want to have to go back and figure out what you're trying to show.

Step 2: Make an Outline

Once you've decided on your topic or opinion, the next step is to write an outline. Come up with three examples to support your points or opinion.

Next, decide the best order in which to present your examples. Is there a logical order to lay out your ideas? How do you want to start your essay? How do you want to end it? Make some notes on your scratch paper so when you start to write, you can glance at them to keep you on track and writing quickly.

Step 3: Write Your Essay

Now you have to write the essay. Follow your outline carefully, but be flexible. Maybe you'll think of another great idea midway through your writing. Should you ignore it, or should you substitute it for the third example you had planned to include? If you think it's better than what you originally came up with, go ahead and write about it instead. Just make sure that any deviation you make from your outline is in fact an improvement over the original idea.

WHAT WAS I THINKING?

"Even if you're feeling rushed, don't skip the Outlining step. Planning your essay will make the entire writing process easier and faster, and it will ensure that your writing is well organized. Remember, wear a watch on test day so you can keep a handle on your pacing."

Step 4: Proofread

Wrap up your writing five minutes before the end of your allotted time. Give your essay a good read-through, making sure you haven't made any spelling mistakes, written any run-on sentences, or forgotten to capitalize a proper name. You won't be able to make any huge changes at this point—after all, you only have five minutes left—but you do want to make sure that you haven't made any egregious errors.

PACING

How much time should you spend on each step? Use your watch and this guideline as you write. You want to give yourself sufficient time for each step, because planning and proofreading will make your essay much stronger. Use the following guidelines for timing:

	SSAT	ISEE
Outlining/ Planning	5 minutes	5 minutes
Writing	15 minutes	20 minutes
Proofreading	5 minutes	5 minutes
Total time:	**25 minutes**	**30 minutes**

BRAINSTORMING IN ACTION

When you get to the essay section, the last thing you want to happen is a *brain freeze*. You know the feeling: You look at the page, you see the words, your brain doesn't register, you stare into space . . . you can't think of a thing to write about.

How do you avoid such a situation? One of the best ways to make sure your brain is in gear and ready to brainstorm on the spot is to practice doing it. Take a look at the following statements. If it is an "agree or disagree" prompt, decide what position you would take and think of three examples you would present in support of your opinion. If it is a "describe" or "explain" prompt, pick your topic and think of three examples you would use to explain or describe your topic. Give yourself about five minutes to do each one.

Sample Topic 1: Free speech on the Internet should be protected at all costs.

Sample Topic 2: We learn more from our mistakes than our successes.

Sample Topic 3: Write about your fondest memory.

SHOW, DON'T TELL

You've probably heard the saying that good writing *shows* rather than *tells*. What does that mean, and what do examples have to do with it?

Take the statement "You can't teach an old dog new tricks." Say you wanted to disagree with it. You could explain why you believe the statement isn't true, what you think about teaching and age, and so forth. Or, you could use examples that *illustrate* the same point. You could discuss the fact that retired people now use the Internet on a regular basis. The fact that people generally considered *old* by society are adapting to a *new* technology in large numbers serves to show that you can, in fact, teach an old dog new tricks.

READING TIPS

"When you read the newspaper, look at the editorial page. You'll see how writers argue their opinions on a variety of topics and what kinds of examples they use. And you might learn something interesting in the process, too."

What makes a good example? A good example illustrates the point you want to make. In addition, it comes from the world at large rather than from your personal life. While it may be true that your grandmother emails you, it's more powerful to say that many retirees use the Internet every day.

If you're not doing so already, try reading the newspaper on a regular basis. Not only will you know more about what's going on in the world and be ready with great examples for your essays, you'll also improve your vocabulary, which will improve your performance on the Verbal section of your test.

JUST THE FACTS

What do you need to do as you write your essay?

- Develop and organize your ideas.
- Use three paragraphs.
- Use appropriate examples.
- Write in standard English.
- Stick to the topic.
- Use proper spelling, grammar, and punctuation.

PRACTICE ESSAY

Work through this topic as though it were the real thing. Brainstorm your ideas, make an outline, write, and proofread. Time yourself (25 minutes if you're taking the SSAT and 30 minutes if you're taking the ISEE).

Essay Topic: Voting is such an important responsibility that all citizens should be required to vote in every election.

Step 1. Brainstorm.

Brainstorm in the space provided below. Do you agree or disagree? What examples might you use to support your argument? (Remember, give yourself only a few minutes to do this!)

Step 2. Make an outline.

Write your outline here. Keep your essay to three paragraphs. Paragraph 1 gives your introduction and an example. Paragraph 2 gives another example, and paragraph 3 gives your final example and your conclusion.

Paragraph 1

Paragraph 2

Paragraph 3

Step 3. Write your essay.

Write your essay below. Give yourself 15 minutes if you're taking the SSAT and 20 minutes if you're taking the ISEE.

Step 4. Proofread.

Go back to your essay and read through it again. Does it make sense? Have you made any spelling or grammar errors? Fix them. Get used to making corrections clearly on your page, since that's how you will do it the day of the test.

CHAPTER 10: INTRODUCTION TO SSAT AND ISEE MATH

Before we dive into the actual math, let's take a step back and think about how to approach math problems in general. You've done math before. In all likelihood, you've already been exposed to most of the math concepts you'll see on your private school admissions test. This begs the question as to why you need to approach SSAT or ISEE math differently than you approach any other math.

The answer is, it's not that you have to do the math *differently*; it's just that you have to do it *deliberately*. You'll be under a lot of time pressure when you take your test, so you need to use your time well.

HOW TO APPROACH SSAT OR ISEE MATH

Ultimately, the best way to take control of your testing experience is to approach every math question the same way. This doesn't mean you'll *solve* every problem the same way. Rather it means that you'll use the same process to *decide* how to solve, or even whether to solve, each problem.

Read Through the Question

Okay, this may seem a little too obvious. Of course, you're going to read the question. How else can you solve the problem? In reality, this isn't quite as obvious as it seems. The point here is that you need to read the entire question carefully before you start solving. When you don't read carefully, it's incredibly easy to make careless mistakes. Consider the following problem:

EXAMPLE

For what positive value of x does $\frac{4}{3} = \frac{x^2}{27}$?

(A) 3

(B) 6

(C) 12

(D) 18

(E) 36

It's crucial that you pay close attention to precisely what the question is asking. The question contains a classic trap that's very easy to fall into if you don't read it carefully. Did you notice how easy it would be to solve for x^2 instead of x? Yes, this would be careless, but it's easy to be careless when you're working quickly.

There are other reasons to read the whole question before you start solving the problem. One is that you may save yourself some work. If you start to answer too quickly, you may assume that a problem is more difficult than it actually is. Or you might assume that it is *less* difficult than it actually is and skip a necessary step or two.

Another reason to read carefully before answering is that you probably shouldn't solve *every* question on your first pass. Taking control of your test experience means deciding which questions to answer, which to save for later, and which to skip (unless you're taking the ISEE, in which case you should NEVER skip a question).

Decide Whether to Do the Question or Skip It for Now

Each time you approach a new math problem, you have the option of answering it immediately or putting it aside. You have to make a decision each time about how best to use your time. You have three options.

1. **If you can solve the question relatively quickly and efficiently, do it!** This is the best option.
2. **If you think you can solve it but that it will take you a long time, circle the number in your test booklet and go back to it later.** Remember that when you go back to the problems you have skipped the first time, you'll want to try your best to fill in an answer. Don't underestimate your ability to eliminate wrong answers even when you don't know how to solve. Every time you rule out a wrong answer choice, you increase your chances of guessing correctly.
3. **If you have no idea what to do, skip the question and circle it.** Save your time for the questions you *can* do.

EXAMPLE

Tamika, Becky, and Kym were investors in a new restaurant. Tamika and Becky each invested one-half as much as Kym invested. If the total investment made was $5,200, how much did Kym invest?

(A) $900
(B) $1,300
(C) $1,800
(D) $2,100
(E) $2,600

Different test takers will have different reactions to this question. Some students may quickly see the algebra—or the backdoor method for solving this problem—and do the math. Others may see a word problem and run screaming from the room. This approach is not recommended. However, if you know that you habitually have difficulty with algebra word problems, you may choose to save this problem for later or make an educated guess.

Here's the algebra, by the way. Kym, Tamika, and Becky contributed a total of $5,200. You can represent this algebraically as $K + T + B = \$5{,}200$. Since Tamika and Becky each contributed half as much as Kym, you can represent these relationships as follows:

$$T = \frac{1}{2}K$$

$$B = \frac{1}{2}K$$

Now, substitute variables so that you can solve the equation.

$$K + T + B = 5{,}200$$

$$K + \frac{1}{2}K + \frac{1}{2}K = 5{,}200$$

$$2K = 5{,}200$$

$$K = 2{,}600 \text{ (E)}$$

Alternatively, you can use the backsolving strategy. Start with **(C)**. If Kym invested $1,800, and Tamika and Becky each invested half of that, or $900 each, then the total investment would have been $1,800 + $900 + $900 = $3,600. But the total investment was $5,200, so our answer isn't large enough. We can rule out **(C)**–and **(A)** and **(B)**.

Now try **(D)**: $2,100 + $1,050 + $1,050 = $4,200. This is still not enough money. Therefore, the answer must be **(E)**.

If you want to check, $2,600 + $1,300 + $1,300 = $5,200, which is the correct total investment. (E) works and is the correct answer.

If you choose to tackle the problem, look for the fastest method.

EXAMPLE

Jenna is now x years old, and Amy is 3 years younger than Jenna. In terms of x, how old will Amy be in 4 years?

(A) $x - 1$

(B) x

(C) $x + 1$

(D) $x + 4$

(E) $2x + 1$

Here is the algebraic solution. If Jenna is x years old, then Amy is $x - 3$ years old, since Amy is 3 years younger than Jenna. So, in 4 years, Amy will be $(x - 3) + 4$, or $x + 1$. The correct answer is (C).

Here is the picking numbers solution. Suppose that $x = 10$. Then Jenna is now 10 years old. Amy is now 7 years old because Amy is 3 years younger than Jenna. In 4 years, Amy will be 11. Now plug 10 for x into all of the answer choices and see which one equals 11. You can eliminate any answer choice that does not equal 11. Since only (C), $x + 1$, equals 11, it must be correct.

With the method of picking numbers, it sometimes happens that more than one answer choice gives you the correct result for the particular number or numbers that you choose. When that happens, go back and pick another number(s) to eliminate the remaining incorrect answer choices.

The lesson here is that you have to know your own strengths. Again, in case you missed the point, *know your strengths and use them to your advantage.*

Some people *see* algebra. Others have a harder time with it. The same is true for geometry, word problems, etc. There's often more than one way to solve a question. The *best* method is the method that will get you the correct answer accurately and quickly.

HELPFUL HINT

"When you skip a question, circle it in your test booklet so that it will be easy to spot if you have time to go back."

Remember, only guess on the SSAT if you can eliminate at least one answer choice. But on the ISEE, don't leave any answers blank. Since there's no penalty for wrong answers, there is no harm in guessing. Of course, the fact that random guessing won't hurt you does not mean that you shouldn't be strategic about guessing. Remember, every answer choice you rule out increases your odds of guessing correctly.

EXAMPLE

What is the greatest common factor of 95 and 114 ?

(A) 1
(B) 5
(C) 6
(D) 19
(E) 38

If you couldn't remember how to find the greatest common factor or were running out of time on the test and wanted to save your time for other questions, you should be able to eliminate at least one answer choice pretty easily. Do you see which one?

Since all multiples of 5 end in 5 or zero, 5 cannot be a factor of 114. Therefore, (B) must be incorrect. Eliminate it and then guess.

Pick Numbers

Sometimes a math problem can appear more difficult than it actually is because it's general or abstract. You can make it more concrete—and easier—by temporarily substituting numbers for the variables. This "picking numbers" strategy can help make the math easier.

EXAMPLE

$3a(2b + 2) =$

(A) $2b + 3a$

(B) $5ab + 2b$

(C) $5ab + 2a + 1$

(D) $6ab + 2a$

(E) $6ab + 6a$

The algebra in this question is pretty straightforward. According to the distributive property, $3a(2b + 2) = (3a)(2b) + (3a)(2) = 6ab + 6a$, or choice (E). Most test takers will probably do the algebra to solve the question.

However, if you have trouble with algebra or simply find that it takes you a long time, you can approach the problem another way. Pick simple numbers for a and b and plug them into the expression $3a(2b + 2)$. If $a = 2$ and $b = 3$, then $3a(2b + 2) = (3)(2)[2(3) + 2] = 6(6 + 2) = 48$. Now you know that if $a = 2$ and $b = 3$, the expression equals 48.

Once you know this, simply plug 2 in for a and 3 in for b in each of the answer choices. Any answer choice that does not equal 48 can be eliminated. Since only (E) equals 48, (E) is the answer.

(A) $2b + 3a = 2(3) + 3(2) = 12$

(B) $5ab + 2b = 5(2)(3) + 2(3) = 36$

(C) $5ab + 2a + 1 = 5(2)(3) + 2(2) + 1 = 35$

(D) $6ab + 2a = 6(2)(3) + 2(2) = 40$

(E) $6ab + 6a = 6(2)(3) + 6(2) = 48$

If two or more answer choices had come out to 48, you would have had to do a little more work. You would have had to pick new numbers for a and b, come up with a new value, and then plug those numbers into the answer choices that came out the same the first time.

In other words, if (B) and (E) had both equaled 48, you could have made $a = 3$ and $b = 4$, discovered that the expression $3a(2b + 2)$ equals 90, and then plugged 3 and 4 into only choices (B) and (E) to determine which one equaled 90.

WORD PROBLEMS

Picking numbers can be extremely helpful when the answer choices to a word problem contain variables. Remember this problem?

BE WARY OF PICKING ZERO OR 1

"Pick small numbers that are easy to use, but not zero or 1. Even though they're small, easy numbers, they often give several "possibly correct" answers."

EXAMPLE

Jenna is now x years old, and Amy is 3 years younger than Jenna. In terms of x, how old will Amy be in 4 years?

(A) $x - 1$
(B) x
(C) $x + 1$
(D) $x + 4$
(E) $2x + 1$

As you saw earlier, there's more than one way to solve this problem. Some test takers will find it easier to solve this question by working with algebraic expressions. Others may feel that this will slow them down. Picking a number for x may be faster and easier.

If you say that $x = 10$, then Jenna is 10 years old and Amy is 7, since she's three years younger. In four years, Amy will be 11. Once you have this value, plug in 10 for x in each of the answer choices to see which ones equal 11. Those answer choices that don't equal 11 can be eliminated.

(A) $10 - 1 = 9$
(B) 10
(C) $10 + 1 = 11$
(D) $10 + 4 = 14$
(E) $2(10) + 1 = 21$

Only (C) equals 11, so (C) must be correct.

PERCENT INCREASE/DECREASE PROBLEMS

If you see a problem that deals with percents, picking 100 is the easiest and quickest way to solve.

EXAMPLE

If the price of a stock decreases by 20 percent, and then by an additional 25 percent, by what percent has the price decreased from its original value?

(A) 40%
(B) 45%
(C) 50%
(D) 55%
(E) 60%

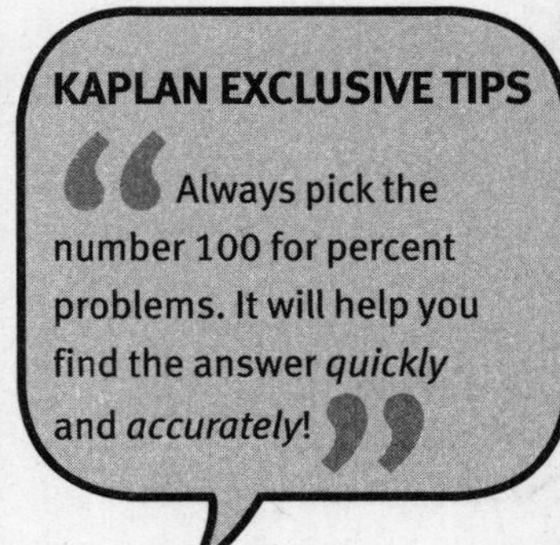

KAPLAN EXCLUSIVE TIPS
"Always pick the number 100 for percent problems. It will help you find the answer *quickly* and *accurately*!"

Make the original price of the stock \$100. The initial 20 percent decrease brings the price down to \$80. (Twenty percent of 100 is 20.) Twenty-five percent of 80 or one-quarter of \$80 is \$20, so the stock price is decreased by an additional \$20, bringing the final price down to \$60. Since the price dropped from \$100 to \$60, the total decrease is \$40 or 40 percent of the original price. (A) is the correct answer.

You may have been able to solve this problem by setting up algebraic equations, but picking 100 is easier and faster here.

Backsolve

Backsolving is another tool to help you get a math answer more quickly. What this means is that you can work backward from the answer choices. Backsolving will work only if your answer choices are all numbers (and they don't include variables).

Here's how it works. When answer choices are numbers—i.e., not variables—you can expect them to be arranged from *small to large* or *large to small.* The test maker does not get creative with the order of the answer choices. What you do is to start with the *middle* answer choice and plug it directly into the problem. If it works, you're set. If it doesn't, you can usually determine whether to try a larger or smaller answer choice. Look at the following problem and explanation.

EXAMPLE

Three consecutive multiples of 20 have a sum of 300. What is the greatest of these numbers?

(A) 60
(B) 80
(C) 100
(D) 120
(E) 140

SPEED TIP

"Always start with the middle answer choice when backsolving. If it's too small, move to the bigger ones."

Begin with the middle answer choice. If 100 is the greatest of the three numbers, the three numbers must be 100, 80, and 60, and 100 + 80 + 60 = 240. The correct three numbers will add up to 300, so the greatest of these numbers must be greater than 100. Try answer (D). If 120 is the greatest, the three numbers must be 120, 100, and 80, and 120 + 100 + 80 = 300. Choice (D) is correct.

It's worth noting that if (D) had also given you a sum less than 300, you would not have had to check choice (E). Think about it. If the numbers are arranged from small to large and the second-largest number gives you an answer that is too small, you know that the largest number has to be correct.

A WORD ABOUT CALCULATORS

This is an easy one. You *cannot* use a calculator on the SSAT or ISEE. Leave your calculator home. End of story.

The rest of the Math chapters in this book deal with Math Content review. Some of this will be familiar; some may be less familiar. Take a look at all of it, but spend more time with the subjects that are less familiar. Even if you don't need to review a particular subject, however, make sure you do the practice set. There's no harm in practicing extra problems.

CHAPTER 11: ARITHMETIC

On the SSAT and ISEE, **arithmetic** means more than addition and subtraction. **Arithmetic** is the umbrella term for a wide range of math concepts, including **number properties, factors, divisibility, fractions, decimals, exponents, radicals, percents, averages, ratios, proportions, rates,** and **probability.** These concepts are summarized in your Math Reference at the end of the book. This section will go over these important concepts and give you a chance to practice problems dealing with these subjects.

DEFINITIONS

Number Type	Definition	Examples
Integers	*Whole numbers including 0 and their opposites (negative whole numbers)*	–900, –3, 0, 1, 54
Fractions	*A **fraction** is a number that is written in the form $\frac{A}{B}$ where A is the numerator and B is the denominator.*	$-\frac{5}{6}, -\frac{3}{17}, \frac{1}{2}, \frac{899}{901}$
Improper fractions	*An **improper fraction** is a fraction whose value is greater than 1 (or less than –1).*	$-\frac{65}{64}, \frac{9}{8}, \frac{57}{10}$
Mixed numbers	*An improper fraction can be converted into a **mixed number**. A mixed number has an integer part and a fraction part.*	$-1\frac{1}{64}, 1\frac{1}{8}, 5\frac{7}{10}$
Positive/Negative	*Numbers greater than 0 are **positive numbers**; numbers less than 0 are **negative**. 0 is neither positive nor negative.*	Positive: $\frac{7}{8}, 1, 5, 900$ Negative: –64, –40, –11, $-\frac{6}{13}$

Number Type	Definition	Examples
Even/Odd	*An **even number** is an integer that is a multiple of 2. Even numbers end in 0, 2, 4, 6, or 8.* *An **odd number** is an integer that is not a multiple of 2. Odd numbers end in 1, 3, 5, 7, or 9.*	Even numbers: –8, –2, 0, 4, 12, 188 Odd numbers: –17, –1, 3, 9, 457
Prime numbers	*A **prime number** is an integer greater than 1 that has exactly two factors: 1 and itself. 2 is the only even prime number.*	2, 3, 5, 7, 11, 59, 83
Composite numbers	*A **composite number** is an integer greater than 1 that has more than two factors.*	12, 35, 84
Consecutive numbers	*Numbers that follow one after another, in order, without skipping any.*	Consecutive integers: 3, 4, 5, 6 Consecutive even integers: 2, 4, 6, 8, 10 Consecutive multiples of 9: 9, 18, 27, 36
Factors	*A positive integer that divides evenly into a given number with no remainder.*	The complete list of factors of 12: 1, 2, 3, 4, 6, 12
Multiples	*A number that a given number will divide into with no remainder.*	Some multiples of 12: 0, 12, 24, 60

ODDS AND EVENS

There are a few things to remember when you're dealing with odd and even numbers:

Even ± Even = Even

Even ± Odd = Odd

Odd ± Odd = Even

Even × Even = Even

Even × Odd = Even

Odd × Odd = Odd

POSITIVES AND NEGATIVES

You will not see many problems that focus specifically on positives and negatives, but you must know the basics because these concepts will show up as part of harder problems.

To **add** any two integers with the **same sign,** keep the sign and add the integers.

EXAMPLES

$$(-3) + (-8) = -11$$

$$9 + 12 = 21$$

To **add** any two integers with **opposite signs,** keep the sign of the integer further from zero, then subtract the integers, ignoring the signs.

EXAMPLES

$$3 + (-8) = -(8 - 3)$$
$$= -5$$

$$-9 + 12 = +(12 - 9)$$
$$= 3$$

To **subtract** two integers, change the subtraction sign to addition, then change the sign of the number being subtracted to its opposite.

EXAMPLES

$$(3) - (-8) = 3 + (+8)$$
$$= 11$$
$$-9 - 12 = -9 + (-12)$$
$$= -21$$

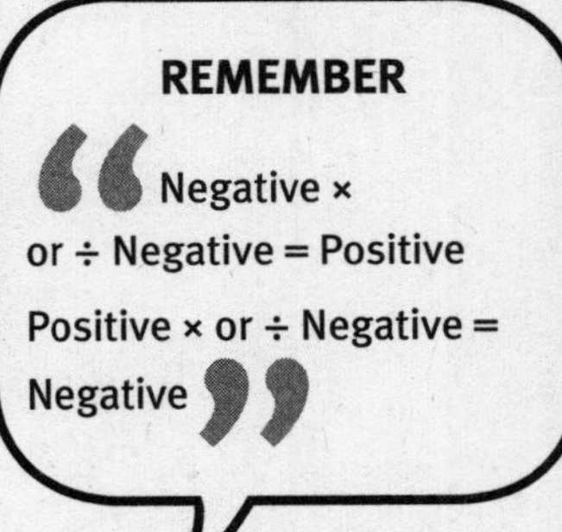

REMEMBER
Negative × or ÷ Negative = Positive
Positive × or ÷ Negative = Negative

Multiplying and **dividing** positives and negatives is like all other multiplication and division, with one catch. To figure out whether your answer is positive or negative, count the number of negatives you had to start. If you had an odd number of negatives, the answer is negative. If you had an even number of negatives, the answer is positive.

$$6 \times (-4) = -24 \text{ (1 negative} \rightarrow \text{negative product)}$$
$$(-6) \times (-4) = 24 \text{ (2 negatives} \rightarrow \text{positive product)}$$
$$(-1) \times (-6) \times (-4) = -24 \text{ (3 negatives} \rightarrow \text{negative product)}$$

Similarly,

$$-24 \div 6 = -4 \text{ (1 negative} \rightarrow \text{negative quotient)}$$
$$-24 \div (-4) = 6 \text{ (2 negatives} \rightarrow \text{positive quotient)}$$

Absolute Value

To find the **absolute value** of a number, simply find the number's distance from zero on a number line. Because distance cannot be negative, the absolute value of a number will always be greater than or equal to zero.

$|4| = 4$*

$|-4| = 4$**

*because 4 is four units from zero

**because –4 is four units from zero

When absolute value expressions contain different arithmetic operations, perform the operation inside the bars first and then find the absolute value of the result.

$$\begin{aligned} |-6 + 4| &= |-2| \\ &= 2 \end{aligned}$$

$$\begin{aligned} |(-6) \times 4| &= |-24| \\ &= 24 \end{aligned}$$

Factors and Multiples

To find the **prime factorization** of a number, keep factoring it until you are left with only prime numbers. To find the prime factorization of 168:

$$\begin{aligned} 168 &= 4 \times 42 \\ &= 4 \times 6 \times 7 \\ &= 2 \times 2 \times 2 \times 3 \times 7 \end{aligned}$$

To find the **greatest common factor (GCF)** of two integers, break down both integers into their prime factorizations and multiply all prime factors they have in common. If you're looking for the GCF of 40 and 140, first identify the prime factors of each integer.

$$\begin{aligned} 40 &= 4 \times 10 \\ &= 2 \times 2 \times 2 \times 5 \\ 140 &= 10 \times 14 \\ &= 2 \times 5 \times 2 \times 7 \\ &= 2 \times 2 \times 5 \times 7 \end{aligned}$$

Next, see what prime factors the two numbers have in common and then multiply these common factors. Both integers share two 2s and one 5, so the GCF is $2 \times 2 \times 5$ or 20.

If you need to find a **common multiple** of two integers, you can always multiply them. However, you can use prime factors to find the **least common multiple (LCM)**. To do this, multiply all of the prime factors of each integer the most amount of times as they appear. This may sound confusing, but it becomes clear once it's demonstrated. Take a look at the example to see how it works.

Common multiple of 20 and 16: $20 \times 16 = 320$

Although 320 is a common multiple of 20 and 16, it is not the least common multiple.

LCM of 20 and 16:

$$20 = 2 \times 2 \times 5$$
$$16 = 2 \times 2 \times 2 \times 2$$
$$= 2 \times 2 \times 2 \times 2 \times 5 = 80$$

Note that there are four factors of 2 in the LCM because there were four factors of 2 in 16, and that's the largest number of 2s present in either number.

THE ORDER OF OPERATIONS

There is a specific order in which arithmetic operations must be performed.

1. **Parentheses:** Simplify all operations inside parentheses first.
2. **Exponents:** Simplify any exponential expressions.
3. **Multiplication and Division:** Perform all multiplications and divisions as they occur in the problem from left to right.
4. **Addition and Subtraction:** Perform all additions and subtractions as they occur in the problem from left to right.

An easy way to help you remember this order is to use the mnemonic "Please Excuse My Dear Aunt Sally" (or **PEMDAS**). This phrase uses the first letter of each operation in the order in which it is to be performed.

$$(3 + 5)^2 - 7 + 4 = (8)^2 - 7 + 4$$
$$= 64 - 7 + 4$$
$$= 57 + 4$$
$$= 61$$

RULES FOR DIVISIBILITY

If you've forgotten—or never learned—divisibility rules, spend a little time with this chart. Even if you remember the rules, take a moment to refresh your memory. Remember, there are no easy divisibility rules for 7 and 8.

Divisible by	The Rule	EXAMPLE: 558
2	The last digit is even.	a multiple of 2 because 8 is even
3	The sum of the digits is a multiple of 3.	a multiple of 3 because 5 + 5 + 8 = 18, which is a multiple of 3
4	The last 2 digits comprise a 2-digit multiple of 4.	NOT a multiple of 4 because 58 is not a multiple of 4
5	The last digit is 5 or 0.	NOT a multiple of 5 because it doesn't end in 5 or 0
6	The last digit is even AND the sum of the digits is a multiple of 3.	a multiple of 6 because it's a multiple of both 2 and 3
9	The sum of the digits is a multiple of 9.	a multiple of 9 because 5 + 5 + 8 = 18, which is a multiple of 9
10	The last digit is 0.	NOT a multiple of 10 because it doesn't end in 0

Hint: To test for 2, 4, 5, or 10, look at the last digit or two. To test for 3, 6, or 9, add all the digits.

FRACTIONS AND DECIMALS

Generally, there are eight operations you should feel comfortable performing with fractions:

1. Simplifying fractions
2. Converting a fraction to one with a different denominator
3. Adding fractions
4. Subtracting fractions
5. Multiplying fractions
6. Dividing fractions
7. Comparing fractions
8. Converting fractions to decimals and vice versa

To **simplify a fraction,** find the GCF of the numerator and denominator of the fraction, then divide both numerator and denominator by this quantity.

EXAMPLE

Simplify $\frac{18}{30}$.

The GCF of 18 and 30 is 6, so divide both 18 and 30 by 6:

$$\begin{aligned}\frac{18}{30} &= \frac{18 \div 6}{30 \div 6}\\ &= \frac{3}{5}\end{aligned}$$

To **convert a fraction to one with a different denominator,** multiply both numerator and denominator by the same quantity.

EXAMPLE

Convert $\frac{3}{7}$ into a fraction with a denominator of 28.

Since $7 \times 4 = 28$, multiply the 3 and the 7 each by 4:

$$\begin{aligned}\frac{3}{7} &= \frac{3 \times 4}{7 \times 4}\\ &= \frac{12}{28}\end{aligned}$$

To **add and subtract fractions with the same denominator,** keep the denominator the same and add or subtract the numerators. Simplify the result if possible.

EXAMPLE

Add.

$$\begin{aligned}\frac{1}{8} + \frac{3}{8} &= \frac{4}{8}\\ &= \frac{1}{2}\end{aligned}$$

To **add and subtract fractions with the different denominators,** find the least common multiple (LCM) of the denominators, convert the fractions so they have this denominator, and then add or subtract and simplify.

EXAMPLE

Subtract.

$$\begin{aligned}\frac{7}{8} - \frac{5}{12} &= \frac{21}{24} - \frac{10}{24}\\ &= \frac{11}{24}\end{aligned}$$

To **multiply fractions,** multiply the numerators and multiply the denominators, then simplify the result. It is also possible to simplify the fractions before multiplying by canceling like factors from the numerators and denominators of the fractions:

EXAMPLE
Multiply.

$$\frac{11}{12} \times \frac{9}{22} = \frac{99}{264} \text{ OR } \frac{{}^{1}\not{11}}{{}_{4}\not{12}} \times \frac{\not{9}^{3}}{\not{22}_{2}} = \frac{3}{8}$$

$$= \frac{99 \div 3}{264 \div 3}$$

$$= \frac{33 \div 11}{88 \div 11}$$

$$= \frac{3}{8}$$

KAPLAN EXCLUSIVE TIPS

"Dividing by a fraction is the same as multiplying by its reciprocal."

To **divide fractions,** multiply the dividend (the first fraction) by the reciprocal of the divisor(the second fraction).

EXAMPLE
Divide.

$$\frac{8}{15} \div \frac{2}{3} = \frac{{}^{4}\not{8}}{{}_{5}\not{15}} \times \frac{\not{3}^{1}}{\not{2}_{1}}$$

$$= \frac{4}{5}$$

To **compare fractions,** convert both fractions to the same denominator and compare the numerators. Or find the cross-products and compare as follows.

EXAMPLE: Which is larger, $\frac{3}{4}$ or $\frac{10}{13}$?

Find the cross-products by multiplying the numerator of the first fraction by the denominator of the second, then multiplying the denominator of the first by the numerator of the second:

3×13 4×10
39   40

Because 39 is less than 40, the first fraction is less than the second. The second fraction is the larger fraction.

To **convert a fraction to a decimal**, divide the denominator into the numerator.

To convert $\frac{8}{25}$ to a decimal, divide 25 into 8.00.

$$\begin{array}{r} .32 \\ 25\overline{)8.00} \\ 0 \\ -7\,5 \\ \hline 50 \\ -50 \\ \hline 0 \end{array}$$

To **convert a decimal to a fraction,** use the place value of the digits in the decimal. Recall that beginning at the decimal point, the first place to the right is the tenths place, followed by the hundredths place, the thousandths place, the ten-thousandths place, the hundred-thousandths place, etc.

EXAMPLES

Convert the decimal 0.4 into a fraction.

Because the last decimal place is the tenths place, the decimal is four tenths, so the fraction is as well:

$$0.4 = \frac{4}{10} = \frac{2}{5}$$

Convert the decimal 0.825 into a fraction.

Because the last decimal place is the thousandths place, the decimal is eight hundred twenty-five thousandths, so the fraction is as well:

$$0.825 = \frac{825}{1,000} = \frac{165}{200} = \frac{33}{40}$$

COMMON PERCENT EQUIVALENCIES

Familiarity with the relationships among percents, decimals, and fractions can save you time on test day. Don't worry about memorizing the following chart. Simply use it to refresh your recollection of relationships you already know (e.g., 50% = 0.50 = $\frac{1}{2}$) and to familiarize yourself with some that you might not already know. To convert a decimal to a percent, multiply by 100 and add a % sign. To convert a percent to a decimal, divide by 100% (drop the percent sign and move the decimal point two spaces to the left).

Fraction	Decimal	Percent
$\frac{1}{20}$	0.05	5%
$\frac{1}{10}$	0.10	10%
$\frac{1}{8}$	0.125	12.5%

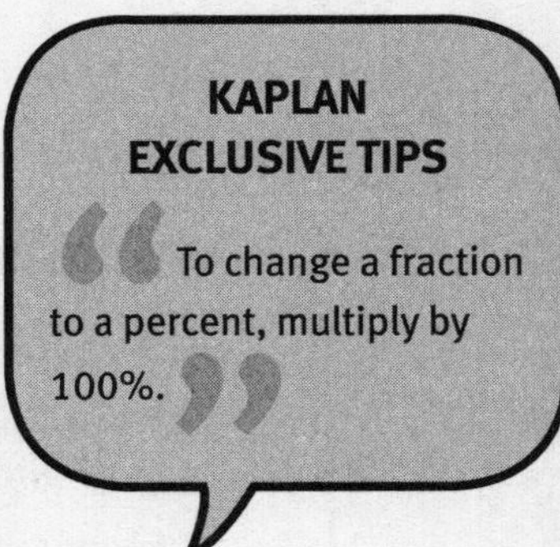

KAPLAN
EXCLUSIVE TIPS
To change a fraction to a percent, multiply by 100%.

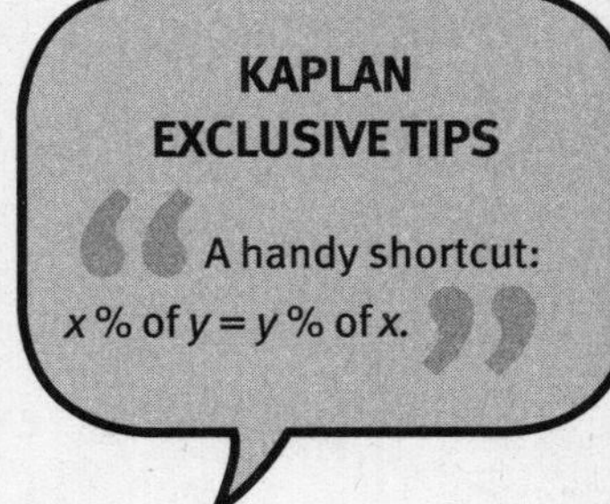

KAPLAN
EXCLUSIVE TIPS
A handy shortcut: x % of y = y % of x.

Fraction	Decimal	Percent
$\frac{1}{6}$	$0.16\overline{6}$	$16\frac{2}{3}\%$
$\frac{1}{5}$	0.20	20%
$\frac{1}{4}$	0.25	25%
$\frac{1}{3}$	$0.33\overline{3}$	$33\frac{1}{3}\%$
$\frac{3}{8}$	0.375	37.5%
$\frac{2}{5}$	0.40	40%
$\frac{1}{2}$	0.50	50%
$\frac{3}{5}$	0.60	60%
$\frac{2}{3}$	$0.66\overline{6}$	$66\frac{2}{3}\%$
$\frac{3}{4}$	0.75	75%
$\frac{4}{5}$	0.80	80%
$\frac{5}{6}$	$0.83\overline{3}$	$83\frac{1}{3}\%$
$\frac{7}{8}$	0.875	87.5%

EXPONENTS AND ROOTS

Exponents are the small raised numbers written to the right of a variable or number. They indicate the number of times that variable or number is to be used as a factor. On the SSAT or ISEE, you'll usually deal with numbers or variables that are squared, but you could see a few other concepts involving exponents.

EXAMPLES

$$2^3 = 2 \times 2 \times 2$$
$$= 8$$
$$-(3^2) = -(3 \times 3)$$
$$= -9$$
$$3(-2)^2 = 3[(-2)(-2)]$$
$$= 3(4)$$
$$= 12$$

A **square root** of a nonnegative number is a number that, when multiplied by itself, produces the given quantity. The radical sign $\sqrt{\ }$ is used to represent the positive square root of a number, so $\sqrt{25} = 5$, since $5 \times 5 = 25$.

To **add** or **subtract** radicals, make sure the numbers under the radical sign are the same. If they are, you can add or subtract the coefficients outside the radical signs.

EXAMPLE

$$2\sqrt{2}+3\sqrt{2}=5\sqrt{2}$$

$\sqrt{2}+\sqrt{3}$ cannot be combined because the quantities beneath the radical signs are not the same.

To **simplify** a radical, factor out the perfect square factor(s) from under the radical, simplify them, and put the result in front of the radical sign.

EXAMPLE

$$\sqrt{32}=\sqrt{16\times 2}=\sqrt{16}\sqrt{2}=4\sqrt{2}$$

To **multiply** or **divide** radicals, multiply (or divide) the coefficients outside the radical. Then, multiply (or divide) the numbers inside the radicals.

EXAMPLE

$$\sqrt{x}\times\sqrt{y}=\sqrt{xy}$$

$$3\sqrt{2}\times 4\sqrt{5}=12\sqrt{10}$$

$$\frac{\sqrt{x}}{\sqrt{y}}=\sqrt{\frac{x}{y}}$$

$$\frac{12\sqrt{10}}{3\sqrt{2}}=4\sqrt{5}$$

To **take the square root of a fraction,** break the fraction into two separate roots and take the square root of the numerator and the denominator.

EXAMPLE

$$\sqrt{\frac{16}{25}}=\frac{\sqrt{16}}{\sqrt{25}}=\frac{4}{5}$$

POWERS OF 10 AND SCIENTIFIC NOTATION

The exponent of a power of 10 indicates how many zeros the number would contain if it were written out. For example, $10^4 = 10{,}000$ (4 zeros) since the product of 4 factors of 10 is equal to 10,000.

When multiplying a number by a power of 10, move the decimal point to the right the same number of places as the number of zeros in that power of 10.

EXAMPLE

$0.0123 \times 10^4 = 123$ (four places to the right)

When dividing by a power of 10, move the decimal point to the left.

EXAMPLE

$43.21 \div 10^3 = 0.04321$ (three places to the left)

Multiplying by a power with a negative exponent is the same as dividing by a power with a positive exponent. Therefore, when you multiply by a number with a positive exponent, move the decimal to the right. When you multiply by a number with a negative exponent, move the decimal to the left.

EXAMPLE

$$28.5 \times 10^{-2} = 28.5 \div 10^2$$
$$= 0.285$$
$$0.36 \div 10^{-4} = 0.36 \times 10^4$$
$$= 3{,}600$$

Scientific notation is commonly used in science and mathematics as a shorthand method for writing very large or very small numbers. A number is in scientific notation if it is in the form $a \times 10^n$ where $a <$ 10 and n is an integer.

To convert a number from **standard notation to scientific notation,** simply move the decimal point in the number to the right if the exponent on 10 is a positive number and to the left if the exponent is negative.

EXAMPLE

$4.23 \times 10^6 = 4{,}230{,}000$ The decimal point is moved to the right six places.

$9.6 \times 10^{-2} = 0.096$ The decimal point is moved to the left two places.

To convert a number from **scientific notation to standard notation,** find the decimal point in the number. If there is no decimal point, put one at the end of the number. Now move the decimal point to the right or to the left until the resulting quantity is a number between 1 and 10. The number of places the decimal point moved indicates the exponent to be placed on the 10. The direction indicates the sign of the exponent; if the decimal point was moved to the left, the exponent will be positive, if the decimal point was moved to the right, the exponent will be negative.

EXAMPLE

$82{,}000{,}000{,}000 = 8.2 \times 10^{10}$ The decimal point moved from the end of 82,000,000,000 to the left 10 places.

$0.00004138 = 4.138 \times 10^{-5}$ The decimal point moved from the front of 0.00004138 to the right five places.

PERCENTS

The key to solving most fractions and percents word problems is to identify the part and the whole. Usually you'll find the **part** associated with the verb ***is/are*** and the **whole** associated with the word ***of.*** In the sentence "Half of the boys are blonds," the whole is the boys ("*of* the boys"), and the part is the blonds ("*are* blonds").

Whether you need to find the part, the whole, or the percent, use the same formula:

Part = Percent × Whole

OR

Percent = $\frac{\text{Part}}{\text{Whole}}$

Let's look at some examples.

EXAMPLE

What is 12% of 25?

Setup: Part = 0.12 × 25

Part = 3

EXAMPLE

15 is 3% of what number?

Setup: $\frac{15}{0.03} = \frac{0.03 \times \text{Whole}}{0.03}$

$500 = \text{Whole}$

EXAMPLE

45 is what percent of 9?

Setup: $\frac{45}{9} = \frac{\text{Percent} \times 9}{9}$

$5 = \text{Percent}$

Move the decimal point two places to the right to convert to a percent: 5.00 = 500%.

To increase or decrease a number by a given percent, **take that percent of the original number and add it to or subtract it from the original number.**

To increase 25 by 60%, first find 60% of 25.

25 × 0.6 = 15

Then, add the result to the original number:

25 + 15 = 40

To decrease 25 by 60%, subtract the 15:

25 – 15 = 10

To find the **original whole before a percent increase or decrease,** set up an equation. Think of a 15% increase over x as being $1.15x$, since it's really 115% of x.

EXAMPLE
A country's population after a 5% increase was 59,346. What was the population *before* the increase?

Setup:
$$\frac{1.05x}{1.05} = \frac{59{,}346}{1.05}$$
$$x = 56{,}520$$

To determine the combined effect of multiple percent increases and/or decreases, **start with 100 and see what happens.**

EXAMPLE
A price went up 10% one year, and the new price went up 20% the next year. What was the combined percent increase?

Setup: First year: 100 + (10% of 100) = 110

Second year: 110 + (20% of 110) = 132

Combined increase = 32%

AVERAGE, MEDIAN, AND MODE

The **average,** or mean, of a group of terms is the sum of the terms divided by the number of terms.

The average of 15, 18, 15, 32, and 20 is $\frac{15 + 18 + 15 + 32 + 20}{5} = \frac{100}{5} = 20$

The **median** is the value of the middle term, with the terms arranged in increasing or decreasing order. Suppose you want to find the median of the terms 15, 18, 15, 32, and 20. First, put the terms in order from small to large. 15, 15, 18, 20, 32. Then, identify the middle term. The middle term is 18. If there is an even number of terms, the median is the average of the two middle terms with the terms arranged in order.

The **mode** is the value of the term that occurs most. Of the terms 15, 18, 15, 32, and 20, the number 15 occurs twice, so it is the mode. If every number occurs only once, there is no mode. If more than one number occurs the most, then both numbers would be the modes.

RATIOS, PROPORTIONS, AND RATES

Ratios can be expressed in two forms. The first form is $\frac{a}{b}$.

If you have 15 dogs and 5 cats, the ratio of dogs to cats is $\frac{15}{5}$. (The ratio of cats to dogs is $\frac{5}{15}$.) Like any other fraction, this ratio can be simplified: $\frac{15}{5}$ can be simplified to $\frac{3}{1}$. In other words, for every 3 dogs, there is 1 cat.

The second form is ***a:b.***

The ratio of dogs to cats is 15:5 or 3:1. The ratio of cats to dogs is 5:15 or 1:3.

Pay attention to what ratio is specified in the problem. Remember that the ratio of dogs to cats is different from the ratio of cats to dogs.

A **proportion** is a statement that two ratios are equal. To solve a proportion, cross-multiply and solve for the variable.

$$\frac{x}{6} = \frac{2}{3}$$

$$3x = 12$$

$$x = 4$$

A **rate** is a ratio that compares quantities measured in different units. The most common example is **miles per hour**. Use the following formula for such problems:

Distance = Rate × Time

Remember that although not all rates are speeds, this formula can be adapted to any rate.

PROBABILITY

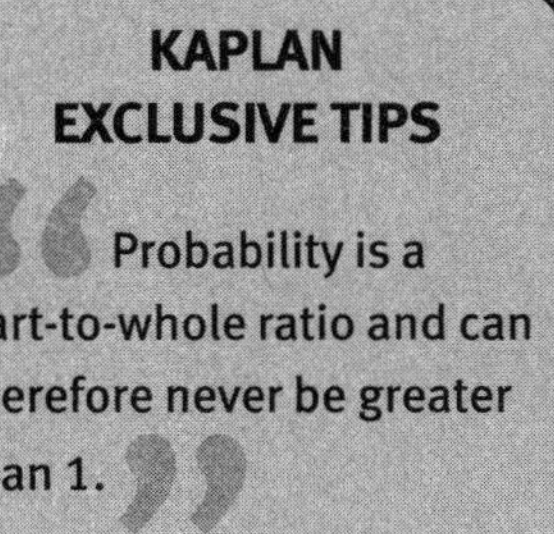

KAPLAN EXCLUSIVE TIPS
Probability is a part-to-whole ratio and can therefore never be greater than 1.

An **event** is a collection or set of possible outcomes. Suppose that a die with faces numbered 1, 2, 3, 4, 5, and 6 is rolled. All the possible outcomes are 1, 2, 3, 4, 5, and 6. Let A be the event that a 1, 3, or 5 is rolled. The event A is made up of the outcomes 1, 3, and 5. Thus A can also be described by saying that the number rolled is odd. A **possible outcome** is the elementary building block from which events are made up.

Of course, it is possible for an event to consist of a single possible outcome. For example, suppose that $B = \{4\}$; that is, the event B is the result that a 4 is rolled. An event consisting of a single possible outcome is called an elementary event. Thus, B, which is $\{4\}$, is an elementary event.

To find the **probability** that an event will occur, use this formula:

$$\text{Probability} = \frac{\text{Number of desirable outcomes}}{\text{Number of possible outcomes}}$$

EXAMPLES

If 12 books are on a shelf and 9 of them are mysteries, what is the probability of picking a mystery?

$\frac{9}{12} = \frac{3}{4}$. This probability can also be expressed as 0.75 or 75%.

To find the probability that two **events** will occur, find the probability that the first event occurs and multiply this by the probability that the second event occurs—given that the first event occurs.

EXAMPLES

If there are 12 books on a shelf and 9 of them are mysteries, what is the probability of picking a mystery first and a non-mystery second if exactly two books are selected?

Probability of picking a mystery: $\frac{9}{12} = \frac{3}{4}$

Probability of picking a non-mystery: $\frac{3}{11}$

(Originally there were 9 mysteries and 3 non-mysteries. After the mystery is selected, there are 8 mysteries and 3 non-mysteries; i.e., 11 books remaining.)

Probability of picking both books: $\frac{3}{4} \times \frac{3}{11} = \frac{9}{44}$

STRANGE SYMBOLISM AND TERMINOLOGY

Some questions will be confusing because you're unfamiliar with the math concept being tested. Others will seem confusing because the math has literally been made up just for the purposes of the test. The test makers make up math symbols and terminology to test your ability to deal with unfamiliar concepts.

These problems aren't as hard as they seem. When you see a strange symbol, the question stem will *always* indicate what the symbol means. And if you see strange terminology, it will *always* be defined. The problems are essentially about following directions, so don't panic when you see them. All you have to do is slow down, read the problem, and follow the directions.

EXAMPLES

If $x{<<>>}y = \sqrt{x+y}$, what is 9<<>>16?

All you have to do here is to substitute 9 and 16 into the defining equation:

$$\sqrt{9+16} = \sqrt{25} = 5$$

To "chomp" a number, take the sum of the digits of that number and divide this value by the number of digits.

What value do you get when you "chomp" 43,805?

$$4 + 3 + 8 + 0 + 5 = 20$$

$$20 \div 5 = 4$$

PRACTICE QUESTIONS

1. Which of the following is not even?
   (A) 330
   (B) 436
   (C) 752
   (D) 861
   (E) 974

2. What is the least prime number greater than 50?
   (A) 51
   (B) 53
   (C) 55
   (D) 57
   (E) 59

3. Which of the following is a multiple of 2?
   (A) 271
   (B) 357
   (C) 463
   (D) 599
   (E) 756

4. $\frac{15\times7\times3}{9\times5\times2}=$
   (A) $\frac{2}{7}$
   (B) $\frac{3}{5}$
   (C) $3\frac{1}{2}$
   (D) 7
   (E) $7\frac{1}{2}$

5. What is the least common multiple of 18 and 24?
   (A) 6
   (B) 54
   (C) 72
   (D) 96
   (E) 432

6. Which of the following is a multiple of 3?
   (A) 115
   (B) 370
   (C) 465
   (D) 589
   (E) 890

7. $-6(3 - 4 \times 3) =$
   (A) −66
   (B) −54
   (C) −12
   (D) 18
   (E) 54

8. Which of the following is a multiple of 10?
   (A) 10,005
   (B) 10,030
   (C) 10,101
   (D) 100,005
   (E) 101,101

9. Which of the following is a multiple of both 5 and 2?
   (A) 2,203
   (B) 2,342
   (C) 1,005
   (D) 7,790
   (E) 9,821

10. Which of the following is a multiple of both 3 and 10?

(A) 103
(B) 130
(C) 210
(D) 310
(E) 460

11. Which of the following is a multiple of 2, 3, and 5?

(A) 165
(B) 235
(C) 350
(D) 420
(E) 532

12. Which of the following is an even multiple of both 3 and 5?

(A) 135
(B) 155
(C) 250
(D) 350
(E) 390

13. Professor Jones bought a large carton of books. She gave 3 books to each student in her class, and there were no books left over. Which of the following could be the number of books she distributed?

(A) 133
(B) 143
(C) 252
(D) 271
(E) 332

14. Two teams are having a contest. The prize is a box of candy that the members of the winning team will divide evenly. If team A wins, each player will get exactly 3 pieces of candy, and if team B wins, each player will get exactly 5 pieces. Which of the following could be the number of pieces of candy in the box?

(A) 153
(B) 325
(C) 333
(D) 425
(E) 555

15. Three consecutive multiples of 4 have a sum of 60. What is the greatest of these numbers?

(A) 8
(B) 12
(C) 16
(D) 20
(E) 24

16. Sheila cuts a 60-foot wire cable into equal strips of $\frac{4}{5}$ of a foot each. How many strips does she make?

(A) 48
(B) 51
(C) 60
(D) 70
(E) 75

17. Which of the following is NOT odd?

(A) 349
(B) 537
(C) 735
(D) 841
(E) 918

18. Which of the following can be the sum of two negative numbers?

(A) 4
(B) 2
(C) 1
(D) 0
(E) –1

19. Which of the following is NOT a prime number?

(A) 2
(B) 7
(C) 17
(D) 87
(E) 101

20. All of the following can be the product of a negative integer and positive integer EXCEPT

(A) 1.
(B) –1.
(C) –2.
(D) –4.
(E) –6.

21. Susie and Dennis are training for a marathon. On Monday, they both run 3.2 miles. On Tuesday, Susie runs $5\frac{1}{5}$ miles and Dennis runs 3.6 miles. On Wednesday, Susie runs 4.8 miles and Dennis runs $2\frac{2}{5}$ miles. During those 3 days, how many more miles does Susie run than Dennis?

(A) 4.8
(B) 4
(C) 3.2
(D) 3
(E) 2.4

22. Which number is a multiple of 60?

(A) 213
(B) 350
(C) 540
(D) 666
(E) 1,060

23. Two odd integers and one even integer are multiplied together. Which of the following could be their product?

(A) 1.5
(B) 3
(C) 6
(D) 7.2
(E) 15

24. If the number 9,899,399 is increased by 2,082, the result will be

(A) 9,902,481.
(B) 9,901,481.
(C) 9,901,471.
(D) 9,891,481.
(E) 901,481.

25. What is the sum of five consecutive integers if the middle one is 13?

(A) 55
(B) 60
(C) 65
(D) 70
(E) 75

26. $\dfrac{4x^5}{2x^2} =$

(A) $2x^2$
(B) $2x^3$
(C) $2x^4$
(D) $4x^2$
(E) $4x^3$

27. $-2^3(1-2)^3 + (-2)^3 =$

(A) -12
(B) -4
(C) 0
(D) 4
(E) 12

28. n is an odd integer and $10 < n < 19$. What is the mean of all possible values of n?

(A) 13
(B) 13.5
(C) 14
(D) 14.5
(E) 15.5

29. $a \triangle b = \dfrac{3a}{b}$. What is $\dfrac{14}{32} \triangle 1\dfrac{3}{4}$?

(A) $\dfrac{1}{4}$
(B) $\dfrac{1}{3}$
(C) $\dfrac{1}{2}$
(D) $\dfrac{3}{4}$
(E) $\dfrac{49}{64}$

30. Jon works 4.5 hours a day, 3 days each week after school. He is paid $7.25 per hour. How much is his weekly pay (rounded to the next highest cent)?

(A) $13.50
(B) $21.75
(C) $32.63
(D) $54
(E) $97.88

31. Zim buys a calculator that is marked 30% off. If he pays $35, what was the original price?

(A) $24.50
(B) $45.50
(C) $47
(D) $50
(E) $62.50

32. A museum records 16 visitors to an exhibit on Monday, 21 on Tuesday, 20 on Wednesday, 17 on Thursday, 19 on Friday, 21 on Saturday, and 17 on Sunday, what is the median number of visitors for the week?

(A) 18.5
(B) 18.75
(C) 19
(D) 19.5
(E) 19.75

33. A bag contains 8 white, 4 red, 7 green, and 5 blue marbles. Eight marbles are withdrawn randomly. How many of the withdrawn marbles were white if the chance of drawing a white marble is now $\frac{1}{4}$?

(A) 0
(B) 3
(C) 4
(D) 5
(E) 6

34. $\sqrt{1,500} =$

(A) $10 + \sqrt{15}$
(B) $10\sqrt{15}$
(C) 25
(D) $100 + \sqrt{15}$
(E) $10\sqrt{150}$

35. $2(3 \times 2)^2 - 27(6 \div 2) + 3^2 =$

(A) 72
(B) 9
(C) 3
(D) 0
(E) –24

36. Which of the following numbers is closest to the product of 48.9 × 21.2?

(A) 10,000
(B) 8,000
(C) 1,000
(D) 100
(E) 70

37. $|16 - 25| + \sqrt{25 - 16} =$

(A) –12
(B) –6
(C) 0
(D) 6
(E) 12

38. Which of the following is 81,455 rounded to the nearest 100?

(A) 81,000
(B) 81,400
(C) 81,500
(D) 82,000
(E) 90,000

39. If 35% of x is 7, what is x% of 35?

(A) 7
(B) 20
(C) 28
(D) 35
(E) 42

40. A number is considered "blue" if the sum of its digits is equal to the product of its digits. Which of the following numbers is "blue"?

(A) 111
(B) 220
(C) 321
(D) 422
(E) 521

41. To "fix" a number, you must perform the following four steps:

Step 1: Raise the number to the 3rd power.

Step 2: Divide the result by 2.

Step 3: Take the absolute value of the result of Step 2.

Step 4: Round off this result to the nearest whole number.

When you "fix" –3, you get

(A) –13.
(B) 4.
(C) 5.
(D) 13.
(E) 14.

42. When D is divided by 15, the result is 6 with a remainder of 2. What is the remainder when D is divided by 6?

(A) 0
(B) 1
(C) 2
(D) 3
(E) 4

43. For any two numbers a and b, $a ? b = (a + b)(a - b)$. For example, $10 ? 5 = (10 + 5)(10 - 5) = (15)(5) = 75$. The value of $7 ? 5$ is

(A) 2.
(B) 12.
(C) 24.
(D) 36.
(E) 48.

44. What is the greatest integer less than $\frac{71}{6}$?

(A) 9
(B) 10
(C) 11
(D) 12
(E) 13

45. Which of the following is NOT less than 0.25?

(A) $\frac{2}{9}$
(B) $\frac{3}{14}$
(C) $\frac{16}{64}$
(D) $\frac{19}{80}$
(E) $\frac{4}{17}$

46. If the average of 5 consecutive odd numbers is 11, then the largest number is

(A) 17.
(B) 15.
(C) 13.
(D) 11.
(E) 9.

PRACTICE QUESTION ANSWERS

1. D

The way to tell if an integer is even is to look at the last digit to the right—the ones digit. If that digit is divisible by 2, or is 0, the number is even. Looking at the choices, only (D) ends in a number that isn't divisible by 2, so only it is not even.

2. B

A prime number is an integer greater than 1 that is divisible by only two different positive integers, itself and 1. Of the choices, only (B), 53 and (E), 59 are prime. You want the least prime number greater than 50, so (B) is correct. Using the divisibility rules would quickly show you that 51 and 57 are divisible by 3, while 55 is divisible by 5.

3. E

If the ones digit of a number is even (0, 2, 4, 6, or 8), the number is even. The only choice whose last digit is even is (E), 756.

4. C

Before you do the multiplication, see which common factors in the numerator and denominator can be canceled. Canceling a 3 from the 3 in the numerator and the 9 in the denominator leaves $\frac{15 \times 7 \times 1}{3 \times 5 \times 2}$. Canceling a 5 from the 15 in the numerator and the 5 in the denominator leaves $\frac{3 \times 7 \times 1}{3 \times 1 \times 2}$. Canceling the 3 in the numerator and the 3 in the denominator leaves $\frac{7 \times 1}{1 \times 2} = \frac{7}{2} = 3\frac{1}{2}$, (C).

5. C

The least common multiple (LCM) of two integers is the product of their prime factors, each raised to the highest power with which it appears. The prime factorization of 18 is $2 \cdot 3^2$ and that of 24 is $2^3 \cdot 3$. So their LCM is $2^3 \cdot 3^2 = 8 \cdot 9 = 72$. You could also find their LCM by checking out the multiples of the larger integer until you find the one that's also a multiple of the smaller. Check out the multiples of 24: 24? No. 48? No. 72? Yes, $72 = 4 \times 18$.

6. C

If a number is divisible by 3, the sum of its digits will be divisible by 3. Checking the answer choices, only (C), 465 works, since $4 + 6 + 5 = 15$, which is divisible by 3.

7. E

According to PEMDAS, start in the parentheses. As per PEMDAS, perform multiplication before subtraction: $-6(3 - 12)$. After the subtraction: $-6(-9)$. Since a negative times a negative is a positive, the answer is 54, (E).

8. B

If a number is divisible by 10, its last digit will be a 0. Only (B) fits this criterion.

9. D

If a number is divisible by both 5 and 2, then it must also be divisible by $5 \cdot 2$ or 10. Since a number divisible by 10 must have a 0 as its last digit, (D) is correct.

10. C

For a number to be divisible by 3 and 10, it must satisfy the divisibility rules of both: Its last digit must be 0, which automatically eliminates (A), and the sum of its digits must be divisible by 3. Checking the rest of the answer choices, only (C) is also divisible by 3, since $2 + 1 + 0 = 3$.

11. D

For a number to be a multiple of both 2 and 5, it must also be a multiple of 2 • 5 = 10. This means it must have a 0 as its last digit, which eliminates all but (C) and (D). To be a multiple of 3, the number's digits must sum to a multiple of 3. (D) is the only of the remaining two choices that fits this requirement, since 4 + 2 + 0 = 6.

12. E

Since an even number is divisible by 2, the question is asking for a number that is divisible by 2, 3, and 5. If the number is divisible by 2 and 5, it must also be divisible by 10, so its last digit must be 0. To be a multiple of 3, its digits must sum to a multiple of 3. Eliminate (A) and (B) since they don't end in 0. Of the remaining choices, only (E) is a multiple of 3, since 3 + 9 + 0 = 12.

13. C

If Professor Jones was able to distribute all the books in groups of 3 without any left over, the number of books she started with was divisible by 3. Whichever choice is divisible by 3 must therefore be correct. For a number to be divisible by 3, the sum of its digits must also be divisible by 3. Only (C) fits this requirement: 2 + 5 + 2 = 9.

14. E

The problem tells you that the number of pieces of candy in the box can be evenly divided by 3 and 5. So the correct answer has a 0 or 5 as its last digit, and the sum of its digits is divisible by 3. Eliminate (A) and (C) since they don't end in either 0 or 5. Of the remaining choices, only (E) is also divisible by 3, since 5 + 5 + 5 = 15.

15. E

Use the answer choices to help find the solution. When backsolving, start with the middle choice, since it will help you determine if the correct answer needs to be greater or less than it. In this case the middle choice is 16. The sum of 16 and 2 numbers that are each smaller than 16 has to be less than 3 • 16 or 48, so it is obviously too small. Therefore, (A) and (B) must also be too small and you can eliminate all three. Try (D), 20. Again, 20 plus two numbers smaller than 20 will be less than 3 • 20 or 60, so it's not correct. The only choice remaining is (E), 24, so it must be correct. To prove it, 24 plus the two preceding consecutive multiples of 4, which are 16 and 20, do indeed sum to 60: 16 + 20 + 24 = 60.

16. E

When you're asked how many strips $\frac{4}{5}$ of a foot long can be cut from a 60-foot piece of wire, you're being asked how many times $\frac{4}{5}$ goes into 60, or what is $60 \div \frac{4}{5}$. Before you do the division, you can eliminate some unreasonable answer choices. Since $\frac{4}{5}$ is less than 1, $\frac{4}{5}$ must go into 60 more than 60 times. Eliminate (A), (B), and (C) because they're all less than or equal to 60. Dividing by a fraction is the same as multiplying by its reciprocal, so $60 \div \frac{4}{5} = 60 \bullet \frac{5}{4} = 75$.

17. E

If a number is odd, its last digit must be odd. (E) ends in an even digit, so it is not odd.

18. E

The sum of two negative numbers is always negative. (E) is the only negative choice, so it must be correct. If you're wondering how two negative numbers can add up to –1, remember that "number" doesn't necessarily mean "integer." It can also mean "fraction." For example, $\left(-\frac{1}{4}\right)+\left(-\frac{3}{4}\right)=-1$. Always read the questions carefully to see what types of numbers are involved.

19. D

A prime number has only two different positive factors, 1 and itself. The numbers 2, 7, and 17 are obviously prime, so eliminate them. Use the divisibility rules to check out the two remaining choices. Both end in an odd number, so neither is divisible by 2. But the digits of 87 sum to 15, which is a multiple of 3, so 87 is divisible by 3 and is therefore not prime.

20. A

The product of a positive integer and a negative integer is always negative. (A) is positive, so it couldn't be the product of a negative and a positive.

21. B

The simplest way to solve this problem is to convert the numbers so that they're all decimals or all fractions: $5\frac{1}{5}=5\frac{2}{10}=5.2; 2\frac{2}{5}=2\frac{4}{10}=2.4$. Now you can more easily compare the distances. On Monday, they ran the same number of miles. On Tuesday, Susie ran 5.2 miles and Dennis ran 3.6 miles. The difference between the two amounts is 5.2 – 3.6, or 1.6, so on Tuesday Susie ran 1.6 more miles than Dennis did. On Wednesday, Susie ran 4.8 miles and Dennis ran 2.4. Then 4.8 – 2.4 = 2.4, so on Wednesday Susie ran 2.4 miles more than Dennis. The total difference for the three days is 1.6 + 2.4 = 4.0 more miles.

22. C

A number that is a multiple of 60 must be a multiple of every factor of 60. The factors of 60 are 1, 2, 3, 4, 5, 6, 10, 12, 15, 20, 30, and 60. (A) and (D) are not multiples of 10. (B) and (E) are not multiples of 3. The answer is 540, (C).

23. C

The product of three integers must be an integer, so eliminate (A) and (D). A product of integers that has at least one even factor is even, so the product of two odd integers and one even integer must be even. The only even choice is 6, (C).

24. B

This question is simply asking for the sum of 9,899,399 and 2,082, which is 9,901,481, (B).

25. C

If the middle of five consecutive integers is 13, the first two are 11 and 12 and the last two are 14 and 15. So the sum is 11 + 12 + 13 + 14 + 15 = 65. You could get to this answer more quickly if you knew that the middle term in a group of consecutive numbers is equal to the average of the group of numbers. In other words, the average of these five integers is 13, so their sum would be 13 • 5 = 65.

26. B

Simplify the expression by first simplifying the fraction $\frac{4}{2}$, which equals 2. Then, to divide the exponential expressions with the same base, subtract the exponents:

$$\frac{x^5}{x^2}=x^{5-2}$$
$$=x^3$$

So $\frac{4x^5}{2x^2}=2x^3$.

27. C

A negative number raised to an odd power is negative. Using PEMDAS,

$$-2^3(1-2)^3 + (-2)^3$$
$$= -2^3(-1)^3 + (-2)^3$$
$$= -8(-1) + (-8)$$
$$= 8 + (-8)$$
$$= 8 - 8$$
$$= 0$$

28. C

The mean (or average) is the sum of the terms divided by the number of terms. The numbers included are 11, 13, 15, and 17. Note that 19 is not in the set, since *n* is less than 19. The average is $\frac{11+13+15+17}{4} = \frac{56}{4} = 14$. The average is an even number although the numbers in the set are all odd.

29. D

Substitute the number on the left for *a* and the number on the right for *b* in the formula given for the strange symbol. First convert *b* to an improper fraction: $\frac{7}{4}$. So the numerator is 3 times $\frac{14}{32}$, or (simplifying the fraction) 3 times $\frac{7}{16}$, or $\frac{21}{16}$. Dividing by $\frac{7}{4}$ is the same as multiplying by $\frac{4}{7}$. So we have $\frac{21}{16} \times \frac{4}{7}$ or $\frac{3}{4} \times \frac{1}{1} = \frac{3}{4}$.

30. E

Multiply the number of hours per day, times the number of days, times the rate per hour. $4.5 \times 3 \times 7.25 = 97.875$, which rounds to \$97.88.

31. D

Let's say the original price is *x* dollars. The price paid is 70 percent of the original price (100% minus 30%). So, $0.7x = 35$; $70x = 3{,}500$; $x = 50$.

32. C

The numbers for the week are 16, 21, 20, 17, 19, 21, 17. Listing them in ascending order, we have 16, 17, 17, 19, 20, 21, 21. There are an odd number of numbers, so the median is the number in the middle of the set: 19.

33. C

By adding the 8 white, 4 red, 7 green, and 5 blue marbles, we have a total of 24 marbles. If 8 are withdrawn, 16 remain in the bag. If the chance of drawing a white marble is now one-fourth, 4 white marbles remain in the bag, so 8 – 4, or 4 must have been drawn out.

34. B

To simplify the square root of a large number, break the number down into two or more factors and write the number as the product of the square roots of those factors. This is especially useful when one of the factors is a perfect square. In this case, break 1,500 down into two factors. $1{,}500 = 15 \cdot 100$, and 100 is a perfect square. So $1{,}500 = \sqrt{100 \cdot 15} = \sqrt{100} \cdot \sqrt{15} = 10\sqrt{15}$.

35. D

This is a basic arithmetic problem, and if you remember PEMDAS, it will be a breeze. PEMDAS tells you the order in which you need to do the different calculations: parentheses, exponents, multiplication and division, addition and subtraction. Take the expression and solve the parts in that order:

$$2(3 \times 2)^2 - 27(6 \div 2) + 3^2$$
$$= 2(6)^2 - 27(3) + 3^2$$
$$= 2(36) - 27(3) + 9$$
$$= 72 - 81 + 9$$
$$= -9 + 9$$
$$= 0$$

36. C

One way to solve this one would be to do the calculation. But this is really a test to see if you understand how to approximate a calculation by rounding off numbers. You could round off both numbers to the nearest whole number, but that wouldn't make the calculation much easier. And besides, the answer choices you're choosing between are pretty far apart, so you can probably round both numbers to the nearest ten. Then 48.9 is close to 50, so round it up to 50. And 21.2 is close to 20, so round it down to 20. Now the multiplication is 50 • 20 or 1,000, choice (C).

37. E

In terms of order of operations, treat absolute value bars and roots just like parentheses: Simplify them first. In this case, first find the value of 16 – 25: 16 – 25 = –9. The absolute value of a number is its distance from zero on the number line. Now –9 is 9 units from zero, so

$$|16 - 25| = |-9|$$
$$= 9$$

Now, simplify $\sqrt{25-16}$. 25 – 16 = 9, so $\sqrt{25-16} = \sqrt{9}$. Because the radical sign is being used, simplify $\sqrt{9}$ by finding only the positive square root of 9, which is 3. The problem becomes 9 + 3, which is 12, (E).

38. C

You're being asked whether 81,455 is closer to 81,400 or 81,500. Logically, because 81,455 is greater than 81,450 (the halfway point between 81,400 and 81,500), it is closer to 81,500. Formally, to round a number to the nearest hundred, consider the tens digit. If the tens digit is 5 or greater, round the hundreds digit up 1. If the tens digit is 4 or smaller, keep the same hundreds digit. Here the tens digit is 5, so round the hundreds digit up 1 from 4 to 5. To the nearest 100, 81,455 is 81,500, (C).

39. A

This problem is a snap if you remember that a% of b = b% of a. In this case, 35% of x = x% of 35, so x% of 35 is 7.

If you didn't remember that a% of b = b% of a, you could also have solved the statement that 35% of x is 7 for x and then found x% of 35. Percent • Whole = Part, so

$$\frac{35}{100}x = 7$$
$$35x = 700$$
$$x = 20$$

So x% of 35 is 20% of 35, which is 7, (A).

40. C

In this type of problem, you're given a rule or definition you've never heard before and then asked a question involving that new rule. In this example, you're given a definition of the term "blue": a number is "blue" if the sum of its digits is equal to the product of its digits. To solve, simply try each answer until you find the one that fits the definition of "blue". Only (C) is blue, because 3 + 2 + 1 = 3 • 2 • 1 = 6.

41. E

This is another invented rule question. This time all you have to do is follow directions. To "fix"–3, you first raise it to the 3rd power: $(-3)^3 = -27$. Then divide this result by 2: $-27 \div 2 = -13.5$. Next take the absolute value of –13.5, which is just 13.5. Finally, round off this result to the nearest integer: 13.5 rounds up to 14, (E).

42. C

One way to do this problem is to realize that the remainder would have to be the same whether D were divided by 15 or 6, since $D = 15 \times 6 + 2$. In other words, D is 2 more than a multiple of both 15 and 6. Hence, the remainder of 2 regardless of whether D is divided by 15 or 6.

Otherwise, find the actual value of D by calculating:

$$D = 15 \times 6 + 2$$
$$= 90 + 2$$
$$= 92$$

Now divide D by 6 to find the remainder: $92 \div 6 = 15$, with a remainder of 2. (C) is correct.

43. C

This is another follow-the-instructions problem. Just replace a with 7 and b with 5. So $7 ? 5 = (7 + 5)(7 - 5) = (12)(2) = 24$, (C).

44. C

$\frac{71}{6} = 11\frac{5}{6}$, so the greatest integer less than $\frac{71}{6}$ is 11.

45. C

$0.25 = \frac{1}{4}$, so just find which choice is NOT less than $\frac{1}{4}$. (C), $\frac{16}{64}$, reduces to $\frac{1}{4}$ so it is equal to, not less than, 0.25.

46. B

The average of an odd number of consecutive numbers is equal to the middle term. Since 11 is the average of these five consecutive odd numbers, 11 is the third and middle term. So the five numbers are 7, 9, 11, 13, and 15. The largest number is 15.

CHAPTER 12: ALGEBRA

Algebra problems will appear in two forms on the SSAT or ISEE: As regular math problems and as word problems. Word problems will be dealt with in another chapter. This chapter will give you a chance to review the basic algebra concepts that you'll see on the test. Chapter 14: Word Problems will build on these concepts and introduce word problem-specific skills.

ALGEBRA CONCEPTS

Vocabulary

Algebra consists of the same basic operations as arithmetic, so in a sense, it can best be defined as abstract arithmetic. The difference is that letters, called *variables,* are often substituted for numbers. Before we discuss algebraic topics, let's review some important definitions.

A **variable** is a letter (usually lowercase) used to represent a numerical value that is unknown. The value of the variable may differ in any particular problem.

A **constant** is a value that does not change its value regardless of the problem. Constants are typically numbers.

A **term** is a variable, a constant, or the product of a constant and one or more variables. The variables may be raised to exponents. A term containing only a number is called a *constant term* because it contains no variable factors.

The **coefficient** of a term is understood to be the numerical factor of that term. If no numerical factor is present, the coefficient is understood to be 1 (or –1).

EXAMPLES

Term	Variable(s)	Coefficient	Constant(s)
$5x$	x	5	5
$-3yz$	y, z	-3	-3
12			12

Like terms are terms that contain exactly the same variables raised to exactly the same exponents. Like terms can be added and subtracted by combining the numerical coefficients and keeping the variable portion of the terms.

Examples:	Can be simplified to:
$7x + 5x$	$12x$
$3xy - 2 - xy$	$2xy - 2$
$8a^2b + 5ab^2 - 4a^2b$	$4a^2b + 5ab^2$ (This expression cannot be simplified further because the exponents on the variables *a* and *b* are not the same.)

In algebra you work with expressions and equations. An algebraic **expression** contains one or more terms separated by addition and subtraction signs.

EXAMPLES

$4x^3 + 12x^2 + 7x + 8$

$18a^3b^4 + 14a^2b^5 + 12a + 56$

An algebraic **equation** is a statement that two expressions are equal. An equal sign, =, is used to indicate that the two expressions are equal.

EXAMPLES

$5x + 10 = 4x + 26$

$x^2 + 5x + 12 = 3y + 4$

FOR ALGEBRAIC EXPRESSIONS

"Make sure you combine only 'like terms.'"

A **polynomial** is an algebraic expression that is the sum of two or more terms. If a polynomial has two terms, it is called a **binomial**. If it has three terms, it is called a **trinomial**. If an expression only has one term, it is called a **monomial**.

EXAMPLES

$16x^3 - 10x^2$	binomial, polynomial
$-3a^3b^4 + 4a + 6$	trinomial, polynomial
$13p^6k^9$	monomial

Substitution

If a problem gives you the value for a variable, just substitute the value into the expression and solve. Make sure that you follow the correct order of operations and are careful with your calculations.

EXAMPLE

If $x = 15$ and $y = 10$, what is the value of $4x(x - y)$?
Substitute 15 for x and 10 for y.

$$4(15)(15 - 10) =$$

Then evaluate.

$$(60)(5) = 300$$

Simplifying Polynomial Expressions

To simplify a polynomial expression, remove all grouping symbols (parentheses) using distribution, simplify each term so that each variable appears no more than once in any one term, then combine like terms.

EXAMPLES

$$6(3b - 4) = 18b - 24$$

$$\begin{aligned} -3(4x + 1) + 2 &= -12x - 3 + 2 \\ &= -12x - 1 \end{aligned}$$

$$\begin{aligned} (2b)^3 - 5b^2(3b) &= 8b^3 - 15b^3 \\ &= -7b^3 \end{aligned}$$

$$\begin{aligned} 3a + 2b - 8a &= 3a - 8a + 2b \\ &= -5a + 2b \text{ or } 2b - 5a \end{aligned}$$

$$\begin{aligned} (4w + 9h) - (3w - 4h) &= 4w + 9h - 3w + 4h \\ &= 4w - 3w + 9h + 4h \\ &= w + 13h \end{aligned}$$

Factoring Polynomial Expressions

The main factoring method you need to master for the test is factoring using the **greatest common factor (GCF)** of an algebraic expression. The GCF of an expression consists of the largest numerical factor and the largest number of variable factors that can be factored out of all terms in the expression.

To find the GCF of an expression, first make sure that the expression is simplified. Second, find the largest factor common to all coefficients in the expression (it is possible to have a numerical GCF of 1). Finally, identify the variable factors common to all terms in the expression. The GCF will contain these factors raised to the lowest exponent given on the variable in any one term.

To write an expression in factored form, use the distributive property to write the GCF followed by the polynomial factor in parentheses.

EXAMPLES

$7y^3 + 14y^2 - 21y = 7y(y^2 + 2y - 3)$

$12ab^3 - 15a^2b^2 = 3ab^2(4b - 5a)$

In the first example, $7y$ is the GCF of the expression. In the second example, $3ab^2$ is the GCF of the expression.

Multiplying and Dividing Monomials and Binomials

To **add** or **subtract** terms consisting of a coefficient (the number in front of the variable) multiplied by a power (a power is a base raised to an exponent), both the base and the exponent *must* be the same. As long as the bases and the exponents are the same, you can add the coefficients.

$x^2 + x^2 = 2x^2$

$3x^4 - 2x^4 = x^4$

$x^2 + x^3$ cannot be combined.

$x^2 + y^2$ cannot be combined.

KAPLAN EXCLUSIVE TIPS

"To multiply powers with the same base, add exponents. To raise a power to an exponent, multiply exponents."

To **multiply** terms consisting of coefficients multiplied by powers having the same base, multiply the coefficients and add the exponents.

$2x^5 \times 8x^7 = (2 \times 8)(x^{5+7}) = 16x^{12}$

To **divide** terms consisting of coefficients multiplied by powers having the same base, divide the coefficients and subtract the exponents.

$6x^7 \div 2x^5 = (6 \div 2)(x^{7-5}) = 3x^2$

To **raise a power to an exponent,** multiply the exponents.

$(x^2)^4 = x^{2 \times 4} = x^8$

When you multiply monomials, multiply the coefficients of each term. (In other words, multiply the numbers that come before the variables.) Then, multiply the variables. Exponents of like variables should be added.

$$(6a)(4b) = (6 \times 4)(a \times b) = 24ab$$

$$\begin{aligned}(6a)(4ab) &= (6 \times 4)(a \times a \times b) = \\ &= (6 \times 4)(a^{1+1} \times b) \\ &= 24a^2b\end{aligned}$$

When you divide monomials, divide the coefficient of the numerator by the coefficient of the denominator. When the same variable appears in both the numerator and the denominator, subtract the exponent of that variable in the denominator from the exponent of that variable in the numerator.

$$24a \div 3b = \frac{24a}{3b} = \frac{8a}{b}$$

$$40x^2y^5 \div 5xy^2z^4 = \frac{40x^2y^5}{5xy^2z^4} = \frac{8x^{2-1}y^{5-2}}{z^4} = \frac{8x^1y^3}{z^4} = \frac{8xy^3}{z^4}$$

Remember that $x^1 = x$.

Use the FOIL method to **multiply binomials.** FOIL stands for **F**irst **O**uter **I**nner **L**ast.

$$\begin{aligned}(y + 1)(y + 2) &= (y \times y) + (y \times 2) + (1 \times y) + (1 \times 2) \\ &= y^2 + 2y + y + 2 \\ &= y^2 + 3y + 2\end{aligned}$$

WORKING WITH EQUATIONS

The key to **solving equations** is to do the same thing to both sides of the equation until you have your variable isolated on one side of the equation and all of the numbers on the other side.

$$12a + 8 = 23 - 3a$$

First, subtract 8 from each side so that the left side of the equation has only a variable term.

$$12a + 8 - 8 = 23 - 3a - 8$$

$$12a = 15 - 3a$$

Then, add $3a$ to each side so that the right side of the equation has only numbers.

$$12a + 3a = 15 - 3a + 3a$$

$$15a = 15$$

Finally, divide both sides by 15 to isolate the variable.

$$\frac{15a}{15} = \frac{15}{15}$$
$$a = 1$$

Sometimes you're given an equation with two variables and asked to **solve for one variable in terms of the other.** This means that you must isolate the variable for which you are solving on one side of the equation and put everything else on the other side. In other words, when you're done, you'll have x (or whatever the variable is) on one side of the equation and an expression on the other side.

Solve $7x + 2y = 3x + 10y - 16$ for x in terms of y.

Since you want to isolate x on one side of the equation, begin by subtracting $2y$ from both sides.

$$7x + 2y - 2y = 3x + 10y - 16 - 2y$$
$$7x = 3x + 8y - 16$$

Then, subtract $3x$ from both sides to get all the x's on one side of the equation.

$$7x - 3x = 3x + 8y - 16 - 3x$$
$$4x = 8y - 16$$

Finally, divide both sides by 4 to isolate x.

$$\frac{4x}{4} = \frac{8y - 16}{4}$$
$$x = 2y - 4$$

Picking Numbers

Picking numbers is a useful strategy for avoiding tedious calculations. Instead of solving the equation and figuring out which answer choice matches your answer, you plug choices back into the equation until one fits.

Some typical questions that can be solved by picking numbers involve the following:

- Age stated in terms of variables
- Remainder
- Percentages or fractions of variables
- Even/odd variables
- Algebraic expressions in the answers

WORKING WITH INEQUALITIES

Solving inequalities is very similar to solving equations—with two important differences:

1. When **multiplying or dividing both sides of an inequality by a negative number, the direction of the inequality must change.**

2. The **solution of an inequality** will be a **range of values for the variable,** rather than just one value.

When solving the inequality $-5a < 10$, for instance, it is correct to divide both sides of the inequality by -5. Because -5 is a negative number, the solution, after simplifying, would be $a > -2$, not $a < -2$.

If this is confusing, consider the rules for multiplying signed numbers. If -5 multiplied by some value must be less than 10, any positive number will do. That's because -5 multiplied by a positive number yields a negative number and ALL negative numbers are less than 10. In addition, some negative numbers like -1 and $-\frac{1}{2}$ will also work; though when multiplied by -5 they yield positive results, the positive product is less than 10. If -5 is multiplied by -2 or smaller numbers, however, the product becomes too large.

EXAMPLES

$$4a + 6 > 2a + 10$$
$$4a - 2a > 10 - 6$$
$$2a > 4$$
$$a > 2$$

$$5(g - 6) \leq 6g + 18$$
$$5g - 30 \leq 6g + 18$$
$$5g - 6g \leq 18 + 30$$
$$-g \leq 48$$
$$g \geq -48$$

PRACTICE QUESTIONS

1. What is the value of $a(b-1)+\frac{bc}{2}$ if $a=3$, $b=6$, and $c=5$?

   (A) 0
   (B) 15
   (C) 30
   (D) 45
   (E) 60

2. If $\frac{c}{d}=3$ and $d=1$, then $3c+d=$

   (A) 3
   (B) 4
   (C) 6
   (D) 7
   (E) 10

3. What is the value of x in the equation $5x-7=y$, if $y=8$?

   (A) –1
   (B) 1
   (C) 2
   (D) 3
   (E) 70

4. What is the value of $x(y-2)+xz$, if $x=2$, $y=5$, and $z=7$?

   (A) 12
   (B) 20
   (C) 22
   (D) 28
   (E) 32

5. If $x=\sqrt{3}$, $y=2$, and $z=\frac{1}{2}$, then $x^2-5yz+y^2=$

   (A) 1.
   (B) 2.
   (C) 4.
   (D) 7.
   (E) 8.

6. If $x+y=7$, what is the value of $2x+2y-2$?

   (A) 5
   (B) 9
   (C) 12
   (D) 14
   (E) 16

7. What is the value of a in the equation $3a-6=b$, if $b=18$?

   (A) 4
   (B) 6
   (C) 8
   (D) 10
   (E) 18

8. If $\frac{x}{y}=\frac{2}{5}$ and $x=10$, $y=$

   (A) 4.
   (B) 10.
   (C) 15.
   (D) 20.
   (E) 25.

9. $-5n(3m-2)=$

   (A) $-15mn+10n$
   (B) $15mn-10n$
   (C) $-8mn+7n$
   (D) $8mn+7n$
   (E) $-2mn-7n$

10. What is the value of $(a + b)^2$, when $a = -1$ and $b = 3$?

(A) 2
(B) 4
(C) 8
(D) 10
(E) 16

11. If $s - t = 5$, what is the value of $3s - 3t + 3$?

(A) 2
(B) 8
(C) 11
(D) 12
(E) 18

12. $(3d - 7) - (5 - 2d) =$

(A) $d - 12$
(B) $5d - 2$
(C) $5d + 12$
(D) $5d - 12$
(E) $8d + 5$

13. What is the value of $xyz + y(z - x) + 2x$ if $x = -2$, $y = 3$ and $z = 1$?

(A) −13
(B) −7
(C) −1
(D) 7
(E) 19

14. If $3x + 7 = 14$, then $x =$

(A) −14.
(B) 0.
(C) $\frac{7}{3}$.
(D) 3.
(E) 7.

15. If x is an integer, which of the following expressions is always even?

(A) $2x + 1$
(B) $3x + 2$
(C) $4x + 3$
(D) $5x + 4$
(E) $6x + 2$

16. If $4z - 3 = -19$, then $z =$

(A) −16.
(B) $-5\frac{1}{2}$.
(C) −4.
(D) 0.
(E) 4.

17. If $3ab = 6$, what is the value of a in terms of b?

(A) 2
(B) $\frac{2}{b}$
(C) $\frac{2}{b^2}$
(D) $2b$
(E) $2b^2$

18. If x and y are integers, in which equation must x be negative?

(A) $xy = -1$
(B) $xy^2 = -1$
(C) $x^2y = -1$
(D) $x^2y^2 = 1$
(E) $xy^2 = 1$

19. If n is an odd number, which of the following expressions is always odd?

(A) $2n + 4$
(B) $3n + 2$
(C) $3n + 5$
(D) $5n + 5$
(E) $5n + 7$

20. If $5p + 12 = 17 - 4\left(\frac{p}{2} + 1\right)$, what is the value of p?

(A) $\frac{1}{7}$

(B) $\frac{1}{3}$

(C) $\frac{6}{7}$

(D) $1\frac{2}{7}$

(E) 2

21. If $\frac{2x}{5y} = 6$, what is the value of y, in terms of x?

(A) $\frac{x}{15}$

(B) $\frac{x}{2}$

(C) $\frac{8}{2}$

(D) $15x$

(E) $\frac{30}{x}$

22. If x is an odd integer and y is an even integer, which of the following expressions MUST be odd?

(A) $2x + y$

(B) $2(x + y)$

(C) $x^2 + y^2$

(D) $xy + y$

(E) $2x + y^2$

23. If $100 \div x = 10n$, then which of the following is equal to nx?

(A) 10

(B) $10x$

(C) 100

(D) $10xn$

(E) 1,000

24. For what value of y is $4(y-1) = 2(y + 2)$?

(A) 0

(B) 2

(C) 4

(D) 6

(E) 8

25. $\frac{3}{4} + x = 8.3$

What is the value of x in the equation above?

(A) 4.9

(B) 6.75

(C) 7.55

(D) 8

(E) 9.05

26. If $2(a + m) = 5m - 3 + a$, what is the value of a, in terms of m?

(A) $\frac{3m}{2}$

(B) 3

(C) $5m$

(D) $4m + 33$

(E) $3m - 3$

PRACTICE QUESTION ANSWERS

1. C

Substitute $a = 3$, $b = 6$, and $c = 5$.

$$3(6-1) + \frac{6\times5}{2} = 3(5) + \frac{30}{2}$$
$$= 15 + 15$$
$$= 30$$

2. E

Since we're told the value of d, we can substitute it into the equation $\frac{c}{d} = 3$ to find the value of c. We are told that $d = 1$, so $\frac{c}{d} = 3$ can be rewritten as $\frac{c}{1} = 3$. Since $\frac{c}{1}$ is the same as c, we can rewrite the equation again as $c = 3$. Now we can substitute the values of c and d into the expression $3c + d$ to get $3(3) + 1 = 10$.

3. D

We are told that $y = 8$, so first we'll substitute 8 for y, and then we can solve for x.

$$5x - 7 = y$$
$$5x - 7 = 8$$

Now we can add 7 to both sides:

$$5x - 7 + 7 = 8 + 7$$
$$5x = 15$$

Next we divide both sides by 5:

$$\frac{5x}{5} = \frac{15}{5}$$
$$x = 3$$

4. B

Here we have three values to substitute. Remember, xz means x times z. After we substitute the values of x, y, and z, we will do the operations in PEMDAS order—parentheses, exponents, multiplication and division, addition and subtraction.

$$x(y-2) + xz = 2(5-2) + 2\times7$$
$$= 2(3) + 2\times7$$
$$= 6 + 14$$
$$= 20$$

5. B

This is another "plug-in" question. Remember, $5yz$ means $5 \times y \times z$. First we will replace x, y, and z with the values given. Then we will carry out the indicated operations using PEMDAS.

$$x^2 - 5yz + y^2 = (\sqrt{3})^2 - 5\times2\times\frac{1}{2} + 2^2$$
$$= 3 - 5\times2\times\frac{1}{2} + 4$$
$$= 3 - 5 + 4$$
$$= -2 + 4$$
$$= 2$$

6. C

If you look carefully at the expression $2x + 2y - 2$, you should see some similarity to $x + y = 7$. If we ignore the -2 for a moment, $2x + 2y$ is really just twice $x + y$. If it helps to make it clearer, we can factor out the 2, making $2x + 2y$ into $2(x + y)$. Since $x + y = 7$, $2(x + y)$ must equal 2(7), or 14. If we replace $2x + 2y$ with 14, the expression $2x + 2y - 2$ becomes $14 - 2$, which equals 12, (C).

7. C

This question is solved the same way as question 3.

Plug in 18 for b in the equation:

$$3a - 6 = 18$$

Isolate a on one side of the equation:

$$3a = 18 + 6$$

$$3a = 24$$

Divide both sides by 3 to find the value of a: $a = 8$.

8. E

Substitute 10 for x in the equation:

$$\frac{10}{y} = \frac{2}{5}$$

Cross-multiply:

$$(10)(5) = (2)(y)$$
$$50 = 2y$$

Divide both sides by 2 to find the value of y:

$$\frac{50}{2} = \frac{2y}{2}$$
$$25 = y$$

9. A

Distribute $-5n$ to each term within the parentheses:

$$-5n(3m - 2) = (-5n)(3m) + (-5n)(-2)$$

Multiply:

$$= -15mn + 10n$$

Note that $(-5n)(-2) = +10n$, because a negative × a negative yields a positive.

10. B

Plug $a = -1$ and $b = 3$ into the expression:

$$(-1 + 3)^2 = (2)^2 = 4$$

11. E

The expression can be rewritten as $3(s - t) + 3$.

Plug in 5 for $s - t$:

$$3(5) + 3 = 15 + 3$$
$$= 18$$

12. D

Distribute the minus sign over the terms in parentheses: $3d - 7 - 5 - (-2d)$. Combine like terms:

$$3d - (-2d) - 7 - 5$$
$$5d - 12$$

$3d$ minus $-2d$ equals $+5d$, because subtraction is equivalent to "addition of the opposite." So $3d - (-2d)$ becomes $3d + (+2d)$ which is equal to $5d$.

13. C

Plug in $x = -2$, $y = 3$, and $z = 1$:

$$(-2)(3)(1) + 3[(1 - (-2)] + 2(-2)$$
$$= -6 + 3(3) - 4$$
$$= -6 + 9 - 4$$
$$= 3 - 4$$
$$= -1$$

14. C

We have to rearrange the equation until the x is alone on one side of the equal sign. You must do the same thing to the both sides of the equation. First we will take away the 7:

$$3x + 7 = 14$$
$$3x + 7 - 7 = 14 - 7$$
$$3x = 7$$
$$\frac{3x}{3} = \frac{7}{3}$$
$$x = \frac{7}{3}$$

15. E

Notice that the question asks which expression is always even. (E), $6x + 2$, is correct because, first, the product of an even number and any integer is even, so $6x$ is even because 6 is even. Then, when two even numbers are added, their sum is also even, so $6x + 2$ is even. (A) and (C) are always odd regardless of what integer is substituted for x. (B) and (D) are even only when x is even.

16. C

We must rearrange the equation until the z is alone on one side of the equal sign. Anything we do to one side of the equation we must also do to the other side. First we'll add 3 to both sides:

$$4z - 3 = -19$$

$$4z - 3 + 3 = -19 + 3$$

$$4z = -16$$

Next we'll divide both sides by 4:

$$\frac{4z}{4} = -\frac{16}{4}$$

$$z = -4$$

17. B

Rearrange the equation until the variable a is alone on one side of the equal sign.

$$3ab = 6$$

$$\frac{3ab}{3} = \frac{6}{3}$$

$$ab = 2$$

$$\frac{ab}{b} = \frac{2}{b}$$

$$a = \frac{2}{b}$$

18. B

Try each answer choice until you find the correct one.

(A) $xy = -1$. If the product of two integers is negative, then one of the two integers must be negative. In this case x could be negative, but it's possible that y is negative and x is positive. We're looking for an equation where x will always have to be negative.

(B) $xy^2 = -1$. The exponent here applies only to the y, not to the x. The square of any non-zero number is positive, so whatever y is, y^2 must be positive. (We know that y isn't zero; if it were, then the product xy^2 would also be zero.) Since y^2 is positive and the product of y^2 and x is negative, x must be negative. (B) is the answer.

19. B

We're told that n is odd, so we don't have to check to see what happens if n is even. We do have to try each answer to see which one represents an odd number. Let's say $n = 3$ and replace all the n's with 3s.

(A) $2n + 4$. $2(3) + 4 = 6 + 4 = 10$. 10 is even.

(B) $3n + 2$. $3(3) + 2 = 9 + 2 = 11$. 11 is odd, so (B) is the answer.

20. A

This equation takes a few more steps to solve than the previous ones, but it follows the same rules.

First we multiply using the distributive law:

$$5p + 12 = 17 - 4\left(\frac{p}{2} + 1\right)$$

$$5p + 12 = 17 + (-4)\left(\frac{p}{2}\right) + (-4)(1)$$

$$5p + 12 = 17 + \left(-\frac{4p}{2}\right) + (-4)$$

$+\left(-\frac{4p}{2}\right)$ is equal to $-2p$, so $5p + 12 = 17 - 2p - 4$

Combine the integers on the right side:

$$5p + 12 = 13 - 2p$$

We can add $2p$ to each side to get all the p's on one side:

$$5p + 2p + 12 = 13 - 2p + 2p$$

$$7p + 12 = 13$$

Now we will subtract 12 from both sides:

$$7p + 12 - 12 = 13 - 12$$

$$7p = 1$$

And lastly, we divide both sides by 7:

$$\frac{7p}{7} = \frac{1}{7}$$

$$p = \frac{1}{7}$$

21. A

We want to rearrange the equation until y is alone on one side of the equal sign. There's more than one way to do this, but here's one way:

$$\frac{2x}{5y} = 6$$

$$(5y)\,\frac{2x}{5y} = 6(5y)$$

$$2x = 30y$$

$$\frac{2x}{30} = y$$

$$\frac{x}{15} = y$$

22. C

This is another "try each answer" problem. We know that x is odd and y is even. Let's say that $x = 3$ and $y = 4$.

(A) $2x + y$. $2(3) + 4 = 6 + 4 = 10$. 10 is even, so this isn't correct.

(B) $2(x + y)$. $2(3 + 4) = 2(3 + 4) = 2(7) = 14$. 14 is even.

(C) $x^2 + y^2$. $3^2 + 4^2 = 9 + 16 = 25$. 25 is odd, so (C) is correct.

23. A

This problem looks harder than it really is. If

$100 \div x = 10n$ then

$(10n)(x) = 100$ or

$10nx = 100$

$nx = 10$, (A)

24. C

Multiply through and solve for y by isolating it on one side of the equation:

$$4(y - 1) = 2(y + 2)$$

$$4y - 4 = 2y + 4$$

$$2y - 4 = 4$$

$$2y = 8$$

$$\frac{2y}{2} = \frac{8}{2}$$

$$y = 4$$

25. C

Isolate x on one side of the equation:

$$\frac{3}{4} + x = 8.3$$

$$\frac{3}{4} + x - \frac{3}{4} = 8.3 - \frac{3}{4}$$

$$x = 8.3 - \frac{3}{4}$$

Then $\frac{3}{4}$ can be rewritten as 0.75, and subtracting 0.75 from 8.3 gives you 7.55.

26. E

Multiply through and find a in terms of m by isolating a on one side of the equation:

$$2(a + m) = 5m - 3 + a$$

$$2a + 2m = 5m - 3 + a$$

$$2a = 3m - 3 + a$$

$$a = 3m - 3$$

CHAPTER 13: GEOMETRY

Like the rest of the math you'll see on your private school admissions test, the geometry will range from straightforward to difficult. You can count on seeing questions that test your knowledge of lines and angles, triangles, circles, and other assorted geometric figures. You will also see a little coordinate geometry. And finally, diagramless geometry can also show up in the form of word problems.

The most helpful thing you can do is review geometry content and practice a whole lot. If you're concerned about your math readiness, spend more time with the subjects that are less familiar to you. Make certain that you do all of the problems in the practice set even if you feel comfortable with the example questions presented.

It's important to know that unless otherwise indicated, *figures are drawn to scale*. That means you can usually eyeball the measurements of a figure.

LINES AND ANGLES

LINE SEGMENTS

Some of the most basic geometry problems deal with line segments. A **line segment** is a piece of a line, and it has an exact measurable length. A question might give you a segment divided into several pieces, provide the measurements of some of these pieces, and ask you for the measurement of a remaining piece.

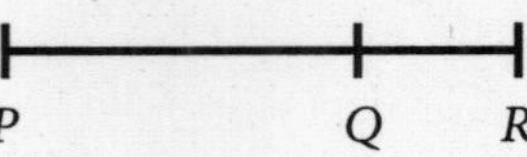

If $PR = 12$ and $QR = 4$, $PQ =$

$PQ = PR - QR$

$PQ = 12 - 4$

$PQ = 8$

The point exactly in the middle of a line segment, halfway between the endpoints, is called the **midpoint** of the line segment. To **bisect** means to cut in half, so the midpoint of a line segment bisects that line segment.

M is the midpoint of AB, so $AM = MB$.

ANGLES

A **right angle** measures 90 degrees and is usually indicated in a diagram by a little box. The figure above is a right angle. Lines that intersect to form right angles are said to be **perpendicular.**

$a°$ $b°$

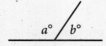

Angles that form **a straight line add up to 180 degrees**. In the figure above, $a + b = 180$.

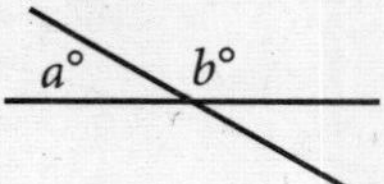

When two lines intersect, **adjacent angles are supplementary,** meaning they add up to 180 degrees. In the previous figure, $a + b = 180$.

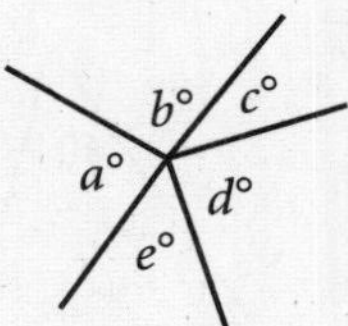

Angles around a point add up to 360 degrees. In the figure above, $a + b + c + d + e = 360$.

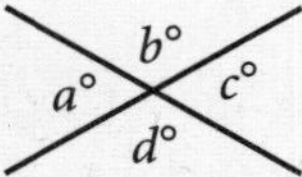

When lines intersect, angles across the vertex from each other are called **vertical angles** and **are equal to each other.** Above, $a = c$ and $b = d$.

PARALLEL LINES

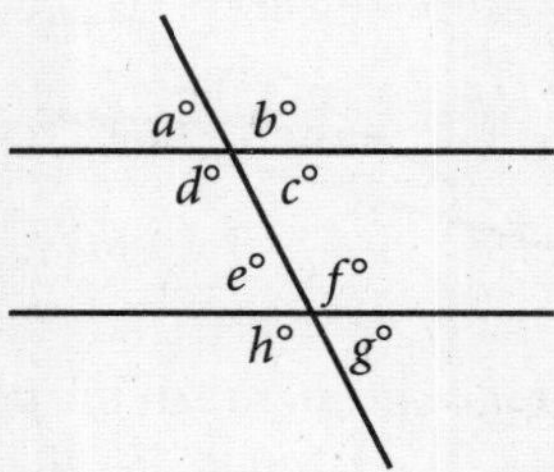

When parallel lines are crossed by a transversal:

- Corresponding angles are equal (for example, $a = e$).
- Alternate interior angles are equal ($d = f$).
- Same-side interior angles are supplementary ($c + f = 180$).
- All four acute angles are equal, as are all four obtuse angles.

TRIANGLES

There are a few basic rules that apply to triangles in general.

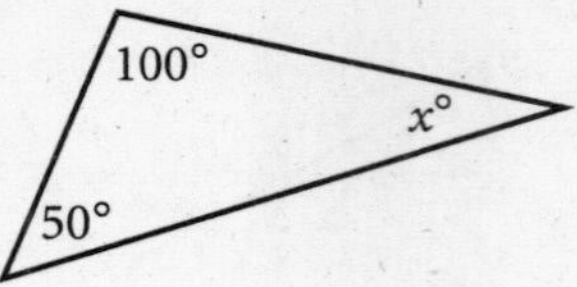

The three interior angles of any triangle add up to 180°. In the previous figure, $x + 50 + 100 = 180$, so $x = 30$.

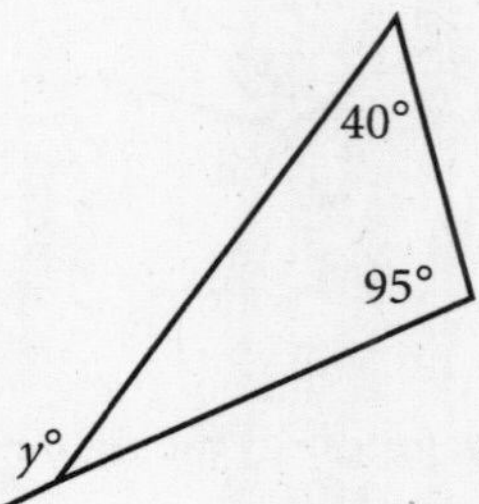

An exterior angle equals the sum of the remote interior angles. In the figure above, the exterior angle labeled $y°$ equals the sum of the remote interior angles: $y = 40 + 95 = 135$.

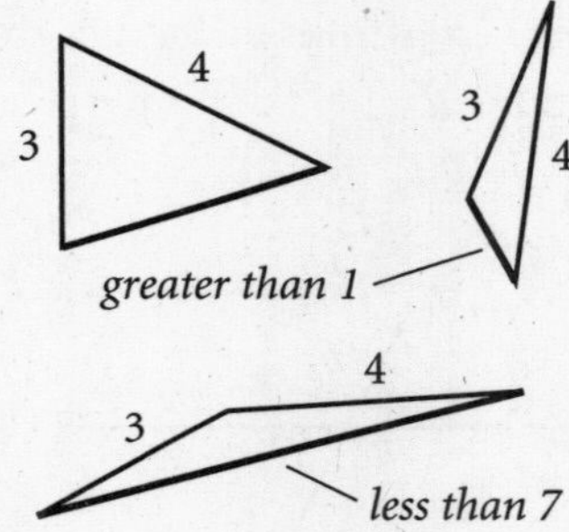

The length of one side of a triangle must be greater than the positive difference and less than the sum of the lengths of the other two sides. If it is given that the length of one side is 3 and the length of another side is 4, then the length of the third side must be greater than $4 - 3 = 1$ and less than $4 + 3 = 7$.

Triangles—Perimeter and Area

The **perimeter** of a triangle is the sum of the lengths of its sides.

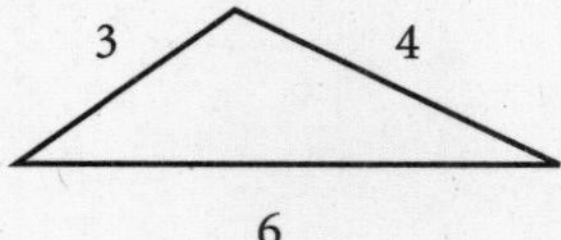

The perimeter of the triangle in the figure above is $3 + 4 + 6 = 13$.

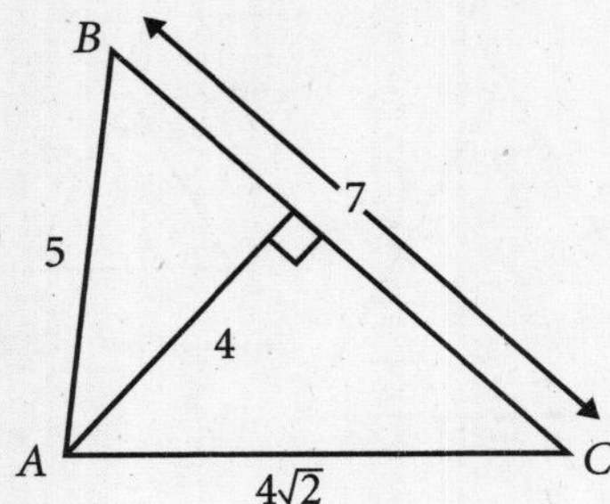

The **area** of a triangle is one-half base times height. The height is the perpendicular distance between the side that's chosen as the base and the opposite vertex. In this triangle, 4 is the height when the 7 is chosen as the base.

$$\text{Area} = \frac{1}{2}bh = \frac{1}{2}(7)(4) = 14$$

Similar Triangles

Similar triangles have the same shape: **Corresponding angles are equal, and corresponding sides are proportional.**

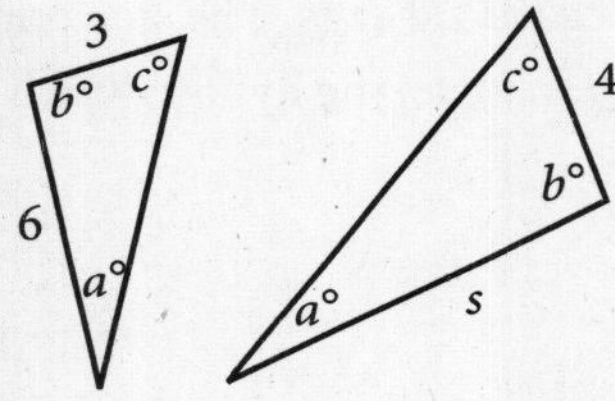

These triangles are similar because they have the same angles. The 3 corresponds to the 4, and the 6 corresponds to the *s*.

$$\frac{3}{4} = \frac{6}{s}$$
$$3s = 24$$
$$s = 8$$

Special Triangles

Special triangles are the isosceles, equilateral, and right triangles.

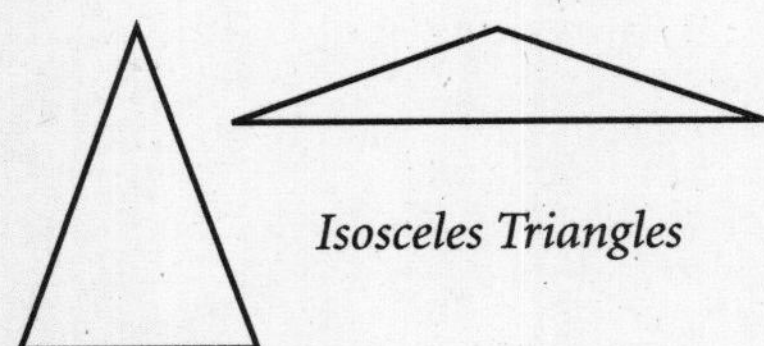

Isosceles Triangles

An **isosceles triangle** is a triangle that has two equal sides. Not only are two sides equal, but the angles opposite the equal sides, called base angles, are also equal.

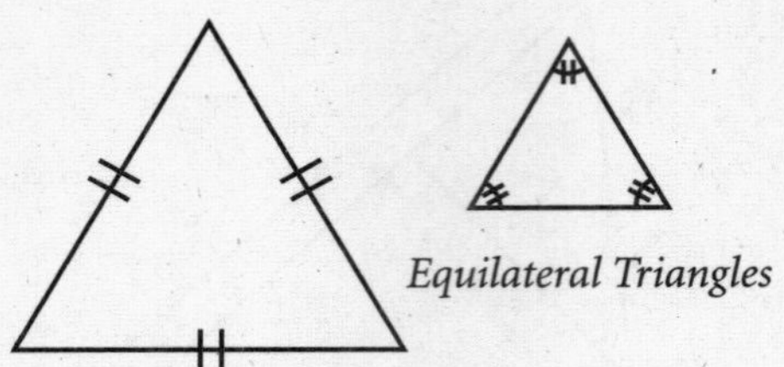

Equilateral Triangles

Equilateral triangles are triangles in which all three sides are equal. Since all the sides are equal, all the angles are also equal. All three angles in an equilateral triangle measure 60 degrees, regardless of the lengths of the sides.

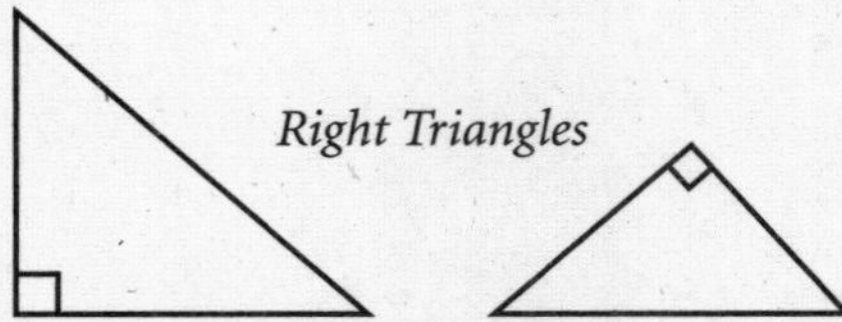

Right Triangles

A **right triangle** is a triangle with a right angle. Every right triangle has exactly two acute angles. The sides opposite the acute angles are called the **legs**. The side opposite the right angle is called the **hypotenuse**. Since it's opposite the largest angle, the hypotenuse is the longest side of a right triangle.

Right Triangles

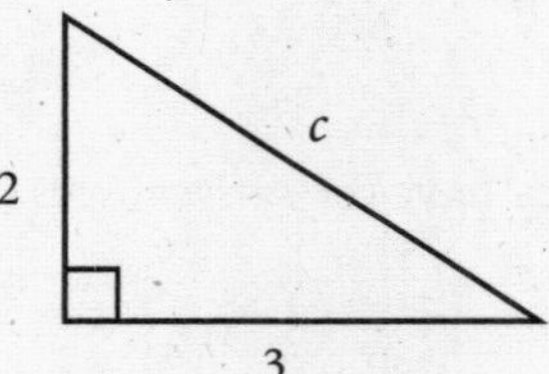

Pythagorean Theorem

The Pythagorean theorem is as follows:

$$(\text{leg}_1)^2 + (\text{leg}_2)^2 = (\text{hypotenuse})^2 \text{ or } a^2 + b^2 = c^2$$

If one leg is 2 and the other leg is 3, then

$$2^2 + 3^2 = c^2$$
$$c^2 = 4 + 9$$
$$c = \sqrt{13}$$

PYTHAGOREAN "TRIPLETS"

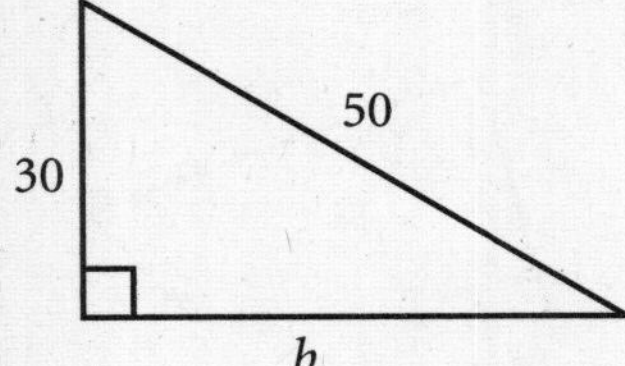

If a right triangle's leg-to-leg ratio is 3:4, or if the leg-to-hypotenuse ratio is 3:5 or 4:5, it's a 3-4-5 triangle and you don't need to use the Pythagorean theorem to find the third side. Just figure out what multiple of 3-4-5 it is. In this right triangle, one leg is 30 and the hypotenuse is 50. This is 10 times 3-4-5. The other leg, *b*, is 40.

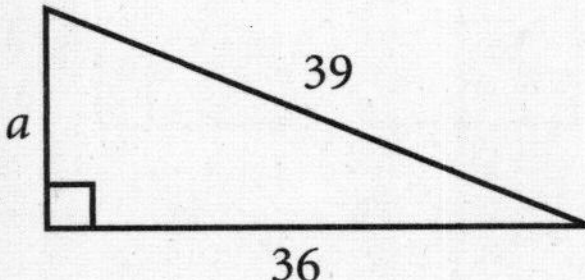

If a right triangle's leg-to-leg ratio is 5:12, or if the leg-to-hypotenuse ratio is 5:13 or 12:13, then it's a **5-12-13 triangle** and you don't need to use the Pythagorean theorem to find the third side. Just figure out what multiple of 5-12-13 it is. Here one leg is 36 and the hypotenuse is 39. This is 3 times 5-12-13. The other leg, *a*, is 15.

SIDE–ANGLE RATIOS

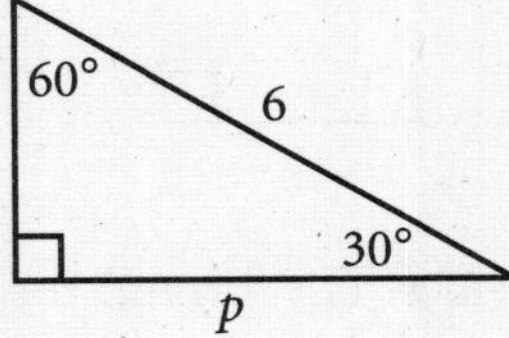

The sides of a 30-60-90 triangle are in a ratio of $x:x\sqrt{3}:2x$. You don't need to use the Pythagorean theorem. If the hypotenuse is 6, then the shorter leg is half that, or 3; and then the longer leg, *p*, is equal to the short leg times $\sqrt{3}$, or $3\sqrt{3}$.

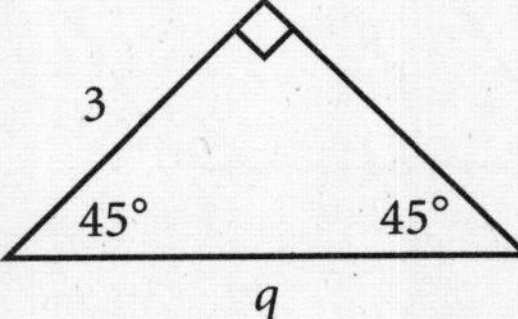

The sides of a 45-45-90 triangle are in a ratio of $x:x:x\sqrt{2}$. If one leg is 3, then the other leg is also 3, and the hypotenuse, *q*, is equal to a leg multiplied by $\sqrt{2}$, or $3\sqrt{2}$.

QUADRILATERALS

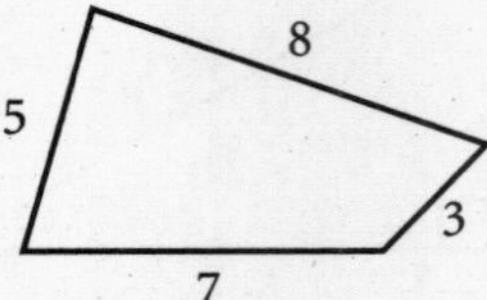

The **perimeter** of a polygon is the sum of the lengths of its sides. The perimeter of the quadrilateral in the figure above is 5 + 8 + 3 + 7 = 23.

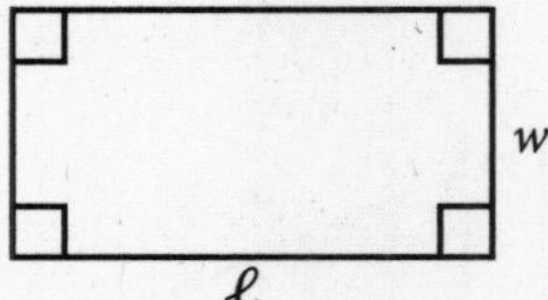

A **rectangle** is a parallelogram containing four right angles. Opposite sides are equal. The formula for the area of a rectangle is

Area = (length)(width)

In the figure above, ℓ = length and w = width, so area = ℓw. Perimeter = $2(\ell + w)$.

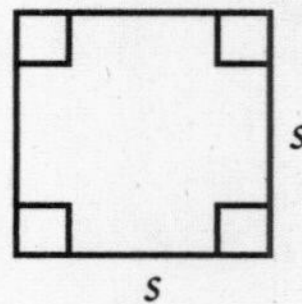

A **square** is a rectangle with four equal sides. The formula for the area of a square is

Area = (side)^2

In the figure above, s = the length of a side, so area = s^2. Perimeter = $4s$.

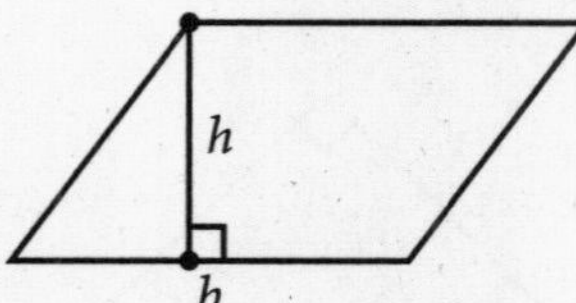

A **parallelogram** is a quadrilateral with two sets of parallel sides. Opposite sides are equal, as are opposite angles. The formula for the area of a parallelogram is

Area = (base)(height)

In the previous diagram, h = height and b = base, so area = bh.

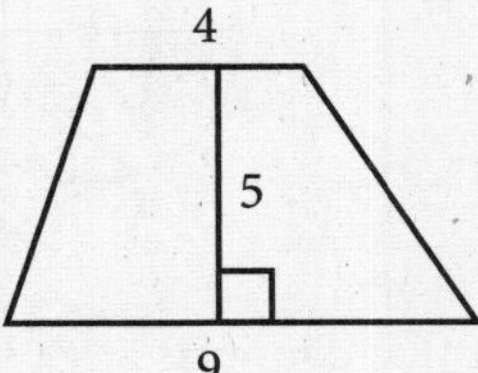

A **trapezoid** is a quadrilateral with one pair of parallel sides. The formula for the area of a trapezoid is

$$\textbf{Area} = \frac{1}{2}\textbf{(sum of the lengths of the parallel sides)(height)}$$

In the figure above, the area of the trapezoid is $\frac{1}{2}(4 + 9)(5) = 32.5$

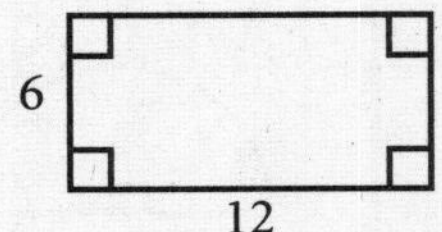

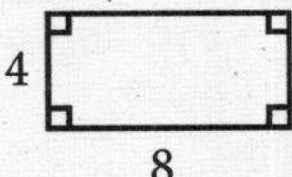

If two polygons are similar, then corresponding angles are equal and corresponding sides are in proportion.

The two rectangles above are similar because all the angles are right angles and each side of the larger rectangle is $1\frac{1}{2}$ times the corresponding side of the smaller.

CIRCLES

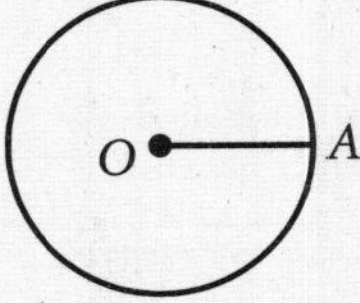

A **circle** is a figure each point of which is an equal distance from its center. In the diagram, O is the center of the circle.

The **radius** of a circle is the straight-line distance from its center to any point on the circle. All radii of one circle have equal lengths. In the previous figure, OA is a radius of circle O.

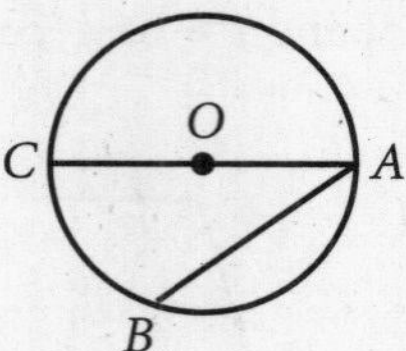

A **chord** is a line segment that connects any two points on a circle. Segments *AB* and *AC* are both chords. The largest chord that may be drawn in a circle will be a diameter of that circle.

A **diameter** of a circle is a chord that passes through the circle's center. All diameters are the same length and are equal to twice the radius. In the figure above, *AC* is a diameter of circle *O*.

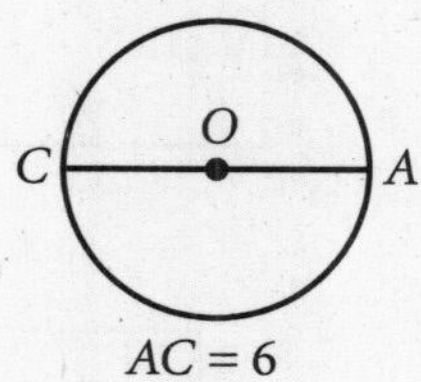

$AC = 6$

WHAT'S π?

"π is an infinite and nonrepeating decimal, but all you need to remember is that it's approximately 3.14."

The **circumference** of a circle is the distance around it. It is equal to πd, or $2\pi r$. In this example, circumference = $\pi d = 6\pi$.

The **area** of a circle equals π times the square of the radius, or πr^2. In this example, since *AC* is the diameter, $r = \frac{6}{2} = 3$, and area = $\pi r^2 = \pi(3^2) = 9\pi$.

COORDINATE GEOMETRY

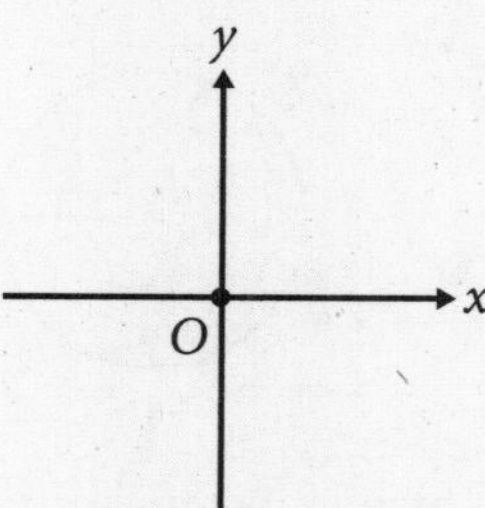

The previous diagram represents the **coordinate axes**—the perpendicular "number lines" in the coordinate plane. The horizontal line is called the ***x*-axis.** The vertical line is called the ***y*-axis.** In a coordinate plane, the point *O* at which the two axes intersect is called the **origin.**

The pair of numbers, written inside parentheses, that specify the location of a point in the coordinate plane are called **coordinates.** The first number is the ***x*-coordinate,** and the second number is the ***y*-coordinate.** The **origin** is the zero point on both axes, with coordinates (0, 0).

Starting at the origin:

to the right:	x is positive.
to the left:	x is negative.
up:	y is positive.
down:	y is negative.

The two axes divide the coordinate plane into four quadrants. When you know what quadrant a point lies in, you know the signs of its coordinates. A point in the upper left quadrant, for example, has a negative x-coordinate and a positive y-coordinate.

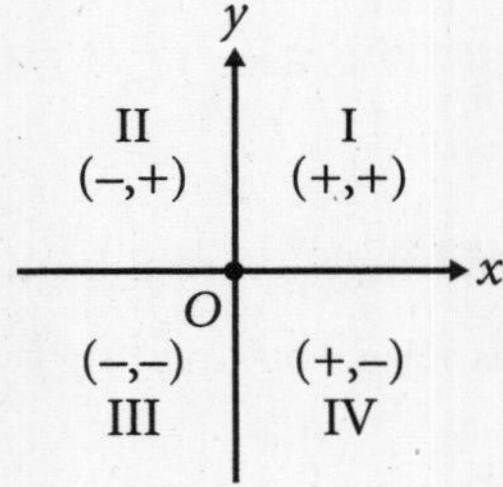

Plotting Points

If you were asked to graph the point (2, –3) you would start at the origin and count 2 units to the right and 3 down. To graph (–4, 5) you would start at the origin and go 4 units to the left and 5 units up.

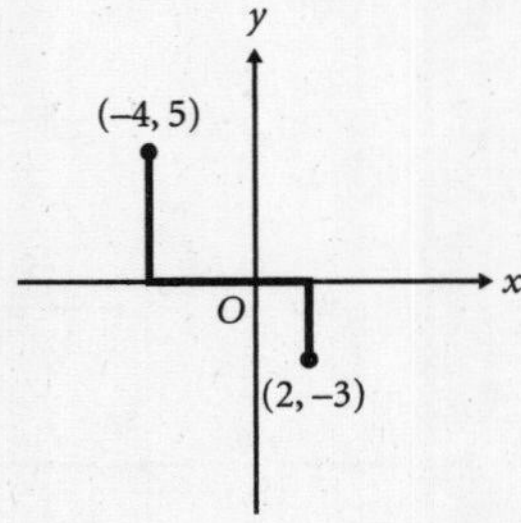

Slope of a Line

To use two points to find the **slope of a line**, use the following formula:

$$\text{Slope} = \frac{\text{change in } y}{\text{change in } x} \text{ or slope} = \frac{\Delta y}{\Delta x} \text{ or } \frac{y_2 - y_1}{x_2 - x_1}.$$

EXAMPLE

Calculate the slope of a line that contains the points $A(4, 6)$ and $B(0, -3)$.

$$\frac{y_2 - y_1}{x_2 - x_1} = \frac{-3-6}{0-4} = \frac{-9}{-4} = \frac{9}{4}$$

To use an equation of a line to find the slope, put the equation into the **slope-intercept form**:

$y = mx + b$, where the slope is m

EXAMPLE

To find the slope of the equation $5x + 3y = 6$, rearrange it:

$5x + 3y = 6$

$3y = -5x + 6$ Subtract $5x$ from both sides of the equation.

$y = -\frac{5}{3}x + 2$ Isolate y by dividing by 3.

The slope is $-\frac{5}{3}$.

Figuring Lengths

To find the length of a line segment **parallel to the *x*-axis** in the coordinate plane, calculate the absolute value of the difference of its *x*-coordinates.

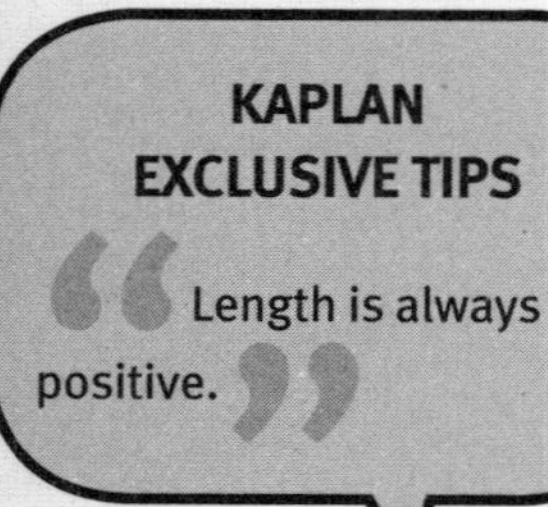

To find the length of a line segment **parallel to the *y*-axis** in the coordinate plane, calculate the absolute value of the difference of its *y*-coordinates.

EXAMPLE

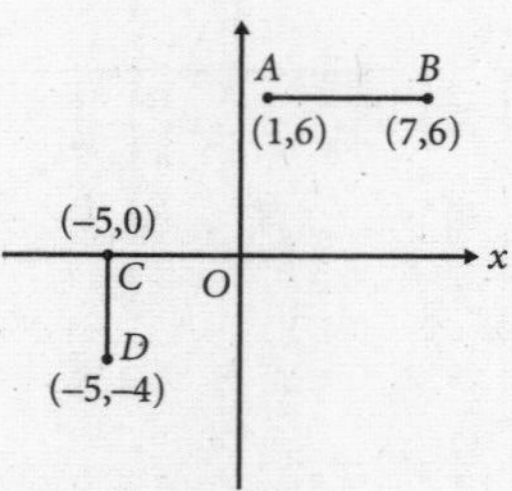

In the figure above, the length of AB is $|7 - 1| = 6$. The length of CD is $|0 - (-4)| = 4$.

Retracing a Geometric Figure

Some geometry questions ask you to determine whether a figure can be drawn without lifting the pencil. There's a simple rule for determining this: In any given figure, if exactly zero or two points have an odd number of intersecting line segments and/or curves, it can be drawn without lifting the pencil or retracing.

EXAMPLE

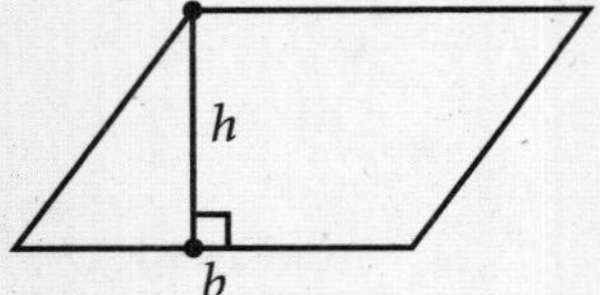

The figure above has two points that have three intersecting lines (an odd number), so it can be drawn without lifting your pencil.

PRACTICE QUESTIONS

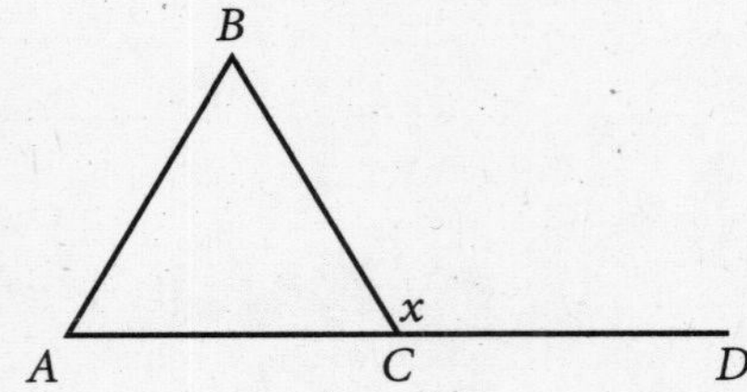

1. In the figure above, segments *AB*, *BC*, *CD*, and *AC* are all equal. What is the value of *x*?

(A) 30
(B) 45
(C) 60
(D) 90
(E) 120

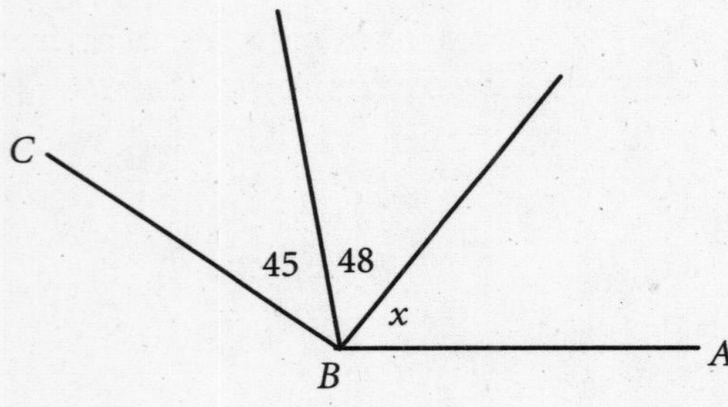

2. If the measure of angle *ABC* is 145°, what is the value of *x*?

(A) 39
(B) 45
(C) 52
(D) 55
(E) 62

3. If the perimeter of a square is 32 meters, what is the area of the square, in square meters?

(A) 16
(B) 32
(C) 48
(D) 56
(E) 64

4. In triangle *XYZ* the measure of angle *Y* is twice the measure of angle *X*, and the measure of *Z* is three times the measure of angle *X*. What is the degree measure of angle *Y*?

(A) 15
(B) 30
(C) 45
(D) 60
(E) 90

5. The perimeter of triangle *ABC* is 24. If $AB = 9$ and $BC = 7$, then $AC =$

(A) 6.
(B) 8.
(C) 10.
(D) 15.
(E) 17.

6. If the perimeter of an equilateral triangle is 150, what is the length of one of its sides?

(A) 35
(B) 35
(C) 50
(D) 75
(E) 100

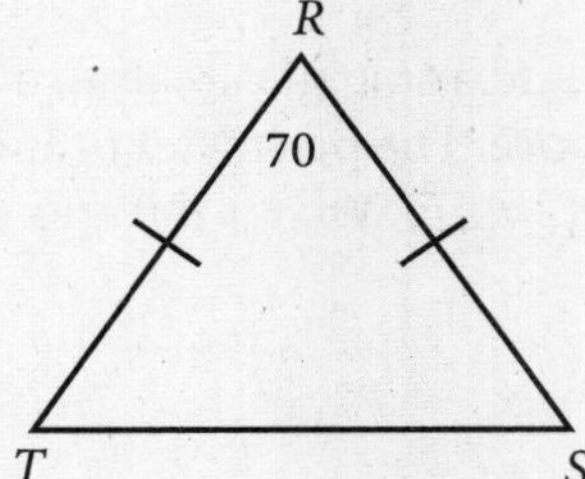

7. In triangle RST, if $RS = RT$, what is the degree measure of angle S?

(A) 40
(B) 55
(C) 70
(D) 110
(E) It cannot be determined from the information given.

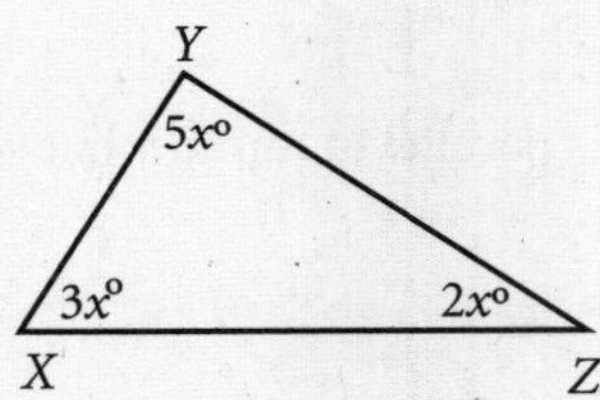

8. In triangle XYZ, what is the degree measure of angle YXZ?

(A) 18
(B) 36
(C) 54
(D) 72
(E) 90

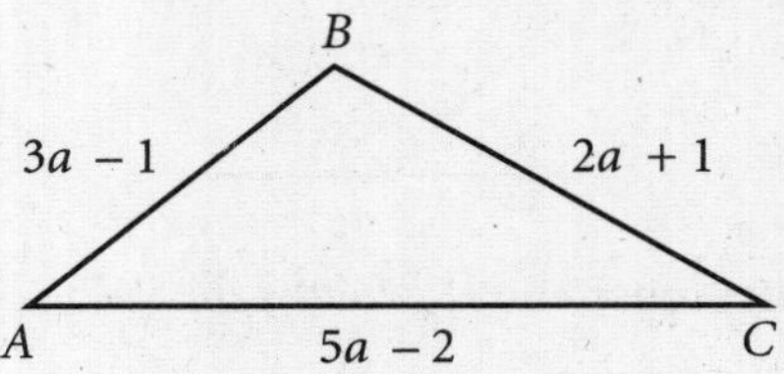

9. If the perimeter of triangle ABC is 18, what is the length of AC?

(A) 2
(B) 4
(C) 5
(D) 6
(E) 8

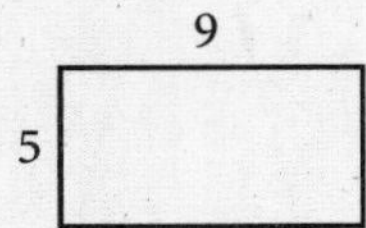

10. What is the area, in square units, of a square that has the same perimeter as the rectangle above?

(A) 25
(B) 36
(C) 49
(D) 64
(E) 81

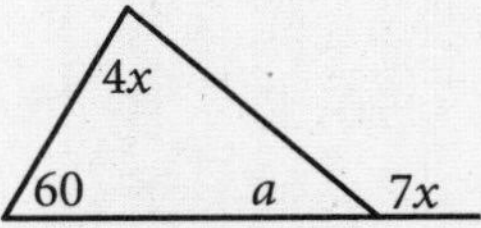

11. What is the value of a in the figure above?

(A) 20
(B) 40
(C) 60
(D) 80
(E) 140

12. In the figure above, what is the value of n?

    (A) 30
    (B) 60
    (C) 45
    (D) 90
    (E) 135

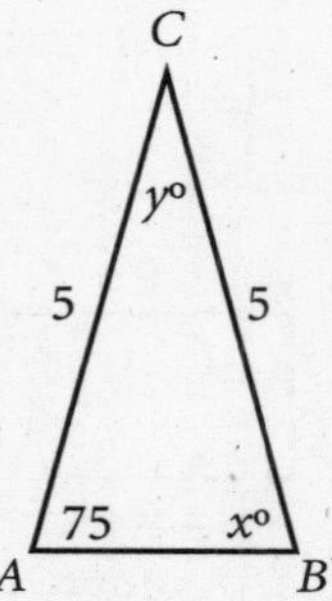

13. In the figure above, what is the value of $x - y$?

    (A) 30
    (B) 45
    (C) 75
    (D) 105
    (E) 150

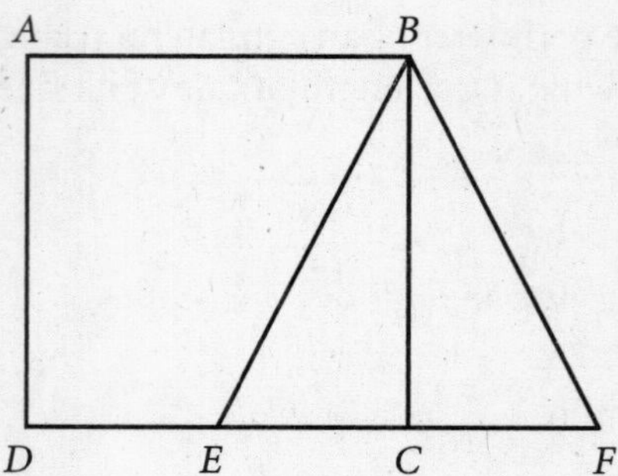

14. A square and a triangle are drawn together as shown above. The perimeter of the square is 64 and $DC = EF$. What is the area of triangle BEF?

    (A) 32
    (B) 64
    (C) 128
    (D) 256
    (E) It cannot be determined from the information given.

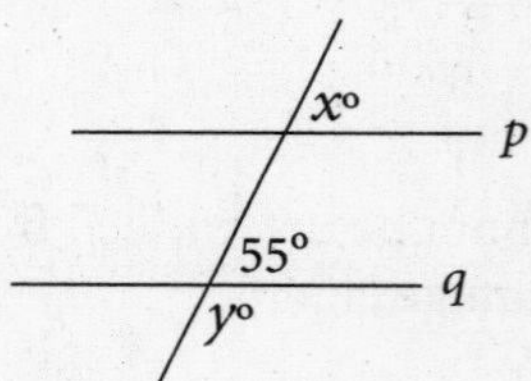

15. If line p is parallel to line q, what is the value of $x + y$?

    (A) 90
    (B) 110
    (C) 125
    (D) 180
    (E) 250

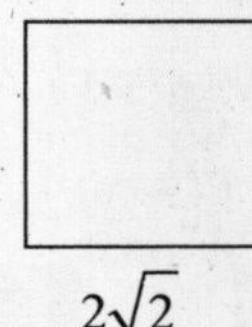

16. What is the area of the square above?

    (A) 4
    (B) $4\sqrt{2}$
    (C) 8
    (D) 16
    (E) 24

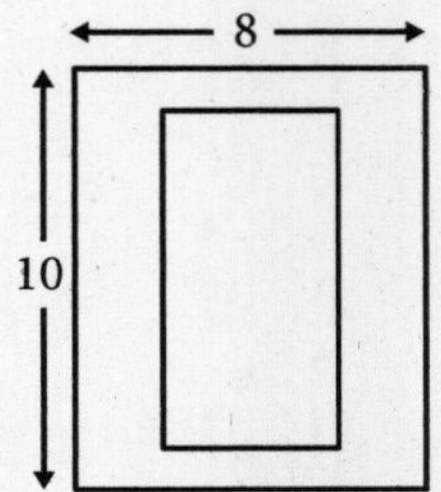

17. What is the area of the frame in the figure above if the inside picture has a length of 8 and a width of 4?

    (A) 4
    (B) 8
    (C) 16
    (D) 24
    (E) 48

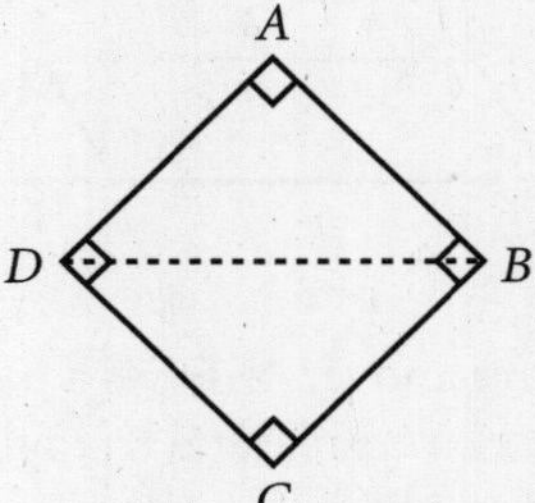

18. In the figure above, *ABCD* is a square, and the area of triangle *ABD* is 8. What is the area of square *ABCD*?

    (A) 2
    (B) 4
    (C) 8
    (D) 16
    (E) 64

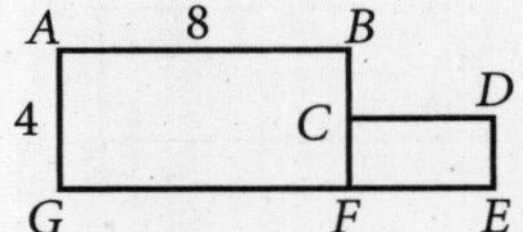

Note: Figure not drawn to scale.

19. In the figure above, *ABFG* and *CDEF* are rectangles, *CD* bisects *BF*, and *EF* has a length of 2. What is the area of the entire figure?

    (A) 4
    (B) 16
    (C) 32
    (D) 36
    (E) 72

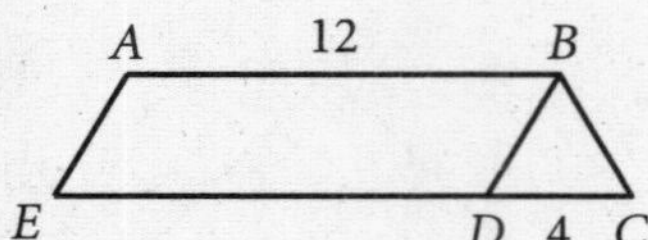

20. In the figure above, *ABDE* is a parallelogram, and *BCD* is an equilateral triangle. What is the perimeter of *ABCE*?

(A) 12
(B) 16
(C) 24
(D) 32
(E) 36

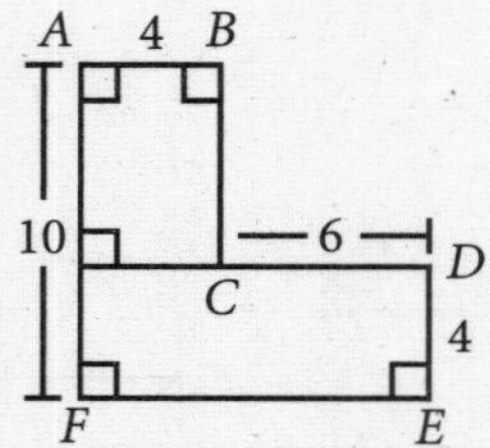

21. In the figure above, what is the perimeter of *ABCDEF*?

(A) 14
(B) 24
(C) 28
(D) 38
(E) 40

22. If the shaded regions are 4 rectangles, what is the area of the unshaded region?

(A) 9
(B) 12
(C) 16
(D) 19
(E) 20

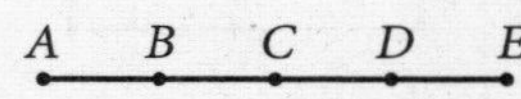

Note: Figure not drawn to scale.

23. In the figure above, *AB* is twice the length of *BC*, $BC = CD$, and *DE* is triple the length of *CD*. If $AE = 49$, what is the length of *BD*?

(A) 14
(B) 21
(C) 28
(D) 30
(E) 35

8 inches

P

24. In the figure above, circle *P* is inscribed in a square with sides of 8 inches. What is the area of the circle?

    (A) 4π square inches
    (B) 16 square inches
    (C) 8π square inches
    (D) 16π square inches
    (E) 32π square inches

25. What is the radius of a circle whose circumference is 36π?

    (A) 3
    (B) 6
    (C) 8
    (D) 18
    (E) 36

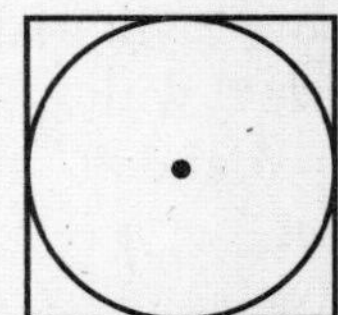

26. If the perimeter of the square is 36, what is the circumference of the circle?

    (A) 6π
    (B) 9π
    (C) 12π
    (D) 15π
    (E) 18π

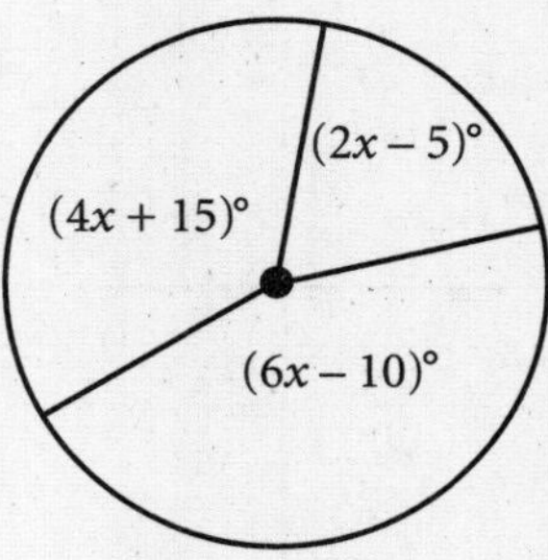

27. In the figure above, what is the value of *x*?

    (A) 15
    (B) 30
    (C) 55
    (D) 70
    (E) 135

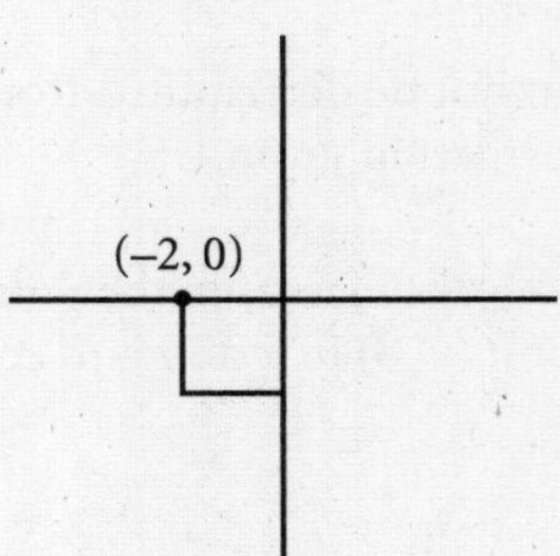

28. In the figure above, a square is graphed on the coordinate plane. If the coordinates of one corner are $(-2, 0)$, what is the area of the square?

    (A) $\frac{1}{4}$
    (B) 1
    (C) 2
    (D) 4
    (E) 16

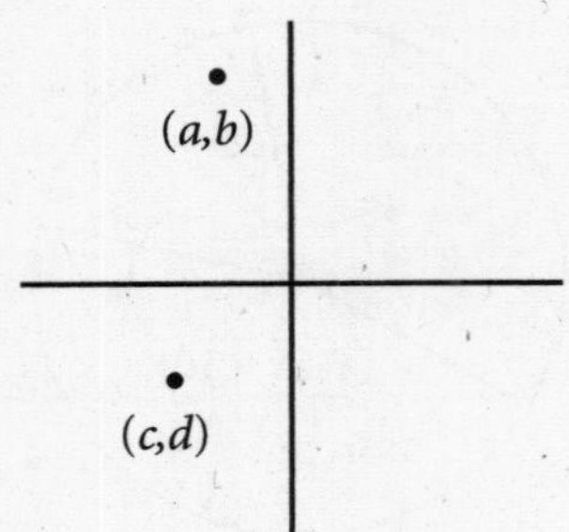

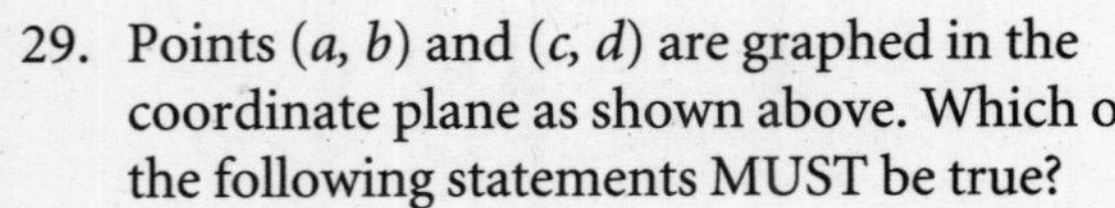

29. Points (a, b) and (c, d) are graphed in the coordinate plane as shown above. Which of the following statements MUST be true?

(A) $bd > ac$
(B) $c > ad$
(C) $b > acd$
(D) $bc > ad$
(E) It cannot be determined from the information given.

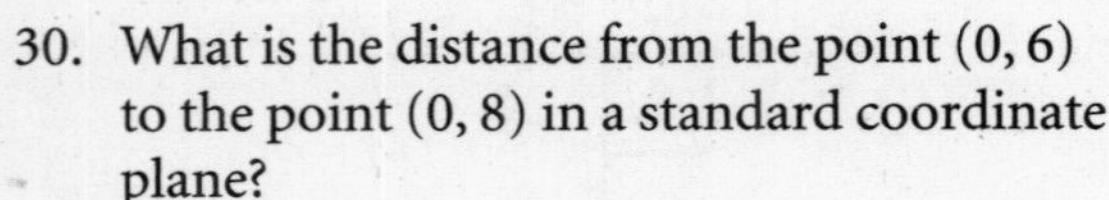

30. What is the distance from the point (0, 6) to the point (0, 8) in a standard coordinate plane?

(A) 2
(B) 7
(C) 10
(D) 12
(E) 14

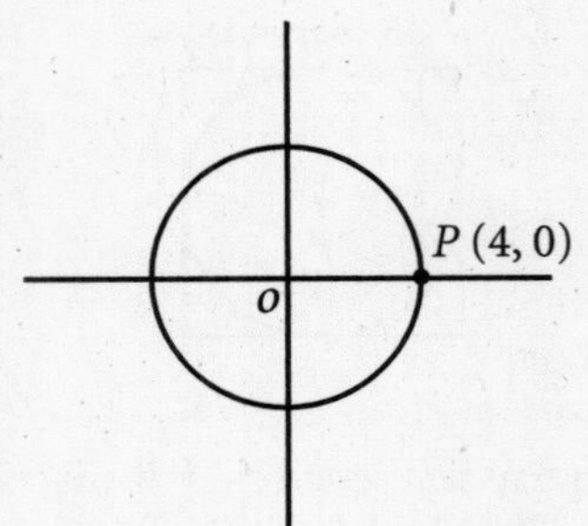

31. Circle O above has its center at the origin. If point P lies on circle O, what is the area of circle O?

(A) 4π
(B) 8π
(C) 10π
(D) 12π
(E) 16π

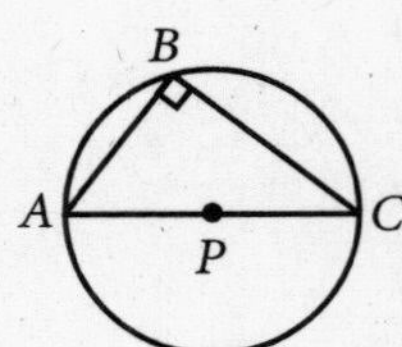

32. In the figure above, right triangle ABC is inscribed in circle P, with AC passing through center P. If $AB = 6$, and $BC = 8$, what is the area of the circle?

(A) 10π
(B) 14π
(C) 25π
(D) 49π
(E) 100π

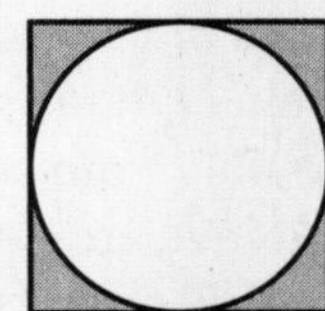

33. In the figure above, a circle is inscribed within a square. If the area of the circle is 25π, what is the perimeter of the shaded region?

(A) $40 + 5\pi$
(B) $40 + 10\pi$
(C) $100 + 10\pi$
(D) $100 + 25\pi$
(E) $40 + 50\pi$

34. What is the slope of the line that contains points $(3, -5)$ and $(-1, 7)$?

(A) -3
(B) $-\frac{1}{3}$
(C) $-\frac{1}{4}$
(D) $\frac{1}{3}$
(E) 3

35. If the circumference of a circle is 16π, what is its area?

(A) 8π
(B) 16π
(C) 32π
(D) 64π
(E) 256π

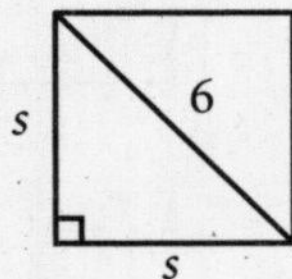

36. What is the area of the square above with diagonals of length 6?

(A) 9
(B) 12
(C) $9\sqrt{2}$
(D) 15
(E) 18

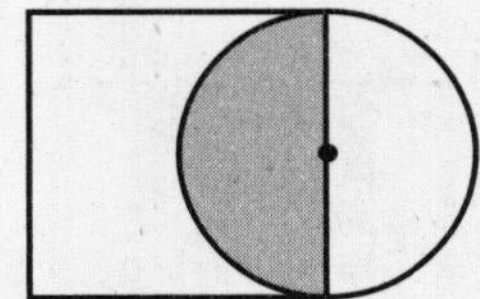

37. A square and a circle are drawn as shown above. The area of the square is 64. What is the area of the shaded region?

(A) 4π
(B) 8π
(C) 16π
(D) 32π
(E) It cannot be determined from the information given.

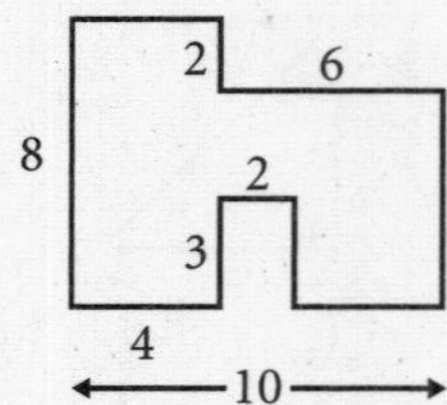

38. What is the area of the polygon above if each corner of the polygon is a right angle?

(A) 40
(B) 62
(C) 68
(D) 74
(E) 80

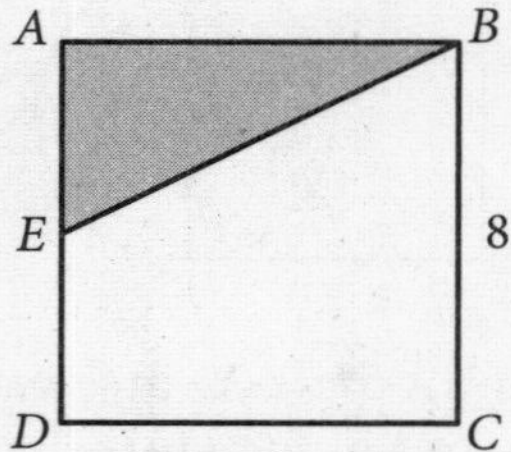

39. *ABCD* is a square. If *E* is the midpoint of *AD*, what is the area of the shaded region?

(A) 8
(B) 12
(C) 16
(D) 24
(E) 32

40. Circle *A* has radius $r + 1$. Circle *B* has radius $r + 2$. What is the positive difference between the circumference of circle *B* and the circumference of circle *A*?

(A) 1
(B) 2π
(C) $2\pi + 3$
(D) $2\pi r + 3$
(E) $2\pi(2r + 3)$

41. Erica has 8 squares of felt, each with an area of 16. For a certain craft project, she cuts the largest circle possible from each square of felt. What is the combined area of the excess felt left over after cutting out all the circles?

(A) $4(4 - \pi)$
(B) $8(4 - \pi)$
(C) $8(\pi - 2)$
(D) $32(4 - \pi)$
(E) $8(16 - \pi)$

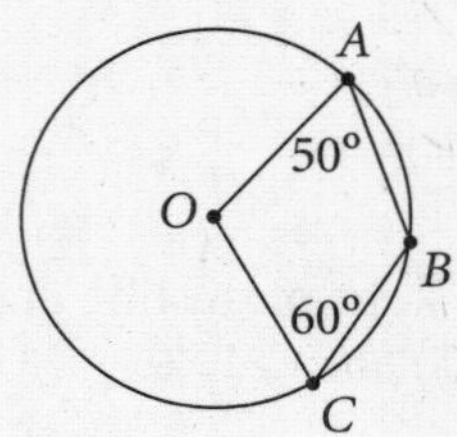

42. In the figure above, points *A*, *B*, and *C* lie on the circumference of the circle centered at *O*. If $\angle OAB$ measures 50° and $\angle BCO$ measures 60°, what is the degree measure of $\angle AOC$?

(A) 110
(B) 125
(C) 140
(D) 250
(E) It cannot be determined from the information given.

PRACTICE QUESTION ANSWERS

1. E

Since $AB = BC = AC$, triangle ABC is equilateral. Therefore, all of its angles are 60°. Since angle BCD or x is supplementary to angle BCA, a 60° angle, the value of x is $180 - 60$ or 120.

2. C

Since the degree measure of angle ABC is 145, $45 + 48 + x = 145$, $93 + x = 145$, and $x = 52$.

3. E

A square has four equal sides, so its perimeter is equal to $4s$, where s is the length of a side of the square. Its perimeter is 32, so its side length is $32 \div 4 = 8$. The area of a square is equal to s^2, so the area of the square is 8^2 or 64.

4. D

In any triangle, the measures of the three interior angles sum to 180°, so $X + Y + Z = 180$. Since the measure of angle Y is twice the measure of angle X, $Y = 2X$. Similarly, $Z = 3X$. So $X + 2X + 3X = 180$, $6X = 180$ and $X = 30$. Since $Y = 2X$, the degree measure of angle Y is $2 \bullet 30 = 60$.

5. B

The perimeter of a triangle is the sum of the lengths of its sides, in this case, $AB + BC + AC$. The perimeter of triangle ABC is 24, so plugging in the given values, $9 + 7 + AC = 24$, $16 + AC = 24$, and $AC = 8$.

6. C

In an equilateral triangle, all three sides have equal length. The perimeter of a triangle is equal to the sum of the lengths of its three sides. Since all three sides are equal, each side must be $\frac{1}{3}$ of 150, or 50.

7. B

Since RS and RT are equal, the angles opposite them must be equal. Therefore, angle T = angle S. Since the three angles of a triangle sum to 180, 70 + angle S + angle T = 180 and angle S + angle T = 110. Since the two angles, S and T, are equal, each must be half of 110, or 55.

8. C

The three interior angles of a triangle add up to 180 degrees, so $2x + 3x + 5x = 180$, $10x = 180$ degrees and $x = 18$. So angle YXZ has a degree measure of $3x = 3(18) = 54$.

9. E

The perimeter of triangle ABC is 18, so $AB + BC + AC = 18$. Plugging in the algebraic expressions given for the length of each side, you get:

$$\begin{aligned}(3a - 1) + (2a + 1) + (5a - 2) &= 18 \\ 10a - 2 &= 18 \\ 10a &= 20 \\ a &= 2\end{aligned}$$

The length of AC is given as $5a - 2$, so $AC = 5(2) - 2 = 8$.

10. C

The perimeter of a rectangle is $2(\ell + w)$, where ℓ represents its length and w its width. The perimeter of this rectangle is $2(9 + 5) = 28$. A square has four equal sides, so a square with a perimeter of 28 has sides of length 7. The area of a square is equal to the length of a side squared, so the area of a square with a perimeter of 28 is 7^2 or 49.

11. B

An exterior angle of a triangle equals the sum of the two remote interior angles. So $7x = 4x + 60$, $3x = 60$, and $x = 20$. So the angle marked $7x°$ has a degree measure of $7(20) = 140$. The angle marked $a°$ is supplementary to this angle, so its measure is $180 - 140 = 40$.

12. C

We are given a right angle, so that is 90°. A straight angle contains 180°, so $2n + 90 = 180$, $2n = 90$, and $n = 45$.

13. B

Since $AC = CB$, the angles opposite these sides are equal as well. So angle CAB = angle CBA, and $x = 75$. The three interior angles of a triangle sum to 180 degrees, so $2(75) + y = 180$ and $y = 30$. The question asks for the value of $x - y$, or $75 - 30 = 45$.

14. C

The area of a triangle is equal to $\frac{1}{2}bh$. In triangle BEF, the height is BC and the base is EF. The square's perimeter is 64, so each of its sides is a fourth of 64, or 16. Therefore $BC = 16$. The question also states that $DC = EF$, so $EF = 16$ as well. Plugging into the formula, the area of triangle BEF is $\frac{1}{2}(16 \times 16) = 128$.

15. D

When parallel lines are crossed by a transversal, all acute angles formed are equal, and all acute angles are supplementary to all obtuse angles. So in this diagram, the obtuse angle measuring $y°$ is supplementary to the acute angle measuring $x°$, so $x + y = 180$.

16. C

The area of a square is equal to the square of one of its sides. In this case, the square has a side length of $2\sqrt{2}$, so its area is $(2\sqrt{2})^2$ or $2 \times 2 \times \sqrt{2} \times \sqrt{2}$ or $4 \times 2 = 8$.

17. E

To find the area of the frame, find the area of the frame and picture combined (the outer rectangle) and subtract from it the area of the picture (the inner rectangle). The outer rectangle has area $10 \times 8 = 80$, the inner rectangle has area $8 \times 4 = 32$, so the area of the frame is $80 - 32 = 48$.

18. D

Diagonal BD divides square $ABCD$ into two identical triangles. If the area of triangle ABD is 8, the area of the square must be twice this, or 16.

19. D

The area of the entire figure is equal to the area of rectangle $ABFG$ plus the area of rectangle $CDEF$. The area of $ABFG$ is $8 \bullet 4 = 32$. So the area of the entire figure must be greater than 32, and at this point you can eliminate (A), (B), and (C). Since BF has length 4, and C bisects BF, CF has length 2. The question states that EF has length 2, so $CDEF$ is actually a square, and its area is 2^2 or 4. So the area of the entire figure is $32 + 4 = 36$, choice (D).

20. E

The perimeter of $ABCE$ is equal to $AB + BC + CD + DE + EA$. Since triangle BCD is equilateral, $BC = CD = BD = 4$. Because $ABDE$ is a parallelogram, $AB = DE = 12$ and $BD = EA = 4$. Therefore the perimeter of $ABCE$ is $12 + 4 + 4 + 12 + 4 = 36$, choice (E).

21. E

Simply add the six sides of the L-shaped figure. Four of them are labeled, and you can use these to figure out the remaining two. The length of side *EF* must be equivalent to the sum of sides *AB* and *CD*, so $4 + 6 = 10$ and $EF = 10$. The length of side *BC* is equivalent to the difference between sides *AF* and *DE*, so $10 - 4 = 6$ and $BC = 6$. Therefore, the perimeter is $10 + 10 + 4 + 6 + 6 + 4 = 40$.

22. A

Each of the shaded rectangles has a side of length 3 opposite the side contributing to the interior unshaded region. So the interior region, a square, has an area of 3^2, or 9.

23. A

Let $BC = x$. *AB* has twice the length of *BC*, so it is $2x$. $BC = CD$, so $CD = x$. *DE* is three times the length of *CD*, or $3x$. Since $AE = 49$, $2x + x + x + 3x = 49$, $7x = 49$, and $x = 7$. *BD* is composed of segments *BC* and *CD*, so its length is $7 + 7 = 14$.

24. D

Since circle *P* is inscribed within the square, its diameter is equal in length to a side of the square. Since the circle's diameter is 8, its radius is half this, or 4. Area of a circle $= \pi r^2$, where *r* is the radius, so the area of circle *P* is $\pi(4)^2 = 16\pi$ square inches.

25. D

Circumference of a circle $= 2\pi r$, where *r* is the radius of the circle. So a circle with a circumference of 36π has a radius of $\frac{36\pi}{2\pi} = 18$.

26. B

The perimeter of the square is 36, and since all four sides are equal, one side has length 9. Since the circle is inscribed in the square, its diameter is equal in length to a side of the square, or 9. Circumference is πd, where *d* represents the diameter, so the circumference of the circle is 9π.

27. B

A circle contains 360°, so:

$$\begin{aligned}(4x + 15) + (2x - 5) + (6x - 10) &= 360\\ 4x + 2x + 6x + 15 - 5 - 10 &= 360\\ 12x &= 360\\ x &= 30\end{aligned}$$

28. D

The area of a square is equal to the square of the length of one of its sides. Since one vertex (corner) of the square lies on the origin at (0, 0) and another vertex lies on the point (–2, 0), the length of a side of the square is the distance from the origin to the point (–2, 0). This can be found by calculating the absolute value of the difference between the *x*-coordinates of the points, namely $|-2 - 0| = |-2| = 2$. Therefore, the area of the square is $2^2 = 4$.

29. C

While there's no way to determine the numerical values of *a*, *b*, *c*, or *d*, from their positions on the coordinate plane, you do know that *a* is negative, *b* is positive, *c* is negative, and *d* is negative. Bearing in mind that a negative times a negative is a positive, consider each answer choice. (C) is indeed true: *b*, which is positive, is greater than the product *acd*, which is negative.

30. A

The points (0, 6) and (0, 8) have the same x-coordinate. That means that the segment that connects them is parallel to the y-axis. Therefore, all you have to do to figure out the distance is subtract the y-coordinate and find the absolute value of the difference. $|8 - 6| = 2$, so the distance between the points is 2.

31. E

OP is the radius of the circle. Since O has coordinates (0, 0), the length of OP is $|4 - 0| = |4| = 4$. The area of a circle is πr^2 where r is the radius, so the area of circle O is $\pi(4)^2 = 16\pi$.

32. C

Right triangle ABC has legs of 6 and 8, so the legs are in a ratio of 3:4 and the triangle is a multiple of the 3-4-5 right triangle. Since the $3 \times 2 = 6$ and $4 \times 2 = 8$, double the hypotenuse length of 5 and the hypotenuse of triangle ABC equals 10. Notice that the hypotenuse is also the diameter of the circle. To find the area of the circle, we need its radius. Radius is half the diameter, so the radius of circle P is 5. The area of a circle is πr^2 where r is the radius, so the area of circle P is $\pi(5)^2 = 25\pi$.

33. B

The area of a circle is πr^2 where r is the radius, and since the area of the circle is 25π, its radius is 5. Circumference is equal to $2\pi r$, or $2\pi(5) = 10\pi$. Only (B) and (C) contain 10π, so you can eliminate (A), (D), and (E). Since the circle is inscribed within the square, its diameter is equal to a side of the square. The diameter of the circle is $2r$ or 10, so a side of the square is 10 and its perimeter is $4(10) = 40$. Therefore the perimeter of the shaded region is $40 + 10\pi$, choice (B).

34. A

Slope of a line is defined by the formula $\frac{y_2 - y_1}{x_2 - x_1}$, where (x_1, y_1) and (x_2, y_2) represent two points on the line. Substitute the given coordinates into the formula (it doesn't matter which you designate as point 1 or point 2; just be consistent):

$$\text{slope} = \frac{y_2 - y_1}{x_2 - x_1} = \frac{7-(-5)}{-1-3}$$
$$= \frac{12}{-4}$$
$$= -3$$

35. D

The circumference of a circle is $2\pi r$, where r is the radius, so a circle whose circumference is 16π has a radius of $\frac{16\pi}{2\pi} = 8$. The area of a circle is πr^2, so in this case the area is $\pi(8)^2 = 64\pi$, (D).

36. E

Since all sides of a square are equal, notice that the diagonal of the square is also the hypotenuse of an isosceles right triangle. Use this information to determine the length of a side of the square, marked s in the figure. The ratio of the sides in such a triangle is $x:x:x\sqrt{2}$. Since $x\sqrt{2}$ represents the hypotenuse, which is equal to 6, solve the equation $x\sqrt{2} = 6$. Divide by $\sqrt{2}$ to get $x = \frac{6}{\sqrt{2}}$. So the length of a side of the square is $\frac{6}{\sqrt{2}}$. The area of a square is therefore

$$\left(\frac{6}{\sqrt{2}}\right)^2 = \frac{36}{2} = 18.$$

37. B

The shaded region represents one-half the area of the circle. Find the length of the radius to determine this area. Notice that the diameter of the circle is equal to a side of the square. Since the area of the square is 64, it has a side length of 8 (because $8^2 = 64$). So the diameter of the circle is 8, and its radius is 4. The area of the circle is πr^2, or $\pi(4)^2 = 16\pi$. This isn't the answer though; the shaded region is only half the circle, so its area is 8π.

38. B

Think of the figure as a rectangle with two rectangular bites taken out of it. Sketch in lines to make one large rectangle (see diagram below):

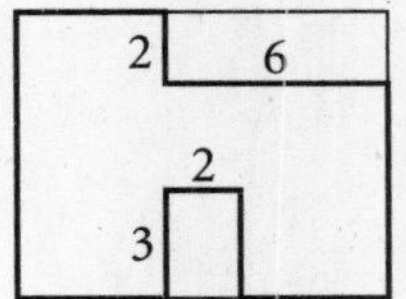

Now find the area of the large rectangle, and subtract the areas of the two rectangular pieces that weren't in the original figure. The area of a rectangle is length times width. Since the length of the large rectangle is 10, and its width is 8, its area is $10 \times 8 = 80$. The rectangular bite taken out of the top right corner has dimensions 6 and 2, so its area is 6×2 or 12. The bite taken out of the bottom has dimensions 2 and 3, so its area is $2 \times 3 = 6$. To find the area of the polygon, subtract the areas of the two bites from the area of the large rectangle: $80 - (12 + 6) = 80 - 18 = 62$, (B).

39. C

Since *ABCD* is a square, all four sides have the same length, and the corners meet at right angles. The area you're looking for is that of a triangle, and since all corners of the square are right angles, angle *EAB* is a right angle, which makes triangle *EAB* a right triangle. The area of a right triangle is $\frac{1}{2}(\text{leg}_1)(\text{leg}_2)$. The diagram shows that *BC* has length 8, so $AB = AD = 8$. Point *E* is the midpoint of *AD*, so *AE* is 4. Now that you have the lengths of both legs, you can substitute into the formula: $\frac{1}{2}(AB)(AE) = \frac{1}{2}(8)(4) = 16$, (C).

40. B

The circumference of a circle is equal to $2\pi r$, where r is the radius. The circumference of circle *A* is $2\pi(r + 1) = 2\pi r + 2\pi$. The circumference of circle *B* is $2\pi(r + 2) = 2\pi r + 4\pi$. So the positive difference between the two circumferences is simply 2π.

41. D

A square with area 16 has sides of length 4. Therefore the largest circle that could possibly be cut from such a square would have a diameter of 4.

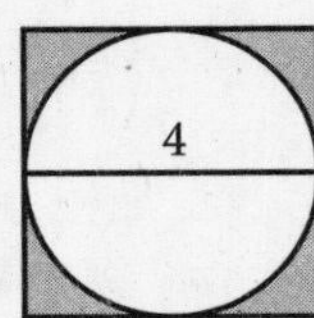

Such a circle would have a radius of 2, making its area $\pi(2)^2 = 4\pi$. So the amount of felt left after cutting such a circle from one of the squares of felt would be $16 - 4\pi$, or $4(4 - \pi)$. There are 8 such squares, so the total area of the left over felt is $8 \times 4(4 - \pi) = 32(4 - \pi)$, (D).

42. C

The key to solving this problem is to draw in *OB*:

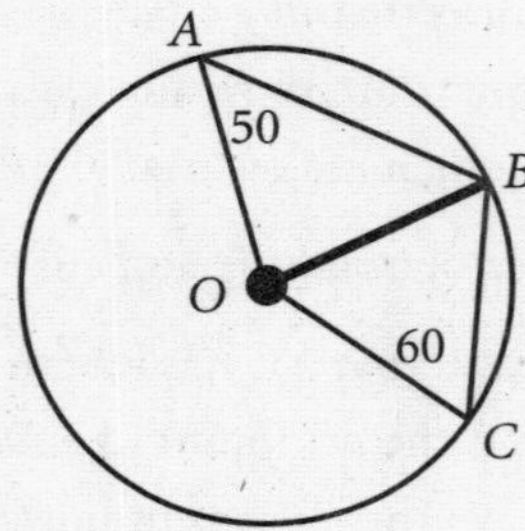

Because *OA*, *OB*, and *OC* are all radii of the same circle, triangle *AOB* and triangle *BOC* are both isosceles triangles, each therefore having equal base angles:

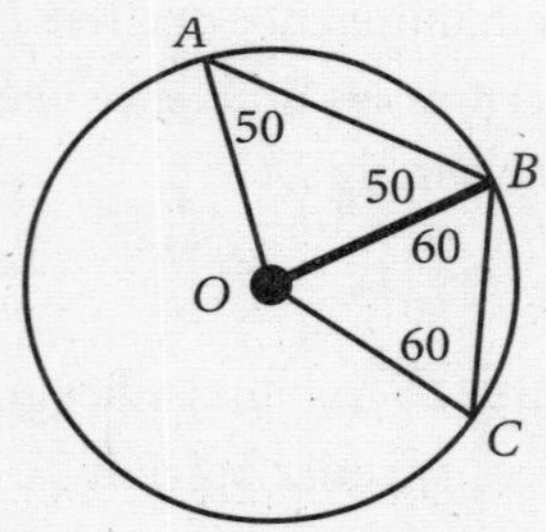

Using the fact that the three interior angles of a triangle add up to 180°, you can figure out that the vertex angles measure 80° and 60° as shown:

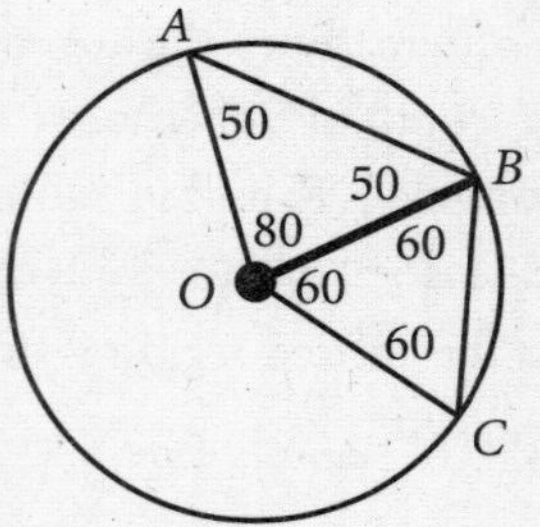

Angle *AOC* measures 80 + 60 = 140, (C).

CHAPTER 14: WORD PROBLEMS

Word Problems. Two simple words that evoke more fear and loathing than most other math concepts and question types combined.

When the subject of word problems arises, you might envision the following nightmare:

> Two trains are loaded with equal amounts of rock salt and ball bearings. Train A leaves Frogboro at 10:00 A.M. carrying 62 passengers. Train B leaves Toadville at 11:30 A.M. carrying 104 passengers. If Train A is traveling at a speed of 85 mph and makes four stops, and Train B is traveling at an average speed of 86 mph and makes three stops, and the trains both arrive at Lizard Hollow at 4:30 P.M., what is the average weight of the passengers on Train B?

The good news is that you won't see anything this ugly. SSAT and ISEE word problems are pretty straightforward. Generally, all you have to do is translate the prose to math and solve.

The bad news is that you can expect to see a lot of word problems on your test. Keep in mind that, while word problems are generally algebra problems, they can contain other math concepts.

TRANSLATION

Many word problems seem tricky because it's hard to figure out what they're asking. It can be difficult to translate English into math. The following table lists some common words and phrases that turn up in word problems, along with their mathematical translations.

When you see:	Think:
sum, plus, more than, added to, combined total	+
minus, less than, difference between, decreased by	−
is, was, equals, is equivalent to, is the same as, adds up to	=
times, product, multiplied by, of, twice, double, triple	×
divided by, over, quotient, per, out of, into	÷
what, how much, how many, a number	*x*, *n*, etc.

Now, try translating the following phrases from English to math.

English	**Math**
1. y is 5 more than x.	________
2. r equals half of s.	________
3. x is twice as great as y.	________
4. 2 less than m is equal to n.	________
5. The product of a and b is 3 more than their sum.	________

TRANSLATE THE STORY

"In some questions, the translation will be embedded within a "story." Don't be put off by the details of the scenario—it's the numbers that matter. Focus on the math and translate."

Now let's look at how you did:

1. $y = x + 5$
2. $r = \frac{1}{2}s$ or $2r = s$
3. $x = 2y$
4. $n = m - 2$
5. $ab = (a + b) + 3$

SYMBOLISM WORD PROBLEMS

KAPLAN EXCLUSIVE TIPS

"If you see a symbol you've never seen before, it's usually a safe bet that the test maker just made it up!"

Word problems, by definition, require you to translate English to math. But some word problems contain an extra level of translation. *Symbolism* word problems are like any other word problem; just translate the English and the symbols into math and then solve.

EXAMPLE

Assume that the notation □ (w, x, y, z) means "Divide the sum of w and x by y and multiply the result by z." What is the value of

□ (10, 4, 7, 8) + □ (2, 6, 4, 5) ?

First, translate the English/symbols into math.

$\square\,(w, x, y, z)$ means $\dfrac{w+x}{y} \times z$

Next, substitute the given values into the expression.

$$\square\,(10, 4, 7, 8) + \square\,(2, 6, 4, 5) = \left(\frac{10+4}{7} \times 8\right) + \left(\frac{2+6}{4} \times 5\right)$$
$$= 16 + 10$$
$$= 26$$

WORD PROBLEMS WITH FORMULAS

Some of the more difficult word problems may involve translations into mathematical formulas. For example, you might see questions dealing with averages, rates, or areas of geometric figures. Since the SSAT and ISEE does *not* provide formulas for you, you'll have to know these going in.

EXAMPLE

If a truck travels at 50 miles per hour for $6\frac{1}{2}$ hours, how far will the truck travel?

(A) 600 miles
(B) 425 miles
(C) 325 miles
(D) 300 miles
(E) 500 miles

To answer this question, you need to remember that Distance = Rate × Time. Once you note the formula, you can just plug in the numbers.

$D = 50 \times 6.5$
$D = 325$ miles, (C).

BACKDOOR STRATEGIES

Word problems are extraordinarily susceptible to backdoor strategies. Here's a quick recap of Kaplan's **picking numbers** and **backsolving** Strategies.

Picking Numbers

Step 1. Pick simple, easy-to-use numbers for each variable.

Step 2. Solve the problem using the numbers you pick.

Step 3. Substitute your numbers into each answer choice. The choice that gives you the same numerical solution you arrived at in step 2 is correct.

Here are a few things to remember:

- You can pick numbers only when the answer choices contain variables.
- Pick easy numbers rather than realistic ones. Keep the numbers small and manageable.
- You have to try all the answer choices. If more than one works, pick another set of numbers.
- Don't pick the same number for more than one variable.
- When picking a number for a remainder problem, add the remainder to the number you're dividing by.
- Always pick 100 for percent questions.

EXAMPLE

The average of four numbers is n. If three of the numbers are $n + 3$, $n + 5$, and $n - 2$, what is the value of the fourth number?

(A) $n - 6$
(B) $n - 4$
(C) n
(D) $n + 2$
(E) $n + 4$

Pick an easy number for n, such as 10. If the average of four numbers is 10, the sum of the four numbers is 40 ($4 \times 10 = 40$). If three of the numbers are $n + 3$, $n + 5$, and $n - 2$, then those three numbers are $10 + 3$, $10 + 5$, and $10 - 2$—13, 15, and 8. Then $13 + 15 + 8 = 36$. The sum of the four numbers must equal 40, so the remaining number is 4. If you plug 10 in for n in each of the answer choices, only (A) gives you 4.

Backsolving

- You can backsolve when the answer choices are only numbers.
- Always start with the middle answer choice, (C).
- If the middle answer choice is not correct, you can usually eliminate two more choices simply by determining whether the value you're looking for must be higher or lower.

EXAMPLE

Mike has n Hawaiian shirts, and Adam has 3 times as many Hawaiian shirts. If Adam gives Mike six Hawaiian shirts, both boys would have an equal number of Hawaiian shirts. How many Hawaiian shirts does Mike have?

(A) 3
(B) 6
(C) 9
(D) 15
(E) 18

Start with the middle answer choice, 9. If Mike has 9 shirts, then Adam has three times as many, or 27. If Adam gives Mike 6 shirts, Adam now has 21 and Mike has 15. This is not equal, so (C) is not correct. Since Adam was left with too many shirts when Mike had 9, Mike must have fewer than 9. Try (B). If Mike has 6 shirts, then Adam has 18. If Adam gives Mike 6, then they both have 12 shirts. Bingo.

ROMAN NUMERAL WORD PROBLEMS

You might see a Roman numeral problem on your test. If you do, keep a few things in mind. In keeping with the problem style, let's lay them out in Roman numerals . . .

I. You don't have to work with the statements in the order they are given. Deal with them in whatever order is easiest for you.

II. If you find a statement that is true, eliminate all of the choices that *don't* include it.

III. If you find a statement that is false, eliminate all of the choices that *do* include it.

EXAMPLE

If the product of the positive numbers x and y is 20 and x is less than 4, which of the following must be true?

I. y is greater than 5.
II. The sum of x and y is greater than 10.
III. Twice the product of x and y is equal to 40.

(A) I only
(B) II only
(C) I and III only
(D) II and III only
(E) I, II, and III

We're told that $xy = 20$ and $x < 4$. Now let's look at the statements. Statement I says that $y > 5$. Since $xy = 20$, $y = \frac{20}{x}$. When $x = 4$, $y = 5$. If we replace x with a smaller number than 4 in $\frac{20}{x}$, then $\frac{20}{x}$, which is y, will be greater than 5. Statement I must be true. Statement I must be part of the correct answer. Eliminate choices (B) and (D). Statement II says that $x + y > 10$. Try picking some values such that $xy = 20$ and $x < 4$. If $x = 3$, then $y = \frac{20}{x} = \frac{20}{3} = 6\frac{2}{3}$. The sum of x and y is not greater than 10. Statement II does not have to be true. It will not be part of the correct answer. Eliminate (E). Statement III says that $2(xy) = 40$, or $2xy = 40$. The question stem says that $xy = 20$. Multiplying both sides of the equation $xy = 20$ by 2, we have that $2(xy) = 2(20)$, or $2xy = 40$. Statement III must be true. (C) is correct.

Now it's time to put all of your skills into play with some practice questions. Remember to translate the English to math, don't get intimidated, and keep your cool. Off you go!

PRACTICE QUESTIONS

1. During a sale, a bookstore sold $\frac{1}{2}$ of all its books in stock. On the following day, the bookstore sold 4,000 more books. Now, only $\frac{1}{10}$ of the books in stock before the sale are remaining in the store. How many books were in stock before the sale?

   (A) 8,000
   (B) 10,000
   (C) 12,000
   (D) 15,000
   (E) 20,000

2. Brad bought an MP3 player on sale at a 20% discount from its regular price of $118. If there is an 8% sales tax that is calculated on the sale price, how much did Brad pay?

   (A) $23.60
   (B) $86.85
   (C) $94.40
   (D) $101.95
   (E) $127.44

3. Sheila charges $5 per haircut during the week. On Saturday, she charges $7.50. If Sheila has six customers each day of the week except Sunday, how much money does she earn in five weekdays and Saturday?

   (A) $150
   (B) $175
   (C) $180
   (D) $195
   (E) $210

4. The original price of a television decreases by 20 percent. By what percent must the discounted price increase to reach its original value?

   (A) 15%
   (B) 20%
   (C) 25%
   (D) 30%
   (E) 40%

5. Ed has 100 dollars more than Robert. After Ed spends 20 dollars on groceries, Ed has five times as much money as Robert. How much money does Robert have?

   (A) $20
   (B) $30
   (C) $40
   (D) $50
   (E) $120

6. A worker earns $15 an hour for the first 40 hours he works each week, and one and a half times this much for every hour over 40 hours. If he earned $667.50 for one week's work, how many hours did he work?

   (A) 40
   (B) 41
   (C) 42
   (D) 43
   (E) 44

7. Liza has 40 less than three times the number of books that Janice has. If B is equal to the number of books that Janice has, which of the following expressions shows the total number of books that Liza and Janice have together?

(A) $3B - 40$
(B) $3B + 40$
(C) $4B - 40$
(D) $4B$
(E) $4B + 40$

8. If $a \bullet b = \frac{ab}{a-b}$, which of the following does $3 \bullet 2$ equal?

(A) $2 \bullet 3$
(B) $6 \bullet 1$
(C) $6 \bullet 2$
(D) $6 \bullet 3$
(E) $8 \bullet 4$

9. If William divides the amount of money he has by 5, and he adds \$8, the result will be \$20. If X is equal to the number of dollars that William has, which of the following equations shows this relationship?

(A) $(X \div 8) + 5 = 20$
(B) $(X \div 5) + 8 = 20$
(C) $(X + 8) \div 5 = 20$
(D) $(X + 5) \div 8 = 20$
(E) $8(X + 5) = 20$

10. If a six-sided pencil with a trademark on one of its sides is rolled on a table, what is the probability that the side with the trademark is not touching the surface of the table when the pencil stops?

(A) $\frac{1}{6}$
(B) $\frac{1}{3}$
(C) $\frac{1}{2}$
(D) $\frac{2}{3}$
(E) $\frac{5}{6}$

11. Yesterday, a store sold 8 times as many hats as it sold coats. It also sold 3 times as many sweaters as it sold coats. What could be the total number of hats, sweaters, and coats that were sold?

(A) 16
(B) 21
(C) 25
(D) 36
(E) 54

12. Five hundred eighty-seven people are travelling by bus for a field trip. If each bus seats 48 people and all the buses are filled to capacity except one, how many people sit in the unfilled bus?

(A) 37
(B) 36
(C) 12
(D) 11
(E) 7

13. Rose has finished $\frac{5}{6}$ of her novel after one week of reading. If she reads an additional tenth of the novel during the next two days, what part of the novel will she have read?

(A) $\frac{1}{10}$

(B) $\frac{7}{15}$

(C) $\frac{4}{5}$

(D) $\frac{14}{15}$

(E) $\frac{29}{30}$

14. A farmer has $4\frac{2}{3}$ acres of land for growing corn and $2\frac{1}{2}$ times as many acres for growing wheat. How many acres does she have for wheat?

(A) $2\frac{2}{3}$

(B) $4\frac{1}{2}$

(C) $8\frac{1}{6}$

(D) $10\frac{1}{2}$

(E) $11\frac{2}{3}$

15. Joyce baked 42 biscuits for her 12 guests. If 6 biscuits remain uneaten, what is the average number of biscuits that the guests ate?

(A) 2

(B) 3

(C) 4

(D) 6

(E) 12

16. The average weight of Jake, Ken, and Larry is 60 kilograms. If Jake and Ken both weigh 50 kilograms, how much, in kilograms, does Larry weigh?

(A) 40

(B) 50

(C) 60

(D) 70

(E) 80

17. If 3 added to 4 times a number is 11, the number must be

(A) 1.

(B) 2.

(C) 3.

(D) 4.

(E) 5.

18. The sum of 8 and a certain number is equal to 20 minus the same number. What is the number?

(A) 2

(B) 4

(C) 6

(D) 10

(E) 14

19. Liz worked 3 hours less than twice as many hours as Rachel did. If W is the number of hours Rachel worked, which of the following expressions shows the total number of hours worked by Liz and Rachel together?

(A) $2W - 3$

(B) $2W + 3$

(C) $3W - 3$

(D) $3W + 3$

(E) $4W - 2$

20. The area of a circle is πr^2, where r is the radius. If the circumference of a circle is $h\pi$, what is the area of the circle, in terms of h?

(A) h^2r^2

(B) $\frac{\pi h^2}{4}$

(C) $\frac{\pi h^2}{2}$

(D) πh^2

(E) $4\pi h^2$

21. If $m \neq 0$, $m \neq 1$, and $m\ddagger = \frac{m}{m^2 - m}$, what is the value of $(6\ddagger) - (-5\ddagger)$?

(A) $\frac{1}{30}$

(B) $\frac{1}{20}$

(C) $\frac{1}{4}$

(D) $\frac{11}{30}$

(E) $\frac{9}{20}$

22. Five less than 3 times a certain number is equal to twice the original number plus 7. What is the original number?

(A) 2

(B) $2\frac{2}{5}$

(C) 6

(D) 11

(E) 12

23. The volume of a sphere is $\frac{4}{3}\pi r^3$, where r is the radius. What is the volume of a sphere with a radius of 3, in terms of π?

(A) 4π

(B) 8π

(C) 16π

(D) 36π

(E) 72π

PRACTICE QUESTION ANSWERS

1. B

Call the original number of books in stock N. On the first day of the sale, $\frac{1}{2}$ of all the books in stock were sold. So on the first day of the sale, $\frac{1}{2}N$ books were sold. After the first day of the sale, $N-\frac{1}{2}N$ books remained. On the next day, 4,000 more books were sold. So after two days of the sale, $N-\frac{1}{2}N-$ 4,000 books remained. We are told that after two days of the sale, $\frac{1}{10}$ of the books in stock before the sale remained in the store. So the number of books that remained in the store after two days of the sale was $\frac{1}{10}N$. Thus $N-\frac{1}{2}N-4{,}000=\frac{1}{10}N$. Solve for N.

$$N-\frac{1}{2}N-4{,}000=\frac{1}{10}N$$
$$\frac{1}{2}N-4{,}000=\frac{1}{10}N$$
$$\frac{1}{2}N-\frac{1}{10}N=4{,}000$$
$$\frac{5}{10}N-\frac{1}{10}N=4{,}000$$
$$\frac{4}{10}N=4{,}000$$
$$\frac{2}{5}N=4{,}000$$
$$N=4{,}000\left(\frac{5}{2}\right)$$
$$=2{,}000\ (5)$$
$$=10{,}000$$

2. D

This problem needs to be done in several steps. First find out the sale price of the MP3 player. The discount was 20%, so the sale price was 80% of the original price.

Percent × Whole = Part
80% × $118 = Sale Price
0.80 × $118 = Sale Price
$94.40 = Sale Price

Now figure out how much tax Brad paid. The tax was 8% of the sale price.

Percent × Whole = Part
8% × $94.40 = Tax
0.08 × $94.40 = Tax
$7.5520 = Tax
$7.55 = Tax

Now just add the tax to the sale price.

$94.40 + 7.55 = $101.95

3. D

Each weekday Sheila earns $5 × 6 haircuts = $30. Each Saturday Sheila earns $7.50 × 6 haircuts = $45. In five weekdays she earns 5 × $30 = $150. In one Saturday she earns $45. So in five weekdays plus one Saturday she earns $150 + $45, or $195.

4. C

It is important to note that while the value of the television decreases and increases by the same dollar amount, it doesn't increase and decrease by the same percent. Let's pick $100 for the price of the television. If the price decreases by 20%, and since 20% of $100 is $20, the price decreases by $20. The new price is $100 – $20, or $80. For the new price to reach the original price ($100), it must be increased by $20. Twenty dollars is $\frac{1}{4}$ of 80, or 25% of $80. The new price must be increased by 25%, choice (C).

5. A

Translate to get two equations. Let E be the amount Ed has and R be the amount Robert has. "Ed has $100 more than Robert" becomes $E = R + 100$. "Ed spends $20" means he'll have $20 less, or $E - 20$. "Five times as much as Robert" becomes $5R$. Therefore, $E - 20 = 5R$. Substitute $R + 100$ for E in the second equation and solve for R:

$$(R + 100) - 20 = 5R$$
$$R + 80 = 5R$$
$$80 = 4R$$
$$20 = R, \text{ so Robert has } \$20$$

6. D

Run the answer choices through the information in the stem to see which one gives a total of $667.50. Since the answer choices are in numerical order, start with the middle choice, (C). If he works for 42 hours, he earns $15 per hour for the first 40 hours, or $600, and he earns $1\frac{1}{2}$ times his normal rate for the two extra hours. So, $\frac{3}{2}$ times $15 is $22.50 per hour, and since he worked 2 hours at that rate, he made an additional $45. The total is $645, which isn't enough. So (C) is too small, as are (A) and (B). Now try (D). He still earns $600 for the first 40 hours, but now you have to multiply the overtime rate, $22.50, by 3, which gives you $67.50. The total is $667.50, which means that (D) is correct.

Another way to approach the question is to see that for the first 40 hours, the worker earns $15 an hour: 40 hours × $15 an hour = $600. For any additional hours, he earns one and a half times $15. So, 1.5 × $15 = $22.50 per hour. If he earned $667.50 in one week, $600 was earned in the first 40 hours and the remaining $67.50 was earned working additional hours. To find out how many additional hours the worker worked, divide the amount earned ($67.50) by the amount earned per hour ($22.50). And $67.50 ÷ $22.50 = 3. So 40 hours + 3 additional hours equals 43 hours.

7. C

This is a straightforward translation problem. You're told that Janice has B books. Liza has 40 less than three times the number of books Janice has, which you can translate as $L = 3B - 40$. The total number they have together equals $B + (3B - 40)$, or $4B - 40$.

8. D

Substitute the given values. Then try the values in each answer choice until you find the one that produces the same result. Substituting 3 and 2 yields $\frac{(3)(2)}{3-2} = \frac{6}{1} = 6$. So you're looking for the answer choice that produces a result of 6. Only (D) does: $\frac{(6)(3)}{6-3} = \frac{18}{3} = 6$.

9. B

This problem asks you to translate English sentences into math.

The amount of money William has is X.
This amount divided by 5: $(X \div 5)$.
Add 8 dollars: $(X \div 5) + 8$.
The result is 20 dollars: $(X \div 5) + 8 = 20$, choice (B).
Since division comes before addition in the order of operations, the parentheses aren't really necessary.

10. E

The probability of an event happening is the ratio of the number of desired outcomes to the number of possible outcomes, or

$$\text{Probability}=\frac{\text{Number of desired outcomes}}{\text{Number of possible outcomes}}$$

One side of the pencil has the trademark on it, and the other 5 sides are blank. When any 1 of the 5 blank sides is touching the surface of the table, the marked side cannot be touching the table. So there are 5 different ways for the pencil to lie on the table without the marked side touching the surface. The total number of possible sides for the pencil to lie on is 6. The probability that the trademark will not be touching the surface of the table when the pencil stops rolling is $\frac{5}{6}$, choice (E).

11. D

Let x be the number of coats that the store sold yesterday. Keep in mind that x must be an integer. The store sold 8 times the number of hats as coats yesterday. So the store sold $8x$ hats. The store sold 3 times the number of sweaters as coats yesterday. So the store sold $3x$ sweaters. The total number of hats, sweaters, and coats that the store sold was $8x + 3x + x = 12x$. Since x is an integer, $12x$ must be a multiple of 12. Only (D), 36, is a multiple of 12 $(36 = 3 \times 12)$.

12. D

There are 587 people traveling, and each bus holds 48 people. Therefore, $587 \div 48 = 12$ with a remainder of 11. So 12 buses are full, and 11 people remain to ride in the unfilled bus.

13. D

Rose read $\frac{5}{6}$ of the novel and plans to read another $\frac{1}{10}$, which will result in her having read $\frac{5}{6} + \frac{1}{10}$ of the novel. Add these two fractions, using 30 as the common denominator: $\frac{5}{6} + \frac{1}{10} = \frac{25}{30} + \frac{3}{30} = \frac{28}{30} = \frac{14}{15}$.

14. E

The farmer has $4\frac{2}{3} \times 2\frac{1}{2}$ acres for growing wheat. Change these mixed numbers to fractions in order to multiply: $\frac{\cancel{14}^{7}}{3} \times \frac{5}{\cancel{2}^{1}} = \frac{35}{3} = 11\frac{2}{3}$ acres.

15. B

If 6 biscuits remain, $42 - 6 = 36$ were eaten by the 12 guests.

$\text{Average} = \frac{\text{Sum of the terms}}{\text{Number of the terms}}$, so the average number of biscuits eaten by the guests is $\frac{36}{12} = 3$.

16. E

$$\text{Average} = \frac{\text{Sum of the terms}}{\text{Number of the terms}}$$

$$60 = \frac{\text{Total weight}}{3}$$

$$60 \times 3 = \text{Total weight}$$

$$180 = \text{Total weight}$$

Jake and Ken each weigh 50 kilograms, so 50 + 50 + Larry's weight = 180 kilograms. Doing the math, Larry must weigh 80 kilograms.

17. B

Let the number be x. Translating gives you $3 + 4x = 11$. Therefore, $4x = 8$ and $x = 2$.

18. C

Translate from English to math. The sum of 8 and b is $8 + b$. The question states that this is equal to 20 minus the same number, or 20 – b. So your equation is 8 + b = 20 – b, and you can solve for b:

$$8 + b = 20 - b$$
$$8 + 2b = 20$$
$$2b = 12$$
$$b = 6$$

19. C

Rachel worked W hours, and Liz worked 3 hours less than twice as many hours as Rachel, or $2W - 3$. Add these expressions to find the total number of hours worked by Liz and Rachel together:

$$W + 2W - 3 = 3W - 3$$

20. B

Circumference of a circle is π times diameter, so a circumference of $h\pi$ means a diameter of h. The radius is half the diameter, or $\frac{h}{2}$. Substitute $\frac{h}{2}$ into the area formula:

$$\pi\left(\frac{h}{2}\right)^2 = \pi\left(\frac{h^2}{4}\right) = \frac{h^2\pi}{4}$$

21. D

Substitute into the expression that defines the symbol ‡:

$$(6‡) - (-5)‡ = \frac{6}{6^2 - 6} - \frac{-5}{(-5)^2 - (-5)}$$
$$= \frac{6}{36 - 6} - \frac{-5}{25 + 5}$$
$$= \frac{6}{30} - \frac{-5}{30}$$
$$= \frac{6}{30} + \frac{5}{30}$$
$$= \frac{11}{30}$$

At two points in your calculation it is crucial to remember that subtracting a negative is the same as adding a positive.

22. E

Call the unknown number x. Five less than 3 times the number, or $3x - 5$, equals twice the original number plus 7, or $2x + 7$. So $3x - 5 = 2x + 7$. Solve for x:

$$3x - 5 = 2x + 7$$
$$x - 5 = 7$$
$$x = 12$$

23. D

Substitute the value of $r = 3$ into the formula and simplify:

$$\text{volume} = \frac{4}{3}\pi(3)^3$$
$$= \frac{4}{3}\pi(27)$$
$$= 36\,\pi$$

CHAPTER 15: MANAGING YOUR STRESS

Is it starting to feel like as though whole life is a buildup to the SSAT or ISEE? You really want to go to a certain school, and you know your parents want you to as well. You have worried about the test for months and spent at least a few hours in solid preparation for it. As the test gets closer, you may find your anxiety is on the rise. Don't worry. After the preparation you've received from this book, you're in good shape for the test.

To calm any pretest jitters you may have, this chapter leads you through a sane itinerary for the last week.

THE WEEK BEFORE THE TEST

- Focus on strategy and backup plans.
- Practice strategies you had the best success rate with.
- Decide and know **exactly** how you're going to approach each section and question type.
- Sit down and do practice problems or complete extra drills you might have skipped the first time through.
- Practice waking up early and eating breakfast so that you'll be alert in the morning on test day.

THE DAYS JUST BEFORE THE TEST

- The best test takers do less and less as the test approaches. Taper off your study schedule and take it easy. Give yourself time off, especially the evening before the exam. By that time, if you've studied well, everything you need to know is firmly stored in your memory bank.
- Positive self-talk can be extremely liberating and invigorating, especially as the test looms closer. Tell yourself things such as "I will do well," rather than "I hope things go well";

"I can," rather than "I cannot." Replace any negative thoughts with affirming statements that boost your self-esteem.

- Get your act together sooner rather than later. Have everything (including choice of clothing) laid out in advance. Most important, make sure you know where the test will be held and the easiest, quickest way to get there. You'll have great peace of mind by knowing that all the little details—gas in the car, directions, etc.—are set before the day of the test.
- Go to the test site a few days in advance, particularly if you are especially anxious. If at all possible, find out what room your part of the alphabet is assigned to and try to sit there (by yourself) for a while. Better yet, bring some practice material and do a section or two.
- Forgo any practice on the day before the test. It's in your best interest to marshal your physical and psychological resources for 24 hours or so. Even race horses are kept in the paddock and treated like royalty the day before a race. Keep the upcoming test out of your consciousness; go to a movie, take a pleasant hike, or just relax. Don't eat junk food or tons of sugar. And, of course, get plenty of rest the night before—just don't go to bed too early. It's hard to fall asleep earlier than you're used to, and you don't want to lie there worrying about the test.

THE NIGHT BEFORE THE TEST

Don't study. Get together the following items:

- Your admission/registration ticket
- Photo ID
- A watch (choose one that is easy to read)
- Slightly dull No. 2 pencils (so they fill in the ovals faster)
- Pencil sharpener
- Erasers
- Clothes you'll wear (Dress in layers! The climate at the test location may vary, as may your body temperature. Make sure you can warm up or cool down easily.)
- Snacks (easy to open or partially unwrapped)
- Money
- Packet of tissues

Relax the night before the test. Read a good book, take a bubble bath, watch TV. Get a good night's sleep. Go to bed at a reasonable hour and leave yourself extra time in the morning.

THE MORNING OF THE TEST

Eat breakfast. Make it something substantial and nutritious, but don't deviate too much from your everyday pattern.

Dress in layers so that you can adjust to the temperature of the test room.

Read something to warm up your brain before the test starts.

Be sure to get there early. Leave enough time to allow for traffic, mass transit delays, your dad getting lost en route, and any other snag that could slow you down.

DURING THE TEST

Don't be shaken. If you find your confidence slipping, remind yourself how well you've prepared. You know the structure of the test; you know the instructions; you've studied for every question type.

The biggest stress monster will be the test itself. Fear not; there are methods of quelling your stress during the test.

- Keep moving forward instead of getting bogged down in a difficult question. You don't have to get everything right to achieve a fine score. So, don't linger out of desperation on a question that is going nowhere even after you've spent considerable time on it. The best test takers skip difficult material temporarily in search of the easier stuff. They mark the ones that require extra time and thought.
- Don't be thrown if other test takers seem to be working more busily and furiously than you are. Don't mistake the other people's sheer activity as a sign of progress and higher scores.
- *Keep breathing!* Weak test takers tend to share one major trait: They don't breathe properly as the test proceeds. They might hold their breath without realizing it, or breathe erratically or arrhythmically. Improper breathing hurts confidence and accuracy. Just as important, it interferes with clear thinking.

  Some quick isometrics during the test—especially if concentration is wandering or energy is waning—can help. Try this:
- Put your palms together and press intensely for a few seconds. Concentrate on the tension you feel through your palms, wrists, forearms, and up into your biceps and shoulders. Then, quickly release the pressure. Feel the difference as you let go. Focus on the warm relaxation that floods through the muscles.

THE NIGHT BEFORE THE TEST, DO NOT

- try to copy the dictionary onto your fingernails.
- stay up all night watching all the *Friday the 13th* movies.
- eat a large double anchovy and pepper pizza with a case of chocolate soda.
- send away for brochures for clown school.
- start making flashcards.
- tattoo yourself.

WHAT ARE "SIGNS OF A WINNER," ALEX?

Here's some advice from a Kaplan instructor who won big on Jeopardy!™ In the green room before the show, he noticed that the contestants who were quiet and "within themselves" were the ones who did great on the show. The contestants who didn't perform as well were those who were cramming facts and talking a lot before the show. Lesson: Spend the final hours before the test getting sleep, meditating, and generally relaxing.

Here's another isometric that will relieve tension in both your neck and eye muscles.

- Slowly rotate your head from side to side, turning your head and eyes to look as far back over each shoulder as you can. Feel the muscles stretch on one side of your neck as they contract on the other. Repeat five times in each direction.

Now you're ready to return to the task.

With what you've just learned here, you're armed and ready to do battle with the test. This book and your studies will give you the information you'll need to answer the questions. It's all firmly planted in your mind. You also know how to deal with any excess tension that might come along, both when you're studying for and taking the exam. You've experienced everything you need to tame your test anxiety and stress. You're going to get a great score.

Even if something goes really wrong, don't panic. If the test booklet is defective—two pages are stuck together or the ink has run—try to stay calm. Raise your hand and tell the proctor you need a new book. If you accidentally misgrid your answer page or put the answers in the wrong section, again don't panic. The proctor might be able to arrange for you to regrid your test after it's over, when it won't cost you any time.

AFTER THE TEST

Once the test is over, put it out of your mind. Start thinking about more interesting things. You might walk out of the test thinking that you blew it. You probably didn't. You tend to remember the questions that stumped you, not the many that you knew.

Part Four

SSAT PRACTICE TESTS AND EXPLANATIONS

SSAT TEST OVERVIEW

Total Time

Approximately two and a half hours, plus two brief breaks.

Questions

Aside from the essay, all questions are multiple-choice in format, with all answer choices labeled (A)–(E).

Content

The SSAT tests Math, Reading, Writing, and Verbal skills. There are two Math sections, one Verbal section, one Reading section, and one unscored Essay.

Pacing

You are not expected to complete all items on the SSAT. This is particularly true if you are at the low end of the age range of test takers for your level. The best approach to pacing is to work as quickly as you can without losing accuracy. Further, if a question is giving you difficulty, circle it and move on. You can always come back to it later, but you shouldn't waste time on a question that is stumping you when you could be gaining valuable points elsewhere.

Guessing

You receive 1 point for each question answered correctly. For those questions you answer incorrectly, you lose $\frac{1}{4}$ point. As a result, guess *only* when you can do so intelligently. In other words, don't guess wildly, but *do* guess if you can eliminate at least one answer choice as clearly wrong.

CHAPTER 16: SSAT PRACTICE TEST 1: UPPER-LEVEL

HOW TO TAKE THIS PRACTICE TEST

Before taking this practice test, find a quiet room where you can work uninterrupted for two and a half hours. Make sure you have a comfortable desk and several No. 2 pencils.

Use the answer sheet provided to record your answers. (You can cut it out or photocopy it.)

Once you start this practice test, don't stop until you've finished. Remember—you can review any questions within a section, but you may not go backward or forward a section.

You'll find answer explanations following the test. Scoring information is in chapter 19.

Good luck.

SSAT Practice Test 1: Upper-Level Answer Sheet

Remove (or photocopy) the answer sheet and use it to complete the practice test.

Start with number 1 for each section. If a section has fewer questions than answer spaces, leave the extra spaces blank.

SECTION 2

1 A B C D E	6 A B C D E	11 A B C D E	16 A B C D E	21 A B C D E
2 A B C D E	7 A B C D E	12 A B C D E	17 A B C D E	22 A B C D E
3 A B C D E	8 A B C D E	13 A B C D E	18 A B C D E	23 A B C D E
4 A B C D E	9 A B C D E	14 A B C D E	19 A B C D E	24 A B C D E
5 A B C D E	10 A B C D E	15 A B C D E	20 A B C D E	25 A B C D E

right in section 2

wrong in section 2

SECTION 3

1 A B C D E	9 A B C D E	17 A B C D E	25 A B C D E	33 A B C D E
2 A B C D E	10 A B C D E	18 A B C D E	26 A B C D E	34 A B C D E
3 A B C D E	11 A B C D E	19 A B C D E	27 A B C D E	35 A B C D E
4 A B C D E	12 A B C D E	20 A B C D E	28 A B C D E	36 A B C D E
5 A B C D E	13 A B C D E	21 A B C D E	29 A B C D E	37 A B C D E
6 A B C D E	14 A B C D E	22 A B C D E	30 A B C D E	38 A B C D E
7 A B C D E	15 A B C D E	23 A B C D E	31 A B C D E	39 A B C D E
8 A B C D E	16 A B C D E	24 A B C D E	32 A B C D E	40 A B C D E

right in section 3

wrong in section 3

SECTION 4

1 A B C D E	13 A B C D E	25 A B C D E	37 A B C D E	49 A B C D E
2 A B C D E	14 A B C D E	26 A B C D E	38 A B C D E	50 A B C D E
3 A B C D E	15 A B C D E	27 A B C D E	39 A B C D E	51 A B C D E
4 A B C D E	16 A B C D E	28 A B C D E	40 A B C D E	52 A B C D E
5 A B C D E	17 A B C D E	29 A B C D E	41 A B C D E	53 A B C D E
6 A B C D E	18 A B C D E	30 A B C D E	42 A B C D E	54 A B C D E
7 A B C D E	19 A B C D E	31 A B C D E	43 A B C D E	55 A B C D E
8 A B C D E	20 A B C D E	32 A B C D E	44 A B C D E	56 A B C D E
9 A B C D E	21 A B C D E	33 A B C D E	45 A B C D E	57 A B C D E
10 A B C D E	22 A B C D E	34 A B C D E	46 A B C D E	58 A B C D E
11 A B C D E	23 A B C D E	35 A B C D E	47 A B C D E	59 A B C D E
12 A B C D E	24 A B C D E	36 A B C D E	48 A B C D E	60 A B C D E

right in section 4

wrong in section 4

SECTION 5

1 A B C D E	6 A B C D E	11 A B C D E	16 A B C D E	21 A B C D E
2 A B C D E	7 A B C D E	12 A B C D E	17 A B C D E	22 A B C D E
3 A B C D E	8 A B C D E	13 A B C D E	18 A B C D E	23 A B C D E
4 A B C D E	9 A B C D E	14 A B C D E	19 A B C D E	24 A B C D E
5 A B C D E	10 A B C D E	15 A B C D E	20 A B C D E	25 A B C D E

right in section 5

wrong in section 5

SECTION 1

Time—25 Minutes

Write an essay on the following prompt on the paper provided. Your essay should NOT exceed two pages and must be written in ink. Erasing is not allowed.

Prompt: What goes up must come down.

Do you agree or disagree with this statement? Use examples from history, literature, or your own personal experience to support your point of view.

GO ON TO THE NEXT PAGE

IF YOU FINISH BEFORE TIME IS CALLED, YOU MAY CHECK YOUR WORK ON THIS SECTION ONLY. DO NOT TURN TO ANY OTHER SECTION IN THE TEST.

SECTION 2

Time—30 Minutes
25 Questions

In this section, there are five possible answers after each problem. Choose which one is best. You may use the blank space at the right for scratch work.

Note: Figures provided with the problems are drawn with the greatest possible accuracy, UNLESS stated "Not Drawn to Scale."

USE THIS SPACE FOR FIGURING.

1. Each member of a club sold the same number of raffle tickets. If the club sold a total of 120 tickets, which of the following CANNOT be the number of tickets sold by each member?

(A) 2
(B) 8
(C) 10
(D) 12
(E) 16

2. According to the graph in Figure 1, about how many students are art majors?

(A) 200
(B) 225
(C) 280
(D) 300
(E) 360

MAJORS OF 900 STUDENTS

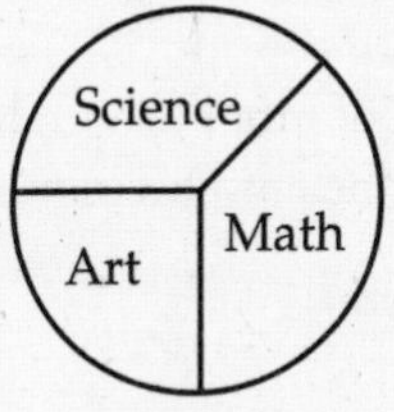

Figure 1

3. Sean arrives home 14 minutes before midnight, and his sister gets home 25 minutes later. When does Sean's sister arrive home?

(A) 11 minutes before midnight
(B) 11 minutes after midnight
(C) 14 minutes after midnight
(D) 25 minutes after midnight
(E) 39 minutes after midnight

4. Which of the following is closest to 0.52×78?

(A) $\frac{1}{5}$ of 70

(B) $\frac{1}{5}$ of 80

(C) $\frac{2}{5}$ of 70

(D) $\frac{1}{2}$ of 70

(E) $\frac{1}{2}$ of 80

USE THIS SPACE FOR FIGURING.

<u>Questions 5–6</u> refer to the graph in Figure 2.

5. Brian's summer savings are greater than James's summer savings by how many dollars?

(A) 3
(B) 4
(C) 100
(D) 150
(E) 200

SUMMER SAVINGS

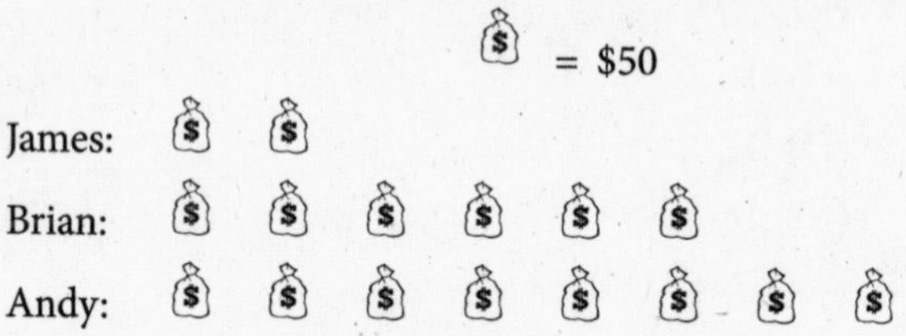

(money bag) = $50

James:	2 bags
Brian:	6 bags
Andy:	8 bags

Figure 2

6. The amount of money saved by Andy is how many times the amount of money saved by James?

(A) 3
(B) 4
(C) 6
(D 300
(E) 400

GO ON TO THE NEXT PAGE

USE THIS SPACE FOR FIGURING.

7. How many students are in a class if 30 percent of the class is equal to 30 students?

   (A) 10
   (B) 90
   (C) 100
   (D) 900
   (E) It cannot be determined from the information given.

8. Each of the following is less than 2 EXCEPT

   (A) $\frac{15}{8}$.
   (B) $\frac{45}{22}$.
   (C) $\frac{99}{50}$.
   (D) $\frac{180}{100}$.
   (E) $\frac{701}{400}$.

9. The sides and angles of triangles *ABC, BDE, BCE,* and *CEF* in Figure 3 are all equal. Which of the following is the longest path from *A* to *F*?

   (A) $A - C - B - D - F$
   (B) $A - B - E - C - F$
   (C) $A - B - C - E - F$
   (D) $A - C - E - F$
   (E) $A - B - D - F$

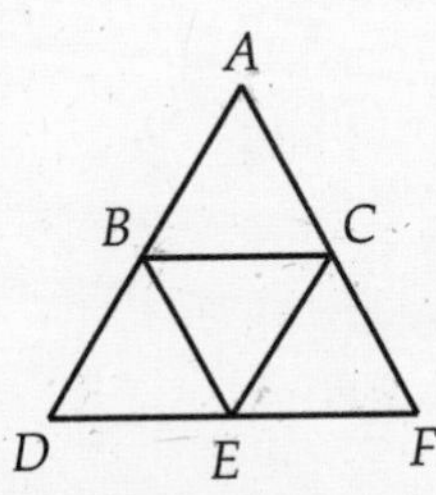

Figure 3

GO ON TO THE NEXT PAGE

USE THIS SPACE FOR FIGURING.

10. Which of the following is closest to 80.08?

(A) 80
(B) 80.01
(C) 80.1
(D) 81
(E) 90

11. If $\frac{1}{3}$ of a number is less than 12, then the number is always

(A) less than 36.
(B) equal to 4.
(C) greater than 4.
(D) equal to 36.
(E) greater than 36.

12. In a basketball game, Team A scored 39 points, and Team B scored more points than Team A. If Team B has 5 players, the average score of the players on Team B must have been at least how many points?

(A) 1
(B) 5
(C) 6
(D) 8
(E) 12

13. In the triangle shown in Figure 4, what is the value of a ?

(A) 4
(B) 6
(C) 8
(D) 9
(E) It cannot be determined from the information given.

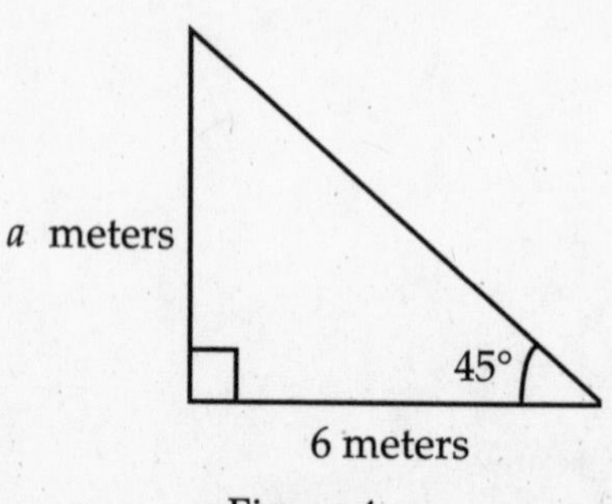

Figure 4

GO ON TO THE NEXT PAGE

USE THIS SPACE FOR FIGURING.

14. A man bought a piece of land for 40 thousand dollars. Then he spent 2 million dollars to build a house on it. The cost of the house is how many times the cost of the land?

(A) 5
(B) 20
(C) 50
(D) 200
(E) 500

15. If $(x - y) + 2 = 6$ and y is less than 3, which of the following CANNOT be the value of x?

(A) -3
(B) 0
(C) $1\frac{1}{2}$
(D) 4
(E) 8

16. In Figure 5, the distance from A to D is 55, and the distance from A to B is equal to the distance from C to D. If the distance from A to B is twice the distance from B to C, how far apart are B and D?

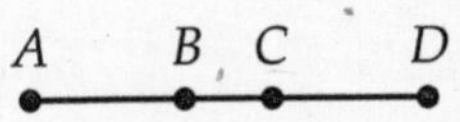

(A) 11
(B) 30
(C) 33
(D) 44
(E) 45

A B C D

Figure 5

GO ON TO THE NEXT PAGE

USE THIS SPACE FOR FIGURING.

17. A book is placed on a flat table surface, as shown in Figure 6. Which of the following best shows all of the points where the book touches the table?

(A) 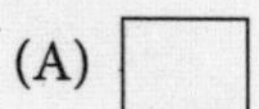

(B) 

(C) 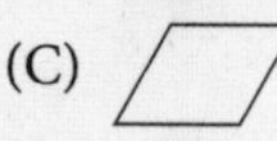

(D) 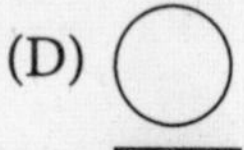

(E) 

Figure 6

18. Which of the following can be expressed as $(J + 2) \times 3$ where J is a whole number?

(A) 40
(B) 52
(C) 65
(D) 74
(E) 81

19. If $a - 7 = 3b + 4$, what does $a + 5$ equal?

(A) $b - 1$
(B) $4b - 1$
(C) $3b + 9$
(D) $3b + 16$
(E) It cannot be determined from the information given.

USE THIS SPACE FOR FIGURING.

20. According to a census report for Country A, 21.5 out of every 100 families live in rural areas. Based on this report, how many of the 2 million families in Country A live in rural areas?

    (A) 430,000
    (B) 215,000
    (C) 43,000
    (D) 4,300
    (E) 430

21. Bob is x years old, and Jerry is 7 years older. In terms of x, what was the sum of their ages, in years, 5 years ago?

    (A) $2x + 3$
    (B) $2x + 2$
    (C) $2x - 3$
    (D) $x - 3$
    (E) $x - 10$

22. A game show contestant answered exactly 20 percent of the questions correctly. Of the first 15 questions, he answered 4 correctly. If he answered only one of the remaining questions correctly, which of the following must be true?

    I. There were a total of 20 questions.
    II. He answered 10 percent of the remaining questions correctly.
    III. He didn't answer 9 of the remaining questions correctly.

    (A) I only
    (B) II only
    (C) I and II only
    (D) II and III only
    (E) I, II, and III

GO ON TO THE NEXT PAGE

USE THIS SPACE FOR FIGURING.

23. If C is the product of consecutive integers A and B, then C must be

(A) greater than $A + B$.
(B) a negative integer.
(C) a positive integer.
(D) an even integer.
(E) an odd integer.

24. A 20 percent discount is offered on all sweaters at Store S. If a cotton sweater is on sale for $48.00 and a wool sweater is on sale for $64.00, what was the difference in price of the sweaters before the discount?

(A) $16.00
(B) $19.20
(C) $20.00
(D) $24.00
(E) $32.00

25. The maximum load that a railway car can carry is $17\frac{1}{3}$ tons of freight. If a train has 36 railway cars, and each of these carries $\frac{5}{9}$ of a ton less than its maximum load, how many tons of freight is the train carrying?

(A) 604
(B) $612\frac{7}{9}$
(C) $640\frac{5}{9}$
(D) 648
(E) 660

IF YOU FINISH BEFORE TIME IS CALLED, YOU MAY CHECK YOUR WORK ON THIS SECTION ONLY. DO NOT TURN TO ANY OTHER SECTION IN THE TEST.

STOP

SECTION 3

Time—40 Minutes
40 Questions

Read each passage carefully and then answer the questions about it. For each question, decide on the basis of the passage which one of the choices best answers the question.

Typical lemurs are primates with bodies similar to those of monkeys but with pointed muzzles and large eyes; most have long, bushy tails. Their fur is woolly and may be colored red, gray, brown, or black. The name of the lemur stems from the Latin *lemures,* the Roman name for vampire-like ghosts of the dead, which these large-eyed creatures were thought to resemble. Found only off the east coast of Africa on the island of Madagascar and neighboring islands, lemurs spend some time on the ground but most often are in the trees, building nests high in the branches. Besides leaves, lemurs eat eggs, fruit, insects, and small animals. They are active throughout the day and night and are reputed to be gentle, friendly creatures. Besides typical lemurs, the lemur family includes avahi, aye-aye, loris, and galogo. However, contrary to popular belief, the so-called flying lemur is not even a primate, much less a true lemur; it is, in fact, a member of an altogether different order of mammals known as *Dermoptera.*

1. The style of the passage is most like that found in a

   (A) biology textbook.

   (B) novel about Madagascar.

   (C) zoologist's diary.

   (D) tourist's guidebook.

   (E) personal letter.

2. Which of the following would be the best title for this passage?

   (A) The Lemur: Friend or Foe?

   (B) Madagascar's Loneliest Hunters

   (C) Facts About Lemurs

   (D) African Vampires

   (E) The Diet of the Lemur

3. According to the passage, all of the following are true about lemurs EXCEPT

   (A) they spend much of their time in trees.

   (B) most have long, bushy tails.

   (C) the flying lemur is not a true lemur.

   (D) they eat only fruits and leaves.

   (E) the body of the lemur resembles the body of the monkey.

4. The passage suggests that

   (A) the typical lemur is a member of an order of mammals known as *Dermoptera.*

   (B) flying lemurs are only active during the night.

   (C) the lemur is not an aggressive animal.

   (D) lemurs spend most of their time on the ground.

   (E) flying lemurs can only be found on Madagascar and neighboring islands.

GO ON TO THE NEXT PAGE

5. According to the passage, it is reasonable to assume that

(A) flying lemurs resemble typical lemurs.
(B) typical lemurs are herbivores.
(C) their large eyes mean that lemurs come out only at night.
(D) aye-ayes are primates.
(E) lemurs' pointed muzzles give them an excellent sense of smell.

Before a joint session of Congress in January 1918, President Woodrow Wilson outlined his plan for a post–World War I peace settlement. Known as the Fourteen Points, Wilson's plan is best remembered for its first point, which declared that international diplomacy should be conducted in the open and that quiet, unpublicized diplomacy should be made illegal. Wilson believed that public diplomacy would end the threat of war by preventing immoral national leaders from secretly plotting aggressive actions against others.

Although Wilson was a highly intelligent and well-meaning man, he lacked insight into the complexities of international politics. Contrary to Wilson's belief, war rarely results from the behind-the-scenes plotting of unscrupulous national leaders. Rather, war usually stems from unresolved disagreements among nations—disagreements over territory, access to resources, and so forth. Even if quiet diplomacy could be eliminated, these disagreements would still remain, as would the threat of war.

6. The second paragraph of this passage is primarily about

(A) a post–World War I peace settlement.
(B) diplomacy's role in international politics.
(C) disagreements among nations.
(D) the actual causes of war.
(E) the first point in Wilson's Fourteen Points.

7. The attitude of the writer toward the subject is

(A) calculating.
(B) suspicious.
(C) opinionated.
(D) cheerful.
(E) apologetic.

8. The author would most likely agree that war between country A and country B would result from which of the following situations?

(A) A dispute over ownership of a piece of land bordering both countries
(B) An agreement by a leader in country A to tax imports from a third country
(C) The capture of a spy from country A in country B
(D) An unpublicized agreement by country A to sell weapons to country B
(E) A secret alliance made between country A and another country

9. Why does the author say that open diplomacy would not prevent war?

(A) Quiet diplomacy will always be a part of international relations.
(B) War breaks out because immoral rulers make decisions in secret.
(C) Open diplomacy is not a solution to the problems which lead to war.
(D) Disagreements over territory and resources rarely lead to conflict.
(E) International relations are too complex to be conducted in the public eye.

GO ON TO THE NEXT PAGE

10. All of the following questions can be answered by the passage EXCEPT:
    (A) Does the author think the Fourteen Points was a good plan?
    (B) According to the author, why does war usually start?
    (C) Did Wilson support public diplomacy or concealed diplomacy?
    (D) Does the author feel he or she understands international politics better than Wilson did?
    (E) How does the author think the threat of war could be eliminated for good?

11. Which of the following is the author most likely to discuss next?
    (A) Wilson's domestic policies in the post–World War I period
    (B) The impact of import taxes on foreign trade relations
    (C) An example of a war that resulted from a territorial or resource dispute
    (D) The events leading up to World War I
    (E) Other examples of Wilson's intelligence

Live thy Life,
Young and old,
Like yon oak,
Bright in spring,
Living gold;

Summer-rich
Then: and then
Autumn-changed,
Soberer-hued
Gold again.

All his leaves
Fall'n at length,
Look, he stands,
Trunk and bough,
Naked strength.

"The Oak," by Alfred, Lord Tennyson.

12. In this poem, the seasons represent different
    (A) kinds of trees.
    (B) times of day.
    (C) stages of life.
    (D) styles of dress.
    (E) periods of history.

13. The "he" mentioned in line 13 refers to
    (A) the poet.
    (B) life.
    (C) the oak.
    (D) autumn.
    (E) the reader.

GO ON TO THE NEXT PAGE

14. What does “Gold again” in line 10 signify?
    (A) The arrival of autumn
    (B) The richness of summer
    (C) The increased wealth of the narrator
    (D) The color of oak trees
    (E) The revival of the past

15. During which season is the oak referred to as “Living gold”?
    (A) Spring
    (B) Summer
    (C) Autumn
    (D) Winter
    (E) This description does not refer to a season.

16. With which of the following statements about life would the speaker be most likely to agree?
    (A) People should live every period of their lives to the fullest.
    (B) It is important to try to accomplish something during one’s lifetime.
    (C) Life is too short to spend time doing unpleasant things.
    (D) The seasons are unpredictable.
    (E) Trees are an integral part of the enjoyment of life.

17. All of the following can describe the tone of the poem EXCEPT
    (A) optimistic.
    (B) passionate.
    (C) pompous.
    (D) hopeful.
    (E) thoughtful.

Tea is consumed by more people and in greater amounts than any other beverage in the world, with the exception of water. The tea plant, from whose leaves tea is made, is native to India, China, and Japan and was first cultivated for use by the Chinese in prehistoric times. The plant, which is characterized as an evergreen, can reach a height of about thirty feet but is usually pruned down to three or four feet for cultivation. It has dark green leaves and cream-colored, fragrant blossoms.

Cultivation of the tea plant requires a great deal of effort. The plant must grow in a warm, wet climate in a carefully protected, well-drained area. Its leaves must be picked by hand. (Cultivation in North America has been attempted, but was found to be impractical because of a shortage of cheap labor.) Today, the plant is cultivated in the lands to which it is native, as well as in Sri Lanka, Indonesia, Taiwan, and South America.

Tea was probably first used as a vegetable relish and for medicinal purposes. In the 1400s Chinese and Japanese Buddhists developed a semireligious ceremony surrounding tea drinking. It was not until after 1700, however, that tea was first imported into Europe. Today, the United Kingdom imports more tea than does any other nation—almost one-third of the world’s production. The United States is also a large importer, but Americans have seemed to prefer coffee ever since the famous Boston Tea Party in 1773.

18. This passage is mainly about
    (A) the tea plant.
    (B) the uses of the tea plant.
    (C) tea drinking throughout history.
    (D) the tea trade.
    (E) the cultivation of the tea plant.

GO ON TO THE NEXT PAGE

19. According to the passage, the tea plant
    (A) was first cultivated in Japan in prehistoric times.
    (B) requires well-drained soil to grow properly.
    (C) is the largest import of the United Kingdom.
    (D) has odorless flowers.
    (E) is native to South America.

20. Why is a large supply of cheap labor important for the cultivation of tea?
    (A) Since the tea plant can reach a height of thirty feet, several workers are required to harvest each plant.
    (B) Since tea is exported all over the world, a lot of people are needed to handle the trade complications that arise.
    (C) Since tea has been around since prehistoric times, many workers are employed to protect it and ensure that it doesn't die out.
    (D) Since England and China are far away from each other, many workers are required to coordinate tea shipments and deliveries.
    (E) Since the tea plant is handpicked, many laborers are needed at harvest time.

21. The style in the passage is most like that found in a
    (A) newspaper article.
    (B) passage in an encyclopedia.
    (C) cookbook.
    (D) journal entry.
    (E) history textbook.

22. Which of the following is the author most likely to discuss next?
    (A) The details and aftermath of the Boston Tea Party
    (B) Other major imports of the United Kingdom and United States
    (C) Current trends in tea consumption
    (D) Other examples of plants that have a medicinal value
    (E) A description of what China was like in prehistoric times

23. The purpose of the second paragraph is to
    (A) describe the role of tea in religious ceremonies.
    (B) explain why Americans prefer coffee.
    (C) discuss historical uses of tea.
    (D) describe the cultivation of tea.
    (E) question the importance of tea.

GO ON TO THE NEXT PAGE

There were moments of waiting. The youth thought of the village street at home before the arrival of the circus parade on a day in the spring. He remembered how he had stood, a small thrillful boy, prepared to follow the band in its faded chariot. He saw the yellow road, the lines of expectant people, and the sober houses. He particularly remembered an old fellow who used to sit upon a cracker box in front of the store and pretend to despise such exhibitions. A thousand details of color and form surged in his mind.

Someone cried, "Here they come!" There was rustling and muttering among the men.

They displayed a feverish desire to have every possible cartridge ready to their hands. The boxes were pulled around into various positions and adjusted with great care.

The tall soldier, having prepared his rifle, produced a red handkerchief of some kind. He was engaged in knitting it about his throat with exquisite attention to its position, when the cry was repeated up and down the line in a muffled roar of sound.

"Here they come! Here they come!" Gun locks clicked.

Across the smoke-infested fields came a brown swarm of running men who were giving shrill yells. They came on, stooping and swinging their rifles at all angles. A flag, tilted forward, sped near the front.

24. In the first paragraph, the youth is primarily concerned with

(A) reliving a fond childhood memory.
(B) describing a turning point in his life.
(C) preparing for the upcoming battle.
(D) planning his day at the circus.
(E) watching a soldier tie a handkerchief.

25. What is meant by the exclamation "Here they come!" in line 12?

(A) A band in a chariot is approaching.
(B) The circus is coming to town.
(C) The enemy soldiers are advancing.
(D) A group of men selling handkerchiefs is on its way.
(E) The youth's family is arriving to save him.

26. The tone of the passage undergoes a change from the first to the second paragraph that can best be described as a movement from

(A) anger to amusement.
(B) reminiscence to anticipation.
(C) informality to formality.
(D) reluctance to fear.
(E) respect to indifference.

27. According to the passage, all of the following are ways the soldiers prepare for battle EXCEPT

(A) gathering cartridges.
(B) positioning ammunition.
(C) priming their guns.
(D) tying handkerchiefs.
(E) saddling horses.

28. Why are the men in the last paragraph carrying a flag?

(A) It is going to be raised in the youth's village.
(B) It needs to be protected from gunfire.
(C) It is going to be burned in a public demonstration.
(D) It represents the side they are fighting for.
(E) It has been damaged and needs to be mended.

GO ON TO THE NEXT PAGE

Acupuncture is a type of medical therapy that has been part of Chinese medicine since ancient times. It involves the insertion of thin, solid needles into specific sites on the body's surface. The belief is that the application of a needle at one particular point produces a specific response at a second point. It is based on the ancient Chinese philosophy that human beings are miniature versions of the universe and that the forces that control nature also control health. These forces are divided between two main principles called the yin and the yang, which have an opposite but complementary effect on each other. For example, one force keeps the body's temperature from rising too high, and the other keeps it from dropping too low. When they are in balance, the body maintains a constant, normal state. Disease occurs when these forces get out of balance.

Although acupuncture had been used in Western countries during many periods, it was not until the 1970s that it gained widespread interest, when it was determined that it could be used to control pain during surgery. The mechanism for its effectiveness is still a mystery, but it has become a very popular technique in many countries for the treatment of various diseases and medical problems.

29. Which of the following is true about acupuncture?

    I. Although originally only a part of Chinese medicine, it is now practiced in many Western countries.

    II. It has been used to control pain during surgery since ancient times.

    III. The mechanism for its effectiveness was discovered during the 1970s.

    (A) I only
    (B) I and II only
    (C) I and III only
    (D) II and III only
    (E) I, II, and III

30. This passage is primarily about

    (A) various diseases that are particularly common among the Chinese.
    (B) the meaning and use of the yin and the yang.
    (C) different types of medical therapies and their relative effectiveness.
    (D) the historical and philosophical background of acupuncture.
    (E) modern uses of acupuncture both in China and in Western countries.

31. According to the passage, acupuncture is based on

    (A) the idea that the human body is a model of the universe and is therefore controlled by the forces of nature.
    (B) a firm belief in the Chinese gods known as the yin and the yang.
    (C) an ancient Chinese religious ceremony that involves the insertion of needles into the body.
    (D) a philosophy of health and disease that originated in China but has been totally changed by Western countries.
    (E) the ideas of an astronomer who was attempting to study the universe in ancient times.

32. According to the passage, the yin and the yang are principles that represent

    (A) high and low extremes of temperature.
    (B) states of health and disease.
    (C) similar treatments for different diseases.
    (D) competing, balancing forces within the body.
    (E) the ideas of comfort and pain.

GO ON TO THE NEXT PAGE

33. The author includes the example of the yin and the yang controlling the extremes of body temperature in order to

(A) back up her claim that the forces within the body mirror the forces of the universe.
(B) clarify how these forces have a complementary effect on each other.
(C) provide proof that acupuncture is an effective medical therapy.
(D) suggest a possible explanation for why people sometimes run high fevers.
(E) highlight a feature of the body that acupuncture has not yet been shown to influence.

34. The author's tone in this passage could best be described as

(A) critical.
(B) admiring.
(C) bitter.
(D) serene.
(E) neutral.

The painter Georgia O'Keeffe was born in Wisconsin in 1887, and grew up on her family's farm. At seventeen she left for Chicago and New York, but she never lost her bond with the land. Like most painters, O'Keeffe painted the things that were most important to her, and she became famous for her simplified paintings of nature. During a visit to New Mexico in 1929, O'Keeffe was moved by the desert's stark beauty, and she began to paint many of its images. From about 1930 until her death in 1986, her true home was in the western desert, and bleached bones, barren hills, and colorful flowers were her characteristic subjects.

O'Keeffe is widely considered to have been a pioneering American modernist painter. While most early modern American artists were strongly influenced by European art, O'Keeffe's position was more independent.

Almost from the beginning, her work was more identifiably American—in its simplified and idealized treatment of color, light, space, and natural forms. Her paintings are generally considered "semiabstract," because, while they often depict recognizable images and objects, they don't present those images in a very detailed or realistic way. Rather, the colors and shapes in her paintings are often so reduced and simplified that they begin to take on a life of their own, independent from the real-life objects they are taken from.

35. According to the passage, all of the following strongly influenced O'Keeffe's paintings EXCEPT

(A) her rural upbringing.
(B) her life in the West.
(C) the work of artists in other countries.
(D) the appearance of the natural landscape.
(E) animal and plant forms.

GO ON TO THE NEXT PAGE

36. O'Keeffe's relationship to nature is most similar to

(A) a photographer's relationship to a model.
(B) a writer's relationship to a publisher.
(C) a student's relationship to a part-time job.
(D) a sculptor's relationship to an art dealer.
(E) a carpenter's relationship to a hammer.

37. O'Keeffe's paintings have been called "semiabstract" because they

(A) involve a carefully realistic use of color and light.
(B) depict common, everyday things.
(C) show recognizable scenes from nature.
(D) depict familiar things in an unrealistic way.
(E) refer directly to real-life activities.

38. According to the passage, O'Keeffe is considered an artistic pioneer because

(A) her work became influential in Europe.
(B) she painted the American Southwest.
(C) her paintings had a definite American style.
(D) she painted things that were familiar to her.
(E) her work was very abstract.

39. The passage's main point about O'Keeffe is that she

(A) was the best painter of her generation.
(B) was a distinctive modern American painter.
(C) liked to paint only what was familiar to her.
(D) never developed fully enough as an abstract artist.
(E) used colors and shapes that are too reduced and simple.

40. It can be inferred from the passage that modern European art of the time

(A) did not depict images of the desert.
(B) was extremely abstract.
(C) did not portray natural shapes in a simple, idealistic manner.
(D) was not influenced by rural landscapes.
(E) approached colors in a semiabstract manner.

IF YOU FINISH BEFORE TIME IS CALLED, YOU MAY CHECK YOUR WORK ON THIS SECTION ONLY. DO NOT TURN TO ANY OTHER SECTION IN THE TEST.

STOP

SECTION 4

Time—25 Minutes
60 Questions

This section consists of two different types of questions. There are directions for each type.

Each of the following questions consists of one word followed by five words or phrases. You are to select the one word or phrase whose meaning is closest to the word in capital letters.

1. PLEAD:
   (A) strike
   (B) cry
   (C) tease
   (D) beg
   (E) try

2. PROWL:
   (A) growl
   (B) sneak
   (C) scrub
   (D) leave
   (E) fight

3. VESSEL:
   (A) blood
   (B) decoration
   (C) car
   (D) account
   (E) container

4. APPROVE:
   (A) withhold information
   (B) regard innocently
   (C) watch attentively
   (D) judge favorably
   (E) consider carefully

5. SEEP:
   (A) ooze
   (B) gurgle
   (C) liquefy
   (D) stick
   (E) fall

6. VEX:
   (A) scribble
   (B) locate
   (C) scream
   (D) play
   (E) irritate

7. DOZE:
   (A) graze
   (B) sleep
   (C) refresh
   (D) bore
   (E) ignore

8. BOUNTY:
   (A) outside border
   (B) new harvest
   (C) woven basket
   (D) upper limit
   (E) generous gift

GO ON TO THE NEXT PAGE

9. COARSE:
   (A) sifted
   (B) sticky
   (C) unpopular
   (D) difficult
   (E) rough

10. MEEK:
   (A) submissive
   (B) old
   (C) tiny
   (D) worried
   (E) quick

11. SATURATE:
   (A) anger
   (B) measure
   (C) soak
   (D) boil
   (E) pour

12. GENTEEL:
   (A) timid
   (B) loud
   (C) stupid
   (D) harmless
   (E) refined

13. WINSOME:
   (A) athletic
   (B) charming
   (C) critical
   (D) small
   (E) shy

14. REPROACH:
   (A) retreat
   (B) blame
   (C) insist
   (D) complain
   (E) whine

15. DEMONSTRATE:
   (A) object
   (B) show
   (C) require
   (D) renew
   (E) imply

16. CAMOUFLAGE:
   (A) jewelry
   (B) outfit
   (C) disguise
   (D) outlook
   (E) helmet

17. AGHAST:
   (A) shocked
   (B) swollen
   (C) irritated
   (D) nasty
   (E) rude

18. RECOLLECT:
   (A) invent
   (B) remove
   (C) discover
   (D) reject
   (E) remember

GO ON TO THE NEXT PAGE

19. INITIATE:
    (A) gather
    (B) try
    (C) start
    (D) command
    (E) celebrate

20. SUFFOCATE:
    (A) give instruction
    (B) pull out
    (C) make willing
    (D) surround completely
    (E) deprive of air

21. PREVAIL:
    (A) triumph
    (B) predict
    (C) entrust
    (D) cover
    (E) enlighten

22. PRANCE:
    (A) boast
    (B) lead
    (C) strut
    (D) pry
    (E) sing

23. PROFOUND:
    (A) stubborn
    (B) unfounded
    (C) perplexing
    (D) absurd
    (E) deep

24. LIMBER:
    (A) supple
    (B) wooden
    (C) skinny
    (D) sober
    (E) sociable

25. TERMINATE:
    (A) extend
    (B) renew
    (C) finalize
    (D) sell
    (E) end

26. CONTEMPLATE:
    (A) ponder
    (B) reject
    (C) founder
    (D) dominate
    (E) deserve

27. CAPRICE:
    (A) idea
    (B) mistake
    (C) whim
    (D) decision
    (E) guess

28. ADAGE:
    (A) permission
    (B) disdain
    (C) humor
    (D) prevention
    (E) proverb

GO ON TO THE NEXT PAGE

29. DIN:
    (A) outline
    (B) clamor
    (C) improvement
    (D) demonstration
    (E) pressure

30. EXPUNGE:
    (A) erase
    (B) handle
    (C) label
    (D) assault
    (E) keep

The following questions ask you to find relationships between words. For each question, select the choice that best completes the meaning of the sentence.

31. Pilot is to airplane as
    (A) team is to players.
    (B) horse is to cart.
    (C) captain is to ship.
    (D) passenger is to train.
    (E) army is to country.

32. Snake is to python as dog is to
    (A) terrier.
    (B) canine.
    (C) pet.
    (D) mammal.
    (E) quadruped.

33. Mayor is to city as
    (A) governor is to state.
    (B) member is to union.
    (C) board is to district.
    (D) secretary is to committee.
    (E) citizen is to legislature.

34. Paper is to novel as
    (A) person is to poll.
    (B) paint is to brush.
    (C) canvas is to portrait.
    (D) back is to chair.
    (E) color is to palette.

35. Refined is to vulgar as
    (A) calm is to placid.
    (B) submissive is to recalcitrant.
    (C) happy is to ecstatic.
    (D) helpful is to victorious.
    (E) tranquil is to forgivable.

36. Whip is to lash as
    (A) stick is to throw.
    (B) shoe is to walk.
    (C) saddle is to sit.
    (D) food is to eat.
    (E) club is to beat.

37. Migrate is to swan as
    (A) hibernate is to groundhog.
    (B) pet is to dog.
    (C) reproduce is to fish.
    (D) sting is to bee.
    (E) pounce is to cat.

GO ON TO THE NEXT PAGE

38. Weather is to meteorologist as vegetation is to
    (A) driver.
    (B) artist.
    (C) oceanographer.
    (D) hunter.
    (E) botanist.

39. Track is to horse racing as
    (A) circus is to elephant.
    (B) court is to tennis.
    (C) net is to basketball.
    (D) goal is to football.
    (E) air is to bird.

40. Director is to actor as coach is to
    (A) executive.
    (B) player.
    (C) chorus.
    (D) airplane.
    (E) officer.

41. Dessert is to meal as
    (A) finale is to performance.
    (B) lunch is to breakfast.
    (C) fork is to spoon.
    (D) plate is to table.
    (E) ocean is to river.

42. Confirm is to deny as
    (A) accept is to reject.
    (B) assert is to proclaim.
    (C) contend is to imply.
    (D) pull is to tug.
    (E) simplify is to organize.

43. Tower is to airport as lighthouse is to
    (A) museum.
    (B) jet.
    (C) park.
    (D) farm.
    (E) shoreline.

44. Fidelity is to unfaithfulness as
    (A) loyalty is to honor.
    (B) friendship is to gossip.
    (C) honesty is to deceit.
    (D) laziness is to slothfulness.
    (E) intelligence is to unconcern.

45. Widespread is to limited as
    (A) encompassed is to surrounded.
    (B) enlarged is to big.
    (C) broad is to narrow.
    (D) unusual is to strange.
    (E) provincial is to international.

46. Saw is to carpenter as plow is to
    (A) banker.
    (B) surveyor.
    (C) farmer.
    (D) physician.
    (E) steelworker.

47. Sword is to fence as glove is to
    (A) box.
    (B) soccer.
    (C) hockey.
    (D) baseball.
    (E) golf.

GO ON TO THE NEXT PAGE

48. Encourage is to demand as
    (A) insinuate is to hint.
    (B) fire is to dismiss.
    (C) suggest is to order.
    (D) motivate is to undermine.
    (E) condemn is to reprimand.

49. Grin is to delight as
    (A) anxiety is to confusion.
    (B) frown is to dismay.
    (C) perspiration is to exhaustion.
    (D) laugh is to happiness.
    (E) resignation is to uncertainty.

50. Mysterious is to understandable as
    (A) unknown is to indefinable.
    (B) doubtful is to incredulous.
    (C) skillful is to swift.
    (D) clouded is to warm.
    (E) obscure is to clear.

51. Injury is to heal as malfunction is to
    (A) repair.
    (B) bandage.
    (C) misinterpret.
    (D) throw.
    (E) disassemble.

52. Jog is to sprint as trot is to
    (A) ramble.
    (B) gallop.
    (C) roam.
    (D) saunter.
    (E) soar.

53. Bone is to body as
    (A) floor is to house.
    (B) motor is to boat.
    (C) driver is to car.
    (D) knob is to door.
    (E) beam is to building.

54. Amorphous is to shape as odorless is to
    (A) appearance.
    (B) weight.
    (C) worth.
    (D) scent.
    (E) anger.

55. Vain is to humble as
    (A) anxious is to boisterous.
    (B) cantankerous is to thoughtless.
    (C) judicious is to lenient.
    (D) authoritative is to discursive.
    (E) extroverted is to shy.

56. Test is to study as
    (A) job is to apply.
    (B) train is to practice.
    (C) play is to rehearse.
    (D) office is to employ.
    (E) income is to work.

57. Smile is to frown as cheer is to
    (A) jeer.
    (B) wince.
    (C) laugh.
    (D) extricate.
    (E) leap.

GO ON TO THE NEXT PAGE

58. Banana is to peel as
   (A) egg is to crack.
   (B) carrot is to uproot.
   (C) apple is to core.
   (D) bread is to slice.
   (E) corn is to husk.

59. Touch is to tactile as
   (A) sound is to noise.
   (B) smell is to olfactory.
   (C) mouth is to oral.
   (D) eye is to visual.
   (E) taste is to sense.

60. Articulateness is to speech as
   (A) etiquette is to society.
   (B) music is to note.
   (C) ballet is to form.
   (D) legibility is to handwriting.
   (E) painting is to palette.

IF YOU FINISH BEFORE TIME IS CALLED, YOU MAY CHECK YOUR WORK ON THIS SECTION ONLY. DO NOT TURN TO ANY OTHER SECTION IN THE TEST. **STOP**

SECTION 5

Time—30 Minutes
25 Questions

In this section, there are five possible answers after each problem. Choose which one is best. You may use the blank space at the right of the page for scratch work.

Note: Figures provided with the problems are drawn with the greatest possible accuracy, UNLESS stated "Not Drawn to Scale."

USE THIS SPACE FOR FIGURING.

1. The crown in Figure 1 is made up of toothpicks that each have the same length. If each toothpick is 2 meters long and each side is equal to one toothpick, what is the perimeter of the crown in meters?

   (A) 5
   (B) 7
   (C) 10
   (D) 12
   (E) 14

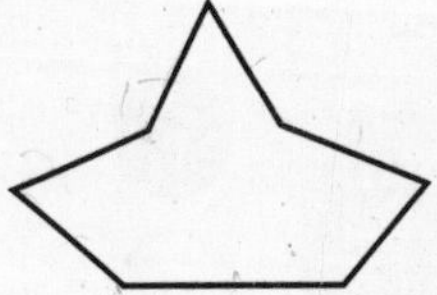

Figure 1

2. *D* is an odd number between 4 and 11. If *D* is also between 7 and 18, what is the value of *D*?

   (A) 5
   (B) 7
   (C) 8
   (D) 9
   (E) 11

3. Gary has a collection of 16 different operas, and his roommate Paul has a collection of 18 different operas. If Paul and Gary have 4 operas common to both record collections, how many different operas do they have between them?

   (A) 18
   (B) 30
   (C) 34
   (D) 36
   (E) 38

GO ON TO THE NEXT PAGE

USE THIS SPACE FOR FIGURING.

4. If $\frac{1}{9}G = 18$, then $\frac{1}{3}G =$
   (A) 6.
   (B) 9.
   (C) 36.
   (D) 54.
   (E) 63.

5. A model sailboat floating on the water is attached to a string 1 meter long, as shown in Figure 2. If the string is tied to a post on the edge of the dock, which of the following best shows the area of water on which the sailboat can float?

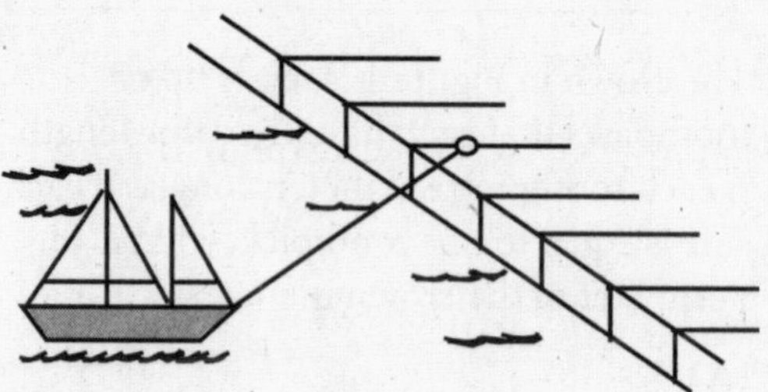

Figure 2

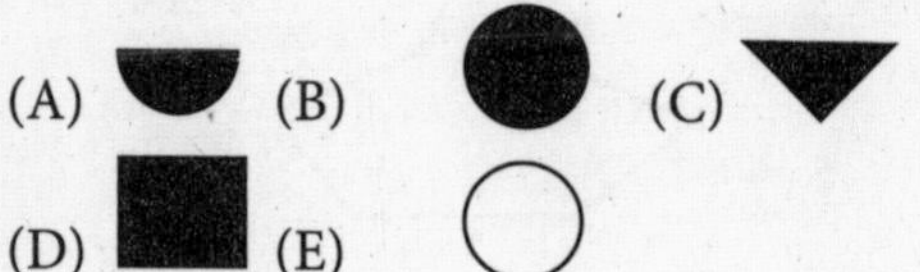

6. At a party, there are exactly 4 times as many adults as children. Which of the following could be the total number of people at this party?
   (A) 14
   (B) 16
   (C) 21
   (D) 25
   (E) 29

7. Using a pair of scissors, which of the following can be made from a 20 cm by 28 cm rectangular sheet of paper by one straight cut?
   I. Triangle
   II. Square
   III. Rectangle

   (A) I only
   (B) II only
   (C) III only
   (D) I and II only
   (E) I, II, and III

GO ON TO THE NEXT PAGE

8. According to the graph in Figure 3, the average number of students taking the swimming class during the four months of March through June was

(A) 50.
(B) 55.
(C) 60.
(D) 65.
(E) 70.

USE THIS SPACE FOR FIGURING.

NUMBER OF STUDENTS TAKING SWIMMING CLASS

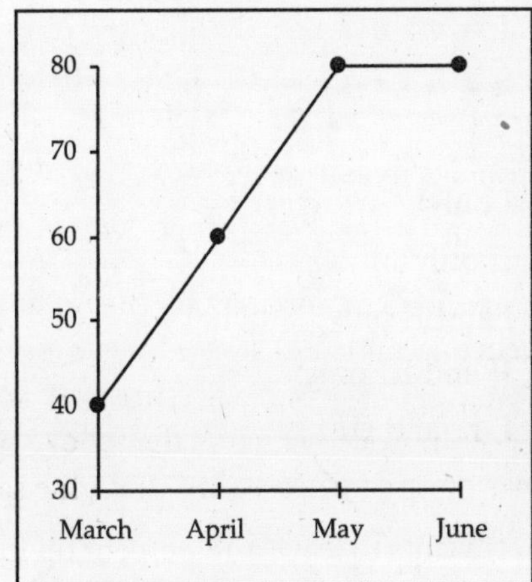

Figure 3

<u>Questions 9–11</u> refer to the following definition.

For all real numbers n and r, $n \clubsuit r = (n-1) - \frac{n}{r}$.

<u>EXAMPLE</u>: $5 \clubsuit 3 = (5-1) - \frac{5}{3} = 4 - \frac{5}{3} = 2\frac{1}{3}$.

9. What is the value of $4 \clubsuit 2$?

(A) 1
(B) 2
(C) 6
(D) 8
(E) 16

10. If $Q \clubsuit 2 = 4$, then $Q =$

(A) 10.
(B) 8.
(C) 6.
(D) 4.
(E) 2.

11. If $n \neq 0$ and $r \neq 0$, which of the following must be true?

USE THIS SPACE FOR FIGURING.

I. $n \clubsuit 1 = -1$
II. $1 \clubsuit n = 0$
III. $n \clubsuit n = r \clubsuit r$

(A) I only
(B) II only
(C) I and II only
(D) II and III only
(E) I, II, and III

12. Robert wants to leave a 15 percent tip for a dinner that costs $20.95. Which of the following is closest to the amount of tip he should leave?

(A) $2.70
(B) $3.00
(C) $3.15
(D) $3.50
(E) $3.75

13. Juan studied from 4:00 P.M. to 6:00 P.M. and finished one-third of his assignments. He is taking a break and wants to finish his homework by 10:30 P.M. If he plans to continue working at the same rate, what is the latest that he can return to his studies?

(A) 6:30 P.M.
(B) 7:00 P.M.
(C) 7:30 P.M.
(D) 8:00 P.M.
(E) 8:30 P.M.

GO ON TO THE NEXT PAGE

USE THIS SPACE FOR FIGURING.

14. Mrs. Brown and her z children each ate 2 peaches. What's the total number of peaches they ate?

(A) $z + 1$
(B) $z + 2$
(C) $2z$
(D) $2z + 1$
(E) $2z + 2$

15. Which figure can be drawn WITHOUT lifting the pencil or retracing?

(A) (B) (C) 

(D) (E)

16. If 0.59 is about $\frac{N}{5}$, then N is closest to which of the following?

(A) 0.3
(B) 1
(C) 2
(D) 3
(E) 30

17. If the largest of 7 consecutive integers is 25, what is the average of the 7 integers?

(A) 24
(B) 22
(C) 21
(D) 20
(E) 16

18. The price of a box of raisins increased from \$0.93 to \$1.08. The increase in price is closest to what percent?

(A) 1%
(B) 14%
(C) 15%
(D) 16%
(E) 20%

USE THIS SPACE FOR FIGURING.

$$21\overline{)Q}\quad \text{quotient } 15$$

$$15\overline{)S}\quad \text{quotient } 21 \text{ remainder } 8$$

19. In the division problems shown above, $S - Q =$

(A) 6.
(B) 8.
(C) 15.
(D) 18.
(E) 21.

20. What is the least number of square tiles with side 6 cm needed to cover a rectangular floor 72 cm long and 48 cm wide?

(A) 14
(B) 72
(C) 96
(D) 144
(E) 192

GO ON TO THE NEXT PAGE

USE THIS SPACE FOR FIGURING.

21. It takes Craig 5 minutes to type n pages. At this rate, how many minutes will it take him to type 20 pages?

(A) $\frac{n}{100}$

(B) $\frac{4}{n}$

(C) $\frac{100}{n}$

(D) $4n$

(E) $100n$

22. The width of a rectangular swimming pool is one-quarter of its length. If the length is 60 meters, what is the perimeter of the pool?

(A) 60 m
(B) 120 m
(C) 150 m
(D) 180 m
(E) 240 m

23. The price of a dress at a department store decreases by 20 percent every month it is not sold. After 3 months, the current price of the unsold dress is approximately what percent of the original price?

(A) 40%
(B) 50%
(C) 60%
(D) 70%
(E) 80%

GO ON TO THE NEXT PAGE

24. If p is a positive integer and n is a negative integer, which of the following is greatest?

(A) $\frac{p}{n}$

(B) $\frac{n}{p}$

(C) $\frac{1}{p-n}$

(D) $\frac{1}{n-p}$

(E) It cannot be determined from the information given.

USE THIS SPACE FOR FIGURING.

25. In a yoga school, $\frac{1}{9}$ of the men and $\frac{1}{3}$ of the women are vegetarians, and twice as many men as women are vegetarians. If there are 84 people in the yoga school, how many men are vegetarians?

(A) 4
(B) 8
(C) 12
(D) 27
(E) 72

IF YOU FINISH BEFORE TIME IS CALLED, YOU MAY CHECK YOUR WORK ON THIS SECTION ONLY. DO NOT TURN TO ANY OTHER SECTION IN THE TEST.

STOP

ANSWER KEY

Section 2

1. E
2. B
3. B
4. E
5. E
6. B
7. C
8. B
9. A
10. C
11. A
12. D
13. B
14 C
15. E
16. C
17. E
18. E
19. D
20. A
21. C
22. D
23. D
24. C
25. A

Section 3

1. A
2. C
3. D
4. C
5. D
6. D
7. C
8. A
9. C
10. E
11. C
12. C
13. C
14. A
15. A
16. A
17. C
18. A
19. B
20. E
21. B
22. C
23. D
24. A
25. C
26. B
27. E
28. D
29. A
30. D
31. A
32. D
33. B
34. B
35. C
36. A
37. D
38. C
39. B
40. C

Section 4

1. D
2. B
3. E
4. D
5. A
6. E
7. B
8. E
9. E
10. A
11. C
12. E
13. B
14. B
15. B
16. C
17. A
18. E
19. C
20. E
21. A
22. C
23. E
24. A
25. E
26. A
27. C
28. E
29. B
30. A
31. C
32. A
33. A
34. C
35. B
36. E
37. A
38. E
39. B
40. B
41. A
42. A
43. E
44. C
45. C
46. C
47. A
48. C
49. B
50. E
51. A
52. B
53. E
54. D
55. E
56. C
57. A
58. E
59. B
60. D

Section 5

1. E
2. D
3. B
4. D
5. A
6. D
7. E
8. D
9. A
10. A
11. A
12. C
13. A
14. E
15. D
16. D
17. B
18. D
19. B
20. C
21. C
22. C
23. B
24. C
25. B

SSAT PRACTICE TEST 1: UPPER-LEVEL: ASSESS YOUR STRENGTHS

Use the following tables to determine which topics and chapters you need to review most. If you need help with your essay, be sure to review Chapter 9: The Essay and Chapter 26: Writing Skills.

Topic	Question
Math I	Section 2, questions 1–25
Reading Comprehension	Section 3, questions 1–40
Verbal: Synonyms	Section 4, questions 1–30
Verbal: Analogies	Section 4, questions 31–60
Math II	Section 5, questions 1–25

Topic	Number of Questions on Test	Number Correct	If you struggled with these questions, study...
Math I	25		Chapters 10–14 and Chapter 25
Reading Comprehension	40		Chapter 8
Verbal: Synonyms	30		Chapters 7 and 24
Verbal: Analogies	30		Chapters 2 and 24
Math II	25		Chapters 10–14 and Chapter 25

ANSWERS AND EXPLANATIONS

SECTION 2: MATH

1. E

We need an answer here that is not a factor of 120. In other words, a number which will not evenly divide into 120. Only (E), 16, is not a factor of 120.

2. B

Recall that all figures on the SSAT are always drawn to scale unless stated otherwise. Extending the vertical line segment boundary of the art slice upward and extending the horizontal line segment boundary of the art slice to the right shows that the art slice is about 25% of the pie. Twenty-five percent or $\frac{1}{4}$ of 900 (the total number of students) is 225 art students.

3. B

Sean's sister must arrive (25 – 14) or 11 minutes after midnight because it takes 14 minutes to reach midnight and 11 more minutes to add up to 25 minutes.

4. E

The key here is to make what you are given look like the answer choices. No calculation is needed. Round off 0.52 to 0.5 or $\frac{1}{2}$ and round 78 to 80.

5. E

Careful! The question asks for dollars. Each sack of money = $50 as is noted in the table. Brian has 4 more sacks than James, so the amount more than James that Brian saved is 4 times $50 which equals $200.

6. B

We must determine how much was saved by Andy and how much was saved by James and compare the two. Andy saved 8 sacks, which is 8 times $50 or $400, and James saved 2 sacks, which is 2 times $50 or $100. Thus, Andy's $400 is 4 times James's $100.

7. C

Using the formula Part = Percent × Whole, 30 = 30% × N (total number of students). We need to isolate the total number of students (N). Thirty percent = $\frac{30}{100}$, so the equation can be written as $30 = \frac{30}{100} \times N$. Now multiply both sides of this equation by $\frac{100}{30}$; the N is now by itself once $\frac{30}{100}$ and $\frac{100}{30}$ cancel out to 1. Multiplying $30 \times \frac{100}{30}$ gives a value of 100 for N.

8. B

Because of the word *except,* we need to determine which fraction is *not* less than 2. So we are looking for a fraction that is greater than or equal to 2. In order to determine this, make all of the fractions improper: With (A), $\frac{15}{8} = 1\frac{7}{8}$. The only fraction where the denominator can be divided into the numerator with a result of at least 2 is (B): $\frac{45}{22} = 2\frac{1}{22}$.

9. A

We are told all the sides are equal. Thus, set each segment = 1 and add. With (A), $A-C-B-D-F$ = 1 (A to C) + 1 (C to B) + 1 (B to D) + 2 (D to E and then E to F) = 5. (B) counts to 4; hence, cross it out. (C) counts to 4 also, so cross it out. (D) counts to 3, and (E) counts to 4. The longest path is 5, so (A) is correct.

10. C

Scan the answer choices. (A), 80, is 80.08 – 80 = 0.08 away from 80.08. (B), 80.01, is 80.08 – 80.01 = 0.07 away from 80.08. (C), 80.1, is 80.1 –80.08 = 0.02 away from 80.08. (D), 81, is 0.92 away from 80.08; and (E), 90, is more than 9 away from 80.08. The question asks for the choice closest to 80.08, and thus (C), 80.1, is correct.

11. A

Call the number *N*. Write an inequality using the information given. Remember, *of* means multiply, $\frac{1}{3} \times N < 12$. We need to isolate *N*, our unknown value. Multiplying both sides by the reciprocal of $\frac{1}{3}$, which is 3, produces a result of $N < 12 \times 3$, and thus $N < 36$. (A) is correct.

12. D

The minimum number of points Team B could have scored is 1 more than Team A, or 40. Using the average formula, Average = $\frac{\text{Sum of the terms}}{\text{Number of terms}}$, we can plug in our given information: Average = $\frac{\text{40 points}}{\text{5 players}}$. Thus the average score of the players on Team B must have been at least 8 points per player.

13. B

The sum of the 3 interior angles of any triangle is 180 degrees. Figure 4 indicates that two of the angles have degree measures of 90 and 45. So the degree measure of the third angle is 180 – 90 – 45 = 45. So this is a 45–45–90 triangle. In any triangle, the sides opposite two equal angles must be equal. Hence, $a = 6$.

14. C

Here, we need to divide 40,000 into 2,000,000: $\frac{2{,}000{,}000}{40{,}000}$. Simply cancel out 4 zeros from the bottom and 4 zeros from the top. We now have $\frac{200}{4}$, which equals 50.

15. E

The question states that *y* is less than 3, and we want the value that *x* cannot equal, so let's solve the equation for *x* in terms of *y* and see if we can conclude something about *x*. The equation is $x - y + 2 = 6$. First subtract 2 from both sides. Then $x - y = 6 - 2$, or $x - y = 4$. Adding *y* to both sides, we have that $x = y + 4$. Since *y* is less than 3, $y + 4$ must be less than 7. Now $x = y + 4$, so *x* must be less than 7. Look for a choice that is not less than 7. Only (E), 8, is not less than 7. So *x* cannot be 8, and (E) is correct.

16. C

Segment $AD = 55$. Because the length of *AB* is 2 times the length of *BC*, let $BC = x$ and let $AB = 2x$. Since $AB = CD$, let $CD = 2x$ also. The total length of $AD = AB + BC + CD = 2x + x + 2x = 5x = 55$. Hence, $x = 11$ and $BD = BC + CD = x + 2x = 3x = 3 \times 11 = 33$.

17. E

The question asks for all the points. (A) is incorrect because it only includes the rectangular boundary of the set of all the points that touch the table; it does not include the points inside this rectangle that also touch the surface of the table. (E) indicates all the points and is correct.

18. E

The question is not asking for a value of *J*. Indeed, *J* could be any whole number. The question is asking for the answer choice that can be written in the form $(J + 2) \times 3$, where *J* is a whole number. Since

3 is a factor of $(J + 2) \times 3$, the choice we're looking for must be a multiple of 3. A whole number is a multiple of 3 if and only if the sum of its digits is a multiple of 3. Looking at the answer choices, only the sum if the digits of (E), 81, is a multiple of 3. That is, the sum of the digits of 81 is $8 + 1 = 9$, which is a multiple of 3. So (E) is correct.

19. D

Using the information given, isolate a: $a = 3b + 4 + 7 = 3b + 11$. Thus, $a = 3b + 11$. Next add 5 to both sides of this equation: $a + 5 = 3b + 11 + 5 = 3b + 16$.

20. A

They give us 21.5 out of 100, which is easily translated into 21.5%. Hence, 21.5% of (multiplication) 2,000,000 is $\frac{21.5}{100} \times 2{,}000{,}000$. Cancel out two zeros from the 100 in the denominator and from the 2,000,000 in the numerator to get $21.5 \times 20{,}000 = 430{,}000$.

21. C

Translate from English into math. Let Bob's current age = x, and let Jerry's current age = $x + 7$. To find their ages 5 years ago, subtract 5 years from each current age: 5 years ago Bob was $x - 5$, and Jerry was $x + 7 - 5 = x + 2$. The sum of Bob and Jerry's ages 5 years ago was $x - 5 + x + 2 = 2x - 3$.

22. D

The contestant answered a total of 5 questions correctly. Using our percent formula, Percent × Whole = Part, 20% × total number of questions = 5. Multiply both sides of the equation by $\frac{100}{20}$ (the reciprocal of 20%), and the total number of questions = 25. Thus, statement I is incorrect so eliminate (A), (C), and (E). For statement II, there were $25 - 15 =$ 10 questions remaining, and 1 of these 10 questions was answered correctly. So he answered $\frac{1}{10}$, or 10% of the remaining questions correctly, so statement II is true. (Also, both remaining answer choices, (B) and (D), contain this Roman numeral.) Finally, statement III is true because 1 of the remaining 10 questions was answered correctly so 9 of these 10 were not answered correctly. Eliminate choice (B). (D) remains and is correct.

23. D

This problem is perfect for our Picking Numbers strategy. $C = A \times B$. Pick two consecutive numbers for A and B such as 2 and 3. Their product is 6 and positive. However, if we selected 1 and 0, the product would be 0, which is neither positive nor negative. Because the integers are consecutive, one of the integers must be even, or a multiple of 2, and hence the product of any two consecutive integers must be even. (D) is correct.

24. C

Be careful here. The question asks for the difference before the discount. The sweaters were sold for 100% – 20% of their old price. Using our percent formula, Part = Percent × Whole, we have that 48 = 80% × old price. Convert 80% to $\frac{80}{100}$ and multiply both sides by $\frac{100}{80}$. We now have $\frac{100}{80} \times 48$ = old price. Canceling yields \$60. Use the percent formula for the wool sweater, and you have the equation \$64 = 80% × old price. You'll find that its original price was \$80. The difference is \$80 – \$60 = \$20.

25. A

The maximum load that a car can carry is $17\frac{1}{3}$ tons. If each car carries the maximum load minus $\frac{5}{9}$ of a ton, then each car carries $17\frac{1}{3} - \frac{5}{9} = \frac{52}{3} - \frac{5}{9} = \frac{52}{3} \times \frac{3}{3} - \frac{5}{9} = \frac{156-5}{9} = \frac{151}{9}$ tons. Next, multiply this amount carried in each car by 36 cars and get $\frac{151}{9} \times 36$ tons. Cancel the 9 into the 36 and get $151 \times 4 = 604$.

SECTION 3: READING COMPREHENSION

Lemurs Passage

This fact-based passage introduces us to the lemur, a monkey-like animal that lives chiefly in Madagascar. We're given various information about lemurs: their physical characteristics, the origin of their name, where they're found, and so on.

1. A

The author's style is straightforward and informative, like the style of a biology textbook. A zoologist's diary would more likely be in the first-person ("June 20: Saw two lemurs in a jungle in southern Madagascar."), and a tourist's guidebook would go into less scientific detail and would place lemurs in a specific location. ("Be sure to check out the lemurs in Avahi National Park.")

2. C

Summarize the passage in your own mind. You might have come up with something like "Things to Know about Lemurs." (C) restates this idea. The passage doesn't mention whether lemurs hunt alone or in groups, so (B) is incorrect, and the rest of the answer choices focus on details.

3. D

You're looking for the detail that's false. The author states that lemurs eat "leaves . . . eggs, fruit, insects, and small animals," so (D) must be incorrect.

4. C

In the second half of the paragraph, the author states that lemurs "are reputed to be gentle, friendly creatures." If they're "gentle" and "friendly," you can infer that they're not very aggressive. (A) is contradicted in the final sentence of the passage. (B) and (D) are refuted when the author says that lemurs "are active throughout the day and night" and are "most often are in the trees." We don't know enough about the flying lemur to infer that it can only be found in and around Madagascar, so (E) is incorrect.

5. D

(A) and (E) cannot be verified using the passage. (B) is incorrect because the passage states that "lemurs eat eggs ... insects, and small animals" (lines 13–14). (C) is incorrect because the passage says that lemurs "are active throughout the day" (line 14). (D) is correct because aye-ayes are in the lemur family and lemurs are primates.

Woodrow Wilson Passage

This historical passage focuses on President Woodrow Wilson and his post-World War I peace settlement—specifically, on the Fourteen-Point Plan, which called for the abolition of secret diplomacy. Wilson considered open negotiations vital for peace, but in paragraph 2 the author disagrees, arguing that Wilson's view was too simplistic.

6. D

The first and second sentences of each paragraph usually reveal the paragraph's topic. In this case, it's the second sentence: Wilson was wrong—war stems not from secret deals by national leaders but from "unresolved disagreements among nations." (A) and (E) summarize the topic of paragraph 1, not paragraph 2. (B) is too general; the paragraph mainly discusses why one form of diplomacy usually fails to avert wars. Not all disagreements among nations lead to war, so (C) is also too broad.

7. C

We're told that Wilson called for an end to secret negotiations as a way to end war and then that Wilson was wrong—that "he lacked insight into the complexities of international politics." Clearly, the author disagrees with Wilson. (A) is tempting, given the author's "realpolitik" attitude, but she isn't being Machiavellian; she's simply stating why Wilson's idea was wrong. (B) and (D) are too emotional, and (E) is incorrect because the author doesn't apologize for criticizing Wilson.

8. A

The scenario in (A) is the closest parallel to the author's thinking. As the next-to-last sentence of the passage puts it, "war usually stems from unresolved disagreements among nations . . . over territory . . . ." (B)'s scenario is an economic trade agreement involving a third country—not very likely to lead to war. The other answer choices involve secret deals or covert activity of the kind that Wilson—not the author—thought would lead to war.

9. C

Look at the last two sentences of the text. According to the author, open diplomacy can't solve the kinds of problems that lead to war. (A)'s assertion that quiet diplomacy will always be with us doesn't explain why open diplomacy won't prevent war.

10. E

To find the correct answer, try to answer each of the questions in the choices. (A) is answered in lines 14–15; the author says Wilson's first point on diplomacy was wrong. (B) is answered in lines 17–19; wars usually result from disagreements among nations. (C) is answered in line 7; Wilson supported open (public) diplomacy. (D) is answered in the second paragraph; the author says Wilson "lacked insight into the complexities of international politics (lines 13–14), and then the author proceeds to present is his or her knowledge or international politics. (E) is the answer because the passage does not tackle ways to eliminate the threat of war.

11. C

To imagine where the author might go next, retrace the steps of the argument: 1) Wilson offered a peace proposal that argued for open diplomacy, which he thought would end wars; 2) Wilson failed to grasp that secret diplomacy is not the cause of most wars, which occur because of unresolved disputes among nations over such things as territory and resources. Having disagreed with Wilson, it's most likely that the author will try to illustrate this last point by giving an example of a war that occurred because of a territorial or resource dispute. (A), (D), and (E) suggest that the author will return to the subjects of President Wilson or World War I, but the text moves beyond Wilson to discuss the cause of war.

Poetry Passage

You are likely to see one poem on the SSAT. When you do, be alert for tone and the use of metaphor. Here, an oak tree is used as a metaphor—for living our lives as an oak tree does, in accordance with nature and the change of seasons. The first three lines of the poem generate its central metaphor: "Live thy life, Young and old, Like yon oak..." ("Yon" is short for "yonder," meaning "that oak over there.") In other words, "Live your life, at all ages, like that oak tree does."

12. C

You're asked to infer the poem's central metaphor. What do the seasons represent? The successive stages of life, (C): Spring is youth, summer is maturity, autumn is middle age, and winter is old age.

13. C

Who is the "he" of line 13? The entire stanza provides clues: "he" has lost his leaves, "he" stands, "trunk and bough, naked strength." "He," then, is the oak tree.

14. A

The second stanza shows the oak tree in summer and in autumn; "gold again" refers to the seasonally changed color of the oak tree's leaves, so (A) is best here. (B), (C), and (E) are pretty easily eliminated, and (D) isn't right because the arrival of autumn signals a change in foliage—and the quoted phrase refers to the latter, not the former.

15. A

This is a detail question. The oak is referred to as "Living gold" in line 5 of the poem; the previous line says, "Bright in spring."

16. A

This question basically asks for the statement that mirrors the poem's Big Idea, which is that we should be like the oak tree, living each season of our lives as well as we can. (A) restates this best. (B) is wrong because "something" can apparently be accomplished at any point in one's life; what about the other "seasons"? (C) makes little sense, and (D) contradicts the poem. (E) dispenses with the poem's central metaphor altogether: It's not that a good life includes the enjoyment of trees; it's that a good life is lived as a tree lives its life.

17. C

Think about how the poem would sound if you read it aloud. It would sound as if the poet were giving you advice on living life to the fullest. That rules out (A), (D), and (E). The poem is optimistic (seeking the best possible outcome), hopeful, and helpful; that leaves passionate (expressing intense feeling) and pompous (arrogant). The poem does sound intense, so the answer is (C).

Tea Passage

This passage is about tea—the plant, and the history of its cultivation and uses. Paragraph 1 describes its universal appeal, its origin, and its description and look. Paragraph 2 describes the difficulties of cultivating tea and where the plant is currently grown. The final paragraph summarizes tea's history, from ancient times to today.

18. A

The choice that best sums up the passage is (A). The other answer choices each touch on only one aspect of the text.

19. B

(A) is wrong because tea was first cultivated in China. (C) distorts lines 25–27: The author states that the United Kingdom is the world's largest importer of tea, not that tea is the United Kingdom's largest import.

20. E

The phrase "cheap labor" in the question stem is also found in paragraph 2, which states that, since tea leaves "must be picked by hand," cultivation in North America "was found to be impractical because of a shortage of cheap labor." In other words, tea cultivation requires a supply of cheap labor because the leaves must be handpicked. (A) contradicts paragraph 1, which says that tea plants are "usually pruned down to three or four feet for cultivation." (B) and (C) are never mentioned, and (D) incorrectly reduces the world's cultivation and consumption of tea to two countries, England and China.

21. B

The author's style is informative, offering an encyclopedic summary of the cultivation and uses of tea.

22. C

Since paragraph 3 summarizes the historic uses of tea, beginning with ancient times and ending with consumption today, it's likely that the author will continue to discuss current consumption trends. (A) temptingly mentions the last detail in the passage, but the Boston Tea Party is only an aside, a lighthearted explanation of why consumption of tea in the United States today lags behind that of coffee.

23. D

Paragraph 2 describes the difficulties of cultivating tea and where it is currently cultivated.

Fiction Passage

This passage reflects the thoughts going through a soldier's mind in the final moments before battle. Notice how the two lines of dialogue toward the end of the passage increase the tension of the imminent attack. Be alert for shifts of tone and perspective and the use of metaphor.

24. A

After the teaser in the opening sentence (moments of waiting for what?), the first paragraph details the youth's childhood memory of the circus in town, (A). The circus's arrival couldn't be called a turning point in his life—it was simply a fond memory—so (B) is incorrect. (D) is incorrect because he wasn't planning his day at the circus; he was simply enjoying the day as a spectator. Neither (C) nor (E) are discussed in the first paragraph, so they are incorrect as well.

25. C

The text jumps from one "scene" to another. That is, the quoted exclamation breaks us away from the youth's daydream of the circus and into the reality of his current situation. A fellow soldier has shouted that the enemy is approaching, (C), and we are jolted into the reality of the situation. (A) and (B) wrongly assume that the exclamation is part of the youth's memory, and (D) and (E) are completely unwarranted inferences.

26. B

As we have just seen in the previous question, the youth reminisces in paragraph 1. As we jump to the next paragraph and to the reality of the battle, the men prepare with anticipation. No other answer choice fits.

27. E

Horses are never mentioned here; all the soldiers are on foot.

28. D

Why do soldiers carry a flag? In the same way flags are raised on ships in the ocean, raising a flag on land is meant to represent one's side or country. (A) is tempting, but true only if the enemy wins. (B) makes no sense, since the flag is carried at the front of a charging line of soldiers.

Acupuncture Passage

This modified science passage discusses acupuncture, an ancient Chinese form of medical therapy. There's very little science in the passage. Instead, the author describes the thinking behind acupuncture and gives a brief history of its use in Western countries.

29. A

A Roman Numeral question. The only true statement, according to the passage, is statement I: Acupuncture was first practiced in China, but it is now practiced in many Western countries as well. Statement II is false: According to the first sentence of paragraph 2, acupuncture was not used to control pain during surgery until the 1970s. And the final sentence of the passage disputes statement III: The mechanism for its effectiveness "is still a mystery."

30. D

The author tells us what acupuncture involves, the ancient Chinese philosophy on which it's based, and how it recently spread to the West. The passage is primarily about the historical and philosophical background of acupuncture, (D). (A) is not mentioned, and (B) focuses too narrowly on the first paragraph. (C) is too general.

31. A

Paragraph 1 states that acupuncture is based on the ancient Chinese belief that "human beings are miniature versions of the universe" and that the same forces control nature and health. Yin and yang are not Chinese gods, (B); they're principles. And contrary to (D), Western countries have not "totally changed" the Chinese philosophy of health and disease. They may have ignored it or failed to understand it, but they did not change it.

32. D

Yin and yang have "an opposite but complementary effect on each other. . . . When they are in balance, the body maintains a constant, normal [i.e., healthy] state." (A) names an example of how the two principles operate, not what they represent. (B) wrongly states that one principle is healthy and the other unhealthy, but it's a balance of both that maintains health and an imbalance that results in sickness.

33. B

When yin and yang are in balance, the body is healthy, but when they're out of balance, disease occurs. These two forces work together, or complement, each other. The claim in (A) was made by ancient Chinese philosophy, and there is no actual proof in the passage for (C). The author does not mention any part of the body that isn't influenced by acupuncture, so (E) is incorrect.

34. B

Are the author's points positive, negative, or neutral? The author sticks to pointing out what acupuncture is and how it has become a popular form of treatment. The author doesn't talk about the negative aspects, so the tone is positive. That rules out (A), (C), and (E), leaving "admiring" and "serene." Next, think about how the passage would sound if you read it aloud. Does it sound as if the author holds acupuncture with high regard and respect (admiring), or does it sound calm and peaceful (serene)? Clearly, the author is excited about acupuncture and admires its effectiveness. (B) is the answer.

O'Keeffe Passage

The final passage is about the American painter Georgia O'Keeffe—her life, her fame, and the subjects of her paintings. The opening sentence of paragraph 2 sums up the main point: O'Keeffe is "widely considered to have been a pioneering American modernist painter."

35. C

(C) is contradicted by paragraph 2, which states that O'Keeffe was "more independent" than most other early modern American artists, who were "strongly influenced by European art." The other choices can be found in the passage as influences on O'Keeffe.

36. A

O'Keeffe was the artist, and nature was her favorite subject. Do this one as you would an Analogy. The relationship of artist to subject is repeated in (A): The model *is* the photographer's subject. Similarly, nature is O'Keeffe's subject.

37. D

Why are the paintings "semiabstract" (line 24)? (B) and (C) are only half the answer: It was her treatment of these objects and scenes—the way she painted them—that made them "semiabstract."

38. C

According to paragraph 2, O'Keeffe was unlike her contemporary American painters—"independent," not influenced by European art. Her work was "identifiably American," which makes (C) correct. (B) and (D) are factually true, but they're not the reason why she's considered a pioneer. And (E) is incorrect since O'Keeffe's work was considered "semiabstract," not very abstract.

39. B

The main point is summed up in the opening sentence of paragraph 2. The author never claims that O'Keeffe was the best painter of her generation, (A), or that she didn't develop a fully abstract style, (D), or even that her colors and shapes were too simple, (E). (C) is plausible (though we never learn that O'Keeffe painted only familiar subjects), but it's not the main point.

40. C

We're told that European art strongly influenced most American artists of O'Keeffe's time. Unlike European art, however, O'Keeffe's paintings offered a "simplified and idealized treatment of color, light, space, and natural forms." Since European art was different from O'Keeffe's art, we can infer that it did not portray natural shapes in a simple, idealistic way, making (C) correct. No other answer choice can be inferred.

SECTION 4: VERBAL

Synonyms

1. D

To plead is to appeal earnestly or desperately—to beg.

2. B

To prowl is to move around secretly, stealthily—in other words, to sneak.

3. E

A vessel, such as a bowl or glass, is a container for holding something.

4. D

To approve means to judge favorably.

5. A

To seep means to flow through little cracks, or to ooze.

6. E

To vex means to anger, or irritate.

7. B

To doze is to sleep lightly. You might doze because someone bores you, but the two words are not synonymous.

8. E

A bounty is a reward or gift.

9. E

Something coarse is harsh or rough.

10. A

Meek means mild mannered or submissive.

11. C

To saturate is to wet something thoroughly or soak it. You saturate a sponge in water, for example.

12. E

Genteel describes something elegant, aristocratic, or refined.

13. B

Winsome means pleasing or charming, such as a winsome smile.

14. B

To reproach means to express disapproval or disappointment in someone. (D) is tempting, but you can complain without blaming anything specific.

15. B

To demonstrate means to explain clearly or show.

16. C

A camouflage is a disguise or a concealment. An outfit, (B), may or may not be a camouflage.

17. A

Aghast is an adjective that means to be struck with amazement or horror—in other words, to be shocked.

18. E

To recollect means to remember.

19. C

To initiate means to begin or start.

20. E

To suffocate is to choke or deprive of air.

21. A

To prevail means to win, overcome, or triumph.

22. C

To prance is to walk in a cocky way or to strut. The closest wrong answer choice, in attitude at least, is (A), but boasting is not a way of walking.

23. E

Profound means deep-seated or intense. A parent has a profound love for his or her child.

24. A

Limber means flexible, lithe, nimble, or supple. (B), wooden, is a good antonym for limber.

25. E

To terminate means to finish or bring to an end.

26. A

To contemplate means to think about or ponder.

27. C

A caprice is a sudden fancy or whim. (A) is tempting, but not all ideas are whims or caprices.

28. E

An adage is a common saying or proverb.

29. B

A din is a loud, confused mixture of noises—in other words, a clamor.

30. A

To expunge is to get rid of, obliterate, erase.

Analogies

31. C

A pilot directs a plane as a captain directs a ship.

32. A

One breed of snake is a python. One breed of dog is a terrier. The relationships in the other answer choices are in the wrong order as compared to the stem words. In other words, a python is a subset of the snake family, and that same relationship is not reflected in (B)–(E). Quadruped, by the way, means four-legged.

33. A

A mayor is the highest official in a city. A governor is the highest official in a state. The suggested bridge easily eliminates (B), (C), and (E). With (D), a secretary is not usually the highest official on a committee—the chairperson is.

34. C

Paper is the material upon which a novel is written. Similarly, canvas is the material upon which a portrait is painted.

35. B

Refined is the opposite of vulgar. In (B), submissive is the opposite of recalcitrant, which means stubbornly defiant. (A) contains synonyms, not opposites. In (C), ecstatic is an extreme state of happiness. And the word pairs in (D) and (E) have no obvious relationship to each other.

36. E

You use a whip to lash something. You use a club to beat something. As for (A), you may throw a stick at someone, but that's not the relationship needed here.

37. A

To migrate is to travel seasonally. In the winter, swans migrate. In the winter, groundhogs hibernate (hide and sleep). Petting is something a person does to a dog, so (B) is incorrect, and (C), (D), and (E) are not specifically done in the winter—even though they all are things these animals do.

38. E

Flip the words: A meteorologist studies weather. Similarly, a botanist studies plants or vegetation.

39. B

Again, flip the pairs: Horse racing is done, or played, on a track. Tennis is played on a court.

40. B

A director tells an actor what to do, the way a coach tells a player what to do.

41. A

The relationship here is one of order or sequence. A dessert is eaten at the end of a meal. A finale is played at the end of a performance. Lunch is eaten after breakfast, but it's a different meal, not part of the same one, so the bridge doesn't fit.

42. A

The words in the stem are opposites. The only pair of opposites among the choices is in (A): Accept is the opposite of reject, as confirm is the opposite of deny.

43. E

A tower is the tall structure that enables planes to navigate safely at an airport. A lighthouse is the tall structure that enables ships to navigate safely near the shoreline.

44. C

Fidelity is the opposite or absence of unfaithfulness. Honesty is the opposite or absence of deceit. The words in (A) and (D) are synonyms, and there's no clear relationship between the words in (B) and (E).

45. C

If something is widespread, it's not limited. If something is broad, it's not narrow. The words in (A) are synonyms, as are the words in (B) and (D). (E) is a little tough: International seems to suggest sophisticated, which is the opposite of provincial, but the words are in the opposite order as those presented in the stem.

46. C

A saw is a tool used by a carpenter. A plow is a tool used by a farmer. No other occupation listed here requires the use of a plow.

47. A

A sword is used against an opponent in fencing just as a glove is used in boxing.

48. C

Here the relationship is one of degree, with the second word being much stronger than the first. You can encourage or suggest that someone do something, and they may or may not do it. But if you demand or order them to do it, then they must. The words in (A) and (B) are synonyms, and the words in (D) are opposites. Condemn in (E) is stronger than to reprimand, not the other way around, so the order is wrong.

49. B

A grin is a facial expression showing delight. A frown is a facial expression showing dismay (dismay is a mixture of fear and discouragement). A laugh in (D) expresses happiness, but it isn't precisely a facial expression.

50. E

Something mysterious is not understandable. Something obscure is not clear.

51. A

When an injury heals, it disappears. When a malfunction is repaired, it disappears. In both cases, the thing that heals or is repaired gets better, which is why (E) is not quite right.

52. B

A jog is a slow run; a sprint is a fast run. A trot is a slow run for a horse, while a gallop is a fast run. (C) means to wander about—not at a great speed, while (D) means to stroll. (E) means flying, not running.

53. E

A bone is one part of the structural system of the body—the system that holds it up. Similarly, a beam—a long piece of timber or steel—is one part of the structural system that holds up a building. (A) may be tempting, but floors don't generally connect to other floors the way beams and bones do.

54. D

Amorphous means "without shape." So amorphous is to shape as odorless is to odor, or scent.

55. E

Another relationship of opposites. A vain person is, by definition, not humble. Similarly, an extroverted or outgoing person is, by definition, not shy. (A) may be tempting since boisterous means noisy and exuberant. But anxious people aren't by definition quiet; one may be anxious and act boisterously—by talking too much out of nervousness, for example. Cantankerous in (B) means bad tempered and quarrelsome, and discursive in (D) means to talk in a rambling way.

56. C

You study for a test the way you rehearse for a play. One is preparation for the other. (A) seems close, but apply is not quite "preparation" for a job.

57. A

You smile when you're happy and frown when you're sad or angry. You cheer to signal your approval and jeer your disapproval of a sports team, for example. Wince, in (B), means to express pain.

58. E

To peel a banana is to pull off its outer covering. To husk an ear of corn is to pull off its outer covering (also called a husk).

59. B

Tactile refers to anything perceptible through the sense of touch, just as olfactory refers to anything perceptible through the sense of smell. If they had been correct, (D) would have read, "sight is to visual," and (C), "taste is to oral."

60. D

Articulateness is the quality of speaking or writing in a clear manner. Similarly, legibility refers to clear, understandable handwriting.

SECTION 5: MATH

1. E

The perimeter of a polygon is the sum of the lengths of its sides. Label each of the sides with a value of 2 and add.

2. D

(C) can be immediately eliminated because it is an even integer and we are looking for an odd. Since D is an odd integer between 4 and 11, D must be one of the integers 5, 7, or 9. Since D is also between 7 and 18, D must be one of the integers 9, 11, 13, 15, or 17. The only choice that meets both requirements is (D), 9. Notice that (E), 11, is not between 4 and 11.

3. B

Gary and Paul have a total of 16 + 18 = 34 operas put together. This number is equal to the number of operas that only Gary has plus the number of operas that only Paul has plus twice the number of operas that they both have in common. The number that they have in common was counted twice: once in the number of operas that Gary has and once in the number of operas that Paul has. Since the number of operas that they have in common should only be counted once, subtract the 4 they have in common from 34, and the result is 30 different operas.

4. D

Solve for G by multiplying both sides by the reciprocal of $\frac{1}{9}$: $G = 18 \times \frac{9}{1} = 162$. Substitute 162 for G into the expression $\frac{1}{3}$ G, and you will get $\frac{1}{3}G = \frac{1}{3} \times 162 = 54$.

5. A

The boat can swing out and around as far as the line extends or the wind can push it anywhere within this semicircle. If you chose (B), you assumed the boat could float onto the dock. You want the choice indicating all the points of the semicircle shaded, which is (A).

6. D

Let x = the number of children. Hence, $4x$ = the number of adults. The total number of people is then $x + 4x = 5x$. The key to solving this is to keep in mind that x must be an integer. It is because of this that $5x$ must be a multiple of 5. Therefore the answer must be a multiple of 5. (D), 25, is correct.

7. E

Draw a figure! With a diagonal cut, triangles can be created. By cutting to decrease the length 28 of the rectangle by 8 with a cut parallel to the sides of length 20, a square can be created, and cutting anywhere parallel to any side of the original rectangle, a rectangle with new dimensions can be created.

8. D

We must note how many students were in the class each month. March = 40, April = 60,

May = 80, and June = 80. Use the formula $\text{Average} = \frac{\text{Sum of the terms}}{\text{Number of terms}}$. Here, the average is $\frac{40 + 60 + 80 + 80}{4} = \frac{260}{4} = 65$.

9. A

The value of n is 4, and the value of r is 2. Simply substitute these values into the equation that defines the symbol: $4 \clubsuit 2 = (4 - 1) - \frac{4}{2} = 3 - \frac{4}{2} = 3 - 2 = 1$, (A).

10. A

Here, you are given $n = Q$ and $r = 2$. Use the equation given in the definition to set $Q \clubsuit 2$ equal to 4 and solve for Q: $(Q - 1) - \frac{Q}{2} = 4$. First, eliminate the denominator by multiplying both sides by 2: $2(Q - 1) - Q = 8$. Then, distribute the 2 through the parentheses: $2Q - 2 - Q = 8$. Third, isolate the Q: $Q = 10$, (A).

11. A

In statement I, $n = n$ and $r = 1$. So $n \clubsuit 1 = (n - 1) - \frac{n}{1} = n - 1 - n = -1$. So $n \clubsuit 1 = -1$, and statement I is true. Eliminate (B) and (D). Statement II: $n = 1$ and $r = n$. According to the definition, $1 \clubsuit n = (1 - 1) - \frac{1}{n} = -\frac{1}{n}$, and $-\frac{1}{n}$ is not equal to 0. Thus $1 \clubsuit n$ is not equal to 0, so eliminate (C) and (E). The answer must be (A). There is no need to go any further, but for argument's sake, $n \clubsuit n = (n - 1)\ 2\ \frac{n}{n} = n - 1 - 1 = n - 2$ and $r \clubsuit r = (r - 1) - \frac{r}{r} = r - 1 - 1 = r - 2$. So $n \clubsuit n = n - 2$ and $r \clubsuit r = r - 2$. Since nothing in the question indicates that n must equal r, n could very well not be equal to r, and statement III does not have to be true.

12. C

Use the percent formula, Part = Percent × Whole. Here, tip = 15% of \$20.95 = 15% × \$20.95. Round the \$20.95 to \$21.00 and evaluate: $\frac{15}{100} \times 21 = \frac{3}{20} \times 21 = \frac{63}{20} = 3\frac{3}{20} = \$3.15$.

13. A

Break down the problem into steps. Juan finishes one-third of his homework in 2 hours. Thus, he has two-thirds still left to do. If it takes 2 hours to do one-third, it must take 4 hours to do two-thirds (twice as much). Finally, subtract 4 hours from 10:30 P.M, and we are left with 6:30 P.M.

14. E

Mrs. Brown ate 2 peaches, plus each child ate 2 peaches. She has z children, so 2 for each of z children and 2 for Mrs. Brown = $2z + 2$.

15. D

You'll recall the rule for geometry questions that ask about drawing figures in one fluid motion without lifting the pencil. In any given figure, if exactly zero or two points have an odd number of intersecting line segments and/or curves, it can be drawn without lifting the pencil or retracing. (A), (B), (C), and (E) are incorrect because they all have four points at which three line segments intersect. Four points is too many. (D) is the answer because it has two points that have three (an odd number) intersecting lines.

16. D

Round 0.59 to 0.6. Now, $0.6 = \frac{N}{5}$. Isolate the N by multiplying both sides by 5. Then $N = 3$. (Be careful placing the decimal point.)

17. B

The consecutive integers must be 19, 20, 21, 22, 23, 24, and 25. The average of an odd number of equally spaced numbers is always the middle one. Consecutive integers are an instance of equally spaced numbers. The answer is 22.

18. D

The percent increase can be found using this formula: $\frac{\text{New price} - \text{Old price}}{\text{Old price}} \times 100\%$. Here, the percent increase is $\frac{1.08 - 0.93}{0.93} \times 100\% = \frac{0.15}{0.93} \times 100\% = \frac{15}{93} \times 100\% = \frac{5}{31} \times 100\% \approx 16\%$.

19. B

To find Q, use the first division problem. $Q = 15 \times 21 = 315$. To find S, use the second division problem. Then $S = 21 \times 15 + 8$. We already know that $15 \times 21 = 315$, so add 8 to the value 315 of Q to get 323. Finally, $S - Q = 323 - 315 = 8$. Notice that this is also the remainder of the second division problem.

20. C

The area of the floor is found by multiplying 72×48. Dividing this result by the area of a single tile, which is 6×6, gives us the number of tiles needed. In the fraction $\frac{72 \times 48}{6 \times 6}$, cancel the 6s, leaving $12 \times 8 = 96$.

21. C

Set up a ratio here. n pages is to 5 minutes as 20 pages is to how many minutes? Let's call x the number of minutes it will take to type 20 pages. Therefore $\frac{n}{5} = \frac{20}{x}$. Cross-multiplying, we get $xn = 100$. Finally, isolate the x by dividing each side by n: $x = \frac{100}{n}$, choice (C).

22. C

Draw a figure. The length is 60, and the width is $\frac{1}{4}$ of 60 or $\frac{1}{4} \times 60 = 15$. The perimeter is simply the sum of the lengths of all the sides: $60 + 60 + 15 + 15 = 150$ meters.

23. B

Pick 100 when dealing with percent problems. If the dress was $100 the first month, the second month it costs 80% of 100 or $80, and the third month it costs 80% of 80, which is $64. After 3 months it costs 80% of $64, which is about $51. So, after 3 months, the cost is about 50% of the original price.

24. C

Picking numbers is your best option here. If $p = 4$ and $n = -2$, then the results are: (A), -2; (B), $-\frac{1}{2}$; (C), $\frac{1}{6}$; (D), $-\frac{1}{6}$. The greatest value is thus $\frac{1}{6}$, making (C) the correct choice. This question can also be solved by realizing that for any positive integer p and any negative integer n, (A), (B), and (D) will be negative, while (C) will be positive.

25. B

This is a challenging problem. Call the number of men in the school m and the number of women in the school w. The first sentence can be translated into $\frac{1}{9}m = 2\left(\frac{1}{3}w\right)$. We also know that $m + w = 84$. Solving the equation for w in terms of m gives us $w = \frac{3}{2} \times \frac{1}{9}m = \frac{3}{18}m = \frac{1}{6}m$. Substituting $\frac{1}{6}m$ for w in the equation $m + w = 84$ gives us $m + \frac{1}{6}m = 84$. Then, $\frac{7}{6}m = 84$. Multiplying both sides by $\frac{6}{7}$, which is the reciprocal of $\frac{7}{6}$, we find that $m = 84 \times \frac{6}{7} = 12 \times 6 = 72$. Hence, there are 72 men in the school, and $\frac{1}{9}$ of these 72 men, or 8 men, are vegetarians.

CHAPTER 17: SSAT PRACTICE TEST 2: UPPER-LEVEL

HOW TO TAKE THIS PRACTICE TEST

Before taking this practice test, find a quiet room where you can work uninterrupted for two and a half hours. Make sure you have a comfortable desk and several No. 2 pencils.

Use the answer sheet provided to record your answers. (You can cut it out or photocopy it.)

Once you start this practice test, don't stop until you've finished. Remember—you can review any questions within a section, but you may not go backward or forward a section.

You'll find answer explanations following the test. Scoring information can be found in chapter 19.

Good luck.

SSAT Practice Test 2: Upper-Level Answer Sheet

Remove (or photocopy) this answer sheet and use it to complete the practice test.

Start with number 1 for each section. If a section has fewer questions than answer spaces, leave the extra spaces blank.

SECTION 2

1 (A)(B)(C)(D)(E)	6 (A)(B)(C)(D)(E)	11 (A)(B)(C)(D)(E)	16 (A)(B)(C)(D)(E)	21 (A)(B)(C)(D)(E)
2 (A)(B)(C)(D)(E)	7 (A)(B)(C)(D)(E)	12 (A)(B)(C)(D)(E)	17 (A)(B)(C)(D)(E)	22 (A)(B)(C)(D)(E)
3 (A)(B)(C)(D)(E)	8 (A)(B)(C)(D)(E)	13 (A)(B)(C)(D)(E)	18 (A)(B)(C)(D)(E)	23 (A)(B)(C)(D)(E)
4 (A)(B)(C)(D)(E)	9 (A)(B)(C)(D)(E)	14 (A)(B)(C)(D)(E)	19 (A)(B)(C)(D)(E)	24 (A)(B)(C)(D)(E)
5 (A)(B)(C)(D)(E)	10 (A)(B)(C)(D)(E)	15 (A)(B)(C)(D)(E)	20 (A)(B)(C)(D)(E)	25 (A)(B)(C)(D)(E)

right in section 2

wrong in section 2

SECTION 3

1 (A)(B)(C)(D)(E)	9 (A)(B)(C)(D)(E)	17 (A)(B)(C)(D)(E)	25 (A)(B)(C)(D)(E)	33 (A)(B)(C)(D)(E)
2 (A)(B)(C)(D)(E)	10 (A)(B)(C)(D)(E)	18 (A)(B)(C)(D)(E)	26 (A)(B)(C)(D)(E)	34 (A)(B)(C)(D)(E)
3 (A)(B)(C)(D)(E)	11 (A)(B)(C)(D)(E)	19 (A)(B)(C)(D)(E)	27 (A)(B)(C)(D)(E)	35 (A)(B)(C)(D)(E)
4 (A)(B)(C)(D)(E)	12 (A)(B)(C)(D)(E)	20 (A)(B)(C)(D)(E)	28 (A)(B)(C)(D)(E)	36 (A)(B)(C)(D)(E)
5 (A)(B)(C)(D)(E)	13 (A)(B)(C)(D)(E)	21 (A)(B)(C)(D)(E)	29 (A)(B)(C)(D)(E)	37 (A)(B)(C)(D)(E)
6 (A)(B)(C)(D)(E)	14 (A)(B)(C)(D)(E)	22 (A)(B)(C)(D)(E)	30 (A)(B)(C)(D)(E)	38 (A)(B)(C)(D)(E)
7 (A)(B)(C)(D)(E)	15 (A)(B)(C)(D)(E)	23 (A)(B)(C)(D)(E)	31 (A)(B)(C)(D)(E)	39 (A)(B)(C)(D)(E)
8 (A)(B)(C)(D)(E)	16 (A)(B)(C)(D)(E)	24 (A)(B)(C)(D)(E)	32 (A)(B)(C)(D)(E)	40 (A)(B)(C)(D)(E)

right in section 3

wrong in section 3

SECTION 4

1 (A)(B)(C)(D)(E)	13 (A)(B)(C)(D)(E)	25 (A)(B)(C)(D)(E)	37 (A)(B)(C)(D)(E)	49 (A)(B)(C)(D)(E)
2 (A)(B)(C)(D)(E)	14 (A)(B)(C)(D)(E)	26 (A)(B)(C)(D)(E)	38 (A)(B)(C)(D)(E)	50 (A)(B)(C)(D)(E)
3 (A)(B)(C)(D)(E)	15 (A)(B)(C)(D)(E)	27 (A)(B)(C)(D)(E)	39 (A)(B)(C)(D)(E)	51 (A)(B)(C)(D)(E)
4 (A)(B)(C)(D)(E)	16 (A)(B)(C)(D)(E)	28 (A)(B)(C)(D)(E)	40 (A)(B)(C)(D)(E)	52 (A)(B)(C)(D)(E)
5 (A)(B)(C)(D)(E)	17 (A)(B)(C)(D)(E)	29 (A)(B)(C)(D)(E)	41 (A)(B)(C)(D)(E)	53 (A)(B)(C)(D)(E)
6 (A)(B)(C)(D)(E)	18 (A)(B)(C)(D)(E)	30 (A)(B)(C)(D)(E)	42 (A)(B)(C)(D)(E)	54 (A)(B)(C)(D)(E)
7 (A)(B)(C)(D)(E)	19 (A)(B)(C)(D)(E)	31 (A)(B)(C)(D)(E)	43 (A)(B)(C)(D)(E)	55 (A)(B)(C)(D)(E)
8 (A)(B)(C)(D)(E)	20 (A)(B)(C)(D)(E)	32 (A)(B)(C)(D)(E)	44 (A)(B)(C)(D)(E)	56 (A)(B)(C)(D)(E)
9 (A)(B)(C)(D)(E)	21 (A)(B)(C)(D)(E)	33 (A)(B)(C)(D)(E)	45 (A)(B)(C)(D)(E)	57 (A)(B)(C)(D)(E)
10 (A)(B)(C)(D)(E)	22 (A)(B)(C)(D)(E)	34 (A)(B)(C)(D)(E)	46 (A)(B)(C)(D)(E)	58 (A)(B)(C)(D)(E)
11 (A)(B)(C)(D)(E)	23 (A)(B)(C)(D)(E)	35 (A)(B)(C)(D)(E)	47 (A)(B)(C)(D)(E)	59 (A)(B)(C)(D)(E)
12 (A)(B)(C)(D)(E)	24 (A)(B)(C)(D)(E)	36 (A)(B)(C)(D)(E)	48 (A)(B)(C)(D)(E)	60 (A)(B)(C)(D)(E)

right in section 4

wrong in section 4

SECTION 5

1 (A)(B)(C)(D)(E)	6 (A)(B)(C)(D)(E)	11 (A)(B)(C)(D)(E)	16 (A)(B)(C)(D)(E)	21 (A)(B)(C)(D)(E)
2 (A)(B)(C)(D)(E)	7 (A)(B)(C)(D)(E)	12 (A)(B)(C)(D)(E)	17 (A)(B)(C)(D)(E)	22 (A)(B)(C)(D)(E)
3 (A)(B)(C)(D)(E)	8 (A)(B)(C)(D)(E)	13 (A)(B)(C)(D)(E)	18 (A)(B)(C)(D)(E)	23 (A)(B)(C)(D)(E)
4 (A)(B)(C)(D)(E)	9 (A)(B)(C)(D)(E)	14 (A)(B)(C)(D)(E)	19 (A)(B)(C)(D)(E)	24 (A)(B)(C)(D)(E)
5 (A)(B)(C)(D)(E)	10 (A)(B)(C)(D)(E)	15 (A)(B)(C)(D)(E)	20 (A)(B)(C)(D)(E)	25 (A)(B)(C)(D)(E)

right in section 5

wrong in section 5

SECTION 1

Time—25 Minutes

Write an essay on the following prompt on the paper provided. Your essay should NOT exceed two pages and must be written in ink. Erasing is not allowed.

Prompt: You don't get a second chance to make a first impression.

Do you agree or disagree with this statement? Use examples from history, literature, or your own personal experience to support your point of view.

GO ON TO THE NEXT PAGE

IF YOU FINISH BEFORE TIME IS CALLED, YOU MAY CHECK YOUR WORK ON THIS SECTION ONLY. DO NOT TURN TO ANY OTHER SECTION IN THE TEST.

SECTION 2

Time—30 Minutes
25 Questions

In this section, there are five possible answers after each problem. Choose which one is best. You may use the blank space at the right of the page for scratch work.

Note: Figures provided with the problems are drawn with the greatest possible accuracy, UNLESS stated "Not Drawn to Scale."

USE THIS SPACE FOR FIGURING.

1. The polygon in Figure 1 has a perimeter of 30. If each side of the polygon has the same length, what is the length of one side?

(A) 3
(B) 4
(C) 5
(D) 6
(E) 7

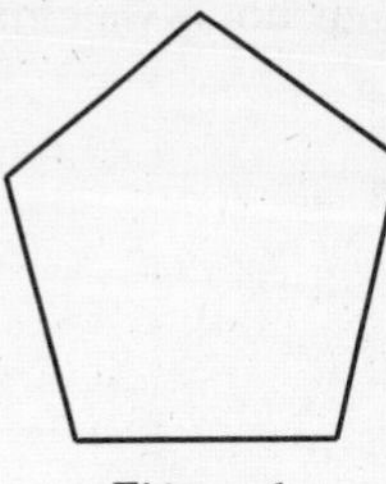

Figure 1

2. Mr. Stuart sold peppermint candy to 25 customers and caramel candy to 17 customers. If 4 of these customers bought both types of candy, how many bought only caramel candy?

(A) 29
(B) 25
(C) 21
(D) 17
(E) 13

3. In a bag of 24 balloons, there is an equal number of balloons of each color. Which of the following CANNOT be the number of different colors in the bag?

(A) 2
(B) 3
(C) 4
(D) 5
(E) 6

GO ON TO THE NEXT PAGE

4. Which of the following is a whole number less than 13 and also a whole number between 11 and 18?

(A) 11
(B) 12
(C) 12.5
(D) 13
(E) 14

USE THIS SPACE FOR FIGURING.

5. According to the graph in Figure 2, Susan spent about how many hours watching movies?

(A) 2
(B) 3
(C) 4
(D) 6
(E) 9

HOW SUSAN SPENT 12 HOURS WATCHING TV

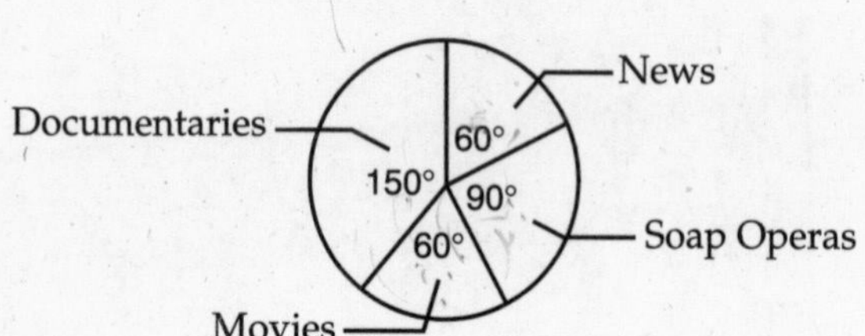

Figure 2

6. If $\frac{1}{2}R = 16$, then $\frac{3}{4}R =$

(A) 24
(B) 20
(C) 16
(D) 12
(E) 8

7. Which of the following is closest to $\frac{1}{4}$ of 59?

(A) 0.26×50
(B) 0.41×50
(C) 0.26×60
(D) 0.41×60
(E) 41×60

GO ON TO THE NEXT PAGE

8. According to the graph in Figure 3, the average sales of Company M from 1993 to 1997 was

(A) \$250,000.
(B) \$260,000.
(C) \$265,000.
(D) \$270,000.
(E) \$275,000.

USE THIS SPACE FOR FIGURING.

SALES OF COMPANY M: 1993–1997

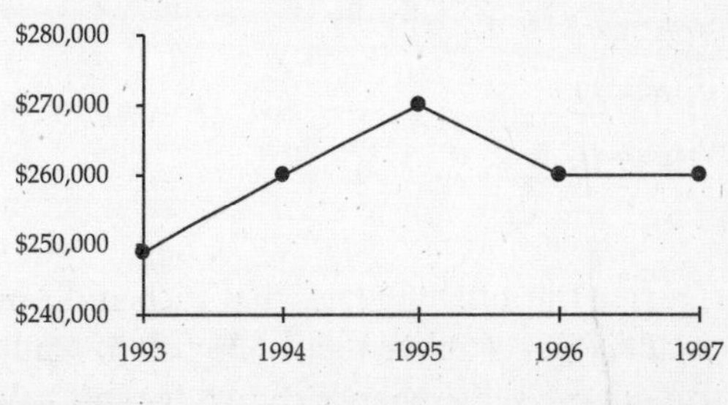

Figure 3

<u>Questions 9–10</u> refer to the following definition.

For all real numbers u and v, $u \o v = u - \left(1 - \frac{1}{v}\right)$.

(Example: $3 \o 2 = 3 - \left(1 - \frac{1}{2}\right) = 3 - \frac{1}{2} = 2\frac{1}{2}$.)

9. Which of the following is equal to $5 \o 5$?

(A) 0
(B) 1
(C) $4\frac{1}{5}$
(D) $4\frac{4}{5}$
(E) 25

10. If $a \o 3 = 4\frac{1}{3}$, then $a =$

(A) $\frac{2}{3}$
(B) 3
(C) 4
(D) $4\frac{2}{3}$
(E) 5

GO ON TO THE NEXT PAGE

11. Twenty percent of 64 is equal to 5 percent of what number?

(A) 16
(B) 20
(C) 64
(D) 128
(E) 256

USE THIS SPACE FOR FIGURING.

12. During the 4 fishing trips that Rich and Andy made, Rich caught a total of 35 fish. If Andy caught more fish than Rich, Andy must have caught an average of a least how many fish per trip?

(A) $8\frac{3}{4}$
(B) 9
(C) 36
(D) 140
(E) 144

13. Jeff, Todd, and Lee were hired by their father to work on the yard, and each was paid at the same hourly rate. Jeff worked 4 hours, Todd worked 6 hours, and Lee worked 8 hours. If the 3 boys together earned $27, how much did Lee earn?

(A) $8
(B) $12
(C) $15
(D) $16
(E) $27

GO ON TO THE NEXT PAGE

USE THIS SPACE FOR FIGURING.

14. Johnny picked apples from 9:00 A.M. to 11:30 A.M. and gathered 200 apples. He wants to pick a total of at least 600 apples before 7:15 P.M. If he plans to pick apples at the same rate, what is the latest time that he can start picking apples again?

    (A) 1:15 P.M.
    (B) 1:45 P.M.
    (C) 2:15 P.M.
    (D) 2:45 P.M.
    (E) 3:15 P.M.

15. If 0.88 equals $8W$, what is the value of W?

    (A) 0.11
    (B) 0.9
    (C) 1.1
    (D) 9
    (E) 11

16. In the triangle shown in Figure 4, what is the value of r?

    (A) 50
    (B) 60
    (C) 70
    (D) 80
    (E) It cannot be determined from the information given.

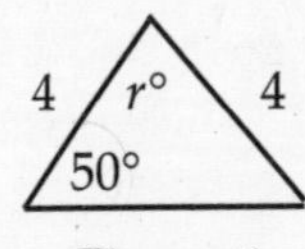

Figure 4

17. A company's income increased from 9 thousand dollars in 1958 to 4.5 million dollars in 1988. Its income in 1988 was how many times its income in 1958?

    (A) 200
    (B) 500
    (C) 2,000
    (D) 5,000
    (E) 20,000

GO ON TO THE NEXT PAGE

USE THIS SPACE FOR FIGURING.

18. Which of the following can be expressed as $(5 \times R) + 2$, where R is a whole number?

(A) 25
(B) 33
(C) 47
(D) 56
(E) 68

19. Which of the following can be drawn without lifting the pencil or retracing?

(A) 
(B) 
(C) 
(D) 
(E)

20. If the population of Country X increased by 10 percent each year over a 2-year period, what was the total percent increase in the population over the entire period?

(A) 2%
(B) 10%
(C) 11%
(D) 20%
(E) 21%

GO ON TO THE NEXT PAGE

21. If $z = y + 2$, what does $2z + 1$ equal?

(A) $y + 3$
(B) $2y + 3$
(C) $2y + 5$
(D) $2y + 6$
(E) It cannot be determined from the information given.

USE THIS SPACE FOR FIGURING.

22. If x is greater than 0 but less than 1, and y is greater than x, which of the following is the LEAST?

(A) $\frac{y}{x}$
(B) $\frac{x}{y}$
(C) xy
(D) $\frac{1}{x-y}$
(E) It cannot be determined from the information given.

23. In a restaurant, there are x tables that can each seat 6 people, and there are y tables that can each seat 5 people. What is the maximum number of people that may be seated?

(A) $5x + 6y$
(B) $6x + 5y$
(C) $11x + 11y$
(D) $11xy$
(E) $30xy$

GO ON TO THE NEXT PAGE

24. Mrs. Smith bought 3 square pieces of fabric. A side of the largest piece is 3 times as long as a side of the middle one, and a side of the middle one is 3 times as long as a side of the smallest one. The area of the largest piece is how many times the area of the smallest piece?

    (A) 112
    (B) 81
    (C) 27
    (D) 9
    (E) 3

USE THIS SPACE FOR FIGURING.

25. Mr. Dali's car uses $\frac{3}{4}$ gallons of gas each time he drives to work. If his gas tank holds exactly 9 gallons of gas, how many tanks of gas does he need to make 18 trips to work?

    (A) $1\frac{1}{2}$
    (B) $2\frac{1}{2}$
    (C) 4
    (D) 6
    (E) 9

IF YOU FINISH BEFORE TIME IS CALLED, YOU MAY CHECK YOUR WORK ON THIS SECTION ONLY. DO NOT TURN TO ANY OTHER SECTION IN THE TEST. **STOP**

SECTION 3

Time—40 Minutes
40 Questions

Read each passage carefully and then answer the questions about it. For each question, decide on the basis of the passage which one of the choices best answers the question.

Scott Joplin composed approximately 60 works during his lifetime, including 41 piano pieces called "rags," many songs and marches, and an opera entitled *Treemonisha*. His most significant creative contribution was to the development of ragtime, a type of instrumental music marked by its distinctive, choppy rhythm. Joplin's rhythmic diversity was very important to the development of ragtime as a genre, a unique musical form. In 1899, his "Maple Leaf Rag" became the most popular piano rag of the time and he was dubbed the "King of Ragtime." Despite all of those accomplishments, he was not considered a serious composer during his lifetime. It was not until 59 years after his death that he was properly recognized: In 1976, he was awarded the Pulitzer Prize for music, at last receiving the praise he deserved.

1. The term "rag," as it is used in the passage, refers to
   (A) a specific piece of operatic music.
   (B) a genre of dance music.
   (C) a piece of piano music known for its unique rhythm.
   (D) a kind of instrumental music played by marching bands.
   (E) a style of songs invented by Joplin.

2. This passage deals primarily with
   (A) the fact that Joplin was not taken seriously during his lifetime.
   (B) the history and development of ragtime music.
   (C) the diversity of styles in which Joplin composed.
   (D) how Joplin came to win the Pulitzer Prize.
   (E) Joplin's contributions to and accomplishments in the world of music.

3. According to the passage, Joplin died in
   (A) 1899.
   (B) 1917.
   (C) 1941.
   (D) 1959.
   (E) 1976.

4. When discussing Scott Joplin, the author's tone in this passage could best be described as
   (A) indifferent.
   (B) amused.
   (C) envious.
   (D) resentful.
   (E) appreciative.

GO ON TO THE NEXT PAGE

5. It can be inferred from the passage that a genre is

(A) a particular type of ragtime music.
(B) a distinct category or style.
(C) a term that Joplin coined when he created ragtime.
(D) a rhythmic style characteristic of Joplin's period.
(E) an early form of "rag."

6. From this passage, it can be inferred that

(A) although people liked Joplin's work, they did not appreciate its value while he was alive.
(B) Joplin died a destitute musician.
(C) ragtime wouldn't have existed had Joplin not written "Maple Leaf Rag."
(D) all of Joplin's piano pieces were rags.
(E) Joplin played a lot of venues to popularize ragtime.

Thousands of species of birds exist today, and nearly every species has its own special courtship procedures and "identification checks." Identification checks are important, because if birds of different species mate, any offspring will usually be sterile or badly adapted to their surroundings.

Plumage often plays a key role in both identification and courtship. In breeding season, male birds often acquire distinctive plumage which they use to attract females who will, in turn, only respond to males with the correct markings. In some species, the females are more brightly colored, and the courtship roles are reversed. Distinctive behavioral changes can also be important aspects of courtship and breeding activity. Aggressiveness between males, and sometimes between females, is quite common. Some birds, like whooping cranes and trumpeter swans, perform wonderfully elaborate courtship dances in which both sexes are enthusiastic participants.

Bird sounds are often a very central part of identification and courtship behavior between individuals in a given species. When a female migrates in the spring to her breeding region, she often encounters numerous birds of different species. By its singing, the male of a species both identifies itself and communicates to females of that species that it is in breeding condition. This information allows a female to predict a male's response to her approach. Later, after mating has taken place, the note patterns of a particular male's song enable a nesting female to continue to identify her own partner.

7. The author implies that a bird engages in identification and courtship procedures mainly in order to

(A) find a better nesting spot.
(B) find the most colorful partner it can.
(C) attract a mate of its own species.
(D) increase its control over its nesting partner.
(E) try to dominate the bird population of a given area.

GO ON TO THE NEXT PAGE

8. According to the passage, a feature of the male songbird is its ability to

I. attract a female of its own species.
II. intimidate rival males.
III. communicate its identity to its mate.

(A) I only
(B) III only
(C) I and II only
(D) I and III only
(E) I, II, and III

9. The author uses the whooping crane as an example of a bird that

(A) seldom participates in courtship procedures.
(B) acquires a distinctive breeding plumage.
(C) behaves in an unusual and noteworthy way during courtship.
(D) reverses the normal male and female courtship roles.
(E) displays unusual aggressiveness while courting.

10. According to the passage, matings between birds of different species

(A) are quite common.
(B) produce more sturdy offspring.
(C) may help to establish a permanent new species.
(D) do not usually result in healthy offspring.
(E) have never happened.

11. The passage is primarily about

(A) causes of aggression between male birds.
(B) several courtship and identification methods used by birds.
(C) the breeding season of birds.
(D) the role of bird sounds in courtship identification.
(E) why birds migrate to particular breeding regions.

12. This passage most likely comes from

(A) a website on identifying birds.
(B) a book on birds and mating.
(C) a personal letter from a bird-watcher.
(D) a novel about breeding birds.
(E) a news article on endangered birds.

More than 1,500 Native American languages have thus far been discovered by linguists. Edward Sapir, a pioneer in the field of Native American linguistics, grouped these languages into six "families" more than three-quarters of a century ago.

Ever since that time, the classification of Native American languages has been a source of controversy. A small group of linguists has recently argued that all Native American languages fit into three linguistic families. These scholars believe that similarities and differences among words and sounds leave no doubt about the validity of their classification scheme. The vast majority of linguists, however, reject both the methods and conclusions of these scholars, arguing that linguistic science has not yet advanced far enough to be able to group Native American languages into a few families. According to these scholars, Native American languages have diverged to such an extent over the centuries that it may never be possible to group them in distinct language families.

GO ON TO THE NEXT PAGE

13. This passage is primarily about
    (A) the classification of Native American languages.
    (B) the six families of Native American languages.
    (C) scholars' views about language.
    (D) the similarities and differences between words of Native American languages.
    (E) linguistic debates about how to group languages.

14. The scholars who believe that Native American languages can be classified into three families apparently believe that
    (A) these languages have diverged significantly over the last 75 years.
    (B) languages can be classified according to the degree of similarities and differences between words.
    (C) linguistic science has not advanced far enough to safely classify languages so narrowly.
    (D) languages are all related by their common origins.
    (E) distinct language families have their own peculiar grammatical rules.

15. The style of the passage is most like that found in a
    (A) personal letter written by a linguistics student.
    (B) textbook about linguistics.
    (C) novel about Native American tribes.
    (D) diary of a linguist.
    (E) biography of Edward Sapir.

16. It can be inferred that the classification of Native American languages has been a source of controversy because
    (A) scholars do not agree on the method for classifying languages.
    (B) languages have split in several directions.
    (C) linguistics is a very new field.
    (D) there is not enough known about Native American vocabulary.
    (E) Native Americans dislike such classifications.

17. Which of the following questions is answered by the passage?
    (A) Did Edward Sapir study languages other than Native American languages?
    (B) How many languages are in a typical linguistic family?
    (C) How many Native American languages are yet to discovered?
    (D) In what ways have Native American languages changed over time?
    (E) Into how many families did Edward Sapir classify Native American languages?

18. As used in the passage, "extent" (line 21) most nearly means
    (A) limit.
    (B) language.
    (C) range.
    (D) time.
    (E) duration.

GO ON TO THE NEXT PAGE

Hope is the thing with feathers
That perches in the soul,
And sings the tune without the words
And never stops at all,

And sweetest in the gale is heard;
And sore must be the storm
That could abash[1] the little bird
That kept so many warm.

I've heard it in the chillest land,
And on the strangest sea;
Yet, never, in extremity,
It asked a crumb of me.

[1]discourage
"Hope" by Emily Dickinson

19. In this poem, hope is compared to
    (A) a gale.
    (B) a sea.
    (C) a storm.
    (D) a bird.
    (E) a song.

20. What is the poet saying in the last stanza of the poem?
    (A) It is terrible to imagine a world without hope, and we must therefore do everything possible to preserve our hopes.
    (B) The bird continues to sing through all conditions.
    (C) Hope can be found anywhere and never asks anything in return for its loyalty.
    (D) The bird is very hungry because it is constantly singing and never takes any time to eat.
    (E) The potential for hope is always present, but it takes a great effort to make it a reality.

21. The lines "the little bird/That kept so many warm" in the second stanza refer to the fact that
    (A) the feathers of birds have traditionally provided protection against the cold.
    (B) hope has comforted a great many people over the years.
    (C) the bird provided protection before it was destroyed in a storm.
    (D) hope has often proven useless in the face of real problems.
    (E) hope is a good last resort when faced with a difficult situation.

22. The attitude of the speaker in this poem can best be described as
    (A) angry.
    (B) unconcerned.
    (C) respectful.
    (D) nervous.
    (E) grateful.

23. The term "sore" (line 6) most nearly means
    (A) hurt.
    (B) angry.
    (C) severe.
    (D) kind.
    (E) wet.

GO ON TO THE NEXT PAGE

Although recycling has taken place in various forms for some time, today we are being asked to regard recycling as not only an important, but even a necessary measure.

Recycling, in its broadest sense, refers to the remaking of waste products and other used materials for practical purposes. For example, an old soda bottle can be returned, washed, and used as a bottle again, or it can be ground down and its glass can be employed for another useful purpose. Since fixing up old things is often cheaper than making brand new ones, this saves money. More importantly, it saves resources and reduces the amount of waste produced.

Businesses have been performing large-scale recycling for some time, based primarily on the goal of saving money. However, the amount of residential waste, that is, the waste produced at home, has been steadily increasing, and the role of the individual in the recycling campaign has been seriously underemphasized. Although it is true that we, as individuals, cannot reduce the overall amount of waste significantly or save large amounts of money and resources on our own, taken collectively, we can have an important impact. Our increased efforts toward recycling can have a dramatic effect on the future availability of resources and the condition of the environment. It is our duty to ourselves and to our fellow human beings to pitch in and help protect what remains of it.

24. According to the passage, which of the following is true?

    I. Recycling increases the amount of waste produced.

    II. Reusing waste products can be very economical.

    III. The amount of waste produced in the home has been continuously growing.

    (A) II only
    (B) I and II only
    (C) I and III only
    (D) II and III only
    (E) I, II, and III

25. The author would most likely agree that

    (A) recycling is a good idea for big businesses but, on an individual level, it makes very little difference.
    (B) although businesses recycle to save money, individuals are motivated to recycle by a desire to serve the general good of society.
    (C) recycling is extremely important and everyone has a responsibility to contribute to the overall effort to preserve our environment.
    (D) although our natural resources are limited, we only live once and we shouldn't concentrate on conservation to such a degree that it interferes with our enjoyment of life.
    (E) recycling is a very expensive process and should be left to the owners of big businesses.

26. All of the following are examples of recycling EXCEPT

    (A) turning old newspapers into cardboard.
    (B) melting down scraps of metal and recasting them.
    (C) washing out empty soda bottles and using them as vases.
    (D) selling a piece of jewelry and using the money to buy a car.
    (E) crushing old cans and reusing the aluminum to make new ones.

27. The tone of this passage is

    (A) insistent.
    (B) relaxed.
    (C) formal.
    (D) amused.
    (E) disinterested.

GO ON TO THE NEXT PAGE

28. Which of the following is the author most likely to discuss next?

    (A) The current problem of toxic waste disposal

    (B) The negative aspects of recycling and the many problems that can develop when it is done too much

    (C) Different ways that an old bottle can be either reused or remade into an entirely different object

    (D) Other important differences between the way businesses and residences are run

    (E) Examples of ways in which people can recycle their own waste and help out on an individual basis

29. What can be said about the author based on lines 15–17?

    (A) She is only interested in the economic aspects of recycling.

    (B) She believes that businesses are motivated to recycle primarily for monetary gain.

    (C) She knows little about the possible financial savings of recycling.

    (D) She is more concerned with the environmental benefits of recycling than the economic rewards.

    (E) She values recycling even though it results in the production of greater amounts of waste.

Most of us who live in relatively mild climates rarely view bad weather as more than an inconvenience, but in certain, less fortunate parts of the world, a change in weather can have disastrous consequences for an entire society. Weather fluctuations along the northwest coast of South America, for instance, can periodically have a dramatic effect on the area's fishing villages.

Under normal circumstances, the cold, steadily flowing waters of the Humboldt Current bring nutrients up from the sea floor along the coast, providing a dependable food supply for fish and squid. For centuries, the fishing villages have depended on this rich ocean harvest for food and trade. Occasionally, however, global weather patterns cause the current to fail, setting off a deadly chain reaction. Without nutrients, the fish and squid die, depriving the villagers of their livelihood. This destructive weather phenomenon, called "El Niño" (The Christ Child) because it occurs at Christmastime, has sometimes forced entire villages to disband and move elsewhere to avoid starvation.

30. According to the passage, the Humboldt Current flows

    (A) only at Christmastime.

    (B) without fail.

    (C) east to west.

    (D) along the northwest coast of South America.

    (E) through warm water.

31. This passage is mainly about

    (A) how the economy of South American villages depends exclusively on fishing.

    (B) the importance of fish and squid in the food chain.

    (C) the advantages of living in a mild climate.

    (D) the undependable nature of the Humboldt Current.

    (E) how changes in weather patterns can have a dramatic effect on the way people live.

GO ON TO THE NEXT PAGE

32. According to the passage, all of the following are true EXCEPT
    (A) the actions of the Humboldt Current help provide nutrients for fish and squid.
    (B) the Humboldt Current affects the survival of fishing on the northwest coast of South America.
    (C) the warm waters of the Humboldt Current affect the climate of nearby land masses.
    (D) the failure of the Humboldt Current can set off a deadly chain reaction.
    (E) the Humboldt Current sometimes fails as a result of global weather patterns.

33. Which of the following would be the best title for this passage?
    (A) An Example of Weather's Social Impact
    (B) Fishing Villages of South America
    (C) El Niño: A Christmas Occurrence
    (D) Fish and Squid: A Rich Ocean Harvest
    (E) The Impact of Fishing on Coastal Villages

34. The author's attitude toward the villagers along the northwest coast of South America can best be described as
    (A) sympathetic.
    (B) unconcerned.
    (C) condescending.
    (D) angry.
    (E) emotional.

35. Which of the following is an example of a chain reaction?
    (A) Forest fires kill off thousands of acres of land, destroying valuable resources.
    (B) When temperatures start to fall, many birds fly south to spend winter in warm climates.
    (C) Earthquakes cause extensive damage to property and often result in the loss of human life.
    (D) Global warming causes glaciers to melt, resulting in rising water levels, which reduce the amount of habitable land.
    (E) The moon revolves around the earth, and the earth revolves around the sun.

World War II left much of Western Europe deeply scarred in many ways. Economically, it was devastated. In early 1948, as the Cold War developed between the United States and the Soviet Union and political tensions rose, U.S. policymakers decided that substantial financial assistance would be required to maintain a state of political stability. This conclusion led Secretary of State George C. Marshall to announce a proposal: European countries were advised to draw up a unified plan for reconstruction, to be funded by the United States.

This European Recovery Program, also known as the Marshall Plan, provided economic and technical assistance to 16 countries. Between 1948 and 1952, participating countries received a combined total of 12 billion dollars in U.S. aid. In the end, the program was seen as a great success; it revived the economies of Western Europe and set them on a course for future growth.

GO ON TO THE NEXT PAGE

36. Which of the following would be the best title for this passage?

    (A) The Aftermath of World War II
    (B) The Marshall Plan: A Program for European Reconstruction
    (C) The Economic Destruction of Europe
    (D) George C. Marshall: The Man behind the Plan
    (E) Western European Recovery

37. The tone of the author toward the Marshall Plan is

    (A) objective.
    (B) excited.
    (C) insistent.
    (D) anxious.
    (E) unfavorable.

38. All of the following are true about the Marshall Plan EXCEPT

    (A) it provided economic assistance to 16 countries.
    (B) it went into action in 1948.
    (C) it supplied economic aid for a period spanning four years.
    (D) it gave each of the participating countries 12 billion dollars.
    (E) it was considered a great long-term success.

39. The passage suggests that the driving force behind the Marshall Plan was

    (A) a formal request for aid by European leaders.
    (B) fear of economic repercussions for the U.S. economy.
    (C) George C. Marshall's desire to improve his political career and public image.
    (D) a joint U.S.-Soviet agreement to assist the countries of Western Europe.
    (E) the increase in tension between the United States and the Soviet Union.

40. Which of the following would the author be most likely to discuss next?

    (A) Developments in the Cold War during and after the years of the Marshall Plan
    (B) The events leading up to Western Europe's economic collapse
    (C) The detailed effects of the Marshall Plan on specific countries
    (D) Other successful economic recovery programs employed throughout history
    (E) How George C. Marshall became the U.S. Secretary of State

IF YOU FINISH BEFORE TIME IS CALLED, YOU MAY CHECK YOUR WORK ON THIS SECTION ONLY. DO NOT TURN TO ANY OTHER SECTION IN THE TEST.

STOP

SECTION 4

Time—30 Minutes
60 Questions

This section consists of two different types of questions. There are directions for each type.

Each of the following questions consists of one word followed by five words or phrases. You are to select the one word or phrase whose meaning is closest to the word in capital letters.

1. HARSH:
   (A) cold
   (B) angry
   (C) poor
   (D) useless
   (E) severe

2. INDICATE:
   (A) meet with
   (B) look at
   (C) help with
   (D) point out
   (E) search for

3. BLEAK:
   (A) unknown
   (B) quiet
   (C) cheerless
   (D) trembling
   (E) timid

4. SECURE:
   (A) unseen
   (B) aware
   (C) secret
   (D) safe
   (E) knotty

5. ALIEN:
   (A) strange
   (B) futile
   (C) valuable
   (D) brutal
   (E) unclear

6. CHRONIC:
   (A) persistent
   (B) difficult
   (C) doubtful
   (D) legal
   (E) elaborate

7. QUENCH:
   (A) complete
   (B) compare
   (C) demean
   (D) satisfy
   (E) withdraw

8. SEVERE:
   (A) frozen
   (B) extreme
   (C) long
   (D) limited
   (E) essential

GO ON TO THE NEXT PAGE

9. RANSACK:
   (A) search thoroughly
   (B) act quickly
   (C) cover completely
   (D) make secure
   (E) denounce publicly

10. SUMMIT:
   (A) plateau
   (B) landscape
   (C) slope
   (D) island
   (E) peak

11. TUMULT:
   (A) annoyance
   (B) commotion
   (C) insignificance
   (D) disagreement
   (E) blockage

12. RETARD:
   (A) turn around
   (B) push apart
   (C) slow down
   (D) change position
   (E) see through

13. ANTIDOTE:
   (A) fantasy
   (B) remedy
   (C) substitute
   (D) award
   (E) decoration

14. SOLITARY:
   (A) mindful
   (B) careless
   (C) friendly
   (D) alone
   (E) troubled

15. CAMOUFLAGE:
   (A) obstacle
   (B) range
   (C) emergency
   (D) disguise
   (E) amount

16. EXPEL:
   (A) finish off
   (B) teach
   (C) question
   (D) scold
   (E) cast out

17. LUNGE:
   (A) pursue
   (B) turn
   (C) thrust
   (D) restore
   (E) startle

18. BREVITY:
   (A) ambition
   (B) consistency
   (C) conflict
   (D) imagination
   (E) shortness

GO ON TO THE NEXT PAGE

19. MARVEL:
    (A) discard
    (B) usurp
    (C) confuse
    (D) point
    (E) wonder

20. CANDOR:
    (A) majesty
    (B) daring
    (C) honesty
    (D) perception
    (E) fatigue

21. CONVENE:
    (A) clarify
    (B) serve
    (C) assemble
    (D) elect
    (E) dignify

22. CATASTROPHE:
    (A) illusion
    (B) disaster
    (C) indication
    (D) warning
    (E) estimate

23. GREGARIOUS:
    (A) sloppy
    (B) sociable
    (C) happy
    (D) intelligent
    (E) talented

24. DEXTERITY:
    (A) secrecy
    (B) equality
    (C) reserve
    (D) nimbleness
    (E) determination

25. IMMINENT:
    (A) intense
    (B) impressive
    (C) proper
    (D) observable
    (E) forthcoming

26. ANIMOSITY:
    (A) doubt
    (B) hatred
    (C) sadness
    (D) illness
    (E) guilt

27. AMEND:
    (A) create
    (B) address
    (C) observe
    (D) exclude
    (E) improve

28. DESPONDENT:
    (A) depressed
    (B) unintended
    (C) artificial
    (D) literary
    (E) unconcerned

GO ON TO THE NEXT PAGE

29. UNFLINCHING:
    (A) uncommitted
    (B) distinct
    (C) uncompromising
    (D) transitory
    (E) invalid

30. REPUDIATE:
    (A) renounce
    (B) impede
    (C) provoke
    (D) divert
    (E) submit

The following questions ask you to find relationships between words. For each question, select the choice that best completes the meaning of the sentence.

31. Sun is to solar as
    (A) earth is to terrestrial.
    (B) pond is to marine.
    (C) ground is to subterranean.
    (D) tower is to architectural.
    (E) planet is to lunar.

32. Botany is to plants as meteorology is to
    (A) weather.
    (B) flora.
    (C) health.
    (D) language.
    (E) style.

33. Hammer is to nail as
    (A) axe is to wood.
    (B) lathe is to molding.
    (C) chisel is to marble.
    (D) nut is to bolt.
    (E) screwdriver is to screw.

34. Bone is to mammal as girder is to
    (A) skyscraper.
    (B) steel.
    (C) rivet.
    (D) crane.
    (E) concrete.

35. Human is to primate as
    (A) kangaroo is to vegetarian.
    (B) snake is to reptile.
    (C) disease is to bacterium.
    (D) bird is to amphibian.
    (E) dog is to pet.

36. Tremor is to earthquake as
    (A) eye is to hurricane.
    (B) desert is to sandstorm.
    (C) faucet is to deluge.
    (D) wind is to tornado.
    (E) flood is to river.

GO ON TO THE NEXT PAGE

37. Amusing is to uproarious as
    (A) silly is to serious.
    (B) dead is to immortal.
    (C) interesting is to mesmerizing.
    (D) humorous is to dull.
    (E) worthless is to valuable.

38. Fickle is to steadfastness as tempestuous is to
    (A) worthlessness.
    (B) openness.
    (C) inspiration.
    (D) peacefulness.
    (E) ire.

39. School is to fish as
    (A) fin is to shark.
    (B) library is to student.
    (C) flock is to bird.
    (D) leg is to frog.
    (E) college is to mascot.

40. Cartographer is to map as chef is to
    (A) flower.
    (B) silverware.
    (C) table.
    (D) meal.
    (E) ingredient.

41. Throne is to monarch as
    (A) miter is to pope.
    (B) bench is to judge.
    (C) lobby is to doorman.
    (D) armchair is to general.
    (E) ship is to captain.

42. Canal is to river as
    (A) boat is to driftwood.
    (B) puddle is to lake.
    (C) hammer is to mallet.
    (D) mine is to cavern.
    (E) telephone is to computer.

43. Milk is to sour as bread is to
    (A) bent.
    (B) stale.
    (C) folded.
    (D) baked.
    (E) hot.

44. Ore is to mine as
    (A) apple is to peel.
    (B) water is to purify.
    (C) batter is to stir.
    (D) grain is to plow.
    (E) oil is to drill.

45. Weight is to scale as
    (A) distance is to speedometer.
    (B) number is to slide rule.
    (C) length is to thermometer.
    (D) reading is to gauge.
    (E) altitude is to altimeter.

46. Porcupine is to quill as
    (A) bat is to wing.
    (B) horse is to tail.
    (C) skunk is to odor.
    (D) oyster is to pearl.
    (E) tiger is to stripe.

GO ON TO THE NEXT PAGE

47. Jar is to contain as pillar is to
    (A) stand.
    (B) ascend.
    (C) prepare.
    (D) support.
    (E) swing.

48. Irrigate is to dry as
    (A) soften is to uneven.
    (B) smooth is to coarse.
    (C) purify is to distasteful.
    (D) depend is to supportive.
    (E) ferment is to salty.

49. Electricity is to wire as
    (A) sound is to radio.
    (B) water is to aqueduct.
    (C) music is to instrument.
    (D) light is to bulb.
    (E) river is to bank.

50. Contempt is to sneer as
    (A) shame is to shrug.
    (B) anger is to laugh.
    (C) enjoyment is to groan.
    (D) agreement is to grimace.
    (E) displeasure is to frown.

51. Building is to foundation as plant is to
    (A) pane.
    (B) grotto.
    (C) primer.
    (D) floor.
    (E) root.

52. Nose is to olfactory as ear is to
    (A) beautiful.
    (B) edible.
    (C) auditory.
    (D) raspy.
    (E) allergic.

53. Irk is to soothing as support is to
    (A) conciliating.
    (B) elevating.
    (C) undermining.
    (D) irritating.
    (E) vilifying.

54. Illegible is to read as
    (A) invisible is to see.
    (B) illegal is to act.
    (C) broken is to fix.
    (D) irreparable is to break.
    (E) intense is to strain.

55. Tact is to diplomat as
    (A) parsimony is to philanthropist.
    (B) agility is to gymnast.
    (C) vulnerability is to victim.
    (D) training is to physician.
    (E) bias is to judge.

GO ON TO THE NEXT PAGE

56. Ravenous is to hunger as
    (A) pliable is to obstinacy.
    (B) agitated is to placidity.
    (C) concerned is to apathy.
    (D) smart is to tenacity.
    (E) furious is to indignation.

57. Amplify is to sound as bolster is to
    (A) smell.
    (B) courage.
    (C) insomnia.
    (D) light.
    (E) silence.

58. Auditorium is to lecture as
    (A) theater is to concert.
    (B) attic is to storage.
    (C) temple is to religion.
    (D) cafeteria is to food.
    (E) target is to arrow.

59. Philanthropic is to benevolence as
    (A) smooth is to surface.
    (B) ostentatious is to reserve.
    (C) miserly is to stinginess.
    (D) devout is to malice.
    (E) realistic is to plan.

60. Spurious is to authenticity as
    (A) lavish is to expense.
    (B) abject is to subjectivity.
    (C) affluent is to character.
    (D) laughable is to seriousness.
    (E) totalitarian is to completeness.

IF YOU FINISH BEFORE TIME IS CALLED, YOU MAY CHECK YOUR WORK ON THIS SECTION ONLY. DO NOT TURN TO ANY OTHER SECTION IN THE TEST. **STOP**

SECTION 5

Time—30 Minutes
25 Questions

In this section, there are five possible answers after each question. Choose which one is best. You may use the blank space at the right of the page for scratch work.
Note: Figures are drawn with the greatest possible accuracy, UNLESS stated "Not Drawn to Scale."

USE THIS SPACE FOR FIGURING.

1. Justine bought a comic book at \$5 above the cover price. A year later she sold the book for \$9 less than she paid. At what price did Justine sell the book?
   (A) \$14 below the cover price
   (B) \$4 below the cover price
   (C) The cover price
   (D) \$4 above the cover price
   (E) \$14 above the cover price

Questions 2–3 refer to the graph in Figure 1.

2. How many fewer boxes of cereal were sold in February than in March?
   (A) 2
   (B) 3
   (C) 20
   (D) 40
   (E) 60

3. The number of boxes sold in January was how many times the number of boxes sold in February?
   (A) 2
   (B) $2\frac{1}{2}$
   (C) 3
   (D) 40
   (E) 60

CEREAL SALES AT STORE X

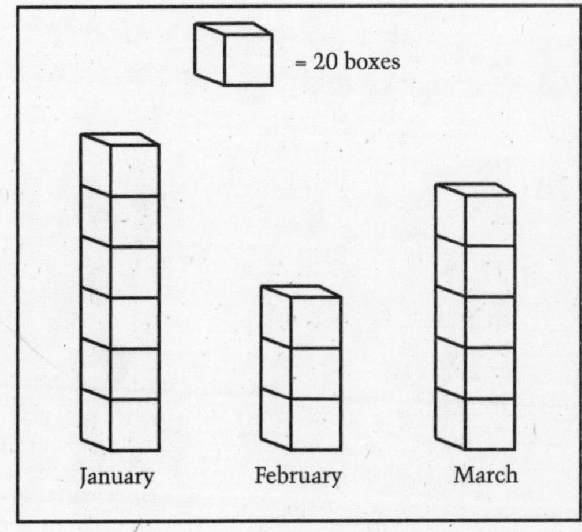

Figure 1

GO ON TO THE NEXT PAGE

USE THIS SPACE FOR FIGURING.

4. Team A has 4 times as many losses as it had ties in a season. If Team A won none of its games, which could be the total number of games it played that season?

(A) 12
(B) 15
(C) 18
(D) 21
(E) 26

5. Figure 2 contains rectangles and a triangle. How many different rectangles are there in Figure 2?

(A) 5
(B) 7
(C) 9
(D) 10
(E) 12

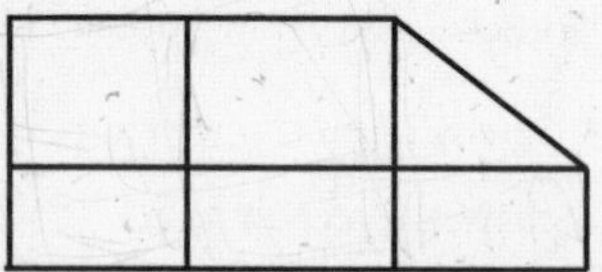

Figure 2

6. Which of the following is NOT less than $\frac{1}{4}$?

(A) $\frac{2}{9}$

(B) $\frac{3}{14}$

(C) $\frac{14}{64}$

(D) $\frac{19}{70}$

(E) $\frac{27}{125}$

GO ON TO THE NEXT PAGE

USE THIS SPACE FOR FIGURING.

7. In Figure 3, the sides of triangles *ABC* and *FGH*, and of squares *BCFE* and *CDGF*, are all equal in length. Which of the following is the longest path from *A* to *H*?
   (A) $A - B - C - F - H$
   (B) $A - B - E - F - H$
   (C) $A - C - D - G - H$
   (D) $A - B - E - G - H$
   (E) $A - C - F - G - H$

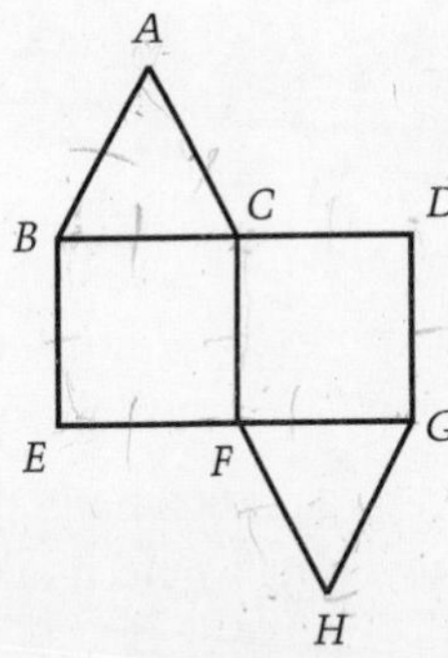

Figure 3

8. If $5\frac{1}{3} \times (14 - x) = 0$, then what does x equal?
   (A) 0
   (B) 1
   (C) $5\frac{1}{3}$
   (D) 14
   (E) It cannot be determined from the information given.

9. Which of the following is closest to 1.18?
   (A) 12
   (B) 2.2
   (C) 1.9
   (D) 1.1
   (E) 1

10. If X is greater than 15, then $\frac{1}{3}$ of X must always be
   (A) less than 5.
   (B) equal to 5.
   (C) greater than 5.
   (D) equal to 45.
   (E) less than 45.

GO ON TO THE NEXT PAGE

USE THIS SPACE FOR FIGURING.

11. Of the following, 35 percent of $26.95 is closest to

(A) $7.00.
(B) $9.45.
(C) $10.50.
(D) $11.15.
(E) $12.25.

12. If a factory can make 600 nails every 3 minutes, how long would it take to make 27,000 nails?

(A) 45 minutes
(B) 1 hour
(C) 1 hour 45 minutes
(D) 2 hours 15 minutes
(E) 3 hours 15 minutes

13. Sally has x dollars and receives $100 for her birthday. She then buys a bicycle that costs $125. How many dollars does Sally have remaining?

(A) $x + 125$
(B) $x + 100$
(C) $x + 25$
(D) $x - 25$
(E) $x - 100$

14. If $\frac{A+B}{3} = 4$ and A is greater than 1, which of the following could NOT be the value of B?

(A) -3
(B) 0
(C) 1
(D) 2
(E) 12

USE THIS SPACE FOR FIGURING.

15. The average of five numbers is 10. If two of the five numbers are removed, the average of the remaining three numbers is 9. What is the sum of the two numbers that were removed?

(A) 17
(B) 18
(C) 21
(D) 22
(E) 23

16. The bottom of the shopping bag shown in Figure 4 is placed flat on a table. Except for the handles, this shopping bag is constructed with rectangular pieces of paper. Which of the following diagrams best represents all the points where the shopping bag touches the table?

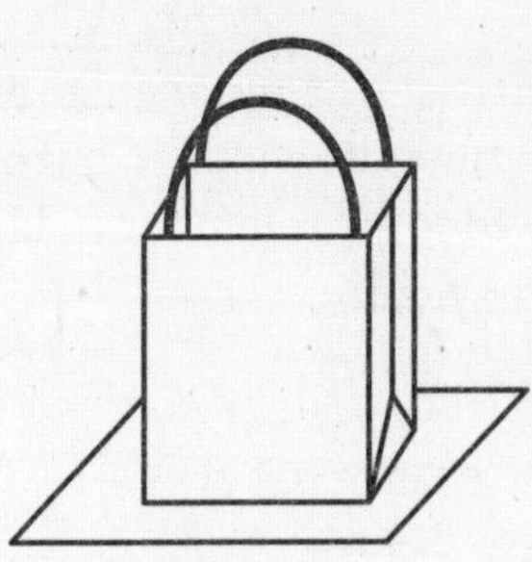
Figure 4

(A) 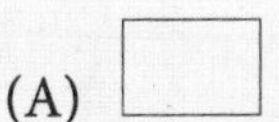   (B) 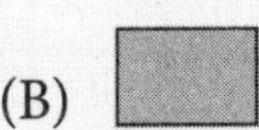   (C) 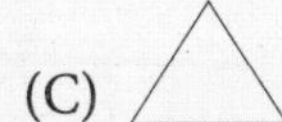

(D) 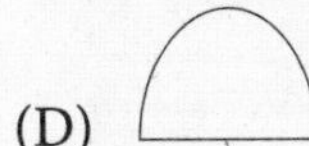   (E) 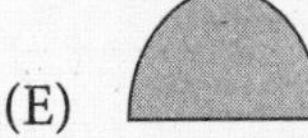

17. The number of students in a certain school is expected to increase from 1,086 students in 2010 to 1,448 students in 2011. What is the expected increase to the nearest percent?

(A) 20%
(B) 33%
(C) 37%
(D) 40%
(E) 45%

GO ON TO THE NEXT PAGE

USE THIS SPACE FOR FIGURING.

18. In Figure 5, the distance between W and Y is three times the distance between W and X, and the distance between X and Z is twice the distance between X and Y. If the distance from W to X is 2, how far apart are W and Z?

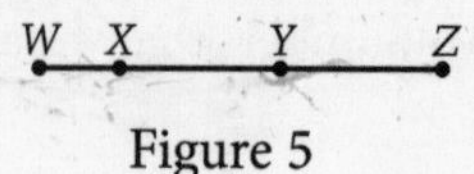

Figure 5

(A) 10
(B) 12
(C) 14
(D) 16
(E) 18

19. A fence surrounds a rectangular field whose length is 3 times its width. If 240 meters of the fence is used to surround the field, what is the width of the field?

(A) 30 m
(B) 40 m
(C) 60 m
(D) 80 m
(E) 90 m

20. Ms. Kirschner receives $50 for every $900 she collects from stock sales. How much does she receive if she collects $18,000 from stock sales?

(A) $100
(B) $180
(C) $1,000
(D) $1,200
(E) $1,800

GO ON TO THE NEXT PAGE

USE THIS SPACE FOR FIGURING.

21. What is the greatest number of rectangles 4 centimeters wide and 6 centimeters long that can be cut from a square piece of paper with a side of 24 centimeters?

(A) 2
(B) 10
(C) 24
(D 36
(E) 48

22. *R* is the sum of consecutive integers *S* and *T*. If *S* and *T* are negative, which of the following is ALWAYS true?

(A) $R = -4$
(B) $R = -1$
(C) *R* is less than either *S* or *T*.
(D) *R* is greater than either *S* or *T*.
(E) $R + S + T$ is positive.

23. Initially, Greg had a total of 60 DVDs and CDs in his collection. He then sold $\frac{1}{8}$ of his CDs and $\frac{1}{2}$ of his DVDs. If the number of DVDs he sold is twice the number of CDs he sold, how many DVDs did he sell?

(A) 4
(B) 5
(C) 8
(D) 10
(E) 20

GO ON TO THE NEXT PAGE

USE THIS SPACE FOR FIGURING.

24. Mary saved exactly 60 percent of the total allowance she received in the last two weeks, and she spent the rest. If she received $20 for allowance each week and spent $12 of her first week's allowance, which of the following MUST be true?

    I. She saved a total of $24.
    II. She spent $6 of her second week's allowance.
    III. She saved 80 percent of her second week's allowance.

    (A) None
    (B) I only
    (C) II only
    (D) I and III only
    (E) I, II, and III

25. Paul and Bill each received a raise of 20 percent. If Paul now earns $4.50 per hour while Bill earns $5.40 per hour, Bill earned how much more per hour than Paul before their raises?

    (A) $0.70
    (B) $0.73
    (C) $0.75
    (D) $0.80
    (E) $0.90

IF YOU FINISH BEFORE TIME IS CALLED, YOU MAY CHECK YOUR WORK ON THIS SECTION ONLY. DO NOT TURN TO ANY OTHER SECTION IN THE TEST.

STOP

ANSWER KEY

Section 2

1. D
2. E
3. D
4. B
5. A
6. A
7. C
8. B
9. C
10. E
11. E
12. B
13. B
14. C
15. A
16. D
17. B
18. C
19. C
20. E
21. C
22. D
23. B
24. B
25. A

Section 3

1. C
2. E
3. B
4. E
5. B
6. A
7. C
8. D
9. C
10. D
11. B
12. B
13. A
14. B
15. B
16. A
17. E
18. C
19. D
20. C
21. B
22. E
23. C
24. D
25. C
26. D
27. A
28. E
29. B
30. D
31. E
32. C
33. A
34. A
35. D
36. B
37. A
38. D
39. E
40. C

Section 4

1. E
2. D
3. C
4. D
5. A
6. A
7. D
8. B
9. A
10. E
11. B
12. C
13. B
14. D
15. D
16. E
17. C
18. E
19. E
20. C
21. C
22. B
23. B
24. D
25. E
26. B
27. E
28. A
29. C
30. A
31. A
32. A
33. E
34. A
35. B
36. D
37. C
38. D
39. C
40. D
41. B
42. D
43. B
44. E
45. E
46. C
47. D
48. B
49. B
50. E
51. E
52. C
53. C
54. A
55. B
56. E
57. B
58. A
59. C
60. D

Section 5

1. B
2. D
3. A
4. B
5. E
6. D
7. D
8. D
9. D
10. C
11. B
12. D
13. D
14. E
15. E
16. B
17. B
18. A
19. A
20. C
21. C
22. C
23. D
24. D
25. C

SSAT PRACTICE TEST 2: UPPER-LEVEL: ASSESS YOUR STRENGTHS

Use the following tables to determine which topics and chapters you need to review most. If you need help with your essay, be sure to review Chapter 9: The Essay and Chapter 26: Writing Skills.

Topic	Question
Math I	Section 2, questions 1–25
Reading Comprehension	Section 3, questions 1–40
Verbal: Synonyms	Section 4, questions 1–30
Verbal: Analogies	Section 4, questions 31–60
Math II	Section 5, questions 1–25

Topic	Number of Questions on Test	Number Correct	If you struggled with these questions, study…
Math I	25		Chapters 10–14 and Chapter 25
Reading Comprehension	40		Chapter 8
Verbal: Synonyms	30		Chapters 7 and 24
Verbal: Analogies	30		Chapters 2 and 24
Math II	25		Chapters 10–14 and Chapter 25

ANSWERS AND EXPLANATIONS

SECTION 2: MATH

1. D

With a perimeter of 30 and 5 sides of equal length, the length of one side is $\frac{30}{5}$, or 6.

2. E

There were a total of 17 customers who bought caramel candy. Subtract from these the 4 who bought both, and you are left with the 13 who bought only caramel.

3. D

Only factors of 24 (numbers that can be divided evenly into 24) can be the number of different colors in the bag. Since 5 is not a factor of 24, (D), 5, is the correct choice.

4. B

Since the whole number is less than 13 and also between 11 and 18, it must be between 11 and 13. We can immediately eliminate (C) because we need a whole number. (D) and (E) are out, too, because 13 and 14 are not "less than 13." And (A) is incorrect because 11 is not "between 11 and 18." Therefore, the number must be 12, choice (B).

5. A

Movies take up 60 degrees of 360 degrees, one-sixth of the pie chart. So Susan spent about one-sixth of 12 hours, or 2 hours, watching movies.

6. A

To solve for R, multiply both sides of the equation by 2; hence, $R = 32$. Plug 32 for R into the expression $\frac{3}{4}R$, and you find that $\frac{3}{4}R = \frac{3}{4} \times 32 = 24$.

7. C

The fraction $\frac{1}{4}$ has a decimal value of 0.25; thus (B), (D), and (E) can be eliminated. Fifty-nine rounded to the nearest ten is 60; indeed, 59 is much closer to 60 than to 50, so (C) is correct.

8. B

There is no calculation necessary on this problem. Three of the five points lie on the horizontal \$260,000 line, and the only other two points are the identical distance above and below the line. Thus, \$260,000 is the correct answer.

9. C

This problem calls for substitution. $u = 5$ and $v = 5$. Plugging these values in yields $5 \o 5 = 5 - (1 - \frac{1}{5}) = 5 - \frac{4}{5} = 4\frac{1}{5}$; (C) is correct.

10. E

This problem calls for substitution. $u = a$, $v = 3$, and $a \o 3 = 4\frac{1}{3}$. Using the definition for the left side of this equation, which is $a \o 3$, we have $a - (1 - \frac{1}{3}) = 4\frac{1}{3}$; then $a - \frac{2}{3} = 4\frac{1}{3}$ and $a = 5$.

11. E

Call the unknown number x and translate the information in the question into math. Remember that *of* means "times." Twenty percent of 64 means $\frac{20}{100}(64)$, and 5% of x means $\frac{5}{100}x$. Then 20% of 64 is equal to 5% of x means that $\frac{20}{100}(64) = \frac{5}{100}x$. Reducing $\frac{20}{100}$ and $\frac{5}{100}$ yields $\frac{1}{5}(64) = \frac{1}{20}x$. Isolate the x by multiplying both sides by 20. Then $x = \frac{1}{5}(64) \times 20 = \frac{64 \times 20}{5} = 64 \times 4 = 256$.

12. B

The minimum number of fish Andy could have caught was 36, or 1 more than Rich caught. Use the average formula, Average = $\frac{\text{Sum of the terms}}{\text{Number of terms}}$. Sum of the terms = 36, and number of terms (or number of fishing trips) = 4. Hence, Andy must have caught an average of at least $\frac{36}{4} = 9$ fish per trip.

13. B

We need to set up an equation here. We know all the boys earned the same amount per hour, so 4 × Rate + 6 × Rate + 8 × Rate = 27. Thus, 18 × Rate = 27 and the Rate = $\frac{27}{18}$ = \$1.50 per hour. Lee worked 8 hours, so Lee earned 8 × \$1.50 = \$12.

14. C

Johnny has already picked 200 apples in 2.5 hours. He must pick an additional 600 – 200 = 400 apples. Call the number of additional hours that Johnny must spend picking apples *x*. To find *x*, set up a ratio and solve for x: $\frac{200 \text{ apples}}{2.5 \text{ hours}} = \frac{400 \text{ apples}}{x \text{ hours}}$. Since the numerator of the fraction on the right is equal to twice the numerator of the fraction on the left, the denominator of the fraction on the right must also be equal to twice the denominator of the fraction on the left. So $x = 2 \times 2.5 = 5$. Since Johnny must work an additional 5 hours, the latest time that he can begin picking apples again is 5 hours earlier than 7:15 PM. So 2:15 p.m. is the latest that Johnny can start picking apples again.

15. A

Set up an equation: $8W = 0.88$. Isolate the W by dividing each side by 8. $W = \frac{0.88}{8} = 0.11$.

16. D

Figure 4 indicates that the legs of two sides of the triangle are equal and thus the triangle is isosceles. Angles that are opposite equal sides must be equal. Thus, each of the two base angles is 50 degrees, and we know that the sum of the three interior angles of any triangle is 180 degrees, so $r = 180 - 50 - 50 = 80$.

17. B

To determine how many times the income of 1958 was in 1988, divide the 1988 income by the 1958 income. Then the number we are seeking is $\frac{4,500,000}{9,000}$. Dividing the numerator and the denominator by 1,000, we have $\frac{4,500}{9} = 500$.

18. C

The correct answer choice, when 2 is subtracted from it, must be a multiple of 5. A number is a multiple of 5 only if its ones digit is a 5 or a 0. Looking at the choices, 25 – 2 = 23 is not a multiple of 5, so eliminate choice (A). 33 – 2 = 31 is not a multiple of 5, so eliminate (B). 47 – 2 = 45, which is a multiple of 5. So (C) is correct.

19. C

Recall Kaplan's strategy: A figure can be drawn without lifting the pencil or retracing if there are exactly 0 or 2 points where an odd number of lines intersect. (C) has no points where an odd number of lines intersect. Hence, this is the correct answer.

20. E

Pick 100 as the initial population of Country X. The increase for the first year was $\frac{10}{100}$ of 100 = 10, and the total at the end of the first year was 100 + 10 or 110 people. The increase for the second year was $\frac{10}{100}$ of 110 = 11, and the total at the end of the second year was 110 + 11 or 121 people. The population increased from 100 to 121 over the two-year period. The increase in the population was 121 – 100 = 21. Hence, the percent increase in the population over the entire two-year period was $\frac{21}{100}$ or 21%.

21. C

The value of z is given to us in terms of y; we need to multiply this value by 2 and add 1. Hence, $2z + 1 = 2(y + 2) + 1 = 2y + 4 + 1 = 2y + 5$, (C).

22. D

Picking numbers for x and y is a foolproof method for solving this problem. Pick a positive fraction for x that is less than 1, such as $\frac{1}{2}$. Then pick a positive value for y that is greater than x, which in this case means that the y that we pick must also be greater than $\frac{1}{2}$. Remember, the question says that y is greater than x and the numbers you pick must always be consistent with the question stem. So let's pick 1 for y. So we're letting x be $\frac{1}{2}$ and y be 1. With these values, (A) is 2, (B) and (C) are both $\frac{1}{2}$, and (D) is –2. Further examining (D), we see that the denominator, $x - y$, has a larger positive number y subtracted from a smaller positive number x. So $x - y$ will always be negative. Therefore $\frac{1}{x-y}$ will also always be negative.

23. B

If 6 people can sit at each of x tables and 5 people can sit at each of y tables, then the maximum number of people that may be seated is $6x + 5y$.

24. B

Draw 3 squares: big, bigger, and biggest. Let the side of the middle fabric piece be 9. The side of the largest fabric piece must be three times this, or 27. Likewise, the side of the smallest square piece must be 3. The area of the largest piece is $27 \times 27 = 729$, and the area of the smallest piece is 9. Now determine the number of times that 9 goes into 729: $\frac{729}{9} = 81$.

25. A

Begin by determining how many gallons of gas it takes to make the 18 trips: $\frac{3}{4} \times 18 = \frac{27}{2} = 13.5$ gallons. If there are 9 gallons in a tank, Mr. Dali will need $\frac{13.5}{9} = 1.5$ tanks of gas.

SECTION 3: READING COMPREHENSION

Scott Joplin Passage

First up is a brief history passage about Scott Joplin, a composer best known for his ragtime music. Don't try to absorb all the details, even in a brief passage like this. Just get a feel for the Big Idea, which is that Joplin was instrumental in developing the ragtime genre but wasn't recognized as a serious composer until almost 60 years after his death.

1. C

Lines 2–3 note that Joplin composed 41 piano pieces known as "rags," the only time the word is used in the passage. (C), then, must be correct. (E) is tempting, but the genre or style of songs Joplin invented is described as "ragtime," not "rag." (A)'s "operatic" is incorrect; Joplin's *Treemonisha* was his only opera. (B) and (D) are incorrect because ragtime is never described as "dance" music or as being played by marching bands.

2. E

Only (E) has the proper scope here. (A) and (B) focus too narrowly on details. It was Joplin's "rhythmic diversity," not his stylistic diversity, (C), that distinguished his composing. The passage doesn't say how Joplin finally won the Pulitzer, (D).

3. B

The passage states that Joplin received the Pulitzer in 1976, "59 years after his death." Subtract 59 from 76 and you get 17, so Joplin died in 1917, choice (B).

4. E

The author discusses Joplin's "significant creative contribution" to music, his great popularity, and how he "at last" received "the praise he deserved." Thus, (E)'s "appreciative" best sums up the author's tone toward Joplin.

5. B

The passage states that Joplin was instrumental in developing ragtime "as a genre, a unique musical form." Therefore, (B) is the correct inference: A genre is a distinct category or style. While ragtime is an example of a musical genre, a genre is not an example of a particular type of ragtime, (A). There's no evidence that Joplin coined the term *genre*, (C).

6. A

Lines 13–14 say "he was not considered a serious composer during his lifetime," even though his "Maple Leaf Rag" was "the most popular piano rag of the time" (lines 10–11). That says his work was liked but people didn't appreciate it as serious music. The last sentence says he wasn't celebrated until 59 years after he died, making (A) correct. (C) is incorrect because line 5 says he made a "contribution" to ragtime; he didn't invent it.

Bird Courtship Passage

Next up is a science passage about the courtship procedures and "identification checks" used by birds during courtship and mating. Paragraph 1 introduces the topic, paragraph 2 details the roles of plumage and aggressive behavior, and paragraph 3 the role of sounds in the birds' courting and mating rituals.

7. C

This Inference question is answered in the opening paragraph. The author states that the bird's identification and courtship procedures are important "because if birds of different species mate, any offspring" will be sterile and have a low chance for survival. Thus, the procedures are important because they help a bird find a mate of its own species. (B) focuses too narrowly on a detail from paragraph 2.

8. D

The answer lies in paragraph 3, which states that a male's singing tells females of its species that "it is in breeding condition," I, and, after mating, enables the nesting female "to continue to identify" her partner, III. The passage does not mention that male birds use sound to intimidate male rivals, II, so I and III only are correct.

9. C

This Detail question focuses on the last sentence of paragraph 2. There we learn that whooping cranes "perform wonderfully elaborate courtship dances."

So the whooping crane is an example of a bird that behaves in an unusual, noteworthy way during courtship, and (C) is correct. (B), (D), and (E) incorrectly mention other details from paragraph 2—plumage, reversed roles, and aggressiveness.

10. D

The answer here is taken from the same sentence—the last of paragraph 1—that answered question 7. If birds of different species mate, "any offspring will usually be sterile or badly adapted to their surroundings." This point is restated in (D). (B) is the opposite of the correct choice. The frequency of interspecies mating, (A), is not mentioned in the passage, but it must happen occasionally, contrary to (E), or the author wouldn't warn against its dangers. The idea of a new species evolving, (C), is not discussed.

11. B

This time the Big Idea question comes near the end of the set. The passage is about the various courtship behaviors and "identification checks" used by birds, which makes (B) correct. (A) and (E) raise issues not debated in the passage. (C) and (D) focus too narrowly on details.

12. B

Think about where you would most likely find this passage. (C) and (D) are incorrect because the passage contains nothing personal or fictional, just facts. (E) is incorrect because the passage does not talk about endangered birds. (A) is incorrect. The passage discusses how birds of the same species identify one another in order to mate, not how you would identify birds, so (B) is correct.

Native American Passage

Next up is a brief passage about the 1,500 Native American languages that have been discovered by linguists. The Big Idea here is simple: A pioneering linguist originally divided these 1,500 languages into six main groups; a recent group of scholars thinks they can all be divided into three broader groups, but other scholars disagree with this new theory.

13. A

(A) is the most specific and accurate, and it's correct here. (B) leaves out the recent debate over the revised classification of Native American languages into three groups. (C) and (E) are too broad; they could be talking about any group of languages, not just Native American languages. And (D) focuses too narrowly on a detail from paragraph 2.

14. B

According to paragraph 2, scholars believe Native American languages can be classified into only three families because of "similarities and differences among words and sounds." (B) can be inferred from this statement. (A) distorts a detail from paragraph 1. (C) is the argument of those who think Native American languages can't be classified into three families. (D) is too broad, and (E) is beyond the scope of the passage.

15. B

Where would you be likely to come upon this passage? In a discussion of Native American languages or a linguistics textbook (B). (A), (C), and (D) are incorrect because there's nothing either personal or fictional in the text; it's just a series of factual statements. And while Sapir pioneered the field of Native American linguistics, the passage doesn't contain any significant biographical information about his life, (E).

16. A

Why is classifying Native American languages controversial? Those who group them into three families have "no doubt about the validity" of their theory. But "the vast majority of linguists" argue that "linguistic science has not yet advanced far enough" to group 1,500 languages into only three families. So the controversy exists because scholars do not yet agree on how to classify languages, and (A) is correct. (B) is a point argued by linguists who think Native American languages might never be properly grouped into families, but it's not the source of the controversy. We don't know when the field of linguistics was founded, but even though it hasn't "advanced far enough," it is not a "very new" field, as (C) suggests. There's no evidence for (D) or (E).

17. E

Paragraph 1 states that Sapir classified Native American languages into six families. None of the other questions is answered in the passage.

18. C

Look at the sentence "extent" appears in. The author says the languages have "diverged" so much that it would be impossible to classify them into three linguistic families. Therefore, the answer needs to mean something close to "wide". (C) is the answer.

Poetry Passage

Next up is a famous poem by Emily Dickinson. The first stanza creates a metaphor of hope as a bird that lives inside us and never stops singing. The second stanza says that the bird of hope sings even in bad weather (i.e., bad times). And in the final stanza, the poet claims that, while she has heard the bird of hope singing in distant places, "It never asked a crumb of me."

19. D

Hope is "the thing with feathers" in stanza 1 and "the little bird" in stanza 2, so (D) is correct. (A), (B), and (C) are trials and dangers that the bird/hope faces; (E) is what the bird sings.

20. C

Paraphrase the final stanza: "I've heard the bird of hope in far-off places, and it never asked me for anything." This points to (C) as correct. (A) is incorrect because the poem says nothing about a world without hope or about preserving hope at all costs. (B) summarizes the second stanza, not the third. (D) takes the poem literally to the point of absurdity; the "crumb" line doesn't mean that the bird is always hungry, but rather that it gives its song of hope freely. And (E) is incorrect because, according to the poet, hope is always present; no great effort is required to make it so.

21. B

Remember you're dealing with metaphor. This poem isn't about a bird; it's comparing hope to a bird that never stops singing. The statement that it "kept so many warm" means that hope has given comfort to a lot of people; therefore, (B) is correct. (A) and (C) take the poem literally. (D) is pessimistic where the poet is optimistic about hope, and (E) implies that hope *only* works in the worst of situations. But the poet is saying that hope is helpful *even* in the worst of situations.

22. E

The poet likens hope to a bird that, thankfully, is always there to help people, never asking anything in return. Her tone is one of gratitude, making choice (E) correct. (C) is the closest character, but "respectful" is too formal, too distancing. Hope in this poem isn't a great person or awesome display of nature; it's a little bird "that perches in the soul."

23. C

Figure out what the poet is saying in the lines "sore" appears in. The poet is saying only the worst of storms could discourage the bird. The only choice that comes close to meaning "worst" is "severe," (C).

Recycling Passage

The next passage is about recycling, the remaking of waste products and materials for practical purposes. In paragraph 1, we learn that recycling is now considered a necessity, that it saves money and resources and reduces waste. In paragraph 2, the author focuses on residential recycling—what we as private citizens can do to reduce waste.

24. D

Statement I is false: Recycling "reduces the amount of waste produced" (lines 13–14). This eliminates (B), (C), and (E). Since statement II is included in both of the remaining answer choices, it must be true, and it is: We're told twice that recycling can save money. Statement III, then, is the crucial one. And it's true: Lines 17–19 state that "the amount of...waste produced at home has been steadily increasing." So only Statements II and III are true, and choice (D) is correct.

25. C

(A) is easily eliminated: The author thinks the individual's role in recycling "has been seriously underemphasized." The first half of (B) is correct: Businesses do recycle to save money. But the second half is incorrect: The author doesn't think individuals are motivated to recycle by a sense of the greater good—but the author does think that we should be so motivated. This point is restated in correct choice (C). (D) says we shouldn't recycle, which the author would certainly disagree with, and (E) claims that recycling is only the responsibility of businesses, which goes against the thrust of paragraph 2.

26. D

You're looking for the choice that is not an example of recycling, which the author defines in lines 5–7 as "the remaking of waste products and other used materials for practical purposes." Using this definition, (A), (B), and (E) are easily checked off as examples of recycling. (C) involves a second use for empty soda bottles, as does the author's example in lines 8–10. This leaves (D): Selling jewelry to buy a car is not recycling, because the jewelry is not a waste product that's being remade.

27. A

The author argues that recycling is "important... even...necessary," that "it is our duty to ourselves and to our fellow human beings." These and similar signals throughout the passage reveal the author's tone as insistent, (A). By the same token, (B), (D), and (E) are easy to eliminate. (C) may be tempting since the author tells us that the future of humanity is at stake, but (A) remains the best choice, because more than being formal, the author is trying to motivate us, to do something (recycle).

28. E

Paragraph 3 argues that individuals can and must learn to recycle their waste products. You can predict, then, that the author will go on to suggest one or more ways in which individuals can pitch in to help the recycling effort, a point restated in (E). There's no evidence to suggest (A) or (B). (C) wrongly suggests the author will return to a detail from the previous paragraph. And (D) doesn't even mention recycling.

29. B

In lines 15–17, the author states that businesses recycle "based primarily on the goal of saving money." So you can infer that the author believes that businesses recycle primarily for financial gain, (B). (A) is incorrect because the economics of recycling are of greatest interest to businesses, not to the author. Nor can it be inferred from the passage that the author's knowledge of the financial aspects of recycling, (C), is limited. And while (D) is probably true, it can't be inferred from lines 15–17.

El Niño Passage

The passage begins with a statement that, although bad weather is usually only an "inconvenience" for us, it can have "disastrous consequences" for communities in other parts of the world. The remainder of the passage describes an example of this disastrous bad weather: El Niño, a change in the Humboldt Current (an ocean current) that disrupts marine life and can thereby threaten villagers on the northwest coast of South America with starvation.

30. D

The Humboldt Current flows off the northwest coast of South America, making (D) correct. Each of the other choices contradicts the passage. El Niño occurs only at Christmastime (A), but the Humboldt Current flows all year long. The Humboldt Current does fail when El Niño occurs (B). The passage does not state the directional flow of the Humboldt Current, (C), but does state that it is a cold-water current, not a hot-water current, (E).

31. E

The bulk of the passage concerns what happens when the Humboldt Current fails, which makes (D) very tempting, but the Big Idea of the passage is really stated in the first sentence: Changes in weather patterns can dramatically affect the way people live, making (E) correct here. Remember, the Humboldt Current–El Niño information is there only to back up this claim by the author. (A), (B), and (C) focus on details and should have been easier to eliminate.

32. C

Here you're looking for the one choice that isn't true. Only (C) is not confirmed in the passage. As we noted in question 30, the Humboldt Current carries cold water, not warm; the passage also never states that the current affects "the climate of nearby land masses."

33. A

If you answered question 31 correctly, you probably answered this one correctly too. This passage is not about El Niño; the El Niño is discussed in order to prove the author's larger point: that bad weather can harm communities. This means that (A), not (C), is the correct answer.

34. A

We're told that bad weather can have a "dramatic effect" on these villages, "depriving" them "of their livelihood." The author's attitude toward the villagers, then, is—what? Not condescending, (C), angry, (D), or emotional, (E). And though the author doesn't express undue alarm, you wouldn't say she was simply unconcerned about the villagers, as (B) puts it. No, the author's attitude is best described as sympathetic, (A). The villagers occasionally have this awful problem, and the author expresses concern about it.

35. D

The "chain reaction" described in the passage is as follows: the current fails, stopping the flow of nutrients to the fish and squid, which die, thereby harming the villagers. A chain reaction then, is not a pair but a series of causally linked occurrences. (A), (B), and (C), concern only a pair—not a chain—of occurrences. The best example of a chain reaction in the choices is therefore (D), where global warming leads to melted glaciers, which lead to higher water levels and then less available land for people. (E) gives two phenomena that occur at the same time.

Marshall Plan Passage

The final passage is a history passage about the Marshall Plan, an American scheme to help rebuild Europe after World War II. Paragraph 1 sets the scene, explaining that the United States believed that Europe's economic devastation needed to be cured in order to keep it from falling under the domination of the Soviet Union. Paragraph 2 explains that in 1948, U.S. Secretary of State George Marshall instituted the Marshall Plan, which distributed 12 billion dollars among 16 different European countries over the next four years.

36. B

The answer will probably mention the Marshall Plan and how it helped Europe; (B) fits this bill nicely. (A) and (E) are way too broad. (C) describes what happened during World War II that made the Marshall Plan so necessary but says nothing about the Plan itself. (D) suggests that the passage is about Marshall himself, when the author actually tells you nothing more than Marshall's name and job—Secretary of State.

37. A

The author's tone is not noticeably positive (B) or negative (E). It betrays no personal feelings such as insistence, (C), or anxiety, (D). Instead, it's objective.

38. D

This is a Detail question that careful readers will get. Paragraph 2 states that the Marshall Plan doled out "a combined total of $12 billion" to the 16 "participating countries." So each country did not get $12 billion. All of the other statements are substantiated in the passage.

39. E

What was the driving force behind the Marshall Plan? Early in paragraph 1, we learn that post-World War II Western Europe was economically devastated and that when tensions between the United States and the Soviet Union escalated, U.S. policymakers felt "substantial financial assistance" was needed in Western Europe "to maintain a state of political stability." This points to (E). None of the other choices draws a correct inference from the passage.

40. C

The first paragraph describes the postwar economic and political problems that the Marshall Plan was intended to solve, and paragraph 2 describes, in general terms, how much money was distributed and how well the plan worked. You can infer, then, that the author will go on to talk about specifics—how the Plan's money was put to work in some or all of the 16 participating countries. (A) wrongly sees the Cold War, not the Marshall Plan, as the focus of the passage. (B) goes back in time, to events before the

Marshall Plan was ever dreamed up. Other economic recovery plans are never mentioned, and (E) is also unwarranted.

SECTION 4: VERBAL

SYNONYMS

1. E

Harsh means rough or overly demanding—in other words, severe, (E). A crime might be punished by a harsh penalty, for example. One can be angry, (B), without being harsh; these words are not synonyms.

2. D

Indicate means to show, state, or point out.

3. C

Bleak means desolate and barren, or cheerless, (C). "We camped out in a bleak wilderness."

4. D

Secure means free from danger or safe.

5. A

Alien means foreign or strange.

6. A

Chronic means frequently occurring, habitual, or persistent, (A), as in a "chronic cough."

7. D

To quench a thirst means to slake or satisfy it, (D).

8. B

Severe, as we saw in question 1, means harsh, overly demanding, or extreme, (B). Severe cold leaves you frozen, (A), but severe and frozen are not synonyms. Don't just think associatively; look for the word that's closest in meaning to the stem word.

9. A

When thieves ransack an apartment, they turn it upside down looking for things to steal. In other words, to ransack is to search thoroughly, (A).

10. E

The summit is the top of something, as in the summit of a mountain peak, which makes (E) correct.

11. B

A tumult is a loud noise, an uproar, or commotion, (B).

12. C

To retard means to delay the progress of, hold back, or slow down, (C).

13. B

An antidote is a cure or remedy, (B), such as an antidote for poison.

14. D

Solitary is the state of being secluded or alone, (D).

15. D

To camouflage means to hide or disguise, (D).

16. E

To expel means to drive out, to reject, or to cast out, (E).

17. C

To lunge is to make a sudden forward stride or leap. A lunge—especially with a weapon—is also called a thrust, (C). To pursue, (A), means to chase, that is, to follow with the intent of overtaking. Pursuit may begin with a lunge, but the two verbs are not synonyms. In similar fashion, a lunge may involve a turn, (B), or startle someone, (E), but these words are not synonyms of lunge, either.

18. E

Brevity is the quality of being brief, which means of short duration—so shortness, (E), is correct.

19. E

To marvel is to feel surprise, amazed curiosity, or wonder, (E).

20. C

Candor is truthfulness, or honesty, (C). To be daring, (B), is to be bold but not necessarily honest.

21. C

To convene is to meet or to assemble, (C). The closest distracters, (B) and (D), are actions associated with meetings that are convened, but they're not synonyms.

22. B

A catastrophe is a great misfortune, a terrible occurrence, or a disaster, (B).

23. B

Gregarious means talkative, outgoing, or sociable, (B).

24. D

Dexterity is mental or physical skill and quickness. The best synonym here is nimbleness, (D).

25. E

To say that something is imminent means that it's about to happen, that it is forthcoming, (E).

26. B

Animosity is hostility, ill will, or resentment. The best synonym here is hatred, (B).

27. E

To amend means to change, alter, or improve, (E).

28. A

Someone who feels despondent is very sad or depressed, (A).

29. C

Unflinching means not flinching or shrinking from; it's the quality of being steadfast. The best synonym here is uncompromising, (C). (A) and (D) are near-antonyms for unflinching.

30. A

To repudiate means to cast off, disown, or refuse to have anything to do with. The choice with the closest meaning to repudiate is renounce, (A). To impede, (B), is to slow or interfere with someone's progress.

Analogies

31. A

Anything having to do with the sun is solar. In the same way, anything having to do with the earth is terrestrial, (A). Marine refers to a sea or ocean, not to a pond. Subterranean refers to what is below the ground, not to the ground itself. You might suspect (E), but lunar refers to anything having to do with the moon, not planets.

32. A

Botany is the study of plants. Similarly, meteorology is the study of weather, (A). Flora is the generic word for plant life or vegetation.

33. E

You use a hammer to *put in* a nail. In the same way, you use a screwdriver to *put in* a screw, (E). You use an axe to chop wood, a lathe to smooth or shape molding, a chisel to chip marble, and a nut to secure a bolt.

34. A

A bone is part of the structural system that supports a mammal. A girder is part of the structural system that supports a skyscraper, (A). The other choices are also part of the structural system that supports a skyscraper, not the skyscraper itself.

35. B

A primate is an order of mammals that includes monkeys, apes, and humans. So a human is one species of the primate order, just as a snake is one species of the order of reptiles. Vegetarians are not an order in the same way as primates and reptiles. A disease is not necessarily bacterial in nature. Birds are mammals, not amphibians; amphibians are a class in the animal kingdom that includes frogs and toads.

36. D

A tremor is a quivering motion of the earth. A powerful tremor may be an earthquake. In the same way, wind is a motion of the air, and a powerful wind may be a tornado, (D). The analogy isn't exact here, but it's better than the other choices. An eye is the calm center of a hurricane, (A); a powerful desert is not a sandstorm, (B). A faucet is a man-made object through which water flows; a deluge, (C), is a great flood. And a powerful flood, (E), is not a river.

37. C

Something tremendously amusing is uproarious; similarly, something tremendously interesting is hypnotic, fascinating, or mesmerizing, (C).

38. D

Being fickle, or inconstant, is the opposite of steadfastness. In the same way, being tempestuous, or stormy, is the opposite of peacefulness, (D). Ire, (E), means anger.

39. C

A group of fish is called a school, just as a group of birds is called a flock.

40. D

A cartographer is a designer of maps, just as a chef is a designer of meals.

41. B

A throne is the official chair for a monarch, just as a bench is the official chair for a judge, (B). A miter, (A), is the headdress worn by bishops.

42. D

A canal is a man-made river, just as a mine is a man-made cavern, (D). It's stretching things to call a boat a manmade piece of driftwood, (A), even though both float.

43. B

When milk goes bad it gets sour; when bread goes bad it gets stale, (B).

44. E

Ore is mined to bring it up out of the earth, just as oil is drilled to bring it up out of the earth, (E). Grain is plowed, (D), but it's not found buried in the earth.

45. E

Weight is measured on a scale, just as altitude is measured on an altimeter. Speed, not distance, is measured on a speedometer (A). (B) is a little tricky: Numbers are measured on a slide rule, but only special kinds of numbers called logarithms.

46. C

A porcupine protects itself with quills. In a similar fashion, a skunk protects itself with odor.

47. D

The purpose of a jar is to contain, just as the purpose of a pillar is to support, (D).

48. B

Irrigate means to flush with liquid. So you irrigate something that is dry, just as you smooth something that's coarse, (B). (A) and (C) are tempting but not as good. You soften something that's hard, not uneven. And you purify something that's impure, or tainted. To ferment something is to induce a chemical process that makes alcohol; this has nothing to do with saltiness.

49. B

Electricity flows through a wire, just as water flows through an aqueduct. Sound is broadcast from a radio, choice (A), which is not the same thing. (C) and (D) have similar problems; in each case the music or light is emitted from the object, it doesn't flow through it. And in (E), a river is contained by its bank.

50. E

You can express contempt with a sneer. In the same way, you express displeasure with a frown, (E). Each of the other actions is inappropriately matched to its emotion.

51. E

The base of a building is its foundation. The base of a plant is its root, (E). If you chose (A), (C), or (D), you were probably confusing the vegetative meaning of "plant" with, say, a manufacturing plant. A grotto is a cave.

52. C

Olfactory refers to anything having to do with the sense of smell. So our bridge could be, *The nose is the organ of the olfactory sense*. Similarly, the ear is the organ of the sense of hearing or auditory sense, (C).

53. C

Irk means to annoy, disgust, or irritate. So the relationship here is of opposites: Something that irks is not soothing. In the same way, something that supports is not weakening or undermining, (C). Irritating, (D), is second-best here; it would go better with soothing than with support.

54. A

Something illegible is impossible to read, just as something invisible is impossible to see, (A). Something broken is not by definition impossible to fix.

55. B

Tact is sensitivity, or the ability to do or say the right thing with people. So tact is a necessary quality for a diplomat. In the same way, agility is a necessary quality for a gymnast, which makes (B) correct. Parsimony, (A), or stinginess, is a quality a philanthropist will not have, since a philanthropist is someone who gives generous amounts of money to charity. Similarly, a judge, (E), should be unbiased, not biased, which means having a declared preference for one side or the other. Victims may be vulnerable, (C), but you wouldn't ordinarily say that vulnerability is a necessary quality for being a victim. And training in (D) is too vague; it's not a quality specific to the practice of medicine.

56. E

Ravenous means extremely hungry. So to be ravenous is to be in an extreme state of hunger. In the same way, to be furious is to be in an extreme state of indignation, (E). None of the other choices has a first word that's an extreme version of the second word. Pliable, (A), means flexible, while obstinacy is stubbornness, so these words are opposites. The same is true for (B) and (C). Tenacity, (D), is stubborn persistence; being smart is not being in an extreme state of tenacity.

57. B

To amplify sound is to make it stronger or louder. To bolster something means to strengthen it. In the same way, then, to bolster courage is to make it stronger. Getting the right answer here depends a little on knowing common usage. You can't bolster a smell, (A), insomnia or sleeplessness, (C), or light, (D), or silence, (E).

58. A

Reverse the order of the stem pair: You attend a lecture in an auditorium. In the same way, you attend a concert in a theater, (A). This bridge clearly doesn't work on (B), (D), or (E). One attends religious services, not religion itself, in a temple, (C).

59. C

Philanthropic means generous, giving; benevolence is the quality of generosity. So our bridge might be, *A philanthropic act is evidence of benevolence.* In the same way, a miserly act is evidence of stinginess, (C). Ostentatious, (B), means showy or extravagant.

60. D

Spurious is simply a fancy word meaning fake. So we've got a relationship of opposites here: Something spurious has no authenticity. Similarly, something laughable has no seriousness, (D). Lavish, (A), means extravagantly expensive. Abject means miserable; subjectivity may or may not be miserable, (B). There's no obvious bridge between the words in (C), and in (E), totalitarian refers to an imposing system of government, so it is not the opposite of completeness.

SECTION 5: MATH

1. B

Begin with \$5 + cover price – \$9 and simplify it: cover price – \$4, which means \$4 below the cover price. (B) is correct.

2. D

Note here that each cube = 20 boxes. February has two cubes less than March, hence 2(20) = 40 boxes less.

3. A

In January, 6 cubes were sold, and in February, 3 cubes were sold. Thus, in January, the number of boxes sold was $\frac{6}{3} = 2$ times the number of boxes sold in February. It is not necessary to perform the calculation using the fact that 20 boxes are represented by each cube.

4. B

Let x = the number of ties for Team A; keep in mind that x is an integer here. Thus, Team A had $4x$ losses. Adding the losses and ties (there were no wins), the number of games the team played was $x + 4x = 5x$. Thus, the correct answer choice must be a multiple of 5 (because x is an integer). Only (B), 15, is a multiple of 5.

5. E

In order to make the discussion simpler, the five rectangles that are in the figure to begin with have been labeled.

A B
C D E

Systematically count the different rectangles in the figure. There are 5 rectangles in the figure to begin with, which we will call basic rectangles. Next, let's count the number of rectangles that are made up of 2 basic rectangles. Rectangles made up of 2 basic rectangles can be formed from basic rectangles A and B, C and D, D and E, A and C, and B and D. There are 5 rectangles made up of 2 basic rectangles. Next, let's count the number of rectangles that can be made up of 3 basic rectangles. There is just one such rectangle. This is the rectangle that is made up of the 3 basic rectangles at the bottom, rectangles C, D, and E. Next, let's count the number of rectangles that can be made up of 4 basic rectangles. There is just one such rectangle, the rectangle that is made up of basic rectangles A, B, C, and D. There are no other rectangles that can be made up of basic rectangles. There is a total of 5 + 5 + 1 + 1 = 12 different rectangles in the figure.

6. D

We are looking for the fraction that is NOT less than $\frac{1}{4}$, that is, a fraction that is greater than or equal to $\frac{1}{4}$. (D) is correct because $\frac{1}{4} = \frac{19}{19 \times 4} = \frac{19}{76}$ is less than $\frac{19}{70}$ because $\frac{19}{70}$ has a smaller denominator. Looking at the other choices, since $\frac{2}{8} = \frac{1}{4}$, $\frac{2}{9}$ must be less than $\frac{1}{4}$ (since 9 is a greater denominator).

Since $\frac{3}{12} = \frac{1}{4}$, $\frac{3}{14}$ must be less than $\frac{1}{4}$ (due to the greater denominator, 14). Reducing $\frac{14}{64}$, we get $\frac{7}{32}$ and since $\frac{8}{32} = \frac{1}{4}$, $\frac{14}{64} = \frac{7}{32}$ is less than $\frac{1}{4}$. Since $\frac{1}{4} = \frac{27}{27 \times 4} = \frac{27}{108}$, then $\frac{27}{125}$ is less than $\frac{27}{108} = \frac{1}{4}$.

7. D

Begin by labeling each side 1. Using the answer choices, count the lengths of 1 in the path: (A) = 4, (B) = 4, (C) = 4, (D) = 5, and (E) = 4. (D) is the longest path.

8. D

No lengthy calculation is needed here. In order for a product of numbers to equal 0, at least one of the numbers must equal zero. Since $5\frac{1}{3}$ is not 0, the other factor, $14 - x$, must equal 0. So $14 - x = 0$, and $x = 14$.

9. D

Since 1.18 has 2 places after the decimal point, write each answer choice with 2 places after the decimal point. (A) and (B) are more than 1.00 away from 1.18. (C), 1.90, is more than 0.70 away from 1.18, (D), 1.10, is 0.08 away from 1.18, and (E), 1.00, is 0.18 away from 1.18.

10. C

Write out the given inequality: $X > 15$. Next multiply both sides by $\frac{1}{3}$ (or divide both sides by 3). We now have $\frac{1}{3}X > \frac{15}{3}$ and $\frac{1}{3}X > 5$, (C).

11. B

Round \$26.95 to 27.00. Then we have $\frac{35}{100} \times 27 = ?$. Canceling yields $\frac{7}{20} \times 27 = \frac{189}{20} = 9.45$.

12. D

Let T be the number of minutes. Set up a ratio:

$\frac{600}{3} = \frac{27{,}000}{T}$. Reduce $\frac{600}{3}$ to $\frac{200}{1}$. Then $\frac{200}{1} = \frac{27{,}000}{T}$. Next cross-multiply: $200T = 27{,}000$. Divide both sides by 100: $2T = 270$, and thus $T = 135$. Put this into the time format of hours and minutes by dividing 135 minutes by 60 minutes per hour and we have $2\frac{1}{4}$ hours, which is 2 hours and 15 minutes.

13. D

Translate what is stated in the question step-by-step. To begin with, Sally has x dollars. After she receives 100 dollars, she has $x + 100$ dollars. She spends 125 dollars, so she has $(x + 100) - 125$ dollars left. Now simplify $(x + 100) - 125$: $(x + 100) - 125 = x + 100 - 125 = x - 25$. Sally has $x - 25$ dollars left, so (D) is correct.

14. E

Begin by multiplying both sides by 3 to eliminate the denominator. Then $A + B = 12$. If A is greater than 1, then B must be less than 11. Thus (E), 12, could not be the value of B.

15. E

Use the average formula, which is Average = $\frac{\text{Sum of the terms}}{\text{Number of terms}}$. Call X the sum of all 5 numbers. Then $\frac{X}{5} = 10$, so $X = 50$. Call Y the sum of the 3 remaining numbers. Then $\frac{Y}{3} = 9$, so $Y = 27$. Subtracting from the sum of all 5 numbers the sum of the 3 numbers that remain leaves the sum of the 2 numbers that were removed. So the sum of the 2 numbers that were removed is $X - Y = 50 - 27 = 23$.

16. B

The bottom surface of the bag is a rectangle and all points are inside the rectangle, so choice (A) can be eliminated. (B) is correct.

17. B

The formula for percent increase is Percent increase = $\frac{\text{New value} - \text{Old value}}{\text{Old value}} \times 100\%$. Here, $\frac{1{,}448 - 1{,}086}{1{,}086} \times 100\% = \frac{362}{1{,}086} \times 100\% = \frac{1}{3} \times 100\% = 33\frac{1}{3}\%$, so (B) is the best choice.

18. A

Let the length of WX be represented by a. Then the length of WY is $3a$. The length of XY must be $3a - a = 2a$. Then, the length of XZ must be $2 \times 2a = 4a$. So $WZ = WX + XZ = a + 4a = 5a = 5(2) = 10$.

19. A

Draw a rectangle. Label its width w and its length $3w$. The perimeter is 240, thus $3w + w + 3w + w = 240$, so $8w = 240$ and $w = 30$.

20. C

The phrase "for every" indicates a ratio is needed. Call the amount she receives from the \$18,000 collection x. Here set up $\frac{50}{900} = \frac{x}{18{,}000}$. After cancellation on the left we have $\frac{1}{18} = \frac{x}{18{,}000}$. Cross-multiply and get $18x = 18{,}000$. Solve for x by dividing each side by 18, and $x = 1{,}000$.

21. C

We need to find out how many 4×6 rectangles fit into a square with a side of 24. Use our area formula $A = L \times W$: $\frac{24 \times 24}{4 \times 6} = 24$.

22. C

Pick numbers. Let $S = -2$ and $T = -3$. Thus, we have $R = -5$. Taking this value for R through our choices, only (C) fits.

23. D

Call the number of DVDs Greg has d and the number of CDs he has c. Our first equation is $d + c = 60$. The second equation is $\frac{1}{2}r = 2(\frac{1}{8}c)$. So $\frac{1}{2}r = \frac{1}{4}c$ and $c = 4 \times \frac{1}{2}r = 2d$. Now, substitute $2d$ for c in the first equation, $d + c = 60$. Then $d + 2d = 60$, $3d = 60$, and $d = \frac{60}{3} = 20$. The problem asks how many DVDs he sold, which is $\frac{1}{2}(20) = 10$.

24. D

Mary received \$20 each week for 2 weeks and saved 60% of this or $\frac{60}{100}(\$40) = \$24$. Since she saved only \$8 the first week, she must have saved \$16 the second week. Looking at the Roman numeral statements, I is true so eliminate (A) and (C). Looking at statement II, $\$20 - \$16 = \$4$ was spent during the second week, not \$6, so it is not true. Eliminate (E). Finally in III, the percent of the second week's allowance that she saved was $\frac{16}{20} \times 100\% = \frac{4}{5} \times 100\% = 80\%$, so statement III is true. (D) is correct.

25. C

First work with Paul: Original wage + 20% of his original wage = \$4.50. Convert this into the equation: $x + 0.20x = 4.50$, $1.2x = 4.50$, and $x = \$3.75$. Set up a similar equation for Bill: $y + 0.20y = 5.40$ and $1.2y = 5.40$, so $y = \$4.50$. Hence, $\$4.50 - \$3.75 = \$0.75$.

CHAPTER 18: SSAT PRACTICE TEST 3: LOWER-LEVEL

HOW TO TAKE THIS PRACTICE TEST

Before taking this practice test, find a quiet room where you can work uninterrupted for two and a half hours. Make sure you have a comfortable desk and several No. 2 pencils.

Use the answer sheet provided to record your answers. (You can cut it out or photocopy it.)

Once you start this practice test, don't stop until you've finished. Remember—you can review any questions within a section, but you may not go backward or forward a section.

You'll find answer explanations following the test. Scoring information can be found in chapter 19.

Good luck.

SSAT Practice Test 3: Lower-Level Answer Sheet

Remove (or photocopy) the answer sheet and use it to complete the practice test.

Start with number 1 for each section. If a section has fewer questions than answer spaces, leave the extra spaces blank.

SECTION 2

1 Ⓐ Ⓑ Ⓒ Ⓓ Ⓔ	6 Ⓐ Ⓑ Ⓒ Ⓓ Ⓔ	11 Ⓐ Ⓑ Ⓒ Ⓓ Ⓔ	16 Ⓐ Ⓑ Ⓒ Ⓓ Ⓔ	21 Ⓐ Ⓑ Ⓒ Ⓓ Ⓔ
2 Ⓐ Ⓑ Ⓒ Ⓓ Ⓔ	7 Ⓐ Ⓑ Ⓒ Ⓓ Ⓔ	12 Ⓐ Ⓑ Ⓒ Ⓓ Ⓔ	17 Ⓐ Ⓑ Ⓒ Ⓓ Ⓔ	22 Ⓐ Ⓑ Ⓒ Ⓓ Ⓔ
3 Ⓐ Ⓑ Ⓒ Ⓓ Ⓔ	8 Ⓐ Ⓑ Ⓒ Ⓓ Ⓔ	13 Ⓐ Ⓑ Ⓒ Ⓓ Ⓔ	18 Ⓐ Ⓑ Ⓒ Ⓓ Ⓔ	23 Ⓐ Ⓑ Ⓒ Ⓓ Ⓔ
4 Ⓐ Ⓑ Ⓒ Ⓓ Ⓔ	9 Ⓐ Ⓑ Ⓒ Ⓓ Ⓔ	14 Ⓐ Ⓑ Ⓒ Ⓓ Ⓔ	19 Ⓐ Ⓑ Ⓒ Ⓓ Ⓔ	24 Ⓐ Ⓑ Ⓒ Ⓓ Ⓔ
5 Ⓐ Ⓑ Ⓒ Ⓓ Ⓔ	10 Ⓐ Ⓑ Ⓒ Ⓓ Ⓔ	15 Ⓐ Ⓑ Ⓒ Ⓓ Ⓔ	20 Ⓐ Ⓑ Ⓒ Ⓓ Ⓔ	25 Ⓐ Ⓑ Ⓒ Ⓓ Ⓔ

right in section 1

wrong in section 1

SECTION 3

1 Ⓐ Ⓑ Ⓒ Ⓓ Ⓔ	9 Ⓐ Ⓑ Ⓒ Ⓓ Ⓔ	17 Ⓐ Ⓑ Ⓒ Ⓓ Ⓔ	25 Ⓐ Ⓑ Ⓒ Ⓓ Ⓔ	33 Ⓐ Ⓑ Ⓒ Ⓓ Ⓔ
2 Ⓐ Ⓑ Ⓒ Ⓓ Ⓔ	10 Ⓐ Ⓑ Ⓒ Ⓓ Ⓔ	18 Ⓐ Ⓑ Ⓒ Ⓓ Ⓔ	26 Ⓐ Ⓑ Ⓒ Ⓓ Ⓔ	34 Ⓐ Ⓑ Ⓒ Ⓓ Ⓔ
3 Ⓐ Ⓑ Ⓒ Ⓓ Ⓔ	11 Ⓐ Ⓑ Ⓒ Ⓓ Ⓔ	19 Ⓐ Ⓑ Ⓒ Ⓓ Ⓔ	27 Ⓐ Ⓑ Ⓒ Ⓓ Ⓔ	35 Ⓐ Ⓑ Ⓒ Ⓓ Ⓔ
4 Ⓐ Ⓑ Ⓒ Ⓓ Ⓔ	12 Ⓐ Ⓑ Ⓒ Ⓓ Ⓔ	20 Ⓐ Ⓑ Ⓒ Ⓓ Ⓔ	28 Ⓐ Ⓑ Ⓒ Ⓓ Ⓔ	36 Ⓐ Ⓑ Ⓒ Ⓓ Ⓔ
5 Ⓐ Ⓑ Ⓒ Ⓓ Ⓔ	13 Ⓐ Ⓑ Ⓒ Ⓓ Ⓔ	21 Ⓐ Ⓑ Ⓒ Ⓓ Ⓔ	29 Ⓐ Ⓑ Ⓒ Ⓓ Ⓔ	37 Ⓐ Ⓑ Ⓒ Ⓓ Ⓔ
6 Ⓐ Ⓑ Ⓒ Ⓓ Ⓔ	14 Ⓐ Ⓑ Ⓒ Ⓓ Ⓔ	22 Ⓐ Ⓑ Ⓒ Ⓓ Ⓔ	30 Ⓐ Ⓑ Ⓒ Ⓓ Ⓔ	38 Ⓐ Ⓑ Ⓒ Ⓓ Ⓔ
7 Ⓐ Ⓑ Ⓒ Ⓓ Ⓔ	15 Ⓐ Ⓑ Ⓒ Ⓓ Ⓔ	23 Ⓐ Ⓑ Ⓒ Ⓓ Ⓔ	31 Ⓐ Ⓑ Ⓒ Ⓓ Ⓔ	39 Ⓐ Ⓑ Ⓒ Ⓓ Ⓔ
8 Ⓐ Ⓑ Ⓒ Ⓓ Ⓔ	16 Ⓐ Ⓑ Ⓒ Ⓓ Ⓔ	24 Ⓐ Ⓑ Ⓒ Ⓓ Ⓔ	32 Ⓐ Ⓑ Ⓒ Ⓓ Ⓔ	40 Ⓐ Ⓑ Ⓒ Ⓓ Ⓔ

right in section 2

wrong in section 2

SECTION 4

1 Ⓐ Ⓑ Ⓒ Ⓓ Ⓔ	13 Ⓐ Ⓑ Ⓒ Ⓓ Ⓔ	25 Ⓐ Ⓑ Ⓒ Ⓓ Ⓔ	37 Ⓐ Ⓑ Ⓒ Ⓓ Ⓔ	49 Ⓐ Ⓑ Ⓒ Ⓓ Ⓔ
2 Ⓐ Ⓑ Ⓒ Ⓓ Ⓔ	14 Ⓐ Ⓑ Ⓒ Ⓓ Ⓔ	26 Ⓐ Ⓑ Ⓒ Ⓓ Ⓔ	38 Ⓐ Ⓑ Ⓒ Ⓓ Ⓔ	50 Ⓐ Ⓑ Ⓒ Ⓓ Ⓔ
3 Ⓐ Ⓑ Ⓒ Ⓓ Ⓔ	15 Ⓐ Ⓑ Ⓒ Ⓓ Ⓔ	27 Ⓐ Ⓑ Ⓒ Ⓓ Ⓔ	39 Ⓐ Ⓑ Ⓒ Ⓓ Ⓔ	51 Ⓐ Ⓑ Ⓒ Ⓓ Ⓔ
4 Ⓐ Ⓑ Ⓒ Ⓓ Ⓔ	16 Ⓐ Ⓑ Ⓒ Ⓓ Ⓔ	28 Ⓐ Ⓑ Ⓒ Ⓓ Ⓔ	40 Ⓐ Ⓑ Ⓒ Ⓓ Ⓔ	52 Ⓐ Ⓑ Ⓒ Ⓓ Ⓔ
5 Ⓐ Ⓑ Ⓒ Ⓓ Ⓔ	17 Ⓐ Ⓑ Ⓒ Ⓓ Ⓔ	29 Ⓐ Ⓑ Ⓒ Ⓓ Ⓔ	41 Ⓐ Ⓑ Ⓒ Ⓓ Ⓔ	53 Ⓐ Ⓑ Ⓒ Ⓓ Ⓔ
6 Ⓐ Ⓑ Ⓒ Ⓓ Ⓔ	18 Ⓐ Ⓑ Ⓒ Ⓓ Ⓔ	30 Ⓐ Ⓑ Ⓒ Ⓓ Ⓔ	42 Ⓐ Ⓑ Ⓒ Ⓓ Ⓔ	54 Ⓐ Ⓑ Ⓒ Ⓓ Ⓔ
7 Ⓐ Ⓑ Ⓒ Ⓓ Ⓔ	19 Ⓐ Ⓑ Ⓒ Ⓓ Ⓔ	31 Ⓐ Ⓑ Ⓒ Ⓓ Ⓔ	43 Ⓐ Ⓑ Ⓒ Ⓓ Ⓔ	55 Ⓐ Ⓑ Ⓒ Ⓓ Ⓔ
8 Ⓐ Ⓑ Ⓒ Ⓓ Ⓔ	20 Ⓐ Ⓑ Ⓒ Ⓓ Ⓔ	32 Ⓐ Ⓑ Ⓒ Ⓓ Ⓔ	44 Ⓐ Ⓑ Ⓒ Ⓓ Ⓔ	56 Ⓐ Ⓑ Ⓒ Ⓓ Ⓔ
9 Ⓐ Ⓑ Ⓒ Ⓓ Ⓔ	21 Ⓐ Ⓑ Ⓒ Ⓓ Ⓔ	33 Ⓐ Ⓑ Ⓒ Ⓓ Ⓔ	45 Ⓐ Ⓑ Ⓒ Ⓓ Ⓔ	57 Ⓐ Ⓑ Ⓒ Ⓓ Ⓔ
10 Ⓐ Ⓑ Ⓒ Ⓓ Ⓔ	22 Ⓐ Ⓑ Ⓒ Ⓓ Ⓔ	34 Ⓐ Ⓑ Ⓒ Ⓓ Ⓔ	46 Ⓐ Ⓑ Ⓒ Ⓓ Ⓔ	58 Ⓐ Ⓑ Ⓒ Ⓓ Ⓔ
11 Ⓐ Ⓑ Ⓒ Ⓓ Ⓔ	23 Ⓐ Ⓑ Ⓒ Ⓓ Ⓔ	35 Ⓐ Ⓑ Ⓒ Ⓓ Ⓔ	47 Ⓐ Ⓑ Ⓒ Ⓓ Ⓔ	59 Ⓐ Ⓑ Ⓒ Ⓓ Ⓔ
12 Ⓐ Ⓑ Ⓒ Ⓓ Ⓔ	24 Ⓐ Ⓑ Ⓒ Ⓓ Ⓔ	36 Ⓐ Ⓑ Ⓒ Ⓓ Ⓔ	48 Ⓐ Ⓑ Ⓒ Ⓓ Ⓔ	60 Ⓐ Ⓑ Ⓒ Ⓓ Ⓔ

right in section 4

wrong in section 4

SECTION 5

1 Ⓐ Ⓑ Ⓒ Ⓓ Ⓔ	6 Ⓐ Ⓑ Ⓒ Ⓓ Ⓔ	11 Ⓐ Ⓑ Ⓒ Ⓓ Ⓔ	16 Ⓐ Ⓑ Ⓒ Ⓓ Ⓔ	21 Ⓐ Ⓑ Ⓒ Ⓓ Ⓔ
2 Ⓐ Ⓑ Ⓒ Ⓓ Ⓔ	7 Ⓐ Ⓑ Ⓒ Ⓓ Ⓔ	12 Ⓐ Ⓑ Ⓒ Ⓓ Ⓔ	17 Ⓐ Ⓑ Ⓒ Ⓓ Ⓔ	22 Ⓐ Ⓑ Ⓒ Ⓓ Ⓔ
3 Ⓐ Ⓑ Ⓒ Ⓓ Ⓔ	8 Ⓐ Ⓑ Ⓒ Ⓓ Ⓔ	13 Ⓐ Ⓑ Ⓒ Ⓓ Ⓔ	18 Ⓐ Ⓑ Ⓒ Ⓓ Ⓔ	23 Ⓐ Ⓑ Ⓒ Ⓓ Ⓔ
4 Ⓐ Ⓑ Ⓒ Ⓓ Ⓔ	9 Ⓐ Ⓑ Ⓒ Ⓓ Ⓔ	14 Ⓐ Ⓑ Ⓒ Ⓓ Ⓔ	19 Ⓐ Ⓑ Ⓒ Ⓓ Ⓔ	24 Ⓐ Ⓑ Ⓒ Ⓓ Ⓔ
5 Ⓐ Ⓑ Ⓒ Ⓓ Ⓔ	10 Ⓐ Ⓑ Ⓒ Ⓓ Ⓔ	15 Ⓐ Ⓑ Ⓒ Ⓓ Ⓔ	20 Ⓐ Ⓑ Ⓒ Ⓓ Ⓔ	25 Ⓐ Ⓑ Ⓒ Ⓓ Ⓔ

right in section 5

wrong in section 5

SECTION 1

Time—25 Minutes

Write an essay on the following prompt on the paper provided. Your essay should not exceed two pages and must be written in ink. Erasing is not allowed.

Prompt: The early bird gets the worm.

Do you agree or disagree with this statement? Use examples from history, literature, or your own personal experience to support your point of view.

GO ON TO THE NEXT PAGE

IF YOU FINISH BEFORE TIME IS CALLED, YOU MAY CHECK YOUR WORK ON THIS SECTION ONLY. DO NOT TURN TO ANY OTHER SECTION IN THE TEST.

SECTION 2

Time—30 Minutes
25 Questions

In this section, there are five possible answers after each question. Choose which one is best. You may use the blank space at the right of the page for scratch work.

Note: Figures are drawn with the greatest possible accuracy, UNLESS stated "Not Drawn to Scale."

USE THIS SPACE FOR FIGURING.

1. Which of the following shapes can be folded to create a cube with no overlapping flaps?

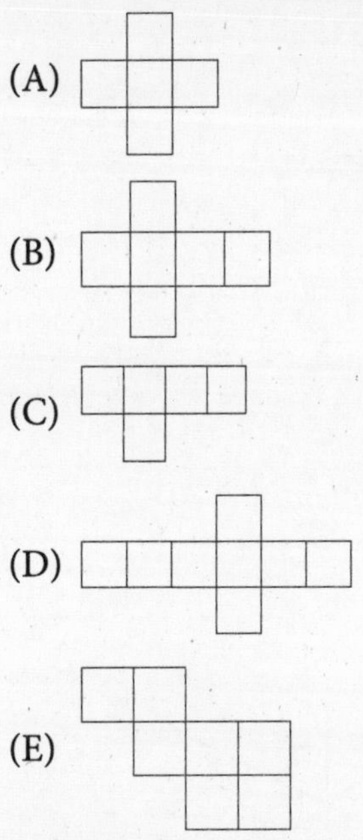

2. Of the following, 20 percent of $19.95 is closest to

   (A) $1.95.
   (B) $2.
   (C) $4.
   (D) $5.
   (E) $20.

GO ON TO THE NEXT PAGE

USE THIS SPACE FOR FIGURING.

3. Dividing 93 by 5 leaves a remainder of

(A) 18.
(B) 5.
(C) 4.
(D) 3.
(E) 2.

4. If 7,000 + ❐ – 500 = 9,500, then ❐ =

(A) 200.
(B) 300.
(C) 2,000.
(D) 2,500.
(E) 3,000.

5. The width of a rectangle is one-third of its length. If the length is 12, what is its perimeter?

(A) 3
(B) 4
(C) 16
(D) 24
(E) 32

6. What is the value of a in Figure 1?

(A) 30
(B) 60
(C) 90
(D) 120
(E) It cannot be determined from the information given.

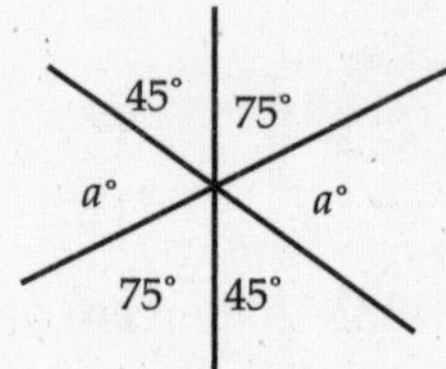

Figure 1

7. Of the following, which number is the greatest?

(A) 0.08
(B) 0.7899
(C) 0.7923
(D) 0.792
(E) 0.79

GO ON TO THE NEXT PAGE

USE THIS SPACE FOR FIGURING.

8. "When 4 is added to three times a number N, the result is 36." Which of the following equations represents this statement?

(A) $4N + 3 = 36$

(B) $36 + 4N = 3$

(C) $36N + 3 = 4$

(D) $3N + 4 = 36$

(E) $36 - 4N = 3$

9. If $N + 5$ is an odd, whole number, then N could be which of the following?

(A) 5

(B) 3

(C) $\frac{1}{2}$

(D) 0

(E) -7

10. A bull is tied to a seven-foot leash in the center of a square pen, as shown in Figure 2. If a side of the pen is 14 feet in length, which figure best shows the shape and size of the area in which the bull can move?

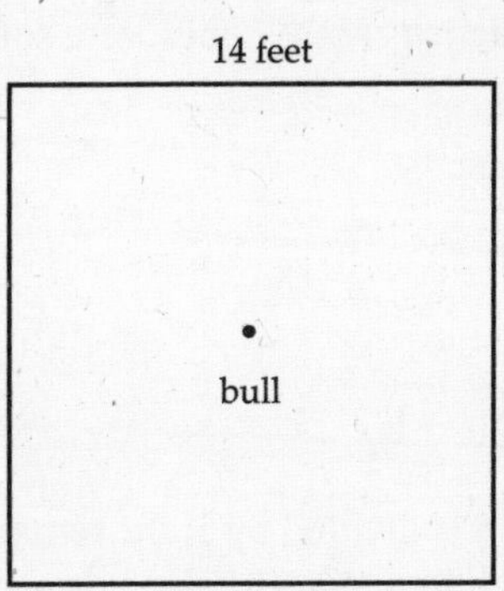

Figure 2

(A)

(B) 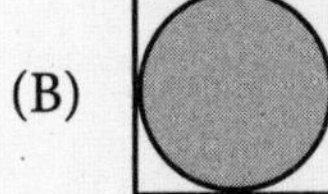

(C) 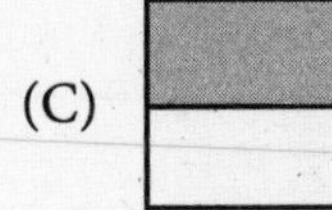

(D) 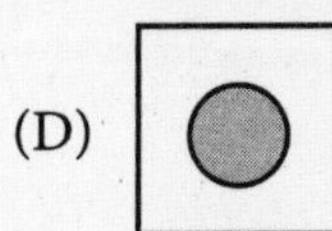

(E) 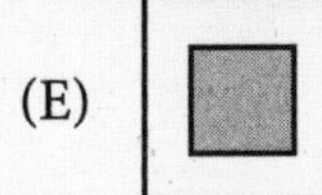

GO ON TO THE NEXT PAGE

USE THIS SPACE FOR FIGURING.

11. $\frac{7}{8} - \frac{5}{8} =$

(A) 0.58
(B) 0.5
(C) 0.375
(D) 0.25
(E) 0.125

12. At sunset the temperature was 20 degrees. By midnight, it had dropped another 32 degrees. What was the temperature at midnight?

(A) 12 degrees below zero
(B) 6 degrees below zero
(C) 0 degrees
(D) 12 degrees above zero
(E) 20 degrees above zero

13. According to the graph in Figure 3, how many chocolate ice cream cones were sold?

(A) 25
(B) 30
(C) 50
(D) 75
(E) 100

Flavors of 300
Ice Cream Cones Served

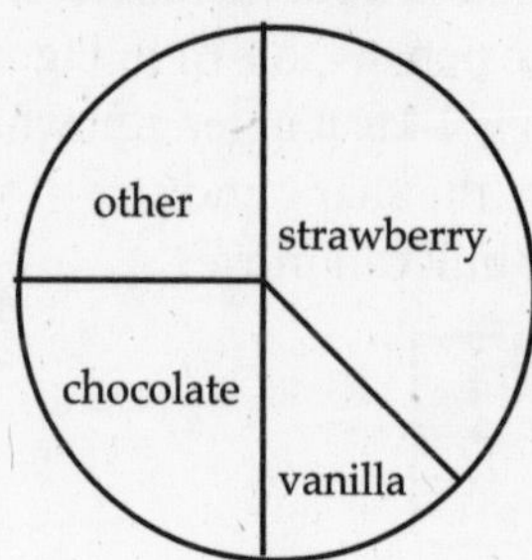

Figure 3

14. When 36 is divided by 5, the remainder is the same as when 65 is divided by

(A) 10
(B) 9
(C) 8
(D) 7
(E) 6

GO ON TO THE NEXT PAGE

USE THIS SPACE FOR FIGURING.

15. According to the graph in Figure 4, what is the average number of 911 calls made from Monday through Thursday, inclusive?

    (A) 500
    (B) 750
    (C) 875
    (D) 1,000
    (E) 1,125

911 Emergency Calls

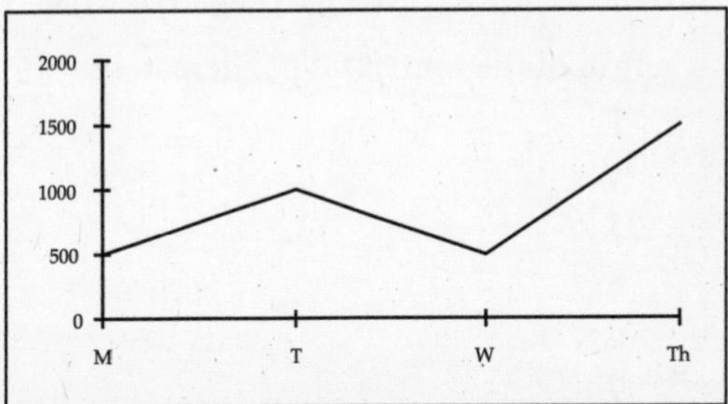

Figure 4

<u>Questions 16–18</u> refer to the following definition.

For all real numbers y and z, let $y @ z = y \times z - 2$.

16. $3 @ 7 =$

    (A) 15
    (B) 19
    (C) 21
    (D) 25
    (E) 27

17. If $y @ 4 = 6$, then y must equal

    (A) 1.
    (B) 2.
    (C) 4.
    (D) 6.
    (E) 12.

18. If $y = \frac{1}{4}$, for what value of z will $y @ z$ equal 0?

    (A) –4
    (B) 4
    (C) 6
    (D) 8
    (E) 10

GO ON TO THE NEXT PAGE

USE THIS SPACE FOR FIGURING.

19. A class of 25 girls and 15 boys built a haunted house for the Halloween carnival. If $\frac{1}{5}$ of the girls and $\frac{2}{3}$ of the boys participated, what fraction of the total class participated?

(A) $\frac{1}{5}$
(B) $\frac{3}{8}$
(C) $\frac{3}{7}$
(D) $\frac{3}{5}$
(E) $\frac{13}{15}$

20. The ratio of 7 to 4 is equal to the ratio of 28 to what number?

(A) 7
(B) 8
(C) 12
(D) 14
(E) 16

21. Which figure CANNOT be drawn without lifting the pencil or retracing?

(A) 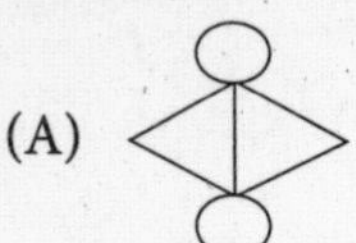

(B) 

(C) 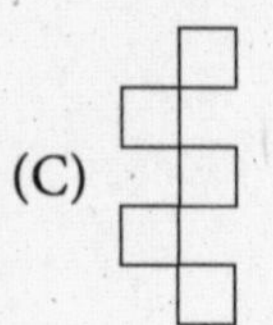

(D) 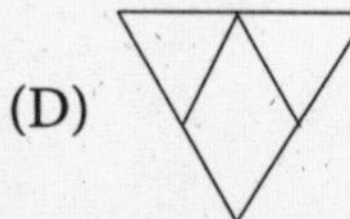

(E) 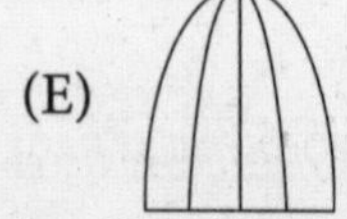

GO ON TO THE NEXT PAGE

USE THIS SPACE FOR FIGURING.

22. Sparkly stickers are \$0.50 and smelly stickers are \$0.60. If Jill buys 5 sparkly stickers and 8 smelly stickers, what is her change from \$10? (Stickers are not taxable.)

(A) \$1.20
(B) \$2
(C) \$2.70
(D) \$3
(E) \$7.30

23. Greg read from 5:00 P.M. to 5:45 P.M and finished one-third of his book. He wants to finish reading his book by 11:00 P.M. If he plans to read at the same rate, what is the latest time he can start reading again?

(A) 7:15 P.M.
(B) 8:00 P.M.
(C) 8:45 P.M.
(D) 9:30 P.M.
(E) 10:15 P.M.

24. The map in Figure 5 shows all the paths that connect X and Y, and all distances are expressed in miles. How many paths are there from X to Y measuring exactly seven miles?

(A) 2
(B) 3
(C) 4
(D) 5
(E) 6

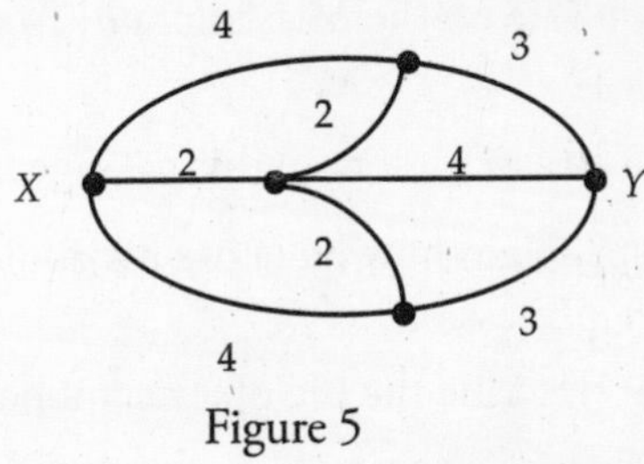

Figure 5

25. A palindrome is a number that is unchanged when the order of its digits is reversed. For example, 232 is a palindrome. Which of the following is one more than a palindrome?

(A) 7,336
(B) 373
(C) 8,337
(D) 7,338
(E) 8,338

IF YOU FINISH BEFORE TIME IS CALLED, YOU MAY CHECK YOUR WORK ON THIS SECTION ONLY. DO NOT TURN TO ANY OTHER SECTION IN THE TEST. **STOP**

SECTION 3

Time—40 Minutes
40 Questions

Read each passage carefully and then answer the questions about it. For each question, decide on the basis of the passage which one of the choices best answers the question.

When I was a boy, there was but one permanent ambition among my comrades in our village on the west bank of the Mississippi River. That was, to be a steamboat-man. We had transient ambitions of other sorts, but they were only transient. When a circus came and went, it left us all burning to become clowns; the first minstrel show that came to our section left us all suffering to try that kind of life; now and then we had a hope that if we loved and were good, God would permit us to be pirates. These ambitions faded out, each in its turn; but the ambition to be a steamboat-man always remained.

From Life on the Mississippi *by Mark Twain*

1. The author's intent in this passage is to

(A) explain how he chose his adult profession.
(B) describe the life of a steamboat-man.
(C) convey some of his childhood aspirations.
(D) compare the merits of several different occupations.
(E) present a social history of the Mississippi.

2. According to the passage, the author considered all of the following as possible careers EXCEPT

(A) steamboat-man.
(B) clown.
(C) minstrel.
(D) writer.
(E) pirate.

3. As it is used in line 5, the word "transient" means

(A) appealing.
(B) relative.
(C) short-lived.
(D) disastrous.
(E) equal.

4. The author most likely uses the phrase "all burning to become clowns" in order to

(A) provide an example of the boys' fleeting ambitions.
(B) illustrate the lack of cultural life in Mississippi.
(C) encourage his readers to follow similar career paths.
(D) clarify why the boys all wanted to be steamboat-men.
(E) show the kind of people that traveled on steamboats.

5. Which of the following best describes the effect of the phrase "if we loved and were good, God would permit us to be pirates"?

(A) Pathos
(B) Humor
(C) Exaggeration
(D) Mockery
(E) Rhyme

GO ON TO THE NEXT PAGE

6. The attitude of the author toward the subject is

(A) nostalgic.
(B) regretful.
(C) optimistic.
(D) cynical.
(E) somber.

7. The reader can infer from the passage that

(A) the author and his friends looked forward to leaving the village.
(B) no girls hoped to navigate the river by steamboat.
(C) the author became a steamboat-man.
(D) the author regrets not becoming a pirate.
(E) the author disliked growing up on the Mississippi River.

Alchemy is the name given to the attempt to change lead, copper, and other metals into silver or gold. Today, alchemy is regarded as a pseudoscience. Its associations with astrology and the occult suggest primitive superstition to the modern mind, and the alchemist is generally portrayed by historians as a charlatan obsessed with dreams of impossible wealth. For many centuries, however, alchemy was a highly respected art. In the search for the elusive secret to making gold, alchemists helped develop many of the apparatuses and procedures that are used in laboratories today. Moreover, the results of their experiments laid the basic conceptual framework of the modern science of chemistry.

8. The passage is mainly about the

(A) early history of a scientific field.
(B) manufacture of gold from other metals.
(C) mystery surrounding the origins of chemistry.
(D) links among chemistry, astrology and sociology.
(E) specific results of alchemists' experiments.

9. According to the passage, alchemists are generally portrayed in history books as

(A) wealthy businessmen.
(B) rogues motivated by greed.
(C) talented but misunderstood individuals.
(D) the ancestors of today's chemists.
(E) brilliant scientists.

10. It can be inferred from the passage that a "charlatan" (line 7)

(A) existed only in the Middle Ages.
(B) is not respected by historians.
(C) practiced an early form of chemistry.
(D) uses his research for criminal purposes.
(E) understood the secret to making gold.

11. The style of the passage is most like that found in a

(A) scientist's diary.
(B) novel about alchemists.
(C) history textbook.
(D) newspaper article.
(E) personal letter.

12. With which of the following statements would the author most likely agree?

(A) Few alchemists ever became wealthy from their work.
(B) Alchemy was a primitive, superstitious field of science.
(C) Alchemy is becoming increasingly respectable among today's chemists.
(D) Astrology and the occult also deserve consideration as legitimate sciences.
(E) Alchemists helped pave the way for scientists today.

GO ON TO THE NEXT PAGE

13. The following questions are all answered by the passage EXCEPT:
    (A) What did alchemists hope to achieve?
    (B) What have alchemists contributed to science?
    (C) How do historians view alchemy?
    (D) How did alchemists turn metals into gold?
    (E) Has the general consensus always been that alchemists were charlatans?

14. Which of these titles is the most appropriate for the passage?
    (A) Alchemy as Art
    (B) Turning Copper to Gold
    (C) In Pursuit of Wealth
    (D) Alchemists: Charlatans or Scientists?
    (E) Alchemy's Contributions to Science

On May 18, 1980, in Washington State, the volcano Mount Saint Helens erupted, sending a cloud of dust 15 miles into the air. The explosion was not unexpected; the earth's crust had shaken for weeks beforehand, providing people in the surrounding area with plenty of advance warning. In spite of these danger signals, no one was prepared for the extent of the blast; over the course of several weeks, the volcano's eruption ripped the top 1,300 feet off the mountain, resulting in a landslide that was the largest in recorded history. 540 million tons of ash from the volcano were spread over three states, altering the earth's weather patterns for several years afterward. One thing missing from the initial eruption was fluid lava usually identified with volcanic activity. Later eruptions emitted a thick and oozing lava. Thick lava is easily outrun because it moves extremely slowly. In addition, thick lava creates taller volcanoes because it often cools and hardens instead of flowing down the volcano's sides.

15. This passage is primarily about
    (A) the geological history of Washington State.
    (B) the difficulty of predicting volcanic activity.
    (C) a contrast between different forms of lava.
    (D) a story of an unusual geological event.
    (E) the factors that cause landslides.

16. As used in line 6, the word "advance" means
    (A) ahead of time.
    (B) moving forward.
    (C) in the past.
    (D) undetected.
    (E) extremely urgent.

17. According to the passage, all of the following were caused by the Mount Saint Helens eruption EXCEPT
    (A) tidal waves.
    (B) streams of lava.
    (C) a massive landslide.
    (D) changes in the earth's climate.
    (E) the emission of clouds of ash.

18. It can be inferred from the passage that fluid lava (lines 15 and 16)
    (A) is very thick.
    (B) creates tall volcanoes.
    (C) is only found in the United States.
    (D) is not easily outrun.
    (E) destroyed many forests in Washington.

GO ON TO THE NEXT PAGE

19. The author's style is best described as

    (A) surprised.
    (B) dramatic.
    (C) skeptical.
    (D) informative.
    (E) mysterious.

20. The author most likely mentions "providing people in the surrounding area with plenty of advance warning" in order to

    (A) show that experts thought they knew what was coming.
    (B) indicate that no one was hurt in the blast.
    (C) criticize people who did not evacuate on time.
    (D) describe how experts were not seeing fluid lava.
    (E) convey the importance of volcano warning systems.

The cowboy of the American West is an enduring icon in popular culture, but Hawaiian cowboys predated their American counterparts by several decades. In 1792, King Kamehameha the Great of Hawaii received gifts of beef cattle, goats, sheep, and horses from Captain George Vancouver. The introduction of these unfamiliar animals caused unrest among the native islanders, because the unruly animals often trampled the crops in their fields. Initially, the king protected his imports from wrathful Hawaiians under kapu laws. But in 1830, Kamehameha III decided to hire a few Spanish vaqueros from California to keep the animals under control. Soon the Hawaiians were riding, roping, and lassoing alongside the Spanish cowboys.

21. It can be inferred from the passage that the American cowboy

    (A) taught the Hawaiians how to ride and lasso.
    (B) accompanied the shipment of horses and cattle to Hawaii.
    (C) did not understand the Hawaiians' opposition to horses.
    (D) emerged in the West later than his counterpart in Hawaii.
    (E) was not able to lasso as well as the Hawaiian cowboy.

22. According to the passage, all of the following are true about horses and cattle EXCEPT

    (A) they were unfamiliar to Hawaiians before 1792.
    (B) they were introduced to Hawaii in the 18th century.
    (C) they were protected by Hawaiian law.
    (D) they were found to be too expensive to import.
    (E) they were destructive to Hawaiian property.

23. According to the passage, the Hawaiian cowboys

    I. were taught to ride by the Spanish vaqueros.
    II. existed earlier than the American cowboys.
    III. proved better at roping and lassoing than their American counterparts.

    (A) I only
    (B) II only
    (C) I and II only
    (D) II and III only
    (E) I, II, and III

GO ON TO THE NEXT PAGE

24. This passage is primarily about
    (A) the roping of cattle.
    (B) the history of King Kamehameha.
    (C) the Spanish relationship with Hawaii.
    (D) the history of horses in Hawaii.
    (E) the introduction of cowboys to Hawaii.

25. The attitude of the writer toward the subject is
    (A) biased.
    (B) condescending.
    (C) neutral.
    (D) elated.
    (E) confused.

26. As it is used in line 11, "wrathful" most nearly means
    (A) tolerant.
    (B) enraged.
    (C) accommodating.
    (D) confused.
    (E) vengeful.

27. Which of the following questions is NOT answered by the passage?
    (A) How did Hawaiians view Capt. George Vancouver's gifts?
    (B) What effect did the vaqueros have on the animals?
    (C) What can be implied about the author's attitude toward the cowboys?
    (D) For how many years did the animals cause unrest in Hawaii?
    (E) How did the king use kapu laws in Hawaii to protect animals?

In recent years, scientific research has done much to alter long-held beliefs about history. This is particularly true of scholarship surrounding the Silk Road. The Silk Road was a trans-Asian trading route that extended across two continents, linking China with the center of European trade in the Mediterranean. Most famous for the transport of silk, this ancient highway was also the conduit for such items as roses, peaches, gunpowder, and paper. Systems of belief were also passed along the road: The spread of Christianity, Buddhism, and Islam was accelerated by the connection between East and West.

Based on historical texts, historians have traditionally believed that the Silk Road was established in 115 B.C.E., yet the recent discovery of a much older piece of silk in Egypt suggests that the road was established at least a thousand years earlier. Through carbon dating, scientists dated the fabric of the newly discovered piece of silk to around 1000 B.C.E. In that period, only the Chinese held the secret to silk manufacturing; Mediterranean countries would not develop the technology to manufacture silk until the sixth century C.E. As a result, historians now believe that Asia and Europe may have traded silk via the Silk Road as long ago as the second century B.C.E.—though exactly how traders navigated the plateaus, mountains, and deserts that lie along the route remains a mystery.

28. This passage is primarily about
    (A) the impact of a new discovery on a historical theory.
    (B) ancient trading routes between East and West.
    (C) the introduction of silk manufacturing to Europe.
    (D) conflict between Chinese and Mediterranean traders.
    (E) the spread of Christianity, Buddhism, and Islam.

GO ON TO THE NEXT PAGE

29. As used in line 10, the phrase "systems of belief" most likely means

(A) travel routes.
(B) organizations.
(C) languages.
(D) religions.
(E) military secrets.

30. According to the passage, all of the following were traded along the Silk Road EXCEPT

(A) fabrics.
(B) explosives.
(C) fruit.
(D) flowers.
(E) jewels.

31. It can be inferred from paragraph 2 that historians believe that

(A) the silk fragment discovered in Egypt was a fake.
(B) most ancient Egyptian garments were made of silk.
(C) the ancient Egyptians were unable to cross plateaus, mountains, or deserts.
(D) carbon dating is not the most accurate method of dating artifacts.
(E) the ancient silk fragment found in Egypt must have been imported from China.

32. The author's style is best described as

(A) surprised.
(B) dramatic.
(C) poetic.
(D) mysterious.
(E) informative.

33. According to the passage, it is reasonable to assume that

(A) civilizations used the Silk Road for more than just trade.
(B) the Silk Road had not been established yet in 200 B.C.E.
(C) historians can't say for sure whether the recent silk discovery was from Asia.
(D) the author believes the Silk Road never existed.
(E) if it weren't for the Silk Road, Mediterranean countries never would have developed silk-producing technology.

During the 15th century, the Belgian city Bruges was the most important commercial city in the north of Europe. Like Florence in Italy, Bruges derived its wealth from wool and banking. Ships brought raw wool there from England and Spain and carried away finished wool cloth, which was celebrated throughout Europe. Bankers came to Bruges on the heels of the wool merchants—among them, representatives of the House of Medici. Soon Bruges became the financial center for all of northern Europe. Merchants from Italy, the Near East, Russia, and Spain all congregated in Bruges. Even though nearby cities such as Ghent and Louvain also flourished, Bruges so outshone them in prosperity that the Duke of Burgundy made that city his capital and moved his court there in the early 15th century.

34. As it is used in line 4, the word "derived" most nearly means

(A) created.
(B) exchanged.
(C) invested.
(D) obtained.
(E) traveled.

GO ON TO THE NEXT PAGE

35. It can be inferred from the text that the arrival of representatives of the House of Medici in Bruges

    (A) improved the quality of life for all residents of Bruges.
    (B) increased the amount of raw wool brought to Bruges.
    (C) required the city to provide official translators.
    (D) secured the status of Bruges as an important financial center.
    (E) lowered the level of market activity in Bruges.

36. It can be inferred from the text that the wool brought to Bruges

    (A) was of the best quality available in northern Europe.
    (B) was not instrumental in Bruges's growth as a financial center.
    (C) was woven into cloth and shipped throughout Europe.
    (D) was also sent to rival towns Ghent and Louvain.
    (E) was as valuable as gold and other precious metals.

37. The author most likely mentions "merchants from Italy, the Near East, Russia, and Spain" in order to

    (A) illustrate the variety of merchants involved in the wool trade.
    (B) convey the excitement of Europe in the 15th century.
    (C) portray the peaceful cooperation of European countries.
    (D) indicate the poverty of trade in those countries.
    (E) demonstrate how successful Bruges became.

38. According to the text, why did the Duke of Burgundy choose Bruges over Ghent and Louvain as the site of his court?

    (A) Ghent was on the verge of a financial crisis.
    (B) Ghent and Louvain were too far away from Burgundy.
    (C) Bruges was unquestionably the most wealthy city.
    (D) Bruges produced a higher quality of wool fabric.
    (E) More painters and musicians lived in Bruges than in other cities.

GO ON TO THE NEXT PAGE

39. Which of the following best states the main idea of the passage?

    (A) The growth of the wool trade transformed commerce in the Renaissance.

    (B) Tired of his court in France, the Duke of Burgundy moved to Bruges.

    (C) Wool and banking made Bruges the commercial center of northern Europe.

    (D) Bruges outshone Florence in prosperity and cultural diversity.

    (E) Most 15th-century cities centered around banking and wool manufacture.

40. All of the following are reasons why Bruges was an important city EXCEPT

    (A) its prosperity brought prosperity to other cities.

    (B) it was a central meeting place for foreign merchants.

    (C) it provided a venue for wool traders to exchange merchandise.

    (D) it became the heart of banking in the region.

    (E) its status as the Belgian capital made it a commercial center.

IF YOU FINISH BEFORE TIME IS CALLED, YOU MAY CHECK YOUR WORK ON THIS SECTION ONLY. DO NOT TURN TO ANY OTHER SECTION IN THE TEST.

STOP

SECTION 4

Time—30 Minutes
60 Questions

This section consists of two different types of questions. There are directions for each type.

Each of the following questions consists of one word followed by five words or phrases. You are to select the one word or phrase whose meaning is closest to the word in capital letters.

1. ALIAS:
   (A) formal relationship
   (B) assumed name
   (C) blatant falsehood
   (D) presumed location
   (E) deep emotion

2. PHOBIA:
   (A) illumination
   (B) retraction
   (C) anxiety
   (D) height
   (E) dismissal

3. PROPEL:
   (A) intend
   (B) belie
   (C) fly
   (D) project
   (E) repel

4. HEADSTRONG:
   (A) foreign
   (B) delicate
   (C) stubborn
   (D) useless
   (E) hysterical

5. CODDLE:
   (A) baby
   (B) waddle
   (C) carry
   (D) riddle
   (E) assume

6. KEEN:
   (A) sharp
   (B) nice
   (C) forgiving
   (D) dense
   (E) rotund

7. MURKY:
   (A) religious
   (B) musty
   (C) sentimental
   (D) gloomy
   (E) forgetful

8. TRYING:
   (A) impossible
   (B) strenuous
   (C) easy
   (D) weathered
   (E) morose

GO ON TO THE NEXT PAGE

9. ADHERE:
   (A) connect
   (B) alter
   (C) stick
   (D) listen
   (E) complete

10. ENIGMATIC:
   (A) attractive
   (B) confused
   (C) happy
   (D) mysterious
   (E) unfortunate

11. POMPOUS:
   (A) flat
   (B) concerned
   (C) arranged
   (D) colorful
   (E) pretentious

12. FATAL:
   (A) childish
   (B) painful
   (C) accidental
   (D) social
   (E) lethal

13. FREQUENT:
   (A) general
   (B) frail
   (C) locomotive
   (D) various
   (E) habitual

14. OSTENTATIOUS:
   (A) prevalent
   (B) confident
   (C) repetitive
   (D) flashy
   (E) elongated

15. DEARTH:
   (A) mortality
   (B) fear
   (C) lack
   (D) consumption
   (E) approval

16. BUFFET:
   (A) toss about
   (B) serenade to
   (C) place upon
   (D) start over
   (E) send back

17. WAIVE:
   (A) fold over
   (B) ride on
   (C) climb under
   (D) urge on
   (E) give up

18. INDUSTRY:
   (A) element
   (B) accusation
   (C) diligence
   (D) phobia
   (E) warehouse

GO ON TO THE NEXT PAGE

19. TREPIDATION:
    (A) fear
    (B) agriculture
    (C) masterpiece
    (D) scarcity
    (E) acumen

20. CONDONE:
    (A) respect
    (B) approve
    (C) give
    (D) stifle
    (E) elevate

21. HARBINGER:
    (A) messenger
    (B) entry
    (C) dock
    (D) lagoon
    (E) consequence

22. SENTRY:
    (A) watch
    (B) beginning
    (C) row
    (D) revolutionary
    (E) companion

23. ORBIT:
    (A) program
    (B) inertia
    (C) revolution
    (D) galaxy
    (E) project

24. PARADOX:
    (A) submission
    (B) contradiction
    (C) dislike
    (D) imperfection
    (E) curse

25. BUFFOON:
    (A) gas
    (B) median
    (C) sphere
    (D) fool
    (E) gift

26. IMMINENT:
    (A) impenetrable
    (B) impossible
    (C) immature
    (D) implicated
    (E) impending

27. TUMULT:
    (A) sustenance
    (B) disorder
    (C) juvenilia
    (D) dossier
    (E) philosophy

28. SPURN:
    (A) unearth
    (B) incinerate
    (C) twirl
    (D) reject
    (E) clash

GO ON TO THE NEXT PAGE

29. PLETHORA:
    (A) compassion
    (B) excess
    (C) waste
    (D) forewarning
    (E) myth

30. DISSEMINATE:
    (A) discourage
    (B) renovate
    (C) broadcast
    (D) clarify
    (E) subside

The following questions ask you to find relationships between words. For each question, select the choice that best completes the meaning of the sentence.

31. Scissors is to cut as pencil is to
    (A) snip.
    (B) write.
    (C) raze.
    (D) turn.
    (E) read.

32. Pasta is to sauce as
    (A) noodle is to dough.
    (B) tomato is to vine.
    (C) napkin is to plate.
    (D) toast is to jam.
    (E) cheese is to milk.

33. Bread is to crust as orange is to
    (A) butter.
    (B) pudding.
    (C) rind.
    (D) tree.
    (E) lemon.

34. Team is to captain as
    (A) sport is to player.
    (B) paper is to reporter.
    (C) republic is to president.
    (D) game to opponent.
    (E) navy is to ensign.

35. Olfactory is to smell as
    (A) sweet is to mouth.
    (B) allergic is to nose.
    (C) heavy is to strength.
    (D) seasonal is to flower.
    (E) tactile is to touch.

36. Ruler is to measure as camera is to
    (A) piano.
    (B) lung.
    (C) soul.
    (D) limb.
    (E) photograph.

37. Tiptoe is to walk as
    (A) whisper is to speech.
    (B) dance is to rhythm.
    (C) tumble is to tree.
    (D) rasp is to throat.
    (E) press is to wrinkle.

GO ON TO THE NEXT PAGE

38. Kernel is to central as trivia is to
    (A) controversial.
    (B) unimportant.
    (C) unleavened.
    (D) harvested.
    (E) productive.

39. Fib is to liar as
    (A) perform is to crew.
    (B) convict is to attorney.
    (C) flatter is to toady.
    (D) campaign is to politician.
    (E) tally is to banker.

40. Nap is to sleep as snack is to
    (A) rest.
    (B) meal.
    (C) biscuit.
    (D) part.
    (E) age.

41. Fossil is to petrified as
    (A) solution is to dissolved.
    (B) wood is to hard.
    (C) snowflake is wet.
    (D) fog is to dense.
    (E) gully is to craggy.

42. Sphere is to round as
    (A) rectangle is to shape.
    (B) protractor is to angle.
    (C) ball is to rubber.
    (D) triangle is to line.
    (E) honeycomb is to hexagonal.

43. Careful is to picky as
    (A) tired is to exhausted.
    (B) alert is to asleep.
    (C) concerned is to grateful.
    (D) forgiving is to peaceful.
    (E) fancy is to short.

44. Cave is to rock as apse is to
    (A) cliff.
    (B) plateau.
    (C) patio.
    (D) church.
    (E) stage.

45. Lemonade is to lemon as
    (A) juice is to cherry.
    (B) berry is to stain.
    (C) glass is to ivory.
    (D) paper is to wood.
    (E) stone is to mud.

46. Frog is to amphibian as whale is to
    (A) mammal.
    (B) toad.
    (C) sea.
    (D) branch.
    (E) fur.

47. Dentist is to drill as
    (A) surgeon is to scalpel.
    (B) doctor is to stretcher.
    (C) farmer is to grain.
    (D) manager is to computer.
    (E) pilot is to wing.

GO ON TO THE NEXT PAGE

48. Mosaic is to tile as
(A) advertisement is to magazine.
(B) tapestry is to thread.
(C) billboard is to chart.
(D) sweater is to wool.
(E) poster is to frame.

49. Pebble is to rock as drop is to
(A) boulder.
(B) fountain.
(C) sand.
(D) liquid.
(E) grain.

50. Levee is to river as
(A) sail is to boat.
(B) bridge is to truck.
(C) train is to track.
(D) path is to forest.
(E) shoulder is to road.

51. Redundant is to necessary as
(A) desirable is to pretty.
(B) original is to needed.
(C) plain is to valuable.
(D) vague is to explicit.
(E) fake is to expensive.

52. Coral is to pink as aquamarine is to
(A) deep.
(B) rosy.
(C) shady.
(D) bland.
(E) blue.

53. Fan is to air as heart is to
(A) power.
(B) heat.
(C) lung.
(D) wind.
(E) blood.

54. Palette is to colors as
(A) kaleidoscope is to glass.
(B) collage is to images.
(C) paint is to canvases.
(D) brush is to pictures.
(E) side is to picture.

55. Salutation is to letter as
(A) postscript is to note.
(B) heading is to stationery.
(C) introduction is to book.
(D) postcard is to picture.
(E) handwriting is to analysis.

56. Quill is to porcupine as
(A) needle is to thread.
(B) wing is to duck.
(C) pouch is to kangaroo.
(D) tail is to pig.
(E) scent is to skunk.

57. Caterpillar is to butterfly as
(A) salmon is to fish.
(B) egg is to dinosaur.
(C) tadpole is to frog.
(D) nest is to chick.
(E) worm is to bait.

GO ON TO THE NEXT PAGE

58. Budget is to cost as
    (A) blueprint is to design.
    (B) ratio is to value.
    (C) demonstration is to argument.
    (D) definition is to vocabulary.
    (E) foundation is to concrete.

59. Juror is to judge as soothsayer is to
    (A) predict.
    (B) soften.
    (C) report.
    (D) punish.
    (E) deny.

60. Buffer is to impact as
    (A) median is to lane.
    (B) boundary is to design.
    (C) antiseptic is to infection.
    (D) bandage is to heal.
    (E) injury is to fault.

IF YOU FINISH BEFORE TIME IS CALLED, YOU MAY CHECK YOUR WORK ON THIS SECTION ONLY. DO NOT TURN TO ANY OTHER SECTION IN THE TEST. **STOP**

SECTION 5

Time—30 Minutes
25 Questions

In this section, there are five possible answer choices after each question. Choose which one is best. You may use the blank space at the right of the page for scratch work.

Note: Figures are drawn with the greatest possible accuracy, UNLESS stated "Not Drawn to Scale."

USE THIS SPACE FOR FIGURING.

1. What is the reciprocal of $\frac{3}{4}$?

(A) $\frac{1}{4}$

(B) $\frac{3}{4}$

(C) $\frac{4}{3}$

(D) 3

(E) 4

2. If $\frac{1}{4}N = 4$, then $\frac{1}{8}N =$

(A) $\frac{1}{2}$.

(B) 1.

(C) 2.

(D) 8.

(E) 16.

3. In Figure 1, the number of shaded triangles is what fractional part of the total number of triangles?

(A) $\frac{1}{3}$

(B) $\frac{2}{5}$

(C) $\frac{2}{3}$

(D) $\frac{4}{5}$

(E) $\frac{3}{2}$

Figure 1

GO ON TO THE NEXT PAGE

USE THIS SPACE FOR FIGURING.

4. If the largest of five consecutive whole numbers is 10, then the average of these numbers is

(A) 6.
(B) 7.
(C) 8.
(D) 9.
(E) 10.

5. $\frac{2}{3} \times \frac{3}{6} \times \frac{2}{4} =$

(A) $\frac{1}{12}$
(B) $\frac{1}{6}$
(C) $\frac{3}{4}$
(D) 1
(E) 2

6. If the perimeter of the polygon in Figure 2 is 24, what is the value of $a + b$?

(A) 5
(B) 7
(C) 9
(D) 10
(E) 15

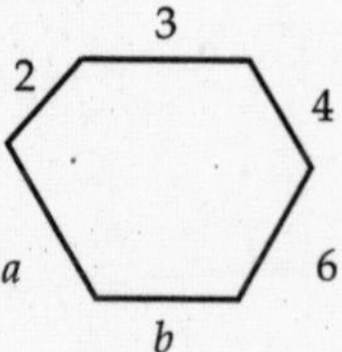

Figure 2

7. Julie's grades for her three math tests were 75, 100, and 89. What is her average grade for these three tests?

(A) 80
(B) 82
(C) 85
(D) 88
(E) 92

GO ON TO THE NEXT PAGE

USE THIS SPACE FOR FIGURING.

8. What is the result when the product of 2 and 6 is subtracted from the sum of 10 and 14 ?

(A) 21
(B) 16
(C) 12
(D) 6
(E) 2

9. N is a whole number between 3 and 6, and also a whole number between 4 and 8. What is the value of N?

(A) 7
(B) 6
(C) 5.5
(D) 5
(E) 4.5

10. All of the following are less than $\frac{3}{4}$ EXCEPT

(A) $\frac{2}{3}$.
(B) $\frac{5}{8}$.
(C) $\frac{14}{16}$.
(D) $\frac{7}{12}$.
(E) $\frac{4}{6}$.

Questions 11–12 refer to the chart in Figure 3.

11. How many more white cars than red cars were sold?

(A) 1
(B) 70
(C) 100
(D) 200
(E) 700

Popularity of Car Colors

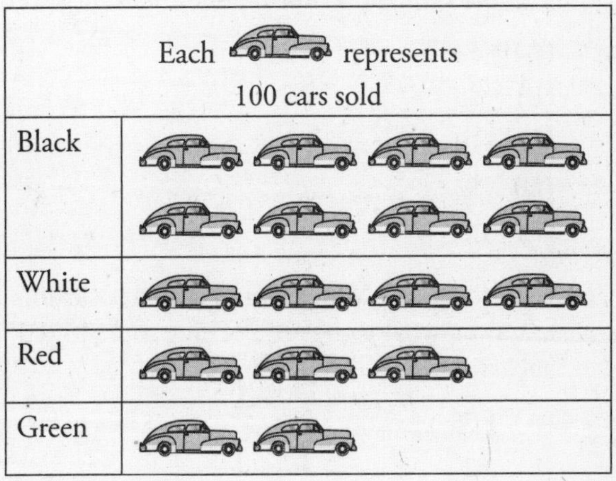

Each represents 100 cars sold

Black
White
Red
Green

Figure 3

GO ON TO THE NEXT PAGE

USE THIS SPACE FOR FIGURING.

12. The number of black cars sold is how many times the number of green cars sold?

(A) 4,000
(B) 440
(C) 400
(D) 40
(E) 4

13. If $3 \times 4 \times N = 6 \times 2$, then $N =$

(A) 0.
(B) 1.
(C) 2.
(D) 12.
(E) 24.

14. If the perimeter of the rectangle in Figure 4 is 20, what is the value of m?

(A) 2
(B) 4
(C) 5
(D) 6
(E) 8

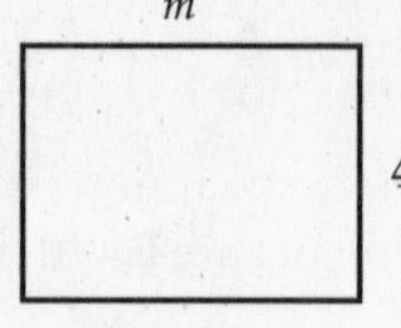

Figure 4

15. A shirt sells for \$40. If Cathy buys the shirt at a 15% discount, how much money does she save?

(A) \$4
(B) \$6
(C) \$10
(D) \$12
(E) \$15

16. If there are 14 blue socks and 21 red socks in a drawer, what is the ratio of blue socks to red socks?

(A) 1:7
(B) 3:2
(C) 2:3
(D) 2:5
(E) 3:5

USE THIS SPACE FOR FIGURING.

17. A bucket is set on a table, as shown in Figure 5. Which of the following describes all of the points where the bucket touches the table?

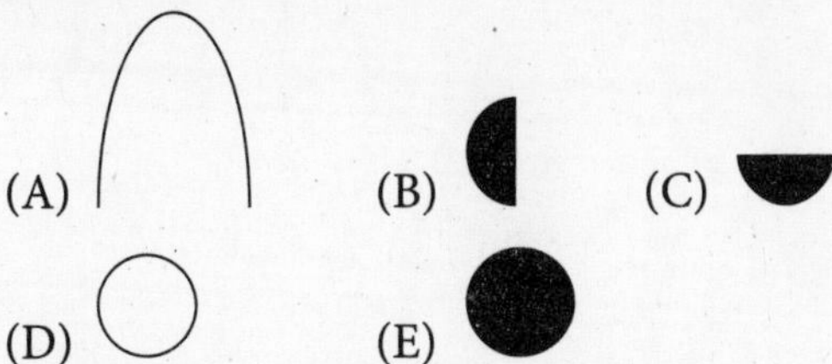

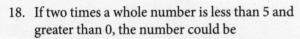

Figure 5

18. If two times a whole number is less than 5 and greater than 0, the number could be

(A) –2.
(B) –1.
(C) 0.
(D) 2.
(E) 4.

19. If Cindy earns $20 per hour, how many hours must she work to earn $420?

(A) 42
(B) 24
(C) 21
(D) 12
(E) 16

20. If 0.73 is about $\frac{N}{8}$, then N is closest to

(A) 100.
(B) 8.
(C) 6.
(D) 4.
(E) 3.

21. In a restaurant, 5 vegetarian meals are ordered for every 7 nonvegetarian meals. What could be the total number of meals sold?

(A) 350
(B) 490
(C) 500
(D) 600
(E) 620

GO ON TO THE NEXT PAGE

USE THIS SPACE FOR FIGURING.

22. If $N \blacklozenge 4 = \frac{1}{4}N$, for which of the following values of N is $N \blacklozenge 4$ NOT a whole number?

(A) 4
(B) 6
(C) 8
(D) 12
(E) 16

23. To which of the following is 1.01 closest?

(A) 0.01
(B) 0.1
(C) 1
(D) 1.1
(E) 11

24. If $\frac{O}{3} = 75$, then $O =$

(A) 75.
(B) 150.
(C) 225.
(D) 300.
(E) 450.

25. When a number is tripled and the result is increased by 4, the number obtained is 25. What is the original number?

(A) 21
(B) 12
(C) 7
(D) 4
(E) 3

IF YOU FINISH BEFORE TIME IS CALLED, YOU MAY CHECK YOUR WORK ON THIS SECTION ONLY. DO NOT TURN TO ANY OTHER SECTION IN THE TEST. **STOP**

ANSWER KEY

Section 2

1. B
2. C
3. D
4. E
5. E
6. B
7. C
8. D
9. D
10. B
11. D
12. A
13. D
14. C
15. C
16. B
17. B
18. D
19. B
20. E
21. E
22. C
23. D
24. C
25. D

Section 3

1. C
2. D
3. C
4. A
5. B
6. A
7. A
8. A
9. B
10. B
11. C
12. E
13. D
14. E
15. D
16. A
17. A
18. D
19. D
20. A
21. D
22. D
23. C
24. E
25. C
26. E
27. E
28. A
29. D
30. E
31. E
32. E
33. A
34. D
35. D
36. C
37. E
38. C
39. C
40. E

Section 4

1. B
2. C
3. D
4. C
5. A
6. A
7. D
8. B
9. C
10. D
11. E
12. E
13. E
14. D
15. C
16. A
17. E
18. C
19. A
20. B
21. A
22. A
23. C
24. B
25. D
26. E
27. B
28. D
29. B
30. C
31. B
32. D
33. C
34. C
35. E
36. E
37. A
38. B
39. C
40. B
41. A
42. E
43. A
44. D
45. D
46. A
47. A
48. B
49. D
50. E
51. D
52. E
53. E
54. B
55. C
56. E
57. C
58. A
59. A
60. C

Section 5

1. C
2. C
3. B
4. C
5. B
6. C
7. D
8. C
9. D
10. C
11. C
12. E
13. B
14. D
15. B
16. C
17. E
18. D
19. C
20. C
21. D
22. B
23. C
24. C
25. C

SSAT PRACTICE TEST 3: LOWER-LEVEL: ASSESS YOUR STRENGTHS

Use the following tables to determine which topics and chapters you need to review most. If you need help with your essay, be sure to review Chapter 9: The Essay and Chapter 26: Writing Skills.

Topic	Question
Math I	Section 2, questions 1–25
Reading Comprehension	Section 3, questions 1–40
Verbal: Synonyms	Section 4, questions 1–30
Verbal: Analogies	Section 4, questions 31–60
Math II	Section 5, questions 1–25

Topic	Number of Questions on Test	Number Correct	If you struggled with these questions, study…
Math I	25		Chapters 10–14 and Chapter 25
Reading Comprehension	40		Chapter 8
Verbal: Synonyms	30		Chapters 7 and 24
Verbal: Analogies	30		Chapters 2 and 24
Math II	25		Chapters 10–14 and Chapter 25

ANSWERS AND EXPLANATIONS

SECTION 2: MATH

1. B

Remember, a cube has six faces. Since you're asked which shape can be folded into a cube with no overlapping flaps, the answer must contain exactly six faces. The only choice that does so is (B).

2. C

You know \$19.95 is close to \$20. Twenty percent of \$20 is \$4, (C).

3. D

Five will divide evenly into numbers that end in five or zero. You are asked to divide 93 by 5. The largest number less than 93 that 5 divides into evenly is 90. This means that five will divide into 93 with a remainder of three.

4. E

This question is essentially an algebra question. Just isolate the ❐ and solve.

$$7{,}000 + \square - 500 = 9{,}500$$
$$7{,}000 + \square = 10{,}000$$
$$\square = 3{,}000$$

5. E

The perimeter of a rectangle is equal to $2(l + w)$, where l and w represent the length and width, respectively. The length of the rectangle is 12, so you need to find its width in order to solve. You're also told that the width of the rectangle is one-third of its length, so $\frac{12}{3}$, or 4, is its width. Plugging in the formula, the perimeter is equal to $2(12 + 4) = 2(16) = 32$, choice (E).

6. B

Angles about a point add up to 360°, so you can write the following equation to solve for a:

$$45 + 75 + a + 45 + 75 + a = 360$$
$$2a + 240 = 360$$
$$2a = 120$$
$$a = 60$$

7. C

The easiest way to solve is to compare each answer choice, looking for the largest digit in each place holder. The largest tenths digit, for example, is 7. Eliminate (A) since its tenths digit is 0. In the hundredths place the largest digit is 9. (B) is out, too, since its hundredths digit is 8. (E) doesn't have a thousandths, so it is understood to be 0, which is less than the 2 that appears in the thousandths places in (C) and (D). (D) doesn't have a digit in the ten-thousandths place, so it is understood to be 0. It can be eliminated since it is less than the 3 in the ten-thousandths place in (C). (C) is the largest.

8. D

Break this question down into parts, translating as you go. You're told that 4 added to 3 times a number N results in 36. Three times N can be represented algebraically as $3N$, and adding 4 to that can be written as $3N + 4$. The result is 36, so $3N + 4 = 36$, (D).

9. D

You are looking for the choice that, when added to 5, will result in an odd, whole number. Try each answer choice to see which does:

(A) $5 + 5 = 10$; not odd
(B) $3 + 5 = 8$; not odd
(C) $\frac{1}{2} + 5 = 5\frac{1}{2}$; not a whole number
(D) $0 + 5 = 5$; an odd, whole number!
(E) $-7 + 5 = -2$; not odd

10. B

Try drawing in the bull's leash to get a sense of how far it can graze. Since the length of the fence is 14 feet, and the length of the rope is 7 feet, the bull will just be able to reach the center of each side but not the corners. In other words, the bull will be able to graze in a circle with radius 7, as shown in (B). Though (D) also represents the region as a circle, it is too small.

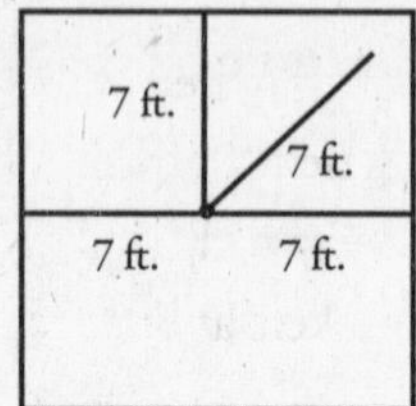

11. D

A quick look at the answer choices tells you that your answer needs to be in decimal form. So, first convert to decimal form, then subtract: $0.875 - 0.625 = 0.25$. Another approach is to subract the fractions to get $\frac{7}{8} - \frac{5}{8} = \frac{2}{8}$. Since $\frac{2}{8} = \frac{1}{4}$, convert $\frac{1}{4}$ to 0.25.

12. A

The temperature was originally 20 degrees. It then dropped 32 degrees, so you need to subtract 32 from 20: $20 - 32 = -12$. So the temperature at midnight was -12, or 12 degrees below zero, (A).

13. D

According to the graph, the slice labeled "chocolate" represents $\frac{1}{4}$ of the entire pie. Since a total of 300 cones were sold, $\frac{1}{4} \times 300 = 75$ chocolate cones were sold.

14. C

First determine what the remainder is when 36 is divided by 5. Five goes into 36 seven times with a remainder of one. So you need to find which choice will divide into 65 and leave a remainder of one. Since $8 \times 8 = 64$, 65 will leave a remainder of one when divided by eight. The answer is (C).

15. C

The average formula is Average = $\frac{\text{Sum of the terms}}{\text{Number of terms}}$.
Look at the graph to find the number of 911 calls made for each of the four days and plug them into the formula:

$$\frac{500 + 1{,}000 + 500 + 1{,}500}{4} = \frac{3{,}500}{4} = 875$$

16. B

This is a straightforward symbolism problem. Plug in the values for y and z and solve.

$$\begin{aligned} y @ z &= y \times z - 2 \\ 3 @ 7 &= 3 \times 7 - 2 \\ &= 21 - 2 \\ &= 19 \end{aligned}$$

17. B

Plug the given information into the equation and solve for y.

$$\begin{aligned} y @ z &= y \times z - 2 \\ y @ 4 &= 6 \\ 4y - 2 &= 6 \\ 4y &= 8 \\ y &= 2 \end{aligned}$$

18. D

Plug the given information into the equation and solve for z.

$$y @ z = y \times z - 2$$
$$\frac{1}{4} @ z = 0$$
$$\frac{1}{4} \times z - 2 = 0$$
$$\frac{1}{4}z = 2$$
$$z = 8$$

19. B

There are 25 girls and 15 boys in the class, a total of 40 students. One-fifth of the girls, or $\frac{25}{5} = 5$, and two-thirds of the boys, or $\frac{2}{3} \times 15 = 10$, ran the haunted house. So a total of $5 + 10 = 15$ students participated. Since the class has 40 students in all, $\frac{15}{40} = \frac{3}{8}$ of all the students participated.

20. E

Set up a proportion, letting N equal the number you are looking for:

$$\frac{7}{4} = \frac{28}{N}$$
$$4 \times 28 = 7N$$
$$112 = 7N$$
$$16 = N$$

21. E

Here is the rule for whether you can retrace a figure without having to lift your pencil: If exactly zero or two points have an odd number of intersecting line segments and/or curves, the figure can be drawn without lifting. So, for example, if a figure has three places where an odd number of line segments intersect, you would have to lift your pencil to retrace it. Also, the number of points a figure has with an even number of intersecting line segments is irrelevant.

Count the number of line segments that meet at each point of intersection. Find all the points that bring together an odd number of line segments. If you find zero or two points that meet this condition, the diagram can be drawn without lifting your pencil.

So, in this question, the only figure that doesn't fit this criteria is (E). There are six points of intersection, four of which have an odd number of intersecting segments.

22. C

To find Jill's change, you need to know how much money she spent. Then subtract that amount from \$10. Jill bought five sparkly stickers at \$0.50 each and eight smelly stickers at \$0.60 each:

$$(5)(0.50) + (8)(0.60) = \$7.30$$
$$\$10 - \$7.30 = \$2.70$$

23. D

Greg spent 45 minutes to finish one-third of the book. He still has two-thirds left to read, twice as much as he has already read. So he'll need to spend twice the time he already spent—an hour and a half. To finish by 11 P.M., he needs to start an hour and a half before 11 P.M., or at 9:30 P.M.

24. C

Work systematically, checking one route at a time and keeping careful track of each path. There is a total of 4 paths from X to Y with a total length 7, as shown in the figures below:

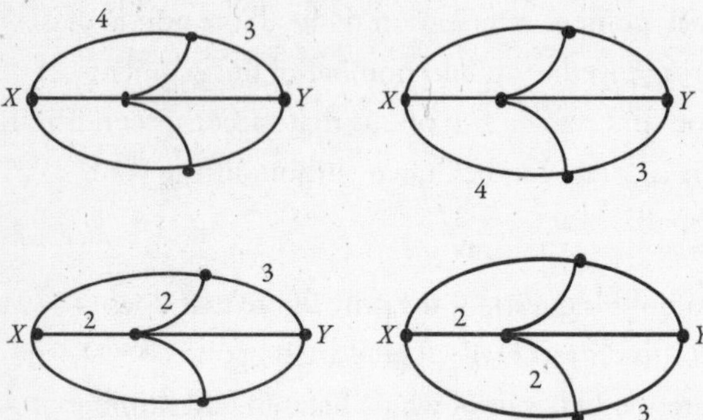

25. D

You need the answer choice that is 1 more than a palindrome, so you should be able to subtract 1 from the correct answer choice and end up with a palindrome. (A) gives you the number 7,336. One less than 7,336 is 7,335, which is not a palindrome. Same thing for (B), (C), and (E). In (D), 1 less than the answer choice is 7,337, which is a palindrome.

SECTION 3: READING COMPREHENSION

Fiction Passage

First up is a narrative passage. The author is reminiscing about his childhood and some of the fantasies that he and his peers had about their future professions. As with all fiction passages, pay close attention to shifts in tone and uses of simile, metaphor, and irony as you read.

1. C

This is a Main Idea question. You first need to summarize what the passage is about. The first two sentences contain the author's main idea: He and his peers wanted nothing more than to be steamboat-men. This is essentially what (C) states.
(A) is tricky; it mentions a profession, but we were never told that the author chose to be a steam-boatman in adulthood.

2. D

We are asked to determine which profession the author did not consider. The easiest way to do this is to eliminate all choices that he did consider. By just looking back at the text, we can identify all choices except (D). Being a writer is never mentioned.

3. C

After the author uses the word "transient," he explains that while he and his friends had other professional aspirations, those desires went away. Only the desire to be a steamboat-man remained. In other words, the other desires were "short-lived" as in (C).

4. A

Immediately before line 6, we are told that the author and his friends had "transient ambitions." In other words, they had ambitions that disappeared very quickly. The phrase "all burning to become clowns" is an example of such a fleeting ambition.

5. B

This question is a little tricky. After the friends considered being clowns and minstrels, they dreamt of becoming pirates. The fact that the boys wanted to become pirates is in itself comical, but with the added reference about God permitting that if they were good, the lightheartedness and humor become evident. If you weren't sure about the answer, try the other choices. It couldn't be (E), because there is no rhyme here, and it couldn't be (D), because Twain isn't making fun of anyone. Pathos means sympathy, sorrow, so (A) is definitely out, too. (C) is wrong since nothing is being exaggerated.

6. A

The author is fondly looking back on his childhood days. Somber, cynical, and regretful are too negative; the author is not saying anything negative. Neither is he hopeful about the future or optimistic. So the only answer choice that makes sense is (A), nostalgic. Nostalgic means reminiscing about the old days.

7. A

The author and his friends dreamed about piloting steamboats. Their "transient ambitions"—clowns with the circus, traveling minstrels, pirates—were all jobs that would have required them to travel away from the village, so (A) is the answer. (B) is incorrect because girls are not mentioned in the passage. (C) and (E) might be true, but they can't be proved with this passage. (D) is incorrect because if the author regrets not becoming something, it's most likely a steamboat-man.

ALCHEMY PASSAGE

Next up we have a science passage about alchemy. The first half describes alchemy and the unfavorable way in which it has been viewed by history. The second half of the passage explains the positive aspects of alchemy and how it paved the way for modern science.

8. A

Remember to summarize the main point to yourself before going to the questions. Here, the passage provides a brief history of alchemy. (A) best restates this idea. (B) is incorrect because gold was never actually manufactured.

9. B

Lines 6–8 state that "the alchemist is generally portrayed by historians as a charlatan obsessed with dreams of impossible wealth." In other words, historians feel that the alchemists were greedy. (B) restates this idea. Be careful of (D): It contains information stated in the passage, but this isn't the view of historians, which is what the question asks for.

10. B

Infer means to draw a conclusion. Read the surrounding lines: They tell you that a "charlatan" was portrayed as obsessively greedy by historians—so you can infer that historians did not respect "charlatans"—(B).

11. C

To determine where this passage most likely came from, you need to consider the author's tone and purpose. Does the passage sound positive, negative, or neutral? Does the author seem to be trying to convince us of something? In fact, the author's tone sounds very detached—as you do when you are explaining something. So a history book is the logical place to find this type of passage. The text doesn't sound like news, so (D) is out.

12. E

To answer this question you need to understand the author's point of view. The author makes it clear that while alchemy was viewed with disdain by historians, it did make a positive contribution to the sciences. (E) reflects this attitude. Watch out for choices that contain information not expressly stated in the passage—(A), (C), and (D). (B) is tricky: Even though the text says that historians felt alchemy was primitive and superstitious, we don't know if the author thinks this is the case.

13. D

To find the answer, try to use the passage to answer each question. (D) cannot be answered using the passage, which says only that alchemists attempted to change metals into gold and makes no mention of successful attempts. It does not say how alchemists make gold. The other choices can be answered by the passage. (A) is answered in lines 2–3: "change lead, copper, and other metals into silver or gold." (B) is answered in lines 11–13: "alchemists helped develop many of the apparatuses and procedures that are used in laboratories today." (C) is answered in lines 6–8: "the alchemist is generally portrayed by historians as a charlatan obsessed with dreams of impossible wealth." (E) is answered in lines 8–10: "For many centuries ... alchemy was a highly respected art."

14. E

This is a Main Idea question. Although the passage talks about what alchemy is and how alchemists were viewed, those were not the goals of the author, so (A), (B), (C), and (D) are not correct. The author spends lines 10–15 supporting alchemy's influences on modern science, making (E) the answer.

Mount Saint Helens Passage

This is a science passage describing the eruption of the volcano Mount Saint Helens and its effects. The first part of the passage focuses on the physical results of the eruption, while the last part describes the kind of lava emitted.

15. D

As you were reading the passage, you should have tried to summarize the point. The text describes Mount Saint Helens, its eruption, and what the eruption produced. (A) is far too broad, and (C) and (E) are too narrow and detailed. The information in (B) is not discussed.

16. A

Lines 3–6 state, "The explosion was not unexpected; the earth's crust had shaken for weeks beforehand, providing people in the surrounding area with plenty of advance warning." In other words, the shaking of the crust warned people of the impending volcano; "advance," therefore, means ahead of time. While "moving forward" (B) is one definition for advance, it is not the meaning that works in this context.

17. A

You need to identify the answer choice that contains information not mentioned in the passage. If something leaps out at you immediately, there's a good chance that it's the answer. If not, eliminate all answer choices that are mentioned in the passage until one remains. Only tidal waves aren't mentioned.

18. D

Fluid lava, in the question stem, is thin, flowing lava. The text states, "Thick lava is easily outrun because it moves extremely slowly." Since thin and thick lava would naturally have opposite characteristics, we can assume that thin lava is not easily outrun—(D).

19. D

The author isn't speaking in praise of something, nor is he trying to persuade his readers of a certain point of view. His tone is informative and balanced. (D) is the best choice.

20. A

The author offers that phrase as a contrast to the next sentence: "In spite of these danger signals, no one was prepared for the extent of the blast." (A) is correct because these lines, to paraphrase, are saying that people were prepared and knew about the blast, but no one expected such as major explosion, which the author goes on to discuss. (D) might be true, that experts were not seeing fluid lava in the blast, but it does not have to do with the phrase in question.

Hawaiian Cowboy Passage

This humanities passage discusses how the cowboy came to Hawaii. The author explains that while the word *cowboy* conjures up an image of the American West, the Hawaiian cowboy actually emerged earlier than his Western counterpart.

21. D

The first sentence of the text tells us that American cowboys emerged later than Hawaiian ones. This is what (D) states. (A) contradicts the text, and (B), (C), and (E) present details not discussed in the text.

22. D

Here you have to research which answer choice was not mentioned in the passage. If something leaps out at you immediately, there's a good chance that that is the answer. If not, use process of elimination by looking back at the text. The only answer choice not mentioned is (D).

23. C

Evaluate each Roman numeral one at a time, eliminating answer choices as you go. I is supported directly by lines in the text, so it is correct. We can now eliminate (B) and (D) because they do not contain I. II is also supported in the text, so it, too, is true. That means (A) can be eliminated. Finally, III is not supported by the passage, so it is not true. The answer must therefore be (C).

24. E

The passage discusses how the cowboy came to Hawaii, which is what (E) states. (A), (B), and (C) don't get the focus of the passage right, while (D) focuses too much on one detail. Even though the introduction of horses is mentioned in the text, it isn't the point of the entire passage.

25. C

The author isn't excited or confused, so (D) and (E) are out right away. Biased means prejudiced toward a point of view, and condescending means negative, and the tone was neither one of these things, so (A) and (B) are incorrect, too. His tone is informative and balanced, so (C) is the answer.

26. E

(A) and (C) are almost antonyms of "wrathful." (D) doesn't make sense in context. (B) is close, but (E) is more accurate. Lines 10–12 say the king felt the need to protect the troublemaking animals from the people. He wouldn't need to protect the animals if the people were merely enraged, or angry.

27. E

Find the right answer by using the passage to answer the questions asked in the choices. (A) is answered in line 9: The Hawaiians found the animals unruly for ruining their crops. (B) is answered in lines 14–16: With the help of the vaqueros, the animals were able to become cowboys and control the animals. (C) is answered in the first lines: The author calls Western cowboys icons but wants to clarify that by the time the West's cowboys entered pop culture, the Hawaiians had already had cowboys for decades. (D) is answered by subtracting line 4's year—1792—from line 12's year—1830. (E) cannot be answered using the passage. Kapu laws are mentioned in lines

12–13, but the passage doesn't say what they were or how they were used.

SILK ROAD PASSAGE

This science passage tells us about the Silk Road, the ancient trading route that connected China to Rome. In the text, we learn about a piece of silk that was discovered in Egypt and how that discovery affected our knowledge about the Silk Road.

28. A

The passage is about the Silk Road and how our knowledge of the Silk Road was affected by the discovery of a piece of silk. This is essentially what (A) states. (B) is incorrect because it fails to mention the fragment of silk discussed in paragraph 2. (C) and (E) are incorrect because they focus too much on details. And (D) introduces material which was never discussed.

29. D

Go to the reference lines and see if you can figure out what the term "systems of belief" means. We're told that "systems of belief" were passed along the road. Immediately after that, the spread of Christianity, Buddhism, and Islam are discussed. So we can assume that these three religions are examples of "systems of belief," making (D) the answer. No other choice fits the context.

30. E

We need to find which item was *not* traded along the Silk Road, so we can eliminate everything that is mentioned in the text. We can definitely eliminate (A), fabrics, since we know that silk was traded. (B) is incorrect as well, since gunpowder is mentioned in the text. (C) and (D) are incorrect as well, since peaches and roses are mentioned.

31. E

The best way to proceed here is to evaluate each answer choice and eliminate anything that doesn't agree with the information in the passage. (A) states that the silk fragment found in Egypt was a fake. But nothing in the passage indicates that this was the case. (B), too, brings up information that we don't know for certain; we aren't told that most Egyptian garments were made of silk. While we are told that it is difficult to know "exactly how traders navigated the plateaus," we are not told that the Egyptians were definitely "unable" to cross plateaus, etc., so (C) is out. Neither is (D) supported by the text. Only (E) makes sense: We are told that only the Chinese knew how to make silk in 1000 B.C.E., so we can assume that the fragment found in Egypt dating back to 1000 B.C.E. must have been made in China.

32. E

As you read the text, ask yourself what the author's tone and purpose are. Does the passage sound positive or negative? Does the author seem to be making an emotional appeal, or is she just presenting information? Since this is a science passage, the author is unlikely to be biased. (A), (B), (C), and (D) are all incorrect because they do not fit the tone or purpose here. Only (E) makes sense.

33. A

Although the passage talks about the trade of such items as silk and "roses, peaches, gunpowder, and paper" (lines 9–11), it also mentions that the Silk Road allowed religions to spread (lines 11–13). (B) is contradicted by lines 17–18: A recent discovery suggests the road existed at least for 1,000 years before 115 B.C.E. (C) is incorrect because lines 21–24 say the silk must have come from Asia because Mediterranean countries hadn't yet developed silk-making technology. (D) is wrong because the author never doubts the existence of the Silk Road. (E) is not something that can be concluded using this passage.

Bruges Passage

This passage discusses the city of Bruges in the 15th century. The first lines set up the author's main idea: "During the 15th century, the Belgian city Bruges was the most important commercial city in the north of Europe."

34. D

Immediately following the word "derived" is the phrase, "its wealth from wool and banking." The text then goes on to say that "ships brought raw wool… to Bruges." We can assume, then, that "derived" means obtained or got its wealth.

35. D

We're told that among those bankers who came to Bruges, "representatives of the House of Medici" also arrived. We are also told that "soon Bruges became the financial center for all of northern Europe." From this we can assume that the arrival of the Medicis influenced the status of Bruges—(D).

36. C

You need to go to the part of the passage that discusses wool. We do not know anything about the quality of the wool from the text; we only know that the finished cloth was famous in Europe. Nor is there anything to support the claims in (D) and (E). (B) contradicts the passage, as wool was very instrumental in the growth of Bruges. (C) is indeed supported by the text.

37. E

This is a Purpose of Detail question: You are asked to determine why a specific detail is mentioned. We are told that Bruges became "the financial center for all of northern Europe." Immediately afterward, we're told about the various merchants who came there, indicating how important a place it had become.

38. C

The text says that Bruges so outshone the other cities in prosperity that "the Duke of Burgundy made that city his capital." The Duke chose Bruges because of its prosperity—(C). (A) is incorrect, since the text says that Ghent was prosperous.

39. C

(A) is too broad; we are only dealing with Bruges, not the entire Renaissance world. (B) and (D) focus only on small details. (E) is out, too, as there's no evidence to support this statement. (C) is the best answer.

40. E

Try finding these details in the passage. (A) is found in lines 13–14: "nearby cities such as Ghent and Louvain also flourished." (B) is found in lines 11–13: "Merchants from Italy, the Near East, Russia, and Spain all congregated in Bruges." (C) is found in lines 4–6: "Ships brought raw wool there from England and Spain, and carried away finished wool cloth." (D) is found in line 10: "Bruges became the financial center." (E) is not true, because lines 14–17 say the capital was moved to Bruges because the city was so prosperous.

SECTION 4: VERBAL

SYNONYMS

1. B

An alias is an assumed name. Superman's alias is Clark Kent.

2. C

To have a phobia is to have great fear or anxiety about something. To have a phobia of snakes is to have a fear of snakes.

3. D

To propel something is to thrust it forward or to project it. A strong wind can propel a ship through the water. Note that *project* is used as a verb here, not as a noun. Your answer must always be the same word form as that of the stem word.

4. C

A headstrong person is stubborn and doesn't like to listen to anyone else. A headstrong horse may refuse to walk when you ask it to.

5. A

To coddle something is to treat it gently or to baby it. Too much coddling of a child, for example, may cause him to be insufficiently prepared to face the harsh realities of life.

6. A

To be keen is to be very smart or sharp. A keen mind is good at solving problems.

7. D

If something is murky, it is dark and mysterious, or gloomy. Murky water is hard to see through.

8. B

The word *trying* isn't used here as a verb, as you might expect. It is used as an adjective. A trying situation is very demanding or strenuous. A trying hike, for example, will make you very tired. Always look at the root word to see what word form you need to use.

9. C

If you adhere to a decision, you stay with it or stick to it. Adhesive tape is sticky tape—it adheres.

10. D

An enigmatic person is difficult to figure out—she is mysterious. Many people thought Howard Hughes was enigmatic because so little was known about him.

11. E

To be pompous is to be stuck up or pretentious. A pompous person feels and acts as though he is more important than he is.

12. E

Something that is fatal will kill you; it is lethal. A fatal blow is a blow that kills a person.

13. E

Something frequent happens regularly; it is habitual. A frequent flyer is a person who flies all the time.

14. D

An ostentatious person is a show-off; he is showy or flashy. An ostentatious outfit might include lots of jewelry and expensive-looking accessories.

15. C

A dearth of something is a lack of something. If an area has a dearth of water, then there's very little water in that area.

16. A

To be buffeted is to be tossed about. A small ship may be buffeted by large waves.

17. E

To waive something is to let it pass or to give it up. If you waive your right to vote, you give up your right to vote.

18. C

Industry is commonly thought of as manufacturing, but it also means hard work, or diligence. A person who possesses great industry is a person who is very diligent.

19. A

Trepidation is the same as fear. To watch a horror movie with great trepidation is to watch it with great fear.

20. B

To condone something is to approve of something or to support it. If one condones a certain type of behavior, then one approves of it.

21. A

A harbinger is a messenger. Dark clouds are often a harbinger of a rainstorm.

22. A

A sentry is a group of people who look out for certain things—a watch. During war, the sentry looks out for the enemy.

23. C

An orbit occurs when one object circles around another object; it is a revolution. When the moon orbits the earth, it makes a revolution. Don't be mislead by the fact that revolution also means a war, as in the American Revolution. If a word has more than one meaning, make sure you consider them all before deciding that an answer choice is incorrect.

24. B

A paradox occurs when one thing is said but another is meant—it's a confusion or a contradiction. The word "bittersweet" is a contradiction: How can something be bitter and sweet at the same time?

25. D

A buffoon is a person who everyone makes fun of—a fool. Clowns often pretend to be buffoons.

26. E

An imminent event is just about to happen—it is impending. For centuries, people have believed that the end of the world is imminent.

27. B

Tumult is havoc, or disorder. When a hurricane goes through towns, it can create a tumult.

28. D

To spurn someone is to scorn or reject someone. A spurned friend is a rejected friend.

29. B

Plethora is the opposite of *dearth* in question 15. A plethora is an abundance or an excess of something. If there's a plethora of corn, there's a great deal of corn.

30. C

To disseminate something is to spread it out or to broadcast it. To disseminate information is to broadcast it.

ANALOGIES

31. B

Scissors are specifically used to cut, just as a pencil is specifically used to write.

32. D

The specific topping for pasta is sauce; the specific topping for toast is jam. A noodle (A) is made out of dough, and tomato (B) grows on a vine.

33. C

The outer shell of bread is the crust. The outer shell of an orange is the rind.

34. C

A captain is the leader of a team, just as a president is the leader of a republic. Watch out for (A)—it mentions the word sports, which fits the subject matter of the stem pair but does not match the bridge.

35. E

Olfactory refers to one's sense of smell, just as tactile refers to one's sense of touch.

36. E

A ruler is a tool used to measure something, just as a camera is a tool used to photograph something.

37. A

Tiptoe is a quiet kind of walk, as whisper is a quiet kind of speech. A rasp (D) is a harsh sound in one's throat.

38. B

A kernel is a central piece of information. Trivia is an unimportant piece of information.

39. C

A liar is a person who fibs, just as a toady is a person who flatters. A politician (D) by definition is not a person who campaigns but, rather, a person who engages in politics. To tally (E) is to count up: A banker may tally money, but she may also do other things like lend money.

40. B

A nap is a short sleep just as a snack is a short meal. A biscuit can be a type of snack, but we are looking for a word that fits the bridge "is a short."

41. A

A fossil is a substance that is petrified. A solution is a substance that is dissolved. Wood (B) is not necessarily hard, nor are snowflakes (C) necessarily wet.

42. E

A sphere is round in shape in the same way that a honeycomb is hexagonal in shape. A protractor (B) is used to measure an angle.

43. A

To be picky is to be extremely careful. Similarly, to be exhausted is to be extremely tired. To be alert (B) is to be awake.

44. D

A cave is the rounded, hollowed-out part of a rock, just as an apse is the rounded, hollowed out part of a church. A plateau (B) is a large, flat rock.

45. D

Lemonade is made from lemons, just as paper is made from wood. Juice (A) may or may not be made from cherries; it can be made from other ingredients as well.

46. A

A frog is a type of amphibian, as a whale is a type of mammal.

47. A

A dentist uses a drill in the way that a surgeon uses a scalpel. A doctor doesn't use a stretcher—his patients do. And though a farmer may harvest grain, he does not by definition use it.

48. B

A mosaic is a picture made up of individual tiles, the way a tapestry is a picture made up of individual threads. A sweater (D) may or may not be made out of wool.

49. D

A pebble is a tiny bit of rock, just as a drop is a tiny bit of liquid.

50. E

A levee is the border of a river, just as a shoulder is the border of a road. A path may or may not go through a forest.

51. D

Something that is redundant, by definition, is not necessary. Something that is vague, by definition, is not explicit. Something that is desirable (A) is not necessarily pretty.

52. E

Coral is a shade of pink, the way aquamarine is a shade of blue. Rosy (B) is another shade of pink, while bland (D) means plain.

53. E

A fan by definition circulates air, and a heart circulates blood.

54. B

A palette is an assortment of colors, and a collage is an assortment of images.

55. C

A salutation is an introductory greeting in a letter, as an introduction is an introductory greeting in a book. A postscript (A) occurs at the end of a letter.

56. E

A quill is a porcupine's means of defense just as a scent is a skunk's means of defense. Wings (B) are a duck's means of flight.

57. C

A caterpillar is an animal that turns into a butterfly. A tadpole is an animal that turns into a frog.

58. A

A budget is used to plan the cost of a project, the way a blueprint is used to plan the design of a project.

59. A

The job of a juror is to judge. The job of a soothsayer is to predict. A soothsayer predicts the future.

60. C

A buffer is used to prevent an impact, as an antiseptic is used to prevent an infection. A bandage (D) may help to heal a wound, but it will not prevent it, which is the bridge we need.

SECTION 5: MATH

1. C

Finding the reciprocal of a number involves flipping its numerator with its denominator. So the reciprocal of $\frac{3}{4}$ is simply $\frac{4}{3}$.

2. C

There are at least two ways to solve this problem. If you recognized that $\frac{1}{8}$ is half of $\frac{1}{4}$, $\frac{1}{8}N$ must be half of 4, or 2. Alternately, you could have solved the first equation for the value of N and then plugged that value into the second expression.

$$\frac{1}{4}N = 4$$

$$\frac{1}{4}N = 4(N = 4)$$

$$N = 16$$

$$\frac{1}{8}N = \frac{1}{8} \times 16 = 2$$

3. B

There are 10 triangles. Four of these are shaded. So $\frac{4}{10} = \frac{2}{5}$ of all the triangles are shaded.

4. C

The average of a group of consecutive integers is equal to the middle term. Since you're told that the largest of the five integers is 10, they must be 6, 7, 8, 9, and 10. So the middle term and average is 8, (C).

5. B

The fastest way to solve this question is to simplify by canceling terms and then to multiply.

$$\frac{2}{3} \times \frac{3}{6} \times \frac{2}{4} = \frac{2}{3} \times \frac{1}{2} \times \frac{1}{2}$$

$$= \frac{1}{3} \times \frac{1}{1} \times \frac{1}{2}$$

$$= \frac{1}{6}$$

6. C

The perimeter is the sum of all the sides of a figure. Set up an equation to solve for the sum of a and b.

$$a + b + 2 + 3 + 4 + 6 = 24$$

$$a + b + 15 = 24$$

$$a + b = 9$$

7. D

The average formula is

$$\text{Average} = \frac{\text{Sum of terms}}{\text{Number of terms}}$$

Plug in Julie's three grades to find her average grade:

$$\frac{75+89+100}{3} = \frac{264}{3} = 88$$

8. C

You are first asked to find the product of 2 and 6, or $2 \times 6 = 12$. You're then asked to subtract that product from the sum of 10 and 14, or $10 + 14 = 24$. So $24 - 12 = 12$, (C).

9. D

N is a whole number between 3 and 6, so it could be 4 or 5. N is also a whole number between 4 and 8, so it could be 5, 6, or 7. The only number that fits both these conditions is 5.

10. C

Evaluate each answer choice and eliminate as you go. Since $\frac{2}{3} = \frac{8}{12}$ and $\frac{3}{4} = \frac{9}{12}$, (A) is less than $\frac{3}{4}$; eliminate (A). Since $\frac{3}{4} = \frac{6}{8}$, $\frac{5}{8}$ is less than $\frac{3}{4}$; eliminate (B). Since $\frac{14}{16} = \frac{7}{8}$ and $\frac{3}{4} = \frac{6}{8}$, (C) is not less than $\frac{3}{4}$ and it is the answer.

11. C

According to the chart, each car icon represents 100 cars. Since there are four icons in the white category, 400 white cars were sold. With three icons in the red category, 300 red cars were sold. So there were $400 - 300 = 100$ more white than red cars sold.

12. E

According to the graph, there were 800 black cars sold and only 200 green cars sold. In other words, the number of black cars sold is 800 divided by 200: 4 times the number of green cars sold.

13. B

Treat this question as a straightforward algebra problem. As you simplify, watch out for careless errors.

$$3 \times 4 \times N = 6 \times 2$$
$$12N = 12$$
$$N = 1$$

14. D

Perimeter of a rectangle is equal to $2(l + w)$, where l and w represent the length and width respectively. The width is 4, the length is m, and the perimeter is 20, so plug these into the formula.

$$20 = 2(m + 4)$$
$$20 = 2m + 8$$
$$12 = 2m$$
$$6 = m$$

15. B

The shirt is originally \$40, but Cathy buys it at a 15 percent discount. You are asked to find out how much money Cathy saves, or 15 percent of \$40.

$$15\% \times \$40 = (0.15)(\$40)$$
$$= \$6$$

16. C

Ratios can be expressed either with fractions or with a colon. A look at the answer choices reveals that the answer will be expressed with a colon. The ratio of 14 to 21 is therefore 14:21. You can reduce this ratio by a factor of 7, so it simplifies to 2:3, (C).

17. E

You only need to be concerned with the bottom part of the bucket—the circular part. Since the entire circular bottom of the bucket touches the table, the figure that most accurately represents all the points where the bucket touches the table is (E).

18. D

Two times a whole number is less than 5 and greater than zero. So our end result must be 1, 2, 3, or 4. Therefore, the whole number could be $\frac{1}{2} = 1$ or $\frac{4}{2} = 2$ (half of 1 or 3 would not be a whole number). Of these, only 2 is listed as an answer choice, so it's correct.

19. C

Think of this as a proportion problem. Cindy earns \$20 for an hour of work. You want to figure out how many hours she needs to work to earn \$420, so set up a proportion, letting x equal the number you're looking for:

$$\frac{20}{1} = \frac{420}{x}$$
$$20x = 420$$
$$x = 21$$

20. C

So 0.73 is close to 0.75, which can be expressed in fractional form as $\frac{3}{4}$. This also equals $\frac{6}{8}$. Of the choices, N is closest to 6, (C).

21. D

For every 5 vegetarian meals, 7 nonvegetarian meals are ordered. This means that the total number of meals ordered must be a multiple of 12 (since $7 + 5 = 12$). The only answer choice that is a multiple of 12 is (D), 600.

22. B

You're asked to find which value of N will not result in a whole number. You can see that the symbol instructs you to take $\frac{1}{4}$ of N, so the number that is not a multiple of 4 will not produce a whole number value. The only number not divisible by 4 is (B), 6. Alternately, you could have plugged each answer choice into the expression to see which did not produce a whole number.

23. C

Because 0.1 is just 0.01 or one hundredth away from 1, it is the closest of the choices.

24. C

This is an algebra problem. You need to treat the O as a variable and isolate it on one side of the equation. Cross-multiplying shows that $3 \times 75 = O$, so $225 = O$, (C).

25. C

Let's set up an equation. Let N equal the original number. Translating, "when N is tripled" means $3 \times N$, or $3N$. "The result is increased by 4" means $+ 4$, or $3N + 4$. "The number obtained is 25" means $3N + 4 = 25$. Now isolate N to solve for it:

$$3N + 4 = 25$$
$$3N = 21$$
$$N = 7$$

CHAPTER 19: SCORING YOUR SSAT PRACTICE TEST

Your SSAT score is calculated by using a formula that cannot be directly applied to your practice tests. Therefore, it is impossible to provide a completely accurate score for your practice tests. Nevertheless, you'll understandably want to get an idea of how well you have performed.

Follow the steps described below to obtain a rough approximation of what your score on the actual SSAT might be. First, add up the number of questions you got right and the number of questions you got wrong. Questions left blank are worth zero points. Then, do the math, based on the following:

	Verbal (60 questions total)	(Quantitative) Math (50 questions total)	Reading Comprehension (40 questions total)
+ 1 point for each right answer	________	________	________
$-\frac{1}{4}$ point for each wrong answer	________	________	________
TOTAL:	________	________	________

This is called your **raw score.** Next, take your raw score and look at the following chart, which *approximates* a conversion to a **scaled score.** A scaled score takes into account the range in difficulty level of the various editions of the test.

Again, while the following scores and percentiles are close approximations, they do not reflect the official scores and percentiles used on the SSAT. Among other contributing factors, your actual test score will take into account the group of students to whom you will be compared to on your test administration.

UPPER-LEVEL SCORES

Upper-level scores are based on a scale of 500–800. Once you have looked up your scaled score, refer to the 50th Percentile score chart below: This will tell you the score at which equal numbers of students scored above and below you. With this information, you will be able to gauge how well you have done with respect to other students.

SCALED SCORES

Raw Score	Reading	Verbal	Math*
60		800	
55		800	
50		779	800
45		752	782
40	800	725	755
35	722	698	725
30	692	671	698
25	662	644	668
20	632	617	641
15	602	590	614
10	572	563	584
5	542	533	557
0	512	506	530
–5 and lower	500	500	500

* Both math sections have been combined. Add together both of your scores for those sections.

MEDIAN SCORE: 50TH PERCENTILE

Grade	Reading	Verbal	Quantitative
8	629	662	647
9	644	683	668
10	647	671	692
11	626	653	689

LOWER-LEVEL SCORES

Lower-level test scores are based on a scale of 440–710. Once you have looked up your scaled score, refer to the 50th Percentile score chart below: That chart will tell you the score at which equal numbers of students scored above and below you. This way, you will be able to gauge how well you have done with respect to other students.

SCALED SCORES

Raw Score	Reading	Verbal	Math*
60		710	
55		710	
50		710	704
45		698	680
40	710	674	659
35	686	650	635
30	656	626	614
25	626	602	593
20	596	578	569
15	566	554	540
10	536	530	527
5	506	506	503
0	476	482	482
–5	446	458	458
–10 and lower	440	440	440

* Both math sections have been combined. Add together both of your scores for those sections.

MEDIAN SCORE: 50TH PERCENTILE

Grade	Reading	Verbal	Quantitative
5	569	584	563
6	593	614	593
7	611	638	614

Part Five

ISEE PRACTICE TESTS AND EXPLANATIONS

ISEE TEST OVERVIEW

Total Time

Approximately 3 hours.

Questions

Aside from the essay, all questions are multiple-choice format, with all answer choices labeled (A)–(D).

Content

The ISEE tests Math, Reading Comprehension, and Verbal skills. There are two scored Math sections, one scored Reading Comprehension section, one scored Verbal sections, and one unscored Essay.

Pacing

You are not expected to complete all items on the ISEE. This is particularly true if you are at the low end of the age range of test takers for your level. The best approach to pacing is to work as quickly as you can without losing accuracy. Further, if a question is giving you difficulty, circle it and move on. You can always come back to it later, but you shouldn't waste time on a question that is stumping you when you could be gaining valuable points elsewhere.

Guessing

There is no guessing penalty on the ISEE. You receive 1 point for each question that you answer correctly. You don't lose any points for questions left blank or for questions answered incorrectly. As a result, it's always to your advantage to guess on questions you don't know. However, it's better to answer questions correctly, so only guess if you try to answer the question and can't figure it out, or if you are running out of time.

CHAPTER 20: ISEE PRACTICE TEST 1: UPPER- AND MIDDLE-LEVEL

HOW TO TAKE THIS PRACTICE TEST

Before taking this practice test, find a quiet room where you can work uninterrupted for three hours. Make sure you have a comfortable desk and several No. 2 pencils.

Use the answer sheet provided to record your answers. (You can cut it out or photocopy it.)

Once you start this practice test, don't stop until you have finished. Remember—you can review any questions within a section, but you may not go backward or forward a section.

You'll find answer explanations following the test.

Note: There are no major differences between the Middle- and Upper-level ISEE tests, and most of the questions on both tests are appropriate to either the middle or upper levels.

The practice test here covers both levels. If you are taking this as a Middle-level test, you may find a few of the questions to be too difficult. Don't worry—just do the best you can, and know that on test day, you will see only those questions that are appropriate to your level. Remember, too, that your scores will be based on how you compare to others taking the Middle-level test.

Good luck.

ISEE Practice Test 1: Upper- and Middle-Level Answer Sheet

Remove (or photocopy) the answer sheet and use it to complete the practice test.

Start with number 1 for each section. If a section has fewer questions than answer spaces, leave the extra spaces blank.

SECTION 1

1	A B C D	9	A B C D	17	A B C D	25	A B C D	33	A B C D
2	A B C D	10	A B C D	18	A B C D	26	A B C D	34	A B C D
3	A B C D	11	A B C D	19	A B C D	27	A B C D	35	A B C D
4	A B C D	12	A B C D	20	A B C D	28	A B C D	36	A B C D
5	A B C D	13	A B C D	21	A B C D	29	A B C D	37	A B C D
6	A B C D	14	A B C D	22	A B C D	30	A B C D	38	A B C D
7	A B C D	15	A B C D	23	A B C D	31	A B C D	39	A B C D
8	A B C D	16	A B C D	24	A B C D	32	A B C D	40	A B C D

right in section 1

wrong in section 1

SECTION 2

1	A B C D	9	A B C D	17	A B C D	25	A B C D	33	A B C D
2	A B C D	10	A B C D	18	A B C D	26	A B C D	34	A B C D
3	A B C D	11	A B C D	19	A B C D	27	A B C D	35	A B C D
4	A B C D	12	A B C D	20	A B C D	28	A B C D	36	A B C D
5	A B C D	13	A B C D	21	A B C D	29	A B C D	37	A B C D
6	A B C D	14	A B C D	22	A B C D	30	A B C D	38	A B C D
7	A B C D	15	A B C D	23	A B C D	31	A B C D	39	A B C D
8	A B C D	16	A B C D	24	A B C D	32	A B C D	40	A B C D

right in section 2

wrong in section 2

SECTION 3

1	A B C D	9	A B C D	17	A B C D	25	A B C D	33	A B C D
2	A B C D	10	A B C D	18	A B C D	26	A B C D	34	A B C D
3	A B C D	11	A B C D	19	A B C D	27	A B C D	35	A B C D
4	A B C D	12	A B C D	20	A B C D	28	A B C D	36	A B C D
5	A B C D	13	A B C D	21	A B C D	29	A B C D	37	A B C D
6	A B C D	14	A B C D	22	A B C D	30	A B C D	38	A B C D
7	A B C D	15	A B C D	23	A B C D	31	A B C D	39	A B C D
8	A B C D	16	A B C D	24	A B C D	32	A B C D	40	A B C D

right in section 3

wrong in section 3

SECTION 4

1	A B C D	11	A B C D	21	A B C D	31	A B C D	41	A B C D
2	A B C D	12	A B C D	22	A B C D	32	A B C D	42	A B C D
3	A B C D	13	A B C D	23	A B C D	33	A B C D	43	A B C D
4	A B C D	14	A B C D	24	A B C D	34	A B C D	44	A B C D
5	A B C D	15	A B C D	25	A B C D	35	A B C D	45	A B C D
6	A B C D	16	A B C D	26	A B C D	36	A B C D	46	A B C D
7	A B C D	17	A B C D	27	A B C D	37	A B C D	47	A B C D
8	A B C D	18	A B C D	28	A B C D	38	A B C D	48	A B C D
9	A B C D	19	A B C D	29	A B C D	39	A B C D	49	A B C D
10	A B C D	20	A B C D	30	A B C D	40	A B C D	50	A B C D

right in section 4

wrong in section 4

SECTION 1

Time—20 Minutes
40 Questions

This section consists of two different types of questions. There are directions for each type.

Each of the following questions consists of one word followed by five words or phrases. Select the one word or phrase whose meaning is closest to the word in capital letters.

1. EXCESS:
   (A) exit
   (B) surplus
   (C) disorder
   (D) end

2. REIMBURSE:
   (A) punish
   (B) divert
   (C) compensate
   (D) recollect

3. ASTOUND:
   (A) stun
   (B) laugh
   (C) suspend
   (D) scold

4. MASSIVE:
   (A) high
   (B) inferior
   (C) huge
   (D) ancient

5. DIN:
   (A) departure
   (B) clamor
   (C) code
   (D) supper

6. SCARCE:
   (A) delicious
   (B) afraid
   (C) thin
   (D) rare

7. DECEIT:
   (A) civility
   (B) trickery
   (C) rudeness
   (D) despair

8. HALLOWED:
   (A) carved
   (B) distinguished
   (C) empty
   (D) sacred

GO ON TO THE NEXT PAGE

9. APPREHENSION:
   (A) appreciation
   (B) worry
   (C) aggravation
   (D) elevation

10. BLEAK:
   (A) charming
   (B) warm
   (C) drowsy
   (D) dreary

11. OFFEND:
   (A) divulge
   (B) betray
   (C) soothe
   (D) insult

12. VIGOROUS:
   (A) robust
   (B) hungry
   (C) destructive
   (D) lovely

13. DESPONDENT:
   (A) heightened
   (B) annoyed
   (C) relaxed
   (D) depressed

14. SATIATE:
   (A) prolong
   (B) elongate
   (C) seal
   (D) satisfy

15. SPONTANEOUS:
   (A) impulsive
   (B) excitable
   (C) ingenious
   (D) dazzling

16. WAN:
   (A) short
   (B) pale
   (C) foreign
   (D) insincere

17. ABHOR:
   (A) despise
   (B) horrify
   (C) avoid
   (D) deny

18. APPARITION:
   (A) clothing
   (B) ghost
   (C) guard
   (D) wall

19. BENEVOLENT:
   (A) disobedient
   (B) charitable
   (C) sensitive
   (D) widespread

20. TOLERANT:
   (A) open-minded
   (B) friendly
   (C) grave
   (D) ambitious

GO ON TO THE NEXT PAGE

Directions: Select the word(s) that best fit the meaning of each sentence.

21. The ____ writer was on her 12th novel.
   (A) myopic
   (B) prolific
   (C) nefarious
   (D) elusive

22. Though underfunded, the school made the best of its ____ resources.
   (A) meager
   (B) emphatic
   (C) acrid
   (D) belittled

23. The advent of the computer chip made Frank's job ______.
   (A) exuberant
   (B) eminent
   (C) belligerent
   (D) obsolete

24. All efforts to save the nature preserve proved ______.
   (A) inextricable
   (B) insular
   (C) glib
   (D) futile

25. Except for periods where they function as "loners," wolves are generally ____ animals, living in packs.
   (A) carnivorous
   (B) fearsome
   (C) social
   (D) wild

26. The company employed many unproductive employees who had a(n) ____ approach to their work.
   (A) creative
   (B) discontented
   (C) independent
   (D) lackadaisical

27. The recent forest fire, which ____ the mountains of Indonesia, was the most severe ____ disaster the region has ever experienced.
   (A) destroyed .. inflammable
   (B) devastated .. environmental
   (C) singed .. intangible
   (D) burned .. scientific

28. Despite his ____ beginnings as the son of a minor tribal chieftain, the warrior became one of the greatest ____ in Asia.
   (A) humble .. rulers
   (B) luxurious .. leaders
   (C) innocent .. monarchs
   (D) regal .. kings

29. Although Angela was an interior decorator, her home was ____ decorated.
   (A) sufficiently
   (B) impressively
   (C) modestly
   (D) amply

30. Beneath the calm surface of the lake, marine creatures ____ continually for food.
   (A) qualified
   (B) survived
   (C) contested
   (D) gathered

GO ON TO THE NEXT PAGE

31. The captain demonstrated his ____ for the crew by bellowing his commands in a harsh voice.

(A) admiration
(B) contempt
(C) reverence
(D) affinity

32. The ballet dancers performed with a grace and ____ that left the audience breathless.

(A) hilarity
(B) ineptitude
(C) elegance
(D) reserve

33. I did not set out to _____ my classmate; I meant well, but my words came across as _____.

(A) irk .. affable
(B) offend .. gauche
(C) ostracize .. sincere
(D) impress .. confused

34. The volunteer association ____ people with a wide range of ____ to staff their offices.

(A) recruited .. attributes
(B) fired .. skills
(C) rejected .. experiences
(D) hired .. tendencies

35. In spite of her ____ work, Joanne did not receive a promotion.

(A) tardy
(B) industrious
(C) irate
(D) occasional

36. The sky jumper was ____ to survive after his parachute operated ____.

(A) unable .. perfectly
(B) anxious .. instinctively
(C) surprised .. adequately
(D) fortunate .. improperly

37. The puppy was ____ to discipline and whined when reprimanded by its new owner.

(A) anxious
(B) unaccustomed
(C) jovial
(D used

38. At one time, historians spoke of ancient Greece as though its cultural and scientific achievements were wholly _____, whereas it is now generally recognized that at least some Greek science and culture was _____.

(A) primitive .. simple
(B) original .. derivative
(C) mistaken .. dubious
(D) successful .. significant

39. Jeremy has a(n) ____ personality and is very uncomfortable in social situations.

(A) jolly
(B) introverted
(C) outgoing
(D) gregarious

40. After the military government banned the opposing political party, its members continued to meet in _____ groups.

(A) clandestine
(B) amicable
(C) sanctioned
(D) elaborate

IF YOU FINISH BEFORE TIME IS CALLED, YOU MAY CHECK YOUR WORK ON THIS SECTION ONLY. DO NOT TURN TO ANY OTHER SECTION IN THE TEST.

SECTION 2

Time—35 Minutes

37 Questions

In this section there are four possible answers after each question. Choose which one is best. You may use the blank space at the right of the page for scratch work.

Note: Figures are drawn with the greatest possible accuracy, UNLESS stated "Not Drawn to Scale."

USE THIS SPACE FOR FIGURING.

1. Two radii of a circle combine to form a diameter if they meet at an angle whose measure in degrees is

(A) 90 degrees.
(B) 120 degrees.
(C) 180 degrees.
(D) 240 degrees.

2. The price of a stock doubled from Monday to Tuesday. What is the percent increase in the price of the stock from Monday to Tuesday?

(A) 50%
(B) 100%
(C) 150%
(D) 200%

3. Which of the following is true?

(A) $0.2 \times 0.2 = 0.4$
(B) $0.2 \times 2 = 0.04$
(C) $\frac{0.2}{2} = 0.1$
(D) $\frac{0.2}{0.1} = 0.01$

4. A square has a perimeter of 8. What is the length of one of its sides?

(A) 2
(B) 4
(C) 8
(D) 16

GO ON TO THE NEXT PAGE

USE THIS SPACE FOR FIGURING.

5. All of the following are equal to $\frac{1}{3}$ EXCEPT
   (A) $\frac{6}{18}$.
   (B) $\frac{10}{30}$.
   (C) $\frac{11}{33}$.
   (D) $\frac{7}{24}$.

6. If N is an integer, which of the following MUST be odd?
   (A) $2N$
   (B) $N + 1$
   (C) $2N + 1$
   (D) $3N + 1$

7. If $\frac{700}{x} = 35$, then $x =$
   (A) 2.
   (B) 5.
   (C) 20.
   (D) 200.

8. Which of the following is closest to 15%?
   (A) $\frac{1}{7}$
   (B) $\frac{1}{5}$
   (C) $\frac{1}{4}$
   (D) $\frac{1}{3}$

9. When A is divided by 5 it leaves a remainder of 3. What is the remainder when $A + 2$ is divided by 5?
   (A) 0
   (B) 1
   (C) 2
   (D) 3

GO ON TO THE NEXT PAGE

USE THIS SPACE FOR FIGURING.

10. The difference between 30% of 400 and 15% of 400 is

(A) 200.
(B) 150.
(C) 60.
(D) 30.

11. If $\frac{x}{3} = \frac{y}{6} = 3$, what is the value of $x + y$?

(A) 27
(B) 21
(C) 18
(D) 9

12. In the triangle in Figure 1, $x =$

(A) 50.
(B) 60.
(C) 80.
(D) 100.

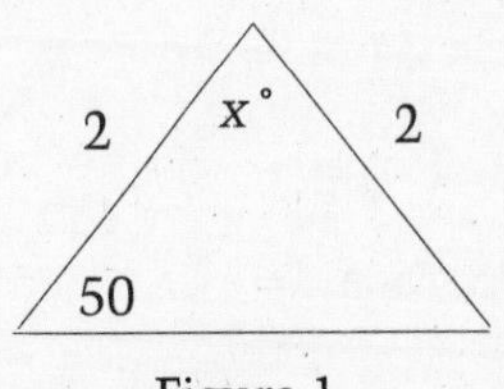

Figure 1

13. In Figure 2, if triangle *ABC* and triangle *CED* are equilateral, then the measure in degrees of angle *BCE* is

(A) 60
(B) 90
(C) 120
(D) 180

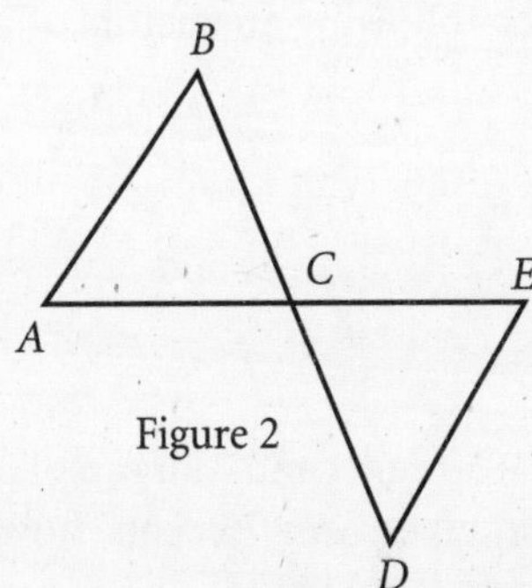

Figure 2

14. If 9 is added to the product of 12 and 4, the result is

(A) 17.
(B) 25.
(C) 57.
(D) 84.

15. If 45 is divided by the product of 3 and 5, the result is

(A) 3.
(B) 5.
(C) 9.
(D) 15.

USE THIS SPACE FOR FIGURING.

16. Joe shoveled snow for $2\frac{1}{3}$ hours in the morning and then for another $1\frac{3}{4}$ hours in the afternoon. How many hours did he shovel in total?

(A) $3\frac{1}{6}$
(B) $3\frac{5}{6}$
(C) $4\frac{1}{12}$
(D) 7

17. All of the following are factors of 27 EXCEPT

(A) 1.
(B) 3.
(C) 7.
(D) 27.

18. Greg has 50 cents and Margaret has $5. If Margaret gives Greg 75 cents, how much money will Greg have?

(A) $1
(B) $1.25
(C) $1.50
(D) $5.50

GO ON TO THE NEXT PAGE

USE THIS SPACE FOR FIGURING.

19. $\frac{1}{2} + \frac{1}{6} =$

(A) $\frac{1}{3}$

(B) $\frac{2}{3}$

(C) $\frac{5}{6}$

(D) $\frac{1}{12}$

20. How many integers are there from 1,960 to 1,980, inclusive?

(A) 10

(B) 20

(C) 21

(D) 30

21. If $n^* = 2n + 4$, what is the value of 10^*?

(A) 14

(B) 24

(C) 40

(D) 44

22. If $a + b = 6$, then which expression is equal to b?

(A) $b = a - 6$

(B) $b = 6 - a$

(C) $b = 6a$

(D) $b = \frac{6}{a}$

Directions: In questions 23–37, note the given information, if any, and then compare the quantity in Column A to the quantity in Column B. Choose on you answer sheet grid

A if the quantity in Column A is greater.

B if the quantity in Column B is greater.

C if the two quantities are equal.

D if the relationship cannot be determined from the information given.

	Column A	Column B
23.	$3 + 4$	3×4
24.	1,000 – 3.45002	1,000 – 3.45601

USE THIS SPACE FOR FIGURING.

The ages of the 5 members of a certain family are 8, 12, 16, 20, and 24.

	Column A	Column B
25.	The average (arithmetic mean) age of the 5 family members	16

The price of one grapefruit is \$0.45, and the price of a bag of oranges is \$2.45.

	Column A	Column B
26.	The price of a grapefruit	The price of an orange
27.	Area of a triangle with a base of 6 and a height of 10	Area of a triangle with a base of 12 and a height of 5
28.	$\frac{1}{4}$ of 12,948	25% of 12,948

GO ON TO THE NEXT PAGE

	Column A	Column B
29.	n	n^2
30.	$2(2x + 1)$	$4x + 4$
31.	$\frac{1}{4} + \frac{5}{8} + \frac{11}{12}$	$\frac{3}{16} + \frac{3}{7} + \frac{2}{9}$
32.	$9.9999 - 2$	$0.99999 + 7$

USE THIS SPACE FOR FIGURING.

$10M + 2 = 32$

	Column A	Column B
33.	3	M
34.	5% of 100	100% of 5
35.	$\frac{1}{4}$	$0.2569 - 0.007$

A sweater sells for $60.

	Column A	Column B
36.	The price of the sweater after a 10% discount	$50
37.	4.23×8	37.2×8

IF YOU FINISH BEFORE TIME IS CALLED, YOU MAY CHECK YOUR WORK ON THIS SECTION ONLY. DO NOT TURN TO ANY OTHER SECTION IN THE TEST.

SECTION 3

Time—35 Minutes

36 Questions

Read each passage carefully and then answer the questions about it. For each question, decide on the basis of the passage which one of the choices best answers the question.

The word "chocolate" is a generic term used to describe a variety of foods made from the seeds, or beans, of the cacao tree. The first people known to have consumed chocolate were the Aztecs, who used cacao seeds to brew a bitter, aromatic drink. It was not until the Mexican expedition of Hernan Cortes in 1519, however, that Europeans first learned of cacao. Cortes came to the New World primarily in search of gold, but his interest was apparently also piqued by the Aztecs' peculiar beverage, for when he returned to Spain, his ship's cargo included three chests of cacao beans. It was from these beans that Europe experienced its first taste of what seemed a very exotic beverage. The drink soon became popular among those wealthy enough to afford it, and over the next century cafes specializing in chocolate drinks began to spring up throughout Europe.

1. As used in line 1, the word "generic" means

(A) scientific.
(B) technical.
(C) general.
(D) obscure.

2. The passage suggests that chocolate foods can be

(A) unhealthy if consumed in excessive quantities.
(B) one of the staples of a society's diet.
(C) made from part of the cacao tree.
(D) made from ingredients other than the cacao tree.

3. It can be inferred from the passage that Cortes journeyed to Mexico mainly in order to

(A) conquer the Aztecs.
(B) increase his personal wealth.
(C) claim new land for Spain.
(D) gain personal glory.

4. The author implies in lines 9–14 that Cortes found the Aztecs' chocolate drink to be

(A) sweet.
(B) relaxing.
(C) stimulating.
(D) strange.

5. The passage suggests that most of the chocolate consumed by Europeans in the 1500s was

(A) expensive.
(B) candy.
(C) made by Aztecs.
(D) made by Cortes.

6. All of the following questions can be answered in the passage EXCEPT:

(A) Did Cortes return to Europe with gold?
(B) How did the Aztecs consume chocolate?
(C) Were cacao beans well received in Europe?
(D) Who were the first people to enjoy chocolate?

GO ON TO THE NEXT PAGE

It has been known for some time that wolves live and hunt in hierarchically structured packs, organized in a kind of "pecking order" similar to that found in flocks of birds. At the top of the hierarchy in any wolf pack are the senior males, dominating the others in all matters of privilege and leadership. As many as three other distinct subgroups may exist within a pack: mature wolves with subordinate status in the hierarchy; immature wolves (who will not be treated as adults until their second year); and outcast wolves rejected by the rest of the pack. Each individual wolf, moreover, occupies a specific position within these subgroups, taking precedence over wolves of lower rank in the selection of food, mates, and resting places and holding a greater share of the responsibility for protecting the pack from strange wolves and other dangers.

7. According to the passage, wolves and birds are similar in that they both

(A) mate for life.

(B) become adults at two years of age.

(C) defer to senior females.

(D) live in structured groups.

8. The passage suggests that our knowledge of the social hierarchies of wolves is

(A) mostly theoretical.

(B) not a recent discovery.

(C) based on observations of individual wolves.

(D) in need of long-range studies.

9. What is implied in the passage about outcast wolves?

(A) They never share the pack's food.

(B) They sometimes kill the pack's young.

(C) Their status is lower than that of immature wolves.

(D) They are incapable of protecting the pack from strange wolves.

10. According to the passage, the structure of a wolf pack is determined by each wolf's share of all of the following EXCEPT

(A) food.

(B) water.

(C) resting place.

(D) mate.

11. The author's attitude toward the subject may best be described as

(A) admiring.

(B) critical.

(C) informative.

(D) indifferent.

12. As used in line 9, the word "subordinate" most nearly means

(A) top.

(B) inferior.

(C) short.

(D) immature.

GO ON TO THE NEXT PAGE

The Romantic poets in nineteenth-century Britain prided themselves on their rejection of many of the traditional practices of English poetry. William Wordsworth, one of the leaders of the Romantic movement, wished to avoid what he considered the emotional insincerity and affectation characteristic of much earlier poetry; instead he attempted to achieve spontaneity and naturalness of expression in his verse. According to Wordsworth, a poet should be "a man speaking to men" rather than a detached observer delivering pronouncements from an ivory tower. John Keats, Wordsworth's younger contemporary, brought a similar attitude to his poetry. Keats tried to make even the structure of his sentences seem unpremeditated. "If poetry," he claimed, "comes not as naturally as the leaves to a tree, it had better not come at all."

13. The passage is primarily concerned with
    (A) describing an artistic movement.
    (B) detailing the achievements of William Wordsworth.
    (C) criticizing traditional English poetry.
    (D) providing information about John Keats.

14. As used in line 3, the word "traditional" means
    (A) conservative.
    (B) formal.
    (C) boring.
    (D) standard.

15. It is implied by the passage that
    (A) the Romantic poets wrote better poetry than their predecessors did.
    (B) Keats imitated Wordsworth's poetry.
    (C) Keats is considered a Romantic poet.
    (D) Keats only wrote poetry about nature.

16. By the statement that a poet should be "a man speaking to men," Wordsworth probably meant that poetry should
    (A) be written in the form of a dialogue.
    (B) always be read aloud to an audience.
    (C) not be written by women.
    (D) have the directness and spontaneity of real speech.

17. All of the following are true about Wordsworth and Keats EXCEPT
    (A) both were Romantic poets.
    (B) both wrote with a naturalness of expression.
    (C) both liked poetry that was told from an angle of a detached observer.
    (D) both wanted to stray from traditional English poetry.

18. Where would this passage most likely be found?
    (A) A review of a book on Romantic poets
    (B) A biography of Wordsworth
    (C) A research paper on Romantic poets
    (D) A love letter from Wordsworth

GO ON TO THE NEXT PAGE

Edward Stratmeyer, the creator of the Hardy Boys, Nancy Drew, and the Bobbsey Twins, did not gain enormous commercial success through luck alone. His books, in which young amateur detectives had fantastic adventures and always saved the day, had a particular appeal in the time they were written. When Stratmeyer himself was a boy, the harsh economics of an industrializing America quickly forced children to become adults. By 1900, however, prosperity began to prolong childhood, creating a new stage of life—adolescence. From 1900 to 1930, the heyday of Stratmeyer's career, adolescence came of age. Child labor laws made schooling compulsory until the age of sixteen. Young Americans, with more free time than the working youth of the previous century, looked to fiction and fantasy for adventure. Stratmeyer, writing under a variety of pseudonyms, responded to the needs of his readers with a slew of heroic super-teens.

19. The passage primarily serves to explain

(A) the universal appeal of Stratmeyer's characters.
(B) the benefits of mandatory schooling for teenagers.
(C) the underlying reason for a writer's popularity.
(D) the economic boom created by child labor laws.

20. The passage suggests that the appeal of Stratmeyer's fictional heroes lay partly in the fact that

(A) they worked long hours in industrial jobs.
(B) their activities were not restricted by fictional parents.
(C) they were the same age as his readers.
(D) they were based on young people Stratmeyer actually knew.

21. According to the passage, children under sixteen during the 1930s

(A) led lives of fun and adventure.
(B) were better off financially than ever before.
(C) began to lose interest in Stratmeyer's books.
(D) were legally required to attend school.

22. According to the passage, Stratmeyer wrote his books

(A) in a single thirty-year span.
(B) using a series of pseudonyms.
(C) to pay off family debts.
(D) without ever gaining commercial success.

23. As used in line 10, "prosperity" most closely means

(A) success.
(B) failure.
(C) medicine.
(D) life.

24. The author's attitude toward Stratmeyer can best be described as

(A) surprised.
(B) tired.
(C) admiring.
(D) scornful.

GO ON TO THE NEXT PAGE

The ventriloquist's "dummy," the wooden figure that a ventriloquist uses to create the illusion of "throwing" his or her voice, was first developed in the 1880s. On the outside, the first dummies looked very much like those used today—with much the same exaggerated mouth and range of movement. On the inside, however, the best of these wooden figures were a curious fusion of engineering feats and sculpture. Underneath the wig, the back of the dummy's head opened up, revealing tangled innards of metal and wire, screws, and levers. Arguably the most mechanically complex figures were made by the McElroy brothers, who together created one hundred figures in the ten years prior to the Second World War. The mechanical brain of the McElroy dummy was assembled from some 300 different springs, pieces of metal, typewriter keys, and bicycle spokes—a synergistic effort comparable to the work of the Wright Brothers.

25. The primary purpose of the passage is to

(A) compare the achievements of two different families of inventors.
(B) relate the history of the ventriloquist's art.
(C) compare the ventriloquists' dummies of the 19th century with those produced today.
(D) describe the complex craftsmanship behind early ventriloquists' dummies.

26. It can be inferred from the passage that the outward appearance of ventriloquists' dummies

(A) is meant to seem as lifelike as possible.
(B) has not changed much since they were invented.
(C) depends on what mechanical devices are inside them.
(D) changed after the work of the McElroy brothers.

27. The passage suggests that the most complex dummies are

(A) created using scientific and artistic craftsmanship.
(B) able to fool the most discerning observer.
(C) those with the widest range of movement.
(D) those made since the end of the Second World War.

28. The author probably argues that the McElroy brothers' dummies were "a synergistic effort" (line 19) because

(A) the McElroys were related to the Wright Brothers.
(B) the McElroys borrowed design concepts from other inventors.
(C) the McElroys worked together on the design.
(D) their dummies required so much energy to operate.

29. The author's attitude toward the McElroy brothers can best be described as

(A) skeptical.
(B) puzzled.
(C) elated.
(D) appreciative.

30. All the following questions can be answered by the passage EXCEPT:

(A) How does a ventriloquist throw his or her voice?
(B) What is a dummy?
(C) How did the McElroy brothers' dummies differ from others?
(D) Did the McElroy brothers start making dummies before or after war?

GO ON TO THE NEXT PAGE

In 1916, James VanDerZee opened a photography studio in New York City's Harlem. It was the eve of the Harlem Renaissance—the decade-long flowering of art and culture that established Harlem as the most artistically vigorous African-American community in the nation. For some 40 years, VanDerZee captured the life and spirit of that burgeoning community, producing thousands of portraits, not only of notables but of ordinary citizens—parents and children, brides and grooms, church groups, and women's clubs. Critics consider these images important today not only for their record of Harlem life, but for their reflection of their subjects' keen sense of the importance of their culture. VanDerZee's carefully staged photographs spotlighted his subjects' pride and self-assurance. His unique vision recorded a time, place, and culture that might otherwise have slipped away.

31. This passage focuses primarily on
    (A) the cultural achievements of the Harlem Renaissance.
    (B) the history of African-American photography.
    (C) the creative influences that shaped one photographer's career.
    (D) the cultural record left by a Harlem photographer.

32. It can be inferred from the passage that VanDerZee opened his studio
    (A) just before the Harlem Renaissance began.
    (B) in order to photograph African-American celebrities.
    (C) without having previous photographic experience.
    (D) with financial support from his community.

33. The passage most likely describes the subjects of VanDerZee's photographs (lines 7–12) in order to
    (A) demonstrate the artist's flair for composition.
    (B) show that his work represented the whole community.
    (C) highlight the self-assurance of Harlem residents.
    (D) reflect upon the nature of photography.

34. The author's attitude toward VanDerZee can best be described as
    (A) neutral.
    (B) condescending.
    (C) admiring.
    (D) generous.

35. Which of the following statements is NOT true?
    (A) VanDerZee helped trigger the Harlem Renaissance.
    (B) If it weren't for VanDerZee, a part of Harlem life would have been forgotten.
    (C) The Harlem Renaissance helped establish the neighborhood as an artistic community.
    (D) VanDerZee captured the lives of a variety of people in Harlem.

36. As used in line 8, "burgeoning" means
    (A) beautiful.
    (B) barren.
    (C) quiet.
    (D) thriving.

IF YOU FINISH BEFORE TIME IS CALLED, YOU MAY CHECK YOUR WORK ON THIS SECTION ONLY. DO NOT TURN TO ANY OTHER SECTION IN THE TEST.

SECTION 4

Time—40 Minutes

47 Questions

In this section there are four possible answers after each question. Choose which one is best. You may use the blank space at the right of the page for scratchwork.

Note: Figures are drawn with the greatest possible accuracy, UNLESS stated "Not Drawn to Scale."

USE THIS SPACE FOR FIGURING.

1. Ralph is twice as old as Howie. If Ralph is x years old, how many years old is Howie, in terms of x?

(A) $0.5x$

(B) $2x$

(C) $x + 2$

(D) $x - 2$

2. A bag contains only blue and red marbles. If there are three blue marbles for every red marble, what fraction of all the marbles is red?

(A) $\frac{1}{4}$

(B) $\frac{1}{3}$

(C) $\frac{1}{2}$

(D) $\frac{3}{4}$

3. On Monday the temperatures of four different cities were 55°, –18°, 25°, and –15°. What was the average (arithmetic mean) temperature on Monday for these four cities?

(A) 103°

(B) 20°

(C) 12°

(D) 11.75°

GO ON TO THE NEXT PAGE

Questions 4–5 refer to the graph in Figure 1.

USE THIS SPACE FOR FIGURING.

4. Approximately how many medium-sized shirts were sold?

(A) 300
(B) 400
(C) 500
(D) 600

5. If each shirt sells for $5.95, approximately how much was spent on small-sized shirts?

(A) $300
(B) $900
(C) $1,800
(D) $3,600

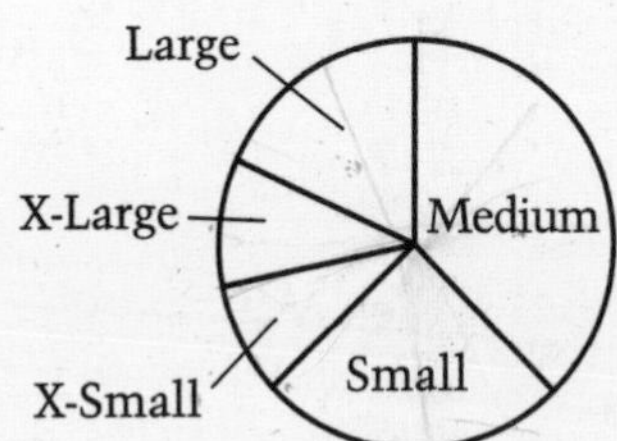

Figure 1

6. How many seconds are there in $\frac{1}{20}$ of a minute?

(A) 2
(B) 3
(C) 20
(D) 30

7. What is the greatest number of squares, each measuring two centimeters by two centimeters, that can be cut from a rectangle with a length of eight centimeters and a width of six centimeters?

(A) 48
(B) 12
(C) 8
(D) 6

8. Five percent of the guests at a Halloween party were dressed as witches. If there were eight witches at the party, how many guests were at the party?

(A) 40
(B) 80
(C) 160
(D) 200

GO ON TO THE NEXT PAGE

USE THIS SPACE FOR FIGURING.

Questions 9–10 refer to the following definition.

For all real numbers a and b, $a@b = (a \times b) - (a + b)$.

Example: $6 @ 5 = (6 \times 5) - (6 + 5) = 30 - 11 = 19$.

9. $9@8 =$

(A) 73
(B) 72
(C) 71
(D) 55

10. If $10@N = -1$, then $N =$

(A) 0.
(B) 1.
(C) 9.
(D) 11.

11. A CD collection was divided among six people so that each received the same number of CDs. Which of the following could be the number of CDs in the collection?

(A) 10
(B) 15
(C) 21
(D) 24

12. At which of the following times is the smaller angle formed by the minute hand and the hour hand of a clock less than 90 degrees?

(A) 1:30
(B) 3:00
(C) 4:30
(D) 6:00

GO ON TO THE NEXT PAGE

USE THIS SPACE FOR FIGURING.

13. Carol spent $\frac{1}{2}$ of her day at work, and $\frac{2}{3}$ of her time at work in meetings. What fraction of her entire day did Carol spend in meetings?

(A) $\frac{1}{2}$

(B) $\frac{1}{3}$

(C) $\frac{1}{5}$

(D) $\frac{1}{6}$

14. If $\frac{1}{2} \times S = 0.2$, then $S =$

(A) $\frac{2}{5}$.

(B) $\frac{1}{4}$.

(C) $\frac{1}{5}$.

(D) $\frac{1}{10}$.

15. If 50% of a number equals 75, then 10% of the number equals

(A) 15.

(B) 30.

(C) 60.

(D) 150.

16. If $\frac{1}{2} + \frac{1}{3} = \frac{M}{12}$, then $M =$

(A) 8.

(B) 9.

(C) 10.

(D) 11.

GO ON TO THE NEXT PAGE

17. The perimeter of a rectangle is 32. If its length is three times as long as its width, what is its width?

    (A) 12
    (B) 8
    (C) 6
    (D) 4

USE THIS SPACE FOR FIGURING.

$$2{,}955 \times A = 35{,}460$$
$$11{,}820 \times B = 35{,}460$$
$$3{,}940 \times C = 35{,}460$$
$$7{,}092 \times D = 35{,}460$$

18. If each of the above equations is correctly solved, which of the following has the greatest value?

    (A) A
    (B) B
    (C) C
    (D) D

19. In a certain garage, 3 out of every 10 cars are foreign. If there are 180 cars at the garage, how many of them are foreign?

    (A) 27
    (B) 45
    (C) 54
    (D) 60

20. If *N*¿= *N* × 10, then 30¿ + 2¿ =

    (A) 32.
    (B) 302.
    (C) 320.
    (D) 3,200.

GO ON TO THE NEXT PAGE

USE THIS SPACE FOR FIGURING.

21. Patricia began reading from the beginning of page 42 of a book and stopped at the end of page 83. How many pages did she read?

(A) 40
(B) 41
(C) 42
(D) 43

22. In Figure 2, if $AB = 8$ and $AC = 14$, how far is the midpoint of AB from the midpoint of BC?

(A) 3
(B) 4
(C) 7
(D) 8

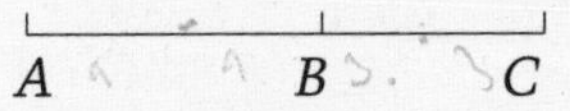

A B C

Figure 2

23. Judy has six more baseball cards than her brother. How many would she have to give him so that they would have an equal number of cards?

(A) 6
(B) 4
(C) 3
(D) 2

24. Fred averaged 168 on the first three games he bowled. What must he score on his fourth game in order to raise his average 5 points?

(A) 158
(B) 163
(C) 178
(D) 188

25. Which of the following equations could NEVER be true?

(A) $N \times 0 = N$
(B) $1 \times N = N$
(C) $N \times N = N$
(D) $N - 1 = N$

GO ON TO THE NEXT PAGE

USE THIS SPACE FOR FIGURING.

26. If X is the set of numbers greater than 6 and Y is the set of numbers less than 11, how many whole numbers exist that are in both sets?

(A) 4
(B) 5
(C) 6
(D) Infinitely many

27. Mary has 30% more money than June has. If June has $65, how much money does Mary have?

(A) $84.50
(B) $80
(C) $50
(D) $45.50

28. If 9 is x percent of 90, what is 50 percent of x?

(A) 5
(B) 10
(C) 15
(D) 18

29. A certain machine caps 5 bottles every 2 seconds. At this rate, how many bottles will be capped in 1 minute?

(A) 75
(B) 150
(C) 225
(D) 300

30. What is five percent of twenty percent of one hundred?

(A) 1
(B) 5
(C) 20
(D) 25

GO ON TO THE NEXT PAGE

USE THIS SPACE FOR FIGURING.

31. If an exam had 10 questions and Keith answered 2 questions incorrectly, what percent of the questions did he answer incorrectly?

(A) 2%
(B) 10%
(C) 12%
(D) 20%

32. The difference between 6,985 and 3,001 is approximately

(A) 3,000.
(B) 3,500.
(C) 4,000.
(D) 4,500.

33. One and one-third minus five-sixths equals

(A) $\frac{1}{4}$.
(B) $\frac{1}{3}$.
(C) $\frac{1}{2}$.
(D) $\frac{3}{4}$.

34. Patty and Liza went out for lunch. Patty paid $3.30 for a drink and two hot dogs. Liza paid $2.15 for a drink and one hot dog. How much did a hot dog cost?

(A) $0.90
(B) $1.15
(C) $1.30
(D) $1.65

GO ON TO THE NEXT PAGE

35. If one-fourth of a number is 3, what is one-third of the same number?

(A) 1
(B) 2
(C) 3
(D) 4

USE THIS SPACE FOR FIGURING.

36. $2 \times 4 \times 7 \times 9$ is equal to the product of 18 and

(A) 8
(B) 14
(C) 28
(D) 36

37. If $12 + P = 20 - 2 \times 3$, then $P =$

(A) 2.
(B) 14.
(C) 36.
(D) 42.

38. One-tenth of 99 is

(A) 0.99.
(B) 9.9.
(C) 99.
(D) 99.9.

39. Twenty percent of 30 is

(A) 6.
(B) 8.
(C) 10.
(D 12.5.

40. $\frac{64}{2 \times 4} =$

(A) 8
(B) 24
(C) 42
(D) 128

GO ON TO THE NEXT PAGE

USE THIS SPACE FOR FIGURING.

41. $\frac{81}{9} + 2 =$

(A) 3
(B) 6
(C) 8
(D) 11

42. In a certain class, there are 6 girls for every 2 boys. What is the ratio of the number of girls to the entire class?

(A) 12:1
(B) 8:6
(C) 6:2
(D) 3:4

43. If $\frac{28}{a} = \frac{48}{12}$, then $a =$

(A) 7.
(B) 8.
(C) 9.
(D) 10.

44. If Set *A* contains all integers greater than 8, and Set *B* contains all integers less than 30, which of the following numbers could be in both sets?

(A) 0
(B) 2
(C) 4
(D) 9

45. $\frac{18+16}{4}$ equals

(A) 8
(B) 8.5
(C) 9
(D) 22

GO ON TO THE NEXT PAGE

46. When an integer is multiplied by itself, it can end in all of the following EXCEPT

(A) 1.
(B) 3.
(C) 5.
(D) 6.

47. If 20 percent of J is 1,500, what is 15 percent of J?

(A) 1,125
(B) 3,000
(C) 5,125
(D) 6,000

USE THIS SPACE FOR FIGURING.

IF YOU FINISH BEFORE TIME IS CALLED, YOU MAY CHECK YOUR WORK ON THIS SECTION ONLY. DO NOT TURN TO ANY OTHER SECTION IN THE TEST.

STOP

SECTION 5

Time—30 Minutes

DIRECTIONS: Write an essay on the following prompt on the paper provided. Your essay should NOT exceed two pages and must be written in ink. Erasing is not allowed.

Prompt: <u>You can't teach an old dog new tricks</u>.

Do you agree or disagree with this statement? Use examples from history, literature, or your own personal experience to support your point of view.

IF YOU FINISH BEFORE TIME IS CALLED, YOU MAY CHECK YOUR WORK ON THIS SECTION ONLY. DO NOT TURN TO ANY OTHER SECTION IN THE TEST.

STOP

ANSWER KEY

Section 1

1. B
2. C
3. A
4. C
5. B
6. D
7. B
8. D
9. B
10. D
11. D
12. A
13. D
14. D
15. A
16. B
17. A
18. B
19. B
20. A
21. B
22. A
23. D
24. D
25. C
26. D
27. B
28. A
29. C
30. C
31. B
32. C
33. B
34. A
35. B
36. D
37. B
38. B
39. B
40. A

Section 2

1. C
2. B
3. C
4. A
5. D
6. C
7. C
8. A
9. A
10. C
11. A
12. C
13. C
14. C
15. A
16. C
17. C
18. B
19. B
20. C
21. B
22. B
23. B
24. A
25. C
26. D
27. C
28. C
29. D
30. B
31. A
32. B
33. C
34. C
35. A
36. A
37. B

Section 3

1. C
2. C
3. B
4. D
5. A
6. A
7. D
8. B
9. C
10. B
11. D
12. B
13. A
14. D
15. C
16. D
17. C
18. C
19. C
20. C
21. D
22. B
23. A
24. C
25. D
26. B
27. A
28. C
29. D
30. A
31. D
32. A
33. B
34. C
35. A
36. D

Section 4

1. A
2. A
3. D
4. B
5. C
6. B
7. B
8. C
9. D
10. B
11. D
12. C
13. B
14. A
15. A
16. C
17. D
18. A
19. C
20. C
21. C
22. C
23. C
24. D
25. D
26. A
27. A
28. A
29. B
30. A
31. D
32. C
33. C
34. B
35. D
36. C
37. A
38. B
39. A
40. A
41. D
42. D
43. A
44. D
45. B
46. B
47. A

ISEE PRACTICE TEST 1: UPPER- AND MIDDLE-LEVEL: ASSESS YOUR STRENGTHS

Use the following tables to determine which topics and chapters you need to review most. If you need help with your essay, be sure to review Chapter 9: The Essay and Chapter 26: Writing Skills.

Topic	Question
Verbal: Synonyms	Section 1, questions 1–20
Verbal: Sentence Completions	Section 1, questions 21–40
Quantitative Reasoning: Word Problems	Section 2, questions 1–22
Quantitative Reasoning: Quantitative Comparison	Section 2, questions 23–37
Reading Comprehension	Section 3, questions 1–36
Mathematics Achievement	Section 4, questions 1–47

Topic	Number of Questions on Test	Number Correct	If you struggled with these questions, study...
Verbal: Synonyms	20		Chapters 7 and 24
Verbal: Sentence Completions	20		Chapter 4
Quantitative Reasoning: Word Problems	22		Chapters 10–14 and Chapter 25
Quantitative Reasoning: Quantitative Comparison	15		Chapter 5
Reading Comprehension	36		Chapter 8
Mathematics Achievement	47		Chapters 10–14 and Chapter 25

ANSWERS AND EXPLANATIONS

SECTION 1: VERBAL REASONING

SYNONYMS

1. B

An excess is an extra amount of something—a surplus.

2. C

To reimburse someone is to pay him back or to compensate him.

3. A

When you astound someone, you greatly surprise or stun her.

4. C

Something that is massive is extremely large or huge.

5. B

Din refers to a large and distracting sound or a clamor.

6. D

When something is scarce there is not a lot of it; it is very rare.

7. B

If you accuse someone of deceit, you are accusing him of being untruthful or of trickery.

8. D

You often hear the expression "hallowed ground," which means sacred ground.

9. B

If you have apprehension about something, you have an acute concern or worry about it.

10. D

When something is bleak, like the weather, it is very harsh or dreary.

11. D

To offend someone is to be extremely rude to her or to insult her.

12. A

Someone who is vigorous is very lively and healthy—robust.

13. D

A despondent person feels hopeless and depressed.

14. D

If you are very hungry and then eat a large meal, you can say that your appetite has been satiated or satisfied.

15. A

Spontaneous actions or behavior occur with no apparent reason or cause—they are impulsive.

16. B

Someone whose face is wan is sickly and pale.

17. A

If you abhor liver or brussel sprouts, you dislike them immensely—you despise them.

18. B

If you see an apparition on Halloween, you are seeing something resembling a ghost.

19. B

A person who is benevolent is kind and giving—charitable.

20. A

A tolerant person does not become angry or intimidated by new and strange ideas because she is open-minded.

SENTENCE COMPLETIONS

21. B

This author has written a lot of novels, so we need a word that describes an author who writes a great deal. Prolific means producing abundant works.

22. A

The school has managed in this situation in spite of a lack of funds. Meager means deficient in quantity or scant. Don't be misled by (D), belittled. True, it has to do with little, but in an emotional sense. One feels belittled by public criticism.

23. D

With the advent, or arrival, of the computer chip, Frank's job became "something." Common sense tells us that his job became outdated or extinct. Obsolete means just that: no longer useful.

24. D

There were efforts to do something to the nature preserve. Whatever those efforts were, we can infer from the word "proved" that they were unsuccessful. Inextricable, (A), looks tempting, as it means incapable of being disentangled (think of extricating yourself from something), but it doesn't make sense here. Futile, (D), means having no useful result or ineffective.

25. C

The clue "except for" indicates that you're looking for the opposite of "loners"—social, (C).

26. D

"Unproductive" is the clue here—it suggests that the company employs people who don't work hard. In other words, they have a lackadaisical approach to their work.

27. B

Environmental, (B), is the only word that fits the second blank—a forest fire "devastated the region" fits the first blank.

28. A

"Despite" is a clue that indicates contrast—in spite of his humble beginnings, the chieftain became one of the greatest rulers.

29. C

Another contrast question—in spite of Angela's job as an interior decorator, her home might be modestly decorated.

30. C

Contested is the only word that fits the context here—you can't gather, qualify, or survive for food if you're a marine creature.

31. B

You're looking for a negative word here—contempt, (B), fits the captain's attitude best.

32. C

Which word goes best with grace? Grace and (C), elegance, are the two words that best describe a ballet dancer.

33. B

You're looking for negative words here for both blanks, so you can eliminate choices (A), (C), and (D).

34. A

The word "staff" indicates that the volunteer association is either (A), recruiting, or (D), hiring. Attributes is the word that best fits the idea of job qualifications.

35. B

The phrase "in spite of" indicates a contrast or paradox—you can tell that Joanne didn't get the promotion even though she worked hard. (B), industrious, is the only word that works.

36. D

The sky diver's reaction has to be consistent with his parachute—if it opened improperly, then he would be fortunate to survive.

37. B

The logic of the sentence suggests that the puppy would only whine if unaccustomed, or unused to, discipline.

38. B

The clue word "whereas" tells you this is a contrast question, so you need a choice with contrasting words. Only choice (B) provides the needed contrast.

39. B

Another word for "uncomfortable in social situations" is (B), introverted.

40. A

You're looking for a word that means secret. You may have heard the word "clandestine" on the news or in spy movies. It means secret, or undercover.

SECTION 2: QUANTITATIVE REASONING

Word Problems

1. C

A diameter is a chord that runs straight through the center of a circle. Two radii will form a diameter if they form a straight line, as shown in the figure below. A straight angle has 180°, so (C) is correct.

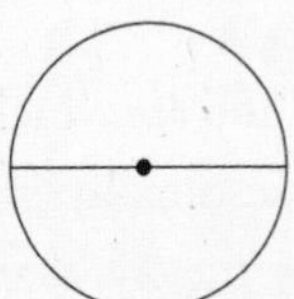

2. B

If the price of the stock doubled, it increased by its full price, or 100%, (B). If this isn't clear, pick a number for the original price of the stock, say $100. On Tuesday it would be twice this, or $200. So the increase is $200 – $100 = $100; $100 is 100% of $100, so again (B) is correct.

3. C

Evaluate each choice to see which is true:

(A) $0.2 \times 0.2 = 0.04$, not 0.4, so (A) is false.

(B) $0.2 \times 2 = 0.4$, not 0.04, so (B) is false.

(C) $0.2 \div 2 = 0.1$, so (C) is true.

(D) $0.2 \div 0.1 = 2$, not 0.01, so (D) is false.

4. A

A square has 4 equal sides, so its perimeter is equal to $4s$, where s represents the length of one of its sides. So $4s = 8$, and a side of the square has length 2.

5. D

Evaluate each choice to see which is not equal to $\frac{1}{3}$:

(A) $\frac{6}{18} = \frac{1}{3}$ (when you factor out a 6)

(B) $\frac{10}{30} = \frac{1}{3}$ (when you factor out a 10)

(C) $\frac{11}{33} = \frac{1}{3}$ (when you factor out an 11)

(D) $\frac{7}{24} \neq \frac{1}{3}$

6. C

Pick numbers for N and see which of the choices must be odd. The question says must, not can, so the correct choice will be the one that is odd no matter what number you pick. Start with $N = 1$:

(A) $2N = 2$; even so eliminate (A). Any integer multiplied by 2 will be even.

(B) $N + 1 = 2$; even, so eliminate (B).

(C) $2N + 1 = 3$; odd. To see if this is always the case, try $N = 2$: $2N + 1 = 5$; odd, so (C) is correct. Since any integer multiplied by 2 will be even, $2N + 1$ will always be odd.

(D) If $N = 1$, $3N + 1 = 4$; even, so eliminate (D).

7. C

You know $\frac{700}{x} = 35$, so $35x = 700$ and $700 \div 35 = 20$. Thus, $x = 20$.

8. A

Fifteen percent $= \frac{15}{100} = 0.15$. Convert each choice to a decimal to see which comes closest to 0.15.

(A) $\frac{1}{7} = 0.142...$

(B) $\frac{1}{5} = 0.2$

(C) $\frac{1}{4} = 0.25$

(D) $\frac{1}{3} = 0.0\overline{33}$

Of the choices, 0.142 is closest to 0.15, so (A) is correct.

9. A

Pick a number for A. Since A leaves a remainder of 3 when divided by 5, let $A = 5 + 3 = 8$. You're asked for the remainder when $A + 2$, or 10, is divided by 5. Because 10 is divisible by 5, it leaves a remainder of 0.

10. C

You could figure out 30% of 400, then figure out 15% of 400, and then find their difference, but it's not necessary. The difference between 30% of a number and 15% of that same number is 30% – 15% = 15% of that number. Then 15% of 400 is 60, so (C) is correct.

11. A

Since $\frac{x}{3}$ and $\frac{y}{6}$ both equal 3, $\frac{x}{3} = 3$, and $x = 3 \times 3 = 9$ and $\frac{y}{6} = 3$, so $y = 3 \times 6 = 18$. So $x + y = 9 + 18 = 27$.

12. C

The triangle in Figure 1 is isosceles, since it has two sides of length 2. Therefore, the angles opposite these sides are also equal, and the unidentified base angle must equal 50°. The interior angles of a triangle sum to 180°, so $50 + 50 + x = 180$, $100 + x = 180$, and $x = 80$.

13. C

Since triangle ABC is equilateral, it has three 60° angles. Therefore, $\angle BCA$ is 60°. $\angle BCE$ is supplementary to $\angle BCA$, so $60 + \angle BCE = 180$ and $\angle BCE = 120$.

14. C

The product of two numbers is the result of multiplying them together, so the product of 12 and 4 is $12 \times 4 = 48$. Adding 9 to 48 gives you 57, (C).

15. A

The product of 3 and 5 is equal to $3 \times 5 = 15$. $45 \div 15 = 3$, (A).

16. C

Joe shoveled for a total of $2\frac{1}{3} + 1\frac{3}{4}$ hours. To add, first convert to improper fractions: $\frac{7}{3} + \frac{7}{4}$. Then find a common denominator: $\frac{28}{12} + \frac{21}{12} = \frac{49}{12}$. Lastly, convert to a mixed number: $= 4\frac{1}{12}$.

17. C

Evaluate each choice to see whether it is a factor of 27:

(A) $1 \times 27 = 27$, so 1 is a factor.

(B) $3 \times 9 = 27$, so 3 is a factor.

(C) 7 is *not* a factor of 27.

(D) $27 \times 1 = 27$, so 27 is a factor.

18. B

Greg has \$0.50 and is given \$0.75, for a total of \$1.25, (B).

19. B

$\frac{1}{2} + \frac{1}{6} = \frac{3}{6} + \frac{1}{6} = \frac{4}{6} = \frac{2}{3}$, (B)

20. C

To find the number of integers in an inclusive range, subtract the first integer from the last integer, and then add 1: $1{,}980 - 1{,}960 = 20$; $20 + 1 = 21$, choice (C).

21. B

Plug in 10 for n in the equation. So, $10^* = 2(10) + 4 = 20 + 4 = 24$.

22. B

If $a + b = 6$, in order to solve for b, you need to move a to the right side of the equation by subtracting it from 6. So, $b = 6 - a$.

Quantitative Comparison

23. B

In Column A, $3 + 4 = 7$. In Column B, $3 \times 4 = 12$. Since Column B is greater, (B) is correct.

24. A

You don't need to figure out the differences to answer this QC. In both cases you're subtracting some number from 1,000. Since you're subtracting more from 1,000 in Column B, the difference in Column B is smaller than the difference in Column A.

25. C

$$\text{Average} = \frac{\text{Sum of terms}}{\text{Number of terms}}, \text{ so here:}$$

$$\text{Average age} = \frac{8 + 12 + 16 + 20 + 24}{5} = \frac{80}{5} = 16$$

You could have saved time if you remembered that the average of a group of consecutive integers is equal to the middle value. The ages of the family happen to be consecutive multiples of 4, so their average is the middle value, or 16.

26. D

You're told that a grapefruit costs \$0.45, so that's the value in Column A. You're told that a bag of oranges costs \$2.45, but you're given no information about the number of oranges in the bag. If there were 2 oranges in the bag, each would cost about \$1.25, and Column B would be greater. But if there were 10 oranges in the bag, each would cost about \$0.25, and Column A would be greater. As it stands, you are not given enough information to determine which column is larger, so (D) is correct.

27. C

Area of a triangle is equal to $\frac{1}{2}$(base)(height). In Column A you have $\frac{1}{2}(6)(10) = 30$. In Column B you have $\frac{1}{2}(12)(5) = 30$. The columns are equal, so (C) is correct.

28. C

In Column A you have $\frac{1}{4}$ of 12,948, and in Column B you have 25% of 12,948. Since $\frac{1}{4} = 25\%$, the columns will be equal. Notice that you didn't need to do any calculation to solve this problem—in fact, calculating would waste time you could use to answer other questions.

29. D

Pick numbers for n. If $n = 1$, Column A is 1 and Column B is $1^2 = 1$, and the columns are equal. But if $n = 2$, Column A is 2, and Column B is $2^2 = 4$, and Column B is greater. Since there is more than one possible relationship between the columns, (D) is correct.

30. B

Multiplying through Column A gives you $4x + 2$. Compare piece by piece: While you may not know the value of $4x$, it will be the same in both columns. Looking at the second piece in each column, 4 is greater than 2, so Column B is greater.

31. A

It's not necessary—and is actually a waste of time—to find common denominators and calculate the sum in each column. Compare piece by piece. The first piece in Column A is $\frac{1}{4}$, and the first piece in Column B is $\frac{3}{16}$; $\frac{1}{4} = \frac{4}{16}$, so the first piece in A is bigger. The second piece in A is $\frac{5}{8}$, which is a little more than $\frac{1}{2}$, and the second piece in B is $\frac{3}{7}$, which is a little less than $\frac{1}{2}$. Therefore the second piece in A is greater. The third piece in A is $\frac{11}{12}$, which is greater than $\frac{1}{2}$, and the third piece in B is $\frac{2}{9}$, which is less than $\frac{1}{2}$. So the third piece in A is also greater, and Column A is greater.

32. B

The value in Column A is 7.9999, and the value in Column B is 7.99999. Column A only shows four places to the right of the decimal place, so any other places are understood to be zeros. Therefore Column A is actually 7.99990. So Column B is 0.00009 greater than Column A.

33. C

$10M + 2 = 32$, so $10M = 30$ and $M = 3$. Therefore the columns are equal.

34. C

This question is a breeze if you remember that a% of $b = b$% of a. If not, work it out. In Column A, 5% of 100 is 5. In Column B, 100% of 5 is 5. The columns are equal, so (C) is correct.

35. A

Put the columns in the same form so that they're easier to compare. In Column A, $\frac{1}{4} = 0.25$. In Column B, $0.2569 - 0.007 = 0.2499$, just less than 0.25 in Column A.

36. A

A 10 percent discount on a price of \$60 is \$6, so the sale price is \$60 – \$6 = \$54. This is greater than \$50 in Column B.

37. B

Comparing piece by piece, you see that the second pieces in both columns, namely 8, are equal. Since $4.23 < 37.2$, the first piece in B, 37.2, is greater, so Column B is greater.

SECTION 3: READING COMPREHENSION

Chocolate Passage

The first passage is about chocolate, which comes from the seeds, or beans, of the cacao tree. You're told that chocolate was first known to have been consumed (in drink form) by the Aztec people of Mexico, that the Spanish explorer Cortes learned of chocolate in 1519 on his expedition among the Aztecs, and that he brought three chests of cacao beans back to Spain. Over the next century, the passage concludes, the chocolate drink became popular with the wealthy throughout Europe.

1. C

Chocolate, we learn, is a "generic" term that describes "a variety of foods." Generic means general or relating to a whole group.

2. C

The passage's first sentence says that chocolate can be "made from the seeds, or beans, of the cacao tree." Since seeds are a part of the tree, (C) is correct. The healthiness of chocolate, (A), is not mentioned; we don't know whether it's a main food or staple of any society, (B); and we don't know what other ingredients, if any, go into making chocolate, (D).

3. B

Stick to what the passage actually says. "Cortes came to the New World primarily in search of gold... ." Therefore, (B) is correct: He came to amass wealth—i.e., to get rich.

4. D

We learn that Cortes's "interest was... piqued by the Aztec's peculiar beverage." The word "peculiar" suggests that Cortes found the Aztecs' chocolate drinks strange, (D). Several lines earlier, we learn that the drink was bitter, so (A) is incorrect. And the passage doesn't say whether the drink was relaxing, (B), or stimulating, (C).

5. A

This question points you to the passage's final sentence. It says there that, in the century after its introduction to Europe, the chocolate drink "became popular among those wealthy enough to afford it," which implies that chocolate was very expensive in Europe at that time, (A). This early European chocolate was a drink, not a candy, (B). As far as we know, Aztecs were not imported to make the drink, (C), only the cacao beans were. And the passage never suggests that Cortes himself made most of the chocolate consumed in Europe during the entire 16th century, (D).

6. A

Find the right answer by using the passage to answer the questions asked in the choices. (B) is answered in line 5; they "used cacao seeds to brew a bitter, aromatic drink." Line 15 says drinks made from cacao beans "became popular" in Europe, so (C) is incorrect. (D) is answered in lines 3–4; the passage says that "the first people known to have consumed chocolate were the Aztecs'. (A) is the answer because the passage does not say whether Cortes returned with gold in his cargo, only that he returned with "chests of cacao beans."

Wolves Passage

The next passage is about the structured packs that wolves live in. These packs are described as hierarchies similar to the "pecking order" of birds. Senior male wolves are at the top of the hierarchy, followed by mature wolves, young or immature wolves, and outcast wolves. We learn that a wolf's place in the hierarchy determines its selection of "food, mates, and resting places" and how much responsibility each wolf is given in terms of protecting the pack from danger.

7. D

Wolves are compared with birds only in the first sentence, where the wolf pack structure is compared to the pecking order of a bird flock. So both species live in structured groups, and (D) is correct. We don't learn whether birds or wolves mate for life, (A), when birds become "adults," (B), or whether either species defers to senior females, (C).

8. B

The passage's opening sentence notes that "it has been known for some time" that wolves live in structured packs; therefore, our knowledge of such packs is not a recent discovery, (B). (A) is incorrect because the information given is not theoretical. (C) is presumably incorrect because information about wolf packs must come from observations of the packs themselves, not individual wolves. And (D) is never suggested.

9. C

Outcast wolves are only mentioned in the third sentence, where we learn that they are fourth in order of importance, behind senior males, mature wolves, and immature wolves. So (C) is correct: The status of outcast wolves is lower than that of immature wolves. (A), (B), and (D) are all plausible statements, but none of them is implied in the passage.

10. B

The passage's final sentence says that the order of the pack determines the selection of "food, mates, and resting places," which eliminates choices (A), (C), and (D). It's plausible that a wolf's share of water, (B), would also be determined by the pack structure, but this is never mentioned, so (B) is correct.

11. D

The author's attitude toward wolf packs may best be described as indifferent because no opinion is expressed, (D).

12. B

Look at the sentence "subordinate" appears in. It talks about hierarchy, and the word modifies "status," so you know that the answer will have something to do with where the mature wolves fall in the hierarchy. That rules out (C) and (D). The sentence also calls the mature wolves a subgroup, putting them below senior males. That means their status is inferior to that of the senior males (B).

Romantics Passage

The third passage is about the Romantic poets, a group of writers in 19th-century England who "prided themselves on their rejection of" earlier English poetry. In other words, the Romantic poets tried to write differently than their predecessors. In support of this thesis, you're told about how two major Romantic poets, Wordsworth and Keats, rejected pre-Romantic poems as insincere and affected and tried to write more spontaneous-seeming poems.

13. A

The best choice is (A): The passage describes an artistic movement, the Romantic movement in British poetry. (B) and (D) are equally incorrect, as each focuses on only one Romantic poet. And while (C) describes how the Romantics felt about earlier English poetry—they were critical of it—it doesn't sum up the passage, which also describes the kind of poetry the Romantics themselves tried to write.

14. D

The word "traditional" is used here to describe earlier British poetry. The Romantics rebelled against what they saw as the usual or standard practices of earlier poets, so (D) is correct. (A), (B), and (C) are all fairly plausible in context, but they don't have the equivalent meaning of "traditional."

15. C

Which of these statements is implied in the passage? (C): Since Keats was Wordsworth's contemporary, and brought a similar attitude to his poetry as this leader of the Romantic movement did, Keats must also be a Romantic poet. (A) isn't implied; all we know about Romantic poetry is that it was different from earlier poetry, not that it was better (even if the Romantics themselves thought it was). Similarly, (B) is incorrect because we only know that Keats brought an attitude to his writing that was similar to Wordsworth's—we don't know if the younger man actually imitated his older contemporary or not. And while Keats said that poetry should be written "as naturally as the leaves to a tree," this is a comment about spontaneity—it doesn't imply that Keats's poems are actually about nature (D).

16. D

In the sentence just before the quoted one, we learn that Wordsworth "attempted to achieve spontaneity and naturalness of expression" in his poems. Therefore, (D) is correct. (A), (B), and (C) all interpret Wordsworth's statement too literally. Wordsworth meant that poetry should *seem* like spontaneous speech, not that it should actually be written in dialogue form, or always read aloud, or only be written by men.

17. C

Try to find facts in the passage to back up each statement. (A) is in lines 4–5 and 12–13. (B) is in line 9. (D) is in lines 2–3. (C) is contradicted in lines 10–11.

18. C

Think about where you would most likely find this passage. (A) is incorrect because a review would most likely include opinions, which are not offered in the passage. (B) is incorrect because the focus of the passage is on Romantic poets in general, not just Wordsworth. (D) is incorrect because the passage has no passion and doesn't take the tone of a love letter. (C) is the most likely answer because the passage offers facts on Romantic poets.

Stratmeyer Passage

The fourth passage is about Edward Stratmeyer, a writer who created those fictional teen heroes and heroines the Hardy Boys, Nancy Drew, and the Bobbsey Twins. The author gives some biographical information about Stratmeyer, but the passage's main thrust is that he was so successful because his career coincided with the growth of a new population segment—adolescents. Labor laws passed early in the 20th century required children to stay in school until the age of 16, which gave them more free time than they'd ever had before. Wanting adventure, they read Stratmeyer's books.

19. C

As noted above, the main thrust of the passage is not the universal appeal of Stratmeyer's characters, (A); how mandatory schooling benefited teenagers, (B); or the boom created by labor laws, (D). Instead, the author is interested in telling us why Stratmeyer was so popular.

20. C

The second sentence describes the adventurous young heroes of Stratmeyer's books as having particular appeal; the final sentence notes that Stratmeyer satisfied his readers' needs with a "slew of heroic super-teens." Since Stratmeyer's readers were mostly teenagers, you can infer that his fictional heroes appealed to them at least partly because readers and heroes were the same age, (C). (A), (B), and (D) are not mentioned in the passage.

21. D

The passage states that, by 1930, adolescence had come of age, because labor laws required children to be in school until the age of sixteen, which makes (D) correct. (A) distorts the passage: By 1930, adolescents had more free time, but it was Stratmeyer's heroes who led lives of fun and adventure. (B) distorts the fourth sentence, which notes that, by 1900, the nation was more prosperous—not that teens themselves were. (C) is tricky. 1930 is described as the end of the heyday of Stratmeyer's career, but that doesn't necessarily mean his reading audience started to drop. It may just as well mean he stopped writing so many books.

22. B

(A) is incorrect because the 30-year span was the heyday, or best part, of Stratmeyer's career. This doesn't mean he wrote all his books within that span. The passage doesn't mention that his family was in debt, (C), and we know from the first sentence that, contrary to (D), he enjoyed enormous commercial success. This leaves correct choice (B): As the final sentence describes in passing, Stratmeyer wrote his books "under a variety of pseudonyms," or false names.

23. A

Look at the sentence "prosperity" appears in. The author says that "prosperity began to prolong childhood." That sounds as if "prosperity" is something positive, meaning (B) is incorrect. (D) doesn't make sense, so it's incorrect. That leaves success and medicine. Medicine is not mentioned in the passage, so the answer is (A).

24. C

Questions about the author's attitude are generally asking about the tone of the passage. Are the author's points positive, negative, or neutral? The author uses phrases such as "did not gain enormous commercial success through luck alone" and responded to the needs of his readers with a slew of heroic super-teens." Those show that the author had a positive attitude, and that rules out (B) and (D). Next, think about how the passage would sound if you read it aloud. Does it sound as if the author didn't think Stratmeyer would be successful, or does it sound as if the author respected Stratmeyer's work? (C) is correct.

Dummies Passage

The fifth passage is about ventriloquists' dummies. The author tells you when dummies were first developed and that early dummies looked much like those of today on the outside but, on the inside, were a complicated mixture of "engineering feats and sculpture." The passage goes on to describe the inside of early dummy heads, especially the dummies made by the McElroy brothers, whose creations are said to have rivaled those of the Wright Brothers—inventors of the airplane—in complexity.

25. D

The author's primary purpose here is to describe early ventriloquists' dummies—the care and craft that went into making them. This point is restated in correct choice (D). The two inventing families mentioned in (A)—the McElroy and Wright Brothers—are only compared briefly in the passage's last sentence, making this a poor choice for a primary purpose question. (B) is too general, and as for (C), the passage compares early dummies with today's dummies only to tell us that both had similar exteriors. But the bulk of the passage is about the interiors of early dummies, and we learn nothing about the insides of today's dummies, so (D) remains best.

26. B

As described in the last question, the outsides of dummies are only mentioned in sentence 2: The outsides of early ones "looked very much like those used today." So you can infer (B), that outwardly, dummies haven't changed much since they were invented. (A) is not indicated, since at least one feature, the mouth, has always been "exaggerated." (C) is wrong because the outward appearance has remained the same even though the insides have changed over the years.

27. A

Correct choice (A) restates sentence 3: The interiors of the best dummies "were a curious fusion of engineering feats and sculpture"—that is, a mix of science and art. With their exaggerated features, even the best-made dummies aren't meant to fool the observer, (B); it's the "throwing" of the ventriloquist's voice that does the fooling. (C) distorts the point, in sentence 2, that dummies from all eras have similar range of movement. And the McElroy brothers' dummies, arguably the best ever made, were constructed before World War II, not after (D).

28. C

A "synergistic effort" describes two things working together so that the effect of the whole is more than the effect of the parts working separately. We know that the McElroy brothers worked together on their puppets, making (C) the correct answer. There's no evidence for (A). (B) and (D) are never mentioned.

29. D

The author clearly admires the work of the McElroy brothers, so (A) and (B) are easily eliminated. Elated, (C), means extremely happy, which doesn't seem fitting in the context of what is essentially a dry, expository passage.

30. A

Find the right answer by using the passage to answer the questions asked in the choices. (B) is answered in lines 1–3. (C) is in lines 12–13. (D) is answered in lines 14–16. (A) is not addressed in the passage.

Photography Passage

The sixth and last passage on this test is about James VanDerZee, a photographer who worked in Harlem. We learn that VanDerZee's career started in 1916, just before an African-American cultural boom known as the Harlem Renaissance, and that, in a career spanning 40 years, he took thousands of photographs of Harlem residents. The passage states that these photographs—of celebrities and unknown citizens alike—are now considered an important cultural record of a proud community.

31. D

The main focus of this passage is clearly on the work of VanDerZee, how he created an important cultural record. (D), which restates this idea, is thus the correct answer. (A) is too broad in scope and too narrow in time frame: VanDerZee was just one artist among many who made up the Harlem Renaissance, and that "decade-long flowering" spanned only one-fourth of his productive career. (B) is similarly too broad, since VanDerZee is the only African-American photographer mentioned in the passage. And (C) is incorrect because we're never told what creative influences shaped VanDerZee's career.

32. A

The passage states that VanDerZee opened his studio in 1916, on "the eve of the Harlem Renaissance." As it does in "Christmas Eve," the word "eve" means, literally or figuratively, the night before. So we can infer that 1916 was just before the beginning of the Harlem Renaissance, and (A) is correct. (B) is unlikely, since the passage states that VanDerZee photographed thousands of noncelebrities. In fact, we really know nothing (and so can infer nothing) of his original intentions, of his experience prior to opening the studio, (C), or of who bankrolled his studio, (D).

33. B

Sentence 3 describes VanDerZee's Harlem subjects as representing "the life and spirit of that burgeoning community." It also notes that they were not only "notables," or celebrities, but also "ordinary citizens." In other words, VanDerZee's subjects represented the entire Harlem community, and (B) is correct. The artist's flair for photographic composition, (A), and the self-assurance of his subjects, (C), are described further down in the passage, not in the lines in question. And (D) is too abstract and theoretical; the author wants to tell you whose pictures VanDerZee took, not to expound on the nature of photography in general.

34. C

The author describes VanDerZee as capturing the life of a community, as an artist respected by critics who had a "unique vision." In other words, the author admires VanDerZee, and (C) is correct. Neutral, (A), implies that the author doesn't feel one way or the other about VanDerZee, which clearly isn't the case. Condescending, (B), is a negative word that means "looking down on," and it's also inappropriate. Generous, (D), seems to imply that the author is somehow giving VanDerZee the benefit of the doubt, looking kindly on a career that really wasn't as great as the author says it was. No such attitude is hinted at in the passage, so (C) is best.

35. A

Try to find facts in the passage to back up each statement. (B) is supported by lines 18–19; the author says that he "recorded a time, place and culture that might otherwise have slipped away." (C) is found in lines 5–7; the author says the Harlem Renaissance "established Harlem as the most artistically vigorous African-American community in the nation." (D) is described in lines 10–12; he produced portraits of "parents and children, brides and grooms, church groups, and women's clubs." (A) is not true because the passage says the photographer opened his studio on "the eve of the Harlem Renaissance," meaning it was on the verge of occurring when he arrived in Harlem.

36. D

Look at the sentence "burgeoning" appears in. "VanDerZee captured the life and spirit of that burgeoning community." That shows that the answer has something to do with something lively, ruling out (B) and (C). That leaves "beautiful" and "thriving." (D) is the answer.

SECTION 4: MATHEMATICS ACHIEVEMENT

1. A

Ralph's age is represented by x. Since Ralph is twice as old as Howie, Howie is half as old as Ralph, or $0.5x$.

2. A

If there are 3 blue marbles for every red marble, 1 out of every 4 marbles is red. Therefore, red marbles represent $\frac{1}{4}$ of all the marbles.

3. D

Average = $\frac{\text{Sum of terms}}{\text{Number of terms}}$, so the average temperature on Monday was

$$\text{Average} = \frac{55° + (-18°) + 25° + (-15°)}{4}$$
$$= \frac{80° + (-33°)}{4}$$
$$= 11\frac{3}{4}° = 11.75°$$

4. B

Looking at the pie chart, you can see that the slice that represents medium shirts represents about $\frac{1}{3}$ of the pie. The entire pie represents 1,200 shirts, so $\frac{1}{3}$ represents 400 shirts, (B).

5. C

The slice that represents small shirts represents about $\frac{1}{4}$ of the pie. Since the whole pie is 1,200 shirts, there were 300 small shirts sold. Each shirt sold for $5.95. The question asks approximately how much was spent on the small shirts, so estimate the price of a shirt to be $6 to make the calculation easier. The choices are pretty far apart, so it's okay to do this. 300 × $6 = $1,800, so (C) is correct.

6. B

There are 60 seconds in a minute, so in $\frac{1}{20}$ of a minute there are $60 \times \frac{1}{20} = \frac{60}{20} = 3$ seconds.

7. B

Sketch yourself a diagram:

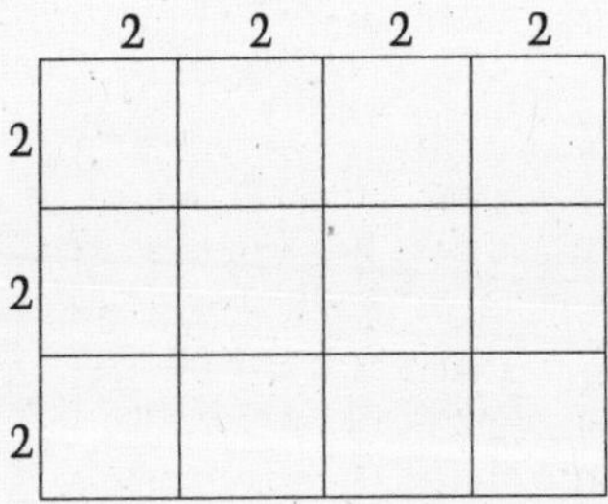

The 8-inch length can be divided into four 2-inch segments, and the 6-inch width can be divided into three 2-inch segments, which gives you a total of 4 × 3 = 12 squares.

8. C

Five percent of the guests at the party were witches. There were 8 witches, so 8 represents 5 percent = $\frac{5}{100} = \frac{1}{20}$ of the guests. The total number of guests is 20 × 8 = 160.

9. D

Just plug into the formula: 9@8 = (9 × 8) – (9 + 8) = 72 – 17 = 55.

10. B

Plug into the formula and solve for N:

$$10@N = -1$$
$$(10 \times N) - (10 + N) = -1$$
$$10N - 10 - N = -1$$
$$9N - 10 = -1$$
$$9N = 9$$
$$N = 1$$

11. D

If a CD collection can be evenly divided among 6 people, the number of CDs must be a multiple of 6. Only (D), 24, is a multiple of 6, since $6 \times 4 = 24$.

12. C

Make yourself a few quick sketches:

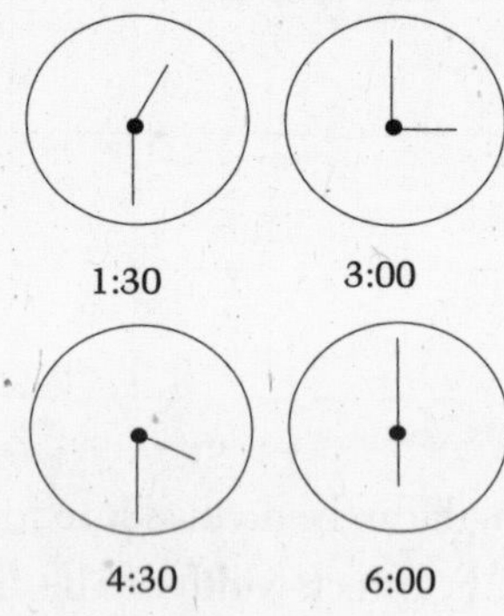

Only at 4:30 is the smaller angle less than 90°, so (C) is correct.

13. B

Carol spent $\frac{1}{2}$ of her day at work and $\frac{2}{3}$ of that time in meetings. So the amount of time she spent in meetings was $\frac{1}{2} \times \frac{2}{3} = \frac{2}{6} = \frac{1}{3}$ of her day.

14. A

If $\frac{1}{2}S = 0.2$, S is twice that, or $2 \times 0.2 = 0.4$. The answer choices are all given as fractions, so convert 0.4 to a fraction: 0.4 is four-tenths, or $\frac{4}{10}$, which reduces to $\frac{2}{5}$, (A).

15. A

Ten percent is one-fifth of 50%, so if 50% of a number is 75, 10% of that same number is $\frac{1}{5} \times 75 = 15$.

16. C

$$\frac{1}{2} + \frac{1}{3} = \frac{M}{12}$$

$$\frac{6}{12} + \frac{4}{12} = \frac{10}{12}$$

So $M = 10$.

17. D

Let w = the width of the rectangle. Its length is three times its width, or $3w$. Perimeter is equal to $2(l + w)$, where l and w represent length and width respectively. The perimeter is 32, so $2(l + w) = 32$. Plug in $3w$ for l: $2(3w + w) = 32$; $8w = 32$; $w = 4$.

18. A

It is possible to solve for each of the four variables, but it is really a waste of time. Note that each of the equations is equal to 35,460. Therefore, the largest variable will be the one with the smallest coefficient, because it takes fewer of a larger number to come up with the same product. Looking at the equations, you see that since 2,955 is the smallest coefficient, A must have the greatest value.

19. C

Let x = the number of foreign cars and set up a proportion.

$$\frac{3}{10} = \frac{x}{180}$$

$$(3)(180) = 10x$$

$$540 = 10x$$

$$54 = x$$

20. C

Plug in and solve.

If N¿ = $N \times 10$, 30¿ + 2¿ = $30 \times 10 + 2 \times 10$

$= 300 + 20$

$= 320$

21. C

To find the number of integers in an inclusive range, subtract the smaller integer from the larger and then add 1: $83 - 42 = 41 + 1 = 42$, (C).

22. C

Looking at the figure, you can see that $AB + BC = AC$. Therefore, $8 + BC = 14$, and $BC = 6$. The midpoint of AB divides it into two segments of length 4, and the midpoint of BC divides it into two segments of length 3. Therefore the distance between their midpoints is $4 + 3 = 7$.

4 4 3 3
A B C

23. C

Judy has 6 cards more than her brother. For each to have an equal number, she would have to split her 6 extra cards between them, that is, give him 3, while keeping 3 for herself. If this isn't clear, pick numbers. Say Judy's brother had 4 cards. That would mean Judy had $4 + 6 = 10$ cards. If she gave him 3, she'd have $10 - 3 = 7$, and he would have $4 + 3 = 7$.

24. D

Since Average = $\frac{\text{Sum of terms}}{\text{Number of terms}}$, Average × Number of terms = Sum of terms. If Fred averaged 168 for his first three games, that means he scored a total of $3 \times 168 = 504$ points. With his last game Fred wants to score enough to raise his average by 5 points, bringing it up to $168 + 5 = 173$. That means he needs to score a total of $173 \times 4 = 692$ for all four games. Since he scored 504 in the first three games, he'd need to score $692 - 504 = 188$ in his last game.

25. D

Evaluate each statement. If you can come up with even one value for N that makes the statement true, eliminate it.

A: If $N = 0$, $0 \times 0 = 0$, and the statement is true—eliminate.

B: If $N = 1$, $1 \times 1 = 1$, and the statement is true—eliminate.

C: If $N = 1$, $1 \times 1 = 1$, and the statement is true—eliminate.

D: $N - 1 = N$, so $N = N + 1$. There is no value of N for which adding 1 to it will result in a sum of N, so this statement can never be true.

26. A

To find the numbers that are in both sets, start listing the integers greater than 6, but stop before you hit 11: 7, 8, 9, 10. There are 4, so (A) is correct.

27. A

If June has \$65, Mary has \$65 + 30%(\$65) = \$65 + \$19.50 = \$84.50.

28. A

Nine is $\frac{1}{10}$, or 10%, of 90, so $x = 10$. Then 50%, or $\frac{1}{2}$, of $10 = 5$.

29. B

Let x = the number of bottles capped in 1 minute and set up a proportion. Be sure to convert 1 minute into 60 seconds.

$$\frac{5}{2} = \frac{x}{60}$$

$$(5)(60) = 2x$$

$$300 = 2x$$

$$150 = x$$

30. A

Take this problem in steps: 20% of 100 is 20; 5% of 20 is (0.05)(20) = 1.

31. D

Keith answered 2 out of 10 questions, or $\frac{2}{10}$, incorrectly. Then $\frac{2}{10} = \frac{1}{5}$, or 20%, choice (D).

32. C

You know 6,985 is approximately 7,000 and 3,001 is approximately 3,000. Therefore the difference between 6,985 and 3,001 is approximately 7,000 – 3,000 = 4,000, (C).

33. C

Convert to improper fractions: $1\frac{1}{3} - \frac{5}{6} = \frac{4}{3} - \frac{5}{6}$.

Find a common denominator: $\frac{16}{12} - \frac{10}{12} = \frac{6}{12} = \frac{1}{2}$.

34. B

Patty bought 2 hot dogs and a soda, and Liza bought 1 hot dog and a soda. Therefore the difference in what they paid, or \$3.30 – \$2.15 = \$1.15, is the price of 1 hot dog.

35. D

If one-fourth of a number is 3, the number is 4 × 3 = 12. One-third of 12 is 4, (D).

36. C

Rewrite 2 × 4 × 7 × 9 as (2 × 9)(4 × 7) or 18 × 28. (C) is correct.

37. A

$12 + P = 20 - 2 \times 3$

$12 + P = 20 - 6$

$12 + P = 14$

$P = 2$

38. B

One-tenth or 0.1 of 99 is 9.9, (B).

39. A

Twenty percent or $\frac{1}{5}$ of 30 is 6, (A).

40. A

$\frac{64}{2 \times 4} = \frac{64}{8} = 8$, (A).

41. D

$\frac{81}{9} + 2 = 9 + 2 = 11$, (D).

42. D

If there are 6 girls for every 2 boys, the ratio of girls to the entire class is 6:(6 + 2) or 6:8, which reduces to 3:4, (D).

43. A

So $\frac{48}{12} = \frac{4}{1}$, so $\frac{28}{a} = \frac{4}{1}$. Cross-multiply to get $28 = 4a$, and $a = 7$, (A).

44. D

For a number to be in both sets, it must be greater than 8 and less than 30. The only choice that falls in this range is 9, (D).

45. B

You can determine $\frac{18+16}{4} = \frac{34}{4} = 8\frac{1}{2} = 8.5$, (B).

46. B

Pick numbers. All of the choices, except (B), can be ruled out by squaring the first few integers. $1^2 = 1$; $5^2 = 25$; $6^2 = 36$. Nothing squared ends in 3.

47. A

If $0.2J = 1{,}500$, then $J = 0.1{,}500 = 7{,}500$. So $0.15J = 0.15(7{,}500) = 1{,}125$.

CHAPTER 21: ISEE PRACTICE TEST 2: UPPER- AND MIDDLE-LEVEL

HOW TO TAKE THIS PRACTICE TEST

Before taking this practice test, find a quiet room where you can work uninterrupted for three hours. Make sure you have a comfortable desk and several No. 2 pencils.

Use the answer sheet provided to record your answers. (You can cut it out or photocopy it.)

Once you start this practice test, don't stop until you have finished. Remember—you can review any questions within a section, but you may not go backward or forward a section.

You'll find answer explanations following the test.

Note: There are no major differences between the Middle- and Upper-level ISEE tests, and most of the questions on both tests are appropriate to either the middle or upper levels.

The practice test here covers both levels. If you are taking this as a Middle-level test, you may find a few of the questions to be too difficult. Don't worry—just do the best you can, and know that on test day, you will see only those questions that are appropriate to your level. Remember, too, that your scores will be based on how you compare to others taking the Middle-level test.

Good luck.

ISEE Practice Test 2: Upper- and Middle-Level Answer Sheet

Remove (or photocopy) the answer sheet and use it to complete the practice test.

Start with number 1 for each section. If a section has fewer questions than answer spaces, leave the extra spaces blank.

SECTION 1

1	A B C D	9	A B C D	17	A B C D	25	A B C D	33	A B C D
2	A B C D	10	A B C D	18	A B C D	26	A B C D	34	A B C D
3	A B C D	11	A B C D	19	A B C D	27	A B C D	35	A B C D
4	A B C D	12	A B C D	20	A B C D	28	A B C D	36	A B C D
5	A B C D	13	A B C D	21	A B C D	29	A B C D	37	A B C D
6	A B C D	14	A B C D	22	A B C D	30	A B C D	38	A B C D
7	A B C D	15	A B C D	23	A B C D	31	A B C D	39	A B C D
8	A B C D	16	A B C D	24	A B C D	32	A B C D	40	A B C D

right in section 1

wrong in section 1

SECTION 2

1	A B C D	9	A B C D	17	A B C D	25	A B C D	33	A B C D
2	A B C D	10	A B C D	18	A B C D	26	A B C D	34	A B C D
3	A B C D	11	A B C D	19	A B C D	27	A B C D	35	A B C D
4	A B C D	12	A B C D	20	A B C D	28	A B C D	36	A B C D
5	A B C D	13	A B C D	21	A B C D	29	A B C D	37	A B C D
6	A B C D	14	A B C D	22	A B C D	30	A B C D	38	A B C D
7	A B C D	15	A B C D	23	A B C D	31	A B C D	39	A B C D
8	A B C D	16	A B C D	24	A B C D	32	A B C D	40	A B C D

right in section 2

wrong in section 2

SECTION 3

1	A B C D	9	A B C D	17	A B C D	25	A B C D	33	A B C D
2	A B C D	10	A B C D	18	A B C D	26	A B C D	34	A B C D
3	A B C D	11	A B C D	19	A B C D	27	A B C D	35	A B C D
4	A B C D	12	A B C D	20	A B C D	28	A B C D	36	A B C D
5	A B C D	13	A B C D	21	A B C D	29	A B C D	37	A B C D
6	A B C D	14	A B C D	22	A B C D	30	A B C D	38	A B C D
7	A B C D	15	A B C D	23	A B C D	31	A B C D	39	A B C D
8	A B C D	16	A B C D	24	A B C D	32	A B C D	40	A B C D

right in section 3

wrong in section 3

SECTION 4

1	A B C D	11	A B C D	21	A B C D	31	A B C D	41	A B C D
2	A B C D	12	A B C D	22	A B C D	32	A B C D	42	A B C D
3	A B C D	13	A B C D	23	A B C D	33	A B C D	43	A B C D
4	A B C D	14	A B C D	24	A B C D	34	A B C D	44	A B C D
5	A B C D	15	A B C D	25	A B C D	35	A B C D	45	A B C D
6	A B C D	16	A B C D	26	A B C D	36	A B C D	46	A B C D
7	A B C D	17	A B C D	27	A B C D	37	A B C D	47	A B C D
8	A B C D	18	A B C D	28	A B C D	38	A B C D	48	A B C D
9	A B C D	19	A B C D	29	A B C D	39	A B C D	49	A B C D
10	A B C D	20	A B C D	30	A B C D	40	A B C D	50	A B C D

right in section 4

wrong in section 4

SECTION 1

Time—20 Minutes
40 Questions

This section consists of two different types of questions. There are directions for each type.

Each of the following questions consists of one word followed by four words or phrases. Select the one word or phrase whose meaning is closest to the word in capital letters.

1. DESECRATE:

(A) defend
(B) deny
(C) describe
(D) defile

2. LAUD:

(A) touch
(B) praise
(C) insult
(D) hear

3. AVERT:

(A) vindicate
(B) prevent
(C) explain
(D) dislike

4. PIETY:

(A) rarity
(B) smell
(C) faith
(D) meal

5. AMORAL:

(A) unethical
(B) lovable
(C) transparent
(D) imaginary

6. CANDOR:

(A) odor
(B) honesty
(C) ability
(D) wealth

7. HAUGHTINESS:

(A) heat
(B) height
(C) rudeness
(D) arrogance

8. VERIFY:

(A) complete
(B) prove
(C) violate
(D) consume

9. DECEIVE:

(A) trick
(B) empty
(C) dye
(D) view

10. FICTION:

(A) presumption
(B) growth
(C) falsehood
(D) wound

GO ON TO THE NEXT PAGE

11. HARDY:
    (A) healthy
    (B) mysterious
    (C) firm
    (D) obese

12. LYRICAL:
    (A) mythical
    (B) bright
    (C) musical
    (D) wet

13. METAMORPHOSIS:
    (A) change
    (B) compliment
    (C) rejection
    (D) meeting

14. LAMENT:
    (A) support
    (B) decline
    (C) solidify
    (D) grieve

15. ARID:
    (A) light
    (B) clean
    (C) worried
    (D) dry

16. PERCEPTIVE:
    (A) confused
    (B) round
    (C) observant
    (D) imbued

17. ADAMANT:
    (A) thin
    (B) enlarged
    (C) admiring
    (D) stubborn

18. NEUTRAL:
    (A) inventive
    (B) foreign
    (C) unbiased
    (D) detailed

19. DOCILE:
    (A) old
    (B) tame
    (C) active
    (D) rare

20. WARINESS:
    (A) extremity
    (B) caution
    (C) superiority
    (D) mobility

Directions: Select the word(s) that best fits the meaning of each sentence.

21. Raccoons are ____ : they come out at night to look for food and sleep during the day.
    (A) nocturnal
    (B) friendly
    (C) precocious
    (D) monolithic

GO ON TO THE NEXT PAGE

22. Normally ____, Jenny lacked her usual ____ when I called her and invited her to a movie.
    (A) absurd .. severity
    (B) scornful .. predilection
    (C) amiable .. enthusiasm
    (D) distraught .. cheeriness

23. The soap opera regularly dwells on the ____ aspects of life; just last week two characters died.
    (A) morbid
    (B) presumptuous
    (C) exciting
    (D) expensive

24. Once a(n) ____ gathering, the Greek festival has, in recent times, become highly ____.
    (A) urban .. contemporary
    (B) religious .. commercialized
    (C) mournful .. gloomy
    (D) parallel .. transformed

25. The candidate changed his positions on so many issues that people began to think he was ____.
    (A) reliable
    (B) dependent
    (C) aloof
    (D) flighty

26. Melanie danced with such ____, that no one could ____ her talent any longer.
    (A) speed.. ascertain
    (B) grace .. affirm
    (C) agility .. question
    (D) melancholy .. deny

27. Sandy showed genuine ____ when she was caught: she cried and promised never to hurt anyone again.
    (A) remorse
    (B) melodrama
    (C) wit
    (D) enthusiasm

28. The ____ journey ____ us all; even my dog sat down to take a rest.
    (A) panoramic .. exhausted
    (B) tortuous .. invigorated
    (C) strenuous .. fatigued
    (D) arduous .. rejuvenated

29. Relying on every conceivable gimmick and stereotype, the latest Hollywood movie is not only ____ but ____.
    (A) dull .. ambivalent
    (B) predictable .. absurd
    (C) complete .. erudite
    (D) boring .. enlightening

30. Lara not only respected her grandfather, she ____ him.
    (A) feared
    (B) retired
    (C) resembled
    (D) revered

31. That Chinese pieces of silk dating over 1,500 years old have been found in Egypt is ____ since the landscape between these two countries includes arid deserts and several ____ mountain ranges.
    (A) known .. required
    (B) impressive .. reduced
    (C) predictable .. steep
    (D) incredible .. massive

GO ON TO THE NEXT PAGE

32. At first the empty house seemed frightening with all its cobwebs and creaking shutters, but we soon realized that it was quite ____ .

(A) benign
(B) deceptive
(C) affluent
(D) obliterated

33. Once a ____ propagated only by science fiction movies, the possibility of life on Mars has recently become more ____ .

(A) wish .. doubtful
(B) myth .. plausible
(C) story .. impossible
(D) hypothesis .. empty

34. Many writers of the 20th century were influenced by Hemingway's ____ writing style and consequently discontinued the ____ language characteristic of the 19th century novel.

(A) sparse .. verbose
(B) dull .. insipid
(C) peaceful .. descriptive
(D) complete .. florid

35. Dave never failed to charm listeners with his ____ stories.

(A) lethargic
(B) wan
(C) insufferable
(D) engaging

36. Screaming and laughing, the students were ____ by their ____ experience on the white-water raft.

(A) amused .. tepid
(B) irritated .. continued
(C) exhilarated .. first
(D) frightened .. secure

37. Highly influenced by Frank Lloyd Wright's principles of design, the architect E. Fay Jones has built homes reputed to equal—and even _____ —Wright's successes at building in harmony with natural surroundings.

(A) echo
(B) question
(C) reconstruct
(D) surpass

38. Weighing more than 70 tons, brachiosaurus was a(n) _____ creature, yet its brain was quite _____.

(A) intelligent .. enormous
(B) gargantuan .. small
(C) minute .. tiny
(D) prodigious .. extant

39. Trumpets, including Pacific conch-shell trumpets, African ivory trumpets, orchestral valve trumpets, and tubas, comprise one of the most _____ categories of wind instruments.

(A) excessive
(B) discordant
(C) coherent
(D) diverse

40. The _____ nature of the platypus makes it difficult to spot, even in the _____ space of a zoological exhibit.

(A) elusive .. confined
(B) crafty .. massive
(C) playful .. structured
(D) slothful .. open

IF YOU FINISH BEFORE TIME IS CALLED, YOU MAY CHECK YOUR WORK ON THIS SECTION ONLY. DO NOT TURN TO ANY OTHER SECTION IN THE TEST. **STOP**

SECTION 2

Time—35 Minutes
37 Questions

In this section there are four possible answers after each question. Choose which one is best. You may use the blank space at the right of the page for scratch work.

Note: Figures are drawn with the greatest possible accuracy, UNLESS stated "Not Drawn to Scale."

USE THIS SPACE FOR FIGURING.

1. If $Q + 7 - 8 + 3 = 23$, what is the value of Q?
   (A) 19
   (B) 20
   (C) 21
   (D) 22

2. A kilogram is equal to how many grams?
   (A) –1,000
   (B) –100
   (C) 100
   (D) 1,000

3. What is the value of $\frac{1}{9} + \frac{7}{12} + \frac{5}{6}$?
   (A) $\frac{9}{13}$
   (B) $1\frac{19}{36}$
   (C) $1\frac{2}{3}$
   (D) 2

4. What is 15% of 60?
   (A) 6
   (B) 9
   (C) 12
   (D) 15

GO ON TO THE NEXT PAGE

USE THIS SPACE FOR FIGURING.

5. If $a + 2 > 5$ and $a - 4 < 1$, which of the following is a possible value for a?

   (A) 2
   (B) 3
   (C) 4
   (D) 5

6. If $2x + 4 = 26$, then $x + 4 =$

   (A) 9.
   (B) 11.
   (C) 13.
   (D) 15.

7. If the perimeter of an equilateral hexagon is 42, what is the sum of the lengths of 2 sides?

   (A) 6
   (B) 7
   (C) 12
   (D) 14

8. If Angelo earns $2,000 per month and spends 30% of his monthly earnings on rent, how much does he pay for rent each month?

   (A) $510
   (B) $600
   (C) $610
   (D) $680

9. A farmer pays $58 for 6 new chickens. How many eggs must the farmer sell at 16 cents apiece in order to pay for the chickens?

   (A) 360
   (B) 361
   (C) 362
   (D) 363

GO ON TO THE NEXT PAGE

USE THIS SPACE FOR FIGURING.

10. A certain moped needs 12 gallons of fuel to go 48 miles. At this rate, how many gallons of fuel are needed to go 60 miles?

(A) 4
(B) 5
(C) 15
(D) 24

11. $1\frac{6}{11} + 1\frac{7}{22}$

(A) $2\frac{13}{33}$
(B) $2\frac{19}{22}$
(C) $2\frac{10}{11}$
(D) $2\frac{21}{22}$

12. If the average of 6 numbers is 9, what is the sum of those numbers?

(A) 15
(B) 30
(C) 54
(D) 96

13. If $\frac{1}{2} > x > 0$ and $\frac{1}{3} > x > \frac{1}{10}$, which of the following is a possible value for x?

(A) $\frac{2}{3}$
(B) 0.47
(C) $\frac{1}{5}$
(D) $\frac{1}{20}$

USE THIS SPACE FOR FIGURING.

14. If $3a + 6a = 36$, what is the value of a?

(A) 1
(B) 2
(C) 3
(D) 4

15. What is $\frac{1}{4}$ of 0.72?

(A) 0.018
(B) 0.18
(C) 1.8
(D) 18

16. In Figure 1, what is the total area?

(A) 10
(B) 24
(C) 28
(D) 45

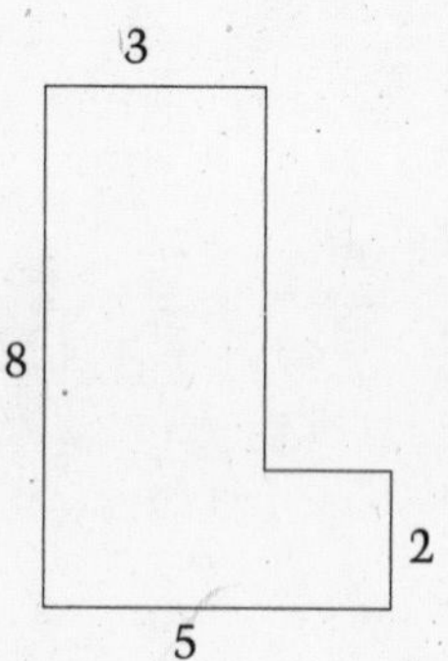

Figure 1

17. How many different prime factors are there of 48?

(A) 1
(B) 2
(C) 3
(D) 4

18. Which of the following is a factor of 36 but not of 48?

(A) 3
(B) 6
(C) 12
(D) 18

19. If Figure 2 is a cube, what is its volume?

(A) 125
(B) 100
(C) 50
(D) 25

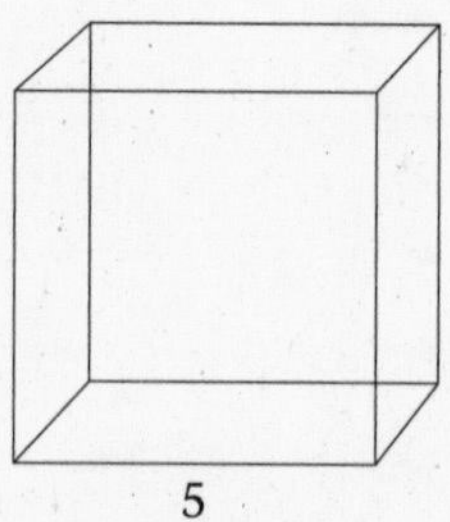

Figure 2

GO ON TO THE NEXT PAGE

USE THIS SPACE FOR FIGURING.

20. While studying for a history test, it took Jake 1 hour 15 minutes to review the first 30 pages. If he continues to study at the same pace, how long will it take him to review the remaining 70 pages?

(A) 2 hours 30 minutes
(B) 2 hours 37 minutes
(C) 2 hours 45 minutes
(D) 2 hours 55 minutes

21. Mary types 12 words every 20 seconds. At this rate, how many words does she type every 2 minutes?

(A) 18
(B) 36
(C) 42
(D) 72

22. If $r = 8$, then $(r + 4)^2 =$

(A) 24.
(B) 64.
(C) 80.
(D) 144.

GO ON TO THE NEXT PAGE

Directions: In questions 23–35, note the given information, if any, and then compare the quantity in Column A to the quantity in Column B. Next to the number of each question write

A if the quantity in Column A is greater.

B if the quantity in Column B is greater.

C if the two quantities are equal.

D if the relationship cannot be determined from the information given.

	Column A	Column B
23.	$\frac{1}{2} + \frac{3}{4} + \frac{7}{8}$	$\frac{2}{5} + \frac{3}{4} + \frac{7}{9}$
24.	$\frac{4}{5} \times \frac{15}{45} \times \frac{3}{16}$	0.05
25.	$\frac{4}{9} \times \frac{18}{6} \times \frac{12}{20}$	$\frac{5}{4}$

USE THIS SPACE FOR FIGURING.

$3x - 12 = 3x - 6x$

	Column A	Column B
26.	$x + 2$	2

$x > 0$

$y > 0$

	Column A	Column B
27.	$x + 1$	y
28.	5% of (3 + 4)	4% of (3 × 4)
29.	0.46	$\frac{9}{20}$

GO ON TO THE NEXT PAGE

	Column A	Column B
30.	The number of 32-cent stamps that can be purchased with \$5	The number of 29-cent stamps that can be purchased with \$5

$$\frac{8}{9} > x > \frac{1}{2}$$

	Column A	Column B
31.	x	$\frac{2}{3}$

$$x < 0$$

	Column A	Column B
32.	$2x$	$(2x)(1x)$

	Column A	Column B
33.	Perimeter of an octagon with sides of equal length	8

	Column A	Column B
34.	The number of prime factors of 21	3

$\frac{5}{7}$ of x is 35.

	Column A	Column B
35.	x	48

	Column A	Column B
36.	98% of 51	51% of 98

	Column A	Column B
37.	20% of \$42	\$9

USE THIS SPACE FOR FIGURING.

IF YOU FINISH BEFORE TIME IS CALLED, YOU MAY CHECK YOUR WORK ON THIS SECTION ONLY. DO NOT TURN TO ANY OTHER SECTION IN THE TEST. **STOP**

SECTION 3

Time—40 Minutes
36 Questions

Read each passage carefully and then answer the questions about it. For each question, decide on the basis of the passage which one of the choices best answers the question.

The heyday of the log cabin occurred between 1780 and 1850, when a great number of settlers forged westward. While early cabins were primitive, with dirt floors and sod roofs, later settlers built fine, two-story, log-hewn farmhouses with rooms for entertaining. By the 1840s, though, the log cabin began fading out. Factors contributing to its decline included sawmills, nails, and the rising popularity of the Greek Revival-style house, with its democratic roots in ancient Greece and its templed front facing the street. Trains brought hardware, manufactured goods, and an end to geographic isolation. Climate and the proximity of the local forest no longer set architectural limits. In hundreds of towns, log homes were gradually sheathed with clapboard or brick or, in many instances, were simply burned. Logs continued to house livestock, but after the 1850s, fewer and fewer people.

1. The passage suggests that the origins of the Greek Revival style
   (A) arose out of a general desire to replace log cabins.
   (B) widely influenced contemporary Greek architects.
   (C) were popular with devoutly religious Americans.
   (D) appealed to democratic-minded Americans.

2. As used in line 3, the word "forged" means
   (A) fled.
   (B) wandered.
   (C) moved.
   (D) returned.

3. It can be inferred from the passage that, unlike Greek Revival homes, log cabins
   (A) did not always face the street.
   (B) lacked indoor plumbing.
   (C) could not have glass windows.
   (D) were built near lakes and rivers.

4. It can be inferred from the passage that a limiting factor in the construction of a settler's log cabin was often
   (A) the availability of nails.
   (B) the location of the nearest forest.
   (C) the opinions of other settlers.
   (D) the laws of the local government.

5. According to the passage, most log structures after 1850 were built
   (A) in wilderness areas.
   (B) in frontier towns.
   (C) as railroad depots.
   (D) to shelter animals.

GO ON TO THE NEXT PAGE

6. Which of the following questions is NOT answered in the passage?

   (A) In their heyday, were log cabins common in the west?

   (B) When did log cabins finally disappear?

   (C) Why was the Greek Revival–style house popular?

   (D) How did log cabins in the 1780s differ from log cabins in the 1840s?

The plague, or Black Death, struck Europe in a series of outbreaks in the 13th and 14th centuries, killing an estimated one-third of the continent's population. The epidemic wrought enormous changes in European society, some of which, ironically, were beneficial. Reform in the medical profession, which had mostly failed to relieve the suffering, was one of the most immediate benefits. A great many doctors died or simply ran away during the plague. By the 1300s, many universities were lacking professors of medicine and surgery. Into this void rushed people with new ideas. In addition, ordinary people began acquiring medical guides and taking command of their own health. Gradually, more medical texts began to appear in everyday languages rather than in Latin, making medical knowledge more accessible.

7. The passage focuses primarily on

   (A) the enormous loss of life caused by the plague.

   (B) the lack of qualified doctors during the plague.

   (C) one positive result of a catastrophic event.

   (D) the translation of medical texts into everyday language.

8. As used in line 4, the word "wrought" means

   (A) caused.

   (B) needed.

   (C) accelerated.

   (D) offered.

9. The passage suggests that, prior to the plague outbreaks, European medicine was

   (A) hampered by a shortage of doctors.

   (B) available only to university students.

   (C) in need of sweeping changes.

   (D) practiced mainly in Latin-speaking countries.

10. It can be inferred from the passage that after the 1300s, medical texts

    (A) included information on how to cure the plague.

    (B) were more easily available to the general population.

    (C) were no longer written in Latin.

    (D) were not written by university professors.

11. Which of the following best describes the tone of the article?

    (A) Mournful

    (B) Sarcastic

    (C) Favorable

    (D) Sensible

12. All of the following are outcomes of the plague EXCEPT

    (A) medical information was made more accessible to people.

    (B) people started learning Latin to understand the medical texts.

    (C) people with new ideas on medicine started teaching medicine and surgery.

    (D) a lot of people died from the plague.

GO ON TO THE NEXT PAGE

In the sport of orienteering, competitors use a map and compass to navigate their way cross-country along an unfamiliar course. The novice quickly finds, however, that the most important question in orienteering is not compass bearing but choice of route. There are almost always several different ways to get from one point to another, and the beeline on a direct compass bearing over a mountain is seldom the best. Indeed, orienteers tend to disdain beelining over obstacles as a crude approach; they aspire to intellectual finesse. If climbing 20 feet in elevation requires the time and energy it would take to travel 250 feet on level ground—the sort of quick calculation orienteers are always making—then it may be better to follow a prominent contour along one flank of the mountain or even to stick to the safety of a trail looping around the base.

13. The passage suggests that a hiker with a map and compass is NOT orienteering if she
   (A) climbs more than one mountain per route.
   (B) travels over a known, familiar route.
   (C) takes more than one route per day.
   (D) follows a direct path over an obstacle.

14. According to the passage, an orienteer places greatest importance on
   (A) maintaining a single compass bearing.
   (B) avoiding hazardous terrain.
   (C) overcoming obstacles as fast as possible.
   (D) choosing the best route available.

15. It can be inferred from the passage that most orienteers would consider a competitor who climbs a mountain in order to take the most direct route to be
   (A) gaining a major advantage.
   (B) lacking sophistication.
   (C) breaking the rules.
   (D) endangering other competitors.

16. The passage suggests that one skill orienteers require is the ability to
   (A) run while carrying a backpack.
   (B) swim long distances.
   (C) set up a campsite.
   (D) make rapid calculations.

17. As used in line 12, "finesse" means
   (A) skill.
   (B) movement.
   (C) inefficiency.
   (D) devotion.

18. Which of the following best describes the author's attitude toward the subject?
   (A) Respect
   (B) Disdain
   (C) Indifference
   (D) Appreciation

Researchers have identified two phenomena that in previous literature were confounded under the category of nightmares. On the one hand, there is the true nightmare, which is an actual, detailed dream. On the other there is the "night terror," from which the sleeper, often a child, suddenly awakes in great fright with no memory of a dream, often screaming and sometimes going off in a sleepwalking trance. Night terrors are seldom of serious consequence, no matter how horrifying they may appear to anxious parents. Outside of taking commonsense precautions—such as making sure a sleepwalker does not go to bed near an open window or on a balcony—there is nothing much to do about them. A child's night terrors can be reduced somewhat with a consistent sleep schedule and by avoiding excessive fatigue. Excessive concern or medication should usually be avoided.

GO ON TO THE NEXT PAGE

19. As used in line 2, the word "confounded" means
    (A) entitled.
    (B) confused.
    (C) written.
    (D) underappreciated.

20. The passage suggests that, until recently, sleep researchers
    (A) knew very little about the nature of dreams.
    (B) studied only adult sleeping habits, not those of children.
    (C) did not differentiate between nightmares and night terrors.
    (D) prescribed medication for children suffering from night terrors.

21. According to the passage, a nightmare is a
    (A) full-fledged dream.
    (B) dream fragment.
    (C) hallucination.
    (D) trancelike state.

22. The passage implies that parents of children who experience night terrors
    (A) tend to dismiss them as inconsequential.
    (B) also suffered night terrors when they were children.
    (C) find their occurrence nearly as frightening as the children themselves do.
    (D) should consult a doctor as soon as possible.

23. Which of the following questions is NOT answered in the passage?
    (A) What is the difference between nightmares and night terrors?
    (B) What are some precautions parents can take to ensure the safety of children who experience night terrors?
    (C) Does a child who is frightened upon waking from a night terror remember dreaming?
    (D) Why does a consistent sleep schedule reduce the incidence of night terrors?

24. According to the passage, how are night terrors different from nightmares?
    (A) One is remembered by the sleeper, and the other is not.
    (B) One happens when the person is asleep, and the other is not.
    (C) One will bring harm to the sleeper, and the other does not.
    (D) One requires hospitalization, while the other does not.

GO ON TO THE NEXT PAGE

The Neanderthal was an early human that flourished throughout Europe and western Asia between 35,000 and 85,000 years ago. Physically, Neanderthals differed from modern humans in many important ways. They had massive limb bones, a barrel chest, thick brow ridges, a receding forehead, and a bunlike bulge on the back of the skull. Yet despite Neanderthals' reputation for low intelligence, there is nothing that clearly distinguishes a Neanderthal's brain from that of modern humans—except for the fact that, on average, Neanderthal versions were slightly larger. Combining enormous physical strength with manifest intelligence, Neanderthals appeared to be supremely well adapted. Nevertheless, around 35,000 years ago, they vanished from the face of the earth. The question of what became of the Neanderthals still baffles paleontologists and is perhaps the most talked-about issue in human origins research today.

25. It can be inferred from the passage that most Neanderthals probably had

(A) big arms.
(B) wide-set eyes.
(C) bowed legs.
(D) narrow feet.

26. According to the passage, Neanderthals lived

(A) in caves and mud dwellings.
(B) by hunting in packs.
(C) in Europe and Asia.
(D) on all the continents.

27. Based on information in the passage, modern humans, when compared with Neanderthals, probably have

(A) superior eyesight.
(B) a better sense of smell.
(C) less physical strength.
(D) more body hair.

28. The passage suggests that modern humans tend to think of Neanderthals as

(A) peaceful.
(B) skilled artists.
(C) farmers.
(D) unintelligent.

29. According to the passage, one question paleontologists are still trying to solve is

(A) what constituted the basic Neanderthal diet.
(B) what were the Neanderthals' migratory patterns.
(C) why the Neanderthal species became extinct.
(D) where the Neanderthals originally came from.

30. Where would this passage most likely be found?

(A) A short story about cavemen
(B) A research paper on early humans
(C) A letter from an explorer's encounter with a Neanderthal
(D) A textbook in health class

GO ON TO THE NEXT PAGE

Coyotes are one of the most primitive of living dogs. According to the fossil record, a close relative of the contemporary coyote existed here two to three million years ago. It in turn seems to have descended from a group of small canids that was widely dispersed throughout the world and that also gave rise to the jackals of Eurasia and Africa. One to two million years ago, a division occurred in North America between the coyote and the wolf. Time passed, and glaciers advanced and receded. Mammoths, saber-toothed tigers, and dire wolves (canids with enormous heads) came and went. Native horses left the continent over land bridges, and others returned on galleons. Through it all, coyotes remained basically the same—primitive in evolutionary terms but marvelously flexible, always progressive and innovative—riding out, adjusting to and exploiting the changes.

31. The primary focus of the passage is on
    (A) the ability of the coyote species to survive unchanged.
    (B) the unfortunate extinction of many prehistoric life forms.
    (C) the changing nature of animal life in prehistoric times.
    (D) the evolutionary division between coyotes and wolves.

32. The passage suggests that modern dogs are
    (A) direct descendants of dire wolves.
    (B) native to North America but not to Eurasia.
    (C) genetically related to coyotes.
    (D) lacking in evolutionary flexibility.

33. According to the passage, a close relative of the coyote existed in North America
    (A) ten million years ago.
    (B) seven million years ago.
    (C) five million years ago.
    (D) two million years ago.

34. The author probably mentions mammoths and saber-toothed tigers in order to give examples of
    (A) the coyote's more distant relatives.
    (B) animals that did not leave North America by land bridge.
    (C) species that the jackal hunted into extinction.
    (D) species that failed to adapt as the coyote did.

35. When the passage states that "others returned on galleons" (line 14), it most probably means that
    (A) some species of horse became extinct, then others appeared.
    (B) horses were reintroduced to North America when Europeans brought them by ship.
    (C) some coyotes were introduced into Africa and Eurasia.
    (D) prehistoric horses and dire wolves became extinct at roughly the same time.

36. All the following are true EXCEPT
    (A) mammoths and dire wolves no longer exist.
    (B) horses were in North America before the Europeans brought them here
    (C) coyotes are related to wolves.
    (D) coyotes are not good at adapting to change.

IF YOU FINISH BEFORE TIME IS CALLED, YOU MAY CHECK YOUR WORK ON THIS SECTION ONLY. DO NOT TURN TO ANY OTHER SECTION IN THE TEST.

SECTION 4

Time—40 Minutes
47 Questions

In this section there are four possible answers after each question. Choose which one is best. You may use the blank space at the right of the page for scratch work.

<u>Note:</u> Figures are drawn with the greatest possible accuracy, UNLESS stated "Not Drawn to Scale."

USE THIS SPACE FOR FIGURING.

1. What are all the values of x for which $(x - 2)(x + 5) = 0$?

(A) –5
(B) –2
(C) 2 and –5
(D) –2 and –5

2. Patty uses 2 gallons of paint to cover 875 square feet of surface. At this rate, how many gallons will she need to cover 4,375 square feet of surface?

(A) 4
(B) 5
(C) 8
(D) 10

3. What is the area of a triangle with a base of 4 inches and a height of 6 inches?

(A) 10
(B) 12
(C) 20
(D) 24

4. An equilateral triangle has sides of lengths $3x + 1$ and $x + 7$. What is the length of one side?

(A) 3
(B) 5
(C) 8
(D) 10

GO ON TO THE NEXT PAGE

5. $(65 \times 10^2) + (31 \times 10^3) + 12 =$

USE THIS SPACE FOR FIGURING.

(A) 375,120
(B) 37,512
(C) 3,751.20
(D) 375.12

6. Mr. Richman purchased a boat for $120,000. If the boat loses 20% of its value when placed in the water, how much did Mr. Richman lose in the value of his boat on its first use?

(A) $2,400
(B) $9,600
(C) $24,000
(D) $96,000

7. A dog is chained by a flexible leash to a stake in the ground in the center of his yard. If the leash is 8 meters long, what is the area in square meters in which he is able to run?

(A) 8
(B) 16
(C) 8π
(D) 64π

8. If Megan needs to drive 328 miles in 4 hours, at what rate of speed must she drive?

(A) 92 miles per hour
(B) 82 miles per hour
(C) 72 miles per hour
(D) 67 miles per hour

GO ON TO THE NEXT PAGE

USE THIS SPACE FOR FIGURING.

9. If a jet travels at a constant rate of 270 miles per hour, approximately how many hours will it take to reach its destination 3,300 miles away?

(A) 23.68
(B) 18.91
(C) 15.38
(D) 12.22

10. If $a = 3$ and $b = 4$, what is the value of $a^2 + 2ab + b^2$?

(A) 14
(B) 24
(C) 49
(D) 144

11. If $x - y = 5$ and $4x + 6y = 20$, then $x + y =$

(A) 3.
(B) 4.
(C) 5.
(D) 6.

12. How many distinct prime factors are there of 726?

(A) 2
(B) 3
(C) 4
(D) 5

13. If n is an odd number, which of the following MUST be even?

(A) $-2n - 1$
(B) $2n + 1$
(C) $2n - 1$
(D) $4n$

GO ON TO THE NEXT PAGE

USE THIS SPACE FOR FIGURING.

14. If Jamie is in school for 6 hours per day, 5 days per week, how many seconds does Jamie spend in school in one week?

    (A) 1,108,000
    (B) 180,000
    (C) 108,000
    (D) 18,000

15. If it is snowing at a rate of 3.5 inches per hour and the storm is expected to continue at the same rate for the next 4 days, how many inches of snow accumulation can be expected?

    (A) 84
    (B) 168
    (C) 226
    (D) 336

16. Nicholas is x years old, and Billy is three times as old as Nicholas. What was the sum of their ages, in years, 5 years ago?

    (A) $x - 5$
    (B) $2x + 2$
    (C) $3x - 10$
    (D) $4x - 10$

17. In a certain class, there are twice as many boys as girls. If the total number of students in the class is 36, how many boys are there?

    (A) 24
    (B) 18
    (C) 12
    (D) 9

GO ON TO THE NEXT PAGE

USE THIS SPACE FOR FIGURING.

18. At a party, $\frac{1}{3}$ of the guests drank only soda, and $\frac{2}{5}$ of the guests drank only juice. If the remaining 16 guests had nothing to drink, then how many guests were at the party?

(A) 60
(B) 50
(C) 45
(D) 30

19. If x and y are consecutive integers such that $xy = 6$ and y is greater than x, which of the following statements MUST be true?

I. $x + y = 5$.
II. x is less than 6.
III. $\frac{x}{y} = \frac{2}{3}$.

(A) I only
(B) II only
(C) I and II only
(D) I and III only

20. Jenny has y baseball cards. She gives 5 cards to each of three different friends and in return receives 2 cards from each friend. How many cards does Jenny have after the exchange?

(A) $y - 9$
(B) $y - 5$
(C) $y + 3$
(D) $y + 5$

GO ON TO THE NEXT PAGE

USE THIS SPACE FOR FIGURING.

21. If two fair coins are tossed simultaneously, what is the probability that two tails are thrown?

(A) 1

(B) $\frac{1}{2}$

(C) $\frac{1}{4}$

(D) $\frac{1}{8}$

22. A photocopier makes copies at a constant rate of 15 copies per minute. A certain copy job requires 600 copies. What fraction of the job will the machine finish in 5 minutes?

(A) $\frac{1}{200}$

(B) $\frac{1}{40}$

(C) $\frac{1}{8}$

(D) $\frac{1}{5}$

23. Which of the following is a possible value of z if $2(z - 3) > 6$ and $z + 4 < 15$?

(A) 3

(B) 6

(C) 7

(D) 11

24. In a certain library there are 3 fiction books for every 8 nonfiction books. If the library has 600 nonfiction books, how many books does it have?

(A) 2,200

(B) 1,400

(C) 825

(D) 800

GO ON TO THE NEXT PAGE

USE THIS SPACE FOR FIGURING.

25. If $x + y$ equals an odd number and $x + z$ equals an even number, each of the following could be true EXCEPT

(A) x is even and y is odd.
(B) y is even and z is odd.
(C) x and z are even and y is odd.
(D) x and y are even and z is odd.

26. On the first test, Ted scored 7 percentage points above the passing grade. On the second test he scored 12 percentage points lower than he did on his first test. His score on the second test was

(A) 19 percentage points below the passing grade.
(B) 12 percentage points below the passing grade.
(C) 5 percentage points below the passing grade.
(D) 2 percentage points above the passing grade.

27. In a class, 70 percent of the students are right-handed, and the rest are left-handed. If 70 percent of the left-handed students have brown eyes, then left-handed students with brown eyes make up what percent of the entire class?

(A) 14%
(B) 21%
(C) 30%
(D) 49%

Questions 28 and 29 refer to the following definition: For all real numbers q and r, let $q//r = (qr) - (q - r)$.

28. $8//2 =$

(A) 6
(B) 8
(C) 10
(D) 16

GO ON TO THE NEXT PAGE

USE THIS SPACE FOR FIGURING.

29. If $P//3 = 11$, then $P =$

(A) 3.
(B) 4.
(C) 6.
(D) 7.

30. If the product of integers a and b is 16 and a is greater than 4, then which of the following MUST be true?

I. $b = 2$.
II. The sum of a and b is greater than zero.
III. a is greater than b.

(A) II only
(B) III only
(C) I and II only
(D) II and III only

31. In Figure 1, what is the value of x ?

(A) 20
(B) 30
(C) 45
(D) 90

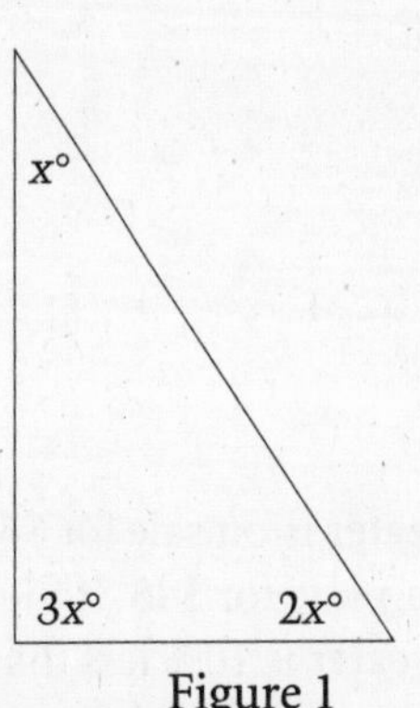

Figure 1

32. In Figure 2, the distance from B to C is twice the distance from A to B, and the distance from C to D is equal to half the distance from A to C. If the distance from B to C is 12, what is the distance from A to D ?

(A) 18
(B) 24
(C) 27
(D) 32

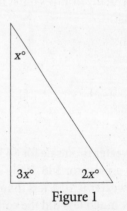

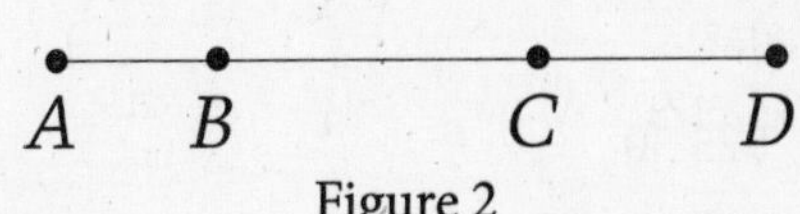

Figure 2

GO ON TO THE NEXT PAGE

USE THIS SPACE FOR FIGURING.

33. What is the greatest number of squares with sides of 2 centimeters that can be cut from a square with an area of 36 square centimeters?

(A) 4
(B) 9
(C) 18
(D) 36

34. If $x = 4y + 3$, then what does $x - 5$ equal?

(A) $4y - 8$
(B) $4y - 2$
(C) $4y + 5$
(D) $5y - 8$

35. A grocer buys oranges at a price of 4 for $1 and then sells them in his store for 40 cents each. How many oranges must he sell to earn a profit of $3?

(A) 2
(B) 10
(C) 15
(D) 20

36. A wool sweater is on sale for $63, and a cotton sweater is on sale for $45. If the sale price for each sweater is 10% less than the original price, how much less did the cotton sweater cost than the wool sweater before either went on sale?

(A) $23.50
(B) $20
(C) $19.80
(D) $18

GO ON TO THE NEXT PAGE

USE THIS SPACE FOR FIGURING.

37. John finished $\frac{1}{3}$ of his homework assignment between 6:00 P.M. and 7:30 P.M. He needs to finish the assignment by 11:00 P.M. If he works at the same rate, what is the latest time that he can return to his homework?

(A) 7:45 P.M.
(B) 8:00 P.M.
(C) 8:30 P.M.
(D) 9:30 P.M.

38. There are twice as many men as women on a track team. Medals were given to $\frac{1}{3}$ of the women. If there are 45 men and women on the team, how many women received medals?

(A) 5
(B) 6
(C) 10
(D) 11

39. If m is greater than n, and n is greater than 4, which of the following is LEAST?

(A) $\frac{1}{4m}$
(B) $\frac{1}{4n}$
(C) $\frac{1}{4 + m}$
(D) $\frac{1}{4 + n}$

GO ON TO THE NEXT PAGE

USE THIS SPACE FOR FIGURING.

40. If $\frac{1}{5}$ of a number is less than 20, the number must be

(A) less than 4.
(B) equal to 4.
(C) greater than 4.
(D) less than 100.

41. A six-story apartment building has x apartments on each of its lower 3 floors and y apartments on each of its upper 3 floors. If 3 people live in each apartment, how many people live in the building?

(A) $3x + 3y$
(B) $3x + 3y + 3$
(C) $9x + 9y$
(D) $3x + 3y + 18$

42. Joe spent 20% of his allowance on CDs. Then he spent 10% of what was left on a movie. After the movie, he was left with what percent of his original allowance?

(A) 65%
(B) 70%
(C) 72%
(D) 75%

43. Each of the n members in an organization may invite up to 3 guests to a conference. What is the maximum number of members and guests who might attend the conference?

(A) $n + 3$
(B) $3n$
(C) $3n + 4$
(D) $4n$

GO ON TO THE NEXT PAGE

USE THIS SPACE FOR FIGURING.

44. A square rug with each side 4 meters long is placed on a square floor. If each side of the rug is one-third the length of one side of the floor, what is the area, in square meters, of the floor?

(A) 144
(B) 96
(C) 64
(D) 16

45. Figure 3 is composed of six squares. How many rectangles are there in the figure?

(A) 20
(B) 18
(C) 15
(D) 12

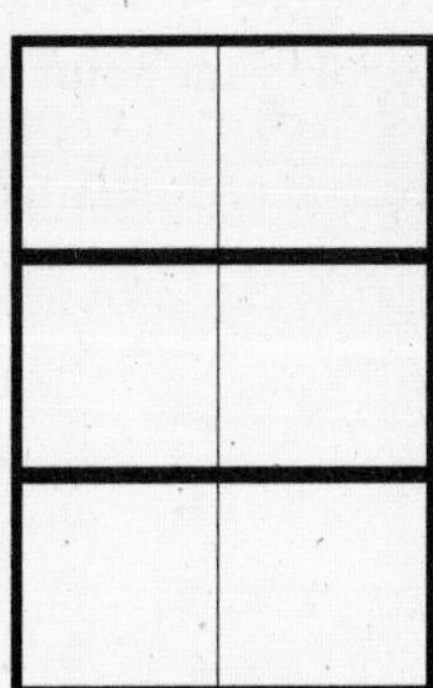
Figure 3

46. When Mr. Jones arrived at the grocery store, there were 8 cases of soda on the shelf. One case contained 11 cans of soda, and each of the others contained 6. If Mr. Jones bought all 8 cases, how many cans of soda did he purchase at this store?

(A) 53
(B) 54
(C) 57
(D) 59

47. When the sum of a set of numbers is divided by the average (arithmetic mean) of these numbers, the result is *j*. What does *j* represent?

(A) Half of the sum of the numbers in the set
(B) The average of the numbers in the set
(C) Half of the average of the numbers in the set
(D) The quantity of numbers in the set

IF YOU FINISH BEFORE TIME IS CALLED, YOU MAY CHECK YOUR WORK ON THIS SECTION ONLY. DO NOT TURN TO ANY OTHER SECTION IN THE TEST.

SECTION 5

Time—30 Minutes

Directions: Write an essay on the following prompt on the paper provided. Your essay should NOT exceed two pages and must be written in ink. Erasing is not allowed.

Prompt: Technology makes the world smaller every day.

Do you agree or disagree with this statement? Use examples from history, literature, or your own personal experience to support your point of view.

GO ON TO THE NEXT PAGE

IF YOU FINISH BEFORE TIME IS CALLED, YOU MAY CHECK YOUR WORK ON THIS SECTION ONLY. DO NOT TURN TO ANY OTHER SECTION IN THE TEST.

ANSWER KEY

Section 1

1. D
2. B
3. B
4. C
5. A
6. B
7. D
8. B
9. A
10. C
11. A
12. C
13. A
14. D
15. D
16. C
17. D
18. C
19. B
20. B
21. A
22. C
23. A
24. B
25. D
26. C
27. A
28. C
29. B
30. D
31. D
32. A
33. B
34. A
35. D
36. C
37. D
38. B
39. D
40. A

Section 2

1. C
2. D
3. B
4. B
5. C
6. D
7. D
8. B
9. D
10. C
11. B
12. C
13. C
14. D
15. B
16. C
17. B
18. D
19. A
20. D
21. D
22. D
23. A
24. C
25. B
26. A
27. D
28. B
29. A
30. B
31. D
32. B
33. D
34. B
35. A
36. C
37. B

Section 3

1. D
2. C
3. A
4. B
5. D
6. B
7. C
8. A
9. C
10. B
11. D
12. B
13. B
14. D
15. B
16. D
17. A
18. A
19. B
20. C
21. A
22. C
23. D
24. A
25. A
26. C
27. C
28. D
29. C
30. B
31. A
32. C
33. D
34. D
35. B
36. D

Section 4

1. C
2. D
3. B
4. D
5. B
6. C
7. D
8. B
9. D
10. C
11. C
12. B
13. D
14. C
15. D
16. D
17. A
18. A
19. B
20. A
21. C
22. C
23. C
24. C
25. D
26. C
27. B
28. C
29. B
30. D
31. B
32. C
33. B
34. B
35. D
36. B
37. B
38. A
39. A
40. D
41. C
42. C
43. D
44. A
45. B
46. A
47. D

ISEE PRACTICE TEST 2: UPPER- AND MIDDLE-LEVEL: ASSESS YOUR STRENGTHS

Use the following tables to determine which topics and chapters you need to review most. If you need help with your essay, be sure to review Chapter 9: The Essay and Chapter 26: Writing Skills.

Topic	Question
Verbal: Synonyms	Section 1, questions 1–20
Verbal: Sentence Completions	Section 1, questions 21–40
Quantitative Reasoning: Word Problems	Section 2, questions 1–22
Quantitative Reasoning: Quantitative Comparison	Section 2, questions 23–37
Reading Comprehension	Section 3, questions 1–36
Mathematics Achievement	Section 4, questions 1–47

Topic	Number of Questions on Test	Number Correct	If you struggled with these questions, study...
Verbal: Synonyms	20		Chapters 7 and 24
Verbal: Sentence Completions	20		Chapter 4
Quantitative Reasoning: Word Problems	22		Chapters 10–14 and Chapter 25
Quantitative Reasoning: Quantitative Comparison	15		Chapter 5
Reading Comprehension	36		Chapter 8
Mathematics Achievement	47		Chapters 10–14 and Chapter 25

ANSWERS AND EXPLANATIONS

SECTION 1: VERBAL REASONING

SYNONYMS

1. D

To desecrate is to commit a sacrilegious act—to defile.

2. B

To laud is to praise in a lavish manner (e.g. "The spectators lauded the efforts of the competing athletes.").

3. B

To avert is to prevent something from occurring (e.g, "The disaster was averted by the air-traffic controller.").

4. C

Piety is another word for religious faith.

5. A

Amoral means without "without moral code." Ethics are a kind of moral code, so unethical is the best choice here.

6. B

Candor means honesty—a "candid camera," for example, is one that shows real-life events.

7. D

Haughtiness means excessive pride—arrogance. (C), rudeness, might have been a tempting distractor, but rude people aren't necessarily haughty.

8. B

To verify means to prove something (e.g., "The existence of UFOs has never been verified.").

9. A

To deceive means to trick.

10. C

Look for secondary definitions—a fiction is a story that is untrue, so one possible meaning for fiction is falsehood (e.g., "His reputation was largely based on the fiction that he had fought in World War II.").

11. A

Something that's hardy is healthy (e.g., "a hardy troop of soldiers").

12. C

Something that's lyrical is like a singing voice—it's musical.

13. A

Use roots here—*meta* means change, and *morph* means shape. So the closest synonym is change.

14. D

To lament for someone or something is to grieve.

15. D

Something that's arid is dry (e.g., an arid desert). Word association could have worked here if you thought of *Arrid* the deodorant.

16. C

A perceptive person is observant—he or she is able to perceive things quickly and understand them.

17. D

An adamant person is convinced, resolute—stubborn (e.g., "Dave was adamant about his decision to buy a Range Rover™.").

18. C

Neutral people or parties are impartial. They don't take sides—they're unbiased.

19. B

Docile means tame (e.g., "The aggressive dog became docile in later life.").

20. B

Wariness means caution—if you're wary, you're apprehensive about a situation.

Sentence Completions

21. A

The clue words "come out at night" indicate that raccoons are nocturnal.

22. C

The two clue words "normally" and "usual" suggest that both blanks mean more or less the same—(C), amiable .. enthusiasm, works best here.

23. A

Death is a morbid subject, making (A) the best choice here.

24. B

You're looking for a contrast here; once a religious festival (B), the event is now commercialized.

25. D

A person who is constantly changing his views is described as flighty.

26. C

You're looking for a positive word for the first blank and a word meaning "deny" or "criticize" for the second blank. (C), agility .. question, fits this description.

27. A

Predict a synonym for "guilt" here—(A), remorse, is the correct answer.

28. C

The first blank should mean "tiring," so rule out (A). The only choice that means "tired" for the second blank is (C), fatigued. So strenuous .. fatigued is the correct answer.

29. B

The phrase "not only . . . but . . ." indicates that the second word is slightly more extreme than the first. Since you're looking for negative-sounding words, (B), predictable .. absurd, fits best.

30. D

Predict a more extreme version of "respect" for the blank here; revered works best in this context.

31. D

The first blank here should express the writer's incredulity—after all, it's pretty amazing that Chinese silk showed up in Egypt. (D), incredible .. massive, best explains why this fact is so amazing.

32. A

"At first" should have clued you into the contrast here—the house seemed frightening, but later proved benign, or friendly.

33. B

You're looking for a contrast—once just a myth, UFO stories are now thought plausible or believable.

34. A

Again, there should be a contrast here—(A), sparse, means terse, brief, minimal, and verbose means excessively wordy.

35. D

The clue "charm his listeners" suggests a positive word here, such as (D), engaging.

36. C

Exhilarated best captures the mixture of fear and enjoyment suggested by the sentence—consistent with a first trip on a raft.

37. D

The key phrase here is "to equal and even—Wright's successes." So we're looking for a word meaning more than equal. Choice (D), surpass, works nicely.

38. B

"Weighing more than seventy tons" leads us to predict a word like large or gigantic for the first blank. The word "yet" sets up a contrast for the second blank. We want a word like small for the second blank. Only (B), gargantuan, and (D), prodigious, work for the first blank. Of these two options, only choice (B), small, works for the second blank. So (B) is correct.

39. D

We are looking for a word that covers the wide variety of trumpets described in this sentence. Look for a word that means "varied" among the answer choices. Choice (D), diverse, works best.

40. A

Take this two-blank sentence one word at a time. For the first blank, we're looking for a word that works with "difficult to spot." Elusive, (A), and crafty, (B), are the only choices that work. For the second blank, we're looking for a word that sets up a contrast with "difficult to spot." Choice (A), confined, works here.

SECTION 2: QUANTITATIVE REASONING

Word Problems

1. C

$$Q + 7 - 8 + 3 = 23$$
$$Q + 2 = 23$$
$$Q = 21$$

2. D

A kilogram is equal to 1,000 grams. Remember, *kilo* means 1,000. A kilometer, for example, equals 1,000 meters.

3. B

To solve this problem, you need to find a common denominator. In this case, the lowest common denominator is 36.

$$\frac{1}{9} + \frac{7}{12} + \frac{5}{6} = \frac{4}{36} + \frac{21}{36} + \frac{30}{36}$$
$$= \frac{55}{36}$$
$$= 1\frac{19}{36}$$

4. B

$$15\% \text{ of } 60 = (15\%)(60)$$
$$= (0.15)(60)$$
$$= 9$$

5. C

To solve this problem, you first need to determine the limits of possible values for a:

$$\begin{aligned} a + 2 &> 5 \\ a &> 3 \\ a - 4 &< 1 \\ a &< 5 \end{aligned}$$

So a is between 3 and 5. The only value from the answer choices that fits in the limits is (C), 4.

6. D

To solve this equation, we first need to find the value of x.

$$2x + 4 = 26$$
$$2x = 22, \text{ so } x = 11.$$

Therefore, $11 + 4 = 15$.

7. D

The key to solving this problem is to take in the information one piece at a time. We're told that we have an equilateral hexagon. *Equilateral* means that all sides are equal. A hexagon has 6 sides. If we divide 6 into 42, we have the measure of one side: 7. So two sides would total 14.

8. B

Angelo earns \$2,000. Of this money, he spends 30% on rent. We can easily turn this information into an equation.

$$\begin{aligned} \text{Rent} &= 30\% \text{ of } \$2{,}000 \\ &= (0.30)(\$2{,}000) \\ &= \$600 \end{aligned}$$

9. D

The eggs cost 16 cents apiece. We need to figure out how many eggs can make up for the cost of 6 new chickens, or 58 dollars. In other words, how many times does 16 cents divide into 58 dollars. Set this problem up as you would any division problem, paying attention to decimal places.

$$0.16\overline{)58.00}$$

$$\begin{array}{r} 362.5 \\ 16\overline{)5800.0} \end{array}$$

Since the famer cannot sell half of an egg, he must sell 363 eggs.

10. C

Notice the use of the word "rate" in this problem. Don't be fooled by the terms "fuel" and "miles"—this is a straightforward rate problem, and you want to set it up as such. Twelve gallons of fuel for 48 miles is the same as how many gallons for 60 miles?

$$\frac{12}{48} = \frac{x}{60}$$
$$48x = 12 \times 60$$
$$x = \frac{720}{48} = 15$$

11. B

To add mixed numbers, add the whole number parts and add the fraction parts. (Sometimes the sum of the fraction parts will be greater than 1, in which case you would need to make some adjustments.) To add the fraction parts, find a common denominator.

$$\begin{aligned} 1\frac{6}{11} + 1\frac{7}{22} &= 2 + \frac{6}{11} + \frac{7}{22} \\ &= 2 + \frac{12}{22} + \frac{7}{22} \\ &= 2\frac{19}{22} \end{aligned}$$

12. C

Use the average formula:

$$\text{Average} = \frac{\text{Sum of the items}}{\text{Number of items}}$$

$$9 = \frac{\text{Sum}}{6}$$

$$\text{Sum} = 9 \times 6 = 54$$

13. C

Let's consider each answer choice. (A) gives us the value $\frac{2}{3}$. But we know that x must be smaller than $\frac{1}{2}$, and since $\frac{2}{3}$ is not, we can eliminate it. (B) proposes 0.47, but x must be smaller than $\frac{1}{3}$, and 0.47 is not. (C) gives us $\frac{1}{5}$, which is smaller than $\frac{1}{3}$ but larger than $\frac{1}{10}$—it fits the given criteria. Since there can only be one correct answer, there is no reason to check the last answer choice. Choice (D) is incorrect because $\frac{1}{20}$ is less than $\frac{1}{10}$ and x can not be less than $\frac{1}{10}$.

14. D

The best way to solve this problem is to solve for a.

$$3a + 6a = 36$$
$$9a = 36$$
$$a = 4$$

15. B

The easiest way to solve this problem is to convert $\frac{1}{4}$ to a decimal, 0.25, and then multiply. Again, make sure that you remember to count your decimal places.

$$(0.72) \times (0.25) = 0.18$$

16. C

The easiest way to solve this problem is to break the diagram on the right into two rectangles. Then solve for each area and add them together.

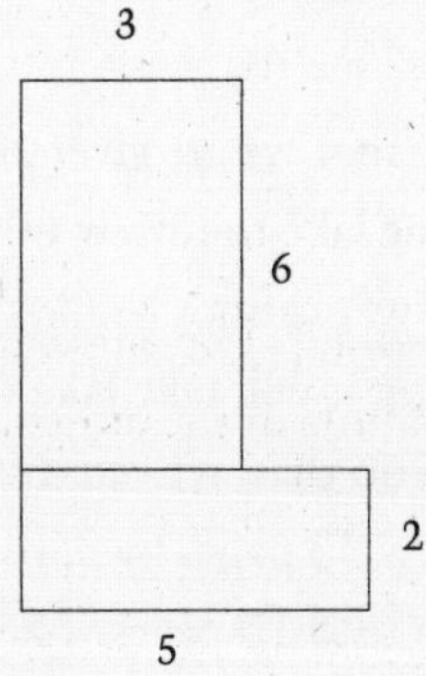

The area of the rectangle on top is 3 × 6 = 18. The area of the rectangle on bottom is 5 × 2 = 10. The total area is 18 + 10 = 28.

17. B

First you need to break down 48 into its prime factors, and then you can determine how may *different* ones there are.

$$48 = 2 \times 24$$
$$= 2 \times 2 \times 12$$
$$= 2 \times 2 \times 2 \times 6$$
$$= 2 \times 2 \times 2 \times 2 \times 3$$

There are only two different prime factors for 48:2 and 3.

18. D

Remember as you do this problem that a factor is a number that divides evenly into another number. Again, the easiest way to solve this problem is to consider each factor individually. (A) cannot be the answer because 3 is a factor of 36 and also 48. Ditto for (B), 6, and (C), 12. The answer must be (D), 18.

19. A

The formula for the volume of a cube is the length of a side cubed. We are told that the length of one side is 5. Five cubed equals 125, (A).

20. D

Doubling the rate that we are given, we have 2 hours and 30 minutes for Jake to review 60 pages. We know that the answer cannot be (A). But we need to figure out how long it will take Jake to review those final 10 pages. To do that, we can divide the rate it takes Jake to review 30 pages by 3; that will give us the rate it takes to read 10 pages. Then 1 hour and 15 minutes is the same as 75 minutes. A third of 75 is 25—we know it will take Jake 25 minutes to read 10 pages. Put it all together: 2 hours and 30 minutes plus 25 minutes gives us 2 hours and 55 minutes for Jake to read his history book.

21. D

If Mary types 12 words in 20 seconds, then she types 36 words in 60 seconds, or 1 minute. Thus, she types twice that, or 72 words, in 2 minutes.

22. D

Just substitute 8 for r in the equation: $(8 + 4)^2 = (12)^2 = 12 \times 12 = 144$.

Quantitative Comparisons

23. A

Remember to compare, not calculate: There is no reason to look for common denominators and solve here. The $\frac{1}{2}$ in Column A is just slightly larger than the $\frac{2}{5}$ in Column B. Both columns contain $\frac{3}{4}$. The $\frac{7}{8}$ in Column A is also larger than the $\frac{7}{9}$ in Column B, so overall, whatever the total value, Column A is larger than Column B.

24. C

Put the expressions in Column A and Column B in the same form so they are easy to compare. First, simplify the value under Column A. It's easy to multiply these fractions together because they cancel easily, giving us a final value of $\frac{1}{20}$, which in decimal form is 0.05. The columns are equal.

25. B

This problem is similar to the one above. First simplify the value under Column A, making sure that you cancel whenever possible. Under Column A we end up with the value $\frac{4}{5}$, which is less than 1. The value under Column B is $\frac{5}{4}$, which is greater than 1. So, the answer is (B).

26. A

The fastest way to solve this problem is to determine the value of x.

$$3x - 12 = 3x - 6x$$
$$-12 = -6x$$
$$2 = x$$

So x equals 2. If you add 2 to x, you get 4, a value larger than the 2 in Column B. So Column A is larger.

27. D

The answer to this problem is (D). All we know about x and y is that both are positive. We don't know their relative values: We don't know if x is greater than y or vise versa. Consequently, we can't determine if adding the number 1 to the value of x would make Column A greater, less than, or equal to the value under Column B. The answer here must therefore be (D).

28. B

Find the value of each column:

$$\begin{aligned} 5\% \text{ of } (3 + 4) &= 5\% \text{ of } 7 \\ &= (0.05)(7) \\ &= 0.35 \\ 4\% \text{ of } (3 \times 4) &= 4\% \text{ of } 12 \\ &= (0.04)(12) \\ &= 0.48 \end{aligned}$$

29. A

The easiest way to solve this problem is to change the value under Column B, a fraction, into a decimal. Thus, $\frac{9}{20}$ is the same as $\frac{45}{100}$ or 0.45. Column A, with a value of 0.46, is larger than Column B.

30. B

This problem requires no math at all. You are given a certain amount of money—5 dollars. Can you buy more expensive items (32-cent stamps) or more cheap items (29-cent stamps) with this money? You can buy more of the cheaper items, so the answer must be Column B.

31. D

You're given that x is between $\frac{8}{9}$ and $\frac{1}{2}$, and you're asked to compare x to $\frac{2}{3}$. The fraction $\frac{2}{3}$ is between $\frac{8}{9}$ and $\frac{1}{2}$, but so are lots of other fractions, some less than $\frac{2}{3}$ and others greater than $\frac{2}{3}$. Column A could be greater than, equal to, or less than Column B, so the answer is (D).

32. B

This is another problem that takes no math at all. We are told that x is negative. Before you start plugging in values for x, you should take a look at the expression under Column B: $(2x)(1x)$. If you multiplied these x's together, whatever the value, the result would be positive. The value under Column A, however, would remain negative. Since a positive is always greater than a negative, the answer has to be (B).

33. D

Don't be fooled by the number 8 under Column B. Column A asks you to find the perimeter of an octagon with sides of equal length. The problem is, we don't know what those lengths are. One side could equal 1, in which case the answer would be (C). One side could be 2, in which case the answer would be (A). We already have two possibilities, which tells us that the correct answer must be (D).

34. B

The factors of 21 are 1, 3, 7, and 21. Of these only two are prime. Compare that to the value under Column B, 3, and the answer is (B).

35. A

Translate the expression into an equation: $\frac{5}{7}$ of x is 35.

$$\begin{aligned} \frac{5}{7}x &= 35 \\ x &= 35 \times \frac{7}{5} \\ x &= 49 \end{aligned}$$

36. C

Remember the saying "A percent of B is equal to B percent of A"? If you do, then this question is a breeze. If not, you want to commit that rule to memory. In this case, 98% of 51 is $0.98 \times 51 =$

49.98, and 51% of 98 is $0.51 \times 98 = 49.98$. The columns are equal.

37. B

There are a few ways to solve this problem. The first is to actually calculate the math. Twenty percent of 42 is the same as (0.20)(42) or 8.4. The other way to do this problem is to realize that 20% of 42 is the same as taking $\frac{1}{5}$ of 42. We know that $\frac{1}{5}$ of 45 is 9, the value under Column B. But we want $\frac{1}{5}$ of 42, which will be less than 9. In either case, the answer must be (B).

SECTION 3: READING COMPREHENSION

Log Cabins Passage

The first passage is about log cabins and the era of their greatest popularity—a period from 1780 to 1850. The author describes early simple cabins and grand later ones and then discusses the factors that led to a decline in the log cabin's popularity, factors like the greater availability of hardware and building materials, the rising popularity of the Greek Revival style of house, and the spread of the railroads. The passage ends with a brief description of what happened to most log cabins as their heyday ended.

1. D

The Greek Revival style is described as becoming increasingly popular, "with [i.e., because of] its democratic roots in ancient Greece...." So the origins of the new style lay in the ancient democracy of Greece—a fact that might well have appealed to the citizens of a young democratic nation like the United States—meaning (D) is the best answer. The passage never suggests that there had been a general desire to replace log cabins, (A), and never mentions contemporary Greek architects, (B), or devoutly religious Americans, (C).

2. C

The first sentence says that "a great number of settlers forged westward." What word plugs in best for "forged"? (C)'s moved. Fled, (A), incorrectly implies that the settlers were running away from something; wandered, (B), implies that their movements were aimless, without purpose. Returned, (D), suggests that the settlers had already been out west, which makes little sense in context.

3. A

The author indicates that Greek Revival houses became more popular than log cabins for two reasons: the democratic roots of the Greek Revival style and the templed fronts of these houses, which faced the street. This last feature—that the fronts of Greek Revival houses faced the street—suggests that log cabins became less popular because they didn't always face the street, which makes (A) correct. The passage doesn't suggest that either style of house had indoor plumbing, (B), or that log cabins could not have glass windows, (C). And while log cabins may well have been built near lakes and rivers, (D), there's no suggestion that Greek Revival homes were not. So (A) is the correct answer.

4. B

The question stem's reference to limiting factors in the architecture of log cabins recalls sentence 6: "Climate and the proximity of the local forest no longer set architectural limits." What does this mean? It means that, with the new railroads bringing lumber and hardware to formerly isolated regions, a settler's choice of which house to build was no longer dictated by local weather and the distance to the nearest forest. (B) restates this latter point, and it's correct. (A) is incorrect because, unlike logs from the local forest, nails were not widely available. (C) and (D) bring up issues that aren't mentioned at all in the passage and so cannot be inferred.

5. D

The passage's final sentence notes that, after the 1850s, log structures housed livestock but "fewer and fewer people." So most log structures built after 1850 housed animals, (D).

6. B

Find the right answer by using the passage to answer the questions asked in the choices. (A) can be answered in lines 1–3; log cabins actually grew in popularity because settlers were moving west. (C) is answered in lines 10–12; the style's "democratic roots in ancient Greece and its templed front facing the street" were desirable. (D) can be answered in lines 3–6; log cabins grew from being primitive to being sophisticated, two-story houses. (B) is the answer because the author does not say log cabins have disappeared.

Plague Passage

Next up is a passage about the plague, an epidemic that killed one-third of the people in Europe in the 13th and 14th centuries. The author says that, ironically, the plague brought about some beneficial changes in European society. One of these changes—the focal point of the passage—was in the medical profession. The plague created a shortage of doctors, allowing people with new ideas to enter the profession. In addition, having been failed by the old doctors with their Latin medical texts, ordinary people began clamoring for medical texts printed in everyday languages. These were eventually published, making medical knowledge more accessible to everyone.

7. C

As noted above, the primary focus of the passage is how at least one good thing came out of the terrible tragedy of the plague. (C) correctly restates this idea. (A) and (B) focus too narrowly on details mentioned in sentences 1 and 4. (D) is closer to the mark, but it too is a detail, not the larger focus of the passage.

8. A

Plug the choices into the sentence in question, and (A) is correct: The epidemic caused enormous changes in European society. The changes were needed, (B), but needed by the society, not by the plague itself. Accelerated, (C), means moved faster, which implies that the changes were already occurring before the plague. But the passage never suggests that this was so. Offered, (D), doesn't work at all.

9. C

Sentence 6 says that, when the plague created a shortage of doctors, "people with new ideas" rushed in to fill the void, bringing needed reform (sentence 3) to the medical profession. This suggests that, prior to the plague, the medical profession was in need of new ideas—sweeping changes—which makes (C) correct. The shortage of doctors, (A), occurred during and after the plague, not before it. As for (B), while sentence 5 says that universities were short on medical professors, there's no evidence that medical care was available only to students in the pre-plague years. And (D) distorts the final sentence, which says that people demanded medical texts printed in their own languages, not the language of Latin. This doesn't mean that, before the plague, medicine was only practiced in Latin-speaking countries. (Latin is, in fact, and was even then, a "dead" language, the language of the long-vanquished Roman Empire.)

10. B

Take another look at the last sentence of the passage. It says that medical texts gradually began to be published in everyday languages instead of in Latin, "making medical knowledge more accessible." You can infer from this that, after the 1300s, easy-to-read medical texts were probably more available to the general public, an idea restated in choice (B). The passage never indicates that a cure for the plague, (A), would soon be found (in fact, it would not be found for several centuries). As for (C), just because more medical texts were published in everyday languages after the plague doesn't mean that, a hundred years later, none were written in Latin. Finally, (D) is completely unsupported by the passage.

11. D

Are the author's points positive, negative, or neutral? The author talks about the negative effects of the plague, but he or she focuses more on the positive results. The author says that medical knowledge became more accessible to people and that it led to medical reform. That rules out (A) and (B), leaving favorable and sensible. Next, think about how the passage would sound if you read it aloud. Does it sound as if the author expresses approval about the outcome of the plague (favorable), or does it sound as if he or she has based his argument on sound reasoning (sensible)? Although, the author recognizes that the plague had positive effects, he or she also points out the negative—one-third of the European population died. (D) is the better answer.

12. B

Try to find each of the choices in the passage. (A) is in lines 15–17; the author says new medical texts in everyday languages made "medical knowledge more accessible." (C) is in lines 10–12; people with new ideas took the place of doctors who died or fled during the plague. (D) is in lines 3–4. (B) is the answer because it is not fully addressed in the passage. The author says in lines 15–17 that medical texts began appearing in languages other than Latin, but that doesn't mean more people did not learn Latin.

Orienteering Passage

The fourth passage is about the sport of orienteering, in which competitors make their way across unfamiliar terrain using only a map and a compass. The author focuses on the notion that the most important element of orienteering is choosing a good route. Why? Because the shortest route from point A to point B is rarely the fastest or easiest way.

13. B

What defines orienteering, if not having a compass and a map? Orienteers have to "navigate their way cross-country along an unfamiliar course." Therefore, a hiker with a map and compass is NOT orienteering if she travels over a known, familiar route, and (B) is correct. (A) and (C) propose rules that are never mentioned in the passage. (D) describes an orienteer who takes the "crude" approach.

14. D

As sentence 2 puts it, "the most important question in orienteering is not compass bearing but choice of route," which eliminates (A) and makes (D) correct. While it is no doubt important to avoid hazardous terrain, (B), and to overcome obstacles quickly, (C), the passage places the highest priority on the choice of route.

15. B

The competitor in question climbs a mountain to take the most direct route, but sentences 3 and 4 say that this is "seldom the best" and that orienteers "tend to disdain" competitors who do so as crude and lacking intellectual finesse, or sophistication, (B). (A) is incorrect because the competitor's beeline approach will probably put him at a disadvantage in terms of both time and energy. The beeline approach may be stupid, but the author never says it's against the rules, (C), or that it can endanger other competitors, (D). So (B) is correct.

16. D

The passage never mentions running or backpacks, (A), swimming, (B), or setting up campsites, (C). So (D) must be correct. In fact, the final sentence of the passage notes that orienteers "are always making" quick calculations of the times and distances involved in various possible routes.

17. A

Look at the sentence "finesse" appears in. The author contrasts "intellectual finesse" with "beelining over obstacles," which means orienteers would rather use their minds before acting, so you know the answer's not (B). (C) is wrong, too, because "intellectual inefficiency" doesn't make sense. That leaves "skill" (ability) and "devotion" (dedication). (A) is the answer.

18. A

Questions about the author's attitude are generally asking about the tone of the passage. Are the author's points positive, negative, or neutral? The passage doesn't discuss downfalls or troubles orienteers might have, but it does talk about their "intellectual finesse" and the "quick calculation orienteers are always making." That rules out (B) and (C), leaving "respect" and "appreciative." Next, think about how the passage would sound if you read it aloud. Does it sound as if the author is holding orienteers in high regard, or does it sound as if the author is showing gratitude to orienteers? (A) is the answer.

Night Terrors Passage

Next up is a passage about two psychological phenomena: first, nightmares, and second, something called night terrors. In the latter the sleeper, usually a child, wakes up in great fright with no memory of having dreamed. The passage begins with the statement that, while nightmares and night terrors used to be confused with each other, researchers now know they are two different phenomena. The rest of the passage focuses on night terrors, noting that they're not really dangerous and that parents should use common sense, taking precautions and not worrying unduly.

19. B

Two phenomena, long "confounded" under one heading, are now known to be separate things. The word in question, then, should mean confused, or mixed up, (B). None of the other words means anything remotely similar to confounded.

20. C

The correct answer, (C), restates the first sentence of the passage. None of the other choices are suggested, not even (D), which is a distorted echo of the passage's final sentence. The author says that children suffering from night terrors should usually not be medicated. This is a far cry from saying that sleep researchers used to prescribe medication for such children but have recently stopped.

21. A

Sentence 2 says that a nightmare "is an actual, detailed dream." (A) correctly restates this fact.

No mention is made of dream fragments, (B), hallucinations, (C), or trances, (D).

22. C

What do we know about the parents of children who suffer from night terrors? That these parents themselves sometimes find their child's experience "horrifying" and that a child suffering from night terrors can make a parent "anxious." We can infer, then, that the parents find night terrors nearly as frightening as the children do, and (C) is correct. (A) is the opposite of what the author says. (B) makes an unwarranted leap; the passage never suggests that these parents also suffered night terrors when they were children. And the last sentence of the passage implies, if anything, that a doctor usually should not be consulted at all, rather than as soon as possible, (D).

23. D

The difference between nightmares and night terrors, (A), is defined in sentences 2 and 3. The question in (B) is answered in the second-to-last sentence of the passage. Sentence 3 notes that the child waking from a night terror does not remember dreaming, (C). This leaves (D) as correct, and indeed, the author merely advises a sleep schedule, never explaining why a sleep schedule helps reduce night terrors.

24. A

How would you answer this question in your own words? Lines 3 and 5 use contrast phrases: "On the one hand" and "On the other." Those are hints to where to find the difference between nightmares and night terrors. (B) is incorrect, and (C) and (D) are not addressed in the passage.

Neanderthals Passage

This passage is about the Neanderthal, an early human that lived in Europe and Asia until about 35,000 years ago. The passage puts forth two ideas: first, that Neanderthals were physically very different from modern humans and second, that despite their reputation to the contrary, Neanderthals were probably quite intelligent. The passage concludes with a teaser: The disappearance of this capable creature mystifies and fascinates scientists and is "perhaps the most talked-about issue in human origins research today."

25. A

All four choices are physical attributes of the Neanderthal. In the author's description of Neanderthals, found in sentence 3, "massive limb bones" are the first item on the list. A "limb" is an arm or a leg, so you can infer from this that most Neanderthals had big arms, (A). You can't infer, however, that their legs were bowed, (C), because "bowed" implies shape, not size. The set of Neanderthal eyes, (A), and the breadth of their feet, (D), are never mentioned.

26. C

The opening sentence says that Neanderthals lived "throughout Europe and western Asia," which makes (C) correct. The passage never says what kind of dwellings they lived in, (A), how they hunted, (B), or whether they lived on all the continents, (D).

27. C

The author says that Neanderthals, unlike modern humans, had "massive limb bones," and "enormous physical strength." Modern humans, then probably have less physical strength than their Neanderthal cousins, and (C) is correct. No information is given on either species' eyesight, (A), sense of smell, (B), or amount of body hair, (D).

28. D

The only reference to what modern humans think of Neanderthals comes at the beginning of sentence 4: "yet despite the Neanderthals' reputation for low intelligence...." (D) is thus the correct inference.

29. C

The word "question" appears only once in the passage, in the final sentence. We know from the previous sentence that Neanderthals vanished or died out around 35,000 years ago. "The question of what became of the Neanderthals...." Therefore, (C) is correct. The questions of the Neanderthals' diet, (A), migratory patterns, (B), and origins, (D), are never raised in the passage.

30. B

Think about where you would most likely find this passage. (A) is incorrect because the passage contains nothing fictional. (C) is incorrect because it is unlikely an explorer would encounter Neanderthals, who lived at least 35,000 years ago. (D) is incorrect because the passage doesn't discuss nutrition, exercise, or any other health topic. (B) is the answer because the passage sticks to facts about Neanderthals.

Coyotes Passage

The final passage is about coyotes. The author's main focus is not on the behavioral habits of living coyotes, but rather on the evolution of the coyote as found in the fossil record. Both the coyote and the wolf, we learn, had a common ancestor living in North America as long as three million years ago. One or two million years ago, the coyote and the wolf became separate species. As time passed, other species such as the mammoth and the saber-toothed tiger lived and became extinct, but the coyote endured—basically the same primitive animal, but still marvelously adaptable to its environment.

31. A

In most passages, the main idea is stated in the first or second sentence. Here the main idea becomes clear only at the end: the coyote has endured for millions of years without evolving into a more advanced species. This point is restated in correct choice (A). (B) focuses on a detail, how other species came and went. But these species are described in order to provide a contrast with the coyote, which not only avoided extinction but did so without evolving. (C) has the same problem: The author's point is that, unlike other animals, the coyote did not change—it survived by staying the same. And (D) is a passing detail found in sentence 4—not significant enough to be the primary focus of the passage.

32. C

"Modern" dogs are mentioned only in the first sentence, which says that coyotes are "one of the most primitive of living dogs." This suggests that modern dogs are relatives of coyotes, as stated in (C). Dire wolves are extinct "canids;" we don't know from the passage whether they're related to modern dogs or not, but it's a pretty safe bet that modern dogs are not "direct descendants of dire wolves," as (A) suggests. Where modern dogs live, (B), is not mentioned, but again, common sense suggests they're found everywhere, not just in North America. The evolutionary flexibility of modern dogs (D) is not discussed in the passage.

33. D

Sentence 2 says that "a close relative of the contemporary coyote existed here two to three million years ago." The choice closest to this estimate is (D), and it's correct.

34. D

Why does the author mention mammoths and saber-toothed tigers? Because they lived and became extinct, while the ever-adaptable coyote endured. In other words, these species died out because they failed to adapt as the coyote did, and (D) is correct. Neither animal in question is described as a relative of the coyote, (A). Unlike wild horses, mammoths and tigers are not described as having left North America by land bridge, (C), but that's beside the point. These species died out because they couldn't adapt—as the coyote did. And the author never says that jackals hunted any species into extinction, (D).

35. B

Here's a word-in-context question that really requires you to know the meaning of the word—the word, in this case, being "galleon." Maybe you've come across it in pirate stories; a galleon is a kind of ship. So the idea that other horses "returned on galleons" means that horses, who had left North America by land bridge, returned to the continent when brought by ship, making (B) correct. None of the other choices picks up on the proper meaning of "galleon."

36. D

Try to find evidence in the passage supporting each of the choices. (A) is found in lines 11–13: "Mammoths ... and dire wolves ... came and went." (B) is in lines 13–14: "Native horses left the continent ... and others returned in galleons." (C) is in lines 8–10: "a division occurred in North America between the coyote and the wolf." (D) is the answer because it is incorrect. The passage says they have existed a long time, living even as "time passed, and glaciers advanced and receded" (lines 10–11) and that they have always adjusted to the changes (lines 17–18).

SECTION 4: MATHEMATICS ACHIEVEMENT

1. C

$(x-2)(x+5)$ will equal 0 when either factor $(x-2)$ or $(x+5)$ is 0. That's when x is 2 or -5.

2. D

Set up a proposition. Here 2 gallons for 875 square feet is the same as x gallons for 4,375 square feet:

$$\frac{2}{875}=\frac{x}{4{,}375}$$
$$875x=2\times 4{,}375$$
$$875x=8{,}750$$
$$x=\frac{8{,}750}{875}=10$$

3. B

Use the formula for the area of a triangle:

$$\text{Area} = \frac{1}{2}\text{(base)(height)}$$
$$= \frac{1}{2}\text{(4 in.)(6 in.)} = 12 \text{ sq. in.}$$

4. D

The sides of an equilateral triangle are equal in length, so $3x+1$ and $x+7$ are equal:

$$3x+1=x+7$$
$$3x-x=7-1$$
$$2x=6$$
$$x=3$$

Plug $x=3$ back into either of the expressions, and you'll find that the length of each side is 10.

5. B

Sixty-five times 10^2 means 65 times 100, or 6,500. Thirty-one times 10^3 means 31 times 1,000, or 31,000. Add 6,500 and 31,000 and 12 and you get 37,512.

6. C

He lost 20% of $120,000, which is 0.20 times $120,000, or $24,000.

7. D

The dog can run in a circular area with radius of 8 meters. Use the formula for the area of a circle:

$$\begin{aligned}\text{Area} &= \pi(\text{radius})^2\\ &= \pi(8 \text{ meters})^2\\ &= 64\pi \text{ square meters}\end{aligned}$$

8. B

Rate is distance divided by time. So 328 miles divided by 4 hours is $\frac{328}{4} = 82$ miles per hour.

9. D

If distance equals rate times time, then time equals distance divided by rate. Here the distance is 3,300 miles and the rate is 270 miles per hour. And 3,300 miles divided by 270 miles per hour is $\frac{3.300}{270} \approx 12.22$ hours.

10. C

Plug $a = 3$ and $b = 4$ into the expression:

$$\begin{aligned}a^2 + 2ab + b^2 &= 3^2 + 2(3)(4) + 4^2\\ &= 9 + 24 + 16\\ &= 49\end{aligned}$$

11. C

Look what happens when you just add the equations as presented:

$$\begin{aligned}x - y &= 5\\ 4x + 6y &= 20\\ \hline 5x + 5y &= 25\end{aligned}$$

Now just divide both sides by 5, and you get $x + y = 5$.

12. B

Break 726 down to its prime factorization by factoring out any prime factor you see one at a time:

$$\begin{aligned}726 &= 2 \times 363\\ &= 2 \times 3 \times 121\\ &= 2 \times 3 \times 11 \times 11\end{aligned}$$

The distinct prime factors are 2, 3, and 11. That's 3 distinct prime factors.

13. D

Plug any odd number in for n and evaluate the answer choices. If you take $n = 3$, you'll find that (A) is $-2(3) - 1 = -7$; (B) is $2(3) + 1 = 7$; (C) is $2(3) - 1 = 5$; and (D) is $4(3) = 12$. Only (D) is even.

14. C

Six hours a day for 5 days is 30 hours; 30 hours is $30 \times 60 = 1{,}800$ minutes; and 1,800 minutes is $1{,}800 \times 60 = 108{,}000$ seconds.

15. D

There are $4 \times 24 = 96$ hours in 4 days. Then 96 hours of snow at 3.5 inches per hour is $96 \times 3.5 = 336$ inches.

16. D

Today Nicholas is x years old and Billy is $3x$ years old. Five years ago Nicholas was $x - 5$ years old and Nicholas was $3x - 5$, so the sum of their ages was $(x - 5) + (3x - 5) = 4x - 10$.

17. A

If there are twice as many boys as girls, then $\frac{2}{5}$ of the students are boys and $\frac{1}{3}$ are girls. Two-thirds of 36 is 24.

18. A

The $\frac{1}{3}$ who drank soda only and the $\frac{2}{5}$ who drank juice only account for $\frac{1}{3}+\frac{2}{5}=\frac{5}{15}+\frac{6}{15}=\frac{11}{15}$ of the guests. The 16 who drank nothing therefore account for the other $\frac{4}{15}$. So you want to find out what number multiplied by $\frac{4}{15}$ will give you 16: $\frac{4}{15}x =$ 16; $x = 16 \times \frac{15}{4} = 4 \times 15 = 60$.

19. B

You might think that x has to be 2 and y has to be 3, but in fact there's another pair of consecutive integers that have a product of 6: –3 and –2. So what you know is that either $x = 2$ and $y = 3$, or $x = -3$ and $y = -2$. All three statements are true in the first case (when x and y are positive), but only statement II is true in the second case (when x and y are negative).

20. A

She starts with y cards. Giving away 5 to each of 3 friends means giving away $3 \times 5 = 15$, leaving her with $y - 15$. Receiving 2 from each of 3 friends means receiving $3 \times 2 = 6$, leaving her with $y - 15 + 6 = y - 9$.

21. C

For each coin the probability of tails is $\frac{1}{2}$. The combined probability is the product of the separate probabilities: $\frac{1}{2}\times\frac{1}{2}=\frac{1}{4}$.

22. C

Five minutes at 15 copies per minute is $5 \times 15 = 75$ copies. Then 75 out of 600 is $\frac{75}{600}=\frac{1}{8}$.

23. C

Simplify each inequality:

$$2(z-3) > 6$$
$$2z - 6 > 6$$
$$2z > 6 + 6$$
$$2z > 12$$
$$z > 6$$
$$z + 4 < 15$$
$$z < 15 - 4$$
$$z < 11$$

So z is between 6 and 11. The only answer choice that qualifies is (C), 7.

24. C

Three fiction books for every 8 nonfiction books means that 8 out of 3 + 8, or $\frac{8}{11}$, of all the books are nonfiction. The 600 nonfiction books are $\frac{8}{11}$ of the number you're looking for, so:

$$\frac{8}{11}x = 600$$
$$x = 600 \times \frac{11}{8} = \frac{6{,}600}{8} = 825$$

25. D

(D) is impossible because if x and y were even and z were odd, then $x + y$ would be even and $x + z$ would be odd.

26. C

If you call the passing grade x, then his second score was $x + 7$, and his third score was $x + 7 - 12 = x - 5$, which is 5 less than x.

27. B

If 70 percent are right-handed and the rest are left-handed, then $100 - 70 = 30$ percent are left-handed. Of that 30 percent, 70 percent have brown eyes. Seventy percent of 30 percent is $(0.70)(0.30) = 0.21$, or 21 percent.

28. C

Plug $q = 8$ and $r = 2$ into the definition:

$$q//r = (qr) - (q - r)$$
$$8//2 = (8 \times 2) - (8 - 2)$$
$$= 16 - 6 = 10$$

29. B

Plug $q = P$ and $r = 3$ into the definition:

$$q//r = (qr) - (q - r)$$
$$P//3 = (P \times 3) - (P - 3)$$
$$= 3P - P + 3$$
$$= 2P + 3$$

Set that equal to 11 and solve for P:

$$2P + 3 = 11$$
$$2P = 11 - 3$$
$$2P = 8$$
$$P = 4$$

30. D

Since a is anything greater than 4, a can be 8 or 16, so b doesn't have to be 2—which eliminates statement I. But you do know that b has to be positive, because a is positive (it's greater than 4) and the product of a and b is positive (it's 16). Therefore the sum of a and b is positive, and statement II is true. And lastly, when $a = 8$, $b = 2$; and when $a = 16$, $b = 1$. Thus, a is greater than b, and statement III is true.

31. B

The three angles have to add up to 180°, so:

$$x + 2x + 3x = 180$$
$$6x = 180$$
$$x = 30$$

32. C

AB is half of BC, which is given as 12, so $AB = 6$, and $AC = 6 + 12 = 18$. CD is half of AC, so $CD = 9$, and thus $AD = AB + BC + CD = 6 + 12 + 9 = 27$.

33. B

A square with an area of 36 square centimeters has sides of length 6 centimeters. Thus each side of the large square gets cut into thirds, and the whole large square gets divided into $3 \times 3 = 9$ smaller squares:

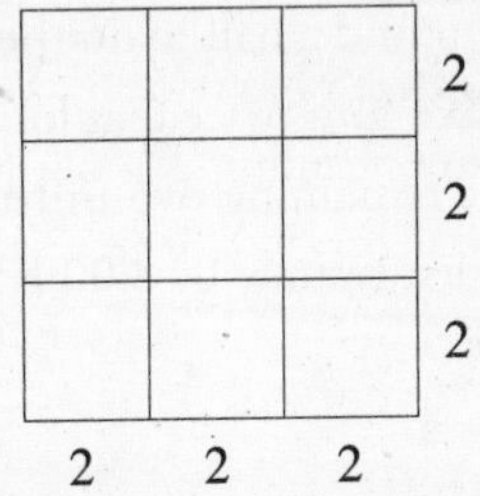

34. B

Just subtract 5 from both sides of the given equation:

$$x = 4y + 3$$
$$x - 5 = 4y + 3 - 5$$
$$= 4y - 2$$

35. D

Four for a dollar means 25 cents each. Selling them for 40 cents each means a profit of 15 cents on every orange sold. To get a total profit of \$3.00, he must sell $\frac{\$3.00}{\$0.15} = \frac{300}{15} = 20$ oranges.

36. B

Each sale price is 90% of the original price. Sixty-three dollars is 90% of what?

$$0.90x = \$63$$
$$x = \$\frac{63}{0.90} = \$70$$

The original price of the wool sweater was \$70. And \$45 is 90% of what?

$$0.90y = \$45$$
$$y = \$\frac{45}{0.90} = \$50$$

The original price of the cotton sweater was \$50. The difference was \$20.

37. B

It took him a hour and a half to do the first one-third, so it will take him twice that long—or 3 hours—to do the remaining two-thirds. To finish by 11:00 P.M., he must resume by 8:00 P.M.

38. A

If there are twice as many men as women on the team, then two-thirds of the team members are men and one-third are women. One-third of 45 is 15, so there are 15 women. One-third of those 15 women received medals, so that's 5 women medal winners.

39. A

The four fractions you're comparing all have the same numerator (1) and they all have positive denominators, so the fraction with the least value must be the one with the greatest denominator. m is greater than n, so $4m$ is greater than $4n$, and $4 + m$ is greater than $4 + n$. That eliminates (B) and (D). And since m is greater than 4, $4m$ is greater than $4 + m$. Thus, (A) has the greatest denominator and therefore the least value.

40. D

Translate into algebra. If one-fifth of a number is less than 20, then:

$$\frac{1}{5}x < 20$$
$$x < 20 \times \frac{5}{1}$$
$$x < 100$$

41. C

The lower three floors have a total of $3x$ apartments. The upper three floors have a total of $3y$ apartments. That's a total of $3x + 3y$ apartments in the building. If there are 3 people in each apartment, then the total number of people is 3 times $(3x + 3y)$, or $9x + 9y$.

42. C

After spending 20% on CDs, Joe had 80% left. He then spent 10% of that, or 8% of the original amount, leaving

100% – (20% + 8%) = 72%.

43. D

If every one of the n members invited 3 guests, that would be a total of $3n$ guests. n members plus $3n$ guests adds up to $n + 3n = 4n$ attendees.

44. A

If each side of the 4-by-4 rug is one-third of the sides of the floor, then it's a 12-by-12 floor, which would have an area of 144 square meters.

45. B

Each of the six squares is a rectangle.

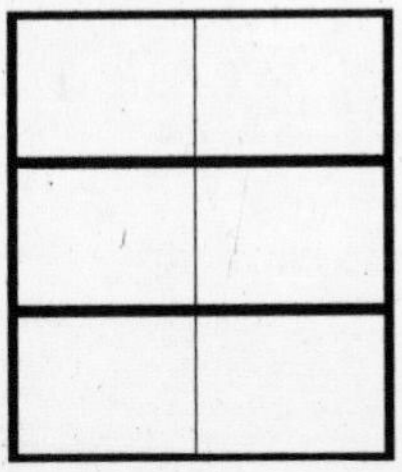

Plus there are these two rectangles:

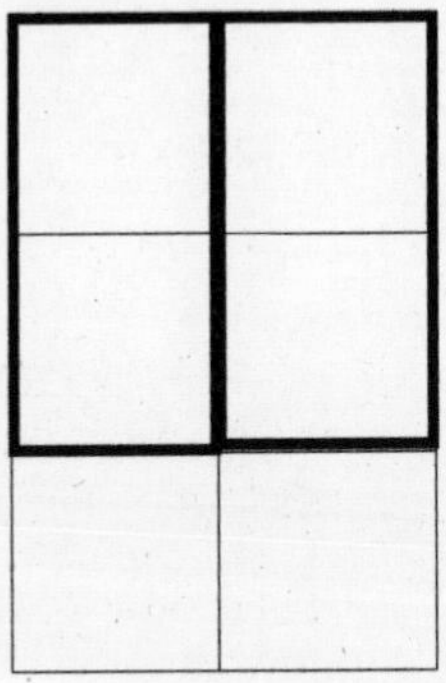

And these two:

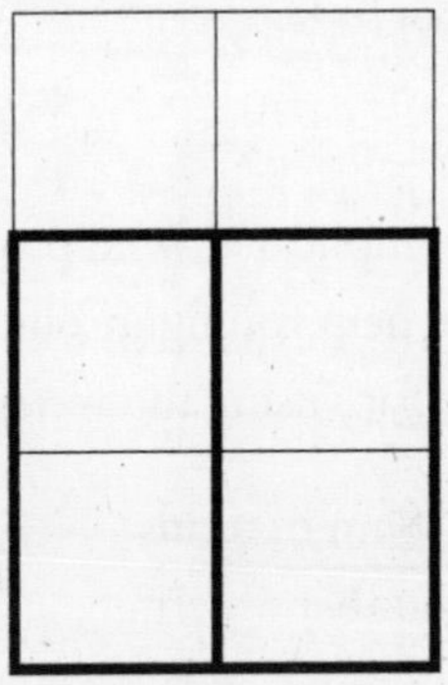

And these two:

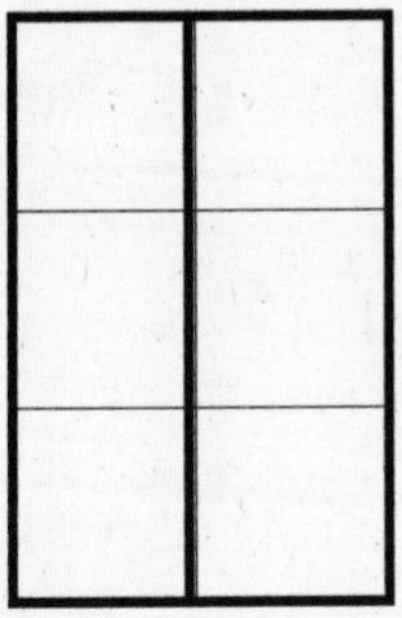

Plus this one:

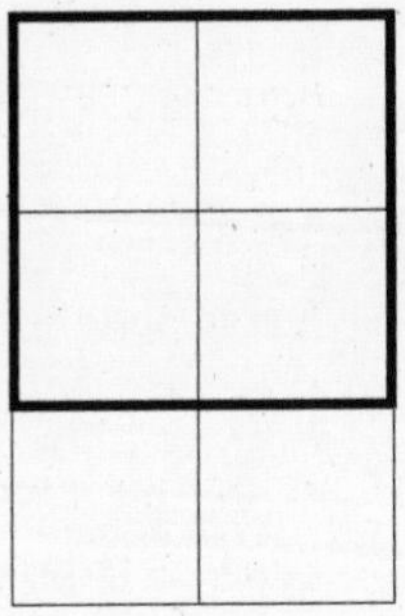

And this one:

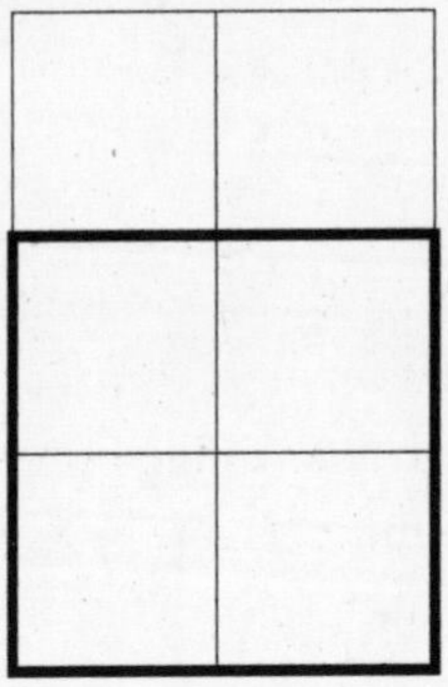

And lastly this one:

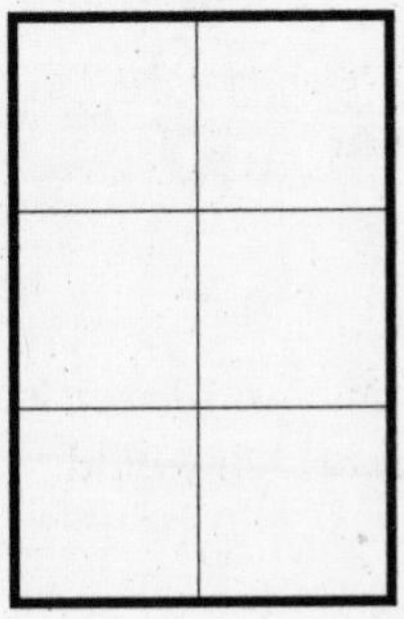

That's a total of 6 + 3 + 2 + 2 + 2 + 1 + 1 + 1 = 18.

46. A

Mr. Jones bought 1 case with 11 cans and 7 cases with 6 cans each, so he bought 1(11) + 7(6) or 11 + 42 = 53 cans of soda.

47. D

Translating complicated word problems into written equations can help you figure out where to get started. Solve for *j* using the average formula:

$$\text{Average} = \frac{\text{Sum of terms}}{\text{Number of terms}}$$

Now, express this as $\frac{\text{Sum of terms}}{\text{Average of terms}} = \text{Number} = j$.

CHAPTER 22: ISEE PRACTICE TEST 3: LOWER-LEVEL

HOW TO TAKE THIS PRACTICE TEST

Before taking this practice test, find a quiet room where you can work uninterrupted for three hours. Make sure you have a comfortable desk and several No. 2 pencils.

Use the answer sheet provided to record your answers. (You can cut it out or photocopy it.)

Once you start this practice test, don't stop until you've finished. Remember—you can review any questions within a section, but you may not go backward or forward a section.

You'll find answer explanations following the test.

Good luck.

ISEE Practice Test 3: Lower-Level Answer Sheet

Remove (or photocopy) the answer sheet and use it to complete the practice test.

Start with number 1 for each section. If a section has fewer questions than answer spaces, leave the extra spaces blank.

SECTION 1

1 A B C D	9 A B C D	17 A B C D	25 A B C D	33 A B C D	☐ # right in section 1
2 A B C D	10 A B C D	18 A B C D	26 A B C D	34 A B C D	
3 A B C D	11 A B C D	19 A B C D	27 A B C D	35 A B C D	
4 A B C D	12 A B C D	20 A B C D	28 A B C D	36 A B C D	
5 A B C D	13 A B C D	21 A B C D	29 A B C D	37 A B C D	☐ # wrong in section 1
6 A B C D	14 A B C D	22 A B C D	30 A B C D	38 A B C D	
7 A B C D	15 A B C D	23 A B C D	31 A B C D	39 A B C D	
8 A B C D	16 A B C D	24 A B C D	32 A B C D	40 A B C D	

SECTION 2

1 A B C D	9 A B C D	17 A B C D	25 A B C D	33 A B C D	☐ # right in section 2
2 A B C D	10 A B C D	18 A B C D	26 A B C D	34 A B C D	
3 A B C D	11 A B C D	19 A B C D	27 A B C D	35 A B C D	
4 A B C D	12 A B C D	20 A B C D	28 A B C D	36 A B C D	
5 A B C D	13 A B C D	21 A B C D	29 A B C D	37 A B C D	☐ # wrong in section 2
6 A B C D	14 A B C D	22 A B C D	30 A B C D	38 A B C D	
7 A B C D	15 A B C D	23 A B C D	31 A B C D	39 A B C D	
8 A B C D	16 A B C D	24 A B C D	32 A B C D	40 A B C D	

SECTION 3

1 A B C D	9 A B C D	17 A B C D	25 A B C D	33 A B C D	☐ # right in section 3
2 A B C D	10 A B C D	18 A B C D	26 A B C D	34 A B C D	
3 A B C D	11 A B C D	19 A B C D	27 A B C D	35 A B C D	
4 A B C D	12 A B C D	20 A B C D	28 A B C D	36 A B C D	
5 A B C D	13 A B C D	21 A B C D	29 A B C D	37 A B C D	☐ # wrong in section 3
6 A B C D	14 A B C D	22 A B C D	30 A B C D	38 A B C D	
7 A B C D	15 A B C D	23 A B C D	31 A B C D	39 A B C D	
8 A B C D	16 A B C D	24 A B C D	32 A B C D	40 A B C D	

SECTION 4

1 A B C D	9 A B C D	17 A B C D	25 A B C D	33 A B C D	☐ # right in section 4
2 A B C D	10 A B C D	18 A B C D	26 A B C D	34 A B C D	
3 A B C D	11 A B C D	19 A B C D	27 A B C D	35 A B C D	
4 A B C D	12 A B C D	20 A B C D	28 A B C D	36 A B C D	
5 A B C D	13 A B C D	21 A B C D	29 A B C D	37 A B C D	☐ # wrong in section 4
6 A B C D	14 A B C D	22 A B C D	30 A B C D	38 A B C D	
7 A B C D	15 A B C D	23 A B C D	31 A B C D	39 A B C D	
8 A B C D	16 A B C D	24 A B C D	32 A B C D	40 A B C D	

SECTION 1

Time—20 Minutes

34 Questions

This section consists of two different types of questions. There are directions for each type.

Each of the following questions consists of one word followed by four words or phrases. Select the one word or phrase whose meaning is closest to the word in capital letters.

1. DECLINE:
   (A) decrease
   (B) promote
   (C) delete
   (D) agree

2. DELICATE:
   (A) strong
   (B) fragile
   (C) low
   (D) delicious

3. JUBILEE:
   (A) confidence
   (B) chaos
   (C) design
   (D) festival

4. LIBERATE:
   (A) release
   (B) work
   (C) chase
   (D) hope

5. TRANSFORM:
   (A) open
   (B) submit
   (C) change
   (D) keep

6. COLLIDE:
   (A) forget
   (B) crash
   (C) amplify
   (D) plan

7. PROCLAIM:
   (A) behave
   (B) preclude
   (C) submit
   (D) announce

8. SYMPATHY:
   (A) understanding
   (B) harmony
   (C) affection
   (D) responsibility

9. INVENTION:
   (A) interpretation
   (B) party
   (C) delegation
   (D) creation

10. AUTHORITY:
    (A) expert
    (B) respect
    (C) bravery
    (D) rivalry

GO ON TO THE NEXT PAGE

11. ILLUSTRATE:

(A) cover
(B) draw
(C) simulate
(D) waste

12. COMMOTION:

(A) happiness
(B) trick
(C) uproar
(D) collaboration

13. EXHAUSTED:

(A) clumsy
(B) tired
(C) accountable
(D) excited

14. TREAD:

(A) scatter
(B) help
(C) alarm
(D) walk

15. MENTOR:

(A) symbol
(B) artist
(C) collector
(D) counselor

16. REACTION:

(A) selection
(B) response
(C) care
(D) achievement

17. DWINDLE:

(A) ridicule
(B) thwart
(C) shrink
(D) tarnish

Directions: Select the word(s) that best fit the meaning of each sentence.

18. Although Mrs. Brown had taught long division to her students numerous times, she decided to take the time to __________ it once more.

(A) admonish
(B) request
(C) explain
(D) employ

19. Keesha's __________ nature would not allow her to ignore others who were feeling sad or lonely.

(A) terse
(B) intellectual
(C) secure
(D) compassionate

20. The toddler was so _________ that he often hid behind his mother's legs when introduced to strangers.

(A) hyper
(B) timid
(C) young
(D) disobedient

21. Alex often felt ___________ after earning a high score on a test.

(A) distressed
(B) proud
(C) helpless
(D) intimidated

GO ON TO THE NEXT PAGE

22. The low, gray clouds made the sky look __________.

(A) trite
(B) ominous
(C) intentional
(D) luminous

23. Judy noticed that the native vegetation created a ____________ over the swamp.

(A) canopy
(B) hazard
(C) reef
(D) lagoon

24. Ling needed to win one more match in order to be the __________ of the tournament.

(A) creator
(B) center
(C) choice
(D) champion

25. Phoebe was __________ after she finished running the Boston Marathon.

(A) conservative
(B) fortunate
(C) jubilant
(D) confused

26. Jeff spilled grape juice on his essay, but it wasn't a big deal since he could just print out a ____________ copy.

(A) duplicate
(B) creative
(C) symbolic
(D) previous

27. A __________ summer day for the young mother and her son included a two-mile walk around the neighborhood.

(A) naïve
(B) typical
(C) confidential
(D) dire

28. Even though Mischa was guilty, she tried to ________ it.

(A) tell
(B) shout
(C) propose
(D) deny

29. Highway traffic was ____________ due to the accident up ahead.

(A) tight
(B) stalled
(C) reinforced
(D) fatigued

30. The police officer told Clay he needed to __________ his speed on the road.

(A) simplify
(B) join
(C) reduce
(D) practice

31. In order to do well in school, the football player had to ___________ his time between his practice and his studies.

(A) balance
(B) entertain
(C) connect
(D) perform

GO ON TO THE NEXT PAGE

32. Allison left a note on the counter to ________ her father to buy more milk.

(A) confront
(B) urge
(C) taunt
(D) remind

33. The puppy looked ____________ when he realized he was going to be left behind.

(A) relieved
(B) dejected
(C) hungry
(D) excited

34. The _________ solution to a problem takes both sides into account.

(A) incredible
(B) malicious
(C) ideal
(D) unexpected

IF YOU FINISH BEFORE TIME IS CALLED, YOU MAY CHECK YOUR WORK ON THIS SECTION ONLY. DO NOT TURN TO ANY OTHER SECTION IN THE TEST.

STOP

SECTION 2

Time—35 Minutes
38 Questions

In this section there are four possible answers after each question. Choose which one is best. You may use the blank space at the right of the page for scratch work.
Note: Figures are drawn with the greatest possible accuracy, UNLESS stated "Not Drawn to Scale."

USE THIS SPACE FOR FIGURING.

1. If $8 - x = 4$, and $10 + y = 12$, then $x - y =$

(A) 2.
(B) 3.
(C) 4.
(D) 5.

2. Twenty students brought animals to school for pet day. Eight students brought dogs, four students brought birds, two brought cats, and the rest brought other animals. What fraction of the students brought other animals?

(A) $\frac{3}{10}$
(B) $\frac{6}{14}$
(C) $\frac{10}{12}$
(D) $\frac{3}{20}$

3. $8 \times 2 \times 6 \times 2$ is equal to the product of 16 and

(A) 4.
(B) 8.
(C) 12.
(D) 16.

4. Jennifer and José each swam five laps in 15 minutes. At the same rate of speed, how long would they need in order to swim 35 laps?

(A) 35 minutes
(B) 75 minutes
(C) 105 minutes
(D) 175 minutes

GO ON TO THE NEXT PAGE

USE THIS SPACE FOR FIGURING.

5. A square has a perimeter of 16. What is the length of one side?

(A) 2
(B) 4
(C) 6
(D) 8

6. Which of the following is the smallest?

(A) 0.0005
(B) 0.005
(C) 0.05
(D) 0.5

7. Which of the following is equal to two-thirds?

(A) $\frac{4}{12}$
(B) $\frac{6}{12}$
(C) $\frac{10}{15}$
(D) $\frac{12}{15}$

8. Which fruit is included in the shaded section of Figure 1?

(A) Apples
(B) Peaches
(C) Grapes
(D) Bananas

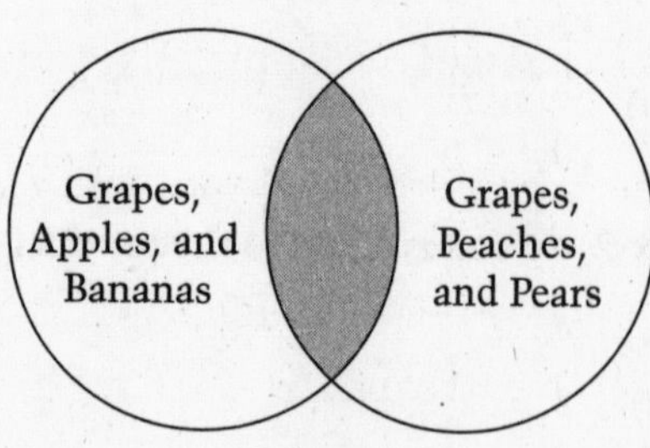

Figure 1

9. Which of the following numbers is NOT a prime factor of 90?

(A) 2
(B) 3
(C) 5
(D) 9

USE THIS SPACE FOR FIGURING

10. In a semester of 40 school days, Mrs. Alvarez was out sick twice. What percent of the time was she out sick?

    (A) 3 percent
    (B) 4 percent
    (C) 5 percent
    (D) 10 percent

11. To which number is the arrow pointing in Figure 2?

    (A) $\frac{3}{8}$
    (B) $3\frac{3}{8}$
    (C) $3\frac{2}{4}$
    (D) $3\frac{5}{8}$

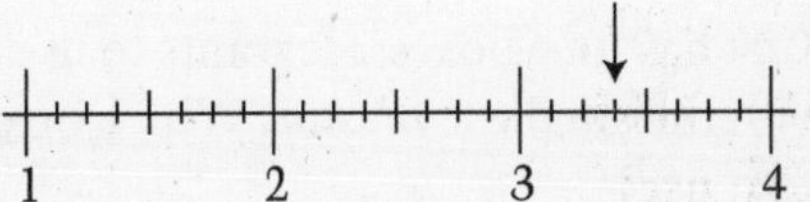

Figure 2

12. In the Venn diagram in Figure 3, the shaded region shows people who drive

    (A) cars and trucks.
    (B) trucks and motorcycles.
    (C) cars and motorcycles.
    (D) cars, trucks, and motorcycles.

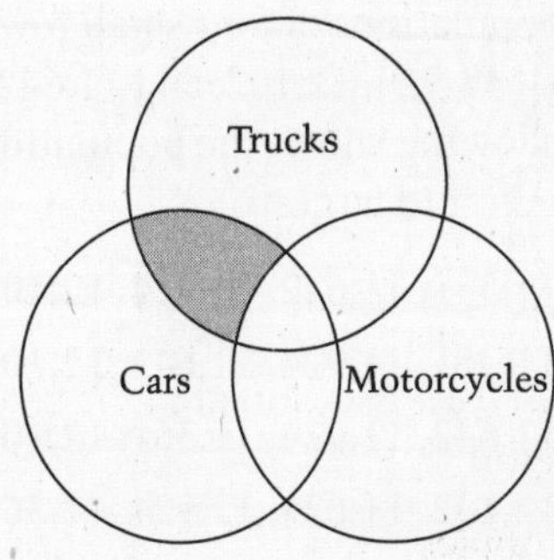

Figure 3

13. The record for the 100-yard dash was 13.71 seconds. Andrew beat the record by a tenth of a second. What was Andrew's time?

    (A) 13.61 seconds
    (B) 13.72 seconds
    (C) 13.82 seconds
    (D) 14.71 seconds

USE THIS SPACE FOR FIGURING.

14. During a 24-hour day, Shannon's cat sleeps $\frac{5}{6}$ of the time. How many hours does the cat sleep?

    (A) 16 hours
    (B) 18 hours
    (C) 20 hours
    (D) 22 hours

15. Kurt has four boxes. He wants to use the box with the smallest volume. Which box should Kurt use?

    (A) 2" high × 3" wide × 4" long
    (B) 2" high × 4" wide × 5" long
    (C) 3" high × 4" wide × 5" long
    (D) 4" high × 5" wide × 6" long

16. The populations of four small towns are 11,361, 11,924, 12,102, and 11,642. Which of the following shows the populations in order of smallest to largest?

    (A) 11,361, 11,642, 11,924, 12,102
    (B) 11,361, 11,924, 11,642, 12,102
    (C) 11,642, 11,924, 11,361, 12,102
    (D) 12,102, 11,624, 11,924, 11,361

17. Which of these numbers is equal to $\frac{65}{100}$?

    (A) 0.065
    (B) 0.65
    (C) 6.5
    (D) 65

18. Look at this series: 1, 3, 7, 15, 31, 63, ...What number comes next?

    (A) 64
    (B) 126
    (C) 127
    (D) 133

GO ON TO THE NEXT PAGE

19. Christopher is nine times the age of his twin 4-year-old sons. How old is Christopher?

    (A) 30 years old
    (B) 32 years old
    (C) 34 years old
    (D) 36 years old

USE THIS SPACE FOR FIGURING.

20. Darby was making a fruit smoothie. The ingredients included 15 percent yogurt, 40 percent ice, and 10 percent bananas. The only other thing she put in was frozen strawberries. What fractional part of the smoothie was made up of strawberries?

    (A) $\frac{7}{20}$
    (B) $\frac{55}{100}$
    (C) $\frac{13}{20}$
    (D) $\frac{65}{100}$

21. What place does the 5 take in 23.654?

    (A) Tenths
    (B) Hundredths
    (C) Thousandths
    (D) Ten-thousandths

22. Ms. Campton's classroom is 15 feet long and 22 feet wide. What is the area of her classroom?

    (A) 37 square feet
    (B) 74 square feet
    (C) 300 square feet
    (D) 330 square feet

GO ON TO THE NEXT PAGE

USE THIS SPACE FOR FIGURING.

23. The O'Malleys have a rectangular pool that is 16' long and 8' wide. Their next-door neighbors want to build a congruent pool. What measurements will the neighbors' pool have?

(A) 8' × 8'

(B) 8' × 16'

(C) 24' × 2'

(D) 16' × 16'

24. Casey makes a 30 percent profit for every sale she makes selling cosmetics. If she sells $300 worth of cosmetics, how much money will she make?

(A) $30

(B) $90

(C) $100

(D) $200

25. Which of the following does NOT equal $\frac{1}{4}$?

(A) $\frac{2}{8}$

(B) $\frac{3}{12}$

(C) $\frac{4}{16}$

(D) $\frac{8}{20}$

26. Approximately how long is the drive from point A to point B in Figure 4?

(A) 12 miles

(B) 14 miles

(C) 16 miles

(D) 20 miles

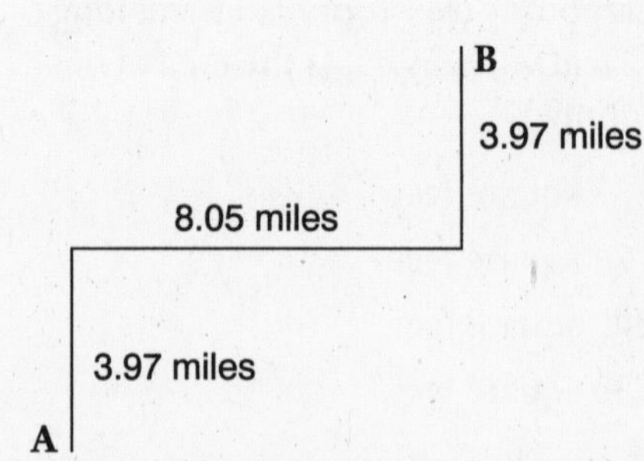

Figure 4

GO ON TO THE NEXT PAGE

USE THIS SPACE FOR FIGURING.

27. Cecile received $10 as an allowance. She spent $1.15 on ice cream and $3.49 on a magazine. How much does Cecile have left?

(A) $4.64
(B) $5.36
(C) $6.51
(D) $8.85

28. The school bus can hold 50 children. Which two classes can use the school bus for their field trip?

(A) A class of 14 and a class of 32
(B) A class of 15 and a class of 36
(C) A class of 25 and a class of 26
(D) A class of 30 and a class of 25

29. Rover's dog food costs $19.85 for a 20-pound bag. Trixie's cat food costs $9.24 for a 10-pound bag. Which of the following costs more?

(A) One bag of dog food
(B) Two bags of cat food
(C) One bag of dog food and two bags of cat food cost the same.
(D) The answer cannot be determined from the information given.

30. In a grocery cart, there is an equal number of vegetables, fruits, and breads. How many items could be in the cart?

(A) 14
(B) 38
(C) 42
(D) 56

31. Which transformation has been applied to the shape in Figure 5?

(A) A reflection
(B) A slide
(C) A turn
(D) A slide followed by a turn

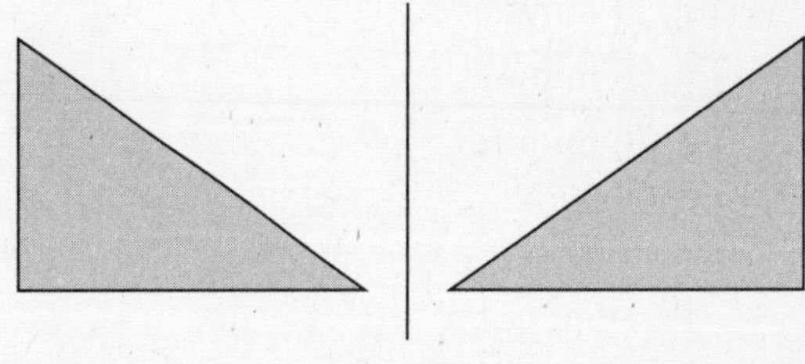

Figure 5

GO ON TO THE NEXT PAGE

USE THIS SPACE FOR FIGURING.

32. Libby types 75 words per minute. How many words does she type per second?

(A) 0.75
(B) 1.25
(C) 2
(D) 7.5

33. In a geography class of 24 students, each student had to select a state on which to give a three-minute report. How long did the presentations last in total?

(A) 1 hour 6 minutes
(B) 1 hour 12 minutes
(C) 1 hour 15 minutes
(D) 1 hour 30 minutes

34. If the shaded section of the circle in Figure 6 signifies 850 types of flowers, how many flowers could the unshaded section represent?

(A) 750
(B) 800
(C) 850
(D) 900

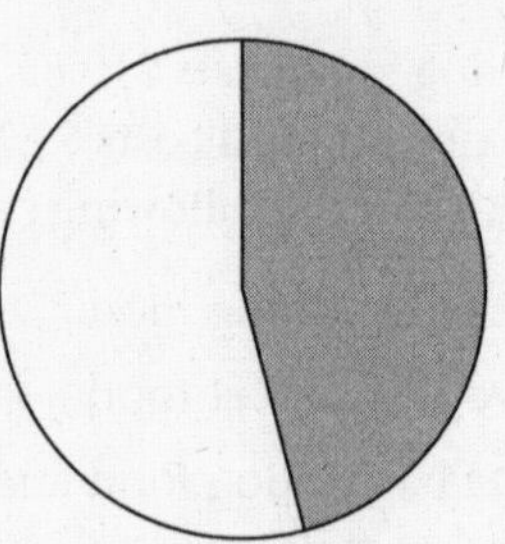

Figure 6

35. Rebecca, Ian, and Clare were driving at the same speed. It took Rebecca 20 minutes to drive 15 miles. How long did it take Ian to drive 30 miles?

(A) 40 minutes
(B) 50 minutes
(C) 60 minutes
(D) 70 minutes

GO ON TO THE NEXT PAGE

USE THIS SPACE FOR FIGURING.

36. In a jar, there are equal numbers of red, green, and yellow marbles. Which of the following could be the number of marbles in the jar?

    (A) 35
    (B) 47
    (C) 58
    (D) 72

37. In a survey of 45 students, twice as many students preferred dogs to cats than preferred cats to dogs. If all students preferred either a dog or a cat, how many people preferred dogs?

    (A) 15
    (B) 20
    (C) 25
    (D) 30

38. Which of these is a whole number greater than 15?

    (A) 14
    (B) 15.5
    (C) $16\frac{1}{2}$
    (D) 18

IF YOU FINISH BEFORE TIME IS CALLED, YOU MAY CHECK YOUR WORK ON THIS SECTION ONLY. DO NOT TURN TO ANY OTHER SECTION IN THE TEST.

STOP

SECTION 3

Time—25 Minutes
25 Questions

Read each passage carefully and then answer the questions about it. For each question, decide on the basis of the passage which one of the choices best answers the question.

Whale sharks (*Rhincodon typus*) are not whales and they are not mammals. They are the largest fish in the world. An average whale shark is around 25 feet long, but they can reach up to 40 feet long. As with most sharks, the females are larger than the males.

You would think that with such a massive body this shark would be a fierce predator, but this mammoth fish is quite mild-mannered. It likes its solitude. Its mouth, which looks quite threatening, can open up to four feet wide and has about 310 rows of teeth, or about 3,000 teeth in all. The interesting thing is, this gentle giant doesn't even really use the teeth. Instead, it filters plankton and krill through its gills for nourishment by simply opening its enormous mouth to take in a large amount of water. The plankton stay in the mouth for nourishment while the water strains through gills in the side of the mouth. Even though a whale shark has a huge body, its gullet is relatively small.So while a whale shark could fit larger food into its mouth, it would not be able to swallow it.

Whale sharks are quite beautiful. Their back and sides are a reddish or greenish-brown. The top of the body has white or yellowish spots and stripes of varying sizes, and the underside is whitish or yellowish-white. A diver looking for such beauty has nothing to fear: Whale sharks are harmless to people, and if met by a diver, would probably ignore him completely. They live in the open seas all over the world, preferring to stay in areas close to the equator for the mild temperatures. They reach adulthood at 25 to 30 years of age, and they may live to be 100 years old.

1. The purpose of this passage is to
   (A) explain why whale sharks are harmless to people.
   (B) explain why whale sharks are fish instead of mammals.
   (C) describe whale sharks.
   (D) explain how divers should deal with whale sharks.

2. Most female sharks are
   (A) larger than the males.
   (B) more beautiful than the males.
   (C) more dangerous than the males.
   (D) smaller than the males.

3. What is a predator?
   (A) A fish
   (B) A hunter
   (C) A mammal
   (D) A gentle giant

4. Which of the following is NOT true about whale sharks?
   (A) They use all 3,000 teeth.
   (B) They have mouths that can open up to four feet wide.
   (C) They cannot swallow a large amount of food.
   (D) They eat mostly plankton and krill.

GO ON TO THE NEXT PAGE

5. If a scuba diver came across a whale shark, the whale shark would probably
   (A) swim away.
   (B) open its enormous mouth.
   (C) keep its eye on the diver.
   (D) pay no attention to the diver.

There is nothing I like so well on a summer day as to hear the ding-ding song of the ice cream truck as it's coming around the corner. That tune of "Do Your Ears Hang Low" makes my heart jump. I race out the door to catch the truck before I miss it, but not before grabbing some change from the kitchen counter that my parents have left. It's something to do—something to cool me off—and it's the highlight of a typical lazy day.

Once I catch the truck, I've got all the time in the world to hem and haw about what to get. I like to read through the entire side-of-the-truck menu, chatting with the girl behind the counter. I usually like an orange push-up, though occasionally I'll get an ice cream sandwich. I have to eat it slowly enough to enjoy it, but fast enough so that it doesn't drip down my arm. Finding this balance is tricky, and sometimes depends on whether the sky is cloudy or clear.

Lots of my neighbors race out of their houses the way I do, hoping to get there in time. I'm usually first since my house is the closest to the corner, and if I can catch the truck, then they are usually all safe. Often, though, if I miss it, they miss it too. If that's the case, imagine how disappointed I am. If there's no change to grab from the counter or if the truck is going too fast, I get outside just in time to see its taillights turn off my street. On those days, I'm not allowed to go that far to catch it. But when I do make it in time, that ice cream song stays with me for the rest of the day.

6. The purpose of the passage is to
   (A) challenge the reader to run to the ice cream truck.
   (B) prove that ice cream is the best treat on a summer day.
   (C) describe a summer treat.
   (D) teach the reader a new song.

7. What does it mean to "hem and haw"?
   (A) To take one's time in choosing
   (B) To buy more than one thing
   (C) To halt
   (D) To choose quickly

8. This passage is written in the
   (A) first person.
   (B) second person.
   (C) third person.
   (D) fourth person.

9. All of the following are true EXCEPT
   (A) the ice cream truck makes this person feel happy.
   (B) this person is not allowed to leave the street where she lives.
   (C) this person always gets an orange push-up.
   (D) other people in the neighborhood enjoy the ice cream truck too.

10. The main character is probably a
   (A) baby.
   (B) toddler.
   (C) parent.
   (D) child.

GO ON TO THE NEXT PAGE

In May, Bailey moved into a new house. His large, fenced-in yard had potential, but the grass needed to be weeded and some flowers needed to be planted. Bailey invited some friends to his house to help. He provided good music, plenty of snacks, and cold drinks. Everyone was amazed how much they were able to accomplish in that one day!

Bailey and Nolan started by weeding the front yard. Then they planted ferns and marigolds underneath the olive tree. They planted a bleeding heart vine and some red impatiens along the front of the fence. Bailey left plenty of room between the impatiens for the roses he would plant in the fall.

Janet focused on the side of the back porch. She filled some holes with dirt, and then she hoed the ground to make it level. She alternated planting gardenias and black-eyed Susans. She knew that gardenia blooms would smell lovely, and the bright yellow flowers would be pleasing to the eye. Together these plants made an attractive garden bed.

Meanwhile, Christina and Akiko worked along the back of the porch. They laid 10 large stepping stones in even spaces, and in between each stone, planted red, orange, yellow, and pink purslane ground cover. They knew that the plants would grow all around the stones to create a charming walkway.

Lilia and Nathan cleared weeds along the whole right-side fence. This was back-breaking work, but the weeds had to go! Then they planted red bougainvillea and blue plumbago bushes. There was still space to plant some smaller annuals, but Bailey would have to do that another day.

After hours of work in the hot sun, the friends were exhausted. They spent the rest of the afternoon resting, talking, and laughing on the porch, surrounded by the results of their hard work. Thanks to the help of so many friends, Bailey's new house looks loved.

11. In paragraph 1, what does it mean that the yard had potential?
    - (A) There was the possibility that the yard would look good.
    - (B) The yard was full of weeds and needed work.
    - (C) The yard had no flowers.
    - (D) Someone had been taking care of the yard.

12. Bailey wants his yard to look
    - (A) unusual.
    - (B) busy.
    - (C) charming.
    - (D) exhausting.

13. Bailey and Nolan
    - (A) weeded the backyard.
    - (B) planted an olive tree.
    - (C) planted roses.
    - (D) planted ferns and marigolds.

14. What did Janet do first?
    - (A) She planted gardenias.
    - (B) She planted black-eyed Susans.
    - (C) She smoothed the ground.
    - (D) She filled in some holes.

15. Lilia and Nathan did all of the following EXCEPT
    - (A) plant some small annuals.
    - (B) plant bougainvillea.
    - (C) plant plumbago bushes.
    - (D) pull out weeds.

GO ON TO THE NEXT PAGE

"Come on, come on," you think. "I can see the top!" You're almost there. The top. The summit. Your goal. The sun is beating down on your back and you are there, in the moment, looking upward. Whatever you do, you cannot look down. Leg muscles shaking, fingertips clutching their hold, you think, "I can do this!"

This is rock climbing at its best. There's the challenge to face, the fear to overcome, the muscles to test, and finally, the exhilaration to feel. But would you rather ride horses? Hike? Do gymnastics? Do you stick your toe in the water first before jumping in? Or do you dive headfirst? Cautious, careful, or crazy, one week at an adventure camp could change your whole attitude about yourself and level of confidence.

Maybe you're thinking that "real kids" don't get to do these things. You're wrong. You don't even have to be an athlete. Today there are thousands of adventure camps across the country. So what are you waiting for? Sign up and go! What you do with your experience will be up to you.

16. What is the purpose of this passage?
    (A) To teach you about backpacking
    (B) To challenge you to change your lifestyle
    (C) To excite you about going to adventure camp
    (D) To encourage you have a better attitude

17. What is "exhilaration" (paragraph 2)?
    (A) Fear
    (B) Heat
    (C) Understanding
    (D) Excitement

18. Which of the following statements is NOT listed as a part of rock climbing?
    (A) The challenge of reaching the summit
    (B) Overcoming your fear
    (C) Testing your muscles
    (D) Spending time with friends

19. Why would someone choose to go to an adventure camp?
    (A) To challenge himself
    (B) To climb a mountain
    (C) To do gymnastics
    (D) To go hiking

20. What kind of person sticks her toe in the water before going in?
    (A) A risk taker
    (B) An adventurous person
    (C) A cautious person
    (D) A mountain climber

Here's what to do for the dogs while we're out of town:

Fido likes to go out first thing in the morning and then before bed. There's no need to go out with her, just open the door and she'll go right into the yard. If she needs to go in the middle of the day, she'll stare at you intently and grunt. Both dogs like a little walk in the morning and again at around 4:30. After the morning walk, you can give them some bread as a treat.

Samson has to take arthritis pills: Two in the morning and one in the evening. Use peanut butter or bread to hide the pills so that he'll eat them. Fido gets two vitamins in the morning, which she loves, so you don't have to camouflage her pills.

I'm leaving peanut butter treats, chew sticks, bacon, and sausages in the fridge. Use anything you want! If you need more food, that's in the garage. We leave the food bowl filled up all day so the dogs can eat whenever they are hungry. Please make sure they always have cold water in their bowls.

Thanks for all of your help! See you on Saturday!

Oh, one last thing: If you decide to take the dogs to your house, don't forget to take the dog bed, along with a blanket, so you can cover up Samson if it starts to thunder.

GO ON TO THE NEXT PAGE

21. What is the purpose of this passage?
    (A) To give directions for feeding two dogs
    (B) To give directions for taking care of two dogs
    (C) To give directions for walking two dogs
    (D) To give directions for giving medicine to two dogs

22. When do the dogs eat?
    (A) Whenever they are hungry
    (B) After their morning walk
    (C) In the afternoon
    (D) After their afternoon walk

23. Why do Samson's pills have to be hidden in peanut butter or bread?
    (A) He will spit them out otherwise.
    (B) He might otherwise try to eat Fido's vitamins.
    (C) He likes peanut butter or bread as a breakfast treat.
    (D) He is spoiled.

24. How does Fido let you know if she needs to go out?
    (A) She barks.
    (B) She only needs to go out during her regular walks.
    (C) She paces around the room.
    (D) She stares and grunts.

25. After their morning walk, the dogs get what treat?
    (A) Sausages
    (B) A piece of bread
    (C) Dog food
    (D) A peanut butter treat

IF YOU FINISH BEFORE TIME IS CALLED, YOU MAY CHECK YOUR WORK ON THIS SECTION ONLY. DO NOT TURN TO ANY OTHER SECTION IN THE TEST. STOP

SECTION 4

Time—30 Minutes
30 Questions

In this section there are four possible answers after each question. Choose which one is best.

Note: Figures are drawn with the greatest possible accuracy, UNLESS stated "Not Drawn to Scale."

USE THIS SPACE FOR FIGURING.

1. Which is fifty-three thousand, nine hundred fourteen?

(A) 53,914
(B) 503,914
(C) 530,914
(D) 539,014

2. Which is the largest fraction?

(A) $\frac{6}{18}$
(B) $\frac{1}{2}$
(C) $\frac{5}{6}$
(D) $\frac{9}{10}$

3. $\frac{1}{5} + \frac{2}{3} =$

(A) $\frac{3}{15}$
(B) $\frac{2}{8}$
(C) $\frac{3}{8}$
(D) $\frac{13}{15}$

4. $400 + 950 =$

(A) 990
(B) 1,350
(C) 4,950
(D) 9,450

GO ON TO THE NEXT PAGE

USE THIS SPACE FOR FIGURING.

5. What is the product of 11 and 3?

(A) 0.273
(B) 3.66
(C) 14
(D) 33

6. What is 5,772 divided by 6?

(A) 662
(B) 912
(C) 962
(D) 1,012

7. ___ + 8 – 19 = 50

(A) 11
(B) 31
(C) 39
(D) 61

8. 15 × 300 =

(A) 45
(B) 450
(C) 4,500
(D) 45,000

9. 53.09 – 9.34 =

(A) 40.31
(B) 42.25
(C) 43.25
(D) 43.75

10. $\frac{?}{15} = \frac{2}{3}$

(A) 2
(B) 4
(C) 5
(D) 10

GO ON TO THE NEXT PAGE

USE THIS SPACE FOR FIGURING.

11. Marla twirls her hair once every six seconds. How many times does she twirl her hair in a minute?

(A) 6
(B) 8
(C) 10
(D) 12

12. __ + 16 – 5 = 40

What is the missing number?

(A) 24
(B) 29
(C) 31
(D) 33

13. A puppy weighed four pounds when he was six weeks old. Now that he is six months old, he has gained 80 percent more weight. How much does the puppy weigh now?

(A) 7 pounds
(B) 7.2 pounds
(C) 12.8 pounds
(D) 32 pounds

14. If $x = 5$, which of these statements is true?

(A) $x + 8 = 11 + 3$
(B) $x + 9 = 6 + 8$
(C) $x + 10 = 15 - 5$
(D) $x + 11 = 14 + 5$

15. What is the missing number in the pattern in Figure 1

(A) 16
(B) 17
(C) 18
(D) 19

–3	9
0	12
3	15
6	?

Figure 1

GO ON TO THE NEXT PAGE

USE THIS SPACE FOR FIGURING.

16. If $n = 9$, which of these number sentences is true?

 (A) $2n - 6 = 14$
 (B) $3(n - 3) = 18$
 (C) $4(n + 5) = 18$
 (D) $5n + 8 = 22$

17. What is the sum of 25 and 30?

 (A) 5
 (B) 55
 (C) 75
 (D) 750

18. Devon bought $8.96 worth of gas. He paid with a 20 dollar bill. How much change did he receive?

 (A) $11.04
 (B) $11.96
 (C) $12.14
 (D) $12.96

19. 500 – 409 = ____

 (A) 91
 (B) 109
 (C) 101
 (D) 191

20. What is the product of 5 and 20?

 (A) 4
 (B) 25
 (C) 75
 (D) 100

GO ON TO THE NEXT PAGE

USE THIS SPACE FOR FIGURING.

21. If $8 + a = 15$ and $6 + b = 14$, then what is $a + b$?

    (A) 12
    (B) 13
    (C) 14
    (D) 15

22. If $a = b$ and $b = c$, then

    (A) $a + b = c$
    (B) $a = c$
    (C) $bc = a$
    (D) $c + b = a$

23. The diameter of the circle in Figure 2 is 8 cm. What is the radius? NOTE: The radius is the length halfway across the circle.

    (A) 4 cm
    (B) 8 cm
    (C) 10 cm
    (D) 16 cm

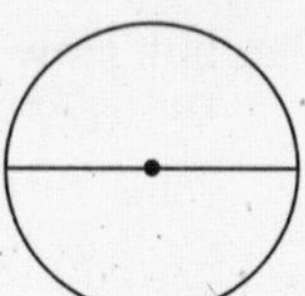

Figure 2

24. What is the perimeter of the rectangle in Figure 3?

    (A) 18 in.
    (B) 30 in.
    (C) 36 in.
    (D) 72 in.

Figure 3

25. When folded on the lines, what will the shape in Figure 4 become?

    (A) Cylinder
    (B) Cube
    (C) Square pyramid
    (D) Sphere

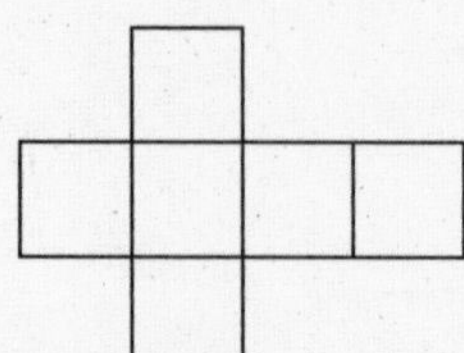

Figure 4

26. What is the volume of the box in Figure 5?

    (A) 12 cubic feet
    (B) 24 cubic feet
    (C) 48 cubic feet
    (D) 60 cubic feet

USE THIS SPACE FOR FIGURING.

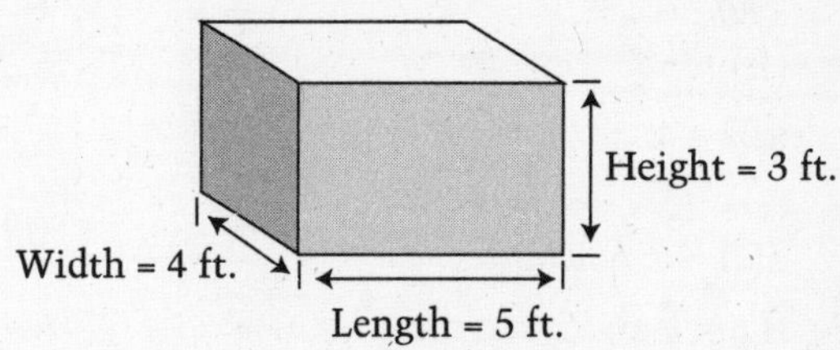

Figure 5

27. $5.123 + 2.627 =$

    (A) 7.65
    (B) 7.743
    (C) 7.749
    (D) 7.75

28. $10{,}000 - 45n =$

    (A) $955n$
    (B) $9{,}955n$
    (C) $99{,}955n$
    (D) The answer cannot be determined from the information given.

29. Which of the following is closest to 100.11?

    (A) 99.11
    (B) 101
    (C) 100.1
    (D) 100

GO ON TO THE NEXT PAGE

USE THIS SPACE FOR FIGURING.

30. $\frac{1}{4} + \frac{5}{8} =$

(A) $\frac{1}{2}$

(B) $\frac{3}{4}$

(C) $\frac{5}{6}$

(D) $\frac{7}{8}$

IF YOU FINISH BEFORE TIME IS CALLED, YOU MAY CHECK YOUR WORK ON THIS SECTION ONLY. DO NOT TURN TO ANY OTHER SECTION IN THE TEST.

STOP

SECTION 5

Time—30 Minutes

Write an essay on the following prompt on the paper provided. Your essay should not exceed two pages and must be written in ink. You must use a black or blue pen. Erasing is not allowed.

Prompt: Write about a time when you made a mistake.

GO ON TO THE NEXT PAGE

IF YOU FINISH BEFORE TIME IS CALLED, YOU MAY CHECK YOUR WORK ON THIS SECTION ONLY. DO NOT TURN TO ANY OTHER SECTION IN THE TEST.

ANSWER KEY

Section 1

1. A
2. B
3. D
4. A
5. C
6. B
7. D
8. A
9. D
10. A
11. B
12. C
13. B
14. D
15. D
16. B
17. C
18. C
19. D
20. B
21. B
22. B
23. A
24. D
25. C
26. A
27. B
28. D
29. B
30. C
31. A
32. D
33. B
34. C

Section 2

1. A
2. A
3. C
4. C
5. B
6. A
7. C
8. C
9. D
10. C
11. B
12. A
13. A
14. C
15. A
16. A
17. B
18. C
19. D
20. A
21. B
22. D
23. B
24. B
25. D
26. C
27. B
28. A
29. A
30. C
31. A
32. B
33. B
34. D
35. A
36. D
37. D
38. D

Section 3

1. C
2. A
3. B
4. A
5. D
6. C
7. A
8. A
9. C
10. D
11. A
12. C
13. D
14. D
15. A
16. C
17. D
18. D
19. A
20. C
21. B
22. A
23. A
24. D
25. B

Section 4

1. A
2. D
3. D
4. B
5. D
6. C
7. D
8. C
9. D
10. D
11. C
12. B
13. B
14. B
15. C
16. B
17. B
18. A
19. A
20. D
21. D
22. B
23. A
24. C
25. B
26. D
27. D
28. D
29. C
30. D

ISEE PRACTICE TEST 3: LOWER-LEVEL: ASSESS YOUR STRENGTHS

Use the following tables to determine which topics and chapters you need to review most. If you need help with your essay, be sure to review Chapter 9: The Essay and Chapter 26: Writing Skills.

Topic	Question
Verbal: Synonyms	Section 1, questions 1–17
Verbal: Sentence Completions	Section 1, questions 18–34
Quantitative Reasoning	Section 2, questions 1–38
Reading Comprehension	Section 3, questions 1–25
Mathematics Achievement	Section 4, questions 1–30

Topic	Number of Questions on Test	Number Correct	If you struggled with these questions, study...
Verbal: Synonyms	17		Chapters 7 and 24
Verbal: Sentence Completions	17		Chapter 4
Quantitative Reasoning	38		Chapters 10–14 and Chapter 25
Reading Comprehension	25		Chapter 8
Mathematics Achievement	30		Chapters 10–14 and Chapter 25

ANSWERS AND EXPLANATIONS

SECTION 1: VERBAL REASONING

SYNONYMS

1. A

To decline is to deteriorate or decrease.

2. B

Something delicate is also fragile, as in a delicate glass vase. Do not be misled by (D) just because its beginning letters are similar to that of the original word.

3. D

A jubilee is a celebration, such as an anniversary or festival.

4. A

To liberate is to set free or release from captivity.

5. C

When you transform your life, you change it.

6. B

When two items collide, they crash into each other.

7. D

To proclaim something means to announce it.

8. A

To show sympathy for another is to express sorrow and understanding of that person's feelings.

9. D

An invention is a new idea or creation.

10. A

An authority is an expert.

11. B

To illustrate is to draw.

12. C

To cause a commotion is to create a fuss or uproar. A collaboration is something that involves the participation of several people.

13. B

When you feel exhausted, you are extremely tired.

14. D

Tread is another word for walk.

15. D

A mentor is a tutor or coach. (D), counselor, is the closest in meaning.

16. B

A reaction is a response.

17. C

To dwindle means to shrink or become steadily less, such as a dwindling bank account.

SENTENCE COMPLETIONS

18. C

The sentence implies that the students need long division to be explained again. "Although" is a key word here: It suggests that you will need to repeat an idea again in the second clause. The verb "had taught" is closely related to explain. Numerous means many, so she had taught them many times before. Admonish means to caution, which does not make sense. Request means to ask for, and employ means to use.

19. D

The blank requires you to fill in a word with the same meaning as *not ignoring others who are feeling sad or lonely*. A compassionate person is concerned for others. A terse person is dismissive or brief, an intellectual person thinks academically, and an insecure person lacks confidence; none of these have anything to do with being concerned for others.

20. B

Hiding behind your mother's legs would suggest you are timid or shy. A toddler would probably be young as well, but being young does not explain why he would hide when meeting strangers. He might also be disobedient, but that, too, does not explain why he would hide.

21. B

Earning a high score is something one would be proud of. Feeling distressed (upset) would be the opposite of how you would feel under these circumstances. Neither would you feel helpless (defenseless). Intimidated means nervous or anxious, so that answer choice is incorrect as well.

22. B

Low, gray clouds are a sign of something—probably something bad or negative. Ominous means threatening and is the correct answer. Trite means commonplace and unoriginal. Intentional means on purpose.

23. A

A canopy is a covering. From the other words in the sentence, we know we need something "created" by the vegetation. No other choice fits.

24. D

Ling is winning "in order to be" something. The only answer choice that makes sense is (D). A champion is a winner in a competition.

25. C

We know that Phoebe finished running the marathon, so she must be very happy. Jubilant means filled with joy, and it is the right answer. She might feel also fortunate (lucky), but between the two answer choices (B) and (C), jubilant is the better choice: We do not know for certain that she would feel lucky, but we can be fairly certain that she would feel happy.

26. A

Jeff needs to print out a new copy of his essay. (A), duplicate (double or identical) copy is what he would need to print. Don't be misled by (D), a previous copy: Previous means earlier or prior, and it is not right here. You wouldn't print out an earlier copy; you would print out an identical copy.

27. B

It seems as though a walk around the neighborhood is something the mother and son do on a daily basis—in other words, on a typical day or a regular day. Naïve means inexperienced or innocent, confidential means private, and dire means terrible.

28. D

"Even though" tells us there must be a contrast here. We are told that Mischa is guilty, so the contrast is probably something that has to do with denying the truth—declaring it untrue.

29. B

An accident on the highway would make traffic come to a standstill. That's another way of saying stalled traffic, (B). You might suspect (A) is correct, but it is not appropriate to say tight traffic. Fatigued means tired, and traffic cannot be tired.

30. C

A police officer would want Clay to lower, or reduce, his speed.

31. A

The football player would have to balance, or divide fairly, his time between practice and studying if he wants to do well in school. Entertain makes no sense here; nor does connect or perform.

32. D

The note is intended to remind her father. Don't be tricked by (B): It seems like it might be acceptable to say that she urged her father to get more milk, but then when you see (D) as an option, you see *remind* is the best possible answer choice.

33. B

Since the puppy was going to be left behind, we probably need a word that means unhappy. Dejected means unhappy. The puppy would not be relieved or excited if he were left behind, so (A) and (D) are incorrect.

34. C

The ideal solution would be the best solution. It means the perfect solution.

SECTION 2: QUANTITATIVE REASONING

1. A

$8 - x = 4$, so $x = 4$. $10 + y = 12$, so $y = 2$. That means $x - y$ is the same as $4 - 2$.

2. A

First, figure out how many students brought other pets. Fourteen students brought dogs, birds, and cats, so that means six students brought other pets. The fraction is $\frac{6}{20}$, which reduces to $\frac{3}{10}$. You might have incorrectly chosen (B) since it has the number 6 in it.

3. C

You have $8 \times 2 = 16$ and $6 \times 2 = 12$. So $8 \times 2 \times 6 \times 2$ equals 16 times 12, (C).

4. C

Five laps in 15 minutes means 3 minutes per lap. If Jennifer and José want to swim 35 laps at 3 minutes each, that would take 105 minutes.

5. B

A square has 4 equal sides. Sixteen divided by 4 is 4. If you divided by 2, you might have gotten an incorrect answer of 8, (D).

6. A

So, 0.0005 is equivalent to $\frac{5}{10{,}000}$, which is the smallest number given. The farther away a digit is to the right of the decimal point, the smaller the place that digit is in.

7. C

Two-thirds is equal to $\frac{10}{15}$ because $2 \times 5 = 10$ and $3 \times 5 = 15$.

8. C

Grapes are the only fruit included in both circles.

9. D

A prime number is a number greater than 1 that can be divided evenly only by itself and by 1. Nine is not a prime number because it can be divided by 3. You might have suspected (D) was incorrect because 90 is divisible by 9, but 9 is not prime.

10. C

Divide 2 by 40 to get 0.05, which is the same as 5 percent. You might have guessed 4 percent since the original number was 40, but that would be incorrect.

11. B

The interval from 3 to 4 is divided into 8 equal segments, so each segment has a length of $\frac{1}{8}$. Since there are 3 segments to where the arrow is pointing, the arrow is pointing to $3\frac{3}{8}$.

12. A

The shaded region shows people who drive cars and trucks. You might have guessed (D), since cars, trucks, and motorcycles are all included in the diagram, but the question asks you to look at the shaded region.

13. A

Since this is a race time, for Andrew to beat the record means his time is 0.1 second less than the record. Line up the decimal points to solve:

$$\begin{array}{r} 13.71 \\ -\ 0.1 \\ \hline 13.61 \end{array}$$

14. C

$\frac{5}{6}$ of 24 is $\frac{5}{6} \times 24 = 20$ hours.

15. A

Volume is length × width × height. The box with the smallest volume is the one in (A), $2 \times 3 \times 4 = 24$ cubic inches.

16. A

(A) shows the numbers from smallest to largest.

17. B

So $0.65 = \frac{65}{100}$ (sixty-five hundredths). (D), 65, is tempting, but you must remember to change your fraction to a decimal.

18. C

The pattern is that each number adds twice the difference between the previous two terms: +2, +4, +8, +16, +32, +64, and so on. $63 + 64 = 127$.

19. D

To find Christopher's age, multiply the twins' age (4) by 9.

20. A

You have 15 + 40 + 10 = 65 percent. Subtract that number from 100 percent and you get 35 percent. Then $\frac{35}{100}$ reduces to $\frac{7}{20}$. If you forgot to subtract from 100, you might have gotten wrong answer (C).

21. B

The 5 is in the hundredths place. From the decimal, moving right, the places are as follows: tenths, hundredths, thousandths.

22. D

Area equals length × width. If you had added instead of multiplied, except for the unit square feet, you would have gotten an incorrect answer of (A).

23. B

Congruent pools have the same measurements. A congruent figure is the same shape and size as the original figure.

24. B

The decimal equivalent of 30% is 0.3. So 0.3 × 300 = $90.

25. D

$\frac{8}{20}$ reduces to $\frac{2}{5}$, not $\frac{1}{4}$. You can use the process of elimination to solve this question.

26. C

Let's approximate: 4 miles plus 4 miles plus 8 miles—the drive is about 16 miles.

27. B

Cecile spent a total of $1.15 + $3.49 = $4.64. From $10.00, that means $5.36 is left. Make sure to line up the decimal points when calculating.

28. A

The number of students cannot exceed 50. (A) is the only combination of classes that is less than or equal to 50.

29. A

One bag of dog food costs $19.85; 2 bags of cat food would cost $18.48.

30. C

The number of items in the cart must be a multiple of 3. Forty-two is divisible by 3 without a remainder, so 42 is a multiple of 3.

31. A

The shape has been reflected (flipped as if in a mirror).

32. B

Divide 75 by 60 to find the answer. (A) and (D) are tricky because you might think you should be dividing by 10 or 100, but they are incorrect.

33. B

Multiply 24 by 3 to get 72 minutes. Since there are 60 minutes in an hour, that's the same as 1 hour 12 minutes.

34. D

More of the circle is unshaded, so the number has to be higher than 850.

35. A

Fifteen miles divided by 20 minutes = 0.75 miles per minute. Thirty miles divided by 0.75 miles per minute = 40 minutes. You could also have realized that if Rebecca and Ian are driving at the same speed, it will take Ian twice as long to drive twice as far. 2 × 20 = 40 minutes. If you had added Rebecca's 20 minutes to her 30 miles, you would have gotten the number in incorrect answer (B).

36. D

The number must be divisible by 3 with no remainder.

37. D

Solve this problem by thinking of three groups: one group that likes cats and two groups that like dogs. Divide 45 by 3 to see that there are 15 students in each group. There are 2 dog groups, so multiply 15 × 2 to get 30.

38. D

A whole number has no fraction or decimal point. Also, the number has to be greater than 15, so (D) is the only possible answer.

SECTION 3: READING COMPREHENSION

Whale Sharks Passage

1. C

This is a descriptive passage. The other three answer choices are details included in the passage, but none gives the purpose or main idea of the passage.

2. A

The passage states that most female sharks are larger than the males. As for (B), the passage does state that whale sharks are beautiful, though it doesn't say anything about the females being more beautiful than the males.

3. B

A predator is a hunter—one that preys or destroys. The meaning is implied by the text: "You would think that with such a massive body this shark would be a fierce predator, but this mammoth fish is quite docile. It likes its solitude." The other three answer choices are words used in the passage, but none of them mean the same thing as predator.

4. A

The whale shark's teeth are largely useless. Since you are asked which answer choice is NOT true, you can go back to the passage to find the three that are true. Then, use the process of elimination.

5. D

You can reread the last paragraph of the passage to find out that whale sharks will probably ignore divers, or pay no attention to them.

Ice Cream Truck Passage

6. C

The function of the passage is to describe a summer treat. It does not challenge, prove, or teach anything.

7. A

To "hem and haw" means to take one's time in choosing. Read the context of the words surrounding this phrase, and you will see that it suggests taking one's time.

8. A

When a passage uses the author's own voice, and when it uses pronouns *I* and *me*, it is written in first person. That means the story is told from the author's perspective.

9. C

You must find the answer choice that is NOT true here. (C) is not true: Though the author usually gets an orange push-up, that's not always the case. The other three answer choices are indeed stated in the passage.

10. D

Since the writer needs permission to grab change and run to catch the truck but is not allowed off of the street, she is probably a child. A baby or toddler would not be able to run out to the ice cream truck, and a parent would not need permission to go to the ice cream truck.

Yard Work Passage

11. A

"The yard had potential" means the yard could look good if some work was done to it. You may have chosen (B) because the yard was indeed full of weeds and it did need work, but since that's not what the question asked, it is incorrect.

12. C

Bailey wanted the yard to look charming. He and his friends were busy all day, but that is not how the yard looked.

13. D

Bailey and Nolan planted ferns and marigolds under an olive tree that was already there. You might have chosen the incorrect answer of (A). Bailey and Nolan did some weeding, but they weeded in the front yard, not the back.

14. D

Janet had to fill in the holes before she could do the rest of her work.

15. A

Lilia and Nathan left room to plant annuals at a later time, but they did not actually do it that day.

Adventure Camps Passage

16. C

The purpose of the passage is to excite you about going to adventure camp. It does not challenge you to change your life, only to try something new.

17. D

The meaning of exhilaration is implied in the sentence. It means excitement or stimulation.

18. D

Use the process of elimination to see that being with friends is not mentioned.

19. A

One might do yoga or climb a mountain or go backpacking while there, but no matter what activity one chose, adventure camp would challenge a kid.

20. C

A cautious person would test the water before jumping into it.

Dog Care Passage

21. B

The passage is intended to give directions for taking care of Samson and Fido. Feeding, walking, and giving medicine are mentioned, but those answers are all details that are part of the overall care. The main idea of the passage is reflected in (B).

22. A

Since the dog food bowl is left full all day, the dogs can eat whenever they are hungry.

23. A

Since the pills have to be hidden in bread or peanut butter, Samson must not like the taste of them. He would probably spit them out if given them plain. Chances are, he likes the taste of peanut butter or bread. He may also be spoiled, but that doesn't explain why he needs his pills hidden in something sweet.

24. D

Fido stares and grunts when she needs to go out. The other three choices are not mentioned in the text.

25. B

The dogs get a piece of bread as a breakfast treat. Though the text does mention the other choices, you are asked to identify the treat the dogs get after their morning walk.

SECTION 4: MATH ACHIEVEMENT

1. A

To solve, read each answer choice individually:

(A) Fifty-three thousand, nine hundred fourteen—YES

(B) Five hundred three thousand, nine hundred fourteen—NO

(C) Five hundred thirty thousand, nine hundred fourteen—NO

(D) Five hundred thirty-nine thousand, fourteen—NO

2. D

You know $\frac{6}{18}$ is less than $\frac{1}{2}$ because the numerator 6 of $\frac{6}{18}$ is less than half of the denominator 18. Also, $\frac{1}{2}$ is less than each of $\frac{5}{6}$ and $\frac{9}{10}$ because the numerator of each of those two fractions is greater than half of the denominator. So we must compare $\frac{5}{6}$ with $\frac{9}{10}$ to find the greatest fraction. The easiest way to compare these fractions is to convert them to decimals: $\frac{5}{6} = 0.8\overline{3}$ and $\frac{9}{10} = 0.9$. So $\frac{9}{10}$ is the largest fraction.

3. D

So, $\frac{1}{5} + \frac{2}{3} = \frac{3}{15} + \frac{10}{15} = \frac{13}{15}$. You might have chosen (C) if you had simply added the numerators and denominators together, but that is not the correct way to solve.

4. B

$400 + 950 = 1{,}350$

5. D

The product is the answer when you multiply: $11 \times 3 = 33$. If you didn't know that product means to multiply, you might have added and gotten (C), which is 14.

6. C

5,772 ÷ 6 = 962.

7. D

To solve, turn the question around: 50 + 19 – 8 = __. If you forgot to change your signs, you would get 39, which is (C). You have to change + to – when you move the numbers across the equal sign. The answer is 61.

8. C

15 × 300 = 4,500. A good rule of thumb is that there are the same number of zeros at the end of a number in the question as in the answer.

9. D

Line up the decimal points before you subtract. You have to borrow in order to find the answer.

```
  12
 4 2.
 5 3.0 9
   9.3 4
 -------
 4 3.7 5
```

10. D

Convert $\frac{2}{3}$ to a fraction with a denominator of 15. Since 3 × 5 = 15, then $\frac{2}{3} = \frac{2\times5}{3\times15} = \frac{10}{15}$ So ? is 10.

11. C

There are 60 seconds in a minute. Sixty divided by 6 = 10. She twirls her hair 10 times in a minute.

12. B

This question would be a good one to backsolve. Plug in the answer choices and see which one works. You could also move the numbers across the equal signs. You have to change + to – and you have to change – to + . So ___ = 40 – 16 + 5. The answer is 29.

13. B

Eighty percent is the same as 0.80. To find out how much weight the puppy has gained, multiply: 4 × 0.80 = 3.2. Add the original weight (4 pounds) to the gained weight (3.2). Then 4 + 3.2 = 7.2.

14. B

Substitute in 5 for *x* and see which answer choice results in a true statement. When you solve, choice (B) becomes 14 = 14, which is the only true statement here.

15. C

The numbers on the right-hand column skip by threes: 9, 12, 15 (and are 12 more than the number in the left column). Fifteen plus 3 is 18 (and 6 plus 12 is 18), so that must be the missing number.

16. B

Plug 9 into each answer choice. For (B), after you have substituted, you must find the value of what is in parentheses first, then multiply by 3. If you tried to multiply before you subtracted, you would have gotten an incorrect value.

17. B

The sum is the result of addition. So 25 + 30 = 55. If you multiplied the numbers, you would have gotten (D), which is incorrect.

18. A

You have \$20 – \$8.96 = \$11.04. You must line up the decimal points and borrow.

19. A

You must borrow to solve this subtraction question.

$$\begin{array}{r} \not{1}0 \\ \not{5}\ \not{0}\ \not{0} \\ 4\ 0\ 9 \\ \hline 9\ 1 \end{array}$$

20. D

The product is the result of multiplication. Here, $5 \times 20 = 100$. If you added you might have come up with (B), which is incorrect.

21. D

If $8 + a = 15$, then $a = 15 - 8 = 7$. If $6 + b = 14$, then $b = 14 - 6 = 8$. $a = 7$ and $b = 8$, so $a + b$ is the same as $7 + 8$.

22. B

If $a = b$ and $b = c$ then it follows logically that $a = c$.

23. A

The diameter is the full length across the circle. The radius is the length halfway across. If we're given that the diameter is 8 cm, the radius is half of that: 4 cm. If you doubled the length of 8 cm, you would have gotten 16, which would have been incorrect.

24. C

To find the perimeter, add the lengths of all four sides: $12 + 6 + 12 + 6 = 36$ inches.

25. B

A cube is made up of six squares. The six squares in the figure can be folded into a cube.

26. D

Volume = Length × Width × Height. The volume in cubic feet is $5 \times 4 \times 3 = 60$.

27. D

Line up the decimal points to add.

$$\begin{array}{r} 5.123 \\ 2.627 \\ \hline 7.750 \end{array}$$

28. D

Since n is unknown, the answer cannot be determined.

29. C

There is only 0.01 difference between 100.11 and 100.1. If you weren't sure, you could subtract for each to solve.

30. D

Find a common denominator. The lowest common denominator is 8. Convert $\frac{1}{4}$ to $\frac{2}{8}$.

Then add: $\frac{2}{8} + \frac{5}{8} = \frac{7}{8}$.

CHAPTER 23: SCORING YOUR ISEE PRACTICE TEST

The ISEE calculates scores by using a formula that compares each student's score against the scores of other students of the same grade level. The governing board of the ISEE does not release any information about how scores are actually calculated, so we are unable to provide you with a scaled score on your practice tests.

So, rather than worrying over what the numbers mean, just concentrate on improving your performance. Look over all the answers and explanations we have provided. Since you won't know how hard the actual test will be on test day, or how other students will do, simply focusing on performing your best in your practice will put you in the right frame of mind to do just that on test day.

Part Six

LEARNING RESOURCES

CHAPTER 24: VOCABULARY REFERENCE

ROOT LIST

ROOT	MEANING	EXAMPLES
A, AN	*not, without*	amoral, atrophy, asymmetrical, anarchy, anesthetic, anonymity, anomaly, annul
AB, A	*from, away, apart*	abnegate, abortive, abrogate, abscond, absolve, abstemious, abstruse, avert, aversion, abnormal, abdicate, aberration, abhor, abject, abjure, ablution
AC, ACR	*sharp, sour*	acid, acerbic, exacerbate, acute, acuity, acumen, acrid, acrimony
AD, A	*to, toward*	adhere, adjacent, adjunct, admonish, adroit, adumbrate, advent, abeyance, abet, accede, accretion, acquiesce, affluent, aggrandize, aggregate, alleviate, alliteration, allude, allure, ascribe, aspersion, aspire, assail, assonance, attest
ALI, ALTR	*another*	alias, alienate, inalienable, altruism
AM, AMI	*love*	amorous, amicable, amiable, amity
AMBI, AMPHI	*both*	ambiguous, ambivalent, ambidextrous, amphibious
AMBL, AMBUL	*walk*	amble, ambulatory, perambulator, somnambulist
ANIM	*mind, spirit, breath*	animal, animosity, unanimous, magnanimous
ANN, ENN	*year*	annual, annuity, superannuated, biennial, perennial
ANTE, ANT	*before*	antecedent, antediluvian, antebellum, antepenultimate, anterior, antiquity, antiquated, anticipate
ANTHROP	*human*	anthropology, anthropomorphic, misanthrope, philanthropy
ANTI, ANT	*against, opposite*	antidote, antipathy, antithesis, antacid, antagonist, antonym

ROOT	MEANING	EXAMPLES
AUD	*hear*	audio, audience, audition, auditory, audible
AUTO	*self*	autobiography, autocrat, autonomous
BELLI, BELL	*war*	belligerent, bellicose, antebellum, rebellion
BENE, BEN	*good*	benevolent, benefactor, beneficent, benign
BI	*two*	bicycle, bisect, bilateral, bilingual, biped
BIBLIO	*book*	Bible, bibliography, bibliophile
BIO	*life*	biography, biology, amphibious, symbiotic, macrobiotics
BURS	*money, purse*	reimburse, disburse, bursar
CAD, CAS, CID	*happen, fall*	accident, cadence, cascade, deciduous
CAP, CIP	*head*	captain, decapitate, capitulate, precipitous, precipitate, recapitulate
CAP, CAPT, CEPT, CIP	*take, hold, seize*	capable, capacious, captivate, deception, intercept, precept, inception, anticipate, emancipate, incipient, percipient
CARN	*flesh*	carnal, carnage, carnival, carnivorous, incarnate, incarnadine
CED, CESS	*yield, go*	cede, precede, accede, recede, antecedent, intercede, secede, cession, cease, cessation, incessant
CHROM	*color*	chrome, chromatic, monochrome
CHRON	*time*	chronology, chronic, anachronism
CIDE	*murder*	suicide, homicide, regicide, patricide
CIRCUM	*around*	circumference, circumlocution, circumnavigate, circumscribe, circumspect, circumvent
CLIN, CLIV	*slope*	incline, declivity, proclivity
CLUD, CLUS, CLAUS, CLOIS	*shut, close*	conclude, reclusive, claustrophobia, cloister, preclude, occlude
CO, COM, CON	*with, together*	coeducation, coagulate, coalesce, coerce, cogent, collateral, colloquial, colloquy, commensurate, commodious, compassion, compatriot, complacent, compliant, complicity, compunction, concerto, conciliatory, concord, concur, condone, conflagration, congeal, congenial, congenital, conglomerate, conjure, conjugal, conscientious, consecrate, consensus, consonant, constrained, contentious, contrite, contusion, convalescence, convene, convivial, convoke, convoluted, congress

ROOT	MEANING	EXAMPLES
COGN, GNO	*know*	recognize, cognition, cognizance, incognito, diagnosis, agnostic, prognosis, gnostic, ignorant
CONTRA	*against*	controversy, incontrovertible, contravene, contradict
CORP	*body*	corpse, corporeal, corpulence
COSMO, COSM	*world*	cosmopolitan, cosmos, microcosm, macrocosm
CRAC, CRAT	*rule, power*	democracy, bureaucracy, theocracy, autocrat, aristocrat, technocrat
CRED	*trust, believe*	incredible, credulous, credence
CRESC, CRET	*grow*	crescent, crescendo, accretion
CULP	*blame, fault*	culprit, culpable, inculpate, exculpate
CURR, CURS	*run*	current, concur, cursory, precursor, incursion
DE	*down, out, apart*	depart, debase, debilitate, declivity, decry, deface, defamatory, defunct, delegate, demarcation, demean, demur, deplete, deplore, depravity, deprecate, deride, derivative, desist, detest
DEC	*ten, tenth*	decade, decimal, decathlon, decimate
DEMO, DEM	*people*	democrat, demographics, demagogue, epidemic, pandemic, endemic
DI, DIURN	*day*	diary, diurnal, quotidian
DIA	*across*	diagonal, diatribe, diaphanous
DIC, DICT	*speak*	diction, interdict, predict, abdicate, indict, verdict, dictum
DIS, DIF, DI	*not, apart, away*	disaffected, disband, disbar, disburse, discern, discordant, discredit, discursive, disheveled, disparage, disparate, dispassionate, dispirit, dissemble, disseminate, dissension, dissipate, dissonant, dissuade, distend, differentiate, diffidence, diffuse, digress, divert
DOC, DOCT	*teach*	doctrine, docile, doctrinaire
DOL	*pain*	condolence, doleful, dolorous, indolent
DUC, DUCT	*lead*	seduce, induce, conduct, viaduct, induct
EGO	*self*	ego, egoist, egocentric
EN, EM	*in, into*	enter, entice, encumber, endemic, ensconce, enthrall, entreat, embellish, embezzle, embroil, empathy
ERR	*wander*	erratic, aberration, errant

ROOT	MEANING	EXAMPLES
EU	*well, good*	eulogy, euphemism, euphony, euphoria, eurythmics, euthanasia
EX, E	*out, out of*	exit, exacerbate, excerpt, excommunicate, exculpate, execrable, exhume, exonerate, exorbitant, exorcise, expatriate, expedient, expiate, expunge, expurgate, extenuate, extort, extremity, extricate, extrinsic, exult, evoke, evict, evince, elicit, egress, egregious
FAC, FIC, FECT, FY, FEA	*make, do*	factory, facility, benefactor, malefactor, fiction, fictive, beneficent, affect, confection, refectory, magnify, unify, rectify, vilify, feasible
FAL, FALS	*deceive*	false, infallible, fallacious
FERV	*boil*	fervent, fervid, effervescent
FID	*faith, trust*	confident, diffidence, perfidious, fidelity
FLU, FLUX	*flow*	fluent, flux, affluent, confluence, effluvia, superfluous
FORE	*before*	forecast, foreboding, forestall
FRAG, FRAC	*break*	fragment, fracture, diffract, fractious, refract
FUS	*pour*	profuse, infusion, effusive, diffuse
GEN	*birth, class, kin*	generation, congenital, homogeneous, heterogeneous, ingenious, engender, progenitor, progeny
GRAD, GRESS	*step*	graduate, gradual, retrograde, centigrade, degrade, gradation, gradient, progress, congress, digress, transgress, ingress, egress
GRAPH, GRAM	*writing*	biography, bibliography, epigraph, grammar, epigram
GRAT	*pleasing*	grateful, gratitude, gratis, ingrate, congratulate, gratuitous, gratuity
GRAV, GRIEV	*heavy*	grave, gravity, aggravate, grieve, aggrieve, grievous
GREG	*crowd, flock*	segregate, gregarious, egregious, congregate, aggregate
HABIT, HIBIT	*have, hold*	habit, inhibit, cohabit, habitat
HAP	*by chance*	happen, haphazard, hapless, mishap
HELIO, HELI	*sun*	heliocentric, helium, heliotrope, aphelion, perihelion
HETERO	*other*	heterosexual, heterogeneous, heterodox
HOL	*whole*	holocaust, catholic, holistic

ROOT	MEANING	EXAMPLES
HOMO	*same*	homosexual, homogenize, homogeneous, homonym
HOMO	*man*	*Homo sapiens*, homicide, bonhomie
HYDR	*water*	hydrant, hydrate, dehydration
HYPER	*too much, excess*	hyperactive, hyperbole, hyperventilate
HYPO	*too little, under*	hypodermic, hypothermia, hypochondria, hypothesis, hypothetical
IN, IG, IL, IM, IR	*not*	incorrigible, indefatigable, indelible, indubitable, inept, inert, inexorable, insatiable, insentient, insolvent, insomnia, interminable, intractable, incessant, inextricable, infallible, infamy, innumerable, inoperable, insipid, intemperate, intrepid, inviolable, ignorant, ignominious, ignoble, illicit, illimitable, immaculate, immutable, impasse, impeccable, impecunious, impertinent, implacable, impotent, impregnable, improvident, impassioned, impervious, irregular
IN, IL, IM, IR	*in, on, into*	invade, inaugurate, incandescent, incarcerate, incense, indenture, induct, ingratiate, introvert, incarnate, inception, incisive, infer, infusion, ingress, innate, inquest, inscribe, insinuate, inter, illustrate, imbue, immerse, implicate, irrigate, irritate
INTER	*between, among*	intercede, intercept, interdiction, interject, interlocutor, interloper, intermediary, intermittent, interpolate, interpose, interregnum, interrogate, intersect, intervene
INTRA, INTR	*within*	intrastate, intravenous, intramural, intrinsic
IT, ITER	*between, among*	transit, itinerant, reiterate, transitory
JECT, JET	*throw*	eject, interject, abject, trajectory, jettison
JOUR	*day*	journal, adjourn, sojourn
JUD	*judge*	judge, judicious, prejudice, adjudicate
JUNCT, JUG	*join*	junction, adjunct, injunction, conjugal, subjugate
JUR	*swear, law*	jury, abjure, adjure, conjure, perjure, jurisprudence
LAT	*side*	lateral, collateral, unilateral, bilateral, quadrilateral
LAV, LAU, LU	*wash*	lavatory, laundry, ablution, antediluvian
LEG, LEC, LEX	*read, speak*	legible, lecture, lexicon
LEV	*light*	elevate, levitate, levity, alleviate

ROOT	MEANING	EXAMPLES
LIBER	***free***	liberty, liberal, libertarian, libertine
LIG, LECT	***choose, gather***	eligible, elect, select
LIG, LI, LY	***bind***	ligament, oblige, religion, liable, liaison, lien, ally
LING, LANG	***tongue***	lingo, language, linguistics, bilingual
LITER	***letter***	literate, alliteration, literal
LITH	***stone***	monolith, lithograph, megalith
LOQU, LOC, LOG	***speech, thought***	eloquent, loquacious, colloquial, colloquy, soliloquy, circumlocution, interlocutor, monologue, dialogue, eulogy, philology, neologism
LUC, LUM	***light***	lucid, illuminate, elucidate, pellucid, translucent
LUD, LUS	***play***	ludicrous, allude, delusion, allusion, illusory
MACRO	***great***	macrocosm, macrobiotics
MAG, MAJ, MAS, MAX	***great***	magnify, magnanimous, magnate, magnitude majesty, master, maximum
MAL	***bad***	malady, maladroit, malevolent, malodorous
MAN	***hand***	manual, manuscript, emancipate, manifest
MAR	***sea***	submarine, marine, maritime
MATER, MATR	***mother***	maternal, matron, matrilineal
MEDI	***middle***	intermediary, medieval, mediate
MEGA	***great***	megaphone, megalomania, megaton, megalith
MEMOR, MEMEN	***remember***	memory, memento, memorabilia, memoir
METER, METR, MENS	***measure***	meter, thermometer, perimeter, metronome, commensurate
MICRO	***small***	microscope, microorganism, microcosm, microbe
MIS	***wrong, bad, hate***	misunderstand, misanthrope, misapprehension, misconstrue, misnomer, mishap
MIT, MISS	***send***	transmit, emit, missive
MOLL	***soft***	mollify, emollient, mollusk
MON, MONIT	***warn***	admonish, monitor, premonition
MONO	***one***	monologue, monotonous, monogamy, monolith, monochrome
MOR	***custom, manner***	moral, mores, morose
MOR, MORT	***dead***	morbid, moribund, mortal, amortize
MORPH	***shape***	amorphous, anthropomorphic, metamorphosis, morphology

ROOT	MEANING	EXAMPLES
MOV, MOT, MOB, MOM	***move***	remove, motion, mobile, momentum, momentous
MUT	***change***	mutate, mutability, immutable, commute
NAT, NASC	***born***	native, nativity, natal, neonate, innate, cognate, nascent, renascent, renaissance
NAU, NAV	***ship, sailor***	nautical, nauseous, navy, circumnavigate
NEG	***not, deny***	negative, abnegate, renege
NEO	***new***	neoclassical, neophyte, neologism, neonate
NIHIL	***none, nothing***	annihilation, nihilism
NOM, NYM	***name***	nominate, nomenclature, nominal, cognomen, misnomer, ignominious, antonym, homonym, pseudonym, synonym, anonymity
NOX, NIC, NEC, NOC	***harm***	obnoxious, noxious, pernicious, internecine, innocuous
NOV	***new***	novelty, innovation, novitiate
NUMER	***number***	numeral, numerous, innumerable, enumerate
OB	***against***	obstruct, obdurate, obfuscate, obnoxious, obsequious, obstinate, obstreperous, obtrusive
OMNI	***all***	omnipresent, omnipotent, omniscient, omnivorous
ONER	***burden***	onerous, onus, exonerate
OPER	***work***	operate, cooperate, inoperable
PAC	***peace***	pacify, pacifist, pacific
PALP	***feel***	palpable, palpitation
PAN	***all***	panorama, panacea, panegyric, pandemic, panoply
PATER, PATR	***father***	paternal, paternity, patriot, compatriot, expatriate, patrimony, patricide, patrician
PATH, PASS	***feel, suffer***	sympathy, antipathy, empathy, apathy, pathos, impassioned
PEC	***money***	pecuniary, impecunious, peculation
PED, POD	***foot***	pedestrian, pediment, expedient, biped, quadruped, tripod
PEL, PULS	***drive***	compel, compelling, expel, propel, compulsion
PEN	***almost***	peninsula, penultimate, penumbra
PEND, PENS	***hang***	pendant, pendulous, compendium, suspense, propensity

ROOT	MEANING	EXAMPLES
PER	*through, by, for, throughout*	perambulator, percipient, perfunctory, permeable, perspicacious, pertinacious, perturbation, perusal, perennial, peregrinate
PER	*against, destruction*	perfidious, pernicious, perjure
PERI	*around*	perimeter, periphery, perihelion, peripatetic
PET	*seek, go toward*	petition, impetus, impetuous, petulant, centripetal
PHIL	*love*	philosopher, philanderer, philanthropy, bibliophile, philology
PHOB	*fear*	phobia, claustrophobia, xenophobia
PHON	*sound*	phonograph, megaphone, euphony, phonetics, phonics
PLAC	*calm, please*	placate, implacable, placid, complacent
PON, POS	*put, place*	postpone, proponent, exponent, preposition, posit, interpose, juxtaposition, depose
PORT	*carry*	portable, deportment, rapport
POT	*drink*	potion, potable
POT	*power*	potential, potent, impotent, potentate, omnipotence
PRE	*before*	precede, precipitate, preclude, precocious, precursor, predilection, predisposition, preponderance, prepossessing, presage, prescient, prejudice, predict, premonition, preposition
PRIM, PRI	*first*	prime, primary, primal, primeval, primordial, pristine
PRO	*ahead, forth*	proceed, proclivity, procrastinator, profane, profuse, progenitor, progeny, prognosis, prologue, promontory, propel, proponent, propose, proscribe, protestation, provoke
PROTO	*first*	prototype, protagonist, protocol
PROX, PROP	*near*	approximate, proximity, propinquity
PSEUDO	*false*	pseudoscientific, pseudonym
PYR	*fire*	pyre, pyrotechnics, pyromania
QUAD, QUAR, QUAT	*four*	quadrilateral, quadrant, quadruped, quarter, quarantine, quaternary
QUES, QUER, QUIS, QUIR	*question*	quest, inquest, query, querulous, inquisitive, inquiry
QUIE	*quiet*	disquiet, acquiesce, quiescent, requiem
QUINT, QUIN	*five*	quintuplets, quintessence

ROOT	MEANING	EXAMPLES
RADI, RAMI	***branch***	radius, radiate, radiant, eradicate, ramification
RECT, REG	***straight, rule***	rectangle, rectitude, rectify, regular
REG	***king, rule***	regal, regent, interregnum
RETRO	***backward***	retrospective, retroactive, retrograde
RID, RIS	***laugh***	ridiculous, deride, derision
ROG	***ask***	interrogate, derogatory, abrogate, arrogate, arrogant
RUD	***rough, crude***	rude, rudimentary
RUPT	***break***	disrupt, interrupt, rupture, erupt
SACR, SANCT	***holy***	sacred, sacrilege, consecrate, sanctify, sanction, sacrosanct
SCRIB, SCRIPT, SCRIV	***write***	scribe, ascribe, circumscribe, inscribe, proscribe, script, manuscript, scrivener
SE	***apart, away***	separate, segregate, secede, sedition
SEC, SECT, SEG	***cut***	sector, dissect, bisect, intersect, segment, secant
SED, SID	***sit***	sedate, sedentary, supersede, reside, residence, assiduous, insidious
SEM	***seed, sow***	seminar, seminal, disseminate
SEN	***old***	senior, senile, senescent
SENT, SENS	***feel, think***	sentiment, sentient, nonsense, assent, consensus, sensual
SEQU, SECU	***follow***	sequence, sequel, subsequent, obsequious, obsequy, non sequitur, consecutive
SIM, SEM	***similar, same***	similar, verisimilitude, semblance, dissemble,
SIGN	***mark, sign***	signal, designation, assignation
SIN	***curve***	sine curve, sinuous, insinuate
SOL	***sun***	solar, parasol, solarium, solstice
SOL	***alone***	solo, solitude, soliloquy, solipsism
SOMN	***sleep***	insomnia, somnolent, somnambulist
SON	***sound***	sonic, consonance, dissonance, assonance, sonorous, resonate
SOPH	***wisdom***	philosopher, sophistry, sophisticated, sophomoric
SPEC, SPIC	***see, look***	spectator, circumspect, retrospective, perspective, perspicacious
SPER	***hope***	prosper, prosperous, despair, desperate
SPERS, SPAR	***scatter***	disperse, aspersion, sparse, disparate
SPIR	***breathe***	respire, inspire, spiritual, aspire, transpire

ROOT	MEANING	EXAMPLES
STRICT, STRING	*bind*	strict, stricture, constrict, stringent, astringent
STRUCT, STRU	*build*	structure, obstruct, construe
SUB	*under*	subconscious, subjugate, subliminal, subpoena, subsequent, subterranean, subvert
SUMM	*highest*	summit, summary, consummate
SUPER, SUR	*above*	supervise, supercilious, supersede, superannuated, superfluous, insurmountable, surfeit
SURGE, SURRECT	*rise*	surge, resurgent, insurgent, insurrection
SYN, SYM	*together*	synthesis, sympathy, synonym, syncopation, synopsis, symposium, symbiosis
TACIT, TIC	*silent*	tacit, taciturn, reticent
TACT, TAG, TANG	*touch*	tact, tactile, contagious, tangent, tangential, tangible
TEN, TIN, TAIN	*hold, twist*	detention, tenable, tenacious, pertinacious, retinue, retain
TEND, TENS, TENT	*stretch*	intend, distend, tension, tensile, ostensible, contentious
TERM	*end*	terminal, terminus, terminate, interminable
TERR	*earth, land*	terrain, terrestrial, extraterrestrial, subterranean
TEST	*witness*	testify, attest, testimonial, testament, detest, protestation
THE	*god*	atheist, theology, apotheosis, theocracy
THERM	*heat*	thermometer, thermal, thermonuclear, hypothermia
TIM	*fear, frightened*	timid, intimidate, timorous
TOP	*place*	topic, topography, utopia
TORT	*twist*	distort, extort, tortuous
TORP	*stiff, numb*	torpedo, torpid, torpor
TOX	*poison*	toxic, toxin, intoxication
TRACT	*draw*	tractor, intractable, protract
TRANS	*across, over, through, beyond*	transport, transgress, transient, transitory, translucent, transmutation, transpire, intransigent
TREM, TREP	*shake*	tremble, tremor, tremulous, trepidation, intrepid
TURB	*shake*	disturb, turbulent, perturbation
UMBR	*shadow*	umbrella, umbrage, adumbrate, penumbra
UNI, UN	*one*	unify, unilateral, unanimous
URB	*city*	urban, suburban, urbane
VAC	*empty*	vacant, evacuate, vacuous

ROOT	MEANING	EXAMPLES
VAL, VAIL	*value, strength*	valid, valor, ambivalent, convalescence, avail, prevail, countervail
VEN, VENT	*come*	convene, contravene, intervene, venue, convention, circumvent, advent, adventitious
VER	*true*	verify, verity, verisimilitude, veracious, aver, verdict
VERB	*word*	verbal, verbose, verbiage, verbatim
VERT, VERS	*turn*	avert, convert, revert, incontrovertible, divert, subvert, versatile, aversion
VICT, VINC	*conquer*	victory, conviction, evict, evince, invincible
VID, VIS	*see*	evident, vision, visage, supervise
VIL	*base, mean*	vile, vilify, revile
VIV, VIT	*life*	vivid, convivial, vivacious, vital
VOC, VOK, VOW	*call, voice*	vocal, equivocate, vociferous, convoke, evoke, invoke, avow
VOL	*wish*	voluntary, malevolent, benevolent, volition
VOLV, VOLUT	*turn, roll*	revolve, evolve, convoluted
VOR	*eat*	devour, carnivorous, omnivorous, voracious

VOCABULARY LIST

WORD	DEFINITION, CONTEXT, SYNONYMS
ABDICATE	to give up a position, right, or power *With the angry mob clamoring outside the palace, the king* abdicated *his throne and fled with his queen.* Synonyms: **quit, resign, renounce, step down**
ABDUCT	to carry, take, or lead away forcefully and wrongfully *The kidnappers planned to* abduct *the child and hold her for ransom.* Synonyms: **kidnap, carry off**
ABHOR	to hate, to view with repugnance, to detest *After repeated failure to learn the Pythagorean theorem, Susan began to* abhor *geometry.* Synonyms: **hate, loathe, abominate**
ABSURD	ridiculously unreasonable, lacking logic *Ironing one's underwear is* absurd. Synonyms: **ridiculous, ludicrous, preposterous, bizarre**
ABYSS	deep hole; deep immeasurable space, gulf, or cavity *Looking down into the* abyss *was terrifying, for I could not see the bottom.* Synonyms: **chasm, pit**
ACCELERATE	to increase in speed, cause to move faster *The new disease has spread like wildfire, causing researchers to* accelerate *their search for a cure.* Synonyms: **speed up, hasten, expedite**
ACCLAIM	(n) praise, enthusiastic approval *The artist won international* acclaim*; critics and viewers all over the world were intrigued by the works.* Synonyms: **praise, approval** (v) to approve, to welcome with applause and praise *The critic was eager to* acclaim *the actress for her performance.* Synonyms: **cheer, applaud, praise, honor**
ACUTE	sharp in some way (as in an acute angle) or sharp in intellect; crucial *There is an* acute *shortage of food will ultimately result in a famine if something is not done soon to increase the food supply.* Synonyms: **perceptive, sharp, keen, shrewd, crucial**
ADAGE	old saying, proverb *"A penny saved is a penny earned" is a popular* adage. Synonyms: **proverb, maxim**

WORD	DEFINITION, CONTEXT, SYNONYMS
ADHERE	to stick fast; to hold to *(1) After we put glue on his pants, John* adhered *to the chair.* *(2) He was a strict Catholic who* adhered *to all the teachings of the Church.* Synonyms: **stick to** (like glue or adhesive tape); **follow**
ADJOURN	to postpone; to suspend (a meeting) for a period of time *Since it was late in the day, the prosecutor moved that the court* adjourn *for the day.* Synonyms: **suspend, recess, postpone**
ADJUNCT	something or someone associated with another but in a defendant or secondary position *An* adjunct *professor is one not given the same full-time status as other faculty members.* Synonyms: **additional, supporting, assisting, accessory**
ADMONISH	to scold (sometimes in a good natured way); to urge to duty, remind; to advise against something *My mother began to* admonish *me about my poor grades.* Synonyms: **warn, caution, scold**
ADORN	to decorate or add beauty to, for instance with ornaments; to make pleasing, more attractive *She* adorned *her hair with flowers.* Synonyms: **decorate, ornament, embellish**
ADVERSARY	opponent or enemy *Democrats and Republicans are usually* adversaries *in the political world.* Synonyms: **enemy, foe, opponent**
AERONAUTIC	relating to aircraft *The Air Force's Stealth plane is reported to be a masterpiece of* aeronautic *design.*
AFFABLE	pleasantly easy to get along with; friendly and warm *He was an* affable *host and made us feel right at home.* Synonyms: **agreeable, amiable**
AFFECTATION	attempt to appear to be what one is not for the purpose of impressing others (for instance, pretending to have a pretentiously cultured accent) *Justin once spent three months in France and has now acquired the silly* affectation *of using French phrases in casual conversation.* Synonyms: **pretension, unnaturalness, artificiality, mannerism, pretense, airs, sham, facade, pose, posture**

WORD	DEFINITION, CONTEXT, SYNONYMS
AGHAST	overcome by surprise, disgust, or amazement; seized with terror; shocked *The investigator was* aghast *at the horrible conditions in the nursing home.* Synonyms: **astounded, dismayed, appalled, astonished, shocked**
AGILITY	condition of being able to move quickly and easily or being mentally alert *Strength and* agility *are important for an athlete.* Synonyms: **skillfulness, dexterity, nimbleness**
AGITATE	to shake or grow excited; to move around a lot, to disturb or excite emotionally *The bat's flight into the classroom managed to* agitate *the teacher so much that he went home early.* Synonyms: **disturb, upset, stir up** (like a washing machine)
AIMLESS	lacking purpose or goals *After its engine died, the boat drifted* aimlessly *for days.* Synonyms: **purposeless, haphazard, accidental**
ALLEVIATE	to make easier to bear, lessen *This medicine will help to* alleviate *the pain.* Synonyms: **relieve, allay, assuage, ease, decrease, lessen, mitigate**
ALLURE	fascination, appeal *Video games have an* allure *that some people find impossible to resist.* Synonyms: **temptation, attraction, fascination**
ALOOF	distant in relations with other people *The newcomer remained* aloof *from all our activities and therefore made no new friends.* Synonyms: **detached, cool, blase, remote**
ALTRUISTIC	concerned for the welfare of others *The* altruistic *woman gave out money to all who seemed needy.* Synonyms: **benevolent, charitable, compassionate, humane**
AMATEUR	(n) someone not paid to engage in a hobby, sport, art, etc. *Since professionals couldn't play, only* amateur *athletes were allowed to participate in the Olympics.* Synonyms: **devotee, dabbler, enthusiast, buff, nonprofessional** (adj) like an amateur *The brilliant author James Joyce was an* amateur *singer.*

WORD	DEFINITION, CONTEXT, SYNONYMS
AMEND	to improve; to alter; to add to, or subtract from by formal procedure *Congress will* amend *the bill so that the president will sign it.* Synonyms: **alter, improve, repair, mend, make better, ameliorate**
AMOROUS	having to do with love *The love-sick young poet wrote many* amorous *poems about his girlfriend.* Synonyms: **romantic, erotic**
AMORPHOUS	lacking a specific shape *In the movie* The Blob, *the creature was an* amorphous *one that was constantly changing shape.* Synonyms: **shapeless, vague**
AMPHIBIAN	animal at home both on land and in the water *A frog, which lives both on land and in the water, is an* amphibian.
ANGULAR	having clear angles or thin and bony facial features. *The figures on the left side of the painting are very* angular, *whereas the figures on the right are rounded.* Synonyms: **lanky, gaunt, bony**
ANIMOSITY	feeling of ill will, intense dislike for someone or something *The deep-rooted* animosity *between them made it difficult for the brothers to work together.* Synonyms: **ill will, ill feeling, bitterness, rancor, acrimony**
ANNIHILATE	to destroy completely *The first troops to land on the beach during the invasion were* annihilated *by the powerful artillery of the enemy.* Synonyms: **destroy, devastate, demolish**
ANTIDOTE	remedy to relieve the effects of poison *The first aid kit included an* antidote *for snake bite.* Synonyms: **remedy, counteragent, neutralizer**
APERTURE	opening *The* aperture *of a camera lens is a circular opening of variable diameter that regulates the amount of light entering the lens.* Synonyms: **hole, gap, space, opening, crack**
AQUEOUS	similar to, or composed of water *The inside of an eyeball is filled with an* aqueous *substance.* Synonyms: **watery, aquatic, hydrous, liquid**

WORD	DEFINITION, CONTEXT, SYNONYMS
ARDENT	characterized by passion or desire *After a 25-game losing streak, even the Mets' most* ardent *fans realized the team wouldn't finish first.* Synonyms: **passionate, enthusiastic, fervent**
ARID	very dry, lacking moisture; unproductive, unimaginative *The* arid *farmland produced no crops.* Synonyms: **dry, parched, barren, dull, uninteresting, insipid**
AROMA	pleasing fragrance; any odor or smell *The* aroma *in the bakery made her mouth water.* Synonyms: **smell, fragrance, odor**
ARTICULATE	(adj) well-spoken, lucidly presented *Joe's* articulate *argument was so persuasive that we all agreed with him.* Synonyms: **eloquent, glib** (v) to pronounce clearly *The great actor* articulated *every word so clearly it was easy to understand him.* Synonyms: **enunciate**
ARTIFICE	(1) trickery, clever ruse *Ralph's use of rubber masks proved to be a brilliant* artifice. Synonyms: **stratagem, trick, ploy, deception, ruse, maneuver** (2) ability to create or imagine *Many question the meaningfulness of Jamie's science fiction novel, but its fantastic images and ingenious plot cannot fail to impress one with his sheer* artifice. Synonyms: **creativity, inventiveness, innovation, resourcefulness, imagination, ingenuity**
ASCERTAIN	to find out or discover by examination *Try though he did, the archaeologist couldn't* ascertain *the correct age of the Piltdown man's skeleton.* Synonyms: **determine, discover, unearth, find out**
ASSAILABLE	able to be attacked or assaulted by blows or words *Carcassonne was widely thought to be an* unassailable *fortress after it resisted a siege by Charlemagne.* Synonyms: **vulnerable, exposed, unprotected**

WORD	DEFINITION, CONTEXT, SYNONYMS
ASTOUND	to overwhelm with amazement *The extent of his great knowledge never ceases to* astound *me.* Synonyms: **amaze, stupefy, stun**
ASTUTE	shrewd and perceptive; able to understand clearly and quickly *The novelist Judy Blume is an* astute *judge of human character.* Synonyms: **keen, discerning, penetrating, incisive, perceptive, crafty, foxy, wily, shrewd**
ATROCITY	horrible act *During the Indian bid for freedom from British colonial rule, a British officer committed the* atrocity *of slaughtering a large congregation of peaceful Indian demonstrators.* Synonyms: **horror, barbarity, outrage**
AUDACITY	boldness or daring, especially with disregard for personal safety *He had the* audacity *to insult the president to his face.* Synonyms: **boldness, daring, impudence**
AUTHORITATIVE	having great authority *J. R. R. Tolkien, who had written many books about Old English poetry, was widely considered to be the most* authoritative *scholar in the field.* Synonyms: **masterful**
BANAL	boringly predictable *A boring conversation is likely to be full of* banal *statements like "Have a nice day."* Synonyms: **boring, dull, bland, insipid**
BANISH	to send away, condemn to exile; drive or put away *After the incident with the food fight, Arthur was* banished *from the lunchroom.* Synonyms: **send away, get rid of, expel, exile, deport**
BARRIER	anything that makes progress harder or impossible; a limit or boundary *(1) The Pythagorean theorem has been a* barrier *to Donald's complete understanding of geometry.* *(2) To discourage visitors, Janet built a* barrier *in front of the entrance to her room.* Synonyms: **obstacle**
BEGUILE	to delude, deceive by trickery Beguiled *by the supernatural songs of the Sirens, Odysseus wanted to abandon all his men and forget his family.* Synonyms: **charm, allure, bewitch, captivate**

WORD	DEFINITION, CONTEXT, SYNONYMS
BELLIGERENCE	aggressive hostility *A soldier can be shocked by the* belligerence *of his enemy.* Synonyms: **aggressiveness, combativeness**
BENEFACTOR	someone giving financial or general assistance *A wealthy alumnus who gives $5 million to his old college would be considered a great* benefactor. Synonyms: **patron, backer, donor**
BENEFICIAL	advantageous, helpful, conferring benefit *Eating vegetables and getting 8 hours of sleep are* beneficial *to your health, but they sure aren't much fun.* Synonyms: **advantageous, favorable**
BENEVOLENCE	inclination to do good deeds *The* benevolence *of the generous donor was recognized by a plaque.* Synonyms: **largess**
BEWILDERED	completely confused or puzzled, perplexed *I was* bewildered *by the complex algebra problem.* Synonyms: **confused, puzzled, perplexed**
BIAS	(n) prejudice, particular tendency *Racial* bias *in employment is illegal in the United States.* Synonyms: **partiality** (v) to cause prejudice in (a person); to influence unfairly *The article is not accurate and may* bias *some readers.*
BILE	ill temper, irritability *Mr. Watkins is harsh when he grades essays; his comments reveal his* bile *and sharp tongue.* Synonyms: **bitterness**
BLISS	supreme happiness, utter joy or contentment; heaven, paradise *For lovers of ice cream, this new flavor is absolute* bliss. Synonyms: **joy, delight, ecstasy**
BOISTEROUS	loud and unrestrained *The* boisterous *party made so much noise last night that I got no sleep.* Synonyms: **loud, noisy, raucous**
BOTANIST	scientist specializing in study of plants *A* botanist *is a scientist who studies plants.*

WORD	DEFINITION, CONTEXT, SYNONYMS
BOUNTY	generosity in giving; reward *The police offered a* bounty *for the capture of the criminal.* Synonyms: **abundance, cornucopia, reward, loot**
BRAVADO	showy and pretentious display of courage *The coward's* bravado *quickly vanished when his captors threatened to hit him; he began to whine for mercy.* Synonyms: **bluster, bombast, swagger**
BREVITY	state of being brief, of not lasting a long time *The* brevity *of your visit to my home implied that you did not enjoy my family's company.* Synonyms: **shortness, fleetness, swiftness**
BRIG	ship's prison *Captain Bligh had the rebellious sailor thrown into the* brig. Synonyms: **jail, prison**
BURNISH	(n) to make shiny by rubbing, as with a cloth *Mr. Jin loved to stand in the sun and* burnish *his luxury car until it gleamed.* Synonyms: **shine, polish, buff, varnish** (n) shininess produced by burnishing *They all admired the* burnish *on the car.* Synonyms: **shine, luster, gleam, brilliance**
CACHE	hiding place for treasures, etc.; anything in such a hiding place *The secret panel hid a* cache *of jewels.* Synonyms: **stash**
CAJOLE	to wheedle, persuade with promises or flattery, coax *The spoiled girl could* cajole *her father into buying her anything.* Synonyms: **coax, wheedle**
CAMOUFLAGE	(n) disguise worn in order to deceive an enemy; for instance, uniforms the color of trees and dirt *The soldiers wore* camouflage *on their helmets.* Synonyms: **disguise** (v) to deceive by means of camouflage *They have* camouflaged *the missile silo in order to deceive enemy bombers.* Synonyms: **disguise, obscure, cloud, hide**

WORD	DEFINITION, CONTEXT, SYNONYMS
CANDOR	frankness and sincerity; fairness *The candor of his confession impressed his parents, and they gave him a light punishment as a result.* Synonyms: **honesty, sincerity**
CANINE	relating to dogs Canine *relates to dogs in the same way as feline relates to cats.*
CANTANKEROUS	quarrelsome and grouchy *The old grouch was always in a* cantankerous *mood.* Synonyms: **grouchy, argumentative, ill-tempered**
CAPRICE	sudden, unpredictable change *With the* caprice *of an irrational man, he often went from rage to laughter.* Synonyms: **impulse, whim, fancy**
CASCADE	(n) waterfall, as in a type of fireworks resembling a waterfall Synonyms: **waterfall, torrent** *The* cascade *of sparks from the fireworks caused the crowd to ooh and aah.* (v) to fall like a cascade *The stream flowed over the cliff and* cascaded *into the valley below.*
CATASTROPHE	disastrous event *The eruption was truly a* catastrophe; *lava and ash buried several towns on the slopes of the volcano.* Synonyms: **disaster, ruin, devastation**
 **CELESTIAL**	relating to the heavens *Venus is a* celestial *body sometimes visible from Earth.* Synonyms: **heavenly, divine, spiritual**
CENSOR	to remove material from books, plays, magazines, etc. for moral, political, or religious reasons *After they* censored *the "dirty" parts out of the book, all that was left was the dedication and half of the cover.* Synonyms: **suppress, delete**
CHASM	gorge or deep canyon *If you look down from the top floor of a New York City skyscraper, it seems as though you're looking into a deep* chasm. Synonyms: **ravine, canyon, abyss**
 **CHOLERIC**	bad-tempered *The grumpy old man was* choleric *whenever he didn't get his morning coffee.* Synonyms: **bad-tempered**

WORD	DEFINITION, CONTEXT, SYNONYMS
CHOREOGRAPHER	person creating and arranging dances for stage performances *After being an innovative dancer, Martha Graham became a* choreographer *and arranged many innovative dance performances for her company.*
CHORUS	group acting together *The* chorus *of over fifty people harmonized as one.* Synonyms: **group, band**
CHRONIC	continuing over a long period of time, long-standing *Joshua suffered from* chronic *tiredness; most days he slept straight through geometry class.* Synonyms: **continuous, constant, persistent, confirmed, settled**
CIRCUMSCRIBE	to encircle with a line; to limit in any way *The Howards' country estate is* circumscribed *by rolling hills.* Synonyms: **limit, outline, bound, define, encompass**
COLLISION	crash, clash, or conflict *The* collision *of the two cars made a terrible sound and tied up traffic for hours.* Synonyms: **crash, clash, impact**
COMMUNICATIVE	talkative and likely to communicate *Despite their limited knowledge of English, the foreigners were eager to be* communicative *with the host family.* Synonyms: **talkative, articulate, vocal, expressive**
COMPASSION	deep feeling of pity or sympathy for others *The jury decided that the cold-hearted killer felt no* compassion *for his victims.* Synonyms: **pity, sympathy, mercy**
COMPEL	to force someone or something to act *Even torture couldn't* compel *the spy to reveal his secrets.* Synonyms: **force, coerce, goad, motivate**
COMPETENT	having enough skill for some purpose; adequate but not exceptional *He was not the most qualified candidate, but at least he was* competent. Synonyms: **qualified, capable, fit**
CONCISE	brief and compact *Barry gave a* concise *speech: he said everything he needed to and was finished in five minutes.* Synonyms: **brief, terse, succinct, compact**

WORD	DEFINITION, CONTEXT, SYNONYMS
CONDONE	to pardon, to forgive, or overlook *"We cannot* condone *your behavior," said Ben's parents after he missed his curfew. "You are grounded for two weeks."* Synonyms: **pardon, excuse, forgive, absolve, overlook, accept, tolerate, allow, permit, suffer, endure, bear, stomach**
CONFIDENTIAL	done secretly or in confidence *The* confidential *memorandum listed everyone's salary.* Synonyms: **secret, covert, off-the-record**
CONSTRICT	to squeeze, make tighter *As my chest became* constricted, *I found it difficult to breathe.* Synonyms: **choke, stifle, contract, smother**
CONTEMPLATION	thoughtful observation *When the philosopher studied complicated issues, he often became so lost in* contemplation *that he forget to eat or sleep.* Synonyms: **thought, deliberation, meditation, reflection**
CONTEND	to fight or struggle against; to debate *Some people* contend *that no boxer past or present would have been able to contend with Muhammad Ali for boxing's World Heavyweight Championship.* Synonyms: **combat, compete, argue, assert**
CONTENTIOUS	eager to quarrel *The* contentious *gentleman angrily ridiculed whatever anyone said.* Synonyms: **quarrelsome, cantankerous, feisty, combative, irascible, pugnacious**
CONVENE	to assemble or meet *The members of the board* convene *at least once a week.* Synonyms: **gather, assemble, meet**
CONVENTIONAL	established or approved by general usage Conventional *wisdom today says that a good job requires a college education.* Synonyms: **customary, well-established, habitual**
COPIOUS	abundant, large in number or quantity, plentiful *The hostess had prepared* copious *amounts of food.* Synonyms: **abundant, plentiful, profuse**

WORD	DEFINITION, CONTEXT, SYNONYMS
COUNTENANCE	(n) face or facial expression, or the general appearance or behavior of something or someone *Jeremy felt quite unsettled about the new Music Appreciation instructor; she seemed to have an evil* countenance. Synonyms: **face, aspect, appearance, bearing, demeanor, air, visage** (v) to approve or support *When Dorothy and Irene started their nightly pillow fight, the babysitter warned them, "I will not* countenance *such behavior."* Synonyms: **sanction, approve, endorse, bless, favor, encourage, condone**
COUPLET	unit of poetry with two rhyming lines *"Rub a dub, dub/Three men in a tub" is an example of a* couplet.
COURIER	person who carries messages, news, or information *The* courier *will deliver the document.* Synonyms: **messenger, runner, carrier**
CUE	hint or guiding suggestion *My mother cleared her throat loudly, which was my* cue *to be quiet and let her speak.* Synonyms: **hint, prompt, signal**
CURVATURE	state of being curved *Someone with* curvature *of the spine usually doesn't stand up straight.* Synonyms: **arc, arch, bow**
DAWDLE	to waste time with idle lingering *If you* dawdle *on your way to school, you'll be late.* Synonyms: **delay, linger, dally**
DEADLOCK	standoff caused by opposition of two conflicting forces *Despite days of debate, the legislature remained at a* deadlock *with 50 votes "yea" and 50 votes "nay".'* Synonyms: **stalemate, standoff, standstill**
DEARTH	scarcity, lack *The* dearth *of supplies in our city made it difficult to hold out for long against the attack of the aliens.* Synonyms: **shortage, lack, scarcity**
DEBRIS	charred or spoiled remains of something that has been destroyed *Scavengers searched for valuables amid the* debris. Synonyms: **trash, rubbish, wreckage, remains**

WORD	DEFINITION, CONTEXT, SYNONYMS
DECADE	period of ten years *The 1960s are known as the* decade *of protest.*
DECEIT	deception or tricky falseness *Morgan Le Fay, the sorceress, used spells and* deceit *to lure Merlin away from Camelot.* Synonyms: **dishonesty, fraudulence, deception, trickery**
DECEIVE	to delude or mislead *A liar often will try to* deceive *you by not telling the truth.* Synonyms: **mislead, delude, trick, dupe, lie**
DECLAMATION	exercise in speech giving; attack or protest *The candidate made a* declamation *against the new tax law.* Synonyms: **long speech, harangue**
DEFICIENT	defective, insufficient, or inadequate *Failing to study will make you* deficient *in your readiness for the test.* Synonyms: **inadequate, defective, insufficient, failing, lacking**
DEHYDRATE	to remove water from *Too much time in the sun will* dehydrate *you.* Synonyms: **dry out, parch**
DEJECTED	depressed, sad *He was too ambitious to become* dejected *by a temporary setback.* Synonyms: **saddened, depressed, discouraged, disheartened**
DELUDE	to deceive, to mislead *After three hours of pouring rain, we stopped* deluding *ourselves that the picnic could go on.* Synonyms: **deceive, dupe, hoax, trick**
DELUGE	(n) flood, large overflowing of water; too much of anything *The president's veto of the housing bill brought a* deluge *of angry calls and letters from people all over America.* Synonyms: **flood, overflow, inundation, torrent** (v) to overflow, to inundate, to flood *The actor was* deluged *with fan mail.* Synonyms: **inundate, engulf, flood, overwhelm**
DEMOTE	to reduce to a lower grade or class *The army will* demote *any soldier who disobeys orders.* Synonyms: **downgrade**

WORD	DEFINITION, CONTEXT, SYNONYMS
DEPLORE	to regard as deeply regrettable and hateful *"I simply* deplore *your table manners," she told him, as he stuck his head into the bowl to lick the last of the oatmeal.* Synonyms: **regret, lament, bemoan, bewail, mourn, denounce, condemn, protest, oppose, despise, loathe, abominate**
DESOLATION	condition of being deserted and destroyed *The terrible flood, which destroyed all the buildings and caused everyone to flee, left only* desolation *in its path.* Synonyms: **barrenness, desertion, bleakness**
DESPICABLE	deserving contempt *Stealing from poor people is* despicable. *In fact, stealing from anyone is* despicable. Synonyms: **hateful, contemptible, base, mean, vile, detestable, depraved**
DESPONDENT	in a state of depression *Mrs. Baker was* despondent *after her husband's death.* Synonyms: **depressed, morose, gloomy, sad, brooding, desolate, forlorn, woeful, mournful, dejected**
DESTITUTE	bereft (of something), without or left without (something); poor Destitute *of friends, Charlotte wandered the streets alone.* Synonyms: **bereft, devoid, lacking; poor, impoverished**
DEVASTATE	to lay waste, make desolate; to overwhelm *News of the death of his beloved wife will* devastate *him.* Synonyms: **ruin, wreck**
DEVOTEE	someone passionately devoted *The opera* devotee *didn't mind standing on line for hours to get a ticket.* Synonym: **enthusiast, fan, admirer**
DEVOUT	deeply religious *Priests and nuns are known to be* devout *people.* Synonyms: **pious, religious, reverent**
DEXTERITY	skill in using the hands or body, agility; cleverness *The gymnast who won the contest demonstrated the highest level of* dexterity *of all the competitors. She was the only one who didn't fall off the balance beam.* Synonyms: **skill, agility**

WORD	DEFINITION, CONTEXT, SYNONYMS
DIMINISH	to become or to make smaller in size, number, or degree *He was once such a beautiful actor, but now his beauty has greatly* diminished! *As has his bank account.* Synonyms: **decrease, lessen, dwindle, shrink, contract, decline, subside, wane, fade, recede, weaken, moderate**
DIN	loud, confused noise *The* din *in the cafeteria made conversation difficult.* Synonyms: **noise, uproar, clamor**
DINGY	dark or drab in color; dirty, shabby, squalid *He lived alone in a depressing,* dingy *apartment.* Synonyms: **dirty, filthy, shabby, dark**
DIPLOMATIC	tactful; skilled in the art of conducting negotiations and other relations between nations *Our host had a very* diplomatic *nature, which enabled her to bring together people who disagreed strongly on many points.* Synonyms: **polite, tactful**
DISCLAIM	to deny ownership of or association with *Francine's statement was so silly that she later* disclaimed *it, pretending that it had been made by someone who looked exactly like her.* Synonyms: **repudiate, reject, disown, disavow, renounce**
DISCURSIVE	covering a wide area or digressing from a topic *The professor, who was known for his* discursive *speaking style, covered everything from armadillos to zebras in his zoology lecture.* Synonyms: **digressive, rambling**
DISMAL	causing gloom; cheerless *Our team made a* dismal *showing in the play-offs; we lost every game.* Synonyms: **miserable, dreary**
DISPUTE	(n) argument or quarrel *The* dispute *between the United States and the Soviet Union arose in part as a result of disagreement over the occupation of Berlin.* Synonyms: **argument, disagreement** (v) to argue or quarrel *There was no way to* dispute *the DNA evidence.* Synonyms: **argue, disagree with**

WORD	DEFINITION, CONTEXT, SYNONYMS
DISSEMINATE	to scatter or spread widely *The Internet* disseminates *information rapidly, so events get reported all over the world shortly after they happen.* Synonyms: **spread (an idea or a message), broadcast, disperse**
DIVERT	(1) to change the course of *Emergency crews tried to* divert *the flood waters by building a wall of sandbags across the road.* Synonyms: **deflect, reroute, turn, detour** (2) to draw someone's attention by amusing them *While their mother napped, Dad* diverted *the twins by playing hide-and-seek.* Synonyms: **amuse, entertain, distract**
DOFF	to remove or take off, as clothing *Baseball players usually* doff *their hats during the National Anthem.*
DOGGED	persistent in effort; stubbornly tenacious *He worked steadily with a* dogged *determination to finish the difficult task.* Synonyms: **stubborn (as a bulldog), obstinate**
DOGMATIC	asserting without proof; stating opinion as if it were fact in a definite and forceful manner *The* dogmatic *professor would not listen to the students' views; she did not allow debate in class.* Synonyms: **absolute, opinionated, dictatorial, authoritative, arrogant**
DOZE	to nap or sleep lightly *I was so tired from working all night that I kept* dozing *off during the next day.* Synonyms: **nap, sleep**
DUNGEON	underground room in fortress often used to keep prisoners *Henry VIII ordered that Anne Boleyn be kept in the* dungeon *of the Tower of London until she was beheaded.* Synonyms: **vault, cellar**
EBULLIENT	overflowing with fervor, enthusiasm, or excitement; high-spirited *The* ebullient *child exhausted the babysitter, who lacked the energy needed to keep up with her.* Synonyms: **bubbling, enthusiastic, exuberant**

WORD	DEFINITION, CONTEXT, SYNONYMS
ECCENTRIC	(n) person who differs from the accepted norms in an odd way *The old* eccentric *was given to burning hundred-dollar bills.* Synonyms: **freak, oddball, weirdo, nonconformist** (adj) *deviating from accepted conduct* *Her* eccentric *behavior began to worry her close friends.* Synonyms: **odd, unorthodox, unconventional, offbeat**
ECSTATIC	deliriously overjoyed *Mortimer was* ecstatic *when he learned of his 2400 SAT scores.* Synonyms: **delighted, overjoyed, euphoric**
EDDY	small whirlpool or any similar current Eddies *can be in the air or water. When water gets pulled down a drain, it forms a small whirlpool, or an* eddy. Synonyms: **swirling water, whirlpool**
EFFECT	(n) result, impression *The* effect *of the new policy will not be known for some time, as it often takes several years for new programs to have a noticeable impact.* Synonyms: **result, impression** (v) *to produce, make or bring about* *We are willing to make any sacrifice in order to* effect *lasting change for the better.* Synonyms: **produce, cause, bring about**
ELUSIVE	hard to find or express *The* elusive *nature of the platypus makes it difficult to spot platypus in the wild. Their ugliness makes it unpleasant.* Synonyms: **slippery, evasive**
EMBELLISH	to add detail, make more complicated *Sanjev's short story is too short: it needs to be* embellished *with more details about life among penguins.* Synonyms: **elaborate, expand, ornament**
EMINENT	distinguished, high in rank or station *They were amazed that such an* eminent *scholar could have made such an obvious error.* Synonyms: **prominent, well-known, famous, distinguished, noteworthy**
EMULATE	to imitate or copy *Hundreds of writers have* emulated *Stephen King, but the result is usually a poor imitation.* Synonyms: **imitate, simulate, copy, follow**

WORD	DEFINITION, CONTEXT, SYNONYMS
ENACT	to make into law *The government wishes to* enact *the new law in January.* Synonyms: **pass (a law), decree, act out**
ENCOMPASS	to form a circle or a ring around *In New York City, Manhattan is an island, so it is completely* encompassed *by water.* Synonyms: **encircle, circumscribe**
ENDORSE	to approve, sustain, support *The principal refused to* endorse *the plan to put a video arcade in the cafeteria.* Synonyms: **accept, approve, authorize, accredit, encourage, advocate, favor, support**
ENIGMA	mystery or riddle *The source of the mysterious hole remained an* enigma. Synonyms: **mystery, riddle, puzzle**
ENIGMATIC	unexplainable, mysterious *The students found the new history teacher to be* enigmatic; *none of them could figure out what he was thinking.* Synonyms: **mysterious, unexplainable, inexplicable, incomprehensible, strange, puzzling, baffling, bewildering, perplexing, cryptic**
ENSNARE	to capture in, or involve, as in a snare *The investigators managed to* ensnare *the corrupt official when they offered him a bribe that he accepted.* Synonyms: **trap**
ENTICE	to lure or attract by feeding desires *Millions of dollars couldn't* entice *Michael Jordan to play basketball in Europe.* Synonyms: **tempt, lure, attract**
ENTOURAGE	group of followers, attendants, or assistants *The movie star was always followed around by an* entourage *of flunkies and assistants.* Synonyms: **group, retinue, coterie**
ERA	period of time *The invention of the atomic bomb marked the beginning of a new* era *in warfare.* Synonyms: **period (of time), age, epoch**

WORD	DEFINITION, CONTEXT, SYNONYMS
ERR	to make a mistake (as in error) *To err is human; we have all made mistakes.* Synonyms: **sin**
ERUDITE	knowledgeable and learned *We were not surprised to read the praises of Mario's history of ancient Greece, for we had expected an* erudite *work from him.* Synonyms: **wise, learned, knowledgeable, informed**
ESSENTIAL	of the innermost nature of something; basic, fundamental; of great importance *Eating vegetables is* essential *to your well-being.* Synonyms: **basic, central, fundamental, important, crucial, necessary, urgent**
ETIQUETTE	code of social behavior *Some people think that* etiquette *forbids eating with your elbows on the table.* Synonyms: **manners, propriety, decorum**
EVACUATE	to empty out, remove, or withdraw *The National Guard had to* evacuate *thousands of people following the catastrophe.* Synonyms: **expel, empty, vacate, remove**
EXOTIC	of foreign origin or character; strange, exciting *The atmosphere of the restaurant was* exotic, *but the food was pedestrian.* Synonyms: **foreign, alien, unfamiliar**
EXPAND	to make greater, broader, larger, or more detailed *Friedrich now sells only scary plastic fangs, but he plans to* expand *his business to include rubber vampire bats with glowing eyes.* Synonyms: **enlarge, increase, augment, extend, broaden, widen, stretch, spread, swell, inflate, dilate, bloat**
EXPUNGE	to delete or omit completely *The censor wanted to* expunge *all parts of Joyce's* Ulysses *he thought were obscene.* Synonyms: **erase, obliterate, strike out**
EXTRACTION	process of removal or something removed *My toothache meant I had to undergo the* extraction *of my wisdom teeth.* Synonyms: **removal**

WORD	DEFINITION, CONTEXT, SYNONYMS
EXTRICATE	to release from difficulty or an entanglement *The fly was unable to* extricate *itself from the flypaper.* Synonyms: **disengage, release, withdraw**
EXTROVERTED	outgoing or interested in people *An* extrovert *wouldn't think twice about going to a party of strangers.* Synonyms: **outgoing, gregarious**
FANATIC	someone with excessive enthusiasm, especially in politics or religion *Unable to listen to differing opinions, the* fanatic *politician screamed at his opponent and ran out of the debate.* Synonyms: **zealous**
FATAL	causing, or capable of causing, death or ruin *The race car driver suffered a* fatal *accident when his car hit a patch of oil on the roadway.* Synonyms: **lethal, deadly, killing, mortal, malignant**
FATIGUE	(v) to exhaust the strength of *The energetic baby* fatigued *me.* Synonyms: **tire out, weary, enervate** (n) weariness, tiredness from exertion *The recruits suffered from* fatigue *after the twenty-mile march.* Synonyms: **exhaustion, weariness**
FAUNA	animals of a given area *Darwin studied the* fauna *of the Galapagos Islands.* Synonyms: **animals, creatures, beasts**
FELICITY	happiness, bliss *She was so good, she deserved nothing but* felicity *her whole life.* Synonyms: **happiness, contentment, bliss**
FEROCIOUS	savage and fierce Ferocious *Arctic wolves will hunt and kill much larger animals in pursuit of food.* Synonyms: **fierce**
FERVENT	showing great warmth, intensity, feeling, enthusiasm; hot, burning, glowing *I am a* fervent *admirer of that author's works; I think she is a genius.* Synonyms: **warm, eager, enthusiastic**
FICKLE	easily changeable, especially in emotions *She earned a reputation for being a* fickle *customer; she always changed her order at least twice.* Synonyms: **inconstant**

WORD	DEFINITION, CONTEXT, SYNONYMS
FIDELITY	faithfulness to duties; truthfulness *A traitor is someone whose* fidelity *is questioned.* Synonyms: **loyalty, allegiance, faithfulness, devotion, truthfulness, accuracy**
FINALE	the final part of some entertainment, often music *The* finale *of the* 1812 Overture *is often accompanied by fireworks.* Synonyms: **end, finish, conclusion, wind-up**
FLAGRANT	outrageously glaring, noticeable, or evident; notorious, scandalous *His* flagrant *disregard for the rules has resulted in his dismissal from the job.* Synonyms: **obvious, glaring**
FLIPPANT	not serious, playful; irreverent *John was* flippant *to the teacher, so she sent him to the principal's office* Synonyms: **frivolous, flip, playful**
FLOW	to move along in a stream or like a stream; to proceed continuously (as in a computer flowchart, which shows how a program flows) *People* flowed *out of the crowded department store through the main doors.* Synonyms: **run, stream** (like water)
FORETELL	to predict the future *Some prophets claim to* foretell *the future.* Synonyms: **forecast, prophesy, auger**
FORMIDABLE	able to inspire awe or wonder because of outstanding power, size, etc. *The steep face of rock we were directed to climb was indeed* formidable. Synonyms: **impressive, awe-inspiring, impregnable, invincible**
FOUNDATION	basis or groundwork of anything, whether a building or idea *The claim that the sun revolves around the earth has no* foundation, *because scientific evidence disproves this claim.* Synonyms: **bottom, groundwork, basis**
FRAGILE	easily broken, or damaged *The Ming dynasty porcelain vase was* fragile *and needed to be handled carefully* Synonyms: **breakable, frail, brittle, delicate**

WORD	DEFINITION, CONTEXT, SYNONYMS
FREQUENT	(adj) happening or occurring at short intervals *He travels so much he's a member of five* frequent *flyer plans.* Synonyms: **repeated, regular, habitual, common** (v) to visit often *My friend loves antique hunting and frequents the local antique shops.*
FUTILE	ineffective, useless; unimportant *Our attempt to reach the shore before the storm was* futile; *the wind blew us back into the middle of the lake.* Synonyms: **useless, hopeless, pointless**
GARRULOUS	talkative and likely to chatter *My* garrulous *friend often talks on the telephone for hours at a time.* Synonyms: **talkative, loquacious**
GERMINATE	to bud or sprout *Three weeks after planting, the seeds will* germinate. Synonyms: **sprout, grow**
GLEE	joy, pleasure, happiness *The child was filled with* glee *at the sight of so many presents.* Synonyms: **joy, elation**
GLIB	able to speak profusely; having a ready flow of words (It often implies lying or deceit.) *The politician was a* glib *speaker.* Synonyms: **flip, fluent, verbose, smooth, smug**
GREGARIOUS	fond of company *For the* gregarious *person, dormitory life is a pleasure.* Synonyms: **sociable, companionable, amiable, convivial**
GROTESQUE	odd or unnatural in some way *The minotaur is a* grotesque *creature out of mythology: part man and part bull.* Synonyms: **bizarre, outlandish, ugly**
GROVEL	to humble oneself, to beg *The dog* groveled *at his owner's feet.* Synonyms: **crawl, beg**
GRUESOME	grisly, horrible *The horror film was filled with* gruesome *scenes.* Synonyms: **frightful, shocking, ghastly**
HALLOWED	regarded as holy; sacred *The Constitution is a* hallowed *document in the United States.* Synonyms: **holy, sacred**

WORD	DEFINITION, CONTEXT, SYNONYMS
HARBINGER	omen, precursor, forerunner *The groundhog's appearance on February 2 is a* harbinger *of spring.* Synonyms: **precursor, forerunner, omen, messenger**
HARSH	stern or cruel; physically uncomfortable; unpleasant to the ear Harsh *words were exchanged during their argument.* Synonyms: **rough, strict, severe**
HASTY	done quickly (often too quickly); rushed, sloppy *Henry was too* hasty *in completing his research paper, and forgot to put his name on it.* Synonyms: **rushed, sloppy, shoddy, careless**
HEED	(n) careful attention, notice, observation *Pay* heed *to his warnings about that place; he's been there enough times to know the dangers.* Synonyms: **attention** (v) to listen to and obey *The naughty children did not* heed *their mothers rules.* Synonyms: **listen to, obey**
HERBIVOROUS	feeding on plants *A cow is an* herbivorous *animal.* Synonyms: **plant eating**
HETEROGENEOUS	not uniform; made up of different parts that remain separate. (Its opposite is *homogeneous.*) *The United Nations is a* heterogeneous *body.* Synonyms: **mixed, unlike, diverse, dissimilar, various**
HEXAGON	polygon having six sides *A* hexagon *has six sides, and an octagon has eight.*
HIBERNATE	to spend the winter in a sleeplike, dormant state *During winter, bears* hibernate *in caves.* Synonyms: **sleep**
HIVE	structure where bees live *My friend Les is so interested in bees that he'll watch them going into and out of one of their* hives *for hours.*
HORRID	something that causes horror, or is at least pretty bad *The weather has been just* horrid*; we've had three storms in a week.* Synonyms: **dreadful, horrible, shocking**
HOVEL	small, miserable shack *In Charles Dickens's novels poor people often live in terrible, dirty* hovels. Synonyms: **shack, shanty**

WORD	DEFINITION, CONTEXT, SYNONYMS
HUMID	moist or damp *It is so* humid *in the jungle that it is advisable to wear light, loose clothing.* Synonyms: **moist, damp, sultry**
IGNITE	(literally) to set on fire; (figuratively) to stir emotionally (light a fire under someone) (1) *If you* ignite *that match, you might burn the whole house down.* (2) *Through his speaking ability, the speaker was able to ignite the people who attended his speeches.* Synonyms: **light, kindle, inflame, rouse, excite, agitate, stir, provoke, prod, inspire**
ILLITERACY	inability to read and write *If everyone learned how to read and write,* illiteracy *wouldn't be a problem.*
IMMACULATE	spotless; free from error *After I cleaned my apartment for hours, it was finally* immaculate. Synonyms: **errorless, faultless, unblemished, impeccable**
IMMINENT	about to happen, on the verge of occurring *Joan was becoming nervous about her* imminent *wedding.* Synonyms: **impending, approaching, near**
IMMORTAL	undying *Someone who never grows old and never dies is* immortal. Synonyms: **undying, eternal**
IMPASSE	(1) road having no exit *A rock slide produced an* impasse, *so we could proceed no further on the road.* (2) a dilemma with no solution *The meeting was at an* impasse *because neither side was willing to compromise.* Synonyms: **deadlock, standoff, stalemate, standstill**
IMPERVIOUS	incapable of being penetrated; unable to be influenced *Superman is* impervious *to bullets.* Synonyms: **impenetrable**
IMPIOUS	lacking piety or respect for religion Synonyms: **irreverent, sacrilegious**

WORD	DEFINITION, CONTEXT, SYNONYMS
IMPLY	to suggest without stating directly *Although Jane did not state that she loved Mr. Rochester, it was clearly* implied *in her look.* Synonyms: **hint, suggest, intimate**
INADVERTENT	unintentional *I wrote my paper in such a hurry that I made many* inadvertent *errors.* Synonyms: **accidental, unintentional**
INCENTIVE	motivation or drive to do a particular task or to go in a given direction *His father's encouragement gave him the* incentive *to try again.* Synonyms: **motive, inducement, stimulus**
INCREDULOUS	not believing *I was* incredulous *about Ismael's wild fishing story about "the one that got away."* Synonyms: **skeptical, disbelieving**
INDICATE	to point out or make known with a good degree of certainty *Recent polls* indicate *that the Democrats will probably be victorious.* Synonyms: **disclose, show, reveal, imply, signify**
INERT	having no power to move or act; resisting motion or action *In the heat of the desert afternoon, lizards are* inert. Synonyms: **sluggish, passive, inactive, dormant, lethargic, lifeless**
INFECTIOUS	able to be passed from one person to another (such as an infection); contagious *Her laughter was* infectious, *and soon we were all laughing.* Synonyms: **catching, contagious**
INGENIOUS	possessing or displaying great creativity and resourcefulness *Luther found an* ingenious *way to solve the math problem.* Synonyms: **brilliant, inspired, imaginative, shrewd, crafty, cunning, resourceful**
INGENUITY	inventive skill or cleverness *Use your* ingenuity *to come up with a new solution to the problem.* Synonyms: **creativity, cleverness, inventiveness**
INHABIT	to reside or live in *Arboreal creatures, such as monkeys,* inhabit *the trees.* Synonyms: **live, occupy, reside, dwell, stay**
INNATE	present at birth *The plan was doomed from the start; there was an* innate *problem with it.* Synonyms: **natural, inborn, inherent, instinctive**

WORD	DEFINITION, CONTEXT, SYNONYMS
INNOCENT	pure, not guilty; someone with the simplicity of a baby *Those accused of practicing witchcraft in Salem were clearly* innocent *of any such act.* Synonyms: **pure, harmless, guiltless, naïve, chaste**
INSINUATION	devious hint or sly suggestion made to cause suspicion or doubts *During the last election, the* insinuation *that the congressman had taken kickbacks cost him thousands of votes.* Synonyms: **hint, suggestion, reference, implication**
INSOMNIA	inability to fall sleep *No matter how tired I am, I continue to suffer from* insomnia. Synonyms: **sleeplessness**
INSURGENT	(n) rebel *When secrets were being leaked to the enemy, we realized we had an* insurgent *among our ranks.* Synonyms: **rebel, mole** (adj) rising in revolt, starting a revolution *The* insurgent *crew staged a mutiny and threw the captain overboard.* Synonyms: **rebellious, mutinous**
IRATE	full of anger, wrathful, incensed *He was* irate *at being wrongly accused of the crime.* Synonyms: **angry, indignant, infuriated, enraged**
JEER	(n) taunting remark *The* jeers *of the crowd were enough to make the performers run off stage crying.* Synonyms: **gibe, taunt** (v) to mock in an abusive way *My brother loved to* jeer *at me because he knew how much it hurt my feelings.* Synonyms: **ridicule, mock, scoff**
JUBILANT	feeling joy or happiness *We were* jubilant *after our victory in the state championships.* Synonyms: **exultant, gleeful, joyful, ecstatic**
JUDICIOUS	having wise judgment *The wise and distinguished judge was well-known for having a* judicious *temperament.* Synonyms: **wise, sage, sagacious**

WORD	DEFINITION, CONTEXT, SYNONYMS
KINETIC	relating to motion *A* kinetic *sculpture is one that moves.* Synonyms: **animated, energetic, spirited, moving**
LAGOON	shallow body of water connected to a much larger one, as a lake or sea *The pirates anchored their ship offshore and rowed into the* lagoon, *where they went ashore.* Synonyms: **inlet, pool**
LENIENT	merciful, not strict *When the commissioner only fined the pitcher fifty dollars for throwing a baseball at a batter, many fans thought the punishment was too* lenient. Synonyms: **merciful, indulgent**
LETHARGY	drowsiness, tiredness, inability to do anything much *A feeling of* lethargy *came over me, and I wanted nothing more than a nice long nap.* Synonyms: **sluggishness, fatigue**
LIMBER	bending and moving easily *The gymnast warmed up for thirty minutes so that she would be* limber *before her routine.* Synonyms: **agile, supple**
LUNGE	to thrust something forward *The toboggan* lunged *forward at the point where the slope became quite steep.* Synonyms: **thrust, plunge**
MAGNANIMOUS	having a great or noble spirit, acting generously, patiently, or kindly *Although at first he seemed cold, Uncle Frank turned out to be a very* magnanimous *fellow.* Synonyms: **big-hearted, generous, noble, princely, forgiving, patient, tolerant, indulgent, ungrudging, unresentful**
MALFUNCTION	(n) an instance of failing to function *The engine* malfunction *prevented the racer from making it to the finish line.* Synonyms: **failure** (v) to fail to function *When my cell phone* malfunctioned, *I had to make all my calls from the land line.* Synonyms: **fail**

WORD	DEFINITION, CONTEXT, SYNONYMS
MALLEABLE	can be molded or shaped *Gold is so* malleable *that it can be beaten into a thin foil.* Synonyms: **soft, flexible, yielding**
MAR	to damage something and make it imperfect *Telephone poles* mar *the beauty of the countryside.* Synonyms: **deform, impair, spoil, disfigure, damage**
MARVEL	(n) amazing thing; something astonishing or marvelous *It was a* marvel *that they survived the crash.* Synonyms: **miracle, prodigy, wonder** (v) to be surprised or full of wonder I marvel *at your ability to remain calm.* Synonyms: **wonder**
MEAGER	very small or insufficient *He rented an expensive apartment and dined at fine restaurants, but he earned a* meager *wage and soon ran out of money.* Synonyms: **slight, trifling, skimpy, puny, scant, inadequate, insufficient, insubstantial**
MEEK	humble and submissive *People who are too* meek *won't stand up for themselves.* Synonyms: **passive, unassertive, docile, compliant**
MELANCHOLY	very sad or depressing *The rainy weather made James feel* melancholy. Synonyms: **gloomy, mournful, somber**
METEOROLOGIST	scientist dealing with weather and weather conditions *Although the* meteorologist *predicted a heat wave, the temperature remained below freezing.*
MIMIC	imitate, copy (not always in a complimentary way) *Mary got in trouble for* mimicking *the teacher.* Synonyms: **mock, impersonate, simulate, counterfeit**
MINUSCULE	tiny, miniature *Dave needed a magnifying glass to read the* minuscule *print on the lease.* Synonyms: **microscopic, minute**

WORD	DEFINITION, CONTEXT, SYNONYMS
MISBEGOTTEN	poorly conceived, poorly planned, based on false assumptions or false reasoning *It came as no surprise when Fred's* misbegotten *scheme proved an utter failure.* Synonyms: **illegitimate, ill-conceived**
MOURN	feel sad for, regret *The family gathered to* mourn *for the dead.* Synonyms: **lament, grieve**
MURKY	dark, dim *Jill groped her way down the* murky *hallway.* Synonyms: **obscure, gloomy**
NAUSEOUS	sickening, makes you feel sick, or turns your stomach *The cook mixed skim milk with green eels and produced a concoction that was truly* nauseous. Synonyms: **revolting, disgusting, nauseating**
NEBULOUS	hazy, not well-defined *During the campaign, the candidate promised to fight crime. But when reporters asked for details, his plan was* nebulous*—he could not say whether he would hire more police or support longer jail sentences.* Synonyms: **hazy, cloudy, ill-defined, unclear, shapeless, vague, unspecific**
NIMBLE	quick and agile in movement or thought *A* nimble *athlete is a well-coordinated one.* Synonyms: **agile, active, quick, clever, cunning**
NOMAD	someone who has no permanent home and wanders *The Berbers are a tribe of* nomads *who travel from place to place searching for grassland for their herds.* Synonyms: **wanderer, vagrant**
NOTIFY	to tell, let know, give notice *The landlord failed to* notify *the tenants of the planned demolition of the building.* Synonyms: **tell, inform, apprise**
OBESE	very fat *Some* obese *people suffer from anxiety-induced overeating.* Synonyms: **fat, corpulent, portly**

WORD	DEFINITION, CONTEXT, SYNONYMS
OBNOXIOUS	offensive and very disagreeable *The last time I went to the movies, an* obnoxious *person sitting beside me talked loudly during the entire movie.* Synonyms: **offensive, repugnant, repellant**
OBSCURE	(adj) hard to see; unknown, uncertain *The references the author made were so* obscure*, I don't think half the readers knew what he was talking about.* Synonyms: **vague, unclear, dubious** (v) to hide or make difficult to find *Because he didn't want to go to jail, he tried to* obscure *the fact that he had been embezzling money for years.* Synonyms: **confuse, becloud**
OBSERVATION	(1) examination *Close* observation *of Arnold led Anne to believe that he was hiding something.* Synonyms: **attention, watching** (2) remark, comment *Damon amused the class with his witty* observation *about the teacher's methods.* Synonyms: **pronouncement, opinion**
OBSOLETE	no longer in use; discarded or outmoded *It's as* obsolete *as a telephone modem.* Synonyms: **outdated, passé, old-fashioned**
OBSTINATE	stubborn *Hal's mother tried to get him to eat his spinach, but he remained* obstinate. Synonyms: **mulish, dogged**
OBSTRUCT	to get in the way of; to block; to hamper *He removed his hat so as not to* obstruct *another's view of the stage.* Synonyms: **block, check, clog, impede**
OBTUSE	not acute; someone who is not smart; thick, dull *Alfred was too* obtuse *to realize that the sum of the angles of a triangle is 180 degrees.* Synonyms: **slow, stupid**

WORD	DEFINITION, CONTEXT, SYNONYMS
OLFACTORY	relating to the sense of smell *In human beings,* olfactory *sensations are perceived with the nose.*
OMINOUS	threatening, menacing, having the character of an evil omen *The sky filled with* ominous *dark clouds before the storm.* Synonyms: **foreboding**
OPPORTUNE	appropriate to time or circumstances: timely, lucky *Dalbert's investment in plastics, made just before the demand for plastics began to rise, was* opportune. Synonyms: **timely, appropriate, lucky**
OPTION	choice, selection, preference *Donna carefully considered every* option *before making her final decision.* Synonyms: **alternative, election**
ORBIT	(v) to move around some object, as a planet; to circle *The moon* orbits *the earth, which in turn* orbits *the sun.* Synonyms: **circle, revolve, circuit** (n) the actual route the thing takes when it goes around the other thing, as in the orbit of the moon around the earth *The German shepherd dog approached the intruder cautiously, circled him and sniffed, made two more* orbits, *and then walked away.* Synonyms: **circuit, revolution**
ORCHID	purple (as in the flower) *The vice principal turned* orchid *with rage.* Synonyms: **lavender**
OSTENTATIOUS	pretentious and flashy *Some think Donald Trump's Taj Mahal casino, which he proudly calls the Eighth Wonder of the World, is really an* ostentatious *display of wealth and poor taste.* Synonyms: **conspicuous, flashy, flamboyant, showy**
PALATABLE	good tasting *Her cooking is quite* palatable. Synonyms: **savory, agreeable, appetizing, delicious, acceptable**

WORD	DEFINITION, CONTEXT, SYNONYMS
PARADOX	contradiction, something that doesn't fit; something that shouldn't be true because it seems to offend common sense, yet is true anyway *The* paradox *of government is that the person who most desires power is the person who least deserves it.* Synonyms: **contradiction**
PASSIVE	not active; someone who lets things happen rather than himself taking action *Ned portrayed himself as the* passive *victim of external forces.* Synonyms: **submissive**
PEDDLE	sell (although usually used in a somewhat bad way) *Bill got a job going door to door to* peddle *vacuum cleaners.* Synonyms: **hawk, vend**
PEDESTRIAN	(adj) common, everyday, usual *The critics called the new restaurant's food* pedestrian; *it never had many customers and eventually closed.* Synonyms: **plodding, prosaic, commonplace, ordinary, plain, mundane, humdrum, trite, banal, drab, colorless, boring, barren, unimaginative, uninspired, undistinguished, unremarkable, unexceptional** (n) one who does not ride but walks *With the way the taxis speed, it can be dangerous to be a* pedestrian *in New York. Of course, it's dangerous to be in the cab too, which leaves little choice but to stay home in bed.* Synonyms: **walker, hiker, stroller**
PERJURY	making deliberately false statements when under oath *Mr. Mason accused the witness of* perjury. Synonyms: **falsehood, fraud, lies**
PERSEVERE	to continue in some course of action despite setbacks and opposition *Although at first the problems looked difficult, Wendy* persevered *and found that she could answer almost all of them.* Synonyms: **continue, struggle, endure, persist**
PETRIFY	(literally) to turn to stone; (figuratively) to paralyze with fear or with surprise *The movie is so frightening that it would* petrify *even the bravest viewer.* Synonyms: **shock, stun, stiffen, paralyze, fossilize**

WORD	DEFINITION, CONTEXT, SYNONYMS
PIOUS	religiously devout or moral *Saul, a* pious *man, walks, to the synagogue on the Sabbath and prays daily.* Synonyms: **devout, religious, God-fearing, reverent, moral, upstanding, scrupulous**
PLAGIARISM	copying of someone else's work and claiming it as your own *The notable scientist lost his job when his* plagiarism *was revealed; years before, he had copied a research paper from a magazine.* Synonyms: **copying, stealing**
PLAUSIBLE	seeming to be true *Joachim's excuse for lateness to class sounded* plausible *at the time, but I later learned that it had been a lie.* Synonyms: **credible, believable, likely, probable, conceivable**
POMPOUS	characterized by stiff, unnatural formality *Gerald began his speech to the class with a* pompous *quote from Julius Caesar.* Synonyms: **stuffy, stiff, affected, mannered, unnatural, pretentious, self-important, conceited**
PROCRASTINATE	to postpone; to put something off to a later time *Don't* procrastinate; *do your homework now.* Synonyms: **delay, postpone, defer**
PROFOUND	deep, wise, serious *Both the* Book of Ecclesiastes *and the* Tao Te Ching *contain* profound *observations about human life.* Synonyms: **wise, deep, sagacious**
PROLIFIC	producing great amounts; fertile *Stephen King, a* prolific *writer, seems to write new books as fast as they are published.* Synonyms: **productive, fertile**
PROPEL	to move, make something go forward *An ill-timed push on the gas pedal* propelled *the car through the plate glass window of the dealership.* Synonyms: **compel, project, drive**

WORD	DEFINITION, CONTEXT, SYNONYMS
PROPHESY	to predict the future using divine guidance *The ancient Greek oracles at Delphi were supposed to be able to* prophesy *the future.* Synonyms: **predict, foretell, forecast, auger**
PUNGENT	sharp, flavorful (sometimes too flavorful) *The soup was so* pungent *that it brought tears to Alice's eyes.* Synonyms: **peppery, hot, piquant, biting, acrid**
PURSUE	to chase, go after *The cat* pursued *the squirrel up the tree.* Synonyms: **trail, tail, dog, follow**
QUELL	to quiet something raucous (often a rebellion); crush, defeat, conquer *The dictator dispatched troops to* quell *the rebellion.* Synonyms: **quash, overpower, overcome, quench, suppress**
QUENCH	to satisfy a need or desire *After coming in from the desert, Ezra needed gallons of water to* quench *his thirst.* Synonyms: **satisfy, extinguish, subdue, sate**
RABBLE	large, disorderly, and easily excited mob *The* rabble *waited anxiously below the king's window for news of the tax decree.* Synonyms: **crowd, mob, multitude, horde**
RABID	(literally) afflicted with rabies, a disease of the nervous system that causes convulsions and wildly irrational behavior Rabid *animals can sometimes be identified by saliva dripping from their jaws and by frantic behavior.* (figuratively) acting fanatically or madly, as if afflicted by rabies *The first speaker was calm, but the second—a wild-eyed man advocating the destruction of all tractors—was positively* rabid. Synonyms: **fanatical, mad, crazy, irrational, wild-eyed, maniacal, lunatic, incoherent**
RANCOR	bad feeling, bitterness *Herbert was so filled with* rancor *that he could think of nothing but taking revenge on those who had humiliated him.* Synonyms: **animosity, resentment, hatred, malice, spite**

WORD	DEFINITION, CONTEXT, SYNONYMS
RANDOM	lacking order, free from order or bias *She conducted a* random *survey of garage mechanics by drawing their names from a hat.* Synonyms: **chance, haphazard, unordered, unbiased**
RANSACK	to search thoroughly and messily *Did the burglars* ransack *your entire house?* Synonyms: **plunder, pillage, search, loot, pilfer, steal**
RATIFY	to approve formally *The Senate* ratified *the treaty after only a brief debate.* Synonyms: **confirm, affirm, endorse, approve, sanction**
RAVENOUS	(literally) wildly eager to eat *The homeless man had not had a bite of food in two days and was* ravenous. (figuratively) hungry for anything *The abandoned puppy was* ravenous *for affection and tenderness.* Synonyms: **hungry, famished, voracious, starved**
RAZE	to destroy (a building, city, etc.) utterly *The house had been* razed: *Where once it had stood there was nothing but splinters and bricks.* Synonyms: **demolish, destroy, wreck, level, flatten**
RECLUSE	someone who lives far away from other people *Anthony left the city and lived as a* recluse *in the desert.* Synonyms: **hermit, loner**
RECUR	to return; to occur again *The problem is bound to* recur *if you don't solve it now.* Synonyms: **return, repeat**
REEK	(literally) giving off a strong, offensive odor; strong smell *Boy! Something really* reeks *in here. Did you bring a dead skunk with you or something?* Synonyms: **stink** (figuratively) to be pervaded by something unpleasant *The legislature, with its history of bribery and cronyism,* reeked *of corruption.*
REFRAIN	to stop or avoid doing something, quit *The librarian insisted that everyone* refrain *from making any noise.* Synonyms: **abstain, cease, desist**

WORD	DEFINITION, CONTEXT, SYNONYMS
REGAL	royal, splendid *Prince Charles was married with full* regal *ceremony.* Synonyms: **kingly, majestic**
REIGN	rule over, govern, dominate *The British monarch used to* reign *over the entire British Empire.* Synonyms: **rule, prevail**
REIMBURSE	to repay someone for their expenses *If you buy me lunch today, I'll* reimburse *you tomorrow.* Synonyms: **repay, compensate**
REINFORCE	strengthen, add to *The purpose of the homework is to* reinforce *what's taught in class.* Synonyms: **support**
REMINISCENCE	memory or act of recalling the past *The old timer's* reminiscence *of his childhood was of a time when there were no cars.* Synonyms: **collection, recall, memory, nostalgia**
RENOWNED	well-known, famous, celebrated *Having spent her whole childhood banging on things, Jane grew up to be a* renowned *drummer.* Synonyms: **famed, distinguished, notable**
REPARTEE	witty conversation, retort *As a master of* repartee, *Bob was the hit of every party he attended.* Synonyms: **banter**
REPUDIATE	to reject what one was once associated with *After Grace discovered that her friends had been spreading false rumors about her, she* repudiated *them and made new friends.* Synonyms: **disown, reject, renounce**
REPUGNANT	something gross, repulsive, or revolting *Bill liked his macaroni and cheese with jelly, a combination that many of his friends found* repugnant. Synonyms: **distasteful, objectionable, offensive**
RESIDUE	something that remains after a part is taken *The fire burned everything, leaving only a* residue *of ash and charred debris.* Synonyms: **remainder, remnant, leftover**

WORD	DEFINITION, CONTEXT, SYNONYMS
REVEAL	show, divulge, expose *Wendy cut through the frog's abdominal wall to* reveal *the internal organs.* Synonyms: **unveil, disclose**
REVEL	celebrate noisily, have a party *The whole school got together to* revel *in the football team's victory.* Synonyms: **celebrate, indulge, enjoy**
ROUT	conquer, defeat, and chase off *The renewed onslaught* routed *the enemy.* Synonyms: **overwhelm, overcome, subdue, scatter**
SATELLITE	moon, a small thing going around a bigger thing *A spy* satellite *can take pictures of the people and things that it passes above as it circles the globe.* Synonyms: **moon**
SATURATE	to fill something to the point where it can hold no more *Reading the entire encyclopedia will* saturate *your mind with facts.* Synonyms: **soak, fill, drench, permeate**
SAUCY	impudent, impertinent, flippant *She always got in trouble with her parents for her* saucy *remarks.* Synonyms: **pert, lively, rude, insolent**
SAVOR	to enjoy something with relish or delight *I* savored *every bite of my father's chocolate cream pie.* Synonyms: **taste, relish, enjoy, appreciate**
SCALD	burn with hot liquid or steam *Sharon was* scalded *when she bumped into a pot of boiling water.* Synonyms: **burn, scorch, boil**
SCARCE	rare, uncommon *Water is* scarce *in the Sahara Desert.* Synonyms: **sparse, infrequent**
SCATHING	overly critical *Walter was depressed by the* scathing *reviews that his play received.* Synonyms: **searing, crushing, harmful**

WORD	DEFINITION, CONTEXT, SYNONYMS
SCHISM	division or separation between groups of members within an organization *Because half of the student council wanted the jukebox in the cafeteria, and the other half wanted it in the library, the council suffered a* schism. Synonyms: **disunity, break, division, conflict, clash**
SCRUPULOUS	(1) acting in accordance with a strict moral code *David could not have stolen Sheila's money; he was too* scrupulous. Synonyms: **moral, upstanding, virtuous, principled, ethical** (2) thorough in the performance of a task *Roger is a* scrupulous *editor who checks every word his reporters write.* Synonyms: **careful, conscientious, thorough, diligent**
SECURE	(v) to fasten, make secure *I had* secured *my suitcase in the overhead luggage rack at the beginning of the journey.* Synonyms: **fasten, bind, clamp** (adj) well-fastened, not likely to fall or come loose *My suitcase seemed* secure *in the luggage rack. But then it fell on me.* Synonyms: **fastened, fixed, bound, safe, stable**
SEETHE	to heave or bubble from great inner turmoil, as a volcano; to boil *Immediately after learning of Roger's gossip about me, I began to boil with anger, and by the time I reached his house, I was* seething. Synonyms: **boil, bubble, steam, foam, surge, heave, swell**
SENTRY	guard, sentinel, watchman *Mitchell stood as* sentry *while the others were in the boys' room goofing off.* Synonyms: **watch, lookout**
SEQUEL	addition or result; story that continues a previous one *I hear they're making another* sequel *to the* Friday the 13th *movies.* Synonyms: **aftermath, outcome, continuation, consequence**
SHREWD	clever, keen-witted, cunning, sharp in practical affairs *He was a* shrewd *businessman and soon parlayed his meager savings into a fortune.* Synonyms: **clever, keen, astute, cunning, wily, sharp, discerning**

WORD	DEFINITION, CONTEXT, SYNONYMS
SIGNIFICANT	meaningful, important, relevant *A good detective knows that something that hardly seems worth noticing may be highly* significant. Synonyms: **consequential, momentous, weighty**
SINISTER	threatening, evil, menacing *His friendly manner concealed* sinister *designs.* Synonyms: **ominous, wicked**
SLACK	(n) lack of tautness or tension; a time of little activity or dullness *There was no wind; the sails hung* slack, *and the boat was motionless.* Synonyms: **lull, relaxation** (adj) sluggish, idle, barely moving, loose, relaxed *The* slack *atmosphere made it unlikely that anyone would work efficiently.* Synonyms: **lax, negligent, remiss, careless, inactive, slow, loose, relaxed**
SOCIABLE	friendly, companionable *Although they maintain their independence, cats are* sociable *creatures.* Synonyms: **gregarious, companionable, friendly, affable, amiable**
SOLICIT	(1) to seek (something) from another *The tennis player disagreed with the first judge's decision, so he* solicited *the opinion of a second judge.* Synonyms: **seek** (2) to make a request of someone *I* solicited *my parents for money, but they said no.* Synonyms: **request, petition, beg**
SPECIFY	to mention, name, or require specifically or exactly *The report* specified *the steps to be taken in an emergency.* Synonyms: **detail, identify, stipulate, itemize, define, state**
SPLICE	to join, bind, attach; in film editing, to join two pieces of film *The editor removed all the scenes with the troublesome actress and* spliced *the remainder together.* Synonyms: **join, bind, connect, attach, link, unite**

WORD	DEFINITION, CONTEXT, SYNONYMS
SPURN	reject with scorn, turn away *When Harvey proposed to Harriet, she* spurned *him; she loved another man.* Synonyms: **refuse, snub**
SQUALID	very dirty or foul; wretched *The* squalid *living conditions in the tenement building outraged the new tenants.* Synonyms: **filthy, sordid, poor, foul**
SQUANDER	to waste (often money) on some worthless purchase or practice *While I have carefully saved money to buy the piano I have always wanted, my friend Sean has* squandered *his earnings on thousands of lottery tickets.* Synonyms: **waste, fritter away, consume, exhaust**
STAUNCH	steady, loyal *A dog is a* staunch *friend.* Synonyms: **firm, sturdy, stable, solid, established, substantial, steadfast, faithful, unfailing**
STEALTHY	sneaky, secret *The children made a* stealthy *raid on the refrigerator during the night.* Synonyms: **sneaky, furtive, clandestine**
STRESS	emphasize, point out *Vanessa wrote on the blackboard the main points that she was going to* stress *in her lecture.* Synonyms: **highlight**
SUAVE	smooth, graceful, and confident in speech and behavior (sometimes insincerely) *Nina was a* suave *young woman who knew exactly how to act in any situation.* Synonyms: **smooth, gracious, courtly, worldly, sophisticated, urbane, cosmopolitan, cultivated, cultured, refined**
SUBDUE	to bring under control; to decrease the intensity of (as in the adjective subdued) *The king's army attempted to* subdue *the rebellious peasants, who were threatening to storm the castle.* Synonyms: **control, vanquish, suppress, repress, master, overcome, tame**

WORD	DEFINITION, CONTEXT, SYNONYMS
SUCCEED	(1) to follow, come after *George Bush* succeeded *Ronald Reagan as president.* Synonyms: **follow, replace** (2) to prosper, do well *Valerie was resolved to* succeed *in her new school.* Synonyms: **flourish, thrive**
SUCCUMB	to give in, to submit *Don't* succumb *to temptation.* Synonyms: **yield, surrender, give in, submit, die, expire**
SUFFICE	to be adequate or enough *"A light dinner should* suffice *the average person," said the thin man, eating his lettuce sandwich.* Synonyms: **satisfy**
SUMMIT	highest level or point *The first people to reach the* summit *of Mount Everest were Tenzing Norgay and Edmund Hillary.* Synonyms: **apex, peak, top, pinnacle**
SUPERB	wonderful, superior, excellent *The main course was merely adequate, but the dessert was* superb. Synonyms: **splendid, magnificent, grand**
SUPPRESS	crush, hold in, hide *The students could hardly* suppress *their excitement on the last day of school.* Synonyms: **quell, contain**
SURFEIT	overly abundant supply, an excess *There certainly is no* surfeit *of gasoline this year.* Synonyms: **excess, glut, overabundance**
SURMISE	(v) to guess, to infer *From his torn pants and bloody nose I* surmised *that he had been in a fight.* Synonyms: **guess, conjecture, speculate, hypothesize, infer** (n) instance of surmising *My* surmise *was correct; he had been in a fight.*

WORD	DEFINITION, CONTEXT, SYNONYMS
SURROGATE	person or thing substituted for another *When I was ill, my friend agreed to act as my* surrogate *and give my speech for me.* Synonyms: **proxy, substitute, alternate**
SUSCEPTIBLE	vulnerable, liable to be affected by something *Because of her weakened state, Valerie was* susceptible *to infection.* Synonyms: **vulnerable, open, exposed**
SUSPENSE	fear or anticipation of waiting for something; something having to do with fear or mystery, as in a suspense novel *Joe was in an agony of* suspense *waiting to find out if he'd gotten the lead part in the school play.* Synonyms: **apprehension, anxiety**
SYNOPSIS	short summary, outline *Oren wrote a 1-page* synopsis *of a 55-page book.* Synonyms: **summary, outline**
TACITURN	quiet, tending not to speak *Lyle is a* taciturn *boy who plays by himself and rarely says a word.* Synonyms: **quiet, shy, reserved, guarded**
TACTFUL	acting with sensitivity to others' feelings *I sent Eva to explain our sudden departure to our rude hosts, for she is the most* tactful *person I know.* Synonyms: **diplomatic, discreet, judicious, sensitive, considerate, thoughtful, politic, delicate**
TAINT	to poison, as a drink; to corrupt, as a person *"I have* tainted *the princess's wine with a potion that will age her horribly in a few short weeks!" the witch proclaimed gleefully.* Synonyms: **poison, contaminate, infect, spoil; corrupt, debase, pervert, stain, blemish**
TAMPER	bother, interfere, meddle *Dan* tampered *with the thermostat and raised the temperature in the room to 85 degrees* Synonyms: **tinker, manipulate**

WORD	DEFINITION, CONTEXT, SYNONYMS
TANGIBLE	can be felt by touching; having actual substance *The storming of the castle didn't bring the soldiers* tangible *rewards, but it brought them great honor. They would have preferred the rewards.* Synonyms: **material, real, touchable, palpable, concrete, perceptible**
TAUT	stretched tightly; tense *The tightrope was* taut. Synonyms: **tight, stretched, tense, strained**
TEMPERATE	(1) denying oneself too much pleasure; avoiding extreme positions, moderate, sensible *Lloyd is the most* temperate *student I have ever met; even on Friday nights he goes to bed early.* Synonyms: **self-denying, sensible, level-headed, rational** (2) a mild climate *The* temperate *weather of California is a welcome change from the harsh winters and muggy summers or New York City.* Synonyms: **mild, moderate**
TENACIOUS	steadily pursuing a goal, unwilling to give up; stubborn *For years, against all odds, women* tenaciously *fought for the right to vote.* Synonyms: **persistent, persevering, untiring, tireless**
TEPID	(1) neither hot nor cold; lukewarm *Roxanne refused to take a bath in the* tepid *water, fearing that she would catch a cold.* Synonyms: **lukewarm, mild, temperate** (2) lacking character or spirit, bland *Neither liking nor disliking Finnegan's film, the critics gave it* tepid *reviews.* Synonyms: **unenthusiastic, halfhearted, indifferent**
TERMINATE	to stop, end *Amy and Zoe* terminated *their friendship and never spoke to each other again.* Synonyms: **cease, finish, conclude**
TERSE	concise, brief, using few words *Kate was noted for her* terse *replies, rarely going beyond "yes" or "no."* Synonyms: **concise, succinct, compact**

WORD	DEFINITION, CONTEXT, SYNONYMS
TETHER	(n) chain or rope tied to an animal to keep it within specific bounds *The cheetah chewed through its* tether *and wandered off.* Synonyms: **rope, chain** (v) to fasten or confine *I have to* tether *my dog to the fence to keep it out of the neighbor's yard.* Synonyms: **tie, fasten**
TOKEN	(n) sign or symbol *I offered him a chocolate bar as a* token *of my gratitude for his help.* Synonyms: **symbol, expression, representation** (adj) existing in name or appearance only, without depth, or significance *He offered me a* token *handshake, but I knew that we were in fact still enemies.* Synonyms: **nominal, superficial, meaningless**
TORRID	extremely hot, scorching *The* torrid *weather destroyed the crops.* Synonyms: **hot, parched, sizzling**
TREPIDATION	fear, apprehension *Mike approached the door of the principal's office with* trepidation. Synonyms: **fright, anxiety, trembling, hesitation**
TRITE	lacking originality, inspiration, and interest *Lindsay's graduation speech was the same* trite *nonsense we've heard a hundred times in the past.* Synonyms: **tired, banal, unoriginal, common, stale, stock**
TUMULT	noise and confusion *The* tumult *of the "no nukes" demonstrators drowned out the president's speech.* Synonyms: **racket, disorder**
TYRANNY	harsh exercise of absolute power *The students accused Ms. Morgenstern of* tyranny *when she assigned them seats instead of letting them choose their own.* Synonyms: **oppression, repression**
ULTIMATE	marking the highest point; cannot be improved upon; final *The new fashions from Paris are the* ultimate *in chic.* Synonyms: **maximum, remotest, final, conclusive, last, elemental, primary, fundamental**

WORD	DEFINITION, CONTEXT, SYNONYMS
UNANIMOUS	approved by everyone concerned *The student council voted* unanimously; *not one person opposed the plan.* Synonyms: **unchallenged, uncontested, unopposed, united, harmonious**
UNKEMPT	messy, sloppily maintained *Sam's long hair and wrinkled shirt seemed* unkempt *to his grandmother; she told him he looked like a bum.* Synonyms: **sloppy, slovenly, ruffled, disheveled, messy, untidy, ragged**
USURP	to seize, take by force (most often used of abstract nouns like "power" rather than concrete nouns like "bathrobe"). *The vice principal was power hungry and tended to* usurp *the principal's power.* Synonyms: **seize, grab, steal, snatch**
VACATE	leave *The police ordered the demonstrators to* vacate *the park.* Synonyms: **depart, go**
VACUOUS	silly, empty-headed, not serious *The book that Victor loved when he was six struck him as utterly* vacuous *when he was twenty. But he still liked the pictures.* Synonyms: **shallow, vapid**
VAGUE	not clear or certain *It took us a while to find John's house because the directions were* vague. Synonyms: **nebulous, imprecise**
VEHEMENT	with deep feeling *Susanne responded to the accusation of cheating with a* vehement *denial.* Synonyms: **passionate, earnest, fervent**
VEND	to sell goods *Every Saturday in the summer, crafts people* vend *their products in the park.* Synonyms: **sell, peddle, merchandise**

WORD	DEFINITION, CONTEXT, SYNONYMS
VEX	to irritate to a great degree, to annoy *Your constant sniveling is beginning to* vex *me.* Synonyms: **tease, irritate, provoke, torment, pester, harass, bother, annoy**
VITALIZE	make something come alive *The government's flagrant acts of injustice* vitalized *the opposition.* Synonyms: **animate, vivify**
VIVACIOUS	lively, full of spirit *Quiet and withdrawn at first, Joan became increasingly* vivacious. Synonyms: **animated, sprightly, spirited**
WAN	unnaturally pale, lacking color *The sick child had a* wan *face.* Synonyms: **pale, ashen, bloodless**
WANTONLY	without a reason *Instead of singling out appropriate targets for his anger, the crazed robot struck out* wantonly. Synonyms: **randomly, indiscriminately**
WRATH	extreme anger *He denounced the criminals in a speech filled with righteous* wrath. Synonyms: **ire, fury, rage**
WRETCHED	miserable, pathetic *Steve felt* wretched *when he failed the test.* Synonyms: **dejected, woebegone, forlorn**
WRITHE	to squirm or twist as if in pain *After the being hit by a car, the pedestrian was* writhing *in pain.* Synonyms: **squirm, twitch, twist**
ZEALOUS	enthusiastic, eager *Serge was a* zealous *supporter of the cause and never missed a rally.* Synonyms: **fervent, fervid, intense, passionate**

CHAPTER 25: 100 ESSENTIAL MATH CONCEPTS

The math on the PSAT covers a lot of ground—from arithmetic to algebra to geometry.

Don't let yourself be intimidated. We've highlighted the 100 most important concepts that you'll need for PSAT Math and listed them in this chapter.

Use this list to remind yourself of the key concepts you'll need to know. Do four concepts a day, and you'll be ready within a month. If a concept continually causes you trouble, circle it and refer back to it as you try to do the questions.

You've probably been taught most of these concepts in school already, so this list is a great way to refresh your memory.

NUMBER PROPERTIES

1. Number Categories Signed

Integers are whole numbers; they include positive and negative numbers and zero, but not fractions or decimals.

A **rational number** is a number that can be expressed as a **ratio of two integers. Irrational numbers** are real numbers—they have locations on the number line—but they **can't be expressed precisely as a fraction or decimal.** For the purposes of the PSAT, the most important **irrational numbers** are $\sqrt{2}$, $\sqrt{3}$, and π.

2. Adding/Subtracting Signed Numbers

To **add a positive and a negative,** first ignore the signs and find the positive difference between the number parts. Then attach the sign of the original number with the larger number part. For example, to add 23 and –34, first ignore the minus sign and find the positive difference between 23 and 34—that's 11. Then attach the sign of the number with the larger number part—in this case it's the minus sign from the –34. So, $23 + (-34) = -11$.

Make **subtraction** situations simpler by turning them into addition. For example, you can think of –17 – (–21) as –17 + (+21).

To **add or subtract a string of positives and negatives,** first turn everything into addition. Then combine the positives and negatives so that the string is reduced to the sum of a single positive number and a single negative number.

3. Multiplying/Dividing Signed Numbers

To multiply and/or divide positives and negatives, treat the number parts as usual and **attach a minus sign if there were originally an odd number of negatives.** For example, to multiply –2, –3, and –5, first multiply the number parts: $2 \times 3 \times 5 = 30$. Then go back and note that there were **three**—an **odd** number—negatives, so the product is negative: $(-2) \times (-3) \times (-5) = -30$.

4. PEMDAS

When performing multiple operations, remember to perform them in the right order: **PEMDAS,** which means **Parentheses** first, then **Exponents,** then **Multiplication** and **Division** (left to right), and lastly **Addition** and **Subtraction** (left to right). In the expression $9 - 2 \times (5 - 3)^2 + 6 \div 3$, begin with the parentheses: $(5 - 3) = 2$. Then do the exponent: $2^2 = 4$. Now the expression is: $9 - 2 \times 4 + 6 \div 3$. Next do the multiplication and division to get: $9 - 8 + 2$, which equals 3. If you have difficulty remembering PEMDAS, use this sentence to recall it: **P**lease **E**xcuse **M**y **D**ear **A**unt **S**ally.

5. Counting Consecutive Integers

To count consecutive integers, **subtract the smallest from the largest and add 1.** To count the number of integers from 13 through 31, subtract: $31 - 13 = 18$. Then add 1: $18 + 1 = 19$.

NUMBER OPERATIONS AND CONCEPTS

6. Exponential Growth

If r is the ratio between consecutive terms, a_1 is the first term, a_n is the nth term, and S_n is the sum of the first n terms, then $a_n = a_1 r^{n-1}$ and $S_n \frac{a_1 - a_1 r^n}{1 - r}$.

7. Union and Intersection of Sets

The things in a set are called elements or members. The union of Set A and Set B, sometimes expressed as $A \cup B$, is the set of elements that are in either or both of Set A and Set B. If Set $A = \{1, 2\}$ and Set $B = \{3, 4\}$, then $A \cup B = \{1, 2, 3, 4\}$. The intersection of Set A and Set B, sometimes expressed as $A \cap B$, is the set of elements common to both Set A and Set B. If Set $A = \{1, 2, 3\}$ and Set $B = \{3, 4, 5\}$, then $A \cap B = \{3\}$.

DIVISIBILITY

8. Factor/Multiple

The **factors** of integer n are the positive integers that divide into n with no remainder. The **multiples** of n are the integers that n divides into with no remainder. For example, 6 is a factor of 12, and 24 is a multiple of 12. Therefore, 12 is both a factor and a multiple of itself, since $12 \times 1 = 12$ and $12 \div 1 = 12$.

9. Prime Factorization

To find the prime factorization of an integer, continue factoring until **all the factors are prime.** For example, to factor 36: $36 = 4 \times 9 = 2 \times 2 \times 3 \times 3$.

10. Relative Primes

Relative primes are integers that have no common factor other than 1. To determine whether two integers are relative primes, break them both down to their prime factorizations. For example: $35 = 5 \times 7$ and $54 = 2 \times 3 \times 3 \times 3$. They have **no prime factors in common,** so 35 and 54 are relative primes.

11. Common Multiple

A common multiple is a number that is a multiple of two or more integers. You can always get a common multiple of two integers by **multiplying** them, but unless the two numbers are relative primes, the product will not be the *least* common multiple. For example, to find a common multiple for 12 and 15, you could just multiply: $12 \times 15 = 180$.

To find the **least common multiple (LCM),** check out the **multiples of the larger integer** until you find one that's **also a multiple of the smaller.** To find the LCM of 12 and 15, begin by taking the multiples of 15: 15 is not divisible by 12, nor are 30 or 45. But the next multiple of 15, 60, *is* divisible by 12, so it's the LCM.

12. Greatest Common Factor (GCF)

To find the greatest common factor, break down the integers into their prime factorizations and multiply **all the prime factors they have in common.** For example, $36 = 2 \times 2 \times 3 \times 3$ and $48 = 2 \times 2 \times 2 \times 2 \times 3$. These integers have a 2×2 and a 3 in common, so the GCF is $2 \times 2 \times 3 = 12$.

13. Even/Odd

To predict whether a sum, difference, or product will be even or odd, just **take simple numbers such as 1 and 2 and see what happens.** There are rules—"odd times even is even," for example—but there's no need to memorize them. What happens with one set of numbers generally happens with all similar sets.

14. Multiples of 2 and 4

An integer is divisible by 2 (even) if the **last digit is even.** An integer is divisible by 4 if the **last two digits form a multiple of 4.** The last digit of 562 is 2, which is even, so 562 is a multiple of 2. The last two digits form 62, which is *not* divisible by 4, so 562 is not a multiple of 4. The integer 512, however, is divisible by 4 because the last two digits form 12, which is a multiple of 4.

15. Multiples of 3 and 9

An integer is divisible by 3 if the **sum of its digits is divisible by 3.** An integer is divisible by 9 if the **sum of its digits is divisible by 9.** The sum of the digits in 957 is 21, which is divisible by 3 but not by 9, so 957 is divisible by 3 but not by 9.

16. Multiples of 5 and 10

An integer is divisible by 5 if the **last digit is 5 or 0.** An integer is divisible by 10 if the **last digit is 0.** The last digit of 665 is 5, so 665 is a multiple of 5 but *not* a multiple of 10.

17. Remainders

The remainder is the **whole number left over after division.** For example, 487 is 2 more than 485, which is a multiple of 5, so when 487 is divided by 5, the remainder is 2.

FRACTIONS AND DECIMALS

18. Reducing Fractions

To reduce a fraction to lowest terms, **factor out and cancel** all factors the numerator and denominator have in common.

$$\frac{28}{36} = \frac{4 \times 7}{4 \times 9} = \frac{7}{9}$$

19. Adding/Subtracting Fractions

To add or subtract fractions, first find a **common denominator,** then add or subtract the numerators.

$$\frac{2}{15} + \frac{3}{10} = \frac{4}{30} + \frac{9}{30} = \frac{4+9}{30} = \frac{13}{30}$$

20. Multiplying Fractions

To multiply fractions, **multiply** the numerators and **multiply** the denominators.

$$\frac{5}{7} \times \frac{3}{4} = \frac{5 \times 3}{7 \times 4} = \frac{15}{28}$$

21. Dividing Fractions

To divide fractions, **invert** the second one and **multiply.**

$$\frac{1}{2} \div \frac{3}{5} = \frac{1}{2} \times \frac{5}{3} = \frac{1 \times 5}{2 \times 3} = \frac{5}{6}$$

22. Mixed Numbers and Improper Fractions

To convert a mixed number to an improper fraction, **multiply** the whole number part by the denominator, then **add** the numerator. The result is the new numerator (over the same denominator). To convert $7\frac{1}{3}$, first multiply 7 by 3, then add 1, to get the new numerator of 22. Put that over the same denominator, 3, to get $\frac{22}{3}$.

To convert an improper fraction to a mixed number, divide the denominator into the numerator to get a **whole number quotient with a remainder.** The quotient becomes the whole number part of the mixed number, and the remainder becomes the new numerator—with the same denominator. For example, to convert $\frac{108}{5}$, first divide 5 into 108, which yields 21 with a remainder of 3. Therefore, $\frac{108}{5} = 21\frac{3}{5}$.

23. Reciprocal

To find the reciprocal of a fraction, **switch the numerator and the denominator.** The reciprocal of $\frac{3}{7}$ is $\frac{7}{3}$. The reciprocal of 5 is $\frac{1}{5}$. The product of reciprocals is 1.

24. Comparing Fractions

One way to compare fractions is to **reexpress them with a common denominator.** For example, $\frac{3}{4} = \frac{21}{28}$ and $\frac{5}{7} = \frac{20}{28}$. Now, $\frac{21}{28}$ is greater than $\frac{20}{28}$, so $\frac{3}{4}$ is greater than $\frac{5}{7}$. Another method is to **convert them both to decimals.** For example, $\frac{3}{4}$ converts to 0.75 , and $\frac{5}{7}$ converts to approximately 0.714.

25. Converting Fractions and Decimals

To convert a fraction to a decimal, **divide the bottom into the top.** To convert $\frac{5}{8}$, divide 8 into 5, yielding 0.625.

To convert a decimal to a fraction, set the decimal over 1 and **multiply the numerator and denominator by 10** raised to the number of digits which are to the right of the decimal point.

To convert 0.625 to a fraction, you would multiply $\frac{0.625}{1}$ by $\frac{10^3}{10^3}$ or $\frac{1{,}000}{1{,}000}$.

Then simplify: $\frac{625}{100} = \frac{5 \times 125}{8 \times 125} = \frac{5}{8}$.

26. Repeating Decimal

To find a particular digit in a repeating decimal, note the **number of digits in the cluster that repeats.** If there are 2 digits in that cluster, then every second digit is the same. If there are 3 digits in that cluster, then every third digit is the same. And so on.

For example, the decimal equivalent of $\frac{1}{27}$ is 0.037037037..., which is best written $0.\overline{037}$. There are 3 digits in the repeating cluster, so every 3rd digit is the same: 7. To find the 50th digit, look for the multiple of 3 just less than 50—that's 48. The 48th digit is 7, and with the 49th digit the pattern repeats with 0. The 50th digit is 3.

27. Identifying the Parts and the Whole

The key to solving most fraction and percent word problems is to identify the part and the whole. Usually you'll find the **part** associated with the verb ***is/are*** and the **whole** associated with the word ***of***. In the sentence, "Half of the boys are blonds," the whole is the boys (*of* the boys), and the part is the blonds (*are* blonds).

PERCENTS

28. Percent Formula

Whether you need to find the part, the whole, or the percent, use the same formula:

$$\textbf{Part} = \textbf{Percent} \times \textbf{Whole}$$

Example: What is 12 percent of 25?
Setup: Part = 0.12×25

Example: 15 is 3 percent of what number?
Setup: $15 = 0.03 \times$ Whole

Example: 45 is what percent of 9?
Setup: $45 =$ Percent $\times 9$

29. Percent Increase and Decrease

To increase a number by a percent, **add the percent to 100 percent,** convert to a decimal, and multiply. To increase 40 by 25 percent, add 25 percent to 100 percent, convert 125 percent to 1.25, and multiply by 40:

$$1.25 \times 40 = 50$$

30. Finding the Original Whole

To find the **original whole before a percent increase or decrease,** set up an equation. Think of the result of a 15 percent increase over x as $1.15x$.

Example: After a 5 percent increase, the population was 59,346. What was the population before the increase?

Setup: $1.05x = 59{,}346$

31. Combined Percent Increase and Decrease

To determine the combined effect of multiple percent increases and/or decreases, **start with 100 and see what happens.**

Example: A price went up 10 percent one year, and the new price went up 20 percent the next year. What was the combined percent increase?

Setup: First year: 100 + (10 percent of 100) = 110. Second year: 110 + (20 percent of 110) = 132. That's a combined 32 percent increase.

AVERAGES

32. Average Formula

To find the average of a set of numbers, **add them and divide by the number of numbers.**

$$\textbf{Average} = \frac{\textbf{Sum of the terms}}{\textbf{Number of terms}}$$

To find the average of the five numbers 12, 15, 23, 40, and 40, first add them: $12 + 15 + 23 + 40 + 40 = 130$. Then divide the sum by 5: $130 \div 5 = 26$.

33. Average of Evenly Spaced Numbers

To find the average of evenly spaced numbers, just **average the smallest and the largest.** The average of all the integers from 13 through 77 is the same as the average of 13 and 77:

$$\frac{13+77}{2} = \frac{90}{2} = 45$$

34. Using the Average to Find the Sum

$$\textbf{Sum} = \textbf{(Average)} \times \textbf{(Number of terms)}$$

If the average of ten numbers is 50, then they add up to 10×50, or 500.

35. Finding the Missing Number

To find a missing number when you're given the average, **use the sum.** If the average of four numbers is 7, then the sum of those four numbers is 4×7, or 28. Suppose that three of the numbers are 3, 5, and 8. These three numbers add up to 16 of that 28, which leaves 12 for the fourth number.

36. Median and Mode

The median of a set of numbers is the **value that falls in the middle of the ordered set.** If you have five test scores, and they are 88, 86, 57, 94, and 73, you must first list the scores in increasing or decreasing order: 57, 73, 86, 88, 94.

The median is the middle number, or 86. If there is an even number of values in a set (six test scores, for instance), simply take the average of the two middle numbers.

The mode of a set of numbers is the **value that appears most often.** If your test scores were 88, 57, 68, 85, 99, 93, 93, 84, and 81, the mode of the scores would be 93 because it appears more often than any other score. If there is a tie for the most common value in a set, the set has more than one mode.

RATIOS, PROPORTIONS, AND RATES

37. Setting Up a Ratio

To find a ratio, put the number associated with the word *of* **on top** and the quantity associated with the word *to* **on the bottom** and reduce. The ratio of 20 oranges to 12 apples is $\frac{20}{12}$, which reduces to $\frac{5}{3}$.

38. Part-to-Part Ratios and Part-to-Whole Ratios

If the parts add up to the whole, a part-to-part ratio can be turned into two part-to-whole ratios by putting **each number in the original ratio over the sum of the numbers.** If the ratio of males to females is 1 to 2, then the males-to-people ratio is $\frac{1}{1+2}=\frac{1}{3}$ and the females-to-people ratio is $\frac{2}{1+2}=\frac{2}{3}$. In other words, $\frac{2}{3}$ of all the people are female.

39. Solving a Proportion

To solve a proportion, **cross-multiply:**

$$\frac{x}{5}=\frac{3}{4}$$
$$4x=3\times 5$$
$$x=\frac{15}{4}=3.75$$

40. Rate

To solve a rate problem, **use the units** to keep things straight.

Example: If snow is falling at the rate of one foot every four hours, how many inches of snow will fall in seven hours?

Setup: $\frac{1 \text{ foot}}{4 \text{ hours}} = \frac{x \text{ inches}}{7 \text{ hours}}$

$$\frac{12 \text{ inches}}{4 \text{ hours}} = \frac{x \text{ inches}}{7 \text{ hours}}$$

$$4x = 12 \times 7$$

$$x = 21$$

41. Average Rate

Average rate is *not* simply the average of the rates.

$$\text{Average } A \text{ per } B = \frac{\text{Total } A}{\text{Total } B}$$

$$\text{Average speed} = \frac{\text{Total distance}}{\text{Total time}}$$

To find the average speed for 120 miles at 40 mph and 120 miles at 60 mph, **don't just average the two speeds.** First figure out the total distance and the total time. The total distance is 120 + 120 = 240 miles. The times are three hours for the first leg and two hours for the second leg, or five hours total. The average speed, then, is $\frac{240}{5} = 48$ miles per hour.

POSSIBILITIES AND PROBABILITY

42. Counting the Possibilities

The fundamental counting principle: if there are ***m* ways** one event can happen and ***n* ways** a second event can happen, then there are ***m* × *n* ways** for the two events to happen. For example, with five shirts and seven pairs of pants to choose from, you can have 5 × 7 = 35 different outfits.

43. Probability

$$\textbf{Probability} = \frac{\textbf{Favorable outcomes}}{\textbf{Total possible outcomes}}$$

For example, if you have 12 shirts in a drawer and 9 of them are white, the probability of picking a white shirt at random is $\frac{9}{12} = \frac{3}{4}$. This probability can also be expressed as 0.75 or 75%.

POWERS AND ROOTS

44. Multiplying and Dividing Powers

To multiply powers with the same base, **add the exponents and keep the same base:**

$$x^3 \times x^4 = x^{3+4} = x^7$$

To divide powers with the same base, **subtract the exponents and keep the same base:**

$$y^{13} \div y^8 = y^{13-8} = y^5$$

45. Raising Powers to Powers

To raise a power to a power, **multiply the exponents:**

$$(x^3)^4 = x^{3 \times 4} = x^{12}$$

46. Simplifying Square Roots

To simplify a square root, **factor out the perfect squares** under the radical, unsquare them, and put the result in front.

$$\sqrt{12} = \sqrt{4 \times 3} = \sqrt{4} \times \sqrt{3} = 2\sqrt{3}$$

47. Adding and Subtracting Roots

You can add or subtract radical expressions **when the part under the radicals is the same:**

$$2\sqrt{3} + 3\sqrt{3} = 5\sqrt{3}$$

Don't try to add or subtract when the radical parts are different. There's not much you can do with an expression like:

$$3\sqrt{5} + 3\sqrt{7}$$

48. Multiplying and Dividing Roots

The product of square roots is equal to the **square root of the product:**

$$\sqrt{3} \times \sqrt{5} = \sqrt{3 \times 5} = \sqrt{15}$$

The quotient of square roots is equal to the **square root of the quotient:**

$$\frac{\sqrt{6}}{\sqrt{3}} = \sqrt{\frac{6}{3}} = \sqrt{2}$$

49. Negative Exponents and Rational Exponents

To find the value of a number raised to a negative exponent, simply rewrite the number, without the negative sign, as the bottom of a fraction with 1 as the numerator of the fraction: $3^{-2} = \frac{1}{3^2} = \frac{1}{9}$. If x is a positive number and a is a nonzero number, then $x^{\frac{1}{a}} = \sqrt[a]{x}$. So $4^{\frac{1}{2}} = \sqrt[2]{4} = 2$. If p and q are integers, then $x^{\frac{p}{q}} = \sqrt[q]{x^p}$. So $4^{\frac{3}{2}} = \sqrt[2]{4^3} = \sqrt{64} = 8$.

ABSOLUTE VALUE

50. Determining Absolute Value

The absolute value of a number is the distance of the number from zero on the number line. Because absolute value is a distance, it is always positive. The absolute value of 7 is 7; this is expressed $|7| = 7$. Similarly, the absolute value of –7 is 7: $|-7| = 7$. Every positive number is the absolute value of two numbers: itself and its negative.

ALGEBRAIC EXPRESSIONS

51. Evaluating an Expression

To evaluate an algebraic expression, **plug in** the given values for the unknowns and calculate according to **PEMDAS.** To find the value of $x^2 + 5x - 6$ when $x = -2$, plug in –2 for x: $(-2)^2 + 5(-2) - 6 = -12$

52. Adding and Subtracting Monomials

To combine like terms, **keep the variable part unchanged while adding or subtracting the coefficients:**

$$2a + 3a = (2 + 3)a = 5a$$

53. Adding and Subtracting Polynomials

To add or subtract polynomials, **combine like terms:**

$$(3x^2 + 5x - 7) - (x^2 + 12) =$$

$$(3x^2 - x^2) + 5x + (-7 - 12) =$$

$$2x^2 + 5x - 19$$

54. Multiplying Monomials

To multiply monomials, **multiply the coefficients and the variables separately:**

$$2a \times 3a = (2 \times 3)(a \times a) = 6a^2$$

55. Multiplying Binomials—FOIL

To multiply binomials, use **FOIL.** To multiply $(x + 3)$ by $(x + 4)$, first multiply the **F**irst terms: $x \times x = x^2$. Next the **O**uter terms: $x \times 4 = 4x$. Then the **I**nner terms: $3 \times x = 3x$. And finally the **L**ast terms: $3 \times 4 = 12$. Then add and combine like terms:

$$x^2 + 4x + 3x + 12 = x^2 + 7x + 12$$

56. Multiplying Other Polynomials

FOIL works only when you want to multiply two binomials. If you want to multiply polynomials with more than two terms, make sure you **multiply each term in the first polynomial by each term in the second:**

$$\begin{aligned}(x^2 + 3x + 4)(x + 5) &=\\ x^2(x + 5) + 3x(x + 5) + 4(x + 5) &=\\ x^3 + 5x^2 + 3x^2 + 15x + 4x + 20 &=\\ x^3 + 8x^2 + 19x + 20\end{aligned}$$

After multiplying two polynomials together, the number of terms in your expression before simplifying should equal the number of terms in one polynomial multiplied by the number of terms in the second. In the example, you should have $3 \times 2 = 6$ terms in the product before you simplify like terms.

FACTORING ALGEBRAIC EXPRESSIONS

57. Factoring Out a Common Divisor

A factor common to all terms of a polynomial can be **factored out.** All three terms in the polynomial $3x^3 + 12x^2 - 6x$ contain a factor of $3x$. Pulling out the common factor yields $3x(x^2 + 4x - 2)$.

58. Factoring the Difference of Squares

One of the test maker's favorite factorables is the **difference of squares.**

$$a^2 - b^2 = (a - b)\ (a + b)$$

$x^2 - 9$, for example, factors to $(x - 3)(x + 3)$.

59. Factoring the Square of a Binomial

Recognize polynomials that are squares of binomials:

$$a^2 + 2ab + b^2 = (a + b)^2$$

$$a^2 - 2ab + b^2 = (a - b)^2$$

For example, $4x^2 + 12x + 9$ factors to $(2x + 3)^2$, and $n^2 - 10n + 25$ factors to $(n - 5)^2$.

60. Factoring Other Polynomials—FOIL in Reverse

To factor a quadratic expression, **think about what binomials you could use FOIL on to get that quadratic expression.** To factor $x^2 - 5x + 6$, think about what **F**irst terms will produce x^2, what **L**ast terms will produce +6, and what **O**uter and **I**nner terms will produce $-5x$. Some common sense—and a little trial and error—lead you to $(x - 2)(x - 3)$.

61. Simplifying an Algebraic Fraction

Simplifying an algebraic fraction is a lot like simplifying a numerical fraction. The general idea is to **find factors common to the numerator and denominator and cancel them.** Thus, simplifying an algebraic fraction begins with factoring.

For example, to simplify $\frac{x^2-x-12}{x^2-9}$, first factor the numerator and denominator:

$$\frac{x^2-x-12}{x^2-9}=\frac{(x-4)(x+3)}{(x-3)(x+3)}$$

Canceling $x+3$ from the numerator and denominator leaves you with $\frac{x-4}{x-3}$.

SOLVING EQUATIONS

62. Solving a Linear Equation

To solve an equation, do whatever is necessary to both sides to **isolate the variable.** To solve the equation $5x-12=-2x+9$, first get all the *x*s on one side by adding $2x$ to both sides: $7x-12=9$. Then add 12 to both sides: $7x=21$. Then divide both sides by 7: $x=3$.

63. Solving "in Terms of"

To solve an equation for one variable **in terms of** another means to **isolate the one variable on one side of the equation,** leaving an expression containing the other variable on the other side of the equation. To solve the equation $3x-10y=-5x+6y$ for x in terms of y, isolate x:

$$3x-10y=-5x+6y$$

$$3x+5x=6y+10y$$

$$8x=16y$$

$$x=2y$$

64. Translating from English into Algebra

To translate from English into algebra, look for the key words and systematically turn phrases into algebraic expressions and sentences into equations. Be careful about order, especially when subtraction is called for.

Example: Celine and Remi play tennis. Last year, Celine won 3 more than twice the number of matches that Remi won. If Celine won 11 more matches than Remi, how many matches did Celine win?

Setup: You are given two sets of information. One way to solve this is to write a system of equations—one equation for each set of information. Use variables that relate well with what they represent. For example, use r to represent Remi's winning matches.

Use c to represent Celine's winning matches. The phrase "Celine won 3 more than twice. . . Remi" can be written as:

$$c = 2r + 3$$

The phrase "Celine won 11 more matches than Remi" can be written as:

$$c = r + 11$$

65. Solving a Quadratic Equation

To solve a quadratic equation, put it in the "$ax^2 + bx + c = 0$" form, **factor** the left side (if you can), and set each factor equal to 0 separately to get the two solutions. To solve $x^2 + 12 = 7x$, first rewrite it as $x^2 - 7x + 12 = 0$. Then factor the left side:

$$(x - 3)(x - 4) = 0$$

$$x - 3 = 0 \text{ or } x - 4 = 0$$

$$x = 3 \text{ or } 4$$

66. Solving a System of Equations

You can solve for two variables only if you have two distinct equations. Two forms of the same equation will not be adequate. **Combine the equations** in such a way that **one of the variables cancels out.** To solve the two equations $4x + 3y = 8$ and $x + y = 3$, multiply both sides of the second equation by -3 to get: $-3x - 3y = -9$. Now add the two equations; the $3y$ and the $-3y$ cancel out, leaving: $x = -1$. Plug that back into either one of the original equations and you'll find that $y = 4$.

A second way to solve for two variables is to use substitution. This is especially useful if one of the variables has a coefficient of 1 or is already solved for. For example, to solve the two equations $5x + 2y = 12$ and $y = x - 1$, we can directly substitute from the second equation into the first one. This gives us $5x + 2(x - 1) = 12$, which becomes $5x + 2x - 2 = 12$. This is simplified to $7x = 14$, or $x = 2$. Now that we know x, we plug it back into the equations to find $y = 1$.

67. Solving an Inequality

To solve an inequality, do whatever is necessary to both sides to **isolate the variable.** Just remember that when you **multiply or divide both sides by a negative number,** you must **reverse the sign.** To solve $-5x + 7 < -3$, subtract 7 from both sides to get: $-5x < -10$. Now divide both sides by -5, remembering to reverse the sign: $x > 2$.

68. Radical Equations

A radical equation contains at least one radical expression. Solve radical equations by using standard rules of algebra. If $5\sqrt{x} - 2 = 13$, then $5\sqrt{x} = 15$ and $\sqrt{x} = 3$, so $x = 9$.

FUNCTIONS

69. Function Notation and Evaluation

Standard function notation is written $f(x)$ and read "f of 4." To evaluate the function $f(x) = 2x + 3$ for $f(4)$, replace x with 4 and simplify: $f(4) = 2(4) + 3 = 11$.

70. Direct and Inverse Variation

In direct variation, $y = kx$, where k is a nonzero constant. In direct variation, the variable y changes directly as x does. If a unit of Currency A is worth 2 units of Currency B, then $A = 2B$. If the number of units of B were to double, the number of units of A would double, and so on for halving, tripling, etc. In inverse variation, $xy = k$, where x and y are variables and k is a constant. A famous inverse relationship is *rate* × *time* = *distance*, where distance is constant. Imagine having to cover a distance of 24 miles. If you were to travel at 12 miles per hour, you'd need two hours. But if you were to halve your rate, you would have to double your time. This is just another way of saying that rate and time vary inversely.

71. Domain and Range of a Function

The domain of a function is the set of values for which the function is defined. For example, the domain of $f(x) = \frac{1}{1-x^2}$ is all values of x except 1 and −1, because for those values the denominator has a value of 0 and is therefore undefined. The range of a function is the set of outputs or results of the function. For example, the range of $f(x) = x^2$ is all numbers greater than or equal to zero, because x^2 cannot be negative.

COORDINATE GEOMETRY

72. Finding the Distance between Two Points

To find the distance between points, **use the Pythagorean theorem** or **special right triangles.** The difference between the xs is one leg and the difference between the ys is the other.

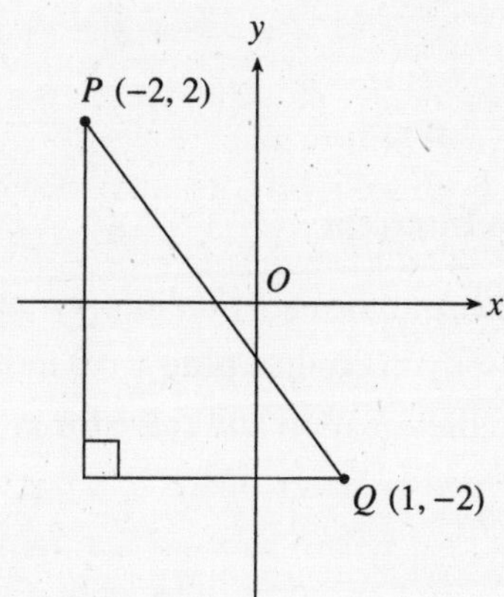

In the figure, *PQ* is the hypotenuse of a 3-4-5 triangle, so $PQ = 5$.

You can also use the **distance formula:**

$$d = \sqrt{(x_1 - x_2)^2 + (y_1 - y_2)^2}$$

To find the distance between $R(3, 6)$ and $S(5, -2)$:

$$\begin{aligned} d &= \sqrt{(3-5)^2 + [6-(-2)]^2} \\ &= \sqrt{(-2)^2 + (8)^2} \\ &= \sqrt{68} = 2\sqrt{17} \end{aligned}$$

73. Using Two Points to Find the Slope

$$\textbf{Slope} = \frac{\textbf{Change in } y}{\textbf{Change in } x} = \frac{\textbf{Rise}}{\textbf{Run}}$$

The slope of the line that contains the points $A(2, 3)$ and $B(0, -1)$ is:

$$\frac{y_A - y_B}{x_A - x_B} = \frac{3-(-1)}{2-0} = \frac{4}{2} = 2$$

74. Using an Equation to Find the Slope

To find the slope of a line from an equation, put the equation into the **slope-intercept** form:

$$y = mx + b$$

The **slope is *m*.** To find the slope of the equation $3x + 2y = 4$, rearrange it:

$$\begin{aligned} 3x + 2y &= 4 \\ 2y &= -3x + 4 \\ y &= -\frac{3}{2}x + 2 \end{aligned}$$

The slope is $-\frac{3}{2}$.

75. Using an Equation to Find an Intercept

To find the *y*-intercept, you can either put the equation into $y = mx + b$ **(slope-intercept)** form—in which case ***b* is the *y*-intercept**—or you can just **plug $x = 0$** into the equation and **solve for *y*.** To find the *x*-intercept, **plug $y = 0$** into the equation and **solve for *x*.**

LINES AND ANGLES

76. Intersecting Lines

When two lines intersect, **adjacent angles are supplementary and vertical angles are equal.**

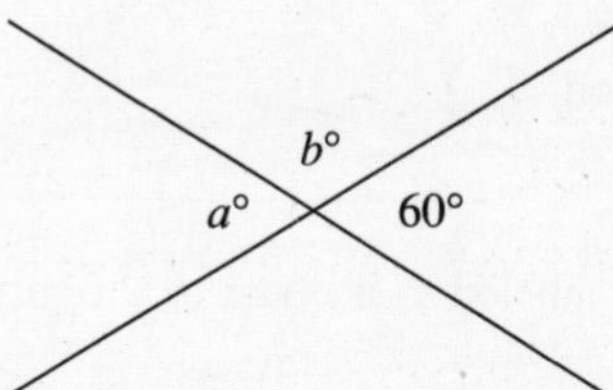

In the figure above, the angles marked $a°$ and $b°$ are adjacent and supplementary, so $a + b = 180$. Furthermore, the angles marked $a°$ and 60° are vertical and equal, so $a = 60$.

77. Parallel Lines and Transversals

A transversal across parallel lines forms **four equal acute angles and four equal obtuse angles.** If the transversal meets the lines at a right angle, then all eight angles are right angles.

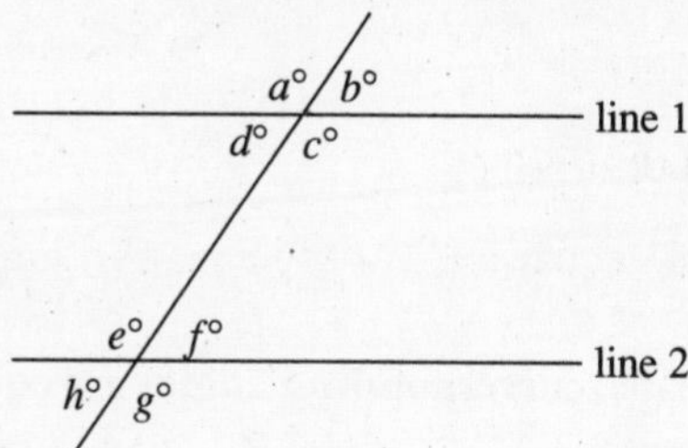

In the figure above, line 1 is parallel to line 2. Angles *a, c, e,* and *g* are obtuse, so they are all equal. Angles *b, d, f,* and *h* are acute, so they are all equal.

Furthermore, **any of the acute angles is supplementary to any of the obtuse angles.** Angles *a* and *h* are supplementary, as are *b* and *e, c* and *f,* and so on.

TRIANGLES—GENERAL

78. Interior and Exterior Angles of a Triangle

The three angles of any triangle **add up to 180 degrees.**

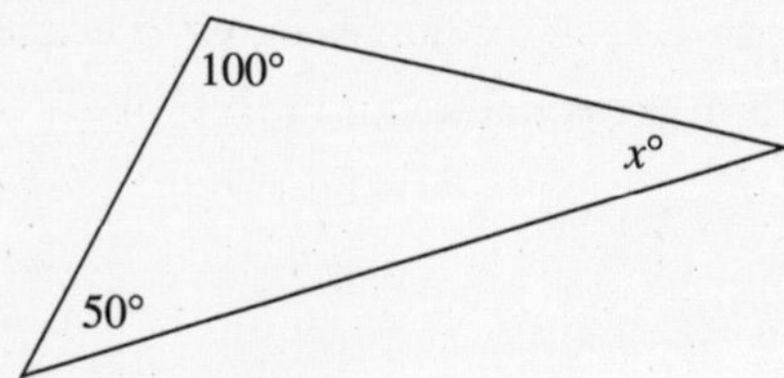

In the figure above, $x + 50 + 100 = 180$, so $x = 30$.

An exterior angle of a triangle is equal to the **sum of the remote interior angles.**

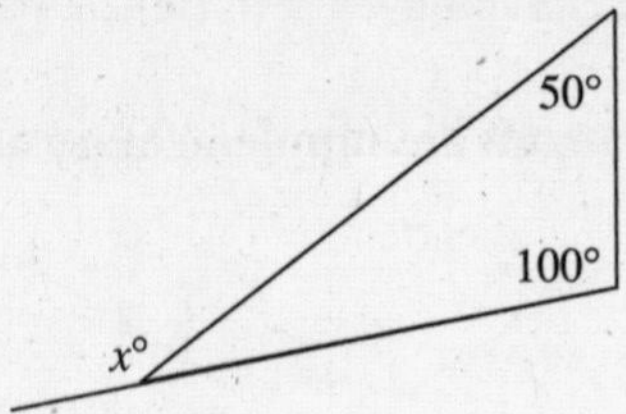

In the figure above, the exterior angle labeled $x°$ is equal to the sum of the remote angles:

$$x = 50 + 100 = 150$$

The three exterior angles of a triangle add up to 360 degrees.

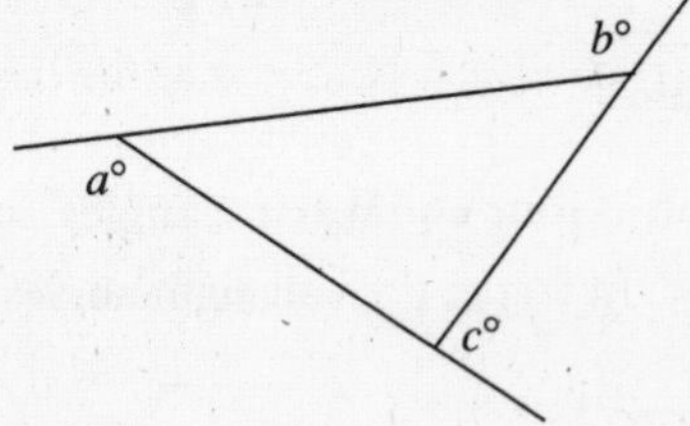

In the figure above, $a + b + c = 360$.

79. Similar Triangles

Similar triangles have the same shape: **corresponding angles are equal and corresponding sides are proportional.**

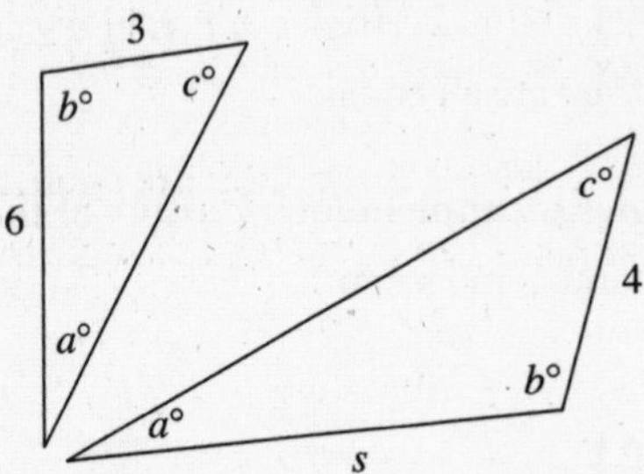

The triangles above are similar because they have the same angles. The 3 corresponds to the 4, and the 6 corresponds to the s.

$$\frac{3}{4} = \frac{6}{s}$$

$$3s = 24$$

$$s = 8$$

80. Area of a Triangle

$$\textbf{Area of Triangle} = \frac{1}{2}\textbf{(base)(height)}$$

The height is the perpendicular distance between the side that's chosen as the base and the opposite vertex.

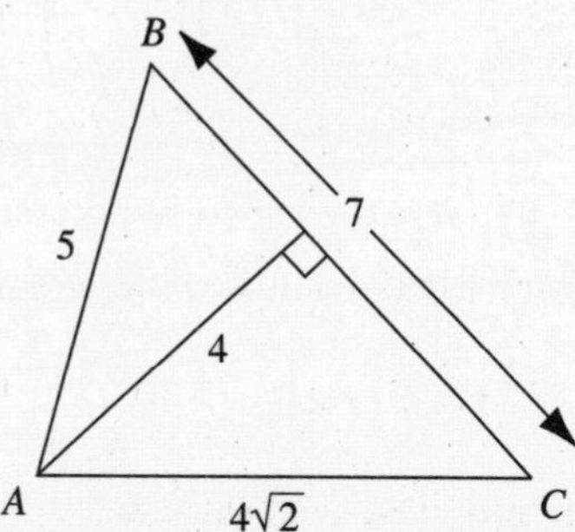

In the triangle above, 4 is the height when the 7 is chosen as the base.

$$\text{Area} = \frac{1}{2}bh = \frac{1}{2}(7)(4) = 14$$

81. Triangle Inequality Theorem

The length of one side of a triangle must be **greater than the difference and less than the sum** of the lengths of the other two sides. For example, if it is given that the length of one side is 3 and the length of another side is 7, then you know that the length of the third side must be greater than $7 - 3 = 4$ and less than $7 + 3 = 10$.

82. Isosceles and Equilateral Triangles

An isosceles triangle is a triangle that has **two equal sides.** Not only are two sides equal, but the angles opposite the equal sides, called **base angles,** are also equal.

Equilateral triangles are triangles in which **all three sides are equal.** Since all the sides are equal, all the angles are also equal. All three angles in an equilateral triangle measure 60 degrees, regardless of the lengths of sides.

RIGHT TRIANGLES

83. Pythagorean Theorem

For all right triangles:

$$\textbf{(leg}_1\textbf{)}^2 + \textbf{(leg}_2\textbf{)}^2 = \textbf{(hypotenuse)}^2$$

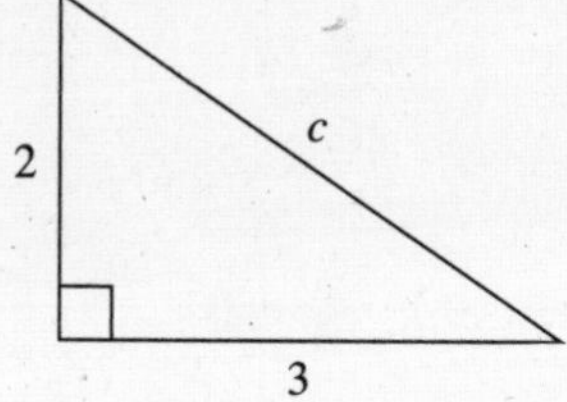

If one leg is 2 and the other leg is 3, then:

$$2^2 + 3^2 = c^2$$
$$c^2 = 4 + 9$$
$$c = \sqrt{13}$$

84. The 3-4-5 Triangle

If a right triangle's leg-to-leg ratio is 3:4, or if the leg-to-hypotenuse ratio is 3:5 or 4:5, it's a 3-4-5 triangle and you don't need to use the Pythagorean theorem to find the third side. Just figure out what multiple of 3-4-5 it is.

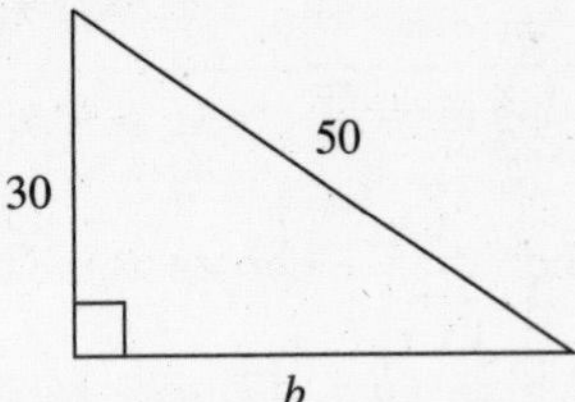

In the right triangle shown, one leg is 30 and the hypotenuse is 50. This is 10 times 3-4-5. The other leg is 40.

85. The 5-12-13 Triangle

If a right triangle's leg-to-leg ratio is 5:12, or if the leg-to-hypotenuse ratio is 5:13 or 12:13, then it's a 5-12-13 triangle and you don't need to use the Pythagorean theorem to find the third side. Just figure out what multiple of 5-12-13 it is.

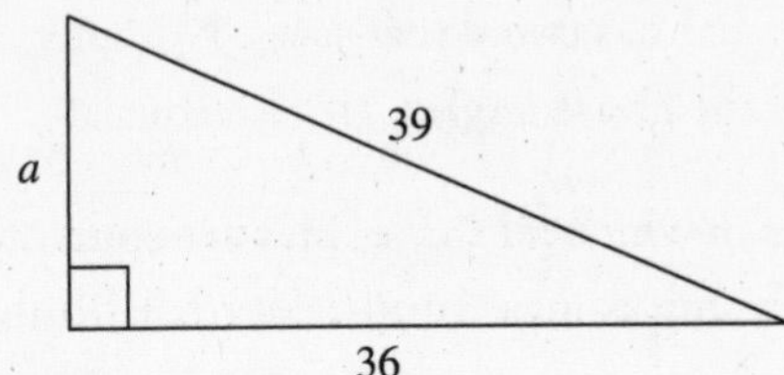

Here one leg is 36 and the hypotenuse is 39. This is 3 times 5-12-13. The other leg is 15.

86. The 30-60-90 Triangle

The sides of a 30-60-90 triangle are in a ratio of $x : x\sqrt{3} : 2x$. You don't need the Pythagorean theorem.

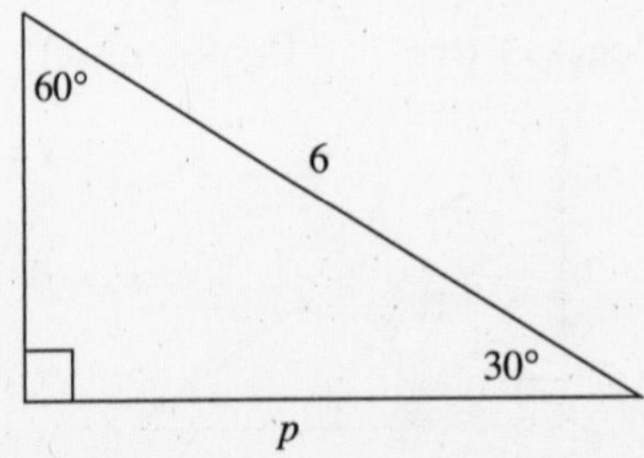

If the hypotenuse is 6, then the shorter leg is half that, or 3; and then the longer leg is equal to the short leg times $\sqrt{3}$, or $3\sqrt{3}$.

87. The 45-45-90 Triangle

The sides of a 45-45-90 triangle are in a ratio of $x:x:x\sqrt{2}$.

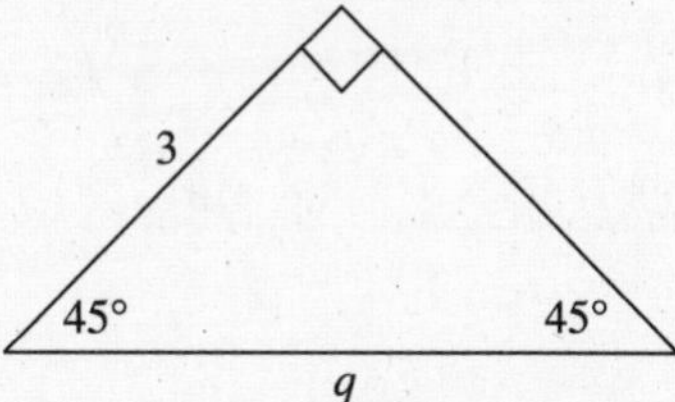

If one leg is 3, then the other leg is also 3, and the hypotenuse is equal to a leg times $\sqrt{2}$, or $3\sqrt{2}$.

OTHER POLYGONS

88. Characteristics of a Rectangle

A rectangle is a **four-sided figure with four right angles.** Opposite sides are equal. Diagonals are equal.

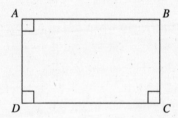

Quadrilateral *ABCD* above is shown to have three right angles. The fourth angle therefore also measures 90 degrees, and *ABCD* is a rectangle. The perimeter of a rectangle is equal to the sum of the lengths of the four sides, which is equivalent to 2(length + width).

Area of Rectangle = length × width

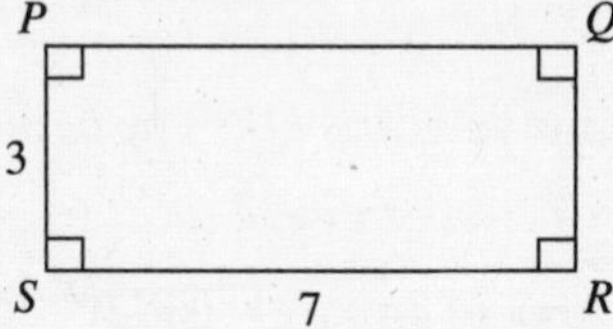

The area of a 7-by-3 rectangle is $7 \times 3 = 21$.

89. Characteristics of a Parallelogram

A parallelogram has **two pairs of parallel sides.** Opposite sides are equal. Opposite angles are equal. Consecutive angles add up to 180 degrees.

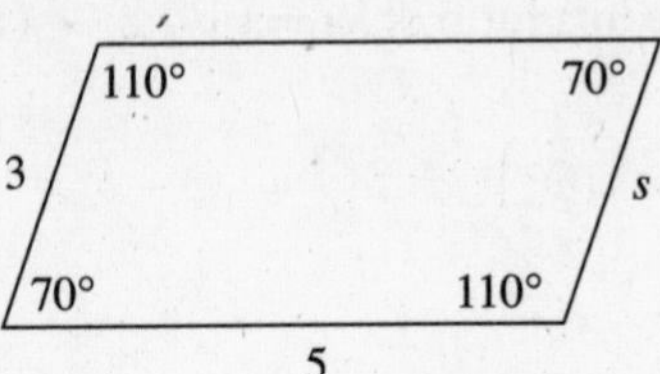

In the previous figure, s is the length of the side opposite the 3, so $s = 3$.

Area of Parallelogram = base × height

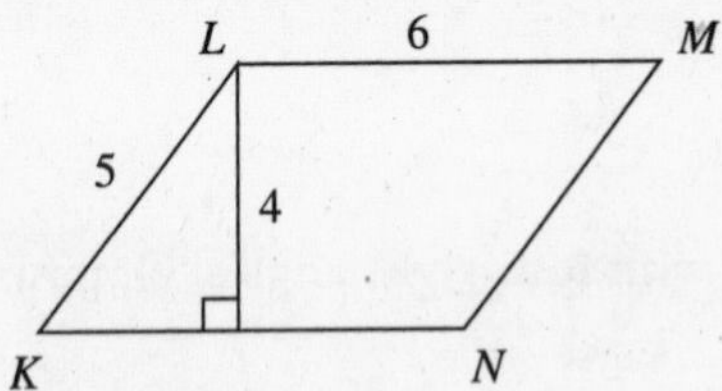

In parallelogram *KLMN* above, 4 is the height when *LM* or *KN* is used as the base. Base × height = $6 \times 4 = 24$.

90. Characteristics of a Square

A square is a **rectangle with four equal sides.**

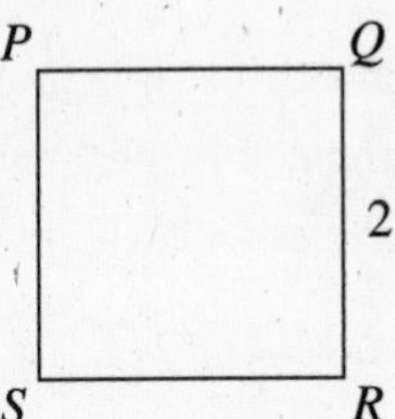

If *PQRS* is a square, all sides are the same length as *QR*. The perimeter of a square is equal to four times the length of one side.

Area of Square = (side)^2

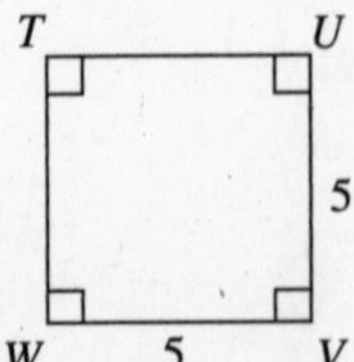

The square above, with sides of length 5, has an area of $5^2 = 25$.

91. Interior Angles of a Polygon

The **sum of the measures of the interior angles of a polygon = $(n - 2) \times 180$,** where n is the number of sides.

$$\textbf{Sum of the Angles} = (n - 2) \times 180$$

The eight angles of an octagon, for example, add up to $(8 - 2) \times 180 = 1{,}080$.

CIRCLES

92. Circumference of a Circle

$$\textbf{Circumference} = 2\pi r$$

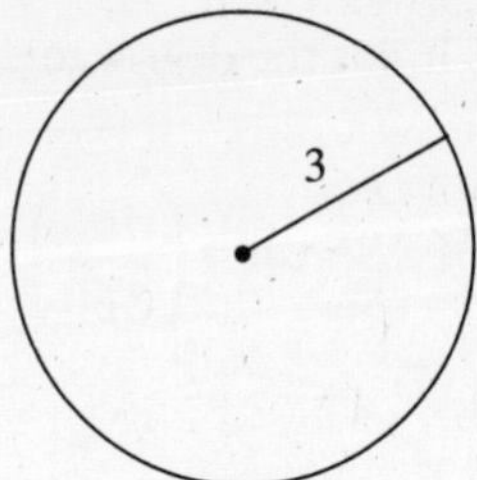

In the circle above, the radius is 3, and so the circumference is $2\pi(3) = 6\pi$.

93. Length of an Arc

An **arc** is a piece of the circumference. If n is the degree measure of the arc's central angle, then the formula is:

$$\textbf{Length of an Arc} = \left(\frac{n}{360}\right)(2\pi r)$$

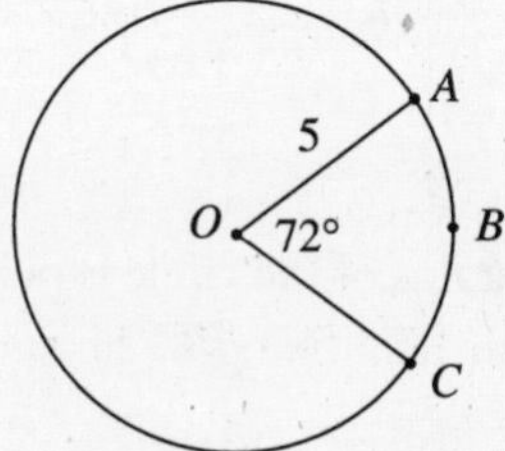

In the previous figure, the radius is 5 and the measure of the central angle is 72 degrees. The arc length is $\frac{72}{360}$ or $\frac{1}{5}$ of the circumference:

$$\left(\frac{72}{360}\right)(2\pi)(5) = \left(\frac{1}{5}\right)(10\pi) = 2\pi$$

94. Area of a Circle

$$\textbf{Area of a Circle} = \pi r^2$$

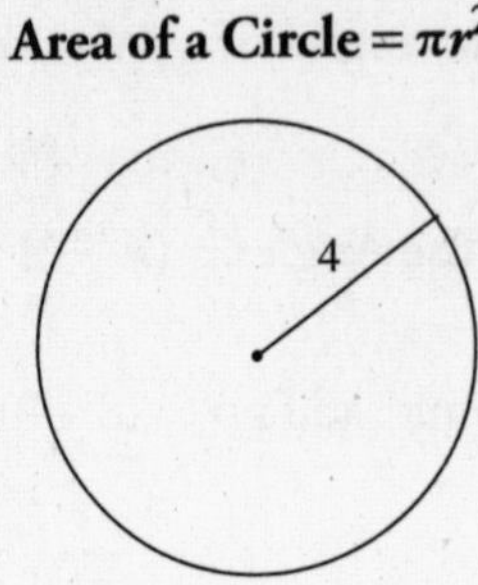

The area of the circle is $\pi(4)^2 = 16\pi$.

95. Area of a Sector

A **sector** is a piece of the area of a circle. If n is the degree measure of the sector's central angle, then the formula is:

$$\textbf{Area of a Sector} = \left(\frac{n}{360}\right)(\pi r^2)$$

In the figure above, the radius is 6 and the measure of the sector's central angle is 30 degrees. The sector has $\frac{30}{360}$ or $\frac{1}{12}$ of the area of the circle:

$$\left(\frac{30}{360}\right)(\pi)(6^2) = \left(\frac{1}{12}\right)(36\pi) = 3\pi$$

96. Tangency

When a line is tangent to a circle, the radius of the circle is perpendicular to the line at the point of contact.

SOLIDS

97. Surface Area of a Rectangular Solid

The surface of a rectangular solid consists of three pairs of identical faces. To find the surface area, find the area of each face and add them up. If the length is l, the width is w, and the height is h, the formula is:

$$\textbf{Surface Area} = 2lw + 2wh + 2lh$$

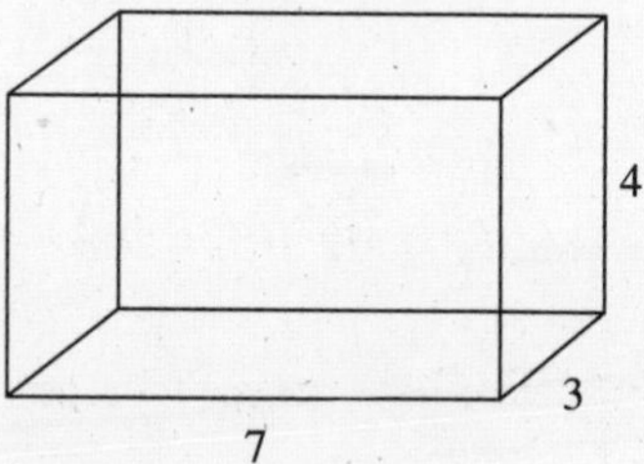

The surface area of the box above is: $2(7 \times 3) + 2(3 \times 4) + 2(7 \times 4) = 42 + 24 + 56 = 122$

98. Volume of a Rectangular Solid

$$\textbf{Volume of a Rectangular Solid} = lwh$$

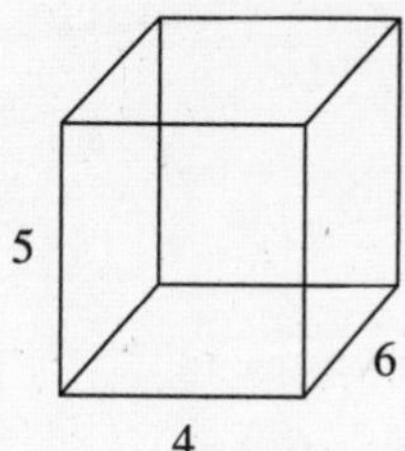

The volume of a 4-by-5-by-6 box is:

$$4 \times 5 \times 6 = 120$$

A cube is a rectangular solid with length, width, and height all equal. If e is the length of an edge of a cube, the volume formula is:

$$\textbf{Volume of a Cube} = e^3$$

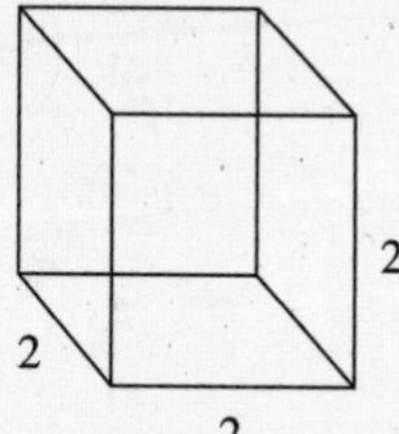

The volume of this cube is $2^3 = 8$.

99. Volume of a Cylinder

Volume of a Cylinder = $\pi r^2 h$

In the cylinder above, $r = 2$, $h = 5$, so:

$$\text{Volume} = \pi(2^2)(5) = 20\pi$$

100. Finding the Midpoint

The midpoint of two points on a line segment is the average of the *x*-coordinates of the endpoints and the average of the *y*-coordinates of the endpoints. If the endpoints are (x_1, y_1) and (x_2, y_2), the midpoint is $\left(\frac{x_1 + x_2}{2}, \frac{y_1 + y_2}{2}\right)$. The midpoint of (3, 5) and (9, 1) is $\left(\frac{3+9}{2}, \frac{5+1}{2}\right)$.

CHAPTER 26: WRITING SKILLS

PUNCTUATION REVIEW

Commas

1. Use commas to separate items in a series

If more than two items are listed in a series, they should be separated by commas. The final comma—the one that precedes the word "and"—may be omitted. An omitted final comma would not be considered an error on the SSAT or ISEE.

> Example: My recipe for buttermilk biscuits includes flour, baking soda, salt, shortening, and buttermilk.
>
> ALSO RIGHT: My recipe for buttermilk biscuits includes flour, baking soda, salt, shortening and buttermilk.

Be watchful for commas placed **before** the first element of a series **or after** the last element.

> WRONG: My recipe for chocolate cake includes, flour, baking soda, sugar, eggs, milk and chocolate.
>
> WRONG: Flour, baking soda, sugar, eggs, milk and chocolate, are the ingredients in my chocolate cake.

2. Use commas to separate two or more adjectives before a noun

> Example: I can't believe you sat through that long, dull movie three times in a row.

It is **incorrect** to place a comma **after** the last adjective in a series.

> WRONG: The manatee is a blubbery, bewhiskered, creature.

3. Use commas to set off parenthetical clauses and phrases

If a phrase or clause is not necessary to the main idea expressed by a sentence, it should be set off by commas.

> Example: Phillip, who never had any formal chef's training, bakes excellent cheesecake.

The main idea here is that Phillip bakes an excellent cheesecake. The intervening clause merely serves to further describe Phillip; it should therefore be enclosed in commas.

4. Use commas after introductory phrases

> Example: Having watered his petunias every day during the drought, Harold was disappointed when his garden was destroyed by aphids.

Example: After the banquet, Harold and Melissa went dancing.

5. Use commas to separate independent clauses

Use a comma before a conjunction (*and, but, nor, yet*, etc.) that connects two independent clauses.

Example: Marta is good at basketball, but she's better at soccer.

Semicolons

Like commas, semicolons can be used to separate independent clauses. As we saw above, two related independent clauses that are connected by a conjunction such as *and, but, nor,* or *yet* should be punctuated by a comma. If the words *and, but, nor,* or *yet* aren't used, the clauses should be separated by a semicolon.

Example: Whooping cranes are an endangered species; there are only fifty of them alive today.

Example: Whooping cranes are an endangered species, and they are unlikely to survive if we continue to pollute their habitat.

Semicolons may also be used between independent clauses connected by words like *therefore, nevertheless,* and *moreover*. For more on this topic, see the section on "Sentence Structure."

Colons

In Standard Written English, the colon is used only as a means of signaling that what follows is a list, definition, explanation, or restatement of what has gone before. A word or phrase such as *like the following, as follows, namely,* or *this* is often used along with the colon to make it clear that a list, summary, or explanation is coming up.

Example: This is what I found in her refrigerator: a moldy lime and a jar of peanut butter.

Example: Your instructions are as follows: Read the passage carefully, answer the questions, and turn over your answer sheet.

The Dash

The dash has two uses. One is to indicate an abrupt break in thought.

Example: The alligator, unlike the crocodile, will usually not attack humans—unless, that is, she feels that her young are in danger.

The dash can also be used to set off a parenthetical expression from the rest of the sentence.

Example: At 32° Fahrenheit—which is zero on the Celsius scale—water will freeze.

The Apostrophe

The apostrophe has two distinct functions. It is used with contracted verb forms to indicate that one or more letters have been eliminated:

Example: The **boy's** an expert at chess. (The boy is an expert at chess.)

Example: The **boy's** left for the day. (The boy has left for the day.)

The apostrophe is also used to indicate the possessive form of a noun.

Example: The **boy's** face was covered with mosquito bites after a day in the swamp.

GRAMMAR REVIEW

SUBJECT-VERB AGREEMENT

The form of a verb must match, or agree with, its subject in two ways: person and number.

1. AGREEMENT OF PERSON

When we talk about "person," we're talking about whether the subject and verb of a sentence show that the author is making a statement about himself (first person), the person he is speaking to (second person), or some other person, place, or thing (third person).

First Person Subjects: **I,** we.

> Example: **I am** going to Paris. **We are** going to Rome.

Second Person Subject: you.

> Example: **Are you** sure you weren't imagining that flying saucer?

Third Person Subjects: he, she, they, it, *and names of people, places, and things.*

> Example: **He is driving** me crazy.

2. AGREEMENT OF NUMBER

When we talk about number, we're talking about whether the subject and verb show that one thing is being discussed (singular) or that more than one thing is being discussed (plural).

> HINT: Subjects and verbs must agree in number.
>
> WRONG: The **children catches** the school bus every morning.
>
> RIGHT: The **children catch** the school bus every morning.

Be especially careful of subject-verb agreement when the subject and verb are separated by a long string of words.

> WRONG: **Wild animals** in jungles all over the world **is endangered**.
>
> RIGHT: **Wild animals** in jungles all over the world **are endangered**.

PRONOUNS

A **pronoun** is a word that is used in place of a noun. The **antecedent** of a pronoun is the word to which the pronoun refers.

> Example: Mary was late for work because she
> ANTECEDENT PRONOUN
> forgot to set the alarm.

Occasionally, an antecedent will appear in a sentence *after* the pronoun.

> Example: Because he sneezes so often, Arthur
> PRONOUN ANTECEDENT
> always thinks he might have the flu.
> PRONOUN

1. PRONOUNS AND AGREEMENT

In clear, grammatical writing, a pronoun must clearly refer to, and agree with, its antecedent.

NUMBER AND PERSON

	Singular	Plural
First Person	I, me my, mine	we, us our, ours
Second Person	you your, yours	you your, yours

Third Person	he, him	they, them
	she, her	
	it	
	one	
	his	their, theirs
	her, hers	
	its	
	one's	

Number Agreement

Pronouns must agree in number with their antecedents. A singular pronoun should stand in for a singular antecedent. A plural pronoun should stand in for a plural antecedent.

> WRONG: The bank turned Harry down when he applied for a loan because **their** credit department discovered that he didn't have a job.

What does the plural possessive *their* refer to? The singular noun *bank*. The singular possessive its is what we need here.

> RIGHT: The bank turned Harry down for a loan because **its** credit department discovered that he didn't have a job.

Person Agreement

Pronouns must agree with their antecedents in person too. A first-person pronoun should stand in for a first-person antecedent, and so on. One more thing to remember about which pronoun to use with which antecedent: Never use the relative pronoun *which* to refer to a human being. Use *who* or *whom* or *that.*

> WRONG: The woman **which** is standing at the piano is my sister.
>
> RIGHT: The woman **who** is standing at the piano is my sister.

2. Pronouns and Case

A more subtle type of pronoun problem is one in which the pronoun is in the wrong case. Look at the following chart:

CASE

	Subjective	Objective
First Person	I	me
	we	us
Second Person	you	you
Third Person	he	him
	she	her
	it	it
	they	them
	one	one
Relative Pronouns	who	whom
	that	that
	which	which

When to Use Subjective Case Pronouns

Use the subjective case for the subject of a sentence.

> Example: **She** is falling asleep.
>
> WRONG: Nancy, Claire, and **me** are going to the ballet.
>
> RIGHT: Nancy, Claire, and **I** are going to the ballet.

Use the subjective case after a linking verb like *to be.*

> Example: It is **I.**

Use the subjective case in comparisons between the subject of verbs that are not stated, but understood.

> Example: Gary is taller than **they** (are).

When to Use Objective Case Pronouns

Use the objective case for the object of a verb.

Example: I called **her**.

Use the objective case for the object of a preposition.

Example: I laughed at **him**.

Use the objective case after infinitives and gerunds.

Example: Asking **him** to go was a big mistake.

Example: To give **him** the scare of his life, we all jumped out of his closet.

Use the objective case in comparisons between objects of verbs that are not stated but understood.

Example: She calls you more than (she calls) **me**.

3. Who and Whom

Another thing you'll need to know is when to use the relative pronoun *who* (subjective case) and when to use the relative pronoun *whom* (objective case: *whom* goes with *him* and *them*). The following method is very helpful when you're deciding which one to use.

Example: Sylvester, (*who* or *whom*?) is afraid of the dark, sleeps with a Donald Duck night-light on.

Look only at the relative pronoun in its clause. Ignore the rest of the sentence.

(Who or whom?) is afraid of the dark.

Turn the clause into a question. Ask yourself:

Who or whom is afraid of the dark?

Answer the question with an ordinary personal pronoun.

He is.

If you've answered the question with a subjective case pronoun (as you have here), you need the subjective case who in the relative clause.

Sylvester, **who** is afraid of the dark, sleeps with a Donald Duck night-light on.

If you answer the question with an objective case pronoun, you need the objective case *whom* in the relative clause.

HINT: Try answering the question with he or him. Who goes with he (subjective case) and whom goes with him (objective case).

Sentence Structure

A **sentence** is a group of words that can stand alone because it expresses a complete thought. To express a complete thought, it must contain a subject, about which something is said, and a verb, which says something about the subject.

Example: Dogs bark.

Example: The explorers slept in yak-hide tents.

Example: Looking out of the window, John saw a flying saucer.

Every sentence consists of at least one clause. Many sentences contain more than one clause (and phrases, too).

A **clause** is a group of words that contains a subject and a verb. "Dogs bark," "The explorers slept in a yak-hide tent," and "John saw a flying saucer" are all clauses.

A **phrase** is a group of words that does not have both a subject and a verb. "Looking out of the window" is a phrase.

1. Sentence Fragments

A **sentence fragment** is a group of words that seems to be a sentence but which is *grammatically* incomplete because it lacks a subject or a verb, **or** which is *logically* incomplete because other elements necessary for it to express a complete thought are missing.

> WRONG: Eggs and fresh vegetables on sale at the farmers' market.

This is not a complete sentence because there's no verb to say something about the subject, *eggs and fresh vegetables*.

> WRONG: Because Richard likes hippopotamuses.

Even though this contains a subject (Richard) and a verb (likes), it's not a complete sentence because it doesn't express a complete thought. We don't know what's true "*because* Richard likes hippopotamuses."

> WRONG: Martha dreams about dinosaurs although.

This isn't a complete sentence because it doesn't express a complete thought. What makes Martha's dreaming about dinosaurs in need of qualification or explanation?

2. Run-On Sentences

Just as unacceptable as an incomplete sentence is a "too-complete" sentence, a run-on sentence.

A **run-on** sentence is actually two complete sentences stuck together either with just a comma or with no punctuation at all.

> WRONG: The children had been playing in the park, they were covered with mud.

> WRONG: The children had been playing in the park they were covered with mud.

There are a number of ways to fix this kind of problem. They all involve a punctuation mark or a connecting word that can properly connect two clauses.

Join the clauses with a semicolon.

> RIGHT: The children had been playing in the park; they were covered with mud.

Join the clauses with a coordinating conjunction (*and, but, for, nor, or, so, yet*) and a comma.

> RIGHT: The children had been playing in the park, and they were covered with mud.

Join the clauses with a subordinating conjunction (*after, although, if, since, while*).

> RIGHT: Because the children had been playing in the park, they were covered with mud.
>
> OR
>
> RIGHT: The children were covered with mud because they had been playing in the park.

And, of course, the two halves of a run-on sentence can be written as two separate, complete sentences.

> RIGHT: The children had been playing in the park. They were covered with mud.

VERBS

English has six tenses, and each has a simple form and a progressive form.

	Simple	Progressive
Present	I work	I am working
Past	I worked	I was working
Future	I will work	I will be working
Present Perfect	I have worked	I have been working
Past Perfect	I had worked	I had been working
Future Perfect	I will have worked	I will have been working

1. USING THE PRESENT TENSE

Use the present tense to describe a state or action occurring in the present time.

Example: I **am** a student.

Example: They **are studying** the Holy Roman Empire.

Use the present tense to describe habitual action.

Example: They **eat** at Joe's Diner every night.

Example: My father never **drinks** coffee.

Use the present tense to describe things that are always true.

Example: The earth **is** round.

Example: Grass **is** green.

2. USING THE PAST TENSE

Use the simple past tense to describe an event or state that took place at a specific time in the past and is now over and done with.

Example: Norman **broke** his toe when he tripped over his son's tricycle.

3. USING THE FUTURE TENSE

Use the future tense for actions expected in the future.

Example: I **will call** you on Wednesday.

We often express future actions with the expression *to be going to.*

Example: I **am going to move** to another apartment soon.

4. USING THE PRESENT PERFECT TENSE

Use the present perfect tense for actions and states that started in the past and continue up to and into the present time.

Example: I **have been living** here for the last two years.

Use the present perfect for actions and states that happened a number of times in the past and may happen again in the future.

Example: I **have heard** that song several times on the radio.

Use the present perfect for something that happened at an unspecified time in the past.

Example: Anna **has seen** that movie already.

5. Using the Past Perfect Tense

The past perfect tense is used to represent past actions or states that were completed before other past actions or states. The more recent past event is expressed in the simple past, and the earlier past event is expressed in the past perfect.

> Example: When I turned my computer on this morning, I realized that I **had exited** the program yesterday without saving my work.

6. Using the Future Perfect Tense

Use the future perfect tense for a future state or event that will take place before another future event.

> Example: By the end of the week, I **will have worked** four hours of overtime.

7. Using the Proper Past Participle Form

If you use the present, past, or future perfect tense, make sure that you use the past participle and not the simple past tense.

> WRONG: I have **swam** in that pool every day this week.
>
> RIGHT: I have **swum** in that pool every day this week.

Irregular verbs have two different forms for simple past and past participle tenses. The following are some of the most common irregular verbs.

IRREGULAR VERBS

Infinitive	Simple Past	Past Participle
arise	arose	arisen
become	became	become
begin	began	begun
blow	blew	blown
break	broke	broken
come	came	come
do	did	done
draw	drew	drawn
drink	drank	drunk
drive	drove	driven
eat	ate	eaten
fall	fell	fallen
fly	flew	flown
freeze	froze	frozen
give	gave	given
grow	grew	grown
know	knew	known
ride	rode	ridden
rise	rose	risen
run	ran	run
see	saw	seen
shake	shook	shaken
shrink	shrank	shrunk
sing	sang	sung
speak	spoke	spoken
take	took	taken
throw	threw	thrown

Adjectives and Adverbs

An **adjective** modifies, or describes, a noun or pronoun.

> Example: A woman in a **white** dress stood next to the **old** tree.
>
> Example: The boat, **leaky** and **dirty**, hadn't been used in years.

An adverb modifies a verb, an adjective, or another adverb. Most, but not all, adverbs end in *-ly*. (Don't forget that some **adjectives**—*friendly*, *lovely*—also end in *-ly*.)

> Example: The interviewer looked *approvingly* at the *neatly* dressed applicant.

Parallel Structure

Matching constructions must be expressed in parallel form. Make sure that when a sentence contains a **list** or makes a **comparison**, the items being listed or compared exhibit parallel structure.

1. *Items in a List*

   WRONG: I love **skipping**, **jumping**, and **to play** tiddlywinks.

   WRONG: I love **to skip**, **jump**, and **to play** tiddlywinks.

   RIGHT: I love to **skip**, **jump**, and **play** tiddlywinks.

   ALSO RIGHT: I love **to skip**, **to jump**, and **to play** tiddlywinks.

   ALSO RIGHT: I love **skipping**, **jumping**, and **playing** tiddlywinks.

2. *Items in a Comparison*

   Comparisons must do more than just exhibit parallel structure. Most faulty comparisons relate to the notion that you can't compare apples and oranges. You don't merely want comparisons to be grammatically similar; they must be logically similar as well.

   WRONG: **To visualize** success is not the same as **achieving** it.

   RIGHT: **To visualize** success is not the same as **to achieve** it.

   ALSO RIGHT: **Visualizing** success is not the same as **achieving** it.

   WRONG: **The rules of chess** are more complex than **checkers**.

   RIGHT: **The rules of chess** are more complex than **those of checkers**.

   ALSO RIGHT: **Chess** is more complex than **checkers**.

STYLE REVIEW

Pronouns and Reference

When we talk about pronouns and their antecedents, we say pronouns refer to or refer back to their antecedents. We noted earlier that pronouns must agree in person and number with their antecedents. But a different kind of pronoun reference problem exists when a pronoun either doesn't refer to any antecedent at all or doesn't refer clearly to one, and only one, antecedent.

Sometimes an incorrectly used pronoun has no antecedent.

> POOR: Joe doesn't like what **they play** on this radio station.

Who are *they*? We can't tell, because there is no antecedent for *they*.

> RIGHT: Joe doesn't like what **the disc jockeys play** on this radio station.

Don't use pronouns without antecedents when doing so makes a sentence unclear. Sometimes a pronoun seems to have an antecedent until you look closely and see that the word that appears to be the antecedent is not a noun, but an adjective, a possessive form, or a verb. The antecedent of a pronoun must be a noun.

WRONG: When you are painting, make sure you don't get **it** on the floor.

RIGHT: When you are painting, make sure you don't get **paint** on the floor.

Other examples of pronoun reference problems:

WRONG: I've always been interested in astronomy and finally have decided to become **one**.

RIGHT: I've always been interested in astronomy and finally have decided to become an **astronomer**.

Don't use pronouns with remote references. A pronoun that is too far away from what it refers to is said to have a **remote antecedent**.

WRONG: Jane quit smoking and, as a result, temporarily put on a lot of weight. **It** was very bad for her health.

RIGHT: Jane quit smoking because **it** was very bad for her health, and, as a result, she temporarily gained a lot of weight.

Don't use pronouns with faulty broad reference. A pronoun with broad reference is one that refers to a whole idea instead of to a single noun.

WRONG: He built a fence to stop people from looking into his backyard. **That's** not easy.

RIGHT: He built a fence to stop people from looking into his backyard. **The fence was not easy to build**.

REDUNDANCY

Words or phrases are **redundant** when they have basically the same meaning as something already stated in the sentence. Don't use two phrases when one is sufficient.

WRONG: The school was **established and founded** in 1906.

RIGHT: The school was **established** in 1906.

RELEVANCE

Everything in the sentence should serve to get across the point in question. Something unrelated to that point should be cut.

POOR: No one can say for sure just how successful the new law will be in the fight against crime (just as no one can be sure whether he or she will ever be a victim of a crime).

BETTER: No one can say for sure just how successful the new law will be in the fight against crime.

VERBOSITY

Sometimes having extra words in a sentence results in a style problem.

WORDY: The supply of **musical instruments that are antique** is limited, so they become more valuable each year.

BETTER: The supply of **antique musical instruments** is limited, so they become more valuable each year.

WORDY: We **were in agreement with each other** that Max was an unsuspecting old fool.

BETTER: We **agreed** that Max was an unsuspecting old fool.

Commonly Misused Words

accept/except

Don't confuse the two. To *accept* means to receive or agree to something, whereas *except* is usually a preposition meaning excluding, although it can also mean to leave out.

WRONG: Can you **except** my apology?

RIGHT: Can you **accept** my apology?

affect/effect

These are easy to confuse. To *affect* means to have an *effect* on something. When the word is being used as a verb, the proper word to use is almost always *affect*; when it's being used as a noun, the proper word to use is almost always *effect*. (It should be noted that *effect* can also be a verb, meaning to bring about or cause to happen.)

WRONG: His affectations **effected** me to no good **affect**.

RIGHT: His affectations **affected** me to no good **effect**.

among/between

In most cases, you should use *between* for two items and *among* for more than two.

Example: The competition **between** Anne and Michael has grown more intense.

Example: He is always at his best **among** strangers.

But use common sense. Sometimes *among* is not appropriate.

Example: Plant the trees in the area **between** the road, the wall, and the fence.

amount/number

Amount should be used to refer to a uncountable quantity. *Number* should refer to a countable quantity.

Example: The **amount** of food he threw away would feed a substantial **number** of people.

as/like

Like is a preposition; it takes a noun object. *As*, when functioning as a conjunction, introduces a subordinate clause. Remember, a clause is a part of a sentence containing a subject and verb.

Example: He sings **like** an angel.

Example: He sings **as** an angel sings.

as . . . as . . .

The idiom is *as . . . as . . .*, **not** *as . . . than . . .*

WRONG: That suit is as expensive than this one.

RIGHT: That suit is as expensive as this one.

fewer/less

Use *fewer* before a plural noun; use *less* before a singular one.

Example: There are **fewer** apples on this tree than there were last year.

Example: He makes **less** money than she does.

neither . . . nor . . .

The correlative conjunction is *neither . . . nor . . .*, **not** *neither . . . or . . .*

Example: He is **neither** strong **nor** flexible.

Avoid the redundancy caused by using *nor* following a negative.

WRONG: Alice's departure was **not** noticed by Debby **nor** Sue.

RIGHT: Alice's departure was **not** noticed by Debby **or** Sue.

its/it's

Many people confuse *its* and *it's*. *Its* is possessive; *it's* is a contraction of *it is* or *it has*:

Example: The cat licked **its** paws.

Example: **It's** raining cats and dogs.

their/they're/there

Many people confuse *their*, *there*, and *they're*. *Their* is possessive; *they're* is a contraction of *they are*:

Example: The girls rode **their** bikes home.

Example: **They're** training for the big race.

There has two uses: It can indicate place and it can be used as an expletive—a word that doesn't do anything in a sentence except delay the subject.

Example: Put the book over **there**.

Example: **There** will be fifteen runners competing for the prize.

Idioms

Some phrases are wrong simply because that's just not the way we say it in English. This is especially true of preposition-verb word combinations. For instance,

WRONG: The fashion police **frowns at** wearing hats adorned with flowers.

RIGHT: The fashion police **frowns upon** wearing hats adorned with flowers.

The first sentence is only wrong because *frowns at* is not the correct idiomatic expression. Either your ear will recognize the correct idiom or it won't.

Idioms

associate *with*
accuse *of*
apologize *for*
arrive *at*
believe *in*
believe *to be*
apologize *for*
attribute *to*
continue *to*
contrast *with*
credit *with*
decide *to*
define *as*
different *from*
discriminate *against*
distinguish *from*
dream *about/of*
forbid *to*
frown *upon*
object *to*
prohibit *from*
substitute *for*
target *at*
use *as*
view *as*
worry *about*